Novell
IntranetWare
the Comprehensive Guide

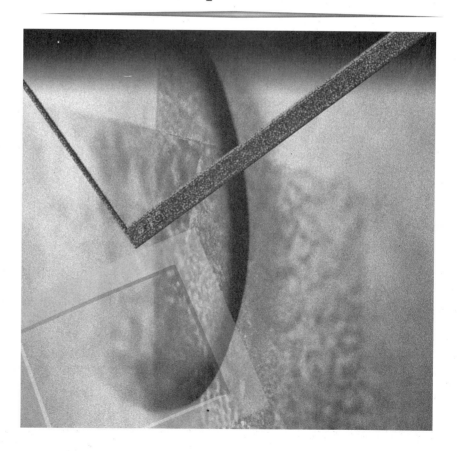

Novell IntranetWare

the Comprehensive Guide

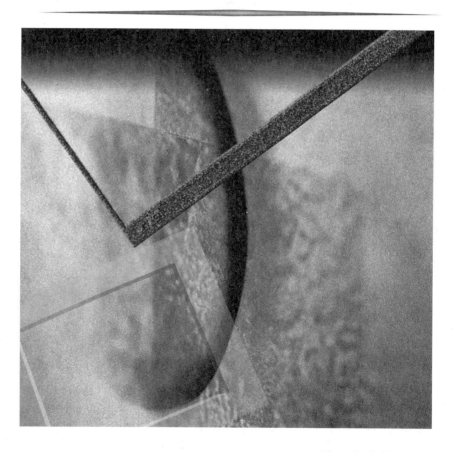

VENTANA

Heath C. Ramsey
Mark R. Bell

Novell IntranetWare: The Comprehensive Guide
Copyright © 1997 by Heath C. Ramsey and Mark R. Bell

Library of Congress Cataloging-in-Publication Data
Bell, Mark R.
The comprehensive guide to Novell IntranetWare/ Mark R. Bell, Heath Ramsey
      p. cm.
  Includes index.
  ISBN 1-56604-666-1
  1. Novell IntranetWare 2. NetWare (Computer file) 3. Intranets (Computer networks)
I. Ramsey, Heath. II. Title
TK5105.8.N65B45 1997
005.3'7682—dc21   97-4288
                                                             CIP

First Edition 9 8 7 6 5 4 3 2 1

Printed in the United States of America

Ventana Communications Group
P.O. Box 13964
Research Triangle Park, NC 27709-3964
919.544.9404
FAX 919.544.9472
http://www.vmedia.com

Ventana Communications Group is a division of International Thomson Publishing.

Limits of Liability & Disclaimer of Warranty
The authors and publisher of this book have used their best efforts in preparing the book and the programs contained in it. These efforts include the development, research, and testing of the theories and programs to determine their effectiveness. The authors and publisher make no warranty of any kind, expressed or implied, with regard to these programs or the documentation contained in this book.

The authors and publisher shall not be liable in the event of incidental or consequential damages in connection with, or arising out of, the furnishing, performance or use of the programs, associated instructions and/or claims of productivity gains.

Trademarks
Trademarked names appear throughout this book and on the accompanying compact disk, if applicable. Rather than list the names and entities that own the trademarks or insert a trademark symbol with each mention of the trademarked name, the publisher states that it is using the names only for editorial purposes and to the benefit of the trademark owner with no intention of infringing upon that trademark.

Screenshots of Yahoo! Web pages are text and artwork copyright (c) 1996 by YAHOO!, INC. All rights reserved. YAHOO! and the YAHOO! logo are trademarks of YAHOO!, INC.

About the Authors

Heath C. Ramsey is the PC/networking guru for the Technical Consulting division of the Duke University Office of Information Technology and is the primary architect of Duke University's NDS tree and Lotus Notes domain infrastructure. He holds both CNE-3 and CNE-4 certification. Heath started working with Novell NetWare during its release as NetWare 3.11 and has been following up on each version ever since. When not geeking out with his computers, he plays volleyball as often as he can and also serves as the volunteer assistant for the Duke women's volleyball team. Go Blue Devils!

Mark R. Bell is the Webmaster and Macintosh Specialist for the Technical Consulting division of the Duke University Office of Information Technology. He is the author of several books, including the *Mac Web Server Book* and the *Mac OS 8 Book*. Mark also writes software manuals for such companies as Maxum Development Corporation and Bare Bones Software. He is married to Virginia D. Smith, a writer and editor, and they live Carrboro, North Carolina with their faithful canine quadruped, Bailey.

Acknowledgments

We would first like to thank our two contributing authors, David McLaurin and David Groth, without whom we couldn't have completed this book on time.

David McLaurin is a former colleague of ours who now lives in Orlando, Florida, and who tirelessly worked to complete Chapter 20 and the Glossary on short notice. Enjoy the sunshine down there, David, and congratulations on your upcoming wedding. Can we at least come to the reception? We hear that you'll be serving orange juice ;).

We met David Groth, who wrote Chapters 17 and 18, via the Internet. David came though for us in spectacular fashion, and once the word got out, publishers began lining up. David has every Novell certification there is, and when he's not putting his knowledge to work on a server, he's restoring Studebakers in Fargo, ND, where he survives the winters very nicely, thank you.

We also would like to thank Neal Paris and our colleagues at Duke University, who put up with our late hours and our occasional lapses in memory. Without their patience, understanding, and support, this book would not have been possible.

Heath would like to thank: all of my friends and family (blood and extended) who helped me and supported me through the authoring of my first book. Many thanks to Anne Beckwith and Sandi Metz for being the voices of reason when I needed them most, to Barbara Wade and Don Eastwood for reviewing chapters or lending an ear when I needed to vent, and to Linda Grensing and Karen Weatherington for understanding why I couldn't be at practice every day ;). Of course, I have to thank Mom, Dad, Judy, Craig, Charlene, Gerry, Chris, and Deirdre for the unconditional love and support from a family no one could replace.

Mark would like to thenk: everyone who put up with my absence while I completed another project, especially Gregg & Mary Catherine, Craig, Angelika, and Erin, my mother and grandmother, Kirk Brodie, and Bailey. I'd also like to thank a few people I should have thanked years ago: Emmett Dozier, Lee Wheeler, Fran Priest, Mr. & Mrs. Johnny Bond, Erma Todd, and Melanie Anderson (again). I wouldn't have been able to do this without their insight and encouragement.

Finally, we would like to thank all the kind and funny people at Ventana with whom we've had the pleasure to work with over the past few months. In particular, we'd like to turn the spotlight on our infinitely patient project editor, Paul Cory; our development editor, Laura Poole; our technical editor, Steven Clegg; our proofreader, Tom Collins, our contract coordinator, Melanie Stepp; and the person with whom this project started, Travis Walsh, the acquisitions editor for this book. Thank you all very much for making this an easy thing to do!

Dedication

I would like to dedicate this book to Tim Cherubini, the most understanding and caring friend a person could have, for putting up with my late nights, mood swings, and general crankiness while I was writing. Now we'll have time to listen to some more dull, soulless dance music...

—HCR

I would to dedicate this, and all other books, to my wife Virginia, who knows what is really important in life, and that sometimes a poodle just has to be a dog.

—MRB

Contents

Introduction xxix

SECTION I
Out of the Box

Chapter 1   **Preparing the Server** 1

Selecting a Server 4
  The Central Processing Unit   5
  Random Access Memory   8
  The Hardware Bus   9
  The Hard Disk Controller   11
  The Hard Disk   12
  The Network Interface Card   13

IntranetWare Hardware Requirements 14
  Hard Disk Capacity & RAM   14
  CD-ROM Drive   15

Preparing to Install IntranetWare 16
  Set Up the Server   17
  Gather Important Server Information   17
  Gather Technical Manuals & Required Software   19
  Create the Server's DOS Partition   20
  Edit the DOS Startup Files   22

Choose the Method of Installation 23
    CD-ROM Installation   23
    NetWare Server-to-Server Installation   24

Applying Concepts: Rambell, Inc. 26

Chapter 2   Installing NetWare 4.11 29

INSTALL.BAT 30

INSTALL.NLM 38
    Server Drivers   38
    Activating the Server Drivers   43
    Configuring the Hard Disks   47
    Volumes   53
    Installing NetWare Directory Services   62
    License Installation   65
    Editing the Server Startup Files   66

Experienced Installer's Guide 66

Applying Concepts: Rambell, Inc. 69

Chapter 3   NetWare 4.11 Concepts 71

The NDS Concept 72

The NDS Structure 74

NDS Object Classes 75
    The [Root] Object   76
    Container Objects   76
    Leaf Objects   78

Context 84
    Current Context   85
    Using CX   85

NDS Object Naming Conventions 88
    Distinguished Naming   89
    Relative Distinguished Naming   89
    Typeful Naming   90
    Typeless Naming   90
    Naming Examples   90

The NetWare Administrator 91
  Navigating the NDS Tree   95
  Manipulating Objects   97
  NetWare Administrator Features   103

Applying Concepts: Rambell, Inc. 106

Chapter 4 Basic NetWare Administration 107

Introduction to NetWare 4.11 Security 108
  Login Security   108
  NDS Security   109
  File System Security   111

User Objects 112
  Creating User Objects   113
  Detailing User Objects   118

Groups 133

Organizational Roles & Aliases 136
  Organizational Role   136
  Aliases   139

Applying Concepts: Rambell, Inc. 140

Chapter 5 Login Scripts 143

Login Script Types 144
  Container Login Script   145
  Profile Login Script   146
  User Login Script   149
  Default Login Script   150

Login Script Commands 152
  # (Execute External Command)   158
  ATTACH   158
  DISPLAY/FDISPLAY   159
  EXIT   159
  FIRE PHASERS   160
  GOTO   160
  IF-THEN   161
  INCLUDE   165

MAP   166
NO_DEFAULT   174
PROFILE   174
REMARK   174
WRITE   175

Identifier Variables 177
Date Variables   178
Time Variables   179
User Variables   179
Network Variables   180
Workstation Variables   181
DOS Environment Variables   181
Miscellaneous Variables   182
Object Properties Variables   182

Applying Concepts: Rambell, Inc. 183

Chapter 6   Managing the File System 185

Servers & Their Volumes 186
The NetWare Server Object   187
The Volume Object   188
File System Organization   197
NetWare 4.11 Default Directories   199
Mapping: A Reprise   201

File System Security 203
File System Rights   203
Trustee Assignments   208
Rights Inheritance & Inherited Rights Filters   213
Effective Rights   217

File System Management 222
Managing File Systems With NetWare Administrator   222
Attributes   225
Salvaging & Purging Files   231

Applying Concepts: Rambell, Inc. 232

Chapter 7 **Print Services** 235

Getting Started With Network Printing 236
Step-by-Step Guide to the Network Print Request   237
Planning the Printing Environment   241
Preparing Hardware for Network Printing   242

Basic NetWare Print Services Configurations 243
Printers Connected to NetWare 4.11 File Servers   243
Printers Connected to Client Workstations   245
Network-Ready Printers   248

Configuring NetWare Printing: Front End 250
Print Queue Object   251
Printer Object   257
Print Server Object   263
NDS Print Object Interaction   269
Front End Setup Recap   269
Printing Environment Quick Setup Option   270
Configuring the Front End With PCONSOLE.EXE   271

Configuring NetWare Printing: Back End 272
The Print Server   273
Printing Station Software   276
NetWare 4.11 Printing & Windows 95   281

Using Print Services at the Workstation 284
Using CAPTURE.EXE   285
Printing to Multiple Network Printers   291
Printing Station Software & CAPTURE.EXE   292

Other Print Services 293
AppleTalk Print Services   293
UNIX Print Services   298

Applying Concepts: Rambell, Inc. 302

SECTION II
NetWare Directory Services

Chapter 8   **NDS Architecture** 307

Learning From the Past: NetWare 3.x 308
   Understanding the Bindery   309
   Limitations of Bindery-Based Networks   311

Applying to the Future: NetWare 4.x 312
   The New Network Concept   312
   Bindery Services   315

NDS Building Blocks 320
   [Root]   320
   Container Objects   320
   Leaf Objects   326

NDS: Key to the Intranet 326
   The Classic LAN: File & Print Services   327
   Expanding the Network   327
   A Complete Set of Network Services   329

Chapter 9   **NDS Security** 331

NDS Rights 332
   Object Rights   333
   Property Rights   335

Trustee Assignments 338
   Granting Trustee Assignments   339
   NDS Special Trustees   344
   Default NDS Rights   345

Rights Inheritance & Filters 347
   Understanding NDS Rights Inheritance   348
   The NDS Inherited Rights Filter   349

NDS Effective Rights 352
   Calculating Effective Rights   354
   Viewing NDS Effective Rights   356
   Troubleshooting Excessive Rights   357

Chapter 10 NDS Partitioning & Replication 363

  Using NDS Manager 364
    Navigating NDS Manager   366
    NDS Manager Tasks   370

  NDS Partitioning 374
    Understanding Partitioning   375
    Dividing the NDS Tree   376
    Managing NDS Partitions   380
    Viewing Partition Information   386

  NDS Replication 387
    Understanding Replicas   387
    Managing NDS Replicas   393
    NDS Replica Synchronization   399
    Viewing Replica Information   406
    Bindery Services (Revisited)   406

Chapter 11 NDS Time Synchronization 409

  Time Synchronization Concepts 410
    The Need for Time Synchronization in NDS   411

  The NDS Time Environment 413
    How Time Is Synchronized   418

  Default Time Synchronization Method 420
    Time Server Communication   422
    Time Server Time Correction   422

  Custom Time Synchronization Method 423
    Custom Time Synchronization Guidelines   426
    Time Server Communication   426
    Time Server Time Correction   428

  Setting Up the NDS Time Environment 429
    Setting & Viewing the Server Time   432
    Configuring Server Time Synchronization Parameters   434
    Saving Your Time Synchronization   443
    Reviewing the TIMESYNC.CFG File   444

Chapter 12 Merging NDS Trees 449

Preparing to Merge 450
  Merging Concepts   450
  Merging Prerequisites   452

Merging NDS Trees With DSMERGE.NLM 456
  Check Servers in This Tree   457
  Check Time Synchronization   459
  Merge Two Trees   461
  Rename This Tree   463

After the Merge 464
  Implications of Merging Trees   464
  Merging Cleanup   466

Chapter 13 NDS Utilities 471

Diagnosing & Repairing NDS 472
  Understanding NDS Inconsistencies   473
  Resolving NDS Inconsistencies With NDS Manager   474
  Monitoring Synchronization With DSTRACE   489
  Repairing the NDS Database With DSREPAIR   494

Protecting Your NDS Database 499
  Understanding SMS Technology   500
  Backing Up NDS With SBACKUP   502

Standardizing User Desktops Through NDS 507
  Defining Network Applications Using NAM   507
  Launching Network Applications Using NAL   514

Chapter 14 NDS Design & Implementation: A Case Study 517

Deciding Upon a Logical NDS Tree Structure 518
  Gathering Preliminary Information   519
  Container Organization Models   520
  Tree Administration Models   524
  Other Structural Considerations   527

Planning NDS Partitioning & Replication 529
    Partitioning Guidelines   529
    Replication Guidelines   533

Planning the NDS Time Environment 538
    Determining the Number of Time Providers   539
    Network Topology Considerations   540
    Time Server Communication Strategies   541

NDS Tree Implementation: Rambell, Inc. 542
    Gather Preliminary Information   543
    Decide Upon a Logical NDS Tree Structure   545
    Plan the Partitioning & Replication Schemes   547
    Plan the Time Synchronization Environment   549

S E C T I O N   I I I

Novell LAN Services

Chapter 15 DOS/Windows Workstation Client 555

Preparing the Client Software for Installation 556

The NetWare DOS Requester 559
    The VLM Workstation Client Architecture   560
    Hardware/Software Requirements   563
    NetWare DOS Requester Installation   564
    Connecting to the NetWare 4.11 Server   566

NetWare Client32 for DOS/Windows 3.x 568
    NetWare Client32 for DOS/Windows Architecture   569
    Hardware/Software Requirements   579
    NetWare Client32 for DOS/Windows Installation   580
    Client32 Windows Utilities   586
    Installing & Configuring Workstation TCP/IP   593

Chapter 16 Windows 95, Windows NT & Mac OS Workstation Clients 597

NetWare Client32 for Windows 95 598
    NetWare Client32 for Windows 95 Architecture   599
    Hardware/Software Requirements   601
    NetWare Client32 for Windows 95 Installation   602
    NetWare Client32 for Windows 95 Configuration   603
    NetWare Client32 for Windows 95 Utilities   605

IntranetWare Client for Windows NT 609
    Hardware/Software Requirements   610
    Preparing the Client Software for Installation   611
    IntranetWare Client for Windows NT Installation   612
    Configuring IntranetWare Client for Windows NT   614
    IntranetWare Client for Windows NT Utilities   616
    Other Products Included With IntranetWare Client
    for Windows NT   619

NetWare Client for Mac OS 624
    Hardware/Software Requirements   625
    Client Installation & Configuring   626
    Logging In   627
    Server Installation & Configuration   629
    Client Utilities   631

Chapter 17 NetWare 4.11 Server Architecture 633

The Core Operating System Files & Their Roles 634
    STARTUP.NCF   636
    AUTOEXEC.NCF   637

NLMs, Disk Drivers & Network Interfaces 639
    Disk Drivers   640
    Name Space Modules   642
    LAN Drivers   642
    Management & Enhancement NLMs   644

Understanding NetWare 4.11 Memory Management 645
    Memory Configuration   645
    Memory Allocation   646

An In-Depth Look at the File System 648

Understanding Volume Configuration   648

Directory Entry Table & File Allocation Table   651

Understanding the NetWare File System   652

The NetWare Core Protocol Suite 656

The IPX & SPX Protocols   656

NetWare Core Protocol (NCP)   657

The RIP & SAP Protocols   658

Chapter 18 NetWare 4.11 Server Management 663

Changing Installation Options & Editing System Files:
INSTALL.NLM 664

Driver Options   665

Disk Options   666

Volume Options   668

License Option   670

Copy Files Option   671

Directory Options   672

NCF Files Options   676

Multi CPU Options   677

Product Options   679

Optimizing Server Performance: SERVMAN.NLM 680

Setting Server Parameters   681

Retrieving Other File Server Information   693

Monitoring Server Performance & Statistics:
MONITOR.NLM 694

Connection Information   698

Disk Information   699

LAN/WAN Information   700

System Module Information   702

Lock File Server Console   702

File Open/Lock Activity   703

Cache Utilization   703

Processor Utilization   704

Resource Utilization   705

Memory Utilization   706
Scheduling Information   707
Multiprocessor Information   708
Server Parameters   708

Network Configuration: INETCFG.NLM 709
Boards   710
Protocols   711
Bindings   717
Manage Configuration   720
View Configuration   722

Other Server Console Tools 724
ALIAS   724
BROADCAST   725
DISPLAY SERVERS   725
DSTRACE   725
MEMORY   726
RCONSOLE   727
REMOTE ENCRYPT   729
REMOVE DOS   729
SECURE CONSOLE   730

Chapter 19 NetWare/IP 731

NetWare/IP Basics 732
NetWare/IP   733
NetWare/IP-Related Services & Concepts   735
Sample NetWare/IP Network Configurations   745

The NetWare/IP Server 749
System Requirements   751
TCP/IP Installation   753
NetWare/IP Installation   755

The NetWare/IP Client 765
NetWare/IP Support in Client32 for DOS/Windows   766
NetWare/IP Support in Client32 for Windows 95   770

Chapter 20 Wide Area Network (WAN) Connectivity 777

What Is a WAN? 777
    Connection Types   778
    Where to Get a Connection   780
    Carrier Services   780

Network Media Options for Connecting WANs 781
    Asynchronous Transfer Mode (ATM)   782
    X.25   782
    Frame Relay   783
    The Decision   783

MultiProtocol Router 784
    What Is a Router?   784
    Installing the MultiProtocol Router   785
    Configuring the MPR   788
    A Simple Example Using IPRELAY   794

NetWare IPX/IP Gateway for Internet Access 795
    The Server Piece   796
    Configuring the IPX/IP Gateway   796
    The Client Piece   799

WAN Extensions 805
    Configuring ATM, Frame Relay & X.25   805

NetWare Link Services Protocol (NLSP) 806
    So Why Should I Use NLSP?   807

SECTION IV

Novell Intranet Services

Chapter 21 Providing Web Services 811

Features of Novell Web Server 3.0 812
    Features New to Version 3.0   812
    HyperText Markup Language Documents   813
    Image & Multimedia Files   813
    Clickable Image Maps   814
    Scripting Support   814

Common Gateway Interfaces   816
Secure Sockets Layer   817
Oracle Database Connectivity   817
QuickFinder Search Engine   817
Virtual Directories   818
Multihoming   818
Server-Side Includes   818
Java Applets   819
Long Filename Support   819
Online Documentation   819

Installing the Server 822
Server Requirements   822
Additional RAM Requirements   823
Installing the Software   824
Reconfiguring & Removing the Software   826
Upgrading the Software   827
Long Filenames   829
DNS Concerns   830

Basic Server Configuration 832
Client Requirements   834
Launching Web Manager   835
Server Tab   837
Directories Tab   839
User Access Tab   841
System Access Tab   843
Virtual Host Tab   844
Interface Tab   846

Chapter 22 Advanced Web Server Configuration 849
Managing Configuration Files 850
HTTPD.CFG   851
SRM.CFG   853
ACCESS.CFG   856
SSL.CFG   859

MIME Management 859
    Understanding MIME Types   860
    Browser Configuration Issues   861
    MIME.TYP   863
    Changing MIME Types   865

File Management 865
    Reviewing Files   866
    File Management Etiquette   873

Logging 874
    Location & Settings   875
    ACCESS.LOG   877
    HTTP Version & Status Codes   879
    ERROR.LOG   880
    Saving, Clearing & Printing   881

Chapter 23   SSL & Web Server Security 883

Secure Sockets Layer 884
    Web Security Issues   884
    Site Certificates & Keys   889
    Enabling SSL   892

Restricting Access 901
    Using Web Manager   903
    Creating Access Files & Using PWGEN.EXE   904
    Restricting Access by User   908
    Restricting Access by Group   911
    Restricting Access by System   913

Browser Configuration 917
    General Configuration Options   917
    Passwords   921
    Personal Certificates   921
    Site Certificates   924

Chapter 24 Providing Web Content 927

    Web Essentials 929

        HTTP Interaction   929

        HTML   933

        URL Anatomy   940

    Directories & Documents 941

        Adding & Removing Directories   941

        User Directories   944

    Images: Inline, Clickable & Maps 948

        Inline Images   948

        Clickable Images   950

        Clickable Image Maps   953

        Server-Side Includes   959

    NDS Browsing 963

        Configuring the Browser   963

        Browsing the Tree   965

Chapter 25 CGI Scripting 971

    What Is a CGI? 972

    HTML Tags & Syntax for CGIs 974

        Searching With <ISINDEX> & GET   975

        Using the POST Method   979

        The NAME Element   980

        The <INPUT> Tag   981

        Single-Line Text Fields   981

        Check Boxes & Radio Buttons   983

        Drop-Down, Scrolling & Multiple-Selection Lists   985

        The <TEXTAREA> Tag   988

        Submit & Reset   989

Supported CGIs 989
    Local Common Gateway Interface   990
    Remote Common Gateway Interface   991
    Perl 5 Scripts   991
    NetBasic Scripts   992
    QuickFinder Search Engine   992
    Loading the NLMs   993

A Few Examples 994
    A Perl Example   995
    A NetBasic Example   999
    A QuickFinder Example   1004
    A Java Applet Example   1007

Chapter 26 FTP Services 1013

Installing FTP Services 1014

Configuring FTP Services 1015
    Set Parameters   1016
    Restrict FTP Access   1019

Client Access 1020

Managing FTP Services 1022
    View Current FTP Sessions   1022
    View FTP Log File   1023
    View Intruder Log File   1023
    Clear Log Files   1024

Linking to Other NetWare Servers 1024
File Types & Compression Schemes 1025

S E C T I O N   V
Appendices

Appendix A Getting Help 1031

Appendix B NetWare 4.11 New Features 1035

Appendix C NDS Error Codes 1045

Appendix D X.500 Country Codes 1049

Glossary 1053

Index 1069

Why Build an Intranet?

Building an intranet isn't an easy task, but it will be worth the effort if you do it the right way. It must be something to which you've already given a lot of thought if you are reading this book, and you therefore must also have some experience with either Novell NetWare or networking in general. Either way, you might want to know what we mean when we use the term *intranet*, and exactly how one goes about building an intranet. Intranets are a natural outgrowth of networked computing that use concepts and technologies popularized by the Internet. Local area networks (LANs) grew into wide area networks (WANs), which in turn grew into metropolitan area networks (MANs), which finally grew into, you guessed it, intranets. In fact, you could argue that the Internet is not a collection of networks, but rather a collection of intranets.

The term *intranet* is sometimes confusing to many people both within the computing industry and to casual users of the tens of thousands of networks around the world. An intranet, simply put, consists of two or more networks connected together using communications protocols popularized by the Internet. Intranets range in size of just a few users in one location connecting to resources located in another location, to multiple groups of several thousand users scattered across the globe. It takes many different types of computer hardware and software working in unison to make the flow of data across these intranets appear seamless to the end user, and IntranetWare is the best glue to bind these many parts together.

The rise of the intranet as a new paradigm for computing is a function of at least three trends. First, network computing continues to play an increasing role in the lives of business and home entertainment. A few years ago it wasn't uncommon for many people to spend time on a networked computer during the work day. These people checked their e-mail, accessed a corporate database, composed documents using a word processor, and perhaps fiddled with a game or new application. Today, however, more and more people are leaving work after spending a significant amount of time using a computer and going home to work and play on another type of computer network—the Internet. In fact, as the number of people accessing the Internet from home continues to grow, computer manufacturers must spend more of their research and development resources pursuing this new market. One result of this changing trend is that home computers are looking more like workstations and less like video games.

A second trend that is having an effect on the move away from local and wide area networks toward intranets is geographic dispersion of corporate employees away from a centralized location. The old model of doing business often had employees of a company located in one building, in one city, on one continent. Now, however, businesses are located in different buildings across towns, countries, and continents. This trend parallels the mobility of the workforce in general, where more people travel longer distances to find employment, and companies open branches or access information from other cities.

A third trend centers around a move away from simplicity towards diversity. In the early days of network computing the typical network was homogeneous, using one model of computer and only one flavor of operating system. Today's economy, however, places a different set of criteria on a computer network: mobility, flexibility, remote access, and platform diversity. Gone are the days of simple networks, and present are the days of complex, heterogeneous, and distant networks. Businesses have discovered that some computers are better at certain tasks than others, and isn't it great if they can all access the same data?

Who Needs This Book?

This book is intended to serve several purposes for a variety of information technology professionals, so it may not be as helpful for someone not familiar with NetWare, networking, or intranets. If you are a NetWare administrator, network engineer, manager of information technology, or a Webmaster, then this book will meet your needs in several areas. You'll learn how NetWare has evolved over the past 10 years into IntranetWare; how to install, configure, and manage IntranetWare; how to configure clients on multiple platforms to access your IntranetWare server; how to allow multiple IntranetWare servers to communicate with one another; how to publish on the World Wide Web; and how to manage intranet services.

Where possible, we'll also give you background information on technologies and trends that may effect the future direction of IntranetWare and intranets. Unlike advances in personal computer technologies, which tend to be regular features on the evening news and in the daily headlines, advances in networking technology tend to happen behind the scenes. Most people are never made aware of them until they are brought to market. As managers of information technology, however, it is our job to notice even the smallest trends because today's trends could easily become tomorrow's standards. Our job will therefore be to make you aware of those trends that may effect your ability to provide intranet services to your customers.

It is no surprise that Novell has created a solid platform on which to build an intranet. As the industry leader in network operating systems, Novell created IntranetWare to take full advantage of its existing NetWare user base and added the protocols and features found on the Internet. The result is a flexible intranet platform with room to expand and grow to meet the needs of networks of all sizes.

Some of you will be installing IntranetWare for the first time, while others will be upgrading from earlier versions of NetWare. In both cases, a little background on Novell and its NetWare line of network operating systems will help us all to understand how NetWare has evolved into an intranet operating system. There have been dozens of books and study guides written on the various versions of NetWare, and as you can image, we won't go into the minute details of each version here. What we will try to do, however, is cover the various protocols and features used by older versions in preparation for comparing them to what you'll find in IntranetWare.

A Brief History of NetWare

Novell NetWare was first introduced as a means of connecting DOS-based clients together to share file and print services. Since then, several versions of Novell NetWare have come and gone, although most of them are still in use. Novell's position is that they will continue to support their products until their revenue generates less than one or two percent of their overall profit. In many cases, a LAN running an old version of NetWare continues to chug away without being upgraded to a newer version. Of course, it makes more sense to not upgrade a network operating system (NOS) as frequently as a workstation's operating system (OS) because of the tremendous amount of work and downtime involved, unless there is a clear benefit or purpose for such an upgrade. For this reason, therefore, many NetWare servers are still running the same version of NOS that was originally installed several years ago. But what are the highlights of the major revisions of NetWare?

NetWare 2.x

Version 2.x of NetWare, according to Peter Dyson's *Novell's Dictionary of Networking* (Novell Press, 1994), is a single processor, 16-bit NOS that was designed to run on the 80286 processor. Pale by today's standards, version 2.x is capable of handling a mere 12MB of RAM and 255MB of disk storage. It is capable of hosting DOS, Mac, and OS/2 clients.

NetWare 3.x

Version 3.x adds many features, including the ability to use up to 4GB of RAM and 32TB of storage. It is a single-processor, 32-bit NOS that supports disk mirroring and uninterruptable power supply (UPS) monitoring for increased safety and security. Support for third-party plug-in-style programs called NetWare Loadable Modules (NLMs) allows other services to be added to the core NetWare operating system. NLMs add such things as backup programs, CD-ROM towers, and active-scanning virus protection programs.

NetWare 4.x

Version 4, introduced in 1993, adds many new features, including support for several types of new storage media such as CD-ROMs and optical disks, which had hitherto been too slow and nonstandardized for use in large networked environments. Other improvements in this version include enhanced security and, most importantly, a new directory service that replaced the bindery. This new service is called the NetWare Directory Service (NDS), and it incorporates the old bindery information into a new type of database built on the X.500 directory services protocol. We'll review this new feature in "A New Generation: NetWare 4.x & NDS" later in this introduction.

LAN-to-WAN Growth

In the early days of network computing, LANs were created to perform two basic tasks: share data files and connect to shared networked devices such as printers. Extremely small, peer-to-peer networks were easily created to perform these tasks, but they were slow, unsecure, and not very flexible. As businesses expanded or turned to computers to perform more and more tasks,

LANs came to rely on a more robust client-server model of computing with a centralized file server that could not only share data and other resources, but could execute shared programs as well.

Understanding Novell's Old LAN Concept

The earlier versions of NetWare helped to prepare the way for an explosion in the LAN population. Some might even argue that if it wasn't for Novell, there might not have been an explosion of LAN growth. The release of version 3.x (still used in tens of thousands of LANs) with the support for NLMs helped LAN administrators tackle specific network-related problems. NLMs enabled administrators to have more flexibility—and therefore control—over their environment, which was growing larger and wider. LANs that started out covering a single room now covered entire floors of buildings, and even buildings themselves. Not too long thereafter, LANs grew into WANs that covered business and college campuses, supporting not just shared files and printers, but mission-critical applications.

The approach Novell took toward coordinating multiple LANs is one that we call their "old" approach of a classic client-server model. Under this model there existed multiple NetWare servers within a LAN, typically separated along departmental lines. For example, users in the accounting department used one server while staff members of the research and development department had their own server. If someone from R & D needed access to data on the accounting server, the administrator would need to create a new user account. In this old approach, then, there existed no easy method to administer one set of user accounts that could be used on multiple servers. This "departmental server" approach wasn't capable of storing security, trustee, and resource information for users across multiple servers.

Fortunately, however, NetWare grew right along with the size and complexity of the LAN, growing and expanding to meet the needs of corporate networked computing. Versions 2.x and 3.x of NetWare performed all the basic tasks of an NOS very well, establishing NetWare as the workhorse of choice among LAN administrators. However, as the explosion of networked computing created a plethora of LANs in the late 1980s, a few years later there was an abundance of WANs that had to be connected as well. Users were often located on different LANs than the information to which they needed access. This scenario created duplication of effort for systems administrators, especially in the areas of account maintenance and password synchronization. The classic model of client/server was no longer working well and a new generation of computing, dubbed the intranet model of computing, was in demand.

A New Generation: NetWare 4.x & NDS

Version 4.x of Novell's NetWare began to address the problems associated with connecting intradepartmental users and multiple WANs, but it wasn't until version 4.11 and IntranetWare that a true intranet platform was developed, one that could meet the needs of businesses and organizations spoiled by the power and ease of use of the Internet.

Version 4.x of NetWare introduced a more powerful replacement to the flat-file bindery of earlier versions. NetWare Directory Services (NDS) is a relational database that functions in a tree-like hierarchy, with roots, branches, and a trunk. It enables access to a theoretically unlimited number of users of a NetWare 4.x or IntranetWare intranet, regardless of their physical location. NDS solves the problems of the old model by sharing the bindery information of multiple NetWare servers across servers, LANs, WANs, and intranets. This not only makes it possible to log in to any of a number of servers without having to create accounts for every user on each server, it also creates a system of fault tolerance among the servers because they each share the information, making a single point of failure impossible.

In addition to NDS, IntranetWare comes with two additional programs that allow you to tightly control incoming IP traffic and outgoing IPX/IP traffic. The IPX/IP Gateway works with NDS to control which nodes on your intranet have access to what services inside and outside your intranet. It also acts as a natural firewall by allowing you to restrict incoming IP access to servers on your intranet. Another feature that ships with IntranetWare is Novell's IP relay, which allows IPX-based segments of your intranet to communicate with one another by "tunneling" IPX packets using IP. This allows you to connect distant segments using leased lines or existing lines provided by your ISP.

The two main parts of the NDS "tree" are partitions and replicas. A partition is the entire tree, called the root partition, as well as the individual branches of the tree. Each partition is replicated on each member server that contains information on both the individual server and the entire tree. The strategy of partition and replication is similar to the strategy behind the creation of the Internet by the Department of Defense. The idea was to create a network divided into segments that could be taken out (as a result of nuclear war) without terminally disrupting the network as a whole. If a NetWare 4.x server is taken off the network, a user may still be authenticated and gain access to data and resources elsewhere on the network. Data contained in the NetWare Directory Database (NDD) includes, for all servers registered on the NDS tree, users' names, personal information, login scripts, password and security data, group information, and volume and printer information.

WAN to Intranet: Our Case Study

Intranets aren't built overnight, and the approach we'll be taking will be to expand an existing WAN into an intranet. We expect that you already have a network infrastructure with which to build your intranet, including a suitable server, workstations, network cabling, and networking devices to connect segments of a WAN across an intranet and onto the Internet. We're also assuming, of course, that you have substantial experience managing either Novell networks or are at least very experienced in networking technology. Most of you will have an existing NetWare-based LAN or WAN with a diverse population of workstations and networked devices.

Novell's Eight-Part Definition of an Intranet

We'll be referring to Novell's eight-part definition of an intranet throughout this book because these elements, when placed in the proper order, provide an excellent progression of all the parts that constitute the classic LAN-turned-intranet. The first of these elements are hallmarks of the traditional LAN:

- **File services:** the sharing of files and management of access rights by users.

- **Printing services:** the management of multiple printer resources.

Other elements point to the traits of a WAN:

- **Directory services:** the management of an intranet's user accounts and resources.

- **Security:** the management of system and user security rights and privileges.

- **Wide-area connectivity:** the ability to remotely access a server's resources.

- **Network management:** the ability to manage the server's resources from one or more locations.

Finally, services hereto associated with the Internet are what set the intranet apart from the WAN:

- **Web services:** the hosting of a Web site, including user accounts, CGI scripting, and security.

- **Messaging:** the hosting of electronic mail and interapplication communication.

Intranet Benefits

The most immediate benefit most people see to building an intranet is the increased capacity to communicate with resources located on distant portions of a network. This may be all that matters to the end user, but for network administrators there are multiple benefits. It may seem that building an intranet is a foregone conclusion, based on all the hype that appears in newspapers and on the evening news. But under the surface of all the clamoring there is a great deal of truth. The benefits include:

- Increased ease of user administration.
- Greater file system security and fault tolerance.
- Lower cost through using Internet standards.
- Expanded capacity for intranetwork communication.
- Greater access to more sources of data.
- Lower support costs.

Global Access: The Intranet/Internet Connection

Perhaps the greatest benefit to building an intranet is the increased access to information and resources available via the Internet. Because intranets built using IntranetWare are based upon open Internet standards and protocols, it is very easy to provide access to the Internet to some or all of your workstations and servers. Of course, your intranet could be a *closed intranet*, where no outgoing or incoming Internet access is afforded, or it could be somewhere in between.

Adding access to the Internet is relatively easy if your intranet is using the same tools and protocols as does the Internet. Sure, there will be a (sometimes large) fee to an Internet Service Provider (ISP), but the main cost for Internet access is the technical assistance provided to users to help them configure their workstations and load the right applications and to instruct them on how to productively use the Internet. Building an intranet provides most of these resources ahead of time, sometimes making the intranet/Internet connection as easy as throwing on a switch in a wiring closet. (It's true; we've seen it happen!)

What's Inside?

This book is designed to serve as a case study of a company, Rambell, Incorporated, that has handed its network management staff the task of building an intranet. Not everything relating to this task falls neatly into logical order for the purpose of this book, however, because the authors of intranet software are typically not authors of books! So, we've created an Introduction followed by five sections that cover everything you'll need to know to build an intranet using Novell's IntranetWare, and arranged the information so it can be easily referenced in the future. The sections are:

Section 1: Out of the Box

This section shows you how to install and configure IntranetWare, as well as explain critical NetWare concepts, create user accounts, log in scripts, and manage file and print services.

Chapter 1 covers everything you need to know to select and prepare an Intel-based computer for use as an IntranetWare server. All the basics are covered, including Intel microprocessor design, RAM configuration issues, bus types, and hard disk preparation.

Chapter 2 covers the actual installation and configuration of IntranetWare, including the requirements of the server and the different methods of installation. Once the installation is complete, you'll learn about the basic capabilities of the default installation.

Chapter 3 helps you get started with the critical concepts of NetWare 4.11 you need to understand, including the nature of network clients, how NetWare Directory Services is used to manage client access, administering IntranetWare using NWADMIN.EXE instead of SYSCON.EXE, and the basics of objects and login scripts.

Chapter 4 covers the basic tasks of NetWare administration including the creation, deletion, and management of users in your network. You will also be able to more easily manage how users interact with your network using other user-related objects such as groups and organizational roles.

Chapter 5 explores the powerful login script abilities built into NetWare 4.11. Through the use of a myriad of login script commands and identifier variables, you can easily customize the network environments for the users on your network through statements executed at login.

Chapter 6 provides you with information necessary to properly administer the file system. This chapter will help you understand how the file system integrates into the NDS tree through the NDS server and volume objects as well as file system security, trustee assignments, and effective rights.

Chapter 7 shows you, step by step, how to provide printing services. In this chapter you'll learn about standalone and network printing basics, including how to create and manage the print environment using Novell and third-party solutions.

Section 2: NetWare Directory Services

This section focuses on the power of Novell's NetWare Directory Services (NDS) as the key to providing intranet management services.

Chapter 8 explores the architecture of NDS, its services, critical concepts, structural design, and conventions.

Chapter 9 discusses NDS and security, including NDS versus file system security, rights, trustees, object and property rights, inheriting security rights, and network auditing of security.

Chapter 10 looks at NDS partitioning and replication. In this chapter we'll discuss the details of database partitioning, the role of NWADMIN.EXE in managing NDS partitions, and the uses for partition replicas, including creating replica rings as a form of fault tolerance.

Chapter 11 discusses the role of NDS and its importance in time synchronization among IntranetWare servers. Time servers, default and custom time synchronization, and time server configuration are all discussed in this chapter.

Chapter 12 shows how to merge NDS trees among NetWare 4.x and IntranetWare servers using the Merge utility.

Chapter 13 discusses the various NDS utilities available to help you manage your NDS trees. You'll learn how to effectively use DSREPAIR.NLM to repair damaged databases, protect your NDS databases using SBACKUP.NLM, as well as how to use Novell's NetWare Application Launcher to manage applications, program groups, and data files for Windows users.

Chapter 14 uses a case study to illustrate the planning of a complex NDS tree. Topics covered include planning the structure, partitioning, replication, and time synchronization of a tree for a large corporate intranet.

Section 3: Novell LAN Services

This section covers the traditional local area network services provided through IntranetWare, including client software installation, NetWare architecture and management, and connecting LANs together to create wide area networks.

Chapter 15 covers the installation and configuration of the 16-bit DOS and Windows 3.x workstation VLM client software.

Chapter 16 covers the installation and configuration of the 32-bit Windows 95, NT, and Mac OS workstation clients.

Chapter 17 explains the architecture of the NetWare 4.11 server, including the role of the core operating system files and additions to the operating system, NetWare Loadable Modules. We'll also cover how disk drivers and network cards interface with the server, as well as how IntranetWare manages memory, details of the file system, and the NetWare Core Protocol Suite.

Chapter 18 shows you how to manage a NetWare 4.11 server using INSTALL.NLM to change the server's installation options and edit system files; how to use SERVERMAN.EXE to optimize the server's performance; how to use MONITOR.NLM to monitor the server's performance and track performance statistics; how to configure your network using INETCFG.NLM, as well as how to utilize other server console tools to manage your IntranetWare server.

Chapter 19 explores NetWare/IP, Novell's TCP/IP stack that allows IPX packets to be encapsulated within TCP/IP for use on, and across, IP-based networks.

Chapter 20 explores wide area network (WAN) connectivity among servers, as well as client access to these servers. Topics include the different network mediums for connecting WANs, Novell's IPX/IP Gateway, and IP Relay.

Section 4: Novell Intranet Services

This section covers how to install and configure Web, FTP, and other additional intranet services.

Chapter 21 explains the features of version 3.0 of the Novell Web Server, then shows you how to install and configure basic Web services. You'll learn how to use the Web Manager program to add directories, enable user directories, restrict access, and create "virtual" Web servers.

Chapter 22 goes into more advanced Web server management tasks, including managing the Web server's configuration files, MIME types, user files, and log files.

Chapter 23 covers how to add Secure Sockets Layers to your Web server to provide industry-standard secure access to your Web server's documents and resources, as well as how to use standard access control to restrict access to your Web server by IP number, host, and domain names.

Chapter 24 explains how to provide quality content to your intranet's Web server. You'll learn all about how the HyperText Transport Protocol works, the different types of URL, the structure of HTML, how, and where, to add documents, how to create clickable image maps and server-side includes, and how to browse your NDS tree over the Web.

Chapter 25 covers how to use Common Gateway Interfaces to add interactivity to your Web server. You'll see how to make forms using BASIC, Perl, Java, and more.

Chapter 26 discusses how to add FTP services to your IntranetWare server so users can upload and download data from their own directories and from public directories. We'll show you how to install, configure, and manage FTP services, as well as protect your FTP server using NDS.

Server Hardware & Software Requirements

IntranetWare servers and clients run on a variety of platforms, and Novell is constantly updating this list. Check the Novell home page at http://www.novell.com for the latest list of supported platforms before purchasing new hardware or installing IntranetWare on your network to ensure compatibility.

Server Requirements

IntranetWare may be run on a variety of IBM PC-compatible clones, but not any other platform at this time. Novell provides a system of approval for hardware manufacturers who want to advertise their servers as NetWare-approved servers, so if you are in the market for a new server ask your hardware vendor for a list of these servers. In general, however, IntranetWare requires the following:

- **Processor:** One to four 80386, 80486, Pentium, or Pentium Pro processors. Intel's MMX technology has not yet been tested for use with IntranetWare at the time of this writing.
- **Data Bus:** Most ISA, EISA, PCI, or Micro Channel busses are compatible with IntranetWare.
- **Network Interface Card:** Dozens of cards have been approved by Novell for use in it servers, including ODI- and NE2000-compatible cards.
- **WAN Adapters:** Any WAN adapter can be used provided it is ODI- or AIO-compatible.

Client Requirements

NetWare has become the industry leader for network operating systems in part because it supports such a wide variety of clients. The following client operating systems and hardware platforms are supported at this time:

Operating Systems

- Mac OS System 7.1 and above
- PC-DOS
- MS-DOS
- Windows 3.x
- Windows 95
- Windows NT 3.51 and above
- OS/2

Hardware Platforms

- Apple Macintosh or Macintosh clone
- IBM XT, AT, PS/2, or compatible clone
- Multiple UNIX platforms from Sun Microsystems, Hewlett-Packard, SCO UNIX, and IBM RS 6000

Conventions Used in This Book

As an experienced computer user, you have no doubt encountered multiple ways that authors of books, software manuals, and magazine articles describe how to complete an operation. Experience tells us that it's better that we tell you up front what we'll be doing so you'll know what it looks like when you read it in print.

- When we are showing you what to type, we'll use boldface type, as in:

```
a:\install.exe
LOAD LONG.NAM
```

- When we're listing computer code or Uniform Resource Locators (URLs), which you may or may not need to type, we'll use a monospaced font and set it apart from the body text as in:

```
<title>This is the Code</title>
require "/local/web/bin/cgi-lib.pl";
http://www.rambell.com/
```

- When describing a menu item to be selected on your computer instead of illustrating it with a screen shot or figure, we'll separate the steps using the filter symbol ("|"), sometime called a "pipe." For example, to describe how to "save a document using a different filename" in Microsoft Word, we'd tell you to choose File | Save As, or press the F12 key.

■ Finally, when listing directory and file names, we'll use all caps to pre-serve the meaning of an example. DOS, Windows 3.x, Windows 95, Windows NT, and the Mac OS all use different capitalization standards throughout their operating systems and applications, and our copy editor and proof reader will probably be glad when this project is over! When referring to volume names and paths on an IntranetWare server, we'll use all caps even though an adjacent screen shot or figure may show the same information using all lower case, or even worse, mixed case. For example, the Web server software will be located in the follow-ing directory:

SYS:WEB

Contacting the Authors

We'd like to hear from you. If you're in the cyberhood, drop us a line at our Ventana e-mail addresses:

■ HeathRamsey@vmedia.com

■ MarkBell@vmedia.com

We both have full-time jobs in addition to writing several books a year, so hearing from our readers is a real surge and helps to keep us going. Rants and raves are both welcomed, but raves are preferred.

Moving On

This book will lead you through a complete installation of IntranetWare from the ground up. But since many of you will be upgrading from an earlier ver-sion of NetWare, we'll endeavor to point out upgrade-specific information where necessary. There are so many new features to IntranetWare, so your best bet might be to read all the way through, instead of skipping to a specific section or chapter. So, without further ado, let's move on to see how Rambell's network manager, John Doe, approaches the task of building an intranet with Novell's IntranetWare.

SECTION I
Out of the Box

1

Preparing the Server

"Hi. My name is John Doe, and I work for Rambell, Inc. We are a small company of 10 employees that sells widgets. We have traditionally been a PC shop, and just recently we have installed a local area network to provide file and printer sharing. This has been adequate for what we need to do, but our business is really growing. We need to look at ways to prepare for growth.

"My boss has given me the charge of upgrading the computer network at Rambell to not only provide the file and printer sharing we have now, but also to provide a suitable infrastructure for the future growth in computing needs we are anticipating, including World Wide Web access, FTP services, and WAN connectivity."

John's situation is not an uncommon one in today's day and age. Many companies large and small are looking for more in a network operating system than the traditional file sharing and print services of yesterday's local area network. Today's local area networks should be able to do much more, such as:

- Provide greater file system security and fault tolerance.
- Allow users to access multiple sources of data transparently.
- Provide centralized network administration and management.
- Interface with other types of networks efficiently using multiple protocols.
- Provide a diverse set of user services from traditional file and print sharing to World Wide Web document serving and File Transfer Protocol services.

Today's network should be able to allow a user to access many different resources regardless of where those resources are located. It should also not matter from where the user is trying to access resources; it should be transparent to the user.

Novell's IntranetWare accomplishes just that. IntranetWare is actually a bundle of several Novell products, which together provide an incredibly flexible and complete network solution. IntranetWare comes packaged with:

- NetWare 4.11
- NetWare Directory Services (NDS)
- NetWare Print Services for UNIX
- FTP services
- NetWare Web Server
- NetWare MultiProtocol Router
- IPX/IP Gateway
- WAN Extensions
- Netscape Navigator
- NetWare/IP
- Client software

Together, NetWare 4.11 and NDS provide a whole new concept of the local area network. With NetWare 4.11's ability to perform the traditional file and print sharing coupled with NDS's advanced security and centralization of network resources, Novell has revolutionized the way people will think about networking. Gone are the days of remembering multiple IDs and passwords; here instead are the days of complete access to network resources with one login.

NetWare Print Services for UNIX and FTP services are integrally intertwined with one another. Since TCP/IP-based file *and* print sharing cannot be done with just one of these products, both are installed on NetWare 4.11 servers to provide this secure and robust networking environment.

NetWare Print Services for UNIX is a bundle in itself. When loaded on the server, it integrates file and print services between the UNIX and NetWare environments. UNIX users are able to print to NetWare printers, and NetWare users are able to print to UNIX printers. Likewise, users needing to share files between NetWare and UNIX platforms will be able to exchange information through FTP services which are provided with NetWare Print Services for UNIX.

The NetWare Web Server provides World Wide Web services on your NetWare server. When loaded, it allows you to host a Web site with HTML document serving, CGI scripting, and user security because it interfaces with NDS. The NetWare Web Server is explored in Section IV, "Novell Intranet Services."

Also included in IntranetWare is a CD-ROM called the Internet Access Server. This CD-ROM in turn includes the NetWare MultiProtocol Router, IPX/IP Gateway, WAN Extensions, and Netscape Navigator. These products serve as the basis for connecting your network to the Internet and providing your users the ability to browse the Internet.

The NetWare/IP product allows workstation clients to communicate with NetWare servers via IPX encapsulated in IP instead of using IPX natively. If running multiple protocols on your network is a concern, NetWare/IP will allow you to run just the TCP/IP protocol, yet still be backward compatible with IPX applications and services. NetWare/IP is discussed in Chapter 19.

IntranetWare comes packaged with the ability to interface with a wide variety of network clients. You can easily connect DOS, Windows 3.x, Windows 95, Windows NT, Mac OS, and OS/2 workstations to your IntranetWare network using the NetWare clients provided with the operating system. The NetWare clients are covered in more detail in Chapters 15 and 16.

Some companies may only require the NetWare 4.11 and NDS portions of IntranetWare to meet their needs. So why purchase the whole package? The cost for just the server component alone (NetWare 4.11, of which NDS is a critical part) is the same as that of the whole package. So in addition to NetWare 4.11, you receive all of the components to add into your system, all at the same cost! To allow for future growth and networking opportunities, it makes sense to buy IntranetWare even though you may not use the complete package. IntranetWare has the capability to fulfill a wide variety of networking needs.

So where do we start? In order to use any of IntranetWare's bundled products, you first need to have a NetWare server installed. The first step is to select your server and ensure that it meets the minimum hardware specifications for NetWare 4.11. Once selected, the server needs to be prepared properly to ready it for the operating system. You also need to choose the method of installation before the operating system can be loaded onto the new server.

Selecting a Server

There are many factors that you should take into account before selecting a server on which to install NetWare 4.11. How many users are you going to connect to the server immediately after you bring it up? How many potential users could you have connecting to the server? What types of services are you going to need from the server? How many types of services are you going to provide with the server? Are the types of network services to be provided solely for internal use, or are external services like World Wide Web and FTP going to be offered as well?

The more services you plan to provide to your network, the more server power you'll need. For example, you'll need a more powerful server to provide both file/print services and Web services than you will for just file/print services alone. This is because you will need more processing power to serve files to your normal users, *and* the large number of potential users from out on the Internet who could request documents at any given time.

The server is the single most important machine you are going to have on your network. It needs to have enough power to handle all of the services you are going to be providing immediately. It also needs to have enough computer power to handle the growth of the network for the near future. It is a good idea to buy the server with the most computing power you can afford.

Unfortunately, most people are limited by their finances and can't buy the top-of-the-line hardware. We all have to make some compromises in server hardware to make the server affordable. There are essentially six major components to a server system that affect the performance of the machine:

- The central processing unit (CPU)
- Random access memory (RAM)
- The hardware bus
- The hard disk controller
- The hard disk
- The Network Interface Card (NIC)

Figure 1-1 shows how these major components interrelate.

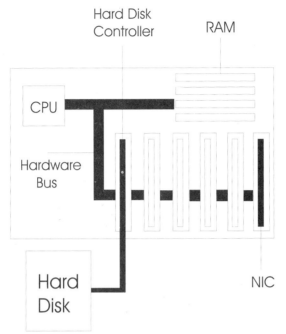

Figure 1-1: Performance-affecting file server components.

The Central Processing Unit

Best summed up, the *CPU* is the brains of the server. All of the tasks that need processing require the services of the CPU. From program execution to mathematical calculations to peripheral device requests, the CPU does it all. Obviously, the faster the CPU, the faster the processing on the server will occur. This does not necessarily mean that the server's overall performance will increase; the other five components on the server factor into that equation. But for the most part, increasing the speed of the processor will increase the performance of the machine.

There have been six generations of IBM-compatible CPUs. It all started with the Intel 8086 processor in 1978. This chip had 16-bit internal registers, a 16-bit data bus, and operated at 10 megahertz speed. It was unlike the other chips of that era, which used an 8-bit internal register, an 8-bit data bus, and operated at 8 MHz clock speed. The 8086 was also very expensive. As a result, Intel provided the alternative 8088 processor with 8-bit registers and an 8-bit data bus. It was with the Intel 8088 processor that IBM introduced the first PC in 1981.

As of today, Intel's most recent CPU is the Pentium Pro processor. It has 32-bit internal registers, a 64-bit data bus, and operates at 150-200 MHz! Table 1-1 provides a history of the six generations of IBM-compatible CPUs. The most important fields to look at in this table are the processor's Clock Speeds and Data Bus. They play a significant role in assessing a processor's performance.

Year	Processor	Internal Registers	Data Bus	Clock Speeds (MHz)
1978	Intel 8086	16-bit	16-bit	4.77-10
1979	Intel 8088	8-bit	8-bit	4.77-8
1982	Intel 80286	16-bit	16-bit	6-12
1985	Intel 80386DX	32-bit	32-bit	16-33
1988	Intel 80386SX	32-bit	16-bit	16-33
1989	Intel 80486DX	32-bit	32-bit	25-50
1991	Intel 80486SX	32-bit	32-bit	25-50
1993	Intel Pentium	32-bit	64-bit	60-133
1995	Intel Pentium Pro	32-bit	64-bit	150-200

Table 1-1: Six generations of PC CPUs.

The SX/DX Difference

You might notice that the 80386 and 80486 have two different flavors. One is the SX chip and the other is the DX chip. Intel first released the DX chip in both the 80386 and 80486 CPU. However, Intel decided to release a less expensive version, the SX chip.

The 80386SX is the same chip as the 80386DX; however, it only has a 16-bit data bus. The 80486SX is the same chip as the 80486DX, but it doesn't have the math coprocessor. Thus, the DX chip will provide much better performance on your server than the SX chip.

The *processor speed* or *clock speed* determines the number of processing cycles per second that the CPU is capable of handling. The higher the rating for the clock speed, the faster the processor is.

The other factor in the performance of the CPU is the data bus. The *data bus* provides the physical path from the CPU to the CPU's immediate peripheral devices (this includes memory). The size of the bus is always a multiple of 8 bits because 8 bits form the smallest recognizable piece of data, the byte.

The data bus is very important because it determines just how fast data can be transferred from the CPU to the other devices in the machine. A larger data bus will provide much faster data transfer than a smaller one. This is analogous to an eight-lane superhighway versus a two-lane country road. If you put the same amount of traffic on the two roads, the traffic is going to flow better on the superhighway.

Let's say you want to transfer 1 kilobyte of data from memory (RAM) through the data bus to the CPU. Since 1 kilobyte of data is 1024 bits of information, it could be moved in 16 processor cycles if the data bus was 64 bits wide; however, it would take 64 processor cycles to move the same amount of data to the CPU using a 16-bit data bus. Remember, this is just for sheer data transfer. That does not even count processing time on that data!

What Is a 486DX-4/100 Processor?

Perhaps you have seen a machine touted as having a 486DX-4/100 processor. It means that the machine's CPU is running at 100 MHz; however, not all is as it seems. That 100 MHz rating is for the internal processing on the CPU. The rating is *not* for the data bus. This means that data transfer will still occur at the regular data bus rate (which in this case is 25 MHz), but the processing on that data once it reaches the internal registers will occur at 100 MHz.

Servers generally don't do much in the way of internal CPU processing. They tend to do much more data transfer over the data bus. This means you will get much better performance out of your server if you purchase a server whose processor has not been doubled.

To recap, higher clock speeds and wider data buses are the key to CPU performance. Note that IntranetWare and its core operating system, NetWare 4.11, will only run on the 80386 CPU and better.

Tip

NetWare 4.11 will run on the 80386, 80486, Pentium, and Pentium Pro processors—it will perform best on the Pentium and Pentium Pro.

Random Access Memory

Random access memory (RAM) is the area of a computer that is often referred to as volatile memory. This is because it is the temporary storage area for data as it travels from the hard disk to the CPU. When data is requested by a program, the data is loaded from the hard drive and stored in memory because it is much faster to read data from RAM than it is to read it from the hard drive. That is why machines with larger amounts of RAM perform better. They can store more information in volatile memory, which results in faster data access times.

In terms of our overall server performance, it is our RAM's speed that impacts us most. Older machines used 80 nanosecond RAM. It is more common today to have machines with 70ns and 60ns memory speeds. This means that to access data stored in memory, there is a delay of x nanoseconds between the lookup request and the time the data is actually put on the data bus, where x is the speed of the RAM.

Parity vs. Non-Parity RAM

Parity is an error-detecting method used to prevent memory corruption. There are two types of parity—odd and even parity. If a byte of data (comprising 8 individual bits that can be set to the value 1 or 0) is stored in parity memory, it actually occupies 9 bits of storage space in RAM. When a byte of data is written to RAM, this parity bit is set based upon the number of 1s and 0s contained in the byte of data. When the data is read from RAM, the byte of data is compared with the parity bit to ensure that no change in data occurred while in volatile memory. This extra bit is built into the hardware on the RAM chip.

RAM chips also come without the extra parity bit. This is called nonparity RAM. Since some machines require that extra bit to check for parity, nonparity RAM usually has a parity generator on the chip. A byte of data is written normally to RAM, but the parity bit is generated on the fly as the byte of data is read from memory.

Because the parity is generated when the data is read, there is no way to tell if the data stored in memory has been corrupted. This could cause unpredictable and undesirable results on your server.

Tip

Since your server is one of your more critical pieces of hardware (if not the most critical), it is generally recommended that you do not purchase nonparity RAM for it.

To get the best performance from your server, parity RAM is recommended along with the fastest RAM available. Also, you should get as much RAM as you can afford because the quantity of RAM definitely impacts the performance of the server.

The Hardware Bus

The *hardware bus* is the component of the server responsible for transferring data between the peripheral expansion slots and the other components in the server (including the CPU and memory). The hardware bus should not be confused with the data bus referred to in "The Central Processing Unit" earlier in this chapter.

The hardware bus is responsible for transferring data from expansion cards like network interface cards (NICs) and disk controllers to the other devices in the machine. Thus the bus plays a critical role in the function of a server. Without it, the data would not be able to get from the network or the disk drive to the CPU. A slow bus can cause poor server performance.

Industry Standard Architecture Bus

Much like CPUs have evolved over time, hardware buses have evolved as well. The first IBM microcomputer (the IBM XT) used an 8-bit bus for data transfer. When IBM released its IBM AT computer with the 80286 processor, it had a 16-bit bus. This bus has pretty much become the standard today. It is called the Industry Standard Architecture (ISA) bus.

The ISA bus has a clock speed of 8 MHz. This clock rating is evaluated the same way that the CPU clock speed is evaluated, which means that the ISA bus is capable of over eight million processing cycles per second.

Remember, the ISA bus is a 16-bit bus and still is a popular bus for many computer systems, including the 80486, Pentium, and Pentium Pro, all of which have much larger data buses. This means that there is a waste of processor time as the CPU waits for the data to be transferred from its local data bus to the peripheral devices via the ISA bus.

Micro Channel Architecture Bus

As processors grew and matured, it was evident that the hardware bus technology needed to grow as well. In 1987, IBM began to manufacture PCs with its own proprietary hardware bus. This bus was called the Micro Channel Architecture (MCA) bus. The MCA bus is better in many ways than the ISA bus because it is a 32-bit bus that operates at 10 MHz. It is also compatible with expansion cards that require a 16-bit bus.

The MCA bus also has a feature called *bus mastering* that it uses to help with the data transfer rates. Although the clock speed of the bus is only 10 MHz, an MCA bus can achieve data transfer rates of up to 40 megabits per second.

Unfortunately, IBM decided to keep this technology proprietary and did not share its design with any of its competitors. The MCA bus has really taken the back seat to another comparable bus that was developed at the same time.

Extended Industry Standard Architecture Bus

Also in 1987, a consortium of PC makers released a new hardware bus technology called the Extended Industry Standard Architecture (EISA) bus. The EISA bus was developed as an alternative to the IBM technology that was prevalent during the 1980s.

EISA's name pretty much describes its basic architecture. It is an extension of the original ISA bus. Like the ISA bus, EISA operates at 8 MHz clock speed, but it is a 32-bit-wide bus. It also uses bus mastering to achieve higher data transfer rates. EISA is capable of a 32 megabits per second data transfer rate despite its 8 MHz clock.

Local Bus Technology

In the past few years, the speed of the CPU has grown at an unbelievable rate. Just 5 years ago in 1991, the fastest chip was 33 MHz. The latest crop of CPUs have broken the 200 MHz mark! But that really doesn't do much good if the hardware bus cannot handle all of that information. Think of a water main 2 feet in diameter through which water is flowing freely. As you travel down the pipe, the diameter suddenly decreases to 4 inches. This is in effect what is happening in today's computers where the hardware bus is meeting the CPU's data bus.

To combat this problem, a technology called *local bus* was developed. Certain expansion slots on the motherboard have direct access to the CPU. In effect, the peripherals in these special slots become directly part of the CPU's data bus. Note that not every expansion slot has this benefit. Local bus technology is used in conjunction with older hardware bus technology to provide a cost-effective solution to the data transfer problem experienced in today's faster machines.

There are two popular local bus technologies that are prevalent today. One is the Video Electronics Standards Association (VESA) bus. It is also called the VL-Bus. The other is the Peripheral Component Interface (PCI) bus. In a NetWare server, the local bus technology can be used for disk controllers and NICs to provide much greater data transfer rates than you could get with an ISA, EISA, or MCA hardware bus.

The Hard Disk Controller

The *hard disk controller* plays a very important role in the overall performance of the server. The controller is responsible for writing data to and retrieving data from the hard disks themselves. There are two key characteristics of the hard disk controller that determine what effect this component will have on the server performance: the controller's bus architecture and hard disk interface.

As discussed in the previous section on hardware buses, the controller's bus architecture will play an important role in server performance. An ISA hard disk controller will transfer data between the hard disk and memory much slower than an EISA or MCA hard disk controller. A PCI or VESA hard disk controller will have the best performance.

The other factor that affects server performance is the hard disk interface that the controller uses to "speak" to the device it controls. NetWare currently supports five of these interface "languages": Modified Frequency Modulation (MFM), Enhanced Small Device Interface (ESDI), Integrated Drive Electronics (IDE), Enhanced Integrated Drive Electronics (EIDE), and Small Computer System Interface (SCSI).

Each of these interface technologies differs in the maximum capacity of the attached device, the number of devices each controller can support, and the transfer rate at which data is transferred from the device.

SCSI and EIDE are the most prevalent interfaces today. Since they can accommodate much larger device capacities, they are the interfaces of choice. EIDE controllers can handle up to 4 devices (depending upon the controller) with a maximum device capacity of 2 gigabytes (GB). SCSI controllers can handle up to 7 or 15 devices (again, depending upon the controller) with a maximum individual device capacity of 9GB. The data transfer rate for SCSI controllers is generally better than that of EIDE controllers. The latest SCSI controllers support data transfer rates of up to 40MB/sec.

For best server performance, you should get the fastest SCSI controller you can get. Not only will this allow you fast data transfer rates, it will allow plenty of room for device expansion. Many other types of peripheral devices come with SCSI interfaces, including tape drives and CD-ROM drives. An SCSI controller will make your server more flexible and will give you more options in the future.

The Hard Disk

The *hard disk* is the physical medium on which all data is stored. Everything is stored on the hard disk from the operating system files to NDS information to user data. All things that are written to the server are written to the hard disk.

As stated in the previous section, the hard disks interface with the hard disk controller to provide a data path for the server. When a read request is issued, the CPU instructs the hard disk controller to retrieve the requested information. The controller then interfaces with the hard disk to retrieve the information required.

In terms of performance, it is much slower to retrieve information from the hard disks than it is to retrieve from RAM. That is why a large quantity of RAM is so important in a server. However, it is inevitable that data is going to need to be retrieved from the hard disk, so it is important to get hard disks that have small access times.

The *access time* is the total time required to retrieve the requested data from the hard drive. It is actually composed of two smaller times—the read time and the seek time. The *read time* is the time it takes to actually read the requested data from the hard drive once the data is located on the physical media.

Because the heads of the hard disk are usually not directly over the data that is requested, there is a delay period while the disks spin and the heads line up over the spot where the data is requested. This is called the *seek time*. Each time data is accessed on the disk drive, there is an initial seek time to locate the data followed by a read time as the data is actually read from the disk. Adding these two times together gives the total access time for the hard drive.

In comparison, the seek time is much greater than the read time. It is so much greater, in fact, that the read time is negligible. In effect, the access time is the seek time necessary to locate the data on the physical media of the hard disk. For best server performance, you should get hard drives that have the lowest access times.

It should be noted that the type of hard disk controller you select will dictate which type of hard disk you should use. An SCSI hard disk controller must use SCSI hard drives. You cannot mix and match hard disk controller and hard disk technology types.

The Network Interface Card

If the server were to be standing alone, the previously defined components would have dictated the performance of the machine; however, the server is an integral part of a computer network. It needs to be connected to the network to accomplish its function, which means an NIC needs to be installed.

Just like the hard disk controller, the NIC will fit into an expansion slot on the motherboard. This also means that the speed of data transfer from the network to the server's memory is dependent upon the hardware bus. Thus, the bus architecture of the network card will greatly affect the performance of the server *as the user perceives it*.

Do you remember the discussion about the data bus/hardware bus interface in "The Hardware Bus" earlier in this chapter? A 16-bit hardware bus cannot take full advantage of a CPU's 64-bit data bus because it would take four processing cycles of the hardware bus to move data from the data bus to the peripheral devices on the machine. The same holds true for the data path at the hardware bus/NIC interface. It is important to get a network card with a wide bus architecture. Preferably, your NIC should be PCI or EISA, at the least.

From the user's perspective, the performance of the server will also be related to the overall speed of your network. In a lot of cases, you will not have control over the network media or topology; however, if you are building the network from scratch, it would be a good idea to research network topologies very carefully before you implement your network.

Even though these six server components are separate entities that perform different machine functions, each component affects the overall performance of the server. If one component is not able to handle the demands of the server, the other components cannot compensate for it. The effect is a degradation in server performance. This is often called a hardware *bottleneck*.

For example, the high performance server with the 8-bit network card described earlier in this chapter has a bottleneck. The bottleneck is the 8-bit network card. Assuming the server had an EISA hardware bus, replacing that component with an EISA network card could drastically increase server performance.

It is important to consider hardware bottlenecks when purchasing the hardware for your server. You want to make sure you get the most performance for your money. Quite often, though, we must sacrifice components we would like to have in our servers because of cost constraints. Do not cut corners with RAM and hard disk technology when trying to decide where you might save money. Get as much RAM as you can along with enough SCSI drives to provide your users with enough disk space to last.

IntranetWare Hardware Requirements

While you are figuring out just which machine to purchase or implement, you need to be aware of the minimum hardware requirements for the IntranetWare server. NetWare 4.11 must be run on the following hardware platform:

- A PC with a 80386, 80486, Pentium, or Pentium Pro processor
- At least 20MB of RAM
- At least one NIC
- A 15MB DOS partition
- A NetWare partition with at least 100MB of disk space

These are the bare minimums; there are, however, a few issues that need to be addressed. The following sections cover those issues.

Hard Disk Capacity & RAM

Ensure that you have enough hard disk capacity for the needs of your network. As mentioned, you need at least 15MB for the DOS partition on the server and 100MB space for the NetWare partition to hold the operating system files. You will need an additional 60MB on the SYS volume if you want to install the online documentation. Beyond that, you will need to provide sufficient capacity for application and user data space on the server. Plan ahead for the needs of your network.

It is also important to know that the hard disk capacity plays a role in just how much RAM you are required to have in the server. Here's how you calculate how much RAM you will need for your hard disk capacity:

1. Multiply your hard disk capacity (in megabytes) by 0.008.

2. Add this number to the minimum RAM required for the NetWare 4.11 server.

3. Add an additional 1-4MB of RAM for optimal performance.

Let's calculate how much RAM would be required for a server with a hard disk capacity of 1GB. Remember that 1GB of disk space equals 1024MB: (1024MB X 0.008) + 20MB + 4MB = 32.192MB RAM.

In calculations with memory, you always round up when you finish because RAM only comes in megabyte quantities. This particular server with 1GB of disk space would require 33MB RAM.

Remember, the calculation is really only a rough estimate of RAM required for a machine. The type of files that are going to be stored on the server will have a direct impact on the memory required, as will the number of other IntranetWare features you are going to load on the server. In this example, you would probably find you needed more than 33MB RAM for the best performance.

CD-ROM Drive

In the past, versions of NetWare 2.x and NetWare 3.x have come on low- and high-density floppy disks. NetWare 3.12 was shipped on CD-ROM as well. With the release of NetWare 4.x, Novell shipped the operating system on CD-ROM only. This holds true for IntranetWare.

To install IntranetWare, access to a CD-ROM drive that can read ISO 9660 formatted CD-ROM disks is required. The CD-ROM does not necessarily have to be connected to your server. In some cases you might be able to install IntranetWare from another server; however, you will initially need to one way or another read the files off the CD-ROM.

Preparing to Install IntranetWare

IntranetWare installation really involves two steps. The first step is installing the network operating system on the server. The second step is installing the client software on the workstation machines. The second step is briefly discussed in Chapter 2. A more thorough discussion of the client software is given in Chapters 15 and 16.

Before you begin installing the core operating system, NetWare 4.11, it is important to make sure that you have some things in place. The following list outlines steps you should take before preparing the server:

1. Install the NIC and connect it to the network.

2. Connect a UPS to the server hardware (optional).

You will need to have the NIC installed in the server to provide network connectivity. You also need to have the physical network media in place. This includes the NICs for the client workstations, the network cabling, and the hubs to connect all of the machine together.

In a large university or corporation, the network infrastructure is often already in place, and the network administrator will only need to plug into the existing cabling. If this is the case, it is important to know what the existing network topology is. This will help you in the purchase of your NIC for the server and the workstations.

Since your server is also a critical piece of equipment, it is a good idea to get an uninterrupted power supply (UPS) for it. A UPS plugs into the wall electrical outlet, and the server plugs into the UPS. The UPS provides a constant power source for the server and protects the server from power surges and spikes. Also, the UPS will provide battery power to the server in the event that the power goes out. Although once activated, the battery will not last forever (on average it is 15 minutes), it lasts long enough to gracefully shut down the server to prevent data corruption.

Before you actually install IntranetWare, there are a few things you need to do. We have provided a short checklist to help you prepare for NetWare 4.11 server installation:

1. Set up the server.

2. Gather important server information.

3. Gather technical manuals and required software.

4. Create the server's DOS partition.

5. Edit the DOS startup files.

Once these steps are complete, it is just a matter of choosing the method of installation you will use to install the core operating system of IntranetWare, NetWare 4.11.

Set Up the Server

Setting up the server is probably the easiest part of the entire installation. You will want to make sure the server works properly before trying to install IntranetWare. If you have not installed the NIC at this point, it is time to do so. Open up the machine and insert the NIC in an expansion slot. Unfortunately, it really is not as easy as that to install a NIC, as many PC users know. There are many things that you need to be aware of when installing a NIC. You will want to make sure that the NIC is configured for a free interrupt (IRQ) and port address. Consult your NIC's manual for help with the card installation. Once the NIC has been installed, turn the server on and bring it up. Make sure the server correctly performs its power on self-test (POST). Verify the hard drives are working properly. Once you are confident the server hardware functions properly, it is time to move on to the next step.

Gather Important Server Information

During the installation of NetWare 4.11, you'll be prompted for certain bits of information concerning your CPU, your hard disk controller, and your NIC. More often than not, the information you need about these cards can be found in the documentation that comes with the server and the NIC. Sometimes, you will need to actually open up the machine to get the information you need. You can always proceed with the installation, reach a point where you don't know a card setting, abort the installation, find the card setting, and start over. This is time consuming, though; it's easier to just gather all the information you need up front.

Tip

Gathering the important server information ahead of time will make the installation of NetWare 4.11 much easier.

Before installing IntranetWare, get the appropriate information from the CPU, disk controller, and NIC. The information you'll need about the CPU is the type (80386, 80486, Pentium, or Pentium Pro) and the speed (33 MHz, 50 MHz, 66 MHz, and so forth). Although this information is not critical to the installation of NetWare 4.11, it is helpful. Through a NetWare server utility called SPEED, you will be able to ascertain if NetWare is using your CPU optimally.

Since your hard disk controller and NIC control the disk and network access on the server, NetWare needs very specific information about them. There is also some other information that NetWare does not necessarily need, but it will be beneficial if you keep it handy.

For the hard disk controller, the most important information to know is:

■ Type of interface (MFM, ESDI, IDE, EIDE, SCSI, etc.)

■ Controller interrupt and port information

■ Slot number

■ Controller manufacturer and model

You must know the type of interface the hard disk controller is using so that you can load the appropriate disk driver in NetWare. Without this information, NetWare will be unable to communicate with the hard disks.

With certain interface technologies, you will be required to provide controller interrupt and port information, which NetWare needs to know in order to communicate with the physical hard disks. Without this information, the physical disks will be inaccessible to NetWare. Consult the documentation that came with the hard disk controller.

The third item, slot number, is really only required for those buses that use bus mastering (like EISA and PCI). However, you may be prompted to input the slot number at some point during installation.

The NIC requires that you know even more information about the hardware. You will need to know certain network information at the same time:

■ Interrupt

■ Port

■ Memory address

■ DMA channel

■ Hardware address

■ NIC manufacturer and model

■ Slot number

■ Network frame type

Most of this information should be provided by the manufacturer in the NIC's documentation. Because most of these settings are configurable, make a note if you have changed any from the default factory setting.

The last two items in the list are pieces of information that are not provided by the manufacturer of the card because they deal with your specific environment. Make note of the slot number if you are using a hardware bus that has bus mastering (EISA, MCA, PCI). Also, if you are plugging your server into an existing network infrastructure, you must find out which network frame type you will be using.

Gather Technical Manuals & Required Software

In addition to all of the information we gathered in the last section, it is a good idea to have by your side all of the documentation that came with the server. We have installed many servers, and more often than not, we have had to reference these manuals during the server installation.

The technical manuals of note are the hard disk controller manual (that should have come with your server) and the NIC manual. They are invaluable as reference tools, and they are often able to provide that one piece of information that will make or break a server install.

The hard disk controller and NIC most likely shipped with some software. This software will include drivers for the hardware on various operating system platforms. NetWare 4.11 already supports many hard disk controllers and NICs out of the box; however, if the driver necessary for your hardware does not come with NetWare 4.11, you will need to load it from the disks that came with the products.

Is My Hardware NetWare Compatible?

Quite often when you purchase hardware, you will see a small red NetWare "yes" label attached to the box or included somewhere in the documentation. The NetWare label will usually say one of three things:

- "It runs with NetWare" means the manufacturer claims this product will run with NetWare. It has been tested by the manufacturer, but it is not supported by Novell.

- "NetWare Tested and Approved" means that Novell has thoroughly tested the product, and it meets Novell's standards for NetWare quality. The results of those tests are available through Novell.

- "NetWare Ready" means that the product has been tested by Novell, and the hardware's drivers are shipped with the NetWare operating system.

Not only should you have the drivers for your hardware handy, you should also gather all of your IntranetWare software at the same time. IntranetWare comes packaged with four CD-ROMs. Additionally, you will need a license diskette to install the IntranetWare license onto the server during the installation process.

Create the Server's DOS Partition

NetWare 4.11 still requires the server executable to be launched from a DOS partition. This means that a DOS partition must be created, and DOS must be installed before NetWare can be installed. MS-DOS version 5.0 or higher is recommended. NetWare 4.11 can also be installed from a Windows 95 partition that has been booted to command-line mode.

Tip

NetWare can also be launched from a Windows 95 partition.

In previous versions of NetWare, it was possible to boot the server from a floppy diskette. The floppy diskette was formatted with DOS, and the necessary files required to start NetWare were placed on that floppy disk. The files included the server executable (SERVER.EXE) and the NetWare disk drivers. This meant no DOS partition needed to be created on the server's hard disk.

With NetWare 4.11, this is no longer an option. Current floppy disk technology does not have the capacity to store all of the files that NetWare needs in the DOS partition. Therefore, a DOS partition must be created on the server's hard disks. To create a DOS partition, just follow these steps:

1. Create a DOS bootable floppy diskette.

2. Use FDISK to create the DOS partition.

3. FORMAT the DOS partition and make it bootable.

Easier said than done! You would not believe the gymnastics you have to go through to create a DOS partition. The first step is to create a DOS bootable floppy diskette. This can be done using the DOS FORMAT utility. After booting the server from the hard drive with DOS, insert a blank floppy diskette into the floppy drive and type **format a: /s** at the command prompt. This will copy the DOS system files to the floppy diskette after it has finished formatting.

Once the diskette is bootable, copy these files from the C:\DOS directory:

- FDISK.EXE
- FORMAT.COM
- EDIT.COM
- QBASIC.EXE

These files will be necessary to create the DOS partition on the server. (EDIT.COM allows you to edit ASCII files and requires QBASIC.EXE to run.) Once the files have been copied, it is time to create the DOS partition on the server.

The partition is created by using the DOS utility FDISK. Boot the server from the floppy diskette, and type **fdisk** at the A:\> prompt. This will bring up a menu like the one shown in Figure 1-2.

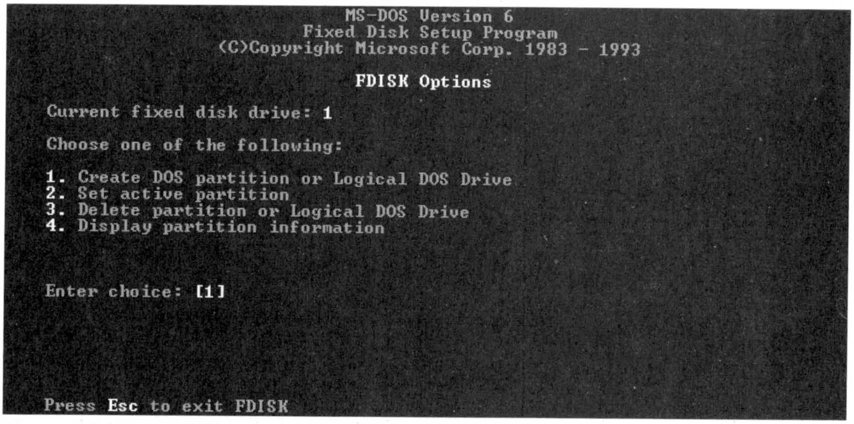

```
                        MS-DOS Version 6
                     Fixed Disk Setup Program
              (C)Copyright Microsoft Corp. 1983 - 1993

                          FDISK Options

   Current fixed disk drive: 1

   Choose one of the following:

   1. Create DOS partition or Logical DOS Drive
   2. Set active partition
   3. Delete partition or Logical DOS Drive
   4. Display partition information


   Enter choice: [1]



   Press Esc to exit FDISK
```

Figure 1-2: The FDISK menu.

The first thing you'll want to do is delete any partitions that exist on the server's hard disks using option three (Delete Partition or Logical DOS Drive) from Figure 1-2. The FDISK utility will allow you to delete both DOS and non-DOS partitions. More than likely, you will only need to delete a primary DOS partition. Make sure that you have retrieved all data you might want from the drive before you delete the partition. This includes any device drivers (like CD-ROM or SCSI drivers) that came with the server. Once the partition is deleted, all of the data on the server's hard disk will be lost.

The next step after deleting the partitions is to create a new DOS partition on the server using option one (Create DOS Partition or Logical DOS Drive) from Figure 1-2. The new DOS partition must be at least 15MB in size; however, it is wiser to make the DOS partition larger. Once the partition is created, it cannot be expanded short of deleting it and recreating a larger one. You will want to make sure that the DOS partition you create will be large enough to handle the NetWare files and any other utilities and files you might want to put on the disk for diagnostic purposes. We recommend that this partition be at least 50MB in size. The rest of the disk will be used for the NetWare partition, which will be created in the installation of the operating system.

If you have multiple hard disks connected to your system, FDISK will display a fifth option (Change Current Fixed Disk Drive) on the main menu. This option will allow you to switch between the physical hard disks connected to your hard disk controller. You do not need to create a DOS partition on every physical disk. Only one DOS partition is required to install or load NetWare 4.11.

Once the partition is created, it must be made active. If the partition is not active, the server will not boot off of the hard disk. Many an hour has been spent with the hard disk controller documentation trying to figure out why the server will not boot. Select option number two (Set Active Partition) from Figure 1-2 to make your DOS partition active.

When you have created the DOS partition and made it active, FDISK will require you to reboot the system. Make sure your bootable floppy diskette is in the floppy drive; then reboot the system. The next thing you need to do is format the newly created DOS partition. Type **format c: /s** at the A:\> prompt to format the fixed disk. This command will also transfer the DOS bootstrap files to the hard drive to make it bootable.

After the formatting is complete, remove the floppy diskette from the server and reboot the machine. The server should boot DOS from its hard disk. The creation of the DOS partition is complete, but we are not quite ready to install NetWare yet.

Edit the DOS Startup Files

When the server reboots after the format, DOS prompts you for a time and date. This is because there are no startup configuration files for DOS to load. When both CONFIG.SYS and AUTOEXEC.BAT are absent, the operating system prompts for the correct time and date.

As you probably guessed by now, we must go back and recreate these two files to finish configuring the machine for the NOS installation. You can create the files using your EDIT.COM. To create a file and open it for editing, type in **edit** *filename*, where *filename* is CONFIG.SYS or AUTOEXEC.BAT. In CONFIG.SYS, you need to include the following lines for the installation of NetWare:

```
FILES=12
BUFFERS=15
```

Be sure *not* to load HIMEM.SYS in your CONFIG.SYS file. NetWare has its own methods of memory management, and it does not need the help of HIMEM.SYS. Although NetWare 4.11 may load properly with HIMEM.SYS loaded, it is not recommended that this memory manager be loaded in the DOS partition.

Use EDIT.COM to create the AUTOEXEC.BAT with a PATH statement and a PROMPT statement. No additional lines are needed at this time, however, once an installation method is chosen, you may need to add some lines to the file.

Choose the Method of Installation

Before Installing IntranetWare (which will be covered in Chapter 2), you will need to decide how you are going to install it: from a CD-ROM drive attached to the server or from another NetWare server. The method of installation impacts how the server needs to be configured for the successful installation of the operating system. We will briefly explore both options.

CD-ROM Installation

If you have a CD-ROM drive attached directly to your server, the installation is really simple. Install the CD-ROM drivers that came with your drive, then open both your CONFIG.SYS and AUTOEXEC.BAT to make sure the drivers are correctly referenced.

A typical line in CONFIG.SYS to load the CD-ROM device file looks like this:

```
DEVICE=c:\CD\IBMIDECD.SYS /D:IBMCD100
```

This is a line taken from a machine that is loading the device driver for an IBM IDE double-speed CD-ROM drive. Not only does this driver need to load, a file needs to load from AUTOEXEC.BAT as well:

```
C:\CD\MSCDEX.EXE /D:IBMCD100 /M:10
```

When this line is loaded from AUTOEXEC.BAT, the server will be able to recognize the CD-ROM drive. A drive letter will be assigned to it. For more information regarding the loading of the CD-ROM drivers, refer to the manual that came with your hardware.

Once the CD-ROM drive is recognized by your server, insert CD1, labeled "NetWare 4.11 Operating System CD," into the drive. You are now ready to install IntranetWare.

Tip

If your installation is interrupted with a "Drive not ready" error, it probably means your CD-ROM driver is not compatible with the NetWare 4.11 installation. Contact the drive manufacturer for the most recent CD-ROM drivers.

NetWare Server-to-Server Installation

The NetWare server-to-server installation can only be performed if your server is connected to an existing network and there is another NetWare server already running on the network. This method of installation will temporarily turn your server-to-be into a NetWare client while it runs the NOS installation program from the existing server.

Setting up the server-to-server installation requires two basic steps:

1. Mount the CD-ROM on an existing NetWare server with a CD-ROM drive, or copy the CD-ROM files from the CD-ROM to the existing NetWare file server.

2. Install the NetWare client software on the new server and log into the existing NetWare server.

If a file copy from the CD-ROM to the existing server is required, make sure there is at least 630MB of disk space available on the server. This is how much data is included on the NetWare 4.11 CD. While the files are copying, set up the NetWare workstation client on the new server. Since this client is only going to be temporary, the 16-bit VLM client will be sufficient for the installation.

The NetWare client software can be obtained from the NetWare 4.11 installation CD as well. Since this is a server-to-server installation, we will assume there is already a NetWare 4.11 server installed on the network, with the client software installation ready to go. This installation needs to be copied to floppy disk so the client software can be loaded on the new server.

The NetWare Requester installation program will copy the necessary files to the server's DOS partition. The files will include a file called STARTNET.BAT that is responsible for loading the network drivers and the NetWare Requester into memory. Once loaded, the server will be able to connect to the network. STARTNET.BAT will contain the following commands in this order (assuming the client was installed to the default directory C:\NWCLIENT):

```
SET NWLANGUAGE=ENGLISH
C:\NWCLIENT\LSL.COM
C:\NWCLIENT\<MLID>
C:\NWCLIENT\IPXODI.COM
C:\NWCLIENT\VLM.EXE
```

These programs must be loaded in this order; otherwise, the client will not load successfully. Each one plays a vital role in the workstation's communication with the network, and each one builds upon the foundation set by the previous.

The third line in the STARTNET.BAT commands is special and tailored specifically for the network card in the server. MLID stands for Multiple Link Interface Driver, and it allows the machine to talk to the network card installed. Each type of network card will have a unique MLID (supplied on floppy diskette by the manufacturer) specifically for use with the NetWare client. If the network card in the server is NetWare Ready, the driver will be installed by the NetWare client installation program. For more information on NetWare client installation and configuration, refer to Chapters 15 and 16.

Once you have installed the NetWare client on the new server, connect to the server from which you will be installing NetWare 4.11 and map a drive to the volume and directory that contain the installation software. When mapping this drive, make it a root mapping to the top level of the CD-ROM files. The NetWare installation will fail if this drive is not mapped properly.

For instance, you copied the CD-ROM software to a subdirectory on the DATA volume of the existing server. The existing path to the CD-ROM software might be *SERVER*/DATA:IW\CD1, where *SERVER* is the name of your existing NetWare server. Instead of just mapping a drive to the DATA volume (map G:=*SERVER*/DATA:), you must map root the drive to the CD1 directory by typing **map root G:=*SERVER*/DATA:IW\CD1**.

Once the new server has connected (as a client) to the existing server and a drive has been root mapped to the CD-ROM software, the server-to-server installation setup is complete. You are ready to install IntranetWare.

Applying Concepts: Rambell, Inc.

So what kind of decisions will John Doe make regarding the hardware for his company's new network? His boss has authorized him to spend up to $3,500 on the new server for Rambell, Inc. While it won't buy a top-of-the-line server for the company, it will provide a respectable one. John just needs to decide which components he is going to sacrifice for the sake of others.

After reviewing the documentation on the minimum hardware requirements for installing IntranetWare and talking to other information technology professionals, John decides on the following configuration for the company's server:

- Intel Pentium 133 MHz processor
- 64MB RAM
- Two-slot PCI hardware bus plus ISA expansion slots
- PCI SCSI hard disk controller
- Two 2GB disk drives for disk mirroring
- SCSI CD-ROM drive
- PCI network interface card

Certainly this machine is in the realm of the $3,500 John was allotted to spend on the server, but has he made logical trade-offs in return for economical spending? It's debatable, but let's look at his thinking for a moment.

John could have spent more money on a CPU for the machine. If he had chosen a bigger and faster processor, he would have had to cut some corners elsewhere—probably either RAM or disk space. That would not have been a wise decision.

The PCI/ISA bus decision is another area in which he could have chosen a better technology, but he sacrificed technology to stay in a budget. Although the PCI-based bus is faster than the EISA bus configuration, there are usually only two to three PCI slots in machines. These slots are occupied by the NIC and hard disk controller. Any further card expansion in the server requires using the ISA slots, which are significantly slower than EISA. However, EISA-based machines cost more than PCI/ISA machines. Again, to get the memory and hard disk space required, this is a good compromise.

The SCSI controller and disks are going to be more expensive than their EIDE counterparts, but SCSI is better able to provide for future expansion of disk space and also has faster access times than EIDE. This machine will have excellent performance with the combination of the SCSI disk technology and the PCI-based SCSI interface.

The remainder of the components are logical as well. John chose the PCI network card because he wants to make sure that the network connection is not the bottleneck in performance on this server. The 64MB of RAM and 2GB of total file capacity on the server (after mirroring) should be enough to get the company started with a stable file and print sharing environment for the 10 users in the company. John has weighed the options carefully and has made a wise purchase.

Now fully prepared, John is ready to immerse himself into the world of network operating systems.

Moving On

After selecting your server hardware and preparing it for IntranetWare, it is time to look at the installation of the operating system itself. NetWare 4.11 comes with an extensive installation program with many features and options to load the operating system on your server. Chapter 2 will help you successfully install the operating system while avoiding the common pitfalls many people encounter.

2

Installing NetWare 4.11

A file server's performance is directly related to the hardware on which it is based. In Chapter 1, we learned the ins and outs of basic hardware architecture and looked into how a file server's hardware components can affect its ability to perform its duties. John Doe took these issues seriously when selecting his server and now has an excellent machine on which to install NetWare 4.11 and provide the services his users need.

Upon receiving the server, John dutifully prepared it for the NetWare installation, and it is ready to go. He has chosen the CD-ROM installation because he has no other server from which to install the operating system. He is at the threshold to a new powerful network environment, and it all starts with the installation of the core operating system, NetWare 4.11.

The NetWare 4.11 installation program can seem unintuitive and complex to those that are not familiar with it. Because the same installation program is used to install a myriad of products, there are many different options from which to choose. Not to worry; after this chapter, you will be a NetWare 4.11 installation pro.

There are essentially two parts to this chapter. The first part deals with the installation program in detail, screen by screen, as we walk through it. It is recommended that you have this book handy and follow along in this part of the chapter as you perform the installation. Please note that the sections "INSTALL.BAT" and "INSTALL.NLM" provide an in-depth discussion of the installation.

The second part of the chapter is for those of you who are familiar with installing NetWare. It provides a brief description of each step in the installation process. Because you are familiar with most of the issues regarding NetWare installation, you will be able to install the network operating system with no trouble by following along. Refer to "Experienced Installer's Guide" near the end of the chapter to skip the in-depth details.

Before we get started with the installation, it is important to note that NetWare 4.11 does not come with its own bootstrap files; it relies upon DOS for its initial boot and installation. Therefore, the installation procedure for the operating system is a two-step procedure. The first step is to run a DOS-based program, INSTALL.BAT, from the DOS partition to lay the foundation for the operating system. Once complete, the NetWare 4.11 operating system is launched. The second step in the installation occurs when NetWare automatically loads INSTALL.NLM, a NetWare utility that will guide the installer through the remainder. Fortunately, the installation program handles the loading of the server and INSTALL.NLM to make these two steps seamless, making it seem like one large installation program.

Once the installation is complete, your server will be up and running. You will have taken your first step towards providing a complete networking environment for your users. So without further ado, let's dive into the installation of NetWare 4.11.

INSTALL.BAT

For the purposes of this book, we will assume that we are installing from a CD-ROM drive on the server. The installation for a server-to-server setup will be very similar, and major differences between the two methods of installation will be noted as they occur. To start the installation, change drives to the CD-ROM drive and type **install**. For server-to-server installation, change drives to the network drive that was map rooted and type **install**. The installation program will load, and you will see the screen shown in Figure 2-1.

The first NetWare Install screen will let you choose the language for NetWare 4.11. NetWare 4.11 comes with the language choices of German, English, Spanish, French, Italian, and Portuguese. Highlight the desired language using the arrow keys and press Enter to select it.

Figure 2-1: Selecting the installation language for NetWare 4.11.

After the language has been selected, the Novell Terms and Conditions will be displayed. It is a software license agreement that outlines the terms by which you agree to use NetWare 4.11. When finished with the first screen of the agreement, press any key to continue on to the next screen. Continue to do this until you have read the entire agreement. Then press any key to continue with the installation of the operating system.

After the license agreement, INSTALL.BAT presents a variety of installations from which to choose as shown in Figure 2-2. The choices for installation are:

- NetWare Server Installation—causes INSTALL.BAT to install the server software on the desired machine.

- Client Installation—installs the various client workstation software to the server. This includes the DOS/Windows, Windows 95, OS/2, and Macintosh clients.

- Diskette Creation—installs the DOS/Windows client workstation files to floppy diskette. This will allow you to create a client workstation that can connect to the server once NetWare 4.11 is installed.

- Readme Files—installs all of the readme files concerning NetWare 4.11 to the desired location.

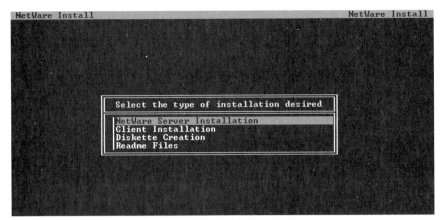

Figure 2-2: Installation options presented by INSTALL.BAT.

The last three options do not have to be performed on a NetWare server. Client software, diskette creation, and readme files can be installed or created on any machine. Just run INSTALL.BAT and choose one of those options on a local machine. To install the NetWare 4.11 operating system, NetWare Server Installation must be chosen from this screen. Highlight it and press Enter.

The next screen (shown in Figure 2-3) will allow you to choose the product that is going to be installed. You have the option of installing NetWare 4.11 or NetWare 4.11 SFT III. NetWare 4.11 SFT III stands for level-three system fault tolerance. It is a method of providing complete hardware redundancy for critical systems by using two file servers that are exact mirror images of one another. Traditionally, the SFT III product had to be purchased separately and was shipped on different media than the NetWare operating system; however, it now comes packaged with IntranetWare.

The NetWare 4.11 SFT III installation requires two things:

- The server on which you want to install SFT III must already have NetWare 4.11 installed.

- You must have a NetWare 4.11 SFT III license diskette purchased through your authorized Novell reseller. Without the license diskette, you cannot successfully install NetWare 4.11 SFT III.

We will choose to install NetWare 4.11. Because NetWare 4.11 SFT III is a highly specialized product with its own set of features, it requires a level of attention beyond the scope of this book.

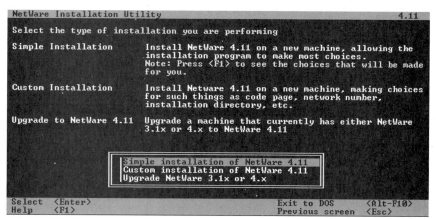

```
NetWare Installation Utility                                          4.11
Choose the product you want to install
NetWare 4.11           Single machine running NetWare 4.11.
NetWare SFT III        Dual machines running dedicated NetWare 4.11 with level 3
                       system fault tolerance.

                  ┌─────────────────────────────────────┐
                  │NetWare 4.11                          │
                  │NetWare 4.11 SFT III                  │
                  │Display Information <README> File     │
                  └─────────────────────────────────────┘




Select   <Enter>                                     Exit to DOS    <Esc>
Help     <F1>
```

Figure 2-3: Selecting a product for installation.

This third screen of INSTALL.BAT (Figure 2-3) has a couple of other features of note. It gives you the option to display the readme files. It is always a good idea to read these files because they contain pertinent information about the operating system. Also, along the bottom of the screen in a gray bar you will notice other commands. On this and many of the other screens throughout the rest of the installation, the options that appear in this bar are extremely important. If you get stuck at any point during installation and are confused about how to continue, look to the options on the gray bar for guidance.

After you have highlighted the NetWare 4.11 option and pressed Enter, you will have to choose which type of installation of NetWare 4.11 you want to perform. There are three types of installations offered, as shown in Figure 2-4.

```
NetWare Installation Utility                                          4.11
Select the type of installation you are performing
Simple Installation        Install NetWare 4.11 on a new machine, allowing the
                           installation program to make most choices.
                           Note: Press <F1> to see the choices that will be made
                           for you.
Custom Installation        Install Netware 4.11 on a new machine, making choices
                           for such things as code page, network number,
                           installation directory, etc.
Upgrade to NetWare 4.11    Upgrade a machine that currently has either NetWare
                           3.1x or 4.x to NetWare 4.11

                  ┌─────────────────────────────────────┐
                  │Simple installation of NetWare 4.11   │
                  │Custom installation of NetWare 4.11   │
                  │Upgrade NetWare 3.1x or 4.x           │
                  └─────────────────────────────────────┘
Select   <Enter>                           Exit to DOS       <Alt-F10>
Help     <F1>                              Previous screen    <Esc>
```

Figure 2-4: Choosing the type of installation.

You can choose a simple installation, a custom installation, or an upgrade to NetWare 4.11. The simple installation makes certain assumptions about your system that will cause the installation program to bypass a lot of steps; it makes the installation easier for the novice installer. The custom installation is for the advanced installer who wants to tweak some settings during the installation of the operating system. Table 2-1 outlines the differences between the simple and custom installations.

The upgrade option will allow you to install NetWare 4.11 on a server that is currently running NetWare 3.x or NetWare 4.x. We will choose the custom installation to show all of the selections that can be made during the installation of NetWare 4.11. In the box near the bottom of the screen, highlight Custom Installation of NetWare 4.11 and press Enter.

After the custom installation is chosen, a new screen appears in which you must name the new server. What you name your server is completely up to you. We generally choose the names of mythological and fictional figures for security reasons. It's pretty easy for a hacker to guess the function of a server called Accounting. It's a lot harder to figure out which department a server named Damocles is serving. If security on your network is a concern, try to avoid naming the server after its function. Type in the name of the server and press Enter.

The next screen is used to give an internal IPX number to the new server. The internal IPX number is an eight-digit hexadecimal number that is used to uniquely define the server on the network. No other server on the network may have this number, and no network segment may have this number, either.

	Simple Installation	Custom Installation
DOS Partition	Requires a 15MB DOS partition on the server hard disk. Also assumes DOS is installed on the DOS partition and server is booting from the DOS partition.	DOS can be booted either from the server's hard disk or floppy.
Hard Disks	Assumes no disk mirroring or duplexing.	Allows disks to be mirrored or duplexed.
NetWare Partitions	All free disk space on a hard drive will be assigned to a single NetWare partition.	Installer performs all NetWare partitioning.
Volumes	Only one volume will exist per NetWare partition. Those volumes will be given default names.	Complete control over volume naming and volume segment assignment.

Startup Files	Assumes AUTOEXEC.NCF and STARTUP.NCF do not need to be edited.	Allows editing of the server startup files.
NetWare Directory Services (NDS)	NDS will be installed with one organization per tree that contains all objects.	Allows specification of multiple NDS containers for the NDS tree.
Protocols	Only the IPX protocol will be installed. The IPX network number will be chosen by the installation.	Multiple protocols can be installed. The IPX network number for the IPX protocol is customizable.
Time Parameters	No modification of time zone parameters allowed.	Can customize time zone information for NetWare Directory Services.
Internal IPX Number	Assigns a randomly generated internal IPX number.	Recommends a randomly generated internal IPX number. This number can be customized.

Table 2-1: NetWare simple versus custom installation.

Internal IPX Number Versus IPX Network Number

The internal IPX number differs from the IPX network number. The network number is also an eight-digit hexadecimal number; however, it is used to reference a specific segment of network cable. All servers connected to the same piece of network cable will reference the same network number. However, each server on that same piece of cable will have a unique internal IPX number that differs from the network number and all other internal IPX numbers.

These numbers are used for routing information packets between servers and workstations. NetWare servers internally keep tables of information concerning just how far away specific pieces of network cable are. The server also keeps track of how far away other servers are through those same tables. By keeping track of network numbers and internal IPX numbers, a server can determine the shortest distance between itself and another server and network cable to achieve the most efficient packet exchange it can.

The NetWare 4.11 installation program will randomly assign an internal IPX number to the server. You can either accept that number or input one of your own. If you are a smaller department on a large company network, you may need to obtain an internal IPX number from your central information systems department. Accept the number by pressing Enter, or press Enter after typing in the customized number.

Once the internal IPX number has been entered, it is time to copy the necessary server files to the DOS partition of the server. The screen that appears should look like the screen in Figure 2-5.

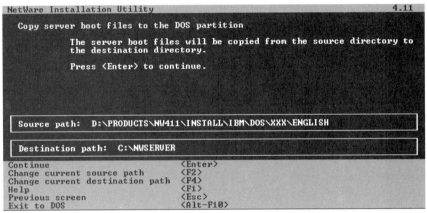

Figure 2-5: Specifying a target directory in the DOS partition for the NetWare 4.11 server files.

The screen in Figure 2-5 displays the source path of the server files and the destination path. The source path is used to determine the location of the NetWare 4.11 installation files. The destination path is the directory on the DOS partition where the operating system files will be installed. By default, the destination path will be the C:\NWSERVER directory on the hard drive's DOS partition. Notice how the gray bar at the bottom of the screen has changed to reflect the different options available on this screen. To change the current source path, press F2. To change the current destination path, press F4. You will be asked to enter the new source or destination. To continue with the installation, press Enter. The files will be copied to the server's hard drive.

After the file copy, a new screen appears (Figure 2-6) in which to provide locale information for your server. If you are in the United States, great. The default locale information is for the United States. If you are outside of the United States, you will need to change the information on this screen. There are three items of information that pertain to locale:

- Country Code—a three-digit number that represents the country location of the server.

- Code Page—a three-digit number that represents the character code set that will be used on the server. Instead of the traditional ASCII character set, NetWare uses the Unicode standard to represent character sets that ASCII is not capable of representing. The standard United States English character set is specified in Unicode set 437.

- Keyboard Mapping—allows you to change to keyboard mapping if you use a keyboard mapping that is different from the standard.

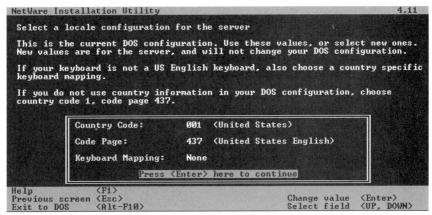

```
NetWare Installation Utility                                          4.11

Select a locale configuration for the server

This is the current DOS configuration. Use these values, or select new ones.
New values are for the server, and will not change your DOS configuration.

If your keyboard is not a US English keyboard, also choose a country specific
keyboard mapping.

If you do not use country information in your DOS configuration, choose
country code 1, code page 437.

        ┌─────────────────────────────────────────────────────────┐
        │ Country Code:          001   <United States>             │
        │                                                          │
        │ Code Page:             437   <United States English>     │
        │                                                          │
        │ Keyboard Mapping:      None                              │
        │          Press <Enter> here to continue                  │
        └─────────────────────────────────────────────────────────┘

Help             <F1>
Previous screen  <Esc>                       Change value  <Enter>
Exit to DOS      <Alt-F10>                    Select field  <UP, DOWN>
```

Figure 2-6: Specifying locale information.

After specifying the locale, continue the installation by highlighting Press Enter Here to Continue and pressing Enter. The next screen to appear will give you the option to add, modify, or delete any special commands from the STARTUP.NCF file.

When your server boots after installation, it follows a specific process (much like DOS does). After DOS boots, the file SERVER.EXE is executed, which starts the NetWare 4.11 server. Upon startup, NetWare 4.11 looks to two files for specific loading information. The first is STARTUP.NCF; the second is AUTOEXEC.NCF. The STARTUP.NCF file is located in the DOS partition in the directory specified as the target for the server files (by default, this is C:\NWSERVER).

During the installation, you can modify the STARTUP.NCF file to load special commands that are needed when the server starts. To add these commands, choose Yes. Otherwise, choose No. Choosing yes will bring up a STARTUP.NCF editing screen in which commands can be modified, added, or deleted. When finished with this screen, press F10 to save the changes and continue.

The next screen in the installation program will give you the option to start the NetWare 4.11 server immediately from the DOS bootstrap file AUTOEXEC.BAT. When the machine is turned on and DOS loads, DOS reads two configuration files—CONFIG.SYS and AUTOEXEC.BAT. This screen asks if you want to add a command to AUTOEXEC.BAT to load SERVER.EXE. If you choose Yes, you will need to specify the path to the existing AUTOEXEC.BAT file. Once modified, SERVER.EXE will automatically load when DOS loads, which will start the NetWare 4.11 server automatically after loading DOS.

Once AUTOEXEC.BAT has been modified (or not modified as the case may be), INSTALL.BAT is finished. The last thing INSTALL.BAT does is load SERVER.EXE from the DOS partition, starting the NetWare server. INSTALL.NLM is then automatically loaded, and the installation of the operating system will continue.

INSTALL.NLM

INSTALL.BAT has laid the foundation for things to come by copying a lot of the files necessary to both start the server and load the necessary drivers to finish the installation of the server. It is INSTALL.NLM, however, that does most of the work during the installation of NetWare 4.11.

Server Drivers

After SERVER.EXE loads, the server console will appear. You can recognize the server console easily because it displays the server's name followed by a colon. This is called the console prompt. After loading, INSTALL.NLM will try to auto-detect the hard disk controller and NIC installed in the server. Those of you who have installed previous versions of NetWare will understand how helpful this is. It takes the confusion out of server driver installation. The majority of the hardware that comes in today's newer servers will be detected during the installation of NetWare 4.11. Figure 2-7 shows the screen during installation after the hard disk controller and network card have been detected.

The server drivers are critical to the successful installation of NetWare 4.11. The hard disk controller driver controls the hard disks connected to your server. Without it, NetWare would be unable to communicate with the hard disks. Likewise, the network driver controls the NIC. If this driver is not loaded properly, the server will not be able to access the network, which will prevent the server from communicating with any other machines via the network. Without these drivers, the server is useless.

If you encounter problems while trying to load the NIC drivers, still continue with the installation. You will be able to add NIC commands after the operating system has been installed. It is generally better to completely install the operating system and retrieve the NIC information later than to interrupt the installation.

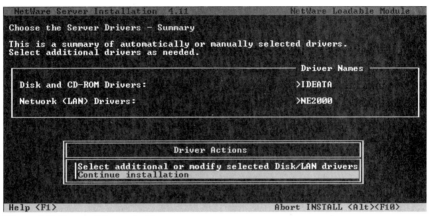

Figure 2-7: Server driver selection.

Selecting the Disk Driver

NetWare is able to communicate with the hard disks through the use of a disk driver. As mentioned, NetWare 4.11 will try to auto-detect the hard disk controller; however, there may be a time when you have to manually select the disk drivers because it was unable to detect the hard disk controller successfully.

To manually select a disk driver for the server when the hard disk controller is not found by the installation program, perform the following steps from the Choose the Server Drivers—Summary screen:

1. Use the arrow keys to highlight the line labeled Disk and CD-ROM Drivers (see Figure 2-7). This line will be blank because the hard disk controller was not detected.

2. Press the Enter key. The Choose the Server Drivers—Disk Driver screen (shown in Figure 2-8) will appear containing the list of the NetWare Ready disk drivers. Notice that these files are named *.DSK and *.HAM. In NetWare, disk drivers always have these extensions.

·3. Find the disk driver you want to install. If your disk controller does not appear on this list, you must provide the NetWare-compatible disk driver supplied by the manufacturer. To install an unlisted driver from another location, press the Insert key. By default, NetWare will look in the floppy drive for the new driver. To change this path, press the F3 key and input the correct path to the driver. The unlisted driver will be found.

4. Select the driver and press Enter.

After selecting the driver, you will be taken to the Additional Driver Actions menu near the bottom of the screen shown in Figure 2-8. Select Continue Installation from the menu to return to the screen shown in Figure 2-7. If you have more than one hard disk controller in your server, you can select multiple disk drivers by choosing Select an Additional Driver from the menu in Figure 2-8. Just repeat the process for each driver that is required.

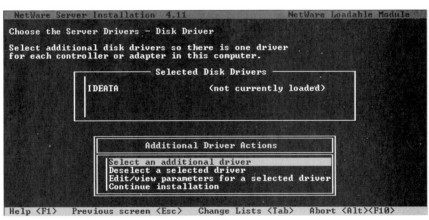

Figure 2-8: Additional driver actions.

Selecting the Network (LAN) Driver

NetWare requires a special driver for the network card installed in your server. Without it, the server is not able to communicate with the network. This driver is essentially the server's link to the outside world. As with the disk driver, you may have to select the network driver manually if NetWare is not able to auto-detect it. The procedure is almost identical to the procedure to select the disk driver.

To manually select a network driver for the server, perform the following steps from the Choose the Server Drivers—Summary screen (see Figure 2-7):

1. Use the arrow keys to highlight the line Network (LAN) Drivers. This line will be blank because the NIC was not auto-detected.

2. Press the Enter key. The Choose the Server Drivers—Network Driver screen will appear containing the list of the NetWare Ready LAN drivers. Notice that all of these files are named *.LAN. In NetWare, network drivers always have the .LAN extension.

3. From the list of LAN drivers, find the network driver you want to install. If your NIC is not included, you must provide the NetWare-compatible LAN driver that came with the card. If it is not there, contact the manufacturer of your NIC. To install an unlisted network driver from another location, press the Insert key. By default, NetWare will look for the new driver on floppy diskette. To change the path, press the F3 key and input the correct path to the driver. The unlisted driver will be found.

4. Select the driver and press Enter.

Tip

Because many cards are NE2000 compatible, try selecting Novell's NE2000 driver from the LAN driver list if your card's driver does not appear.

After selecting the driver, you will be taken to the Additional Driver Actions menu. It will be similar to the one on the screen shown in Figure 2-8. Select Continue Installation to return to the main server driver screen shown in Figure 2-7. If there is more than one NIC installed in your server, you will need to select additional drivers for the other NICs by choosing Select an Additional Driver from the Additional Driver Actions menu (Figure 2-8). Repeat the procedure to install all of the LAN drivers required by your server.

Setting Disk Driver Parameters

If NetWare 4.11 was unable to auto-detect the hardware, you will most likely have to manually configure the driver to match the settings of the hardware components in the system. The information you recorded before the server installation will be invaluable. This will include the applicable interrupt setting, port setting, memory address range, and/or slot number required for the successful loading of the disk driver.

To modify the parameters for the hard disk controller, perform the following steps:

1. Highlight the Disk and CD-ROM Drivers line in the Choose the Server Drivers—Summary screen (Figure 2-7) using the arrow keys.

2. Press Enter. The Additional Driver Actions menu will appear (Figure 2-8).

3. Choose Edit/View Parameters for a Selected Driver from the Additional Driver Actions menu and press Enter.

4. Highlight the desired disk driver from the Selected Disk Drivers list, and press Enter. The screen shown in Figure 2-9 will appear and will allow you to specify any parameters that may be needed to load the disk driver successfully.

5. When finished modifying parameters, select Save Parameters and Continue. This will return you to the Additional Driver Actions menu.

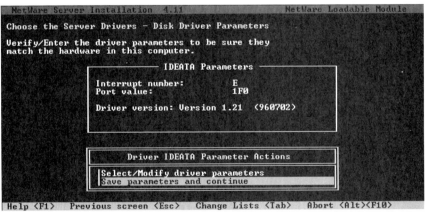

Figure 2-9: Modifying server driver parameters.

Setting LAN Driver Parameters

With older network cards, it's likely that the NIC will not be auto-detected by NetWare 4.11. In the event this occurs, you will have to manually specify the parameters used to load the LAN driver. To do this, complete the following steps:

1. Highlight the Network (LAN) Drivers line in the Choose the Server Drivers—Summary screen (Figure 2-7) using the arrow keys.

2. Press Enter, and the Additional Driver Actions menu will appear (similar to Figure 2-8).

3. Choose Edit/View Parameters for a Selected Driver from the Additional Driver Actions menu and press Enter.

4. Select the desired LAN driver from the Selected Network Drivers box and press Enter. A new screen will appear that is similar to Figure 2-9, which will allow you to specify any parameters that may be needed to load the network driver successfully.

5. When done modifying the LAN driver parameters, select Save Parameters and Continue. The Additional Driver Actions menu will appear.

The network card parameters that may need to be specified include the interrupt setting, port address setting, memory address range, and transceiver type. For the LAN driver to load successfully, this information must be provided to the operating system.

Once all server drivers have been selected and configured for the server, highlight the Continue Installation option from the Choose the Server Drivers—Summary screen (Figure 2-7) using the arrow keys. Press Enter.

Activating the Server Drivers

After continuing with the installation of the operating system, INSTALL.NLM will attempt to load the drivers that were selected with the parameters that were specified. If you did not specify any parameters for drivers not detected, NetWare probably will not be able to load the drivers by itself. Fortunately, INSTALL.NLM will notify you if it fails to load a server driver. Hold down the Alt key and press Esc to switch to the server console.

The server console will display any errors the server encountered while attempting to load the driver. From this point, you will have to load the driver manually. To load the driver from the system console, type:

`load <driver> <parameters>`

For example, to load the driver for an NE2000 card set to interrupt 10 and port 300, type:

`load ne2000 int=10 port=300`

at the console prompt. If you need more information on how to load these drivers, Chapters 17 and 18 deal with disk and LAN drivers more thoroughly.

Once the disk driver has loaded, it does not need any more attention. The same cannot be said for the network driver. Loading the network driver is only half of what is required to get the server talking to the network. The LAN driver gives the server the ability to talk to the network; it must, however, speak the same language as the other machines on the network. This is where the concept of network protocols comes into play.

A *protocol* is a communication standard a computer uses to facilitate its interaction with other machines. For a machine to be able to talk to another machine, both need to be using the same protocol.

By default, NetWare will attempt to communicate with other machines using the Internetwork Packet Exchange (IPX) protocol. NetWare 4.11 also supports the AppleTalk protocol and Transmission Control Protocol/Internet Protocol (TCP/IP) out of the box; however, to talk with other NetWare servers and NetWare clients, it must be using the IPX protocol.

To get the server talking to the network, you must *bind* a protocol to the network driver. To bind a protocol to the LAN driver, you need to specify the frame type that protocol will use as well as the network number of the cable to which the server is connected. Protocols will only be able to run over specific frame types.

Frame Types

A frame type is another standard that computers use to communicate with one another. The *frame type* defines how the physical packets the computers put on the network wire are structured. Different network architectures have different frame types; there are also multiple frame types supported within one network architecture.

Well, we now know about frame types and protocols, but how do they relate? Some protocols may only be communicated over specific frame types. Thus, multiple frame types may need to be supported by both the NIC in the server and the physical network cable. Fortunately, this is possible. Table 2-2 summarizes some popular communication protocols and which Ethernet and Token Ring frame types are supported.

Protocol	Frame Types Supported
IPX	Ethernet_802.2, Ethernet_802.3, Ethernet_II, Ethernet_SNAP Token Ring, Token Ring_SNAP
TCP/IP	Ethernet_II Token Ring_SNAP
AppleTalk	Ethernet_SNAP Token Ring_SNAP

Table 2-2: Frame types and protocols.

Not only must machines on the same network be speaking the same protocol, they must also communicate using the same frame type. If one machine is using the Ethernet_II frame type and another is using Ethernet_802.3, they will still be unable to talk to one another, even though both are using the IPX protocol.

Tip

By default, NetWare 4.11 uses the Ethernet_802.2 frame type. Older versions of NetWare (2.x and 3.x) use Ethernet_802.3 as the default frame type. If you have an integrated environment, make sure all your servers are using the same frame type.

Because the frame type is protocol related, one would expect this information to be specified when binding the protocol to the network card at the server console. Unfortunately, this is not the case. The frame type is actually specified when loading the LAN driver *manually from the console prompt*. For each type of frame type that is to be used by the server, a separate LAN driver must be loaded with the specified frame type. Thus, running the IPX protocol over both Ethernet_802.3 and Ethernet_802.2 frame types would require the LAN driver to be loaded two times:

```
load ne2000 int=10 port=300 frame=ethernet_802.\3 name=ne2000_1
load ne2000 int=10 port=300 frame=ethernet_802.\2 name=ne2000_2
```

This is called loading the LAN driver *re-entrantly*. Two drivers are used to control the same network card; unfortunately, this is necessary if multiple frame types are to be supported. The name parameter in the specified lines is also required for binding the protocol and its frame type to the appropriate card. Remember, this is done only if the LAN driver needs to be loaded from the console prompt!

Network Number

As we discussed previously, the *IPX network number* is the eight-digit hexadecimal number that is used to identify a physical piece of network cable. All servers connected to this network cable will use the same network number when binding a specific protocol and frame type to the LAN driver.

Different frame types will require different network addresses as well. This is because the network number is a logical number that refers to a physical piece of cable. If a network is running the frame types Ethernet_802.3 and Ethernet_802.2, both of the frame types are running on the same physical network wire; however, logically they are two different networks. Think about it—even though both machines may be using the IPX protocol, if they are using different frame types, they will still be unable to communicate with one another. Thus, there really are two different logical networks on the same piece of physical network cable.

If you are in charge of a small network, you should be able to define a network number. Just keep track of the network numbers you have chosen for the various frame types. If you are a member of a larger network with a central network systems administrator, you may need to obtain the network number from him/her.

If the NIC has been auto-detected and the network driver loaded, INSTALL.NLM will present the Protocol Selection screen asking you which protocols you would like to bind to the LAN driver. To accept what NetWare has proposed, select Continue With Installation from the Protocol Options.

To view or modify the protocol settings proposed by NetWare, perform the following:

1. Highlight the View/Modify Protocol Settings option in the Protocol Options menu and press Enter.

2. Select the network board to be reviewed from the Protocols Selected box. The screen in Figure 2-10 will appear.

3. Toggle selections by using the Enter key. Any box that contains an X will cause NetWare to bind the protocol to the network board. Enter the appropriate network numbers, network ranges, and IP addresses.

4. When finished, press the Escape or F10 key to return to the Protocol Selection screen.

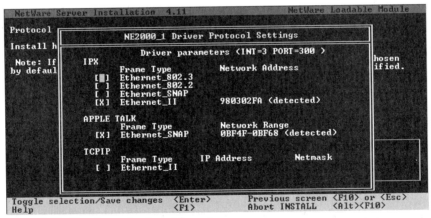

Figure 2-10: Choosing protocols and frame types.

If NetWare is not able to bind the protocols automatically, you will need to bind them yourself. To bind the protocols, switch to the server console screen by holding down the Alt key and pressing the Esc key. At the colon prompt, bind the protocol to the driver. The syntax will look like the following line:

```
BIND IPX TO NE2000_1 NET=11111111
```

In this example, the IPX protocol is being bound to the NE2000 LAN driver using the Ethernet_802.3 frame type from our previous example, and the network number is 11111111. This is the syntax that is used for binding protocols to LAN drivers. The command used to bind IPX to the network board using the Ethernet_802.2 frame type from our previous example would look like this:

```
BIND IPX TO NE2000_2 NET=22222222
```

Other protocols will require different parameters for the bind command. For example, to bind TCP/IP to the LAN driver, you would need to type something like the following after loading support for the TCP/IP protocol:

```
BIND IP TO NE2000 ADDR=<ip_address> MASK=<ip_ne\tmask> GATE=<ip_router>
```

Again, these bind statements are only used if you are required to load and bind the LAN drivers and protocols from the server console. NetWare 4.11 comes with an improved LAN driver and protocol configuration utility called INETCFG.NLM. This utility is explained in Chapter 18.

Configuring the Hard Disks

Once the server drivers have been selected and activated and the network protocols are bound, you are ready to configure your hard disks. Because the disk driver is loaded, NetWare 4.11 is now able to see the physical hard disks. However, the hard disks are not ready to hold any data. The NetWare partitions must be created on them, and the volumes must also be created and configured to store information. Fortunately, the installation program will help you accomplish these tasks so that the operating system files can be installed on the server.

Configuring the hard disks on your server involves three general steps (which will take you through myriad menus). These steps are as follows:

1. Create the NetWare partitions.

2. Adjust the size of the Hot Fix areas.

3. Assign mirrored or duplexed sets of hard disks.

We will look at each general step and describe the process required to successfully configure your hard disks.

Creating Partitions

Before the server was ready for the installation, we had to create a DOS partition on the bootable hard disk for NetWare. When the partition was created, it used a small amount of space in comparison to the overall capacity of the hard disks. The remaining capacity of the disks is still unassigned to any type of file system. That space needs to be appropriated by NetWare for the operating system to be able to use it.

After activating the server drivers, the installation program will ask you if you want to create the NetWare disk partitions automatically or manually, as shown in Figure 2-11. If you allow the installation program to automatically create the NetWare partitions, it will make all available free space into NetWare partitions. Automatic NetWare partitioning does not allow you to change the Hot Fix areas or the mirroring configuration of the hard disks.

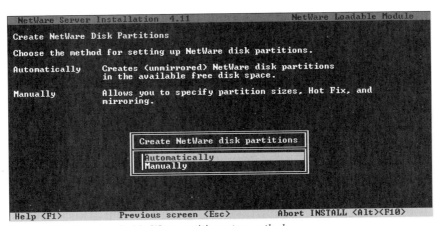

Figure 2-11: Choosing the NetWare partition setup method.

The custom creation of NetWare disk partitions gives the installer complete flexibility to customize the configuration of the hard disks. Through custom creation, you will be able to mirror or duplex your hard disks for fault tolerance and redundancy. We will choose the custom creation of NetWare partitions. Highlight Manually from the Create NetWare Disk Partitions menu, and press Enter.

After choosing custom creation, the Disk Partition and Mirroring Options menu will appear as in Figure 2-12. Through this menu, you will be able to create, delete, and modify disk partitions as well as mirror and unmirror partition sets. To create the NetWare partitions, choose the Create, Delete, and Modify Disk Partitions option from the menu, and press Enter. A list of available disk drives will appear.

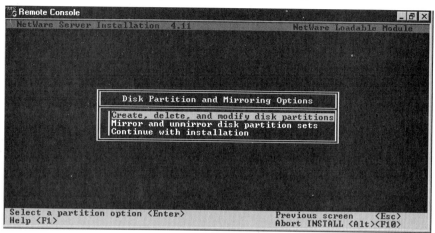

Figure 2-12: The Disk Partition and Mirroring Options menu.

Select the disk drive on which you want to create the NetWare partition by using the arrow keys to highlight the desired drive. Press Enter, and the partition information for that drive will appear.

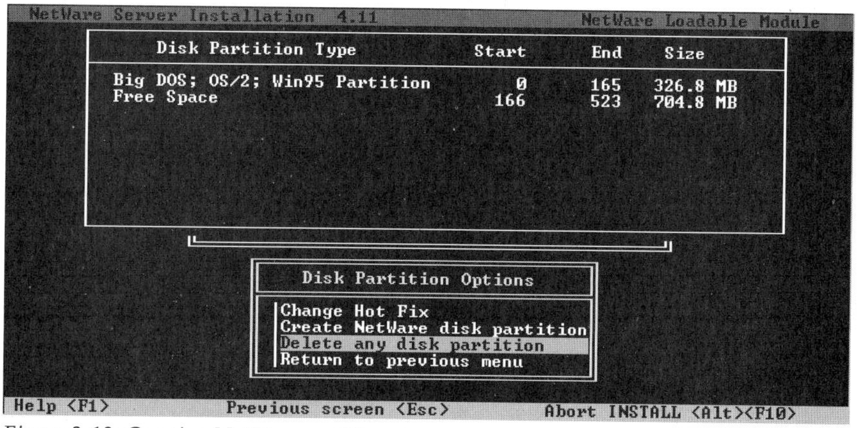

Figure 2-13: Creating NetWare partitions.

In Figure 2-13, we can see this particular hard drive has a 326.8MB DOS partition, and the remainder of the hard disk is listed as Free Space. This means there is no partition information defined for that portion of the hard drive. To make this free space a network partition, choose Create NetWare Disk Partition from the Disk Partition Options menu. Information about the new partition will be displayed, including the partition type, partition size, and Hot Fix information. You can modify this information as you want. When done, press Escape or F10 to save the partition information and continue.

Also note that the menu in Figure 2-13 can be used to delete partitions that exist on the hard drive. You can not only delete NetWare partitions, you can delete any partition that exists on the hard drive (including the DOS partition that was previously created!). Choose Delete Any Disk Partition from the Disk Partition Options menu to select and delete the desired partition.

Hot Fix

As you are creating the NetWare partitions, you might want to change the Hot Fix area of the physical disk. The Hot Fix area of the hard disk is used for fault tolerance. When NetWare writes a piece of data to the hard disk, it will immediately reread the block of data it has just written. It will compare what it has just read with the information it has stored in memory to determine if they are equal. If they are not equal, the operating system assumes the block on the physical disk is bad. It will then redirect the data in memory to a block in the Hot Fix area. This write-and-verify method prevents data corruption that can be caused by physical imperfections on the surface of the hard disk.

When a NetWare partition is created, 2 percent of the disk is reserved for the Hot Fix area. This can be modified using the Change Hot Fix option from the Disk Partition Options menu shown in Figure 2-13. The Hot Fix area can be made larger or smaller, depending on your needs. It should be noted the Hot Fix area is a reserved area of the hard disk. Data will only be written to it in the event a normal data block goes bad. Increasing the Hot Fix area will decrease the data storage capacity of your drive.

Once you have created the NetWare partition with an appropriate Hot Fix area, repeat the creation of the NetWare partition on all available disk drives using the Available Disk Drives screen and the Disk Partition Options screen. Once all of the partitions have been created, you will then be able to mirror or duplex the hard drives if you want that level of fault tolerance as well.

Mirroring & Duplexing

You can provide data redundancy for your server with both mirroring and duplexing. When you mirror hard disks, you cause them to be exact replicas of one another. Any data that is written to one disk is also written to the other disk. Thus, any data that is stored on the server is stored in two separate locations. If one of the mirrored hard disks fails, the other is still there with all of the information.

Duplexing is another method to provide data redundancy for your file server. When you duplex data across two hard disks, the data is written to both of them. Thus, the data is stored in two separate locations on the file server. If one of the duplexed hard disks fails, the data from that hard disk is not lost because it is stored on the other hard disk as well.

Now the two sound like they're the same, right? In essence, they are; there is, however, one major difference. Mirroring uses two hard disks that are both attached to the same hard disk controller. This configuration still has one point of failure—the hard disk controller. If it fails, your file server will be down because it cannot serve the data to the network (even though the data is intact on the disk drives).

Duplexing uses two hard disk controllers with a hard drive attached to each one. In this configuration, there are two complete data paths to the information stored on the hard drive. Both hard disks or both controllers have to fail before the file server will go down. Obviously this solution is more expensive because it requires an extra hard disk controller; however, it does provide a higher level of hardware redundancy. Figure 2-14 illustrates the difference between mirroring and duplexing. Notice the mirrored machine still has one single point of failure. If the hard disk controller fails, the data will not be accessible. Duplexing provides hard disk controller redundancy.

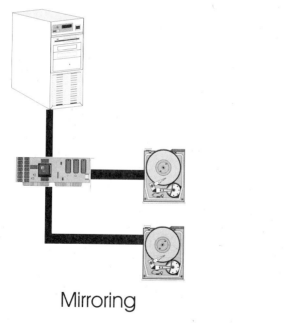

Mirroring

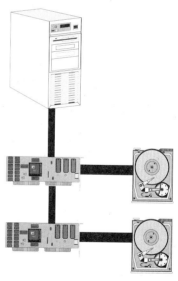

Duplexing

Figure 2-14: Mirroring versus duplexing.

There is a disadvantage to mirroring or duplexing. They both require that the total hard disk capacity be twice as much as the total amount of mirrored or duplexed space you want. For instance, if you want to have a total of 2GB mirrored disk space for your server, you need to have 4GB of total hard drive capacity (2GB will be used for the data; the other 2GB is used for the mirroring). The same is true for duplexing. If you have two 1GB hard drives in a duplexed configuration, you will only have 1GB available for data on your server.

Partitions that are mirrored or duplexed should be the same size. A 1GB partition should be mirrored with another 1GB partition. If you mirror or duplex partitions of different capacities, NetWare will only use the capacity of the smaller partition. A 500MB partition can be duplexed with a 1GB partition; however, only the first 500MB of the 1GB partition will be used by NetWare. The extra 500MB will be wasted space. If you don't have identical partitions, try to match them in size as best you can to reduce the amount of wasted space.

Whether you mirror or duplex your hard drives, NetWare handles them both the same way. Mirroring and duplexing can only be done on hard disks that have had NetWare partitions created on them. To mirror disks, choose the Mirror and Unmirror Disk Partition Sets selection from the Disk Partition and Mirroring Options menu in Figure 2-12. The Disk Partition Mirroring Status menu will appear as shown in Figure 2-15.

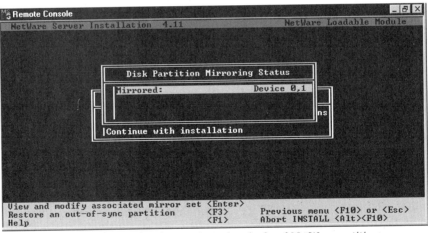

Figure 2-15: Viewing the status of your mirrored or duplexed NetWare partitions.

The hard disks recognized by the operating system are listed in the menu. Mirrored sets are listed as mirrored; nonmirrored sets are listed as not mirrored. To mirror a set of drives, select a device that is not mirrored and press the Enter key. The Mirrored Disk Partitions menu will be displayed.

To add a drive for mirroring, press the Insert key on the keyboard. A list of drives available for mirroring will be displayed. Select the desired device, and the drives will begin to mirror themselves. It will take time for the devices to become completely mirrored; when they do, a message will appear on the server console informing you that the mirrored partitions are in sync.

Duplexing is done the same way mirroring is done. The only difference is that you as the installer need to keep track of the devices. To achieve mirrored sets on hard drives that are attached to different controllers, you must manually choose the devices as they appear. NetWare will treat them as if they are mirrored drives; however, they will be duplexed by virtue of the fact they are connected to different controllers.

Let's say you have four identical hard drives, two of which are attached to controller #1. The other two hard drives are attached to controller #2. A single NetWare partition occupies the full space of each hard drive. NetWare will recognize these devices as devices 0, 1, 2, and 3. Devices 0 and 1 will be controller #1's devices. Devices 2 and 3 will be controller #2's devices. To duplex the drives, create two mirror sets. One set will consist of devices 0 and 2; the other set will be made from devices 1 and 3. NetWare will treat them like it treats any other set of mirrored drives; however, because devices 0 and 2 are on different controllers, they are duplexed by definition.

Once the NetWare partitions are created, the Hot Fix areas have been determined, and the drives have been mirrored or duplexed, it is time to create the NetWare volumes on the drives. Creating these volumes will allow you to store data on the server's hard disks. Select Continue With Installation from the Disk Partition and Mirroring Options menu to continue.

Volumes

Volumes are the primary means for organizing data on a NetWare server. You can create a volume for every department that is going to use your server. You can create a volume specifically for software applications; you can create a volume specifically for user data. In NetWare 4.11, multiple volumes can be created on a single NetWare partition; conversely, a single volume can span multiple NetWare partitions (physical hard disks). There are advantages and disadvantages to each type of volume implementation.

NetWare 4.11 can support a single volume with a maximum capacity of 32 terabytes (TB). That's over 33 million megabytes worth of information! A single volume may also span a maximum of 32 hard disks. Splitting volumes across multiple hard disks can greatly increase the performance of your file server. This is because multiple data requests to the same volume can be handled by multiple disk drives at the same time. Unfortunately, volumes that span multiple hard disks are more susceptible to failure. If one hard disk fails in the volume, all data will be lost on that volume (unless the disk is mirrored or duplexed).

How you design your volume scheme is completely up to you; however, there is always going to be a volume called SYS. NetWare creates this volume by default, and it stores all of the operating system files. NDS information is also stored in the SYS volume.

In the NetWare 3.x world, many network administrators enjoyed the luxury of spanning the SYS volume on their servers across many hard disks to stay with a one-volume setup. With the advent of NetWare 4.x and NDS, this scheme is no longer a good idea. The NDS database is a dynamic database that is constantly growing and shrinking in size. It must have the room to expand and shrink. Should the SYS volume ever run low on space and prevent proper NDS database updates from occurring, it can seriously corrupt the database for the entire network. We recommend that you create a smaller SYS volume for just the network operating system files and NDS database with enough extra space for any operating system expansion that may occur in the future. A 300-400MB SYS volume should be sufficient for IntranetWare. You can then create other volumes to store the production data for your users.

By default, the NetWare 4.11 installation will create a volume for every NetWare partition that is created. It will cause SYS to occupy the entire capacity of the first NetWare partition. The second NetWare partition will contain a volume called VOL1. Likewise, the third NetWare partition will be named VOL2 by the installation program. You can go with this default naming scheme, or you can modify the volume sizes and names to fit your network's needs.

After activating the server drivers, the installation program will display the Manage NetWare Volumes screen with the proposed new volumes on the server (see Figure 2-16). To create the proposed volumes list, it uses the scheme mentioned earlier where each NetWare partition gets a volume that occupies the entire partition space.

To see the volume parameters for a specific proposed volume, use the arrow keys to highlight the volume and press Enter. The Volume Information box will appear with statistics concerning that volume, as shown in Figure 2-17. Five of the six options can be changed on the proposed volume during the initial installation of NetWare 4.11.

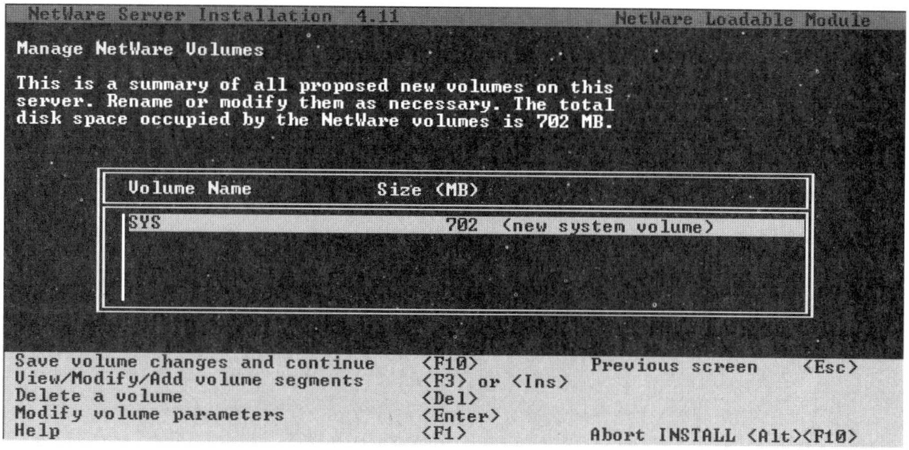

Figure 2-16: Proposed new volume list.

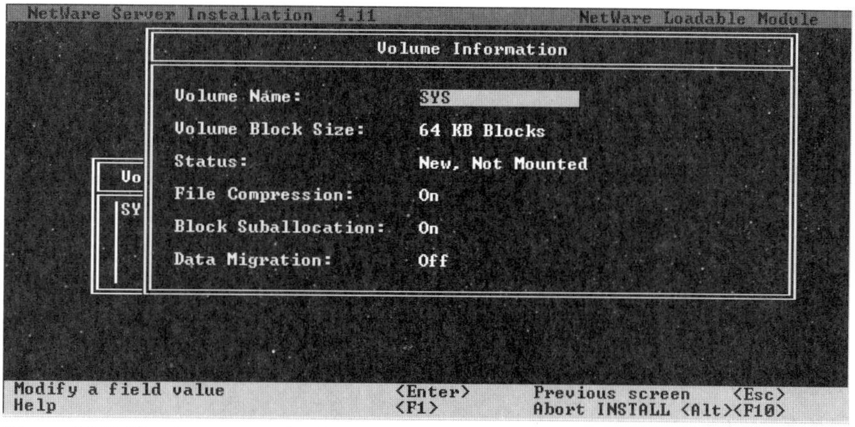

Figure 2-17: Viewing proposed volume parameters.

Because volumes play such a critical role in the organization of the NetWare 4.11 file system, it is important that they be set up appropriately. We will explore each of the options presented in Figure 2-17 to help you make informed decisions when configuring your NetWare volumes.

Volume Name

The NetWare installation program will propose a name for the specified volume using the naming system described in the previous section. The first NetWare partition will be named SYS, and successive partitions will be named VOL1, VOL2, and VOL3. This will continue until all NetWare partitions have proposed volumes.

Using the Volume Information screen (Figure 2-17), the installer can change the name of the proposed volume. There must always be a SYS volume; it is used to store the operating system files. The remaining volumes can be re-named using the following naming conventions:

- The volume name must be 2 to 15 characters in length.

- The name cannot include spaces or the following characters:
  " * + , / \ | : ' = < > ? [ ]

To rename the volume, highlight the Volume Name option using the arrow keys. Type in the desired volume name, and press Enter.

Volume Block Size

A *volume block* is the minimum unit of data that NetWare will read or write from a volume during a data request. If the volume block size is 4KB, any single read or write request performed by NetWare will be 4KB. Even if the information that is requested is only 1KB in size, it will be written, stored, and read in a 4KB block on the volume.

The installation program will provide a default volume block size. This is the block size that should provide the most efficient disk access and memory usage for your server's configuration. The default volume block size is determined by the size of the volume that is proposed. See Table 2-3 for a listing of the default volume block size.

Volume Size	Default Block Size
1-31MB	4KB
32-149MB	16KB
150-499MB	32KB
500MB+	64KB

Table 2-3: Default volume block sizes.

Most people do not have any reason to change the default volume block size. We recommend that you accept the default value. The block size does not have as much of an impact on your true data capacity as it did in NetWare 3.x because of a technique called block suballocation. For more information on block suballocation, refer to Chapter 17.

To change the block size on the server, highlight the Volume Block Size parameter (see Figure 2-17). Press Enter to change the value of the volume block size.

Status

The status parameter is not a parameter that is modifiable during the initial installation of the operating system. Once a volume has been completely installed, this parameter can be used to either mount or dismount the volume. For the server to be able to access the data in a volume, the volume must be mounted. After the proposed volumes have been accepted, the installation program will automatically mount the volumes for you.

File Compression

By default, NetWare 4.11 enables file compression on all volumes that are created. When file compression is enabled, files are not compressed immediately after being written to the volume. NetWare will compress the files if they have not been accessed for a specific period of time. NetWare 4.11's file compression will help maximize the use of the space on a volume.

File compression is enabled on a per-volume basis. One of your volumes may have file compression enabled; another volume may not have file compression. It is not useful to enable compression on a volume that is going to store data that has already been compressed by an external program or data that is constantly going to be used. NetWare is not capable of compressing previously compressed data, and data that is perpetually open will not compress because it will be frequently accessed.

If file compression has been enabled on a volume and data has been written to that volume, the file compression cannot be removed from the volume. Once you make the decision to compress, there is no going back.

To change the status of the new volume's file compression, highlight the File Compression parameter using the arrow keys (see Figure 2-17). Press the Enter key to toggle the setting between On and Off.

Block Suballocation

Block suballocation is another technique used by NetWare to maximize the use of the volume's disk space, and it is closely related to the volume block size. As mentioned earlier, the data on the volume is stored in blocks. The minimum size of the blocks is determined by the volume block size parameter. A piece of data less than the volume block size will still require one complete volume block. For example, if the data that needs to be stored is 9KB in size and the volume block size is 8KB, it will be written to two 8KB blocks. The first block will be completely filled with the first 8KB of the data. The second block will contain only 1KB of data, leaving the other 7KB unused.

This is where block suballocation is useful. When block suballocation is enabled on a volume, the data that will not completely fill a block is stored in 512-byte suballocation blocks. In the example in the preceding paragraph, the remaining 1KB of data would be stored in two 512-byte suballocation blocks. This is a much better alternative than wasting 7KB of volume space. Suballocation is explained in more detail in Chapter 17.

NetWare 4.11 has suballocation blocks enabled by default when the volume is created. Unless there is a compelling reason not to do so, leave this option enabled; however, if you do want to turn suballocation blocks off, highlight the Block Suballocation parameter by using the arrow keys (see Figure 2-17). Press Enter to toggle between On and Off.

Data Migration

Data migration is a method of increasing the capacity of your server. It involves using a high-capacity storage subsystem (HCSS), such as an optical jukebox or online tape device, with third-party management software to provide a "near-line" device to store data. The management software uses an algorithm to determine which data should be migrated from the volume to the HCSS. Data stored on the HCSS is much slower to access; however, it is still available to the user who needs it. Generally, files that are the least recently used (LRU) are the files that are migrated to the HCSS. It is less likely these files are going to be needed, which makes space for the files that are used frequently.

To change the data migration status for a volume, highlight the Data Migration option using the arrow keys (see Figure 2-17). Press the Enter key to toggle the option between On and Off. By default, NetWare 4.11 has data migration disabled for all volumes.

After the properties for the volume have been modified, press the Escape key to return to the Manage NetWare Volumes screen that was shown in Figure 2-16. From this screen, we can modify the sizes of the volumes and create new ones if desired. Volumes can also be deleted using this screen. To delete a volume, highlight it and press the Delete key. To modify, view, or create volumes, press the F3 key. The Volume Disk Segment List will appear.

Managing Volume Segment Size

A *volume segment* is space on a NetWare partition that has been appropriated for a volume's use. A volume segment can be the size of the NetWare partition, or the single NetWare partition can be broken up into multiple volume segments. Volume segments are flexible, and together they will define the sizes of the volumes once they are created.

When the Volume Disk Segment List appears, as shown in Figure 2-18, all of the volume segments for the server appear in tabular form. There are five columns to the table:

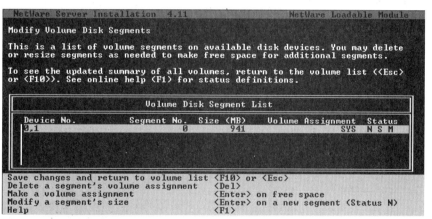

Figure 2-18: Modifying volume segments.

- Device Number—provides information concerning the physical location of the volume segment. The number displayed indicates the number of the physical disk on which the segment exists.
- Segment Number—displays which segment it is on the device.
- Size—shows the size of the volume segment in megabytes.
- Volume Assignment—assigns the specific segment to a volume. If the segment has not been assigned to a volume, it appears as free space.
- Status—displays the status of the volume segment.

The Status column is capable of displaying four letters, which are described in Table 2-4.

Status Letter	Meaning	Description
N	New	The volume segment has not been used yet.
S	Sys	The volume segment is part of the SYS volume.
M	Mirrored	The segment is a mirrored volume segment.
E	Existing	The segment is part of an already existing volume.

Table 2-4: Determining the status of a volume segment.

Volumes and volume segments are really different entities. Volume segments are the physical segments of the hard disk that compose the volume. The volume itself is a logical data structure that is composed of physical volume segments. Logically, a volume can span multiple NetWare partitions; however, it requires multiple volume segments on those partitions to make the single spanned volume.

Modifying Volume Segment Size

Changing the volume segment size is accomplished through the Volume Disk Segment List screen. You can get to this screen by highlighting the volume you want to modify and pressing Enter on the Modify Volume Disk Segments screen. To change the size of the volume segment from this new screen, perform the following steps:

1. Highlight the volume segment by using the arrow keys.

2. Press Enter to display the window showing the segment's current size.

3. Use the Delete key to delete the current size. Enter the desired size of the volume segment and press Enter. If you decrease the size of the segment, a new segment will be created and assigned to free space in the Volume Disk Segment List screen. You can increase the size of the segment only if there is existing free space in the Volume Disk Segment List.

4. Press the Escape key until you to return to the Volume Disk Segment List screen.

It is important to note only new volume segments (with the status N) can be modified in size. Existing volumes' sizes may not be modified using this method.

Deleting a Volume Assignment

If you don't like the default volume assignments that NetWare 4.11 created during installation, you can get rid of them easily. Do the following from the Modify Volume Disk Segments screen (Figure 2-18):

1. Highlight the segment you want to delete by using the arrow keys.

2. Press the Delete key.

The segment is not deleted (you can't delete a physical structure); however, the volume assignment is deleted. The assignment now becomes free space. With this free space, you can create new volumes or assign the space to be part of another volume.

Creating a Volume Assignment

If you want to create a new volume from the volume segments available, you need to have a segment that is marked as free space (it has no volume assignment). To assign a segment marked as free space to a new volume, perform the following steps from the Modify Volume Disk Segments screen (Figure 2-18):

1. Highlight the free space volume segment by using the arrow keys.

2. Press Enter. The What Would You Like to Do With This Free Segment? menu appears.

3a. To make the free segment part of a new volume, choose the Make This Segment a New Volume option from the menu. You will be prompted to enter a name for the new volume and to specify the size of the new volume.

or

3b. To make the free segment part of an existing volume, choose the Make This Segment Part of Another Volume option from the menu. A list of existing volumes appears. Highlight the volume you want to expand and press Enter.

When all the volume segment assignments are satisfactory, choose the Escape key to return to the Manage NetWare Volumes screen (Figure 2-16). We are ready to continue with the installation. If you are satisfied with the volume setup, press the F10 key to save the volume information and continue. You will be asked to confirm the settings. Select Yes, and the volume information is saved. NetWare will then attempt to mount the volumes.

After the volumes are mounted, the server is ready for the preliminary copy of the operating system files. The volumes must be mounted in order to access the file system on them. INSTALL.NLM will do one of two things at this point, depending upon which method of installation you chose. If you installed from CD-ROM, the drivers for the CD-ROM drive will automatically be loaded to continue with the installation.

If you are performing a server-to-server installation, the network connection was lost when you loaded the LAN driver for the network card. NetWare must reestablish the server-to-server connection. You will be prompted to input the password for the other server. Input the password and press Enter. NetWare will attempt to reconnect to that server and continue with the installation.

Installing NetWare Directory Services

When the preliminary file copy is complete, it is time to install NetWare Directory Services (NDS) on the server. NDS is the centralized database that stores all information about the network, including server and user information. It is analogous to the bindery in NetWare 3.x, but it is much more than that. NDS is discussed in detail in Section II of this book.

If the installation program is unable to detect other NDS trees on your network, it will ask you if this is the first NetWare 4.x server. Selecting Yes will bring up a prompt to type in the name of the NDS tree as it will be known. All NDS trees have names that identify them uniquely on the network. Answering No to this question will let you join this server to an existing NDS tree.

If other NDS trees are detected on the network by the installation program, the Choose a Directory Tree screen will appear. To join this server to an existing NDS tree, select the tree name from the Existing Directory Trees box and press Enter. Even if there are other trees on the network, it is possible to create your own tree. To create a brand-new tree, press the Insert key.

A new tree should be created only if there are no existing trees on the network or if there is compelling reason why multiple trees should exist. A large organization with highly autonomous departments may have multiple trees. If you are on a large network with a central information systems department, discuss this decision with them.

After pressing the Insert key, the Create a New Tree? box appears. Select Yes to confirm the creation of a new NDS tree. The Enter a Directory Tree Name screen will appear with a prompt for the tree name. Type in the name of the tree and press Enter. The tree name must be unique; it cannot be the same name as the server. For purposes of this book, we will assume a new NDS tree is being created for this server. Select the method that will install a brand-new NDS tree on the network.

After joining an existing tree or creating a new one, INSTALL.NLM will bring up the Choose Time Zone screen. Select the appropriate time zone from the list of time zones available. If your time zone is not listed, press the Insert key to enter the parameters for your time zone. After highlighting the appropriate time zone, press Enter.

The next screen is Verify/Enter Time Configuration Information for This Server, shown in Figure 2-19. This screen allows modifications to be made to the time zone parameters. The information from this screen and the previous one is important because it defines the time parameters for your network.

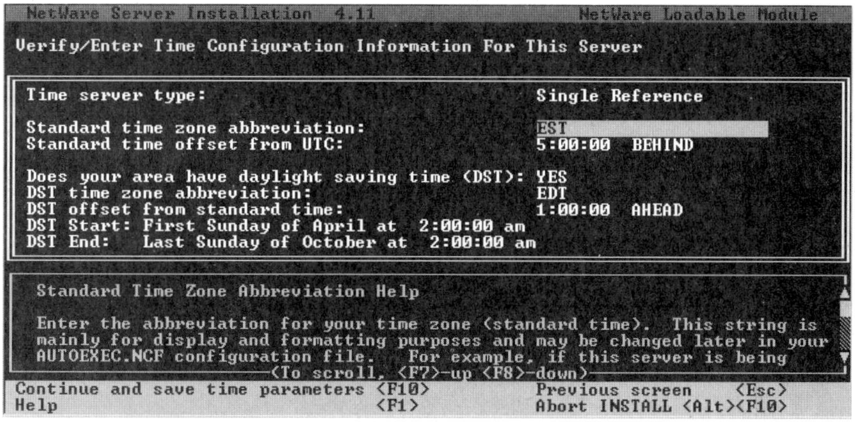

```
NetWare Server Installation  4.11                NetWare Loadable Module

Verify/Enter Time Configuration Information For This Server

Time server type:                        Single Reference

Standard time zone abbreviation:         EST
Standard time offset from UTC:           5:00:00   BEHIND

Does your area have daylight saving time (DST): YES
DST time zone abbreviation:              EDT
DST offset from standard time:           1:00:00   AHEAD
DST Start: First Sunday of April at  2:00:00 am
DST End:   Last Sunday of October at  2:00:00 am

 Standard Time Zone Abbreviation Help

  Enter the abbreviation for your time zone (standard time).  This string is
  mainly for display and formatting purposes and may be changed later in your
  AUTOEXEC.NCF configuration file.   For example, if this server is being
                   (To scroll, (F7)-up (F8)-down)
Continue and save time parameters (F10)          Previous screen    (Esc)
Help                              (F1)            Abort INSTALL (Alt)(F10)
```

Figure 2-19: Modifying time zone parameters.

NDS is dependent upon a highly synchronized network because by nature it is a dynamic, distributed database that is constantly changing. When these changes are made, they are registered with a time and date stamp. If objects making changes are not synchronized, it is possible for modifications to be lost. This is because the most recent time and date stamp for a database record is the record that is kept.

At the top of the screen in Figure 2-19, the Time Server Type parameter is shown. There are four types of time servers in NetWare 4.11:

■ Single Reference

■ Reference

■ Primary

■ Secondary

If you have created a new tree, leave the Time Server Type set to the default Single Reference. If you have joined an existing tree, consult with the NDS coordinator to determine how the time parameters should be set. Besides setting the Time Server Type screen, you must also set the time zone in which the server resides along with any special time considerations, such as Daylight Savings Time. You will also notice an abbreviation called UTC. It stands for Universal Time Coordinated, and it means the same thing as Greenwich Mean Time (GMT). For more information on NDS time synchronization, refer to Chapter 11.

When the time parameters are set, press F10 to save the time parameters and continue with the installation. You will see the Specify a Context for This Server and Its Objects screen in Figure 2-20. This is where the preliminary structure for the new NDS tree is created. Enter a name for the organization. If desired, enter the names for any organizational units to be created beneath the organization. What is being specified here is the location in the NDS tree where the server is going to exist. Note the Server Context parameter and the Administrator Name parameter.

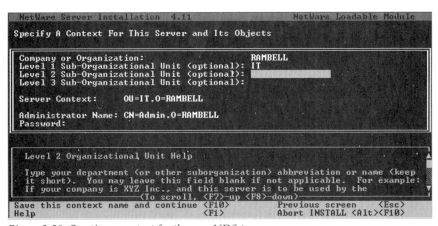

Figure 2-20: Creating a context for the new NDS tree.

As you create an organization and optional organizational units, the Server Context parameter will change to reflect this. It is not too important to understand this right now because what you type here is not set in stone. Just write down the server context for future reference. The Administrator Name also changed when the organization was created. This is the account that will be used to initially provide access to the network. Write down the information next to the Administrator Name parameter.

When the organization and organizational units are created, use the arrow keys to highlight the Password parameter. Type in the password for the Admin account. After typing it in, you will be prompted to verify the password. Type in the password again. Do not forget this password. If you do, you will have to reinstall NDS! After typing in the password, press F10 to continue with the installation.

After continuing with the installation, NetWare will remind you of the NDS tree name, the server context, and the administrator name. It is important to remember these. Press Enter to dismiss the screen, and NDS will be installed on the server.

License Installation

After installing NetWare Directory Services, the next step is the installation of the NetWare 4.11 license. NetWare 4.11 can be installed without a license file, but it will be limited to a two-user connection. Only two workstations will be able to concurrently connect to the file server. This is obviously very limiting if you have many users who need to have access to the server.

There should be a diskette labeled LICENSE with your IntranetWare package. This diskette contains a file called SERVER.MLS that INSTALL.NLM will use to set the number of concurrent users to the appropriate level. IntranetWare licenses are purchased in specific user quantities. Licenses can be purchased to allow concurrent connections for 5, 10, 25, 50, 100, 250, 500, or 1,000 users.

People who are familiar with NetWare 3.x will remember how limiting these licenses are. If you had 75 users that needed to use your server, but only a 50-user license, you had to upgrade to the 100-user license to connect all your users. This is not the case with NetWare 4.11. The licenses are stackable. If you only have a 50-user license and you need to connect 75 users, you only need to purchase an additional 25-user license and add the two licenses together.

At this point in the installation, INSTALL.NLM will ask you to insert the floppy diskette with the server license file. Insert the disk and press Enter to load the license. If the license is located in a different location, press the F3 key and specify the path for the SERVER.MLS file.

The license is also serialized. The serial number is unique, and all NetWare servers on the network are scanning to see if other servers have that serial number. Your license agreement specifies that you may only install the license on one server. If you use that license file on another server, you break the terms of your license agreement. If a NetWare server finds another server operating with the same license serial number, it will alert you to your copyright violation frequently.

Editing the Server Startup Files

When a NetWare 4.11 server loads, it looks for two files for commands to load and parameters to set. These files are the STARTUP.NCF file and the AUTOEXEC.NCF file. STARTUP.NCF is read first. After the installation of the license, INSTALL.NLM brings up a screen to edit the STARTUP.NCF file. Review the commands that are going to be placed in the new file, modify or add any commands as appropriate, and press F10 to save the file. For more information on commands included in the STARTUP.NCF and AUTOEXEC.NCF files, refer to Chapter 17.

After STARTUP.NCF is saved, another edit screen will appear. This time it will be for AUTOEXEC.NCF. Again, review the commands that are going to be placed in the file, modify or add any specific commands you want, and press F10 to save the file. Again, for a thorough discussion of the server startup files, refer to Chapter 17.

After the startup files are saved, the main copy of the operating system files occurs. Sit back, relax, and have a few cups of coffee. It will take a few minutes to finish copying the files. When the file copy is complete, the Other Installation Options screen will appear.

This screen lists other components of the NetWare 4.11 system that can be installed. These items will be discussed throughout the book, however, you will not be installing any of them at this time. For now, just choose Continue Installation by highlighting it and pressing Enter. Congratulations! The installation of the operating system is now complete. It is recommended you down the server and restart it after installation is complete. This will ensure the operating system has installed properly.

Experienced Installer's Guide

For people who are comfortable with installing NetWare, here is a condensed step-by-step installation procedure. It provides a brief overview of the installation process that does not get bogged down in the details of the actual menu selections on the various screens throughout the installation.

Once the server has been prepared and the method of installation chosen, install NetWare 4.11. The following steps assume that NetWare 4.11 is being installed with a custom installation:

1. From the CD-ROM or file server prompt, type **INSTALL.BAT**.

2. Select the file server language.

3. View the Novell software license agreement.

4. Choose Server Installation from the installation options.

5. Select the operating system to be installed. To install NetWare 4.11, select NetWare 4.11 from the menu.

6. Choose the type of installation to be performed. Select the custom installation option to customize the installation of NetWare 4.11.

7. Enter a name for the file server.

8. Provide an internal IPX number for the file server.

9. Specify the target location for the required server files in the DOS partition. The files will be copied once the destination is entered.

10. Provide server locale information.

11. Add, modify, and delete commands from the STARTUP.NCF file displayed. Press F10 to save information and continue the installation.

12. Decide if NetWare 4.11 will load from the AUTOEXEC.BAT file.

13. After step 12, the NetWare installation program will launch the operating system (SERVER.EXE). Once NetWare 4.11 is up, INSTALL.NLM will be loaded to finish the installation of the operating system.

14. Select the disk driver and LAN driver for the server. NetWare will attempt to auto-detect this information; however, these drivers may need to be manually selected.

15. Modify disk driver and LAN driver load parameters by selecting the desired driver and pressing Enter. A new menu will be displayed in which the options to view and edit the driver parameters are given.

16. After the drivers are selected, NetWare will attempt to load the server drivers. If any drivers are not loading properly, switch to the system console and load them manually.

17. Select the protocols and frame types to bind to the network card. NetWare 4.11 will attempt to auto-detect the protocols and frames on the network; however, protocols may need to be bound manually if NetWare is unable to perform this auto-detection.

18. Create the NetWare partitions on the hard disks. This assumes the disk driver(s) for the server have loaded properly.

19. If desired, create mirrored or duplexed sets of partitions.

20. Review the proposed volume list and make any necessary changes to the volume segments. Sizes of volumes can be reduced or enlarged, and new volumes can be created from free space. Press F3 from the Manage NetWare Volumes screen to modify the proposed volumes.

21. Once volume segments are configured for the appropriate volumes, review the volumes' pertinent information. These volume parameters include the volume's name, block size, file compression, block suballocation, and data migration. Select the volume and press Enter on the Manage NetWare Volumes screen to view these parameters.

22. Save volume information by pressing F10. The installation program will mount the volumes and perform the preliminary operating system file copy.

23. After the files have been copied, select the NDS tree this server is going to join. If a new NDS tree is to be created, press the Insert key and type in a name for the new tree.

24. Choose the time zone from the list of time zones displayed. To enter parameters for a time zone not listed, press the Insert key.

25. Verify the time zone parameters and the NDS Time Server Type. Press F10 to save the time information.

26. Create the organization and organizational units in the NDS tree. Also specify the Admin account password. Press F10 to save the NDS container and Admin information.

27. Provide the NetWare license diskette to transfer the license from the floppy disk to the server.

28. Edit the proposed STARTUP.NCF file. Press F10 to save the file and continue.

29. Edit the proposed AUTOEXEC.NCF file. Press F10 to save the file and continue.

30. Down the server and restart it to ensure the operating system was installed correctly.

After the AUTOEXEC.NCF file is saved, the main operating system file copy will be performed. This copy will take longer than the previous two copies have. When complete, the Other Installation Options screen will appear. Select Continue Installation from this screen. Once chosen, the custom installation of NetWare 4.11 is complete.

Applying Concepts: Rambell, Inc.

From the beginning, John Doe knew that he had some special considerations concerning his NetWare 4.11 installation. He knew he was going to mirror drives on his server for fault tolerance; a custom installation was in order.

John decided to name his server Damocles and accepted the internal IPX number generated by the installation program. Because the server was new, INSTALL.NLM was able to detect the hard disk controller and network card present in the machine. He did not need to add any additional parameters for the server drivers to load successfully.

Because it is a brand-new network, John did have to provide an IPX network number for the IPX protocol. He also accepted the default Ethernet_802.2 frame type. After the protocol was bound to the LAN driver, it was time to move onto the volumes.

With this server, the NetWare partitions were created out of the remaining free space on the drives. The two drives on the machine were mirrored using the mirroring options; however, John was a bit concerned. He received an error message about the NetWare partitions being different sizes. He thought, "But the hard drives are both the same size!"

After consulting with other information technology professionals, he realized that one of the drives had a 50MB DOS partition that the other drive did not. Thus, the NetWare partition on the hard disk which also contained the DOS partition required for booting the server was 50MB smaller in size than the NetWare partition on the hard drive without the DOS partition. The partitions were mirrored, but 50MB of space on the second drive was not being used because mirroring unlike partitions causes the smaller of the partitions to be used.

John created two volumes out of his free NetWare partition space. A 300MB SYS volume was created to store the NetWare 4.11 operating system files and some applications he is going to install on the server. It will have enough remaining space to handle NDS information, and users will not be allowed to deposit data on this volume. The remainder of the space was given to a volume called VOL1, which is going to be used to house all of the user data.

After creating the volumes, a new NDS tree was created. John decided to call his company's tree Willow. After specifying time zone information and time server parameters (the defaults were accepted), an organization was created in the NDS tree called RAMBELL, and an organizational unit beneath that called IT was created. John made note of the administrator account information as well as the context in which Damocles resides.

John installed the user license he purchased, saved the startup files, and finished copying the operating system files from the CD-ROM to the server. He downed Damocles and restarted it. He breathed a sigh of relief as the server came up without a hitch.

Moving On

Now that the server has been installed, we have touched upon a lot of concepts that may seem vague, and rightly so! NDS trees and server contexts are confusing if you are not familiar with them. Chapter 3 will provide an overview of concepts that are critical to the understanding of the NetWare 4.11 environment. Now that the server has been installed, we can begin to get into the meat of operating and managing the NetWare environment.

3

NetWare 4.11 Concepts

John Doe now has NetWare 4.11 installed on his server, but he has only done half of the work involved in setting up a basic computer network. Client/server computer networking involves just that. One machine needs to be the server, which implies that there must be some client workstations. In addition to being the main interface to the network for the users, client workstations are also of particular importance to the network administrator. Most network administration tasks are performed from the client workstation.

But before we get to the heart of network administration, it is important to understand the concept behind the NetWare 4.11 computer network. The cornerstone of this network is a new creature called NetWare Directory Services (NDS). NDS is a distributed, object-oriented database that stores all of the information concerning your network. NDS is discussed in great detail in Section II of this book; however, it is necessary to provide an overview of the concept of NDS before we can perform the basic tasks of network administration in NetWare 4.11.

This overview will include a discussion of the structure and composition of NDS. NDS has a treelike hierarchical structure that is composed of many objects. The objects represent your network resources. To access these resources, you must know their positions in the tree and their names. In this chapter, you will learn about these objects, their contexts, and how to derive NDS names for them.

Once the conceptual foundation is laid, we will explore the NetWare Administrator. This is the utility that comes with NetWare 4.11 that allows the network administrator to navigate the network and enter all of the appropriate information about the network, including users, groups, and printers. The NetWare Administrator utility will allow you to provide centralized management to all NDS objects in your NetWare network. The days of having to administer file servers individually are gone!

The NDS Concept

Back in the days of NetWare 3.x, the concept of a local area network (LAN) was server-centric. Things like user accounts, groups, and printers were created on a server and pertained only to that server. Users were expected to authenticate to this server and use its associated resources. Those resources did not, however, carry over to any other servers.

If a user had a need to access the resources on another server, he or she was required to separately authenticate to that other server even if the user IDs and passwords were identical on both servers. If the user had a need to access another server, a third authentication process would occur.

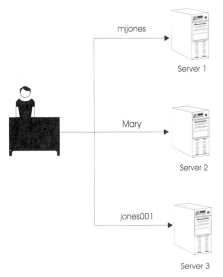

Figure 3-1: A user needs to authenticate to three servers individually because no security information is shared.

In the NetWare 3.x world, the user in Figure 3-1 was connected to three separate LANs. Any changes to the user account usually involved modifying the user's record three times—once for each server. If the user was required to change a password on one of the servers, he or she either needed to remember the different passwords for the three servers or spend the time changing the password on all three to achieve password synchronization. If the user left the company, the user account would need to be removed from three separate locations.

It is inefficient to have to have to go through the same process three times just to maintain the information on one user. To combat this problem and address the needs of growing networks where users quite often need a diverse set of resources from many different servers, Novell has created NDS and made it the foundation of the NetWare 4.x operating system.

With NDS, everything on the network (servers, user IDs, printers, groups, and so on) is brought together and viewed as one giant resource pool. All of the information on the various components of the resource pool is kept in a central database maintained by NDS. This information includes security information to ensure that only the appropriate users have access to these objects (Figure 3-2).

All the NetWare 4.x servers in the resource pool have a copy of the central database, which gives them all the same information about every resource on the network. This commonality provides a single, unified network in which every user requires only one point of entry to access the entire network.

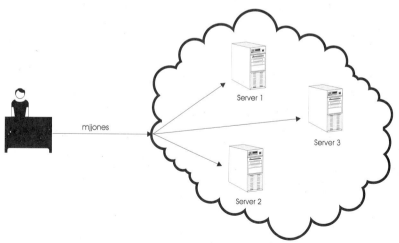

Figure 3-2: A user needs to authenticate only once to the resource pool because all resources share the same security information.

The entire scenario has changed from when the user had to authenticate three separate times to gain access to all the network resources he or she needs. The user is now only required to log in once to access the resource pool. Because there is a unique record for every user in NDS, the network administrator only needs to modify the user's record once. Every server will know the change has occurred because the change will be made to the common database.

The NDS Structure

Although the concept is accurate, it would be extremely hard for a network administrator to keep track of NDS if it was represented as a resource pool. The pool concept lacks the hierarchical structure that would provide the logical organization necessary to administer NDS. To help ease the administration, a much more understandable concept was required. Thus, NDS is organized in a tree structure.

All of the network resources from our resource pool become part of the tree. They take their place in the tree as distinct objects. An *object* is a discrete NDS unit representing a unique resource that exists on the network. Objects are the building blocks of the NDS tree, and each one contains information about the specific network resource it represents.

An object itself comprises properties and values. A *property* describes a particular quality of the object. The specific information that describes the property is the property's *value*. For example, a user has the properties name and department. Their values might be Mary Smith and accounting. All NDS objects of the same type will have the same properties; however, they will not all have the same values. Likewise, objects of differing types will have different properties and values.

Object: User	
Property	Value
Login Name	mjjones
Password	changeme
Telephone No.	555-1324
Location	417 Any Bldg.

Object: Printer	
Property	Value
Name	Laserprt
Location	312 Any Bldg.
Queue(s)	ACCT

Figure 3-3: Different object types have different properties and values.

In Figure 3-3, the difference between objects, properties, and values is illustrated. Some properties for the user object are login ID, password, telephone number, and location. These are general categories that help describe the user object. The values of these properties—mjjones, changeme, 555-1324, and 417 Any Building—provide specific data about the defined properties.

It is important to note that some properties are mandatory and some are multivalued. A *mandatory* property is a property that must contain a value. NDS will not permit an object to exist without the mandatory properties defined. These properties must have a value before the object is created, and the values cannot be deleted once the object exists (although they can be changed).

A *multivalued* property is a property that can contain more than one value. For instance, the Location property of the User object is multivalued. If a user works in multiple locations, each location can be recorded in this one property. Group Membership is also a multivalued property of the User object. In NetWare 4.11, a user can be a member of multiple groups.

All objects that can be created in NDS have predefined properties. Many objects come with a large number of properties for which the network administrator can provide values; however, it is not necessary to fill every object property with a value. A balance should be struck between populating the properties with useful information and spending large quantities of time maintaining the information in NDS.

NDS Object Classes

As we know, the NDS tree is made up entirely of objects; however, there are three distinct classes of objects that exist in NDS that help in the organization of the tree:

- The [Root] object
- Container objects
- Leaf objects

It is these object classes that actually define the structure of the tree. [Root] is the object class that exists at the top of the tree, and immediately below it are containers that hold other objects. Containers may hold other containers or leaf objects. Leaf objects cannot hold any other objects; they are the objects that define specific network resources like users, groups, and printers. Through the use of these object classes, it is possible to create a logical tree structure for your network.

The [Root] Object

[Root] always exists on every NDS tree, and it always exists at the top of the tree. Unlike most trees, which grow upward, the NDS tree starts with [Root] at the top and grows downward. There is only one [Root] per NDS tree, and it is created during the installation of NDS. Because of its importance and uniqueness in NDS, you need to use brackets ([]) when referring to the [Root] object in the NDS tree.

Since [Root] is the top-level structure in the tree, it follows that other objects will be added beneath [Root]; however, only container objects may be created directly beneath the [Root] object. A leaf object cannot exist in NDS directly beneath [Root].

Container Objects

Container objects can hold either other container objects or leaf objects. In the tree analogy, the containers are the branches of the tree and graphically give NDS its treelike structure. The main purpose of containers is to provide organization in the NDS tree.

Container objects are often named for specific departments or divisions of an organization to provide a logical structure for your computer network. All network resources that exist in a company's accounting department might be grouped into a container called ACCT. By judiciously using container objects, you can create an efficient network structure.

To help with this grouping of network resources, NDS provides three types of container objects:

- Country objects
- Organization objects
- Organizational Unit objects

Each one of these container objects provides the same type of service (to hold leaf objects or other containers), but each one has its own particular nuances and restrictions about how and where you can use it in the NDS tree. For more information on these objects and how to use them in your NDS tree, refer to Chapter 8.

Country Objects

The Country object was intended for large international companies. It is helpful to immediately divide the NDS tree into the international divisions that exist in these types of companies. The names of Country objects are always two characters in length. Care should be taken in naming them; your NDS country name should match the X.500 two-character code standard for that country. That will ensure that your NDS naming scheme is compatible with other existing directory service standards. Refer to Appendix D for a complete listing of X.500 country codes.

There are a couple of restrictions when using the Country object in your NDS tree:

- The Country object may exist only in the first level of the tree—directly below [Root].

- The Country object may only contain the Organization container object or the Alias leaf object.

Organization Objects

Organization objects (also called organizations) help to give the NDS tree an identity in relation to the company for which it is providing services. An NDS tree with an organization object named Rambell would help identify that tree with Rambell, Inc.

Organizations are the first container object that can contain all leaf objects. They also can contain other container objects, but there are restrictions in how you can use Organizations:

- An organization may exist only beneath [Root] or a country object. They may not exist in another organization.

- Organizations can contain an organizational unit or any leaf object. They may not contain another organization.

- Every NDS tree must have at least one organization in it.

- An organization name is limited to a maximum of 64 characters.

Small companies using NDS may only have one organization in the tree with all of the leaf objects directly beneath it. Larger companies will probably have an organization at the top with many organizational units beneath it to represent the various departments within the company.

Organizational Units

Organizational units provide another level of organizational detail for your NDS tree. Quite often, organizational units represent a department, group, or division within a company. They help refine the tree structure and provide for the logical grouping of leaf objects within your tree. Of all the container objects, organizational units are the most flexible because they can be layered two and three deep in the tree.

Here are the restrictions pertaining to the organizational unit:

- An organizational unit may exist only beneath an organization or organizational unit. They may not exist beneath a country or [Root].

- Organizational units may contain all leaf objects and other organizational units. They may not contain any other container object.

- An organizational unit name is limited to a maximum of 64 characters.

Organizational units provide great flexibility to the design of the NDS tree because they may contain other organizational units. For example, a company may have an information technology department. Within the information technology department, there may be a group responsible for the network backbone of the company while another group provides application support. It makes sense to create a tree design like the one in Figure 3-4 for this situation. The organizational unit is the key to creating this type of structure.

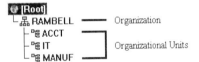

Figure 3-4: Organizational units may be layered to refine the tree organizational structure.

Leaf Objects

Leaf objects are the items in the NDS tree that represent the network resources that exist physically or logically. These resources include users, printers, servers, print queues, and volume objects. The version of NDS that ships with NetWare 4.11 provides for 23 different types of leaf objects. They are grouped into nine different categories that help describe their function.

Some of the leaf objects described in the following sections get created automatically in the NDS tree by various installation programs. This is most often true during the installation of the actual NetWare 4.11 operating system. However, many objects need to be created manually (like the user-related leaf objects). When creating objects manually, remember that leaf objects are subject to restrictions just like container objects:

- Leaf objects may exist only in organizations or organizational units. The one exception is the Alias leaf object, which may exist in a country as well.

- Leaf objects may not contain any other objects.

- Leaf object names are limited to a maximum of 64 characters.

Figure 3-5 shows a typical NDS tree with [Root], container, and leaf objects.

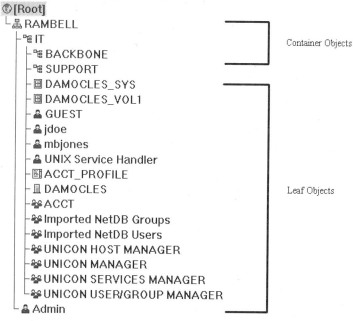

Figure 3-5: Objects in an NDS tree.

Parent & Child Objects

Quite often you will see the terms parent and child when discussing objects. If you don't know what a parent object or child object is, don't panic. It is not a difficult concept to understand. A child object is an object that exists within another object. Likewise, a parent object is an object that contains other objects.

In Figure 3-5, the RAMBELL organization is the parent of the IT organizational unit. IT is the child of RAMBELL. It should also be noted that RAMBELL is both a parent and a child at the same time. RAMBELL is the child of [Root].

By definition, [Root] is only a parent object because there is nothing above it. All leaf objects are only children because they may not contain any other objects.

As mentioned, there are 23 distinct types of leaf objects which are grouped into nine general categories which help describe their function. The nine categories and their component leaf objects are briefly described in the next sections.

Application Leaf Object

The Application leaf object (there is only one type of leaf object in this category) is related to the NetWare Application Manager (NAM). When this object is used in conjunction with NAM, it lets the network administrator manage network-based software applications as objects in the NDS tree. For more information on NetWare Application Manager and Application leaf objects, refer to Chapter 13.

Auditing Leaf Object

This category of leaf object has only one member. It is the Auditing File Object (AFO), and it is critical in providing the auditing capabilities included with NetWare 4.11.

Informational Leaf Object

This category of leaf object has only one member, the computer leaf object. Informational leaf objects provide just that—information. By creating a computer leaf object in the NDS tree, the network administrator is representing a foreign computer that exists on the network. Computer leaf objects are useful if the network administrator wants to keep track of all of the workstations connected to the network. Each workstation could have a computer leaf object created to represent it in the tree. Each one of the objects would be used to store information about that specific workstation.

Message-Related Leaf Objects

If Novell's Message Handling Services (MHS) are installed on the NetWare 4.11 server, message-related leaf objects will be installed in the NDS tree. By using these objects, the network administrator will be able to provide electronic mail services to users on the network. MHS is no longer included with IntranetWare and must be purchased with Novell's GroupWise.

Message-related leaf objects include:

- Distribution List
- External Entity
- Message Routing Group
- Messaging Server

NetWare Licensing Services Leaf Object

This category of leaf object has one member. It is the License Service Provider (LSP) server object. This object is created when the NetWare Licensing Services (NLS) NetWare Loadable Module (NLM) is loaded on a NetWare server. NLS allows you to manage the software licenses on your network from a central location. This way, your users will not be able to run 20 copies of an application on your network when you only have 10 licensed copies available.

Printer-Related Leaf Objects

Like previous versions of NetWare, NetWare 4.x comes with a flexible and robust printing environment. It is an environment that relies heavily on the printer objects that are created in the NDS tree. For a thorough discussion of NetWare 4.11 printing, see Chapter 7. Printer-related leaf objects include:

- Print queue
- Print server
- Printer

Server-Related Leaf Objects

These leaf objects represent the NetWare server and its related components in the NDS tree. Server-related leaf objects include:

- **The AFP server object** shows where on the NDS tree a server has the AppleTalk Filing Protocol (AFP) installed. This object is not automatically created in the NDS tree when AFP is installed on a server. The network administrator needs to create it manually to store information about the server.

- **The Directory Map object** functions much like the Alias object does. It provides a pointer to a specific directory on any NetWare file server. Many login scripts point to Directory Map objects in the NDS tree. That way, if the specific directory changes, only the Directory Map object needs to be modified—not every login script.

- **The NetWare Server object** is also referenced in many places as the NetWare Core Protocol (NCP) Server object; they are one and the same. This object obviously represents a server that is running NetWare. When NetWare 4.11 is installed, it automatically creates a NetWare Server object in the NDS tree. Without this object, it would not be possible to access the server's file system.

- **A volume object** is created in the NDS tree automatically for every volume that is created during the installation of NetWare 4.11. This object points to physical NetWare volumes that exist on the network.

User-Related Leaf Objects

Users are the main reason that network administrators exist. Without them, we wouldn't have a job. User-related objects allow us to provide users with access to all of the network resources. These objects include:

- **The group object** allows the network administrator to reference many users that may exist in different contexts with just one object. By doing so, the network administrator can grant mass trustee rights to a specific network resource. Any modification to the level of rights the group needs is made once to the group object, and the network administrator just adds and removes user objects from the group as he or she sees fit.

- **The organizational role object** is used to define a specific position that exists within your organization. A user then occupies this role and inherits its security privileges for the duration that user is the occupant of the organizational role object.

    An excellent example to describe the use of this object is network administration itself. An organizational role is set up with the appropriate rights to administer the network (this usually requires some form of supervisory privilege). A user is then designated as the occupant of this role, and as the occupant, inherits all of the rights associated with it. When the user is removed from the role, the security privileges are gone as well. The user receives all of the necessary rights from being in the organizational role, not from his or her individual user object.

■ **The profile object** is incredibly useful because it contains the profile login script. When a user's object references a profile object, the associated profile login script is executed upon login along with any other login scripts that are pertinent. This is a way to provide a common login script to users who are scattered across different containers in the tree. The different types of login scripts (including the profile login script) are discussed in detail in Chapter 5.

■ **The user object** represents a user on your network. This is probably the most important object that exists in NDS. Through the 55 predefined properties associated with this object, a network administrator can set such things as login restrictions, intruder lockout detection, passwords, and security rights.

Miscellaneous Leaf Objects

As implied by their title, miscellaneous leaf objects don't fit any of the other eight categories, so they were grouped together. Miscellaneous leaf objects include:

■ **The Alias object** provides a pointer to another leaf object in the NDS tree by actually appearing to be that object. Most often, it is used to provide access to NDS objects that exist in different locations in the NDS tree.

■ **The bindery object** is placed in the NDS tree by an upgrade or migration utility for backward compatibility purposes. Without this object in the tree, old bindery-based utilities would not be able to function.

■ **The bindery queue object** is also placed in the NDS tree by an upgrade or migration utility for backward-compatibility purposes. These objects refer to old bindery-based print queues and allow users using bindery services to print.

■ **The unknown object** appears when an existing NDS object can no longer be identified as one of the other 22 types of leaf objects. Usually when you see this object, you know there is something amiss. If unknown objects begin to appear on your NDS tree, it is time to start doing some detective work to discover the root of the problem.

Now that you are familiar with the types of objects which can exist in the NDS tree, you can create them at will. Obviously, container objects are required to hold the leaf objects in your NDS tree, and the leaf objects are used to represent network resources; however, how do you actually identify these objects in the tree once they are in place? Through a concept called context, you will be able to locate all of the objects which exist in your NDS tree.

Context

As a network administrator begins to populate the NDS tree with objects, it is important to note exactly where in the tree they fall. When a resource is requested, the position in the tree must be indicated in order for NDS to find the object. The position of the object in the NDS tree is its *context*. In Figure 3-6, a user object named Mike is in the MANUF organizational unit while a different Mike user object is in the organizational unit ACCT. These objects have the same name (and may be for the same user), but because they exist in different positions in the tree, they have different contexts.

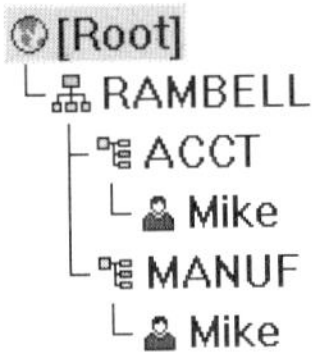

```
⊛[Root]
└ 品 RAMBELL
   ├ ᵈᵈ ACCT
   │   └ ♟ Mike
   └ ᵈᵈ MANUF
       └ ♟ Mike
```

Figure 3-6: Same username, but different contexts.

To correctly specify an object's context, locate the object in the NDS tree and trace the path back to [Root]. As you are tracing this path in the tree, list every container object you go through on the way up and separate each object by a period. Do not include [Root] in the context. Looking back at Figure 3-6, the contexts for the two Mike user objects are different:

- The context for the Mike user object in the organizational unit ACCT is ACCT.RAMBELL.

- The context for the Mike user object in the organizational unit MANUF is MANUF.RAMBELL.

Note that when context is specified, only the container objects are listed. This is important to understand. When the leaf object's name is included with its context, it is no longer a context; it is an object name. (See "NDS Object Naming Conventions" later in this chapter.)

Current Context

The *current context* is the present position of a client workstation in the NDS tree. Unlike the context of an existing object, which is static, a user may navigate the workstation around the NDS tree freely, changing contexts at will. A workstation's context is dynamic, and its current position in the tree is its current context.

The current context is the default point of reference the workstation uses when trying to access the resources requested by the user. If the resource requested exists in the workstation's current context, only the resource's name needs to be specified; however, if the requested resource exists outside of the current context, the resource's name and context need to be supplied.

This is just like executing a program from the DOS command prompt. If the program is in your current directory, you can execute it by merely typing the name. If the program exists outside of your current directory, you must provide not only the name of the program but the path to the file as well. That's how DOS is able to find programs. It is also how NDS is able to locate objects.

Here's another way to look at current context. We've all seen the "You Are Here" directory maps in shopping malls with the colored dot that points out where we are. When we approach one map, the colored dot tells us where we are standing. As we travel through the mall and get to another directory, the position of the dot has changed, but it still tells us where we are standing. Current context is the colored dot. It's value (position) changes, but it always tells us where we are currently located.

Using CX

When the client workstation is set up, the network administrator will set a default context. The default context should be set to the container whose resources the user of that workstation will use most often. This way, only the resource names need to be specified by the user. However, there may be times when a user from a context other than the default wants to use the workstation. In these cases, it is useful to change the current context of the workstation.

There are many ways to change the current context of a workstation. Two of the most common methods are through the NetWare Administrator and the CX command in DOS. The first method will be discussed in "Navigating the NDS Tree" later in this chapter, but exploring the CX command now will help you understand context in NetWare 4.11. CX will allow a user to both determine his or her current context and change that current context.

By typing **cx** at the DOS prompt, this utility will return your current context. If your current location in the tree is [Root] and you type **cx**, it will display the following:

```
[Root]
```

This command gives you a quick and simple way to determine where you are in the tree.

Changing context using CX requires more thought and more knowledge of the structure of the NDS tree itself. There are two conventions that are used to change context with CX:

- **cx <context>**

- **cx .<context>**

The first convention allows you to change to a context that exists below your current context. CX determines the new context by taking the context you typed in and appending your current context to it. For example, if your current context is IT.RAMBELL, and you type **cx support**, CX will switch your context to SUPPORT.IT.RAMBELL *if that context exists*. Otherwise, your current context will remain unchanged.

When you use CX, it is similar to using CD to navigate the DOS file system. For example, if the directory SUPPORT existed as a subdirectory of your current directory, you could type the command **cd support** to get to that directory. Use the same logic in the NDS tree.

When you use the first CX convention, there is one important thing to remember. Context is specified from the bottom up, not the top down. This is where context differs from directory structure. Assume that the current position is the root of the tree. We are trying to get to SUPPORT, as described in the preceding paragraph. If this were a directory structure, you would type **cd rambell\it\support**. However, with NDS and CX you would type **cx support.it.rambell**.

The second convention will let you change to a context relative to [Root]. CX will not try to append your current context to the end of what you type if you begin the context with a period. Typing **cx .acct.rambell** will change your context to ACCT.RAMBELL regardless of your current context *if that context exists*. Otherwise, your current context will remain unchanged.

CX is a powerful tool that helps you navigate the NDS tree. It also comes with other options. Table 3-1 lists some of the common options used with CX. When using CX, it is useful to imagine the structure of your NDS tree. Although you must traverse the tree from bottom to top to identify the context, using CX requires that you think in a normal top-down mentality.

Command	Action
cx .	Change your current context to the context of the parent container.
cx ..	Change your current context to the context of the container two levels above your present location.
cx /r	Change your current context to [Root].
cx <context> /r	Change your current context to the context specified, relative to [Root]. Equivalent to cx .<context>.
cx /t	Display the NDS structure below your current context. Only container objects are shown.
cx /t /a	Display the NDS structure below your current context, including all leaf objects.

Table 3-1: Command options for CX.

For example, we could use CX to navigate the sample NDS tree shown in Figure 3-7. If our current context was the organization RAMBELL, we could get to the context IT.RAMBELL by typing **cx it** at the DOS prompt. Notice that although the context name is specified as IT.RAMBELL, we actually used the inherent top-down structure of the NDS tree to navigate it using CX.

Figure 3-7: Keep the structure of the NDS tree in mind when using CX to navigate contexts.

Now that we understand context and how to navigate the NDS tree, we will be able to determine the names of the objects that we create and put in the tree. NDS and NetWare 4.11 provide different types of naming conventions, and each one has its own subtlety.

NDS Object Naming Conventions

Every leaf object that exists in an NDS tree has a common name. A *common name* is the name that identifies a particular user object within its context. Looking back to Figure 3-6, earlier in this chapter, there were two user objects in the tree named Mike. Mike is the common name for both user objects.

Common names do not necessarily need to be unique. It is acceptable for two objects to have the same common name within a single NDS tree. This is because the uniqueness of the object does not depend solely upon its common name; it also depends upon its position in the tree. As we have learned already, an object's context specifies its position in the tree. Thus, the object's uniqueness is defined as a combination of its common name and its context.

It should also follow that no two objects in the same context are allowed to have the same common name. This is true even for objects of different types, and the reason for this is obvious. Each name within the NDS tree must be unique. The combination of an object's common name and its context must identify exactly one object; otherwise, the NDS tree will not be able to determine which object is being referenced.

The naming itself is probably the easiest part. To find an object's NDS name, start with the leaf object and trace the path back to [Root] while writing down the name of every container you pass through. Separate each object's name in this path with a period. Sometimes this is easier said than done. There are actually two types of naming conventions used in NDS:

- Distinguished naming
- Relative distinguished naming

When you are writing these types of names, there are two methods of expressing them:

- Typeful naming
- Typeless naming

Distinguished Naming

A *distinguished name* is the combination of an object's common name and its context. When writing distinguished names, there are a couple of rules to follow:

- Distinguished names are always written with a leading period.

- Periods are used to separate the objects in the distinguished name.

Relative Distinguished Naming

When the NDS tree has many different containers and objects, distinguished naming can become cumbersome. As you begin to trace back through the tree, you might encounter numerous objects that you would be required to list in the distinguished name. For convenience sake, NDS has another type of naming. A *relative distinguished name* traces an object's path back to your current context and lets NDS take care of the rest.

NDS creates a distinguished name from a relative distinguished name by appending the current context to the relative distinguished name that was supplied. For example, if your current context is IT.RAMBELL and the relative distinguished name Mary.SUPPORT is given, NDS will create the distinguished name .Mary.SUPPORT.IT.RAMBELL to identify the object in the tree.

When writing relative distinguished names, there are some guidelines to follow:

- Relative distinguished names are *never* written with a leading period.

- Periods are used to separate the objects in the relative distinguished name.

- Relative distinguished names can be written with a trailing period.

A trailing period in a relative distinguished name causes NDS to remove one container from the left side of your current context. If your current context is IT.RAMBELL and you enter the relative distinguished name Admin., NDS will remove one object from the left side of the current context and then append the remainder to create the distinguished name to identify the object. In this case, the IT organizational unit will be removed, and RAMBELL will be appended to create the distinguished name .Admin.RAMBELL.

Typeful Naming

Typeful names include the object attribute type abbreviations in the naming of the NDS object. They are listed in Table 3-2.

Attribute Type Abbreviation	Object
C	Country
O	Organization
OU	Organizational Unit
CN	Common Name

Table 3-2: Object attribute type abbreviations.

When you are writing distinguished names and relative distinguished names, each object is preceded by the attribute type abbreviation and an equal sign (−). A typeful description of a user object might be CN=JDoe.

Typeless Naming

Most of the naming examples that have been used already have been typeless names. As you can probably guess, typeless names do not use the object attribute type abbreviation in the naming of the NDS object. Typeless names provide a more concise way of expressing NDS names; however, typeful names are more explicit and reference the tree structure at the same time.

Naming Examples

To better understand the differences between the types of NDS object naming conventions, consider the following examples. In each example, we are using a specific naming convention to identify the user object Mike. This user object exists in the NDS tree in the current context ACCT.RAMBELL (refer to Figure 3-6 for a graphical representation):

- Typeful distinguished name: .CN=Mike.OU=ACCT.O=RAMBELL
- Typeless relative distinguished name: Mike
- Typeful relative distinguished name with trailing period: CN=Mike.OU=ACCT.

No naming convention is more right or wrong than any other one; how-ever, people new to NDS should use typeful distinguished names at first to avoid confusion. As you grow more accustomed and familiar with the NDS tree and its object naming conventions, feel free to use any of the concise methods that save time by reducing the amount of typing you have to do in referencing an object.

It is important to understand naming conventions because you must know how to uniquely identify an object within the NDS tree. Quite often, NDS tries to take care of naming objects automatically for you; however, there are times when you will need to explicitly provide the unique name for an object to a NetWare utility. Understanding naming conventions will allow you to provide the utility with the appropriate name.

The NetWare Administrator

As we all know, DOS is not a user-friendly operating system. In the NetWare 3.x environments, Novell used a DOS-based menuing program to provide all of the user interfaces. Many network administrators will remember FILER and SYSCON, which were clunky to use but much better than the DOS command line alternative.

With the release of the virtual loadable module (VLM) client for NetWare, Novell provided a graphical user interface (GUI) for user login and drive mapping. This was a sign of things to come (and none too soon!). In NetWare 4.11, Novell still provides a DOS menu program called NETADMIN to per-form the basic network administrative tasks, but NetWare 4.11 also comes with an advanced GUI application called the NetWare Administrator that makes NDS management very user-friendly.

NetWare Administrator is the utility through which a vast majority of network administration tasks are performed. It will allow you to create user objects and groups to manage the users on your network. It will also allow you to create and configure your network printing environment. File system security and NDS security are other administrative features performed through this versatile program. It is important to be familiar with the utility's interface; the myriad functions of this utility will be discussed in Chapter 4 and other places throughout the remainder of this book.

Unlike the NetWare User Tools application that gets installed with the VLM client, the NetWare Administrator requires some setup on the network administrator's part. The application itself resides on the NetWare 4.11 server and requires that an icon be created. In the DOS/Windows 3.x environment, you must connect to the network using the VLM workstation client (also called the NetWare DOS Requester). For more detailed information on installing and connecting with the VLM client, see Chapter 15. Once you are connected to the NetWare environment, log in to the NDS tree and start Windows.

Once in the Windows environment, create a program icon. The NetWare Administrator for the Windows 3.x environment resides in the PUBLIC directory of the SYS: volume on your NetWare 4.11 server:

1. Select the program group in which you want to create the icon.

2. Select File | New from the menu bar in the Program Manager.

3. Choose Program Item from the New Program Object dialog box and click OK.

At this point, the Program Item Properties dialog box should appear. You will need to input the information about the NetWare administrator into this box. If the SYS: volume on your NetWare 4.11 server is mapped to drive F:, the dialog box should look like the one shown in Figure 3-8.

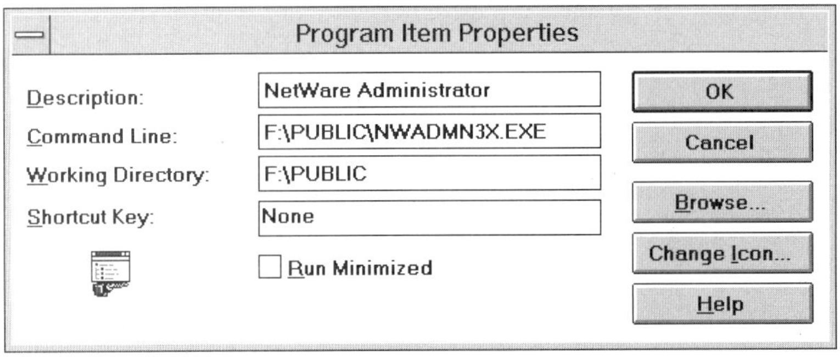

Program Item Properties		
Description:	NetWare Administrator	OK
Command Line:	F:\PUBLIC\NWADMN3X.EXE	Cancel
Working Directory:	F:\PUBLIC	Browse...
Shortcut Key:	None	Change Icon...
	Run Minimized	Help

Figure 3-8: Creating an icon in Windows 3.x for the NetWare Administrator.

Once you have filled in the text editing box specifying the path to the program and clicked OK, the icon will be created in the specified program group. You can now double-click on the new icon to start NetWare Administrator.

In previous versions of NetWare 4.x, the NetWare Administrator was contained in a file called NWADMIN.EXE. In NetWare 4.11, the NetWare Administrator can also be run with the NWADMN3X.EXE executable. Your workstation's operating system and NetWare client will determine which NetWare Administrator you will run. Refer to Table 3-3 for guidance.

Workstation Operating System	NetWare Client	NetWare Administrator Version
DOS/Windows	Client for DOS/Windows (VLMs) version 1.2	NWADMIN.EXE
DOS/Windows	Client for DOS/Windows (VLMs) version 1.25	NWADMIN.EXE or NWADMN3X.EXE
DOS/Windows	Client32 for DOS/Windows	NWADMIN.EXE or NWADMN3X.EXE
Windows 95	Client32 for Windows 95	NWADMN95.EXE
Windows NT	Client32 for Windows NT	NWADMNNT.EXE

Table 3-3: Which NetWare Administrator to use.

Each client that is shipped with NetWare 4.11 comes with the appropriate version of NetWare Administrator. The location of the specific NetWare Administrator file will vary depending upon the client used. As mentioned, NetWare Administrator for Windows 3.x is automatically installed during the installation of the operating system, and it is always stored in SYS:SYSTEM.

It should be noted that for the DOS/Windows client, NetWare 4.11 only comes supplied with NWADMN3X.EXE. The older version of NetWare Administrator (NWADMIN.EXE) is shipped with earlier versions of NetWare 4.x. NetWare 4.11 and NDS are still compatible with the older versions of NetWare Administrator, which can be used without ill effect.

NWADMN3X.EXE vs. NWADMIN.EXE

What is the benefit of using the newer version of NetWare Administrator? Even though both executables can accomplish the same thing, NWADMN3X.EXE has some added features that make it more powerful.

The most important difference is that NWADMIN.EXE comes packaged with its own partition manager to manipulate the NDS partitions and replicas. NWADMN3X.EXE does not have this feature; however, NetWare 4.11 comes with a sister application called NDS Manager (NDSMGR16.EXE) that provides more comprehensive NDS partition and replica management. Really, NetWare 4.11 has replaced one large application (NWADMIN.EXE) with two separate applications (NWADMN3X.EXE and NDSMGR16.EXE) to provide a better user interface and easier network management. NDS Manager and its functions will be discussed in detail in Section II of this book.

NWADMN3X.EXE also comes with other features that NWADMIN.EXE lacks. The newer version has support for concurrent, multiple NDS tree access, software license options, NetWare 3.x-to-4.x migration utilities, and print services quick setup. By far, NWADMN3X.EXE offers much more than the older NWADMIN.EXE.

Once the icon has been installed in Windows, it is time to run the application. To start the NetWare Administrator, double-click on the icon you just created. You should see a window appear that looks like the one shown in Figure 3-9.

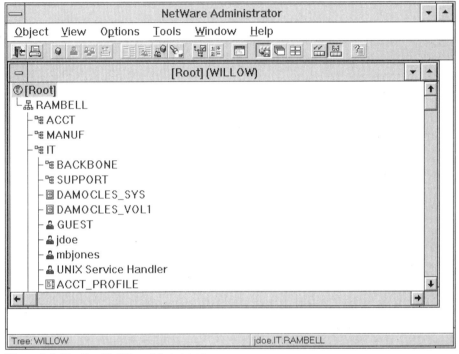

Figure 3-9: Starting NetWare Administrator.

Because it's a Windows application, the NetWare Administrator has all of the features of Windows we have grown accustomed to. It has the customary title bar, a menu bar, a toolbar, and a default subordinate window. In the subordinate window, your current NDS tree is displayed from the perspective of your current context. In Figure 3-9, the current context is set to [Root]; that is why [Root] appears at the top of the tree. If the current context was IT.RAMBELL, the tree would be truncated, and the organizational unit IT would be displayed at the top left of the subordinate window. Your current context and tree are also displayed on the title bar of the subordinate window. We can see that our current context and tree is [Root](WILLOW).

Navigating the NDS Tree

We learned about the DOS command utility CX earlier in the chapter. However, we need to have a keen understanding of NDS and its structure in order
to use it. NetWare Administrator provides an easier way to navigate the NDS
tree. It is much more intuitive and requires a lot less thought than CX does.

If you want to expand a branch of the tree to see which objects are in a
particular container, just double-click on that container object. To collapse that
branch once you have seen what you want, double-click on that container
object a second time. By default, NetWare Administrator will show you every
object that exists in the tree. As we will learn later, we can apply filters so that
we see only specific object types in the tree as we view it.

Changing your context in the tree is just as easy. From the menu bar, choose
View | Set Context. From the Set Context dialog box (see Figure 3-10), you can
choose your current context not only in your present tree but also from other
NDS trees that may exist on your network.

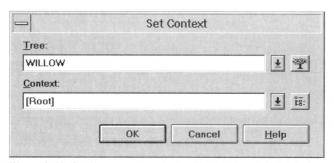

Figure 3-10: Setting current context with NetWare Administrator.

The Set Context dialog box will allow you to switch your current context to a
different NDS tree. To see the other trees on the network, just click on the Tree
button. To select the context in the desired tree, either type in the context or click
on the Select Object button to the far right of the Context text editing box.

If you type the desired current context in the Context box, do not worry
about distinguished versus relative distinguished naming conventions. Any
context that is entered in the Context box is taken as a distinguished name
whether or not a leading period is entered. This means that any context typed
in will be referenced from [Root].

Clicking on the Select Object button to the far right of the Context box will bring up another dialog box. The Select Object dialog box provides a GUI for browsing the NDS tree and selecting an object (see Figure 3-11). The Browse Context (right-hand) box allows you to navigate the tree by double-clicking on the objects that appear. If you want to see the objects contained in the RAMBELL organization object, double-click on that object *in the box on the right*. To select an object and make it your current context, click on it once in the Available Objects (left-hand) box; then click OK. To change the current context from [Root] to RAMBELL, click on the RAMBELL organization *in the box on the left*, and click OK. Get familiar with the Select Object dialog box; you will be using it frequently in NetWare Administrator.

Tip

The Select Object dialog box will appear in many locations throughout the NetWare Administrator. Remember the right-hand box is for NDS tree browsing; the left-hand box is for object selection.

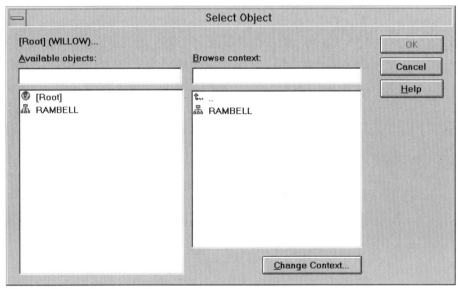

Figure 3-11: Graphically selecting current context.

For small trees, we generally find it useful to set the current context to [Root] so that we can see all of our tree at the same time. For large trees, this will quickly become cumbersome because there will be many containers and many objects. In this case, it will be useful to specify a current context to isolate a portion of the tree in a NetWare Administrator window. For especially large trees, it may be useful to create more than one window to display multiple contexts within an NDS tree.

Trying to manage two NDS trees at the same time is another instance in which you might want to have multiple windows open in NetWare Administrator. Although it is not recommended that you have more than one NDS tree, many organizations find multiple trees on their network. If you are a network administrator responsible for merging trees, it will be helpful to have both trees displayed at the same time. To create another window, choose Window | New Window from the NetWare Administrator menu bar. A new current context can then be set in this new window to provide the view of the NDS tree desired.

Manipulating Objects

Besides being able to move around the NDS tree, it is important to learn the basics of creating and manipulating objects within it. Most of the tasks you will perform with objects in the NDS tree will be done with NetWare Administrator. The only things you won't do with NetWare Administrator are container manipulations (like moving), NDS database partitioning, and NDS database replication. These are done with the NDS Manager, which will be explained in Section II, "NetWare Directory Services."

There are essentially five different object manipulations that a network administrator will want to do through NetWare Administrator:

- Creating objects
- Renaming objects
- Moving objects
- Detailing objects
- Deleting objects

The key to NDS and understanding NetWare Administrator is to remember that everything in NDS is an object. Generally, if you know how to manipulate one object, you can manipulate every object in the tree the same way. In the following sections, we will learn how to perform these basic functions on objects in the NDS tree. Learning how to manipulate objects with NetWare Administrator is crucial to managing the network.

Creating Objects

The first logical step a network administrator would take after installing the server would be to create user accounts. Every user that is going to access the network needs to have a user object created for them by the network administrator. Users are not the only types of objects that need to be created. Printers will be needed, users will be put in groups, and other organizational units will be added to the NDS tree. Most objects that will end up in the NDS tree will be created by the network administrator using NetWare Administrator.

To create an object in the NDS tree, click once on the container object that will contain the new object you are going to create. The desired container will then be highlighted. Choose Object | Create from the menu bar. The New Object dialog box will appear, as shown in Figure 3-12. Notice the parent container is displayed for the object being created.

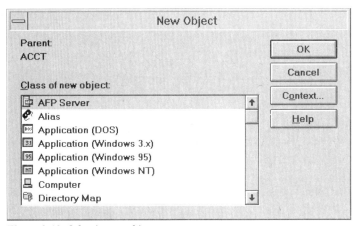

Figure 3-12: Selecting an object to create.

In the Class of New Object box, you can select the type of object you want to create in the NDS tree. Click once on the desired object, then click OK. It should be noted that the list of available objects will change depending upon which container you initially select. Creating an object in [Root] will produce a different list of objects than creating an object in an organizational unit. This is where the container rules discussed earlier in this chapter are enforced.

The New Object dialog box also gives you the option of displaying the context of the container in which you are creating the object. To see the context, click on the Context button. It will display another dialog box that will show you the context of the container that will be the parent of this new object.

Besides using the menu bar, there are two other ways to create an object through NetWare Administrator. The first method is to highlight the container that will be the parent of the new object and press the Insert key on your keyboard. The second method is to click once on the container with the right mouse button. Choose Create from the pop-up menu. Both methods will bring up the New Object dialog box.

Renaming Objects

There may be times when you want to rename an object in the NDS tree. This is easily accomplished. To rename an object, select it by clicking once on the object. Choose Object | Rename from the menu bar. A Rename dialog box will appear. Type in the new name for the object and click OK. Be careful when renaming objects; renaming an object that a user is currently using will cause an interruption in service. For example, if user Mike is logged in to the network and his user object is renamed to MikeB, his current network session will be terminated because NDS will no longer recognize Mike as a valid user.

Moving Objects

Let's say you have a network printer that is serving the accounting department of your company. Accounting purchases a new printer and gives their old one to the manufacturing department. Instead of deleting the old printer object in the ACCT organizational unit and creating a new one in the MANUF organizational unit, it would be easier to move the printer object from one context to the other. This can be accomplished using NetWare Administrator.

To move an object from one container to another, highlight the object by clicking on it once with the left mouse button. Choose Object | Move from the menu bar to make the Move dialog box appear. In the From box, you will see the object that you want to move. In the Destination box, type in the destination container to which you want to move the object. Click OK.

If you are not certain of the destination context, you can browse the NDS tree by clicking on the Select Object button to the right of the Destination box. This will bring up the same dialog box that we saw when we were setting our current context (the Select Object dialog box in Figure 3-11). We can navigate this dialog box the same way we did when setting our current context. The Browse Context (right-hand) box can be used to navigate the NDS tree to find container objects. The Available Objects (left-hand) box is used to select the destination container. After selecting the destination container, click OK.

You can also use a shortcut to bring up the Move dialog box; select the object and press the F7 key on your keyboard.

Detailing Objects

As we discussed previously, objects have properties and values associated with them. Once an object is created, the network administrator will need to give the object's properties their associated values. For example, when a new printer is installed in the tree, the network administrator will want to provide information concerning which print queues it is going to service, the location of the printer, and the printer configuration. All this is done through the NetWare Administrator detailing option.

To detail an object, select the object by clicking on it once with the left mouse button to highlight it. Choose Object | Details from the menu bar. A dialog box will appear with important information about the object in the title bar (see Figure 3-13).

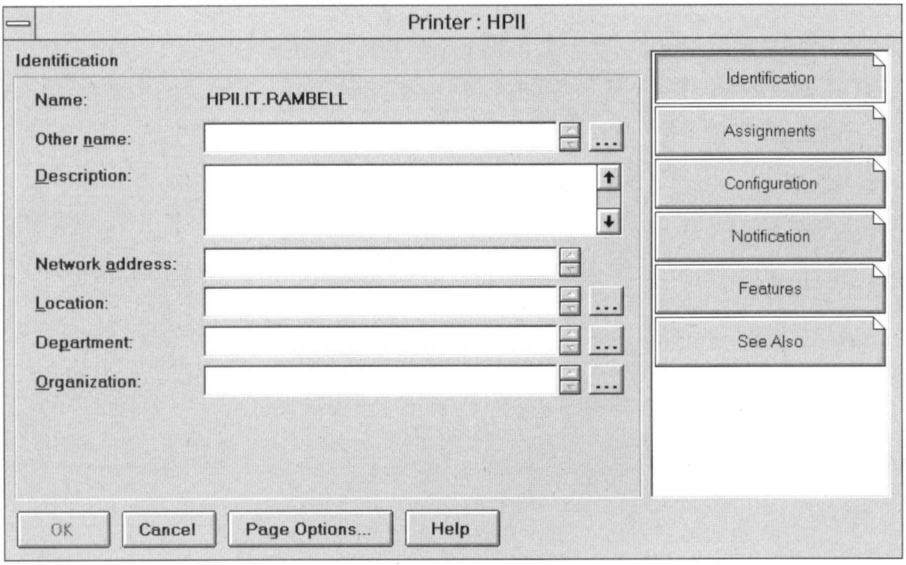

Figure 3-13: Detailing an object with NetWare Administrator.

From the title bar, we can see that this is indeed a printer object. We can also see that the name of the printer is HPII. The detailing dialog box is split up into two sections. Tabs are listed toward the right of the box, and there are specific properties associated with the tabs on the left side of the dialog box. In this particular case, the Identification tab is selected, and you see the properties associated with it. If you want to see the properties associated with the Assignments tab, just click on that tab with the left mouse button. The properties on the left side of the box will change to reflect the properties associated with printer assignments.

By default, all property tabs associated with an object are displayed for the administrator; however, not every tab will be used on a frequent basis. Fortunately, Novell has created a way for the administrator to customize the display of the object properties. This can be done through the Page Options button at the bottom of the dialog box. Click on it to bring up the Page Options dialog box, shown in Figure 3-14.

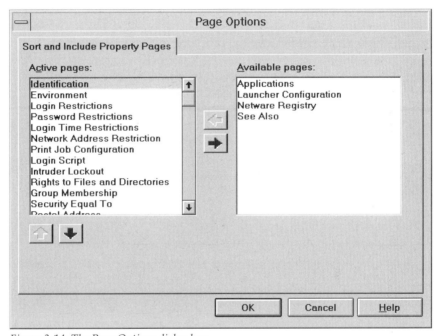

Figure 3-14: The Page Options dialog box.

The left-hand box in the Page Options dialog box is labeled Active Pages. It contains all of the property tabs that will be displayed on the details page of a particular NDS object type. The right-hand box is the Available Pages box. This is the list of property tabs that you can add to your current display. By default, all of the property tabs for the selected object appear in the Active Pages box. To remove a property tab from the display, select the title of the property tab and click on the right-pointing arrow in the center of the screen. The tabs that were removed will then appear in the right-hand box. To add a tab to the display, select the page from the Available Pages box and click on the left-pointing arrow. In the configuration shown in Figure 3-14, the property tabs for Applications, Launcher Configuration, NetWare Registry, and See Also will not appear when viewing the details of the user object.

The Page Options dialog box can also be used to order the display of the property page tabs for the user object. As seen in Figure 3-14, the Identification tab is the first tab displayed for the user object when the properties are examined. If you want the Environment tab and its properties to be displayed initially when you detail the user object, select Environment in the Active Pages box and click on the Up arrow near the bottom of the page. The tab is promoted to the top of the list. Likewise, tabs can be demoted by selecting them and clicking on the Down arrow.

After you have customized the property page views, it is time to look at the properties themselves. In the properties portion of the dialog box, properties are listed with a text entry box to input the value associated with them. Some of these properties have a button with three dots to the right of their text entry box, as seen in Figure 3-13. These properties, such as Location, Department, and Organization, are the multivalued properties discussed in "The NDS Structure" section earlier in this chapter. To enter more than one value for a property, click on the button.

Two shortcuts are provided to detail objects with NetWare Administrator. To use the first method, select the object by clicking on it once with the left mouse button and press the Enter key on your keyboard. The second method is to click once on the desired object with your right mouse button. Choose Details from the menu that appears. Both methods will cause NetWare Administrator to display the details box associated with that particular object.

In the special case of the user object, you have the option to change the values for properties on multiple user objects concurrently. To do so, make sure a user object is selected by clicking on it once with the left mouse button. Choose Object | Details on Multiple Users from the menu bar. A special dialog box will appear with most of the tabs and properties for the user object. Modifications can be made to any of the properties' values in this box. After that, choose the users that will be affected by this change. Once this is completed, any value changes made to the properties will be propagated to all users selected in the user list. This is a convenient way to change specific information on many user objects at the same time.

Deleting Objects

There always comes a time when a network administrator must delete objects from the NDS tree. Whether a user has left the company or a printer has died, the object must be removed. NetWare Administrator is used to remove objects from the tree. Take care when deleting objects. Once they are gone, they cannot be retrieved and must be re-created from scratch.

To delete an object from the NDS tree, select the object in NetWare Administrator by clicking on it once with the left mouse button. This will highlight the selected object. From the menu bar, choose Object | Delete. NetWare Administrator will ask you to confirm that you do indeed want to delete the object. If you are sure the object is to be removed, choose Yes. It will then be removed from the tree.

When the object you are trying to remove is a container, it may not be deleted from the tree while it contains subordinate objects. All objects within that container must be moved or deleted before the container itself can be deleted. This is to ensure an entire branch of your NDS tree is not deleted by accident.

There are two shortcuts that will help you get rid of objects even more quickly. The first method is to select the object by clicking on it once with the left mouse button; then press the Delete key on your keyboard. The second method is to right-click on the desired object. Choose Delete from the menu that appears. Both methods will cause the object to be deleted from the NDS tree.

NetWare Administrator Features

Large NDS trees will contain a large number of objects. They will also contain many different *types* of objects. Viewing these trees with NetWare Administrator can become cumbersome because there may be a lot of information displayed that is not necessarily needed for the current session.

There are many different times when a network administrator might be looking for very specific information on the network. He or she might also want to view only a specific type of object on the NDS tree or find an object that has a specific value for one of its properties. NetWare Administrator comes with built-in view filtering and object searching capabilities to help the network administrator perform day-to-day tasks.

View Filtering

By default, NetWare Administrator displays every object that has been created in your NDS tree. This can provide a cluttered view of your tree. You can tell NetWare Administrator exactly which types of objects you want displayed by implementing a view filter for your NDS tree. Even though the objects will not be displayed after applying a filter, the objects will still be in the tree. The filter just needs to be removed before they can be seen.

To remove the filter, choose View | Sort and Include from the menu bar. The Browser Sort and Include dialog box appears, as shown in Figure 3-15.

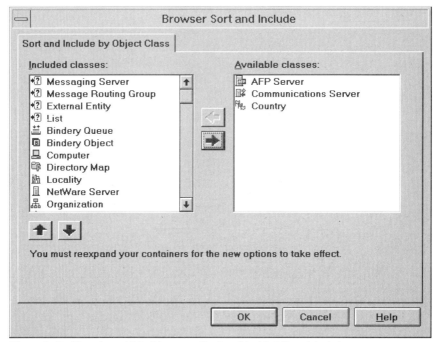

Figure 3-15: Choosing which objects are displayed in NetWare Administrator.

The dialog box is separated into two boxes. On the right-hand side is the Available Classes box; on the left-hand side is the Included Classes box. Any object type listed in the Included Classes box will be displayed by NetWare Administrator. Object types listed in the Available Classes box will *not* be displayed. The dialog box in Figure 3-15 indicates that the AFP Server, Communications Server, and Country objects will not be displayed in the NDS tree by NetWare Administrator.

To remove an object type from the display, find the object type in the Included Classes box, select it by clicking on it once with the left mouse button, and click on the right-pointing arrow to the right of the Included Classes box. The object type will move from the Included Classes box to the Available Classes box. To make an object type visible, select it in the Available Classes box and click on the left-pointing arrow.

Not only will the Browser Sort and Include dialog box provide view filtering, it will also provide view sorting. You can specify in which order objects are displayed in the NDS tree by modifying the order of the object types in the Included Classes box. Objects listed at the top of the Included Classes box will be displayed in the tree ahead of objects listed toward the bottom of the list. In Figure 3-15, you can see that Computer objects in a specific container will be displayed ahead of the NetWare Server objects in that container. To move an object up or down in the list, click on it once with the left mouse button to select it. Then click on the Up or Down arrow below the Included Classes to move the object accordingly. This powerful option will allow you to completely customize the look and feel of NetWare Administrator.

Searching

NetWare Administrator also comes with a search engine that will allow you to find objects in the tree whose properties equal a specific value that you set. For example, if you want to find every user in the NDS tree who belongs to the accounting department, you can use the search utility.

To start the search utility, a container object must be selected. Click on the container with the left mouse button. Choose Object | Search from the menu bar to display the Search dialog box (see Figure 3-16).

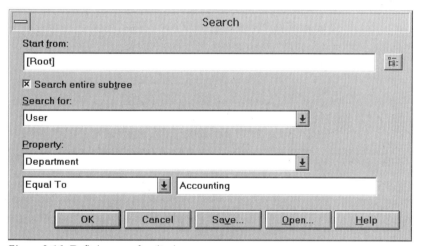

Figure 3-16: Defining search criteria.

In the Search dialog box, the context from which the search is starting is displayed in the Start From box. To change the context, click on the Select Object button to the right of the Start From box. The search feature gives you the option to search a specific container or all containers within that subtree. Specify the target object type of the search from the drop-down list in the Search For box. Beneath that, define the property and value criteria.

In Figure 3-16, we are specifying a search that will search the entire NDS tree. It will look for user objects whose department property is equal to accounting. When we execute this search by clicking OK, the search engine will find every user on our network that works in the accounting department. This is a fast, efficient way to retrieve specific data about your network.

Applying Concepts: Rambell, Inc.

The last time we checked in on John Doe at Rambell, he had just finished installing NetWare 4.11 on his server and was ready to begin creating the user objects for his network. His client workstation is installed, and he has connected to the network using the Admin account. Because he is using a DOS/Windows workstation, he is using NWADMN3X.EXE in the SYS:PUBLIC directory to run NetWare Administrator.

But before creating any user objects, John is taking some time to plan out his network. He wants to ensure that the NDS tree is set up properly and login security is created and enforced across the network. Because Rambell is not a large company, it does not make sense to deviate from the default NDS structure. He decides to stay with the NDS structure created when NetWare 4.11 was installed on the server. This means he has one organization called RAMBELL with one subordinate organizational unit called IT. For now, every network resource will exist in this organizational unit as an object. As the company grows, more organizations and organizational units will be created to accommodate the networking needs.

Moving On

In this chapter, we learned some fundamental concepts about the NDS tree that we need to perform basic network administration. You should now have a conceptual understanding of NDS, including its structure and object composition. You know how to identify your location in the tree as well as name objects that exist in the tree.

You have been introduced to the NetWare Administrator utility that is used to navigate and manipulate objects in the NDS tree. You also learned that it is capable of performing some powerful searches on the data contained in the NDS database. But this is not the last we will see of the NetWare Administrator.

In the next chapter, you'll learn how to use the NetWare Administrator to help you with our day-to-day user management. You will need to build on your newfound knowledge of NDS and your skills in using NetWare Administrator to get the network running smoothly.

4

Basic NetWare Administration

Now that you know all the terminology or "buzzwords" concerning NDS, its time to learn just how to use it. Chapter 3 dealt with NDS in an abstract way; Chapter 4 will provide more detail about creating, detailing, and managing objects in the NDS environment. Using the NetWare Administrator, you will be able to perform the day-to-day tasks of the typical network administrator.

Before any objects are created in the NDS tree, it is important to understand the types of security offered in NetWare 4.11, including NDS security. Objects cannot be created by just anybody in the NDS tree; to create and modify the objects, a user must have the appropriate rights. By restricting access to manipulate objects in the NDS tree, the network administrator can provide a unified and secure network environment.

After you have sufficient rights, your next step is the creation of users and user-related objects. All users that will be accessing the NetWare network will need an NDS user object. Without it, a user will not be able to use any resources on the network. Once it is created, the user object also needs to be detailed. This involves providing values for the many different properties it holds. From login restrictions to file system security assignments, the user object stores all of the specific information and security clearances the user has.

There are many instances when a large number of users need the same level of access to the network. It would be time consuming to modify the user objects individually to reflect this. It is more convenient to lump all of the users together in one category from which they could derive their network privileges. This can be accomplished through the creation of group objects where rights are granted through association with a specific group. In this chapter, we'll discuss the creation and configuration of group and other user-related objects.

Besides user and group objects, there are some other user-related objects that will provide users with the appropriate access to network resources. We mentioned them in Chapter 3, and in this chapter, we will take a closer look at them. Those objects are the organizational role and alias.

After this chapter, you will be thoroughly versed in the user-related NDS objects. In addition to being able to deftly create and configure specific objects for your users, you will be able to make administration of the network easier through the judicious use of groups and other user-related NDS objects.

Introduction to NetWare 4.11 Security

Security is one of the key components of computer networking. Networking allows multiple users access to the same resources; sharing resources, however, can lead to problems. Someone may unintentionally view a sensitive document on the network or someone may maliciously deletes information out of spite. Regardless of the intent, there must be a way to secure the information on the network. In this section, we will provide you with an overview of the types of security built into NetWare 4.11. This will acquaint you with the concepts necessary for the successful administration of your network.

To help network administrators deal with potential problems, NetWare 4.11 provides three different levels of security:

- Login security
- NDS security
- File system security

Using these three types of security, you can ensure the integrity of the information contained in your network.

Login Security

Login security provides a first level of defense for your network. To even begin to access the network, a person must have a login name and password. Once entered, that name and password are checked against the NDS database. If they match what is contained in the NDS database, the user is granted access to the network.

Although login security is a simple type of security conceptually, there are some modifiable parameters that make it more robust. The network administrator can customize parameters to further restrict login capabilities:

- **Login restrictions** allow the network administrator to give user accounts expiration dates. The number of simultaneous connections to the network can also be restricted.

- **Password restrictions** force users to have passwords to access the network. Passwords can have a mandatory minimum length and users can be required to change them periodically.

- **Login time restrictions** can limit the time periods that users have access to the network. If desired, the network may only be accessed by users between 8:00 A.M. and 5:00 P.M. on weekdays.

- **Network address restrictions** require users to access the network from a particular workstation. If he or she tries to access the network from another workstation, access will be denied.

- **Intruder lockout capabilities,** when enabled, will alert the network administrator to any unauthorized attempts to access user accounts. If too many unsuccessful login attempts are made on a user account during a specific window of time, the account is locked to prevent an unauthorized user from gaining access to the network.

A consistent login security implementation across your network is recommended. It is not a good idea to grant a lesser degree of login security to one user unless there is compelling reason to do so. Login security parameters are set by the network administrator through the individual user objects in the NDS tree and will be discussed more thoroughly in "User Objects," later in this chapter.

NDS Security

Once a user has logged in to the NDS tree successfully, the next type of security is applied—NDS security. Because all of the network resources are congregated into one giant pool now, this type of security is required. NDS security defines the level of access to the objects, properties, and values contained in the NDS tree. NDS security is granted through the concept of trustee assignments. When a user or object is made a trustee of another object, the trustee object is granted a specific level of rights to the other object. Within NDS security, there are two flavors of rights.

Object rights determine what a trustee can do with an object. There are five rights associated with the object rights:

- **Supervisor** gives all object right privileges to the trustee. It not only gives all object rights, it also grants all property rights.
- **Browse** allows the trustee to see the object in the NDS tree.
- **Create** grants the ability to create new objects in the NDS tree. The Create object right applies only to container objects.
- **Delete** allows the trustee to remove the object from the NDS tree.
- **Rename** gives the trustee the ability to change the name of the object.

Object rights give trustees access to the object; they do not give trustees control over the properties and values associated with the objects. Someone with the right to delete objects (a trustee) can delete a user object from the NDS tree. That same trustee cannot, however, modify any properties of that user object unless he or she also has the appropriate property rights to that object.

As mentioned, *property rights* grant trustees the ability to work with the information stored in the NDS object (the properties and values). Through property rights, trustees may browse, search, or modify information contained within the object. There are five types of property rights:

- **Supervisor** gives all property rights to the trustee.
- **Compare** allows the trustee to compare any value against the value of the property. This does not give the trustee the ability to view the value; comparing a value against the value of the property will return a Boolean true or false.
- **Read** grants the trustee the right to read the values of the object's properties. When the Read right is granted, compare is included.
- **Write** gives the right to add, modify, or delete property values. Granting the Write right also grants the add self right.
- **Add Self** allows the trustee to add or delete him- or herself as a value of the property. This right pertains only to those properties that use object names for values.

To perform the tasks of network administration discussed in this chapter, you must be working with a user object that has sufficient rights to create and modify NDS objects and properties. The Admin account that is created during the installation of NDS will provide these rights. Otherwise, use the Admin account initially to create a user object for yourself. Grant this user account the Supervisor object rights at the [Root] of the tree; it will give you the ability to administer the NDS tree. A thorough discussion of NDS security and security trustee assignments will be provided in Chapter 9.

File System Security

File system security is the third level of security in NetWare. This last line of defense protects the critical information on your servers. Even though someone may have access to the network and have the appropriate NDS security rights to see the server and the volumes on the server, it does not mean that person will have access to the file systems associated with those volumes. NDS security and file system security are two completely separate entities.

Like NDS security, file system security is based on trustee assignments. Users are given a specific level of rights to the file system through an explicit assignment. There are eight different kinds of file rights pertaining to security:

- **Supervisor** grants the trustee complete control over that portion of the file system.

- **Read** allows the trustee to open, read, and execute files.

- **Write** gives the trustee the ability to open and change the contents of the files.

- **Create** lets a trustee create files and subdirectories.

- **Erase** allows the trustee to delete files and directories.

- **Modify** grants the trustee the ability to change the name or file attributes associated with the file or directory.

- **File Scan** gives the right to see the files and directories in the file system.

- **Access Control** allows the trustee to make other trustee assignments and modify the Inherited Rights Filter.

Through the use of these file rights, a network administrator can grant users complete access to one directory while hiding another one from view completely. Flexible by nature, file system security allows the network administrator to completely customize the network environment for the users for whom he or she is providing network services. Only users with sufficient rights to the file system are able to access the data on the network. File system security and administration will be discussed thoroughly in Chapter 6.

Of the three types of NetWare security, NDS security has the most relevance for user administration. The person responsible for managing the user and user-related objects must have sufficient NDS rights to create, modify, and delete those objects. There are cases where sufficient NDS rights and file system rights are required to be able to fully administer the network. For example, creating a file system trustee assignment for a user requires sufficient NDS rights to modify the user object and sufficient file system rights to grant the trustee assignment. However, there is a clear distinction between the two types of securities.

There is one specific place NDS security and file system security overlap—at the NDS server object. Any trustee of the server object that has Supervisor NDS rights is also given Supervisor file system rights for all volumes on that server. This is the only time that an NDS security assignment will affect the file system.

It is important that you be familiar with the types of security available in NetWare. The level of security you implement on your network affects how your users will be able to utilize network resources. As you begin to create users in your NDS tree, you must decide just how much access you are going to give them. Keep this in mind as we begin the next section.

User Objects

User management in the NDS world requires an understanding of the various types of objects users on your network might be able to access. In IntranetWare, there are four different objects in the tree that directly affect the user. These four objects determine the level of access and the resource mappings a user will have when he or she logs into the network:

- User object
- Group object
- Organizational Role object
- Alias object

The two most common types of objects that a network administrator will use for user management are the user and group objects. Every user who wants access to the network needs a user object in the NDS tree. Now, rather than managing each user account individually to provide the proper security in the NDS tree and related file systems, a group object will allow the network administrator to group together users that need the same level of security clearance or require the same network resources. It makes the administration of the network easy because any modifications that need to be made to the group only need to be made once to the group object instead of having to change each individual user. It is crucial to understand the user and group objects to effectively administer the NetWare 4.11 network.

Creating User Objects

During the installation of NetWare 4.11, only one user object is created in the NDS tree. This is the Admin account, which has complete security access over both the NDS tree and the newly installed server's file system. During the installation of the NDS tree, it is important to write down the context and password for this account. Because the Admin account is all-powerful, it is a good idea to use it only when necessary. This will prevent accidents from happening. However, since it is the only user object in the tree that will allow access to the NetWare network after installation, you must use this account the first time you log in to the NDS tree. You can then create a personal user account for yourself and one for each user on your network.

Being able to create and manage user objects in the NDS tree requires three basic things. The first thing is a workstation that has had the NetWare client installed and is connected to the network. The second thing is a basic understanding of how to set up and use NetWare Administrator on that machine. The third thing is a user account with the rights to create and edit NDS objects. The Admin account has the rights that are necessary to manage objects in the NDS tree. Without these three things, you will not be able to administer the network.

NETADMIN

NETADMIN is a DOS-based utility that is located in the SYS:PUBLIC directory of the NetWare 4.11 server. It provides the same functionality as the NetWare Administrator; however, its user interface is cumbersome and often confusing. Use NETADMIN only if a Windows-based machine is unavailable.

Once the NetWare Administrator has been started, the user accounts can be created. To create a user object, click once with the left mouse button on the container that will hold the object. Choose Object | Create from the menu bar and select User from the dialog box that follows. Another dialog box entitled Create User will appear, as in Figure 4-1.

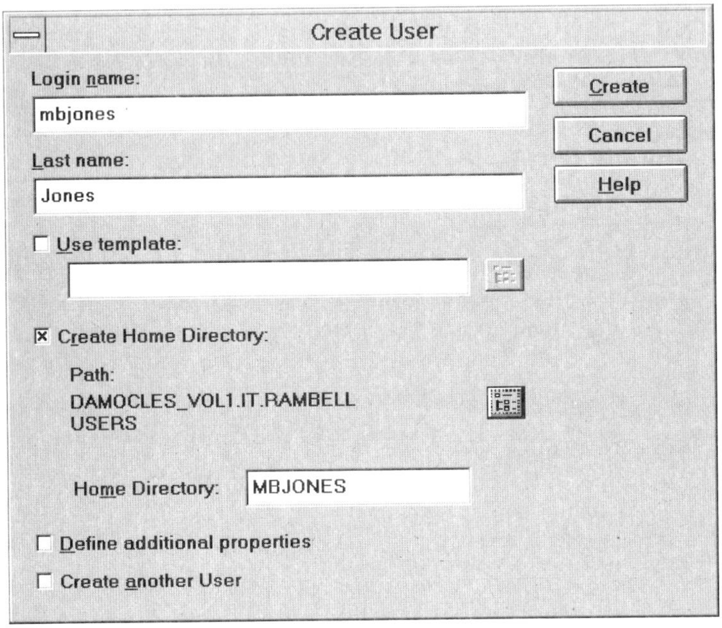

Figure 4-1: Creating a user object.

The Create User dialog box shows the mandatory properties for the user object. If no values are specified for the properties, the user object *cannot be created*. The mandatory properties are the Login Name and Last Name properties. Only when both boxes have been filled in will the option to create the user object be given.

Login Name

The Login Name is one of the mandatory fields that appear in the Create User dialog box. It is obviously an important item to every user because this is how he or she will be known to the network. Great care should be taken when devising a scheme for login names because they will have a great impact on you as the network administrator.

The first thing you should consider is the user-friendliness of the login name. Many users really want to log in to the network using their first name or last name. It is easy for them to remember and makes the computer environment more personal than it would be with a login name like 0816542. That might make people feel criminal. A memorable login name will prevent the network administrator from receiving support calls from people who have forgotten theirs.

While using first names or last names might be feasible for smaller networks, that scheme does not scale well for large networks with many users. NDS is capable of handling two users with the login name Mike, providing they exist in different containers; however, it cannot handle two user objects named Mike in the same container—just like it cannot handle multiple Smiths in the same container if the user's last name is used as a login name. Larger networks obviously beg a better login name convention.

Here are a couple of suggestions for a login name convention that is both user-friendly and scalable:

- Use a combination of a user's first and middle initial and the first six characters of the last name to create an eight-character login name. Heath C. Ramsey would have the login name HCRAMSEY, and Mark R. Bell would be MRBELL.

- Use a combination of the first characters of a user's last name and a series of numbers. If the first five characters of a user's last name were chosen using this convention, Heath C. Ramsey would be RAMSE001. The second Ramsey in the organization would be RAMSE002. Mark R. Bell's login name might be BELL001 or BELL0001, if a consistent eight-character login name was desired.

Both of these conventions result in a login name that is memorable yet still provides unique login names for every user on the network. Of course, both of the conventions have limitations. What happens if two people's login names are both HCRAMSEY, and they needed to exist in the same container? What happens if there are over 999 Smiths in your organization? These are probably extremes, but they are things that should be considered when devising a login name convention.

Last Name

The Last Name property is self-explanatory. Once the person's last name is entered along with the login name, the Create button will no longer be grayed out. You then click on Create to create the user object.

Besides the mandatory properties associated with the user object, there are some options included in the Create User dialog box that aid in the administration of the user object.

Use Template

The Use Template option will allow the network administrator to use a previously defined template to help create the user. Templates are useful if the network administrator creates many users that have similar network resource needs. The template predefines many of the properties of the user object, including login scripts and restrictions, group membership, and trustee information. When a template is used in the creation of the user object, the object is created with the specified login name and last name plus all of the predefined properties included in the user template. This saves time that would normally be required to detail each user object individually.

For example, a user object is being created with the login name Mary and last name Smith. The Rambell user template is being used to help create this object. In this template, a login script has been defined. When the object is created, it has the login name Mary and the last name Smith as well as the Rambell login script. The network administrator does not need to manually detail Mary's user object and create a login script for it because a template was used.

You can create a template object the same way you create a user object. Right-click on the container that will hold the template and select Create from the menu that appears. Choose the Template object from the New Object dialog box that appears and click OK. The Create Template in Figure 4-2 will be displayed.

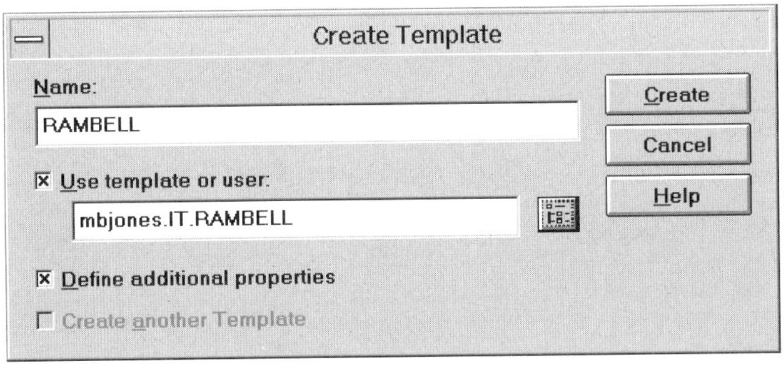

Figure 4-2: Creating a template object.

After naming the template object, check the Define Additional Properties check box and click on the Create button. The Template properties box will be displayed, in which the properties for the template can be modified. As seen in Figure 4-2, you can associate a template with an existing user object. If this option is chosen, the object properties for the template object will be the same as the user object selected. In our case, the template RAMBELL will have the same properties as the user object mbjones.

To use a template when creating a user object, check the Use Template check box in the Create User dialog box (Figure 4-1) and specify the name of the template object that will be used to define the user. To browse the NDS tree for the template object, click on the Select Object button to the right of the Use

Template text box. This will allow you to navigate the NDS tree and select the desired template object. This template object *must already exist in the NDS tree* to be able to use it in the creation of a new user object.

Tip

> *Do you remember the Select Object dialog box from Chapter 3, "NetWare 4.11 Concepts"? As we mentioned, it will be used often in NetWare Administrator. Become familiar with this dialog box because it is invaluable in searching for and selecting objects in the NDS tree. The Select Object dialog box is also used to navigate the various file systems on the network.*

Create Home Directory

A user's home directory is the directory on a file server to which that user has complete access to store personal information (important stuff like games). The home directory is restricted so that no other user is able to see or access its contents without the permission of the owner. This allows the user to keep sensitive information on the network in a private location to which no one else has access (except the network administrator).

By default, the name of the user's home directory will be the same as his or her login name. Just where this directory exists is completely up to the network administrator. Many people like to create a directory on one of the server volumes called USERS under which all of the home directories exist. This provides a clean method of organization, and as a network administrator, you will be able to find the users' home directories easily.

To create a home directory for a user, mark the Create Home Directory check box in the Create User dialog box (Figure 4-1). You will then be allowed to enter a path and home directory name for the user. To select a path, click on the Select Object box to the right of the Path section. This will allow you to navigate the NDS tree to find the appropriate server volume. On that server volume, select the desired target directory that will contain the user's home directory and click OK. You will be returned to the Create User dialog box. The name of the user's home directory can also be changed in the Create User dialog box; however, we recommend you keep the default name.

The last two options in the Create User dialog box are Define Additional Properties and Create Another User. Either one or the other can be checked, not both. The Define Additional Properties check box, when checked, will take you immediately to the properties screen where the user object can be detailed more thoroughly. The Create Another User check box, when checked, will create the user as specified and immediately bring up another Create User dialog box.

Once all of the appropriate fields are filled out in the Create User dialog box, click on Create to create the user object. If NetWare Administrator does not blacken the Create button, the information has been entered incorrectly. Once the user object has been created, it is important to detail it. Detailing allows the network administrator to further customize the user object.

Detailing User Objects

Now that the user object has been created in the NDS tree, it is time to customize it for the user. This involves filling out general information about the user along with information regarding the user's interaction with the network. From the user's physical location at the company to the login and password restrictions, all modifications to the information concerning the user are accomplished through detailing the user object.

To configure the user object using NetWare Administrator, click on the desired user with the right mouse button. Choose Detail from the menu that appears. The User dialog box will appear.

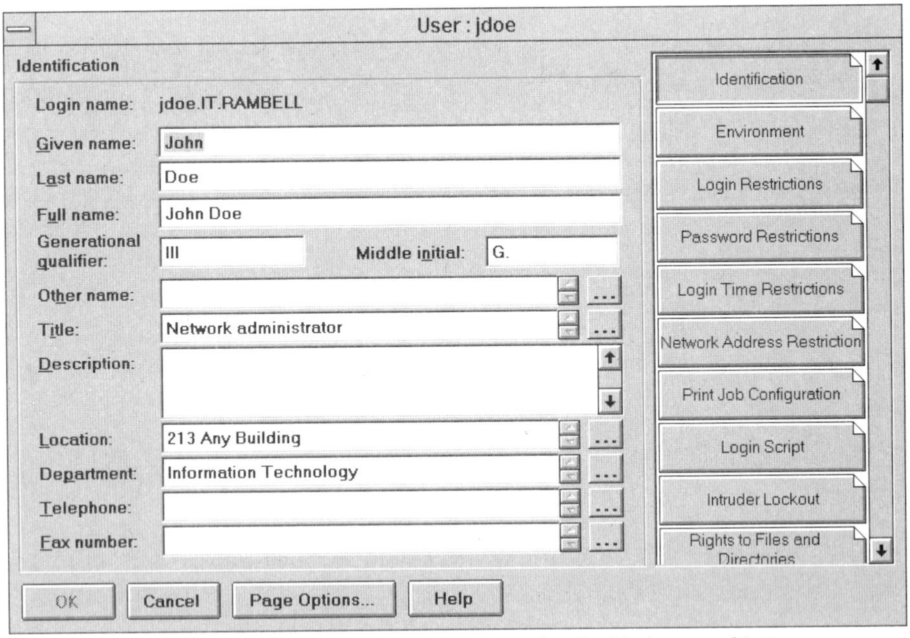

Figure 4-3: The User dialog box displays properties associated with the user object.

Along the right-hand side of the dialog box, the various categories of properties are listed. To fill out the properties of a category, click once on the appropriate tab with the left mouse button. The depressed tab is the tab whose properties are currently showing. The properties of Identification for the user object jdoe are shown in Figure 4-3.

The Identification properties tab allows the network administrator to input information about the user. Among the information that can be stored in NDS is the user's first name, last name, title, department, location, and phone number. Although this information has no real "function" in NetWare (it does not affect the network in any way), it does provide a way to store administrative information concerning the company's employees in one central location. Coupled with NetWare Administrator's powerful searching capabilities, this database can provide quick information about company demographics.

Another tab that provides this type of information is the Postal Address tab. The properties in this tab provide the network administrator with a way to store the user's postal address and mailing label information. They can be used to print labels for mass employee mailings. The Environment tab also displays generic user information like the network address of the workstation he or she is using and the home directory of the user.

In addition to general information about the user and his or her physical location, there are properties that directly affect how the user interacts with the network. These properties determine things like the password requirements, login restrictions, and trustee assignments. By customizing these properties of the user object, the network administrator begins to define the security and administration policies for the users of the network.

The most important user object properties associated with network administration can be broken down into three main topics:

- **Login properties** allow the network administrator to customize the login security of the NetWare network.

- **Security properties** allow the users to inherit security privileges from object association (like groups).

- **Trustee properties** give the user explicit security assignments to file systems around the network.

In Figure 4-3, you cannot see all of the property tabs associated with the user object. You will notice a scroll bar to the right of the property tabs. If we mention a tab you do not initially see, use the scroll bar to scroll down the list of property tabs. You will then be able to see the tab to which we refer.

Login Properties

The tabs dealing with the login properties allow the network administrator to customize the login for a user. These properties help determine login restrictions, password requirements, and intruder detection services. The settings for login restrictions and passwords should be determined by the network administrator beforehand and applied to all users. It is not a good idea to whimsically set values to these properties. The login properties are defined by tabs of the User dialog box.

Login Restrictions   Clicking on the Login Restrictions tab once with the left mouse button will display the login restriction properties. The network administrator can disable the account or force the account to have an expiration date (after which no one will be able to use the account to log in). This option is useful for temporary employees who will be using the network for a finite period of time.

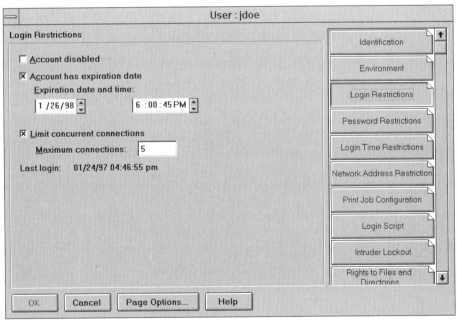

Figure 4-4: Defining user login restrictions.

Through the Login Restrictions property tab, shown in Figure 4-4, the network administrator can use the Limit Concurrent Connections property to severely restrict a user's access to the network. This will allow the user to sustain only a specific number of simultaneous network sessions. For example, setting the Maximum Connections to 1 forces the user to use only one workstation at a time. It is common for a user to walk away from a machine without logging out of the network. However, the user will not be able to access the network from another machine until the previous network session is terminated.

The Login Restrictions property tab can also be used to display information concerning the last time the user logged in to the network. In addition, the user's account can be disabled with the click of a button.

Password Restrictions   The Password Restrictions tab is important in terms of login security. Through the properties on this tab, the network administrator can require a password for a user (as well as specify a minimum length for the password). The administrator can also allow the user to change his or her own password. When a password is required for an account, the network administrator determines whether or not the password will expire after a certain period of time.

Inevitably, a user will forget his or her password, and the administrator will have to change it. This password change is accomplished through the Change Password button on the Password Restrictions tab.

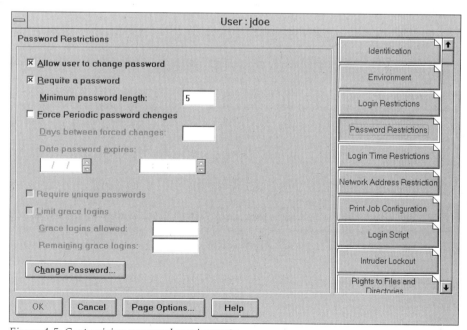

Figure 4-5: Customizing password requirements.

Figure 4-5 shows the Password Restrictions tab of the user object. When a password is required for an account, the network administrator is given the options to force periodic password changes, require unique passwords, and limit grace logins. The Force Periodic Password Changes option makes a password valid only for a specific number of days. After that time, users are required to change their passwords. This is where the grace logins come into play.

Grace logins are used after a user's password has expired. When the user logs in to the network after password expiration, he or she is asked to change the password. If the user does not change the expired password, the Remaining Grace Logins total is decremented by one. If the user continues to refuse the password change and the total reaches zero, the user will not be able to log in without the help of the network administrator.

If the Require Unique Passwords property is enabled, when users change their password, they will be forced to always think of a new one. NetWare archives password information on users and remembers past passwords so that users must create different passwords every time they change them. NetWare 4.11 keeps track of the last 20 passwords a user has entered.

Login Time Restrictions   The Login Time Restrictions tab allows the network administrator to limit the times during the day the user can be logged in to the network. When this tab is chosen, a grid will be displayed with the days of the week listed in rows. The columns are half-hour increments of a 24-hour period. The grid represents an entire week broken down into half-hour slots. Using the grid, the network administrator can specify when a user is and is not allowed to be authenticated to the network.

Figure 4-6 shows that the user mbjones is not able to access the network on Saturday or Sunday because those days have been blacked out. By default, every block in the grid starts out white. A white block means the user is able to log in during that period of time. Clicking on a box with the left mouse button will turn it black. A black box indicates the user is unable to use the network during that time block. For instance, to prevent a person from using the network on Sunday, make every box in the Sunday row black.

The administrator may find it useful to keep users off of the network at night. This is especially true if a server backup is being run during the evening hours. If a user is connected to the network during the day and a blackout period approaches, the user is warned and will be disconnected when the blackout period arrives.

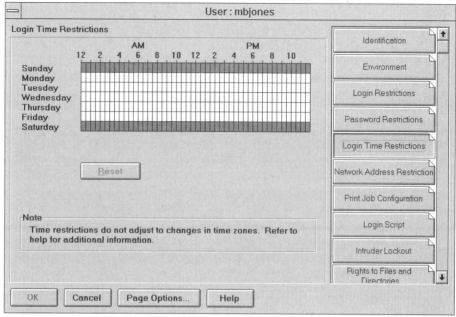

Figure 4-6: Login time restriction grid.

Network Address Restriction   The Network Address Restriction tab allows the network administrator to restrict users to specific workstations for their network use. The user can be restricted by network address, network number, and protocol type. This is an advanced security feature that prevents users from using other people's workstations for network access. Click on the Add button to add a network number or address restriction for the protocol specified. By default, a user can access the network from any workstation that is connected to the network.

Figure 4-7 shows that mbjones may only access the network from a specific network number. This means he is able to access the network from any workstation connected to the physical cable segment with the IPX network number AAAAAAAA. The node address of FFFFFFFFFFFF indicates mbjones may use any workstation on the cable segment to connect to the NDS tree. This security can be taken to an even higher level. The access for a user can be restricted to one specific machine on the network by specifying the hardware address of the network card in his or her machine in addition to the IPX network number. When the user tries to log in from a machine other than the one specified, NDS will deny access.

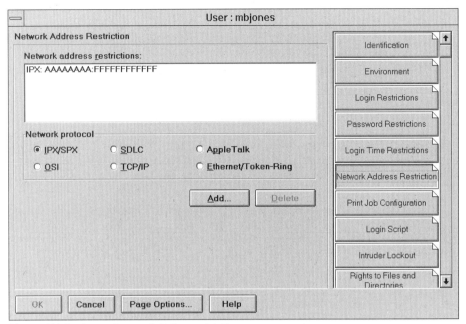

Figure 4-7: Implementing workstation restrictions.

To remove a network address restriction, highlight the desired restriction and click on the Delete button. A user can be restricted to a small subset of workstations on the network. The removal of a restriction will limit the user's access even more. Only when all restrictions are removed (the Network Address Restrictions box in Figure 4-7 would be blank) will the user be able to log in to the network from any location.

Login Script   The Login Script tab allows the network administrator (or the user) to create a user login script. This script is executed at the time of login to provide specific drive and print queue mappings for that user. The user login script is used to provide a specific customization of the network environment for that user only. Type in the user login script commands in the large text editing box (labeled Login Script) displayed in Figure 4-8. To understand the commands listed in this figure, refer to Chapter 5.

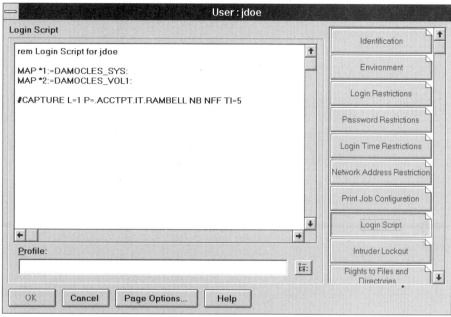

Figure 4-8: Creating a user login script.

One item of note on this page is the Profile box at the bottom. It will allow the network administrator to associate the user with an NDS profile object. The profile will contain more login script commands that will be executed when the user logs in to the network. To find a profile for the user, click on the Select Object button to the right of the Profile box to browse the NDS tree. Select the profile and click OK. The profile name will appear in the Profile box. A more detailed discussion of user and profile login scripts, as well as the profile object itself, is given in Chapter 5.

Intruder Lockout   Intruder lockout protection comes built in to NetWare 4.11 just like it has to all of NetWare 4.11's predecessors. It allows network administrators to set limits on the number of unsuccessful login attempts a user may make before the intruder lockout flag is set for that user. The network administrator also determines what happens when this flag is set.

Intruder lockout protection is actually a container-based service. To enable it, right-click on the desired container and choose Details from the menu that appears. Click on the Intruder Detection tab on the right-hand side of the container properties dialog box.

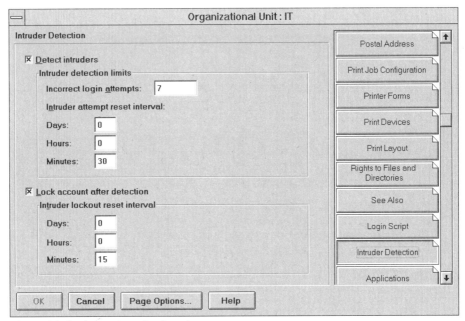

Figure 4-9: Setting up intruder detection.

Figure 4-9 shows the container properties box for Intruder Detection. Remember this is in the container's properties, not the user's! Check the Detect Intruders check box to enable intruder detection for that container. At this point, the network administrator can set the detection limits for the account. This is the window of time during which the intruder detection is going to count the number of incorrect login attempts. By default, it is set to 30 minutes, with the number of incorrect login attempts set to 7. This means that if a user has 7 unsuccessful login attempts within 30 minutes, the intruder detection flag will be set. The counter does not get reset when the user successfully logs in to the network.

The network administrator can set the window of time and number of unsuccessful attempts to whatever values he or she desires. The network administrator can also set the Lock Account After Detection property and its associated values. Enabling the features will cause the user account to be disabled for a specified length of time after the intruder detection flag is set. By default, the account will be disabled for 15 minutes. When disabled, the user may not log in to the network. This helps prevent hackers from trying to crack passwords on your network.

Once intruder detection is enabled, the Intruder Lockout tab in the User dialog box becomes important. This page shows the information concerning the intruder detection feature. It lets you know if the account is locked and the number of unsuccessful login attempts during the specified window of time. If the account is locked, it will also show you the account reset time (when the account becomes enabled again) and the network address of the workstation that caused the account to be locked.

In Figure 4-10, mbjones's user account has been locked due to intruder detection. Here we can see that the account is indeed locked and the time the account will become active again. The offender's address is shown so the network administrator can verify whether or not it was mbjones that forgot or mistyped his password. If it was not mbjones that caused the intruder detection, the network administrator has a lead on the hacker who is trying to get into the network.

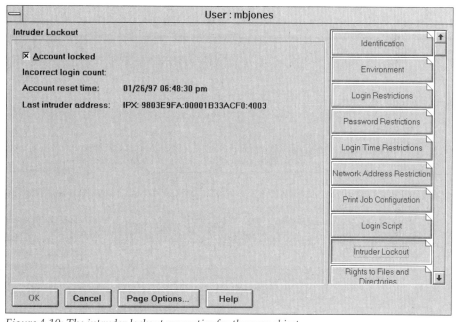

Figure 4-10: The intruder lockout properties for the user object.

If a user's account has been disabled, the Intruder Lockout properties tab will show the account has been locked (if it has been set up to do so). To enable the account again before the default period of time elapses, click on the Account Locked check box. The *X* will be removed, and the user will be able to access the network again.

Together, the login properties provide a first line of defense in the security of your computer network. By placing restrictions at the point of entry to your network, you can ensure that people who do not belong on your network will be unable to gain access. Login security is something that should be devised by the network administrator ahead of time and applied consistently across groups of users.

Security Properties

The security properties tabs allow the network administrator to provide users a level of rights above and beyond what their individual user objects give them. This is accomplished by associating the user object with another object that exists in the NDS tree. To remove extra rights from the user, you only need to remove the object association. The individual user object's rights are not modified in any way. This makes for efficient network administration. There are two security property tabs—Group Membership and Security Equal To.

Group Membership   The Group Membership tab allows the network administrator to associate a user with a group. Through group objects, network administrators can group together users that need the same level of access to network resources. When modifications to the rights of the group need to be made, they are made once to the group object instead of individually to every user. Groups are discussed in more detail later in this chapter. Figure 4-11 shows the Group Membership property tab.

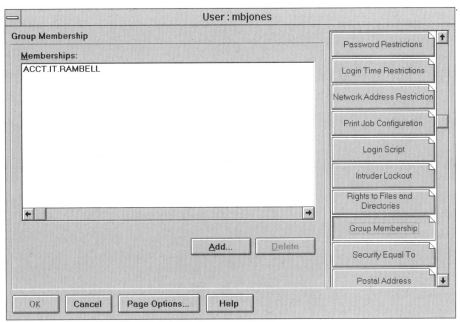

Figure 4-11: Defining user group membership.

To add a user to a group's roster, click on the Group Membership tab once with the left mouse button. Click on the Add button to bring up the Select Object dialog box. Browse the NDS tree to find the desired target group, select it, and click OK. The user is then added to that group.

To remove a user from a group, highlight the group name in the Memberships box by clicking on it once with the left mouse button. Click on the Delete button, and the user will be removed from the group's membership. As discussed in the next section, it may be easier to add and remove users from the group using the properties of the group object itself rather than modifying the Group Membership property of each individual user object.

Security Equal To   The Security Equal To property allows the network administrator to easily give a user the same level of rights another object in the NDS tree has. One common instance of this in NetWare 4.x is making a user the security equivalent of the Admin object. This is an old concept left over from the NetWare 3.x days.

It is generally not a good idea to use this property to grant security equivalencies because it is based on object association. Instead of creating another account on the network with the appropriate rights necessary to administer the network, let's say that you make your user account the security equivalent of Admin. Accidentally, the Admin account is deleted. There will no longer be an object in the NDS tree that has sufficient rights to administer the network. Admin is gone, and since your account was equivalent to Admin, you no longer have those rights!

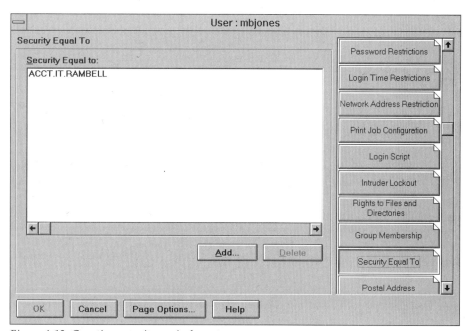

Figure 4-12: Granting security equivalence to users.

To create a security equivalence, choose the Security Equal To tab in the User dialog box by clicking on it with the left mouse button. The screen in Figure 4-12 will appear. Click on the Add button. The Select Object dialog box will appear. Browse the NDS tree to find the security equivalence desired. Select it, and click OK.

Notice in Figure 4-12 that the security equivalence is the same as the group membership from Figure 4-11. When a user is made the member of a group, he or she is automatically given the security equivalence of the group, which is reflected in the Security Equal To property tab. If the group security equivalence is removed, the user is still a member of the group; however, he or she no longer inherits the file system and NDS rights associated with the group object.

To remove a security equivalence, select the equivalence you want to remove by clicking on it once with the left mouse button in the Security Equal To box. Click on the Delete button to remove the association.

Trustee Properties

A user object can be given a specific security assignment to the file system. This is called a *trustee assignment*. One instance of a trustee assignment is the user's home directory in the file system. When the object is created, the user is granted explicit rights to that directory. This will allow that user to read files, write files, create files, and modify files in that directory. The extra rights are granted through a specific trustee assignment when the user object is created and the home directory object is chosen.

The trustee property tab in the User dialog box is the most complex. It offers the network administrator a graphical interface to the file system security. To get to these properties, click on the Rights to Files and Directories tab once with the left mouse button.

In Figure 4-13, we can see that the properties are split into three distinct sections. There are Volumes, Files and Directories, and Rights. Each section plays an important role in making trustee assignments. Also note the Effective Rights button on the bottom of the Rights section. It helps the network administrator determine which rights the user has for that particular file or directory.

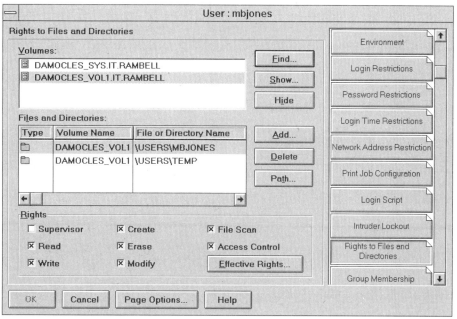

Figure 4-13: Making file system trustee assignments.

Volumes   The Volumes portion of the Rights to Files and Directories property tab (Figure 4-13) is used to find existing trustee assignments for the user in question. Clicking on the Find button to the right of the Volumes box will bring up the Search Context dialog box. Enter the context in which you want to search for the user's trustee assignments. All of the trustee assignments for that user in that specific context will now appear on the screen.

By using the Volumes portion of the property tab, the network administrator can easily find and verify a particular user's trustee assignments. The volumes found in the searched context appear in the Volumes portion; the actual trustee assignments the user has are displayed in the Files and Directories portion of the screen. The rights associated with the trustee assignment are shown in the Rights portion at the bottom of the screen.

The trustee assignments display is also customizable for easier browsing of a user's rights. If NetWare finds more than one volume in a searched context, all trustee assignments for the multiple volumes are displayed. However, if the network administrator only wants to see the trustee assignments for one specific volume, the other volumes' trustee assignments can be hidden by selecting those volumes and clicking on the Hide button. When finished, they can be viewed again by clicking on the Show button.

Files & Directories   The Files and Directories portion of the Rights to Files and Directories property tab is where the trustee assignments are actually made. To make a trustee assignment for a user, click on the Add button to the right of the Files and Directories box. The Select Object dialog box appears. Use it to navigate the file system and select the desired file or directory for the trustee assignment. Click OK. The file or directory will now be displayed in the Files and Directories box with the default rights of Read and File Scan.

To delete a trustee assignment for a user, select the assignment by clicking on it with the left mouse button. It becomes highlighted. Click on the Delete button to the right of the Files and Directories box to remove the highlighted trustee assignment.

The Path button to the right of the Files and Directories box is used to display the full path to the file or directory of the highlighted trustee assignment. If no trustee assignment is highlighted, the Path button will be unavailable. The full path to the file or directory is often too long to be displayed in the Files and Directories box. Use the Path button to find this information easily without having to resort to scroll bars or modifying the width of the columns in the box.

Rights   The Rights portion of the screen is where specific rights are assigned for the trustee assignments that were created in the Files and Directories section. To see the rights granted through the trustee assignment, click on the assignment with the left mouse button to highlight it. The Rights box at the bottom of the screen will display the rights granted for that trustee assignment. In Figure 4-13, the trustee assignment to MBJONES is highlighted, so the Rights box will display the rights to that directory.

The rights that have an X in the box to the left of them are the rights that are given for the trustee assignment. By default, NetWare will assign Read and File Scan rights for all file and directory trustee assignments. To grant more rights, click on the unmarked boxes; an X will appear to show the right is granted. To remove rights, click on the marked boxes; the X will disappear to show the right has been revoked.

The process should be repeated for all trustee assignments to ensure that the user has been granted the appropriate rights. The Rights portion of the box will always show the granted rights for the trustee assignment that is highlighted in the Files and Directories box.

The three sections of the Rights to Files and Directories property tab have distinct and separate functions. When used in conjunction with one another, they allow the network administrator to manipulate users' trustee assignments. The Volumes section allows the network administrator to find all of the user's trustee assignments in a specified context. The Files and Directories section facilitates the creation of the trustee assignments. The Rights section grants and revokes file system rights for the trustee assignments that were created.

There is one more button to note on this page—the Effective Rights button. It will help the network administrator determine the rights a user has to the file system. The concept of effective rights will be discussed in Chapter 6 but remember this button exists in the Rights to Files and Directories property tab. We will come back to it in that chapter.

While user objects will play an important role in your NDS tree, they are not the only user-related objects in the NDS world. Another useful object is the group object which allows the network administrator to grant rights and manage users with similar networking needs.

Groups

One of the most useful objects to help manage users in NetWare 4.11 is the group object. The group object does just what its name implies; it allows the network administrator to group users together to provide them with the same network resources. When a change in network resources is required for users in the group, the change needs to be made only to the group object. Users inherit rights as members of the specified group.

For instance, the manufacturing department at Rambell, Inc., which consists of 10 users, needs to have access to a directory on the departmental file server that contains the production schedule information they use on a daily basis. Instead of granting 10 users trustee rights to that particular directory for file access, one group object can be created and given the trustee rights. The network administrator only needs to make the 10 users members of that one group to give them the rights necessary to access that directory.

Groups are created in the same manner that users are; however, instead of choosing a user object to create, choose the group object instead. To create a group object in NetWare Administrator, right-click on the container which will

hold the group object and select Create from the menu which appears. The
New Object dialog box will be displayed. Choose the group object from the
Class of New Object box and click on the OK button. The Create Group dialog
box will appear.

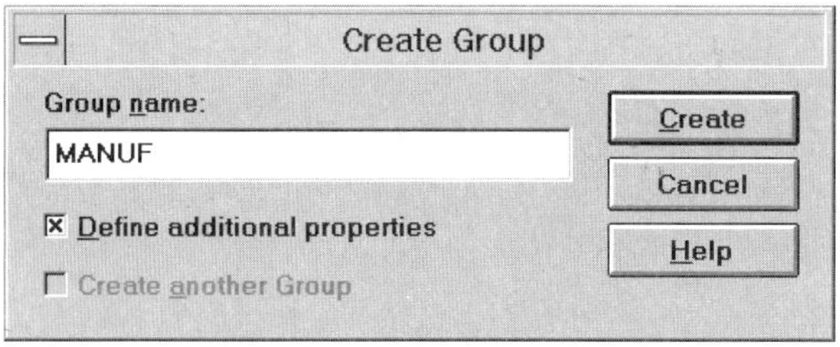

Figure 4-14: Creating a group in NetWare 4.11.

In the Create Group dialog box, specify the name of the group that will be
created. You can then choose whether you want to define additional properties
for this group immediately or create another group. Once the name has been
given and the options chosen, click on the Create button to create the group in
the NDS tree. Eventually, additional properties must be defined to provide
information about the object. A group that has not been detailed is useless.

To detail a group object, click on the group once with the left mouse button
so it is highlighted. Select Object | Details from the menu bar in NetWare Ad-
ministrator. The Group dialog box will appear. Notice at the right are the
property tabs associated with the group object. By default, the Identification
properties are the first to be displayed when detailing the group object. This
property page is similar to the user object's Identification tab; it displays
pertinent information about the group. However, it does not list who is a
member of the group itself. To view the list of members in the group, click on
the Members tab once with the left mouse button. Figure 4-15 shows the
Members property tab of the group object.

When detailing group objects, the most important tabs to look at are the
Members tab and the Rights to Files and Directories tab. These properties are
used to add or delete members from the group and provide trustee assignments to the file system. When a change is made to the trustee rights on the
group object, all of the users listed on the Members page will be affected
accordingly.

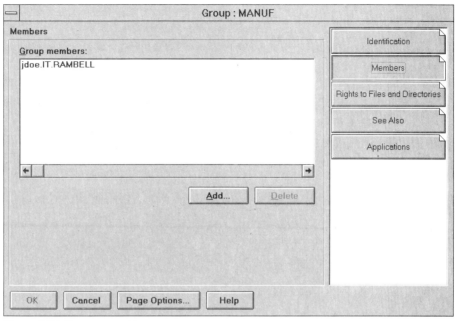

Figure 4-15: Group properties.

To make a user a member of the group, click on the Members tab to see the associated properties. The current members of the group are listed in the Group Members box. To add a user, click on the Add button on the Members tab. This will bring up the Select Object dialog box. Navigate the NDS tree and select the user object. Once selected, click OK; the user is now a member of the group. To remove a user from the group, select the user from the Group Members box by clicking on it once with the left mouse button. Click on the Delete button, and the user will be removed from the group.

Earlier in this chapter, we showed you a way to associate a user with a group using the Group Membership property of the user object (see "Group Membership"). Using the Members property tab of the group object is a second way of accomplishing the same task. Since each method accomplishes the same goal, it is a matter of choice as to which method is used. If you are performing group memberships en masse, it is easier to use the group object. If you are adding or removing just one member, it may be easier to edit the user object.

Group trustee assignments to the file systems on the network are made the same way that user trustee assignments are made. Use the Volumes, Files and Directories, and Rights portions of the Rights to Files and Directories tab exactly the same way you would for the user. The only difference is that all members of the group receive the trustee assignment instead of one individual user.

Groups are useful in the organization of your directory tree. They provide a way to give multiple users the same access to network resources. The best part is that users do not need to be in the same container as the group object to inherit the rights and privileges of that group. Users who are part of a group can be located anywhere in the NDS tree. Thus, it is possible for thousands of users halfway around the world from each other to be members of the same group and have the same network privileges. And all these users' rights can be managed through that one group object.

Besides users and groups, there are also new mechanisms for helping you efficiently manage your network. NDS comes with two new objects, the organizational role and the alias, which allow the network administrator to make user interaction with the network easier. In the next section, we will discuss these two helpful user-related objects.

Organizational Roles & Aliases

While users and groups are the most common user-type objects in the NDS tree, organizational roles and aliases also play key parts in user management. Like groups, these objects allow users to inherit rights through object association. When modifications in access rights need to be made, they are made to the objects instead of the individual user objects themselves. Judicious use of organizational roles and aliases (along with groups) will allow the network administrator to affect the rights of many users through the modification of a small number of NDS objects. This reduces the amount of time and effort necessary to effectively manage the network.

Organizational Role

We briefly covered the organizational role when we discussed the various leaf objects in Chapter 3; however, we did not do the organizational role justice. The organizational role is a powerful object that makes a job or network task independent of the user who is currently performing that job or task. The rights necessary to accomplish the task are defined in the Organizational Role object, and the user object is made the occupant of the organizational role. The user then inherits the rights defined in the Organizational Role object that allows him or her to accomplish the job.

Organizational roles are helpful in ensuring your network is secure. By creating a centralized object with a specific level of network access, the security of the network is managed through this object—not through the individual user objects. Too often, an individual user's object is modified to provide an excessive level of rights to the network. Sometimes, that person needs to have a backup. If that person is unavailable, a third person's user object may need to be modified. The network administrator needs to keep track of exactly who has been modified to prevent someone from having a level of access to the network that isn't appropriate.

Instead of modifying three user objects, the three users can be made occupants of a specific organizational role. Through this role, the users will inherit the extra rights necessary; when they no longer need those rights, they are removed from the organizational role. The network administrator does not need to be bothered with worrying about who may or may not have rights on the network. All rights are granted from an easily managed central location.

To create an organizational role in NetWare Administrator, select the container in which you wish to create the object and choose Organizational Role from the list that appears. A dialog box called Create Organizational Role will appear. Specify the name of the organizational role and choose whether or not you want to define additional properties or create another organizational role. To fill the organizational role with occupants, you must define additional properties.

When defining additional properties, there are two main items of note. The first is the trustee assignments. They will provide the object the level of rights necessary to perform the job function. To modify the trustee assignments, click on the Rights to Files and Directories tab. The second item is making users occupants of the organizational role. To do this, click on the Identification tab; the property page in Figure 4-16 will appear.

In the Identification box on the left-hand side of the page, there is a property labeled Occupant. This is a multivalued property; thus, multiple users can be occupants of the organizational role. To make a user an occupant, click on the button to the right of the Occupant property box with the three dots on it. This will bring up the Occupant dialog box, shown in Figure 4-17.

Clicking on the Add button in the Occupant dialog box will cause the Select Object dialog box to appear. In the Select Object dialog box, find the user you want to occupy the organizational role. Click OK. To remove a user from occupying an organizational role, highlight the user in the Occupant dialog box and click on the Delete button.

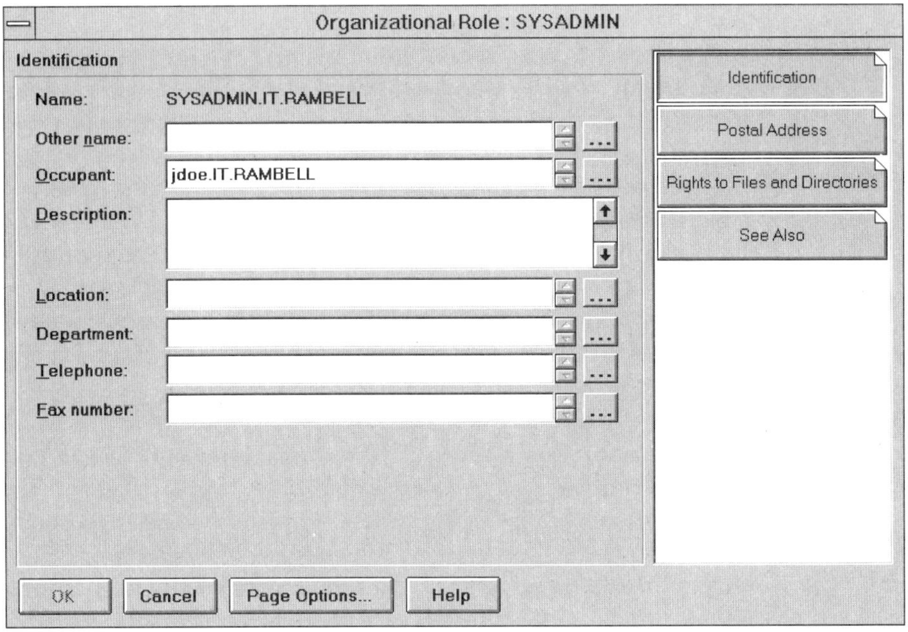

Figure 4-16: Defining organizational role properties.

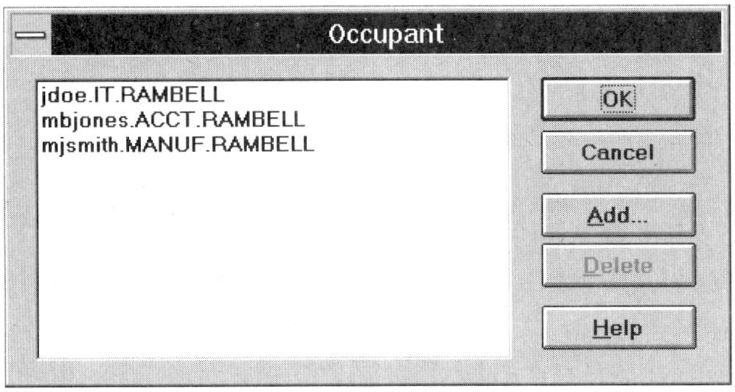

Figure 4-17: Occupants of an organizational role.

You might think that groups and organizational roles are similar. They really are. A group object can be used to perform the same function the organizational role object performs (and vice versa). However, there is a difference that is subtle, yet distinct. A group is used to provide many users the same level of access to resources on the network. Groups are a method of commonality. An organizational role is used to provide specific users with a greater level of access to resources on the network to perform one specific task or job.

Aliases

An alias in the NDS tree is a leaf object that is created to point to another object that exists in the NDS tree. Aliases are not only used to point to other user objects, they can also point to container and other leaf objects as well. The real object in the NDS tree the alias refers to is called the *aliased object*. An alias object can be created to point to a specific server volume that exists on the network. However, aliases are most often used as pointers to other users.

If a company has a user that travels from office to office and accesses the network from many different locations, it may be useful to have one alias for this person in a top level of the tree. The real user object will be located in the "home" container for that person; however, there will be an alias in the NDS tree that the user actually uses for login. When the user uses the alias for login, it will be just as if the user were logging in from his or her "home" container using the real user object. The user will have the same rights, drive mappings, and login script because the alias is just a pointer to that real object.

Aliases are used so users do not have to worry about remembering their context. The aliases will point directly to their appropriate user objects. Regardless of where they log in to the network, they log in with the same name (context independent). Because of the alias, they will have access to resources just as if they had logged in as the user object in their "home" container.

To create an alias in NetWare Administrator, select the target container for the alias object by clicking on it once with the left mouse button. Select Object | Create from the menu bar in NetWare Administrator. The New Object dialog box will be displayed. Choose Alias from the list of objects. The Create Alias dialog box will appear. Name the alias and have it point to the desired object in the NDS tree. In Figure 4-18, the name of the alias is mbjones, and it points to the user object mbjones located in the ACCT.RAMBELL container. Once you have finished inputting the information, click on the Create button to create the alias object.

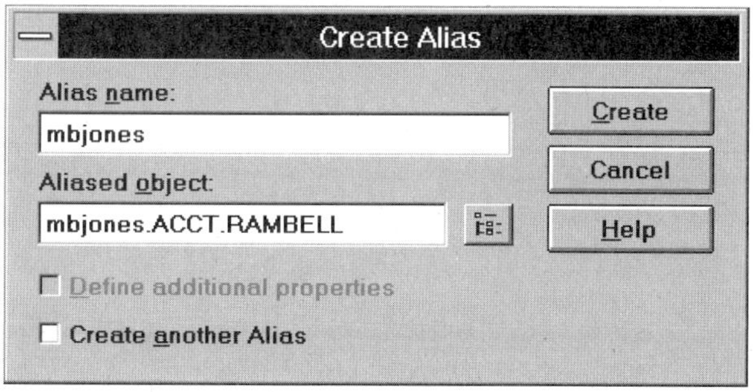

Figure 4-18: The Create Alias dialog box.

Within NetWare Administrator, note that if you right-click on the alias object in the NDS tree and choose Details from the menu that appears, the properties you are seeing are the properties for the real object. Any modifications made to the alias properties are made to the aliased object. The alias truly is just a pointer to another object that exists in the NDS tree. No tangible object is created when an alias is made.

For example, John Doe creates an alias for the user mbjones in the RAMBELL container. The user object for mbjones really exists in the ACCT.RAMBELL container. John then changes the Department property of the alias from Manufacturing to Accounting. If John were to then look at the properties of the real mbjones user object, the user object would now show the Department of mbjones to be Accounting. Any modifications made to the properties of the alias directly affect the object it is referencing. This is an important concept to understand.

Now that we have discussed the many different types of user-related objects you can have in your NDS tree, you will be able to effectively administer your NetWare network. In the next section, we will see how John Doe is handling his user administration from a conceptual level to give you an idea of how you might want to set up the users in your NDS tree.

Applying Concepts: Rambell, Inc.

When we last left John Doe at Rambell, Inc., he had decided upon his NDS tree structure. He wanted to maintain the default structure for his NDS tree because the company is small. Having decided this, John now turns his attention to login security for his network. He decides to implement this security with the following features:

- Users will be limited to one concurrent network connection.
- All users will be required to have a password at least five characters in length. The password will expire every 90 days, and users are required to use unique passwords that they themselves can change at any time.
- Users will not be able to access the network between 10:00 P.M. and 5:00 A.M. This is when the server backup will run.

John takes this information and creates an NDS template object to make the creation of the user objects easier. The template will be used for all users, including himself. The next step is to decide on a login name scheme for his network.

Rambell only has 10 users right now. However, it is likely the company is going to be acquiring another company in the near future. Business is booming, and it looks like more employees are going to be hired. John wants to ensure that his login name scheme is going to scale well should the number of employees begin to increase rapidly. He is going to use the employee's first and middle initial and the first six letters of the last name. Thus, John G. Doe will have a login name of jgdoe.

Now that the login security and name policies have been decided, it is time to create the user objects in the NDS tree. John creates one user object for every employee. He uses the template he previously created so he does not have to manually define properties for each user. All users are created in the IT organizational unit of the NDS tree.

Rambell as a company really consists of two main groups of people. The majority of them belong to the manufacturing group. The remainder (except for John, the network administrator) take care of the bills and finances of the company. Each set of people is going to need access to a different set of files. To facilitate this easily, John creates two groups in the NDS tree. One group is called ACCT for accounting, and the other group is called MANUF for manufacturing. John plans to assign a specific set of rights to the file system for each group. Members of each group will inherit the rights of the user object for their group.

Finally, John realizes that he should not use the Admin account indiscriminately; however, his user object does not have sufficient rights to administer the network. He decides to create an organizational role object in the NDS tree that will function as the network administrator. He names the organizational role SYSADMIN and creates an NDS trustee assignment to [Root] with supervisory rights. By placing his own user object as an occupant of this role, he is able to administer the network using his own jgdoe account.

Moving On

Now that the user objects have been created in the tree, users are able to access the network; however, that is about all they can do. Their network environment has not been customized, and when they log in to the network, none of their resources are going to be available to them unless they type commands. The next step to making network use easier for your users is the creation of the login script. It provides a powerful and flexible way to customize the user environment so that the user can access the network efficiently. The various types of login scripts and their commands will be discussed in the next chapter.

5

Login Scripts

In Chapter 4, we learned about users and user-related objects in the NDS tree. These objects are critical to users' interactions with the network, and managing them obviously plays an important role in the appropriate use of the network. But exactly how do users get to the network resources? The answer is easy. Every time a user logs in to the network, he or she is required to manually input the commands that will provide access to the network resources needed for that session. That means that a ritual to map the appropriate resources after login would have to be performed every day.

This is obviously not an acceptable solution; fortunately, NetWare 4.11 comes with a built-in login scripting environment. Most users on the network will use the same file server, the same network printer, and the same network resources day after day. Thus, the commands necessary to customize the user's network environment after login would be the same day after day. Login scripts automate these repetitive commands and execute them for the user upon login. All users' environments are immediately set for them when they access the network.

Generally, login scripts are used to map network drives and connect the users to network print queues; however, they can do much more. NetWare's login script environment is a powerful scripting language that can be used to provide drastically different environments for different users that execute the same login script. Through variables and programming conditionals, different users will get different environments depending upon their specific circumstances.

After this chapter, you will be able to identify the various types of login scripts available in NetWare 4.11 and determine in which order they will run for users. You will be able to program login scripts to perform advanced functions and use the built-in NetWare environment variables to effectively customize the networking environment for all users on your network.

Login Script Types

Because NetWare 4.11 is a distributed networking environment, there are many different places a user can obtain login script commands. The user may require certain login commands due to his or her location in the NDS tree. Other users may require special commands because of the association with a group. There also may be individual circumstances where a single user needs specific network customization. Regardless of the reason, NetWare 4.11 allows the network administrator (and sometimes the user) to customize users' environments through a variety of login scripts. There are four different types of login scripts that can be executed for a particular user upon login, and they are executed for the user in this order:

1. Container login script

2. Profile login script

3. User login script

4. Default login script

At login, NetWare looks to see if a container login script exists in the user's container. If one does, NetWare executes it. NetWare then looks for an associated profile login script for the user, executes it if it exists, and then follows the same procedure for an individual user login script. If there is no user login script, the default login script is executed for the user.

Even though they are executed in this order, not every type of login script is run for every user. For instance, users that have not been associated with an NDS profile object will not run a profile login script. If a user does not have an individual user login script, it will not execute. The login scripts run in this order *only if they are applicable* to the specific user. If a particular login script does not exist for a user, NetWare searches for the next applicable one in the list.

How you, as the network administrator, organize and maintain your login scripts is left completely to your discretion; however, there are some general guidelines to follow when thinking about implementing login scripts:

- Container login scripts should be used to provide global login script commands for all users immediately beneath a specific container. These commands are usually very general.

- Profile login scripts should be used for groups of people who need the same type of access to network resources. This login script is independent from NDS context and provides a much more efficient way of handling login script commands.

- The user login script should be used to provide specific user commands.

Login scripts are usually maintained by the network administrator. Having many login scripts will require more maintenance and upkeep. Try creating as few login scripts as possible through thoughtful placement and use of container and profile login scripts in your NDS tree.

Container Login Script

The container login script is the first login script to run for a user who is logging in to the network. This script is dependent upon the user's location in the NDS tree. Every organization and organizational unit in the NDS tree can have a container login script. NetWare determines the container in which the user object exists and looks to see if that container has a container login script to be executed.

The container login script is created and maintained by the network administrator. Users will not have the ability to modify the login script unless given a trustee assignment to the container object with sufficient NDS property rights. The container login script is used to execute common commands all users in the container (organization or organizational unit) require. Most often, they are used to map network drives to server volumes to allow access to the file system. Container login scripts are analogous to the system login script in the NetWare 3.x environment.

It is important to understand that only users contained immediately within the container execute the container login script. Users of subordinate containers will not execute the container login scripts of any other containers higher up in the NDS hierarchy. They will execute only the container login script of their specific container. For example, the Rambell NDS tree, WILLOW, has one organization (RAMBELL) with one subordinate organizational unit (IT). The context of any user that exists in the IT container will be IT.RAMBELL. When users from this context log in to the network, only the IT container login script is executed for them. No commands from the RAMBELL container login scripts will be used.

Container login scripts are optional; not every container will have one. To create or modify the container login script, you must be using the NetWare Administrator utility. Bring up the container's properties by clicking on the container once with the right mouse button and choosing Details from the menu that appears. When the container property window appears, click on the Login Script property tab to display the container login script, as shown in Figure 5-1. This screen is essentially one large text editing box that is used to input login script commands.

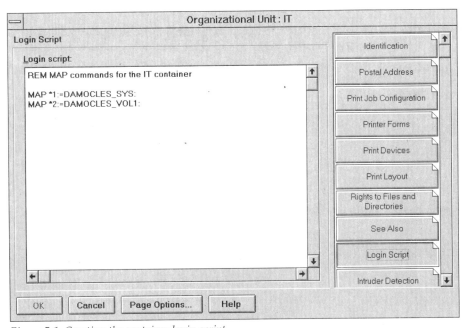

Figure 5-1: Creating the container login script.

Profile Login Script

After the container login script, the profile login script executes. This login script is associated with a particular profile object that exists in the NDS tree. Before we actually discuss the login script associated with this object, we need to learn about the NDS profile object itself.

The main reason the profile object exists in NetWare 4.11 is for the use of the login script. The profile object allows the network administrator to execute the equivalent of a group login script. Through the association of the user object with the profile object, another set of login script commands can be run. However, the profile object does more than that. The profile object can be assigned trustee rights to file systems and other NDS objects. Through the use of security equivalence, users can inherit the rights to other objects through the profile object.

To create an NDS profile object, right-click on the container in NetWare Administrator that will contain it. Select Create from the menu that appears. The New Object dialog box will be displayed. Select Profile from the list. Once the Profile object has been selected, click on the OK button. The Create Profile dialog box will appear. Type the name of the profile object in the Profile Name box and click Create to continue. To immediately detail the object after creation, make sure the Define Additional Properties box is checked, as shown in Figure 5-2.

Figure 5-2: Creating a profile object.

If the Define Additional Properties box is checked, the properties for the profile object will appear. You will notice that this object only has four property tabs as in Figure 5-3. The customary Identification tab is there along with Rights to Files and Directories, See Also, and Login Script. The Rights to Files and Directories property tab can be used to create file system trustee assignments for the profile object.

To create these trustee assignments, follow the same procedures we used to make trustee assignments for user objects (see "Trustee Properties" in Chapter 4). Note that users who are associated with the profile object through the login script property of the user object *do not inherit* file system rights from the profile like they would a group. For the profile object rights to affect the user's rights, you would make the user a security equivalent of the profile object through the Security Equivalence property tab of the user object.

The most important property of the profile is the Login Script tab. The profile login script is usually created and maintained by the network administrator. It is used to provide users located in different areas of the NDS tree the same login script. Where the container login script is executed on the basis of a user's location in the NDS tree, the profile login script is executed independent of location. All that is necessary is an association with the profile object. The profile login script is useful for providing both a global system login, through which all users on your network execute a standard login script, and a group login script for group-specific login commands.

Profile login scripts are optional, like container login scripts. A user is not required to be associated with a profile object; however, it is a convenient way to provide groups of people with the same login script. To modify the profile login script, right-click on the profile object in the NDS tree using NetWare Administrator and choose Details from the menu that appears. When the Profile properties window appears, click on the Login Script property tab with the left mouse button. Figure 5-3 shows the text editing box used to edit the profile login script.

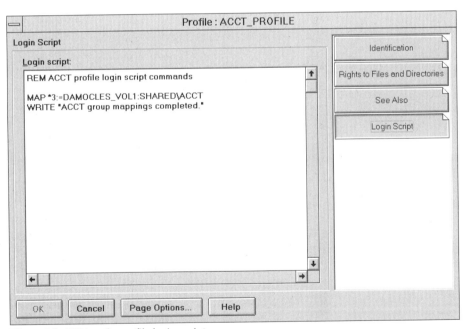

Figure 5-3: Editing the profile login script.

When you are using profile login scripts on your network, there are two important things to remember:

■ A user may only be associated with one profile in the NDS tree. This association occurs through modifying the properties of the individual user object.

■ To execute the profile login script, the user must be a trustee of the NDS profile object. This trustee assignment must include both the Browse object right and the Read property right to the Login Script property of the profile object. These rights will allow the user to see the object in the NDS tree and read the login script associated with that object.

Although a user can only be formally associated with one profile, he or she is able to execute additional profile login scripts if necessary. This can be accomplished executing LOGIN.EXE with a command-line parameter. Using the /P option and the profile object's distinguished name at the LOGIN.EXE command line, another profile login script can be run in addition to another profile login script specified for that user.

For example, mjsmith is associated with the profile object AUDIT; however, she sometimes also needs to execute the login script associated with the .PAYROLL.ACCT.RAMBELL profile object. It could be accomplished typing **login mjsmith /p .payroll.acct.rambell** when logging in to the network instead of the customary **login mjsmith**.

User Login Script

Some users have special needs that require completely different types of access to network resources. This is where the user login script comes in handy. It is the third login script to execute, and it is associated with the user object itself. A user login script will only be executed for that particular user.

Generally, user login scripts are created and maintained by the individual user, although they can be maintained by the network administrator as well. Users are automatically given the right to modify their own login scripts. To edit a user login script using NetWare Administrator, right-click on the user object and select Details from the menu that appears. When the user property window appears, click on the Login Script property tab. Figure 5-4 shows the screen that appears under the Login Script property tab.

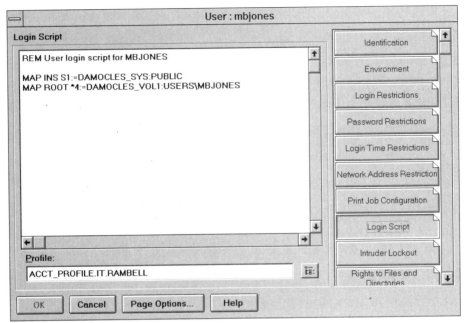

Figure 5-4: Modifying the user login script.

At the bottom of the screen shown in Figure 5-4, there is a box labeled Profile. This is the place where a user's association with a profile object occurs. To create this link, either type the distinguished name of the profile object in the Profile box or use the Select Object button to the right of the Profile box to browse the NDS tree and select the desired profile object.

Like the two login scripts previously discussed (container and profile), the user login script is optional. Only if the user login script is present will it be executed for the user. Many network administrators prefer not to use user login scripts on their network and instead rely on container and profile login scripts to suit their users' needs.

Default Login Script

The last of the login scripts to be executed at login is the default login script. This is the login script that is compiled into LOGIN.EXE and contains the essential commands necessary for performing basic NetWare network commands; it does this by mapping drives immediately to the root of the SYS volume and to SYS:PUBLIC. This will allow the execution of utilities like MAP.EXE, LOGIN.EXE, and LOGOUT.EXE. The first time the network was accessed after the installation of NetWare 4.11, the Admin account was used for login. Because there were no other login scripts defined on the network, the default login script was the only login script to execute. The actual commands issued in the default login script will be examined later in this chapter in the section "Login Script Commands."

If a user object has a login script, the default login script will not execute. It will only execute for users who have only a container and/or profile login script. There is a special command that can be used in a container or profile login script to prevent the default login script from executing. It is the NO_DEFAULT command. When the NO_DEFAULT command is used, the default login script will not be run regardless of whether or not the user has a user login script.

Even though there are only four types of login scripts which can be executed during login, it can be confusing trying to figure out which scripts will execute for a particular user. The best way to determine which scripts will run is to imagine where the user exists in the NDS tree. Because login script execution depends upon NDS tree context, knowing the user's location in the tree will help.

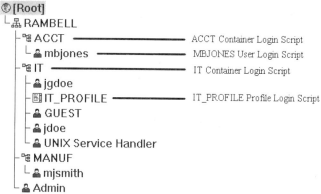

Figure 5-5: Determining which login scripts are executed.

In Figure 5-5, a sample NDS tree is displayed with multiple organizational units and users. User jgdoe is a member of the IT profile in the tree that contains a login script. Jgdoe also has sufficient NDS rights to read the login script. The organizational units IT and ACCT both have container login scripts. The following is true for the NDS tree shown in Figure 5-5:

■ When jgdoe logs in to the network, the IT container login script is executed. Upon completion, the IT_PROFILE profile login script is run. Lastly, the default login script executes because jgdoe does not have a user login script.

- When mbjones logs in to the network, the ACCT container login script is executed. When completed, the individual user login script of the mbjones user object is run. Mbjones is not associated with any profile; no profile login scripts run.

- When mjsmith logs in to the network, only the default login script is executed. This is because there is no container login script for MANUF. Mjsmith is not associated with a profile for a profile login script and has no user login script, either.

Now that you understand the different types of login scripts that exist in NetWare 4.11 and the order in which they are executed upon login, it is time to learn about the specific login commands that are used in these scripts. NetWare 4.11 provides a variety of login script commands that allow the network administrator to completely customize users' network environments.

Login Script Commands

NetWare's login script environment comes with its own syntax, much like a programming language. You must use the specific NetWare commands to automate the login script properly. These commands are used in login scripts to provide four different types of services for users when they log in to the network:

- To map network drives to the file systems and connect the users to network print queues.

- To display messages from the network administrator to the users.

- To set user environment variables.

- To execute external programs or menus for the user.

Login scripts really are a convenience for both the network administrator and the user. The user does not have to be concerned with setting up his or her own environment every day after logging in to the network; it is all automated. The network administrator does not have to worry about users setting up their own environments and the technical support they will need to do so. Network administrators are also able to communicate important information concerning network events such as directory structure modifications and server downtime.

Login scripts are made up of commands that are executed in order, one after another. As the script runs, it is generally processed line by line from top to bottom with one command per line. Only in special cases will this script deviate from the line-by-line approach; commands that alter this pattern are discussed later in this section. For a first look at some login script commands, here is the default login script that is compiled into LOGIN.EXE (the lines are numbered for purposes in this book; actual login scripts do not contain any line numbers):

```
1.  MAP DISPLAY OFF
2.  MAP ERRORS OFF
3.  MAP *1:=SYS:
4.  MAP *1:=SYS:%LOGIN_NAME
5.  IF "%1"="ADMIN" THEN MAP *1:=SYS:SYSTEM
6.  MAP P:=SYS:PUBLIC
7.  MAP INS S1:=SYS:PUBLIC
8.  MAP INS \ S2:=SYS:PUBLIC\%MACHINE\%OS\%OS_VERSION
9.  MAP DISPLAY ON
10. MAP
```

As we mentioned before, the first time the Admin account was used to access the network, the default login script was executed. We will use the line numbers to help describe each line of the default login script. Here's what actually happened when the Admin account logged in for the first time:

1. Normally, MAP commands are displayed on the screen during the login script. This line causes those commands to not be displayed; the ability has been turned off.

2. By default, login scripts will display any errors that occur when executing the MAP command to the screen. This command causes the login script to turn off the displaying of mapping errors.

3. The workstation's first network drive is mapped to the root directory of the SYS volume on the server to which the workstation is attached.

4. The workstation's first network drive is mapped to the user's home directory if the home directory matches the LOGIN_NAME identifier variable. If this home directory does not exist directly off of the root of SYS, this command is ignored and does not replace the mapping from line three. Identifier variables and their use will be discussed later in this chapter in the section "Identifier Variables."

5. If the person accessing the network is logged in as Admin, the workstation's first network drive is mapped to SYS:SYSTEM instead of the home directory or root of SYS. The IF-THEN statement used in this line is a programming conditional. Conditionals will be discussed later in this section.

6. If the user is logging in from an OS/2 workstation, the drive P: is mapped to the SYS:PUBLIC directory. This command is not included for non-OS/2 workstations logging in to the server. DOS/Windows workstations will not execute this line.

7. If the user is logging in from a DOS/Windows machine, the first search drive is mapped to the SYS:PUBLIC directory.

8. If the user is logging in from a DOS/Windows workstation, the second search drive is mapped to the directory below SYS:PUBLIC specified by the identifier variables MACHINE, OS, and OS_VERSION. If this directory does not exist, this command is not executed. Default login script lines seven and eight are actually incorporated into one line separated by a semicolon. These commands are only run for DOS/Windows workstations.

9. This turns on the map display commands.

10. This line shows a list of all drive mappings the user's workstation currently has.

The default login script really only uses the MAP login script command. It does use the conditional IF-THEN statement once to test for a certain condition; however, when the condition is satisfied, it executes a MAP command. Do not be tempted to think the login script environment is limited because of the default login script's simplicity. Login scripts are much more flexible and offer a wider variety of commands that can be executed.

As mentioned earlier, when login scripts are run, the script starts at the first line and executes each command one at a time in order from the top of the file to the bottom of the file. The only exception to this is the GOTO script command that has the potential to change the order of execution (through the concept of a programming loop). NetWare's login script commands are listed in alphabetical order in Table 5-1 with a brief explanation of the command, the command's syntax, and an example of how the command might be used in a login script.

For the purposes of this chapter, we will use a specific syntax convention to help describe these login commands. When reading the Syntax column in Table 5-1, use the following guidelines to understand the login script command's use:

■ Anything typed in all capital letters is a login script command or option that must be spelled as it is in the Syntax column. When actually using the command in a login script, it does not matter if it appears in upper- or lowercase letters; however, it must look exactly like it does in the table.

■ A vertical bar | means *or*. The option to the left of the bar can be used, or the option to the right of the bar can be used. When you see a vertical bar, you cannot choose both options.

■ Optional items associated with the login script command are contained in square brackets []. These items may be omitted from the login script command.

■ Words in *italics* are variables that pertain specifically to your environment. Replace these words with appropriate values when you use the login script command.

■ Nested square brackets [[]] are sometimes used in the Syntax column. Although all of these commands are optional, if you use options that are enclosed in a second level of square brackets, you must also use the options enclosed in the first level. For example, the command EAT [*meal*[*dessert*]], would mean you can't have *dessert* unless you EAT *meal* as well.

Login Script Command	Explanation	Syntax/Example
#	Executes an external program.	**# [*path*]*filename* [*parameters*]** #C:\RUNME.BAT
ATTACH	Connects users to bindery-based servers.	**ATTACH [*server*[/*username*[;*password*]]]** ATTACH oldserver/jgdoe
BREAK	Enables or disables the user's ability to terminate the execution of the login script. Default is BREAK OFF.	**BREAK ON|OFF** BREAK OFF
CLS	Clears the screen.	**CLS** CLS
COMSPEC	Sets the location from which the DOS command interpreter loads while the workstation is logged in to the network.	**COMSPEC=[*path*]COMMAND.COM** COMSPEC=C:\DOS\COMMAND.COM
CONTEXT	Changes the current context of the user in the NDS tree. Functions just like the CX utility discussed in Chapter 3.	**CONTEXT *context*** CONTEXT .IT.RAMBELL
DISPLAY	Displays the contents of an ASCII file.	**DISPLAY [*path*]*filename*** DISPLAY SYS:PUBLIC\MOTD.TXT

➡

Login Script Command	Explanation	Syntax/Example
DOS BREAK	Enables or disables the ability to terminate DOS programs.	**DOS BREAK [ONIOFF]** DOS BREAK ON
DOS SET	Used to set DOS environment variables.	**DOS SET** *variable_name="value"* DOS SET TEMP="C:\WINDOWS"
DOS VERIFY	Enables or disables read-after-write verification.	**DOS VERIFY [ONIOFF]** DOS VERIFY ON
DRIVE	Changes the workstation default drive.	**DRIVE [***drive:***I****n:***]** DRIVE F:
EXIT	Terminates execution of the login script with the option of executing an external program.	**EXIT ["***filename[***parameters***]***"]** EXIT "WIN"
FDISPLAY	Displays contents of a word-processed text file to the workstation screen.	**FDISPLAY [***path***]***filename* FDISPLAY SYS:PUBLIC\FORM.DOC
FIRE PHASERS	Makes sound to draw attention. The number of sounds made is specified in the command.	**FIRE *n*** FIRE 5
GOTO	Forces login script to execute a portion of script out of the normal sequence.	**GOTO *label*** GOTO LOOP
IF . . . THEN	Programming construct used to perform actions only when certain conditions are met.	**IF *conditional* [ANDIOR [*conditional*]] THEN commands [ELSE command] [END]** IF DAY_OF_WEEK="Monday" THEN FIRE 1
INCLUDE	Executes login script commands specified in an external ASCII file or another object's login script property.	**INCLUDE [***path***]***filename*I*object_name* INCLUDE .PAYROLL.ACCT.RAMBELL
LASTLOGINTIME	Displays user's most recent time and date.	**LASTLOGINTIME** LASTLOGINTIME
MACHINE	Sets the DOS machine name; up to 15 characters in length.	**MACHINE=***name* MACHINE=MY_PC
MAP	Maps network and search drives.	**MAP [***option***] [***drive:=path***]** MAP ROOT *1=DAMOCLES_SYS:PUBLIC
NO_DEFAULT	Prevents the default login script from executing.	**NO_DEFAULT** NO_DEFAULT

Login Script Command	Explanation	Syntax/Example
NOSWAP	Prevents login utility from being swapped to disk or extended/expanded memory.	**NOSWAP** NOSWAP
PAUSE	Waits for user to press a key before continuing.	**PAUSE** PAUSE
PCCOMPATIBLE	Allows IBM-compatible machines to use the EXIT login script command.	**PCCOMPATIBLE** PCCOMPATIBLE
PROFILE	Replaces a user's normal profile login script with the specified profile login script.	**PROFILE** *profile_object_name* PROFILE .PAYROLL.ACCT.RAMBELL
REMARK	Allows network administrator to comment login scripts.	**REM** *text* REM This is a comment.
SCRIPT_SERVER	Reads bindery login script from specified server for NetWare 2.x and 3.x users.	**SCRIPT_SERVER** *server_name* SCRIPT_SERVER oldserver
SET	Sets DOS or OS/2 environment variables.	**SET** *name="value"* SET PATH="C:\DOS"
SET_TIME	Enables or disables the synchronization of the workstation time to the network time.	**SET_TIME ON|OFF** SET_TIME ON
SHIFT	Changes the position of the login command-line parameters.	**SHIFT [*n*] (n is a number)** SHIFT 3
SWAP	Swaps login utility out of conventional memory to extended/expanded memory or disk.	**SWAP [*path*]** SWAP C:\
TEMP SET	Sets a DOS or OS/2 environment variable for only the duration of the login script.	**TEMP SET** *name="value"* TEMP SET PATH="C:\"
WRITE	Displays messages on workstation screen.	**WRITE "*text*"** WRITE "This will be displayed."

Table 5-1: Login script commands.

There is a specific subset of login script commands that are the most frequently used. They include the commands that allow the execution of external programs, the mapping of network drives, the displaying of messages, and the programming conditionals. In the following sections, we will examine these login script commands in detail along with some other commands that require more explanation.

(Execute External Command)

The # command is used to run a program that is external to the login script. This is useful for running DOS batch files or other small programs that the user might need. It is also useful for running other NetWare utilities that are not included in the login script syntax, such as the utility for capturing network printing devices.

If a search drive has already been mapped to SYS:PUBLIC, you can capture the workstation's first parallel port to a network print queue called PRINTQ1 by typing **#capture l=1 q=printq1 nb nff ti=30** in the login script. A path is necessary because the external capture program is located in a search drive.

To execute a DOS batch file called RUNME.BAT located in the BATCHES directory on the workstation's hard drive, just add the command **#C:\BATCHES\RUNME** to the login script.

ATTACH

The ATTACH login script command will allow the user to connect to a bindery-based NetWare server (NetWare 2.x or NetWare 3.x) or any NetWare 4.x server that has had bindery services set up on it. Among the optional arguments for this login script command are the server name, the user's ID, and the password for the user.

It is not a good idea to place a user's password in the login script because the password is stored in clear text. Any person who has the NDS rights to examine the login script would be able to obtain the user's password. To attach the user Mike to the server ACCT, type **attach ACCT/Mike**. Because no password is specified, Mike would be prompted to enter a password to complete the attachment to the server. If Mike's password was bubbles, the login script could provide an attachment without any input from Mike by including the line **attach ACCT/Mike;bubbles** in the login script.

DISPLAY/FDISPLAY

The DISPLAY and FDISPLAY login script commands accomplish the same ends; however, each one is used in a different circumstance. The DISPLAY login script command is used to display a straight ASCII text file to the screen. All characters in the file are displayed regardless of whether or not they are understandable text. These characters include any printer or word processing codes that might be contained in the file. When these types of codes are interpreted by DISPLAY, they come across the screen as gibberish.

The FDISPLAY login script command is used to display a word-processed file to the screen. FDISPLAY filters out any special word processing characters in the file so only the text in the file appears on the screen. FDISPLAY will not display tabs to the screen; any special text formatting used involving tabs will be lost using this login script command.

Many network administrators like to present a message of the day to their users. DISPLAY and FDISPLAY make it very easy to do so. The message only needs to be created in a file specified by DISPLAY or FDISPLAY in the login script. Every user who logs in to the network will see the contents of the file. This is useful for informing users about specific network events or happenings. When the message changes, the network administrator only needs to modify the text file, not the login script. For example, to display a message of the day contained in the file MOTD.TXT in the SYS:PUBLIC directory, type the command **DISPLAY sys:public\motd.txt**.

There is one important thing to remember when using DISPLAY or FDISPLAY to display a file's contents to users. The user reading the file must have Read and File Scan file rights to that file. Otherwise, the login script command will not be able to display the file for the user, and no error message will be displayed.

EXIT

The EXIT login script command is a powerful one because it will force the immediate termination of the login script. When executed, the login script stops; any commands that exist after EXIT are not executed. The EXIT command will only work for IBM-compatible workstations running DOS. To ensure that this command runs for users, EXIT is often preceded by the login script command PCCOMPATIBLE.

EXIT can be used to run a program immediately after terminating the login script. To do this, enclose the name of the program and any command-line parameters in quotation marks and place it after EXIT. Be sure the enclosed string does not exceed 15 characters; excess characters are truncated by EXIT and not passed to the DOS command prompt.

FIRE PHASERS

This particular login script command really does not need much explanation, but it does have some significance. When this command is executed, it causes the workstation to make a phaser-like sound. Although this sound can be annoying, it is incredibly useful in grabbing a user's attention.

Many users let the message of the day scroll by without giving it so much as a casual glance. But sometimes the network administrator has critical information that needs to be shared (like server downtime). Displaying this message in conjunction with an audible sound will alert the user. It really causes users to take a second look at the screen.

To make the phaser-like sound three times upon login, type **fire 3**. Three can be replaced with any desired number. Usually after five times, the sound becomes more annoying than attention grabbing.

GOTO

The GOTO login script command is special because it allows the login script execution to deviate from the standard line-by-line order. Computer programmers will immediately recognize this command as a loop construct. It can force the login script to literally go in circles until specific criteria are met.

When a GOTO command is used in a login script, it is always followed by a label. The label tells the login script from where exactly the execution of the login script should continue. GOTOs are most frequently used in conjunction with the IF-THEN conditional construct; together they can be used to form an iterative loop in your login script. A GOTO statement is used in the following example:

```
MAP DISPLAY OFF
BREAK ON
IF DAY_OF_WEEK="MONDAY" THEN GOTO MONDAY
DISPLAY SYS:PUBLIC\OTHERDAY.TXT
EXIT
MONDAY:
DISPLAY SYS:PUBLIC\MONDAY.TXT
```

On all days of the week except Monday, the login script will display OTHERDAY.TXT and terminate the login script; however, on Monday, the login script will display MONDAY.TXT and continue with any other login script commands that happened to follow the display command. This is because of the GOTO statement. It caused the login script to jump ahead to the section of the login script labeled Monday.

There are some things to remember when using GOTO:

- Any label that exists in the login script must be followed by a colon. This is how a label is distinguished.

- When using GOTO commands, it is a wise idea to preface the login script with the command BREAK ON. This will allow you to break out of the login script if by accident an infinite loop is created.

- GOTO commands should not be used to exit out of nested IF-THEN statements. This can cause unpredictable results. Remember, login scripting is not a true programming environment; it is a scripting language that has limitations.

IF-THEN

The real flexibility and customization of the login script is achieved through the use of the IF-THEN command. This login script command is a programming conditional. It will execute a certain command providing a specific condition is met:

```
IF DAY="15" THEN
        WRITE "BEWARE THE IDES."
END
```

This login script command will display "BEWARE THE IDES." on the 15th day of every month when a user logs in to the network. The expression DAY="15" is the *conditional* of the IF-THEN statement. It is testing to see if the current day is the 15th day of the month. The WRITE statement is the *command* after the condition. If the conditional returns a true value, all commands following THEN are executed.

The general syntax of the IF-THEN statement can be quite confusing; however, with some explanation, you should be able to understand it easily. Once you become familiar with using it, you will wonder how you ever got along without it! The IF-THEN statement will always look something like this:

```
IF conditional THEN
        command(s)
[ELSE
        command]
[END]
```

There are essentially three main components to the IF-THEN statement. The conditional statements, the command statement, and the ELSE portion together comprise the full IF-THEN login command. You will notice from the syntax convention that the ELSE portion is optional along with the END statement. To better understand this powerful login script command, let's take a closer look at its three main portions.

Conditional Statement

The conditional statement of the IF-THEN expression is the key to determining if the command statements are executed. When an IF-THEN construct is used, NetWare evaluates the expression contained in the conditional statement. This evaluation will return a true or false value for the login script. A true value will cause the commands after THEN to be executed; a false value will cause the commands associated with the ELSE portion to execute. NetWare allows a variety of expressions that can be used to test for relationships between items. They are summarized in Table 5-2.

Relationship	Acceptable Symbols for Expressing Relationship
Equals	EQUALS[,]IS[,]= [,]= =
Not Equal to	NOT EQUAL TO[,]DOES NOT EQUAL[,]IS NOT[,]!= [,]<> [,]#
Greater Than	IS GREATER THAN[,]>
Greater Than or Equal to	IS GREATER THAN OR EQUAL TO[,]>=
Less Than	IS LESS THAN[,]<
Less Than or Equal to	IS LESS THAN OR EQUAL TO[,]<=
Member of	MEMBER OF
Not Member of	NOT MEMBER OF

Table 5-2: Symbols to express conditional relationships.

The last two expressions (MEMBER OF and NOT MEMBER OF) are actually identifier variables used to test if a user is a member of a specific NDS group. They apply only to group objects. If a group called ADMINS existed in the NDS tree and a test was required to determine if a user was a member of this group, the following line could be used in the login script:

```
IF MEMBER OF "ADMINS" THEN . . .
```

The group name is always enclosed in quotation marks when using this identifier variable. In Table 5-2, some relationships have more than one symbol associated with them. Any one of the symbols is acceptable in the login script. In the following example, both of these statements are evaluated in exactly the same way in the login script and will produce the same result:

```
IF DAY_OF_WEEK="MONDAY" THEN . . .
IF DAY_OF_WEEK IS "MONDAY" THEN . . .
```

In this example, the value of the identifier variable DAY_OF_WEEK is compared to the string "MONDAY", but how is it being compared? This IF-THEN statement is testing for equality. Are the two equal? The conditional statement is evaluated to see if this relationship exists. If it does, the value that is returned is true; the remainder of the IF-THEN statement is executed. If this relationship of equality does not exist, the remainder of the login script command is ignored.

Command Statement

The command statement of the IF-THEN construct contains a specific login script command that is executed if the relationship expressed in the conditional statement is true. Any valid login script command can be used in the command statement. The only time this is not true is when IF-THEN statements are nested; the GOTO command cannot be used in the command portion of nested IF-THEN statements.

Multiple commands can be executed in the command statement. This is quite common when using the IF-THEN construct, and it is often called the *command statement block*. When using a command statement block, the first command in the block should start on a different line than the IF-THEN statement itself. Because it occupies multiple lines in the login script, the statement block must also be immediately followed by an END statement on a separate line. The login utility needs to know where the IF-THEN statement ends; the explicit END tells the login utility exactly where that termination is.

ELSE Option

This option is useful because it sets up an either/or scenario in the login script. If the evaluation of the conditional statement returns a true value, the commands contained in the login script after THEN are executed. If the evaluation returns a false value, the remainder of the login script is ignored, *unless* there is an ELSE option. If an ELSE option exists, the commands contained in this portion of the IF-THEN construct are executed when the false value is returned.

When the ELSE option is used in the IF-THEN construct, the keyword ELSE must exist on its own line after THEN and its associated command statement block. The first command associated with the ELSE keyword must start on a separate line immediately below ELSE.

Syntactic Rules of the IF-THEN Statement

Even though it is the most powerful command, the IF-THEN login script command is also the most tricky to learn and use. There are some specific syntactic rules that exist for the IF-THEN statement that have to be learned before the construct can be used properly. If you are going to use IF-THEN statements, here are the rules to remember:

1. An IF-THEN statement can accommodate a compound conditional. Separate the conditionals with AND or OR.

2. An IF-THEN statement has an optional ELSE statement that may be used. If the conditional statement returns a false value, the ELSE statement is executed instead of the THEN statement.

3. When values are used to express relationships in conditional statements, they must be surrounded by quotation marks. In the "Beware the Ides" example, the values 15 and March must be enclosed in quotation marks.

4. An IF-THEN statement and its associated command statement can be one line in length. In this case, no END command is necessary. An IF-THEN statement that occupies more than one line must be followed by an END command.

5. A WRITE command used in an IF-THEN statement must be on a separate line.

6. When using IF, ELSE, and END, each command must be on its own separate line. THEN usually is included on the same line as IF.

7. IF-THEN statements can exist inside other IF-THEN statements. This is called *nesting*. In NetWare 4.11, IF-THEN statements can be nested up to 10 levels.

The example shown in Figure 5-6 incorporates all of the syntactic rules to demonstrate how they work. Some lines of this example incorporate multiple syntactic rules.

```
IF-THEN STATEMENT EXAMPLE                                          RULES APPLIED
--------------------------------------------------------------------------------------
IF MEMBER OF "ACCT" THEN                                               3,6
    MAP K:=SERVER1_ACCT
    IF DAY_OF_WEEK="MONDAY" AND AM_PM="AM" THEN                    1,3,6,7
        WRITE "Happy Monday Morning!"                                  5
    END                                                               4,6
ELSE                                                                  2,6
    MAP K:=SERVER1_DATA:GAMES
END                                                                   4,6
```

Figure 5-6: Applying the syntactic rules to the IF-THEN statement.

The numbers to the right of the lines in Figure 5-6 refer to the numbered syntactic rules. For example, the line in the example with the number 5 to the right refers to IF-THEN syntactic rule number 5, which states a WRITE command used in an IF-THEN statement must be written on a separate line. Lines with multiple numbers incorporate multiple syntactic rules.

Now that we see how the example relates to the rules, let's look at what the example actually does. If the user logging in to the network is a member of the group ACCT, the K: drive is mapped to the ACCT volume on the server. Furthermore, if the day is Monday and the time is AM, the message about Monday morning is displayed; however, if the user logging in to the network is not a member of the ACCT group, drive K: is mapped to the GAMES directory on the DATA volume no matter what day of the week it is. Because the drive mapping to DATA:GAMES exists in the ELSE portion of the statement, users who are members of the group ACCT will never have this statement executed during the login script.

INCLUDE

When we discussed the types of login scripts that can be executed in NetWare 4.11 we saw a user could only be associated with one profile object. However, we were able to execute multiple profile login scripts using command-line parameters with LOGIN.EXE. The INCLUDE login script command accomplishes the same thing; however, the user does not need to be concerned with command-line parameters when logging in to the network.

INCLUDE is not limited to just profile login scripts, either. It can be used to execute the login script of any other NDS object or a text file that contains login script commands. It effectively spawns a sub-login script that is executed. When the INCLUDE command is encountered by the login utility it pauses the current login script, executes the sub-login script, and then returns to the original login script and continues.

The syntax for the INCLUDE command is INCLUDE [*path*]*filename* | *object_name*. What is specified after the INCLUDE statement is either the path and filename to a file containing login script commands or an NDS object whose login script will be executed. When you are using INCLUDE, be aware of the following things:

- The INCLUDE command can be nested. A login script can spawn a sub-login script which can spawn another sub-login script. The only limit to this nesting ability is the available memory on the workstation.

- If INCLUDE points to a file on a file server, the user must have Read and File Scan file rights to that file to execute the commands.

- If INCLUDE points to another NDS object, the user must have the Browse object right to the NDS object and the Read property right to the Login Script property to execute the login script of that object.

If you wanted a user to execute the login script contained in the profile object PAYROLL in the context ACCT.RAMBELL, you could type **include .payroll.acct.rambell** in the user's login script.

MAP

The MAP command is probably the most important command that is used in the login script. It provides a way for workstations to interface with the file systems that exist on the network. Through the concept of network drives, a workstation is able to treat servers' volumes as though they were physical hard drives attached directly to the machine. The MAP command is employed to allow users on the network to access the data on the network file servers easily.

Tip

If you choose not to use the default login script, your login script must contain MAP commands to allow your users to access the file systems on your servers.

MAP is a versatile command. What it does is determined by the command-line parameters passed to the command. The syntax for the MAP command is MAP [*option*] [*drive:=path*], where *drive* can be replaced with a local drive letter, a network drive letter, or a search drive number. The *path* variable in the command can be replaced with a drive letter, a directory path (including volume name), or an NDS Directory Map object. The general options available for the MAP command are broken down into three main categories:

- Display options
- Error options
- Drive mapping options

Display Options

The display options for the MAP command allow the network administrator to enable or disable the display of drive mappings on the screen. In the default login script, the display options are turned off at the beginning and turned on at the end. To set the display options, use one of the following commands:

```
MAP DISPLAY OFF
MAP DISPLAY ON
```

By default, NetWare 4.11 enables the display of drive mappings during the execution of the login script (MAP DISPLAY ON).

Error Options

Error options enable or disable the display of MAP error messages on the screen during the execution of a login script. To turn error messages on or off, use the following commands in the login script:

```
MAP ERRORS ON
MAP ERRORS OFF
```

By default, NetWare 4.11 will display map error messages (MAP ERRORS ON). To avoid any error messages appearing, the MAP ERRORS OFF command must be used in the login script before any other MAP statements are executed.

Drive Mappings

It is the NetWare 4.11 servers on your network that store all of the data on their hard drives. For organizational purposes, the space on the servers' hard drives is separated into volumes, and the volumes themselves are composed of files and directories. But how does the workstation actually use these files and directories? It is able to interact with the various file systems on the network through the use of drive mappings. A drive mapping will fool the workstation into thinking the network is just another hard disk. The NetWare client then takes the data that is mapped to the network and creates packets of data that are put out onto the network and arrive at the appropriate server, which writes the data to its hard disk.

For a DOS workstation, there are two types of drive mappings that can be made. These are the network drive mapping and the search drive mapping. A *network drive mapping* assigns a workstation drive letter to a server volume on the network. This will give the local workstation's operating system access to the volume. For example, if your users need data on the ACCT volume of the file server Damocles, you could include the following statement in your login script:

```
MAP I:=DAMOCLES/ACCT:
```

At the prompt, the user could change the current drive to I: and access the file system on that volume, assuming he or she has enough file system rights to do so. Each drive mapping uses up one drive letter on the workstation. Since the workstation often uses drive mappings A-E, usually only drives F-Z are available for network drive mappings. Because drive letters are limited on the workstation, be thoughtful when using the MAP command to map drives to network resources.

A *search drive mapping* adds the specified path to the local workstation's PATH DOS environment variable. Search drives are only applicable for the DOS workstation. When a command is executed at the DOS prompt, the operating system looks for the command in the directories specified in the DOS PATH environment variable. Essentially, a search drive mapping tells the operating system to look for executables not only on the local workstation but also on the network.

If users needed to access batch files located in the BATCHES directory of the ACCT volume on the file server Damocles, you could add the following statement to your login script:

```
MAP S1:=DAMOCLES/ACCT:BATCHES
```

When a command is executed at the prompt now, the workstation will also look in this particular directory for the batch file. Search drive mapping assignments are always made with the drive assignment Sn, where n is the search drive number. NetWare then finds an open drive letter and assigns it to the search drive mapping. Search drive mappings start at the end of the alphabet and work their way back toward the beginning. The first search drive would be assigned to the Z: drive. The second would be assigned to Y:. A maximum of 16 search drive mappings are allowed on a DOS workstation.

Be careful when using search drive mappings on your DOS workstation. Because search drives take longer to search when looking for executables, a lot of search drives in your PATH environment variable will adversely affect the performance of your machine. Try to keep search drives limited to essential directories like SYS:PUBLIC, SYS:SYSTEM, or SYS:LOGIN. More than three search drive mappings for a workstation is usually too many.

Although the MAP command can be used with only the *drive* and *path* variables specified, MAP is much more flexible and useful when the *options* are exercised. The options for the MAP command are summarized in Table 5-3. We will discuss the more common options in detail in the following sections.

MAP Option	Meaning	Use
INS	Inserts a search drive mapping between existing search drives.	MAP INS S*n*:=*path*
DEL	Deletes a network drive or search drive mapping.	MAP DEL *drive*:
ROOT	Fools the local operating system into thinking the network drive mapping is the root of the file system.	MAP ROOT *drive*:=*path*
C	Toggles the drive mapping between a network drive mapping and a search drive mapping.	MAP C *drive*:
P	Forces the mapping to the physical volume of the server rather than the NDS volume object name.	MAP P *drive*:=*physical_volume*:*path*
N	Maps the next available drive letter when no letter or number is specified.	MAP N *path*

Table 5-3: MAP drive mapping options.

MAP INS   Using the INS option in conjunction with a search drive mapping will cause the workstation to insert the new search drive mapping in between two existing ones so that no search drive is lost by accident. The best way to illustrate this is with an example.

Let's say the DOS PATH environment variable is set to C:\; C:\WINDOWS; C:\DOS. This means there are three directories that are searched when a command is issued at the DOS prompt. When a search drive is mapped, the three directories in the PATH are treated as three separate search drives. C:\ is search drive one; C:\WINDOWS is search drive two; C:\DOS is search drive three. In the login script, the following command is issued:

```
MAP S1:=SYS:PUBLIC
```

The first search drive is being mapped to SYS:PUBLIC. The NetWare client finds an available drive letter (let's say Z:) and creates the search drive mapping. Now when PATH is viewed in DOS, it is set to Z:.; C:\WINDOWS; C:\DOS. The first search drive really has been set to SYS:PUBLIC—at the expense of C:\!

This can be avoided by using the INS command. If the same search MAP command was executed in the login script with the INS option (MAP INS S1:=SYS:PUBLIC), Z: would be inserted into the front of the list. The DOS PATH variable would then be Z:.; C:\; C:\WINDOWS; C:\DOS.

Tip

Use the MAP INS command to insert drive mappings at your workstation. This command will not supercede any existing drive mapping.

MAP DEL   The MAP DEL option is used to remove a drive mapping during a network session. Either a network drive mapping or a search drive mapping can be removed. Just specify the drive letter to be removed, and it will be gone. It can always be re-created using another MAP command.

MAP ROOT   The MAP ROOT option can be a confusing one. This option fools the operating system into thinking the path specified by the mapped drive is the root of the file system. There are many DOS programs that can only be executed from the root of the file system; the NetWare 4.11 installation program is one of them. When they are run from a place other than the root, they fail. To trick these programs into execution, use the MAP ROOT option. Let's look at two MAP commands, both mapped to the same place, to see just what the ROOT option does:

```
MAP I:=ACCT:BATCHES
MAP ROOT J:=ACCT:BATCHES
```

When the user switches to the I: drive from the workstation, the prompt would appear as I:\BATCHES>. The workstation understands that BATCHES is a subdirectory that exists directly off of the root directory on the volume ACCT. If the user were to type **cd ..** from this prompt, he or she would be able to access the root of the file system.

If the user were to switch to the J: drive, the prompt that appears would be J:\>, even though the user would be in the BATCHES directory. The workstation believes this directory is the root of the file system. Executing a DIR command from both the I:\BATCHES> and J:\> prompts would produce the same list of files. The difference is that the workstation thinks the J: drive is the top level of the file system. A program in BATCHES dependent upon being at the root of the file system would execute from the J: drive but *not* the I: drive.

Tip

Use MAP ROOT when you want to hide the upper branches of the file system from the user. Because the workstation believes the root of the file system exists at a lower level, the user will not be able to access those directories which exist at a higher level in the file system.

Other MAP Command Issues

MAP commands are most often used in connection with explicit drive assignments. Network administrators generally like the concept of static drive mappings. Whenever they go to a workstation, they know the F: drive is always SYS:PUBLIC, for instance. However, there is a disadvantage to explicitly assigning drive letters in the login script. Let's say the login script maps the following drives:

```
MAP E:=SERVER_SYS:PUBLIC
MAP ROOT F:=SERVER_VOL1:DATA
MAP ROOT G:=SERVER_VOL1:USERS\%LOGIN_NAME
```

In most cases, these drives would map just fine without interfering with any local workstation file systems. The E: drive would map to the PUBLIC directory on the SYS volume. The F: drive would map to the DATA directory on the VOL1 volume. The G: drive would map to the user's home directory (as specified by the LOGIN_NAME identifier variable) on VOL1.

Unfortunately, there may be machines on your network that use drives E: and F: to access local devices. A workstation that has three hard drives and a CD-ROM drive would need to use drives C:, D:, E:, and F: for local devices. After the mapping statements in the login script, the workstation would no longer be able to access the drive E: and F: local devices until the network drive MAP statements were removed.

NetWare 4.11 comes with a way to avoid this dilemma. When assigning drives for network drive mappings, the convention *n can be used (where *n* is a number) for the *drive* variable in the MAP command. This causes NetWare to dynamically assign drive letters based upon the first network drive specified in the NetWare Requester. If the first network drive was set to F:, the following MAP command would assign a network drive mapping to the I: drive:

```
MAP *4:=SERVER_SYS:PUBLIC
```

NetWare starts with drive F: and counts off four letters to get to I:. On the machine with three hard drives and a CD-ROM drive, the network drive mapping would be assigned to drive J:, assuming the first network drive is set to G:. If you use this method, you can map drives without having to worry about those mappings conflicting with local devices.

In conjunction with expressing drives in different ways, referencing volumes in the drive mapping can also be expressed in multiple ways. The volume can be referenced through either its NDS volume object name or its complete server and physical volume name. To access the ACCT physical volume on the server Damocles, which has the NDS object name DAMOCLES_ACCT, either one of the following MAP commands could be used:

```
MAP *1:=DAMOCLES/ACCT:DATA
MAP *1:=DAM_ACCT:DATA
```

The first example explicitly specifies the server name and physical volume. The second references only the NDS volume object that represents the physical volume; however, both achieve the same result. When using the NDS volume object, remember this: if the volume object exists in the same context as the user, only the common name of the volume needs to be given in the MAP command. For users in a different context, the full distinguished name of the volume object needs to be expressed.

If only the name of the volume is used in the MAP command (instead of server and volume), the NetWare client assumes the workstation is trying to access a volume on the server to which it is currently attached. When omitting server names from the MAP commands in login scripts, the network administrator must be sure the user has attached to the appropriate file server.

Besides referencing server volumes, the MAP command can also be used to map drives to an NDS Directory Map object. Remember that the Directory Map object contains a mapping to a directory on a volume's file system. Mapping drives through Directory Map objects is an efficient way to use the MAP command. If the directory changes, only the Directory Map object needs to be modified instead of all login scripts that reference that directory. To map a drive to a Directory Map object, use the distinguished name of the object as the *path* variable.

The MAP command can also be used without any options. When used this way, it displays a list of the current drive mappings for the workstation. This is a useful command to show just exactly what has been mapped during a login script. Many network administrators add MAP to the end of the login script to verify the accuracy of the login script.

If for some reason a user needs to map additional drives after the login scripts have been executed, it is not a problem. Not only is MAP a login script command, it is also a DOS command-line executable that can be run from any system prompt. However, there are a few differences between the login script command and the executable:

- MAP DISPLAY and MAP ERRORS options are used only in the login script command.

- The MAP command-line utility has an extra option called no prompt (NP). When it is used, MAP will not prompt the user before deleting or overwriting an existing drive mapping.

```
MAP NP DEL G:
```

This example will cause NetWare to delete the drive mapping without prompting the user to confirm the deletion. Apart from these two differences, the command-line utility and the login script command function exactly the same.

MAP can also make use of identifier variables. This is useful for mapping drives to users' home directories. Instead of having to create a user login script for all users with an explicit drive mapping, just type the following in the container login script:

```
MAP *3:=SERV_DATA:USERS\%LOGIN_NAME
```

This will cause MAP to map the third network drive to the directory specified by the user's login name, if that directory exists; otherwise, an error will be returned, and the drive will not be mapped. When referencing identifier variables with the MAP command, the variables must be preceded by the percent sign (%).

Tip

Using identifier variables in conjunction with the MAP will save you a lot of effort. Instead of having to create an individual login script for each user, you can accomplish the same thing with one MAP command using an identifier variable. For more information on identifier variables, refer to the section "Identifier Variables" later in this chapter.

The MAP command plays a critical role in allowing your DOS/Windows and OS/2 workstations to access the data stored on your file servers. You will become very familiar with it as you begin to create login scripts. But as we know, MAP is not the only command you can use in the login script. Let's resume our discussion of some of the common login script commands in NetWare 4.11.

NO_DEFAULT

The NO_DEFAULT login script command will prevent the default login script from executing. As we have learned, when there is no individual user login script, the default login script will run. To prevent the default login script from running, add the NO_DEFAULT statement to the container or profile login script.

PROFILE

The PROFILE login script command can be used to force an association with a profile login script. If the user object has not been linked to an NDS profile object and a profile login script needs to run, use the PROFILE command to set the script into action. For users who already have a profile login script set to run, the PROFILE command will override that script.

For example, a user is already supposed to execute the login script of the profile object PAYROLL.ACCT.RAMBELL; however, in the container login script, the following command exists:

```
PROFILE .IMPORTANT.IT.RAMBELL
```

Because PROFILE replaces any existing profile login script set to run, the user logging in to the network will execute the login script associated with the IMPORTANT object instead of the PAYROLL object. This is different from the INCLUDE login script command, which will allow you to run a profile login script in addition to any existing one.

REMARK

As we have mentioned, the login script environment is very similar to a programming language. As such, it is a good idea to comment your login scripts so that you can go back to them at a later date and remember what you have done. Also, you are not going to be the network administrator forever; another person is going to have to look at your work and try to figure out what you have done. This is where commenting a login script comes in handy. It explains exactly what the commands are doing.

All comment lines begin with the REMARK command. This command tells the login utility to ignore any text that follows on that line. Comments also do not appear on the workstation screen. They are essentially invisible; they appear only on the login script editing screen. The following are some examples of comments in login scripts:

```
REMARK THIS IS THE IT CONTAINER LOGIN SCRIPT
REM CREATED 07JUL96
* BY JOHN DOE
; THIS SECTION PROVIDES DRIVE MAPPINGS
```

The REMARK command can also be represented in login scripts as the string REM, an asterisk, or a semicolon. All four representations can be used in the same login script. They are treated in exactly the same way by the login utility.

The REMARK command should occupy its own line in the login script. Do not try to combine REMARK on the same line as other login script commands. It may cause unpredictable results. Take the time to comment your login scripts. You will thank yourself at a future date.

WRITE

The WRITE login script command is used to display text to the workstation screen when the user logs in to the network. Its function is similar to that of DISPLAY and FDISPLAY; however, it is a little more flexible, and it has some other features DISPLAY and FDISPLAY do not have.

To display the text to the workstation screen, use the WRITE command followed by the text in quotation marks. To print "Hello world!" to the screen, type **WRITE "Hello world!"** in the login script. It's as simple as that. There are some instances where special characters are required to perform actions not specified by text alone. These special characters are described in Table 5-4.

Special Character	Result
\r	Creates a carriage return.
\n	Creates a new line of text.
\"	Causes the quotation mark to be displayed on the screen instead of ending the text string.
\7	Produces a beep.

Table 5-4: WRITE special characters.

Together, \r and \n produce the effect of the Enter key on a keyboard. Alone, \r would return the cursor to the left edge of the screen without advancing the display to a new line, causing all of the text to be written on the same line. A \n by itself would advance the cursor to a new line but would not return the cursor to the left. If we wanted to display Edgar Allen Poe's famous quote on our screen, we would type the following in our login:

```
WRITE "Quoth the Raven:\r\n\"Nevermore!\"\7"
```

This would produce the output:

```
Quoth the Raven:
"Nevermore!"
```

This display would be followed by an audible beep. Because the quotation mark is the character that delineates the beginning and end of the text to be displayed, the special character \" is used if a quotation mark needs to be displayed on the screen. The \ tells the WRITE command that the following quotation mark is meant for display; it does not mean the end of the string.

WRITE statements that appear on separate lines in the login script will appear on separate lines of the screen when displayed. To force two or more separate WRITE statements to display output on the same line, follow them with a semicolon (;). The following commands:

```
WRITE "THE SERVER WILL BE DOWN FOR ";
WRITE "SERVICE AT 5:00PM."
```

would appear on the workstation screen as:

```
THE SERVER WILL BE DOWN FOR SERVICE AT 5:00PM.
```

Although WRITE can be used to display simple text to the workstation screen, it is much more useful than that. The WRITE statement can be used to display information contained in system identifier variables. For instance, the greeting for each user could be customized by using the identifier variables GREETING_TIME and FULL_NAME:

```
WRITE "Good %GREETING_TIME %FULL_NAME.";
WRITE "Today is %DAY_OF_WEEK."
```

If John Doe logged in to the network on Tuesday morning, he would be greeted with the message "Good MORNING JOHN_DOE. Today is TUESDAY." If Mary Smith logged in to the network on Thursday afternoon, she would see the message "Good AFTERNOON MARY_SMITH. Today is THURSDAY." Through the use of identifier variables, WRITE offers a much more flexible way to display current information for users on your network.

If these login script commands were your only available resources in creating your login scripts, you would have a rigid environment that would not be customizable to your specific situation. Fortunately, the login script environment allows you to use variables to test for such things as membership and equivalence so you can use conditional statements. These identifier variables, covered in the next section, will help you customize your login scripts so you can customize the network environment for all of your users.

Identifier Variables

As we have seen in the previous section, identifier variables can be used to customize login scripts. Instead of having to create individual login scripts with specific commands for users, identifier variables can be used in more general container and profile login scripts to provide the same specialized user mappings and environments.

One prime example of this is the mapping of a user's home directory. Without identifier variables, the only way to do this is to create an individual login script for every user with one MAP command. John Doe's user login script would contain a command like the following:

```
MAP N VOL1:USERS\JGDOE
```

Mary Smith would have an equivalent command in her user login script, except JGDOE would be replaced with her login name. The network administrator would then be responsible for maintaining many login scripts. The use of identifier variables can help this problem tremendously. Instead of all the individual user login scripts with one command, you could have a container login script that contains the following command:

```
MAP N VOL1:USERS\%LOGIN_NAME
```

Every user that logs in to the network would get a customized drive mapping to his or her home directory, and the network administrator would only have to maintain one login script. This is why the use of identifier variables makes login scripts efficient.

NetWare 4.11 provides myriad identifier variables that can be used in the various login scripts on the network. There are some guidelines to follow when using these identifier variables in login script commands:

- When the identifier variable is being used for comparison in an expression, type the variable in all capital letters:

```
IF NDAY_OF_WEEK="2" THEN
    WRITE "IT'S MONDAY AGAIN!"
END
```

- When the identifier variable is being used for the value it contains, it is preceded with a percent sign (%). This is how identifier variables are used in MAP commands:

```
MAP *4:=SERV_VOL1:USERS\%LOGIN_NAME
```

- When identifier variables are placed inside quotation marks, they must be preceded by a percent sign (%) and typed in all capital letters:

```
WRITE "GOOD %GREETING_TIME, %FULL_NAME."
```

Identifier variables are most frequently used with the login script commands IF-THEN, MAP, and WRITE. Use the examples in the preceding guidelines to help you determine whether or not the percent sign (%) needs to be used with the identifier variable. The percent sign is generally required for the WRITE and MAP commands; it is not used in the conditional of the IF-THEN statement.

Identifier variables can be organized into eight general categories. The categories describe the type of information that is stored in the variable. The next sections describe the general categories and the identifier variables that are available in NetWare 4.11.

Date Variables

The identifier variables pertaining to the current date get their data from the workstation time. Identifier variables holding date information are shown in Table 5-5; values that follow in parentheses are the valid values for that identifier variable.

Identifier Variable	Description	Valid Values
DAY	Holds the day number of the month.	01-31
DAY_OF_WEEK	Stores the day name of the week.	Monday, Tuesday, Wednesday, etc.
MONTH	Holds the month number of the year.	01-12
MONTH_NAME	Stores the month name of the year.	January, February, March, etc.
NDAY_OF_WEEK	Contains the day number of the week.	1 (Sunday)– 7 (Saturday)
SHORT_YEAR	Stores the last two digits of the year number.	95, 96, 97, etc.
YEAR	Holds the four-digit year number.	1995, 1996, 1997, etc.

Table 5-5: Date identifier variables.

Time Variables

The time identifier variables also store information read from the workstation's current time. The identifier variables holding this information are shown in Table 5-6.

Identifier Variable	Description	Valid Values
AM_PM	Stores the day or night clock setting.	AM, PM
GREETING_TIME	Contains the qualitative time of day.	MORNING, AFTERNOON, EVENING
HOUR	Stores the numeric hour for a 12-hour clock.	1-12
HOUR24	Stores the numeric hour for a 24-hour clock.	00-23
MINUTE	Holds the minute of the hour.	00-59
SECOND	Contains the second of the minute.	00-59

Table 5-6: Time identifier variables.

User Variables

The variables that pertain to the user are retrieved from the user object and its context in the NDS tree. When the user logs in to the network, the login utility examines the user's user object and stores pertinent information about that user. These variables are the most often used to customize NetWare login scripts, as seen in Table 5-7.

Identifier Variable	Description	Valid Values
CN	Stores the common name of the user object.	Any
FULL_NAME	Retrieves the value from the Full Name property of the NDS user object.	Any
LAST_NAME	Stores the user's last name from the Last Name property of the NDS user object.	Any
LOGIN_ALIAS_CONTEXT	Holds a Y if the REQUESTER_CONTEXT identifier variable is an alias object.	Y, N

➡

Identifier Variable	Description	Valid Values
LOGIN_CONTEXT	Contains the context where the user object exists.	Any valid context in the NDS tree
LOGIN_NAME	Holds the information from the Login Name property of the NDS user object (truncated to eight characters).	Any
MEMBER OF "group"	Used to verify group membership.	Y, N
NOT MEMBER OF "group"	Used to verify group nonmembership.	Y, N
PASSWORD_EXPIRES	Returns the number of days before the user's password expires.	Numeric value
REQUESTER_CONTEXT	Contains the workstation's current context.	Any valid context in the NDS tree
USER_ID	Stores the NetWare-assigned user number.	Numeric value

Table 5-7: User identifier variables.

Network Variables

The network identifier variables store information about your network environment. These variables can be used to return important information about your particular network. Network variables are given in Table 5-8.

Identifier Variable	Description	Valid Values
FILE_SERVER	Returns the name of the file server to which the workstation is currently attached.	Any
NETWORK_ADDRESS	Holds the IPX network number of the workstation's physically attached network cable.	8-digit hexadecimal value

Table 5-8: Network identifier variables.

Workstation Variables

Identifier variables pertaining to the workstation gather information about the physical machine, the operating system, and the NetWare client shell. One particularly useful variable returns the hardware address of the client workstation. It is often useful to write commands in the login script to display workstation information because machine configuration is important to track. Refer to Table 5-9 for workstation variables.

Identifier Variable	Description	Valid Values
MACHINE	Holds the long name of the computer.	Any
NETWARE_REQUESTER	Stores the version of the NetWare Requester.	Any valid NetWare Requester version
OS	Returns the operating system of the workstation.	MSDOS, OS2, etc.
OS_VERSION	Stores the version of the work- station's operating system.	Numeric value
P_STATION	Contains the hardware address of the workstation's network interface card.	12-digit hexadecimal number
PLATFORM	Retrieves the operating system platform of the workstation.	DOS, OS2, WIN, WNT, W95
SHELL_TYPE	Stores the NetWare shell version of the workstation.	Any valid NetWare shell version number
SMACHINE	Holds the short machine name of the workstation.	Any
STATION	Retrieves the user's server connection number.	Numeric value

Table 5-9: Workstation identifier variables.

DOS Environment Variables

All DOS environment variables can be used as identifier variables in login scripts as well. To use a DOS environment variable in a login script, enclose the variable name in angled brackets (<>). For example, the local PATH variable for the workstation could be displayed using a WRITE command:

```
WRITE "Your current path is %<PATH>."
```

Miscellaneous Variables

Because they do not fall into any particular group, these last identifier variables fall into the miscellaneous category. They include information about access servers, error levels, and command-line parameters:

- **The ACCESS_SERVER** variable displays the status of the access server. If the server is up, ACCESS_SERVER holds the value TRUE. If the server is down, ACCESS_SERVER holds the value FALSE.

- **The ERROR_LEVEL** variable stores the error level as set by the previous external command executed using the # login script command. If no error was returned, ERROR_LEVEL will hold the value zero.

- **LOGIN.EXE** command-line parameters can be used as identifier variables as well. In login scripts, they are described by the variables %0–%9.

The command-line identifier variables are useful for passing information to a login script through the command line of LOGIN.EXE. If a user logged in to the network typed the command login jgdoe noscript, the command-line identifier variables would be set. The identifier %0 would be assigned the value jgdoe; %1 would store the value noscript. This information could then be used in the login script:

```
IF "%1"="noscript" THEN EXIT
```

Because the value of the second command-line parameter equaled "noscript", the EXIT command would immediately cause the login script to terminate. Command-line parameters are most often used in conjunction with the SHIFT login script command. Together they can filter through any parameters that are passed to the script through the login utility.

Object Properties Variables

The list of available identifier variables does not end with those mentioned in this chapter. Many NDS object properties can be used as identifier variables. To do so, use the property name just as you would use any other variable. For example, you could use the Department property of the user object to display information during the execution of the login script:

```
WRITE "Verify your phone number: %Telephone"
```

The login scripting capabilities provided with NetWare 4.11 are extremely flexible. A well thought-out login script scheme will provide your users with a customized network environment with small administrative overhead. With all of the options provided, the possibilities are endless.

Applying Concepts: Rambell, Inc.

Now that John Doe has his users and user-related objects created, he needs to figure out how he is going to organize the login scripts on his network. He only has one organization in his NDS tree, RAMBELL; it contains only the Admin object and an organizational unit, IT. It is IT that contains all of John's users and groups. Because of his current NDS structure, any container login script IT has will be executed for all users (except the Admin account).

John decides to create a basic login script for the container login script that will map network drives to provide access to the file system on Damocles and allow users to print to the network printer. He also realizes the two groups he has in his network (ACCT and MANUF) will need to have special drives mapped to areas of the file system that belong specifically to them. Instead of using IF-THEN statements in his container login script, John decides to create two profile login scripts for those groups of users.

There are going to be some objects that require user login scripts. One of them is John's own user object, which will not be associated with any group, and the SYSADMIN Organizational Role object. Besides those two individual scripts, no other user is going to need individual customization. John is not going to encourage the creation of user login scripts for others. If individual users want to create and maintain these scripts themselves, that is fine; however, John is not going to be the person responsible for them. The customization of their network environments will be complete through the container and profile login scripts.

Moving On

Now that John has finalized how the network environments are going to be set for users, he is halfway finished with the task of providing users access to a shared file system. The next step is to examine the structure and security of the file system and learn how users gain rights and privileges to files and directories on the server. The next chapter will discuss the hierarchical structure of the file system and the implementation of file system security.

6

Managing the File System

In the previous two chapters, you have learned how to manage the users on your network. User objects in the NDS tree allow the users to access the network. The login scripts associated with the containers, profiles, and users customize the network environment for users at login. They provide mappings to the various file systems on the network. But how do we manage those file systems and implement the necessary security for file sharing?

Generally, the main reason to set up a computer network is to allow people to share files and data easily and efficiently. NetWare 4.11 allows you to accomplish this; however, to ensure the integrity of the data on your file servers, you need to have a thorough understanding of the file system. This chapter will help you achieve that understanding so that you can have a secure file sharing environment for your users.

Because NetWare 4.11 is based upon the concept of the NDS tree, the tree plays a role in the management of the file systems. The file systems installed on the various NetWare 4.11 servers are incorporated into the NDS tree to provide a central point of entry. The file systems of many servers can be accessed through the NDS tree without having to authenticate to each server. This link between the file systems on the server and the NDS tree is accomplished through the use of NDS server and volume objects which will be discussed in the section "Servers & Their Volumes."

Once you understand how NDS and the file systems are related, we will look at the structure of the file system. Data is organized on NetWare servers through the use of volumes and directories. This hierarchical structure will allow you, as a network administrator, to group files together logically. Attributes for files and directories can also be set to enhance the security of your file system.

Besides specific file and directory attributes, NetWare 4.11 has an advanced method for file system security as described in the section "File System Security." You will learn about file system rights and how users are granted rights to the file systems on NetWare servers. Much like the files and directories themselves, NetWare file system security is a hierarchical scheme through which users obtain rights by trustee assignment and rights inheritance. You will learn about these important concepts to ensure your file system is secure.

Finally, we will discuss other file utilities that come packaged with NetWare 4.11 in the section "File System Management." When a file is deleted in DOS, it is gone for good. The same is not true for NetWare. When a file is deleted, the network administrator might be able to retrieve it by using the SALVAGE utility. You will learn about recovering and purging deleted files in your NetWare file system.

Servers & Their Volumes

As we mentioned in our overview of security in Chapter 4, NDS security and file system security are two separate entities in the NetWare world; however, they are also integrally linked. It is through the NDS tree that users are able to access the file systems of different servers on the network. The NDS tree brings all of the systems together into one central location through which the security can be managed to allow users rights to many different network resources. Thus, the NDS tree and file systems are intertwined with one another.

The file systems are incorporated into the NDS tree through two NDS objects. These objects are the NetWare server object (NCP server object) and the volume object. It is through them that users are able to access the file systems of the NetWare 4.x servers on your network. When multiple servers are installed in the NDS tree, each server has its own file system; however, a user object that has been granted sufficient rights to each file system will be able to access all file systems through the NDS tree.

The file system of a server is directly linked to its volume objects installed in the NDS tree. Through the volume objects, trustee assignments and user rights can be granted, but before we actually get to file system security and administration, let's examine the NDS server and volume objects.

The NetWare Server Object

When a NetWare 4.11 server is created, a NetWare server object is installed in the NDS tree. INSTALL.NLM does this when it installs NetWare Directory Services onto the server. Once this object has been placed in the NDS tree, not much else is done with it. Generally, this object is used to keep track of information about the server itself, including its network address, physical location, status, and version of NetWare.

Using NetWare Administrator, you can see all of the pertinent information about the server. You can also input other useful server information by detailing the properties of the server object. From the main windows of NetWare Administrator, right-click on the server object of interest and choose Details from the menu that appears. The NetWare Server properties box will appear, as shown in Figure 6-1.

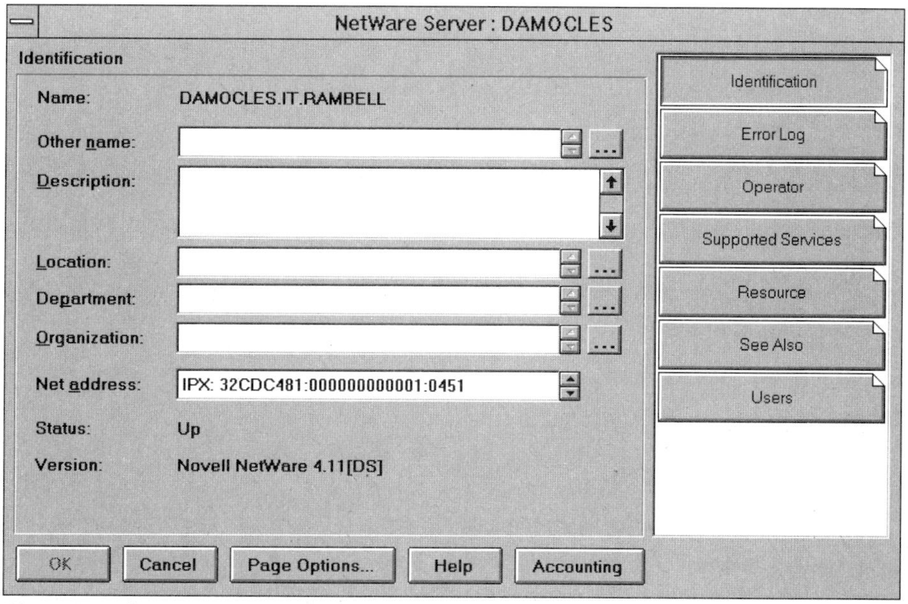

Figure 6-1: The NetWare Server properties box.

Here, we see the properties for the file server Damocles. The server is located in the IT.RAMBELL context. It is a NetWare 4.11 server, and it is also currently up and running. We could also enter other information about the server, such as its physical location and the department that it serves.

Another property tab of interest in this dialog box is the Error Log tab. Clicking on this tab will display the current error log for the server. This log is contained in the file SYS$LOG.ERR, which is located in the SYS:SYSTEM directory. It is important to look at the error log from time to time to ensure that nothing is going wrong with the server. The messages also appear on the server console screen but are tracked using this file.

The other tabs associated with the server do not have any impact on the network. They are there for informational purposes only. These properties will allow the network administrator to drill down to information about the computer network if he or she so desires, but information placed in these fields does not affect the security or performance of the network.

There is one critical item concerning the NetWare server object. It is the only place in the NDS tree where NDS rights affect file system rights. Having the the NDS Supervisor object right to the server object grants you the Supervisor file system right to all volumes on that server. This is the only instance where NDS and file system security overlap.

The Volume Object

The volume object is NDS's representation of the server's file system. It is a special object as well because it contains properties pertaining to both the file system and the NDS tree. It is important to understand the difference between the volume as an NDS object and the volume as a file system. Because the volume object is an object that straddles the two worlds of NDS and file systems, it is treated like both an NDS object and the root of the file system.

As we discussed in Chapter 4, there are actually three types of security in NetWare 4.11. There is login security, file system security, and NDS security. The file system security pertains specifically to the file system of the server. Each server (and its volumes) has its own file system security that exists independent of other servers on the network. On the other hand, NDS security for a tree applies to the tree and to all objects contained in it. File system security and NDS security are completely separate and overlap in only one place. They meet at the server object. The implications of this are discussed in the chapter on NDS security (Chapter 9).

Knowing that there is a difference between NDS security and file system security, it is important to realize the volume exists as an NDS object with its own set of NDS security rights. However, the volume object also represents the file system, and through it, the file system security can be administered. A user with NDS object rights to the volume object does not get any file system rights. File system rights have to be granted separately. It is a subtle but critical distinction in the understanding of NetWare 4.11.

Generally, you will not have to create new volume objects in the NDS tree. During a new installation of NetWare 4.11 on a file server, any volume that was created will automatically have an object created in the tree for it. If a NetWare 3.x file server has been upgraded to NetWare 4.11 or if you increase the storage capacity of a file server to create a new volume, you will have to create a new volume object in the NDS tree manually to manage the file system on that volume.

To create a new volume object, make sure there is already an existing physical volume on the server for the volume object to reference. Right-click on the container that will hold the new volume object and choose Create from the menu that appears. Select the volume object from the New Object dialog box, and the Create Volume dialog box will appear.

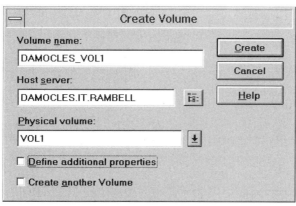

Figure 6-2: Creating a NetWare volume object.

In Figure 6-2, we are creating the volume object for VOL1 on the file server Damocles. When naming the volume, it is a good idea to follow the default naming convention NetWare uses for volume objects. This name includes the file server's name followed by an underscore followed by the name of the volume (e.g., DAMOCLES_VOL1). This will allow you to distinguish between volumes of the same name on different servers.

After naming the volume object, specify the server that holds the physical volume in the Host Server box. To browse the NDS tree for a server object, click on the Select Object button to the right of the Host Server text box. In Figure 6-2, the host server is Damocles. The final item that needs to be input is the Physical Volume property. Once the host server has been selected, the downward-pointing arrow to the right of the text box will blacken. This provides a drop-down list of available volumes on that server. Select the appropriate server volume from this list. Click on the Create button to create the volume object.

There is a definite difference between the volume object name and the physical volume name. The physical volume was created during the installation of the operating system on the server. During the installation, volume segments were used to create volumes on which to store data. The volume object and its name provide NDS with a way to reference that physical volume on the server. The volume object is not the physical volume. If the volume object is deleted from the NDS tree, it does not affect the physical volume on the server; however, users will not be able to access the data on the volume through NDS.

The volume object really is the key to accessing the file system through NDS. When the properties are defined for the volume object, the administration of the file system begins. We encourage everyone to peruse all of the property tabs associated with the volume object because there is much information to be learned about your file system. We will look at a subset of those property tabs in detail.

To view the properties associated with the volume object, click on the desired volume object in NetWare Administrator once with the right mouse button and choose Details from the menu which appears. The property dialog box for the volume object will be displayed. Notice this property dialog box looks similar to the property dialog boxes of other NDS objects. The property tabs are listed at the right of the screen. Figure 6-3 shows a typical volume object property dialog box with the properties associated with the Statistics tab displayed.

Identification

The Identification property tab displays the association of the volume object with the physical volume on a server. The properties specified when the volume was created are displayed but are unchangeable on this screen. These are the name of the volume object, the host server, and the actual name of the physical volume. The version of NetWare running on the server is also shown, and it quite obviously cannot be changed. Remember, the volume object name and the actual volume name can be different; the Identification tab shows the relationship between those two items.

Also on this screen are properties that can be modified by the network administrator. They include the location of the volume, the department, and the organization that the volume serves.

Statistics

Clicking on the property tab marked Statistics will cause the Statistics properties to appear. This property tab will provide the most information concerning the file system of the volume in question.

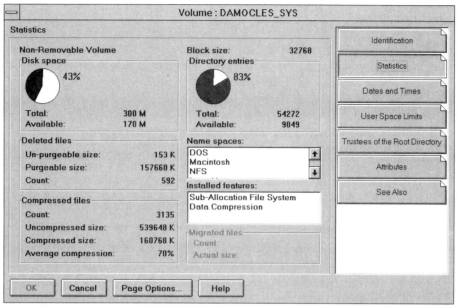

Figure 6-3: Viewing volume file system information.

Figure 6-3 displays the statistics for the SYS volume on the file server Damocles. This particular volume is a nonremovable volume (a hard disk). A volume may be removable; a CD-ROM volume is an example of a removable volume. The file system on this volume is composed of 32K blocks for files. The block size for the volume is always displayed at the top of the screen. After the block size, the Statistics properties screen is then broken up into seven separate sections.

Disk Space   The Disk Space area of the screen displays the total data capacity of the volume. It also shows the amount of available space left for storing files. In Figure 6-3, there is 170MB of free space available on the volume that has a total data capacity of 300MB. The pie graph in this box displays the percentage of space on the volume taken up by existing files. In this case, 43 percent of the volume is already occupied by files.

Deleted Files   The Deleted Files box shows the number of files that have been deleted on the volume and are still salvageable. When a file is deleted from the volume, it is not gone forever immediately. NetWare stores the file once it is deleted, and it may be recovered. This section of the screen will display the number of files and the size of the deleted files that may be purged from the system. Deleted files, salvaging, and purging will be covered later in this chapter (see "Salvaging & Purging Files").

Compressed Files   The Compressed Files area only has statistics if file compression was enabled when the physical volume was created. This box shows the number of files that have been compressed, the cumulative total of those files before and after compression, and the average compression percentage for those files. In Figure 6-3, 3,135 files have been compressed. Without compression, those files would have occupied 539,648K of disk space; however, after compression, they only take up 160,768K of space—that's 70 percent less space after compression!

Directory Entries   The Directory Entry Table on the volume keeps track of information concerning the file system. It stores information concerning file and directory names, the owner, the date and time of the last update of the file, and the physical location of the file's first block of data on the volume. It acts like an index to the information stored on the volume.

The Directory Entries properties for the volume displays the total number of directory entries allotted for that volume. The number of still-available entries is also displayed. In Figure 6-3, there are 54,272 total directory entries available for the SYS volume. However, only 9,049 of these entries are still available. The pie chart shows that 83 percent of the total number of directory entries for the volume are being used.

Name Spaces   The Name Spaces box reflects any name spaces that have been added to the file system. NetWare allows DOS files to be stored on the server, but it can also accommodate other file systems' files, including Macintosh, UNIX, OS/2, and Windows 95/NT. Adding the capacity to store these other files is called *adding name space*.

Any name spaces that have been installed on the volume are shown in the Name Spaces box. For the SYS volume on the server Damocles (Figure 6-3), DOS, Macintosh, NFS (UNIX), and Long (Windows 95/NT) name spaces have been added; however, not all of the name spaces can be seen. Use the scroll bars to the right of the box to view additional name space information.

Installed Features   Any additional features concerning the file system appear in the Installed Features box. These features include data compression, block suballocation, and data migration. All of the features are installed during the creation of the physical volume; they cannot be installed from the volume object. In Figure 6-3, both block suballocation and data compression have been enabled on the server object.

Migrated Files   The Migrated Files area of the screen only has values when data migration has been installed on the volume. This area displays the number of files that have been migrated to the high-capacity storage subsystem (HCSS) and their size. Because data migration was not enabled on the SYS volume of Damocles (Figure 6-3), there is no information displayed.

User Space Limits

Users have a tendency to store a lot of junk on a file server. From data that is old and in need of archiving to games and personal applications, users can occupy a ton of disk space that could be used for more important things. To help combat this problem, NetWare 4.11 comes with the ability to limit the amount of space a user may occupy on a particular volume. To view the current space restrictions, click on the User Space Limits property tab. The screen in Figure 6-4 will appear.

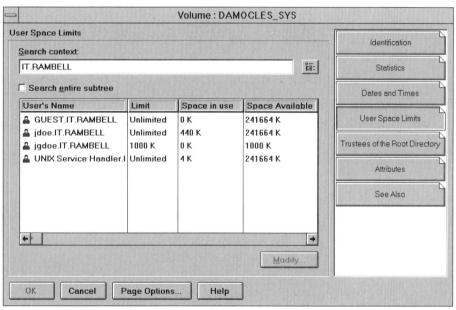

Figure 6-4: Setting user volume space restrictions.

Once the screen is displayed, the context for the search must be entered. Click on the Select Object button to the right of the Search Context box to find the desired context. When the context is specified, NetWare Administrator will display all user objects in that context, the space limit for the users, the amount of disk space used by the users, and the remaining space available to the users. By default, there are no disk space restrictions on any users that are created. Checking the Search Entire Subtree box will not only find all user objects that exist in the specified context, but also all user objects that exist in subordinate containers of the specified context.

After the context has been specified, you can create or modify a user's space limit. To do so, perform the following steps:

1. Select the user object in the User's Name box by clicking on it with the left mouse button.

2. Click on the Modify button below the user space limit table. The Volume Space Restriction dialog box will appear.

3. Check the Limited Volume Space box so it contains an X.

4. Specify the Volume Space Limit in kilobytes.

5. Click OK.

Removing the limit is just as easy. Get to the Volume Space Restriction dialog box by completing steps 1 and 2. Remove the X from the Limited Volume Space check box. The user's space restriction will be removed.

Trustees of the Root Directory

File system security in NetWare 4.11 is based on a hierarchical structure. A user or group receiving rights at the root of the file system will inherit those rights down all of the branches of the tree unless blocked by a filter. The Trustees of the Root Directory property tab of the volume object allows the network administrator to create trustee assignments for a user or group at the root of the directory tree, providing a level of rights that will be inherited throughout the file system.

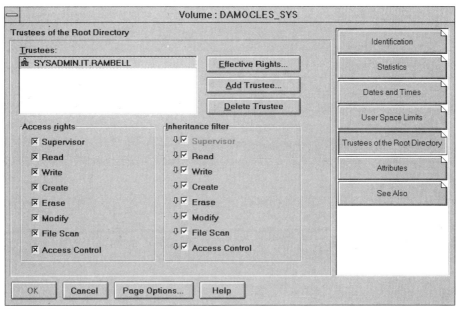

Figure 6-5: Assigning trustee rights to the root of the volume.

To make a trustee assignment to the root directory of the volume, click on the Trustees of the Root Directory property tab. The screen shown in Figure 6-5 will be displayed. Perform the following steps to grant a user or group file system rights:

1. Click on the Add Trustee button. The Select Object dialog box will appear.

2. Select the desired object and click OK. The NDS tree can be browsed using this dialog box if the desired object does not exist in the current context.

3. Using the Access Rights box, grant file system rights for the selected trustee.

4. Using the Inheritance Filter box, specify an Inherited Rights Filter, if desired. For more information on the Inherited Rights Filter and its function, refer to the section "File System Security" later in this chapter.

To delete a trustee assignment, select the trustee to be deleted and click on the Delete Trustee button. A user's or group's effective rights to the root of the volume can be determined using the Effective Rights button. Trustee assignments, file system rights, Inherited Rights Filters, and effective rights will be discussed in more detail later in this chapter in the section "File System Security."

When a trustee assignment to the file system is desired, make sure the assignment is made using this method. Do not grant privileges to the NDS volume object by accident. Making a user a trustee of the volume object does not give the user rights to the file system. It allows them to control that particular NDS object. This is where understanding the difference between the volume as an NDS object and as a link to the file system is crucial.

Attributes

The directory attributes for the root directory of the volume are set using the Attributes property tab. To set the attributes, click on the Attributes tab with the left mouse button. You will see a list of directory attributes. Check the desired attributes by clicking on the check box with the left mouse button. A checked attribute indicates that it is set for the root directory. File and directory attributes will be discussed later in this chapter (see "Attributes").

The volume object is the main link between the NDS tree and the file system. It is important to understand that the volume is an NDS object as well as the logical representation of the root of the file system. When you use the right mouse button to click on the volume object, the normal NDS menu appears. Any trustee assignments made using this menu are NDS object trustee assignments. Giving someone supervisory rights through this method will grant NDS rights to the volume object, which allows the person to modify or delete the volume object itself; it will not grant any rights to the file system. This is how the volume object acts like an NDS object (which it is).

The one option in this menu that does not perform an NDS-related function is the Create option. We know the NDS volume object is a leaf object; no other NDS objects can exist beneath it. Therefore, the Create option must be a file system function. It will create a directory that exists immediately below the root in the file system because the volume object logically represents the root of the file system. To make file system trustee assignments at the root directory level, you must use the Trustees of the Root Directory property tab associated with the NDS volume object.

Now that the entry point to the file system has been established in the NDS tree, it is time to take a closer look at the structure of the file system. Data contained in the file system is organized through the use of directories. The file system itself mimics the structure of the NDS tree. Understanding the structure of the NDS tree will help you gain some insight into the structure of the file systems on your network.

File System Organization

As mentioned before, the volume object is the logical representation of a NetWare server's file system. The volume object really serves as the root directory of the file system for that physical volume. Root directory trustee assignments and directory attributes made through the properties of the NDS volume object affect the root directory of the file system. From there, the file system branches out in a treelike structure. This structure is analogous to the NDS tree and its construct.

As it is with the NDS tree, a logical organization is the key to successful file system management. Whereas the NDS tree has a variety of container objects that can be used for organization, there is only one organizational structure for the file system—the directory. A directory can contain files or other directories that further classify and organize your file system.

Think of the server and its volumes as a filing cabinet. Each drawer in the cabinet is a volume on the server. Within each drawer is an assortment of folders that contain both papers and other folders. Inside those other folders might be more papers and still more folders. The file system works in exactly the same way. The folders are directories, and the papers are the files themselves. For logical organization of paper files, it is useful to have folders within folders coexisting with papers. The same is true for the file system. Figure 6-6 shows a typical file system directory tree.

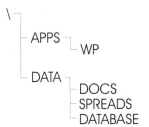

Figure 6-6: File system structure.

The top-most level of the file system is called the *root directory*. Directly off of the root directory in Figure 6-6 are the directories APPS and DATA. Directly beneath APPS, there exists another directory called WP. WP is a *subdirectory* of APPS. As there are with NDS, there are parent and child directories in the file system. The directory that exists immediately above a subdirectory is the subdirectory's *parent*. APPS is the parent directory of WP. A subdirectory that exists immediately below a directory is the directory's *child*. APPS, besides being a parent directory, is also the child of the root directory.

Directory structures are also often described in terms of levels. The root of the file system is the top level. The directories APPS and DATA are the second level of the file system because they exist directly off of the root directory. The third level comprises WP, DOCS, SPREADS, and DATABASE because they are subdirectories of second-level directories. Any directories that existed beneath these would be considered the fourth level due to their position relative to root.

The overall structure of the directory tree can be classified one of two ways. The file system's structure can be flat, or it can be deep. A flat directory tree has many directories that exist directly off of the root. These directories in turn do not contain many levels of subdirectories; a flat file system does not have a lot of third-level directories. On the other hand, a deep directory tree is a file system with many levels. Deep trees often have sixth- and seventh-level directories. Flat directory trees generally result in better file system performance. We recommend that your directory structure not be more than five levels deep.

In the directory structure, files can exist in any directory. There are no restrictions to where files can exist in the file system. They may reside directly in the root directory; however, for security reasons, it is not recommended that you store user files in the root directory of a volume's file system. As we will see, a user's rights flow down the directory structure; any rights granted at the root directory will be inherited all the way down the directory tree.

The file system has a specific naming convention for identifying files within the file system, just as NDS does. Files with the same name can coexist in the same file system; however, they may not exist in the same directory. The filename is like the common name for an NDS object. There is an equivalent for the NDS context in the file system as well. It is called the *path*. A file's unique name is specified as a combination of the name of the file and its path.

The file's path is found by starting at the root of the directory tree and tracing down through the directories until the file is reached. Each directory that is gone through is recorded in the path of the file. All of the directory names are separated by a backslash (\). In Figure 6-6, if a file named LETTER.TXT existed in the WP directory, it would have a unique name of \APPS\WP\LETTER.TXT. This is contrary to the naming convention for NDS objects. The full distinguished name for an NDS object starts at the object and follows the containers back to the root. The unique name for a file starts at the root and follows its way down the directories to the file. This naming convention ensures that every file in the file system can be uniquely identified.

NetWare 4.11 Default Directories

NetWare 4.11 starts organizing the file system for you upon installation of the operating system. As we saw in Chapter 2, NetWare will always create a SYS volume on the server. Not only is the SYS volume created, but there is also a standard set of default directories created during installation. These directories begin to provide a logical structure to the files on the server. Figure 6-7 shows the standard directory structure after the SYS volume is created.

SYS Volume

```
\
 ├── DELETED.SAV
 ├── DOC
 ├── ETC
 ├── LOGIN
 ├── MAIL
 ├── PUBLIC
 └── SYSTEM
```

Figure 6-7: NetWare default directories.

Depending upon which options are chosen during the installation, NetWare will create either six or seven directories to store the operating system files and utilities. We strongly recommend against changing the initial directory structure. NetWare looks for operating system files in these specific places, and unpredictable results could occur if the basic directory structure changes. The default directories are:

- **SYS:DELETED.SAV** stores files that have been deleted but not yet purged by the operating system. It is a directory that has the HIDDEN directory attribute set. This directory and its function will be discussed in more depth later in this chapter (see "Salvaging & Purging Files").

- **SYS:ETC** holds sample server configuration files. The files help the network administrator configure different services, from protocol configuration to FTP server configuration.

- **SYS:LOGIN** contains all the programs required for users to be able to log in to the server successfully. This directory contains a subdirectory, LOGIN\OS2, which holds the necessary login files for OS/2 workstations.

- **SYS:MAIL** will be remembered by NetWare 3.x administrators. It was the place where a user's login script was stored. This is no longer the case with NetWare 4.x. The user's login script is part of the user object; however, this directory and its subdirectories are used by NetWare-compatible mail programs. Be default, a subdirectory is created for the Admin user object on the first NetWare 4.x server in the NDS tree.

- **SYS:SYSTEM** holds the NetWare operating system files. The files include the NetWare Loadable Modules (NLMs) loaded from the server console as well as other DOS and OS/2 administrative utilities to help with network management.

- **SYS:PUBLIC** stores the general NetWare utilities that allow users to perform their daily tasks. This directory includes such utilities as MAP and CAPTURE, which let users access the various file systems and printing resources on the NetWare network.

- **SYS:DOC** is not created by default during the installation of NetWare 4.11; however, if the option to install the NetWare online documentation is chosen, this directory is created, and the NetWare manuals are installed to it.

There is also one more hidden directory created during the installation of NetWare 4.11. NetWare Directory Services is installed into a directory called SYS:_NETWARE. It exists, but it is very difficult to gain access to it. We will look at this mysterious directory in Chapter 8.

As we mentioned before, it is a good idea to keep SYS a static volume. Install NetWare 4.11 to this volume and leave it alone. If SYS runs out of space, it could cause NDS corruption that can spread to your entire network. Create other volumes for applications and user data. This will lead to a more secure file system because users will not have security trustee assignments to the same volume that stores the operating system files.

Mapping: A Reprise

In Chapter 5, we learned about the MAP command used in NetWare login scripts. This command is essential to accessing the file systems around the network. Now that we understand the structure of the file systems, we can examine how MAP relates to the NetWare 4.11 file system.

We know that on DOS/Windows and OS/2 workstations, network drives are mapped, which allows the workstation to think it is writing data to a local drive when it is really writing data to the server's hard disks. When a network drive at a workstation is mapped to a server volume, it assigns a drive letter to that volume. The drive letter provides a point of entry for the workstation to the file system. For example, the command **map f:=damocles/vol1:** would map the F: drive on the workstation to the volume SYS on the server Damocles.

Similarly, the command **map root g:=damocles/vol1:apps\wp** would map the G: drive to the WP subdirectory on the volume VOL1; however, it would also make the workstation think the WP subdirectory was the root of the file system. Regardless, this would provide another point of entry to the server's file system. The VOL1 file system could be accessed, through either drive F: or G: on the workstation. But more importantly, these drive letters are critical in helping the workstation determine a file's unique name in the file system.

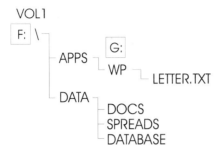

Figure 6-8: Mapping drives to the file system.

Figure 6-8 illustrates the points of entry the MAP commands provide to the workstation. The F: drive allows us to specify filenames from the true root of the file system. The full name of the file LETTER.TXT in the WP directory would be F:\APPS\WP\LETTER.TXT. We start at the point of entry to the file system (in this case, the true root of the volume) and traverse the directory tree down to the file.

For drive G:, the unique name of the file is completely different because the workstation thinks WP is the root of the file system. The full name of the file would be G:\LETTER.TXT. Both of these full names (from the F: drive and G: drive) specify the same exact file; however, the unique name of the file is different depending upon which drive mapping you use. This can get awfully confusing.

The MAP command provides a way for the workstation to have a point of entry to volumes' file systems. How you use this command affects how the workstation interacts with the file system. Using the MAP ROOT command will change how the workstation specifies the unique name of the files. The filename will be determined by the point of entry (what the workstation thinks is root) and any remaining directories in the tree down to the file. Thus, drives pointing to the same file system can obtain completely different, unique filenames for the same exact file.

Of course a logical file system structure is essential for users to interact with the data on your file server; however, it also plays a critical role in the security of your file system. The tree-like structure of the file system provides a mechanism for file system security through which users are granted rights to specific areas of the file system. Those rights then flow down the structure of the file system. In the next section, we will discuss just how users are granted rights to the data on your file servers and how those rights are inherited down the file system.

File System Security

A centralized location for storing data brings up many different issues. The network administrator needs to be sure that space is being distributed evenly and fairly among the users. However, just because users have the space to store files on the file server does not mean they will use it. There are often times that users have confidential or sensitive data that needs to be stored. They are often worried that other people may be able to read that data because it is located in a place to which other users have access.

When you have a centralized file system that serves many different users, it is important to guarantee that data will be available only to those users who are authorized to access it. NetWare does just that. Through a comprehensive method of file system security, the network administrator can ensure the integrity of the data on the file server. To implement this level of security, it is critical to understand how file system security works with NetWare 4.11.

File System Rights

In Chapter 4, we explored the basic file system rights in NetWare 4.11. Here we will examine them in more detail. Users obtain privileges to the file system through a specific set of file system rights granted to them by the network administrator. These rights determine just exactly what the user is or isn't able to do with the files and directories in the file system.

There are eight basic file system rights that can be assigned to users. Usually, file system rights are applied to the directories of the file system to grant users access to all files and directories contained within the specified directory. The eight rights are summarized in Table 6-1.

Right	Abbreviation	Significance
Read	R	Allows the user to read the contents of the files contained in the directory.
Write	W	Allows a user to add or change data in an existing file.
Create	C	Permits a user to create a new file or directory.
Erase	E	Lets the user delete a file or subdirectory.
Modify	M	Enables the user to modify file and directory names.
File Scan	F	Provides the ability to browse the file system.
Access Control	A	Gives the user the ability to grant other users rights to files and directories. It also allows the modification of the Inherited Rights Filters.
Supervisor	S	Gives the user all of the other file system rights by default.

Table 6-1: File system rights.

Read

The Read file system right, when granted, provides the ability to read the contents of the files in the file system. If someone were to use the DOS TYPE command to display the contents of a file, he or she must have the Read right to that file in order to have its contents displayed. Without this right, the user would not be able to see a file's data. When using the DISPLAY or FDISPLAY login script commands, the user executing the login script must have the Read right granted for the file being displayed; otherwise, DISPLAY will not be able to show the contents of the file.

Write

Write permits users to change or add data to existing files in the file system. If a user is working with a spreadsheet and needs to modify the data contained in it, he or she must have the Write right to that file. The DOS EDIT utility would also require the user to have the Write right before the user could access the file. Write does not give the user the ability to create a new file; it only allows the modification of data in an existing file.

Create

Create does what Write cannot. It allows the user to create a new file or directory in the file system. If a user tries to copy a file from one place to another, he or she must have the Create right at the destination of the copy. This right is also needed if a file is being saved in an application for the first time. Because a new file is being created, the Create right is required.

Here is an example to clarify the difference between Create and Write. You open up your word processor and start to type in a brand-new document. When you are done typing, you save the file to the network drive. At this point, you need the Create right because the file does not exist on the server's file system. It is being created by the word processor and placed on the server.

Later on that day, you start up your word processor again to work on the document. This time, you open up the existing file on the server. You make some changes and want to save it again. The right required for this process is Write. This is because the file already exists; you are only making modifications to it.

Erase

This right should probably be called Delete because that is what it lets the user do—delete a file or directory in the file system. Be careful when granting this right to users. Files and directories have an annoying habit of disappearing when this right is granted.

Modify

Do not confuse this right with the Write file system right. Modify does *not* allow the user to change or edit the data in a file. It allows the user to modify the name of the files and directories. A user with the Modify right could change the name of a file called LETTER.TXT to MYLETTER.TXT. Although the name of the file has changed, the contents of the file have not.

Modify also allows the user to change the attributes of the files and directories. Attributes provide yet another level of file system security and will be discussed later in this chapter (see "Attributes"). Just remember that to change the attributes of a file or directory, the Modify right is needed.

File Scan

Even though a user may have the Read right to a file, it does not mean that he or she will be able to see if the file exists in the file system. It is the File Scan right that allows this browsing ability. However, with this right, the user can only see the names of the files in the file system; it does not give users access to the contents of the files.

The DOS command DIR is the best way to illustrate how File Scan works. To allow a user to see the files in the file system using the DIR command, the user must have File Scan rights. Without this right, the DIR command will not display any files, even though they exist in the file system. Revoking this right from a user effectively hides the file from sight.

Access Control

Access Control does not give the user the ability to directly affect the files and directories on the file server; however, it does allow users to grant file system rights to other users. It also allows the user to modify files' and directories' Inherited Rights Filters. This right is useful if you want to give a user complete control over a portion of the file system. With this right, the user can control the access other users have to the files and directories in that portion.

For instance, Mary has the Access Control right to the directory APPS. Mike only has Write access to the files in that directory; however, he needs the Create right because he needs to create some new files in that directory. Because Mary has the Access Control right, she would be able to grant Mike the Create right so he could accomplish his task.

Even though having the Access Control right will not give users direct access to the files and directories of the file system, it is not a right to give out lightly. The user could grant himself or herself other file system rights that would provide direct access to the files and directories. With Access Control, Mary could just as easily give herself all other file system rights, which lets her do anything she wants to the file system's files and directories at or below the level of this trustee assignment.

Supervisor

This right is equivalent to all the other file system rights rolled up into one. A user with the Supervisor file system right is granted all of the other file system rights regardless of any trustee assignment or Inherited Rights Filter that may be present. If a user has been granted the Read, File Scan, and Supervisor rights to the file system, he or she would still have complete control over the file system even though the remainder of the rights were not explicitly granted. This is because of the Supervisor right.

Be careful when granting the Supervisor right to the file system. File system security flows down the directory tree structure, and the Supervisor right cannot be blocked. If a user is granted Supervisor rights to the root directory, he or she will have Supervisor rights to all files and directories in the file system. No specific file system rights can be revoked in a subdirectory below the directory in which the Supervisor right was granted.

In Table 6-1, we saw the abbreviations associated with the file system rights. From now on we will use the abbreviations to specify these rights. A user with the file system rights [_RWCEMFA] would have all of the file system rights except for Supervisor. Another user with the rights [_R____F_] would have only Read and File Scan rights. NetWare uses these abbreviations to represent the file system rights. A right represented by an underscore (_) means the user does not have that particular file system right. When using abbreviations, NetWare always uses the order [SRWCEMFA].

When file system rights are applied to directories, the user is given the rights to all files and subdirectories contained in the directory. For example, there is a directory DATA that contains subdirectories called DOCS and SPREADS. Also contained in this directory are some text files. Mary is given the Read, File Scan, and Modify rights to the DATA directory. With these rights, she will be able to see the text files and the directories DOCS and SPREADS. She will be able to display the contents of the text files. She will also be able to rename the text files as well as the DOCS and SPREADS directories. Granting file system rights at the directory level gives the user the same rights to the files and directories contained therein.

Not only can these file system rights be granted at the directory level, they can also be granted at the file level. A user can be given a trustee assignment to a specific file. When applied to files, the file system rights act a little differently than when they are applied to directories. The file system rights for files are summarized in Table 6-2.

File Right	Significance
Read	Lets the user read the contents of the file.
Write	Permits the user to add or edit the contents of the file.
Create	Allows the user to recover the file after deletion.
Erase	Enables the user to delete the file.
Modify	Lets the user change the name of the file or the attributes of the file.
File Scan	Allows the user to see the file even if the File Scan right has not been granted at the directory level.
Access Control	Permits the user to grant other users rights to the file. Also allows the user to modify the Inherited Rights Filter to the file.
Supervisor	Grants users all rights to the file.

Table 6-2: File system rights when applied to individual files.

Any file system rights that are assigned to files take precedence over rights assigned to the directory that contains the file. In Figure 6-9, we see that Mary has been given the rights [_RWCEMF_] to the directory WP; however, to the file LETTER.TXT she has been explicitly granted the rights [_R____F_]. To the file HIDDEN.TXT, she has no rights [_____]. Even though she has all rights except Supervisor and Access Control to all other files in the directory WP, she would only be able to browse and read the file LETTER.TXT. She would not be able to edit it in any way because those rights have been stripped by the specific rights assignment to the file. Mary cannot even see the file HIDDEN.TXT because all file system rights have been revoked!

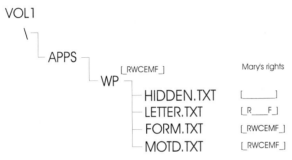

Figure 6-9: Directory rights versus file rights.

Trustee Assignments

Rights play an important role in the security of the file system. It is through rights that network administrators are able to lock down files and directories and ensure that only the appropriate users have access to the data on the file system. We know that rights can be granted at both the directory and file level with the file rights taking precedence over any directory rights assigned. But how do users get these rights?

Rights to the file system can be explicitly granted to a particular user or group. This is called a *trustee assignment*. A user is said to be a trustee of a file or directory if he or she has specifically been given rights to that file or directory. In Figure 6-9, Mary is a trustee of the WP directory. She has been given the rights [_RWCEMF_] to the directory. She is also a trustee of the files LETTER.TXT and HIDDEN.TXT. Her trustee assignments give her the rights [_R____F_] and [_____] to those files, respectively.

Not only can users be granted trustee rights to a file or directory, other user-related objects can be trustees as well, including groups and organizational roles. These trustee assignments are made the same way trustee assignments are granted for individual users. When groups and organizational roles are given trustee assignments, the members or occupants of that object are immediately granted the same rights. Thus, if the group ACCT was given a trustee assignment to the directory APPS with the rights [_RWCE_F_], all members of that group would have those rights as well.

Granting Trustee Assignments

In Chapter 4, we were introduced to trustee assignments with the user and user-related objects. Using NetWare Administrator, we learned how to make trustee assignments for users. That is not the only place where trustee assignments can be made; they can be made at the specific files and directories as well, using NetWare Administrator.

Files and directories are much like NDS objects when managed with NetWare Administrator. They have properties and values just like NDS objects do. To see the properties and values of a file or directory in the NetWare file system, click on that file or directory in NetWare Administrator with the right mouse button and choose Details from the menu that appears. The property dialog box will appear; it will look similar to the NDS object property dialog box. The property tabs for the file or directory are listed at the right of the dialog box. To see a specific set of properties, click on the desired tab with the left mouse button. To see the trustee information for a file, click on the Trustees of This File tab. Directories will have a Trustees of This Directory property tab to view trustee information.

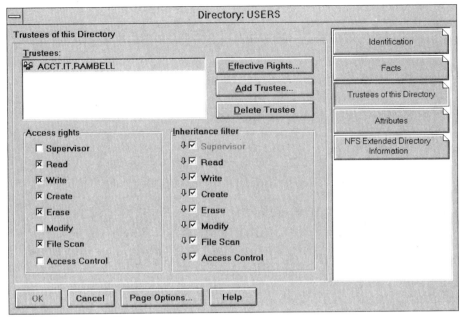

Figure 6-10: Viewing directory trustees.

In Figure 6-10, the trustee information for the directory USERS is displayed. At the top of the screen, the Trustees box displays the current trustees of the directory. To the lower left, the Access Rights box displays all of the current rights for the selected trustee. In this case, the group ACCT is a trustee to the USERS directory, and its file system rights are [_RWCE_F_]. To the lower right is the Inheritance Filter box. These rights determine how rights to this directory are inherited. Rights inheritance and Inherited Rights Filters will be discussed later in this chapter (see "Rights Inheritance & Inherited Rights Filters").

To make a trustee assignment to this directory, click on the Add Trustee button to the right of the Trustees box. The Select Object dialog box appears. Browse the NDS tree to find the NDS object that will be the directory trustee and select it. Click OK. This object now appears in the Trustees box. By default, a new trustee will only be given the rights [_R____F_]. To see the rights granted to a trustee, select that trustee by clicking on it once with the left mouse button. It will become highlighted.

The Access Rights box will display the rights granted for the selected trustee. In Figure 6-10, ACCT is the selected trustee; therefore, the Access Rights box displays the rights for ACCT. To grant other rights to the selected trustee, click on the check boxes in the Access Rights box. Rights with an X in the check box are granted; rights with a blank box are not granted. To give the ACCT group the rights [_RW___F_], make sure the boxes for Read, Write, and File Scan have an X in them. Any modifications made to the Access Rights box affect *only* the highlighted trustee; they do not apply to any other trustees in the Trustees box.

To remove a trustee assignment from the file or directory, select the trustee to be removed by clicking on it with the left mouse button. The trustee will then be highlighted. Click on the Delete Trustee button to remove the NDS object from the Trustees box.

File system trustee assignments can be made in two places using NetWare Administrator. They can be made through the properties of the file and directories using the Trustees of This File or Trustees of This Directory tab. They can also be assigned through the NDS object itself. NDS objects that can be made file system trustees will have a Rights to Files and Directories property tab. Trustee assignments to the file systems on the NetWare network can be made through this property tab. This procedure was discussed in Chapter 4 in the section "Trustee Properties."

Special Trustees

User and user-related objects are not the only NDS objects that can be given file system trustee assignments. There are some other special trustees that can be granted rights to the file system. NDS container objects can be made trustees of files and directories as can the special trustee [Public]. Making either one of these objects a trustee of a file or directory has serious implications.

Container Objects as File System Trustees   When a container object is made the trustee of a file or directory, all objects in the container, including users, groups, organizational roles, and profiles, are also granted the same rights. In Figure 6-11, a typical NDS structure is displayed. There is an organizational unit called IT that contains another organizational unit called BACKBONE. There are users in the IT container as well as in the BACKBONE container. If IT is made the trustee of the directory USERS on VOL1 of the file server Damocles and given the rights [_R___F_], all objects contained in the organizational unit IT are also granted those rights.

Figure 6-11: An organizational unit and its subordinate objects.

The user jgdoe, whose context is the IT organizational unit, would be granted the same [_R____F_] rights to the USERS directory because his parent organizational unit was made a trustee of the directory. These rights apply not only to objects in the immediate container but also to all objects beneath the trustee container, including objects in subordinate containers. Thus, the user account mjsmith in the BACKBONE organizational unit would also be granted [_R____F_] rights to the USERS directory because mjsmith is a subordinate object of the IT organizational unit.

[Public] as a File System Trustee   Those of you who administered NetWare 3.x servers will remember a group called Everyone. This group allowed the network administrator to grant rights to all users on the server. There is an equivalent in NetWare 4.11. It is called the [Public] trustee. When [Public] is granted a file system trustee assignment, every NDS object in the NDS tree is also given those same rights. [Public] allows the network administrator to grant global rights to the file system.

[Public] can only be given trustee assignment through the Trustees of This File or Trustees of This Directory tabs. By default, [Public] is given only [_R____F_] file system rights. The default rights can be modified in the same way other trustees rights can be modified. Highlight [Public] in the Trustees box and check the appropriate rights in the Access Control box. [Public] is treated like any other trustee in NetWare 4.11. The difference is that [Public] is not a true NDS object. It represents all NDS objects collectively.

Rights Inheritance & Inherited Rights Filters

Trustee assignments are not the only way users and objects are given rights to the file system. It is true that rights start with the trustee assignment, but NetWare also eases the administration of file system security by allowing users to inherit rights down the file system. Thus, the network administrator does not have to explicitly grant users rights to every file and directory on the server. One trustee assignment can be made to a directory, and those rights are inherited by subsequent levels of directories in the directory tree.

Understanding Rights Inheritance

In dealing with NetWare file system security, you will often hear the phrase "rights flow down the file system." This phrase refers to the concept of rights inheritance. When a user is granted a trustee assignment to a directory, those rights obviously apply to the immediate directory. However, the rights do not stop there. They also apply to all directories beneath the directory in which the trustee assignment was made.

Figure 6-12 illustrates rights inheritance. We see a branch of the file system starting at the root directory. The user is granted a trustee assignment at the root of the file system and is given the rights [_R____F_]. Through inheritance, the user also gains the [_R____F_] rights to all directories beneath the root. The rights flow down the directory structure until another trustee assignment is encountered.

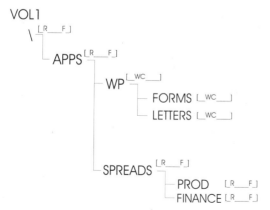

Figure 6-12: File system rights inheritance.

If a trustee assignment is made to the WP directory in Figure 6-12, the rights override any rights that might be inherited through a previous trustee assignment. If the user is granted the rights [__WC____] to the WP through a trustee assignment, those are the only rights the user has to that directory. The [_R____F_] rights are not inherited in the WP directory because the new trustee assignment supersedes the inherited rights. Rights inheritance then flows down the tree from that trustee assignment. Thus, the user inherits the rights [__WC____] to the LETTERS and FORMS directories. Because no trustee assignment was made in SPREADS, the user still has [_R____F_] rights to this directory and any directories and files beneath it.

As we see, one way to block a user from inheriting rights in a portion of the file system is to create a trustee assignment that revokes rights. This could get cumbersome because a user would have many different trustee assignments to grant and revoke rights as necessary. Fortunately, NetWare 4.11 comes with a way to block inherited rights—the Inherited Rights Filter.

Inherited Rights Filters

While the concept of inheritance makes network administration easier, it also complicates it. How do you prevent a user from inheriting rights to a directory when a trustee assignment was made at a higher level? As we saw in the previous section, creating another trustee assignment to the lower directory revoking the rights inherited from a higher level is an inelegant, time-consuming answer to the problem. It is much easier to use the Inherited Rights Filter (IRF) that all directories and files have.

The IRF determines which rights can be inherited. Figure 6-13 shows how the IRF works to filter out inherited rights.

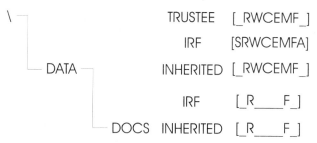

```
\ ─┐                      TRUSTEE    [_RWCEMF_]
   │                         IRF     [SRWCEMFA]
   └─ DATA ─┐            INHERITED   [_RWCEMF_]
            │               IRF      [_R____F_]
            └─ DOCS  INHERITED   [_R____F_]
```

Figure 6-13: Filtering out inherited rights.

The user mbjones was given a trustee assignment to the root directory with the rights [_RWCEMF_], as shown in Figure 6-13. As a result, mbjones inherits those rights in the DATA directory because the IRF for DATA is [SRWCEMFA]. However, the subdirectory DOCS has an IRF of [_R____F_]. Because of this IRF, mbjones only has the rights [_R____F_] to the files and subdirectories in the DOCS directory. Write, Create, Erase, and Modify have been effectively filtered out by DOCS's IRF.

The filtering applies not only to mbjones, but also to every trustee of the file system. Any trustee assignments made higher than the DOCS directory will have the rights blocked by the DOCS directory's IRF. By default, the IRF for all directories is [SRWCEMFA]. This means that all rights are inherited down the directory tree. The network administrator must specify a custom IRF for a file or directory in order for rights to be filtered.

Modifying the Inherited Rights Filter

The Inherited Rights Filter for a file or directory can be modified using NetWare Administrator. Earlier in this chapter, we learned how to make a trustee assignment (see "Trustee Assignments"). The IRF for a file or directory is modified from this same screen (see Figure 6-14). To edit the IRF for a file or directory, right-click on it and choose Details from the menu that appears. When the properties of the file or directory appear, click on the Trustees of This File or Trustees of This Directory tab.

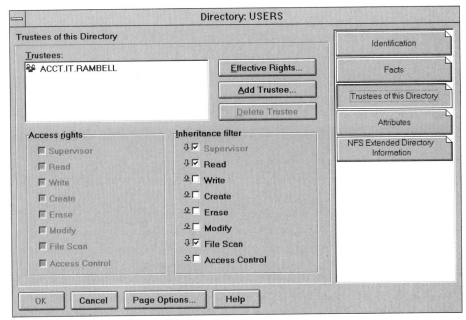

Figure 6-14: Setting the Inherited Rights Filter.

Figure 6-14 displays the trustee and IRF information for the USERS directory on VOL1 of the file server Damocles. In the Inheritance Filter box, we can see the IRF for this directory is [_R____F_]. Rights with a check mark ( ) to the left of them are rights that pass through the IRF. Rights with a blank box are effectively blocked. To the left of the check box, notice the status of the downward-pointing arrow. For the Supervisor, Read, and File Scan rights, the arrow is unimpeded. This indicates those rights are passed down the file system through inheritance. The remaining rights have their arrow blocked. This obviously indicates those rights are not inherited.

The Supervisor Right & the IRF

One special case regarding rights inheritance is that of the Supervisor file system right. This right is all-powerful. You may have noticed when we modified the IRF in the previous section that the Supervisor right was grayed out in the Inheritance Filter box. This is because the Supervisor right cannot be blocked by an IRF. Once a user has the Supervisor right to a directory, he or she has the Supervisor right to all files and directories beneath it.

Be extremely careful when assigning the Supervisor right to users. Once granted, it cannot be revoked either through the IRF or another trustee assignment. The only way a user can be stripped of the Supervisor right is to remove that right from the original trustee assignment that granted it.

Remember, IRFs exist for both files and directories. This provides a finer granularity for file system security. A user may inherit rights to a specific directory yet still not be able to affect files in that directory if the appropriate file IRFs are in place.

Effective Rights

Understanding file system security is the first step to determining an object's rights to files and directories. We now know rights are determined first by trustee assignment, then by inheritance down the directory tree. If rights were associated with only a single object, it would be easy to determine an object's rights; however, this is not the case.

One of the great advantages to NetWare is its ability to associate objects with other objects. Users are members of groups; they can also be occupants of organizational roles. A container can be a trustee of a file or directory, which grants those same rights to all objects in that portion of the NDS tree. Objects are going to gain rights to the file system not only through explicit trustee assignments and inheritance, but also through association with other objects.

Understanding Effective Rights

The *effective rights* of an object are the total sum of all security privileges granted. These rights can be gained by direct trustee assignments or inheritance or achieved through the object's association with another object. For example, a user's effective rights to the USERS directory would be determined by calculating the rights gained from the user's NDS object plus any rights granted through association with other objects like groups or organizational roles.

Network administrators often find instances of users with a set of rights that is greater than what was supposed to be assigned. This is common because of the complexity of NetWare file system security. To calculate (and troubleshoot) the effective rights to a file or directory for an object in the NDS tree, use the following steps:

1. Determine the rights granted to the primary object at the desired file or directory. A trustee assignment to the file or directory will immediately determine the object's rights. If there is no trustee assignment at the file or directory in question, the primary object's rights will come from rights inheritance.

2. Determine any extra rights the primary object receives through associations with other NDS objects. If a user is a member of a group, any trustee assignment that group has to the file or directory in question will be passed on to the user. If the group does not have a trustee assignment, the user may still inherit rights from a group trustee assignment at a higher-level directory.

3. Determine any security equivalencies the primary object has. Rights gained from a security equivalence are applied to the file or directory in question.

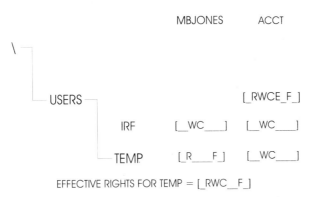

EFFECTIVE RIGHTS FOR TEMP = [_RWC__F_]

Figure 6-15: Determining effective rights for mbjones in the directory TEMP.

Suppose we want to find the effective rights for the user mbjones in the directory TEMP, as shown in Figure 6-15. We see that mbjones has a trustee assignment of [_R____F_] in the TEMP directory. The group ACCT, of which mbjones is a member, has a trustee assignment to the USERS directory of

[_RWCE_F_]. The TEMP directory itself has an IRF of [__WC____]. What are the effective rights for the user mbjones? Let's follow the three steps to determine the user's effective rights:

1. Because we are trying to find the effective rights for mbjones in the directory TEMP, mbjones is the primary object. This object has an explicit trustee assignment to the directory in question; thus, the rights gained from the primary object are [_R____F_]. Trustee assignments supersede any rights inheritance for that object.

2. Since mbjones is a member of the group ACCT, he will gain rights to the TEMP directory through the group object. ACCT does not have a trustee assignment to TEMP; however, there is a trustee assignment of [_RWCE_F_] to USERS, which is higher in the directory tree. ACCT has rights to TEMP through inheritance. Because of the IRF on the TEMP directory, the rights inherited by ACCT are only [__WC____].

3. The object mbjones does not have any other security equivalencies from NDS objects. No extra rights are gained here.

We now take the rights obtained from the primary object and add any rights gained through object association to determine the effective rights. From the primary object, we have the rights [_R____F_]. Through object association, mbjones has gained the rights [__WC____]. Thus, the effective rights for the user mbjones in the directory TEMP are [_RWC__F_].

Determining Effective Rights With NetWare Administrator

Fortunately, we do not have to go through this process every time we want to figure out the effective rights for an object. NetWare Administrator will do all the calculating for us. The effective rights for an object can be determined with just a few clicks of the mouse buttons.

There are two ways to determine the effective rights using NetWare Administrator. The first method is to calculate the rights using the properties associated with the primary object itself. Let's say you wanted to determine the effective rights for mbjones to the TEMP directory using the mbjones NDS user object. To do this, perform the following steps:

1. Right-click on the user object in the NDS tree using NetWare Administrator and select Details from the menu that appears. The properties of the user object will be displayed.

2. Click on the Rights to Files and Directories tab with the left mouse button. This is where the trustee information for the user object is shown.

3. Click on the Effective Rights button. The Effective Rights dialog box is displayed, as shown in Figure 6-16. In the File/Directory box, type in the file or directory for which you want to determine the effective rights. The Select Object button to the right of this box can also be used to browse the file systems on the NDS tree to select the desired file or directory.

4. When the file or directory is selected, rights at the bottom of the Effective Rights dialog box may blacken. Those rights that are blackened are the effective rights for the primary object. In Figure 6-16, the effective rights for the TEMP directory are [_RWC__F_].

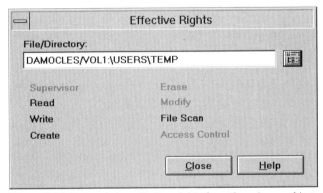

Figure 6-16: Determining effective rights from the primary object properties.

This method of determining effective rights will only allow you to calculate the rights for the particular object you are using. The properties for the mbjones object will calculate effective rights only for mbjones; however, it will determine the rights mbjones has for any file or directory in the NDS tree. This method is useful if you are trying to determine effective rights for a single primary object in many different files or directories.

On the other hand, if you want to determine the effective rights many different objects have to a single file or directory, you will want to use the other method. This method of determining effective rights is accomplished through the properties of the file or directory in question. To do this, perform the following steps:

1. Using NetWare Administrator, right-click on the file or directory in the NDS tree and choose Details from the menu that appears.

2. Click on the Trustees of This Directory or Trustees of This File property tab. The trustee information will be displayed.

3. Click on the Effective Rights button to the right of the Trustees box. The Effective Rights dialog box will appear, as shown in Figure 6-17. In the Trustee box, type in the distinguished name of the trustee for which you want to determine the effective rights. The Select Object button to the right of this box can be used to browse the NDS tree and select a primary object.

4. When the trustee has been selected, the rights in the Effective Rights box may blacken. Rights that are blackened are the effective rights for the trustee. In Figure 6-17, the effective rights for mbjones are [_RWC__F_].

Figure 6-17: Determining effective rights from the target file or directory.

Using NetWare Administrator to display the effective rights for trustees is essential to efficient network administration. It prevents the network administrator from having to sit down and calculate effective rights by hand as we did in the previous section; however, understanding how to calculate effective rights is important. If NetWare Administrator shows a greater level of effective rights than expected, you must go back and troubleshoot to find out why the trustee has these extra rights. The only way you are going to be able to do that is to sit down and calculate the effective rights by hand.

Understanding file system security is important because it controls the data your users can (or can't) view on your file server. To protect the integrity of your data, you should review your file system security scheme frequently. Once this scheme is set, you are ready to start managing the files in your file system. The next section, "File System Management," will discuss the creation and deletion of files and directories along with file and directory attributes which help refine the security of your file system.

File System Management

Now that we understand file system security, we can focus on the management of the file system. File system rights provide the necessary permissions to manipulate files and directories; performing manipulations falls in the realm of file system management. Once a person has sufficient rights, he or she can create, delete, rename, and modify files and directories.

Usually, the file systems for NetWare 4.11 servers are managed through the operating system on your desktop. For instance, the Windows File Manager can be used to perform file system management tasks. Directories can be created or deleted. Files can be copied from one directory to another. All of the tasks associated with managing the file system can be accomplished through your client workstation just as if the server's volumes were a hard drive of the local machine. In addition to using the management tools of your particular operating system, you can also use NetWare Administrator to manage NetWare 4.11 file systems.

Managing File Systems With NetWare Administrator

The advantage of using NetWare Administrator over the operating system-based file management tool is its understanding of the NDS tree and the NetWare network. Often with the other file management tools, network drives need to be mapped to the various file servers on the network to administer the file system. This is not the case with NetWare Administrator. As long as you have sufficient rights, all you need is NetWare Administrator to perform the file system management on all of the file servers on your network.

Besides the advantage of central file system administration, NetWare Administrator also understands another level of NetWare file system security, the attributes that accompany every file and directory in volumes' file systems. File and directory attributes will be discussed later in this section (see "Attributes"). So although it is not as elegant as some other file system management tools, NetWare Administrator does have the inside advantage of being closely linked with the NetWare 4.11 NOS.

Creating Directories

With NetWare Administrator, files and directories are treated somewhat like NDS objects. They can be moved and detailed in the same manner as every other NDS object; directories can be created using the same method used to create NDS objects in the NDS tree. To create a directory, select the directory or volume object that will contain the new directory by clicking on it with the left mouse button. Choose Object | Create from the menu bar of NetWare Administrator. The Create Directory dialog box will appear. Type in the name of the directory and click the Create button. The new directory will be created. Files cannot be created using NetWare Administrator.

Moving & Copying Files & Directories

Files and directories can be easily moved and copied using NetWare Administrator. To move or copy a file or directory in NetWare Administrator, click on it once with the left mouse button in the NDS tree. It will become highlighted. To move it, choose Object | Move from the menu bar. To copy it, choose Object | Copy from the menu bar. Both choices will cause the Move/Copy dialog box to appear.

In the Move/Copy dialog box, the original file or directory will be displayed, and the Destination box at the bottom will be blank. Type in the destination to which the file or directory will be copied or moved. Click OK when finished. There is a Select Object button to the right of the Destination box that can be used to browse the NDS tree for a destination.

Renaming Files & Directories

To rename a file or directory, highlight it by clicking on it with the left mouse button. Choose Object | Rename from the menu bar. The Rename dialog box will appear. Type in the new name for the file or directory in the New Name box and click OK.

Deleting Files & Directories

To delete a file or directory, click on it once with the right mouse button. Choose Delete from the menu that appears. You will not be able to delete a directory that still contains files or other directories. You must delete all subordinate items in that directory before it can be removed.

Viewing File & Directory Information

Another important part of file system management is keeping track of file and directory information. This is data that includes the owner of the file or directory, its creation date, its last modification date, and its last archive date, all of which NetWare Administrator is able to provide. To see the data, right-click on the desired file or directory and choose Details from the menu that appears. The file or directory property dialog box will appear. Click on the Facts property tab.

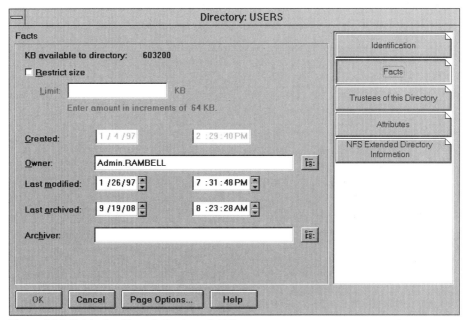

Figure 6-18: Retrieving file and directory statistics.

Figure 6-18 displays information about the directory USERS. Notice that the owner of the directory can be changed as well as the archiver. Because this is a directory, the space its files occupy can also be restricted. To limit the size of a directory, mark the Restrict Size check box and input a space limit for it. This number must be in increments of the block size of the volume. VOL1, which contains the USERS directory, has a block size of 64K; thus, the space limit for that directory must be a multiple of 64K.

Information concerning files is a little bit different. Obviously, the space for a file cannot be restricted like that of a directory. That portion is omitted from the Facts tab of a file; however, in addition to the date the file was last modified, NetWare Administrator names the person who modified the file last. Also, the Facts tab for files contains a last accessed date. A file that is opened but not modified will not be listed as modified; it will be listed as accessed.

Because NetWare Administrator is so closely linked to NDS and NetWare 4.11, using it for file system management has some advantages. It is able to keep track of some file information that other file system management tools cannot. If this information is critical to your network, then NetWare Administrator is the key to your file system management.

Attributes

Every file and directory stored on a NetWare volume has some extra bits associated with them. These bits define the attributes of the file or directory. The *attributes* define another level of security by describing the characteristics of the file or directory. Through attributes, a file or directory might be described as READ ONLY. Files or directories marked as such cannot be modified or deleted unless the attribute is removed.

Those of you who have used DOS will be familiar with the concept of file attributes. In DOS, there are four basic attributes that can be used to describe a file. They are READ ONLY, HIDDEN, SYSTEM, and ARCHIVE. They can be turned on and off using the ATTRIB command from the DOS prompt.

Attributes override any file system rights a person might have to a file or directory. Even though a person might have the rights [SRWCEMFA] to the file system, he or she still would not be able to delete a file with a READ ONLY attribute. The attributes are the final layer in the security structure of NetWare. Files have a larger set of attributes that can be applied; directories have only eight attributes that can be set.

File Attributes

Unlike DOS, which has only 4 file attributes, NetWare comes with 20 separate attributes that can be applied to files. Some of them cannot be set by the user; they can only be set by NetWare. Table 6-3 provides a list of the NetWare file attributes and their abbreviations.

File Attribute	Abbreviation
Archive	A
Can't Compress	Cc
Compressed	Co
Copy Inhibit	Ci
Delete Inhibit	Di
Don't Compress	Dc
Don't Migrate	Dm
Don't Suballocate	Ds
Execute Only	X
Hidden	H
Immediate Compress	Ic
Migrated	M
Normal	N
Purge	P
Read Only	Ro
Read Write	Rw
Rename Inhibit	Ri
Shareable	Sh
System	Sy
Transactional	T

Table 6-3: File attributes.

- **ARCHIVE (A)**—set when a file is modified. It indicates a file has been changed since the last time a backup program was run. When a backup program runs, it resets this attribute after the file is stored successfully. Once the file is modified, ARCHIVE is set again.

- **CAN'T COMPRESS (Cc)**—set by NetWare (not by a user) and signifies the file cannot be compressed because the space savings it would gain are negligible. CAN'T COMPRESS only applies to volumes on which file compression has been enabled.

- **COMPRESSED (Co)**—set by NetWare. This flag indicates the file has been compressed. COMPRESSED applies only to volumes on which file compression has been enabled.

- **COPY INHIBIT (Ci)**—prevents Macintosh users from copying the file. It applies only to Macintosh workstations and is incredibly useful if you have license-sensitive files that cannot be distributed around the network.

- **DELETE INHIBIT (Di)**—prevents a file from being erased even if the user has the ERASE file system right to the file. This flag is automatically set when the READ ONLY attribute is set for a file; however, files that are not marked as READ ONLY can be marked DELETE INHIBIT to prevent users from deleting them.

- **DON'T COMPRESS (Dc)**—applies only to volumes on which file compression has been enabled. If you don't want a file to be compressed, set the DON'T COMPRESS attribute.

- **DON'T MIGRATE (Dm)**—applies only to volumes on which data migration has been enabled. The DON'T MIGRATE attribute will prevent the file from being migrated to an online high-capacity storage system (HCSS) such as an optical disk or tape drive.

- **DON'T SUBALLOCATE (Ds)**—prevents a file from being stored using the NetWare block suballocation technique. This attribute applies only to volumes that have block suballocation enabled.

- **EXECUTE ONLY (X)**—sets a file so that it can only be run. This attribute applies only to executable files on your NetWare server (.EXE or .COM files). Not only does this attribute make the file run only, it prevents users from copying it. This is useful for files that are license sensitive and cannot be distributed freely across the network.

    EXECUTE ONLY can only be set by a person with Supervisor file system rights. Once set as an attribute, it cannot be removed. Make sure there is a backup copy of the file before you set the EXECUTE ONLY attribute. Also be warned: some executables will not run properly if the EXECUTE ONLY attribute is set.

- **HIDDEN (H)**—prevents most people from being able to see the file in a directory listing. Users using the DOS or OS/2 DIR command will not be able to see a file marked as HIDDEN. However, users with the File Scan file system right using the NetWare NDIR command will be able see a HIDDEN file.

- **IMMEDIATE COMPRESS (Ic)**—applies only to volumes on which file compression has been enabled. It tells NetWare to compress the file as soon as it can. NetWare does not wait the default period of time before compressing the file.

- **MIGRATED (M)**—cannot be set by users; it is set by NetWare itself. It indicates the file has been migrated to an HCSS. It applies only to volumes on which data migration has been enabled.

- **NORMAL (N)**—not an attribute that can be set. It means that no other attributes have been set for the file.

- **PURGE (P)**—purges a file from the file system immediately when it is deleted. It cannot be recovered using the SALVAGE utility.

- **READ ONLY (Ro)**—indicates the file is read-only. The data contained cannot be changed or modified. By default, when READ ONLY is set as an attribute, DELETE INHIBIT and RENAME INHIBIT are also set; however, these attributes can be removed. Thus, a READ ONLY file can be deleted or renamed if those extra attributes are reset.

  When READ ONLY is set, it supersedes any file system rights a user might have to a file. A user with the WRITE right will not be able to write to a READ ONLY file because attributes override any file system rights a person may have.

- **READ WRITE (Rw)**—indicates the absence of READ ONLY. When the READ ONLY attribute is not set, NetWare lists the file as READ WRITE. This attribute cannot be set.

- **RENAME INHIBIT (Ri)**—prevents a user from renaming a file even if he or she has the MODIFY file system attribute. A file is automatically marked RENAME INHIBIT when the READ ONLY attribute is set.

- **SHAREABLE (S)**—allows files to be shared on the network. This means that more than one user can access it at any given time; however, marking the file as SHAREABLE does not guarantee that it can be shared properly. Some applications will not be able to access the file if it is already opened by another user.

- **SYSTEM (Sy)**—marks a file as an operating system file. People who are familiar with DOS have seen the SYSTEM attribute before. When this attribute is set, the file is hidden from directory listings, and it cannot be deleted, renamed, or copied. Generally, you will not need to set the SYSTEM attribute for files on your server.

- **TRANSACTIONAL (T)**—used in conjunction with NetWare's Transaction Tracking System (TTS). TTS is a mechanism that prevents files from receiving partial updates. It is used heavily in conjunction with databases that rely on the entire transaction being completed before the data is committed to the database. If the transaction is interrupted (due to power loss, for instance), none of the data is modified. The application must be designed for TTS for the TRANSACTIONAL attribute to work properly.

As we have mentioned before, file system rights do play a role in the ability to affect the file attributes on the NetWare server. A user must have the Modify file system right to the file to affect the file's attributes. To change the attribute settings for files, use the NetWare administrator.

Right-click on the file for which you want to change the attributes and select Details from the menu that appears. The file properties dialog box will appear. Click on the Attributes property tab with the left mouse button to see the attributes, as shown in Figure 6-19.

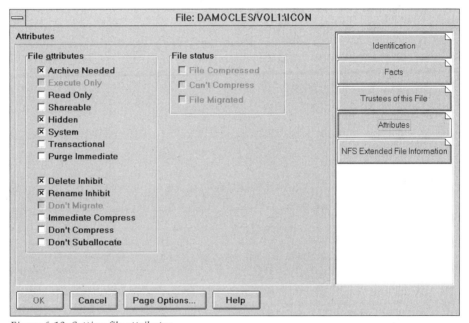

Figure 6-19: Setting file attributes.

Along the left-hand side of the screen are the attributes that can be set by the user. They are listed in the File Attributes box. There is another box on this screen called the File Status box. These are the attributes that are set by NetWare to describe the status of the file. To set an attribute for a file, make sure there is an X in the box to the left of the desired attribute. Cleared boxes indicate the attribute is not set for the file.

Directory Attributes

Like files, directories also have attributes in NetWare; however, there are not as many attributes available for directories. They function similarly to the file system attributes. The directory attributes are listed in Table 6-4.

Directory Attribute	Abbreviation
Delete Inhibit	Di
Don't Compress	Dc
Don't Migrate	Dm
Hidden	H
Immediate Compress	Ic
Purge	P
Rename Inhibit	Ri
System	S

Table 6-4: Directory attributes.

Four directory attributes apply to the directory exactly like they apply to the file. They are HIDDEN, SYSTEM, DELETE INHIBIT, and RENAME IN-HIBIT. A directory with the attribute DELETE INHIBIT cannot be deleted by a user even if that user has the ERASE file system right to the directory.

Where those four attributes apply to the directory itself, the remaining four have the effect of applying to every file contained within the directory. The attributes with this property are DON'T COMPRESS, DON'T MIGRATE, IMMEDIATE COMPRESS, and PURGE. When a directory is marked as DON'T COMPRESS, all files within that directory will not be compressed.

The directory attribute does not apply to subdirectories. If a directory called APPS has a subdirectory WP and the DON'T COMPRESS attribute is set for the APPS directory, all the files contained within APPS will not be compressed; however, files contained in WP are not affected because the attributes are not inherited by subdirectories.

To set the attributes for a directory, the user again must have the MODIFY file system right. Right-click on the directory whose attributes will be modified and select Details from the menu that appears. The directory properties dialog box will appear. Click on the Attributes tab with the left mouse button to display the directory attributes.

Attributes that have an X in the box to the left of them are set for that directory. A cleared box indicates the attribute is not set. Click on the box to toggle the attribute between set and cleared. When finished, click OK.

Salvaging & Purging Files

When users delete files from a NetWare server, they are not immediately gone forever. NetWare stores deleted files, and they can be recovered using the SALVAGE utility within NetWare Administrator. Before we get to actually recovering the data, however, we need to understand where the file is stored after it is deleted.

If a particular file is deleted from a directory, it is stored in that directory. To retrieve it, you must currently be in the directory from which it was deleted. If an entire directory is deleted, the files are stored in a special directory called DELETED.SAV. Every NetWare volume has a DELETED.SAV directory expressly for this purpose. Let's say there is a directory called DOCS on VOL1. A file called LETTER.TXT is deleted from this directory. To salvage this file, you need to be in the DOCS directory; however, if the entire DOCS directory and its files were deleted, you need to search DELETED.SAV to retrieve the files.

To retrieve deleted files, use the SALVAGE utility found in NetWare Administrator. When retrieving files from a specific directory, select that directory by clicking on it once with the left mouse button. Then choose Tools | Salvage from the menu bar to start the SALVAGE utility. This utility is shown in Figure 6-20.

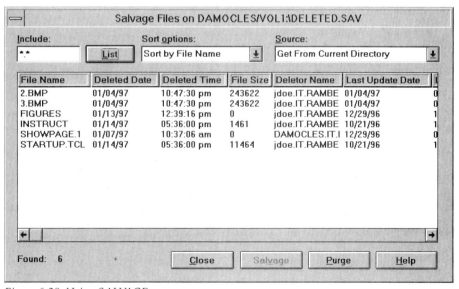

Figure 6-20: Using SALVAGE.

To see if any files are salvageable, click on the List button. Assuming the Source box is set to Get From Current Directory, NetWare will look to see if there are any files that can be retrieved. If there are, they will be listed in the main box on the screen. From this list, select the file to be salvaged and click on the Salvage button at the bottom of the screen. The file will be retrieved and placed in the current directory.

If you need to retrieve files from deleted directories, click on any directory in the file system and start the SALVAGE utility. In the Source box, set the option to Get From Deleted Directories. This will force SALVAGE to look in the DELETED.SAV directory of the current volume. Click on the List button to see all retrievable files. When files are retrieved using this option, they are placed in the DELETED.SAV directory; they are *not* placed in the current directory.

There is some important information associated with the SALVAGE utility that will be of use to the network administrator. Files that can be retrieved are listed with the time they were deleted and by whom. The network administrator can pinpoint who was responsible for erasing the file and take appropriate measures, if necessary.

Files can also be deleted permanently using the SALVAGE utility. To do so, select the file that was deleted just like you would if you were going to retrieve it. Once the file is selected, click the Purge button. This will delete the file from the system. Use the purge option carefully. Once a file is purged, it can never be retrieved.

Applying Concepts: Rambell, Inc.

Last time we checked in on John Doe, he had just completed setting up the network environment for his users. The user and user-related objects had been created, and the login scripts were written. Now John has to pay attention to the file system and the security that will be set up for his users.

John has two volumes on his NetWare server. One is called SYS and the other is VOL1. SYS will be used strictly for NetWare 4.11 operating system files. No applications or user data will be placed on it. For administration purposes, John creates a trustee assignment for the organizational role SYSADMIN at the root directory of the SYS volume. He grants the rights [SRWCEMFA] to this object. Thus, he does not have to use the Admin user object as long as his own user object is an occupant of the organizational role.

So that users can access the NetWare utilities on the SYS volume, John creates two more trustee assignments. The IT organizational unit is given the rights [_R____F_] to both the LOGIN directory and the PUBLIC directory on the SYS volume. This way, they will be able to perform the basic network functions like MAP and CAPTURE for their drive mappings and network printing.

VOL1 is a completely different story. This is the volume that will contain the network applications and user data. John is going to need to grant more rights to users, so he has to think carefully about the security implementation. Again, the organizational role, SYSADMIN, is granted the rights [SRWCEFMA] to the root of VOL1 for administrative purposes. It gives the role complete access to the file system.

Initially, VOL1 is going to have three main directories that exist directly below the root directory—USERS, APPS, and SHARED. The USERS directory will contain the home directories for all users, and they will be created by NetWare when the user objects are created. APPS will contain all of the network applications. SHARED will contain subdirectories for data that will be shared by groups of people on the network.

In the creation of the user object, NetWare creates the appropriate trustee assignments for each user to his or her home directory. This assignment grants the user the rights [_RWCEMFA] to the home directory. To provide the correct security to the APPS directory, John grants the IT organizational unit the rights [_R____F_]. The IRFs of any directories below APPS will allow these rights to pass, so users will be able to execute the network applications, but they will not be able to modify any data or delete any applications in this portion of the file system.

The SHARED directory in turn will contain two subdirectories—ACCT and MANUF. The group ACCT will have a trustee assignment to the ACCT directory with the rights [_RWCEMF_]. The MANUF group will have a trustee assignment to the MANUF directory, also with the rights [_RWCEMF_]. This allows all members of those groups to have complete file access to their pertinent directory. People in the groups will be able to share data efficiently by using their special shared directory.

John doesn't have any need right now to modify the attributes of the files in either volume of the server. However, he keeps this level of security in mind for future use. Now that John has the file system and the user objects squared away, his users will be able to use the file server. He will keep track of the growth and security of the file system to ensure users have an appropriate level of access.

Moving On

The next step to providing complete network services is network printing. In the next chapter, we will explore the NetWare printing environment that gives users the ability to print the files they are now able to share.

7

Print Services

In the previous chapters, we have discussed the steps necessary for implementing file sharing across your local area network. Using a combination of NDS objects and a comprehensive file system security scheme, you were able to allow your users to concurrently access data on the network making their work easier and more efficient. However, to provide a complete set of basic network services, another component needs to be added.

It is one thing for users to be able to share data, but not every user on the network has his or her own printer to print the data that is shared. Users would have to be able to access the machine to which the printer is connected, and if it happened to be another user's machine, the potential for wasted time and resources is obvious. Another solution might be a dedicated printing workstation, which could be cost prohibitive because it would involve devoting a computer full time to printing. There must be a better solution.

With NetWare 4.11, Novell provides a way to share printers across the network. A user who needs data printed can sit at his or her own workstation (which may not have a printer) and route a print job across the network to a printer connected to another machine or the file server itself. There is no need to dedicate hardware specifically to the purpose of printing, and users need not share their workstations to let other users print. The only thing that needs to be shared is the printer.

In this chapter, we will learn about the ins and outs of NetWare printing. We will start with an overview of network printing by discussing just how a print job is created and serviced by a printer across the network. We will also discuss the key components of network printing—the print server, the print queue, and the printer itself. Before we begin to discuss setting up the printing environment in NetWare, we will look at planning the printing environment for your network. These are all issues that are important to understand before we get into the details of NetWare printing.

Once the foundation has been laid, we will discuss the creation and configuration of the printing environment itself. There are two main components to printing in NetWare. The front end involves setting up the appropriate objects in the NDS tree. The back end involves loading the appropriate software on the file server and workstations, which is done by the network administrator. Together, they provide the printing environment that allows users to print across the network.

Network printers will not be useful without user interaction. Once we have covered the configuration of the printing environment, we'll discuss the user interaction with the printers. Through the DOS-based utility CAPTURE.EXE, network administrators and users will be able to send print jobs out to the network and have them print on the newly installed network printers. We will also discuss Windows-based utilities for the network printing environment.

Finally, IntranetWare comes packaged with the ability to interface with the UNIX print environment. Through UNIX Print Services for NetWare, you can have NetWare clients print to UNIX printers as well as have UNIX machines print to NetWare printers. We will discuss the installation and configuration of this platform-integrating product at the end of this chapter.

Getting Started With Network Printing

Before we can discuss the NetWare printing environment in detail, it is important to understand the fundamental principals of network printing. With a single computer and an attached printer, the printing process is very simple. Generally, printers are attached to computers via the parallel port on the back of the machine. The printer cable consists of a 25-pin parallel interface on one end and a Centronix connector at the far end that plugs into the printer. Printers can also be connected to computers via the serial port.

Network printing is considerably more involved—there are many different components to set up and configure, and a lot more software is required to make sure the print job gets to the appropriate place on the network to be printed. Network printing involves the use of print servers, print queues, and network printers to accomplish the printing cycle. Understanding this process not only will provide insight into setting up the NetWare printing environment, it will also help you troubleshoot it when errors occur.

Step-by-Step Guide to the Network Print Request

Unlike the printer attached to the workstation and serving that workstation's printing needs only, network printing requires that either the printer itself is directly attached to the network (in the case of network-ready printers) or the workstation to which the network printer is attached is connected to the network. Either way, there must be an already established network connection. This provides the physical path from the start of the print job to the end of the print job (the user wanting to use network print services must also be working from a workstation connected to the network). Any break in this physical path will prevent network printing.

   This stated, let's take a look at the steps that are executed from beginning to end when a network printing request is issued. The basic components of network printing are illustrated in Figure 7-1. Here we see that the workstation generating the print job is physically connected to the network as well as to the workstation to which the printer is attached. In between, the network cable provides the physical path for the print job to reach the printer from the user's workstation.

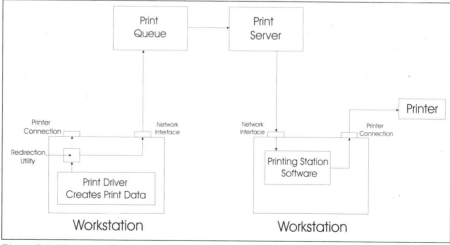

Figure 7-1: The network printing method.

Using the diagram in Figure 7-1, we can follow the printing process from the initial printing request to the actual output from the printer. The network printing process can be summarized by the following steps:

1. A print request is issued.
2. Print data is redirected to a print queue.
3. The print server services the print queue.
4. The printer station receives the job and prints the data.

A Print Request Is Issued

The first step in the print process is a print request issued by the user. The request can be from any application he or she happens to be using. Whether the application is a word processing or spreadsheet application, the method is the same. The user chooses to print data to the printer (whether it be a local or network printer).

Once the print request is given, the application itself gathers the data to be printed and performs the necessary steps to get it ready to be printed; however, no print data itself is generated yet. When the application is done gathering the data, it is then handed off to the print driver, which resides on the workstation itself.

The print driver is the software necessary to translate the data into a format the printer can understand. It is the print driver that generates the *print data*, the data that actually can be printed by a printer. Usually, each printer has its own custom print driver, which is required to format the print data properly for that particular model of printer. For example, the Hewlett-Packard LaserJet III printer will require a different print driver than the Hewlett-Packard LaserJet 5 printer. This is because each printer has a specific set of printing commands; it is up to the print driver to know them and format the data from the application accordingly.

Keep in mind that the type of data being printed will affect how quickly the print driver is able to generate the print data for the printer. A text file will have print data created for it much quicker than a graphics file would. In fact, a print driver will often take a long time to generate the print data for a graphics file due to the complexity of the print data that must be created to print it properly.

Print Data Is Redirected to a Print Queue

Normally, if a printer is attached directly to the workstation, the print job will go out the physical port on the back of the machine (parallel or serial, depending upon how the printer is connected). It is the print driver's responsibility to direct the print data toward the appropriate physical port.

In the case of network printing, a special utility resides on the workstation that diverts the print data from the intended physical port destination. This utility takes the print data and redirects it to the network. A destination print queue to which the printer data will be passed is specified. Once redirected, the print data is sent out the network card to the file server that contains the print queue specified by the network printing utility. The most common network printing utilities in NetWare are CAPTURE.EXE and NPRINT.EXE, but other utilities may be used. These specific utilities are critical in sending the print data to the appropriate print queue on a NetWare file server.

A *print queue* is a temporary holding place for print jobs. When a job is in the queue, it is waiting to be serviced by another component called a print server. Once serviced, the job is taken from the queue and printed. In NetWare 4.11, network print queues are located on the volumes of the NetWare server. This central location for the print queue provides several advantages for network printing:

- Once the job has been spooled to the print queue, the user can continue working. No longer does the user have to wait for the entire print job to complete before resuming his or her duties.

- One print queue can be used for many users; thus, many users will be able to use a single network printer. All users who use the print queue deliver their jobs to the print queue, and the jobs are processed in the order in which they are received. The print queue is a First-In, First-Out (FIFO) structure.

- Print jobs can be assigned a priority. Print jobs with a higher level of priority will be processed through the queue quicker than others. This gives the network administrator the flexibility to determine the importance of specific printing jobs. If a job needs to be processed immediately, it can be assigned the highest priority, and it will be serviced first assuming there are no other jobs ahead of it with the same level of priority.

- Different queues can be serviced by different printers. Thus, users can print to many different network printers just by changing the queue to which they send the print job.

The print queue provides order in the network printing environment. All users using the print queue deliver the jobs, and the print queue places them in order and waits for the jobs to be serviced by the print server. As the queue receives more print jobs, it keeps putting them in line and rearranging them in terms of their priorities. It acts as a barricade as well as an intermediate holding tank for print jobs. Once in the print queue, the print job will not go anywhere unless taken out of the queue and serviced by the print server.

Think of a network printing environment in which people print directly to the printer. If one job is in the middle of being printed, and another job gets to the printer, the new job will overprint any data that is currently being printed. Thus, the original print job, as well as the new print job, will be ruined because they will collide at the printer. The print queue helps to alleviate this situation by providing a place to store the print jobs so they can be processed by the print server and printer in an orderly manner that eliminates colliding print jobs.

Print Server Services Print Queue

When a print job reaches the print queue, it waits. Without the print server, the job would wait in the print queue indefinitely. The print server acts as a traffic cop to direct the print job from the print queue to the printer on which it will print. The *print server* is the software mechanism through which the statuses of the network printers are monitored and the print jobs are ushered from the print queue to the printer itself. In essence, the print server is responsible for managing both the print queues and the printers on the network.

In NetWare 4.11, a print server can service many different print queues, and it can deliver the print jobs stored in those queues to many different printers. In fact, the print server is not limited to the number of queues it can service on the network. A single NetWare 4.11 print server (PSERVER.EXE) can support up to 255 printers on your network. This is a large increase over the 16 printers that could be supported with the NetWare 3.x version of PSERVER.EXE.

A print server will monitor the print queues it services at a default interval of five seconds. If no jobs are found in the queue, the print server will check back after the default sampling period. If a job is found in the queue, the print server processes it and immediately checks the queue again for another job. The default sampling time for the print queue can be changed. This will be explored later in this chapter.

The print server takes the job with the highest priority from the print queue and transmits it to the printer station and printer. The print server also monitors the status of the job once it is transmitted to the printer station to determine if any errors occur. If errors do occur, the print server will display the error messages and wait for input from the print server manager.

Printer Station Receives Job & Prints Data

The printer station is the workstation or machine on the network to which the printer is directly attached. The machine has some special software loaded that enables the printer to be a "networked" printer (even though it is physically attached to a single workstation and not the network). The special software (in most cases a NetWare utility called NPRINTER) processes the print job that is received from the print server and readies the information from the printer. This utility then sends the information to the printer one byte at a time across the physical printer cable (most likely a parallel cable with a Centronix interface at the printer) to the printer.

The printer receives the data one byte at a time, and when enough data is received to print a page, the printer will do so. The print data that is received by the printer (remember the data generated by the printer driver at the source machine?) is translated by the hardware on the printer and formatted appropriately on the page. When the print data is ready, the printer prints the pages as they are received from the printer station. When finished, the print job has successfully navigated the network and been printed through the combined efforts of the print queue, the print server, and the printer.

Planning the Printing Environment

Now that we know the fundamental process a network print job goes through to be printed, we can begin to plan our network printing environment. An efficient printing environment can only be achieved through careful preparation. How many users need to have network printing? How many printers are available for network printing? How many print queues need to be created? How many print servers can be run? These are all questions that need to be answered to provide the best performance for your printing environment.

The most important issues to keep in mind when thinking about printing are network printing performance, hardware requirements, the needs of the users, and general user satisfaction. Each one of these items has a significant impact on you as a network administrator. You need to provide the best network printing performance at the lowest possible cost. The printing environment needs to reflect the needs of the users on your network and be convenient at the same time.

Try to make network printing as user-friendly as possible. If 10 people are in close geographical proximity to a printer and are light printer users, one network printer may be sufficient. If these 10 people are heavy printer users, even though they are in close proximity to one another, they still may need more than one network printer to handle the load. Likewise, if people have to walk halfway across a building to pick up their print jobs at a network printer, you might want to consider setting up another network printer closer to them. If you have the resources to do so, provide the best network printing service you can for your users. They will appreciate it immensely.

Preparing Hardware for Network Printing

Earlier, we talked a bit about the physical path that is necessary from the source machine that generates the print job to the destination printer station to which the printer is attached. This physical path is incredibly important; without it, we would not be able to accomplish any network printing. Apart from the software required for printing (the print driver, the print queue, and the print server), there are hardware requirements that must be met for network printing. You'll need the following:

■ Workstations with network interface cards physically connected to the network.

■ A NetWare 4.11 file server to act as an intermediate storage space for the print jobs, which are stored in the print queues located on the server.

■ A place to load a print server. This may be PSERVER.NLM on the NetWare 4.11 file server. It can also be a third-party external print server that can service NetWare print queues.

■ A machine with a printer connected to it. The machine must also have a network interface card and be physically connected to the network to receive the data sent to it by the print server. This is the printer station.

■ A printer to print the print data when it is received by the print station. The printer must be physically connected to the print station. In the case of some third-party print servers, the print server, print station, and printer are all rolled into one hardware entity.

Make sure all of these hardware components are functioning properly before attempting to set up the network printing environment in NetWare. The workstations and print stations should be able to talk to the file server. The print station should be able to print a job directly to the printer across the printer cable. This will verify the printer is working properly. For third-party print servers, run the diagnostic test that comes with them. Ensuring the hardware runs properly will make troubleshooting the software configuration of the network printing environment much easier.

We have looked at the life of a network print job from beginning to end. We have also done some preliminary planning for our network printing environment and tested the hardware that will be used. It is now time to look at how NetWare in particular handles network printing. In the next section, we will look at the basic NetWare printing configurations that exist and outline the pros and cons of each configuration.

Basic NetWare Print Services Configurations

When we talk about NetWare print services and its configurations, we are generally talking about printing in a DOS or Windows environment. Although NetWare 4.11 supports both Macintosh and UNIX printing, most workstations that connect to Novell servers are DOS- and Windows-based workstations. Thus, we will concentrate on network printing in relation to the DOS- and Windows-based workstations on the network.

There are essentially four main ways NetWare print services can be configured on the network. They are as follows:

- A printer can be connected directly to a NetWare file server.
- A printer can be connected to a client workstation.
- A printer can be network ready.
- A printer can use an external print server to provide printing services.

Each method has its own set of advantages and disadvantages. How you configure your network printing environment is completely up to you; however, knowing the pros and cons of each method should help you make an informed decision about your particular network setup.

Printers Connected to NetWare 4.11 File Servers

The first configuration for network printing involves a printer attached directly to a NetWare 4.11 file server. When a workstation prints to the network printer, the job is redirected to the file server, which stores the print queue. The file server also has the print server loaded on it. In effect, the file server acts as the queue holder, print server, and printing station all in one. This is shown in Figure 7-2.

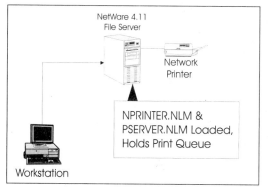

Figure 7-2: A network printer attached to the file server.

In this scenario, the print server and the printing station are actually the same machine. NetWare 4.11 relies upon both PSERVER.NLM and NPRINTER.NLM to perform the network printing. PSERVER.NLM is the print server software responsible for servicing the print queue and directing the print jobs to the printing stations. NPRINTER.NLM is the software loaded on the server to turn it into a printing station.

Note that PSERVER.NLM and NPRINTER.NLM do not need to be concurrently loaded in all situations. One file server may act as the print server while another file server acts as the printing station, as shown in Figure 7-3. In this case, server A has PSERVER.NLM running on it and holds the print queues on one of its volumes. Server B is running the NPRINTER.NLM software. The print job is directed to the print queue on server A. The print server on server A looks to see if there are jobs in the print queue. If there are, they are transmitted to server B, which is the effective printing station. Server B is then responsible for transmitting the data across the printer cable to the printer. Server A does not have NPRINTER.NLM loaded because no printer is physically attached to the server. Server A does not need to be a printing station.

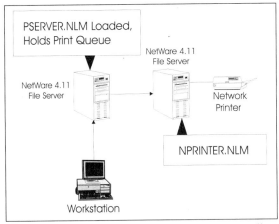

Figure 7-3: File servers can be printing stations as well.

There are some distinct advantages to using a Novell file server as a printing station:

- **The network printing environment will be faster.** Print jobs on servers running both PSERVER.NLM and NPRINTER.NLM do not have to traverse the network from the print queue to the printing station. The majority of the printing environment is located on one machine.

- **The printer will be available at all times.** Generally, file servers stay up and running 24 hours per day. Thus, NPRINTER.NLM will always be available to service print requests.

- **Server performance will be unaffected.** For servers running NPRINTER.NLM, there is generally no change in the machine's performance. Because NetWare 4.11 is a multitasking operating system that runs on a machine with more memory and processing power, a file server's performance will generally not be affected by concurrently using it as a printing station when printing loads are light.

There are also some disadvantages to using a Novell file server as a printing station:

- **High print loads can slow the server down.** Too many print jobs can eventually choke even a Netware 4.11 server, eventually affecting network performance.

- **The number of printers is limited.** The number of printers that can be connected to the file server is limited physically by the number of ports on the back of the server. Thus, if you plan on using printers connected to the server as your only network printers, the number you will be able to have is limited.

- **The server location may not be convenient for users.** Users may need to travel far to retrieve print jobs if they are not physically located near the file server. Because the printer cables are limited in the length they may be, network printers will need to be in close proximity to the file server itself.

Printers Connected to Client Workstations

A second configuration for network printing is connecting the printer to a client workstation on the network. After the print job is delivered to the print queue, the queue is serviced by the print server. The print server transmits the print job to the printing station (the client workstation), which transmits the job to the connected printer. This configuration is shown in Figure 7-4.

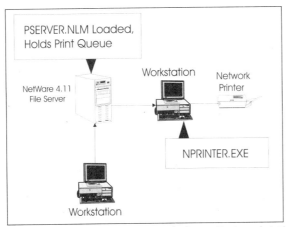

Figure 7-4: A network printer attached to a client workstation.

In this case, NetWare 4.11 relies upon a software program called NPRINTER.EXE. This program is loaded on the workstation, and the print server communicates with it to deliver the print job to the printer station. NPRINTER.EXE then processes the job and transmits it to the printer that is physically connected to the workstation. Note that PSERVER.NLM is still loaded on the server. A print server is required to send the jobs from the print queue to the printing station.

Using a workstation's printer as a network printer is oftentimes a more flexible printing solution with a distinct set of advantages:

- **There is no extra hardware cost.** A workstation with a locally connected printer that is used only for local print jobs can be turned into a network printer at no additional cost. The only modification that needs to be made is to software on the client workstation.

- **It provides distributed printing services to remote locations.** When your network is spread out over a large geographical area, it is much more efficient to set up network printers that are spread out to the various places print services are needed. This could not easily be accomplished when printing to printers connected directly to the file server.

- **The network printing load is distributed across more machines.** When one file server acts as both a print server and a printing station, high print loads can cause adverse network performance. Because the file server will be spending so much time printing, it will not be able to serve files as effectively. Using client workstations as printing stations helps to distribute this load across the network.

Likewise, there are some disadvantages to using workstations as printing stations. Consider these carefully before fully implementing this print service configuration:

■ **Network printing is slower.** Because the print job spends more time on the network, it will take longer to print. This is especially true if the print job is going through a lot of routers and bridges to get to the printing station.

■ **The printer may not always be available.** To use the printer, the attached workstation must be on and have NPRINTER.EXE loaded. Quite often, people will turn off machines without thinking. They may turn off the printing station, which prevents all users from printing to that printer.

■ **The performance of the workstation is affected.** Generally, people will be using the printing station as a client workstation as well. NPRINTER.EXE poses a lot of overhead for the DOS/Windows workstation on which it is loaded. When a print job is received by the printing station, NPRINTER.EXE has to take control of the machine to process the job and transmit it to the printer. The person using the workstation will definitely see a decrease in the machine's performance (in relation to their task at hand) as the workstation is processing the print job.

NPRINTER.EXE is a DOS-based program. Since DOS is not a multitasking environment, only one process can be in control at any time. This is true even if Windows is running on the workstation with NPRINTER.EXE. When the printing station receives the print job from the print server, it must suspend all activities and attend to the print job. Only one process may run at a time, and NPRINTER.EXE will take precedence on the client workstation when a print job is delivered.

The two network printing configurations we've covered (connecting a printer to the NetWare 4.11 file servers and connecting it to client workstations) are the two supported methods under NetWare 4.11. They involve the use of PSERVER.NLM and NPRINTER.EXE or NPRINTER.NLM to provide printing services. These services are accomplished using the NetWare Core Protocol (NCP) suite, which includes IPX/SPX transmissions; however, there are some other solutions to network printing.

Network-Ready Printers

Many new models of printers on the market today come network ready. This means they can plug directly into a network and be configured to support the network's printing environment. In the case of NetWare 4.11, network-ready printers fall into one of two categories—external print server or remote printer. When the network-ready printer is set up as a remote printer, it is not connected physically to a client workstation. It only acts like it is attached to the network in this manner.

Generally, a network-ready printer will come with hardware that gives it the ability to talk to the network. Older printers can become network-ready printers through the use of an external hardware device that connects to the printer or a special device that fits into an existing port on the printer. These devices allow the printer to talk directly to the network without the intervention of a client workstation machine acting as an interpreter.

External Print Server Mode

When we refer to an external print server, we mean a print server that is functioning on a network that does not require the services of PSERVER.NLM on a file server. This print server is not running on a NetWare 4.11 file server and is usually proprietary software that emulates PSERVER.NLM. Figure 7-5 shows how the network printing process is accomplished with an external print server.

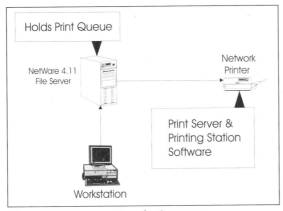

Figure 7-5: Using an external print server.

The manufacturer will provide information about configuring the print server to function with a NetWare network. Follow the instructions to set up the printing environment. Using an external print server may offer some advantages over the traditional printing environment:

■ **No PSERVER.NLM is required to provide the transition from the print queue to the printing station.** It is all built into the external print server. The file server will not be affected by any printing load on the network because the external print server will be responsible for routing the print jobs.

■ **No NPRINTER.EXE is required.** The external print server and the printing station software are all wrapped up into one device that attaches to the printer. No workstation's or server's performance is affected by performing the printing station's duties.

There are also some disadvantages to using an external print server:

■ **An extra network connection is necessary.** External print servers must connect directly to the network. They cannot be hung off of any other device on the network.

■ **External print servers cost more than standard printers.** There is a cost involved with obtaining the hardware necessary to convert a non-network-ready printer into a network-ready printer. Printers with this capability built in are often already more expensive than their non-network-ready counterparts.

■ **Fewer users will be able to access the network.** The print server device will use up a license connection on your NetWare 4.11 license count. Thus, if you have 5 external print servers and a 25-user license for NetWare, only 20 users will be able to concurrently use the network at any given time.

Remote Printer Mode

The remote printer mode functions as if the printer were physically attached to a client workstation. The print queue and print server reside on a NetWare 4.11 file server. When a print job is serviced by the print server, it is sent to the network-ready printer instead of to the printing station. In effect, the network-ready printer becomes the printing station and printer combined. This is shown in Figure 7-6.

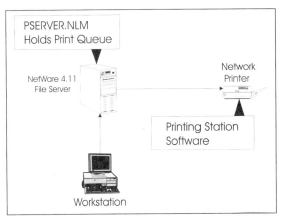

Figure 7-6: Remote printer mode for network-ready printers.

Again, instructions for setting up the remote printer mode on a network-ready printer should be included with the network-ready printer. Use the manufacturer's suggestions for making the printer compatible with the NetWare 4.11 printing environment. The benefits of using the remote printer mode are the same as using the printer connected to the client workstation; however, NPRINTER.EXE is not required because the network-ready printer performs the function of the printing station. The disadvantages to using this method are the same as the external print server; however, no license counts are taken up by the network-ready printer.

Configuring NetWare Printing: Front End

Understanding the network printing procedure is the key to being able to create and configure the NetWare 4.11 printing environment. We have learned about the concepts of the print queue, the print server, the printing station, and the printer. We will use that knowledge here to set up the printing environment. As we do so, think back to the network printing method and see how each part fits into the overall process.

Setting up the printing environment in NetWare 4.11 actually consists of two main parts. There is a front end to the printing environment as well as a back end. The front end consists of setting up the appropriate objects in the NDS tree. Once the objects are created, they must be correctly configured so that the queues, servers, and printers interact properly.

Just because the objects are set up in the NDS tree does not mean that users will immediately be able to print. The tree does not affect the main software components that need to be loaded on the server and workstation. After the front end is configured, the network administrator must set up the back end of the printing environment. This involves the loading of the print server software (PSERVER.NLM) and the printing station software (NPRINTER.EXE). Once these software components are loaded, they work in conjunction with the objects in the NDS tree to provide the print services to users on the network. Configuring the back end of the printing environment will be discussed in the next section of this chapter.

As we have learned, when we are manipulating the NDS tree, we need to use NetWare Administrator. Thus, to set up the front end of the printing environment, start NetWare Administrator from Windows by double-clicking on the program's icon. To complete the front end of the printing environment, we will need to create at least three objects in the NDS tree:

- Print Queue
- Printer
- Print Server

It is recommended you create the objects for the printing environment in the order in which they appear on the preceding list. Once created in the NDS tree, each object must be configured to properly interact with the other objects to form the complete network printing path. A print server that is not configured to service a print queue will cause a print job to sit in the queue forever. It takes the network administrator's hand to point each object in the right direction initially.

Remember, these objects are NDS objects. To create them and modify the properties associated with them, you must have sufficient NDS rights!

Print Queue Object

The print queue object in the NDS tree represents a network print queue. It is a temporary storage area for print jobs waiting to be serviced by the network printing environment. When a user creates a print job, it is delivered to the print queue. Creating the NDS print queue object causes a physical queue to be created on the specified volume of a NetWare file server.

To create a print queue object, right-click on the container that will hold the object in NetWare Administrator. Choose Create from the menu that appears. From the New Object dialog box, select the Print Queue object. The Create Print Queue dialog box will appear as shown in Figure 7-7.

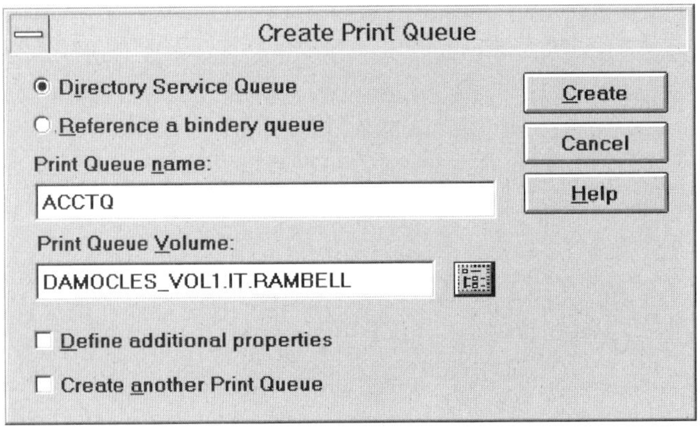

```
┌────────────────────────────────────────────────┐
│ ──│              Create Print Queue              │
├────────────────────────────────────────────────┤
│ ● Directory Service Queue          ┌──────────┐ │
│ ○ Reference a bindery queue        │  Create  │ │
│ Print Queue name:                  └──────────┘ │
│ ┌────────────────────────────┐     ┌──────────┐ │
│ │ ACCTQ                      │     │  Cancel  │ │
│ └────────────────────────────┘     └──────────┘ │
│ Print Queue Volume:                ┌──────────┐ │
│ ┌────────────────────────┐ ┌──┐    │   Help   │ │
│ │ DAMOCLES_VOL1.IT.RAMBELL│ │▦ │    └──────────┘ │
│ └────────────────────────┘ └──┘                 │
│ □ Define additional properties                  │
│ □ Create another Print Queue                    │
└────────────────────────────────────────────────┘
```

Figure 7-7: Creating a print queue object.

When you create a print queue, you have the option of making it a NetWare 4.x print queue (Directory Service Queue) or a NetWare 3.x print queue (Reference a Bindery Queue). Referencing a bindery queue will allow you to support printing outside of your current NDS tree. To print to a print queue that exists in another directory tree, you need to create a reference to that queue in the other tree. Also, to provide printing support for people who are using your tree through Bindery Services, a reference to the bindery queue must be created using the Reference a Bindery Queue option.

When you choose the Reference a Bindery Queue option, the Print Queue Volume text box you see in Figure 7-7 becomes the Server\Queue text box. In Server\Queue text box, you must input the server and queue name of the queue that will be referenced by this NDS object. Setting up a print queue as a reference to a bindery queue merely makes it a pointer to an existing bindery queue on your network.

To create a print queue that uses all the benefits of the NDS tree and allows all your NetWare 4.x clients to print, select the Directory Service Queue radio button. Name the queue object by typing the name in the Print Queue Name box. This is the name by which the print queue will be known. In the Print Queue Volume box, type in the volume on which the print queue will be created.

In NetWare 3.x, print queues always existed on the SYS volume of a file server. This is not the case with NetWare 4.11. The print queue can be created on any file server volume. We recommend print queues not be placed on the SYS volume. Print queues are dynamic; they are always growing and shrinking in size. If there are many print jobs in the print queue that require a lot of disk space, SYS could run out of disk space. This could cause NDS corruption because Directory Services is also stored on SYS. Create your print queues on another volume.

To browse the NDS tree to find a server volume, click on the Select Object button to the right of the Print Queue Volume box. The Select Object dialog box will appear, through which you can browse the NDS tree and find the volume object on which the print queue will reside. Once all the appropriate information has been entered, click on the Create button to create the print queue.

What Happens When I Create a Print Queue?

When a print queue is created in NetWare 4.11, NetWare Administrator makes some changes to the file system on the volume that was selected in the creation of the object. If it is the first time a queue has been created on a volume, a new directory called QUEUES will be created immediately off the root directory. NetWare Administrator then creates a directory specifically for that print queue.

For example, creating the PRINTQ1 object in the NDS tree and specifying VOL1 as the Print Queue Volume box will create the QUEUES directory on VOL1. Immediately beneath QUEUES, you will see a strange-looking directory with an eight-digit name and the extension .QDR. The eight-digit name is the actual object ID of PRINTQ1 as assigned by NDS, and the .QDR extension signifies the directory as a print queue. This is the place on the file system where print jobs are stored when they are received by the print queue.

NetWare Administrator will not provide you with the object ID of the print queue if you need that information. To retrieve the object ID and associate these strange directories with the actual print queue objects, use the PCONSOLE.EXE program from the DOS prompt and choose Print Queues|<print_queue_name>|Information. The object ID is displayed there.

Once the print queue has been created, the network administrator must detail the object to ensure it will work appropriately on the network. To detail the print queue object, click on the object in the NDS tree with the right mouse button and choose Details from the menu that appears. The print queue properties dialog box will appear. The screen will look familiar because it is similar to all other objects' properties dialog boxes; the properties are on the left side of the screen and the properties tabs are on the right side of the screen. There are five main property tabs for the print queue object:

- Identification
- Assignments
- Operator
- Users
- Job List

Identification

To see the identification properties of the print queue object, click on the Identification tab once with the left mouse button. These properties display information concerning the name and volume on which the print queue resides. There are also some text editing boxes for you to provide more information about the print queue, including the department and organization that uses the print queue.

Down at the bottom of the Identification page are operator flags that enable or disable the abilities of the print queue. Through these flags, a print queue operator can allow users to submit print jobs to the queue, allow the print server to service the print queue, and allow new print servers to attach to the print queue to service it. Only operators of the print queue are able to change the flags.

Assignments

The Assignments properties page displays the print servers and printers that are interacting with this queue. Think back to our discussion of the network printing method. The print queue is serviced by the print server and sent to the appropriate printer. Through this screen, you can see exactly which print server will be servicing the queue and to which printer the job will be sent. No modifications to these assignments can be made through this screen. The actual assignments are made through the other NDS objects.

Operator

The Operator properties screen displays the print queue operators. The operators of the print queue are the people who are going to be managing it. These are the people who are able to change the operator flag settings on the Identification screen. Print queue operators have complete control over all print jobs that are submitted to the print queue. They can also add users to the print queue, which enables a person to place a print job in the print queue.

To add an operator to the list, click on the Add button. The Select Object dialog box will appear. Browse the NDS tree and find the object that will be the operator of the print queue. Select the object and click OK. The object's name will be placed in the list of operators. By default, the creator of the print queue is automatically an operator. To remove an operator from the list, select the operator and click on the Delete button.

Users

Users of the print queue are the people who are allowed to submit jobs to it. If a user is not included in this list, he or she will not be able to use this print queue to print. To see the users of the print queue, click on the Users tab once with the left mouse button. The Users box appears with all of the users.

By default, the container object in which the print queue is located is made a user of the print queue. This means that all objects contained in the print queue's container are users of the print queue. All objects contained in subordinate containers are users of the print queue as well. However, other objects in the NDS tree are not granted rights immediately.

To add objects to the print queue users list, click on the Add button. The Select Object dialog box appears. Browse the NDS tree and find the object that will be a user. Select it and click OK. The object appears in the users list. To remove a user, select it by clicking on the user's name with the left mouse button once. Then click on the Delete button. The user will be removed. Only queue operators are allowed to modify the user list of the print queue.

Job List

The job list shows all of the current printing jobs that are waiting in the print queue. To see the job list, click on the Job List tab once with the left mouse button. At the top of the screen, the print queue name and number of print jobs in the print queue will be displayed. All of the current print jobs are listed in the table immediately below that information.

Any operator or user is able to see the print jobs of all print queue users. However, only a print queue operator is able to modify the status of a print job that is not his or her own. Only the people who are authorized to manage the queue are able to manipulate the print jobs of all users.

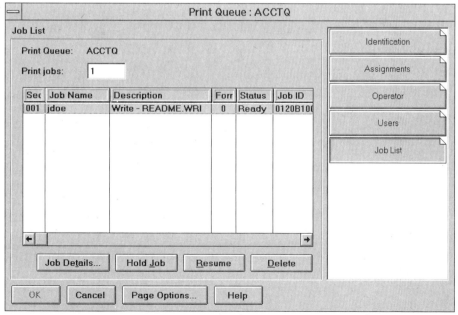

Figure 7-8: Viewing a print queue's job list.

In Figure 7-8, we see a typical job list for a print queue. To view a job, select it by clicking on it once with the left mouse button and clicking on the Job Details button at the bottom of the properties box. The details for that particular print job are displayed, including the print job ID number, the size of the print job file, and the owner of the file. Figure 7-9 shows a sample Print Job Detail screen.

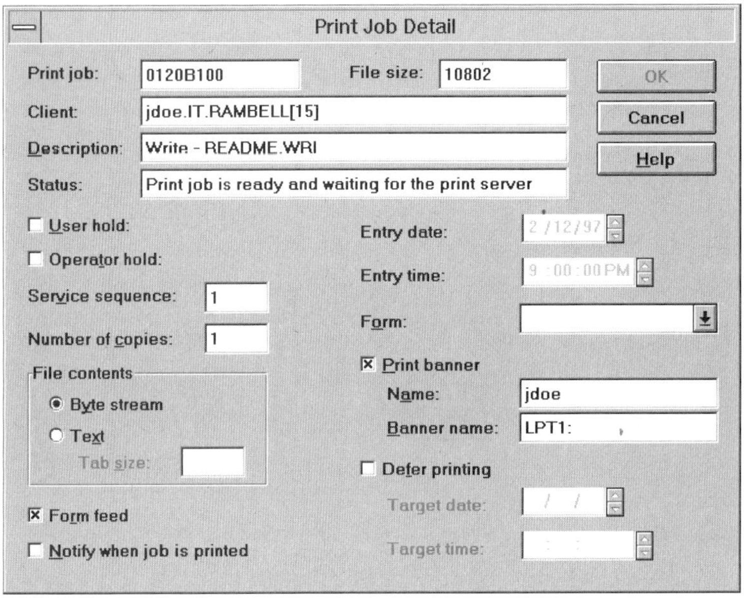

Figure 7-9: Displaying print job details.

You can also perform tasks that involve the status of the print job from the job list (Figure 7-8). To affect one of the print jobs, it must be selected by clicking on the job once with the left mouse button. Once highlighted, press one of the following buttons:

- **Hold Job.** Causes the print job to be held in the print queue. A job that is held in the print queue will not be serviced by a print server until the hold status is removed. Only the queue operator can put jobs on hold.

- **Resume.** Makes a job that is held in the print queue ready again for the print server. Only a queue operator is able to remove the hold status on a print job in the queue.

- **Delete.** Removes a print job from the print queue. Users can delete their own print jobs in the queue. Only a queue operator is able to delete other users' print jobs.

Printer Object

The printer object in the NDS tree represents a physical printer on your network that will be used for network printing. Every network printer must have an associated NDS printer object. When the print server sees a job in the print queue, it will be able to associate the print queue with a physical printer to which the print job will be sent. The NDS printer object should be the second object created in the setup of the printing environment.

To create the printer object in NetWare Administrator, click once on the container that will hold the printer object with the right mouse button and choose Create from the menu that appears. Select Printer from the New Object box and click OK. The Create Printer dialog box will appear. Type in the name of the printer and click on the Create button.

When naming your printer object, try to make the name as descriptive as possible. This will make your job as the network administrator easier because you will be able to quickly identify the physical printer the NDS printer object is associated with. For example, the printer name HP314_ANY is much more descriptive than LASER_PRINTER.

Once the printer object has been created, it must be configured properly. To detail the properties of the printer object, click on the object once with the right mouse button and choose Details from the menu that appears. The properties dialog box for the printer will be displayed. Like all other properties dialog boxes, the property tabs for the NDS object are displayed at the right of the screen.

Identification

The Identification properties page displays general information about the printer on the network, including the name, location, department, and network address of the printer. Fill out as much information as possible concerning the printer. If you need to search over NDS later for specific printer information, having filled out these data fields will help you complete your searches quickly and efficiently.

Assignments

To display the assignments properties for a printer, click on the Assignments tab with the left mouse button. This is the place where a printer is associated with a specific print queue (which was just created in the previous step). The Assignments tab is displayed in Figure 7-10.

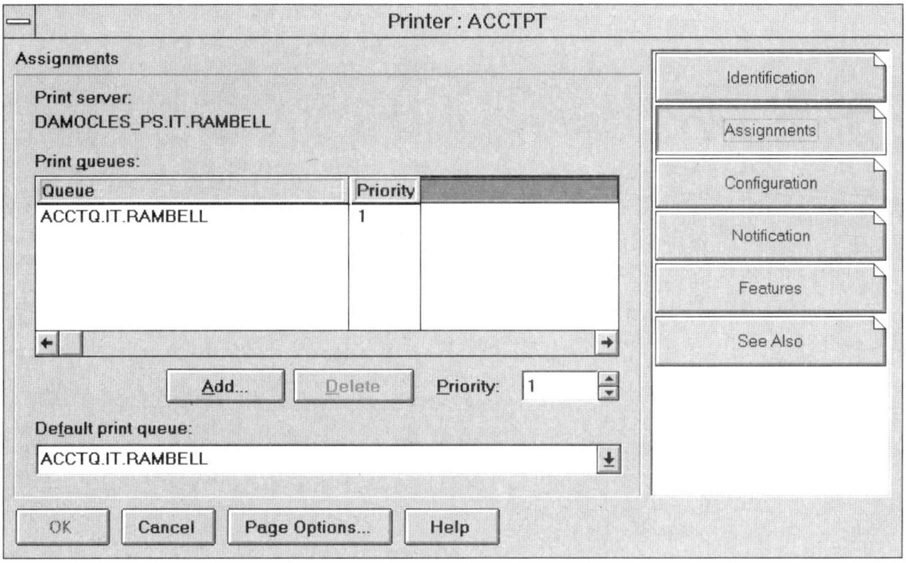

Figure 7-10: Assigning a printer to a print queue.

At the top of the screen, the print server is displayed. If no print server has been set up, this area will be blank. Print server assignments are not made from this screen. In the middle of Figure 7-10, we see the Print Queues box. This box displays the print queues that are currently associated with the printer object. In this case, the ACCTQ.IT.RAMBELL queue is being serviced by this printer with a queue priority of one.

To add a print queue to be serviced by this printer, click on the Add button below the Print Queues box. The Select Object dialog box will appear. Browse the NDS tree to find the appropriate print queue object, select it, and click OK. The print queue will then appear in the Print Queues box. To remove a print queue from being serviced by the printer, highlight it by clicking on it once with the left mouse button. Click on the Delete button to remove the print queue from the printer.

The Default Print Queue box at the bottom of Figure 7-10 determines which print queue the printer will service by default. To select the default print queue, use the drop-down list by clicking on the arrow to the right of the text editing box to select from the list of current queues. The significance of the default print queue will be discussed later in this chapter in the section "Using CAPTURE.EXE."

Priority   In the event that one printer is servicing print jobs from a lot of queues, there are instances when multiple print queues may be competing for the same resource (in this case, the printer). *Priority* allows the network administrator to determine which queue is more important and is thus served first.

The priority of a print queue can be set from 1 to 10 with 1 being the highest priority. Let's assume there are two print queues, ACCTQ and MANUFQ, with priorities of 2 and 3, respectively, that are being serviced by the same printer. When print jobs are submitted and waiting in both queues concurrently, the printer (through the print server) will service ACCTQ before MANUFQ. Thus the first job in MANUFQ will be forced to wait until all of the jobs in ACCTQ are printed before being serviced.

To modify the priority of a print queue, highlight it in the Print Queue box by clicking on it once with the left mouse button. Use the Priority box to then set the priority of the queue. It is a good idea to set all your queues initially with a priority of 2 or 3. This way, there is room to add queues with a higher priority without having to modify the priority of all print queues to make room.

Configuration

The physical configuration of the printer is another crucial group of properties that needs to be set correctly. These properties tell the print server exactly how it needs to communicate with the physical printer itself. The Configuration properties page for the ACCTPT printer is shown in Figure 7-11.

In the Configuration properties tab, we can see that the printer type is set to parallel, the banner type is text, and the service interval is 5. These properties, along with the network address restriction property, must be set correctly for the printing environment to function properly. Many a long hour has been spent trying to make the printing environment work only to find out the configuration parameters are the culprits.

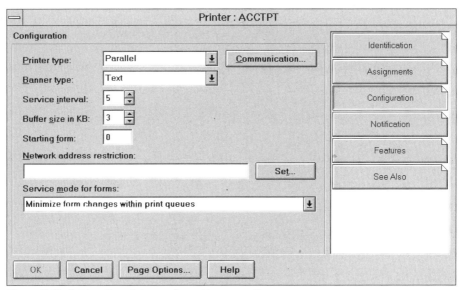

Figure 7-11: Setting the printer configuration properties.

Printer Type   The Printer Type property tells the print server just what type of printer it is. The most common type will be the parallel printer, which connects physically to the back of the workstation or file server. Another common type is the serial connection, which connects to the serial port on the back of the workstation or file server. NetWare 4.11 also supports other types of printers, including AppleTalk, XNP, and UNIX. Generally, these types of printers require additional software. To select the printer type, click on the drop-down button to the right of the Printer Type box. A list of available printer types will appear.

In Figure 7-11, we can see that ACCTPT is a parallel-type printer. This, however, does not completely define the printer type. There are more parameters to be configured, and they can be reached using the Communication button to the right of the Printer Type box. The communication parameters specific to the printer type will appear. Thus, a serial printer will have different communication parameters than a parallel printer. An AppleTalk printer will have its own set of communication parameters as well. Figure 7-12 shows the communication parameters for the parallel printer.

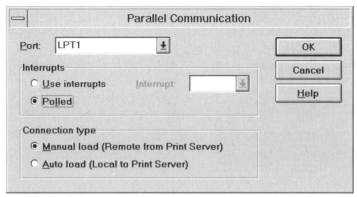

Figure 7-12: Setting parallel printer communication parameters.

In Figure 7-12, we can see that ACCTPT is connected to a machine using LPT1. The printing station software (NPRINTER.EXE or NPRINTER.NLM) will be using the polled mode to communicate with the printer. The Connection Type area at the bottom of the screen determines whether or not the printer is local to the print server. If the printer is connected to a workstation, you must choose the Manual Load option. The Auto Load assumes the printer is attached directly to the file server running PSERVER.NLM.

Once the communications parameters have been set, click on the OK button to return to the Configuration properties page of the printer object.

Polled Mode vs. Interrupt Mode

On the Communications screen for parallel printers, you are given the option of using interrupts to communicate with your printer or using polled mode. Polled mode causes the software on the printing station (NPRINTER.EXE or NPRINTER.NLM) to poll each interrupt to look for the attached printer. This mode helps to prevent interrupt conflicts that may occur on the workstation.

Interrupt mode lets the network administrator explicitly specify which interrupt on the workstation or file server the printer is using. Because the printing station software does not need to poll the interrupts, the printing process is faster; however, if the interrupt is incorrect, the workstation could lock up.

Banner Type The banner type allows the network administrator to choose which type of banner is printed as a header for the print job. When a banner is printed, it can either be in text form or in postscript form. To choose the appropriate banner type, click on the drop-down list button to the right of the Banner Type box and select the desired banner.

Service Interval The Service Interval property was touched on briefly earlier in this chapter. This property tells the print server how often to check the print queue for new jobs. By default, the value is set to 5; thus, every five seconds, the print server will look in the print queue for new print jobs. In the event there is a print job, the print server processes the job from the print queue and immediately checks the queue again for another job. The print server only waits the service interval before checking again when it finds no print job waiting.

Network Address Restriction Like users accessing the network, the printer can be restricted to a specific network address. Through the Network Address Restriction property, the specific network address to which the printer is connected can be entered. To restrict the printer to a network address, click on the Set button and enter the network and node information for the printer. Click OK to have the restriction be reflected in the Network Address Restriction box.

Notification

Another important property page for the printer is the Notification page. On this page, the network administrator can specify which parties are sent notice when the printer is having problems printing the print job. By default, the print job owner is notified when a problem occurs, but other people can be added to this notification list. To add an object to this list, click on the Add button. The Select Object dialog box will appear. Browse the NDS tree to find the object, select it, and click OK to add it.

To remove an object from the notification list, select the object by clicking on it once with the left mouse button. Click on the Delete key; the highlighted object will be removed. You can remove the print job owner from the list by clicking on the Notify Print Job Owner check box. When this check box is clear, the print job owner is not notified when printing problems arise.

Print Server Object

The final object that needs to be created in the NDS tree is the print server object. This object represents the print server that is loaded on the NetWare file server (PSERVER.NLM). It is the object responsible for servicing the print queue and sending the print job to the appropriate printer. Without the print server, the job would never leave the print queue.

To create the print server object in the NDS tree, click with the right mouse button on the container that will hold the object and choose Create from the menu that appears. Select Print Server from the New Object dialog box. Type in the print server name and click on the Create button. The print server object will be created in the NDS tree.

Even though the print server object has been created, it still needs to be configured properly. It needs to know which printers (and thus which print queues) to service. To detail the print server object, click on it with the right mouse button and choose Detail from the menu that appears. This will bring up the properties of the print server object. Like all NDS objects, the various property tabs for the object are shown on the right side of the screen.

What Happens When I Create a Print Server?

Just as there are with a print queue, there are modifications made to the file system when a print server object is created. For each print server, there will be a directory in SYS:SYSTEM created with an eight-digit name. These eight digits reflect the object ID of the print server as defined by the NDS tree when the object was created.

Unlike the volume for the print queues, the volume on which the print server directory is created cannot be changed. Be aware of this when creating audit log files to monitor the print server. Those logs will grow in size. It is the network administrator's responsibility to ensure the SYS volume will not run out of space because of files placed in the print server directory.

Identification

The Identification properties page provides descriptive information about the print server object. At the top of the screen is the print server name as specified when the object was created. This information cannot be changed. Information that *can* be edited on this screen is the network address of the machine on which the print server is loaded, the location of said machine, the department, and the organization.

To secure the print server, a password can be enabled. This prevents unauthorized people from loading the PSERVER.NLM on the file server. If a password has been enabled, PSERVER.NLM will prompt for a password as it is being loaded on the NetWare file server. If the password is incorrect, the print server will not load. To set the password for the print server, click on the Change Password button. If a password already exists, type it in the Old Password box. Type the new password in the New Password box. Retype the new password in the Retype New Password box and click OK.

The operator of the print server can also down the print server through the print server object. When the print server is running and needs to be unloaded, click on the Unload button. The Unload Print Server dialog box will appear. Choose whether you want to down the print server immediately or down it after the current jobs have been processed. Click OK to down the print server. This function is especially useful if the server console is not immediately available and the print server needs to be unloaded.

Assignments

When we looked at the printer object, we had to assign a print queue to the printer in the Assignments property page. For the print server, we have to use the Assignments page to assign the printers to service. This step completes the print queue, print server, and printer association. Once specified, the front end of the printing environment will be set. To reach the Assignments page, click on the Assignments tab with the left mouse button.

In the Printers box are the printers that have been assigned to this particular print server. The printer name is listed along with the printer number. The Assignments properties are shown in Figure 7-13.

To add a printer to the print server's list, click on the Add button at the bottom of the screen. The Select Object dialog box will appear. Use it to browse the NDS tree for the desired printer. Select the printer and click on OK. The printer name will appear in the Printers box. To remove a printer from the print server list, select the printer by clicking on it once with the left mouse button. Click on the Delete button at the bottom of the screen. The highlighted printer will be removed from the Printers box.

As we mentioned earlier in this chapter, PSERVER.NLM can support up to 255 printers. Each printer is assigned a number by which PSERVER.NLM recognizes it. These numbers range from 0 to 254. When a printer is added to the Printers box, the next number available is automatically chosen for the printer. However, you can change the number assigned to the printer by selecting the printer and clicking on the Printer Number button. The Change Printer Number dialog box will appear. Enter the new printer number for the printer and click OK. The printer number in the Printers box will reflect this change.

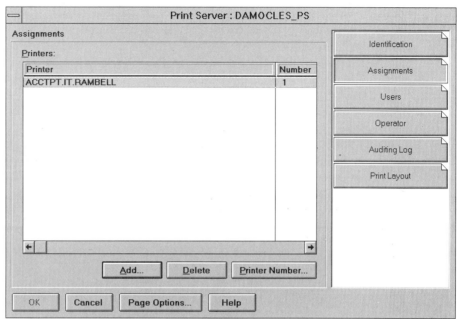

Figure 7-13: Assigning printers to a print server.

Whenever changes are made to the print server object, those changes are not reflected in PSERVER.NLM. For the changes to be registered properly, PSERVER.NLM must be unloaded from the file server and reloaded. Only then will the changes take effect.

Users

Like the print queue, the print server has a list of users. Unlike the print queue, being a user of the print server is not necessary to be able to print to a network printer. The users list merely reflects the list of users who are able to monitor the status of the print server using NetWare Administrator or the DOS-based utility PSC.EXE. To see the list of users, click on the Users tab with the left mouse button.

To add a user to the list of print server users, click on the Add button at the bottom of the screen. The Select Object dialog box will appear. Browse the NDS tree for the desired object and click OK. The object will be added. To remove a user from the print server user list, select the user by clicking on it once with the left mouse button. Click the Delete button, and the user will be removed. By default, the container in which the print server is located will be made a user of the print server. This means all objects in the container and in subordinate containers will be able to monitor the status of the print server.

Operator

Also like the print queue, a print server has a list of operators. These are the people who can manage the print server. Aborting a printing job in progress, restarting the printer, stopping the printer, and checking printer status are among the duties a print server operator is able to perform. People who are not print server operators are able to do the same things *from the print server console* on the file server; however, they will not be able to perform those duties remotely.

To see the list of operators for the print server, click on the Operator tab with the left mouse button. To add an operator, click on the Add button at the bottom of the Operator properties page. The Select Object dialog box will appear. Browse the NDS tree for the desired object and click OK. To remove an operator, select the object in the Operators box by clicking on it with the left mouse button. Then click on the Delete button at the bottom of the screen.

Auditing Log

For accounting purposes, an auditing log can be enabled on the print server. This log records information about all print jobs that are serviced by the print server. The following information is contained in the auditing log file:

- The printer used for the print job.
- The print job owner.
- The name of the print job.
- The print job ID.
- The printing form used.
- The print queue used.
- The time the print job was submitted.
- The time the print job was printed.
- The total number of pages printed.
- The total number of bytes printed.
- The total duration of printing.

By default, the auditing log for the print server is disabled. The print server operator must turn on the audit log to begin the recording of print information. To do so, click once on the Auditing Log property tab with the left mouse button to bring up the Auditing Log properties page. Then click on the Enable Auditing button at the bottom of the screen, as shown in Figure 7-14.

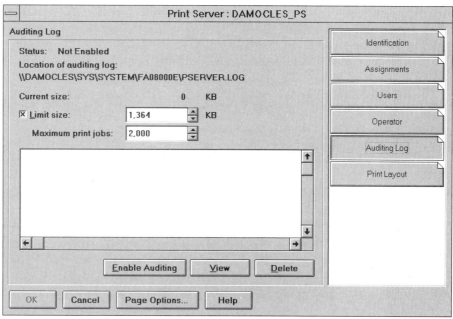

Figure 7-14: Print server auditing log properties.

The auditing log file will be created in the print server directory that was created for the print server on the SYS volume. The path for the file is displayed at the top of the screen. The name of the file will be PSERVER.LOG. The size of the file is displayed next to the Current Size property. Keep a close watch on the size of this file; left unnoticed, it could occupy all free space on the SYS volume. Fortunately, the size of the log file can be limited by checking the Limit Size check box. The size can be limited by file size or number of print jobs recorded. Enter the desired size limit in the appropriate box.

The auditing log file can be deleted at any time. To delete it, just click on the Delete button. To view the log file once it has been enabled, click on the View button at the bottom of the screen. The log file will be displayed in the large text editing window on the screen. The auditing log is helpful if you are billing for network print services; enable it only if you need the information that is recorded by the auditing process.

Print Layout

Just how successfully you've configured your network printing environment can be seen using the Print Layout property tab. Here, the print server is displayed along with all of the print queues and printers associated with the print server. This property box displays a graphical format of the printing environment, as shown in Figure 7-15.

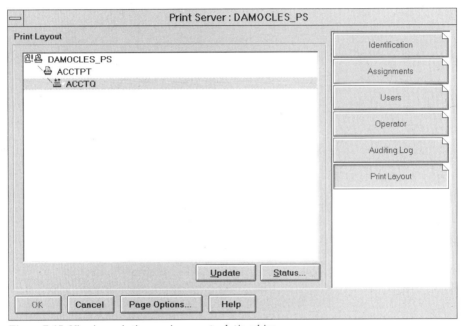

Figure 7-15: Viewing printing environment relationships.

The print server is displayed at the top level of this diagram. The next level shows the printers that are able to service the network print environment. Finally, the third level of the diagram comprises the print queues. They hang directly off of the printers they service. If multiple queues are serviced by the same printer, they both hang off of the printer object. This diagram displays the associations between the NDS objects. If the objects are configured correctly, you will see a line from the print server to the printer. You will also see a line from the printer to the print queue. These lines represent the physical paths that we discussed earlier in this chapter in the section "Step-by-Step Guide to the Network Print Request." Once in place, the stage is set for network printing.

There are two buttons at the bottom of the Print Layout screen—the Update button and the Status button. To immediately update the Print Layout screen, click on the Update button. The screen will be refreshed. The status of the print server, print queue, and printers can also be seen. Select the desired object by clicking on it once with the left mouse button. Click on the Status button to bring up a dialog box showing the status of the highlighted object.

The Print Layout screen will provide a first indication that something is wrong with the printing environment. If one of the components is not working properly, a symbol with a red exclamation point will be displayed to the left of the problem object. Highlight the object and click on the Status button to see what NetWare thinks the problem is. Generally, the information provided is not incredibly helpful; it will, however, give you an indication of where you need to begin troubleshooting the printing problem.

NDS Print Object Interaction

Network printing in NetWare 4.11 takes advantages of the distributed nature of the NDS tree. The three objects required for network printing need not exist in the same container. They can exist anywhere in the NDS tree. As long as they are properly configured to provide the physical path from the workstation creating the print job to the printing station and printer, they are location independent. Thus, a person in the United States could print to a printer in Denmark if the network was set up and configured properly.

Another thing to remember is that the print server and the print queues do not need to exist on the same file server. Server A can hold the print queues while server B acts as the print server. As we saw earlier in the chapter, server C could be the machine that has the printer physically connected to it. Thus, three physical servers could be distributing the load of the printing environment. We also saw that all three components could be loaded on a single file server. Again, the NetWare 4.11 printing environment is incredibly flexible and can be customized to fit the needs of your network easily.

Front End Setup Recap

Before we leave the discussion of setting up the front end of the printing environment, let's quickly recap the configuration:

1. Create the print queue object in the NDS tree.

2. Create the printer object in the NDS tree. Specify the hardware communication parameters and assign a print queue for the printer to service.

3. Create the print server object in the NDS tree. Assign printers to the print server using the Assignments property tab of the print server object.

Even though the printing environment is much more complex than that, the initial setup and key components boil down to those three steps. Novell is well aware of that, too, and has a method for you to set up your printing environment quickly and efficiently.

Printing Environment Quick Setup Option

Through NetWare Administrator, you can quickly set up the front end of the printing environment. This method assumes that you want to create the print server object, print queue object, and printer object all in the same container. This is fine because the objects can be moved after they are created.

To create the objects in a container, select the container by clicking on it once with the left mouse button. It will become highlighted. Then choose the Tools | Print Services Quick Setup option from the menu bar. Once selected, the Print Services Quick Setup dialog box will appear (see Figure 7-16).

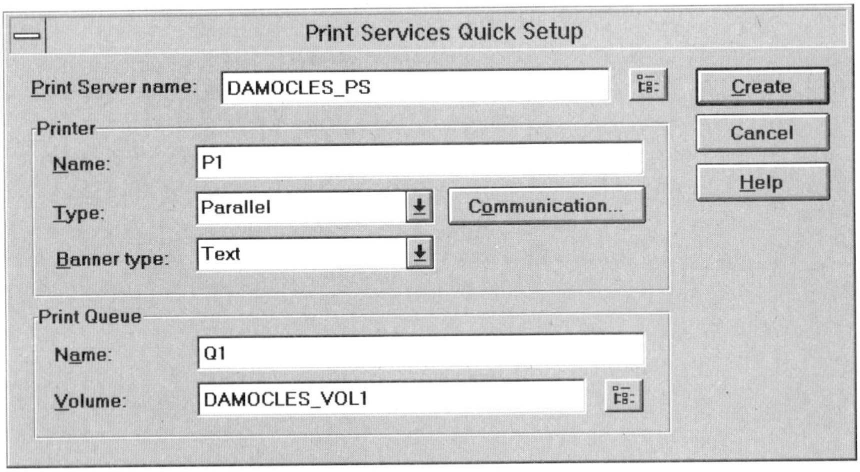

Figure 7-16: Print Services Quick Setup dialog box.

This dialog box is essentially broken up into three sections—one for each print object. Type in the name of the print server in the Print Server Name box. You can use the Select Object button to browse the NDS tree and find an existing print server to associate with the print queue and printer that will be created.

In the Printer section of the dialog box, type in the name of the printer and configure the communication parameters as discussed in the "Printer Object" section earlier in this chapter. Finally, type in the name of the print queue and associate the queue with a volume object on the network. This will be the volume on which the print queue directory will be created. When you are satisfied with the objects, click on the Create button. The NDS objects will be created in the container that was selected. At this point, the only thing that needs to be configured is the back end.

The Print Services Quick Setup option provides a simple way to quickly configure the network printing environment. However, it only works for simple printing setups. For more complex network printing environments, you will need to resort to creating and configuring the NDS print objects manually.

Configuring the Front End With PCONSOLE.EXE

People who are familiar with NetWare 3.x will remember the DOS-based utility PCONSOLE.EXE fondly. It was the only way to configure the network printing environment. Novell has included an updated version of the PCONSOLE.EXE program that can also be used to configure the front end of the network printing environment.

To start PCONSOLE.EXE, make sure the client workstation has a search drive mapped to SYS:PUBLIC on the NetWare server. Once the search drive is mapped, type **pconsole** at the DOS prompt. The program will be launched. You can perform the same functions with PCONSOLE.EXE that you can perform with NetWare Administrator. By understanding the concepts used to configure the printing environment with NetWare Administrator, you will be able to navigate the PCONSOLE.EXE environment as well.

One disadvantage PCONSOLE.EXE has is that it's based in the DOS environment. It is easy to get confused as to where you are in the NDS tree while using it. Printer objects you thought were created might not appear; if that happens, it is probably because you are in a different context in the tree. NetWare Administrator provides the advantage of graphical NDS tree display. In PCONSOLE.EXE, your current context is displayed at the top of the screen, as shown in Figure 7-17. Keep note of exactly where you are in the NDS tree when configuring the printing environment.

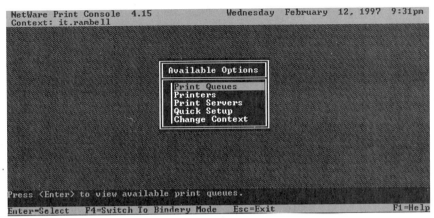

Figure 7-17: PCONSOLE main menu.

If you are more comfortable with the DOS environment, you might find PCONSOLE.EXE easier to use than NetWare Administrator. PCONSOLE.EXE is also able to provide some functions that NetWare Administrator doesn't have. These functions include the display of the IDs for the NDS objects (as we saw with the print queues and print servers). For more information on PCONSOLE.EXE, consult the Print Services manual in the NetWare 4.11 System and Services collection of the online documentation.

Configuring NetWare Printing: Back End

Configuring the front end of the network printing environment is only half of what is necessary to provide network print services. The NDS objects have been created and configured, but there is still the matter of software to be loaded on the machines on the network. As we discussed in the first section of this chapter, both the print server and printing station are run through additional software on the appropriate machines. Configuring the back end of the printing environment involves loading and configuring the software that will actually perform the printing functions.

Which software you load will depend upon your specific print service configuration, but you will generally have two pieces of software to load on network machines. They are the print server software (PSERVER.NLM) and the printing station software (NPRINTER.NLM or NPRINTER.EXE). If you have network-ready printers, the process may be a little different; however, there will be software associated with that network-ready printer that must be loaded and/or configured.

The Print Server

Assuming you are going to be using the standard print server included with NetWare 4.11 (PSERVER.NLM), the loading of the print server software is very easy. To load it, go to the file server console and type the following command:

`LOAD PSERVER <print_server_name>`

In this case, *<print_server_name>* is the name of the print server object you created in the NDS tree. If the print server object exists in the same context as the NDS file server object, you only need to specify the common name of the print server. If the print server object exists in a different context, you must type in the full distinguished name for *<print_server_name>*.

For example, the file server Damocles and the print server object DAMOCLES_PS exist in the container IT.RAMBELL. To load the print server, you would only have to type **load pserver damocles_ps**. However, if Damocles was in IT.RAMBELL and the print server object was in the ACCT.RAMBELL container, you would need to type **load pserver .damocles_ps.acct.rambell** to load the print server software.

After entering the load command at the console prompt, PSERVER.NLM will load on the file server. When you set up the front end, if you specified a password for the print server, you will be required to enter that password as PSERVER.NLM is loading. Type in the password to complete the loading of the software. When the software is has finished loading, the main menu for PSERVER.NLM will appear (see Figure 7-18).

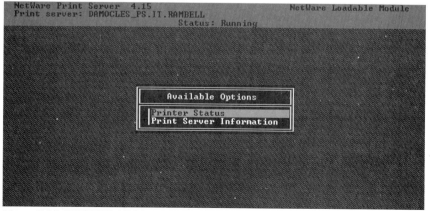

Figure 7-18: PSERVER.NLM main menu.

At the top of the screen, the print server version number, the name of the print server, and the print server's status will be displayed. In Figure 7-18, you can see that we are running version 4.15 of the print server. The print server's name is DAMOCLES_PS, and it is in the IT.RAMBELL container. In the center of the screen, you'll see the Available Options menu. Through this menu, you are able to display information concerning the print server as well as view the printer status.

To display the information about the print server, select the Print Server Information option by highlighting it and pressing Enter. The Print Server Information and Status screen will be displayed. Essentially, this window reiterates the information displayed at the top of the screen; it does, however, include some more information, including the number of printers serviced by the print server, the current queue service mode, and the current status of the print server.

Only one modification can be made to the Print Server Information and Status screen; the current status of the print server can be changed. To change it, make sure Current Status is highlighted and press Enter. The Print Server Status Options menu will appear. If you need to take down the print server, you would do it through this menu; you can unload the print server immediately or after the active print jobs are serviced. You can also opt to leave the print server running.

Tip

*The print server can also be downed by typing **unload pserver** at the server's console prompt.*

From the main menu (Figure 7-18), you can also view the status of the printers the print server is servicing. To so do, highlight the Printer Status option in the Available Options menu and press Enter. The Printer List window is displayed and shows the full distinguished name of all printers defined for the print server and their associated printer numbers. To see the information regarding a specific printer, highlight the printer and press Enter.

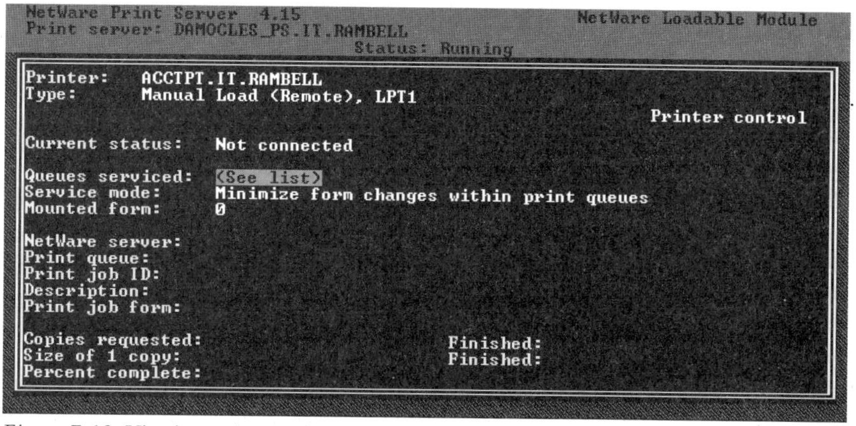

```
NetWare Print Server 4.15                        NetWare Loadable Module
Print server: DAMOCLES_PS.IT.RAMBELL
                            Status: Running
Printer:    ACCTPT.IT.RAMBELL
Type:       Manual Load (Remote), LPT1
                                                       Printer control
Current status:    Not connected

Queues serviced:   <See list>
Service mode:      Minimize form changes within print queues
Mounted form:      0

NetWare server:
Print queue:
Print job ID:
Description:
Print job form:

Copies requested:                    Finished:
Size of 1 copy:                      Finished:
Percent complete:
```

Figure 7-19: Viewing printer status through PSERVER.NLM.

In Figure 7-19, we can see the printer status for the ACCTPT printer, which exists in the ACCT.RAMBELL container. The printer type is also displayed next to the Type field near the top of the screen. The current status of the printer is also displayed. This is where you can determine whether or not the printer has connected properly to the print server. For printers that are ready, Waiting for Job will be displayed in the Current Status field. There are two important items that can be modified using the printer status screen: Printer Control and Queues Serviced.

Printer Control

The Printer Control option in the upper right portion of the printer status screen (Figure 7-19) can be used to control the printer. Select the Printer Control option by using the arrow keys to highlight it. Press Enter to reach the control option. From this menu, you can do the following things:

- **Abort the current print job on the printer.**
- **Pause the printer.**
- **Start the printer.** You can restart a printer after it has been stopped using the Start Printer command. The print server will resume distributing print jobs to the selected printer.
- **Stop the printer.** You can prevent a printer from printing any print jobs by using this option. The print server will just not send any more print information to the printer until it is started again.

These functions can also be accomplished by using the Printer Status tab of the NDS printer object. To choose one of these options, highlight the desired option and press Enter.

Queues Serviced

To see the list of queues serviced by the print server, highlight the (See List) option next to the Queues Serviced heading. Press the Enter key. The current list of queues serviced by the print server are displayed in the Print Queues Serviced by Printer window along with the print queue priority. You can add queues to be serviced by pressing the Insert key. The print server will prompt you for a context to begin searching for queue objects.

Browse the NDS tree to find the queue you want serviced by the print server and select it. You will then be asked to enter the priority of the print queue. Type in a number from 1 to 10, and the print queue is added to the list of queues serviced by the print server. This method can only be used to add existing queues in the NDS tree to the print server. It cannot create print queue objects in the NDS tree.

When you are finished with the printer status screen, press Escape twice to return to the print server main menu. There are cases where the print server console will provide more accurate information concerning the status of printers than NetWare Administrator or PCONSOLE.EXE will. If you are concerned about the status of a printer, it is best to check with the print server console.

Printing Station Software

Printers that are physically connected to network machines need the assistance of a software program to allow them to become network printers. As we discussed earlier in this chapter, these printers can be connected either to a client workstation or file server. A specific software program will be required to communicate with the print server depending upon which operating system the machine with the local printer is running. Once the printing station software is loaded and the communication is established with the print server, the network printing environment is completely configured.

NPRINTER.NLM

If the printer is attached to a NetWare file server, the NPRINTER.NLM program must be loaded to facilitate communication between the printing station and the print server. It must be loaded even if the printing station and print server are the same machine! Thus file server A, which will be the print server and has a printer locally attached, must run both PSERVER.NLM and NPRINTER.NLM.

In the event the network printer is physically attached to the file server that will be running PSERVER.NLM, you do not need to worry about manually loading NPRINTER.NLM. When the printer object was configured through NDS, the printer should have been specified as Local to Print Server (Auto Load). When PSERVER.NLM is loaded on a file server with printers directly attached, NPRINTER.NLM will automatically load and connect to the attached printers. To verify NPRINTER.NLM has loaded, type **modules** at the server console prompt. This will display a list of all NLMs loaded on the file server. NPRINTER.NLM should appear in this list after PSERVER.NLM is loaded.

If the network printer is physically connected to a file server that is not running PSERVER.NLM, the printer should have been specified as a Remote from Print Server (Manual Load) connection type. NPRINTER.NLM needs to be loaded manually. To do so, go to the console of the file server that has the printer connected. Type the following command:

```
LOAD NPRINTER <print_server_name> <printer_number>
```

Here, *<print_server_name>* is the name of the print server as defined by the object in the NDS tree. The *<printer_number>* is the number the print server associates with that particular printer. This number can be displayed through the Assignments property tab of the print server object. Just as when you load PSERVER.NLM, the *<print_server_name>* can be just the common name if the print server object and the file server object exist in the same context. If they exist in different contexts, the full distinguished name of the print server must be specified.

Once NPRINTER.NLM is loaded, the print server printer status screen should display the comment Waiting for Job. If it doesn't, the print server and the printing station software are not communicating properly or there is something wrong with the printer itself (it might not be connected or ready for a print job). If the front end of the printing environment is not configured properly and you try to load NPRINTER.NLM, it will return an error message. This will indicate you need to review the front end configuration.

NPRINTER.EXE

When a printer is connected to a client workstation and that workstation is running the DOS or OS/2 operating system, you need to load NPRINTER.EXE on the workstation to make the printer a network printer. NPRINTER.EXE works on the workstation just like NPRINTER.NLM does on the server. It provides the printing station software that will allow the print server to communicate with the workstation and transmit print jobs to the local printer.

To load NPRINTER.EXE on the workstation, type the following at the command prompt:

```
NPRINTER <print_server_name> <printer_number>
```

Just like with NPRINTER.NLM, the *<print_server_name>* is the name of the print server running on the NetWare 4.11 file server. If the print server object and the local printer exist in the same context, only the common name needs to be substituted for *<print_server_name>*. If the printer exists in a different context from the print server, you must specify the full distinguished name of the print server. The *<printer_number>* is the number assigned to that particular printer through the Assignments property tab of the print server object.

Workstations have multiple ports to which printers can be attached, and there will be machines with more than one local printer. In these cases, a copy of NPRINTER.EXE must be loaded for each individual printer. For example, a workstation with three network printers attached must have NPRINTER.EXE loaded three times, each time with a different *<printer_number>*. This will tell the print server which printer NPRINTER.EXE is servicing.

In addition to the print server name and printer number, there are some other options that can be used on the command line in conjunction with NPRINTER.EXE. These options would be specified after the *<printer_number>* on the command line. Table 7-1 summarizes the command line options for NPRINTER.EXE.

Option	Description	Example
/b=<3-60>	Specifies memory buffer size from 3K to 60K. Default is 3K.	nprinter *<printer_name>* /b=30
/s	Displays the status of all printing station software.	nprinter *<printer_name>* /s
/t=<1-9>	Controls the strobe signal duration from 1 to 9. A higher number gives more priority to the workstation's foreground tasks.	nprinter *<printer_name>* /t=5
/u	Unloads the most recently loaded NPRINTER.EXE from the workstation memory.	nprinter /u
/ver	Displays version information about the current version of NPRINTER.EXE.	nprinter /ver
/? or /h	Shows on-line help.	nprinter /?

Table 7-1: NPRINTER.EXE options.

NPRINTER.EXE can also be loaded by specifying the NDS printer object name on the command line instead of specifying the print server name and printer number. If the printer exists in the workstation's current context, just type the following to load the .HPIII314_ANY.IT.RAMBELL printer:

```
NPRINTER HPIII314_ANY
```

If the printer object exists outside of the current context, the full distinguished name of the printer object must be specified to load NPRINTER.EXE. NPRINTER.EXE will return an error message if it is not able to load successfully.

By default, NPRINTER.EXE is in the SYS:PUBLIC directory. Thus, a user must be logged in to the network to use NPRINTER.EXE, and a search drive must be mapped to SYS:PUBLIC. This method can be prohibitive. What if the user who uses the workstation is out sick? What if there is no one to log in to the network so that NPRINTER.EXE can run? Fortunately, NPRINTER.EXE can be run locally without logging in to the network. This means the workstation only needs to be turned on and NPRINTER.EXE loaded to use network printing on that workstation.

Running NPRINTER.EXE From a Local Workstation   NPRINTER.EXE relies on some supporting files when it is loaded. These files must be copied to the local drive and placed in the directory that contains NPRINTER.EXE on the local workstation. To see the list of supporting files necessary for your particular version of NPRINTER.EXE, type the following at the command prompt:

```
NPRINTER.EXE /VER
```

This will cause NPRINTER to display the supporting files you need to copy to the local workstation. For example, NPRINTER.EXE version 4.15 needs the files listed in Table 7-2. Copy these files along with NPRINTER.EXE into a directory on the local workstation to run it locally.

File Required	Version Number
NPRINTER.MSG	4.10
NPRINTER.HEP	4.10 (for context-sensitive help only)
SCHEMA.XLT	4.11
NWDSBRWS.MSG	4.13
TEXTUTIL.MSG	4.05
TEXTUTIL.HEP	4.02
TEXTUTIL.IDX	(no version specified)
???_RUN.OVL	(e.g., IBM_RUN.OVL)

Table 7-2: Files required for NPRINTER.EXE version 4.15.

Once the files are copied to the local workstation, NPRINTER.EXE can be run while the workstation is *not* logged in to the network. This is the best way to run NPRINTER.EXE because the workstation does not have to be attended by a user for network printing services.

If you are running Windows on this machine in conjunction with NPRINTER.EXE, there may be some steps you need to take to ensure the stability of the workstation. First, NPRINTER.EXE must be loaded before Windows is started. It is not recommended that NPRINTER.EXE be started from a DOS box inside Windows. Second, when the NDS printer object is created, the printer should be set to polled mode under the communication parameters.

If you need to provide a specific interrupt for the printer (the printer is not in polled mode), you will need to make some modifications to the SYSTEM.INI file using any ASCII text editor. Under the [386Enh] section of the SYSTEM.INI file, add the following lines:

```
LPT1AutoAssign=0
LPT1irq=-1
```

If your printer happens to be connected to a different port than LPT1, replace that port in the lines with the correct port (LPT2, COM1, COM2, and so on).

Auto-Loading NPRINTER.EXE at the Workstation   NPRINTER.EXE can be configured to load automatically when the workstation is started. To do so, just add the command you would normally type at the command prompt to a batch file. The **nprinter** *<printer_name>* command should be added to either AUTOEXEC.BAT or STARTNET.BAT using an ASCII text editor like EDIT.COM.

In either case, the Novell client workstation software must be loaded before NPRINTER.EXE can successfully load. Because NPRINTER.EXE must communicate with the print server via the network, the IPX/SPX protocol stack must be loaded on the workstation before the NPRINTER.EXE command is executed. A sample client workstation STARTNET.BAT file with NPRINTER.EXE loading might look like the following:

```
SET NWLANGUAGE=ENGLISH
C:\NWCLIENT\LSL.COM
C:\NWCLIENT\NE2000.COM
C:\NWCLIENT\IPXODI.COM
C:\NWCLIENT\VLM.EXE
C:\NWCLIENT\NPRINTER.EXE .HPII.ACCT.RAMBELL
```

For more information about the DOS/Windows workstation client, refer to Chapter 15.

NetWare 4.11 Printing & Windows 95

Windows 95 presents a new dilemma in terms of network printing with NetWare. The printing station software used by NetWare (NPRINTER.NLM and NPRINTER.EXE) relies upon the Novell standard IPX/SPX protocol stack. If Windows 95 is configured with the Microsoft network shell and Microsoft's IPX/SPX-compatible protocol, printers locally attached to the workstation cannot be used as network printers. This is because NPRINTER.EXE will not be able to communicate with the print server. The protocol stacks in this case are incompatible.

However, with the advent of NetWare Client32 for Windows 95, there is now a network printing solution for Windows 95 clients. The printing station software for Windows 95 is NPTWIN95.EXE. It is located in the SYS:PUBLIC\WIN95 directory of your server where the Windows 95 client software is installed.

Using NPTWIN95.EXE

To start the software, double-click on the NPTWIN95.EXE file in the Windows Explorer. The first time NPRINTER Manager for Windows 95 is started on the local workstation, the Add Network Printer dialog box is displayed. This screen prompts you to define the NDS-based or Bindery-based printer attached to the Windows 95 workstation. Select the desired type of printer and click on the button to the right of the NDS or Bindery selection, as shown in Figure 7-20.

This button is the familiar Select Object button. Use it either to browse the NDS tree (for the NDS-based printer option) or to specify the print server and printer (for the Bindery-based printer option). Once the printer has been selected, NPRINTER Manager will display the information in the Add Network Printer dialog box.

Before clicking OK, notice the Activate Printer When NPRINTER Manager Loads check box. This box determines whether or not your printer definition will load the next time NPRINTER Manager is started. If this option is not checked, the printing station software will only be loaded for this session of Windows 95. If the machine is rebooted, the local printer will not be a network printer. When this box is checked, the printing station software is loaded when NPRINTER Manager is started. Click OK after verifying the status of this box.

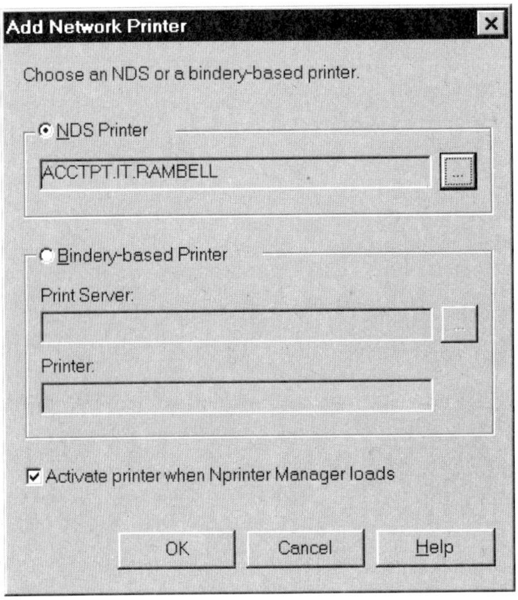

Figure 7-20: Adding a new printer in NPRINTER Manager.

Once the printer has been created, the printer status will appear in the main window of NPRINTER Manager. The name of the printer and the print server are specified along with the printer number, the printer port, and the statuses of both the printing station software and the printer itself. Once the printing station software has been loaded, minimize the NPRINTER Manager window. NPRINTER Manager can be closed once the printing station software is loaded; however, you will not get the benefit of monitoring the status of the software or printer.

It may be useful to display the properties of the printer. To do so, choose Printers I Properties from the menu bar in NPRINTER Manager. The Properties dialog box for the specified printer will appear (Figure 7-21). This dialog box displays the port, interrupt, and memory buffer of the network printer. The properties cannot be modified from this screen; they must be modified at the printer object using NetWare Administrator. The one property that can be modified on this screen is the Activate Printer When NPRINTER Manager Loads check box.

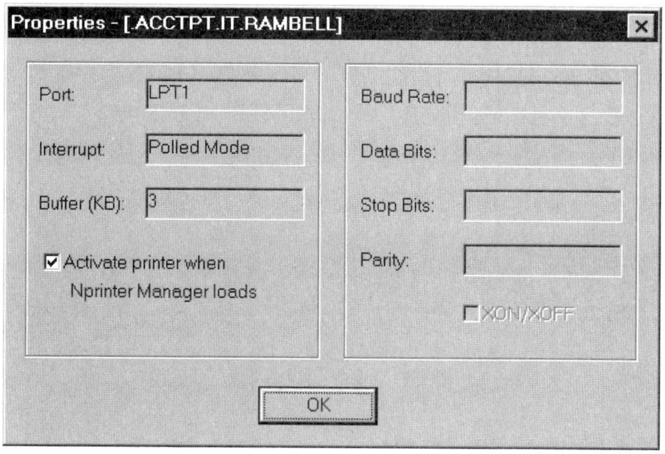

Figure 7-21: Displaying printer properties in NPTWIN95.EXE.

To add more printers to the workstation network printing configuration, choose Printers | Add from the menu bar in NPRINTER Manager. To remove the printing station software for a printer and temporarily down the network printer, choose Printers | Remove from the menu bar for the printer specified. To temporarily down all network printers attached to the workstation, choose Printers | Remove All from the menu bar. To return the machine to its original state as if NPTWIN95.EXE had never run, choose Printers | Clear from the menu bar. All printer definitions for the workstation will be removed.

Running NPTWIN95.EXE at Startup

Just like NPRINTER.EXE, you must manually load the printing station software every time the machine is started. If you do not, the printer will remain a local printer until NPTWIN95.EXE is run. However, NPTWIN95.EXE can be configured so that it runs every time the workstation is started.

With a DOS/Windows machine, there are a specific set of batch files that are executed whenever the machine boots. Windows 95 has a similar feature. There is a program folder called Startup that acts as this "batch file." All programs or program shortcuts stored in this program folder are executed when Windows 95 starts.

Use the Task Bar Manager in Windows 95 to create a shortcut in the Startup program folder that points to NPTWIN95.EXE in the SYS:PUBLIC\WIN95 directory of your NetWare 4.11 server. When this shortcut is created, NPRINTER Manager will load whenever Windows 95 is started.

Running NPTWIN95.EXE Locally

NPTWIN95.EXE can also be run locally just as NPRINTER.EXE can, with the same benefits. To do this, you must create a directory on the hard drive of the local machine for NPTWIN95.EXE and all of its supporting files. For example, you might create a directory off of the root called NPRINTER to which you would copy the following files:

- NPTWIN95.EXE
- NPTWIN95.DLL
- NPTR95.NLM
- NPTDRV95.NLM
- NPTDRV95.MSG
- NRDDLL95.DLL
- NWADLG95.DLL
- NWADMR95.DLL
- NWCOMN95.DLL
- BIDS45F.DLL
- CW3215.DLL
- OWL252F.DLL

If you want to run NPTWIN95.EXE locally and at system startup, make sure the shortcut for NPRINTER Manager in the Startup program group points to this new directory created on your local machine. Running it locally will allow network printing services access to the Windows 95 workstation when it doesn't have a user authenticated to the network.

Using Print Services at the Workstation

To this point, we have merely discussed the process involved with setting up the network printing environment. Now that the setup has been completed, it is time to configure all of the client workstations to use network printing. Setting up the network printing clients is not nearly as complicated as setting up the actual printing environment. Most client workstations will be correctly configured once the CAPTURE.EXE command is executed.

Looking back on our discussion of the network printing method, we saw the print job generated on the user's workstation. Normally, the print data is created by the printer driver on the workstation and directly sent out a physical port on the back of the machine such as LPT1 or LPT2. This is because the applications creating the print job are not network aware. To facilitate network printing for these applications, the job cannot go to these physical ports; the job needs to be redirected to the network. It is the CAPTURE.EXE program that performs this function.

Using CAPTURE.EXE

When CAPTURE.EXE is used at the workstation, it sets flags within the NetWare DOS Requester, the client shell. These flags tell the network shell to redirect any data sent to a specific parallel port out to the network where it can be processed correctly. Thus, CAPTURE.EXE is not a Terminate and Stay Resident (TSR) program; it is utilizing the programs that have already been loaded to provide network services for the client workstation.

Tip

CAPTURE.EXE cannot be used to redirect print jobs sent to a serial port. Only parallel ports can be redirected.

The CAPTURE.EXE program is in the SYS:PUBLIC directory by default. To run it, make sure there is a search drive mapped to SYS:PUBLIC for the workstation. At the command prompt, type the following:

```
CAPTURE [P=<printer_name>/Q=<queue_name>] [L=n] [options]
```

For CAPTURE.EXE, you must specify either the name of the printer or the name of the queue to which the data is being sent and the parallel port number that is being redirected. These options are required to successfully redirect data to the network printing environment. For example, to redirect data sent to LPT1 to the print queue ACCTQ, you would type the following:

```
CAPTURE Q=ACCTQ L=1
```

All data on that workstation sent to LPT1 would be sent to the ACCTQ print queue instead. The name of the printer can also be specified directly in the CAPTURE.EXE command. This is a feature that was not supported in NetWare 3.x. To redirect data sent to LPT2 to the printer ACCTPT, type the following:

```
CAPTURE P=ACCTPT L=2
```

Just as they are when you are loading the print server and printing station software, the names of the print queue and printer to which you are redirecting data are sensitive to your current context. If the print queue or printer are in your current context, only the common name of the NDS object needs to be specified in the CAPTURE.EXE command; however, if the print queue or printer object exists in a different context, the full distinguished name must be used. In the previous example, suppose this printer exists in the .ACCT.RAMBELL context, but your current context is .IT.RAMBELL. You would need to type the following to redirect the data to LPT2:

```
CAPTURE P=.ACCTPT.ACCT.RAMBELL L=2
```

Default Queue Option

Remember the Default Queue option when we made the queue assignments in the section "Printer Object"? This is where that piece of information has significance. When the printer object is used with CAPTURE.EXE, it does not know which queue it needs to send the data to. The printer object's default queue ensures the data is delivered to the appropriate print queue on the network.

Besides the mandatory options of printer/queue and redirected port for CAPTURE.EXE, there are other options that can be used to customize the printing environment for the workstation user. These commands are summarized in Table 7-3. Some options will be used more often than others. We will examine those more closely.

Option	Abbreviation	Description
All	ALL	Used with the End Capture option to end the redirection of all LPT ports. Can also be used with the /? option to display all online help screens.
Autoendcap	AU	Closes the captured data and sends it to the printer when the application is exited. Enabled by default.
Banner	B=<text>	Creates a customized banner to appear on the lower half of the banner page.

Cancel	CA	Must be used with the End Capture option; it ends the capturing of the data to the parallel ports and discards data being captured.
Copies	C=<1-65,000>	Sets number of copies to be printed up to 65,000 copies. Default is one copy.
Create	CR=<filepath>	Sends print data to a file specified by <filepath> instead of to a printer. Can only be used with Timeout, Autoendcap, or No Autoendcap options.
Details	D	Displays print job parameters. Also shows print job configuration used.
End Capture	EC	Ends the capturing of data to an LPT port.
Form	F=<name> or F=<number>	Specifies the form the printer will use. Form must be defined using NetWare Administrator.
Form Feed	FF	Sends form feed signal to printer after job is completed.
Help	/? or /H	Displays online help.
Hold	HOLD	Holds the print job when it gets to the print queue. Hold can be released using NetWare Administrator.
Job Configuration	J=<name>	Specifies print job configuration.
Keep	K	Forces NetWare server to keep all data received from the workstation.
LPT	L=<1-9>	Specifies parallel port to be redirected. LPTn can also be used.
Name	NAM=<text>	Specifies the name that will appear on the banner page. The login name is used by default.
No Autoendcap	NA	Captured data is not closed when application is exited. Allows more data to be added to the print job. The Timeout option will close the captured data after a specific period of time.
No Banner	NB	When used, banner page is not printed.
No Form Feed	NFF	When used, form feed signal is not sent to the printer after the print job.

➡

Option	Abbreviation	Description
No Notify	NNOTI	User is not notified when print job is finished. The No Notify option is the default for CAPTURE.EXE.
No Tabs	NT	Enables "byte stream" mode for printing. This ensures tabs in your print data arrive unchanged; they are not converted to spaces. No Tabs is the default setting.
Notify	NOTI	Print job owner receives a notification message when print job is finished.
Printer	P=*<printer_name>*	Redirects data to a specific NDS printer object. Cannot be used with the Qucuc option.
Queue	Q=*<queue_name>*	Redirects data to a specific NDS queue object. Cannot be used with the Printer option.
Server	S=*<server_name>*	Specifies the server name on which the bindery queue exists. This option is not used for Directory Services print queues.
Show	SH	Displays the current status of port capturing. Not used with other options.
Tabs	T=*<1-18>*	Determines the number of spaces to be substituted for each tab encountered in the print data. Default value is 8 spaces per tab. Range is from 1 to 18 spaces.
Timeout	TI=*<0-1000>*	Determines the number of seconds to wait before closing the print job after the last data is received. Value can be between 0 (zero) and 1000 seconds. Default is 0 (zero) seconds.
Version	/VER	Shows version information about CAPTURE.EXE. Also displays all supporting files that must be present to run the utility.

Table 7-3: CAPTURE.EXE options.

Banner

When using the Banner option with CAPTURE.EXE, you are able to provide a message that will appear on the lower half of the banner page. The message can be up to 12 characters in length, and text with spaces must be enclosed in quotation marks. For example, to print "John's job" on all banner pages, type the following at the DOS command prompt:

```
CAPTURE Q=ACCTQ L=1 B="John's job"
```

End Capture

This option is used to end the capturing of data to a parallel port. If this option is used in conjunction with the L=n option, the capture is ended on that specific port. When no port is specified, this command will stop redirecting data for LPT1. To end capturing on all ports, use the ALL parameter at the command prompt.

```
CAPTURE EC ALL
```

When this option is used with the Cancel option, the capturing of data to the parallel ports will be stopped and data that was being captured will be thrown out.

Form Feed

This option will enable form feed after the print job has been completed. This means the next print job will start on a new page; however, most applications today already send the form feed command after a print option. Using this command with an application that already sends a form feed will cause the printer to print a blank page. If you are using Windows, disable the form feed on a port by using the following command at the DOS prompt:

```
CAPTURE Q=ACCTQ L=1 NFF
```

Keep

When the Keep option is specified, the NetWare server stores the data it receives from the workstation. This is to prevent data loss if for some reason the workstation loses its connection with the file server. When the connection drops, the data already received is sent to the print queue for printing. When this option is not enabled and the connection to the file server is lost, the print data already received is discarded. To keep the data, type the following command at the DOS command prompt:

```
CAPTURE Q=ACCTQ L=1 K
```

Notify

To give the print job owner notification that the job has been printed, use the Notify option. Once the printer has finished with the job, the owner of the job is sent a message. Do not confuse this option with the Notification property tab of the printer object. The notify option associated with CAPTURE.EXE does *not* inform the print job owner about printer problems. To enable notification, use the following command at the command prompt:

```
CAPTURE Q=ACCTQ L=1 NOTI
```

Show

This option is not used with any other option. It displays the current status of all parallel ports. It not only specifies to which queue or printer the port is being redirected, it also shows option information such as tabs, notifications, and banners. To display this information, type the following command at the DOS prompt:

```
CAPTURE SH
```

CAPTURE.EXE will then display information that might look like the following:

```
LPT1 Capturing data to print queue\ACCTQ.IT.RAMBELL

Notify:          Disabled
Automatic End:   Enabled
Timeout Count:   15 seconds
Name:            (None)
Form Feed:       Disabled
Banner:          (None)
Keep:            Disabled
Copies:          1
Tabs:            No conversion
Form:            Unknown
User hold:       Disabled

LPT2 Capturing is not currently active.

LPT3 Capturing is not currently active.
```

Even though CAPTURE.EXE is only a DOS utility, it is the most powerful NetWare tool for configuring the workstation client printing environment. Use this command in login scripts to automatically redirect print data to the network printing environment. To include this command in a login script, simply precede the capture statement by a pound sign (#) and type the command just as if you were at a DOS prompt. A login script command might look like the following:

```
#CAPTURE L=1 Q=ACCTQ NFF NB TI=15
```

The pound sign tells the login script environment that CAPTURE.EXE is an external command. Without the pound sign, the command won't be processed properly in the login script. Not only does the login script command capture print data for DOS workstations, it will do the same thing for OS/2, Windows 95, and Windows NT workstations that can process the NetWare 4.11 login scripts.

CAPTURE.EXE can also be executed from a DOS box on Windows 3.x, Windows 95, and Windows NT. This statement will make a change to the printing environment that will last even after the DOS box has been closed. Just verify the applications are printing to the parallel port that was redirected. For example, if the first parallel port was redirected using CAPTURE.EXE, make sure applications are printing to LPT1.

Printing to Multiple Network Printers

One of the advantages to using network printing is the ability to print to any printer on the network. Through the capture statement, a user may send data to one printer down the hall. He or she may then execute another capture statement and print a document halfway around the world! The possibilities are endless.

Many users need to print to multiple network printers often. Half of the documents a user prints might be needed in the accounting department while the other half might be used by the manufacturing department. Instead of the user having to issue many capture commands to route the print job to the right place, a user may print to multiple network printers through the use of the other local ports available through CAPTURE.EXE.

CAPTURE.EXE supports up to nine logical parallel ports. Even though a machine may only have a limited number of physical ports on the back, CAPTURE.EXE is able to support more because the data never actually reaches the physical parallel port. All of the print data is redirected to the network. Thus, a network printer in accounting could be specified as LPT1, and another network printer in manufacturing could be specified as LPT2. When the user wants to send the data to the accounting printer, he or she would just direct the data toward LPT1; CAPTURE.EXE takes care of the rest.

For each port that is redirected, a separate CAPTURE.EXE statement is required (whether through the login script or at the command prompt). Thus, redirecting three local ports would require three separate CAPTURE.EXE statements. This makes network printing efficient because time is not wasted issuing commands that toggle network printers back and forth on one port.

Printing Station Software & CAPTURE.EXE

When a workstation has printing station software loaded, CAPTURE.EXE plays a special role in the network printing environment. As we know, CAPTURE.EXE takes data that is sent to a physical port on the back of the machine and redirects it to the network where it is processed by the network printing environment. However, workstations with network printers attached have a physical connection out the back of the machine. Why not print directly to the parallel port for print jobs on that workstation?

Because the printer is a network printer, do not consider it locally attached. Jobs should not be sent to the printer directly by the user of that workstation. A local print driver will not understand that the printer is acting as a network printer. If NPRINTER.EXE is processing a print job from the network and transmitting the data to the printer at the same time the local print driver sends print data out the parallel port, the two print jobs will collide. The print data that results will be useless, and two print jobs will have been ruined.

The user of the workstation must have his or her print data redirected to the network to properly use the printer that is attached locally. Even though this may seem like a roundabout solution for this user (it has to go to the network and back just to print), it is required to ensure the integrity of all print data that is sent to that network printer. When the local port to which the printer is attached is redirected to the network, NPRINTER.EXE has complete control over the port and is not competing with any local print drivers for the printer's attention. CAPTURE.EXE for the user at the printer workstation is a must!

Tip

Make sure the user at a workstation with a network printer has had CAPTURE.EXE executed for the port to which the printer is attached. It will ensure that the printing station software is not competing for control of the parallel port.

Other Print Services

Besides supporting the standard NetWare printing environment as discussed in this chapter, NetWare 4.11 is also able to support printing in other environments. Two popular environments for which you might need to configure NetWare 4.11 are AppleTalk networks and TCP/IP networks. Through separate products that come packaged with IntranetWare, you can install and configure the software necessary to provide printing services to clients on different types of networks.

AppleTalk Print Services

For networks that have multiple workstation client platforms, printing can become complex. It is quite common to have both PCs and Macintosh computers connected to your network. Unfortunately, Macintosh computers use a network protocol to communicate with the NetWare file server that is different from the one PCs use. The NetWare server speaks IPX, while the Macintosh native network protocol is AppleTalk.

The printers Macintosh computers use also communicate with the network using the AppleTalk network protocol. This means that PCs will be unable to use these printers on the network because they cannot support the AppleTalk protocol. Likewise, Macintosh computers cannot use PC printers connected to the NetWare environment because they do not speak IPX. However, there may be times when you want all users on the network to share an Apple printer or a PC printer. NetWare 4.11 will allow you to accomplish this.

By installing a package called NetWare for Macintosh, you are able to make your NetWare 4.11 server compatible with an AppleTalk network. Thus, PCs and Macs can communicate with one another via the NetWare server. They can also share their printing environments. Macintosh machines can use the NetWare printing environment to print to PC printers. PCs can print to Apple printers by placing their print jobs in a print queue that is serviced by an Apple printer.

To install NetWare for Macintosh, use the INSTALL.NLM utility. For more information on using INSTALL.NLM, refer to Chapter 18. In INSTALL.NLM, choose Product Options from the Installation Options menu. The Other Installation Actions menu will appear. From the Other Installation Items/Products list at the top of this screen, select Install NetWare for Macintosh.

You will be asked to provide the path to the installation files for this product. NetWare for Macintosh is located on the same CD-ROM from which you installed NetWare 4.11. Specify the path for the files and install the product following the steps displayed in INSTALL.NLM. For more information concerning the installation and configuration of NetWare for Macintosh, refer to the NetWare for Macintosh File and Print Services manual in the NetWare 4.11 System and Services collection of the online documentation.

Tip

Using the NetWare Client for MacOS will allow the Macintosh to take advantage of NetWare's native printing environment. Because this client is NDS aware and uses the IPX/SPX protocol for network communications, you will not need to set up a special printing environment for the Macintosh workstations on your network if you use it. A separate printing environment is only required if you are using the AppleTalk protocol to connect to the NetWare environment.

Using AppleTalk Print Services (ATPS)

AppleTalk Print Services (ATPS) is a NetWare Loadable Module that can be loaded on the NetWare server; it will allow all network clients to print to Apple printers on the network using the AppleTalk protocol. The configuration is displayed in Figure 7-22. By using ATPS.NLM, you bypass the NetWare front-end printing environment. Printing objects are not created and configured in the NDS tree; all configuration for the printing environment is done through an NLM called ATPSCON.NLM.

ATPS.NLM is a print server unto itself. It replaces the PSERVER.NLM print server necessary for the classic NetWare printing environment. However, ATPS.NLM is limited to printing only to printers connected to an AppleTalk network. The ATPS.NLM back end cannot print to printers on a non-AppleTalk network.

ATPS.NLM & PSERVER.NLM

For Macintosh clients that need to print to printers connected to non-AppleTalk segments, something else is needed. PSERVER.NLM provides the services necessary for Macintosh computers to print to the NetWare 4.11 printing environment. Figure 7-23 shows this configuration.

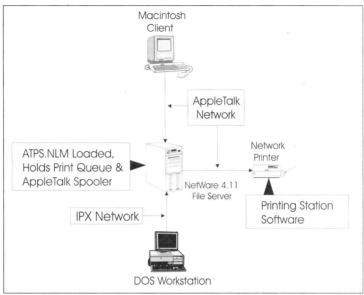

Figure 7-22: Using AppleTalk Print Services.

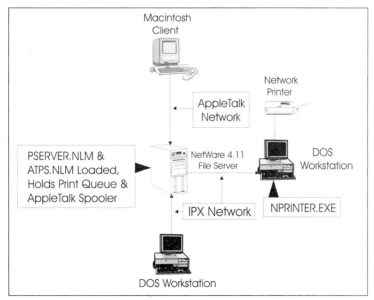

Figure 7-23: Using ATPS.NLM and PSERVER.NLM.

The ATPS.NLM front end will allow the Macintosh computer to spool a job to the AppleTalk spooler. However, since ATPS.NLM cannot communicate with the printer itself, it relies upon PSERVER.NLM to do so. Once the print job is in the spooler, PSERVER.NLM will service the job and print it to the printer that services that particular print queue.

To configure this type of printing, you must have the printing environment configured just as if you were setting it up for non-Macintosh clients. You must use NetWare Administrator or PCONSOLE.EXE to create the printing objects in the NDS tree and configure them correctly. The only difference is that ATPS.NLM must be loaded for the Macintosh client to be able to spool the job. Using ATPSCON.NLM, you can configure the AppleTalk spooler so that it is affiliated with a NetWare print queue. When a job is sent to the spooler, it will be placed in the NetWare print queue and serviced by PSERVER.NLM just like any other job.

Tip

Macintosh computers using AppleTalk printing can only print to PostScript- and QuickDraw-type printers. They cannot print to Printer Control Language (PCL) printers using ATPS or PSERVER.

Using ATPS.NLM, PSERVER.NLM & ATXRP.NLM

The ATPS.NLM can be completely replaced by PSERVER.NLM and ATXRP.NLM to allow network clients to print to printers connected to AppleTalk network segments. This is the best configuration if you have both AppleTalk and non-AppleTalk printers in your network printing environment. It also supports all of the print management features of PSERVER.NLM. Thus, all print objects are created, configured, and maintained in the NDS tree. The entire printing environment (AppleTalk and non-AppleTalk) can be managed using the native printing services for NetWare 4.11.

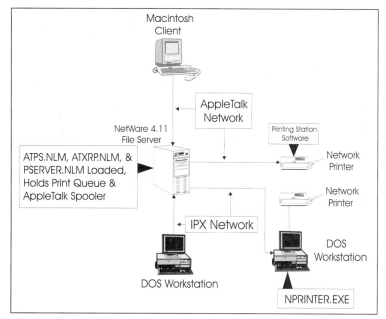

Figure 7-24: Providing AppleTalk printing services with PSERVER.NLM and ATXRP.NLM.

In Figure 7-24, we see that ATXRP.NLM provides the communication necessary for the NetWare print server to communicate with the AppleTalk printers on the network. ATXRP stands for AppleTalk Extended Remote Printer. It acts as the printing station software that allows the print server to connect the print queue and the printer together. Using the AppleTalk Printer Access Protocol (PAP), ATXRP.NLM sends the print job to the printer after it is processed by PSERVER.NLM.

ATPS.NLM still plays a key role here. For Macintosh clients to be able to print to this environment, they still must print to an AppleTalk print spooler. Using ATPSCON.NLM, you can configure a print spooler that is associated with a NetWare print queue. When a print job is sent to the spooler, the job is deposited in the print queue and serviced by PSERVER.NLM like any other print job.

Remember, because you are using the native NetWare printing environment, you must set up the front end and back end as discussed earlier in this chapter. For an AppleTalk printer object, you must specify the printer as an AppleTalk printer in the Configuration property tab of the printer object. This is how PSERVER.NLM will know it has to load ATXRP.NLM to communicate with the AppleTalk printer.

Use the Communication button on the Configuration property tab page to bring up the AppleTalk Communication dialog box. Specify the name of the printer (the name by which the printer is known on the AppleTalk network), the type of printer, and the AppleTalk zone in which the printer is located. Click OK once the information has been entered. If applicable, reload the print server on the NetWare 4.11 server for the changes to take effect.

UNIX Print Services

Macintosh computers are not the only other types of computers that might need to take advantage of the NetWare printing environment. Highly diverse networks will have other types of machines connected to them, including UNIX boxes. UNIX hosts and their associated devices communicate with one another using the TCP/IP protocol. Since NetWare and its clients use the IPX protocol by default, they are not able to take advantage of UNIX printers connected to the network. Likewise, UNIX machines could not print to the NetWare printers.

Fortunately, another product, called NetWare UNIX Print Services, comes bundled with IntranetWare. However, this package not only provides print services in the UNIX environment, it also provides complete UNIX Network File System (NFS) support as well as print service support. To install NetWare UNIX Print Services, you will need to use the INSTALL.NLM utility. At the file server console prompt, type **load install** to start this NLM.

The first screen displayed by INSTALL.NLM is the Installation Options menu. Choose Product Options from this menu and press Enter. The Other Installation Actions menu will be displayed. From here, select Install a Product Not Listed. You will be prompted for the location of the files. Press F3 to specify a different path. NetWare UNIX Print Services comes on the fourth IntranetWare CD-ROM. Thus, if the CD-ROM is mounted as the NWUXPS volume on the server, to provide NetWare with the location of the files, you would type the path **NWUXPS:\NWUXPS** after pressing F3.

NetWare UNIX Print Services relies upon the TCP/IP protocol. TCP/IP must be loaded and bound on your file server to install NetWare UNIX Print Services successfully. For more information on installing and configuring protocols, refer to Chapter 18. Follow the instructions displayed on the screen to finish the installation. For more information, refer to the Installation Guide manual in the NFS20 collection of the online documentation. NetWare UNIX Print Services online documentation is provided on the same CD-ROM as the program files.

Printing From NetWare to UNIX

There might be times when a NetWare user needs to print to a UNIX printer on the network. This can be accomplished through NetWare UNIX Print Services. Using additional software loaded on the server, a NetWare user can submit a print job through the normal NetWare printing environment, and the print job will be routed to the UNIX host and serviced by the UNIX print environment.

UNIX printing relies upon a process called the Line Printer Daemon (lpd). When a person sitting at a UNIX workstation submits a print job, it is submitted to the print queue that sits on a UNIX machine. This queue is then serviced by the lpd, which processes the job and sends it to the network printer. The network printer receives the job and prints it out.

The software loaded on the NetWare server just takes the job from the NetWare print queue, interfaces with the UNIX host, and delivers the print job to the UNIX print queue. From that point it is serviced just like a regular UNIX print job. They key is the interface between the NetWare server and the UNIX host. The network printing path for a print job being routed to a UNIX environment is shown in Figure 7-25.

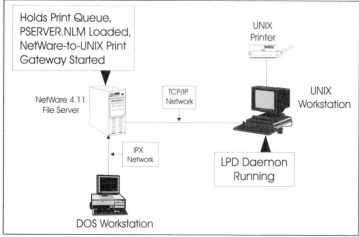

Figure 7-25: The NetWare-to-UNIX print job.

The user at the DOS/Windows workstation generates a print job and submits it to the NetWare print queue just like he or she normally would. However, in the configuration of the printing environment, this queue has been configured to be serviced by the NetWare NFS print server. This print server communicates with the NetWare-to-UNIX Print Gateway, which is responsible for establishing a connection to the UNIX host with the UNIX print queue. Once the print job is delivered to the UNIX print queue, it is serviced by the lpd on the UNIX host and sent to the UNIX printer.

The NetWare-to-UNIX Print Gateway is started and configured in NetWare using UNICON.NLM. From the Main menu in UNICON.NLM, choose Manage Services. The Manage Services menu will appear. Select Print Services from the list that appears, and the Print Administration menu is displayed. Choose Manage NetWare-to-UNIX Printing from the Print Administration menu to configure the printing environment.

The successful configuration of NetWare-to-UNIX Printing is dependent upon a few key things:

■ The NetWare server and the UNIX host must be known to one another. Each machine should have the other listed in its HOSTS file. On the NetWare server, this file is located in SYS:ETC. On most UNIX machines, TCP/IP hosts are specified in the /etc/hosts file.

■ The NetWare server must have the rights to access the UNIX host. It needs to have a login ID on the UNIX host machine to deliver the print job to the UNIX print queue. The NetWare server must also have rights to deliver the print job to the UNIX print queue. The NetWare server should have an entry in the UNIX machine's /etc/host.lpd file (or whatever file necessary to access the UNIX print queue).

■ The print server and printer object in the NDS tree must be correctly set up. The printer needs to be configured as a UNIX printer in the NDS tree. This printer object must also be configured in the Manage NetWare-to-UNIX Printing menu of UNICON.NLM

■ The NetWare-to-UNIX Print Gateway must be started on the NetWare 4.11 server. To do so, choose Start/Stop Services from the Main menu of UNICON.NLM. When the Running Services screen appears, press the Insert key. Choose NetWare-to-UNIX Print Gateway from the Available Services menu.

Printing From UNIX to NetWare

NetWare UNIX Print Services is a bidirectional package. Users on a UNIX machine can print to NetWare printers though the NetWare printing environment with the help of additional software loaded on the NetWare 4.11 server. The print job gets routed through the network to the NetWare 4.11 server and printed using the normal NetWare print server PSERVER.NLM.

When a UNIX user prints a print job, he or she executes an lpr command that places the print job in a UNIX print queue. Once in the print queue, it is serviced by an lpd that directs the print job to the UNIX printer. To print to the NetWare environment, a modification is made to the UNIX print queue that causes the lpd to redirect the print job to the NetWare server instead of the UNIX printer.

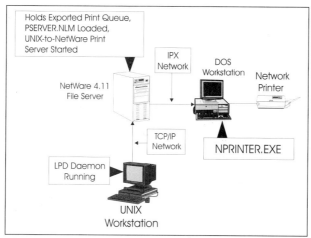

Figure 7-26: Printing to NetWare from a UNIX workstation.

In Figure 7-26, we can see the process as a print job is generated at the UNIX workstation and sent through the network to the NetWare printing environment. The queue in which the print job is placed is a special print queue that is treated differently than the normal UNIX print queues. The lpd sees the print job in the special print queue and establishes a connection with the NetWare server. The NetWare server itself is running an LPD Server, which takes the job from the UNIX lpd and submits it to the exported NetWare print queue. This print queue is then serviced by the NetWare print server just like any other print queue, and the job is printed on the NetWare printer.

The UNIX-to-NetWare Print Server is started and configured in much the same way the NetWare-to-UNIX Print Gateway is configured. From the Main menu in UNICON.NLM, choose Manage Services. The Manage Services menu will appear. Select Print Services from the list that appears, and the Print Administration menu is displayed. Choose Manage UNIX-to-NetWare Printing from the Print Administration menu to configure the printing environment.

The successful configuration of UNIX-to-NetWare Printing is dependent upon a few key things:

- The NetWare server and the UNIX host must be known to one another. Each machine should have the other listed in its HOSTS file. On the NetWare server, this file is located in SYS:ETC. On most UNIX machines, TCP/IP hosts are specified in the /etc/hosts file.

- The UNIX machine must be configured to access the print queue on the NetWare server. Most UNIX systems use a printcap file to define how a print job is handled. Often this file is named /etc/printcap on the UNIX machine.

- The NetWare print server, print queue, and printer object in the NDS tree must be correctly set up using the method discussed earlier in this chapter in the section "Configuring NetWare Printing: Front End." For UNIX-to-NetWare printing, the native NetWare printing environment is used.

- A NetWare print queue must be exported. This readies the NetWare print queue for UNIX print jobs.

- The UNIX-to-NetWare Print Server must be started on the NetWare 4.11 server. To do so, choose Start/Stop Services from the Main menu of UNICON.NLM. When the Running Services screen appears, press the Insert key. Choose UNIX-to-NetWare Print Server from the Available Services menu.

Applying Concepts: Rambell, Inc.

After he set up his file system, John Doe's users were happy because they could share files easily and efficiently. Floppy disks practically disappeared from the office! However, people still needed to be able to print across the network. John took up the task of setting up an appropriate network printing environment for his users.

There were only two printers available for people to use at Rambell, Inc. To maximize the use of these machines, John wanted to set up one printer for the people in accounting and the other for use by manufacturing group. They would be connected to DOS/Windows client workstation machines. Thus, John would have to use PSERVER.NLM on the server and NPRINTER.EXE on the workstations.

The first step was the configuration of the front end of the printing environment. Using NetWare Administrator, John created a print queue for the people in accounting called ACCTQ. Another print queue, called MANUFQ, was created for manufacturing. Both were in the .IT.RAMBELL container. Since the NDS tree has only one container, all users will be able to use these print queues. By default, a container is given rights to use the print queues created inside it.

John then created two printer objects in the .IT.RAMBELL container. They were called ACCTPT and MANUFPT and were assigned to the ACCTQ and MANUFQ print queues, respectively. John defined the printers as parallel printers set to manual load for the printing station software. They would be functioning remotely from the print server. He connected the printers to LPT1 on both machines, and set the mode to polled mode.

He created a print server called DAMOCLES_PS. The printers were associated with the print server. ACCTPT was given printer number zero while MANUFPT was assigned printer number one. He also checked the Print Layout property tab to ensure the printing environment was set up correctly. Once completed, it was time to set up the back end of the printing environment.

At the server, John loaded the print server software. The print server came up on the NetWare 4.11 file server, and it appeared ready to go. He then went to the client workstations and loaded the appropriate printing station software. John also added the NPRINTER.EXE command to the STARTNET.BAT file so it would load automatically whenever the machine booted. He copied all of the necessary files to the local hard drive so a user did not have to log in from the workstation for the network printer to be activated.

When the printing environment was completely set up, all John needed to do was to add some commands to the appropriate profile login scripts so that people's parallel ports would be redirected to the network. This allows both groups to send print jobs to the other printer on the network in the event they have reason to send a job to the other group or their printer is broken.

Moving On

John now has a comprehensive network environment set up at Rambell, Inc. His users now have both file and print services at their fingertips. Looks like he can sit back and rest awhile, right? Probably not. There is so much more to learn about IntranetWare, including an in-depth look at NetWare Directory Services. We will talk about the ins and outs of the heart of IntranetWare in Section II.

NetWare Directory Services

8

NDS Architecture

In Section I, "Out of the Box," we presented the main concepts associated with setting up file and print services on your network. Starting with the selection of the server hardware and the installation of NetWare 4.11, you embarked on a journey that will allow you to provide your users with a complete set of network services. At the center of these network services is NetWare Directory Services (NDS).

NetWare Directory Services is the glue that binds all of the different features of IntranetWare together. From file and print services to World Wide Web and FTP services, each component depends directly upon NDS to provide critical information concerning the network and its users. Without this central source of information, the integration of services would not be possible.

Section II, "NetWare Directory Services," explores the heart of the IntranetWare NOS. There are many key components to NDS that must be understood by the network administrator so it can be implemented effectively and efficiently. Concepts like NDS partitioning, replication, and time synchronization will be discussed along with all of the security features that come built into NDS.

We were introduced to NDS when we were setting up file and print services for our users. We used NDS to create our users and login scripts. NDS was essential for setting up the printing environment. We saw the relationship between NDS and the servers' file systems. But our experience with NDS is still limited; we have only scratched the surface of NDS's capabilities.

In this chapter, we will look at the previous version of Novell's NOS, NetWare 3.x, to provide a historical point of reference in terms of network design. It all started with a database called the bindery, which was effective for providing simple network services for a limited number of users; however, as networks grew and matured, they outgrew this technology.

Novell's current concept of a network involves this core technology, NDS. NDS breaks the constraints of the bindery and allows us to provide a complete set of network services to a large number of users. We will examine the NDS database, understand the concepts of schema, and see how NDS can provide backward compatibility with the old NetWare 3.x bindery.

We have already looked at the structure of NDS; it is a hierarchical tree-like structure composed of containers and leaf objects. We will dive a bit deeper into the structure of NDS and explore the properties associated with the container objects as well as reprise the leaf objects and their function in the NDS tree.

Finally, we will conclude this chapter with a discussion of how NDS promotes Novell's definition of an intranet. This new concept of network design is integrally intertwined with NDS and its features. The scalability of NDS and the products that can be installed to make use of the NDS tree make NDS critical in the implementation of an intranet.

Learning From the Past: NetWare 3.x

Novell NetWare 3.11 was released in 1989; it was the beginning of a long tenure of dominance in the NOS market. With its (at the time) state-of-the-art technology, it quickly became an industry leader. Companies and organizations that required file and print services for their users turned to NetWare as a solution for their needs. NetWare 3.11 is also called NetWare 386; a more current version was released to fix bugs and enhance features of the NOS. This version was NetWare 3.12.

As with NetWare 4.11, NetWare 3.x provided an excellent means of centralized file storage and sharing along with its network printing capabilities. When installed on an Intel-based machine and connected to a network infrastructure, user accounts could be created to provide people with access to the file server. The data on the file server was secured through a database called the bindery.

Understanding the Bindery

The *bindery* is a security implementation used to restrict a user's level of access to the data residing on a NetWare 3.x file server. When a user logs in to a NetWare 3.x server, the user's ID and password are checked against the bindery to determine if he or she is even capable of accessing the data on the server. If the ID and password match what is contained in the bindery, the user is given access to the file system. However, the level of access is also restricted through the bindery.

When a user requests data from the server or tries to access another portion of the file system, the request is sent to the bindery. The request is matched against the level of security specified for that user. If the bindery determines the user does have access to the data or area of the file system, the user will continue on as normal; however, if the user does not have the level of security required, the bindery will deny that user access.

Bindery Architecture

We know that the bindery is used for security in NetWare 3.x, but how does it work? The bindery is a set of files existing in the SYS:SYSTEM directory of the NetWare 3.x server. Together, these files make up a flat database containing information about the users and groups for a specific file server. These three files are:

- NET$OBJ.SYS
- NET$PROP.SYS
- NET$VAL.SYS

They are hidden system files that are used to store objects, properties, and values about users and groups for that file server (hence their names). Using the SYSCON utility in NetWare 3.x, the information contained in the bindery can be modified and configured for your particular environment. A new user or group can be created or deleted, a user can be added to the membership of a group, the full name of the user can be input, or station restrictions can be enforced. These tasks may sound familiar because you do the same thing in NetWare 4.11; however, how the information is stored is completely different.

When we refer to a flat database file, we mean a data structure that has a rigid definition of how the information is stored in the database. Each record contained in the database has a discrete number of fields that can be detailed. These fields, however, cannot be modified without changing the complete structure of the database.

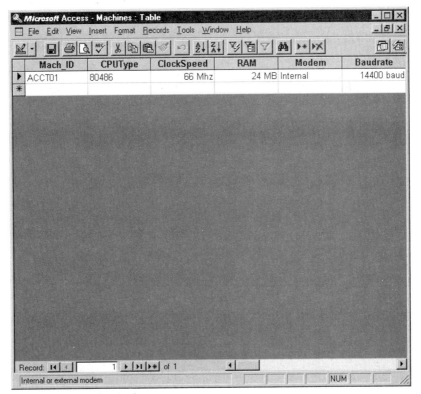

Figure 8-1: A flat-file database.

For example, Figure 8-1 shows a sample database file used to store information about computers on a network. Some of the fields (or properties) used to describe the computers are name, processor, and modem type. Notice there is only one entry available for each field in the record. What happens when a computer has two modems installed? What if there are two processors in the machine? A flat-file database cannot handle this type of information which may have multiple entries easily; you are stuck with the data field definitions that you specify.

Another thing about flat-file databases is their scalability. They work well with small quantities of data; however, as the number of records grow within the database, the file becomes very large. Searching for information through a large database takes longer and becomes more cumbersome due to the sheer volume of information that must be loaded into memory to perform the search. Finding information in a 100-record database will be much quicker than finding information in a 10,000-record database.

When NetWare 3.x stores information about the network and its users in the bindery, it stores them in this flat-file database that comprises three files. As the number of users and objects in the network grows, so does the size of the bindery. As more and more users make requests that require the services of the bindery, the performance of the network will slow because it takes more time to search through the bindery and retrieve the security information necessary for user data access.

Limitations of Bindery-Based Networks

As we have just discussed, the lack of scalability is a serious limitation of bindery-based networks. Although the bindery is capable of handling networks of 500-1,000 users, it would have a much more difficult time serving the needs of 5,000-10,000 users. Granted, not everyone is going to have that size network, but it is a serious problem for people who need a network that can accommodate a larger number of users and network resources.

Another disadvantage to the bindery-based network is the fact it is server-centric. The bindery stores only information about the users, groups, and resources pertaining to the server on which it is housed. This means only requests for security concerning the current server can be handled. No information about other servers on the network and their security is stored.

While a server-centric security scheme is acceptable for a network that has only one server, it is not acceptable for networks with more than one NetWare server. User accounts, group information, and network resources need to be defined for each server. A user that requires the service of both servers would need to have a user account on each file server and authenticate to both file servers just to be able to access the information he or she needs.

From an administrative standpoint, bindery-based networks with multiple NetWare servers pose extra overhead. When a user has an account on two separate servers, each account must be created by the network administrator. Double the work has to be done to completely set up one user to access the network resources he or she needs. Extrapolate this to 100 users, and the network administrator is performing the tasks necessary to create and maintain 200 users (100 users times two servers). Not only is it inconvenient for the user to remember two user IDs and passwords, it is inconvenient for the network manager to administer this type of setup.

Applying to the Future: NetWare 4.x

As the saying goes, "Those who don't learn from history are doomed to repeat it." Novell did learn from the limitations of its NOS and released a new one to completely rehaul the concept of a computer network. In 1993, Novell introduced NetWare 4.0, which was built upon the concept of the NDS tree. While not incredibly successful, it did begin to make people aware of NetWare 3.x's limitations. In 1995, Novell released NetWare 4.1 which fixed a lot of the problems of NetWare 4.0 and made the new version of NetWare more attractive.

NetWare 4.x still provides the file and print services that made NetWare 3.x so successful. Information should be stored in a central location to which users have access. However, this concept was extended to an all-new level. Novell took the security information that was stored in the bindery and centralized it so that there was a central repository of security information that could be used by the entire network. No longer would the authentication and security information be applicable to only one server on the network. All servers on the network could use the same information regarding users, groups, and network resources.

In 1996, Novell released NetWare 4.11 and IntranetWare to extend the services provided by the NOS. NetWare was no longer file and print services alone. It was the foundation for creating an intranet through which all users could access a complete set of network services.

The New Network Concept

As we discussed in Chapter 3, "NetWare 4.11 Concepts," NDS is viewed as a pool of network resources. File servers, users, groups, and printers belong to the network as a whole. Any user can access any resource on the network through NDS. This eliminates the need for a user to have multiple login IDs to access multiple network resources. As long as the user has the appropriate level of rights to the network, he or she can access any resource in the network as it is defined in NDS.

Think of the benefits of having this type of network scheme. When a user requires access to multiple file systems, he or she can easily access all file systems on the network that are part of the NDS tree. A user can print to any printer on the network regardless of whether it is down the hall or in another building. Group membership rights can be applied across many servers and network resources. All things incorporated into NDS can be accessed by a user through one single sign-on. It is a way to provide network services through a unified login scheme.

Also, think of it from the network administrator's point of view. No longer do multiple accounts need to be maintained for users across a number of servers. Servers can be managed centrally through NDS and its associated management tools. From an administrative standpoint, NDS removes a lot of redundancy and duplication of effort required in implementing a network.

The Architecture of NDS

Like the bindery, NDS is a database composed of multiple files. Unlike the bindery, the NDS database is an object-oriented distributed database. The database can be broken up into pieces and spread out across the network so it is stored on multiple servers. This is called *partitioning*. To add fault tolerance, these pieces can be replicated; the replicas can be stored on different servers as well. As you might expect, this is called *replication*. Thus, if one copy of a portion of a database is destroyed, there are still other copies out on the network.

Partitioning also has the benefit of making NDS scalable. As a database grows in size, it can become less manageable, as we saw with the bindery database. However, when the NDS database becomes unwieldy in size, it can be broken up and distributed across multiple servers. Each partition is smaller than the original database, yet the partitions are able to communicate with each other across the network to provide the services they could provide if they were still combined into one large database. Thus, the database can be incredibly large, yet manageable at the same time.

As we saw, the bindery is stored in SYS:SYSTEM on the NetWare 3.x server. The NDS database is also stored on the SYS volume of the file server; however, there is now a dedicated system directory employed to hold the database. This directory, _NETWARE, exists directly off of the root of the file system on SYS and is incredibly hard to access. People who do not know of its existence will never know it is there.

Four files contain the NDS database on a NetWare 4.11 server:

- BLOCK.NDS
- ENTRY.NDS
- PARTITIO.NDS
- VALUE.NDS

To see these files, you need to use the DOS RCONSOLE.EXE utility. It can be run from NetWare Administrator using the Tools | Remote Console option. For more information on using RCONSOLE.EXE, refer to Chapter 18. Once you are authenticated to the server, perform the following steps:

1. Press Alt+F1. This will bring up the Available Options menu.

2. Choose Directory Scan from the menu. The Enter Directory to Scan dialog box will appear.

3. Type SYS:_NETWARE in the box and press Enter.

After completing these steps, the contents of this hard-to-reach directory will be displayed on the screen. You will see the four files used to store the NDS database. Among the information listed is the size of the NDS database files. Using this information, you can gauge how much space is required for your NDS database. Remember, running out of space on your SYS volume is bad because the NDS database will not be able to dynamically grow as necessary. This can have a negative effect on your network.

Obviously, as more NDS information is stored on the server, the NDS database files will increase in size. The same was true with the bindery. However, the bindery was based upon records stored in a flat-file database. NDS is able to keep track of information about your network in a completely different manner.

NDS makes use of the concept of objects to store network information. Each physical network resource is represented in the database as an NDS object. The NDS object is composed of properties and values, as we discussed in Chapter 3. Since this database is not a flat-file database, the object definitions are not set in stone. They can be modified. Properties can be added or deleted to an object to provide more functionality. This customization of objects can enhance your network and the services it provides.

Understanding Schema

One of the "buzzwords" you will hear concerning NDS is the word *schema*. Simply put, the *schema* are the NDS object and property definitions for the network. The schema define the types of objects that can be created in the NDS tree and also define the properties associated with those objects. For example, the user object and all of the properties associated with it are defined in the schema of the NDS tree.

The schema for the NDS tree also define the rules for the relationships between the NDS objects. From our discussion of container objects in Chapter 3, we learned that [Root] could only hold a country, organization, or Alias object. This restriction is defined in the NDS schema and enforced through NetWare Administrator. The schema provide the guidelines to be followed when objects interact.

The NDS schema apply across all servers in the same tree. No server that joins a tree or exists in the same tree can have a different schema than the rest of the servers in the tree. This ensures a uniform set of objects and properties in the tree as well as a consistent set of rules regarding the objects' relationships. It would be extremely confusing to have servers with different schema in the NDS tree.

The set of objects and their properties that come with NetWare 4.11 and its version of NDS is called the *base schema*. The common objects we have used, such as users, groups, and printers, are defined in the base schema. However, this is not the limit of the types of objects that can be created. As we mentioned, the objects and their properties can be customized. This is called a *schema extension*.

With a schema extension, you can expand the capabilities of your NDS tree. You can design a brand-new object with its own set of properties that has relevance and meaning for your network. You decide what the object is going to be and how it is going to relate to the other objects. You declare the rules concerning what this object can do; in effect, you lay the blueprint for the data that will be contained in the object.

While the benefits of schema extension are obvious—you can customize NetWare in a way you never have before—there are some things to consider before implementing these new objects. Just because the object is created does not mean you will be able to use it right away. The object exists with a new set of properties and a new set of rules, but you do not have any applications that understand what those properties or rules are. You must create the software application to use the new object the way you want it used. In other words, the new object will not magically appear in NetWare Administrator where you will be able to manipulate it.

The other thing to consider is the maintenance and upgrade of your schema extension. Just because it is compatible with this version of NDS does not mean it will be compatible with the next version. With each new version of NDS, you may have to redefine the schema extension and reprogram the utility you created to use the extension. This can create an unanticipated resource cost in terms of time and money. While some schema extensions will be absolutely necessary for your organization, think about the long-term investment before you create them.

To create a schema extension, you must use Novell's Directory application programming interface (API). From time to time, Novell will release a schema extension with a product; however, they will also provide the appropriate snap-ins for NetWare Administrator so you will be able to manage the new objects specified in the schema extension. You can also create your own snap-ins for NetWare Administrator to manage the new objects you create.

Bindery Services

Because NDS is a distributed database composed of objects, it represents a complete shift in paradigm from the old NetWare 3.x days. Any old NetWare 3.x client workstations out on the network will not be able to interface with this new technology because it just won't understand it. Fortunately, Novell built backward compatibility into NDS to allow older network clients to still be able to use the network.

Workstation clients that use bindery connections to connect with the server will be able to access a NetWare 4.11 server assuming Bindery Services has been set up on the server. Bindery Services allow the server to view a portion of the NDS tree as if it were a bindery-type database. The 16-bit NETX.EXE shell and the built-in Microsoft NetWare client for Windows 95 and Windows NT require this bindery service to access the server's file system.

The NDS Tree as a Bindery

Since the older clients are expecting a flat-file bindery, Bindery Services takes a section of the NDS tree and treats it like a bindery database. This section of the tree is a container object. When the objects in a container are used as a bindery, that container becomes the bindery context for which Bindery Services is set. When the bindery context is set, all objects in that container can be referenced by a bindery-based utility. In fact, the objects in the bindery context are treated like a flat-file bindery.

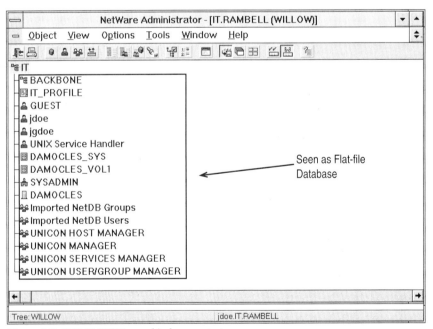

Figure 8-2: IT.RAMBELL as a bindery context.

Bindery context is specified at the server console. In Figure 8-2, it is assumed that the file server Damocles has had the bindery context set to IT.RAMBELL. When user jgdoe accesses the network using an old NETX.EXE shell, Damocles is able to view the objects in the IT.RAMBELL container as if it were a flat-file bindery. Because the user ID jgdoe exists in this bindery context, Damocles will be able to authenticate the user and give him access to the server's file system. The NETX.EXE shell does not understand anything about NetWare 4.11 or NDS, and it interacts with the file server as if it were a NetWare 3.x server.

If the user object jgdoe in the NDS tree existed in a context other than the bindery context, the server would have refused the authentication request from the NETX.EXE client. Even though the user exists in the NDS tree, the user object does not exist in the "bindery" as it was specified.

Bindery Services is server-centric. The bindery contexts are defined at the server level. Each server can have its own bindery context; in this case, servers are independent of one another. Multiple bindery contexts can be specified for a particular server. This enables multiple NDS containers to be viewed as one bindery.

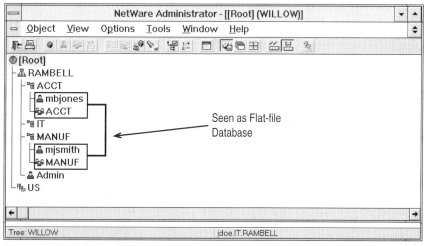

Figure 8-3: Viewing multiple containers as one bindery.

When the bindery context is set to multiple containers, all of the objects in both containers are viewed as if they were one bindery database. In Figure 8-3, the bindery context on Damocles has been set to MANUF.RAMBELL and ACCT.RAMBELL. Even though the user objects exist in different containers, any user object in either container could access the file server using a bindery-based utility. Up to 16 bindery contexts can be set for a single server.

Issues Concerning Bindery Services

While using Bindery Services might be necessary to provide backward compatibility for older workstation clients, network administrators must be aware of issues surrounding the use of Bindery Services. It adds a level of complexity to the NDS tree and its administration.

Object Collision   Object collision occurs when working with multiple bindery contexts. Two NDS objects that have the same common name can be uniquely identified in the NDS by providing the full distinguished name of each object. Unfortunately, there is no way to tell the difference between the two objects when a user is using Bindery Services.

If the user object jgdoe exists in the containers IT.RAMBELL and ACCT.RAMBELL and both containers are set as bindery contexts (with IT.RAMBELL being specified first), jgdoe will appear twice as the server views the bindery. Only the user object in the first specified bindery context will be found. Thus, if the two jgdoe objects pertain to different people, only the jgdoe whose object is in the IT.RAMBELL container will be able to access the server using Bindery Services. When the jgdoe from the ACCT.RAMBELL container tries to log in to the network, Bindery Services will check his password against the wrong user object and always deny him access.

Container Limitations   When a container is specified as a bindery context, only the objects in that container are treated like bindery objects. If that container has subordinate containers, the objects contained in those subordinate containers are not considered part of the bindery. In Figure 8-3, setting the bindery context to RAMBELL would not let users in the containers IT or ACCT use Bindery Services.

Also, there is a limitation on the types of containers to which the bindery context can be set. Only organizations and organizational units can be set as bindery contexts. [Root] and country containers *cannot* be set as bindery contexts.

Object Limitations   Utilities using Bindery Services will not be able to access all of the objects contained in the bindery context. Only bindery-type objects will be accessible to the bindery utilities. Thus, they will be able to recognize and use user and group objects; however, they will not be able to understand container or profile objects and their associated login scripts.

SYSCON vs. NetWare Administrator   When bindery properties need to be changed for a particular object, you must use the old NetWare 3.x SYSCON.EXE utility. This will modify the bindery properties for the object. Adding a system login script through SYSCON.EXE will allow people accessing the server using Bindery Services to execute a login script. However, any modifications made with the SYSCON.EXE utility will affect only the bindery users on the network. It will not affect any of the people accessing the network using NDS. Those modifications must be made using NetWare Administrator.

Setting Up Bindery Services

Bindery Services can be set up on a server one of two ways. The first is at the server console. The second is using a utility called SERVMAN.NLM loaded at the server console. Either way will accomplish the job.

To set the bindery context from the server console, type the following line at the server console prompt:

```
SET BINDERY CONTEXT = <context>
```

In this case, *<context>* is the container that will be viewed as a bindery. Once entered, the context specified will be the bindery context until you enter another bindery context or until the server is reset. To set the bindery context when the server boots, add the preceding line to the AUTOEXEC.NCF file using INSTALL.NLM.

Using SERVMAN.NLM takes a little longer than setting the bindery context at the server console; however, you can tell SERVMAN.NLM to make the modification to AUTOEXEC.NCF automatically so the bindery context is set when the server boots. To set the bindery context using SERVMAN.NLM, perform the following steps:

1. Load the utility into server memory by typing **LOAD SERVMAN** at the server console prompt (the colon prompt on the server).

2. Select Server Parameters from the Available Options menu.

3. Choose Directory Services from the Select a Parameter Category menu.

4. At the bottom of the Directory Services Parameters menu, you will see an option for Bindery Context (you will need to use the down arrow key to get to it). Press the Enter key when this parameter is highlighted.

5. The Bindery Context box will appear. Type in the desired bindery context and press Enter.

6. Press Escape twice to reach the Update Options menu. Select the Update AUTOEXEC.NCF and STARTUP.NCF option from this menu to start Bindery Services when the server boots.

With either method, multiple contexts can be set by separating the contexts with a semicolon. For example, to set the bindery context to both IT.RAMBELL and ACCT.RAMBELL, type the following at the server console:

```
SET BINDERY CONTEXT = IT.RAMBELL;ACCT.RAMBELL
```

Up to 16 bindery contexts can be set per server. Separate each context with a semicolon. To disable Bindery Services, set the bindery context to an invalid context or leave the context field blank. If you do not have any users needing Bindery Services, it is a good idea to disable it.

There is one last requirement to setting up Bindery Services. The server must have a Read/Write replica of the partition that holds the container specified in the bindery context. If IT.RAMBELL and ACCT.RAMBELL existed in the same NDS partition, Damocles would need a Read/Write replica or the Master replica of that partition to provide Bindery Services. If each container existed in a separate partition, Damocles would need a Read/Write or Master replica of both partitions to provide Bindery Services. For more information about NDS partitioning and replication, refer to Chapter 10.

NDS Building Blocks

In Chapter 3, we provided an overview of the structure of NDS. We saw that a pool of network resources is not very manageable. There needs to be some sort of structure to NDS to provide convenient management of the network and its resources. To accomplish this, NDS is organized in a treelike structure. The hierarchical scheme provides a method of logical groupings so you can organize your network efficiently.

[Root]

The [Root] object is a special object in the NDS tree. It acts much like a container object (it holds other objects); however, you cannot manipulate the [Root] object like you can a container object. There is only one [Root] per NDS tree, and it always exists at the top of the NDS tree.

You cannot create a [Root] object. It is created during the installation of NetWare 4.11 when a new tree is created. The name of the tree pertains to [Root], which serves as the origin of the NDS tree. You cannot view the details of the [Root] object but trustee assignments can be made to [Root], and objects can be created to exist immediately beneath [Root]. For more information on the types of objects that can exist immediately beneath [Root], refer to Chapter 3, "NetWare 4.11 Concepts."

Container Objects

The key to the organization of your NDS tree is the container objects. Container objects exist to provide a mechanism for holding other objects in your NDS tree. Container objects can generally hold leaf objects and other container objects. A good analogy for container objects in the NDS tree is directories in a file system. They provide organization for the structure and act as a recursive storage system; container objects can be nested inside one another to provide layer-by-layer organization of the NDS tree.

There are three main types of container objects in the NDS tree:

- Country

- Organization

- Organizational Unit

Each one has its own set of properties and rules about how it can relate to other objects in the NDS tree. They are defined in the base schema. The country and organization objects usually provide container organization for the high levels in the NDS tree (near [Root]) while organizational unit objects are containers that help you refine the lower structure of the NDS tree. Figure 8-5 shows how you might use countries, organizations, and organizational units in your NDS tree.

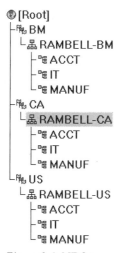

Figure 8-4: NDS tree sample structure.

Country Objects

As we mentioned in Chapter 3, the Country object is intended for companies that have international organizations. It is useful to immediately divide the NDS tree into international divisions for logical organization. This way, each division can have its own branch of the NDS tree. They can administer their own branch in terms of security; however, they would share the benefits of database partitioning and replication as well as time synchronization across the entire corporation.

To create a Country object, perform the following steps in NetWare Administrator:

1. Click on [Root] once with the right mouse button. Choose Create from the menu that appears.

2. In the New Object dialog box, select Country from the Class of New Object box by clicking on it once with the left mouse button.

3. Click on the OK button.

4. Type in the name of the Country object and click Create.

The base schema defines some restrictions when using the Country object in your NDS tree:

- The Country object may only exist immediately beneath [Root].

- The Country object may only contain an Organization container object or an Alias leaf object.

- The names of Country objects are always two characters in length.

Care should be taken in naming these objects; your NDS country name should match the X.500 two-character code standard for that country. That will ensure that your NDS naming scheme is compatible with other existing directory service standards. Appendix D provides a list of country codes as established in ISO 3166.

Since Country objects can only contain organizations and aliases, there are not many properties associated with the object. Their function really is to hold other containers. You can view the properties of the Country object by clicking on it once in NetWare Administrator with the right mouse button and choosing Details from the menu that appears. The properties for the object will appear.

You will note that the Country object has only two property pages associated with it. The first is Identification. Here you can specify a description of the Country object. The second property tab is Rights to Files and Directories. Here, you can grant an entire country rights to a server's file system. When you make a trustee assignment using the Country object, all objects contained in the Country object, including objects in all subordinate containers, are granted rights to the file system. It is an easy way to grant a large number of objects access to files and directories.

Organization Objects

Organization objects are used to identify a company or corporation that owns a portion of the NDS tree. An NDS tree with an Organization object named Rambell would immediately associate Rambell, Inc., with the tree.

To create an organization in your NDS tree, perform the following steps in NetWare Administrator:

1. Click on [Root] or the target Country object once with the right mouse button. Choose Create from the menu that appears.

2. In the New Object dialog box, select Organization from the Class of New Object box by clicking on it once with the left mouse button.

3. Click on the OK button.

4. Type in the name of the Organization object and click Create.

Organizations refine the top-level tree organization and are the first container objects that can contain any leaf object. They can also contain other container objects, but the base schema again defines how you use organizations:

- An organization may only exist in [Root] or a Country object. It cannot exist beneath another organization.

- Organizations may contain an organizational unit or any leaf object. They cannot contain another organization.

- All NDS trees must have at least one Organization object.

- An organization object name is limited to a maximum of 64 characters.

To see the properties associated with the Organization object, click on the organization once with the right mouse button and choose Details from the menu that appears. The properties dialog box will be displayed, as shown in Figure 8-5.

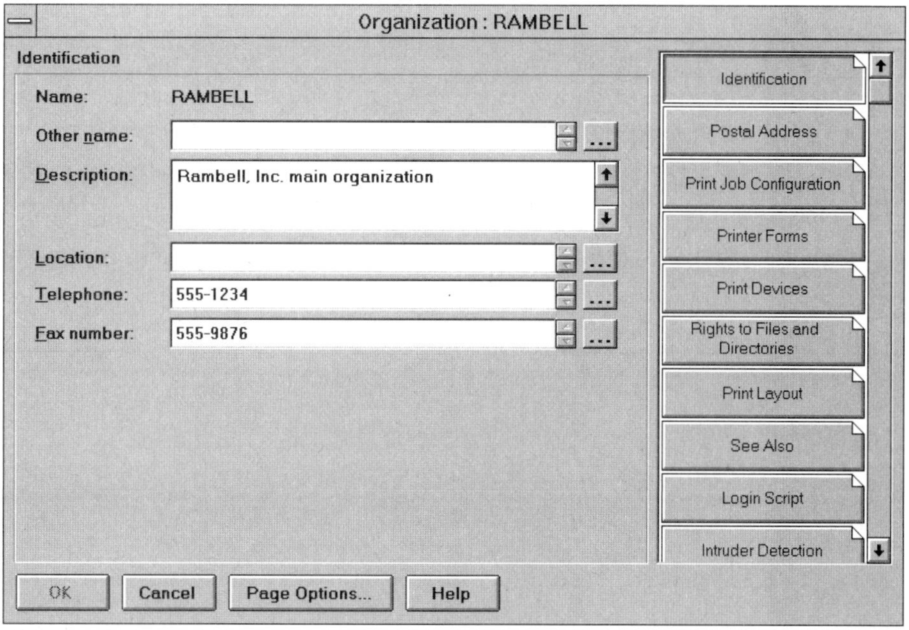

Figure 8-5: The NDS organization object properties dialog box.

The properties of the Organization object are used to control the behavior of all objects that it contains. Any rights granting or restricting done to the Organization object affects all of the subordinate leaf objects. For example, granting a file system trustee assignment to an Organization object will grant those same rights to all subordinate leaf objects. The container properties control the following attributes of the subordinate leaf objects:

- **File system trustee assignments.** Rights to file systems on the network can be granted through these properties.

- **Intruder detection services.** Intruder detection and lockout services can be enabled for a container using this property tab.

- **Container login scripts.** The container login script can be written for users in the container.

- **Print jobs, forms, and devices configurations.** Customized printing configurations can be created. You can also view the current printing environment layout by clicking on the Print Layout property tab.

Organizational Units

Organizational units are used to refine the structure of your NDS tree. Quite often, organizational units represent departments, groups, or divisions within your company or corporation. They help with the logical grouping of leaf objects within your tree. Organizational units are the most flexible of the container objects because they can be nested two and three deep in the tree.

To create an Organizational Unit object in the tree, perform the following steps in NetWare Administrator:

1. Click on the container that will hold the Organizational Unit object once with the right mouse button. Choose Create from the menu that appears.

2. In the New Object dialog box, select Organizational Unit from the Class of New Object box by clicking on it once with the left mouse button.

3. Click on the OK button.

4. Type in the name of the Organizational Unit object and click Create.

As with all other objects in the NDS tree, the base schema define the relationships between the objects. Here are the restrictions pertaining to the Organizational Unit object:

- An Organizational Unit object may only exist in an organization or organizational unit. They cannot exist in [Root] or a Country object.

- Organizational Unit objects may contain any leaf object or other organizational unit.

- An Organizational Unit object name is limited to a maximum of 64 characters.

Organizational units add flexibility to the design of the NDS tree because they may contain other organizational units. This nesting allows the structure of the tree to go many levels deep. Large organizations may have five or six levels of organizational units; small companies may only have one organizational unit in their NDS tree. Use the organizational unit logically to separate out groups of people who have a common goal within your organization and generally need access to the same type of network resources.

The properties associated with the organizational unit are the same as those associated with the Organization object. The organizational unit can be modified to provide the following services for the leaf objects it contains:

- File system trustee assignments
- Intruder detection services
- Container login scripts
- Print jobs, forms, and devices configurations

To view the properties of the organizational unit, click on it once with the right mouse button and select Details from the menu that appears. The properties dialog box for the object will be displayed.

Other Container Objects

Besides the three main container objects, the NDS schema define two more container objects that can hold other NDS objects. You may use one of these objects in the course of your network administration. The other object may be used in a later release of IntranetWare. They are the Licensed Product object and the Locality object.

The Licensed Product object is created in the NDS tree when a license certificate is installed that utilizes the license metering features of IntranetWare. The Licensed Product object can exist in any of the container objects and [Root] mentioned previously. When a software application is installed that uses these licensing services, a License Certificate leaf object is placed in the Licensed Product container object. The object type attribute abbreviation for typeful naming of the Licensed Product object is LP.

The Locality object allows you to specify the location of your network and provides another level of structure to the NDS tree. Its primary use is to help your network comply with the X.500 specification, if needed. But even though this object is defined in the base schema, there are no utilities that are able to manipulate it. The Locality object can exist in any container object except the Licensed Product container object. The object attribute type abbreviation for typeful naming of the Locality object is L.

Leaf Objects

While the container objects in the NDS tree provide the overall structure, it is the leaf objects that do all the work in keeping track of the network resources you have. Every physical device and user that interacts with your network will have a leaf object through which this interaction occurs. The base schema for IntranetWare provides for 23 types of leaf objects. They are summarized in Table 8-1.

AFP Server	Alias	Application	Auditing File
Bindery	Bindery Queue	Computer	Directory Map
Distribution List	External Entity	Group	Licensed Certificate
LSP Server	Message Routing Group	Messaging Server	NetWare (NCP) Server
Organizational Role	Print Server	Printer	Profile
Unknown	User	Volume	

Table 8-1: IntranetWare leaf objects.

For more detailed information about the leaf objects included in the IntranetWare base schema, refer to Chapter 3, "NetWare 4.11 Concepts." By definition, leaf objects cannot hold any other NDS objects. They represent the end of the branch of the tree.

NDS: Key to the Intranet

Thus far, we have covered setting up file and print services on your network. We have also discussed the architecture of the NDS tree. Structurally, we know how it works through [Root], container objects, and leaf objects. We also know a bit about the back end in terms of NDS being an object-oriented distributed database. But how does NDS relate to the implementation of an intranet?

In the Introduction, we discussed Novell's definition of an intranet. It consists of eight parts with each component providing an integral part to a complete set of network services. The eight components are:

- File services
- Print services
- Directory services

- Security

- Wide-area connectivity

- Network management

- World Wide Web services

- Messaging services

When implemented, these eight components together will give your users a comprehensive set of network services. NDS, when used in conjunction with the other products that come packaged with IntranetWare, is the critical element involved in all of these services. Without NDS, a corporate intranet would not be possible.

The Classic LAN: File & Print Services

In Section I, we thoroughly discussed the process for setting up file and print services for users on your network. Using NetWare 4.11, you can provide a central location for the storage of important data that many users can access. Users are also able to share printers connected to their workstations through the use of additional software loaded on their machines.

While the NetWare 4.11 NOS provided a lot of the muscle necessary to provide file and print services for users, it was NDS that did a majority of the work. You needed to create user objects in the NDS tree for people to be able to access the network. File systems integrated with the NDS tree to allow users to be able to access the data. Setting up the printing environment for users was accomplished using the NDS. Without NDS, we would be facing the same bindery-based limitations we saw with NetWare 3.x.

Expanding the Network

With the help of NDS, NetWare 4.11 can provide the same services to users that NetWare 3.x did. However, with NDS, the network can scale to much larger dimensions. We are not limited to server-centric networks anymore; all network resources can be consolidated into a single unified structure to make it easier for network administrators to manage. This scalability allows NDS to be used as the basis for an intranet.

Directory Services

As its name implies, NDS provides directory services for the users on your network. With all of the resources tracked in a central location, NDS becomes a repository of useful information. Not only does it keep track of the rights users have to access file systems, it also stores other information that may be critical for your company's daily work processes.

When you enter all of the information you can on the various identification pages throughout the leaf objects, you enable your organization to use NDS as a searchable database. Anybody on the network could have easy access to information such as employees' departments, phone numbers, fax numbers, and physical locations. This personnel information can be invaluable to a company.

NDS also has the inherent ability to keep track of all your network resources. You can create objects for all users in your organization along with every computer, printer, and server. With sufficient rights, you can retrieve information concerning the hardware connected to your network as well as information concerning your users. The object-oriented nature of NDS provides a powerful tool for directory services.

Security

NDS is the basis for security on your network. All security information is stored in NDS whether that information is NDS object security, file system security, or login security. NDS allows network administrators to control how people use the network and what data people are allowed to see.

Through the use of trustee assignments and rights inheritance, network administrators grant NDS objects explicit rights to resources on the network and make sure those rights are inherited by other objects in the tree. It is the treelike hierarchical structure that makes this security possible. Users can be completely blocked from one portion of the tree and yet have a high level of rights to another branch. The security is completely customizable and each user's rights can be tailored to fit his or her specific situation. Without NDS, every server on the network would need to store the security information for both network users and the servers' file systems to provide the same type of service. NDS security will be discussed in more detail in Chapter 9.

Wide-Area Connectivity

Although not directly responsible for the wide area network (WAN) links themselves, NDS is able to take advantage of them once they are established. The network resources on both sides of the WAN link can be incorporated into a single tree providing all users common network services independent of their physical location. Users halfway around the world from each other will be able to share files easily and efficiently through NDS.

Network Management

Network management is the service that network administrators love. Because NDS is a centralized service that tracks all network resources, all of those resources can be managed from anywhere on the network. No longer do network administrators need to authenticate to multiple servers to perform administrative tasks. All of the security rights necessary to manage the network can be granted to one object.

NDS also reduces the volume of work a network administrator must do to maintain users' accounts on the network. As we saw with NetWare 3.x, users who needed access to multiple servers caused more administrative overhead because the account management had to be done on all servers. This is no longer the case with NDS. Once the account is modified, it is modified for all resources on the network.

NetWare Administrator also comes packaged with remote server management tools. With this application, you can accomplish server management independent of physical location. You can also manage your network resources at the same time. NDS plays an integral part in network management in the IntranetWare world.

A Complete Set of Network Services

All networks large or small have a need for other types of services in today's world. Gone are the days of plain old file and print services. Users not only need access to timely data, they need access to each other. The last two services that make up the intranet provide just those things, and NDS plays a key role in both of them.

World Wide Web Services

When most users think of the World Wide Web, they immediately think of the Internet. Using a Web browser to "surf the net" is often viewed as an entertaining pastime, but it also has many practical applications to the business world. It can be a mechanism to provide timely data to the employees of your company in an efficient manner. For instance, instead of having someone review a spreadsheet using a spreadsheet application (with which they need to be proficient), they can just use their Web browser to view the information and send any changes that need to be made to the owner of the document.

The actual software used to provide Web services is installed on both the NetWare 4.11 server and the client workstations; however, the security employed in providing Web services comes directly from the NDS tree. NDS can allow or restrict a user's access to the data that can be viewed through the Web server. The Web server product integrates nicely with NDS and depends upon the services NDS provides to ensure a secure environment for Web browsing.

Messaging Services

Messaging services across your intranet are actually provided by another package that is sold separately from IntranetWare; however, this package relies upon NDS to provide the central services necessary for your users to take advantage of messaging services.

Users will be able to e-mail one another, but all of the mail accounts and messaging servers will be tracked using NDS. NDS will be able to send the electronic mail where it needs to go and allow users to read their mail. Its security will also prevent other users from seeing messages they do not have the right to see.

Although it's not able to provide all of the intranet services single-handedly, NDS has a pivotal role in each one. All of the other software loaded on the servers and workstations rely upon NDS to provide a central source of information they can use to provide these eight key services of an intranet. Without NDS, these services would not be possible.

Moving On

It is important to understand the NDS tree structure because it inherently lends itself to the security employed on the network. This object-oriented centralized database provides a unified networking environment that is both scalable and flexible. This is a must for an enterprise network operating system. In the next chapter, we will see how this structure relates to NDS security and how these NDS rights flow down the structure of the tree just like file system rights flow down the file system.

9

NDS Security

Any time you have a centralized resource to which many people have access, you will need to deal with security issues. NDS is no exception. Its very nature begs the question of security since the objects stored in the tree grant and deny access to the data on the network. Who is allowed to create objects in the NDS tree? Who is allowed to modify the resources those objects use? Who is allowed to delete NDS objects? Obviously, access to NDS objects and their properties needs to be restricted.

In Chapter 6, we looked at both the structure and the security of the NetWare file systems. The file system security in NetWare 4.11 is directly related to the file system structure. Rights flow down the directory tree. The NDS security scheme is similar. We've already discussed the NDS structure; in this chapter, we will see how that structure is related to the security of the objects stored in the tree.

The first item to explore regarding NDS security is the type of rights available. There are two types of NDS rights—object rights and property rights. Both sets of rights apply to NDS objects, but there is a subtle difference in the way each specifies how a user may modify the object. Once the NDS rights are explained, we will see how they differ from file system rights. Both security schemes offer a comprehensive security package, but both are completely separate from one another.

Once we've covered the types of rights that can be granted in the NDS tree, we will talk about assigning rights to users on your network. Through the concept of trustee assignments, users can be granted an explicit level of rights to a particular leaf object or container in the NDS tree. We will learn how to grant these rights to users, view the assignments we have made using NetWare Administrator, and talk about the special NDS trustee objects that exist.

To ease the task of network administration, security rights flow down the structure of the NDS tree. Once a trustee assignment is made in the NDS tree, the user has the same level of access down that tree branch. This is rights inheritance. We will discuss rights inheritance in detail along with its counterpart, the inherited rights filter, which prevents this downward flow of security rights.

Like the file system, the overall rights a user has to a portion of the NDS tree is calculated from the combination of trustee assignments and rights inheritance. We will see how to calculate a user's effective NDS rights manually to gain a thorough understanding of how NDS rights work. We will also see how to view the user's effective rights through the NetWare Administrator tool.

If a lot of the information in this chapter looks familiar to you, it should. Although NDS security and file system security are two completely separate security systems, they are similar to one another. Having an understanding of file system security concepts gives you a head start in understanding NDS security.

NDS Rights

In Chapter 4, we touched upon the basic sets of rights that exist in the NDS tree. These rights control a user's access to other objects within the NDS tree. Not just anyone can create, delete, and manipulate NDS objects. That type of scheme would cause chaos. There must be some mechanism by which privileges to objects in the tree are assigned. That is accomplished through NDS rights.

There are two basic sets of NDS rights to control a user's access to the NDS tree. Each set of rights applies to a different attribute of the NDS object:

- Object rights
- Property rights

While both sets of rights pertain to the security of NDS objects, they have vastly different functions. Object rights determine the level of access someone has to the NDS object itself. Property rights grant or restrict access to the properties of the object in question. For example, object rights would determine whether or not a user would be able to create or delete a user object. Property rights would determine whether or not a person would be able to change the value of that user object's department or address properties. It's a subtle distinction, yet it must be understood to completely comprehend NDS security.

Here's another example to help explain the difference between object rights and property rights. Think of them in terms of a Rolodex. A Rolodex is made up of individual cards that are labeled with a person's name and contain that person's address, phone number, and e-mail address. Object rights pertain to the cards themselves. Having object rights would allow you to add another card to the set, remove a card from the set, relabel the card (let's say the person gets married), or just plain look at the card.

The property rights for the Rolodex would allow you access to the information contained in the card—the person's address, phone number, and e-mail address. You might be able to read this information, change it, or compare it with information contained in other Rolodex cards. Property rights pertain to the actual data stored within the object.

Object Rights

As mentioned, object rights grant control over NDS objects themselves. There are five basic types of object rights that can be granted in NDS security. They are summarized in Table 9-1.

NDS Right	Abbreviation	Description
Supervisor	S	Grants all object rights.
Browse	B	Allows the object to be seen in the NDS tree.
Create	C	Grants the right to create an NDS object.
Delete	D	Grants the right to remove an NDS object.
Rename	R	Grants the right to change the common name of the object.

Table 9-1: Five types of NDS object rights.

Supervisor

Granting NDS Supervisor object rights is equivalent to granting all NDS object rights. It allows the browsing, creation, deletion, and renaming of the NDS object without each right being explicitly granted. A user that has been granted only the Supervisor and Browse rights to a specific object will still be able to delete or rename that object. As with the Supervisor file system right, great care should be taken when granting this right.

Granting the Supervisor object right also grants all property rights for the object. This is the only place where object and property rights overlap. Thus, a person with the Supervisor object right would be able to modify all of the properties of the object as well. This makes sense; in effect, the person with the Supervisor object right "owns" the object. The Supervisor object right can be blocked with an Inherited Rights Filter (IRF).

Tip

When the Supervisor object right is granted for the NDS file server object, the Supervisor file system right is also granted for the server's file system. This is the only instance where NDS rights and file system rights overlap.

Browse

The Browse object right allows an object to be seen in the NDS tree. Using a utility like NetWare Administrator or NETADMIN.EXE, a user can verify that an object exists; however, he or she would not be able to do much more with it. If you want to hide an object in the NDS tree from users, remove the Browse right from the object. Then, only those users with the NDS Supervisor object right will be able to see the object in the NDS tree.

Create

The Create object right is only available for container objects. It grants the ability to create a new NDS object in the specified container. Obviously, leaf objects would not have the Create right associated with them because they are not allowed to contain any subordinate objects.

Delete

The Delete right allows the user to remove the object from the NDS tree. This right should also be granted with great care. When the Delete right is too freely granted, NDS objects have an annoying habit of disappearing from the NDS tree. And unlike files in the file system, the objects cannot be retrieved once they are deleted.

Rename

Although this is the only object right that directly affects the properties of an NDS object, it makes sense that it is an object right. The Rename object right allows a user to change the common name (CN) of the NDS object. This is the name that appears in the NDS tree when it is browsed. Since it is associated with the object and how it is viewed, it is logical to make it an object right, but it is actually modifying a property of the object. For example, a user with the Rename object right could rename the user account "jdoe" to "jgdoe." That person also might be able to change the name of a container from IT to CIS.

Remember when we were working with file system rights and we had a set of abbreviations we used to refer to them? The same is true for NDS object rights. Novell abbreviates the object rights for an object as [SBCDR]. This particular example would indicate that all rights have been granted for the trustee. If a trustee had only been granted the Create right to a container, it would be abbreviated [__C__].

Property Rights

We saw that some object rights have an impact on an object's property rights. The Rename object right allows the trustee to change the common name of the object; however, that is the only property that can be modified by an object right. The Supervisor object right grants all property rights to the object as well. Except for these two object rights, it takes property rights to change the values of the properties an object has.

There are five types of NDS property rights that can be granted to a trustee. They are summarized in Table 9-2. These are the rights that grant access to the information contained in an object. Changing a user's e-mail address, modifying group membership, and editing the location property of an object require property rights.

Property Right	Abbreviation	Description
Supervisor	S	Grants all property rights.
Compare	C	Allows the property value to be compared with another value.
Read	R	The property value can be read.
Write	W	Value can be added, removed, or changed.
Add Self	A	Grants right to add or remove self from a property.

Table 9-2: Five types of NDS property rights.

Supervisor

Granting the Supervisor property right is equivalent to granting all of the other property rights. Thus, a trustee that was granted only the Supervisor property right would still be able to read, compare, write, and add self to the property. The Supervisor property right can be blocked by an Inherited Rights Filter (IRF).

While granting the Supervisor object right to a trustee also gives all property privileges, the same is not true for the Supervisor property right. The Supervisor property right does *not* grant any object rights to the trustee. It pertains only to the properties of the NDS object.

Compare

The Compare property right is probably one of the most confusing rights there is. It allows the trustee to compare a value against a property's value. The answer returned is a Boolean TRUE or FALSE. For example, your friend thinks of a number between 1 and 100. You guess the number is 49, and your friend says, "No." That is the equivalent of the Compare property right. You do not know what the value is, but you can query against the value to see if you are correct.

When the Read property right is granted to a trustee, the Compare property right is also given. Obviously, if you can see the value of the property, you can also compare other values against it.

Read

The Read property right does just what you think it would. It allows you to see the value of the property. The Read right is often important because it can play a key role as to whether a user will be able to perform a function. For example, all users associated with a profile object must have the Read property right to the login script property to execute the login script. If they do not have access to the value of the property, they will not be able to read the login script commands.

Write

The Write property right grants the privilege of adding, changing, or removing values for a property, which can be either a text-type property (a telephone number) or an object-type property (adding members to a group). To make any changes to the values of a property, you must have the Write property right. Thus, for users to edit their login scripts, they must have the Write property right to the login script.

Having the Write property right also grants the Add Self property right. Obviously, if you can add, change, or modify the values of a property, you can add or remove yourself from the property.

Add Self

The Add Self property right is a curious one. It allows the trustee to add him- or herself to the value of a property. This applies only when the property takes an object as a value. For instance, if you had the Add Self property right for the Members property of an NDS group object, you would be able to make yourself a member of the group. You could also remove yourself as a member of the group. Add Self grants the ability to add and delete only your object to the property; you cannot add or remove anyone else. If the property does not take object values, then the Add Self property right has no meaning. You cannot add yourself to a text field.

Access Control List & Property Rights

Every object has one property that controls both the trustees and the rights of the trustees. It is called the Object Trustees property or the Access Control List (ACL). When a trustee assignment is made and rights are granted, that trustee is added to the ACL. Since the ACL is a property of every object, it is subject to the property rights of the object.

If a user were granted the Write or Add Self property right to the ACL, that user gains access to the trustee list for the object. The user could add him- or herself to the ACL and gain complete control over the NDS object. Be careful when assigning property rights to the ACL of an object.

Like object rights, property rights are also abbreviated. A user who has been granted all property rights is said to have the rights [SCRWA] to the object. The abbreviation for another user with just the compare property right would be [_C___]. This is just a convenient method of expressing the level of rights assigned.

Trustee Assignments

We now understand the basic rights that are available to us in the NDS tree and how they affect the objects. One set of rights pertains to the object itself; the other set of rights applies to the values of the object. Through these rights, a network administrator is able to ensure the security of his or her network and restrict the level of access objects have to other objects in the NDS tree. But how do we use these rights?

Object and property rights to an NDS object can be explicitly granted to another NDS object. This is called a trustee assignment. An NDS object is said to be a trustee of another object if it has been specifically assigned a level of rights to the object. In Figure 9-1, the user jgdoe is a trustee of the Damocles file server object. He has been granted the object rights [_BCDR] and the property rights [_CRWA] to the NDS file server object.

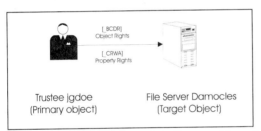

Figure 9-1: Jgdoe is a trustee of the file server Damocles.

User objects are not the only objects that can be NDS trustees of another object. All objects in the NDS tree are eligible to be trustees of other objects. That is why trustee assignments can be so confusing. A print server can be a trustee of a user. A print queue can be the trustee of a file server. Not all of these trustee assignments make sense; however, you have the ability to make one object the trustee of any other existing object in the NDS tree.

All rights in the NDS tree start with a trustee assignment. If there were no trustee assignments granted in the NDS tree, no one would have any rights to any object. The Admin account is granted a trustee assignment to the NDS tree that starts the rights and allows you to create other objects after you install NDS for the first time. The default trustee assignments for the NDS tree will be discussed later in the section "Default NDS Rights."

Granting Trustee Assignments

The bottom line is that we want to grant one object (the trustee) rights to another object (the target). But how do we accomplish this using NetWare Administrator? It depends; there are multiple ways to grant trustee assignments. The first method is from the trustee's point of view. It involves granting NDS rights through the trustee object to the target object in the NDS tree. The second method is from the target's point of view. It involves granting rights through the target object to the trustee.

From the Trustee

To grant an NDS trustee assignment using the trustee object itself, click once with the right mouse button on the trustee object in the NDS tree and choose Rights to Other Objects from the menu that appears. This will cause the Select Context dialog box to be displayed.

In this box, enter the context in which NetWare Administrator will search for trustee assignments. To browse the NDS tree for a context, click on the Select Object button to the right of the text editing box. Once the context has been entered, click OK. The Rights to Other Objects dialog box will appear (Figure 9-2).

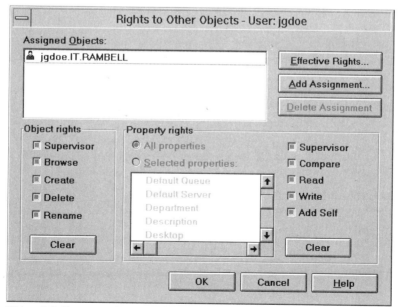

Figure 9-2: Trustee assignments from the trustee point of view.

This dialog box is broken down into three main areas. The area at the top of the box is the Assigned Objects box. It lists all of the current trustee assignments for the trustee in the context specified when the dialog box was opened. For example, if you entered the context IT.RAMBELL when the Select Context box appeared, only the trustee assignments granted to the trustee in that context would appear. In Figure 9-2, we see that jgdoe is a trustee of himself.

Beneath this portion of the dialog box are the remaining two sections. In the bottom left, we have the Object Rights portion of the dialog box. In the bottom right, the Property Rights appear. Once the trustee assignment is granted, this is the portion of the screen used to specify the exact rights granted in the trustee assignment.

To add a trustee assignment for the trustee, perform the following steps:

1. Click on the Add Assignment button to the right of the Assigned Objects box. The Select Object dialog box will be displayed.

2. Browse the NDS tree to find the target object, select it, and click OK. The target object will be added to the Assigned Objects box.

Granting the assignment is as simple as that; however, you are not finished with the trustee assignment. You need to specify the level of rights the trustee has to the target object. To do this, click on the target object in the Assigned Objects box once with the left mouse button to highlight it. The Object Rights and Property Rights sections will show the current rights for the trustee. When the box contains a checkmark, it means the right is granted for the trustee. When the box is clear, that right has been revoked.

In the Property Rights section of the box, you will notice selections for All Properties and Selected Properties. With these options, you can grant a level of rights to all properties associated with the target object, and you can allow a different set of rights to specific properties. When the All Properties radio button is marked, the property rights specified apply to every property of the target object. In Figure 9-3, jgdoe (the trustee) is granted the [_CRWA] property rights to all properties of MBJONES.ACCT.RAMBELL (the target).

When the Selected Properties radio button is marked, you can grant rights for a specific property of the target object. These rights override any rights granted through the All Properties option. In Figure 9-4, jgdoe has been granted the [_CR__] property right to the Department property of the user object MBJONES.ACCT.RAMBELL. Even though jgdoe was granted the [_CRWA] property rights through All Properties, he is still only able to read or compare the value of mbjones's Department property. This is because the Selected Properties option supersedes the property rights granted through the All Properties option.

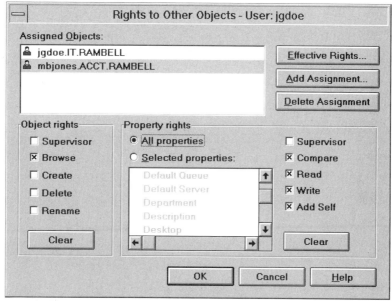

Figure 9-3: Granting rights to all properties of the target object.

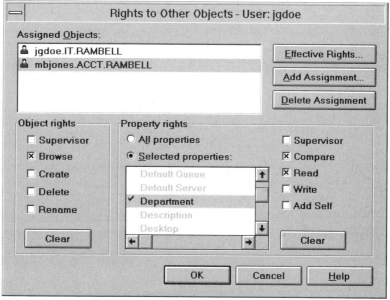

Figure 9-4: Granting property rights to specific object properties.

This Selected Properties trustee assignment also applies to the Supervisor property right. If jgdoe was granted [SCRWA] property rights through All Properties, he would be able to do anything to any property. However, if he is also granted [_CR__] to the Department property through Selected Properties, he would still only be able to read or compare the value of the object's department. The Supervisor property right granted through All Properties can be overridden through a Selected Properties rights assignment.

To remove a target object from the Assigned Objects list, highlight the target object by clicking on it once with the left mouse button. Click the Delete Assignment button to the right of the Assigned Objects box to remove the object. To view the rights the trustee has to the target object, click on the target once with the left mouse button to highlight it. The rights for the target will be displayed in the object and property rights portions of the dialog box.

Tip

The rights displayed in the Object Rights and Property Rights sections of the dialog box apply only to the highlighted target object. If no object is highlighted, no rights will be displayed.

From the Target

To grant a trustee assignment using the target object, click on the target object once with the right mouse button and select Trustees of This Object from the menu that appears. NetWare Administrator will search for all trustees of the object and display them in the Trustees dialog box shown in Figure 9-5.

The Trustees dialog box should appear to be very familiar because it is similar to the Rights to Other Objects dialog box we just discussed. The Trustees dialog box is also broken down into three main sections. At the top of the box is the Trustees list. It displays all of the trustees of the target object. At the bottom of the box are the object and property rights sections where rights are granted to trustees. One difference between the Trustees dialog box and the Rights to Other Objects dialog box is the Inherited Rights Filter (IRF) button in the lower left corner. This allows the IRF for the object to be set. For more information on the IRF, refer to the section "The NDS Inherited Rights Filter" later in this chapter.

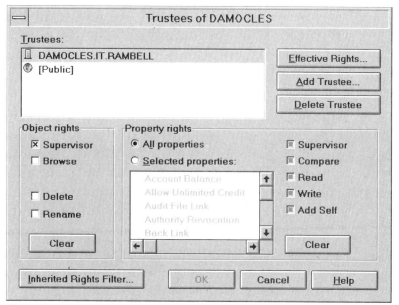

Figure 9-5: Trustee assignments from the target point of view.

To make a trustee assignment to the target object, perform the following steps:

1. Click on the Add Trustee button. The Select Object dialog box will appear.

2. Browse the NDS tree for the trustee object, select it, and click OK. The trustee will be added to the Trustees list at the top of the screen.

When the trustee assignment is made, the new trustee will be highlighted, and the rights for that trustee will be displayed at the bottom of the dialog box. To set the rights for the trustee, check the rights to be granted. Object and property rights that do not have a check mark next to them will be revoked. As with the Rights to Other Objects dialog box, you can grant All Properties and Selected Properties property rights for the trustee as well.

To remove a trustee assignment from the target object, highlight the trustee by clicking on it once with the left mouse button. Click on the Delete Trustee button; the trustee will be removed from the list. To view the rights for a trustee, click on the trustee once with the left mouse button. The rights for the highlighted trustee will be displayed at the bottom of the screen.

Tip

Only the highlighted trustee's rights are displayed at the bottom of the dialog box. The rights shown do not apply to any other trustee of the object.

There are a couple of advantages to granting trustee assignments through the target object. The first involves the modification of the IRF. The IRF for the target object can only be modified through the Trustees dialog box. It cannot be modified using the Rights to Other Objects dialog box. The second advantage is that the Trustees dialog box displays all trustees of the object. This is convenient for network administrators because you immediately see a list of all objects that have explicit rights to the target object.

NDS Special Trustees

As we have learned, any NDS object in the tree can be a trustee of another NDS object. A user can be a trustee of a printer. A group can be a trustee of a container. An organizational role can be a trustee of a file server. The possibilities are endless; however, there are some special trustees of note. These special trustees are [Root] and [Public]. As the network administrator, you need to be aware of them because they affect the security of your network.

The first special trustee is [Root]. As we have seen previously, when a container is made the trustee of an object, it implicitly grants its rights to all of the objects in the container. This also applies to objects in all subordinate containers. Thus, if the container IT.RAMBELL were granted the object rights [SBCDR] to a file server, all objects within IT.RAMBELL would also have those rights to the file server. This also applies to all objects in the container BACKBONE.IT.RAMBELL because BACKBONE is a subordinate container of IT.RAMBELL.

Since [Root] is a special container object, when [Root] is made the trustee of an object, it grants those rights to everyone in the NDS tree. This is because all leaf objects and containers are subordinate to [Root]. [Root] is at the top of the tree; nothing else is higher.

The other special trustee in the NDS tree is [Public]. [Public] is a system-owned trustee; when it is made a trustee of an NDS object, all objects in the NDS tree inherit the same rights. Thus, if the [Public] trustee was granted the object rights [_BCDR] to the file server object Damocles, all objects in the NDS tree would get those same object rights.

To make [Public] (yes, it is always written with brackets like [Root]) a trustee of an object, you must grant the trustee assignment from the target object. Click on the target object once with the right mouse button and select Trustees of This Object from the menu that appears. Click on the Add Trustee button. Navigate the Select Object box to the top of the NDS tree (click on the double-dot in the right-hand box until you can't go any higher). In the left-hand box you will see [Root], any first level container objects, and [Public]. Select [Public] and click OK. [Public] will be added to the Trustees box.

Tip

[Public] rights are granted to anyone merely attaching to your network; they do not have to be logged in to your network to have access. Rights inherited from [Root] are only granted after authentication.

The [Public] trustee is equivalent to the group Everyone in NetWare 3.x. It will let you grant rights to all objects in the NDS tree quickly and efficiently. Just use this trustee with care; many a security hole has developed because [Public] has been granted too many rights.

Default NDS Rights

We've mentioned that rights in the NDS tree start with trustee assignments. They provide an initial point of rights entry to the network. But where do these rights come from? When certain events occur in the NDS tree, default NDS rights are granted to start the rights process. Obviously, when the tree was first installed, there were not user objects or rights available in the tree. The default rights were installed and used when NDS was installed on the first server in your NDS tree. This is how all of the rights in the tree are born.

There are four general events in NDS that cause default NDS rights to be installed. These events have to do with the creation of a new tree, a new file server object, a new user object, and a new container object. When these events occur, certain objects are granted rights to objects within the tree. It is important to understand the default rights because they have an impact on the security of the network.

Creation of a New NDS Tree

When your NDS tree was originally created, NDS was installed on the first server of your network. When this occurred, the NDS installation caused two things to happen in terms of NDS security:

- The user object Admin was created as specified during the installation of the operating system. Admin is a trustee of [Root] with the object rights [S____]. This allows the Admin user to have full run of the NDS tree.

- The trustee [Public] was created in the tree. It was granted the object rights [_B___] to [Root]. This allows everyone in the NDS tree to see every other object in the NDS tree unless this right is blocked out by an IRF or the [Public] trustee assignment is modified.

You might not want just anybody viewing all of the objects in your NDS tree. Consider removing the [Public] trustee from [Root] to prevent unwanted spying by overly curious folk. As the network administrator, you have the right to restrict the access to your network as you see fit.

Installation of a New Server

Installing NetWare 4.11 server in your NDS tree will cause more NDS default rights to be created. For every server added to the tree, the following will occur:

- The creator of the server object (Admin in most cases) will be granted the [S____] object right to the server object. This is logical since someone needs to administer the server.

- The server object is made a trustee of itself with the [S____] object right. With this set of rights, the server is able to manage itself (don't we wish!). Really, if for some reason your Admin account were to be deleted, you could still gain supervisor access to your server by making yourself the security equivalent of the server object.

- [Public] is made a trustee of the file server object with the [_CR__] property right to the Messaging Server property of the file server object. This is required if you are going to be using Message Handling Services (MHS) on your intranet.

Creation of a New User Object

When a new user object is created in the NDS tree, modifications are made to the default NDS rights. The following trustee assignments are made to the user object when a new user is created:

- The user object is made a trustee of itself. This allows the user general access to the network. First, the user is granted the [_CR__] property rights to All Properties. The user is able to see information about his or her user object. Second, the user is also granted the [_CRW_] property rights to the Selected Properties of Login Script and Print Job Configuration. This allows the user to read and modify his or her own login scripts. The user can customize the network environment by him/herself with these rights.

■ [Root] is made a trustee of the new user object as well. It is granted the [_CR__] property right to the Selected Properties of Network Address and Group Membership.

■ [Public] is also made a trustee of the new user object. It is granted the [_CR__] property right to the Selected Property of Default Server. This allows all objects in the tree to identify the default server of the new user.

Creation of a New Container

When a new container is created in the NDS tree, default NDS rights assignments are made. The container is made a trustee of itself and granted the [_CR__] property rights to the Selected Properties of Login Script and Print Job Configuration. This allows all objects within the container to read and execute the container login script and use any print job configuration defined for the container.

As we have said, whenever an explicit rights assignment is made, it is accomplished with a trustee assignment. Whether it's object rights or property rights are granted, a trustee assignment must be made to associate the rights of the trustee to the target object.

Rights Inheritance & Filters

If trustee assignments were the only method by which NDS rights were granted in the tree, implementing security would take a tremendous amount of effort. Every object would have a large number of trustee assignments to establish the appropriate level of NDS rights. This would result in a lot of extra effort for the network administrator. Fortunately, there is another way NDS objects can get NDS rights.

In Chapter 6, we discussed the file system rights. We saw that file system rights were inherited down the directory structure of the file system. The same is true for NDS. NDS rights are inherited; they "flow down," the NDS tree structure. This rights inheritance makes security administration easier for the network manager.

Understanding NDS Rights Inheritance

All rights in the NDS tree start with a trustee assignment. However, once the NDS trustee assignment is made, security is inherited down the structure of the NDS tree. Thus, an NDS trustee assignment made to a container grants the trustee a level of rights to the container object. Through inheritance, that trustee also gains rights to all of the objects in the container as well as rights to subordinate containers and all objects contained in that subordinate container.

It is like granting rights to a branch of the NDS tree. When the trustee assignment is made to a container, the rights are inherited to all objects and branches beneath it. Due to inheritance, a trustee assignment made to [Root] would give the trustee NDS rights to all objects in the tree.

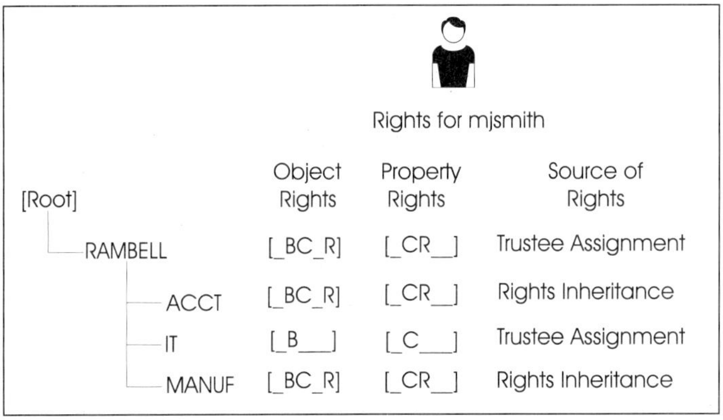

	Object Rights	Property Rights	Source of Rights
[Root]			
RAMBELL	[_BC_R]	[_CR__]	Trustee Assignment
ACCT	[_BC_R]	[_CR__]	Rights Inheritance
IT	[_B___]	[_C___]	Trustee Assignment
MANUF	[_BC_R]	[_CR__]	Rights Inheritance

Rights for mjsmith

Figure 9-6: NDS rights inheritance.

In Figure 9-6, we see a sample NDS tree with [Root] at the top. If mjsmith was made a trustee of the RAMBELL organization with the NDS object rights [_BC_R] and property rights [_CR__], she would have explicit rights to the RAMBELL container. She also gains these rights to all objects in the container through NDS rights inheritance. This gives her the [_BC_R] object rights and [_CR__] property rights to the ACCT container and the MANUF container.

Notice mjsmith is granted another trustee assignment to the IT.RAMBELL container. This assignment gives her the NDS object rights [_B___] and property rights [_C___]. Explicit trustee assignments supersede any rights that might be inherited in the NDS tree. Because of a higher level trustee assignment, it seems she should inherit the [_BC_R] object rights and [_CR__] property rights to the IT container in Figure 9-6, but she does not. Because of an

explicit trustee assignment to the IT organizational unit, she has only the
[_B___] object right and [_C___] property right to the container and all of its
subordinate objects.

It is important to understand this hierarchy of security. Trustee assignments
take precedence over rights inheritance. The same thing is true for file system
rights. Thus, one way to block NDS rights to a particular container or object is
to grant an explicit trustee assignment. However, this could get confusing, and
again you may have to create a large number of trustee assignments to implement the level of security desired.

The NDS Inherited Rights Filter

There is another way to block NDS rights from being inherited down the NDS
tree. It is called the Inherited Rights Filter (IRF). Every object in the NDS tree
has two IRFs associated with it. There is one IRF for NDS object rights and a
second IRF for NDS property rights. The functions of the IRFs are to block
rights inheritance.

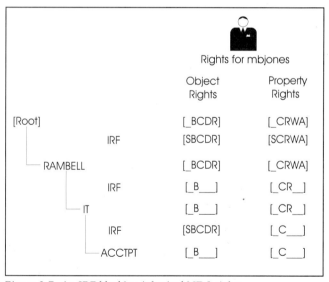

Figure 9-7: An IRF blocking inherited NDS rights.

In Figure 9-7, we see that mbjones has been given a trustee assignment to [Root] with object rights [_BCDR] and property rights [_CRWA]. Because of rights inheritance, mbjones has those NDS rights to all objects in the tree; however, there is an IRF on the IT.RAMBELL container of [_B___] and [_CR__] for the object and property rights. Because of this IRF, mbjones will only have the [_B___] object right and [_CR__] property rights to the container and its subordinate objects.

There is another layer of refinement available with IRFs. They can be used for leaf objects as well as container objects. In Figure 9-7, we saw that mbjones has the object right [_B___] and property rights [_CR__] to the objects in the IT.RAMBELL container. However, the printer object ACCTPT has a property right IRF of [_C___]. Even though mbjones has the rights [_B___] and [_CR__] to all other objects in the container, because of the object specific IRFs he would only have the rights [_B___] and [_C___] to the printer object ACCTPT.

Note that the IRFs for object and property rights are actually two separate filters. If the object rights IRF for an object was [_____], it would not filter out any property rights that might be inherited. To completely filter all rights, both the object *and* property rights IRF must be [_____]. The IRF applies to all objects' rights inheritances; IRFs cannot be used to filter rights for a subset of objects. By default, the IRFs for NDS object rights and NDS property rights are [SBCDR] and [SCRWA], respectively.

Modifying the NDS IRF

The Inherited Rights Filter for an NDS object can be modified using NetWare Administrator. In "Granting Trustee Assignments" earlier in the chapter, we saw how to create a trustee assignment from the target object's point of view. This is the same method used to change the object's IRF:

1. In the NDS tree, click on the target object once with the right mouse button and select Trustees of This Object from the menu that appears. The Trustees dialog box will be displayed.

2. Click on the Inherited Rights Filter button in the lower left corner of the dialog box. The Inherited Rights Filter dialog box will appear.

3. Modify the NDS object rights IRF and the NDS property rights IRF. Click OK to commit to the changes.

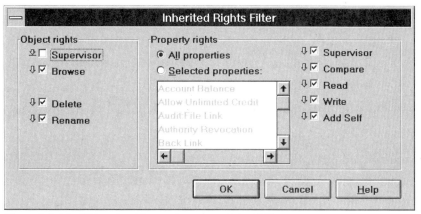

Figure 9-8: Modifying the object and property rights IRFs.

Figure 9-8 displays the Inherited Rights Filter dialog box for NDS rights. On the left-hand side of the dialog box is the object rights IRF; on the right hand side is the property rights IRF. A box with a check mark in it means the right is passed through the filter. A blank box blocks the inheritance for that right. Notice the status of the downward pointing arrow to the left of the check boxes. When the arrow is fully extended, the right passes through the IRF and is inherited. When the arrow is blocked, as it is for the Supervisor object right, it indicates that right is not inherited.

For the property rights, the IRF can get a little complicated. There are selections for All Properties and Selected Properties just as there were for the trustee assignments. IRFs can be applied generally for every property of the NDS object. A property can also be singled out and given a separate IRF through the Selected Properties option. This behavior resembles that of the trustee assignment. An IRF applied to a specific property supersedes the IRF specified for the All Properties option.

The NDS Supervisor Rights & the IRF

When we worked with file system rights, we saw that the Supervisor right was all powerful. It also could not be blocked with a file system IRF. The NDS Supervisor object and property rights *can* be blocked by an appropriate IRF. However, this can lead to trouble.

Let's say the file server object Damocles exists in the NDS tree. All trustee assignments to the object have been removed; however, the Admin user object has the Supervisor object right to the file server through inheritance. By accident, an object rights IRF of [_____] is placed on the file server object. This prevents anyone from administering the server because no object will have rights to the server. There are no explicit rights granted through trustee assignments, and no rights are inherited because of the IRF. This can not only happen with server objects, it can happen with containers as well. You can be effectively cut off from an entire branch of your NDS tree!

Fortunately, NetWare Administrator will allow you to block the Supervisor object right with an IRF if and only if there is a trustee of the target object with the Supervisor object right. This effectively prevents any accidental blocking of NDS rights to an NDS object because there is an explicit assignment of rights that will not be overridden by rights inheritance. Although this provides good protection against "dead" leaves and branches, there are still ways that objects can be cut off from the NDS tree.

Think back to our example of the file server object Damocles. The user mbjones is given a trustee assignment to the file server with the object rights [SBCDR]; his user object is the only NDS object with a trustee assignment to the file server. An object rights IRF of [_____] is also applied to Damocles. This can be done because of the explicit trustee assignment mbjones has; however, if the user object mbjones is deleted from the tree, there is no object remaining with the rights to administer the file server. Anyone up for a reinstall?

Tip

Block the Supervisor object and property rights with an IRF only when necessary. If you must block these rights, be certain there are multiple trustee assignments to the target object. This will prevent the object from being cut off from the NDS tree.

NDS Effective Rights

Trustee assignments are what grant objects an initial level of rights to the NDS tree. From there, rights flow down the NDS tree until another trustee assignment is encountered or an IRF blocks the rights. But many objects not only get security privileges through trustee assignments and inheritance, they also get those privileges through associations with other NDS objects.

We saw with the file system security that users can be members of groups. Because of this group affiliation, the users gain the security equivalents of the group. Any rights the group has to the file system are granted to the user due to this association. The same is true for NDS rights. Objects not only receive NDS rights through trustee assignments and inheritance, they also receive those rights through associations with other NDS objects.

Security Equivalence

As we learned in Chapter 4, an object can be made the security equivalent of another NDS object. When this association is made, the object is implicitly granted the same level of rights as its security equivalent. Using security equivalents is not a good idea; if the security equivalent object is deleted, the other object loses the rights gained through security equivalence.

One place security equivalence plays an important role is with the container object. All objects within a container (including subordinate containers and their objects) are considered to be security equivalents of the container. Thus, when a container is granted a trustee assignment to an object, all of the objects in the container also gain those rights.

The effective rights an NDS object has to the target object are the combination of all rights received from the following sources:

- Explicit trustee assignment
- Rights inheritance
- Security equivalence

Those three things together form a bottom line of NDS rights an object has to a target object. *Effective rights* are the total sum of all security privileges obtained from the three sources. Because NDS rights can come from many different sources, it is important to understand the process used to calculate effective rights in the NDS tree. Many times network administrators don't realize the level of NDS rights an object may have because a rights inheritance or security equivalence was overlooked.

Calculating Effective Rights

The calculation of effective rights for an NDS object is much easier said than done. It takes an intimate knowledge of your network and a remembrance of object associations you have installed in your NDS tree. To calculate an object's NDS effective rights, perform the following steps:

1. Determine the rights granted to the primary object at the target object. Any trustee assignment the primary object has immediately determines the object's rights.

2. If the primary object is not a trustee of the target object, the primary object's NDS rights to the target object will be gained through rights inheritance. Determine the inherited rights for the primary object when no trustee assignment exists.

3. Determine any extra rights the primary object receives through a security equivalence with another NDS object. For example, if a user is a member of a group, any trustee assignment that group has to the target object will be passed on to the primary object. Also, any inherited rights that group has to the target object will be passed on to the primary object. Repeat this step for every object association.

This procedure might be a little reminiscent of some math courses you have taken because it is a manual process that will probably require pencil and paper to complete. However, it is important that you thoroughly understand how effective rights are calculated in the NDS tree because it will help you troubleshoot security holes. Later in this chapter, in the section "Viewing NDS Effective Rights," we will use NetWare Administrator to view effective rights for objects in the NDS tree.

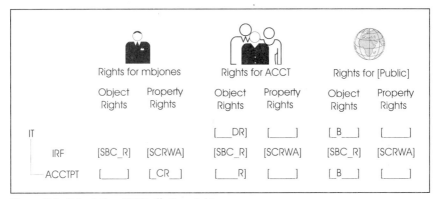

Figure 9-9: Calculating NDS effective rights.

Suppose we want to find the NDS effective rights for the user mbjones to the printer object ACCTPT in the IT.RAMBELL container. He has been given the object rights [_____] and property rights [_CR__] to the printer through explicit trustee assignment. The group ACCT, of which mbjones is a member, has a trustee assignment to the IT.RAMBELL container with the object rights [___DR] and property rights [_____]. The printer object itself has IRFs of [SBC_R] and [SCRWA]. What are the NDS effective rights for mbjones? Let's follow our steps from the previous list to find out:

1. Because we are trying to determine the effective rights of mbjones, mbjones is the primary object. The printer ACCTPT is the target object. The primary object does have a trustee assignment to the target object. Thus, the rights gained from the primary object are the [_____] object rights and the [_CR__] property rights.

2. No NDS rights are inherited because of the explicit trustee assignment the primary object has to the target object.

3. Because mbjones is a member of the group ACCT, he gains rights to the printer object. ACCT does not have a trustee assignment to ACCTPT; however, the group does have a trustee assignment to the IT.RAMBELL container with the object rights [___DR] and property rights [_____]. These rights are inherited; but the printer itself has IRFs of [SBC_R] and [SCRWA]. Thus, the rights mbjones inherits at the ACCTPT printer object from the group ACCT are the object right [____R] and property rights [_____].

4. Through default NDS rights, [Public] has been granted a trustee assignment to [Root] with the object right [_B___] and property rights [_____]. These rights are inherited through the tree. The printer itself has IRFs of [SBC_R] and [SCRWA]. The rights mbjones inherits at the ACCTPT printer object from [Public] are the object right [_B___] and property rights [_____].

To finish the calculation of effective rights, we take all of the rights gained through trustee assignment, inheritance, and security equivalence and add them all together. From the primary object, mbjones, we have the [_____] object rights and [_CR__] property rights. Through object association with the group ACCT, mbjones gains the object right [____R] and property rights [_____]. From [Public], mbjones gains the object right [_B___] and property rights [_____]. Thus, the NDS effective rights for mbjones at the printer object ACCTPT.IT.RAMBELL are [_B__R] object rights and [_CR__] property rights.

Viewing NDS Effective Rights

If you had to go through that process every time you wanted to calculate the effective rights for an object, it would be incredibly inconvenient and time-consuming. Fortunately, there is a way to determine an object's effective rights easily using NetWare Administrator. However, it is important to understand the process so you can see how the built-in utilities arrive at the level of effective rights.

There are two ways to view the effective rights for an object—from the point of view of the primary object and the point of view of the target object. To calculate the NDS effective rights mbjones has to the printer object ACCTPT.IT.RAMBELL, you would perform the following steps:

1. From NetWare Administrator, click on the primary object in the NDS tree (in this case, mbjones) once with the right mouse button. Choose Rights to Other Objects from the menu that appears. The Search Context dialog box will be displayed.

2. Enter the context to be searched. All trustee assignments for the primary object will be found in the specified context. Click OK. The Rights to Other Objects dialog box will appear.

3. Click on the Effective Rights button to the right of the Assigned Objects list. The Effective Rights dialog box will appear (Figure 9-10).

4. In the Effective Rights dialog box, click on the Select Object button to the right to the Object Name text box. Browse the NDS tree to find the target object and click OK.

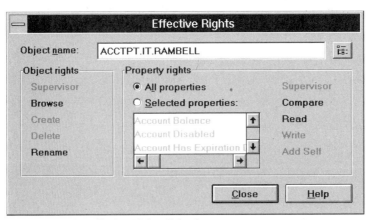

Figure 9-10: The Effective Rights dialog box.

When you are finished, the target object will appear in the Object Name text box, and the effective rights the primary object has to the target object are displayed toward the bottom of the dialog box in the Property Rights and Object Rights sections. Rights that are blackened are rights the primary object has to the target object. In Figure 9-10, mbjones has the [_B__R] object rights and [_CR__] property rights to the ACCTPT.IT.RAMBELL printer object.

This method of determining effective rights will allow you to calculate effective rights only for the primary object. It is useful if you are trying to determine the effective rights for the primary object across many other objects in the NDS tree. However, there are times when you might need to calculate effective rights from the target object. To do so, perform the following steps:

1. From NetWare Administrator, click on the target object in the NDS tree once with the right mouse button and choose Trustees of This Object from the menu that appears. The Trustees dialog box will be displayed.

2. Click on the Effective Rights button to the right of the Trustees list. The Effective Rights dialog box will be displayed.

3. Click on the Select Object button to the right of the Object Name text box to browse the NDS tree for the primary object. Select the primary object and click OK.

When this process is completed, the primary object will appear in the Object Name text box. At the bottom of the dialog box, the rights the primary object has to the target object will be displayed. The object and property rights that are blackened are the NDS effective rights for the primary object. In both methods, you can view either All Property or Selected Property effective rights by choosing the appropriate radio box in the Effective Rights screen.

Always rely upon what NetWare Administrator reports in terms of effective rights for a primary object. Although you might think the effective rights are different than what is displayed, the rights shown using these two methods *are* the effective rights the primary object possesses. Quite often, NetWare Administrator displays more effective rights than the network administrator expected. It is when this happens that it is important to understand how effective rights are calculated; it will help you determine from where the excessive effective rights are coming.

Troubleshooting Excessive Rights

So, NetWare Administrator is reporting that a primary object has more effective rights than you think it should have. Worse, you can't figure out where the primary object is getting these extra rights, and one of them is the Supervisor object right. What do you do?

First of all, calm down and take a deep breath. These types of things happen. Fortunately, you are proactive enough to be monitoring the security of your network (kudos!) and have caught this hole before any damage has been done. With all of the intricacies of NDS security, it is common for objects to obtain excessive rights. Although most situations are not as drastic as the one we just described, we often forget about default NDS rights and security equivalents objects might have. Troubleshooting these excessive rights requires a structured and organized method of combing over the NDS tree to determine their origin. It is easy to do; it may just be time consuming.

The first thing to keep in mind are the three methods through which an object obtains NDS rights:

- Trustee assignment
- Rights inheritance
- Security equivalence

The first two are pretty easy to rule out as culprits of excessive rights. In NetWare Administrator, right-click on the primary object once and select Rights to Other Objects from the menu that appears. The Search Context dialog box will be displayed. In the Begin Search in Context box, type **[Root]**. Mark the Search Entire Subtree box and click OK. This will find every trustee assignment the primary object has in the NDS tree. Use these trustee assignments and the concept of rights inheritance to determine if this is the source of the primary object's excessive rights.

If the excessive rights are not coming from a trustee assignment or the inherited rights of the primary object, the second thing to do is view the trustees of the target object. If the primary object has excessive rights at the target object, it is possible the primary object is getting those rights as a security equivalent of a target object trustee. Click on the target object once with the right mouse button and choose Trustees of This Object from the menu that appears. The Trustees dialog box will appear; it displays all of the trustees of the target object.

Because you are looking for objects that are security equivalents of the primary object, look for the most likely suspects from which the primary object might be obtaining excessive rights. The most likely suspects are [Root], [Public], and the container in which the primary object resides. Also look for groups, organizational roles, and other NDS objects with which the primary object might be associated. Often, rights are granted to these objects and we forget that our primary object is the security equivalent of them.

If that doesn't help identify the source of the excessive rights, the excessive rights are probably inherited from the trustee assignment of a security equivalent higher in the tree. The next step in troubleshooting excessive rights involves tree backtracking. In tree backtracking, you look at the effective rights of the primary object at the next higher container in the NDS tree. This process locates the level of the container at which the excessive rights were introduced.

Looking back on the effective rights example from before, let's suppose mbjones has excessive rights to the ACCTPT.IT.RAMBELL object. With tree backtracking, we would examine mbjones's effective rights at the IT.RAMBELL container. If the excessive rights still existed there, we would backtrack up the tree another level to examine mbjones's effective rights at the RAMBELL container. If mbjones no longer had excessive rights at this level, we would conclude he was getting the excessive rights at the IT.RAMBELL container and would focus our efforts there. Otherwise, we would backtrack again up to [Root] and check mbjones's effective rights there. Figure 9-11 shows the backtracking process.

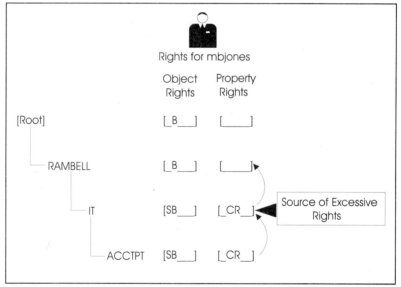

Figure 9-11: Using tree backtracking to troubleshoot excessive rights.

Once the source of the excessive rights is located, you must examine the trustees of the container to determine the origin of the excessive rights. However, if tree backtracking does not help you isolate the excessive rights, you still have one more place to check. If the primary object is a user object, double-click on the user object in the NetWare Administrator. Select the Security Equal To property tab to display the explicit security equivalents of the object. There may be a security equivalent in this list you have forgotten about that is causing the excessive rights.

To recap, here are the steps you should take to troubleshoot NDS excessive rights:

1. View all of the primary object's trustee assignments in the NDS tree. Use this information to determine if the excessive rights are coming from a trustee assignment or rights inheritance.

2. View the trustees of the target object. Excessive rights can come from a security equivalent that is a trustee of the target object.

3. Use tree backtracking to find the container where the excessive rights start. Once the container is located, view the trustees of the container to find the source of the excessive rights.

4. For user objects, view the Security Equal To property tab to view security equivalents that may have been forgotten. Also remember that objects are automatically security equivalents of containers located higher up in the NDS tree and the [Public] trustee.

Like we said, it can be time consuming, but taking an organized approach to locating the source of the excessive rights is the only way you will be successful in troubleshooting these security holes. Be persistent!

Moving On

In this chapter, you learned all you need to know about NDS security. You understand the NDS rights that can be granted in the NDS tree, and you also understand the difference between NDS object rights and property rights. The rights define what can be done to an NDS object in the tree.

Rights are given to objects through trustee assignments. A trustee assignment is an explicit granting of rights to a specific NDS object. All rights in the NDS tree start with a trustee assignment somewhere. Without an initial trustee assignment, there would be no rights present in the tree.

Once trustee assignments are introduced, rights inheritance follows. Rights inheritance is the method by which rights flow down the structure of the NDS tree. When a trustee assignment is made at a high-level container in the NDS tree, that trustee is also granted rights to all subordinate objects and containers through rights inheritance. However, this inheritance can be blocked by an IRF.

Finally, you learned a lot about effective rights. You understand how an object can obtain NDS rights through trustee assignments, rights inheritance, and security equivalence. Although NDS rights can be complicated, you are also now able to troubleshoot any excessive rights an object might have in your NDS tree.

Now that security has been covered, it is time to move toward the infrastructure of the NDS tree. Whether your network has a small number of servers or a large number of servers, organizing how the NDS database is partitioned and replicated is important for the efficiency and fault tolerance of your network. In the next chapter, we will discuss the concepts of NDS partitioning and replication.

NDS Partitioning & Replication

There are two distinct portions of NetWare Directory Services a network administrator must deal with. NDS has both a front end and a back end. The front end deals with the overall structure of the NDS tree, the security implementation of the NDS tree, and the maintenance of objects created in the tree. You can think of it as the part of the tree with which the user interacts. We have covered these portions of NDS in Chapters 3, 4, and 9.

There is another side to NDS, the back end, which the users never see; but to you, as the network administrator, it is incredibly important. It deals with the physical structure of the NDS database, breaking it up into pieces and distributing those pieces across the network. It also encompasses copying those distributed pieces and maintaining their synchronization. It is the network administrator's job to understand the back end of NDS, which is critical to the health of the NDS tree.

We have learned about the utility used to manage the front end of NDS, the NetWare Administrator. The back end also has its own management utility. It is called NDS Manager and it's brand-new to NetWare. In this chapter, we will become familiar with the NDS Manager interface by discussing how to navigate the environment. We will also look at the types of tasks you can accomplish using NDS Manager.

As we have discussed, NDS is an object-oriented distributed database that can be broken up into pieces and distributed across servers on the network. This is called partitioning, and it is one of the main features of the NDS back end. You can enhance the performance of your network by dividing it into logical partitions to even out the load. We will discuss partitioning, how to view the partition information, and how to perform partition management using NDS Manager.

One of the benefits of partitioning is achieved when it is coupled with the concept of replication. With NDS replication, you make copies of the pieces of the database (the partitions) and distribute them across the network as well. This provides a level of fault tolerance; if one partition gets destroyed, there is another copy of it on the network that can be used to restore the destroyed copy. NDS replication and replication management will also be discussed in this chapter.

NDS partitioning and replication are critical elements of the successful implementation of an NDS tree. Understanding these concepts will help you to both provide the best network performance for your users and implement a fault-tolerant network that will be able to continue operation when errors and disaster arise. But before we discuss these critical concepts, we must learn about the tool we will use to manage the NDS back-end environment.

Using NDS Manager

As we have mentioned, NDS Manager is the utility used to administer the back end of the NDS environment. Like NetWare Administrator, NDS Manager is a Windows utility that takes full advantage of its graphical user interface (GUI) to present the back end of the NDS in an easy-to-use-and-understand manner. There are multiple views of the back end that can be provided by NDS Manager, one of which mimics the front end. This establishes a point of reference between the front end and back end that makes the initial use of this new utility more comprehensible.

The Windows 3.x version of the NDS Manager executable resides in the SYS:PUBLIC directory of the NetWare 4.11 server. It is called NDSMGR16.EXE. There are also versions of NDS Manager for Windows 95 and Windows NT called NDSMGR32.EXE and NDSMGRNT.EXE, respectively. They are located in their appropriate client directories off of SYS:PUBLIC. Before launching NDS Manager, it is helpful to set up a shortcut to the application in your Windows environment.

To create the shortcut in Windows 3.x, select the program group that will store the icon. Choose File | New from the menu bar of Program Manager. Select New Program Item from the dialog box displayed. You will be prompted to enter information about NDS Manager. Figure 10-1 displays the information required when NDS Manager is in SYS:PUBLIC and the F: drive has been mapped to the SYS volume. Substitute your drive-letter mapping if it is different.

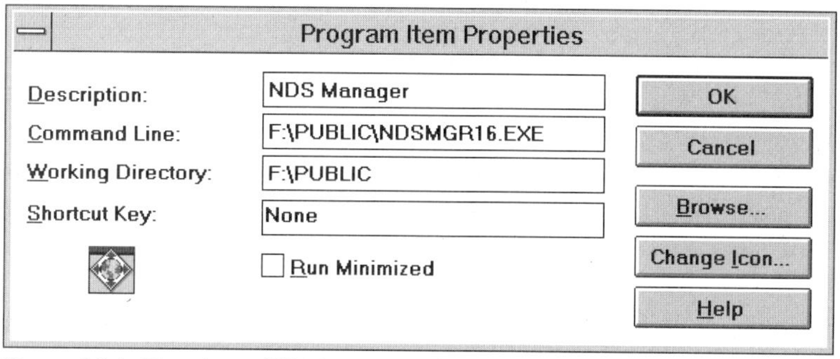

Program Item Properties	
Description:	NDS Manager	OK
Command Line:	F:\PUBLIC\NDSMGR16.EXE	Cancel
Working Directory:	F:\PUBLIC	
Shortcut Key:	None	Browse...
	☐ Run Minimized	Change Icon...
		Help

Figure 10-1: Creating a Windows icon for NDS Manager.

Once the icon has been created, double-click on it to start NDS Manager. The main screen of NDS Manager will appear. Like all other Windows applications, the NSD Manager window has the obligatory title bar and control boxes at the top. The menu bar appears immediately beneath the title bar, and the NDS Manager toolbar is directly underneath the menu bar. The meat of the application is presented in the subordinate window. This is where your interaction with the back end of the NDS environment occurs, as seen in Figure 10-2.

Using NDS Manager With NetWare Administrator

NDS Manager can also be configured with a NetWare Administrator snap-in. To incorporate both applications into one, you need to modify the NWADMN3X.INI file in the WINDOWS directory of your local machine. In the [Snapin Object DLLs WIN 3X] section of the file, add the following line:

```
NDSMGR = NMSNAP16.DLL
```

The next time you open NetWare Administrator, NDS Manager will appear as an option under the Tools menu.

Navigating NDS Manager

In the subordinate window of the NDS Manager utility, you can choose one of two different views of the NDS back end. The first view (the default view) is the NDS Tree view. The point of reference for this view is the logical NDS tree structure. This point of reference is helpful for beginners to the NDS Manager utility because it creates a familiar environment for the network administrator. However, there is another view, the Partitions and Servers view, that provides a compact and concise view of the NDS back end. Each view has its own set of benefits. Choose the one with which you feel most comfortable.

Tree View

The Tree view for NDS Manager appears in Figure 10-2. The subordinate window is broken up into three main sections. Just below the tool bar is another informational bar. This area displays your current context, the partition viewed, and the server from which the information was read. In our example, our current context is [Root], the partition being viewed is [Root], and the server read is the file server Damocles in the IT.RAMBELL container.

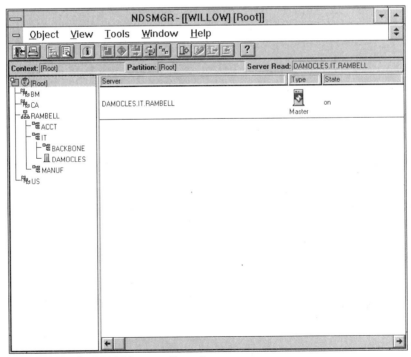

Figure 10-2: The NDS Manager Tree view.

On the left side of the subordinate window, you see the logical tree structure, which is similar to what you would see in NetWare Administrator; however, only container objects and server objects are displayed in the tree. This is because they are the only types of objects that can be manipulated using NDS Manager. You will notice the symbol immediately to the left of [Root]'s globe symbol; it indicates an NDS partition. This happens to be the [Root] partition of the tree Willow.

Since our current context in the tree is [Root], as seen in the information bar, we can see the entire NDS tree in the left-hand window. You can change your current context and limit the size of the tree displayed if you have a very large tree. To change your current context, choose View | Set Context from the menu bar. Once your context is changed, the context specified becomes the top container displayed on the left-hand side of the subordinate window.

If not all of the subordinate containers are displayed in the tree, you can expand a branch of the tree by double-clicking on a container in NDS Manager. The subordinate containers existing underneath that container will be displayed. To shrink a branch of the tree, double-click on the container. All subordinate containers will be hidden.

On the right-hand side of the window, the replicas for the partition are displayed. In Figure 10-2, Damocles holds the only replica of the [Root] partition. We are able to see these replicas only because [Root] has been highlighted in the NDS tree. If RAMBELL were highlighted, we would not see any replica information because RAMBELL is not a partition; it is merely a subordinate container.

When a server is highlighted in the NDS tree on the left-hand side of the window, the right-hand side displays all of the partitions contained on that server. Figure 10-3 shows the file server Damocles highlighted and the information concerning the partitions stored on the server. Thus, you can display information about a single partition by highlighting the partition, or you can display information about a single server by highlighting it in the NDS tree.

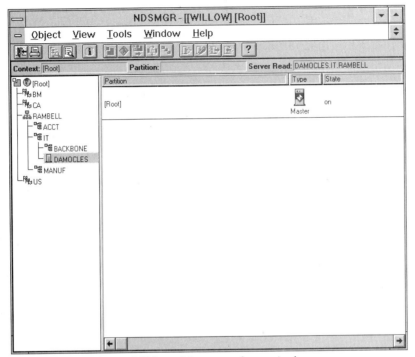

Figure 10-3: Displaying NDS partitions stored on a single server.

Notice the split between the left- and right-hand sides of the subordinate window. This split can be moved by dragging it with the mouse. If your tree is large and the width can't be fully seen, you can drag the split to the right to enlarge the left-hand side.

Tip

To get to Tree View mode, choose View | Tree from the menu bar or press the Tree View button on the toolbar. It is located immediately to the right of the Printer button.

Partitions & Servers View

The Partitions and Servers view takes all of the pertinent back-end NDS information and displays it concisely on one screen. All the partitions in the NDS tree are displayed along with all of the servers. The Partitions and Servers view is shown in Figure 10-4.

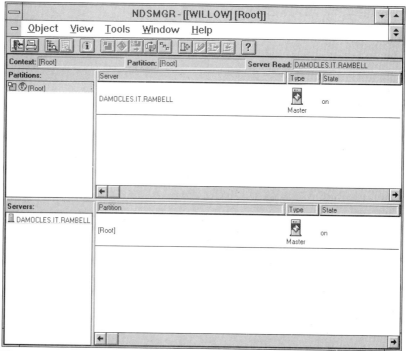

Figure 10-4: NDS Manager Partitions and Servers view.

With this view, the subordinate window is broken up into five main areas. Across the top of the subordinate window, just underneath the toolbar, is the information bar. It appears and functions exactly like the information bar in Tree view. It displays your current context, the partition being viewed, and the server being read.

At the top of the subordinate window is the partition information. The partitions are displayed to the left, and the replica information appears to the right. This is the same information that is gained by clicking on the partition itself in the Tree view; however, all partitions in the NDS tree are listed for convenient access. To view the replica information for a partition, just click on the partition once with the left mouse button.

Toward the bottom of the subordinate window is the server information. The servers are displayed to the left, and the partitions stored on that server are shown to the right. Again, this is the same information that can be viewed by clicking on the server in the Tree view; however, all of the servers in the tree are displayed in a manner that makes them easy to locate. To view partition information stored on a server, click on the server once to highlight it.

As it is in the Tree view, the display of the subordinate window is customizable. You can drag both the horizontal and vertical splits to adjust the size of the four main panes of the subordinate window.

Tip

To get to the Partitions and Servers view in NDS Manager, choose View | Partitions and Servers from the menu bar. You can also select the Partitions and Servers View button located immediately to the right of the Tree View button on the toolbar.

Each view of the NDS back end has its own set of advantages. Which one you choose is up to you. The Tree view is useful for seeing the hierarchy of your partitions and how one partition relates to the others. The Partitions and Servers view is useful for displaying all partitions and servers concisely. You do not need to navigate the NDS tree to get to a partition or server. Assume you can accomplish any task mentioned in this chapter using either view unless we specifically state you can only do it from one particular view.

NDS Manager Tasks

Now that we know how to get around in NDS Manager and what kind of views of our NDS back end we have, we'll take a look at what types of tasks you can perform with NDS Manager. Because it deals with the back-end environment, NDS Manager is not used for everyday NDS administration like user management and security. There is a very specific subset of NDS administrative duties that are accomplished with the utility.

There are four general categories of NDS back-end tasks that are done with NDS Manager:

- Container operations
- Server operations
- Partition operations
- Replication operations

Container Operations

You may have noticed that you are not able to move containers in the NDS tree with NetWare Administrator. What you can do is delete all of the objects in the container, delete the container itself, re-create it in the appropriate place in the tree, and re-create all of the deleted objects. Obviously, this is not a viable solution when you need to move a container; fortunately, there is an easier way to move containers in the NDS tree.

Containers can be moved through NDS Manager using the Tree View mode. Before a container can be moved, it must be made its own partition. Once it is a partition, it can be moved using the partition-moving utilities. We will discuss partition operations later in this chapter in the section "Managing NDS Partitions"; however, you should note that to move a container, you must make it its own partition before doing so.

Server Operations

NetWare Server objects straddle the front-end and back-end worlds. This is because they are responsible for the security of the network and the interface with users, but also because they store partition and replica information about your NDS tree. There are some server operations that cannot be accomplished using NetWare Administrator.

Although a server object can be created, managed, and moved using NetWare Administrator, it cannot be deleted using this method. NetWare Server objects in your NDS tree can only be deleted using NDS Manager. To remove a server from the NDS tree, right-click on it once and choose Delete from the menu that appears.

Tip

When you remove a server object from the NDS tree, it is gone permanently. All information about the server, including resources and file system information, will be removed from your network. Only delete a server object if you are sure it needs to be removed.

Be careful when deleting server objects from your NDS tree. It can cause serious database corruption. Before removing the server object, make sure it is not storing any partition information. If it is, remove all replica information from the server using NDS Manager. When a server is removed from the tree, only a reinstall of NDS on that server will allow it to rejoin. You should only remove a server object from the tree if the server is taken down permanently or it has failed (the hard drives have crashed).

Another server operation that can be accomplished using NDS Manager is the Directory Services (DS) update. From time to time, Novell will release a new version of NDS to enhance the functionality and fix the bugs in a previous version. When this happens, it is recommended you update the version of NDS on your servers to the most current version. To accomplish this, you can go to each server individually and upgrade the version of DS, or you can centrally manage the DS update using NDS Manager.

To update the DS version on a server, select the server by clicking on it once with the left mouse button. Choose Object | NDS Version | Update from the menu bar. The NDS Version Update dialog box will appear (Figure 10-5).

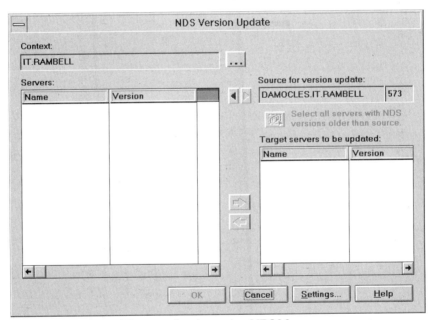

Figure 10-5: Updating Directory Services using NDS Manager.

In the upper right portion of the dialog box, you will see the Source for Version Update box. This is the server that acts as the "master" for the update. Its version of NDS will be sent to the target servers. On the left side of the screen, you specify the context in which the NDS Update program will look for servers. When it finds servers in the specified context (in this case, IT.RAMBELL), it will list names of the servers and their version of NDS. Use the smaller arrows between the Servers box and Source for Version Update box to specify the NDS master. Clicking on the right-pointing arrow will move the highlighted server from the Servers list to the Source for Version Update box.

There is another box on the right side of the screen where the target servers are listed. Use the larger arrows between the two boxes to move servers back and forth. Once the master server and target servers have been specified, click on the OK button. The NDS Update program will update the target servers *and* reset Directory Services to put the new version in effect. You don't have to manually update NDS on each server anymore; it can all be managed centrally. It is a very cool utility.

Tip

The version of Directory Services released with IntranetWare is DS 5.73 for NetWare 4.11. This version will only work with other NetWare 4.11 servers. You cannot place this version of DS on older NetWare 4.1 servers. They have their own NetWare 4.1 version of DS. Consult the Novell Web site (http:// support.novell.com) for more information on the latest release of DS for your version of NetWare.

With NDS, you can also view server information by double-clicking on the server object, as seen in Figure 10-6. You can also manage servers remotely by using the Remote Console utility. Choose Tools | Remote Console from the menu bar. You can only use this feature on servers that have had REMOTE.NLM set up on them. For more information on Remote Console, refer to Chapter 18.

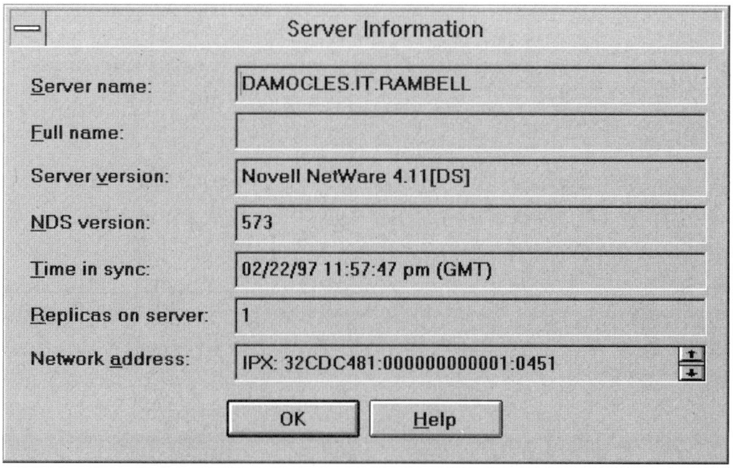

Figure 10-6: Viewing server information in NDS Manager.

Partitioning Operations

All NDS partitioning operations are accomplished using NDS Manager. You can create new partitions, merge existing partitions, move partitions, and synchronize partitions with this utility. NDS partitioning and using NDS Manager to perform these partition operations will be discussed in the next section of this chapter, "NDS Partitioning."

Replication Operations

All NDS replica operations are also accomplished using NDS Manager. You can place new replicas on servers in the NDS tree, remove replicas from selected servers, push replica information to other servers, and pull replica information from other servers. NDS replication and using NDS Manager to accomplish these tasks are discussed in "NDS Replication" later in this chapter.

NDS Manager is your tool for administering the NDS back-end environment. Get familiar with the interface because you will need to use it to maintain the health of your network.

NDS Partitioning

As we have said many times, NDS is an object-oriented distributed database. We can easily see the object-oriented part. The information stored in the database is composed of objects. Every network resource is represented as an object with a specific subset of properties and values. But what about the distributed part?

The distributed nature of NDS comes from the fact the NDS database can be broken up into smaller pieces. These smaller pieces can be stored in separate places across the network. The pieces are distributed across the various servers on your network. This is a great advantage because it makes the NDS database extremely scalable. Unlike with NetWare 3.x, where the entire bindery must be stored on one server, with NetWare 4.11, the workload required for storage and maintenance of the NDS database can be distributed across multiple machines.

There is a drawback to this increased flexibility. The network administrator has more concepts to understand and more work to perform to ensure the integrity of the databases; it is, however, worth it. The distributed database is able to unify your network resources into one central location, which eliminates other network administration work you might have to do. As the network administrator, you make out better in the trade-off.

Even though the pieces of the database can be separated and placed on different servers, all of the pieces still act together to make it look like one big database for the user. Thus, the user has no idea the database has been broken down for scalability. He or she just sees it as a central repository of network resources.

Understanding Partitioning

The best way to describe NDS partitioning is to go back to our Rolodex example from Chapter 9. Remember we said the database was like a Rolodex made up of cards labeled with the person's name and storing a specific set of information on them? Together, all of these cards make up a database of your personal contacts. Many Rolodex filers come with separators that divide your contacts into alphabetical groupings.

Our Rolodex has now been partitioned into 26 smaller pieces; a partition exists for every letter of the alphabet. Each partition contains all of the database information in the grouping. The A partition contains all of your contacts whose last name begins with the letter A. Most of us keep these partitions in the same Rolodex for convenience; however, the As could be moved to a different location, as could the Bs and Cs. NDS partitioning works similarly.

The NDS database is grouped together in a logical manner. The database is broken down in terms of containers. Each container contains objects that need to be stored. The database partition stores all objects the container happens to contain. For instance, in Figure 10-7, the US partition stores the information about all objects underneath it. This includes the organization object RAMBELL-US and the organizational units ACCT, IT, and MANUF. It also stores information about all the leaf objects contained in those subordinate containers.

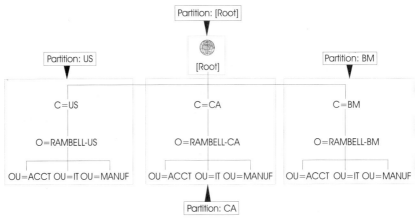

Figure 10-7: Partitions in an NDS tree.

Just because the NDS database is partitioned does not mean it is automatically distributed across your network. That is a process that you must perform using NDS Manager. Obviously, if you have only one server in your NDS tree, you can't distribute the database. Partitions can only be stored on NetWare 4.x servers.

Dividing the NDS Tree

The NDS tree starts with one partition. It is called the [Root] partition, and it is created during the installation of the NDS tree when you bring up your first NetWare 4.11 server. This server stores the NDS database in the SYS:_NETWARE directory, which contains all objects you create using NetWare Administrator. Often, the [Root] partition is called the *default partition* because it is created upon installation and exists in every NDS tree.

Once container objects are placed in the NDS tree, you can begin to partition it using NDS Manager. When a new partition is created, a container object must be the topmost NDS object in the partition. The partition is named for this object, and this object is called the *partition root*. Do not confuse this with the [Root] partition, which is so named because [Root] is the topmost object in the NDS tree. Figure 10-8 shows a partitioned NDS tree with the partition roots labeled.

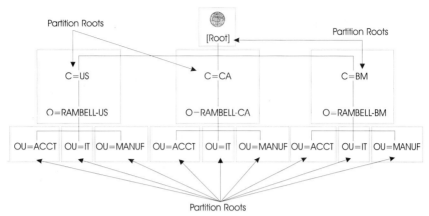

Figure 10-8: NDS partition roots.

Parent/Child Partitions

We can also see from Figure 10-8 that certain partitions seem to exist above others. At the same time, partitions appear to exist directly beneath other partitions. There is a relationship among NDS partitions called the parent/child relationship. When multiple partitions exist in an NDS tree, there are always parent and child partitions.

In Figure 10-8, the [Root] partition is the parent of the US, CA, and BM partitions. This is because it is the partition immediately above those partitions in the NDS tree. The US, CA, and BM partitions are the child partitions of [Root]. They also happen to be parent partitions as well because other partitions exist directly beneath them. For instance, the US partition is the parent of the IT.RAMBELL-US.US partition.

Note that the BM partition is *not* the parent of the IT.RAMBELL-US.US partition. The parent/child relationship is not based upon the relative level of the NDS tree. The relationship is dependent upon the direct association of container objects in the NDS tree. When a partition exists directly above another partition, it is that partition's parent. The parent/child relationships of the partitions in Figure 10-8 are shown in Figure 10-9.

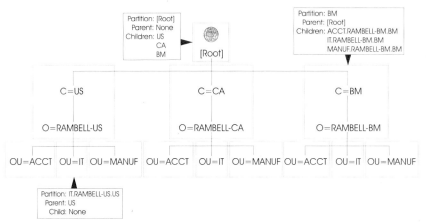

Figure 10-9: Parent/child partition relationships.

Tree Walking

The parent/child partition relationship is critical for a process called tree walking. When a user requests a resource from the tree, that resource may not be stored in the partition with which the user is interfacing. It may have to come from another partition in the tree. Instead of the user having to find it, NDS initiates the process of *tree walking* to locate the resource. This occurs in the background and unbeknownst to the user.

When the request for a resource is initiated, the server to which the user is connected is queried by NDS for the location of the resource. If the server does not hold the information, NDS looks back up the NDS tree to the parent partition, which will hold the next clue concerning the location of the resource. If that partition doesn't have the resource information, then the next parent is searched. It looks like a process similar to the one seen in Figure 10-10.

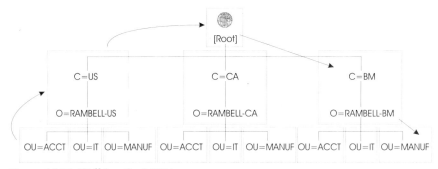

Figure 10-10: Walking the NDS tree.

This is also where our discussion of NDS naming conventions comes into play. Remember, a resource request is always issued from the workstation as a full distinguished name. If you do not provide the full distinguished name, the client workstation software appends your current context to achieve the full distinguished name for the resource. Thus, NDS has a concept of where that resource exists.

In Figure 10-10, a resource request is issued from the ACCT.RAMBELL-US.US container for a resource in the MANUF.RAMBELL-BM.BM container. Because the resource does not exist in the ACCT.RAMBELL-US.US partition, a process of tree walking is initiated to find the resource. When it gets to the [Root] partition, it sees a reference, which exists in the full distinguished name, to the container BM. Tree walking proceeds down the tree to the partition storing the information on the resource. In this case, the resource is located in the MANUF.RAMBELL-BM.BM partition. Once it finds the resource, the information is sent back to the workstation client.

The full distinguished name is incredibly important to NDS. It uniquely identifies the object in the NDS tree and provides a source of information by which the resource can be located.

Partitioning Rules

When you are creating new partitions, there are some rules you must follow. These rules will help you determine where you can and can't create a partition:

- The topmost object in a partition must be a container. It is called the partition root. The partition takes its name from the partition root.

- Partitions may not overlap. If you were to draw out the entire structure of the NDS tree on paper and draw boxes representing the partitions in the diagram, none of those boxes would intersect with another. This means that every NDS object in the NDS tree will exist in one and only one NDS partition.

- There can only be one partition root. Two containers may not coexist as partition roots. Again, if you were to graphically represent the tree on paper, each partition would have only one container at the highest level in the partition. In Figure 1011, we can see a violation of this rule because two containers exist at the top-most level of the partition. *The partition configuration in Figure 10-11 is not valid!*

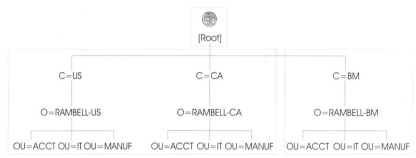

Figure 10-11: A violation of NDS partitioning rules.

Now that we understand partitions and how they relate to the NDS tree, let's talk about partitioning in terms of NDS Manager. In the next section, we will discuss the partition operations that can be accomplished using NDS Manager.

Managing NDS Partitions

As we mentioned earlier in this chapter, all NDS partition operations are accomplished using NDS Manager. There are three main partition operations you will use most frequently:

- Creating new partitions
- Merging partitions
- Moving partitions

Once you understand these operations, you will be well on your way to implementing a scalable and flexible NDS environment that will suit your networking needs.

New Partition Guidelines

Just because you know how to create a new partition in your NDS tree does not necessarily mean that you will *want* to create one. Small networks with one or two servers may only need the default partition. Large networks will have many partitions. Novell does give some guidelines for planning your partitioning scheme that take into account both partition location and size considerations.

Location   Partitioning should take into account the physical layout of your network resources. Servers and resources far apart from each other should exist in separate partitions. For example, partitions should not span WAN links; make each side of the WAN link a separate partition.

The NDS tree should also not be top-heavy with partitions. Reduce the number of partitions at the top of the tree and partition more at the bottom.

Size   Generally, partition sizes should be small. Don't be afraid to create new partitions when warranted. It increases the efficiency of your network because the database is segmented. A partition should not contain more than 4,000 or 5,000 NDS objects. It should also not contain less than 100 objects.

The number of partitions in your tree is also important. Each partition will generally have less than 20 subordinate partitions; however, it should not have more than 50 subordinate partitions unless it cannot be avoided. Only the largest of networks will approach this value of 50 subordinate partitions.

Creating New Partitions

Creating a new partition in your NDS tree actually causes the database to split into more pieces. All of the objects stored underneath the partition root become part of this new, smaller piece of the NDS database puzzle. Using NDS Manager, you can create a new partition only in the Tree view. You have to actually see the container that will be the partition root for the new partition.

Using the Tree view in NDS Manager, perform the following steps to split a new child partition from its parent partition:

1. Select the partition root in the left side of the Tree View screen by clicking on it once with the left mouse button. It will become highlighted.

2. Choose Object I Create Partition from the menu bar. You can also click on the Create Partition button immediately to the right of the Information button in the toolbar. The Create Partition dialog box will appear.

3. If you want to create the new partition using the partition root specified, click on the Yes button.

4. If the preconditions for the operation are met (see Sidebar), click on the Yes button to split the new child partition from its parent.

When the new partition is created, the partition root will have a partition symbol immediately to the left of the container icon in the left-hand pane of the Tree View screen. The database will now have a new piece, and the new partition's Master replica is stored on the server that has the Master replica of the parent partition. If any replicas of the parent partition exist on other servers, those servers will also have replicas of the new partition stored on them. The replica for the new partition will be of the same type as that of the parent partition. Thus, if a server has a Read/Write replica of the parent partition, it will also receive a Read/Write replica of the new child. For more information on replicas, refer to "NDS Replication" later in this chapter.

What Does "Preconditions Have Been Met" Mean?

Before every NDS operation in NDS Manager, you will receive a message indicating that "preconditions have been met" for the operation. This means that NDS is ready for the operation to take place. If there is something wrong with the partitions or the synchronization of the replicas among multiple servers, you will receive an error message in NDS Manager, and you will not be able to perform any NDS operations.

Servers that store partition information must always be running when you perform NDS operations. Before you down a server for an extended period of time, you should remove all partition information from that server so you can perform the back-end functions of the NDS environment. If you leave the information on the server and down it, you will not be able to perform any NDS operations.

In Figure 10-12, a new partition has been created in the tree Willow. The partition root is CA. From the Partitions and Servers view, we can see the new partition listed, and we can see that its Master replica is stored on the file server Damocles. Notice the server portion of the screen at the bottom; the replica information for all partitions on Damocles is displayed. We do, in fact, see that Damocles holds the Master partition for both the [Root] partition and the CA partition.

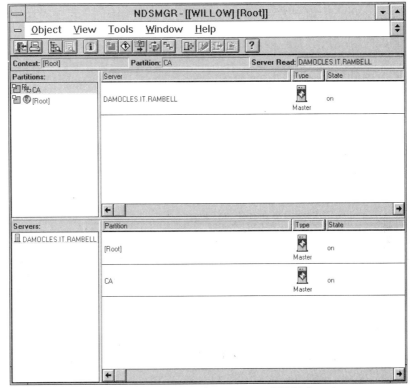

Figure 10-12: Viewing a newly created partition in NDS Manager.

To create a new partition in the NDS tree, you must have the Supervisor object right to the partition root. You can also create a new partition if you have the Write property right to the Object Trustees (ACL) property of the container object. Lack of sufficient rights will prevent you from creating a new partition.

Merging Partitions

Well, if you create partitions, you can delete them, right? Not exactly. Remember, a partition is actually a piece of the NDS database. When you want to remove a partition, you can't delete it because you would also be deleting all of the objects stored in it. The process for creating a partition is reversed when you are *merging* a partition. When a partition is merged, the child becomes part of the parent again. Two pieces of the database are put back together into one piece.

Generally, you will create partitions more often than you will merge them. You may use this operation frequently if you have to move containers in the NDS tree. After the move has occurred, you will probably want to merge the partitions together to return the NDS tree to its original state.

To merge a child partition into its parent partition, perform the following steps in NDS Manager:

1. Select the partition to be merged by clicking on it once with the left mouse button. It will become highlighted.

2. Choose Object | Partition | Merge from the menu bar or click on the Partition Merge button immediately to the right of the Create Partition button on the toolbar. The Merge Partition dialog box will be displayed, as seen in Figure 10-13.

3. If the parent and child partitions are correct in the Merge Partition dialog box, click on the Yes button. If the preconditions for the NDS operation have been met, click on the Yes button in the second Merge Partition dialog box displayed.

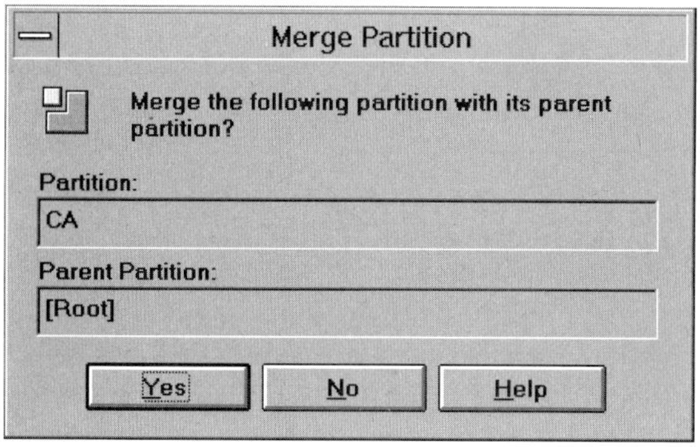

```
 ┌─────────────────────────────────────────────────┐
 │ ═      │        Merge Partition                   │
 ├─────────────────────────────────────────────────┤
 │  ▢⊓     Merge the following partition with its parent │
 │  └┘     partition?                                │
 │                                                   │
 │ Partition:                                        │
 │ ┌───────────────────────────────────────────────┐│
 │ │CA                                              ││
 │ └───────────────────────────────────────────────┘│
 │ Parent Partition:                                 │
 │ ┌───────────────────────────────────────────────┐│
 │ │[Root]                                          ││
 │ └───────────────────────────────────────────────┘│
 │                                                   │
 │   ┌─────────┐  ┌─────────┐  ┌─────────┐          │
 │   │  Yes    │  │   No    │  │  Help   │          │
 │   └─────────┘  └─────────┘  └─────────┘          │
 └─────────────────────────────────────────────────┘
```

Figure 10-13: The Merge Partition dialog box.

When the procedure is complete, the two databases will be merged into one single database again. The child partition will no longer appear in the Partitions and Servers view, and the container icon in the Tree view will no longer have a partition icon to the left of it.

To merge partitions in the NDS tree, you must have the Supervisor object right to the partition root and its parent container. You can also accomplish partition merging if you have the Write property right to the Object Trustees (ACL) properties of the container objects. Lack of sufficient rights will prevent you from merging partitions.

Moving Partitions

When we talk about moving partitions, we are not talking about changing the server on which the partition information is stored. That is a replica operation. Moving a partition means changing the location of the partition root in the NDS tree. This move can only be done when the following are true:

■ The partition being moved does not have any subordinate partitions. Subordinate partitions must themselves be merged back into the partition that will be moved before the move can actually occur.

■ The partition root's destination cannot violate any containment rules. For example, you cannot move a country underneath an organization. That would violate the basic rules of containment.

But why would you want to move a partition? As we mentioned earlier in this chapter, if you want to move a container in your NDS tree, you must make it a partition root and move the partition. To move a partition in the NDS tree, perform the following steps using NDS Manager:

1. Select the partition to be moved by clicking on it once with the left mouse button. It will be highlighted.

2. Select Object | Partition | Move from the menu bar or click on the Move Partition button immediately to the right of the Merge Partition button on the toolbar. The Move Partition dialog box will appear.

3. In the Move Partition dialog box, verify the partition being moved and the destination context. Use the Select Object button next to the To Context box to change the destination context.

4. Decide if you want an alias to be created for the container object being moved. If so, check the check box for creating an alias.

5. Click OK to move the partition. If the preconditions for the NDS operation have been met, click on the Yes button in the second Move Partition dialog box.

When the process is complete, the partition will be moved to the new context. This is also the same procedure used to move a container. Before you can move a container, it must be made a partition root. Once it is, use the Move Partition operation to move the container and its subordinate objects to the desired container. After the move, merge the partition back into the parent if so desired. Simple, right?

To move a partition in the NDS tree, you must have the Supervisor object rights to all containers in the partition. You can also accomplish this move if you have the Write property right to the Object Trustees (ACL) property of the container objects. Lack of sufficient rights will prevent you from moving a partition.

Tip

If you are in the middle of any partition operation, you might be able to abort it. Choose Object | Partition | Abort Operation after clicking on the selected partition once with the left mouse button.

Viewing Partition Information

The information concerning partitions can easily be viewed using NetWare Administrator. To view the information about a partition, perform the following steps:

1. Click on the desired partition once with the left mouse button. The partition will be highlighted.

2. Select Object | Information from the menu bar or click on the Information button immediately to the right of the Partitions and Servers View button on the toolbar. The information for the partition will be displayed, as seen in Figure 10-14.

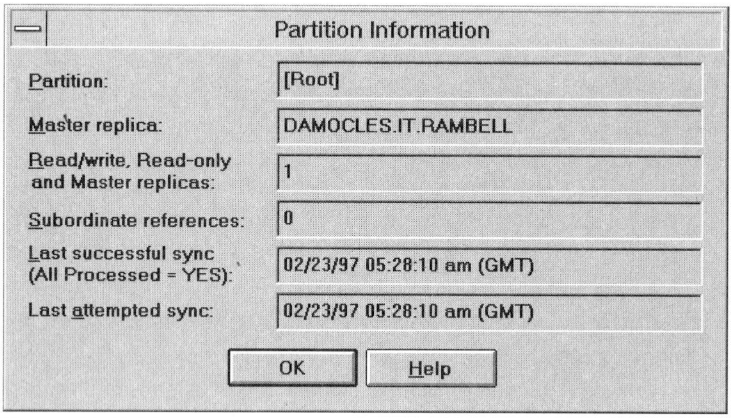

Partition Information	
Partition:	[Root]
Master replica:	DAMOCLES.IT.RAMBELL
Read/write, Read-only and Master replicas:	1
Subordinate references:	0
Last successful sync (All Processed = YES):	02/23/97 05:28:10 am (GMT)
Last attempted sync:	02/23/97 05:28:10 am (GMT)

OK   Help

Figure 10-14: Viewing NDS partition information.

In the dialog box in Figure 10-14, we see the name of the partition and the server on which the Master replica of the partition is stored. We also see information that includes the total number of replicas for this partition, the number of subordinate references for the partition, and synchronization efforts. The final four fields also give replica information and will be discussed in the next section of this chapter.

Although important, partitioning is only a part of the NDS back-end environment. Its partner, NDS replication, expands upon the concept of a distributed database and allows you to distribute the NDS database pieces across the servers on your network.

NDS Replication

The concept of the distributed database relies more upon database replication than it does on database partitioning. However, for maximum efficiency of your database, this distributed nature does rely on *both* partitioning *and* replication. While partitioning makes it possible to break a large database up into smaller, more manageable pieces, it is the replication process that allows those pieces to be moved from place to place on the network. Without replication, you would have separate pieces of a single database all stored in one central location. It really defeats the purpose of distribution.

While replication increases the efficiency of your network, it also does one other thing. It creates more work for the network administrator. It is your responsibility to plan the replication scheme for your network and maintain it. While not a difficult task, it does require you to understand the concepts and features of NDS replication. But, of course, the first question to ask about NDS replication is: What is a replica?

Understanding Replicas

Simply put, a *replica* is a physical copy of a partition. In the process of partitioning, we saw that you could logically divide the NDS database into smaller pieces. When this happened, NDS went through a partitioning process in which the database itself split into pieces. These physical pieces are the replicas of the NDS database. A partition is a logical division of the database; a replica is a physical piece of the NDS database.

Don't be confused by the term *replica* as it pertains to NDS. It usually implies a copy or reproduction of an original; however, in NDS terms, the original piece of the database itself is also called a replica. The original piece of the database is a physical reproduction or copy of the logical partition you created.

The first piece of the database is called the Master replica. When you perform any partition operation, you must have access to the Master replica of the partition. Other replicas of the Master replica can be created. The extra copies of the database piece are placed on other servers in your network. This benefits your network in two ways:

- **It provides a level of fault tolerance to your NDS database.** If for some reason your Master replica becomes damaged or lost, you have other copies of the physical database located on the network. These other pieces can take over the duties of the Master replica in the event of an emergency.

- **It increases the performance of your network.** With other copies of the NDS database on other servers, the workload required for network resource requests is distributed across multiple servers on your network.

Once the replicas of the Master replica have been created, they can be moved to other servers on the network. To take full advantage of partitioning and replication, you really need to have multiple NetWare 4.11 servers on your network. If you only have one server, you will probably only need one database partition, and you will not have the ability to distribute the NDS replicas across multiple servers.

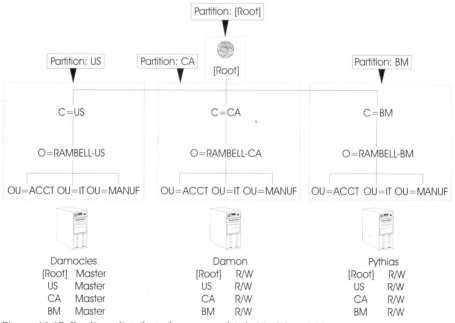

Figure 10-15: Replicas distributed across multiple NetWare 4.11 servers.

Figure 10-15 displays an example of a network that has multiple servers with the replicas of the NDS database distributed amongst them. Originally, there was one partition in this tree, the [Root] partition, and its Master replica was stored on the file server Damocles. The network administrator created three new partitions in the NDS tree due to WAN link considerations. After the partitioning, Damocles held four Master replicas—one Master replica for each partition. To provide fault tolerance, the network administrator placed copies of each of these Master replicas on the NetWare 4.11 servers Damon and Pythias. This distribution of replicas will also help the performance of the network because users will be able to locate network resources through the server on their portion of the WAN. The tree-walking process does not have to span the WAN link.

Figure 10-15 also introduces two new concepts about NDS replicas that need to be explored. The first involves the copies of the replicas themselves as they exist on Damon and Pythias. In the figure, they are labeled as Read/Write replicas. There are actually four different types of NDS replicas. They will be covered in the next section.

The second concept represented in Figure 10-15 is that of the *replica ring*. When there are multiple copies of a single database partition, that partition is said to have a replica ring. For example, Damocles, Damon, and Pythias each have a copy of the [Root] partition. These three replicas compose the replica ring of the [Root] partition.

NDS Replica Types

There are four types of NDS replicas that can be placed on a server for NDS database storage. The network administrator has direct control over the first of three of these types and indirect control over the last type:

- Master replica
- Read/Write replica
- Read-Only replica
- Subordinate Reference replica

The Master, Read/Write, and Read-Only replicas are the three types of replicas the network administrator is able to place on a server using NDS Manager. The fourth, the Subordinate Reference replica, is automatically placed on a server by NDS when certain conditions in your NDS tree exist.

Master Replicas   The Master replica is the critical replica for every partition. By definition, it is the replica that maintains the most accurate data about the partition in your NDS tree. There is only one Master replica for every partition in the NDS tree.

The Master replica is responsible for all partition operations. When a new partition is created, the Master replica for the new partition is created from the Master replica of the parent partition. Thus, you must have access to the Master replica of the parent partition to create a new partition. The same is true for merging and moving partitions. To perform these functions, you must have access to the Master replica of the partition.

Not only is the Master replica used for creating, moving, and merging partitions, it is also in charge of replica synchronization and updates. It initiates the synchronization process between itself and any other replicas of the partition. Because the Master replica is responsible for updates in NDS information and stores all of the information about the partition, it is used for user authentication as well as for the modification of NDS data by users (if they have the rights to modify data).

Read/Write Replicas   The Read/Write replica is second in line in importance in the NDS replication scheme. Although it's not the Master replica, it still has a lot of responsibility in providing the fault tolerance for your network. You can use the Read/Write replica to create extra copies of your database to distribute across the network. Even though there can only be one Master replica for an NDS partition, there can be an unlimited number of Read/Write replicas for that same partition.

As the name implies, the Read/Write replica can also be used to accept updates and changes to the information stored in the NDS tree. This information is then communicated to other replicas of the partition through a process called synchronization. Thus, the Master replica of the partition does not have dominance over the other replicas; both Master and Read/Write replicas can be used to modify NDS data, and they share their knowledge with one another. However, if there is a discrepancy, the Master replica is seen as being more accurate.

Because the Read/Write replica is used for fault tolerance and can be used for user authentication into the NDS tree, it is the most-used type of replica in the NDS world. Without it, NDS replication would be very limited in its ability to serve the needs of the network.

Read-Only Replica   Just like its name implies, the information stored in a Read-Only replica is all outgoing information. You can retrieve a piece of information about the NDS tree from this replica; you cannot, however, change any of the information. When users log in to the NDS tree, the system automatically makes changes to their user object. Thus, a Read-Only replica cannot be used for user authentication. Read-Only replicas are hardly ever used and are often ignored in favor of the Read/Write replica.

Subordinate Reference Replica   The Subordinate Reference replica is not a true replica like the previous three types. It does not contain information about the entire partition; it only holds information about the partition root object. It essentially acts as a pointer reference in the NDS tree. But how is it created, and what is its use?

A Subordinate Reference replica is created by NDS when specific conditions in the NDS partitioning and replication scheme are met. If a server stores a replica of a parent partition and does not store a replica of that parent partition's children, NDS will automatically place a Subordinate Reference replica of each child partition on the server. It may seem very confusing at first, but we will explore this situation to clarify it. Just remember the phrase "where the parent is but *not* the child."

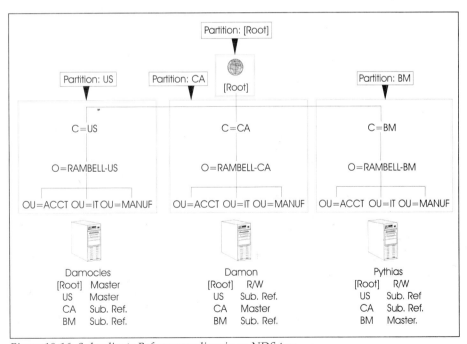

Figure 10-16: Subordinate Reference replicas in an NDS tree.

Figure 10-16 is just a modification of our previous replica example; in this case, however, the Master replicas of the partitions BM and CA have been moved from the file server Damocles to Damon and Pythias, respectively. The replicas of those partitions are then removed from Damocles and are replaced by Subordinate Reference replicas. This is because Damocles is storing a copy of the [Root] partition; however, it does not have a copy of [Root]'s children partitions BM and CA. Because Damocles has a copy of the parent partition but not the child partition, it gets Subordinate Reference replicas of those child partitions.

Subordinate Reference replicas are used by NDS to provide a liaison between parent and child partitions. Because the Subordinate Reference stores the information about the partition root, NDS is able to retrieve information about how partitions are related to one another.

A large number of Subordinate Reference replicas can adversely affect the performance of your network. Try to limit the number of Subordinate Reference replicas by using sound partitioning of your NDS tree. A lot of Subordinate Reference replicas on your servers is a sign of an inadequate partitioning scheme.

Subordinate Reference replicas are managed completely by NDS. You cannot create or remove a Subordinate Reference replica directly, but you can indirectly affect them. By placing another type of replica of the child partition on the server that has the Subordinate Reference replica, you will cause NDS to remove the Subordinate Reference replica from that server. Likewise, if you remove a replica from a server that still has a replica of the parent partition, NDS will create a Subordinate Reference replica of the child partition.

Replica Rings

All of the replicas that exist on your network for a specific partition constitute that partition's *replica ring*. Replica rings provide fault tolerance because having multiple copies of a database on the network will protect against data loss. It is recommended that you have at least 3 replicas in the replica ring for each partition; however, you should not exceed 15 replicas in a replica ring. A high number of replicas in a partition's replica ring can cause excessive network traffic.

Refer back to the diagram in Figure 10-15; we saw a replication scheme that used replica rings to provide fault tolerance for the four partitions. Table 10-1 displays the replica ring for the US partition in that figure.

Server Storing Replica	Replica Type
DAMOCLES.IT.RAMBELL-US.US	Master
DAMON.IT.RAMBELL-BM.BM	Read/Write
PYTHIAS.IT.RAMBELL-CA.CA	Read/Write

Table 10-1: The replica ring for the US partition in Figure 10-15.

Managing NDS Replicas

The theory behind NDS replication might be a bit daunting, but it will become much clearer as we look at how NDS Manager helps us understand and configure this component of the NDS back-end environment. All replication in NDS is done with NDS Manager, and there are essentially four main replica operations:

- Adding replicas to servers
- Removing replicas from servers
- Changing replica types
- Updating replicas

Performing these replica operations will allow you to completely customize your networking environment to provide the most efficient and fault-tolerant network you can have. It lets you have control over your replication strategy and even force manual updates if you require them.

Adding Replicas to Servers

You can increase the number of replicas in a partition's replica ring using NDS Manager. Remember, when a partition is created for the first time, a Master replica is created; therefore, when you add replicas to a replica ring, you are creating a Read/Write or Read-Only copy of the Master replica and placing it on another server in your NDS tree.

Creating replica rings for your partition is beneficial to the health of your NDS tree. It provides fault tolerance for your network. If one replica of a partition becomes corrupted in the replica ring, the remaining replicas will be able to continue providing network services while you fix the damaged one. After you have determined which servers will store the replicas for a partition's replica ring, you will want to add the replica to the server.

To create a new replica in a partition's replica ring, perform the following steps in NDS Manager:

1. Click on the partition once with the left mouse button. The partition will become highlighted.

2. Choose Object | Add Replica from the menu bar or click on the Add Replica button on the toolbar (the button looks like a server with a plus sign next to it). The Add Replica dialog box will appear (Figure 10-17).

3. Select whether the new replica will be a Read/Write or Read-Only replica.

4. Click on the Select Object button to find the server in the NDS tree on which the replica will be stored. Once selected, click OK.

5. If preconditions for this NDS operation have been met, click on the Yes button in the second Add Replica dialog box to place the new replica on the target server.

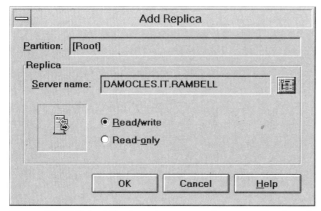

Figure 10-17: Select the target server and new replica type in the Add Replica dialog box.

Once the process is completed, the new replica will be stored on the target server, and you will be able to see it in NDS Manager. You cannot create a new replica on a server that already holds a replica of the partition.

Removing Replicas From Servers

There may be times that you want to remove a partition replica from a NetWare 4.11 server. For example, if you need to remove a corrupted replica from the replica ring, you will need to perform this task using NDS Manager. To remove a replica from a server, perform the following steps:

1. Click on the server object once with the left mouse button. It will become highlighted.

2. From either the Partitions and Servers view or the Tree view, select the replica to be deleted by clicking on the replica in the right-hand side of the subordinate window in NDS Manager. The replica to be deleted will be highlighted.

3. Press the Delete key or choose Object | Delete from the menu bar. The Delete Replica dialog box will appear (Figure 10-18).

4. Make sure the partition replica and the server are correct in the dialog box and press the Yes button. If preconditions have been met for this NDS operation, click on the Yes button in the second Delete Replica dialog box to remove the replica.

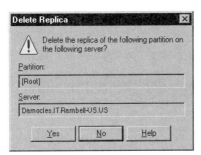

Figure 10-18: Deleting a partition replica.

You cannot delete a Master replica with NDS Manager. If you want to delete a Master replica on a server, you must promote another replica in the replica ring to Master status. The original Master will be demoted to Read/Write status and can then be deleted.

Changing Replica Types

Sometimes there is a need to change the type of replica that is being stored on a server. For example, if the Master partition is unavailable, you can promote another replica in the partition's replica ring to Master status. Or, if you need a replica to perform NDS authentication, you can change a Read-Only replica to a Read/Write replica. To change a replica's type, do the following in NDS Manager:

1. Click on either the partition or server object once with the left mouse button. It will become highlighted.

2. Click on the replica in the right-hand side of the NDS Manager subordinate window once using the left mouse button. It will become highlighted.

3. Choose Object | Replica | Change Type from the menu bar or click on the Change Replica Type button immediately to the right of the Add Replica button on the toolbar. The Change Replica Type dialog box will appear (Figure 10-19).

4. Select the new replica type for the replica and click OK. If the preconditions for the replica operation have been met, click on the Yes button in the second Change Replica Type window.

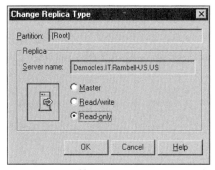

Figure 10-19: Changing a partition replica type in NDS Manager.

You cannot change the replica type of the Master partition. This is logical because if you were able to change the Master replica to a Read/Write replica, there would be no more Master replica for the partition. It is possible to change a Read/Write replica to a Master replica; the original Master replica then gets demoted to a Read/Write replica.

Updating Replicas

The replicas within a replica ring contact each other periodically to exchange information about database modifications. This process is critical in ensuring that the database contains the most current information about the network. As the network administrator, you have no control over how often this process occurs; however, you can manually force this synchronization to occur. For more information on replica synchronization, refer to the section "NDS Replica Synchronization" later in this chapter.

Because the NDS database is loosely consistent, you might want to manually cause the replica synchronization process to occur. This will update all of the replicas in the replica ring to reflect the most current information. When you want to force an update of the replicas in a replica ring, you can select one of two options:

- You can have the selected replica send updates to all other replicas in the replica ring. This is comparable to a database push operation. You are pushing information from one server to the copies of the partition stored on other servers.

- The selected replica can be forced to receive all updates from the Master replica of the replica ring. This is comparable to a database pull operation. The information is being pulled from the server, which stores the Master partition, to the selected replica.

Send Updates   To send updates to all other replicas, perform the following steps in NDS Manager:

1. Select the partition by clicking on it once with the left mouse button. It will become highlighted.

2. Select the replica in the right-hand side of the subordinate window by clicking on it once with the left mouse button. It will become highlighted.

3. Choose Object | Replica | Send Updates from the menu bar or click on the Send Replica Updates button immediately to the right of the Change Replica Type button in the toolbar. The Send Updates dialog box will appear (Figure 10-20).

4. Verify that the source server and the partition are correct and click on the OK button. If the preconditions for the operation have been met, click on the Yes button in the second Send Updates dialog box.

If there is an error in one of the replicas in your partition's replica ring, you might want to initiate a send update; however, take care when doing so. You need to make sure you have the most accurate replica of the partition sending out the information. Sending out information from a corrupt replica will cause major problems for your NDS database. Most often, you will choose the Master replica as the replica from which you send the information to the other replicas in the replica ring.

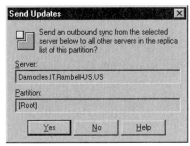

Figure 10-20: Verify the source server and partition are correct before sending replica updates.

Tip

The Send Update option forces a synchronization of all replicas. You cannot choose which copy of a replica will get the update; every replica in the replica ring will be updated.

Receive Updates   To force a replica to receive an update from the Master replica of the partition, perform the following steps in NDS Manager:

1. Select the partition by clicking on it once with the left mouse button. It will become highlighted.

2. Select the replica that will receive the update from the Master replica by clicking on it once with the left mouse button. It will become highlighted.

3. Choose Object I Replica I Receive Updates from the menu bar or click on the Receive Updates button immediately to the right of the Send Updates button on the toolbar. The Receive Updates dialog box will appear (Figure 10-21).

4. Verify that the server storing the replica and the partition are correct and click on the Yes button. If the preconditions for the operation have been met, click on the Yes button in the second Receive Updates dialog box.

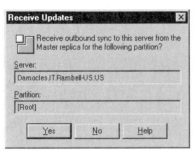

Figure 10-21: Verify the target server and partition in the Receive Updates dialog box.

The Receive Updates option is a selective way to update specific replicas in your partition's replica ring. You can manually select the partitions that will receive the information from the Master replica. It does not force a synchronization of all replicas in the replica ring.

Now that we know about the basic replica operations that can be performed using NDS Manager, we need to shift our focus. We have all of these replicas out there on servers on our network, but how do we know that the information they contain is valid? Fortunately, the replicas have a way of communicating with one another on a periodic basis to exchange information. This replica synchronization is an important part of NDS replication and will be covered next.

NDS Replica Synchronization

We have all of these pieces of the NDS database distributed across the network, and each of them has multiple copies also distributed across the network. Some of the pieces can be modified by users or network administrators; how does NDS keep track of which information is the correct information?

An excellent question. Any time you deal with a distributed database with multiple copies, this issue arises. Each replica in a partition's replica ring represents the database partition; however, when a modification is made to the NDS database, it is made to only one replica of the partition. The other replicas in the replica ring are not aware of the change. Over time, you could have vastly different information among the replicas of your partition.

To combat this dilemma, replicas in the partition's replica ring undergo a frequent process of contacting one another to exchange data. This process of *replica synchronization* ensures that changes made to one replica are reported and distributed to all of the other replicas in the replica ring. During the synchronization, every server in the replica ring for the partition contacts every other server that stores a replica and exchanges information. Figure 10-22 shows four servers that must communicate with one another during each replica synchronization. Imagine the diagram if it had 10 or 20 servers in the replica ring. That would be a lot of synchronization traffic.

The network administrator has no control over when this synchronization occurs. NDS takes care of it on a periodic basis. Unfortunately, there seems to be no consistency as to when NDS synchronizes the partitions. Yes, it is done regularly, but not at consistent intervals. This can lead to delays between a modification in the database and the receipt of information about the modification by the other replicas. Fortunately, you can manually issue a synchronization command to stimulate the process. To do this, refer to the previous section, "Updating Replicas."

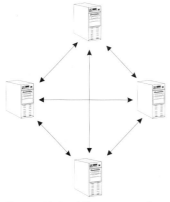

Figure 10-22: All servers in the replica ring contact one another during the synchronization process.

During the synchronization process, the replicas do not exchange every piece of information contained in their database. This would be too time consuming. They only inform the other replicas of any modifications that have been made. The process of incremental updates cuts down the amount of traffic required for replica synchronization.

There is another NDS component which aids in the successful synchronization of partition replicas. This component is the time synchronization environment which ensures the integrity of the distributed NDS database. For more information on time synchronization and its impact on replica synchronization, refer to Chapter 11.

Replica Synchronization Traffic & Performance

Fortunately, the speed and efficiency of replica synchronization on your network can be controlled with a bit of thought and planning. There are five main parameters that affect the speed of replica synchronization:

- Normal partition activity
- Number of replicas in the replica ring
- Server performance
- Network architecture
- Number of Subordinate Reference replicas

While you might not be able to control each parameter, you can control some of them to both reduce the amount of synchronization traffic on your network and increase the efficiency of the NDS replica synchronization process.

Normal Partition Activity The baseline amount of traffic on your network will affect the performance of your replica synchronization. Partitions that have a lot of normal network traffic and updates to the NDS database will take longer to synchronize than partitions that have very little activity. If a partition's traffic is adversely affecting the replica synchronization process, you might want to consider breaking the partition up into smaller pieces.

Normal partition traffic may also be a direct result of the partition size. A large partition will take longer to synchronize than a small one because of the sheer volume of updates that must occur with a large partition. Again, if your partitions are too large, you might consider breaking them up into smaller pieces.

Number of Replicas in the Replica Ring The number of replicas in a partition's replica ring will obviously affect the time required to synchronize a partition. More replicas mean more servers have to communicate with each other to exchange information about the most current updates. In Figure 10-22, we saw four servers in a replica ring that need to communicate with each other. This setup requires six separate communications sessions to synchronize the partitions (each graph edge between the servers represents a communications session).

Five servers in the replica ring would require 10 separate communications sessions to exchange update information. One extra server in this case causes four extra sessions. Having 10 servers in your replica ring would require 45 separate sessions. See how this number grows as you begin to add servers? You can see for yourself; just draw a graph like the one in Figure 10-22 with the desired number of servers in the ring. And don't forget, that's just for one partition. Other partitions may have comparable replica rings that need to synchronize.

Server Performance   The performance of the server also affects the efficiency of the replica synchronization process. If all of the servers in your tree that are storing replicas are high-end, high-speed servers, the synchronization process will not take long at all because each server will be able to process the information quickly.

Unfortunately, one slow server in your replica ring will break down the whole process. This is because each server in the ring must talk with the slow server and wait on it to serve up its updates. So although the rest of the servers might be fast, one slow one will cause a replica synchronization bottleneck.

Another point that should be considered in terms of server performance is the number of replicas stored on an individual server. The synchronization process can become burdensome for the server if there are too many replicas stored on it because usually the server has some other things to do as well (like file and print services, remember?). Unless your server is going to be a dedicated NDS workhorse, try not to store more than 10-15 replicas on it.

Network Architecture   This parameter is probably the one over which you have the least control; however, you can plan around it to increase the efficiency of replica synchronization. The most notorious culprits for affecting your synchronization performance are WAN links. Generally, the WAN links on your network are the weak links. If servers are forced to synchronize across these slower connections, they will take much longer to complete the process.

The way to plan for this is to both partition and replicate around WAN link boundaries. Try to minimize the traffic going across the WAN link. Some traffic is unavoidable, but you can decrease the amount with a smart partitioning and replication scheme. Keep the replication traffic isolated to one side of the link.

Number of Subordinate Reference Replicas   Even though Subordinate Reference replicas are not full replicas, they still have an impact on the efficiency of the synchronization process. They do count toward the number of replicas in the replica ring, and they do participate in the synchronization process. If the number of Subordinate References gets away from you, it will adversely affect your network.

Viewing Synchronization Information

There are multiple ways to view the synchronization of partitions in the NDS tree. One of those methods is the server console utility DSTRACE, which provides detailed information about the synchronization process. DSTRACE and its options will be covered in Chapter 13. While DSTRACE is comprehensive and will provide a slew of information, you can also use NDS Manager to view the synchronization status of partitions.

To see the synchronization status of partitions, select the Partitions and Servers view in NDS Manager and perform the following steps:

1. Click on the desired partition with the left mouse button. It will become highlighted.

2. Choose Object | Check Synchronization from the menu bar or click on the Check Synchronization button immediately to the right of the Move Partition button on the toolbar. The Check Synchronization dialog box will appear.

3. Choose whether you want to see the synchronization status for the desired partition or all partitions in the partitions list. The All Partitions option is not available from Tree view. Click OK.

4. If the preconditions for the operation have been met, click on the Yes button in the Check Partition Synchronization dialog box. The Partitions Synchronization Check dialog box will appear (Figure 10-23).

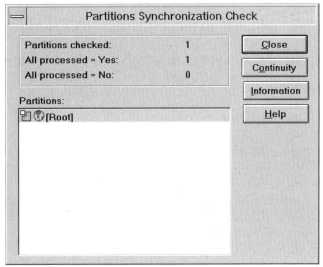

Figure 10-23: Viewing partition synchronization status in NDS Manager.

In the Partitions Synchronization Check dialog box, you will see the status of the synchronization process. The number of partitions checked will be displayed along with the results of the synchronization check. A result of All Processed = Yes means the partition is synchronized. All Processed = No means there is something wrong with the partition. If the status of synchronization is All Processed = No, you must figure out the source of the error and correct it. For more information on DSTRACE and NDS errors, refer to Chapter 13.

Partition Continuity

If the synchronization check has returned an All Processed = No status, you will want to check the partition continuity. The partition continuity will give you a graphical representation of the replica ring and show you the status of the individual replicas. This will help you identify the replica that is causing the error. From the Partitions Synchronization Check dialog box, click on the Continuity button. The Partition Continuity screen will be displayed (Figure 10-24).

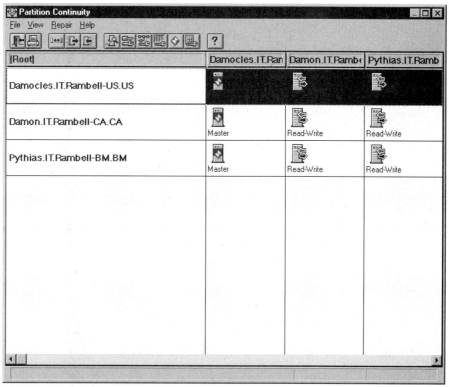

Figure 10-24: View the partition continuity to identify individual replica errors.

In the Partition Continuity screen, you are shown the name of the partition and all of the servers that hold a replica of the selected partition. Listed in the first column below the name of the partition are the servers themselves. The columns to the right of the column with the partition name also list the servers that hold the replicas of the partition. A grid is formed through which you will be able to identify where the synchronization errors are occurring.

To understand the grid, start with a horizontal row and read across the columns. The horizontal row is the server's view of the world and how it "sees" the replicas on the other servers. If the replicas show up without any errors, the synchronization is fine (as in Figure 10-24); however, if a replica appears with an exclamation point in a yellow triangle, it is an alert that there is a synchronization error on the replica as that particular server sees it. When there is an error, double-click on the error replica to see the type of error returned by NDS. For more information on error diagnostic codes, refer to Chapter 13.

Viewing Replica Information

As we have just seen, you can double-click on a replica from anywhere in NDS Manager to see the statistics concerning a specific replica stored on a server. Another way to see replica statistics is to click on the replica once with the left mouse button and choose Object I Information from the menu bar. The Replica Information dialog box will appear (Figure 10-25).

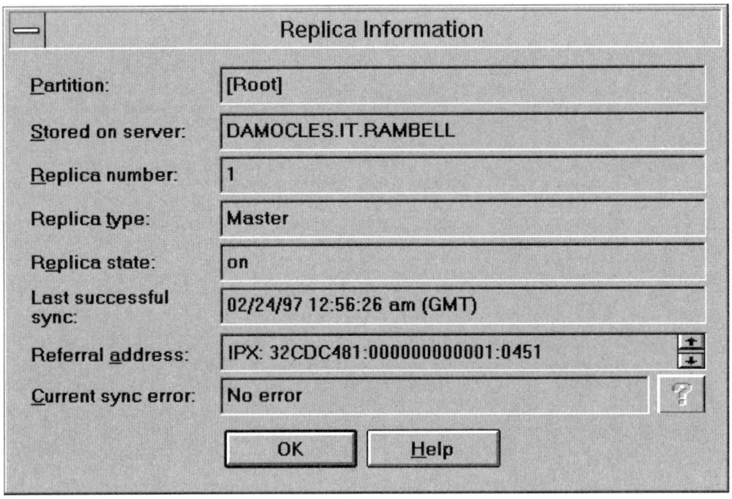

```
┌────────────────────────────────────────────────────────────┐
│ ─│              Replica Information                          │
├────────────────────────────────────────────────────────────┤
│                                                              │
│  Partition:         [Root]                                   │
│                                                              │
│  Stored on server:  DAMOCLES.IT.RAMBELL                      │
│                                                              │
│  Replica number:    1                                        │
│                                                              │
│  Replica type:      Master                                   │
│                                                              │
│  Replica state:     on                                       │
│                                                              │
│  Last successful    02/24/97 12:56:26 am (GMT)               │
│  sync:                                                       │
│                                                              │
│  Referral address:  IPX: 32CDC481:000000000001:0451    [±]   │
│                                                              │
│  Current sync error: No error                          [?]   │
│                                                              │
│              [    OK    ]    [   Help   ]                    │
└────────────────────────────────────────────────────────────┘
```

Figure 10-25: Viewing replica statistics in NDS Manager.

In the Replica Information dialog box, you will see the name of the partition and the name of the server on which the replica is stored. You will also see information about the number of the replica, the type of replica, and the state of the replica. Synchronization statistics are also shown in this informational box. It is extremely helpful in diagnosing synchronization errors. When a synchronization error occurs, the error number will be displayed in the Current Sync Error box at the bottom of the dialog box.

Bindery Services (Revisited)

Now that we know a little more about replicas, we can better understand Bindery Services in NetWare 4.11. As we stated earlier, for a server to provide Bindery Services, it must store a Read/Write or Master replica of the partition that holds the container to which that server's bindery context is set. The reason for this should be obvious at this point.

When a bindery-based workstation client connects to a server, it is expecting that server to contain all of the information necessary to authenticate to the network. The workstation also expects the server to contain all of the appropriate file system and rights information for that server. Unfortunately, the NDS world doesn't work that way, but the bindery-based client does not know any better.

When the server holds a replica of the partition that contains its bindery context container, the server has all of the information necessary to satisfy the bindery-based client. If it does not have the information right at hand, the NetWare 4.11 server knows where to find it in the NDS tree because of this stored replica. Unfortunately, the bindery-based workstation cannot tree walk, so it is necessary for the server to have this information directly on-hand. Thus, a little bit of NDS back-end magic provides a transparent front-end service to the most important part of the network—the user.

Moving On

In this chapter, you learned a lot about the NDS back-end environment. Two main pieces of this back-end environment are partitioning and replication. Although partitioning and replication are somewhat complicated, they make the object-oriented distributed NDS database more scalable and more efficient. They are essential for providing a unified database that keeps track of all your network resources.

You also learned about the various types of operations that you can perform on partitions and replicas, including the creation of new partitions, merging of existing partitions, and moving partitions. We talked about replica rings and providing fault tolerance on your network at the cost of increased network traffic due to the replica synchronization process. It's a reasonable trade-off for a comprehensive networking environment.

Although we have discussed a major portion of the NDS back-end environment, there is still more to talk about. Replica synchronization actually has a partner piece to it that is critical in maintaining the integrity of the data stored in the NDS database. This partner piece is network time synchronization, and it will be discussed thoroughly in the next chapter.

11

NDS Time Synchronization

In the previous chapter, we learned a lot about the back-end NDS environment that the user never sees. The partitioning and replication of the NDS database allows the network administrator to provide a scalable, flexible, and fault-tolerant network transparently to the user. While it takes a lot of extra effort, back-end administration is essential to the health of an NDS network.

When we discussed NDS replication, we introduced the concept of creating multiple copies of a single partition and distributing them across the network. If one replica becomes corrupted, it can be removed and replaced by a fresh copy stored on another server. However, this raises another whole set of issues concerning the synchronization of these replicas.

To provide a tight synchronization method that ensures the integrity of your NDS database, IntranetWare (and NDS) relies upon a scheme called time synchronization. Time synchronization forces all of the servers on your network to be reporting the same time so all transactions that occur on the network will have a uniform point of reference in the time continuum. Think about what would happen if 20 different servers on your network reported 20 different times. It would cause a lot of confusion.

In the last chapter, we discussed the concept of replica synchronization. This process was required to ensure the information in the NDS database is the most current across all copies of the partition. Time synchronization is replica synchronization's partner process. While each process functions independently of one another, replica synchronization is dependent upon time synchronization because all of the servers must be reporting the same time to ensure that the information disseminated in the replica synchronization process is the most accurate information available.

In this chapter, we will discuss this need for time synchronization in a unified networking environment and how it relates to both the integrity of the NDS database and general file transactions between users. We will also learn how time is kept in the NDS environment and what it means to be "time synchronized" in Novell terms.

IntranetWare comes with a built-in time synchronization environment called the *default configuration*. However, this environment is completely customizable; it can be configured for your specific networking environment. We will discuss the default configuration, its advantages, and its disadvantages. We will then look to the custom configuration to show how you might set up your own time synchronization environment to suit your network needs.

Finally, we will discuss the actual implementation of the time synchronization environment in IntranetWare. Once you have decided upon a configuration, you must set up the individual servers on your network to reflect it and get them talking to one another about the network time. Through the set of parameters on the server called the TIMESYNC parameters, we will be able to accomplish this.

While time synchronization in your NDS tree is not hard to implement, it is crucial to a successful tree implementation. When an NDS tree is not configured properly, the NDS database can be corrupted and the results of your modifications to the tree can be unpredictable. A unified set of network resources requires a unified time environment.

Time Synchronization Concepts

Not only is NDS an object-oriented and distributed type of database, it is also a transactional database. A *transaction* is the entire process that occurs when a piece of data in the database is going to be modified. First, the modification is set up. NDS determines which data in the database will be changed. Second, NDS begins a process to secure those portions of the database that will need to be modified. Only when those portions are secured will the change to the database be made. This method of transaction is used to prevent two processes trying to change the same data from writing over one another.

Because these transactions are asynchronous (they can occur at any time), they are unpredictable as to when they will occur. Thus, a method needed to be devised to keep a record of them to ensure that the data is the most current and the most accurate. This is where time synchronization plays a key role.

The Need for Time Synchronization in NDS

In a single server NDS tree, time synchronization is trivial. There is only one server entity whose time needs to be maintained, and there is no partition synchronization. The NDS replicas reside directly on that server, and any changes made to the NDS database are made to those replicas. There are no other copies that can be modified. The server's time is absolute and applies to the data contained on the server.

Unfortunately, the same is not true for an NDS tree with multiple servers. Since there are multiple server entities, great care must be taken to ensure that the data on the network is current and accurate. Each one of those servers could potentially report a different time. Which one is the correct one? This timing uncertainty could have major ramifications for the following data environments:

- General file information
- NDS database transactions

General File Information

We have all seen in DOS that files are kept with time and date stamps. You can determine the last time the file was modified by looking at the DOS time and date stamp. The same thing is true in NetWare 4.11. We even have the added feature of determining when the file was last accessed and by which user. All of this information is important from both a data freshness and security standpoint.

By default, when a workstation authenticates to a server, the workstation sets its own local time to that of the server. If different servers on your network are reporting different times, the workstations connected to those servers will report different times as well. In Figure 11-1, the workstations connected to Damocles believe the correct time is 3:00 P.M. on 2/25/97. The workstations connected to Damon believe it is 2:00 P.M. on 2/25/97. Workstation A creates a text file, and it is time stamped as 2/25/97 3:00P.M. Fifteen minutes later, workstation B accesses the file. It stamps the last access time for the file as 2/25/97 2:15 P.M. However, this time of last access is before the time the file was created! See how this can lead to problems? It can be very confusing if for some reason you needed an audit trail or security information concerning the data on your network.

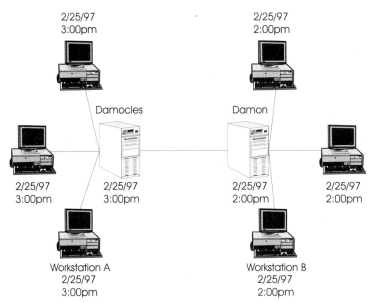

Figure 11-1: Workstations receive their local time from the server to which they are connected.

NDS Database Transactions

If general file information can be that confusing, the problem is tenfold for the critical NDS database transactions that occur on your network. When a transaction takes place in the NDS database, the following procedure is performed:

1. The transaction is requested and set up for the local NDS partition replica the user is accessing.

2. Once the transaction is set to go and the resources are locked, the data is recorded in the NDS partition replica. This change also receives a time and date stamp from the server on which the replica resides.

3. The change is placed in a queue used for replica synchronization. The next time the replica synchronization process occurs, this change in information must be reported for the change to propagate to all replicas on the network.

4. When the replica synchronization occurs, only the data with the *most recent* time and date stamp are kept. Old transaction information is discarded.

Let's go back to our diagram in Figure 11-1 to see how servers with different times can cause unpredictable results. For our purposes, Damocles and Damon each hold a Read/Write replica of the US partition. A network administrator is sitting at workstation A, and she makes a change to a trustee assignment of the user object mjsmith. A half an hour later, she realizes she has made a mistake in modifying the trustee assignment. She makes another change to the user object mjsmith; however, this time the modification is made from workstation B.

As we have seen from the previous example, Damocles believes the time is 3:00 P.M. on 2/25/97 while Damon thinks it is 2:00 P.M. on the same day. Thus, workstation A thinks the time is 3:00 P.M., and workstation B believes the time is 2:00 P.M. When the first modification is made, the transaction is stamped 2/25/97 3:00 P.M. and recorded in the NDS database replica on Damocles. One half hour later, the next modification is made. It gets the time stamp 2/25/97 2:30 P.M. (because workstation B is one hour behind workstation A), and it is recorded in the NDS database replica on Damon.

When these two replicas synchronize, they will exchange data about the trustee assignments of the mjsmith user object. One database transaction will be seen as 2/25/97 3:00 P.M. while the other transaction will be seen as 2/25/97 2:30 P.M. The transaction marked 2/25/97 3:00 P.M. will be the information that is kept in the database because it is the most recent *even though it is incorrect information*. The transaction marked 2/25/97 2:30 P.M. is discarded because it is regarded as old data. All replicas in the replica ring will then receive this incorrect information through the replica synchronization process.

This is just one minor example of how incorrect data can be recorded in the NDS database and spread across the network. Imagine having 20 servers reporting different times and making these database transactions. The integrity of the NDS database data could be seriously compromised because of the lack of time synchronization between the servers. Fortunately, there is a way to combat this problem in NetWare 4.11.

The NDS Time Environment

In our example, Damocles and Damon may be in different rooms of an organization. Or, they may be in two different time zones separated by a WAN link. A large-scale enterprise network needs to be able to handle the time environment independent of the physical locations of the servers. NetWare 4.11 is able to do this through a method called Universal Time Coordinated (UTC).

Also, when you have a large number of servers as part of your NDS tree, it can be cumbersome to be responsible for maintaining the accurate time on all of the servers. You would have to hire a person full time just for time maintenance. Fortunately, there is a hierarchical structure to the NetWare 4.11 time environment so that only key servers are time providers on the network. This concept of time servers is an essential part of your NDS time environment.

Universal Time Coordinated (UTC)

As we know, machines that are geographically dispersed will have their local times set very differently. A server in Boston, MA, will be set three hours ahead of a server in Vancouver, BC. This is because the local times for the two cities are different. *Universal Time Coordinated (UTC)* is a way for NDS to maintain a standard time for the network while adjusting for the time zone in which the server is located.

Calculating the UTC for the network is just like setting the time to Greenwich Mean Time (GMT). There is a general formula for calculating the UTC: local time +/- time zone offset (- daylight saving time offset) = UTC.

When UTC is used, it does not mean the server's time is set for Greenwich mean time. UTC is just a method used for NDS database transactions. When a transaction is made to the database, NDS takes the server's local time, adjusts it for the time zone, and also adjusts for any daylight saving time. When the transaction is stamped in the database, it is stamped with a UTC time; however, the server's time still reflects the local geographical time.

For example, in Figure 11-2, Damocles is located in Boston, MA, Damon is located in Vancouver, BC, and Pythias is located in Hamilton, BM. For Damocles, the server time is set for 3:00 P.M. For Damon and Pythias, it is 12:00 P.M. and 4:00 P.M., respectively. When transactions are made in the NDS database from any of these locations at this time, the transactions are recorded as 9:00 P.M. UTC in the NDS database. UTC takes into account any differences for the servers' time zones and daylight saving time (DST) adjustments if applicable.

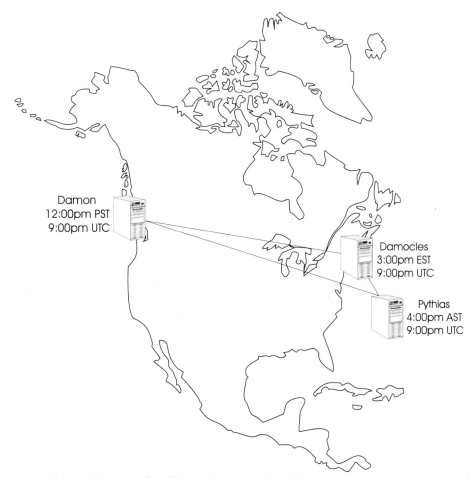

Figure 11-2: UTC accounts for differences in servers' local times due to time zones.

NetWare Time Servers

Every NetWare 4.11 file server on your network is also a time server. When queried, it will provide UTC time to any workstation or NLM requesting time information.

Besides providing time information, the time server has some other responsibilities. Every time server is capable of determining the time synchronization status of your network. If the time environment is out of synch, the time server will be able to tell you. The time servers are also responsible for maintaining time synchronization on the network. If its time is out of synch with the rest of the network, it must correct its own time to get back to network UTC synchronization.

There are two general ways your NetWare 4.11 servers can be configured as time servers. There are time servers that are responsible for dictating the correct UTC time to other servers. They are called *time providers*. Servers that are not time providers are called *time consumers*. They set their own clock to what the time providers dictate.

There are three different types of time providers. Which ones you use will depend upon your specific network configuration:

- Single Reference time server

- Primary time server

- Reference time server

There is only one type of time consumer. It is called the Secondary time server. Most of the NetWare 4.11 servers on your network will be configured as time consumers. Now that we know the difference between time providers and time consumers, let's examine each type of time server in more detail.

Single Reference Time Server

The Single Reference time server is used in the default time server configuration that is implemented when NetWare 4.11 is installed. It is a time provider that has complete control over the network time environment. It will never change the value of its internal clock; it is the sole source of time. All other time servers on your network must be time consumers (Secondary time servers) when you have a Single Reference time server.

Tip

Single Reference time servers cannot coexist with any other time providers in your NDS tree. You cannot use Reference or Primary time servers when you have a Single Reference time server in your NDS tree.

Because the Single Reference server is the single source of accurate time for all machines on the network, all Secondary time servers must be able to communicate with it. The Single Reference server should be located in a place where the other servers will be able to communicate with it cleanly and efficiently.

Primary Time Server

The Primary time server is used only in the custom time environment. It provides a more democratic approach to time synchronization. This time provider queries all other time providers in the NDS tree (Primary and Reference time servers) to determine the network time. All of the time providers then "vote" on the correct network time. The Primary time servers then adjust their own clocks accordingly, depending upon the outcome of the vote. We will discuss how these time providers vote on a correct network time and adjust their own clocks in the next section.

The Primary time server is able to provide the network time to all time consumers. Thus, Secondary time servers and network clients are able to obtain the correct network time from the Primary time server. Primary servers cannot exist in the default time environment.

Tip

Primary time servers can only coexist in the NDS tree with other Primary time servers and Reference time servers.

Reference Time Server

Like the Primary time server, the Reference time server is only used in the custom configuration of the time environment. This time provider should not be confused with the Single Reference time server. They are distinctly different providers of time although they perform the same type of function.

The Reference time server acts just like a Primary time server except it will not adjust its own clock after the result of the time provider vote. It participates in the polling process and votes on a correct network time, but it will not change its clock. This will cause a convergence of network time, as we will see in the next section. The Reference server's main function is to provide an accurate network time; however, it does not solely dictate the time to the network as the Single Reference server does.

Time consumers can get their time from the Reference time server, and in effect, the Primary time servers also get their time from this source. If you have a Reference time server in your tree, you must also have at least one Primary time server.

Tip

If you have a Reference time server in your NDS tree, you must have at least one Primary time server in the tree as well. Reference time servers and Single Reference time servers cannot coexist in the same NDS tree.

Secondary Time Servers

As the only type of server time consumer on the network, the Secondary time server gets its time from time providers on your network. Most of your NetWare 4.11 servers will be Secondary time servers since they will not need to participate in the time voting process. They will just accept the time given to them and adjust their own clocks to the network time if they are out of synch.

By default, once the first Single Reference time server is installed in your NDS tree, all other NetWare 4.11 servers you install will be configured as Secondary time servers. If you have a customized time environment, you must configure the time server type parameter on the NetWare 4.11 server manually to implement your time environment correctly.

We've talked about the different types of time servers that can exist in your NDS tree and whether or not they are in synchronization; however, how does a server know if it's in or out of synch? Good question, and of course, there is a good answer.

How Time Is Synchronized

The specific time server configuration for your network will determine how an overall network time is established; however, how the server determines whether or not it is synchronized to the network time is a different story. The server is able to determine whether or not it is synchronized through a concept called the synchronization radius.

No set of servers in any NDS tree is going to agree on an exact time. Due to limitations in network communications and server clock drift, there is always going to be some discrepancy between the agreed-upon network time and the server's actual time. The margin for acceptable error is called the *synchronization radius* for the server. This value is configurable by the network administrator and determines how far off a server's time can be from network time and still be in synchronization with the network.

The value of the synchronization radius is set in milliseconds, and its value can be set from 0 to 2147483647 milliseconds (ms). The default value for the synchronization radius is 2000ms (2 seconds). It does not matter if the server's time is two seconds faster or slower than the agreed-upon network time. If the server's time falls within the synchronization radius set for it, the server is still considered to be in synch with the rest of the network.

Figure 11-3 shows some examples of network times in relation to the server time and the individual synchronization radii of the servers. The reported network time falls within 2000ms of the server's locally reported time for Damocles and Damon. The difference between the local time and network time for Pythias is larger than the synchronization radius; Pythias is out of synch.

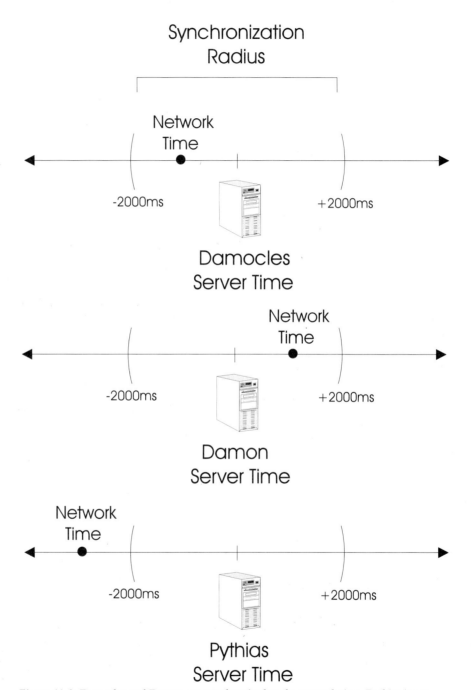

Figure 11-3: Damocles and Damon are synchronized to the network time. Pythias is not.

If the synchronization radius is set to be too small, the network may never get synchronized. If it is set to be too large, you may get corruption in your NDS database. Try not to change the synchronization radius from the 2000 milliseconds default unless you have a compelling reason to do so.

The synchronization radius plays a key role in the adjustment of the servers' internal clocks. How the server adjusts its clock is determined by the type of time server it is. In the next sections of this chapter, we will discuss both the default and custom time environments. Each environment has a specific method to how it calculates the network time and how the network reacts when servers find themselves out of synch.

Default Time Synchronization Method

When NetWare 4.11 is installed on the first server and the NDS tree is created, the installation program assumes you will want the most simple time environment possible. Thus, the first server in the tree is made a Single Reference time server by default. All other servers that are added to the tree become Secondary time servers and accept the network time from the Single Reference time server.

Figure 11-4 shows us the basic default time synchronization method. There is one single time provider on the network that dictates the network time to the time consumers. The Single Reference server can distribute the time to both Secondary time servers and client workstations as seen in Figure 11-4. It is a simple and efficient method of providing time synchronization to your network.

There are some definite advantages to using the default time synchronization environment:

- The configuration is straightforward and easy to understand.

- It does not require a lot of extra maintenance on the part of the network administrator.

- Installing a new server into the NDS tree does not require a reconfiguration of the time synchronization environment.

- No server configuration file is necessary to set up the time synchronization environment.

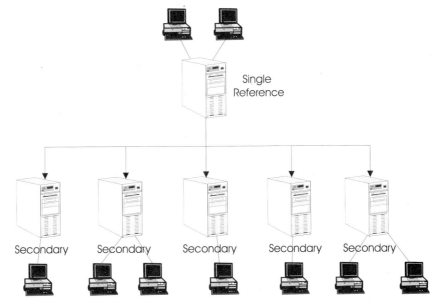

Figure 11-4: The default time synchronization environment.

For beginning network administrators or network administrators with small networks, the default time synchronization is ideal; however, it does have some disadvantages that need to be considered:

- The Single Reference server must be in a location where it can be easily and readily contacted by every other time server on the network.

- Because the default method uses Service Advertising Protocol (SAP) to communicate between time servers, the time synchronization process produces extra network traffic.

- The use of SAP for time configuration may cause some Secondary servers to adjust their time to the wrong time server on the network.

- The Single Reference server poses a single point of failure in the time synchronization environment. If the Single Reference server goes down or is unreachable, the Secondary time servers do not have a time source for the network.

Generally, the default time synchronization environment is recommended if you have less than 30 servers on your network and you do not have any WAN connections to consider. WAN connections generally require a custom configuration that will reduce the amount of time synchronization traffic and provide fault tolerance in case the WAN link is unavailable for a period of time.

Two important issues for any time synchronization environment are how time servers communicate with one another and how time servers correct themselves when they find they are out of synch with the network time. Let's look at how the default time synchronization environment handles these issues.

Time Server Communication

As we have mentioned, the default time synchronization environment uses Service Advertising Protocol (SAP) to allow the servers to communicate with one another. SAP is a broadcast protocol used to advertise a server's services to the network. A server SAPs frequently to the network, and other servers on the network receive that information and build internal databases about the topology of the network and the other server entities on the network.

The Single Reference server uses SAP to broadcast its time information to all of the Secondary time servers on the network. The Secondary time servers see this information on the network and are able to set their times accordingly. If for some reason SAP packets are not reaching a Secondary time server, that server will not be able to synchronize its time with the rest of the network.

SAP will increase the amount of baseline traffic on your network. This level of increase is generally negligible except on WAN links. You may run into some adverse performance conditions across WAN links if you use SAP as your time server communication method.

SAP is also not configurable by the network administrator. It is a self-configuring protocol. If this configuration is disturbed by a misconfigured time server, you can lose the entire time synchronization environment.

Time Server Time Correction

How a time server handles being out of synchronization is very simple in the default time synchronization environment. There is only one time provider whose time never changes. The Single Reference server never considers itself out of synchronization; therefore, the network time is *always* what the Single Reference server specifies.

When a Secondary time server receives the time synchronization information from the Single Reference server, it checks the time against its own time. If the time received from the Single Reference server is outside of the Secondary server's synchronization radius, the Secondary server adjusts its clock to match that of the time server.

For example, the file server Damocles is set up as a Single Reference server in the NDS tree. Damon is set up as Secondary time server with a synchronization radius of 2000ms. Damocles reports the time to Damon as 1:10:34 P.M.; however, Damon thinks the time is 1:10:37 P.M. Because this time falls outside of Damon's synchronization radius, Damon immediately resets its clock to 1:10:34 P.M. to get back in synch with the network time.

While the default time synchronization environment is easy to configure and administer, it is not the appropriate choice for every network. There are many networks that will need a custom time synchronization environment to meet their demands. This custom configuration is discussed in the next section.

Custom Time Synchronization Method

The custom time synchronization method assumes that your network requires special time synchronization considerations. No Single Reference servers are used in the custom method; the network time is calculated by a time provider group. The *time provider group* is the Primary and Reference time servers in your NDS tree. Together, they calculate the overall network time.

The remaining time servers in your tree are set as Secondary time servers, and they set their times according to the time calculated by the time provider group. Generally, the time provider group is a small number of highly visible and highly accessible servers that have the added responsibility of maintaining the network time. Figure 11-5 shows an example of the custom time synchronization method.

The custom time synchronization environment really has a hierarchical structure to it. At the top level is the time provider group, which is responsible for determining the network time. At the second level are the Secondary time servers, which receive their time from the time provider group. With the custom method, the time is calculated and then distributed.

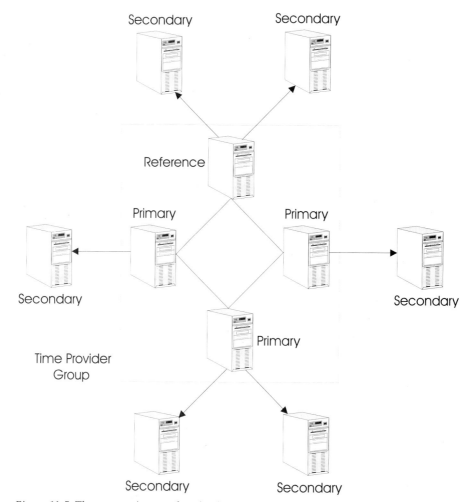

Figure 11-5: The custom time synchronization environment.

The custom time environment is different from the default environment because the servers are carefully configured to reduce the total amount of time synchronization traffic on your network. A Secondary server is configured to talk to a specific Primary or Reference time server to obtain the network time. The Primary and Reference servers must also be configured to point to each other for calculating the network time. Without this configuration, the servers in the time provider group would not be able to communicate with each other and arrive at a calculated network time.

To implement the custom method, the network administrator must first consider a couple of things concerning the environment:

- Select the servers that will be in the time provider group. There should be at least three servers in this group, one of which is a Reference time server.

- Determine how the servers are going to communicate with one another. Time providers need a list of other time providers to be able to calculate the network time. Time consumers need a list to obtain network time. This configured list is kept in a file called TIMESYNC.CFG on the server; it will be discussed later in this chapter.

Once the time servers have been selected and the configuration laid out, the custom time synchronization environment has some distinct advantages over the default configuration:

- The network administrator has control over the entire time synchronization environment.

- The custom time synchronization environment and its time provider group provides a fault-tolerant method for time synchronization. If one server goes down in the time provider group, the other servers can still act to provide a unified network time. Secondary servers can be configured to obtain their time from more than one source as well.

- The time servers can be distributed around the network in a manner that reduces the amount of time synchronization across the network (especially over WAN connections). Large networks will also be able to distribute the time synchronization load across multiple servers.

While this customizable environment is attractive because it can meet the needs of any network, there are also some disadvantages associated with the added flexibility:

- Implementing the custom time synchronization environment requires forethought and planning. You should lay out the environment on paper before you configure it with your servers.

- The custom time synchronization environment requires a configuration file that must be maintained by the network administrator.

- Whenever new servers are introduced into the NDS tree, the time environment will need to be manually configured to reflect the new change. Adding new Primary servers will also add more complexity to the polling process for calculating network time.

The custom time synchronization environment is recommended for large networks or networks with WAN connections. Fault tolerance is also a factor in deciding if you need the custom environment. The custom environment makes the time synchronization process more efficient and flexible.

Custom Time Synchronization Guidelines

When planning your custom time synchronization environment, certain guidelines should be followed for a robust and efficient time environment. Generally, you will have only one Reference time server in your NDS tree. This is the time server responsible for dictating the time to the rest of the network.

When there is a Reference time server in the NDS tree, you also need to have Primary time servers to complete the custom environment. You should try to limit the number of Primary time servers on your network. A large number of Primary time servers will significantly increase the amount of time traffic on your network when the time polling process occurs. You will rarely need to have more than five to seven Primary time servers in addition to the Reference time server. The remaining file servers will be set as Secondary time servers.

Tip

> *Due to WAN link considerations, some network environments may need multiple Reference time servers for the time synchronization environment. If multiple Reference time servers are used in a single NDS tree, they must all be synchronized to the same external time source.*

In planning your time synchronization environment, you should also take into account your network topology. You want to minimize the amount of traffic across slower network links. For more details on the design of the time synchronization environment, refer to Chapter 14.

As with the default environment, two important issues surrounding the custom time synchronization environment are time server communication and time server correction. We'll need to take a look at these to really understand the custom time synchronization environment.

Time Server Communication

Unlike in the default environment, time servers in the custom time synchronization environment rely upon a specific list of servers to contact so they can receive network time information. This authorized list, stored in the file TIMESYNC.CFG, is provided configured by the network administrator and specifies the servers from which the time server is allowed to get time information.

If the time server is a member of the time provider group, the list of servers should include all of the other members of the time provider group. This list constitutes the list of servers that will calculate the time for the network. In Figure 11-6, there are three servers in the time provider group. Each one should be configured to speak to the other two to determine the time for the network. For example, Damocles (the Reference time server) would be configured to communicate with Damon and Pythias about the network time. Damon would be configured to communicate with Damocles and Pythias. Pythias would be configured to communicate with Damocles and Damon. Together, these three servers would then be able to calculate the time for the network based upon a voting process.

When it comes time to vote upon the network time, the servers communicate with one another. The times reported by the time providers are averaged together to arrive at the network time. Once agreed upon, the Primary servers adjust their clock by 50 percent of the difference between their individual reported time and the agreed upon network time. Reference servers do not adjust their time after the vote. This causes a slow, systematic procession of the network time towards the time reported by the Reference server.

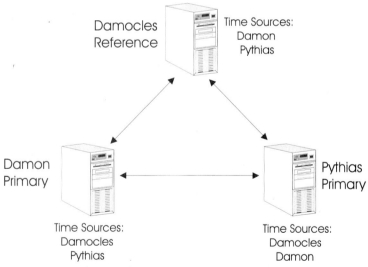

Figure 11-6: Configuring the time provider group.

If the time server is a time consumer, the list determines from which server(s) the Secondary server will retrieve network time information. The servers specified in the Secondary server's list should also be the Primary or

Reference time servers for the network. The Secondary server will contact the first server in the list for time information. If that server is unavailable, the Secondary server will contact the second server in the list and so on until it successfully contacts a time server or reaches the end of the list.

Tip

It is possible for a Secondary time server to contact another Secondary time server for network time information; however, it is not reliable and not recommended. Only use it as a last resort for an extra layer of fault tolerance.

The configuration file used in the custom method is called TIMESYNC.CFG and is located in the SYS:SYSTEM directory of the NetWare 4.11 server. We will discuss this file in detail along with the configured lists of time servers later in this chapter in the section "Setting Up the NDS Time Environment."

Time Server Time Correction

How a server handles being out of synch with the network is a bit more complicated with the custom environment than it is with the default environment. How a server corrects itself depends upon which type of time server it is. The time providers have a way of changing themselves that is different from the way the time consumers do.

Time Provider Correction

As we have seen, when network time is being determined by the time provider group, the servers in the time provider group communicate with one another to vote on the correct network time. Once the network time has been established, Primary time servers that have found themselves out of synch (the time falls outside of the server's synchronization radius) will adjust their clock by 50 percent of the difference between their time and the network time. The Reference server never changes its time even if the network time falls outside of its synchronization radius.

The Reference server provides the central source of time for the network, and the Primary servers in the NDS tree converge upon this time slowly in incremental steps. Although this may not seem logical at first, think about it carefully. If the Primary time servers were to unconditionally set their time to that of the Reference server, you would be giving up the fault-tolerance benefit you attained by setting up the custom environment.

Imagine you had a time provider group with a Reference server and three other Primary time servers. It's functioning correctly and the network time is in synch. Then something happens to the Reference server, and it is reporting an incorrect time. Instead of the entire network time shifting dramatically to this new time reported by the Reference server, the network time will drift slowly to that of the Reference server. This will give you, the network administrator, more time to detect the Reference time server's error and correct the problem.

Because the Reference server ultimately determines the network time, it should be synchronized itself to some reliable source. Using dial-up capabilities or third-party NLMs if you are connected to the Internet, you can configure your Reference server to regularly communicate with an external time source, like the U.S. Naval Observatory, to keep your network time accurate.

Time Consumer Correction

Just like the Secondary servers in the default configuration, the Secondary servers in the custom configuration adjust their clocks to exactly match the network time when they find themselves to be out of synch with the rest of the network. This obviously makes sense because you have provided a two-level hierarchy for time synchronization. Your top level painstakingly calculates the time and ensures that the network time is correct. The second level can just set itself to the determined network time if it falls out of the synchronization.

Now that we have learned about the theory behind time synchronization in NetWare 4.11, we need to learn how to actually set up the time environment. In the next section, we will discuss how you can initially set the time on your servers, how you can configure the many time parameters on your time server, and how you can view time information once the time environment has been configured.

Setting Up the NDS Time Environment

Once the time synchronization environment for your NDS tree has been planned, you must then go through the process of configuring the environment on the NetWare 4.11 servers themselves. The default time synchronization environment is easy to set up; it is the custom configuration that requires more work on the part of the network administrator.

When the NetWare 4.11 server is started, it automatically loads a program called TIMESYNC.NLM, which is responsible for maintaining the time synchronization of your network. This is the NLM that calculates the UTC and time stamps all NDS database transactions along with maintaining the correct local server time. It provides the time-related services in the NetWare 4.11 environment.

The other key to the time synchronization environment is a file located in SYS:SYSTEM called TIMESYNC.CFG. This file is responsible for storing additional time synchronization parameters for the local server. It tells the server what type of time server it is, the server's time zone, and the server's synchronization radius, among other things. It is comparable to an initialization file (.INI) in Windows.

Time synchronization parameters are also specified in the server's AUTOEXEC.NCF file. These parameters are read when the server is booted; however, they might not be the parameters that are retained by the server for time synchronization. Let's look at why this is the case; it depends upon your time synchronization environment.

The default time synchronization file does not have a TIMESYNC.CFG file to configure the time environment. This is because NetWare 4.11 takes care of the time synchronization for you. The first server in your NDS tree is the Single Reference server, and each subsequent server in the tree is a Secondary time server. You need to specify a small number of extra information to properly configure the time environment. All of this information is stored in AUTOEXEC.NCF and read when the server is booted. Figure 11-7 shows a sample AUTOEXEC.NCF from a default time synchronization environment.

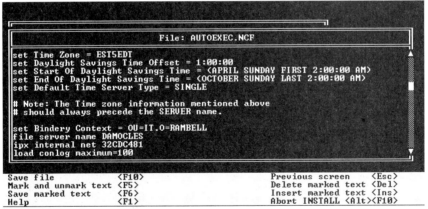

Figure 11-7: Time synchronization parameters are stored in the server's AUTOEXEC.NCF and read when the server is booted.

After AUTOEXEC.NCF has loaded and the time synchronization parameters have been read, TIMESYNC.NLM is loaded. It looks for a companion TIMESYNC.CFG; however, it does not find one because the default time synchronization environment is being used, so it uses the parameters set in the AUTOEXEC.NCF.

Tip

In AUTOEXEC.NCF, time synchronization parameters must always be specified before the file server name.

In the custom time synchronization environment, however, there is a TIMESYNC.CFG file. When TIMESYNC.NLM is loaded, it reads the TIMESYNC.CFG file and sets the time synchronization parameters accordingly. Thus, for a custom time synchronization environment, the following procedure occurs during server boot:

1. Time synchronization parameters are set to the values only specified in AUTOEXEC.NCF. These parameters include the time zone in which the server is located, Daylight Saving Time information, and the Default Time Server Type.

2. TIMESYNC.NLM is loaded and looks for the TIMESYNC.CFG file in SYS:SYSTEM.

3. When the TIMESYNC.CFG file is found, the time synchronization parameters set in it are loaded. Values found in this file may replace the values already set through AUTOEXEC.NCF.

The moral of the story is the time synchronization parameters you see in AUTOEXEC.NCF can be overridden by the parameters in TIMESYNC.CFG. We will discuss TIMESYNC.CFG in detail later in this section.

There are essentially three main components to the configuration of the network time synchronization environment:

- Setting and viewing the server time
- Configuring server time synchronization parameters
- Reviewing the TIMESYNC.CFG file

Without further ado, let's get into the how to of setting up your network time synchronization environment.

Setting & Viewing the Server Time

The first thing that needs to be done at the server is to set the server's local time. Initially, the server reads its time from its own system clock. Once the server establishes connection with the remainder of the time servers on the network, it begins to adjust its clock according to what type of time server it is.

Before the server boots, you should set the server clock by using the DOS TIME command. After booting to DOS but before loading SERVER.EXE, you should type **time** at the DOS prompt. DOS will display the current system time and ask you for a new time. To accept the current time, just press Enter.

The only servers you should be concerned with setting the correct time on are the time providers. It really does not matter what the Secondary time servers' system clocks read because they will adjust their time to exactly match the network time when they establish time synchronization.

There may be some critical applications on your network that are dependent upon an accurate network time. Setting the time at the DOS prompt is a one-shot deal that cannot account for clock drift that may occur on your time providers. There are other ways to maintain an accurate network time once the servers have been booted and time synchronization has been established in the NDS tree.

Reference servers often get their time from an external time source like the U.S. Naval Observatory. If you are connected to the Internet, you can use a third-party NLM like RDATE or CADENCE. These products are loaded on the server and force the time server to periodically query an external time source. Once the server receives the time, it sets its own clock to that of the accurate external source. Reference servers are the obvious candidates for this type of service because they dictate the network time to the rest of the servers on the network.

If you do not have direct access to the Internet, the same thing can be accomplished through a dial-up connection. There are third-party products on the market that will allow your NetWare 4.11 server to utilize a modem to call up the U.S. Naval Observatory and retrieve the correct time. If you have an application that is dependent upon an accurate network time, your Reference time server should have some form of contact with an external time source to maintain its accurate time.

If you do not have access to an external time source, it may be necessary for you to manually adjust your network time upon occasion. This can be done by using the SET TIMESYNC TIME ADJUSTMENT parameter. We will discuss the time parameters in more detail in the next section, "Configuring Server Time Synchronization Parameters."

Tip

Adjusting the network time is a task that should not be taken lightly. Change the time of your network only if it is necessary. Careless time adjustments can cause NDS database corruption.

Once the time has been set, you can see the time information for your server by typing the command **TIME** at the server console prompt (the colon prompt). The current time zone for the server, DST information for the server, time synchronization status, and the current time for the machine both local and UTC will be displayed when you use this command. Figure 11-8 shows a sample display of a server after a TIME command has been issued.

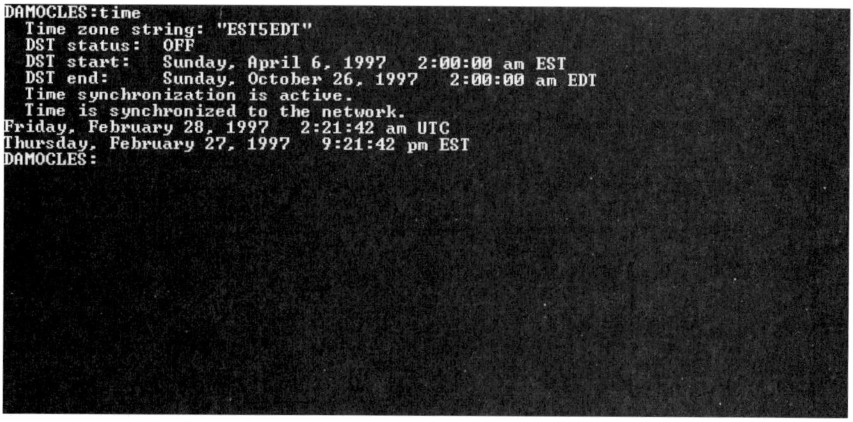

```
DAMOCLES:time
    Time zone string: "EST5EDT"
    DST status:   OFF
    DST start:    Sunday, April 6, 1997   2:00:00 am EST
    DST end:      Sunday, October 26, 1997   2:00:00 am EDT
    Time synchronization is active.
    Time is synchronized to the network.
Friday, February 28, 1997   2:21:42 am UTC
Thursday, February 27, 1997   9:21:42 pm EST
DAMOCLES:
```

Figure 11-8: The server TIME command.

Periodically, you should issue the TIME command at the server console to monitor the time synchronization status of your network. Although NDS will display an alert if time is not synchronized, it is a good idea to be proactive in terms of monitoring the status of your network.

Once the time has been set, you need to look at how your specific network time synchronization environment is configured. The configuration is accomplished using the time synchronization parameters on the server. These parameters define the characteristics of the individual server on which they are set. Let's take a closer look at how you can configure your network time environment.

Configuring Server Time Synchronization Parameters

As we have already discussed earlier in this chapter, how your server's time synchronization environment is configured at boot depends upon whether you are using the default environment or the custom environment. With the default environment, all of the time synchronization parameters are loaded from the server's AUTOEXEC.NCF file. The custom time synchronization environment relies upon additional settings stored in TIMESYNC.CFG for a successful configuration.

Regardless of which environment is used, time synchronization parameters are modified on the NetWare 4.11 server using a SET command. The SET command in NetWare 4.11 is equivalent to the SET command in DOS. It changes the value of a system environment variable to the value you specify. The following example would change the value of the TIME ZONE environment variable to EST5EDT:

```
SET TIME ZONE = EST5EDT
```

All server environment variables that can be modified in NetWare are modified using the SET command. The time synchronization parameters happen to be a subset of these environment variables. To use the SET command, you must issue the command from the server console command prompt (colon prompt). Here is the general syntax of the server SET command:

```
SET <VARIABLE_NAME> = <VALUE>
```

The drawback to using the server SET command is that you must know the exact name of the environment variable to be able to set it correctly. If you do not know the name of the variable, you must look it up before you issue the command. Fortunately, with NetWare 4.x, Novell has provided a more graphical interface to the environment variables. It is called SERVMAN.NLM, and it is loaded at the server console prompt. For more information on SERVMAN.NLM, refer to Chapter 18.

For the default time synchronization environment, we can see the SET commands listed in the server's AUTOEXEC.NCF file (Figure 11-7). There are five server time parameters that are set in the AUTOEXEC.NCF file for the default configuration that are not duplicated in TIMESYNC.CFG:

- Time Zone
- Daylight Saving Time Offset (if applicable)
- Start of Daylight Saving Time (if applicable)

■ End of Daylight Saving Time (if applicable)

■ Default Time Server Type

To create the custom time synchronization environment, you must change these time parameters and others using the server SET command or SERVMAN.NLM. We will use SERVMAN.NLM to discuss the time synchronization parameters because it is easier to use, especially since it lets you set the parameters for both AUTOEXEC.NCF and TIMESYNC.CFG at the same time. SERVMAN.NLM will also create a TIMESYNC.CFG file if one is not present. Remember, however, that any of these parameters in SERVMAN.NLM can be set using the server SET command.

To start SERVMAN.NLM and view the time synchronization parameters for your server, perform the following steps:

1. At the server console prompt (colon prompt) type **LOAD SERVMAN**. The NetWare 4.x Server Manager main screen will appear.

2. From the Available Options menu, choose Server Parameters.

3. From the Select a Parameter Category menu, choose Time. The Time Parameters screen will appear (Figure 11-9).

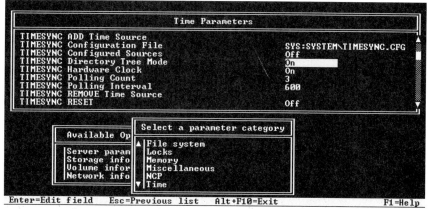

Figure 11-9: Setting server time parameters using SERVMAN.NLM.

From the Time Parameters screen, you can modify all of the time parameters on the local server. All of the parameters and their descriptions are listed in Table 11-1. Each one will also be discussed individually.

Time Parameter	Valid Values	Description
TIMESYNC ADD Time Source	Any NetWare 4.11 server name	Adds a name to the list of time sources.
TIMESYNC Configuration File	Any valid file path	Specifies the location of TIMESYNC.CFG on your server.
TIMESYNC Configured Sources	On, Off	Determines whether or not the server will listen to SAP packets for time information.
TIMESYNC Directory Tree Mode	On, Off	When On, the time server only listens to other time servers in its NDS tree.
TIMESYNC Hardware Clock	On, Off	Determines hardware clock synchronization for the server.
TIMESYNC Polling Count	1-1000	Number of time packets exchanged during time server queries.
TIMESYNC Polling Interval	10-2678400	Number of seconds in between time server queries.
TIMESYNC REMOVE Time Source	Any NetWare 4.11 server name	Removes a name from the list of time sources.
TIMESYNC RESET	On, Off	Resets TIMESYNC.NLM to its default values and clears TIMESYNC.CFG.
TIMESYNC Restart Flag	On, Off	Controls the restart of TIMESYNC.NLM.
TIMESYNC Service Advertising	On, Off	Controls the server's SAP advertising status.
TIMESYNC Synchronization Radius	0-2147483647	Determines the server's synchronization radius in milliseconds.
TIMESYNC Time Adjustment		Adjusts the network time.
TIMESYNC Time Source	Any NetWare 4.11 server name	Adds a name to the list of time sources.
TIMESYNC Type	Single, Primary, Reference, Secondary	Specifies the type of time server.
TIMESYNC Write Parameters	On, Off	Causes time parameters to be written to TIMESYNC.CFG.
TIMESYNC Write Value	1-3	Controls the types of parameters written to TIMESYNC.CFG.
Time Zone		Specifies the time zone for the server and its offset from UTC.
Default Time Server Type	Single, Primary, Reference, Secondary	Specifies time server default type.

➡

Time Parameter	Valid Values	Description
Start of Daylight Saving Time		Controls date when time is corrected for the beginning of daylight saving time.
End of Daylight Saving Time		Controls date when time is corrected for the end of daylight saving time.
Daylight Saving Time Offset		Specifies the daylight saving time offset used to calculate UTC.
Daylight Saving Time Status	On, Off	Displays whether or not daylight saving time is in effect. Used only in the calculation of UTC.
New Time With Daylight Saving Time Status	On, Off	Causes the local time on the server to change as a result of daylight saving time.

Table 11-1: NetWare 4.11 server time parameters.

TIMESYNC ADD Time Source

The TIMESYNC ADD Time Source parameter will let you add a time source to your configured list of time sources in the custom time synchronization environment. For time providers, this list determines the other servers that will be contacted to vote upon a network time. For time consumers, it specifies the time providers that will be contacted to obtain the correct network time.

When adding names to the Time Source list, you only need to enter the common name of the NetWare 4.11 server. You do not need to provide a full distinguished name to the configured list. A full distinguished name will confuse TIMESYNC.NLM and prevent network time synchronization.

TIMESYNC Configuration File

The TIMESYNC Configuration File parameter specifies the location of the server's TIMESYNC.CFG file. By default, TIMESYNC.NLM will look to the SYS:SYSTEM directory for TIMESYNC.CFG. To change the location of TIMESYNC.CFG and have TIMESYNC.NLM recognize this change, you must add the following line to AUTOEXEC.NCF:

```
SET TIMESYNC CONFIGURATION FILE = <path\filename>
```

If you do not instruct TIMESYNC.NLM to look in another location through this line in AUTOEXEC.NCF, it will search SYS:SYSTEM for TIMESYNC.CFG instead of your custom configuration file.

TIMESYNC Configured Sources

When the TIMESYNC Configured Sources parameter is set to On, the time
server will not listen to time information distributed through SAP packets on
the network. It will only contact those servers listed in the configured list of
Time Sources for network time information. In the custom time synchronization environment, this value should be set to On. It will reduce the time synchronization traffic on your network. The default setting is Off.

TIMESYNC Directory Tree Mode

The TIMESYNC Directory Tree Mode parameter determines whether or not a
time server will listen to and use time information from time servers not in the
NDS tree. When set to On, the time server will only communicate with other
time servers in its own NDS tree. For networks with multiple NDS trees, this is
an important parameter to prevent network time corruption. The default value
is On.

TIMESYNC Hardware Clock

When the TIMESYNC Hardware Clock parameter is set to On, the time server
will synchronize with its own hardware clock as well as network time. Single
Reference and Reference servers read their own hardware clock before they
poll the other time servers on the network. Primary and Secondary time servers set their hardware clock at the end of the polling loop to the network time
when this parameter is On. When TIMESYNC Hardware Clock is set to Off, no
hardware clock synchronization occurs. The default value is On.

TIMESYNC Polling Count

The TIMESYNC Polling Count value sets the number of packets that are
exchanged during the polling process. The default value is 3 packets; however,
this can be increased up to a maximum of 1000 packets. Increasing the number
of packets exchanged during polling will increase the traffic on your network.
It is not recommended that you change this value.

TIMESYNC Polling Interval

The TIMESYNC Polling Interval determines the amount of time between
polling processes. By default, 600 seconds (10 minutes) passes between polling
sets. Once time synchronization is established and the environment is stable,
you might want to increase the value to 1200 or 1800 seconds between polls
(20 or 30 minutes). You can set this value to a maximum of 31 days in between
polling sets.

TIMESYNC REMOVE Time Source

The TIMESYNC REMOVE Time Source parameter will allow you to remove a server from your list of configured sources. Just type in the name, and it will be removed from TIMESYNC.CFG once all of the parameters are written to the file.

TIMESYNC RESET

Turning the TIMESYNC RESET parameter On will completely reset TIMESYNC.CFG to the default configuration. If you turn this On and choose to update TIMESYNC.CFG, you will lose all of the information stored in it including your Configured Time Source List. Use this parameter carefully. After you set this parameter to On, it will automatically reset itself to Off (its default value).

TIMESYNC Restart Flag

When the TIMESYNC Restart Flag is set to On, TIMESYNC.NLM will restart and reread the values stored in TIMESYNC.CFG. It is a way of "rebooting" your time environment without bringing down your servers. After you set this parameter to On, it automatically resets itself to Off (its default value). Any time you make a modification to TIMESYNC.CFG and want the changes to take effect, you must set the TIMESYNC Restart Flag to On or reboot the server.

TIMESYNC Service Advertising

The TIMESYNC Service Advertising parameter determines whether or not your servers will use SAP to communicate time information. The default value is On. If you are using a configured list of time servers in the custom environment, you should set it to Off. It will reduce the amount of time synchronization traffic on your network.

TIMESYNC Synchronization Radius

We discussed the TIMESYNC Synchronization Radius for a server earlier in this chapter. It determines how much a server's time can differ from the network time and still be considered synchronized. The default value is 2000 milliseconds (2 seconds). You may need to increase this value if there is considerable communication lag on your network (due to WAN links or excessive network traffic).

TIMESYNC Time Adjustment

The TIMESYNC Time Adjustment parameter allows you to change the network time. The time can be changed immediately, or it can be scheduled in the future. The syntax for using the TIMESYNC Time Adjustment parameter specifies an amount of time by which the network time is to be adjusted and the target time it is going to take place:

```
SET TIMESYNC Time Adjustment = +00:01:00 at 2/28/97 07:29:00PM
```

Typing in the previous example at the server console prompt would cause the network time to advance one minute on Feb. 28, 1997 at 7:29 P.M. Time adjustments can only be issued from a time provider. Take care in issuing network time adjustments. It should be done infrequently and only when absolutely necessary.

TIMESYNC Time Source

The TIMESYNC Time Source parameter serves the same function as the TIMESYNC ADD Time Source parameter described earlier in this section. It's just another way to add time sources to your configured list in the custom time synchronization environment.

TIMESYNC Type

To specify the TIMESYNC Type of time server a server is, use the TIMESYNC Type parameter. By default, this value is set to Secondary. To make the server a member of a time provider group, set this value to Single (for Single Reference), Primary, or Reference.

TIMESYNC Write Parameters

The TIMESYNC Write parameter causes the changed values to be written to TIMESYNC.CFG. If you have made any modifications to the server's time values, you must set TIMESYNC Write Parameters to On for the changes to be saved. Otherwise, the changes you made will be lost when the server is downed. Once it is set to On, it will automatically reset itself to Off.

TIMESYNC Write Value

The TIMESYNC Write Value parameter determines which modifications are written to TIMESYNC.CFG when the TIMESYNC Write Parameters are set to On. The default value is 3, which means all modifications made are written. A value of 1 indicates only internal time parameter information is saved; a value of 2 means only configured time source information is saved to TIMESYNC.CFG. Leave this value at 3. It will ensure that you do not lose any modifications you made to the file.

Time Zone

The Time Zone time parameter specifies the geographical location of the time server. It is also used by NetWare 4.11 to calculate the server's offset from UTC and the name by which the time zone is known when Daylight Saving Time is in effect. The Time Zone parameter is specified by a three-letter code by which the time zone is normally known. The three-letter code is followed by the time zone's offset from UTC, which is followed by the three-letter code by which the time zone is known during Daylight Saving Time.

For example, a server located in Boston, MA, would have the Time Zone variable set for EST5EDT for the following reasons:

- Boston is in the Eastern Standard Time zone (EST).

- The eastern standard time zone is five hours behind Greenwich mean time (UTC).

- During daylight saving time, this time zone is known as eastern daylight time (EDT).

Together, these three components create the value for the Time Zone time parameter. For locations whose time is ahead of UTC, the number must be prefaced by two minus signs (– –). For example, the Time Zone variable for mid-European time would be specified as MET– –1. Time zones that do not observe daylight saving time would have the last three letters omitted.

Default Time Server Type

The Default Time Server Type is the value that is set in AUTOEXEC.BAT to designate the type of time server. Although this value is set early in the boot process for the server, it can be overridden by the TIMESYNC Type parameter in TIMESYNC.CFG. The default value for the Default Time Server Type is Secondary.

Start of Daylight Saving Time

The Start of Daylight Saving Time parameter allows the network administrator to specify the time when Daylight Saving Time takes effect. You can insert the date and time the server needs to adjust for Daylight Saving Time in this field. You can also insert a rule so that this adjustment takes place year after year without any prompting. For example, to set the Start of Daylight Saving Time to the first Sunday in April at 2:00 A.M. every year, you would type the following in SERVMAN next to this parameter:

```
(APRIL SUNDAY FIRST 2:0:0 AM)
```

Tip

Rules for the Start of Daylight Saving Time parameter are always surrounded by parentheses. A specific date like April 6 1997 2:0:0 AM would not use parentheses.

End of Daylight Saving Time

The opposite of the previous time parameter, the End of Daylight Saving Time parameter allows the network administrator to specify the time when Daylight Saving Time ends. You can also specify a specific date or create a rule for the server so the adjustment takes place automatically. The following example will tell your server the end of Daylight Saving Time occurs on the last Sunday of October at 2:00 A.M.:

```
(OCTOBER SUNDAY LAST 2:0:0 AM)
```

Daylight Saving Time Offset

The Daylight Saving Time Offset parameter determines the amount of offset that will be calculated into UTC when it is Daylight Saving Time. By default, this value is one hour; however, it is customizable for those regions that have a different DST than the default.

Daylight Saving Time Status

The Daylight Saving Time Status is a display field for the benefit of the network administrator. When this variable is set to On, it means that the Daylight Saving Time Offset is being used to calculate UTC time stamps for NDS database transactions. This field does not affect the server's local time; it just informs the administrator whether or not the offset is being used in UTC calculations.

New Time With Daylight Saving Time Status

The New Time With Daylight Saving Time Status is the time parameter you probably thought the previous one was. When this is set to On, the server's local time also reflects the DST offset that is being used to calculate UTC. When this parameter is On and the transition to DST occurs, the local time the server displays will jump ahead one hour (if the default one hour offset is being used).

Saving Your Time Synchronization

Once you are finished configuring your custom time synchronization in SERVMAN, you should set the TIMESYNC Write Parameters to On and the TIMESYNC Restart Flag to On. They will both immediately reset themselves to Off; however, it will cause all of your modifications to be written to TIMESYNC.CFG, and it will force TIMESYNC.NLM to reset itself and load the new time parameter values.

To exit SERVMAN, press the Escape button twice. The Update Options menu will appear, as seen in Figure 11-10. Depending upon which modifications were made to the time parameters, you may get the option to Update TIMESYNC.CFG Now and/or Update AUTOEXEC.NCF and STARTUP.NCF Now. These options will commit any changes you have made to the appropriate files.

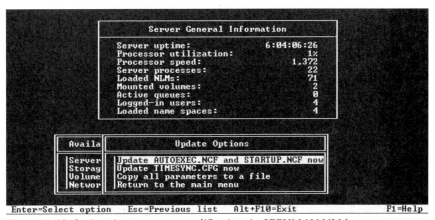

Figure 11-10: Saving time parameter modifications in SERVMAN.NLM.

For TIMESYNC.CFG, the Update TIMESYNC.CFG Now option is the equivalent to setting the TIMESYNC Write Parameters to On. If you forgot to do this in the Time Parameters screen, you have another option to save your changes. To save your changes to either locations shown, select the option and press Enter. To prevent the changes from being committed to file, press the Escape key again. You will be returned to the main screen of SERVMAN.NLM.

To quit SERVMAN.NLM, keep pressing Escape until you reach the menu Exit SERVMAN?. Select Yes to unload this NLM from server memory. Once you have finished configuring and saving the time parameters, your time synchronization environment is complete. The last step is to review the configuration to ensure it is correct.

Reviewing the TIMESYNC.CFG File

As we have learned, the TIMESYNC.CFG file is read by TIMESYNC.NLM to determine the time synchronization environment for your server. If the TIMESYNC.CFG file does not exist or is not locatable by TIMESYNC.NLM, the time synchronization environment reverts to the default environment as specified by the time parameters in AUTOEXEC.NCF.

When you are finished configuring the time server parameters in SERVMAN.NLM, it is a good idea to review the configuration to make sure it is accurate. To view the TIMESYNC.CFG file, type the following command at the server console prompt (colon prompt):

`LOAD EDIT SYS:SYSTEM\TIMESYNC.CFG`

If your TIMESYNC.CFG file is located in a different place, substitute that path for the default path in the above example. This command will cause the NetWare text editor to load and display the TIMESYNC.CFG file. This file should reflect all of the changes you made to the time parameters in SERVMAN.NLM.

```
                 Current File "SYS:SYSTEM\TIMESYNC.CFG"

# Configuration Parameters from server DAMOCLES

Configured Sources =    ON
Directory Tree Mode =    ON
Hardware Clock =    ON
Polling Count =    3
Polling Interval =    600
Service Advertising =    OFF
Synchronization Radius =    2000
Type =    REFERENCE

# Configured time source list from server DAMOCLES

Time Source = DAMON
Time Source = PYTHIAS
```

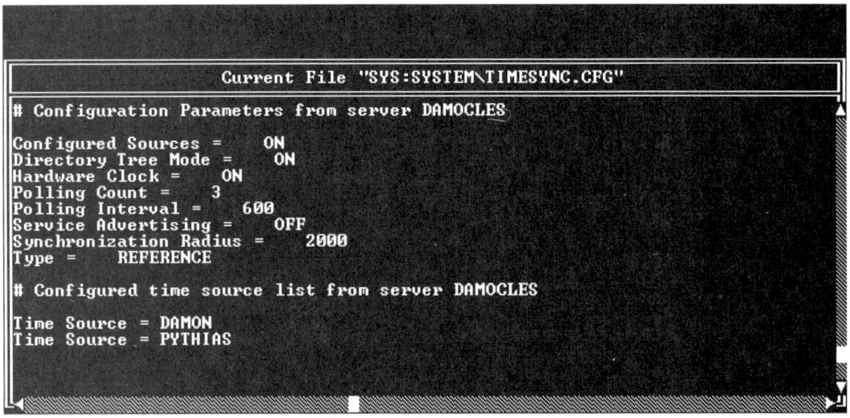

Figure 11-11: TIMESYNC.CFG file for the Reference time server Damocles.

In Figure 11-11, we see the TIMESYNC.CFG file for the Reference time server Damocles. The TIMESYNC.CFG file is located in the SYS:SYSTEM directory on the file server. For this section of the chapter, the examples will refer to our custom time synchronization environment where Damocles is a Reference time server for the Willow NDS tree. Damon and Pythias are both

Primary time servers in the time provider group. In Figure 11-11, we can see the time parameters required to set up Damocles as a Reference time server. Here are some of the more important parameters:

- **TIMESYNC Configured Sources** is set to On. This means Damocles will only talk to the time servers specified in the Configured Time Source List for time information.

- **TIMESYNC Directory Tree Mode** is set to On. Damocles will only receive time information from other servers in the Willow NDS tree.

- **TIMESYNC Service Advertising** is set to Off. Damocles will not accept SAP packets for time information. Only the servers in the Configured Time Source List will be contacted.

- **TIMESYNC Type** is set to Reference. Damocles is the Reference time server for the network.

- **The Configured Time Source List** displays all of the servers Damocles will contact to determine the correct network time. Both Damon and Pythias are included in this list.

The Time Zone and Daylight Saving Time parameters were specified in AUTOEXEC.NCF. They are not specified in TIMESYNC.CFG. However, the TIMESYNC Type parameter in TIMESYNC.CFG will override the TIMESYNC Default Time Server Type parameter specified in AUTOEXEC.NCF. This is one instance where the time parameter value set in AUTOEXEC.NCF is super-seded by the value in TIMESYNC.CFG.

When you are finished reviewing the file, press Escape twice to exit the NetWare text editor. Because it is a text editor, you can also use it to modify TIMESYNC.CFG. Instead of loading SERVMAN.NLM to change the time parameters, you can just change them in the text editor and save the changes. However, if you do so, you must type the following command at the server console prompt (colon prompt):

`SET TIMESYNC RESTART FLAG = ON`

Remember, for changes made to the TIMESYNC.CFG file to take effect in your time synchronization environment, you must restart TIMESYNC.NLM. Issuing the above command at the server console prompt will restart the time environment so your changes will take effect.

The TIMESYNC.CFG files for the file servers Damon and Pythias are going to look very similar to the one for Damocles. The only differences are going to be the TIMESYNC Type and the Configured Time Source List. Figures 11-12 and 11-13 show the TIMESYNC.CFG files for Damon and Pythias, respectively.

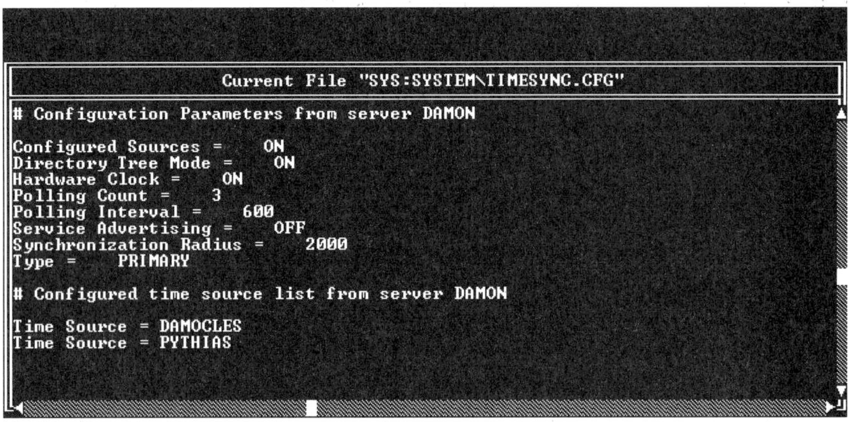

```
                    Current File "SYS:SYSTEM\TIMESYNC.CFG"

# Configuration Parameters from server DAMON

Configured Sources =    ON
Directory Tree Mode =    ON
Hardware Clock =    ON
Polling Count =    3
Polling Interval =    600
Service Advertising =    OFF
Synchronization Radius =    2000
Type =    PRIMARY

# Configured time source list from server DAMON

Time Source = DAMOCLES
Time Source = PYTHIAS
```

Figure 11-12: TIMESYNC.CFG file for the Primary time server Damon.

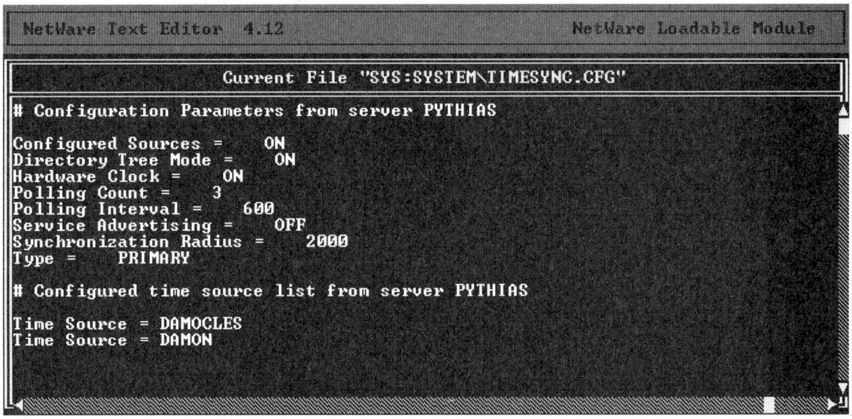

```
 NetWare Text Editor  4.12                    NetWare Loadable Module

                    Current File "SYS:SYSTEM\TIMESYNC.CFG"

# Configuration Parameters from server PYTHIAS

Configured Sources =    ON
Directory Tree Mode =    ON
Hardware Clock =    ON
Polling Count =    3
Polling Interval =    600
Service Advertising =    OFF
Synchronization Radius =    2000
Type =    PRIMARY

# Configured time source list from server PYTHIAS

Time Source = DAMOCLES
Time Source = DAMON
```

Figure 11-13: TIMESYNC.CFG file for the Primary time server Pythias.

The sample TIMESYNC.CFG files in Figures 11-11, 11-12, and 11-13 should provide a guide for you when setting up the custom time synchronization environment. Your files, when finished, will look similar to these. Once the environment has been configured on all of the time servers and the TIMESYNC Restart Flag has been reset, the network time should be synchronized. The following message displayed on the file server console screen will mean you have successfully configured the time synchronization environment:

`Time synchronization has been established.`

Congratulations!

Moving On

Once you have set up the time synchronization environment, you have finished configuring the NDS back end. The foundation has been laid for the eight services provided in Novell's definition of an intranet. Through time synchronization, you can be sure your critical NDS data is accurate and current across your entire network.

In the last few chapters, we have talked about NDS in terms of a single tree. That obviously is the goal to achieve on your network because it provides one central location for the storage of network resource information. If you happen to be part of a larger network environment, though, multiple NDS trees may exist on your network. To achieve the goal of unification, you can merge two trees together while maintaining the integrity of the NDS objects in both trees. In the next chapter, we will explore the process of merging and renaming NDS trees.

12 Merging NDS Trees

The issues we have discussed so far about NDS trees have assumed there is only one tree in your organization. If you are fortunate enough to be the network administrator of a small organization, you can create one tree and maintain it. However, some larger companies or organizations may have multiple NDS trees. Whether this is caused by WAN link considerations or a loose conglomeration of smaller information technology departments, multiple NDS trees can cause inefficiencies in your users' day-to-day networking tasks.

The goal of NDS is to provide a unified networking environment. All of the network resources are stored in a single database, and all security information about those resources is stored in the same place. Users no longer need to deal with multiple user IDs and multiple authentications to obtain access to the network resources they need. Unfortunately, having multiple NDS trees on your network defeats this purpose if users need to access resources in both trees.

But fortunately, there is a way to merge two separate NDS trees into one single tree to achieve the overall goal of network resource centralization. This is done through an NDS utility called DSMERGE.NLM. Once the merge is completed, you will be left with an NDS tree that contains all of the objects from the two original trees.

For example, multiple trees might exist at Rambell, Inc. if different divisions created their own NDS trees before the central information technology department was able to create one for the entire company. This would mean that users within the same company would have to authenticate to two different trees to share resources. Merging these trees into one single unit would allow all of the users in the company to access all network resources using one single login.

A lot easier said than done, right? The process actually is not too difficult to perform. It is done in three distinct phases. First, you must prepare the two trees that will be merged. There are some preconditions that need to be met before the trees can be merged. We will discuss both the prerequisites and the general concepts with which you must be familiar for merging NDS trees.

The second step in the merge deals with the DSMERGE.NLM utility itself. With it, you make one final check of the servers in both trees and synchronize the time environments between them. You can also rename the NDS trees before the merge. Finally, when you are ready, DSMERGE.NLM will perform the actual merging of the two NDS trees.

Once the merging of the trees is complete, there will probably be some cleanup to do. We will discuss the implications of merging the trees, including partitioning and context considerations. We will also talk about what needs to be done to "massage" the merged tree structure into the final structure for your single NDS tree.

Preparing to Merge

Before the actual merging of the two NDS trees takes place, you must make sure they are ready to be merged. There are certain restrictions involved with the process, and the first thing to identify is whether or not your trees *can* be merged. If they cannot, you must upgrade your systems so that merging is a possibility. Once the stage has been set for merging, you can then proceed with the merge.

But before we talk about the requirements that must be met, it is important to have an overview of the merging process. We will define some terms that we will use throughout the rest of this chapter and give you an overview of the merging process.

Merging Concepts

From the onset, merging NDS trees seems like a fairly simple task. But sometimes what appears simple on the surface can be quite complex underneath. That is the case with NDS tree merging. First, we start with two separate NDS trees on a network. The goal is to take those two trees and unite them into one single structure. Fair enough.

There are certain terms we will use to distinguish these two trees from one another. The *source tree* is the NDS tree that will be merged. When the merging process is complete, the source tree will no longer exist. It is also often called the *local tree* or *local source tree*. These three terms are used interchangeably. We will only use the term *source tree* to avoid confusion.

The *target tree* is the destination NDS tree; it will absorb the source tree and be the remaining structure when the merging process is complete. Generally, the target tree will be the larger (or more established) of the two trees. The source tree should be the tree with the least number of objects existing directly below [Root].

When the source and target trees are merged together, all of the objects in the source tree become members of the target tree. Objects that were direct subordinates of the source [Root] become direct subordinates of the target [Root]. It is as if the source tree's [Root] is removed and the remainder of the source tree is placed directly under the target tree's [Root]. Figure 12-1 shows a sample source and target tree before the merge and the remaining target tree after the merge. Notice where the source tree's objects exist in the target tree relative to [Root] after the merge.

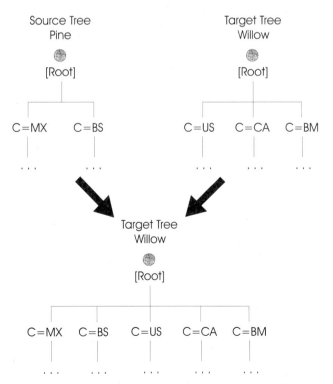

Figure 12-1: After the merge, the source tree's objects are in the same position relative to [Root].

As we see in the figure, the tree is only affected at the [Root] level. The rest of the tree remains intact. Thus, no object's context in either the source tree or target tree changes after the merge. This is important to know. The merging of the trees can be done without any users even knowing that it happened. As we will discuss later, you will not want to leave the tree in this state; however, immediately after the merge, there has been no change in NDS tree context.

Another aspect of this vein of transparency for the end user is that the NDS and file system security for the tree is not changed for objects in the source tree or the target tree. Any trustee assignments or rights inheritance that existed before the merge will exist after the merge. This is an added benefit because you do not need to re-administer the network security after the merge.

As we can see in Figure 12-1, the fundamental changes to the NDS database are taking place at the [Root] level in the [Root] partition of both the source and target NDS tree. Thus to accomplish the merge, you must have access to the Master replica of the [Root] partition on the source NDS tree. If you do not have this access, you cannot merge the two trees. The Read/Write replica on the source tree cannot be used to facilitate the merging process. You must also have the Supervisor NDS object right to the [Root] object in both the source and target NDS trees.

However, it is not enough to have the necessary access and rights. But before we can actually merge the source and target trees, we have to meet all of the prerequisite conditions necessary for merging.

Merging Prerequisites

Merging two NDS trees affects the integral structure of both trees. It is not a trivial process. Both trees must be checked thoroughly for possible errors before the merge can ever take place. The probability of success in merging two trees is directly related to the stability of the two trees before the merge takes place. A tree that is not stable can cause the merge to fail.

Another item that needs to be verified is the compatibility of the two trees before the merge. If the two trees differ in their versions of NDS or their schemas, they cannot be merged. If you think about it, this is logical. When we discussed schema in Chapter 8, we talked about it being the set of rules by which NDS must live. If two trees live by two different sets of rules, which set of rules is the correct one? Only when there is one set standard of rules for both trees can they then be merged.

There are essentially six topics that must be verified before the merging can take place. If your particular situation does not meet these prerequisites, take the necessary corrective steps before the merge:

- User connections
- Unique NDS object identification
- [Root] subordinates
- NDS version compatibility
- Replica status
- Schema compatibility

User Connections

When the merge takes place, no one can be logged in to the NDS tree. Verify that no users are connected to the tree. Use MONITOR.NLM to view the connection status and disconnect users who are still attached to either tree. The person performing the merge does not even need a server connection because DSMERGE.NLM is loaded at the server console.

Tip

To prevent users from logging in to the network when you are merging, issue the **DISABLE LOGIN** *command at the server console prompt. When you are finished with the merge, type* **ENABLE LOGIN** *at the server console prompt to allow your users access to the network again.*

Unique NDS Object Identification

In Chapter 3, "NetWare 4.11 Concepts," you learned that each object in the NDS tree can be uniquely identified through a combination of its common name and its context. Two objects with the same common name can exist in the NDS tree, but they must be located in separate containers. Two objects with the same common name cannot exist in the same container *even if they are different types of objects.*

Before you merge the two trees, you must determine if the resulting tree would cause any violations of this NDS law. Imagine what the tree will look like after the merge (or write it out on paper) and verify that each object in the resulting tree will still be uniquely identified using its common name and container. Rename or move objects whose names would conflict in the final tree structure.

[Root] Subordinates

In the source tree, only container objects may exist directly off of [Root]. Delete aliases or any other leaf objects that may exist as a direct subordinate of [Root]. You will have to re-create these later in the target tree after the merge is completed.

NDS Version Compatibility

Both the source and target trees must be running the same version of NDS for the trees to successfully merge. If you do not have compatible versions of NDS on your servers, upgrade all of your servers to the same version. It is a good idea to keep current versions of NDS on all of your servers, so this should not be a problem.

People who have both NetWare 4.1 and NetWare 4.11 servers in their tree need to be careful. NDS is tailored for a specific version of NetWare. Thus, NDS for NetWare 4.11 version 5.73 cannot be run on a NetWare 4.1 server. However, the source and target trees can still be merged in this environment. The key here is the servers with the replicas of the [Root] partition.

To merge trees in this mixed environment, store the replicas of the [Root] partition in the source and target trees on NetWare 4.11 servers. Remove the replicas of [Root] from the NetWare 4.1 servers. The merge can take place as long as no servers with older versions of NDS are involved in the database transactions. You do still need to ensure, however, that the NetWare 4.11 servers storing the replicas of the [Root] partitions are all running the same version of NDS for NetWare 4.11.

Replica Status

Because merging the NDS trees affects the [Root] partition on both the source and the target tree, all of the replicas of the [Root] partition in both trees must be available. If your replica ring spans a WAN link, make sure the WAN link is stable before the merge takes place or temporarily remove the replicas on the other side of the WAN link to ensure the stability of the merge.

Schema Compatibility

As we mentioned previously, schema compatibility is critical to the successful merging of the NDS trees. Trees with different schemas cannot be merged because it would cause great confusion. There must be one set of standard rules for both trees before the merge will be allowed to happen. If the schemas for the two trees are different, you must make them the same. Fortunately, NDS comes with a process for importing schemas from remote locations.

To import the target tree schema to the source tree, perform the following steps:

1. At the server console prompt (colon prompt) of the server with the master replica of [Root] in the source tree, type **LOAD DSREPAIR**. The main menu of the DS Repair utility will load.

2. From the Available Options menu, choose the Advanced Options Menu. The Advanced Options box will appear.

3. From the Advanced Options box, choose Global Schema Operations.

4. Type in the Administrator name and password for the source tree. Use the full distinguished name of the Admin user account for access. Highlight Press <Enter> to Continue and Log In and press Enter.

5. From the Global Schema Options menu, choose Import Remote Schema.

6. The Import Remote Schema From Another Tree box will appear. Press Enter to see a list of trees and select the target tree from the list.

7. Press F10 to import the schema from the target tree.

When you are finished, a log of the modifications will appear on the screen. This is the log created by the DSREPAIR utility, and it is stored in a file in SYS:SYSTEM called DSREPAIR.LOG. Review this file for any errors. When finished, press the Escape button and you will be returned to the Global Schema Options menu.

Tip

*You can view the DSREPAIR.LOG file in the SYS:SYSTEM directory by using the EDIT.NLM utility. From the server console prompt (colon prompt), just type **load edit sys:system\dsrepair.log**.*

Importing the schema in this manner is a one-way exchange of information. You are importing from the target tree to the source tree. No information is sent from the source tree to the target tree. If there have been schema modifications on the source tree, those modifications are not reported to the target tree. After the import, the schemas for the two trees may still be different.

To ensure schema compatibility, also import the schema from the source tree to the target tree. This will create a two-way exchange of schema information. To completely synchronize the schemas of the two trees, you may have to perform the import process multiple times.

Once the schemas have been synchronized and all of the other prerequisites have been met, it is time to get to the heart of the merging process. The tree merge is accomplished using a utility called DSMERGE.NLM, which is loaded at the server console in the source tree. We still have a few more steps to go before the merge actually takes place, but the remainder of the tasks are accomplished using DSMERGE.NLM.

Merging NDS Trees With DSMERGE.NLM

DSMERGE.NLM is a utility that comes packaged with IntranetWare. It allows you to merge two separate NDS trees together into one unified structure. Assuming that all of the previously discussed prerequisites for the merge have been met, it is time to load DSMERGE.NLM on the servers of the source and target trees that contain the Master replicas of the [Root] partitions. While some of our next procedures can be done with Read/Write replicas, you will need to have access to the Master replicas when the merge occurs. To avoid any confusion, it is a good idea to start working with the Master replicas right from the beginning.

Using an RCONSOLE session or at the server console itself, type the following line at the console prompt (colon prompt) to start DSMERGE.NLM: **LOAD DSMERGE**.

This will load the DSMERGE software, and the main menu for this utility, which is shown in Figure 12-2, will appear. You will note that there are four options available from the DSMERGE main menu. You will need to use these options in the process of the tree merge in this order:

- Check Servers in This Tree
- Check Time Synchronization
- Merge Two Trees
- Rename This Tree (optional)

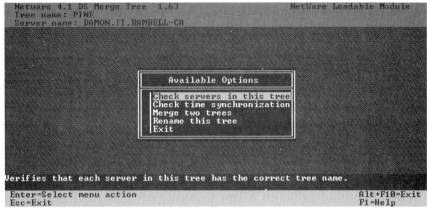

```
Netware 4.1 DS Merge Tree  1.63                    NetWare Loadable Module
Tree name: PINE
Server name: DAMON.IT.RAMBELL-CA




                       ┌──────────────────────────────┐
                       │      Available Options        │
                       ├──────────────────────────────┤
                       │Check servers in this tree     │
                       │Check time synchronization     │
                       │Merge two trees                │
                       │Rename this tree               │
                       │Exit                           │
                       └──────────────────────────────┘



Verifies that each server in this tree has the correct tree name.

   Enter=Select menu action                              Alt+F10=Exit
   Esc=Exit                                               F1=Help
```

Figure 12-2: The DSMERGE main menu.

The first two options in the main menu of DSMERGE, Check Servers in This Tree and Check Time Synchronization, involve more stability tests to prepare for the tree merge. The third option, Merge Two Trees, will actually perform the tree merge. The last option, Rename This Tree, allows you to change the name of your tree. Let's examine these options one at a time during our merging of two trees.

Check Servers in This Tree

The first thing you must do in DSMERGE before merging the trees is check the status of the servers in the source NDS tree. All of the servers in the source tree will be contacted to ensure they are up and running. They will also have their tree name verified at the same time. You must have the Supervisor NDS object right to the source tree [Root] to check the servers in the source tree.

To check the status of the servers in the NDS tree, you must have already loaded DSMERGE.NLM on a server that stores at least a Read/Write replica of the [Root] partition; however, we recommend you load DSMERGE.NLM on the server that stores the Master replica of the [Root] partition in the source tree because you will need this replica to actually perform the merge. From the DSMERGE main menu, choose Check Servers in This Tree by highlighting it and pressing Enter. DSMERGE will proceed to check the status of all of the servers in the NDS tree. Once completed, it will generate a simple report for you and display it on the server's screen.

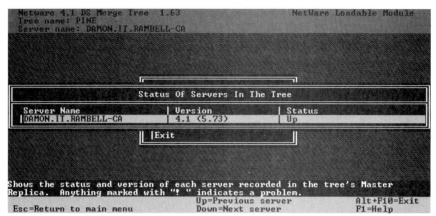

Figure 12-3: DSMERGE verifies the status of the servers in the NDS tree and generates a report.

In Figure 12-3, we can see the report generated for the NDS tree Pine. It contains one server called Damon, which exists in the IT.RAMBELL-CA container of the tree. It is a NetWare 4.11 server, and it is currently up and running. View the status area of this report very carefully. A status of Up means the server is ready. Displayed statuses of Error, Unknown, or Wrong Tree indicate you must identify and fix the problems before the trees are merged. For more information on troubleshooting NDS problems, refer to Chapter 14.

You will also notice in Figure 12-3 that Damon is being reported as a NetWare 4.1 server instead of a NetWare 4.11 server. Next to the version of NetWare in the Version column, you will see the version of NDS on the server in parentheses (in this case it is NDS version 5.73). To determine the type of server it is, look to the NDS version and *not* the NetWare version. Because Damon is running NDS version 5.73, we know that it must be a NetWare 4.11 server; as this book is being written, the most recent version of NDS for NetWare 4.1 is 5.06. So although the display may report the incorrect version of NetWare being run on the server, it will report the correct version of NDS being used. With this information, you can verify it has detected the server correctly.

Once the status of all of the servers has been verified, you can press the Escape key to return to the main menu of DSMERGE. You are now ready to progress to step 2 of the NDS tree merging process.

Check Time Synchronization

As we discussed in the previous chapter, an accurate network time plays an important role in the health of your network. When two trees exist, they more than likely have two distinct time synchronization environments. When the trees are merged, there will only be one time synchronization environment; therefore, you must merge the time synchronization environments of the two trees before you can actually merge the two trees.

If you are using the default time synchronization environment in both the source and target trees, the merging of the two environments is fairly simple. The Single Reference server in the source tree must be made a Secondary time server. If you are using configured time source lists, you must modify the lists on all of the servers in the source tree so that they point to the Single Reference server in the target tree in order to establish the time environment.

The custom time synchronization environment will take a little more effort to merge. You must reorganize your time synchronization environment in the target tree to include the new servers that will be joining. Determine which servers will be the Reference server and Primary servers in the time provider group. Reconfigure the rest of the servers as Secondary servers. On each server, you must also make changes to the configured time sources list to reflect the changes in the time synchronization environment structure.

Once changes have been made to TIMESYNC.CFG, you must restart the time environment in each tree. This change will effectively merge the two time synchronization environments together into one. Once this has been accomplished, you are ready to test the time synchronization environment for the resulting tree after the merge. For more information on setting up the time synchronization environment, refer to Chapter 11.

When time synchronization has been established after the reconfiguration of the time environment, use DSMERGE to test the synchronization. To test the synchronization, DSMERGE.NLM must already be loaded on a server that contains at least a Read/Write replica of the [Root] partition. Again, we recommend using the server that stores the Master replica of the source tree because that is the replica required to perform the actual merge.

From the DSMERGE main menu, choose Check Time Synchronization by highlighting it and pressing Enter. DSMERGE will perform a check of the time environment and display the results for you in the Time Synchronization Information for Tree window, which is shown in Figure 12-4. This box consists of four columns that display information about the time synchronization environment:

- **Server Name.** Displays a list of all servers in the NDS tree. In this case, Damon is the only server in the NDS tree Pine.

- **Type.** Shows the type of time server in the NDS tree. Damon, which used to be the Single Reference server for the source tree Pine, has been reconfigured to be a Secondary server in the target tree once the two trees are merged.

- **In Sync.** Displays the status of the time synchronization environment as that server sees it. Damon is in sync with its configured time source, which happens to be the Single Reference server Damocles in the NDS tree Willow. If the In Sync status of all servers in the tree is Yes, then the two trees are ready to be merged.

- **Time Delta.** Shows the time difference between the server and the configured time source. In our example, there is no difference between Damon's reported time and Damocles's reported time. They are completely in sync with one another.

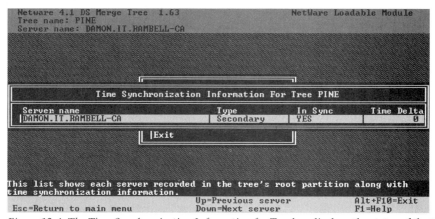

Figure 12-4: The Time Synchronization Information for Tree box displays the status of the time environment.

Merging larger time synchronization environments may take time; it may not happen immediately. Give yourself enough time before the tree merge to establish the time synchronization environment between the two trees. If the time synchronization does not occur after waiting a few hours, you should begin to examine how you have reconfigured the time environment and look for errors in your setup.

You must perform the time synchronization check in both the source tree and the target tree. Remember, DSMERGE needs to run on servers that store at least a Read/Write replica of the [Root] partitions in both trees. You must also have the Supervisor NDS object right to the [Root] object in the source and target trees.

Once the two time environments have been merged successfully, and the time synchronization has been verified, you have successfully completed the preparations of the two trees. It is now time to merge the two NDS trees.

Merge Two Trees

At this point, all of the preparations for the tree merge have been completed. It is time to perform the actual merge using DSMERGE. Once you merge the two trees, you cannot split them again without reinstalling the operating systems on all of the servers in the source tree. After the merge, you have reached the point of no return.

To perform the merge, you must have done the following things:

- DSMERGE.NLM needs to be loaded on the server in the source tree with the Master replica of the [Root] partition.

- You must have the Supervisor NDS object right to the [Root] object in both the source tree and the target NDS tree.

- The time synchronization environments of the two separate trees must have been merged and synchronized to one single time source.

- You should have a current backup of the NDS database for both individual trees.

If you have a backup of the NDS database and for some reason the merge fails or corrupts your NDS database, you will be able to restore your network environment. Having a backup lets you perform the merge with a safety net. If you do not have a backup, merge at your own risk.

To perform the merge, choose the Merge Two Trees option from the main menu of DSMERGE. In the Merge Trees Information box, you will be asked to supply the Admin user object for the source tree and the target tree. You will also need to specify the target tree name. Figure 12-5 shows the Merge Trees Information box before the merge with the source tree Pine and target tree Willow.

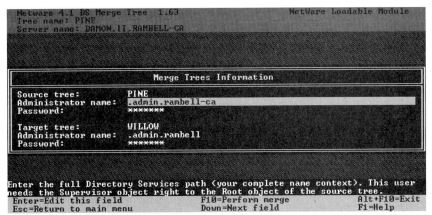

Figure 12-5: The Merge Trees Information box is where you provide information to DSMERGE about the source and target NDS trees.

Once the information has been supplied, press F10 to perform the merge. DSMERGE will provide you with some information concerning the merging process that includes all of the preparation information we have already discussed. Read the information and press Enter to continue through the screens. After the information screens, DSMERGE will perform another last check to verify the trees can be merged. If it finds any errors, it will tell you where you need to look to correct the problem. In Figure 12-6, we can see that the schemas for the two trees are not compatible. We must go back and make them compatible before we can merge the trees.

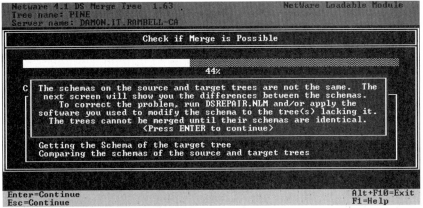

Figure 12-6: DSMERGE reports any errors in the final check of the two trees and tries to help you correct the problem.

Once the final check of the source and target trees has been completed, you will be asked if you want to merge the trees. Highlight Yes and press Enter to merge the source and target trees. DSMERGE will merge the trees and keep you informed of the progress throughout. Once the merge has been completed, press Enter. You will be returned to the main menu of DSMERGE.

At this point, there is only one NDS tree, and it has the name of the target tree. The source tree has effectively disappeared; however, all of its objects now exist in the target tree in the same context they had before the merge. All that's left to do now is the general cleanup and customization of the new NDS environment.

Rename This Tree

The DSMERGE utility also gives you the option to rename an NDS tree. This option can be used at any time; you do not have to merge a tree to be able to rename it. To rename the NDS tree, load DSMERGE on the server in the tree that contains the Master replica of the [Root] partition. Choose Rename This Tree from the main menu. The Rename Tree Information box will appear (Figure 12-7).

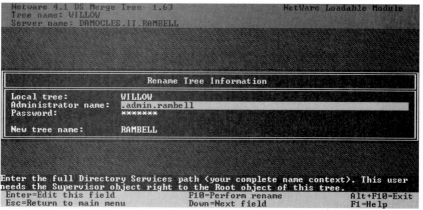

Figure 12-7: To rename an NDS tree, you must log in as the Admin of the tree and specify the new name of the tree.

Once you have filled in the information, press F10 to rename the tree. Do not change tree names lightly. Client workstations may be looking for a specific tree when they boot. If the workstation cannot locate the tree, your users may not be able to log in correctly, which may end up causing you extra work.

To ensure that your users are able to access the tree after you name it, you must change the Preferred Tree option in the NET.CFG file of each workstation to reflect the new name of the NDS tree. For more information on client workstation setup, refer to Chapters 15 and 16.

Once you are done with the DSMERGE utility, you can press Escape at the main menu to exit it. The trees have been successfully merged, but the work of the network administrator is not done yet. We still need to examine the results of the merge and "massage" the new NDS tree so it fits into our overall organizational structure and purpose.

After the Merge

Once the merge is complete, you have one united structure that contains all of the objects originally contained in two trees. But how does it affect our NDS environment from both a front-end and back-end perspective? It is important to understand just what has happened to the NDS tree in the merging process. There may be some security and partitioning/replication changes that could compromise the integrity of your tree. The new structure needs to be reviewed thoroughly.

Implications of Merging Trees

Merging NDS trees has a significant impact on the front-end and back-end environments of NDS. After the merge, there will be changes to your security scheme and to the partitioning and replication of the NDS tree itself. As a network administrator, you must be aware of these changes and take the appropriate measures to return the tree to its original state of security and fault tolerance.

After the merge, three main areas of NDS will be fundamentally changed:

- NDS partitioning and replication
- NDS security
- NDS tree name

NDS Partitioning & Replication

As we have seen, only the [Root] partition of the tree has been affected by the merging process; however, merging trees will change your partitioning scheme and modify the replica ring of the [Root] partition. Both of these changes can compromise the fault tolerance of your network.

During the merge, all of the replicas of the [Root] partition in the source tree are removed from the servers. This is logical because that [Root] partition no longer exists. However, the server that did contain the Master replica of the source tree's [Root] partition will receive a Read/Write replica of the target tree's [Root] partition. This will most likely cause Subordinate Reference replicas to be created on that server.

The merge process will also create new partitions in your tree. Those objects that existed directly below [Root] in the source tree will be the partition root of a new partition. This can cause the creation of many small partitions, which may affect the performance of your network. Figure 12-8 shows two trees and their partitioning schemes before a tree merge and after. The source and target tree each only have one partition—[Root]. However, the target tree after the merge has three partitions because the two subordinate containers in the source tree become partition roots.

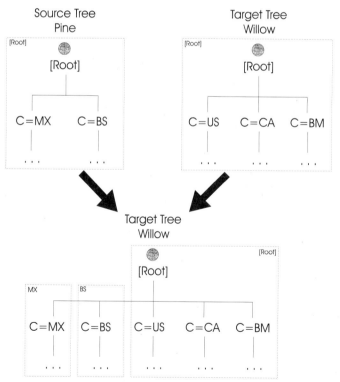

Figure 12-8: Containers directly subordinate to [Root] in the source tree are made partition roots of new partitions in the target tree.

By understanding the changes made to the partitioning and replication of the NDS tree, you will be able to make the necessary adjustments to your NDS back end to re-create a robust and fault-tolerant partitioning and replication design.

NDS Security

When NDS objects are brought from the source tree into the target tree, they keep the same context. The Admin object from the old tree will have the same context in the new tree. Also, all of the NDS objects' trustee assignments are brought over into the new tree. This has some obvious security implications.

In every tree that is created, the Admin user object is granted a trustee assignment to [Root] with the Supervisor NDS object right. This gives the Admin object complete control over the NDS tree. When the two trees are merged together, there will be two Admin objects in the resulting tree (one from the source tree and one from the target tree). Since both were given the Supervisor object right to [Root] in their respective trees, both will have the Supervisor object right to [Root] in the resulting tree.

The same is true for any other objects in the source tree that were granted trustee assignments to [Root]. Those trustee assignments will be intact in the target tree after the merge. If these rights are not appropriate in the new tree, you must change them immediately after the merge to prevent the security of your network from being compromised.

NDS Tree Name

There is only one tree structure after the merge is complete, and it retains the name of the target tree. The source tree no longer exists on your network. Any workstations that were set to connect to the source tree must be modified to connect to the target tree after the merge. To do this, change the Preferred Tree statement on each workstation. For more information on the Preferred Tree setting for workstations, refer to Chapters 15 and 16.

Merging Cleanup

Since there have been some changes to the NDS environment of your target tree, there are some steps you should take after the merging of the two trees to ensure the stability of your network and reestablish workstation client connectivity. After the clean-up process, the merge will be complete, and you will have a single NDS tree to provide a central pool of network resources for all users on your network.

After you have exited DSMERGE on the server, you will want to address the following topics concerning your new NDS environment:

- Container placement
- NDS partitioning and replication
- NDS security
- Workstation connectivity issues

Container Placement

When the two trees are merged, the source tree's NDS objects do not have their contexts changed. This means you may have multiple containers existing directly off of [Root]. If this is not where you want them to exist in the NDS tree, they must be moved to a different location in the tree.

You can accomplish these container moves by using NDS Manager. Remember that each container must be made a partition root before it can be moved; fortunately, DSMERGE has already done this for you during the tree move. It should be a trivial matter to move the containers to their new locations in the NDS tree.

If you move a container in the tree, the context of the objects in that container will change. If this move involves user objects, you must notify the users that their NDS context has been changed and modify their workstations to reflect this change. For DOS/Windows workstations, you will need to change the Name Context variable in the NET.CFG file to the new context for the user object. For more information on configuring the NET.CFG file, refer to Chapter 15.

NDS Partitioning & Replication

As we mentioned in the previous section, some fundamental changes are made to your NDS partitioning and replication scheme when trees are merged. You need to review the new partitions that were created. You also need to review the replica rings of all the partitions in the tree. An increase in the number of Subordinate Reference replicas in your tree is likely after merging NDS trees because a new replica of the [Root] partition is created.

Adjust the replica rings according to your original plan for the target tree. If you removed replicas from non-NetWare 4.11 servers in the preparation process, you should replace them. Merge any small partitions that were created by the merge process but not needed. By doing so, you will decrease the amount of network traffic generated by the replica synchronization process and increase the efficiency of your network.

NDS Security

Because the trustee assignments for both trees are preserved after the merge, the security of your resulting NDS tree may be compromised. Review the trustee assignments at the [Root] level of the tree to ensure that no inappropriate people have rights to [Root]. Review objects' security equivalencies as well. It is important that you carefully examine the security of your new NDS tree to maintain the integrity of the tree and the data stored on the various file servers.

Tip

After the two trees are merged, there will be two Admin accounts. We recommend you delete one of these accounts to maintain the security of your network.

Workstation Connectivity Issues

The people who are affected most by the merging of the trees are the users. After two trees have been merged, you must address the workstation connectivity issues so that users will be able to access the network again once the process is complete. In many cases, this involves modifying each individual workstation's configuration to reflect the network change.

Look for three general items concerning workstation connectivity to the network after two trees have been merged. For more information on specifically configuring these parameters at the workstation, refer to Chapters 15 and 16:

- The Preferred Tree variable in the workstations' NET.CFG files should be changed to the name of the target tree. Only workstations that connected to the source tree will need to be modified.

- The Name Context variable in the workstations' NET.CFG files should be changed if the context of the user object has changed from the source tree to the target tree. Only those users' workstations whose contexts have changed need to be modified.

- If your users require Bindery Services, you need to verify the bindery context on the servers providing Bindery Services. If the bindery contexts in the tree have changed, this change must be reflected in the servers' AUTOEXEC.NCF files.

Tip

To minimize the amount of cleanup necessary after two trees are merged, use the NDS tree with the lesser number of workstation clients connecting to it as the source tree.

If you have disabled the login ability for the network in order to perform the merge, type the following command at the console prompt after you have finished with the clean-up process. It will allow your users to access the network again:

```
ENABLE LOGIN
```

Moving On

Merging two NDS trees really involves three separate steps. The first step is the preparation of the two trees. The second step is the merging of the time synchronization environments, the final checking of tree compatibility, and the actual merge. The last step involves the clean-up process after the merge and ensuring that your users can connect to the network again.

DSMERGE is an effective tool to integrate NDS trees into one larger unified structure. It is a utility that is loaded and used to enhance the features and scope of NDS in your organization. Other NDS utilities exist that also help you in your goal to maintain the health of your NDS network. In the next chapter, we will discuss some of these utilities and how they are used in the NDS world.

13

NDS Utilities

NetWare Directory Services is essentially the glue that holds your entire intranet together. It is the central repository of information for your network, and it plays a key role in the daily network interactions of your users. Fortunately, your users do not have to understand all of the intricacies of NDS—only the network administrator does.

It is the back-end environment of NDS that requires most of the network administrator's attention. A robust and healthy NDS database relies on carefully planned methods of partitioning, replication, and time synchronization on your network. We have covered these topics in Chapters 10 and 11, and you are well on your way to implementing an ordered and stable NDS tree. Once this structure is in place, it really is the foundation for more things to come. Other software and packages will be able to take advantage of the benefits of NDS.

IntranetWare already comes bundled with many NDS utilities that will enhance the functionality of your network. Among them are tools that will allow you to maintain the health of your network. We touched upon some of this diagnosing technology in Chapter 10 when we used NDS Manager.

With NDS Manager, Novell has provided a new tool for you to monitor the status of your NDS tree. You are able to view the status of the various partitions in your database along with the replica and time synchronization of the network. If there are problems, you also have the ability to repair NDS databases. All this can be done with one utility on your desktop.

In conjunction with NDS Manager for maintaining the health of your NDS tree, there are two other utilities that run on the servers themselves to provide a more in-depth look at the status of the NDS processes on your network. People familiar with NetWare 4.1 will remember the DSTRACE and DSREPAIR utilities used to view and correct NDS problems. DSTRACE and DSREPAIR are more comprehensive utilities that provide the network administrator more information about the NDS tree and more powerful features to repair NDS problems. IntranetWare still comes with these utilities as well as NDS Manager to diagnose and repair your NDS tree. We will cover all three of them in this chapter.

As we all know, we can prepare for disaster, but we cannot prevent it. Although replication allows you to provide a fault-tolerant NDS design in case one of the servers in your tree fails, it cannot prevent data corruption in your tree. If one replica gets corrupted and that corruption gets replicated to all of the other replicas, you cannot recover without a fresh copy of the database. That is why it is important to back up your NDS tree regularly to a tape or some other storage media. In this chapter, we will learn about IntranetWare's own backup utility, called SBACKUP, which allows you to prepare for the disaster we know will inevitably come.

We will also talk about a new NDS utility that allows you, as the network administrator, to control a user's desktop. This utility, called NetWare Application Manager, allows you to customize all of your users' desktops on their machines to control which network applications they use. Gone are the days of going to each workstation to install network application icons. Desktop control can now be done centrally with minimal effort.

When used in conjunction with NDS, these utilities will extend the capabilities of your network. You will be able to be proactive when you monitor your NDS tree, protect the data stored within the database, customize your users' desktops, and supervise all network transactions. NDS is the foundation on which most NetWare functionality is based.

Diagnosing & Repairing NDS

As we know, NDS is an object-oriented distributed database. Just like all other types of databases, there is the possibility that the data may become corrupt. Regardless of what types of error detection and correction you build into a system, there is always the possibility the data may be written to the database incorrectly. The sign of a robust system is one that will handle these inconsistencies with grace.

NDS is one of those systems. It is a self-correcting database that will try to resolve inconsistencies the best it can. In the course of your monitoring the system, you might see an NDS error; however, if you just wait and don't do anything, many errors will seem to disappear over the course of time. This is because NDS is constantly working to correct itself and maintain the integrity of the data in the database.

Unfortunately, there will be times when NDS is not able to correct itself. This is when the network administrator must step in and provide the system with the attention necessary to resolve the problem. When you must intercede as a network administrator, you will want to follow a specific set of steps in both diagnosing and repairing the NDS database.

Understanding NDS Inconsistencies

NDS is called a *loosely consistent* database. When changes are made to one piece of the database, those modifications are eventually replicated to all other copies of that piece; however, there is no set time table as to when that synchronization will occur. NDS needs time to distribute modifications to other replicas stored on the network. Thus, there is no guarantee a modification you made at one location in the network will appear in another location immediately.

Loose consistencies lead to errors in the database. However, a lot of these errors are temporary. Once the database synchronizes all of the replicas of the partitions, the error will probably go away because the correct information will be written to the database during the synchronization process. If a problem seems to persist, you might have a database inconsistency.

When the pieces of the database (the partitions) cannot synchronize properly, the data in the replicas of those partitions will be different, as we have already discussed. Changes are made to the various replicas, and when that information is not exchanged between the replicas, the data they contain can be very different. If the replicas of a partition cannot exchange information for a significant period of time, the data may be too dissimilar or corrupted. When replicas contain different information that cannot be resolved through a synchronization process, it is said to be an *NDS database inconsistency*.

A database inconsistency will generally make itself known in one of the following ways:

- **Unknown objects in the NDS tree.** Using NetWare Administrator, you may see a leaf object that appears to be a question mark in the tree. Here, NDS is telling you it has a reference to an object; however, it does not have enough information to determine what the object is. Unknown objects may go away after a period of time. Persistent unknown objects are a good indication of database inconsistencies.

- **Client workstation abnormalities.** We usually call these gremlins; however, their source may be rooted in an NDS inconsistency. Look for weird things like disappearing NDS rights, login problems, and network performance problems. If these problems appear to be NDS related and have a habit of "coming and going," you may have an NDS database inconsistency.

- **NDS errors.** Using any one of the NDS diagnostic tools, you will be able to identify NDS errors as they are being reported by the system. Again, some of these errors are normal and may disappear over time; however, persistent problems are an indication of an NDS database inconsistency.

If you think you have a database inconsistency, you will need to use an NDS diagnostic utility to determine its source. Once you have actually located the inconsistency, you will be able to take measures to resolve it using these same utilities. However, the first step is always locating the inconsistency, and this can be accomplished through a utility we have already used—NDS Manager.

Resolving NDS Inconsistencies With NDS Manager

In Chapter 10, we introduced you to a utility called NDS Manager. We used it to set up and configure our back-end NDS environment. We were able to partition the database and create replica rings to provide a flexible and scalable fault-tolerant network design. In addition to these functions, NDS Manager comes with a wide variety of NDS diagnostic and repair tools so you can monitor the NDS environment from your workstation.

Traditionally, if you wanted to diagnose or repair the NDS database, you needed to load DSREPAIR.NLM on each server in your network and run it. You could establish an RCONSOLE session to remotely access the server console; however, it still meant you had to attend each server individually. NDS Manager allows you to access the NDS databases on each server from your desktop, assuming you have the sufficient rights to do so.

With NDS Manager, you will be able to both identify and resolve most inconsistencies in an NDS database. It provides a graphical environment for locating inconsistencies, which is easier to understand than the traditional utilities like DSTRACE and DSREPAIR. To identify the inconsistencies with NDS Manager, you will want to check both the NDS synchronization and the NDS partition continuity.

NDS Replica Synchronization

The key to a healthy NDS database is the replica synchronization of the NDS environment. When the synchronization of the NDS environment is disrupted, the data in the replicas can be corrupted, causing the database inconsistencies and performance problems you may be experiencing on your network. Let's take a closer look at how the particular type of synchronization can cause an NDS inconsistency and how we can verify the replica synchronization status using NDS Manager.

When replicas are not able to synchronize properly, the information in the replicas of the partition may differ greatly. This is due to the distributed nature of the NDS database. The database is broken up into pieces and spread across the network. For fault tolerance, those pieces of the database are copied and stored on other servers on the network. Every once in a while, the replicas must synchronize with one another to make sure they contain the same information—after all, they are supposed to be copies of one another.

Since some of these copies are allowed to accept modifications to objects in the partition, changes to the partition take place in multiple locations. A change to an object may be made to Replica A while a modification to another object in the partition may be made on Replica B. If the replicas are unable to synchronize, the changes made to the partition will not be distributed across the network to all replica locations. The changes in information will be isolated. Over time, the information stored in Replica A may look very different than the information stored in Replica B even though they are supposed to be exact copies of one another!

It is important to make sure the replicas are synchronizing consistently and properly to maintain the health of your network. You can monitor this synchronization using NDS Manager. You can either view the last time a particular server synchronized its replica information with other servers in the NDS tree, or you can view the synchronization status of a replica ring for a particular NDS partition. Both types of information are useful to have in diagnosing NDS problems.

Single Server Synchronization Information   To check the replica synchronization information for a particular server on your network, you can use NDS Manager. After starting NDS manager, double-click on any server object in the Tree view or the Partitions and Servers view to bring up information about that particular server.

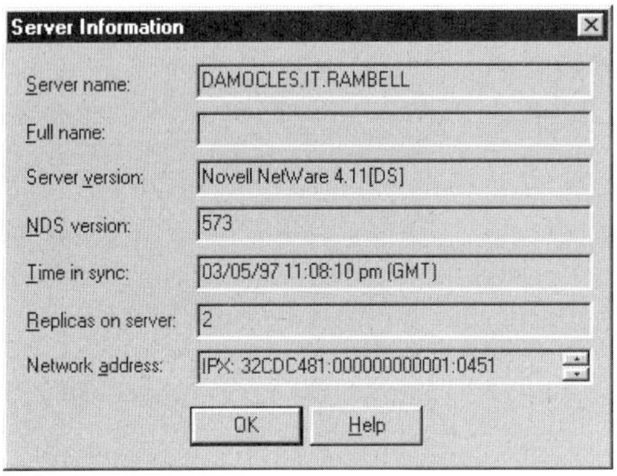

Figure 13-1: NDS Manager will display the last time the server exchanged replica information with other servers in the NDS tree.

In Figure 13-1, we can see the server information for the file server Damocles. Besides information about the server's name and the version of the operating system, we can also see how many replicas the server is storing and the last time replica information was exchanged with other servers in the NDS tree. This is an introductory check to see if the server is staying current in its replica information.

Replica Ring Synchronization Information   Instead of viewing the synchronization for a single server, it is often more useful to monitor the status of an entire replica ring. NDS Manager will allow you to check the synchronization of all replicas for a particular partition. This is better because a server may be synchronizing its replicas for one partition but not another.

With NDS Manager, you can check the synchronization for a specific partition, or you can monitor the synchronization status for all partitions in the NDS database. To do so, perform the following steps:

1. Using NDS Manager, switch to the Partitions and Servers view. This can be done by choosing View | Partitions and Servers from the menu bar in NDS Manager.

2. On the left-hand side of the screen, click on the partition for which you want to view the synchronization information. It will become highlighted.

3. Choose Object | Check Synchronization from the menu bar or click on the Check Synchronization button on the toolbar on top of the NDS Manager subordinate window. The Check Synchronization dialog box will appear (Figure 13-2).

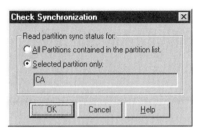

Figure 13-2: Choose to view the partition information for a single partition or all partitions in the NDS database.

4. Choose the appropriate radio box to see synchronization information about a specific partition or all partitions in the NDS database. Click OK.

5. If the preconditions for the operation have been met, click Yes in the Check Partition Synchronization dialog box. The Partitions Synchronization Check dialog box will appear.

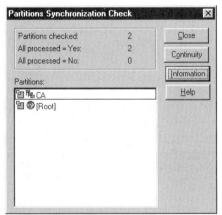

Figure 13-3: The Partitions Synchronization Check dialog box displays the synchronization status of the partitions' replica rings.

Figure 13-3 shows the Partitions Synchronization Check dialog box for all of the partitions in the Willow NDS tree. There are two partitions, CA and [Root], both of which are synchronized. You can view information about a particular partition by clicking on it once to highlight it and clicking on the Information tab. It will display the following statistics:

- **Partition.** The name of the NDS partition.

- **Master Replica.** The server on which the Master replica is stored.

- **Read/Write, Read-Only, and Master Replicas.** The total number of full replicas in the partition's replica ring.

- **Subordinate References.** The number of Subordinate References the partition has.

- **Last Successful Sync.** The last time the replica ring was able to synchronize successfully.

- **Last Attempted Sync.** If the replica ring is not synchronized, the last time the replica ring attempted to synchronize itself.

While all of this information is useful, it does not tell us a whole lot if the replica is not synchronized. It just tells us the last attempted synchronization. What happens if the replica ring is not in sync? The first thing you want to do is wait to see if the problem resolves itself. NDS is a self-correcting database and may be able to fix itself if there is a problem. If the problem persists, you will have to get more aggressive in determining the cause of the problem.

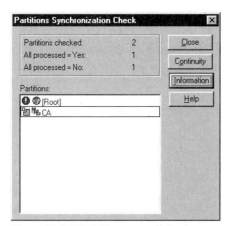

Figure 13-4: NDS Manager will display an error if a partition is not synchronizing properly.

Figure 13-4 shows an example of a partition that is not synchronized. Notice how an exclamation point appears next to it. At this point, we will need to check the continuity of the partition to determine the cause of the NDS database inconsistency. This is also done using NDS Manager.

Tip

The Partitions Synchronization Check may not provide accurate statistics about the synchronization status of the partition because it checks only the first server in the replica ring list. If that server believes the replica ring is synchronized, it will not report an error.

Partition Continuity

Because the Partitions Synchronization Check does not always provide an accurate assessment of the partition, NDS Manager provides another way to check the synchronization status of a partition. It is called *partition continuity.* The partition continuity checks the status of the replicas on *all* servers in the replica ring. It displays the results in tabular format so you can see the status of all replicas in a partition's replica ring.

To view the partition continuity for a specific partition, perform the following steps in NDS Manager:

1. Click on the desired partition in NDS Manager once with the left mouse button. It will become highlighted.

2. Choose Object | Partition Continuity from the menu bar in NDS Manager or click on the Partition Continuity button on the toolbar. The Partition Continuity dialog box will appear.

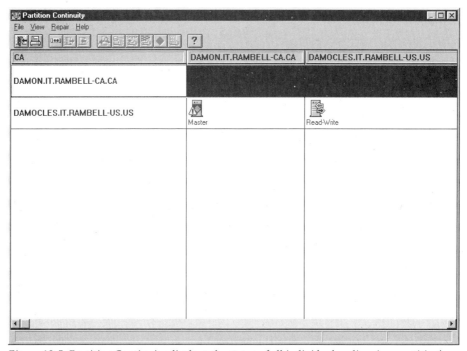

Figure 13-5: Partition Continuity displays the status of all individual replicas in a partition's replica ring.

In Figure 13-5, the Partition Continuity dialog box is displayed for the partition CA in the NDS tree Willow. As you can see, the information about the replicas is displayed in a tabular format. The servers in the replica ring are listed as the headings for both the columns and the rows. Thus, the Partition Continuity dialog box shows you each server's view of the network.

To read the Partition Continuity table correctly, you need to understand the difference between the rows and the columns. Start with the server in the first row of the table. You are viewing the network from the perspective of this server. As you follow this server across the row, you see each replica as the server sees it. In Figure 13-5, if we start with Damon, we can see that the replicas stored on that server cannot be read by NDS Manager.

After reading that server, proceed to the next server in the next row and read across the table. Damocles believes that the file server Damon stores the Master replica for the CA partition. Damocles also thinks the replica on

Damon is generating an error. This error is shown in the table by the exclamation point on the replica. Proceeding along the row, Damocles believes it is storing a Read/Write replica of the CA partition, and the replica it has stored on itself seems to be fine.

If you encounter an error on one of the replicas (or, if you just want to retrieve information about one), double-click on it; the Replica Information dialog box will display. From our example in Figure 13-5, we would double-click on the Damon replica in the Damocles row to retrieve information about the error.

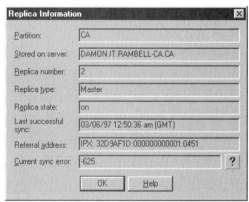

Figure 13-6: Double-clicking on any replica in the table will display information about that particular replica.

Figure 13-6 shows the Replica Information dialog box. It displays important information about the replica of the CA partition stored on the file server Damon, including the number of the replica, the type of replica, the state of the replica, and the last successful replica synchronization. It also displays any NDS error codes that will help you figure out what might be causing NDS database inconsistencies. In our example, the replica is displaying an NDS error code -625.

An error code -625 really does not tell us very much about the error or how to go about correcting the problem. Fortunately, NDS Manager has a list of error codes built into the online help. To view more information about the error, click on the question mark immediately to the right of it with the left mouse button. The online help for that particular error will be displayed.

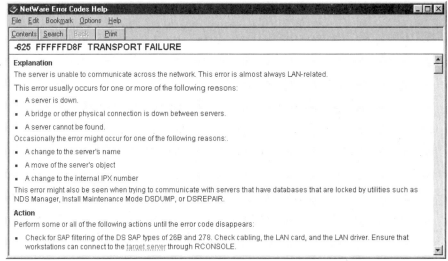

Figure 13-7: NDS Manager displays the error code, possible causes for the error, and steps to take to correct the problem.

Included in this help screen is the number of the error, the name of the error, possible causes for the error, and possible corrections for the error. These help pages are an invaluable resource of information in troubleshooting NDS database inconsistencies. They give you some basic steps to take to rectify the problem.

Tip

Use the NDS Manager online help to display information concerning NDS error messages. It will provide you with a basic course of action to rectify the NDS database inconsistency.

For our example, can you tell what the problem with this partition is? NDS Manager is not able to read any information about the replicas stored on Damon. The NDS error -625 tells us that Damocles is unable to communicate with Damon. Putting these two facts together, it is pretty easy to see that the file server Damon is down. If we bring it back up, the problems should go away.

Unfortunately, not all problems in your NDS tree are going to be as easy to solve as this one. Sometimes the course of action recommended by the online help includes repairing the NDS database. You don't have to do this by hand; there are database maintenance utilities included with NDS Manager that will allow you to repair the NDS database.

NDS Database Maintenance & Repair

After you have identified the source of the NDS database inconsistency and consulted the error codes associated with it, you might have to perform some repairs on the NDS database itself. A scary prospect at first, but it's really not as painful as it sounds. NDS Manager gives you the ability to perform most of the database maintenance and repair tasks required.

Logically enough, you can access these features of NDS Manager from the Partition Continuity screen. You will notice that the toolbar across the top of the screen is different than the one on the main screen of NDS Manager. This is to make the NDS database maintenance and repair features readily accessible to you. There is a block of six buttons at the top of the screen that represent the various features. Notice that there are pictures of wrenches and screwdrivers on these buttons. They will be the tools you use to repair your NDS database.

There are seven general repair and maintenance tasks you can accomplish using NDS Manager. Six of them are represented as buttons on the toolbar. You have to manually select the seventh, Remove Server, from the menu bar. The tasks, in button order from left to right on the toolbar, are as follows:

- Verify Remote Server IDs
- Repair Replica
- Repair Network Addresses
- Repair Local Database
- Assign New Master
- Repair Volume Objects

Verify Remote Server IDs   A server is able to locate an object in the NDS tree by virtue of its ID number. The ID number that is used to represent an object is unique for that server; however, different servers in the NDS tree will have a different ID number for the same object. Thus, the file server Damocles is known to file server Damon as object 1234, while Pythias uses the object ID 5678 to uniquely identify Damocles.

Damocles itself will keep track of how it is known throughout the network on the various servers. It keeps a database and knows that Damon uses 1234 and Pythias uses 5678 for identification purposes. When you choose Verify Remote Server IDs, the server selected will go out on the network and contact each server to which it is known. Damocles contacts Damon to verify Damon is using the ID 1234 to uniquely identify Damocles. Damocles then follows up with Pythias to ensure Pythias is using 5678 to uniquely identify Damocles. If there is an error, NDS Manager will attempt to reconcile the error.

The selected server also keeps a list of servers in the partitions' replica rings. The list represents the other servers the selected server needs to contact when performing replica synchronizations. The Verify Remote Server IDs verification process will ensure that the replica lists on the selected server are current and the server IDs are valid to facilitate communication between the servers. When the process runs, it not only checks the partition selected in the Partition Continuity screen, it also checks the replica rings for all other partition replicas stored on the server. Thus, multiple partitions are checked at the same time.

To start the Verify Remote Server IDs process, click on the Verify Remote Server IDs button on the toolbar or choose Repair | Verify Remote Server IDs from the menu bar in the Partition Continuity screen.

Repair Replica   The Repair Replica operation affects only the chosen replica on a server. It does not affect any other replicas in the NDS tree, and the process is applied to only the partition selected. It performs the same duties that Verify Remote Server IDs does; however, it verifies the information only for the partition selected through Partition Continuity. It, too, ensures that the server is able to communicate with all other servers in the partition's replica ring by correcting the replica lists and server ID table for the selected server.

To start the Repair Replica process, click on the Repair Replica button on the toolbar or choose Repair | Repair Replica from the menu bar in the Partition Continuity screen.

Tip

If you have not run the Repair Local Database tool, you should run it first before running the Repair Replica tool.

Repair Network Addresses   When computers using the Internetwork Packet Exchange (IPX) protocol want to communicate with one another, they rely upon the hardware address of the machine to address the packet so that it goes where it needs to go. Every Network Interface Card (NIC) has a unique 12-digit hexadecimal address so it can be identified on the network. It is also called the machine's *network address*. This information about the servers on your network is stored in multiple places on your network. One important place this information is stored is in the NDS database as the value of the Net Address property of the NetWare Server object in the NDS tree.

Another important place where the hardware addresses for all servers on the network are stored is in the Service Advertising Protocol (SAP) tables on each server. SAP is a broadcast protocol issued by every server on a frequent basis to advertise itself to the network. All servers on the network read these broadcasts and store the information in an internal table. Through this table, the server is able to locate other servers on the network and communicate with them.

The Repair Network Addresses feature of NDS Manager compares the information about the server's hardware address contained in the SAP table (which is updated once per minute) with the value stored in the NDS database. This ensures that the servers can communicate with one another during the replica synchronization process. If you are experiencing a lot of -625 errors in your tree and no servers are down, you might need to use this tool to repair the network addresses of the servers.

To reconcile the hardware addresses stored in the NDS database with those located in the SAP tables, click on the Repair Network Addresses button on the toolbar or choose Repair | Repair Network Addresses from the menu bar in NDS Manager. The network addresses will be repaired for the selected server.

Repair Local Database   Sometimes, the information in the NDS database will become corrupt. When this happens, the Repair Local Database tool might be able to fix the problem. It runs only on the server selected and repairs any NDS inconsistencies it finds in all replicas stored on that server. If you cannot access the data stored in a replica, Repair Local Database should fix the error and allow you to access the stored data.

After the process is completed, a log file will be generated to show you exactly what errors were detected and corrected by the tool. It may not be able to fix every error, but it will tell you if there is any additional work that needs to be completed. This tool does for the NDS database on a server what VREPAIR.NLM does for the file system on a server.

When Repair Local Database runs, it needs to lock the NDS files on that server to perform the analysis and repair. When the files are locked, no users will be able to access any NDS data on that server. Thus, they will be restricted in what they are able to do. Keep this in mind if you have to use this tool.

To run Repair Local Database on a server, select that server in the Partition Continuity screen by clicking on it once with the left mouse button. Click on the Repair Local Database button on the toolbar or choose Repair | Repair Local Database from the menu bar in the Partition Continuity screen.

Assign New Master   We learned in Chapter 10 how to change the replica type for a particular replica. To perform any NDS operations, you need to have access to the Master replica of the partition. Unfortunately, there may be times when the server holding the Master replica has crashed or the Master replica itself is corrupted. In these cases, the normal process to change a replica type will not work to promote a Read/Write replica to the Master replica of a partition.

The Assign New Master tool is the last-ditch effort to gain control over the partition that is misbehaving. When you are unable to promote a replica to the Master replica using the normal methods, use the Assign New Master option. It will force the promotion of another replica to Master status even if the Master replica is unavailable.

To promote a replica to the Master status, select the server that will store the new Master replica by clicking on it once with the left mouse button in the Partition Continuity screen. Click on the Assign New Master button on the tool bar or choose Repair | Assign New Master from the menu bar in NDS Manager.

Tip

Before using this option, try to change the replica type using the normal method in NDS Manager. The Assign New Master tool should only be used as a last resort if the Master replica is unavailable or corrupted.

Repair Volume Objects As we know, all volume objects in the NDS tree represent physical volumes on a NetWare 4.x file server. If, for some reason, one of these objects gets deleted or is corrupted, you can use the Repair Volume Objects tool to repair it.

The Repair Volume Objects tool verifies that the physical volumes for the server selected exist in the NDS tree. If a volume object does not exist for a physical volume, NDS Manager will look in the file server's context for the volume. If it does not exist there, it will try to create a new volume object to represent the server's physical volume.

To use this feature, select the file server to be repaired by clicking on it once with the left mouse button. Click on the Repair Volume Objects button on the toolbar or choose Repair | Repair Volume Objects from the menu bar in the Partition Continuity screen. The Repair Volume Objects dialog box will appear (Figure 13-8). Notice the option to Validate Trustee IDs.

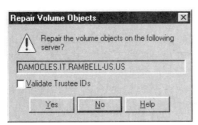

Figure 13-8: The Repair Volume Objects feature allows you to
validate file system trustee assignments as well as repair volume objects.

The Validate Trustee IDs option is a powerful option that allows you to reconcile the trustee assignments for the file system with the NDS objects in the NDS tree. When this feature is checked, each file system trustee is checked against the appropriate object in the NDS tree. If the trustee object no longer exists in the NDS tree, the file system trustee assignment is removed from the volume. Whether or not you choose this option, click on Yes to begin the Repair Volume Objects process.

Remove Server   The Remove Server option should not be confused with the Delete Server option in NDS Manager. The Delete Server option is used to permanently remove a NetWare Server object from the NDS tree. The Remove Server option is used to remove the selected server from the replica list for a particular partition.

There may be times when you remove a replica from a server, but other servers in the replica list are still trying to contact that server to exchange replica information. This is usually an indication of an NDS environment that is on the verge of widespread corruption. If this is the case, your only option may be to manually remove the server from the replica list yourself.

If you have removed a replica from a server, and it still shows up on the Partition Continuity screen, you can manually remove it from the replica list using the Remove Server option. To remove the server, click on the server that is still trying to contact the removed replica once with the left mouse button. The server will be highlighted. Choose Repair | Remove Server from the menu bar in the Partition Continuity screen. The Remove Server dialog box will appear (Figure 13-9).

*Figure 13-9: The Remove Server dialog box will allow
you to manually remove a server from the replica list.*

In this dialog box, verify the information specified. The name of the server
that still holds the replica of the partition should be in the top box. In the
bottom box, use the drop-down list to select the server to be removed from the
replica list. When the information is accurate, click on the Yes button at the
bottom of the dialog box.

NDS Manager will attempt to perform a Delete Replica operation, which is
the normal method of removing a replica from a server; however, if this operation is unsuccessful, it will forcibly remove the selected server from the replica
list. If it does so, a log file will be generated and displayed for you.

Only use the Remove Server option if you have no other choice. Indiscrimi-
nate use of this option can cause serious NDS corruption. Be absolutely sure
you want to perform this option before you do it.

As we can see, NDS Manager can be used to identify NDS database inconsistencies and repair most of them. Rely upon the Partition Continuity screen
to help you isolate the cause of the problem and use the online help to guide
yourself through the resolution of the NDS error. It is an invaluable resource
for maintaining the health of your NDS database. There are times, however,
when NDS Manager will not be able to resolve a particular inconsistency. If
you need more information to track down the inconsistency and repair it, you
will have to use the NDS utilities DSTRACE and DSREPAIR. DSTRACE and
DSREPAIR are discussed in the next sections of this chapter.

Monitoring Synchronization With DSTRACE

Sometimes you might not be able to completely diagnose an NDS database inconsistency with NDS Manager. You need a more powerful tool to understand the nuances of the replica synchronization. This tool is the DSTRACE utility, and it is used at the server console itself. The function of DSTRACE is to monitor NDS traffic between the selected server and all other servers on the network.

DSTRACE is not an NLM that is loaded at the server. It is actually a server SET parameter that you enable. When enabled, the NetWare 4.11 server will display all of its NDS traffic to the monitor. To start DSTRACE, type the following at the server console prompt (colon prompt):

```
SET DSTRACE = ON
```

From the server console screen, nothing will appear to have happened, but you have actually created another screen on the server that will begin to display NDS information. You need to switch server screens to actually view the information. When you hold down the Alt key at the server console, notice the bar that appears at the top of the screen. It tells you which server screen is currently active. While holding down the Alt key, press Escape to get to the next available server screen. Toggle through these screens and look for the Directory Services screen to see the DSTRACE information.

When DSTRACE is first enabled, it will display a minimal amount of NDS information. By default, DSTRACE will not show all NDS information. It only shows you the partition synchronization process. But being a flexible tool, DSTRACE has some options that will customize the display of the NDS information or actually force some NDS actions to occur. These options are summarized in Table 13-1.

DSTRACE Option	Function
SET DSTRACE = ALL	Shows all NDS traffic.
SET DSTRACE = +AUDIT	Shows only NDS audit information on the network.
SET DSTRACE = +AUTHEN	Shows only time stamp information as users authenticate to the network.
SET DSTRACE = +BACKLINK	Shows NDS backlink information.
SET DSTRACE = +INSPECTOR	Shows NDS inspection process, which prepares for the janitor process.
SET DSTRACE = +JANITOR	Shows information about the cleanup of deleted NDS objects.
SET DSTRACE = +LIMBER	Shows the verification process of the server's name, network address, and replica list with other servers on the network.
SET DSTRACE = PART	Shows partition information as partition operations take place.
SET DSTRACE = +SYNC	Shows the replica synchronization process for all replicas on the server.
SET DSTRACE = SCHEMA	Shows the schema synchronization information.
SET DSTRACE = *F	Starts the flatcleaner and janitor processes. You can force an immediate cleaning of the database using this command.
SET DSTRACE = *H	Starts the replica synchronization process.
SET DSTRACE = *L	Starts the server limber process, which causes the server to verify its name, network address, and replica list with other servers on the network.
SET DSTRACE = *P	Shows the current settings for all of the NDS processes.
SET DSTRACE = *R	Resets the log file to zero length.
SET DSTRACE = *SS	Starts the schema synchronization process.
SET DSTRACE = *U	Sets all servers in the replica list to the Up status.
SET DSTRACE = *.	Resets NDS on the server. Forces the local NDS database to close and reopen itself.

Table 13-1: DSTRACE options.

Notice that some options are preceded by a plus sign (+). These options are filters that cause DSTRACE to display only a specific type of NDS traffic. To enable the filter, use it with the plus sign. To disable the filter, precede the option by a minus sign (-). For example, to set DSTRACE to display NDS authentication traffic, you would type **SET DSTRACE = +AUTHEN** at the server console prompt. To disable this feature, type the command **SET DSTRACE = -AUTHEN**.

In Table 13-1, there are also DSTRACE commands that are preceded with an asterisk (*). These are actual NDS commands, which force the server to perform an NDS function. For example, the SET DSTRACE = *. command will effectively "reboot" NetWare Directory Services on your server without actually downing the server. So besides monitoring traffic, DSTRACE can also be used to start some NDS processes that may help you correct NDS database inconsistencies.

Instead of having DSTRACE display its information to the server monitor, it might be more useful to have it create a log file that captures the NDS information. By typing the following line at the server console prompt (colon prompt), you can force DSTRACE to write the NDS traffic to a file:

```
SET TTF = ON
```

When this option is enabled, the file SYS:SYSTEM\DSTRACE.DBG will be created. You can examine this file at your leisure to see the NDS traffic. To disable the log file, type **SET TTF = OFF** at the server console prompt. Typing **SET DSTRACE = *R** at the server console prompt will restart the log file by setting the length of DSTRACE.DBG to zero.

Understanding DSTRACE Messages

When you enable DSTRACE for the first time, it is automatically set to display a minimal amount of tracking information. The NDS information displayed concerns the synchronization process of the partitions. This is particularly useful information if you are experiencing NDS database inconsistencies because you will be able to identify the individual replicas, trace the exchange of replica modifications, and view any NDS errors that might occur.

The Directory Services screen on the server console displays the partition synchronization information to the screen in a color-coded format. Green text represents successful partition synchronization actions. Red text tells you the partition synchronization was not successful. The blue text displays the name of the partition. You will be able to immediately pick out the important information on the screen.

Buried in the noncolored portion of the text is the really useful information. The block of NDS information starts with the time and date of the synchronization attempt. Immediately following this line is the current status of the replica on the server. You will see the replica state and replica type for the replica stored on that server. The replica state and type are given as numeric codes, which will help you identify the health of that particular replica. The replica states are given in Table 13-2, and the replica types are shown in Table 13-3.

Replica State Number	Replica State	Description
0	On	All partition operations have been completed. On is the general "OK" state for the replica.
1	New	The replica is being created and added to the replica list.
2	Dying	The replica is marked for removal from the replica list.
3	Locked	The replica is locked and cannot be used for partition operations.
4	Change Replica Type State 0	The replica type on the server is in the process of changing.
5	Change Replica Type State 1	If a new Master replica is being assigned, the old Master will temporarily be made this replica state.
6	Transition State On	During the process of creating a new replica, a replica will be set to Transition State On just before it is set to On.
48	Split State 0	The Master replica's initial state after a create new partition request is issued.
49	Split State 1	The second stage of the create new partition operation; the Master replica of the parent partition ensures the synchronization of the new partition.
64	Join State 0	The initial state for merging a child partition back into its parent.
65	Join State 1	After the partitions have merged, Join State 1 commences the process of erasing the boundaries between the parent and child partition.
66	Join State 2	The final stages of the merge partition request. It is the last state before all replicas are returned to the On state.
80	Move State 0	Represents a partition move in the NDS tree.

Table 13-2: DSTRACE replica state codes.

Replica Type Number	Replica Type
0	Master replica
1	Read/Write replica
2	Read-Only replica
3	Subordinate Reference replica

Table 13-3: DSTRACE replica type codes.

The next line in DSTRACE after the status of the replica on the server is the replica the server is trying to contact for synchronization. In this line, you will see the number, the state, and the type of the replica and the server on which the replica is stored. Here, you will be able to identify if there is a synchronization error between the current server and another server in the replica list.

You can use Tables 13-2 and 13-3 to decipher the replica state and type in the DSTRACE screen. If you are not able to perform a particular partition operation, you might want to monitor DSTRACE to determine if the replica is in a state other than On. Only when all replicas in a partition are set to On can you perform a partition operation. DSTRACE can provide you with diagnostic information about your NDS environment and help you pinpoint the source of NDS database inconsistencies.

Viewing NDS Error Codes in DSTRACE

In the course of viewing the NDS information through DSTRACE, you may see some NDS error codes appear. When DSTRACE encounters an NDS error, it will display this information to the screen. The NDS error codes for DSTRACE are the same error codes we saw with NDS Manager; however, there is no online help for DSTRACE like there is in NDS Manager.

Use the NDS error codes displayed in DSTRACE to help diagnose and correct any NDS database inconsistencies on your network. Appendix C provides you with a condensed list of NDS error codes and what they represent. For more comprehensive information, consult the online help in NDS Manager.

The only types of NDS processes DSTRACE can initiate are synchronization processes. It can cause a partition synchronization. It can begin the janitor process to clean up the replicas; however, it cannot actually repair the database like NDS Manager can. If NDS Manager was not capable of identifying and repairing the NDS database inconsistency and you used DSTRACE to locate it, you will need to use another NDS utility, DSREPAIR, to repair the NDS database and resolve the inconsistency.

Repairing the NDS Database With DSREPAIR

With NDS Manager, we were able to perform some basic NDS database maintenance and repair procedures to resolve NDS database inconsistencies. NDS Manager is the optimal way to resolve these inconsistencies because you can repair the database on any server in the tree assuming you have sufficient NDS rights to do so.

There is another database repair utility called DSREPAIR, which is the comprehensive utility used to repair NDS databases. It is an NLM that provides more repair options and will help you both diagnose and correct NDS inconsistencies in your NDS tree. The drawback to DSREPAIR is that it is run on the server itself, and it can only repair the NDS replicas on that server. To repair all of the replicas on your network, you would need to run DSREPAIR on each server.

To run DSREPAIR on the server, go to the server console. At the console prompt (colon prompt), type the following command:

`LOAD DSREPAIR`

When you load DSREPAIR at the server, the main menu will appear. On the top of the screen it will display the name of the server, the name of the tree, the version of NDS, and the version of DSREPAIR. In the main menu, you will see the five main functions you can execute using DSREPAIR.

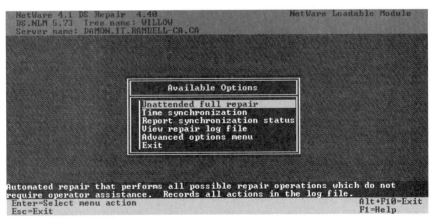

Figure 13-10: The DSREPAIR main menu.

From the main menu, as seen in Figure 13-10, select the option you want to perform. Use the arrow keys to move the highlight bar to the desired selection and press the Enter key. The five functions from which you can choose are:

- Unattended Full Repair
- Time Synchronization
- Report Synchronization Status
- View Repair Log File
- Advanced Options Menu

We will review each one of these choices in detail to provide you with a better understanding of the DSREPAIR utility.

Unattended Full Repair

When the Unattended Full Repair option is selected, DSREPAIR will perform every database maintenance procedure that does not require user intervention. The procedure executes the following tasks:

- Checks all records of all replicas stored on the server for consistency.
- Examines the structure of the NDS tree.
- Examines the schema for the NDS tree.
- Examines the objects within each replica.
- Checks the server's remote IDs as stored on other servers.
- Performs a volume object repair.

This procedure will also attempt to correct any inconsistencies or errors it finds in the database. Upon completion, a log file is displayed to show you the types of inconsistencies encountered and whether or not it was able to correct the problem.

If you are experiencing problems with inconsistencies and DSREPAIR finds errors in your database, you should immediately run the Unattended Full Repair option again. Keep doing this until it reports no errors in the NDS database. If, for some reason, DSREPAIR is unable to resolve an inconsistency, you might have to manually attend to some of the errors. This can be accomplished using the Advanced Option feature, which will be discussed later in this section.

Even if you are not experiencing problems, it is still a good idea to run the Unattended Full Repair occasionally. You will be able to detect inconsistencies before they start causing problems for your network. It will help you maintain a healthy NDS database.

Time Synchronization

Besides diagnosing partition and replication inconsistencies, you can also use DSREPAIR to check the time synchronization on your network. To do so, select Time Synchronization from the main menu of DSREPAIR, as seen in Figure 13-10. When selected, DSREPAIR will assess your time synchronization environment and generate a log file for you to inspect.

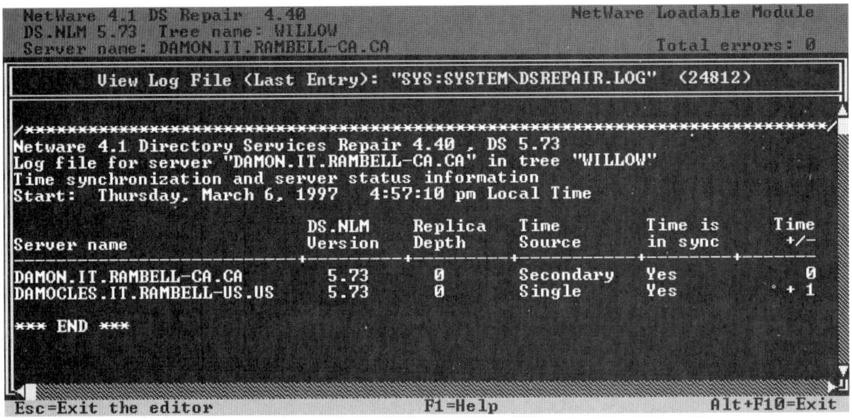

Figure 13-11: Viewing the status of the time synchronization environment in DSREPAIR.

In Figure 13-11, we can see a sample log file, which was generated after DSREPAIR examined the time synchronization environment for the NDS tree Willow. The names of all servers in the network are displayed along with the following items of information:

- NDS version
- Replica depth
- Time source type
- Time synchronization status
- Time deviation from network time

When your network time is in sync, all of the servers should be within one second of each other, by default. If you have changed the synchronization radius, the Time +/- field in Figure 13-11 may have values larger than one second. If your network time is not in sync, this screen will identify the offending servers.

For networks that are not in sync, look to the time provider group if you have a custom time synchronization environment. Once the time provider group is synchronized, the Secondary servers on the network should synchronize soon after.

Report Synchronization Status

This DSREPAIR option will check the synchronization status of all replicas in all partitions on your network. Note that it does not actually perform a replica synchronization; it only tells you if your partitions are synchronizing successfully. When the Report Synchronization Status option is chosen, the server will contact every server in its replica list to determine the status of partition synchronization. When it is finished, it generates a log file for you to examine.

```
NetWare 4.1 DS Repair  4.40                    NetWare Loadable Module
DS.NLM 5.73   Tree name: WILLOW
Server name: DAMON.IT.RAMBELL-CA.CA                     Total errors: 0

      View Log File (Last Entry): "SYS:SYSTEM\DSREPAIR.LOG"  (26280)

/*******************************************************************************
Netware 4.1 Directory Services Repair 4.40 . DS 5.73
Log file for server "DAMON.IT.RAMBELL-CA.CA" in tree "WILLOW"
Start:  Thursday, March 6, 1997  11:02:43 pm Local Time
Retrieve replica status

Partition: CA
  Replica: DAMON.IT.RAMBELL-CA.CA            1997/03/06 22:51:32
  Replica: DAMOCLES.IT.RAMBELL-US.US         1997/03/06 22:52:16
All servers synchronized up to time:         1997/03/06 22:51:32

Partition: [Root]
  Replica: DAMON.IT.RAMBELL-CA.CA            1997/03/06 22:51:32
  Replica: DAMOCLES.IT.RAMBELL-US.US         1997/03/06 22:52:15
All servers synchronized up to time:         1997/03/06 22:51:32

Esc=Exit the editor              F1=Help                Alt+F10=Exit
```

Figure 13-12: The DSREPAIR Report Synchronization Status option generates a log file to display the results of the check.

In Figure 13-12, we see a sample log file, which was generated after the Report Synchronization Status option was run. You see the name of the server on which DSREPAIR is running and the name of the NDS tree. Beneath the introductory information, the synchronization status of all partitions is displayed.

View Repair Log File

When the log file is generated with DSREPAIR, it creates a file called DSREPAIR.LOG, which is stored in SYS:SYSTEM. Whenever you perform a DSREPAIR operation, the results are appended to the end of this file. Thus, it can grow without bound, and you will need to periodically check its size so it does not cause the SYS volume to run out of space.

When this option is chosen, DSREPAIR will display the entire log file. If you have not deleted any portions of it using another text editor, you will have a complete history of every DSREPAIR process that has run on the server. If you run multiple processes, you will be able to review the results of all of them at one time using the View Repair Log File option.

The log file is optional, and it can be turned off. To turn off the logging mechanism for NDS repair, perform the following steps:

1. From the Available Options menu (main menu) in DSREPAIR, select Advanced Options Menu.

2. From the Advanced Options menu, select Log File and Login Configuration.

3. In the Log File/Login Configuration Options dialog box, set the Log Output to a File option to No. This will prevent DSREPAIR from writing to the log file every time an NDS process is run.

Notice that this dialog box also displays the current size of the DSREPAIR.LOG file. You can also reset the log file, change the name of the log file, and select whether or not DSREPAIR appends to the end of DSREPAIR.LOG when an NDS process is run.

Advanced Options Menu

Sometimes the Unattended Full Repair will not be able to resolve the NDS inconsistencies that exist in your NDS tree. When this happens, you might have to roll up your sleeves and get dirty. DSREPAIR allows you to perform NDS processes manually if you need to resolve a problem that NDS Manager, DSTRACE, and the Unattended Full Repair cannot fix. When this occurs, you will need to be familiar with the Advanced Options Menu in DSREPAIR.

The Advanced Options Menu allows you to perform the same type of maintenance you can perform with NDS Manager, but it also lets you do much more than that. Besides performing the normal partition- and replication-type services, the Advanced Options Menu will allow you to perform schema operations, replica list operations, and partition operations. It is the quintessential utility for maintaining the health of your NDS network.

Do not enter the DSREPAIR Advanced Options Menu lightly. There are operations in there that can permanently destroy your NDS environment. The only way you will be able to recover is through a reinstallation of NDS or a restoration from a backup. Consult the Novell online documentation carefully before you perform any NDS maintenance with which you are not familiar.

In this section, we have learned much about the NDS tree and the problems that might affect it. Because of its distributed nature, NDS is susceptible to database inconsistencies. When these inconsistencies arise, it can adversely affect the performance of your network. Fortunately, Novell has provided a way for you to detect and correct NDS inconsistencies.

The process for dealing with NDS database inconsistencies includes:

1. Identifying the source of the inconsistency.

2. Determining the best tool for resolving the inconsistency.

3. Using the tool to fix the error.

Start first with NDS Manager because it is easier to use and displays the NDS environment in a more comprehensible format. If you are unable to determine the source of the inconsistency this way, you may need to use DSTRACE to track the root of the problem. Once the problem is discovered, use DSREPAIR to correct it. If it cannot be corrected with DSREPAIR, it cannot be corrected.

But what happens if it cannot be corrected? You will need to reinstall NDS on your network and input all of the data into the NDS database again. This is obviously not an acceptable option. Fortunately, NetWare 4.11 comes with a way to protect your NDS database through a backup utility that comes bundled with IntranetWare. In the next section, we will learn about this utility and how to use it to protect our NDS database.

Protecting Your NDS Database

Even if you have 10 different servers, all with replicas of every partition, you do not have a completely fault-tolerant network. The probability of your network failing is very slim; however, the entire NDS database can get corrupted. At this point, the only course of action is to completely reinstall NDS and enter all of your NDS database information again.

You can give yourself a safety net by backing up your NDS database to some form of removable media like a tape. This way, if your database ever becomes corrupted, you can restore the NDS environment from the tape. Obviously, your tape backup is only as good as the last time you backed up the NDS environment. An outdated backup serves no purpose because you will have to reenter the objects in the NDS tree anyway.

Tip

Make sure your tape backup is current. An old backup is no good if there have been a lot of changes made to the NDS database since the last successful backup.

To help facilitate backups in your NDS tree, Novell has included a technology called Storage Management Services (SMS). It is a concept based upon the modularity of the backup process. There is always a host and a target. The most important thing about SMS is that it allows you to have a copy of the NDS database from which you can restore your entire NDS tree if there is a catastrophic failure.

Understanding SMS Technology

As mentioned, SMS is a modular type technology, which makes it flexible. It can back up a number of types of data to a number of types of media storage devices. And it's all done through the SMS engine. In Figure 13-13, we see the three components of SMS technology:

- Target
- SMS software
- Device

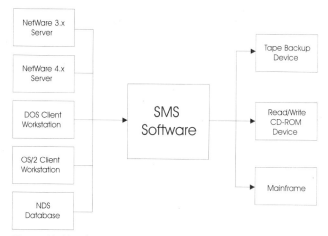

Figure 13-13: There are three main components to SMS technology—the target, the software, and the device.

The target contains the information that is being backed up. On the target, a specific piece of software, called the Target Service Agent (TSA), is loaded, which enables the SMS software to back up the information. The TSA is tailored for a particular target. Thus, one TSA is loaded on the target to back up a client workstation while a different TSA is required on the NetWare 4.11 server to back up the NDS database.

The advantage to this is evident. When a new device is created, only the TSA needs to be written for it. The SMS software will be able to interface with the new TSA to back up the information stored on the new device.

The SMS software is the actual software that performs the backup. It is responsible for interfacing with the TSA on the target and transferring the appropriate data to the device. It is also used to configure the type of backup to be performed, the specific device on which the data will be stored, and the target that will be backed up. Without the SMS software, the data would not be able to get from the target to the device.

The final piece of the SMS puzzle is the devices themselves. The devices are responsible for storing the data that is being backed up. Again, there is a specific piece of software loaded for each type of device called a device driver. The device driver understands how the device is supposed to operate. Each device will usually have its own device driver. When a new device is introduced to the world, only the device driver needs to be written for it before it can be integrated into the SMS world. Again, this makes the SMS environment flexible.

Now that we understand the basic concept behind SMS, let's look at the SMS software included in IntranetWare. It is called SBACKUP.NLM, and it is run from the NetWare 4.11 server that has an appropriate backup device attached to it (like a SCSI tape drive). SBACKUP will be able to back up our NDS database so we can recover gracefully in the event of a catastrophic failure.

Backing Up NDS With SBACKUP

Before we actually back up the NDS database, we need to understand some terms related to SBACKUP. Whenever we run a backup, there is always a *host machine* and a target. The host machine is the machine to which the SMS device is attached. If you have a SCSI tape drive that will be used to back up the NDS database, and the tape device is connected to a NetWare 4.11 server, the NetWare 4.11 server is the host machine.

The *target* is the information that is being backed up. This can be a NetWare 4.x server, a NetWare 3.x server, a DOS client workstation, an OS/2 client workstation, or the NDS database itself. The TSA must be loaded on the target for the SMS software to interface and transfer the desired data from the target to the device on the host machine.

Before SBACKUP can be run, the SMS environment needs to be prepared. Three things need to be done:

- The TSA must be loaded on the target machine that contains the information to be backed up.

- The device driver must be loaded on the host machine so SBACKUP can transfer the data from the target to the device.

- SBACKUP must be loaded on the host machine.

Once these three steps are complete, you will be able to back up your NDS database or any other data on your network you desire.

Loading the TSA on the Target Machine

The first step in preparing the SMS environment is to load the TSA on the target machine. The information you are backing up will determine which TSA needs to be loaded. Table 13-4 shows the type of information to be backed up and the particular TSA that needs to be loaded on the target machine.

Information to Be Backed Up	Target Machine	TSA(s) to Load
NetWare 4.x file system	NetWare 4.x file server	TSA410 *or* TSA400
NetWare 3.x file system	NetWare 3.x file server	TSA312 *or* TSA311
NDS database	NetWare 4.x file server	TSANDS
DOS file system	DOS workstation	TSASMS (TSADOS must also be loaded at the host.)
OS/2 file system	OS/2 workstation	TSAOS2 (TSAPROXY must also be loaded at the host.)

Table 13-4: The information to be backed up determines the TSA that needs to be loaded.

To back up the NDS database, you need to load TSANDS on the target server. This will allow SBACKUP to transfer the NDS database to the media on the storage device. The TSANDS.NLM is located in the SYS:SYSTEM directory. To load it at the host server, type the following command at the server console prompt:

```
LOAD TSANDS
```

Tip

Notice that you can back up entire file systems using SBACKUP.NLM. However, backing up the NDS database will not back up any files on the host server.

Loading the Device Driver

Once the TSA for the NDS database has been loaded, you need to load the device driver for the storage device connected to the host server if it has not been done. NetWare 4.11 comes with some device drivers for common devices. Consult the documentation that came with your storage device or device controller for more information on the proper device driver to be loaded.

If you have a generic ASPI-compatible SCSI controller with a tape backup unit, you can use the generic tape device driver included with IntranetWare. It is called TAPEDAI.DSK, and it is located in the SYS:SYSTEM directory on the host server. To load the device driver, type the following line at the server console prompt (colon prompt) on the host server:

`LOAD TAPEDAI`

This will cause the device driver to load on the server; however, it does not guarantee that SBACKUP will be able to see the physical device attached to the host server. After loading the device driver, you must also type the following line at the server console prompt (colon prompt) on the host server:

`SCAN FOR NEW DEVICES`

This will force the host server to scan the SCSI chain and look for the tape drive. When it is complete, you will be returned to the server console prompt. Don't worry if you do not see an acknowledgment message; the server console will not tell you it has found the tape drive. However, you can check for the new device once you load SBACKUP.

The target machine and the host server can be the same machine. For example, if you want to back up the NDS database from the same server that has the storage device attached to it, you would load the TSA as well as the device driver and SBACKUP on the server. The backup procedure can be run even when there is only one machine involved.

Loading SBACKUP

After the target and the device have been prepared, it is time to load the SMS software itself. In our case, this is SBACKUP.NLM, and it is loaded on the host server that has the storage device attached to it. To load SBACKUP on the server, type the following line at the server console prompt (colon prompt):

`LOAD SBACKUP`

Once the program is loaded, the SBACKUP Main Menu will appear on the host server. It will present the list of options from which you can choose the target and the device to be used in the backup process. The Main Menu for SBACKUP is displayed in Figure 13-14.

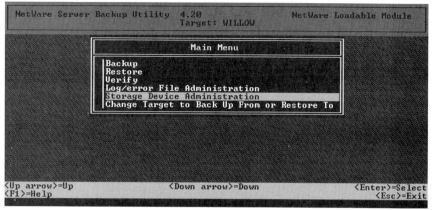

```
NetWare Server Backup Utility  4.20          NetWare Loadable Module
                        Target: WILLOW

                         Main Menu
        Backup
        Restore
        Verify
        Log/error File Administration
        Storage Device Administration
        Change Target to Back Up From or Restore To




<Up arrow>=Up                    <Down arrow>=Down        <Enter>=Select
<F1>=Help                                                   <Esc>=Exit
```

Figure 13-14: The SBACKUP Main Menu.

Performing a Backup Using SBACKUP

To perform the NDS backup, insert the media in the storage device and follow these steps:

1. Select the Change Target to Back Up From or Restore To option from the Main Menu to select the target. The list of servers running TSAs will appear in the list. Select the appropriate server. You will be asked to provide a username and password to use for the backup. You must provide a username with sufficient rights to back up the information desired.

2. Select Storage Device Administration from the Main Menu. This will display a list of available devices you can use to store the information from the backup. Select the desired device.

3. Select Backup from the Main Menu. Follow the instructions on the screen to proceed immediately with the backup or schedule it for later.

When the backup is complete, you will have a copy of your NDS database on the media in the storage device. Guard this media carefully (whether it is a tape, CD-ROM, hard disk, etc.) because it is the only copy of the NDS database you have if the network gets corrupted. Back up frequently to keep your safety net current.

Performing a Restore Using SBACKUP

If the time comes when you need to use that spare copy you made with SBACKUP, you can also restore the NDS information with it. It can both back up and restore information stored on the storage device.

Before you can actually perform the restore, you must prepare the SMS environment just like you did for the backup. The TSA must be loaded on the target machine, the device driver must be loaded on the host server, and SBACKUP must be loaded on the host server as well. Once this is done, to perform the restore, just follow these steps:

1. Select Change Target to Back Up From or Restore To option from the main menu to select the target. The list of servers running TSAs will appear in the list. Select the appropriate server. You will be asked to provide a username and password to use for the backup. You must provide a username with sufficient rights to back up the information desired.

2. Select Storage Device Administration from the Main Menu. This will display a list of available devices you can use to restore the information from the previously successful backup. Select the desired device.

3. Select Restore from the Main Menu. Follow the instructions on the screen to perform a particular type of restore. You can also specify whether the restore should happen immediately or later.

In our example, we have only backed up the NDS database. The information backed up does not include any file or directory information from any server. However, the backup and restore processes can be generalized so you can back up many different types of information using the same procedure. That is the benefit of the modularity of SMS. Only the appropriate TSAs and device drivers need to be loaded. The procedure for backing up and restoring is exactly the same.

Tip

Don't get caught short! Always verify your tape backups by performing a test restoration regularly. A tape backup does no good if you cannot restore the information after a catastrophic failure.

There are some disadvantages to using SBACKUP as your primary backup utility. It does not have a true unattended backup feature. It always requires user intervention. There are some other third-party vendors who sell backup software that is NDS-aware. Whatever package you choose, just make sure it is SMS compliant. This will allow the application to be compatible with the modular backup and restore environment of IntranetWare.

Standardizing User Desktops Through NDS

One of the benefits of having a centralized file system is the ability to run applications over your network. Multiple users can share the same application off of the file server, which means the network administrator only has to install the application once. However, it also means the network administrator needs to set up an icon on the users' workstations to use that application (or instruct his or her users how to set it up themselves). This can be a frustrating and time-consuming process.

Compounding that dilemma is the fact the application may be upgraded or removed or its location on the file server may change. Any time one of these events occurs, the icon on every user's workstation needs to be modified to reflect the change. Again, either the network administrator needs to take the time to attend to every machine, or the users must be notified to make the modification. So although you have the benefit of maintaining the application in one central location, you gain the nuisance of maintaining the icons for the application on your users' desktops.

IntranetWare comes with a utility that will help you, as a network administrator, combat these nuisances. You can control access to network applications from a central location through an NDS utility called NetWare Application Manager (NAM). This utility allows you to treat network applications as NDS objects and allow users access to those objects so the applications can be run. Through NDS, you define the application, any required drive mappings, and required scripting.

On the user workstation, the user executes an application called NetWare Application Launcher (NAL). This application reads the information contained in the NDS tree (as defined by NAM) and presents the user with a set of appropriate icons from which he or she can launch the network applications. When the applications change, the modifications need to be registered with NAM once, and the next time the user starts NAL, he or she will get the new set of icons. No longer does the network administrator need to manually modify icons on each user's desktop.

Defining Network Applications Using NAM

The first step to setting up network applications starts with the NDS utility NetWare Application Manager (NAM). Once the application has actually been installed on the file server and is ready to be run, its information needs to be registered with NDS so users will be able to access it with NetWare Application Launcher (NAL).

NetWare Application Manager (NAM) is a utility that has been included as a snap-in in the latest releases of NetWare Administrator. It extends the schema of your NDS tree to provide for the creation of a new type of NDS object—the application object. The application object holds all of the information necessary to run the application, including its path, required drive mappings, and required scripts. You can create these objects with NetWare Administrator just like you would any other object.

Once the schema for the tree has been extended, new property page tabs will appear for certain NDS objects in the NDS tree. The new property pages will allow you to define the network applications your users will be able to access on your network. By adding application objects in the NDS tree, you can allow your users to access network applications without having to provide drive mappings or paths to the local operating system to be able to execute them. NDS takes care of it all.

With NetWare Application Manager (NAM), there are three basic steps that are required to get the application ready for NetWare Application Launcher (NAL) to use:

1. You must create and configure an application object in the NDS tree to define the network application.

2. The new application object must be associated with other NDS objects so users have the ability to run the application using NetWare Application Launcher (NAL).

3. The users must be granted sufficient rights to the file system where the application is actually located.

Once these steps are completed, you will be able to set up and configure NAL to display the network application icons on the users' desktops so they will be able to execute the network applications.

Tip

To use NAM, you must be running the versions of NetWare Administrator that came with IntranetWare. Older versions of NetWare Administrator, such as NWADMIN.EXE, will not have the appropriate snap-ins to manipulate NDS application objects.

Creating Application Objects

When the schema of the tree was extended to accommodate NAM, the following objects were added to the object definitions in your NDS tree:

- DOS application
- Windows 3.x application
- Windows 95 application
- Windows NT application

To create an application object in your NDS tree, make sure you are running an appropriate version of NetWare Administrator. For Windows 3.x, you will want to be running NWADMN3X.EXE. This will allow you to create the new objects because it already contains the snap-ins that manipulate them. To create the application object, perform the following steps:

1. From NetWare Administrator, click once with the right mouse button on the container that will hold the new application object. Select Create from the menu that appears. The New Object dialog box will be displayed.

2. Select the appropriate type of application (DOS, Windows 3.x, Windows 95, or Windows NT) from the Class of New Object window. Click OK.

Tip

The type of NDS application object plays an important role in NAL. If you create a Windows 3.x application object, only users running Windows 3.x workstations will be able to run that application using NAL. If you want to create icons for network applications across multiple platforms, you must create an application object for each platform.

3. The Create Application dialog box appears. Type in the name of the new application object and the path to the application. The Select Object button to the right of the text box can be used to navigate the NDS tree and file systems to find the executable. Once the path has been specified, click on the Create button.

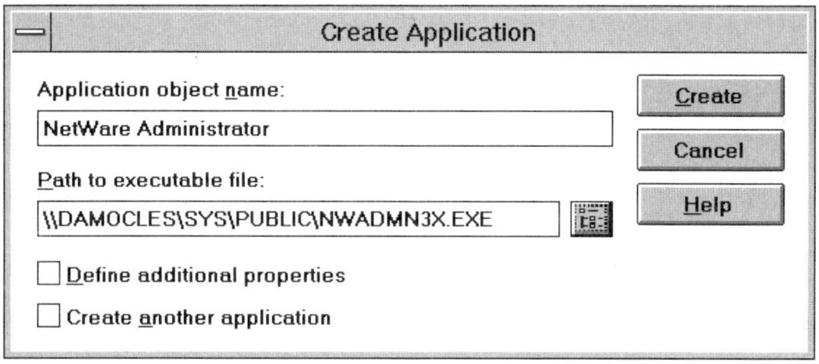

```
┌─────────────────────────────────────────────────────────────────┐
│  ─             Create Application                                 │
├───────────────────────────────────────────────┬─────────────────┤
│  Application object name:                       │  ┌───────────┐  │
│  ┌───────────────────────────────────────────┐ │  │  Create   │  │
│  │ NetWare Administrator                     │ │  └───────────┘  │
│  └───────────────────────────────────────────┘ │  ┌───────────┐  │
│                                                 │  │  Cancel   │  │
│  Path to executable file:                       │  └───────────┘  │
│  ┌─────────────────────────────────────┐ ┌──┐  │  ┌───────────┐  │
│  │ \\DAMOCLES\SYS\PUBLIC\NWADMN3X.EXE   │ │▒▒│  │  │   Help    │  │
│  └─────────────────────────────────────┘ └──┘  │  └───────────┘  │
│  ☐ Define additional properties                 │                 │
│  ☐ Create another application                   │                 │
└─────────────────────────────────────────────────────────────────┘
```

Figure 13-15: Creating a new application object in the NDS tree.

Notice in Figure 13-15 that the path to the executable file does *not* include a mapped drive. The path is defined using the Universal Naming Convention (UNC), which specifies the server, volume, and path to the executable file. This is necessary because NAM functions independently of drive mappings. Because the application is defined with a UNC path, the user does not actually need to have a drive mapped to the application to run it.

Once the application object has been created in the NDS tree, you can customize it to fit your network's needs. To detail the NDS object, double-click on the application object with the left mouse button. The properties for the NDS object will be displayed. As always, the property page tabs are displayed at the right of the screen, and the properties for the selected tab are displayed at the left. Figure 13-16 shows the Identification property tab for a Windows 3.x Application object in the NDS tree.

In the Identification property tab, you can modify the path of the executable for the application and the icon that are displayed by NAL on the user desktop. You can change the title of the icon as it will be seen by the user as well. For example, the application object in Figure 13-16 will cause an icon titled NetWare Administrator to be displayed on a Windows 3.x machine running NAL.

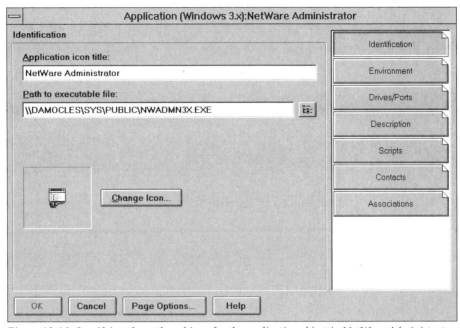

Figure 13-16: Specifying the path and icon for the application object in NetWare Administrator.

Besides the Identification property tab, there are also some other important property tabs that are used to define information about the application and that might be necessary to run the application. These tabs are as follows:

- **Environment.** Allows you to specify any command-line parameters the application might need. You can also specify a working directory for the application.

- **Drives/Ports.** Lets you dynamically map drives and capture printer ports for an application. These drive mappings and printer ports are only in effect when the application is open and are removed when the user closes it. Although a drive mapping is not required for the user to run the application, you may need to map drives to data that exists in another location on the network.

- **Scripts.** Defines any script commands that need to be run prior to the launching of the application and after the application's termination. These script commands use the same syntax as the login script commands we learned about in Chapter 5.

- **Contacts.** Lists people the user can contact in the event he or she encounters a problem with the application. This property tab is purely informational and has no bearing on the NDS tree; however, it may be useful from a user-support standpoint.

After the application object has been detailed, you can click OK at the bottom of the dialog box to accept the changes you made to the properties. Press Cancel to discard any modifications. You will be returned to the NDS tree in NetWare Administrator.

Associating NDS Application Objects With Users

Even though the application object has been created in the NDS tree, it does not mean that users will be able to access its associated network application with NAL. Users must be configured to use that application through user objects, group objects, and container objects. Only after the users on your network configure will NAL display the icon for the network application to them.

To allow a user to access a network application using NAL, you must use one of the new property tabs associated with the user object. In NetWare Administrator, double-click on the user you are configuring with the left mouse button to display the properties for his or her user object. Click on the Applications property tab once with the left mouse button. The Applications properties of the user object will appear.

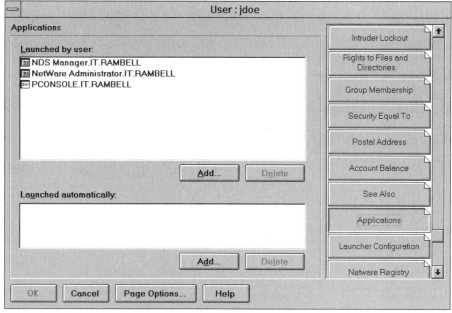

Figure 13-17: To allow a user to access a network application, it must be listed in the Applications tab of the user's user object.

In Figure 13-17, the user jdoe has been configured to use the NetWare Administrator, NDS Manager, and PCONSOLE application objects. We can see these are Windows 3.x and DOS application objects, which means that whenever jdoe logs in to the network from a Windows 3.x machine and uses NAL, he will be able to launch these three applications through the icons that are displayed.

You will notice that the Application property tab is broken up into two windows. The top window contains applications that are launched by the user through NAL at the client workstation. The bottom window shows the applications that are run automatically when NAL is started at the workstation. This is equivalent to putting an icon in the Startup group of a Windows machine.

To add an application to either one of these windows, click on the appropriate Add button (as seen in Figure 13-17). The Select Object dialog box will appear. Navigate the NDS tree to find the appropriate application object, select it, and click OK. The object will be listed in the box. You can remove an application from the list by clicking on it once with the left mouse button to highlight it and clicking on the Delete button.

The application objects listed in this property page will be the applications that are displayed at the user's client workstation when NAL is launched. This is how you can customize your users' workstation desktops. Each user can be given a specific list of network applications that he or she can run through NAL. If the set of applications for the user changes, you only need to change the list of applications in the Applications property tab to affect what the user sees on his or her desktop.

Other NDS objects can be used to distribute network application icons with NAL. Both group and container objects also have an applications tab associated with them. When you associate an Application object with an NDS object, you allow all users who are members of the object access to the network application. Thus, if you associate a network application with the IT container, all objects contained in that container will be able to access the application through NAL.

Tip

Use the Application property tab associated with an NDS container or group object to grant multiple users the ability to run a network application.

Granting Sufficient File System Rights to Users

For users to be able to use the applications defined for them in NAM, they must also have sufficient file system rights to the directory in which the network application resides. Most of the time, the rights required are the Read and File Scan file system rights; however, the documentation provided with the application should contain some information about the NetWare file system rights required by users to successfully run the application on your network.

Once the users have been granted sufficient rights, they will be able to launch the application at their workstation using NAL. For more information on granting file system rights and understanding file system security, refer to Chapter 6.

Once the application objects have been created and defined for your network applications, it is time to set up the client workstations to use NAM's companion, NAL, to actually run the network applications.

Launching Network Applications Using NAL

While NAM is required on the NDS side to define the applications that will run on your network, it is up to NAL to deliver the application icons to the user desktop. Every user who will be accessing the network applications will need to run NAL at his or her client workstation. This means you need to initially set up NAL on each workstation. After the initial investment of time, any changes in network applications only need to be made through NAM. NAL will reflect the changes the next time it is launched at the client workstation.

You run NAL at the client workstation through a simple executable program. It is located in the SYS:PUBLIC directory of your NetWare 4.11 file server. For Windows 3.x workstations, you will want to run NALW31.EXE. You can run it through the File I Run menu option in Program Manager, or you can create an icon for NAL. Either way, if you have the F: drive mapped to SYS:PUBLIC, the path for NAL would be F:\NALW31.EXE.

Tip

Users with Windows 95 workstations would use the NAL executable written specifically for Windows 95. It is also located in the SYS:PUBLIC directory of your NetWare 4.11 server; however, it is called NALW95.EXE.

If you created an icon in Windows for NAL, just double-click on the icon with the left mouse button to launch it. When a user launches NAL, it retrieves the list of applications appropriate for that user from the Applications tab of the user object. It then displays a new window on the user's desktop that contains icons for all of the application objects listed. From this window, the user can double-click on the desired network application to launch it.

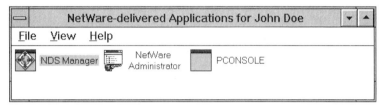

Figure 13-18: NAL displays a new window on the user's workstation desktop from which the network applications can be started.

In Figure 13-18, the user John Doe has launched NAL from Windows 3.1. In this window are all of the applications listed in his user object's Applications property tab as we saw in Figure 13-17. He can launch NetWare Administrator by double-clicking on the NetWare Administrator icon with the left mouse button. To add new icons to this window, the network administrator would only have to add new application objects to the list in the Applications property tab of the user object.

Using NAL as a Windows Shell

If you really want to control your users' desktops, you can use NAL to replace the Windows 3.x Program Manager or Windows 95 Explorer interface. When your user starts Windows, instead of getting the normal display and all of their icons, only those icons created with NAM and NAL are shown. Those are the only applications the user is able to launch from the workstation. It truly gives the network administrator control over what programs a user is and isn't able to use.

To use NAL as the Windows shell on a Windows 3.x workstation, copy the files NALW31.EXE, NALRES.DLL, NALBMP.DLL, and NAL.HLP to the local hard drive. Edit the SYSTEM.INI file with an ASCII editor so the shell line in the [boot] section of the file reads SHELL=C:\<*path*>\NALW31.EXE. Save the modifications and restart Windows.

The next time the user logs in to the network, he or she will only be able to use those applications you specified through NAM and NAL.

Using NAM and NAL to distribute the icons for your network applications can greatly reduce your work as a network administrator because you will not need to modify the icons on every workstation if there is a change to the application. You can centrally administer and distribute the icons representing your network applications to all of your users' desktops. All you need to do is initially configure the applications through NAM and set up NAL on each workstation.

Moving On

In this chapter, we have learned about some utilities that come packaged with IntranetWare that enhance the functionality of your network. The health of your NDS tree can be monitored and maintained using NDS Manager, DSTRACE, and DSREPAIR. SMS technology and SBACKUP allow you to protect yourself in the event your NDS database becomes completely corrupt, and NAM and NAL provide a way to centrally administer your network applications efficiently.

While the previous chapters have talked a lot about the "how to" of NDS, we will digress a little in the next chapter to talk about some more NDS theory. We understand how to partition and replicate the NDS database, and we know how to set up the time synchronization environment. But there are guidelines you should follow before implementing your NDS environment. In the next chapter, we will talk about planning your NDS tree and the guidelines you should follow before you even begin to use any of the applications we have already discussed.

14

NDS Design & Implementation: A Case Study

Throughout this entire section, we have been focusing on the "how to" aspects of NDS. We understand how security works in the NDS tree. We know how to partition and replicate the NDS database. We can successfully set up a time synchronization environment. Obviously, all of this information is required to implement an NDS network environment in your organization; however, we have only touched upon planning the NDS environment.

People who are going to use NDS with a limited number of objects and network resources will benefit from the default configuration NDS provides when it is installed. If you are going to have only one organization and one organizational unit in your NDS tree, it does not make sense to have a complex partitioning and replication scheme. Time synchronization should be kept simple as well. The default time synchronization environment will suit the needs of your network.

However, people who have a large network will want to carefully consider and plan their NDS tree before it is actually implemented in the workplace. Large companies or organizations that require the true enterprise capabilities that NDS offers also beg for a customized partitioning and replication environment to accommodate the number of servers and the topology of the network. For traffic considerations, the time synchronization environment should also be customized.

Which brings us back to planning the NDS environment. For a large-scale rollout, you should start with a planning process to formulate the general structure of the NDS tree so that it will fit with your organization's overall networking goals and objectives. Will the container objects you provide in the NDS tree fit your company's work model and work flow? Should you model the NDS tree after your company's organizational chart? An efficient logical design to your tree will make your network easier to use and more efficient for both you and your users.

The second step in planning a large NDS tree involves the partitioning and replication scheme. You want to provide a fault-tolerant network through partitioning and replication, but you also want to minimize the network traffic that is generated through partitioning and replication operations. Into how many partitions should the NDS database be split? How many replicas should be placed in a partition's replica ring? How many partition replicas should be stored on an individual server? How does my network topology affect the partitioning and replication of the NDS tree? These are all considerations that will be discussed in this chapter.

The time synchronization environment plays an important role in NDS. It is responsible for maintaining the consistency and accuracy of the data in your NDS database. Having a sound time synchronization environment will make your NDS tree more efficient; however, how many time sources should there be in a large NDS tree? How should those time sources communicate with one another? What kind of impact does time synchronization traffic have on the performance of the network? Too many time servers can be overkill and can adversely affect the performance of your network. The time synchronization environment should also take into account the topology of your network. We will discuss the main issues you should consider when setting up your time synchronization environment.

Before deploying NDS in your organization, you should sit down and plan the tree, taking into account the many factors that can affect the performance and efficiency of your network. With careful planning and forethought, you can provide a sound NDS structure that will be suited for your networking environment and your users' needs.

Deciding Upon a Logical NDS Tree Structure

The first step in designing your NDS tree is to plan the logical tree structure your company or organization will use. Because it will have an impact on how your users interact with the NDS tree, it is important to consider their needs when deciding upon the overall structure. But before you even begin to pencil in anything concerning the structure of the NDS tree, you should gather some preliminary information so you can make some informed decisions to balance users' needs with the current network environment you have.

After gathering this information, you will also want to grab a pencil and some paper because you will want to create some hand-drawn diagrams to help you plan the NDS environment as well. Having a working model of your system on paper will help you see any limitations you may be inadvertently building into the system as you proceed through the planning process.

Gathering Preliminary Information

Because the reason for implementing a network in your organization is to provide services for your users, you should take into account their needs and desires. How will they be using the network? Are there specific groups who exchange data on a regular basis? Understanding the workflow of your organization can help you design an NDS structure that is efficient from a human resource point of view.

Besides dealing with users, there are physical limitations in the types of services you can provide on your network. The network topology can affect how you might structure the NDS tree. You will want to isolate WAN links so there is a minimal amount of network traffic flowing across them. Links that are not cluttered with administrative NDS information will help facilitate the transfer of user information between the sides of your WAN.

Finally, you will want an informal inventory of the resources you will be connecting to the network. By knowing the number of printers you have available, the number of servers with which you will be working, and the number of users you will be administering, you will be able to group them into a logical structure in your NDS tree in order to provide efficient communication.

Before you start any planning for the NDS tree, gather the following information about your network and the people who will be using your network:

- A company organizational chart and general workflow process diagram

- The topology of the network, including high-speed connections and WAN links

- An inventory of the number of users, machines, servers, and printers you will have connected to the network

Don't be afraid to get input from the managers in your company. You are providing this network for their use, and you want them to get the most use out of it. By understanding their needs and how they interact with other groups in the company, you will be able to design a logical NDS structure that suits their needs best. You may also want to contact your human resources department (if you have one) or any other person at your company who might be able to provide insight into the present organizational chart and workflow processes.

Once you have all of the preliminary information to help you make the informed decisions concerning the structure of your NDS tree, you'll be ready to get started with the planning process. From here, we will discuss the overall structure of the tree and the models you might want to follow in the implementation of that structure.

Container Organization Models

For your users, the key to the efficiency of the NDS tree is the container organization model upon which you decide. Users and network resources should be grouped together logically for the easiest access. Put yourself in your users' shoes when deciding upon a container organization model for your NDS tree. Use the following points to plan the tree from the users' perspective:

- With which parties does the majority of the data exchange take place?
- How are the network resources going to be accessed?
- Will users be able to find other users on the network easily?

The answers to these questions will help you plan a tree structure that is both efficient and logical from the users' point of view. When your users are happy, you are happy as a network administrator. If you create a tree structure that is confusing and inefficient, you will create more work for yourself.

Gather the answers to those three questions as they pertain to each individual user. From there, you will be able to decide upon a tree structure that will accommodate the most people in your company or organization. You might want to consider one of the four following models to help you design and create a structure for your NDS tree that meets your company's needs:

- The organizational chart structure
- The workflow structure
- The geographic structure
- The combinational structure

The Organizational Chart Structure

As you probably have guessed, the organizational chart structure closely follows the organizational chart of your company or organization. This is a logical structure to follow because presumably your company's organizational chart is a well-thought-out structure that reflects the management of your company.

If the majority of your users' interactions with other people take place within their own division, it is a good idea to follow the organizational chart structure. Users in that department will be able to easily share the resources amongst themselves, and other users in the company will be able to easily locate company resources and people in the NDS tree. By knowing and understanding the company's organizational chart, they will be able to navigate the NDS tree. Figure 14-1 shows a sample NDS tree design based upon a company's organizational chart.

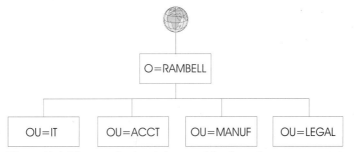

Figure 14-1: The organizational chart model reflects the management structure of your company.

The Workflow Structure

There are times when the organizational chart model is not effective in describing the interactions your users have. Many companies today have project-type focuses in which users from many different departments form teams to work together on a common goal. The users in these teams tend to have more interaction with each other than they do with the users in their assigned division or department. It makes more sense to group the NDS tree by goals or projects instead of by management structure.

When you implement the workflow structure, the similarities in users' tasks are highlighted. Because these users interact with each other and perform the same types of functions in the company or organization, it is logical to group them together. At the same time, this will lead to the more logical grouping of network resources. Figure 14-2 shows a sample NDS tree structure based upon the workflow structure.

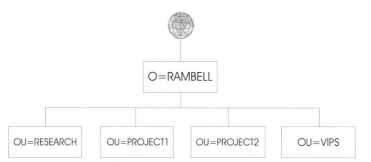

Figure 14-2: The workflow model reflects the project and goal focus of your company or organization.

The Geographic Structure

For large companies that have multiple locations throughout the country or throughout the world, the geographic structure will help break down the organization into more manageable pieces. In the geographic structure, the NDS tree is initially segmented by the divisions' physical locations. Figure 14-3 shows a sample NDS tree based upon the geographic structure.

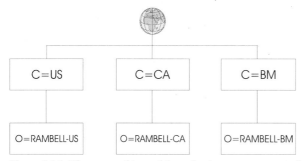

Figure 14-3: The geographic model emphasizes your company's physical plant locations for a more logical, easier-to-manage structure.

How you divide your company along geographic lines is up for debate; however, this is where the NDS Country object can really help you out. If you have an international organization, consider using the Country object as the first level of your NDS tree. It will help you segment your network logically as well as structurally isolate the WAN links in your organization.

The Combinational Structure

Generally, no single one of these structures will accommodate your organization's needs. You will want to use a combination of models to create the most efficient structure. This is called the combinational structure. Its most common use is to combine the geographic structure and the organizational chart structure to achieve a final NDS tree. Figure 14-4 shows a sample NDS tree that employs these two models into one tree structure.

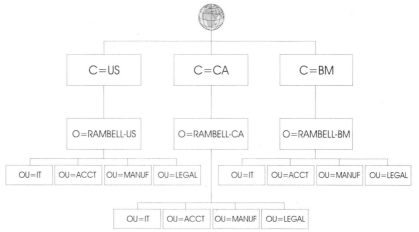

Figure 14-4: The combinational model uses a mix of the other models to achieve a customized NDS tree structure.

Remember your focus when designing the overall structure of your NDS tree. You want a structure that will be logical and easy to use from a user's standpoint. It should reflect how your users interact and work with one another. If your NDS tree structure helps them accomplish their jobs better and more efficiently, you have implemented a sound structure.

While your users are an important part of your network, large companies with large NDS trees will have more than one network administrator. The structure of the tree should also reflect their needs and the security implementation of the network. In the next section, we will discuss some administrative models you might want to integrate into the structure of your NDS tree to facilitate efficient administration as well as to make it easy and efficient for the people in your organization to use.

Now that you have some suggestions concerning the structure of your NDS tree, you will want to create a diagram of a tree structure appropriate to your company or organization. This will be your working model of your NDS tree. Creating this diagram will make the actual creation of the NDS tree in NetWare Administrator much easier when you are ready to implement it.

Tree Administration Models

As we have seen in Chapter 9, you have a certain amount of flexibility when setting up the administrative aspects of the NDS tree. You can provide someone with sufficient rights to create and delete objects in the tree. You can also give that person the ability to modify the properties of objects. You can even grant other people the Supervisor object right to the [Root] of the NDS tree. Besides the default Admin user object, other users can be granted rights to perform NDS administrative tasks.

Whether or not you choose to grant administrative rights to other users is a different story. In addition to deciding upon a structural model for your NDS tree, you should decide upon an administrative model. This decision may have an impact on how you structure your NDS tree as well. Small companies may not need more that one user to administer the NDS tree; large organizations with many departments or divisions may need a network administrator for each department.

There are two general paradigms for NDS administration:

- Centralized administration
- Distributed administration

Centralized administration, which is the default model for IntranetWare, relies upon one user (or a group of users with sufficient rights) to administer the entire tree. This user or group of users is given the Supervisor NDS object right to all objects in the NDS tree and is responsible for maintaining the network resources, creating new objects, and implementing security. The administrator(s) do it all.

Centralized administration is an excellent option for companies with small NDS trees. There generally will not be a need to distribute the administration of the NDS tree. Centralized administration is easier because there does not have to be coordination between multiple administrators to accomplish certain administrative tasks.

Distributed administration relies upon special users who are given sufficient NDS rights to administer entire branches of the NDS tree. The day-to-day tasks of user creation and object maintenance are taken away from the central person and given to administrators distributed throughout the organization.

In large organizations, distributed administration has some definite advantages. Because the administrators are located within a specific department or division, they will be able to deal with users' needs and problems quicker than a centralized administrator would.

As we learned in Chapter 9, the Inherited Rights Filter for NDS rights can filter out the Supervisor object and property rights. This fact plays an important role in your NDS tree administration. You can set up the distributed administration so that a central administrator still has NDS rights over all branches of the tree. The central administrator can function as a backup to the distributed administrators in the event of an emergency.

You can also set up the distributed administration so that the distributed administrator has exclusive rights over a branch of the tree. The central administrator's rights are completely blocked through an Inherited Rights Filter. This kind of distributed administrator is called the *exclusive distributed administrator* because he or she has sole control of the tree branch. Figure 14-5 shows the relationship between the central administrator, the distributed administrator, and the exclusive distributed administrator.

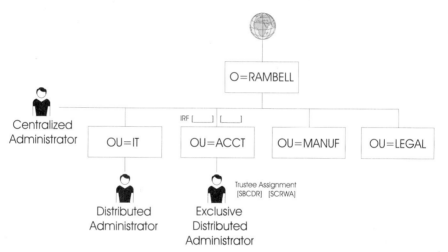

Figure 14-5: An exclusive distributed administrator has sole control over a branch of the NDS tree.

Because the administration model of the NDS tree is so flexible, it can easily be tailored to your specific environment. Use the distributed model in large organizations where it is not feasible for one user or group of users to be responsible for the administration of the entire network. Use the exclusive distributed administrator feature for departments that have confidential or sensitive information that cannot be viewed by anyone else in the network.

Tip

When using the exclusive distributed administrator feature, make sure there is an NDS object that has the Supervisor object right to the container where the IRF exists to block the NDS rights from the central administrator. Do not delete this object or you will lose control over that branch of the NDS tree.

For large organizations, you will usually want to combine features of the centralized and distributed administration models to facilitate the efficient administration of your NDS tree. Generally, you will want to have a central administrator perform the following tasks:

- Initially installing NDS and naming the NDS tree.
- Creating the logical structure of the NDS tree, especially the first layers.
- Partitioning and replicating the NDS database.
- Creating and managing the time synchronization environment.
- Troubleshooting and resolving NDS inconsistencies.
- Providing a central backup of the NDS database.
- Assigning distributed administrators in the NDS tree.

The types of tasks that should be administered by a central information systems department are the tasks that should be performed by a central administrator. He or she should be responsible for database infrastructure decisions and maintaining the health of the NDS tree. On the other hand, the distributed administrator will need to perform the following types of tasks:

- Creating and maintaining user accounts.
- Setting up and maintaining intruder detection services.
- Setting up and maintaining the printing environment.
- Protecting file system data through regular backups.
- Creating file system trustee assignments to the servers over which he or she has control.
- Installing new servers in his or her branch of the tree.

The reason your administrative model may have an impact on the logical structure of your NDS tree is because you need to have the appropriate containers set up for distributed administration. If distributed administration must fall along management lines, you are more likely to choose the organizational chart structure for your NDS tree. If your company has multiple loca-

tions, each with its own central information systems department, you will
want to set up distributed administration across geographical boundaries.

Once you have factored the administration of the NDS tree into the logical
structure, there are a few more items to consider. In the next section, we will
cover the other issues that may have an impact on how you organize the
structure of your NDS tree.

Other Structural Considerations

Besides user and administrator needs, there are some other factors you should
consider when planning your NDS tree. They deal with the physical structure
and backward compatibility of your network. Not accounting for these items
in the structure of your NDS tree can lead to an inefficient tree structure that
hampers the use of your network.

Network Topology

The first factor that will have a direct effect on your NDS tree structure is the
topology of your network. Remember that network diagram we acquired in
"Gather Preliminary Information" earlier in this chapter? The information
about your network's topology on that diagram will be used to help you plan
your network. Users and network resources that are isolated from the rest of
the network via a WAN link should also be isolated in their own container in
the NDS tree. Generally, people on one side of a WAN link tend to exchange
information locally. You can take advantage of this fact and reduce the amount
of traffic flowing across the WAN link by grouping those users and resources
together.

It is important that you understand and account for the physical structure
of your network in the logical structure of the NDS tree. With careful planning,
you can maximize the efficiency of the slower WAN links by limiting the
amount of network traffic that crosses it.

Bindery Services

If you are integrating the NetWare 3.x and 4.x environments on your network,
you will need to contend with Bindery Services. As we have previously mentioned, Bindery Services allows NetWare 4.11 to provide backward compatibility to bindery clients who do not understand the concept of NDS.

When Bindery Services is enabled, it allows bindery clients to view portions
of the NDS tree as a flat-file database. The portions of the tree that are viewed
in this manner are set in the bindery context environment variable of the

NetWare 4.11 server. Because the server's bindery context is directly related to the structure of the container objects in your NDS tree, you will want to plan for Bindery Services before you finalize the structure of your NDS tree.

Identify those users who need Bindery Services on your network and group them together as much as possible. Try not to distribute Bindery Services users across the NDS tree; you will create a situation where each server providing Bindery Services will have multiple bindery contexts to maintain. This can lead to naming collisions in your NDS tree because a name must be unique across all bindery contexts within the tree.

Once you have accounted for all of the different factors that can affect the logical structure of your tree, you are ready to create the structure using NetWare Administrator. Create the appropriate container objects in your NDS tree, and you have built the general infrastructure for the rest of the objects that will be created. The next step is to organize and create the individual objects in the tree using NetWare Administrator. For more information on creating objects in the NDS tree, refer to Chapter 3.

Naming Standards

As you create the objects in your NDS tree to represent the users and the network resources on your network, you will want to institute some sort of naming standard that all administrators on the network will follow. There are some distinct benefits to implementing a naming standard in your NDS tree:

- Users will be able to find network resources quickly and easily.

- Users will be able to remember the object names.

- A naming standard provides a general guideline for distributed administrators to follow.

- Limited time is wasted thinking up names for objects.

For example, if one of your guidelines is that every print queue object's name will end in the letter Q, users will be able to find all of the print queues on your network quickly and easily because they only have to look for that one letter at the end of the object's name. When administrators are naming print queue objects, they have enough flexibility to uniquely identify their print queue while still maintaining order on the network.

Try to keep your container and object names as short and descriptive as possible. Remember, an object's full distinguished name is a combination of its common name and its context. Users who must enter it as a requirement in specific instances will appreciate a short and easy-to-remember name. Also, the distinguished name for an object cannot exceed 256 characters. For more information on naming standards and conventions, refer to Chapter 3.

After the naming standards have been chosen and the infrastructure laid, go ahead and organize the objects in your NDS tree as specified by your working model on paper. When you are finished, you will have an NDS tree that has been customized specifically for your networking environment. The users and administrators on your network will have an efficient system with which they will be able to increase their productivity and perform their work like never before!

At this point, the front end of the NDS environment has been properly planned. But as we know, there is another whole side to NDS that still needs attention. It has to do with the NDS database itself and how it is broken up into pieces, distributed across the network, and synchronized. In the next sections, we will discuss the planning of the back-end environment to create a back end that is as efficient as the front end.

Planning NDS Partitioning & Replication

In Chapter 8, we discussed the basic architecture of NDS. We know it is an object-oriented distributed database. It can be broken up into pieces that can be distributed across the network. This makes NDS flexible and scalable, which is achieved through partitioning the NDS database. Pieces of the database can be copied and stored on other servers in your network. This replication allows you to make your network fault tolerant. Through partitioning and replication, you can provide an incredibly stable and flexible network for your users.

However, you must balance accessibility and fault tolerance with the performance of your network. With partitioning and replication, it's possible to have too much of a good thing. Too many partitions and too many replicas can adversely affect the performance of your network. Because there is administrative overhead traffic required for the maintenance of partitioning and replication, you can flood your network with unnecessary traffic and reduce the bandwidth your users can use for their tasks.

Partitioning Guidelines

Just as you did for the logical structure of your NDS tree, you want to plan your partitioning scheme. A logical partitioning scheme will increase the efficiency and performance of your network. Servers will be able to search the smaller pieces of the database more quickly. The scalability you can achieve through the partitioning of the NDS database is a distinct benefit NDS has over a lot of other network operating systems.

When planning you partitioning scheme, you will want to take into account the following issues:

- Placement of partition boundaries
- Network topology
- Partition size
- Number of partitions

If you follow the guidelines as they are described in the next sections, you will be on your way to implementing an efficient partitioning scheme.

Placement of Partition Boundaries

We discussed the rules associated with partitioning in Chapter 10. When you are planning your partitioning scheme, you must follow the partitioning rules. As a reminder, here are the partitioning rules we have previously stated:

- The topmost object in a partition must be a container. This is called the partition root. The partition takes its name from the partition root.
- Partitions may not overlap. Every NDS object in the NDS tree will exist in one and only one NDS partition.
- There can only be one partition root. Two containers may not coexist as partition roots.

As long as you follow these rules, you can partition wherever you like; however, it might not be efficient to create a partition everywhere in the tree. Generally, you will want to create a small number of partitions at the top of the tree. Toward the bottom of the tree, you will want more partitions. When drawn out, your partitioning scheme should resemble a pyramid.

It's important to follow these guidelines so that you reduce the number of Subordinate Reference replicas that are created. A large number of Subordinate Reference replicas is a sign of a poor partitioning scheme. Having too many partitions toward the top of your tree is likely to result in more Subordinate References because there will be more instances of servers storing a replica of a parent partition but not all of its child partitions.

By reducing the number of Subordinate Replicas, you reduce the overall total number of replicas that must be synchronized. It will cut down on the overhead administrative traffic and increase the overall performance of your network.

Network Topology

The topology of your network will also factor into your partitioning scheme. At this point, it's important to study the diagram of your network because you do not want to partition across a WAN link. This will adversely affect the performance of your WAN link because there will be a baseline of traffic necessary to facilitate user requests concerning partition information.

It is better to isolate partitions on opposite sides of the WAN connection. Since you have already accounted for the WAN connection in the logical structure of the NDS tree, users and resources should already be isolated. Follow suit with the partitioning scheme and isolate it. This will keep partitioning information from flooding the WAN link and decreasing its performance. Figure 14-6 shows a sample NDS tree that has been partitioned. Notice that the organizational unit MANUF has been given its own partition. This is because that group depends upon a WAN link for network connectivity.

On the map of your network topology, you may want to pencil in some proposed NDS partitions. This will allow you to create partitions which accurately reflect the physical layout of your network. Again, this planning will make the implementation of the NDS environment more efficient. Remember that the partitions must also reflect the structure of the tree upon which you already decided. If you need to adjust the structure of the tree to make the networking more efficient, just return to your working model and make modifications.

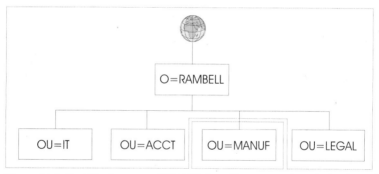

Figure 14-6: Partitioning around WAN links will prevent a degradation in performance by isolating partitioning traffic.

Partition Size

When partitions get too large, it takes more time to locate the information requested by the users. As a general rule, keep the partition sizes small, especially the [Root] partition. Now when we say small, we are not talking about 20 objects in the partition as a maximum. We are in the realm of thousands.

Generally, a partition should have fewer than 1,000 objects in it. Conversely, a partition should not have more than 5,000 objects in it. Once a partition reaches over 2,500 subordinate objects, it becomes a candidate to be split into multiple partitions.

Obviously, network topology takes precedence over the number of objects in the partition. Do not be afraid to partition a container with only 50 objects if that container is across a WAN link. It is more important to reduce the partitioning traffic across that expensive WAN line than to make sure you meet some "minimum" number of objects in a partition.

Number of Partitions

Having too many partitions in your NDS tree can also adversely affect the network performance. Do you remember when we discussed tree walking in Chapter 10? When a user issues a request for resources not contained in his or her partition, NDS initiates a process of tree walking to find the resource. A large number of partitions in your NDS tree will cause the tree walking process to take a longer amount of time, which affects how quickly NDS is able to return the information to the user.

Also remember that each partition must initiate a synchronization process to maintain the consistency of the NDS database. When there is a large number of partitions, you increase the amount of synchronization traffic required to keep your database current. That number compounded with a large number of replicas in each replica ring can bring a network to its knees.

Each partition in the NDS tree should have fewer than 10 subordinate partitions. This makes the partitioning overhead manageable. There are times, however, when you need to have more than 10 subordinate partitions. You should try not to exceed 50 subordinate partitions for a single partition. This should be within the realm of reason. If we take the maximum number of partitions with the maximum number of objects in a partition, each partition should have less than 250,000 subordinate objects in the NDS tree beneath the partition root. This should be an attainable goal for most organizations.

Table 14-1 summarizes the partitioning guidelines we have just discussed. Refer to this table as a reference during the planning of your partitioning scheme. Once you have decided upon a partitioning scheme, you'll need to consider the replica rings you are going to implement for the partition. Replica rings also have an impact upon network performance because there is a constant synchronization process to ensure the consistency of your NDS database. In the next section, we will discuss how you might replicate your NDS partitions.

Partitioning Guideline	Recommendation
Placement of partition boundaries	Keep the number of partitions small at the top of the NDS tree. The partitioning scheme should look like a pyramid.
Network topology	Partition around WAN links. Do not "span the WAN."
Partition size	Keep partition sizes small. A partition should have fewer than 1,000 objects but no more than 5,000 objects.
Number of partitions	Partitions should have fewer than 10 subordinate partitions but no more than 50 subordinate partitions.

Table 14-1: Guidelines for planning your NDS partitioning scheme.

On the network topology map where you penciled in the proposed partitions, you might want to also include the types of information specified in Table 14-1. This will help you create the appropriate partitions for your NDS environment.

Replication Guidelines

You replication scheme should also be planned out before it is implemented on your network. Replication allows you to provide a fault-tolerant network to your users. If the user's preferred server is down, he or she will still be able to authenticate to the NDS tree because another replica of the user's partition can be used to log in to the network. Although the user will not be able to reach the data on the server that is down, he or she will still be able to use all of the other resources on the network. But this can happen only if there is a sound replication scheme in place.

As we have already mentioned, you need to balance this fault-tolerance and accessibility issue with the performance of your network. Too many partitions and replicas will adversely affect network performance because there will be a lot of synchronization traffic required to maintain the consistency of your NDS database. Without synchronization, your database would quickly become corrupt and unusable.

When planning your replication scheme, you will want to take into account the following issues:

- Network topology
- Number of replicas in a replica ring
- Types of replicas in a replica ring
- Number of replicas stored on a single server
- Replica administration

Once you have accounted for these factors on your network, you will have maximized its fault tolerance while minimizing the impact of the partition synchronization traffic.

Network Topology

Once again, you are going to need the diagram of your network to plan an appropriate replication scheme. You want to account for the WAN links in your network. This seems like a recurrent theme, doesn't it? In terms of a replication scheme, you want to minimize the amount of synchronization traffic across the WAN link.

To minimize this traffic, isolate the replication to local sides of the WAN link. Try not to replicate across a WAN link. Generally, WAN links are expensive lines. You do not want to waste their bandwidth with synchronization traffic. You want to preserve as much bandwidth as possible for user data and transactions.

Figure 14-7 shows a sample replication scheme that accounts for a WAN link. Notice that there are multiple servers on each side of the link, and a replica ring can be established for each partition to provide a fault-tolerant network for the users. However, it is not always possible to completely isolate replication because there may only be one server on a given side of a WAN connection. In these cases, minimize the number of partition replicas that are stored on that server to minimize the synchronization traffic across the WAN link.

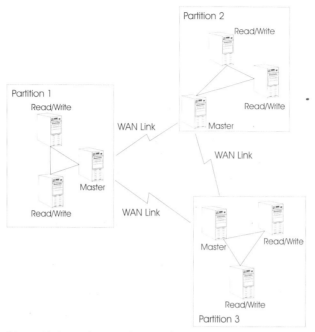

Figure 14-7: Partition replication should be isolated to separate sides of a WAN connection.

Number of Replicas in a Replica Ring

The total number of replicas in a partition's replica ring will determine how fault tolerant your network is. A network with a large number of replicas in the replica ring will be able to tolerate multiple servers going down simultaneously. Again, the users will not be able to access the file systems of servers that are down, but they still will be able to authenticate to the network and use network resources that are still available.

Conversely, placing a larger number of replicas in a partition's replica ring will increase the amount of synchronization traffic required to maintain the consistency of your NDS database. Back in Chapter 10, we discussed the impact of a large number of replicas on your network. Each server in the replica ring must contact every other server in the replica list to exchange information about the latest NDS modifications. A replica ring consisting of 10 replicas would require 45 separate communication sessions per synchronization attempt. Multiply this by the number of partitions on your network, and you could be looking at a significant reduction in the bandwidth of your network.

You should have at least three replicas of a partition stored on your network as a replica ring. This number will provide a minimum amount of fault tolerance. You may want to have more than three servers in your replica ring, but we do not recommend exceeding 10 replicas per replica ring. At this point, you will probably begin to notice a degradation in your network performance as the number of partitions begins to grow.

Types of Replicas in a Replica Ring

In addition to planning for the number of replicas in a replica ring, you also need to determine which types of replicas will be present in the replica ring. There are no real guidelines for the types of replicas you might employ for use on your network. Keep in mind, however, the roles the types of replicas may play.

Of course, every partition has a single Master replica, which is responsible for dictating the synchronization of the partition and is also considered to be the most accurate replica on the network. The Read/Write replicas serve to provide an authentication mechanism on your network and are also used for Bindery Services. Read-Only replicas cannot perform authentication services. They are only able to give information; they cannot make changes to the NDS database.

Obviously, you want to distribute the Master and Read/Write replicas across your network to provide distributed authentication on your network. With well-placed replicas, you can isolate authentication traffic as the users request access to your network. On a final note, try to reduce the number of Subordinate Reference replicas on your network. With a good partitioning scheme, this number should already be close to a minimum.

Number of Replicas Stored on a Single Server

As we have already mentioned, NDS partitioning and replication causes administrative overhead for your servers and network. There will be a baseline of synchronization traffic on your network to maintain the consistency of the NDS database. Servers that hold replicas of partitions will also be forced to use some processing time on the synchronization process. While this should not really hurt the performance of your server, it is something to keep in mind as you are planning your replication scheme.

A server that is providing file and print services for your users should be able to handle 10 partition replicas. Once the number of replicas stored on that server begins to exceed 10, you may start to notice a decrease in its performance. Unless partitioning and replication is the server's only job, try not to store more than 10 partition replicas on a single server.

Replica Administration

Replica administration will create network traffic as well. This is because the replicas need to contact one another to make sure they are updated properly. Multiple users concurrently performing replica administration and manipulation can greatly increase the amount of traffic on your network. It is recommended that there be one person (or a small group of people) responsible for partition and replica administration. The administration will be more efficient, and the network traffic will be minimized.

Table 14-2 summarizes the guidelines we have discussed for planning your replica scheme. Refer to this table as you are planning to maximize the efficiency of your network. Once you have planned the partitioning and replication scheme for your network, it is time to move on to the other portion of the NDS back-end environment, time synchronization. Time synchronization will also have an impact on the performance of your network, and you will want to carefully plan this environment to minimize the amount of time synchronization traffic.

Replication Guideline	Recommendation
Network topology	Isolate replication to local sides of a WAN link. Do not "span the WAN."
Number of replicas in a replica ring	Keep at least three replicas in each partition's replica ring. Try not to exceed 10 replicas in a single replica ring.
Types of replicas in a replica ring	Strategically place the Master and Read/Write replicas to provide efficient user authentication.
Number of replicas stored on a single server	Unless the server is devoted to partitioning and replication, try not to exceed 10 replicas on a single server.
Replica administration	Minimize the number of people on your network who perform replica administration. Replica administration should be performed by a central information systems department.

Table 14-2: Guidelines for planning your NDS replication scheme.

To help you plan your replication environment, you might want to use your trusty pencil and paper again to create a new diagram. You can list each partition in your proposed partitioning scheme. Beneath each partition, list each server which will hold a replica of the partition and indicate the replica type for that server as well. This list beneath the partition will be the replica ring for the partition. This will help you determine the effectiveness of your replication environment.

Planning the NDS Time Environment

In Chapter 11, we discussed the time synchronization environment. We learned that time synchronization plays a crucial role in maintaining the consistency and accuracy of the data in your NDS database. Without a sound time synchronization environment, your NDS database could easily become corrupt, forcing you to reinstall NDS on your network.

You should plan the time synchronization environment before you deploy your network. Understanding which servers will be time providers and which will be time consumers will save you time later in the rollout of your enterprise network. You will be able to easily configure your environment and make informed decisions about how new servers fit into your overall time synchronization environment.

For small networks, the default time synchronization environment is adequate for providing time services. We recommend using the default environment if you can; however, if you have more than 30 servers in your NDS tree or have a WAN link connecting two sites, you should move to a custom time synchronization environment.

In the custom time synchronization environment, there are three types of time servers—Reference, Primary, and Secondary. The Reference and Primary time servers are also called *time providers* because they dispense time to the rest of the network. Secondary time servers are *time consumers* because they unconditionally accept the network time from the time providers on your network. In planning the time synchronization environment for your network, you should determine which servers will be time providers and which servers will be time consumers.

As you think about the time provider/time consumer relationship, you should keep the following issues in mind:

- Determining the number of time providers
- Network topology considerations
- Time server communication strategies

These issues can have an impact on the overall performance of your network. Like partitioning and replication, time synchronization creates extra traffic on your network. Your job is to understand how the time traffic flows on your network and customize the time environment to minimize the amount of time traffic required.

Determining the Number of Time Providers

In the custom time configuration environment, the time providers need to contact one another on a periodic basis to vote on the correct network time. The Reference server and all of the Primary servers poll each other and through a voting process are able to arrive at an agreed-upon time, which is considered to be accurate. After this network time is agreed upon, the time providers then adjust their clocks accordingly.

The polling process between the time providers on your network generates the majority of the time synchronization traffic. To minimize this traffic, you want to minimize the number of time providers. Generally, you should not have more than five Primary time servers in addition to the Reference time server on your network. The remainder of the servers then become Secondary time servers that will accept the network time as it is broadcast to the network. Figure 14-8 shows a sample custom time synchronization environment with four servers in the time provider group. The remainder of the servers are Secondary time servers.

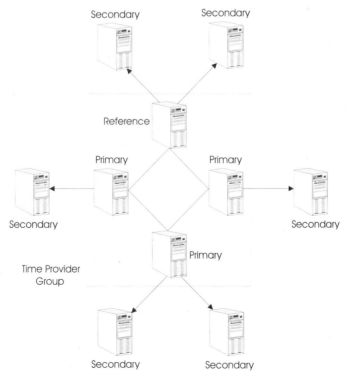

Figure 14-8: A small time provider group disseminates network time to your entire network.

Network Topology Considerations

Just like in everything else we have planned so far, the topology of your network factors into the design of your time synchronization environment. Because WAN links tend to be expensive, you want to maximize their available bandwidth for your users' traffic. You do not want to waste WAN link bandwidth on time synchronization traffic. Design your time synchronization environment to isolate the bulk of the time traffic to local sides of the WAN link.

To do this, you should place a time provider on each side of the WAN link. The Secondary time servers on each side of the WAN link should look to the local time provider for the network time. Do not configure a Secondary time server to get its network time from a time provider across the WAN link. This configuration will isolate a majority of the time traffic to a specific side of the WAN link. Figure 14-9 shows a sample custom time synchronization environment that accounts for the WAN links on the network. Notice that the Secondary servers retrieve their network time from the local time provider. The only time they would get network time from a different time source is when their local time provider is not available.

On the diagram of your network topology, you can pencil in the physical locations of your servers to help you plan your time synchronization environment. It will help you determine how your servers physically communicate with each other over the network and help you isolate time synchronization traffic to local areas instead of distributing it across WAN links.

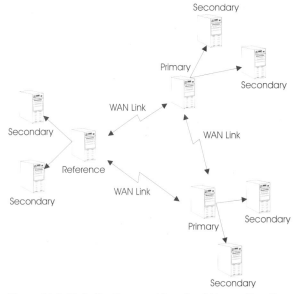

Figure 14-9: Only the time providers should be sending time synchronization traffic across the WAN link.

Time Server Communication Strategies

The default time synchronization environment relies upon a protocol called Service Advertising Protocol (SAP) to relate time information to the various time servers on the network. SAP is a broadcast protocol that is transmitted to every physical network segment. SAP is considered a "chatty" protocol because of its broadcast nature. Even if the information contained in the SAP packet is intended for only a small number of machines in a certain area of the network, the SAP packet still gets broadcast to every segment of the network and every machine will examine its contents.

SAP is fine for networks that do not have slower links. The amount of SAP traffic generated by the time synchronization environment will not adversely affect a standard LAN; however, when WAN links are involved, SAP traffic can greatly reduce the amount of available bandwidth for user data and transactions.

In the custom time synchronization environment, SAP is still used as the default communications mechanism. The machines in the time provider group will contact one another through SAP. Once the network time is agreed upon, the time provider group broadcasts the network time to all of the Secondary time servers on the network. If the amount of network traffic overhead is a concern, you will want to move away from SAP as the main form of communication.

Fortunately, IntranetWare comes with another mechanism that allows time servers to contact one another. Through the use of configured time sources, a time server is instructed to contact only those time servers explicitly specified in the Configured Time Source List. Time information will no longer be broadcast to the network.

You will want to use the Configured Time Source List for your time servers if you need to reduce the amount of time synchronization traffic on your network. This is especially true when you have WAN links to connect remote sites. Referring back to Figure 14-9, we see that this environment is using a Configured Time Source List for each time server. Because the Secondary servers are getting their time from the local time provider, the only time synchronization traffic on the WAN links is the communication between the time providers to determine the network time.

When using the Configured Time Source List for your time environment, you will want to include multiple servers in case the preferred time server is unavailable. This way, the time synchronization can be preserved even if one of the time providers happens to be down. This should be the only instance when the Secondary servers retrieve their network time from a time provider across the WAN. For more information on setting up the custom time synchronization environment, see Chapter 11.

Table 14-3 summarizes the guidelines for the time synchronization environment. Use this table as you are planning the location of the time servers for your network. To maximize the performance of your network, you should reduce the amount of time synchronization traffic through the strategic placement of the time servers and their method of communicating with one another.

Time Environment Guideline	Recommendation
Number of time providers	Keep the number of time providers on your network small. You should not have more than five time providers unless you have many WAN links.
Network topology	Locate a time provider in each WAN site of your network. Isolate time traffic by configuring Secondary time servers to get the network time from the local time provider.
Communication strategy	Reduce the amount of time traffic by using Configured Time Source Lists.

Table 14-3: Guidelines for planning your NDS time synchronization environment.

On the network topology map where you indicated the location of the servers, you can also specify the type of time server each one is along with its associated Configured Time Source List. This will allow you to more easily create the custom time synchronization environment.

Up to this point, we have provided you with some general guidelines that should help you plan your NDS environment; however, it is more helpful to see the planning of the NDS tree in action. In the next section, we will see how John Doe at Rambell, Inc., is doing. The last time we checked in with him, he had just brought up his first server and set up file and print services. Business has grown since then, and John is looking at implementing an enterprise network.

NDS Tree Implementation: Rambell, Inc.

In Section I, "Out of the Box," we monitored John Doe's progress as he installed his first NetWare 4.11 server and provided basic file and print services for the employees of Rambell, Inc. In the meantime, the demand for widgets has increased exponentially, and business is booming! Business is doing so well, in fact, that Rambell has grown into an international manufacturer of widgets.

In the expansion, Rambell has acquired plants in two other locations. Besides the headquarters located in Boston, Massachusetts, Rambell now has sites in both Vancouver, British Columbia, and Hamilton, Bermuda. These three sites are connected via WAN links so there can be one unified network between the remote locations.

John has been made the director of the Information Technology division of Rambell. This division consists of three groups; each location has its own Information Technology group to service the computer needs of the users in the company. Three other divisions have been created in the same manner. There is an Accounting division, a Manufacturing division, and a Legal division.

Now that John is the director, he has been given the charge of implementing an enterprise NDS tree to provide the efficient and timely exchange of data between the three Rambell sites. At this point, John needs to sit down and plan out the NDS environment using the following steps as a guideline for creating the NDS tree:

1. Gather preliminary information.

2. Decide upon a logical NDS tree structure.

3. Plan the partitioning and replication schemes.

4. Plan the time synchronization environment.

We will follow John's progress as he plans his NDS tree, named Willow, from beginning to end. When he is finished, he will have a network that will provide the best performance for the users at Rambell, Inc.

Gather Preliminary Information

The first thing John needs to do is gather information about the company so he can make some informed decisions concerning the front-end and back-end NDS environments. He obtains a copy of the company's organizational chart to determine the management structure. This will help him decide upon a logical structure for the NDS tree.

John also creates a diagram of the topology of the network in relation to the geographic layout of the three Rambell sites. This will provide him with information concerning WAN links, which he will have to account for in all parts of the planning process. By taking these links into account, he can minimize the administrative network traffic on them and maximize the throughput for the users.

Figure 14-10 shows the organizational chart John received. As mentioned, there are four main divisions to Rambell—Information Technology, Accounting, Manufacturing, and Legal. At first, John's inclination was to just divide the NDS tree along those lines; however, he decided to talk to the directors of the other divisions to better understand the workflow at Rambell.

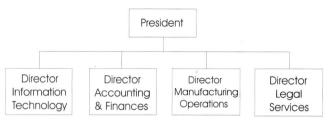

Figure 14-10: The Rambell, Inc. organizational chart.

Much to his surprise, it seems that the three Rambell locations function independently of one another. Almost all of the interaction between people takes place locally. It is not often that groups interact outside of their location. Thus, the Accounting group in Boston tends to work most with other people in Boston. They do not work often with the Accounting group in Vancouver or Hamilton. This will play a key role in determining the logical structure of the NDS tree.

Because John is the director of the Information Technology division, he is well aware of the network topology. After all, he helped to implement it. He draws a basic network diagram to illustrate the relation of the physical locations of the tree sites to one another. Each site is based upon an Ethernet backbone, and each site is connected to the other two sites by a WAN link to provide fault tolerance. If one WAN link goes down, all three sites are still able to communicate with one another. Figure 14-11 shows the network topology map that John drew.

Figure 14-11: The Rambell, Inc. network topology map.

As a last item, John takes a general inventory of the network resources that need to be implemented in the NDS tree. Each Rambell site consists of about 500 employees, each of which will need a computer. He researches the number of network printers that will be necessary to accommodate the print loads of the various divisions. He also realizes that there will be nine servers required to handle the workload of the three remote sites.

At each individual plant, the Information Technology group has a server that is used for research and development. Accounting and Manufacturing share a file server. Due to the confidential nature of the information kept by the Legal department, that division has its own server at each site. Knowing this information, John is ready to get started in planning the enterprise NDS tree.

Decide Upon a Logical NDS Tree Structure

John originally thought he was going to be able to choose the organizational chart model for the NDS tree. After talking with the directors of the other divisions and their subordinate managers, John realized this would not be an efficient solution.

The first overriding concern is the WAN links present on the network. John wants to split the NDS tree along those WAN links to provide efficient communication and to logically group the network resources. Fortunately, the workflow patterns for Rambell, Inc. follow a model where containers split across geographical locations are in the company's best interest.

Once the tree is initially split using the geographic model, each subdivision can then proceed along the organizational chart lines. Thus, each site will have its own container at the first level in the NDS tree. Beneath that container will be the four divisions for that site. Figure 14-12 shows the combinational structure of Rambell's NDS tree. It blends the initial division of the geographical structure with the container refinement of the organizational chart structure.

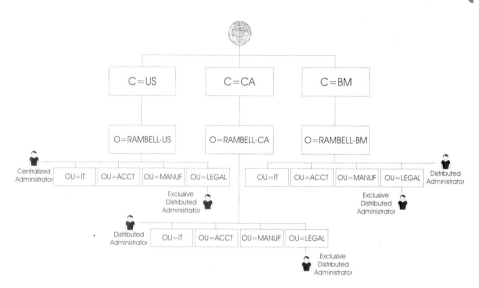

Figure 14-12: The Rambell NDS tree is a combinational structure that blends the geographic and organizational chart NDS tree models.

Notice the placement of the server objects in the Rambell NDS tree. The IT.RAMBELL-US.US group has its own file server, IT_US. The file server Damocles is shared by the ACCT.RAMBELL-US.US and MANUF.RAMBELL-US.US groups. The LEGAL.RAMBELL-US.US division has its own file server, LEGAL_US. This model is replicated at the other two Rambell locations. Pay careful attention to the placement of these servers. They will play a vital role in the partitioning, replication, and time environments in the next sections.

From a tree administration standpoint, Rambell is going to use a combination of the centralized and distributed models. Each Rambell site will have a distributed administrator to perform the day-to-day tasks required, like user creation and maintenance, printer environment configuration, and file system trustee assignments. However, all partitioning and replication of the NDS tree and the maintenance of the time synchronization environment will be performed by the IT.RAMBELL-US.US group. This way, the distributed administrators will not have to worry about the fault tolerance of the network.

Since Rambell started with NetWare 4.11, there are no legacy systems of concern. There are no bindery clients on the network, so Bindery Services are not a concern in the planning of the logical NDS tree structure. After deciding upon the structure for the NDS tree, John is ready to move onto the planning of the NDS back-end environment. He will rely upon this tree structure to appropriately partition and replicate the NDS database.

Plan the Partitioning & Replication Schemes

Again, John's main focus when planning the partition and replication of the NDS database is the WAN links. He wants to provide a fault-tolerant system that increases his users' accessibility; however, it needs to be balanced with network performance. Too much administrative traffic flowing across the WAN links is costly for the company.

Following our guidelines from earlier in this chapter, John is going to create a small number of partitions at the top of the tree. Figure 14-13 shows how John has partitioned the NDS database. There are three partitions—[Root], CA, and BM. Notice that these partitions reflect the physical topology of the network at the same time. John's partitions *do not* span the WAN links.

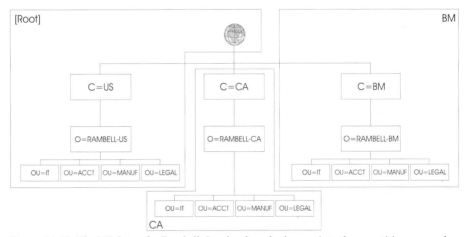

Figure 14-13: The NDS tree for Rambell, Inc. has been broken up into three partitions around the WAN links.

As we have already mentioned, each of Rambell, Inc.'s sites has about 500 employees. This means that each partition should not exceed 1,000 NDS objects. This falls in line with our recommendations concerning partitioning of the NDS database. There is no need to create more partitions because the partitions are small, and there are no more WAN links to accommodate. Partition traffic should be pretty well isolated to local sides of the WAN links.

In terms of replication for the partitions, John again follows the rules for the WAN links. He replicates in such a manner that partition synchronization traffic is localized to a specific site. There is a limited amount of synchronization traffic propagating across the WAN links. Table 14-4 shows the replication scheme John has designed for the NDS tree Willow. The names of the servers in the tree are listed by row, and the partitions are specified by column.

	[Root]	CA	BM
Damocles	Master	Subordinate Reference	Subordinate Reference
IT_US	Read/Write	Subordinate Reference	Subordinate Reference
LEGAL_US	Read/Write	Subordinate Reference	Subordinate Reference
Damon	No Replica	Master	No replica
IT_CA	No Replica	Read/Write	No replica
LEGAL_CA	No replica	Read/Write	No replica
Pythias	No replica	No replica	Master
IT_BM	No replica	No replica	Read/Write
LEGAL_BM	No replica	No replica	Read/Write

Table 14-4: Replication scheme for the partitions in the Willow NDS database.

Notice there are Subordinate Reference replicas for both the CA and BM partitions stored on three file servers—Damocles, IT_US, and LEGAL_US. This is because all three servers have a replica of [Root] but do not have a replica of the child partitions of [Root]. Thus, NDS places Subordinate Reference replicas on these servers. This means there is partition synchronization traffic flowing across the WAN link; however, this is not all bad because the Subordinate Reference replicas do not store all of the information about their partitions. They only store information about the partition root object. Since there will not be many changes to the Country objects or their immediate subordinates, the synchronization traffic propagating across the WAN links should be minimal.

In his scheme, John has created a replica ring with three replicas for each partition. This should provide users with an acceptable level of accessibility. In addition, no server stores more than three replicas. John is well within the established guidelines for replication. The replica types John has chosen also allow for user authentication on all servers in the NDS tree.

John has successfully balanced fault tolerance and accessibility with the performance of the network. Partition information has been isolated locally around the WAN links, and there is a minimal amount of replica synchronization traffic propagating across them. The next thing John needs to do is to ensure that user bandwidth is maximized to configure the time synchronization environment.

Plan the Time Synchronization Environment

The last thing John needs to do in planning the implementation of the NDS tree Willow is create the time synchronization environment. Because Rambell has less than 30 servers, it is a good candidate for the default time synchronization environment; however, there are WAN links to consider. Because of these WAN links, John really needs to implement a custom time synchronization environment, which will minimize the time synchronization traffic.

To implement the custom configuration, the first thing John needs to do is create the time provider group. He is going to keep the time provider group as small as possible. The time provider group is also going to span the WAN links to minimize the amount of time synchronization traffic. Figure 14-14 shows the custom time synchronization environment. Notice the placement of the Reference and Primary time servers. There are only three time providers on this network. The remaining six servers are all Secondary time servers.

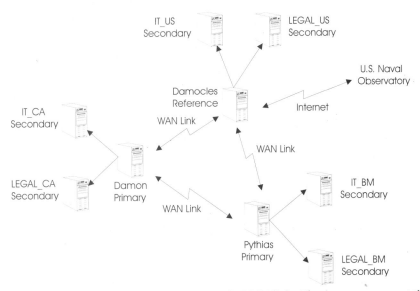

Figure 14-14: The time provider group spans the WAN links. The time consumers get their network time from the local time provider.

Because Damocles is the Reference server, it gets its network time from an external time source. In this case, John has configured Damocles to retrieve the network time from the U.S. Naval Observatory via the Internet. Damon and Pythias, being Primary time servers, slowly adjust their clock to the time reported by Damocles.

The other thing John will do to minimize the amount of time synchronization traffic is to disable the SAP communication feature of the time servers. They will each have a Configured Time Source List specifying the time servers from which they are allowed to get the network time. Damocles will be configured to contact both Damon and Pythias. This is necessary because the time provider groups must be able to speak with each other to vote upon the correct network time.

The remaining time consumers will get their network time from the local time provider. Thus, IT_US will get its network time from Damocles. IT_US will also have Damon and Pythias in its Configured Time Source List; however, they will appear lower in the list than Damocles. This way, if Damocles is down, IT_US will still be able to get the network time from a time provider. IT_US only gets its network time across a WAN link when its local time provider is unavailable. All of the Secondary time servers in the NDS tree Willow are configured in this manner. Figure 14-15 displays the TIMESYNC.CFG file IT_US uses with the Configured Time Source List to achieve this redundancy.

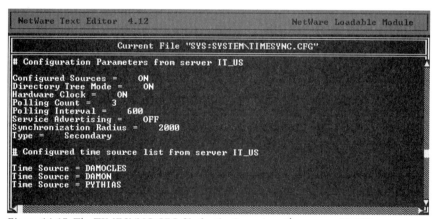

Figure 14-15: The TIMESYNC.CFG file for the Secondary time server IT_US.

The TIMESYNC.CFG file for the other Secondary time servers at the other Rambell sites will be similar; however, the first time server in the Configured Time Source List will be the time provider that is local. For example, IT_CA would have Damon listed as the first time provider in the Configured Time Source List. For more information on the Configured Time Source List and the custom time synchronization environment, refer to Chapter 11.

John has now successfully planned the NDS environment for the NDS tree Willow. All he has to do now is to implement it, as discussed in Chapters 9-12. While this in itself will be a time-consuming process, he already has the infrastructure thoughtfully planned. He will be able to save time in the long run because he will not need to interrupt the implementation to consider the consequences of his actions. Once implemented, John will have provided his company with an efficient network environment that maximizes the throughput across the WAN links while being sufficiently fault tolerant.

Moving On

This concludes our discussion of NDS. NDS is a subject on which volumes and volumes of information could be written; however, we have presented you with enough information to design and implement a thoughtfully planned NDS environment. You know how to create the security in your tree, partition and replicate the NDS database, and configure the time synchronization environment. You also know the general guidelines for providing the most efficient NDS environment for your company or organization.

In the next section of this book, we will regress a bit. Before we can implement an intranet using NDS, we need to fully understand how to manage the NetWare 4.11 server and configure the client workstations on the network. These components will play key roles in the creation of your intranet. Once we master the basics of LAN services, we will be able to discuss the services that can be added to NDS to provide a comprehensive intranet for your company.

Novell LAN Services

15

DOS/Windows Workstation Client

So far, we have concentrated on the NetWare 4.11 server and the network environment itself, NDS. These components of your network obviously play a key role in the successful implementation of network resource sharing at your place of work; however, the components cannot be used unless the client workstations are able to access the network.

In order for clients to connect to the network, the workstation must be set up with the Novell NetWare client software. The client software causes drivers to be installed on the workstation, which allows the workstation to talk to the network and communicate with the NetWare 4.11 server and the NDS tree. This client software must be loaded on the machine before your user can have access to the network.

Each workstation platform has its own specific software package that must be loaded to access the NetWare network. In this chapter, we will discuss the Novell client workstation software for the DOS/Windows 3.x client. There are two different clients that you can install on a DOS/Windows 3.x box to provide NetWare connectivity.

The 16-bit client, called the NetWare DOS Requester (also called the VLM client), is the older generation of NetWare clients. Although popular when NetWare 4.x was first released, it is becoming old technology. While Novell still supports this client for connecting to the NetWare environment, they will be dropping support for it in the future in favor of the new 32-bit client.

The 32-bit client, called NetWare Client32 for DOS/Windows, is another client packaged with IntranetWare for DOS/Windows-based machines. It makes use of the 32-bit Intel processor architecture and maximizes the efficiency of your workstation's memory as it provides you access to the NetWare environment.

In this chapter, we will discuss the hardware and software requirements needed at the workstation to install the software, the architecture of the workstation client, and the installation of the workstation client. We will briefly discuss the NetWare DOS Requester client and spend more time on the NetWare Client32 for DOS/Windows because it is the client that is recommended for installation.

But before we can install any client workstation software, we must set up the client workstation software installation files. This can be done during the initial installation of a NetWare 4.11 server, or it can be done later. We will show you how to install the installation files to the file server so you can set up your client workstation machines.

Preparing the Client Software for Installation

As we just mentioned, the client software for your workstations does not just come out of thin air. The client software is proprietary Novell software that comes packaged with IntranetWare. You must install the client installation software to a server, or set of floppy disks, before the client software can be installed to the local workstation.

The client workstation setup files are provided on the first CD of the IntranetWare package, labeled NetWare 4.11 Operating System. To install the installation files for the different NetWare clients, perform the following steps:

1. At the server console prompt, type **load install**. INSTALL.NLM will be loaded, and it will appear on the screen.

2. From the Installation Options menu of INSTALL.NLM, select Product Options by highlighting it and pressing Enter. The Other Installation Items/Products menu will appear (Figure 15-1).

3. From the Other Installation Items/Products list in Figure 15-1, select Create Client Installation Directories on Server by highlighting it and pressing Enter. INSTALL.NLM will prompt you for the location of the NetWare 4.11 installation files.

4. If you are installing the files from the same location you installed NetWare 4.11 on the server, press Enter. If you need to modify the default location, press F3 and type in the new location.

5. INSTALL.NLM will prompt you to select the clients you want to install on the NetWare 4.11 server, as shown in Figure 15-2. Clients that are marked with an X in the associated box will be installed to the server.

6. Mark the clients to be installed and press F10 to install the software. INSTALL.NLM will install the clients to the server and return you to the Other Installation Actions menu (Figure 15-1).

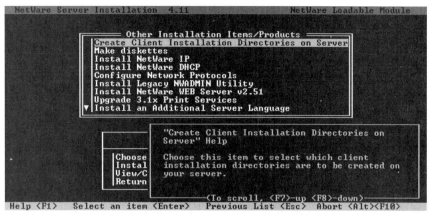

Figure 15-1: INSTALL.NLM allows you to install the client workstation setup programs to the NetWare 4.11 server.

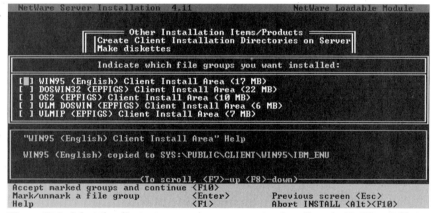

Figure 15-2: Select the client setup programs you want to install on the NetWare 4.11 server.

Currently, INSTALL.NLM allows you to install the clients for five different platforms on your NetWare 4.11 server. These clients are summarized in Table 15-1. Remember, just because you have installed the clients to the server does not mean the workstations will be able to connect. What you have installed with INSTALL.NLM is just the setup files for the client workstation software. You must run the actual client installation at each individual workstation to install the client software in the proper location.

File Group	NetWare Client Installed
WIN95	Client32 for Windows 95
DOSWIN32	Client 32 for DOS/Windows
OS2	NetWare Client for OS/2
VLM DOSWIN	NetWare DOS Requester
VLMIP	NetWare/IP client for NetWare DOS Requester

Table 15-1: INSTALL.NLM allows you to install five types of NetWare clients for your different workstation platforms.

Note the VLMIP file group in Table 15-1. The NetWare DOS Requester requires this extra file group to support NetWare/IP. Client32 for DOS/Windows and Client32 for Windows 95 comes with NetWare/IP support built in. You only need the VLMIP file group if you are using the older NetWare DOS Requester and you need NetWare/IP support at the client.

When INSTALL.NLM installs these file groups on your NetWare 4.11 server, they are installed to the SYS:\PUBLIC\CLIENT directory that is created at the time of installation. Each client will be given its own subdirectory in the CLIENT directory so you can easily locate it. To actually install the client software on the workstation, you must run the installation program from the appropriate client subdirectory.

Of course, if you do not have any clients currently connected to the network, you will not be able to run the client installation program off of the server. You will need to install the client software from floppy disks. INSTALL.NLM also comes with the ability to create floppy disks for client software installation. To create floppy disks, perform the following steps:

1. At the server console prompt, type **load install**. INSTALL.NLM will start, and the main menu will appear.

2. From the Installation Options menu, select Product Options by highlighting it and pressing Enter. The Other Installation Actions menu will appear.

3. From the Other Installation Items/Products list, select Make Diskettes by highlighting it and pressing Enter. INSTALL.NLM will prompt you for the location of the NetWare 4.11 installation files.

4. Specify the location and press Enter. To change the default location, press F3 and type in the new location.

5. INSTALL.NLM will prompt you for the products you want to install onto floppy disks. It also tells you the number of floppy disks required for a particular product. Select the desired products by marking them with an X in the appropriate box, as shown in Figure 15-3.

6. Press F10 to continue. By default, INSTALL.NLM will attempt to copy the necessary files to the server's floppy drive. You can change the path by pressing F3 and typing in a new path.

7. After the floppy disks are created, you will be returned to the Other Installation Actions menu of INSTALL.NLM.

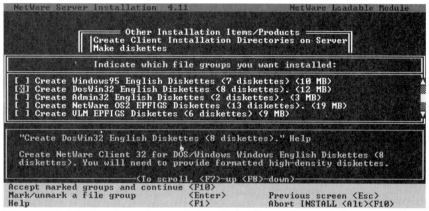

Figure 15-3: Selecting the products to be installed on floppy diskette.

Once you have copied the installation programs for the clients to the server or created the installation floppy disks, you are ready to set up your client workstations. In the next sections, we will discuss the clients for the DOS/Windows workstation. For more information on the Macintosh, Windows 95, and Windows NT clients, refer to Chapter 16.

The NetWare DOS Requester

The NetWare DOS Requester is the traditional client used to connect DOS/Windows 3.x machines to NetWare file servers. It is also responsible for authenticating the user to the NDS tree on your network. It has been around for a number of years and has been frequently updated by Novell. It is also the successor to the old bindery-based client shell NETX.EXE, which was used in the NetWare 3.x environment.

The advantage to using the NetWare DOS Requester with NetWare 4.11 is its NDS awareness. It understands the concept of the NDS tree and allows you to access it. You do not need to run Bindery Services on your NetWare 4.11 servers to provide access to users using this client.

But how does the client actually work? The NetWare DOS Requester, when installed, relies on the Open Datalink Interface (ODI) specification. Files are loaded at the workstation to allow the machine to talk to the network through the NIC installed in the machine. We will take a closer look at the architecture of the NetWare DOS Requester to help us understand how the workstation is able to communicate with the network.

The VLM Workstation Client Architecture

The advantage to using the VLM client on your workstation is that it has been built around the Open Datalink Interface (ODI) specification. This specification was developed jointly by Novell and Apple in 1989 as a means of standardizing adapter driver specifications. It allows manufacturers to develop drivers for their NICs that will be compatible with any network environment using the ODI specification.

There are two features of the ODI specification that are important to note. First, it gives a workstation the ability to support multiple adapters running the same or different protocols. Second, multiple protocols and frame types can be loaded and supported by a single network adapter.

For example, a workstation may need to use the IPX/SPX protocol to communicate with NetWare servers on your network. At the same time, the workstation may need TCP/IP services to communicate with the Internet. A workstation using the ODI interface will be able to communicate multiple protocols while using only one network card.

The NetWare DOS Requester employs the ODI interface when it loads the software to connect to the network. There are four programs that are loaded to facilitate the workstation's communication with the network. These programs are usually started by a file on the workstation called STARTNET.BAT. The following example shows a sample STARTNET.BAT from a workstation running the NetWare DOS Requester:

```
SET NWLANGUAGE = ENGLISH
C:\NWCLIENT\LSL.COM
C:\NWCLIENT\<MLID>
C:\NWCLIENT\IPXODI.COM
C:\NET\BIN\TCPIP.EXE
C:\NWCLIENT\VLM.EXE
```

When loaded, these files take up a significant amount of your conventional memory. You should use a memory manager (like MEMMAKER, included with MS-DOS 6.0 and above) to help you keep enough conventional memory free to run your normal DOS applications. By default, many of these network drivers will attempt to load into high memory to reduce the impact on conventional memory.

The software must be loaded in the prescribed order at the workstation for the NetWare DOS Requester to load successfully. But what do these files actually do? Let's take a closer look at each one to examine the role they play in connecting the client workstation to the network.

Figure 15-4 shows graphically how the NetWare DOS Requester works on the machine. At the bottom is the Multiple Link Interface Driver (MLID). On top of that is the Link Support Layer (LSL). Above the LSL is the IPXODI stack. Finally, at the top, you have the NetWare DOS Requester (VLM shell), which interfaces with the DOS operating system. Although the components are not loaded in this order at the workstation, this is how the components interact with one another.

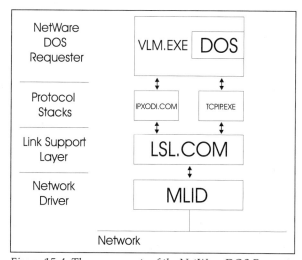

Figure 15-4: The components of the NetWare DOS Requester.

Multiple Link Interface Driver (MLID)

The Multiple Link Interface Driver (MLID) is the driver that is loaded to interface with the network card in the machine. It is a proprietary driver that is specific to the network card in the client workstation. For instance, the old Novell NE2000 network cards use the NE2000.COM MLID to enable the workstation to use the network card. The 3Com Etherlink III cards use the 3C5X9.COM MLID.

If you do not have the specific MLID for you network card, try loading NE2000.COM as your MLID for the NetWare DOS Requester. All network cards that are NE2000-compatible should be able to be interfaced using this particular driver; otherwise, contact the manufacturer of your card for the appropriate MLID.

Link Support Layer (LSL)

The Link Support Layer is one of the components that is critical in implementing the ODI interface on the NetWare client. To enable a single network card to handle multiple protocols, the LSL is required. It essentially acts as a traffic director for the incoming packets from the network. If a packet is picked up off the network, LSL will examine it and determine what kind of packet it is (TCP/IP packet, IPX packet, etc.). It will then route the packet to the appropriate protocol stack above it, as seen in Figure 15-4.

For example, if we picked up a TCP/IP packet off of the network, LSL would examine it and identify it as a TCP/IP packet. It would then forward that packet to the TCP/IP protocol stack (TCPIP.EXE), which would be able to appropriately interpret the packet and carry out the necessary function. If the TCP/IP protocol stack is not loaded on the workstation, the packet would be discarded. It is the function of the LSL to identify the nature of the packet and forward it to the appropriate place.

All of the protocol stacks are loaded on your workstation interface with LSL because it acts as the interpreter between the protocol stack and the network card driver (MLID). It must be loaded first in STARTNET.BAT.

Protocol Stacks

Sitting on top of the LSL are the protocol stacks themselves. These components are responsible for composing the network packets for information on its way out of the machine. The protocol stack takes data from a network application and adds additional information to it (like the source/destination address of the physical machines) to create a network packet. Once created, the network packet is then put out on the network.

The protocol stacks are also responsible for interpreting the incoming network packets after LSL has passed the packet to the protocol stack. At the target machine, the protocol stack removes the information the source machine added to the network packet. Once the application information has been extracted by the protocol stack, it is passed up to the NetWare DOS Requester for higher-level processing.

Each protocol you require on your workstation needs its own protocol stack. The component IPXODI.COM allows your workstation to communicate with the network via the IPX/SPX protocol. The TCPIP.EXE component allows your machine to communicate using the TCP/IP protocol. This modularity of the ODI interface allows you to load only the protocols you need on your workstation.

The NetWare DOS Requester

The NetWare DOS Requester is initiated by the VLM.EXE. VLM.EXE is actually a module manager that loads the virtual loadable modules (VLMs) on the client workstation to handle network services. The modules are broken down by specific network function, and you can configure which ones you want to load through the NET.CFG file. By default, all VLMs will load when VLM.EXE is loaded.

The NetWare DOS Requester actually surrounds the DOS kernel like a vise and enhances the features of DOS with respect to networking. Unlike the old NETX.EXE shell, DOS and the NetWare DOS Requester are actually able to share resources like the drive mapping tables to provide a more efficient and logical network environment.

When the NetWare DOS Requester is loaded at the client workstation, it relies upon a file called NET.CFG, which is located on the machine, for configuration information. This file contains parameters concerning the network card, the protocols used by the workstation, and the VLM manager. To customize your workstation, you must modify this file. For more information on NET.CFG and the NetWare DOS Requester, refer to the NetWare Client for DOS and Windows Technical Reference manual located in the NetWare 4.11 Clients collection of your online documentation.

Hardware/Software Requirements

Before you load the client software on your client workstation, you should be sure your client workstation is able to be a NetWare client. Table 15-2 summarizes the hardware and software requirements for the workstation. Make sure your workstation meets these minimum requirements before attempting to install the NetWare DOS Requester on the machine.

Hardware/Software Category	Minimum Requirement
Processor	IBM-PC compatible with an Intel 8088 or later CPU (80286, 80386, 80484, Pentium, or Pentium Pro).
Hard Disk Space	1.2MB free space for DOS files only. 4MB free space for additional Windows support.
Memory	640KB conventional memory.
Network Card	NetWare-compatible network card installed in the machine.
Network Cable	Client workstation must be connected to your physical network by a network cable attached to your network card.
Operating System	The DOS operating system is required. You must be running MS-DOS 3.3 or later, PC-DOS 3.0 or later, Novell DOS 7 or later, or DR-DOS 5 or later.
Windows	For Windows support, Windows 3.x must be running on the workstation.

Table 15-2: Hardware/software requirements for the NetWare DOS Requester.

Windows is actually optional on the workstation. You can run the NetWare DOS Requester on a machine without Windows 3.x; however, if your client workstation is running Windows 3.x, the NetWare DOS Requester provides Windows support and utilities.

Once you are sure your machine meets the minimum hardware and software requirements, you are ready to install the software. You can install it from the server if you have already connected to the server with an earlier shell (like the bindery-based NETX.EXE shell), or you can install it from floppy disks if you have created the disks as outlined earlier in this chapter.

NetWare DOS Requester Installation

To install the NetWare DOS Requester on your client workstation, you will need to use the installation program provided by Novell. It is either on the NetWare 4.11 server (if you installed the client files to the server) or on the floppy disks you created using INSTALL.NLM.

To begin the installation, run INSTALL.EXE from the SYS:PUBLIC\CLIENT\VLM\IBM_6 directory on the server or from the floppy drive. Windows must not be running when you execute this program. From the DOS prompt, change to the appropriate directory (or drive) and type **install**. After the install utility is started, the client installation menu will appear (Figure 15-5).

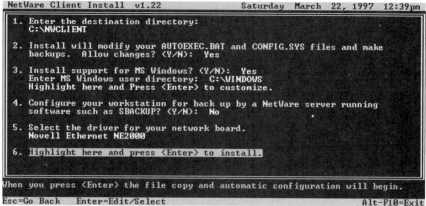

Figure 15-5: The client installation main menu.

Table 15-3 summarizes the options available in the main menu of the NetWare DOS Requester installation screen. Using this screen, you can customize the installation of the NetWare client to suit your needs.

Option Number	Option	Description
1	Destination Directory	Specifies the location where NetWare DOS Requester will be installed on the local hard drive.
2	Modify Startup Files	Lets the installation program make the appropriate changes to the workstation startup files. The command LASTDRIVE=Z will be added to CONFIG.SYS, and STARTNET.BAT will be called from AUTOEXEC.BAT.
3	Support for Windows	Allows you to install Windows support for the NetWare DOS Requester. When Yes is chosen, you must also specify the directory in which Windows is located.
4	Configure Workstation Backup	Installs SMS support on the workstation to facilitate workstation backup.
5	Select Network Board Driver	Allows you to select the appropriate MLID for the workstation from a list of available drivers. Press Enter to configure the MLID.
6	Begin Installation	Starts the installation of the NetWare DOS Requester on the workstation.

Table 15-3: Options for the NetWare DOS Requester installation program.

By default, the installation program will copy the files to the C:\NWCLIENT directory as well as update the Microsoft Windows settings. It will also create the STARTNET.BAT and NET.CFG file in the C:\NWCLIENT directory.

When the startup files are modified by the installation program, STARTNET.BAT is called from the AUTOEXEC.BAT file to load the network drivers during workstation boot. As the network drivers load on the workstation, the NET.CFG is located for configuration information. The following example shows a typical NET.CFG file:

```
Link Driver NE2000
    PORT 300
    INT 10
    MEM D4000
    FRAME ETHERNET_802.3

NetWare DOS Requester
    FIRST NETWORK DRIVE = F
    NETWARE PROTOCOL = NDS BIND
    NAME CONTEXT = "OU=MANUF.O=RAMBELL"
    PREFERRED SERVER = DAMOCLES
```

Connecting to the NetWare 4.11 Server

Once the NetWare DOS Requester has been installed on the client workstation and the network drivers are loaded, you will be able to connect to the NetWare environment. In the previous example of the NET.CFG file, you will notice the line First Network Drive = F. This specifies the drive that can be used to access the network. In this example, you would type **f:** at the DOS prompt to get to the network drive.

When the network drivers have successfully loaded, the client workstation sends out a packet looking for the nearest NetWare server. If the NetWare server is configured to respond to this Get Nearest Server packet, it will respond to the client workstation. The workstation is then *attached* to that particular NetWare server and has access to the server's LOGIN directory. That is the *only* directory to which the client workstation has access when not authenticated to NDS.

At the F:\LOGIN> prompt, you can log in to the network by typing **login**. This will cause the LOGIN.EXE program located in the SYS:LOGIN directory to be executed. When run, it prompts you for your login name and password to the NDS tree. Enter your name and password, and NDS will attempt to authenticate you to the NDS tree.

Unlike the NetWare 3.x LOGIN utility, the NetWare 4.11 LOGIN utility is also NDS-aware and looks for your particular user object in the NDS tree when you authenticate. If you type in your user object's distinguished name (with the beginning period), NDS will attempt to explicitly locate this object in the tree. If you use only a common name or a relative distinguished name to log in to the NDS tree, your workstation's current context is appended to the name, and NDS attempts to find that object in the tree.

If NDS cannot find the object you have specified as your login name, it will look for your user object in the same context as the NetWare 4.11 server. If it does not find the object there, it will deny you access to the tree. It is important you understand NDS naming techniques when you log in to the NDS tree or else you will have a difficult time gaining access to your NetWare environment. For more information on naming conventions, refer to Chapter 3.

For example, John Doe is trying to access the file server Damocles after installing the NetWare DOS Requester on his client workstation. His user object's distinguished name is .jdoe.it.rambell. The server's context is ACCT.RAMBELL, and the workstation's current context is MANUF.RAMBELL, as it was set in the Name Context field of the NET.CFG file. After the network drivers are loaded, John switches to the F: drive and tries to log in to the NDS tree.

At the prompt for his login name, he types jdoe. The first thing the workstation client does is append its current context because John did not specify a distinguished name. Thus, the object name passed to NDS is .jdoe.manuf.rambell. Of course, John does not exist in this context, so NDS attempts to locate the user object jdoe in the same context as the server, ACCT.RAMBELL. It cannot find John's user object here either, so John is denied access to the NDS tree. In this example, John needs to type .jdoe.it.rambell at the login name prompt to successfully access the NDS tree. Once NDS finds the specified user object, he will be prompted for his password.

In an NDS tree with multiple servers or NDS trees, you can specify which server or tree you want to access using the command-line parameters of the LOGIN utility. The syntax for the command-line parameters is as follows:

```
LOGIN [server_name|tree_name/][user_name] [/options]
```

For example, if you wanted to log in to the file server Damon as jdoe, you could type **login damon/.jdoe.it.rambell** at the F:\LOGIN> prompt. The LOGIN utility will attempt to authenticate you to Damon as the specified user. LOGIN also has some command-line options that can be used when the utility executes. These commands are summarized in Table 15-4.

LOGIN Option	Description
/NS	LOGIN is executed without running any login scripts.
/CLS	Clears the screen before executing the login scripts.
/S filename	Forces the login script specified by filename to run.
/B	Forces a bindery-mode connection to the NetWare server.
/TREE	Authenticates to the tree name specified.
/SWAP path	When running login script commands, forces the machine to swap LOGIN to different memory or to the hard drive with the path specified.
/NB	Causes login banner to not be displayed.
/VER	Displays LOGIN utility version information.

Table 15-4: Command-line options for the LOGIN utility.

Once you are authenticated to the NDS tree using the LOGIN utility, you will be able to access the network resources. For more information on LOGIN and the scripting ability associated with LOGIN, refer to Chapter 5.

As we have mentioned, the NetWare DOS Requester, while supported by Novell, is not the recommended client for connecting to the NetWare 4.11 server. The NetWare Client32 for DOS/Windows is a better client in terms of workstation memory management and provides you with extra features not included with the NetWare DOS Requester. In the next section, we will discuss Client32 for DOS/Windows 3.x and how it is used to connect to the NetWare environment.

NetWare Client32 for DOS/Windows 3.x

There are many differences between Novell's 32-bit clients and the older DOS Requester. The newer 32-bit client technology, which is available for all three platforms (Microsoft Windows 3.x, Windows 95, and Windows NT) has many more features, is faster, and requires fewer system resources to run.

Some of the advantages of the IntranetWare client over the DOS Requester are:

- Runs in protected mode. The client uses NetWare Loadable Modules (NLMs) similar to those that run on the NetWare server. Because the client is in protected mode, other programs cannot interfere with the memory that the client has reserved.

- A Windows GUI login utility. Users can log in after entering Windows using this tool or from within DOS using the traditional LOGIN.EXE. This feature gives users the opportunity to log in and log out of the network without closing down Windows. This was not supported with the VLM client.

- Authentication to multiple NDS trees using the NetWare User tool. This is another feature that was not supported in the VLM client. With the VLM client, the only way to authenticate to resources in other NDS trees simultaneously was to attach to the additional file servers using bindery emulation. The Client32 architecture allows users to authenticate to multiple trees through NDS.

- Automatic reconnection to the network if the network goes down. When the network itself is restored, Client32 will restore the connections to the network resources automatically so the machine does not need to be rebooted.

- Lower memory requirements (less than 4KB of conventional memory). The lower memory requirements free up needed system resources, which will alleviate memory problems associated with loading multiple Terminate and Stay Resident (TSR) programs, as in the VLM client.

- Larger network cache sizes at the local workstation that speed up access to NetWare services.

- 32-bit LAN drivers in .LAN format that use the same format as 32-bit LAN drivers that NetWare servers use. These are protected mode drivers that are more stable than the 16-bit real mode drivers.

- Support for multiple network cards in the client workstation. You can connect the machine to multiple networks or provide fault tolerance by configuring the multiple cards to connect to the same network.

Just as we did for the NetWare DOS Requester client, we will discuss the architecture of the NetWare Client32 for DOS/Windows to give you a better understanding of how the client works and which files are invoked to establish the network connection. Client32 is made up of more components than the NetWare DOS Requester, which are layered one on top of the other to provide the network client.

NetWare Client32 for DOS/Windows Architecture

While similar in its layered architecture to the NetWare DOS Requester, NetWare Client32 for DOS/Windows represents an advance in technology. The use of protected mode drivers and extended memory helps the performance of the client and removes the majority of the client software from conventional memory. This improves the stability of the machine.

NetWare Client32 for DOS/Windows also marks a change in the types of modules that are loaded at the client workstation. It used to be that NetWare Loadable Modules (NLMs) were only loaded on the server. That is no longer true. An executable called NIOS.EXE is responsible for loaded 32-bit NLM drivers at the client workstation. These are the drivers that provide network connectivity for the workstation.

Client32 Required Files: STARTNET.BAT

NetWare Client32 for DOS/Windows is normally started from a file called STARTNET.BAT. This file is responsible for containing all of the necessary components required to successfully load the NetWare client. A sample STARTNET.BAT file is shown in Figure 15-6.

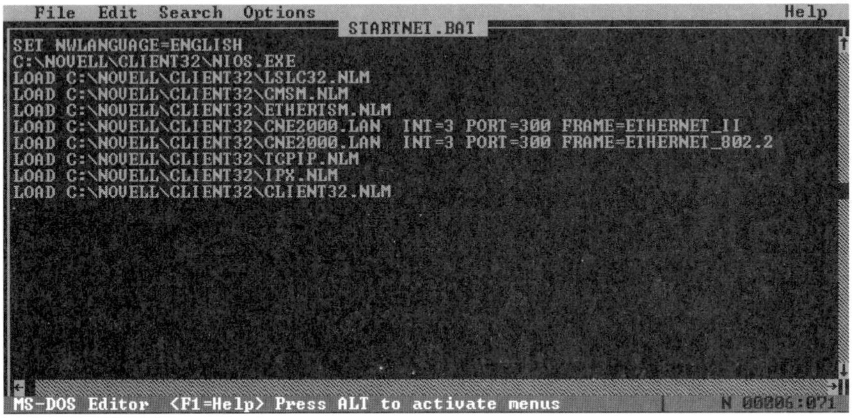

```
 File   Edit   Search   Options                                    Help
                              STARTNET.BAT
SET NWLANGUAGE=ENGLISH
C:\NOVELL\CLIENT32\NIOS.EXE
LOAD C:\NOVELL\CLIENT32\LSLC32.NLM
LOAD C:\NOVELL\CLIENT32\CMSM.NLM
LOAD C:\NOVELL\CLIENT32\ETHERISM.NLM
LOAD C:\NOVELL\CLIENT32\CNE2000.LAN   INT=3 PORT=300 FRAME=ETHERNET_II
LOAD C:\NOVELL\CLIENT32\CNE2000.LAN   INT=3 PORT=300 FRAME=ETHERNET_802.2
LOAD C:\NOVELL\CLIENT32\TCPIP.NLM
LOAD C:\NOVELL\CLIENT32\IPX.NLM
LOAD C:\NOVELL\CLIENT32\CLIENT32.NLM



MS-DOS Editor   <F1=Help> Press ALT to activate menus          N 00306:071
```

Figure 15-6: A sample Client32 for DOS/Windows STARTNET.BAT file.

Notice that the driver for the network card now has a .LAN extension. These network drivers are the same drivers that are loaded on the server itself, which ensures compatibility with currently released LAN drivers. If you do not have the specific LAN driver for your network board, contact your manufacturer and request the 32-bit ODI LAN driver for NetWare servers and load it on your workstation.

Like the NetWare DOS Requester, the drivers for Client32 must be loaded in a specific order. This order is reflected in the sample STARTNET.BAT file in Figure 15-6. Let's examine each line and discuss the purpose of the specific driver or command.

SET NWLANGUAGE=ENGLISH

This line is responsible for establishing the language support for the NetWare Client32. In our example, we are setting up the client to provide messages in English. Novell provides support for many different languages, and you can configure the client to display a number of languages assuming the appropriate language support was installed on the server. This line is necessary for the successful loading of Client32.

C:\NOVELL\CLIENT32\NIOS.EXE

This is the NetWare Input/Output Subsystem that manages the Client32 modules. It is responsible for loading and unloading the 32-bit drivers for the remainder of the STARTNET.BAT file. You will notice that each successive line after the line that executes NIOS.EXE starts with the command LOAD. This command is the same LOAD command that is used to load NLMs at the server.

To load any of the 32-bit drivers for Client32, you must start NIOS.EXE first. Then you can use the LOAD command at the DOS prompt to load any of the drivers you want. You can also use the UNLOAD command at the DOS prompt to remove a driver from memory.

NIOS.EXE also allows you to perform some other commands at the DOS prompt to display information about your Client32 setup. Once NIOS.EXE is loaded, you can type **modules** at the DOS prompt to see all of the Client32 modules loaded on the workstation. You can also enable logging of network client events by typing **enable logging** at the DOS prompt.

This feature will create a log file called NIOS.LOG in the Client32 working directory. You can stop Client32 from logging network events by typing **disable logging** at the DOS prompt.

LOAD C:\NOVELL\CLIENT32\LSLC32.NLM

LSLC32.NLM is the 32-bit Link Support Layer module, which allows the NIC to run multiple protocols. It serves the same function in Client32 that the 16-bit Link Support Layer provided in the NetWare DOS Requester. It essentially directs the incoming network packets to the appropriate protocol stack for further processing.

LOAD C:\NOVELL\CLIENT32\CMSM.NLM

The relationship between the network card driver and the LSL is a complex one. As they communicate with one another, the data they exchange can be grouped into one of two categories. The first category of information exchanged between the network card driver and the LSL is generic information like initialization and run-time issues. These issues are common to all network drivers regardless of manufacturer or network topology.

CMSM.NLM is the Media Support Module, which manages the communication of this common information between the network card driver and the LSL.

LOAD C:\NOVELL\CLIENT32\ETHERTSM.NLM

The other type of information exchanged between the network card driver and the LSL is information that is network topology specific. This module is called the Topology Specific Module (TSM). The TSM you load for your network will depend upon your network topology.

In our example, we are connecting to an Ethernet network, so we need the Ethernet TSM called ETHERTSM.NLM. There are TSMs for other network topologies. You must select the appropriate TSM for your network topology. A list of currently available TSMs is given in Table 15-5.

Tip

You must select the appropriate TSM for your network. If you have a Token Ring network, you cannot use ETHERTSM.NLM in your STARTNET.BAT file. You must use TOKENTSM.NLM at the client workstation.

Network Topology	Required Client32 TSM
Ethernet	ETHERTSM.NLM
Token Ring	TOKENTSM.NLM
FDDI	FDDITSM.NLM

Table 15-5: Topology Specific Modules for Client32.

LOAD C:\NOVELL\CLIENT32\CNE2000.LAN

The next thing to load in STARTNET.BAT is the Multiple Link Interface Driver (MLID). This is the 32-bit network card driver that is responsible for providing the workstation information about how to use the network card to communicate with the network. In our example, we are using a Novell NE2000 NIC to communicate with the network. Thus, we need to load the CNE2000.LAN driver for the machine to communicate with the network card.

The 32-bit driver you will load at your workstation is specific to your network card. If you have a 3Com Etherlink III network card installed in your machine, you would need to load the 3C5X9.LAN driver in your STARTNET.BAT.

You will notice from Figure 15-6 that the CNE2000.LAN driver has some extra parameters following it. This is a new development in the Client32 architecture that applies specifically to 32-bit LAN drivers. When you load the driver, you also need to specify the parameter information about the network card. This information includes interrupt used, address port used, and frame type of the network.

Those of you who are familiar with the NetWare DOS Requester will immediately identify these parameters as the information specified in the Link Driver section of the NetWare DOS Requester NET.CFG file. For 32-bit LAN drivers, you do not need a Link Driver section in your NET.CFG file. You specify these parameters on the command line when loading the LAN driver. Table 15-6 lists some common parameters for the 32-bit LAN driver and provides a brief description of each one.

LAN Driver Parameter	Description
INT	Specifies the interrupt used by the network card.
PORT	Specifies the address port used by the network card.
FRAME	Specifies the network frame type with which the network card will be communicating.

Table 15-6: Common command-line parameters for the 32-bit LAN driver.

In our example in Figure 15-6, you will see that the CNE2000.LAN driver is loading with some command-line parameters. These parameters specify the network card's interrupt to be 3, the address port to be 300, and the frame type to be Ethernet_II. You will also notice that CNE2000.LAN is loaded more than once in STARTNET.BAT. The LAN driver must be loaded once for each frame type you will be using on your network.

In our example, we are connected to a network that is using both the Ethernet_802.2 and Ethernet_II frame types. They are used to communicate with the network via IPX and TCP/IP respectively. CNE2000.LAN must be loaded once for each frame type being used. In Figure 15-6, you see CNE2000.LAN loaded first with the Ethernet_II frame type. It is then loaded again with the Ethernet_802.2 frame type.

LOAD C:\NOVELL\CLIENT32\SROUTE.NLM

Although this line is not shown in our example, it is still an important line to know about. If you are running a Token Ring network and you need to provide source routing, you can use SROUTE.NLM to do so. SROUTE.NLM can only be used with 32-bit LAN drivers. If you are using a 16-bit LAN driver, you must use ROUTE.COM at the client.

LOAD C:\NOVELL\CLIENT32\TCPIP.NLM

Loading TCPIP.NLM allows your machine to communicate with the network using the TCP/IP protocol. If you need to provide Internet access to your client workstations or are setting up NetWare/IP services, this NLM will need to load in STARTNET.BAT after the LAN driver is loaded. For more information on installing and configuring TCP/IP at the workstation, refer to "Installing & Configuring Workstation TCP/IP" later in this chapter.

`LOAD C:\NOVELL\CLIENT32\IPX.NLM`

IPX.NLM allows your machine to communicate with the network using the IPX protocol. This protocol stack is responsible for generating the IPX packets necessary to communicate with the NetWare environment. It also decodes the IPX packets as they come into the machine. You need to load IPX.NLM after the MLID has been loaded.

`LOAD C:\NOVELL\CLIENT32\CLIENT32.NLM`

The CLIENT32.NLM is what provides network services for the user at the workstation. It acts as the liaison between the DOS operating system and the network drivers. Much like VLM.EXE with the NetWare DOS Requester, CLIENT32.NLM is the interface the user sees and uses when using NetWare network resources. This module must be loaded last. Once loaded, it establishes a connection with the nearest NetWare server that replies to its request. When CLIENT32.NLM is loaded, the user can log in to the NDS tree and use the network.

Understanding Client32 File Relationships

Just like with the NetWare DOS Requester, the order the files load does not accurately reflect their relationships with one another. Figure 15-7 shows how the required files build upon one another to provide network services at the workstation.

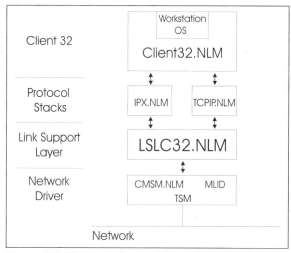

Figure 15-7: NetWare Client32 for DOS/Windows file relationships.

At the bottom of the stack are the three files that facilitate communication with the network card. These are the LAN driver, the Media Support Module, and the Topology Specific Module. They work at the lowest level of the client to provide physical network connection to the network.

On top of those modules is the Link Support Layer. Again, this layer is responsible for acting as a traffic director. It redirects the packets coming from the network card to the appropriate protocol stack. Thus, a TCP/IP packet coming into the machine will be directed to the TCP/IP protocol stack by the LSL. An IPX packet will be directed to the IPX protocol stack.

Sitting on top of the LSL are the protocol stacks. These are the "languages" that the computer can speak. A protocol stack is loaded for each protocol the workstation will be using. The most common protocols used by Client32 are IPX and TCP/IP.

Sitting on top of the protocol stack is Client32 itself. It provides the layer between the workstation's operating system and the network drivers necessary to communicate with the network. Client32 is critical in providing NetWare services to the client workstation.

To this point, we have explored the Client32 files that are necessary to provide NetWare services at the client workstation. Besides the STARTNET.BAT file, which is responsible for loading the client at the workstation, there is another file called NET.CFG, which holds the configuration information for Client32. This file is read when Client32 loads; it helps you customize Client32 for your particular network environment.

The Role of NET.CFG in Client32

During the installation of the NetWare Client32 for DOS/Windows, a file called NET.CFG is created. The NET.CFG file is an ASCII text file that can be opened and edited by any ASCII text editing utility (such as the DOS EDIT.COM utility or Windows Notepad). If you were to open this file, you would see that it is broken up into sections marked by headers. Each header is followed by a list of parameters and values.

The purpose of the NET.CFG file is to provide configuration information for the various Client32 modules you load on the workstation. When the module is loaded, it looks in this NET.CFG file for its particular section. If it finds it, it reads the list of variables and their values and uses them in the network environment. You can customize how a module initializes and functions by editing the appropriate section of the NET.CFG file. Figure 15-8 shows a sample NET.CFG file from a workstation using Client32.

```
  File   Edit   Search   Options                                    Help
                                    NET.CFG
Link Support
         MAX BUFFER SIZE 4736

Protocol IPX
         IPX SOCKETS 40

NetWare DOS Requester
         FIRST NETWORK DRIVE F
         SHORT MACHINE TYPE IBM
         NETWARE PROTOCOL NDS BIND
         NAME CONTEXT "OU=IT.O=RAMBELL"
         SHOW DOTS ON
         PREFERRED TREE WILLOW
         FILE HANDLES 120

Protocol TCPIP
         PATH TCP_CFG C:\NOVELL\CLIENT32\TCP
         IP_ADDRESS 204.32.75.5
         IP_ROUTER 204.32.75.250
         IP_NETMASK 255.255.255.0

MS-DOS Editor  <F1=Help> Press ALT to activate menus        N 00016:009
```

Figure 15-8: The NET.CFG file is composed of sections, each with a list of variables.

As we have mentioned, each section is specific to a Client32 module loaded at the workstation. In our example in Figure 15-8, when the IPX protocol stack loads, it sets the number of IPX sockets for the workstation to 40. Likewise, when CLIENT32.NLM loads, it looks for the NetWare DOS Requester section and sets the values for the variables accordingly. For instance, the preferred NDS tree to which we will attach is Willow.

You will notice that each section starts with a specific key word(s), which appears next to the left margin. The variables are then indented underneath the section header. A new section starts when there is a new section header. For example, the NET.CFG file has four sections. They are Link Support, Protocol IPX, NetWare DOS Requester, and Protocol TCP/IP.

While the NET.CFG file is simple in structure and easy to comprehend, there are many sections and variables that can be specified in the file. Table 15-7 summarizes the sections you can have in the NET.CFG file and provides a brief description for each section.

As a network administrator, you will probably never use half of the section headers to configure your client workstations. You will generally use a specific subset of headers to customize your network environment. Most often, you will use the NetWare DOS Requester, Protocol IPX, and Protocol TCP/IP sections to configure Client32. Tables 15-8, 15-9, and 15-10 provide a list of the most commonly used variables associated with the NetWare DOS Requester, Protocol IPX, and Protocol TCP/IP sections, respectively.

NET.CFG Section Header	Description
Desktop SNMP	Provides client Simple Network Management Protocol (SNMP) support at the workstation.
Host MIB	Provides information concerning local machine resources (hardware/software) for Host Resources Management Information Base (MIB).
Link Driver	Sets parameters for network boards using a 16-bit ODI driver. *This section is not used for 32-bit LAN drivers.*
Link Support	Sets parameters for the 32-bit version (LSLC32.NLM) and 16-bit version (LSL.COM) of the Link Support Layer.
Named Pipes	Provides information concerning the Named Pipes protocol.
NetBIOS	Provides information concerning the NetBIOS protocol.
NetWare DOS Requester	Customizes the client networking environment. Includes settings for preferred NDS tree, current context, and first network drive. This section is used by CLIENT32.NLM.
NetWare DOS TSA	Provides information concerning the SMS-backup Target Service Agent (TSA) for the DOS client workstation.
NIOS	Configures the NetWare Input/Output Subsystem. Used by NIOS.EXE when it is loaded.
NWIP	Provides information concerning the NetWare/IP client. For more information on this section, refer to Chapter 19.
Protocol IPX	Configures the IPX protocol stack. This section is used by IPX.NLM when it is loaded.
Protocol TCP/IP	Provides information concerning the TCP/IP protocol. The information includes workstation IP address, IP gateway, and subnet mask.
SNMP Transport Provider	Provides information concerning the trap target addresses for workstations configured to use SNMP.

Table 15-7: Available section headers for the NET.CFG file.

NetWare DOS Requester Variable	Valid Settings (Default)	Description
First Network Drive	A-Z (first available drive)	Determines the first drive letter that can be used for mapping network resources.
Name Context	Any valid NDS tree context	Sets the current context for the workstation in the NDS tree.
NetWare Protocol	NDS BIND *or* BIND NDS (NDS BIND)	Specifies NetWare connection preference. When BIND is listed first, the client tries to make a bindery connection to the server first. NDS first means the workstation prefers NDS connections.
Network Printers	0-9 (3)	Determines the number of LPT ports that can be assigned to network printers by Client 32.
Preferred Server	Any valid NetWare server name	Determines the server to which the client workstation will first attach.
Preferred Tree	Any valid NDS tree name	Determines the NDS tree to which the client workstation will first attach.
Set Station Time	On, Off (On)	Determines whether the workstation will synchronize its time to that of the NDS tree when it attaches.
Short Machine Type	Any valid string 1-4 characters in length (IBM)	Specifies the value of the variable Short Machine Type.
Show Dots	On, Off (On)	Determines whether or not Client32 shows the dots for parent directories in the navigation of the file system.

Table 15-8: Frequently used variables in the NetWare DOS Requester section of the NET.CFG file.

Protocol IPX Variable	Valid Settings (Default)	Description
IPX Diagnostics	On, Off (On)	Enables or disables the IPX diagnostics function.
IPX Retry Count	0-65535 (20)	Determines the number of times the workstation will attempt to contact its destination before aborting.
Net Bind	Any valid frame type	By default, IPX binds to all network boards and their associated frame types. You can limit the boards to which IPX binds by using this variable.

Table 15-9: Frequently used variables in the Protocol IPX section of the NET.CFG file.

Protocol TCPIP Variable	Valid Settings (Default)	Description
IP_address	Any valid IP address	Determines the IP address of the workstation.
IP_netmask	Any valid IP subnet mask	Determines the IP subnet mask of the workstation.
IP_router	Any valid IP address	Specifies the default router IP address. Up to three default routers can be specified.
Path TCP_CFG	Any valid local file system path (none)	Determines the location of the required TCP/IP configuration files.

Table 15-10: Frequently used variables in the Protocol TCP/IP section of the NET.CFG file.

This concludes our discussion of the architecture of the NetWare Client32 for DOS/Windows. The two main files used to load and configure the client are STARTNET.BAT and NET.CFG. These files are created during the installation of Client32 on the workstation. But before we get to the actual installation of Client32, we need to make sure your workstation meets the minimum requirements for running Client32.

Hardware/Software Requirements

Table 15-11 summarizes the hardware and software requirements for Client32. Make sure your workstation meets these minimum requirements before attempting to install the NetWare Client32 for DOS/Windows on the machine.

Hardware/Software Category	Minimum Requirement
Processor	IBM/PC compatible with an Intel 80386 or later CPU (80484, Pentium, or Pentium Pro).
Hard Disk Space	At least 3MB free disk space.
Memory	At least 4MB RAM.
Memory Manager	Memory manager required—HIMEM.SYS, EMM386.EXE, QEMM, or 386MAX.
Network Card	A NetWare-compatible network card installed in the machine with an appropriate LAN driver.
Network Cable	Client workstation must be connected to your physical network by a network cable attached to your network card.
Operating System	MS-DOS 5.0 or later, PC-DOS 5.0 or later, Novell DOS 7 or later.
Windows	For Windows support, Windows 3.x must be running on the workstation.

Table 15-11: Hardware/software requirements for the NetWare Client32 for DOS/Windows.

Windows is actually optional on the workstation. You can run the NetWare Client32 for DOS/Windows on a machine without Windows 3.x; however, if your client workstation is running Windows 3.x, the NetWare Client32 for DOS/Windows provides Windows support and utilities.

You will notice a memory manager is required for Client32 in addition to 4MB of RAM. This is because Client32 will use Extended Memory (XMS) for its modules. Only NIOS.EXE requires conventional memory. Thus, less than 5KB of conventional memory is used by Client32, which makes the client workstation more efficient. It also prevents Client32 from competing with other TSR programs for system resources.

Once you are sure your workstation can handle the Client32 software, it is time to install it. There are actually two separate installation programs for NetWare Client32 for DOS/Windows. One is DOS based and the other is Windows based. We will cover the Windows-based installation in the next section.

NetWare Client32 for DOS/Windows Installation

To install NetWare Client32 for DOS/Windows, you must already have pre-pared the installation files. They should be sitting on your NetWare 4.11 server or have been installed to floppy disk. If you have not done this, refer to "Pre-paring the Client Software for Installation" earlier in this chapter. Once you have the client installation program ready, it is time to install Client32.

There are two separate installation programs you can use to install NetWare Client32 for DOS/Windows. One is a DOS-based program (INSTALL.EXE), and the other one is a Windows-based program (SETUP.EXE). Both will install the client software, and both installation programs will also install Windows support files.

If you are running Windows on your workstation, you should run the Windows-based installation program. It will provide a cleaner installation. In this section, we are only going to discuss the installation process for SETUP.EXE; however, the installation using INSTALL.EXE is very similar. In fact, the options are the same; you do not have the nice GUI you do in the Windows-based SETUP.EXE.

Tip

If you are only using DOS on your workstation, use INSTALL.EXE. If you have Windows and plan to use Client32, use SETUP.EXE.

To install Client32 for DOS/Windows, prepare your workstation to use whatever installation media you are providing. For instance, if you are running the installation off of a file server, you should have connected to the server and mapped a drive to the installation directory. If you are using a floppy, the floppy disk should be in the floppy drive. Perform the following steps to install Client32 for DOS/Windows:

1. Make sure Windows has been started. From Program Manager, choose File | Run and specify the path to the SETUP.EXE file for the Client32 installation. If you have installed the installation files on a server, SETUP.EXE will be located in the SYS:PUBLIC\CLIENT\DOSWIN32\IBM_6 directory of the NetWare file server. Click OK once the path has been specified. The installation program will start.

2. On the first screen, you will be prompted to choose a language for Client32. Select the desired language and click on the OK button.

3. The Client32 welcome screen will appear. Read the information on the screen and click on Continue when finished.

4. The Software License Agreement dialog box will appear. Read the license agreement and click on Yes to accept the terms of the agreement. The Directory Locations dialog box will appear.

5. In the Directory Locations dialog box, specify the locations for the target directory and the Windows directory. The target directory is the place where the actual Client32 program files will be installed. By default this is C:\NOVELL\CLIENT32. The Windows directory is required for the Windows support files. Its default is C:\WINDOWS. Specify the directories and click on the Next button. The ODI Driver Selection dialog box will appear.

6. In the ODI Driver Selection dialog box, shown in Figure 15-9, use the Board drop-down list to select the type of network adapter that is installed in your workstation. You have the option to select 32-bit or 16-bit LAN drivers for your workstation. We recommend you use the 32-bit LAN drivers. Modify the parameters for the LAN driver by clicking on the Driver Settings button.

   Clicking on the Driver Settings button will allow you to set the network adapter's interrupt, port, and frame type. These settings will be associated with the MLID driver load line in the STARTNET.BAT file. For more information on command-line options associated with the 32-bit LAN driver adapters, refer to "NetWare Client32 for DOS/Windows Architecture" earlier in this chapter.

Clicking on the Other Boards button will allow you to select an adapter that is not listed. Usually, the manufacturer supplies a driver with the adapter card on an installation disk, or it may be possible to download the driver from the manufacturer's site on the Internet. For Client32, you will need the 32-bit driver, which is normally loaded on the server.

Once you have selected the MLID for your network adapter, click on the Next button in the ODI Driver Selection dialog box. This will cause the Additional Options dialog box to appear.

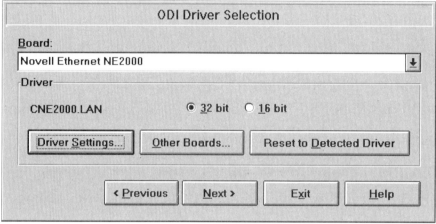

Figure 15-9: The ODI Driver Selection dialog box is used to select the LAN driver for your workstation.

Tip

It bears repeating that if a 32-bit driver is available for the adapter installed in the workstation, it is the driver that should be used. The 32-bit drivers are faster and more reliable than the 16-bit drivers.

7. In the Additional Options dialog box, shown in Figure 15-10, select the extra options you would like installed with Client32. You have the choice to install TCP/IP (with or without NetWare/IP support), SNMP, TSA for SMS, and NetWare IPX/IP Gateway support. A box with an X in it will cause the installation program to install support for that particular product. Table 15-12 provides a brief description of the options available from the Additional Options dialog box. You also have the option to load Client32 automatically when the machine boots. To select this option,

make sure the box to the left of Update AUTOEXEC.BAT to Load NetWare Client 32 is checked. By default, IPX support is always installed during the installation of Client32. Click on the Next button once you are finished.

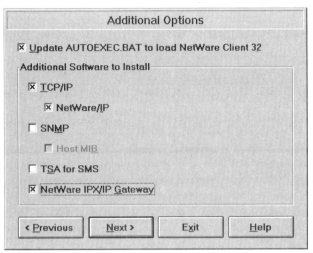

Figure 15-10: The Additional Options dialog box allows you to select additional products to install.

Software Option	Description
TCP/IP	Installs the Client32 TCP/IP files, which allow your workstation to communicate with the network using the TCP/IP protocol.
NetWare/IP	Installs the NetWare/IP client software on the workstation. For more information on this product refer to Chapter 19.
SNMP	Installs support for Simple Network Management Protocol (SNMP), which allows you to manage the computer remotely. Only use it if you have SNMP set up on your network.
Host MIB	Installs Host Resource Management Information Base (MIB) support on the client workstation.
TSA for SMS	Installs the workstation Target Service Agent (TSA) to enable workstation backups using a Storage Management Services (SMS)-backup-compliant package.
NetWare IPX/IP Gateway	Installs support for the NetWare IPX/IP Gateway. For more information on this product, refer to Chapter 20, "WAN Connectivity."

Table 15-12: Software options in the Additional Options dialog box.

8. If you have installed TCP/IP, the TCP/IP Configuration box will appear. Type in the information concerning the TCP/IP environment for the workstation. This information includes IP address, default router IP address, subnet mask, domain name, and the IP address of the DNS server on your network. Click on the Next button when you are finished.

9. If you have chosen to install NetWare/IP support, the NetWare/IP Configuration dialog box will appear. You will be prompted for the information concerning your NetWare/IP environment, including NetWare/IP domain name, preferred Domain SAP/RIP Server (DSS), and nearest NetWare/IP server. For more information on the NetWare/IP environment, refer to Chapter 19. After providing this information click on the Next button.

10. If you have chosen to install SNMP support, the SNMP Configuration dialog box will appear. You will be prompted for information concerning your SNMP environment, including workstation name, workstation location, contact name, and trap target addresses. After providing this information, click on the Next button.

11. If you have chosen to install Host MIB support, the Host Resources MIB Configuration dialog box appears. You will be prompted to enter information about your local hardware and software resources. When you are finished inputting this information, click on the Next button.

12. If you have chosen to install TSA for SMS, the TSA for SMS Configuration dialog box will appear. You will be prompted to input information concerning your SMS environment, including TSA server name, workstation name, password, local drives to be backed up, and the number of transfer buffers. Click on the Next button when you have finished configuring the SMS environment.

13. After you have configured all of the environments you have chosen, the installation program will begin to install NetWare Client32 for DOS/Windows. You will see a progress bar indicating the status of the installation program. When it is complete, the Installation Complete dialog box will appear (Figure 15-11). Click on the desired option and then click OK. It is recommended that you restart your computer to use the features of Client32.

Figure 15-11: The Installation Complete dialog box notifies you of the successful installation of Client32.

Once the machine reboots, you will be able to connect to your NetWare environment using NetWare Client32 for DOS/Windows. You are able to connect using the DOS-based utility LOGIN.EXE, or you can use the Windows login feature of Client32 to authenticate to the network after you have started Windows. This is a feature not available with the NetWare DOS Requester.

After the installation of NetWare Client32 for DOS/Windows, there have been some changes made to your workstation. The following files have been modified by the installation program to provide support for Client32:

- **CONFIG.SYS**   The command LASTDRIVE=Z is added for Client32 support.

- **AUTOEXEC.BAT**   The directory in which the Client32 files were installed is added to the PATH variable. If you specified Client32 to start when the computer is booted, there is a call to STARTNET.BAT in this file as well.

- **WIN.INI**   The command LOAD=NWPOPUP.EXE is added to the [Windows] section of the WIN.INI file.

- **SYSTEM.INI**   The installation program modifies the [386Enh] section of SYSTEM.INI to support Client32.

- **PROGMAN.INI**   A new program group called NetWare Tools is added to Program Manager.

In addition, the STARTNET.BAT files and NET.CFG files have been created in the directory to which Client32 was installed. By default, this is the C:\NOVELL\CLIENT32 directory. For more information on the changes made to the files on the client workstation, refer to the online help that comes with Client32. There is an icon for it in the NetWare Tools program group called Client 32 Help. The default location for this file is C:\NOVELL\CLIENT32\NLS\ENGLISH\SETUP.HLP.

The advantage to using NetWare Client32 for DOS/Windows is its advanced Windows support. In the next section, we will discuss this new support, which did not exist with the NetWare DOS Requester.

Client32 Windows Utilities

People familiar with the old NetWare 3.x environment will remember all of the DOS commands you need to remember to customize the network environment. To initially authenticate to the network, you needed to use a DOS utility. To map drives, you needed to use a DOS utility. There was very little NetWare client support offered through Windows. Client32 provides much more robust Windows support through a couple of Windows GUI utilities:

■ NetWare User Tools

■ NetWare Login

When SETUP.EXE was run to install NetWare Client32 for DOS/Windows, these Windows utilities were automatically installed. Icons were also created for them in a program group called NetWare Tools. By double-clicking on this program group in Program Manager, you will be able to access these utilities.

NetWare User Tools

The NetWare User Tools utility allows you to customize your network environment without having to use those old DOS-based utilities. You can now map network drives, capture network print queues, and access multiple servers using one utility. To start the NetWare User Tools utility, double-click on the NetWare User Tools icon. You can also start this utility be choosing File | Run from the menu bar of program manager and typing **C:\WINDOWS\SYSTEM\NWUSER.EXE** in the Command Line box.

Once the utility has been started, you will see the NetWare User Tools window appear (Figure 15-12). By default, the NetWare Drive Connections button is active, showing your current NetWare drive mappings and connections. Using the other buttons along the top of the screen, you can also customize the network printing environment and manage NetWare connections to servers and NDS trees.

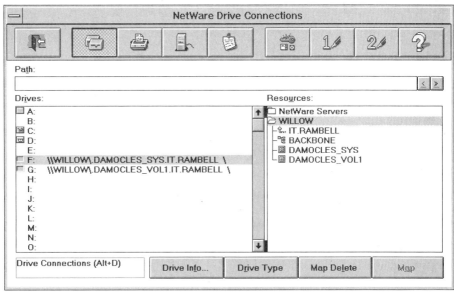

Figure 15-12: The NetWare User Tools Drive Connections management screen.

For more information on using the NetWare User Tools, refer to the online help provided with the NetWare User Tools utility. It can be accessed by clicking on the button with the question mark once with the left mouse button. This button is located at the upper right corner of the NetWare User Tools window shown in Figure 15-12.

NetWare Login

NetWare Client32 for DOS/Windows also has a Windows-based LOGIN utility that makes connecting to the network easier. People familiar with the old NetWare clients remember the limited Windows support. If you wanted to log in to another server, you had to quit Windows and run LOGIN.EXE from DOS. It was not a convenient setup.

Fortunately, you can now authenticate to multiple NetWare servers or multiple NDS trees using the Windows-based LOGIN utility. An icon for it was created in the NetWare Tools program group when Client32 was installed. To use the LOGIN utility, double-click on the NetWare Login icon in this program group. You can also start the utility by choosing File I Run from the Program Manager menu bar, typing **C:\NOVELL\CLIENT32\ LOGINW31.EXE** in the Command Line box and clicking on the OK button.

You can use this utility to authenticate to the NetWare environment. Figure 15-13 shows the Windows-based NetWare Login utility.

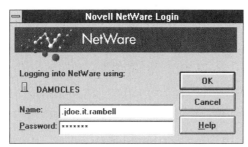

Figure 15-13: NetWare Login is a GUI utility for logging in to the network.

Just type your login name and password into the Name and Password boxes, respectively. As shown in Figure 15-13, you can enter your NDS distinguished name in the Name box if you so desire. Notice that this particular login limits the network resources to which you can authenticate. In fact, you can only authenticate to the server to which your workstation is attached. Fortunately, NetWare Client32 for DOS/Windows can be customized to increase the network client functionality.

Customizing NetWare Client32 for DOS/Windows

When Client32 is installed with Windows support, you can customize how it appears to the user when he or she is working with the machine. To configure Client32, you will need to access the Network Control Panel. To do this, start from Program Manager. Double-click on the Main group to expand it. From the Main group, double-click on the Control Panel icon. This will display the Windows control panels. Now double-click on the Network Control Panel; the NetWare Settings dialog box will appear (Figure 15-14). Notice that Client32 has replaced the normal Windows Network control panel.

There are four main tabs to the NetWare Settings dialog box. In Figure 15-14, you see the UserTools tab. This tab will let you customize the environment for the NetWare UserTools. The NetWare and Startup tabs will let you customize other settings, such as network broadcast, print manager options, and startup options for when Windows first loads. To switch to one of these other tabs, just click on the tab once with the left mouse button.

The most important tab in the NetWare Settings dialog box is the Login tab. This tab lets you configure the NetWare Login utility. Click on the Login tab once with the left mouse button. The Login properties page will be displayed (Figure 15-15).

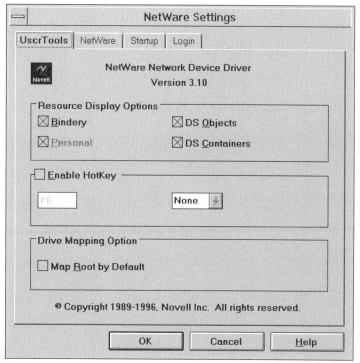

Figure 15-14: The NetWare Settings dialog box.

There are three main sections to this page. By checking the box to the left of a section title, you cause another page to appear in the NetWare Login utility when it is started. There is the Connection Page, the Script Page, and the Variables Page. From the screen shown in Figure 15-15, you can enable the display of these pages and configure them for the user. We have decided to enable all of the pages in the NetWare Login utility, thus, all of the boxes for the sections are checked.

One important item to note is in the Display Script Page section. You will notice that the box to the left of Run Scripts is checked. This allows the execution of login scripts when the user authenticates to the network using the Windows NetWare Login utility. If this box is not checked, the login scripts will not run, and you will have to customize the network environment manually.

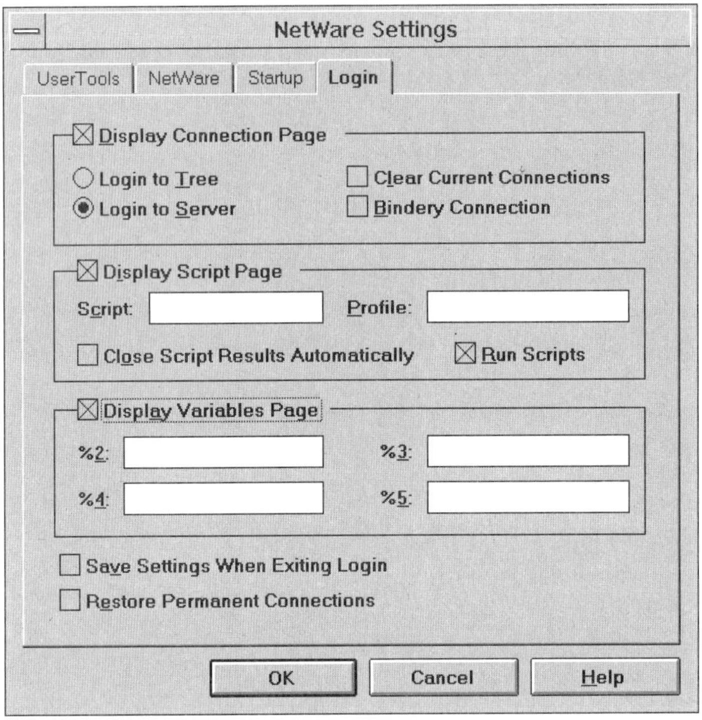

Figure 15-15: Customizing the NetWare Login utility.

Now that we have checked all of the boxes, we can run the NetWare Login utility again to see the changes that have taken effect. You will notice in Figure 15-16 that there are now four tabs associated with the NetWare Login utility. In addition to the original Login page seen in Figure 15-13, there are three additional pages. These three new pages directly correlate with the three sections we checked off in Figure 15-15.

You can now switch through the pages and authenticate to the network using customized settings. To switch through the pages, just click on the appropriate tab once with the left mouse button, and the page will appear. For example, we can click on the Connection tab once with the left mouse button, and the Connection page will appear (Figure 15-17).

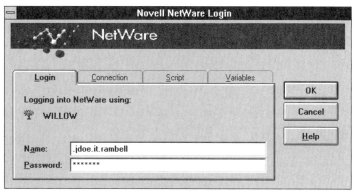

Figure 15-16: The newly configured NetWare Login utility.

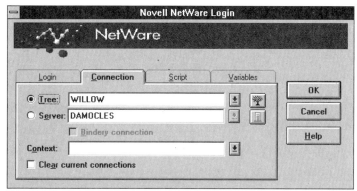

Figure 15-17: The Connection tab allows you to specify a different server or NDS tree.

On the Connection page, you can pick the NDS tree you want to access. Or you can choose to authenticate to a specific server instead. You can specify a bindery connection to a server, and you can also specify your context in the NDS tree. You may need to authenticate to multiple servers or NDS trees in your network environment. The Connection tab is invaluable in helping you make these multiple connections.

The next available page, the Scripts page, show the scripting features available when you log in to an NDS tree or NetWare server. To get to the Scripts page, click on the Scripts tab once with the left mouse button. The Scripts page will appear (Figure 15-18).

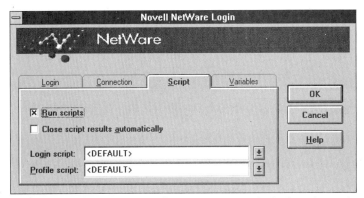

Figure 15-18: The Scripts page allows you to customize login script settings.

From the Scripts page, you can determine whether the login script is going to run when you authenticate. You can also choose to close the result of the login script automatically so it executes transparently to the user. Besides these options, you can use the text edit boxes to select a specific login script or profile login script to execute. For more information on login scripts and login script commands, refer to Chapter 5.

The final page is the Variables page. You'll remember from Chapter 5 that you can pass command-line variables from the LOGIN utility to the login script environment. It was easy to do from the DOS-based LOGIN.EXE, but it is a little more difficult with the Windows NetWare Login. The Variables page allows you to specify the command-line variables to be processed by the login script environment. The Variables page is shown in Figure 15-19.

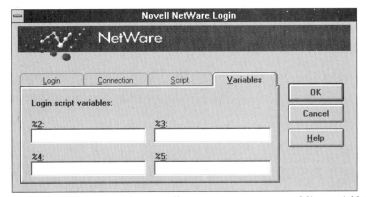

Figure 15-19: The Variables page allows you to pass command-line variables to the login script environment.

Once you have customized your Client32 environment, the workstation is ready to authenticate to the network and use the NetWare resources. Remember that Client32 automatically installs IPX for the network client to connect to the NetWare servers on your network. If you want to install other products, you must specify them during the installation of NetWare Client32 for DOS/Windows. Once the Client is installed, you can use the new Windows utilities that come packaged with the client and customize the Client32 environment at the workstation to reflect your network's needs.

Installing & Configuring Workstation TCP/IP

One important item we want to recap is the installation of TCP/IP on your client workstations. IPX is required to provide NetWare services to your client workstations, and many intranets require that TCP/IP be loaded on the workstations as well. If you plan on using World Wide Web browsing services, FTP services, and NetWare/IP, or to provide Internet access, you will need TCP/IP on the client workstations. In this section, we will briefly cover the installation of TCP/IP using Client32.

Refer back to "NetWare Client32 for DOS/Windows Installation" earlier in this chapter. During the installation, you were given the option to install TCP/IP when the Additional Options dialog box appeared. If you are going to install TCP/IP at the workstation, you need to make sure that box is checked.

After you check the box during the installation, you need to provide TCP/IP with information specific to the client workstation. The information includes the following items, and it is required to successfully configure TCP/IP at the workstation:

- **IP address.** The IP address the workstation will be using. It must be a unique address, especially if you have a direct Internet connection.

- **IP router.** The IP address of the default router the workstation will be using. If a TCP/IP packet needs to leave the workstation's local network, the default router is the machine that will direct the packet to the next place it needs to go.

- **Subnet mask.** The subnet mask applies to your specific network. Generally, if you have a Class C IP address, you will use the subnet mask 255.255.255.0. If you have a Class B IP address, you will use the subnet mask 255.255.0.0. However, if you are part of a larger network at your company, you may want to consult with your central Information Systems department.

- **Domain name.** This is the name of your IP domain. For example, if Rambell, Inc. had their own domain registered with the Internet Network Information Center (InterNIC) as rambell.com, that would be the domain name for the IP network.

- **Domain Name System (DNS) server.** The DNS server resolves host names into IP addresses. To use Domain Name System services, you must have a DNS server on your network.

Once you have input this information, the installation of Client32 will continue and complete as you have configured it. When TCP/IP is installed, certain changes are made to your workstation. First, STARTNET.BAT will be configured to load the TCPIP.NLM module. This loads the TCP/IP protocol stack so that your machine can "speak" TCP/IP. It must be loaded after the 32-bit ODI driver but before CLIENT32.NLM.

Second, the NET.CFG file will have a section added to it, the Protocol TCP/IP section, and it will have the following variables listed in it:

- **IP_ADDRESS.** Specifies the IP address of the machine.

- **IP_ROUTER.** Determines the default router the workstation uses.

- **IP_NETMASK.** Specifies the subnet mask for your IP network.

- **PATH TCP_CFG.** Determines the location of the required TCP/IP files.

These required TCP/IP files are critical in the successful installation and configuration of TCP/IP at the client workstation. By default, the files are copied into C:\NOVELL\CLIENT32\TCP. The main file in this directory is RESOLV.CFG, which holds the information concerning your domain name and the IP address of the DNS server on your network. As you can see, all of the information you input during the installation of Client32 has been placed in one of two files. It has gone into either NET.CFG or RESOLV.CFG.

In addition, the file WINSOCK.DLL was copied to the C:\NOVELL\CLIENT32 directory. This file is critical in providing Windows support for TCP/IP. Any Windows application that needs to access to the TCP/IP protocol stack invokes WINSOCK.DLL to create a TCP/IP socket. Without this file, applications like Netscape Navigator and WS_FTP would not work.

If you are planning to provide Internet connectivity or NetWare/IP services on your network to your clients, you must have TCP/IP installed. For more information concerning TCP/IP on your network, refer to the NetWare 4.11 TCP/IP Reference manual. It can be found in the NetWare 4.11 Communication collection of the online documentation.

Moving On

This chapter has highlighted how to install and configure the appropriate driver software to enable you to connect DOS and Windows 3.x users to your intranet, as well as how to install advanced client and application management utilities such as NAL. Having to configure these clients may seem a bit outdated or old-fashioned to you, but you might be surprised at the number of very old computers in use on NetWare and IntranetWare networks. It can be more time-consuming than configuring the clients for Mac OS, Windows 95, and Windows NT, which we will discuss in the next chapter. They are much easier to configure because of the plug-and-play capabilities that were created on the Mac OS and later spread to the 32-bit version of Windows. But you will eventually need to configure one of these older clients to connect to your intranet, so keep this chapter in mind as a reference.

16

Windows 95, Windows NT & Mac OS Workstation Clients

In the last chapter, we discussed the client software for workstations that use the DOS operating system. These same machines might be running Microsoft Windows 3.x as well. Novell has created two clients for the DOS-based machine. One is built upon a 16-bit architecture, the NetWare DOS Requester, and the other is built upon a 32-bit architecture, NetWare Client32 for DOS/Windows. However, not everyone has a DOS/Windows PC sitting on their desktop. People run a wide array of operating systems at the desktop, and the DOS/Windows client is not going to suit them all.

Fortunately, Novell has created NetWare client software for other operating systems as well. In today's age of powerful desktop computers, a user is able to use more advanced operating systems to help them do their job. Microsoft has released Windows 95 and Windows NT as the successor to the DOS/Windows operating system, and Apple has been regularly upgrading the Mac OS.

All of these operating systems have built-in support for NetWare; however, using this built-in support does not allow you take advantage of all of the features of IntranetWare. For instance, the Microsoft Client for NetWare is not NDS-aware. Currently, when you log in to a NetWare 4.11 server using Windows 95 Microsoft Client for NetWare, you establish a bindery connection to the server. This obviously has some serious drawbacks.

To combat this problem, Novell has created NetWare clients for each operating system so that they can take advantage of the features of IntranetWare. The clients are the NetWare Client32 for Windows 95, the IntranetWare Client for

Windows NT, and the NetWare Client for Mac OS. In this chapter, we will discuss the installation and configuration of each client so you can enhance the networking functionality of these powerful operating systems.

However, be warned before you begin this chapter. We are assuming that you are already familiar with these operating systems. Before you can install any one of the client software packages, you must have already configured the client workstation's networking environment. For more information on setting up the native networking for a particular operating system, consult the online documentation that comes with it.

NetWare Client32 for Windows 95

For many reasons, you are probably beginning to convert your workstation machines from Windows 3.x to Windows 95, if you have not done so already. While the Microsoft Client for NetWare is able to provide basic NetWare services to the Windows 95 machine, it is lacking in its ability to support all of the features of IntranetWare.

The Microsoft Client for NetWare can only support bindery-type connections to NetWare file servers. This means that Windows 95 machines cannot take advantage of NDS and its centralization of network resources. It's comparable to buying some really cool toys but not being able to use them.

The NetWare DOS Requester is compatible with Windows 95. It does not, however, allow you to take advantage of other Windows 95 features, which are probably the reason you upgraded to Windows 95 in the first place. Fortunately, Novell has packaged the NetWare Client32 for Windows 95 with IntranetWare to enable you to take full advantage of the IntranetWare and Windows 95 environments.

The NetWare Client32 for Windows 95 includes all of the modularity and stability of the NetWare Client32 for DOS/Windows. It also has the following benefits:

- Provides the ability to authenticate to, browse, and access NDS resources on your NetWare network using Windows NT network utilities like Network Neighborhood and Windows NT Explorer.

- Enables support for concurrent connections to multiple NDS trees on your network.

- Allows access to IntranetWare file and print services using Windows 95 native applications such as Windows Explorer, Network Neighborhood, and Printer Control Panel.

- Enables support for long filenames.

- Is compatible with the Microsoft Client for Microsoft networks and allows you to use Microsoft's TCP/IP stack for TCP/IP-based communications.

- Provides the ability to administer the IntranetWare environment using NetWare Administrator for Windows 95.

It is clear that the NetWare Client32 for Windows 95 is essential if you are going to be connecting Windows 95 machines to an IntranetWare environment. It will allow you to fully utilize IntranetWare features that the Microsoft Client for NetWare is unable to provide.

NetWare Client32 for Windows 95 Architecture

The architecture of NetWare Client32 for Windows 95 is very similar to its DOS/Windows counterpart. In fact, the only difference is that the NetWare Input/Output Subsystem is a virtual device driver in Windows 95 instead of an executable. Otherwise, the architecture of the clients are the same.

When the Windows 95 workstation is booted, Windows 95 is loaded. Windows 95 then automatically loads Client32 for Windows 95 to establish the connection to the IntranetWare environment. This automatic load alleviates the need for a STARTNET.BAT file. An added benefit already!

Like the NetWare Client32 for DOS/Windows, the modules necessary to establish the network connect must be loaded in a specific order. Once Windows 95 starts, the modules for NetWare Client32 for Windows 95 are loaded in the following order:

1. **NIOS.VXD.** Provides the NetWare Input/Output Subsystem, which is responsible for loading and unloading the NetWare Loadable Modules (NLMs) that the client comprises.

2. **LSLC32.NLM.** Establishes the Link Support Layer, which is the module responsible for directing incoming network packets to the appropriate protocol stack.

3. **CMSM.NLM.** Installs the Media Support Module, which helps facilitate communication between the Link Support Layer and the network card.

4. **ETHERTSM.NLM.** Loads the Topology Specific Module. ETHERTSM.NLM is loaded if you have an Ethernet network; however, if you have a different type of network (Token Ring or FDDI), NIOS.VXD will load the appropriate module.

5. **CNE2000.LAN.** Loads the MLID for your network card. In this case, this is the LAN driver for an NE2000 network card.

6. **IPX.NLM.** Establishes the IPX protocol stack, which is required for your workstation to communicate with a NetWare file server.

7. **CLIENT32.NLM.** Creates the workstation client shell. This shell allows you to use the IntranetWare environment.

Even though the files load in this order, it is not how they relate to one another. Figure 16-1 shows how the modules required for NetWare Client32 for Windows 95 interact with one another to provide network connectivity. For more information on these modules and their roles, refer to Chapter 15.

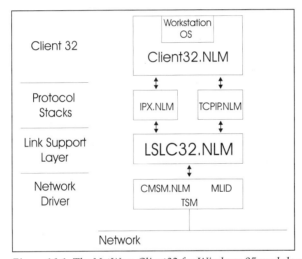

Figure 16-1: The NetWare Client32 for Windows 95 module relationships.

The other nice thing about NetWare Client32 for Windows 95 is the fact that you do not have to maintain a NET.CFG file for the client software. All of the configurable parameters are stored in the Windows 95 Registry. Every time you load Windows 95, the settings are automatically loaded for the client software. To modify these files, you just need to modify the properties of the client. We will discuss the configuration of NetWare Client32 for Windows 95 later in this chapter.

But before you can install the client software on your Windows 95 workstation, you must be sure your workstation is capable of handling it. There is a set of minimum hardware and software requirements that must be met before the client can be installed.

Hardware/Software Requirements

Before you load the Client32 software on your workstation, you should be sure it is capable of being a NetWare client. Table 16-1 summarizes the hardware and software requirements for NetWare Client32 for Windows 95. Make sure your workstation meets the minimum requirements before attempting to install the software on the machine.

Hardware/Software Category	Minimum Requirement
Processor	IBM-PC compatible with an Intel 80386 or later CPU (80484, Pentium, or Pentium Pro)
Hard Disk Space	At least 6MB free disk space
Memory	At least 6MB RAM
Memory Manager	Memory manager required—HIMEM.SYS, EMM386.EXE, QEMM, or 386MAX
Network Card	NetWare-compatible network card installed in the machine with an appropriate LAN driver
Network Cable	Client workstation connected to your physical network by a network cable attached to your network card

Table 16-1: Hardware/Software requirements for the NetWare Client32 for Windows 95.

Tip

If you are connecting Windows 95 machines to your NetWare 4.11 servers, the servers should have the name space LONG.NAM loaded on their volumes. This will allow the client workstations to take advantage of their long filename features.

Once you are sure your workstation can handle the Client32 software, it is time to install it. In the next section, we will discuss the installation of NetWare Client32 for Windows 95.

NetWare Client32 for Windows 95 Installation

Installing NetWare Client32 for Windows 95 is simple. It involves running one executable program. However, before you can run this program, the installation files for NetWare Client32 for Windows 95 must be prepared. For more information on preparing the installation files, refer to "Preparing the Client Software for Installation" in Chapter 15.

Once the installation files for the client software have been installed on a server or floppy disk, it is time for the installation of the client. Before you install the client, we recommend that you already have your Windows 95 networking environment configured. This means you should have the network adapter set up in the Network Control Panel along with the necessary protocols to connect to the IntranetWare environment. This will make the installation of NetWare Client32 for Windows 95 much easier.

If you have put the installation files for NetWare Client32 for Windows 95 on your file server, the setup program, SETUP.EXE, will be located in the SYS:PUBLIC\CLIENT\WIN95\IBM_ENU directory. If you are installing from a floppy disk, SETUP.EXE will be on your first floppy disk. To install NetWare Client32 for Windows 95 on your machine, perform the following steps:

1. Starting from Windows Explorer in Windows 95, double-click on the icon for SETUP.EXE, which will be located where you placed the client installation files.

2. The software license agreement will appear. Read the license agreement and click on the Yes button if you accept the terms. Clicking on the Yes button will display the NetWare Client 32 Installation dialog box.

3. In the NetWare Client 32 Installation dialog box (Figure 16-2), click on the Start button to begin the installation. If you want to upgrade the Windows 95 NDIS drivers for your network card to Novell's 32-bit ODI drivers, make sure the Upgrade NDIS Drivers box is checked.

4. After clicking on the Start button, the installation of the client will begin. You can monitor the progress of the installation through the various indicator bars that will be presented.

5. When the installation is complete, a second NetWare Client 32 Installation dialog box will appear, which will inform you that the installation has been successful. At this point, you can either reboot the machine so the new NetWare client can take effect by clicking on the Reboot button, or you can configure the newly installed client by clicking on the Customize button.

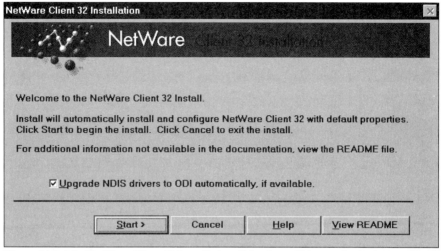

Figure 16-2: The NetWare Client 32 Installation dialog box will let you begin the installation of the client software.

By default, the installation program will place the client software files in the C:\NOVELL\CLIENT32 directory of your local workstation. We do not recommend installing these files to a different location.

If you immediately customize the client configuration, you will be taken to the Network Control Panel. We will cover the configuration of the client in the next section. If you customize the configuration from the second NetWare Client 32 Installation dialog box, you must reboot your machine after you are finished for the new client software to be loaded. You will not be able to use NetWare Client32 for Windows 95 until you reboot.

NetWare Client32 for Windows 95 Configuration

One of the great features of all the NetWare client software is its ability to be customized. You can easily and efficiently specify your preferences for things such as your preferred NDS tree and preferred context. Once these values are set, you don't have to reset them every time you use the client. The client is able to remember the settings and help you reconnect to your network resources with a minimum of effort.

As we mentioned before in the section on the architecture of the client, the ASCII NET.CFG file is not required for NetWare Client32 for Windows 95. All of the parameter settings for the client are stored in the Windows 95 Registry.

When you modify the values of these parameters, Windows 95 automatically edits its Registry to reflect the changes. You are no longer required to maintain workstation preferences in an ASCII text file.

You can configure the NetWare Client for Windows 95 through the Network Control Panel built into the operating system. To get to the necessary screen to modify client parameters, perform the following steps:

1. From the desktop in Windows 95, click on Network Neighborhood once with the right mouse button. Choose Properties from the menu that appears. The Network Control Panel will be displayed.

2. In the Network Control Panel, click on Novell NetWare Client 32 in the list of installed network components once with the left mouse button. It will be highlighted. Click on the Properties button to display the Novell NetWare Client 32 Properties dialog box shown in Figure 16-3.

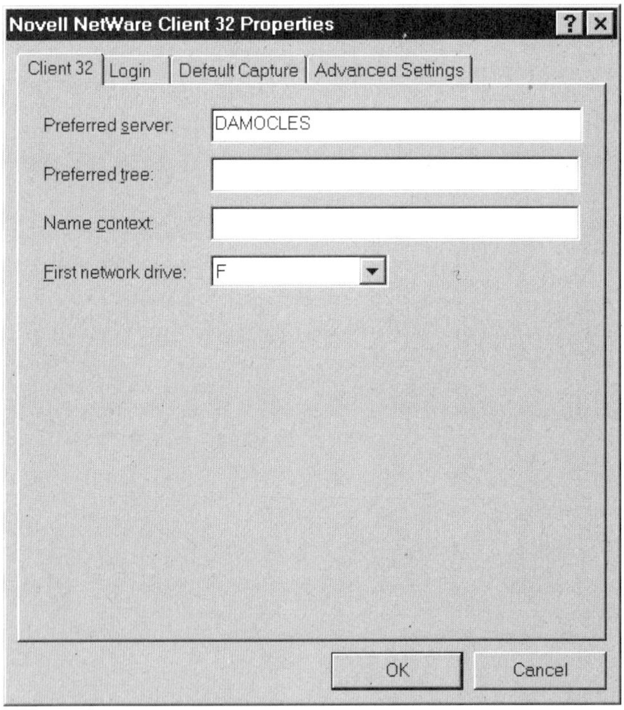

Figure 16-3: The Novell NetWare Client 32 Properties dialog box.

From the dialog box shown in Figure 16-3, you can customize the NetWare Client32 for Windows 95. The first property tab displayed is the Client 32 tab.

The properties associated with this tab allow you to specify information about the network environment and how you will interact with it. You can specify the Preferred Server, Preferred Tree, and Name Context parameters for the workstation. You can also specify the network drive you want to be available first.

In addition to the Client 32 property page, the Novell NetWare Client 32 Properties dialog box has three other pages through which you can configure the IntranetWare environment:

- **Login.** Allows you to customize the NetWare Login utility. Like NetWare Client32 for DOS/Windows, NetWare Client32 for Windows 95 has a GUI login utility to provide authentication to the IntranetWare environment.

- **Default Capture.** Specifies default settings for your NetWare printing environment. These settings can be overridden with other manually issued commands; however, using the property page is an easy way to customize the printing environment without using a lot of login script commands.

- **Advanced Settings.** Lets you specify values for advanced IntranetWare client parameters such as Alert Beep and DOS Name.

When you are done configuring NetWare Client32 for Windows 95, click on the OK button in the Novell NetWare Client 32 Properties dialog box. You will be returned to the Network Control Panel. Click on OK in the Network Control Panel to dismiss it.

After installing and configuring NetWare Client32 for Windows 95, you are ready to use the utilities included with the client. The utilities will help you both access and administer the network. In the next section, we will discuss the basic utilities that help you take full advantage of your IntranetWare environment.

NetWare Client32 for Windows 95 Utilities

Once you install NetWare Client32 for Windows 95 and reboot your machine, you will be able to use some utilities that were packaged with the client. In addition to the benefits of the client software itself, you have the ability to use the following programs:

- NetWare Login
- NetWare Administrator for Windows 95
- NetWare Application Launcher

NetWare Login

NetWare Client32 for Windows 95 has a GUI login utility that makes connecting to the network easier. To access this utility, click on the Start button and choose Programs | Novell | NetWare Login. This will launch the GUI login utility, allowing you to authenticate to the network. The NetWare Login utility is shown in Figure 16-4.

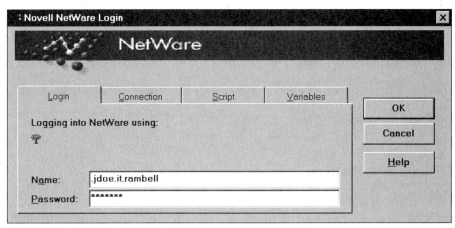

Figure 16-4: The Novell NetWare Login utility for Windows 95.

By default, the first tab of the NetWare Login utility, Login, is always displayed when the program is launched. On this page, you can enter your user ID and password in the Name and Password boxes to gain access to the NDS tree. Fortunately, if the tree you want to access is not the one specified on the Login page, you can change it with the Connection page.

The Connection page allows you to manage which NetWare file server of the NDS tree you want to access. You can specify an NDS connection with a tree or an individual file server. When the Server radio box is selected, you can also specify a bindery connection by checking the Bindery Connection box in Figure 16-5.

You also can specify the current context of your workstation on the Connection page. Instead of having to type your distinguished name into the Name box on the Login page, you can specify the current context of the machine on the Connection page and use just your common name on the Login page.

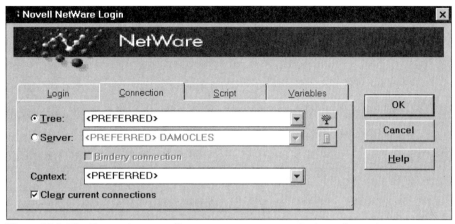

Figure 16-5: The Connection page allows you to manage your login configuration.

The third tab, Script, allows you to customize your login script environment. You can specify alternate login scripts to run during the login process. You can also configure the NetWare Login utility so it does not run any login scripts at all.

The last tab in the NetWare Login utility, Variables, allows you to specify the command-line variables that are passed to the login script environment. You may never use all of these tabs; however, they are available to help make the NetWare Login utility flexible and useful.

Depending upon your networking environment, you might not want your users to have access to all of the tabs in the NetWare Login utility. You can specify which tabs are displayed for the user by customizing the client software environment. To restrict the tabs displayed by the NetWare Login utility when it is run, you need to access the Novell NetWare Client 32 Properties dialog box (Figure 16-3) through the Network Control Panel.

In this dialog box, click on the Login tab to display the properties associated with the NetWare Login utility. The screen in Figure 16-6 will be displayed. You will notice that this page is split up into three sections. Each section of the dialog box pertains to the corresponding tab in the NetWare Login utility. To prevent a specific tab from being displayed, make sure the Display box next to the appropriate section in *not* checked. When you are finished configuring the NetWare Login utility preferences, click on the OK button. You will be returned to the Network Control Panel. Click on the OK button again to accept the changes.

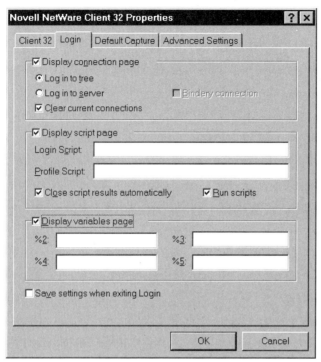

Figure 16-6: The Login tab of the Novell NetWare Client 32 Properties dialog box.

Tip

Notice that there is no section for the Login tab of the NetWare Login utility. This tab is always present because it is required for authentication. By default, Login is the only tab displayed by the NetWare Login utility after NetWare Client32 for Windows 95 is installed.

NetWare Administrator for Windows 95

The NetWare Administrator for Windows 95 functions just like the NetWare Administrator for Windows 3.x. It is located in the SYS:PUBLIC\WIN95 directory, and it is called NWADMN95.EXE. A version of NDS Manager for Windows 95 is also located in this directory, and it is called NDSMGR32.EXE. We recommend using these executables for managing your NDS tree if you are using a Windows 95 machine as your IntranetWare client workstation.

For more information on using NetWare Administrator to manage your IntranetWare environment, refer to Chapter 3. There you will be able to review the NetWare Administrator interface.

NetWare Application Launcher

Just like Windows 3.x has its own version of NetWare Application Launcher to facilitate the central administration of network applications, Windows 95 has *its* own version. The Windows 95 version of NAL, called NALW95.EXE, is located in the SYS:PUBLIC directory of your NetWare 4.11 server. When you use this powerful interface in conjunction with NetWare Application Manager, you can distribute access to network applications to your users. For more information about NetWare Application Manager and NetWare Application Launcher, refer to Chapter 13.

As you can see, the Windows 95 GUI makes the installation and configuration of the NetWare client much simpler. You no longer have to tinker with ASCII files to configure your workstation the way you want. Also, there are some features built into the client which allow it to interface with the NetWare environment better than the native Microsoft client software.

IntranetWare Client for Windows NT

The PCs of today are becoming more powerful by the moment. Their price is also decreasing rapidly, which means you can have, for example, a Pentium Pro CPU with 64MB RAM and all the trimmings for a reasonable cost. These types of machines are well-suited for running Windows NT Workstation because it is a more powerful and more robust operating system than Windows 95. Fortunately, Novell has created a NetWare client for that platform as well.

The IntranetWare Client for Windows NT allows you to take the first step toward integrating your Windows NT and NetWare environments. As we have mentioned, the Microsoft Client for NetWare does not support certain IntranetWare features, including NDS. When you log in to a NetWare 4.11 server using the Microsoft Client for NetWare, you are only able to establish bindery connections to the server. This means you must have Bindery Services set up on the NetWare server for Windows NT to connect to the NetWare environment out of the box.

By installing IntranetWare Client for Windows NT on your Windows NT Workstation machine, you achieve full NetWare support that includes features with which you can:

- Provide the ability to authenticate to, browse, and access NDS resources on your NetWare network using Windows NT network utilities like Network Neighborhood and Windows NT Explorer.

- Enable support for concurrent connections to multiple NDS trees on your network.

- Allow access to IntranetWare file and print services using Windows NT native applications such as Windows NT Explorer, Network Neighborhood, and Printer Control Panel.

- Enable support for long filenames.

- Administer the IntranetWare environment using NetWare Administrator for Windows NT.

Because of its many benefits, it just makes sense to install IntranetWare Client for Windows NT on your Windows NT workstation if you are going to be using IntranetWare on your network. You will get the benefit of using a powerful and robust operating system on your desktop in conjunction with a powerful and robust network operating system.

Tip

For the purpose of this discussion, we are assuming that you are installing IntranetWare Client for Windows NT on a Windows NT Workstation version 4.0 machine. If you are installing this client on Windows NT Workstation version 3.51, the screens and procedures will be different.

Hardware/Software Requirements

Before you load IntranetWare Client for Windows NT on your Windows NT workstation, you should check to see if it meets the following minimum hardware and software specifications:

- A machine running Windows NT Workstation version 4.0 or Windows NT Workstation 3.51 with Service Pack 4 installed.

- At least 25MB of hard disk space if you are going to install the client and all of its associated utilities.

- A network card and a physical connection to your network.

You should also have the Windows NT networking environment already configured before you install the client software. Once you have reviewed your machine, you are ready to install the IntranetWare Client for Windows NT.

Tip

If you are connecting Windows NT Workstation machines to your NetWare 4.11 servers, the servers should have the name space LONG.NAM loaded on their volumes. This will allow the client workstations to take advantage of their long filename features.

Preparing the Client Software for Installation

At the time of this writing, IntranetWare Client for Windows NT is not packaged with IntranetWare. So, you need to get the client software from Novell before you can install it on your workstation. If you have an Internet connection, you can go to the Novell Support Connection home page at http:// support.novell.com/ and download IntranetWare Client for Windows NT. The most recent version of IntranetWare Client for Windows NT at this writing is version 4.1, which is the version we'll use in this discussion.

At the Novell Web site, you have the option of downloading IntranetWare Client for Windows NT in one of two forms. You have two options for downloading the software as a *network installation*, which means you will place the client installation files on your NetWare server just like you would the other NetWare clients. Or, you can download the software as a *diskette installation*. This means you will create floppy disks with which you will install the client on the workstation.

When you download the software, it will come in the form of a self-extracting archive. All you have to do is double-click on the file in Windows NT Explorer, and it will expand itself. We recommend you put the downloaded file in its final destination directory before you unpack it. This prevents having to move the entire directory structure that is created when the utility extracts.

If you download a network installation, create a directory on the SYS volume of your NetWare 4.11 server called SYS:PUBLIC\CLIENT\WINNT. Place the downloaded file in this directory, and then double-click on the file in Windows NT Explorer. The self-extracting archive will create the directory structure for the IntranetWare Client for Windows NT installation files on your file server. If you download a disk installation, you will be prompted to insert floppy disks on which the self-extracting archive will place the installation files.

Once you have the installation files for the client software in place, you are almost ready to install IntranetWare Client for Windows NT on your Windows NT workstation. As we mentioned earlier, you need to make sure your machine is capable of having the client software installed on it.

IntranetWare Client for Windows NT Installation

The installation of IntranetWare Client for Windows NT is actually very easy. To start the installation of the client software, log in to the file server on which the installation files reside or get the floppy disks you created ready. From the SYS:PUBLIC\CLIENT\WINNT directory or the floppy drive (depending upon where the installation files are located), just double-click on the NWSETUP.EXE file in Windows NT Explorer.

Double-clicking on the file's icon will start the IntranetWare Client for Windows NT installation program. The first screen of the installation is shown in Figure 16-7. From this screen, you have the option of viewing the readme file, browsing the online help, canceling the installation, or continuing the installation. To continue the installation, click on the Continue button in the bottom right corner of the dialog box.

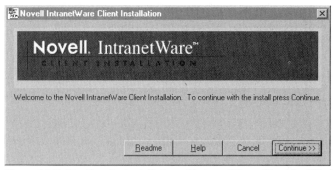

Figure 16-7: Starting the installation of IntranetWare Client for Windows NT.

Once you click on the Continue button, IntranetWare Client for Windows NT will install. You will see several progress bars indicating the status of the installation. When the installation is complete, the Installation Complete dialog box will appear. You can either close this box or reboot your machine. We recommend you reboot your machine so the IntranetWare client can load on the workstation.

That's all there is to it! Pretty simple, right? Once you reboot your machine, though, you're in for some changes right away. You will notice that the normal screen to log in to Windows NT has been replaced with the screen in Figure 16-8. This will let you know immediately that the IntranetWare Client for Windows NT has successfully installed. To log in to the Windows NT machine, just press Ctrl+Alt+Delete like you normally would.

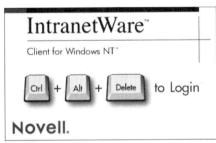

Figure 16-8: After the installation of IntranetWare Client for Windows NT, the welcome screen has changed.

When you press Ctrl+Alt+Delete, you will be greeted with a new Windows NT login screen. You no longer have the simple Windows NT login where you specify the username, machine, and password. IntranetWare Client for Windows NT replaces this screen with a new dialog box that features five tabs. This allows you to customize the client environment for IntranetWare as well as Windows NT.

To switch between the various pages of this new login dialog box, just click on the appropriate tab once with the left mouse button. The properties associated with that tab will be displayed. Table 16-2 lists the five tabs and briefly describes their function.

Tab Name	Function
Login	Allows you to authenticate to your NetWare environment. Enter the information concerning your user ID, NDS tree context, and password.
IntranetWare	Allows you to choose the type of connection to be established. Under NDS Login, you can choose a preferred tree and server. Under Bindery Login, choose the NetWare server. When Bindery Login is chosen, the Login tab will reflect this choice.
Windows NT	Allows you to specify the Windows NT Workstation user account and Domain/Workstation settings like the normal Windows NT login dialog box did. When the Windows NT Login Only box is checked, you are only authenticated to the Windows NT machine.
Script	Allows you to specify IntranetWare scripts to be run at login.
Variables	Allows you to specify command-line variables to be passed to the login script environment.

Table 16-2: The five pages of the new Windows NT login dialog box.

Once you successfully log in to the IntranetWare environment and your Windows NT environment, the installation is complete. If you click on the Start button in the taskbar and choose Programs | IntranetWare (Common), you will notice that the installation program has created shortcuts to some new utilities—the IntranetWare Login utility and the IntranetWare Send Message utility. We will discuss these utilities later in this chapter.

After installing IntranetWare Client for Windows NT, you will want to customize the IntranetWare client software to suit your environment's particular needs. In the next section, we will cover the configuration of IntranetWare Client for Windows NT.

Configuring IntranetWare Client for Windows NT

Just like all of the other clients we have discussed so far, IntranetWare Client for Windows NT is a configurable client that can be customized at each workstation. You can specify your preferences for things such as the preferred NDS tree and preferred context.

With the DOS/Windows versions of the NetWare client, all of the configuration parameters were stored in a file called NET.CFG. This file is not necessary for the IntranetWare Client for Windows NT. All of the settings for the client are stored in the Windows NT Registry. When you modify the values of these client parameters, Windows NT automatically edits the Registry to change them. You do not need to maintain your preferences in an ASCII text file any more.

You can configure the IntranetWare Client for Windows NT through the Network Control Panel. To get to the necessary screen to modify client parameters, perform the following steps:

1. From the desktop in Windows NT Workstation 4.0, click on Network Neighborhood once with the right mouse button. Choose Properties from the menu that appears. The Network Control Panel will be displayed.

2. In the Network Control Panel, click on the Services tab once with the left mouse button. The properties associated with the Services tab will be displayed.

3. In the Network Services box, click on Novell IntranetWare Client for Windows NT service once with the left mouse button to highlight it. Once it is highlighted, click on the Properties button. The Novell IntranetWare Client Services Configuration dialog box will be displayed (Figure 16-9).

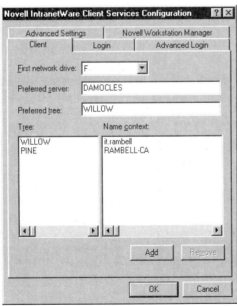

Figure 16-9: The Novell IntranetWare Client Services Configuration dialog box.

From the dialog box shown in Figure 16-9, you can customize the IntranetWare Client for Windows NT. The Client tab is the first property tab displayed. This page allows you to specify information about the network environment and how you will interact with it. You can specify the First Network Drive, your Preferred Server, and your Preferred Tree properties. You can also maintain tree and name context information pairs in the Client tab if you need to access multiple NDS trees in your NetWare Environment.

In addition to the Client property tab, the Novell IntranetWare Client Services dialog box has four other tabs through which you can configure the IntranetWare environment:

- **Login.** Allows you to customize the IntranetWare Login utility. Like NetWare Client32 for DOS/Windows, IntranetWare Client for Windows NT has a GUI login utility to provide authentication to the IntranetWare environment.

- **Advanced Login.** Allows you to set preferences concerning the Windows NT Workstation environment, including Windows NT roaming profiles, policy files, and the Windows NT welcome screen.

- **Advanced Settings.** Lets you specify values for advanced IntranetWare client parameters such as Large Internet Packets (LIP) and Packet Signing.

- **Novell Workstation Manager.** Allows you to enable Novell Workstation Manager on trusted NDS trees. Novell Workstation Manager is a new utility that allows you to integrate the Windows NT and IntranetWare environments. We will cover Novell Workstation Manager briefly later in this chapter

When you are done configuring the IntranetWare Client for Windows NT, click on the OK button in the Novell IntranetWare Client Services Configuration dialog box. You will return to the Network Control Panel. Click on OK in the Network Control Panel to dismiss it.

Now that you have installed and configured IntranetWare Client for Windows NT, let's take a quick look at some of the utilities that are included to help you utilize your IntranetWare environment.

IntranetWare Client for Windows NT Utilities

When you install IntranetWare Client for Windows NT, you can immediately use some utilities that were included with the client software. The utilities include a GUI login utility so you can access your IntranetWare network quickly and efficiently, and a messaging utility so you can send messages to other users on the network. These are features that have always been included in NetWare; however, they have been rewritten to use the Windows NT interface, which makes them more attractive and useful.

IntranetWare Login Utility

The IntranetWare Login utility is a GUI login utility that allows you to log in to the IntranetWare environment. As we have mentioned, you can start this utility by clicking on the Start button and choosing Programs | IntranetWare(Common) | IntranetWare Login. This causes the login utility to start. The screen in Figure 16-10 is displayed.

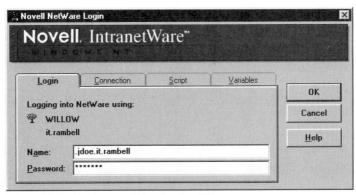

Figure 16-10: The IntranetWare Login utility.

Just like its counterparts in the DOS/Windows 3.x and Windows 95 clients, the login utility has four tabs—Login, Connection, Script, and Variables. For more information on the login utility, refer to the section on the Windows 95 client earlier in this chapter.

Just like with the other clients, the tabs displayed by the utility can be controlled. You can show them or hide them at will, depending on your network environment. To control the display of these pages, you will need to access the IntranetWare Client for Windows NT configuration parameters. The Login tab in the Novell IntranetWare Client Services Configuration dialog box will allow you to customize the display of the IntranetWare Login utility.

IntranetWare Send Message Utility

The IntranetWare Send Message utility allows users on your network to send messages to other users or groups of users by way of their NetWare clients. This utility is not an e-mail package. It simply sends real-time messages from one user logged in to the network to another user who is also attached. When the message is sent, it appears on the recipient's screen, and the recipient must then perform a key stroke combination to clear the message from his or her screen.

To start the IntranetWare Send Message utility, click on the Start button in Windows NT Workstation. Choose the Programs I IntranetWare(Common) I IntranetWare Send Message shortcut. The Send Message dialog box will appear, in which you must select a NetWare file server. Click on the desired file server once with the left mouse button to highlight it and click on the Select button. A second Send Message dialog box will appear (Figure 16-11).

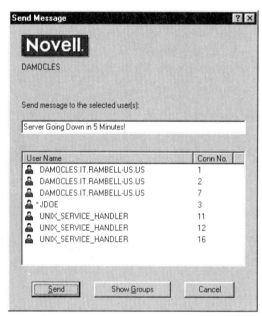

Figure 16-11: The IntranetWare Send Message utility.

With the second dialog box, you can send messages to other users connected to the file server you selected. The names of all users currently logged in to the server will be displayed in the bottom box. To send a message, click on the target user's (or users') name in the bottom box, type in the message in the top box, and click on the Send button. A message will appear on the screen of the target user(s), as shown in Figure 16-12. You must click on the Clear button to dismiss this box from the screen.

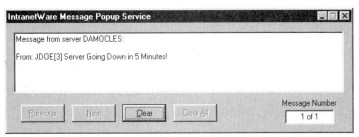

Figure 16-12: Receiving a message from the IntranetWare Send Message utility.

The sender of the message will then see a status box displaying the status of the messages he or she sent. Unfortunately, there may be instances where the target user(s) does not want to receive any messages, as the message service can be intrusive and annoying. Fortunately, the message service is configurable through the Novell IntranetWare Client Services Configuration dialog box.

To customize the messaging service, click once with the left mouse button on the Advanced Settings tab in the Novell IntranetWare Client Services Configuration dialog box. You will see a list of parameters. Click on the Receive Message Broadcast parameter once with the left mouse button to highlight it. The current value for this parameter will be displayed in the Setting box. Use the drop-down menu in the Setting box to configure the messaging service. You can configure the client to receive all messages, messages from the server only, or no messages at all.

The login and messaging utilities are included when you install IntranetWare Client for Windows NT. However, they are not the only utilities you get from the installation files. IntranetWare Client for Windows NT also includes some other useful products, which must be installed separately from the software that provides connectivity to the NetWare environment.

Other Products Included With IntranetWare Client for Windows NT

You may have noticed another executable file in the I386 subdirectory of the IntranetWare Client for Windows NT. This file is responsible for installing other useful utilities that come packaged with the IntranetWare Client for Windows NT, including the following tools:

- NetWare Administrator for Windows NT
- NetWare Application Launcher
- Novell Workstation Manager

When you install these products, the installation program extends the schema of your current NDS tree to accommodate the new objects they need. Make certain you are installing the products into the appropriate tree. To check your current tree, click on Network Neighborhood icon (located on the Desktop) with your right mouse button and select IntranetWare Connections from the list that appears. The Current IntranetWare Resources dialog box will be displayed showing you all attached resources. The NDS tree symbol with the asterisk (*) to the left of it is your current tree.

To install the software on a server in your preferred tree, perform the following steps:

1. Locate the installation files for IntranetWare Client for Windows NT through Windows NT Explorer. Double-click on the ADMSETUP.EXE file to start the installation of the additional products. For example, if the IntranetWare Client for Windows NT installation files have been placed on a file server as described previously, ADMSETUP.EXE will be located in the SYS:PUBLIC\CLIENT\WINNT\I386 directory.

2. The software license agreement will appear. Read the license agreement and click on the Yes button to accept it. The Novell IntranetWare Admin Installation dialog box will appear.

3. To install the software on a server and create objects for the applications in your NDS tree, click on the Continue button in the IntranetWare Admin Installation dialog box. The Setup Selections dialog box will appear.

4. In the Setup Selections dialog box, choose the products you wish to install and the server on which the products will be installed. After you have selected the products and the server, click on the OK button. When the installation is complete, the Installation Complete dialog box will appear.

5. Read the information contained in the Installation Complete dialog box and click Close to continue. If you have installed it, you can also run NetWare Administrator for Windows NT from this dialog box.

After these products are installed, you will need to start NetWare Administrator to extend the schema of the tree. Once you start NetWare Administrator for Windows NT, the IntranetWare Client for Windows NT Snap-In dialog box will appear. You must select the tree for which you want to modify the schema and click Modify. Once you do, you will receive another dialog indicating that the schema has successfully been extended. You can now use NetWare Administrator to manage these new products.

NetWare Administrator for Windows NT

The NetWare Administrator for Windows NT functions just like the NetWare Administrator for the other client workstation platforms. After installing it, you can run it from the SYS:PUBLIC\WINNT directory. Both NetWare Administrator for Windows NT and NDS Manager for Windows NT are installed there. We recommend using this executable file (NWADMNNT.EXE) for managing your NDS tree if you are using Windows NT Workstation as your IntranetWare client workstation.

For more information on using NetWare Administrator to manage your IntranetWare environment, refer to Chapter 3. You will be able to review the NetWare Administrator interface.

NetWare Application Launcher

When the NetWare Application Launcher is installed on a server and the schema for the NDS tree is extended, you are able to centrally manage network applications through NetWare Administrator. You use NetWare Application Manager to create application objects in the NDS tree and associate users with them. After the user has been associated with the application object, he or she will be able to access the network application.

At the client workstation, the user executes NetWare Application Launcher to access the network applications. For more information about NetWare Application Manager and NetWare Application Launcher, refer to Chapter 13.

Novell Workstation Manager

A recently added feature of the IntranetWare Client for NT is the Novell Workstation Manager, which allows a network administrator to manage all user account information, for both Windows NT and IntranetWare, centrally through NDS. This eliminates the need to maintain Windows NT Domain controller, user accounts, and NDS user information within the NT Domain.

Novell Workstation Manager stores Windows NT user information in an NDS object. If a user's user object is associated with this new NT Configuration object in NDS, that user will be allowed to log in and access the network through a Windows NT workstation. The client workstation must also be configured to use the IntranetWare Client and have the Workstation Manager feature turned on. This can be accomplished through the Novell IntranetWare Client Services Configuration dialog box (Figure 16-9). To get to this dialog box, follow the steps listed in the section "Configuring IntranetWare Client for Windows NT" earlier in this chapter.

From this dialog box, click on the Novell Workstation Manager tab once with the left mouse button. The tab's properties, as seen in Figure 16-13, allow you to enable or disable Novell Workstation Manager on a Windows NT client workstation. It also lets you specify which trees should be considered trusted trees. The Windows NT workstation will only allow a trusted NDS tree to make modifications to its user and security database; any attempt by a non-trusted tree to make modifications to the Windows NT security database will be rejected by the workstation. To add an NDS tree to the Trusted Tree list, type the name of the tree into the top text editing box and click on the Add button.

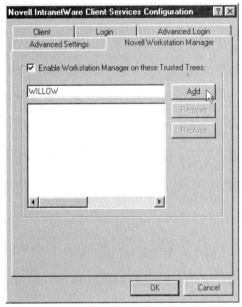

Figure 16-13: Enabling Novell Workstation Manager at the Windows NT client workstation.

After the schema of your NDS tree has been extended using NetWare Administrator, you can create a new type of object in your NDS tree, called an NT Configuration object, to manage the Windows NT workstations on your network. To create one of these objects, perform the following steps:

1. In NetWare Administrator, click once with the right mouse button on the container that will hold the new object and choose Create from the menu that appears. The New Object dialog box will appear.

2. From the Class of New Object window, select NT Configuration by clicking on it once with the left mouse button to highlight it. Click on the OK button to bring up the Create NT Configuration dialog box.

3. In the Create NT Configuration dialog box, type in the name of the NT Configuration object and click on the Create button. The object will be created in the NDS tree.

Once the object has been created, you can double-click on it with the left mouse button to configure it. Just like with every other object in NDS, the NT Configuration has properties and values that can be modified using NetWare Administrator. When you double-click on the NT Configuration object with the left mouse button, you open up the properties dialog box shown in Figure 16-14.

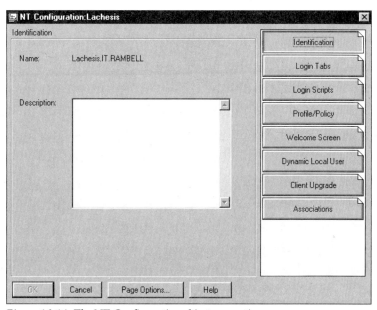

Figure 16-14: The NT Configuration object properties page.

In order for the NT Configuration object to work properly, you must associ- ate users with it. This can be done through the Associations property tab of the NT Configuration object. If the user does not have an account on the NT workstation at the time of login, the Workstation Manager can create an ac- count according to the associated NT user information in the NDS object.

Once the user is attached to the network, an associated individual profile and policy can be downloaded to the workstation to provide a consistent desktop on each NT workstation being used. Normally, this feature of Win- dows NT would only be available if the organization set up and maintained an NT Domain.

IntranetWare Client for Windows NT uses a module called NWGINA to collect the ID and password with which the user accesses IntranetWare and then authenticates the user to NDS. It then creates a Windows NT user account, if necessary, to provide the user with access to the local Windows NT workstation. The Windows NT user account is created dynamically by NWGINA and exists only for the duration of the IntranetWare session. When the user logs out from the NDS tree, the Windows NT account is deleted as well.

NWGINA is a dynamic link library that is installed on the Windows NT Workstation during the installation of Novell Workstation Manager. In order to dynamically create and delete Windows NT user accounts, this DLL is given the security equivalence of the Administrators groups on the Windows NT workstation.

With Novell Workstation Manager, you will be able to begin the integration of the Windows NT and IntranetWare environments. You can incorporate Windows NT objects into your NDS tree and administer user accounts from one central location. If you deploy Windows NT Workstations in your IntranetWare environment, you will want to explore the Novell Workstation Manager product.

To this point, we have focused mainly on clients for Intel-based PCs. However, there are other types of machines on people's desktops that allow them to gain access to the IntranetWare environment. One is the Macintosh. In the next section, we will look at the NetWare Client for Mac OS, which allows your Macintosh computers to access the IntranetWare environment using the IPX protocol.

NetWare Client for Mac OS

The NetWare Client for Mac OS provides a powerful means of integrating Mac OS users into your intranet by allowing them to connect to, and share, your network's resources. The version of the NetWare Client that ships as part of IntranetWare (version 5.11) supports the native IPX protocol as well as AppleTalk, whereas the older NetWare for Macintosh client could only connect to NetWare servers using the AppleTalk protocol. The newer client eliminates the need for NetWare for Macintosh services to be installed and running on the NetWare servers who host Macs or Mac OS clones. Some of the key advantages of the NetWare client over the native Mac client are that it:

- Uses the IPX/SPX or TCP/IP protocol to communicate with NetWare services. Administrators can remove NetWare for Macintosh services from the server if all of their clients are upgraded to the IntranetWare client. This will free up memory and resources from the server and the network.

- Uses Packet Burst and Large Internet Packets (LIP) technologies for faster network performance. Packet Burst will reduce network traffic by transferring multiple packets before requiring a response. All of NetWare's clients now support this technology. LIP increases the maximum packet size that can be sent over bridges or routers.

- Provides access to the NDS and its objects directly. The client includes a tool called NetWare Directory Browser, which allows the user to navigate the NDS tree and search for objects and resources such as volumes and printers. The user can then drag and drop the objects onto their desktop.

- Provides the ability to log in and access multiple NDS trees simultaneously.

- Provides the ability to manage servers remotely through a Mac version of Remote Console. This utility is similar to the one in the DOS version.

- Supports NetWare IP, allowing organizations that are migrating to TCP/IP as their single network protocol to continue to do so with all of their NetWare clients. It also allows users to access NetWare and NDS services through the Internet.

There are two steps to installing the NetWare Client for Mac OS:

1. Install and configure the client software for each Mac-OS-based computer that will access your IntranetWare server.

2. Install the NetWare Client for Mac OS server component.

Each of these options are described in detail in the following sections.

Hardware/Software Requirements

Check to see that the following hardware and software recommendations are met prior to installing the NetWare Client for Mac OS:

- A 68030 or higher processor.

- System 7.1 or later, although Mac OS 7.5.x is needed to fully implement the features of the client.

- 5 MB of available application memory, 8MB for Mac OS 7.5.x users.

As with all other Mac OS applications, the NetWare Client will perform much better with a PowerPC microprocessor and is completely compatible with Mac OS clones.

Client Installation & Configuring

The first step is to install the client software on the Macintosh workstation. The software can be found on the NetWare 4.11 CD-ROM, or downloaded from Novell's Web site, http://support.novell.com. To begin the installation, click on the NW Client Installer, which will prompt for either an easy install or a custom install. The custom install will allow you to add the Remote Console utility or upgrade a previous version of the client. The installation utility informs the user that the machine will need to be rebooted after the installation, and then it proceeds to copy the files to the workstation.

After the client installation is complete and the workstation has been restarted, a new icon of the directory tree will appear in the right-hand corner of the desktop menu bar, shown in Figure 16-15.

Figure 16-15: The Directory Tree icon is added by the NetWare Client installation process.

The Easy Install assumes that your network supports multiple frame types, so you might have to change this option. Figure 16-16 shows the MacIPX Control Panel opened and the Ethernet option selected. To change the frame type, double-click the Ethernet icon, select the correct frame type, and choose OK.

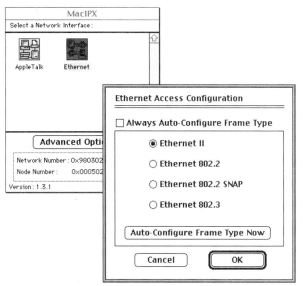

Figure 16-16: Changing the frame type may be necessary to properly configure the NetWare Client for your network.

There are dozens of configuration options available in the MacIPX Control Panel's Advanced Options and the Directory Tree. However, the default options should suffice for most networks; proceed cautiously if you need to make changes.

Logging In

The Directory Tree utility is used to authenticate and log in to the network. It is not an alternative to the standard method of connecting to an AppleShare server through the Chooser, which is located under the Apple Menu. To log in and be authenticated to an IntranetWare server once the NetWare Client has been installed, follow these steps:

1. Select the Log In option from the Directory Tree icon in the menu bar. If you are not already logged in, the icon will resemble a tree without its leaves (as in Figure 16-15).

2. Enter the name of your default tree and the context, username, and password; then click the Log In button. Figure 16-17 shows what the login process looks like.

Figure 16-17: Logging in to an IntranetWare server through the Directory Tree.

Once logged in (authenticated to the NDS tree), a user has several options on how to actually connect to an IntranetWare or NetWare server. First, a user may open the Chooser and log in as usual. The only difference now is that the Chooser detects that the NetWare Client has been installed and presents the user with a new choice, shown in Figure 16-18.

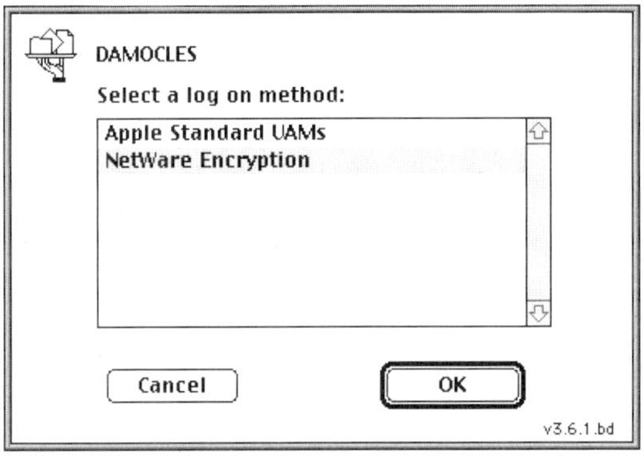

Figure 16-18: Logging in to an IntranetWare server through the Chooser.

The Chooser allows a user to proceed and log in to a server using the standard method of access. However, once a user has been authenticated by NDS, there is no need to present the user with a dialog box requesting a username and password. Selecting NetWare Encryption negates this requirement and presents the user with the standard volume selection, shown in Figure 16-19.

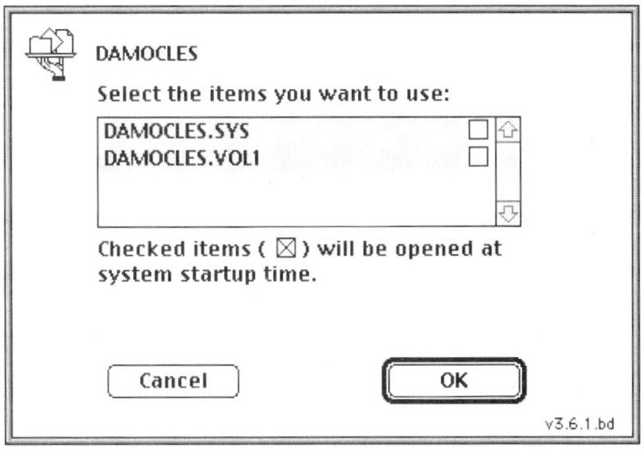

Figure 16-19: Selecting a volume.

If this is the first IntranetWare Client for the Mac OS to be configured on the network, then the server also has to be set up and configured to support Mac IPX. This second step of the installation may be run from the server console or a Remote Console session from a Mac or a PC.

Server Installation & Configuration

The server component installation of the NetWare Client for Mac OS provides several important services to Mac OS users on your intranet. The client installation provides the ability to access NetWare and IntranetWare servers, but your IntranetWare server will need to provide full support to Mac OS users to make them as productive as possible. The server components of the NetWare Client for Mac OS include:

- Long filename support for Mac OS users.
- Custom volume names.
- Multiple client and server languages.
- Mac OS file system support.

To begin the installation process, open a Remote Console session or go to the server console and type **LOAD INSTALL** to bring up the installation utility. Then follow these steps:

1. Select Product Options.

2. If this is the first installation of this product, choose Install a Product Not Listed.

3. Enter the path to the software. Note: You cannot install software from the floppy drive of a Mac because it is not known to the OS as A:\.

4. An installation screen will appear and the software will be installed.

The process used to install the server components provides both an Easy Install option and a Custom Install option, just like the client installation. If you have previously installed Macintosh long filename support (MACNAM.NLM), then you'll need to choose the Custom Install option because the installation program will attempt to install Macintosh long filename support on the SYS volume. If not, choose the Easy Install option, shown in Figure 16-20 through the Remote Console program on the Mac OS.

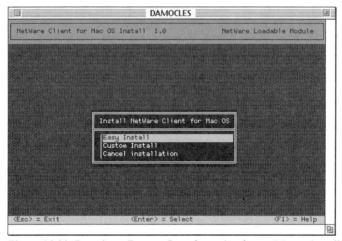

Figure 16-20: Running a Remote Console session from a Mac to install the server component of the NetWare Client for Mac OS.

If you are performing a custom installation, keep these tips in mind as you make your selection choices:

■ Add Macintosh Name Space to all volumes to which you want Mac OS users to have full access. Without this support, Mac OS users will have to follow the 8.3 rule of naming their files. They will also be restricted to using your server as a storage device only, as long filenames and the ability to have blank spaces and special characters (except the colon) will not be permitted. Users will not be able to install, launch, or store applications, only files.

■ Many Mac users name their disks using special characters, as well as a mix of upper- and lowercase letters and blank spaces. Consider naming your server's volumes accordingly.

Client Utilities

The NetWare Client for Mac OS installation provides several useful utilities, like the Remote Console program shown in Figure 16-20. A folder entitled NetWare Client Utilities, shown in Figure 16-21, is installed on the root of the boot drive that contains these utilities, the number of which depends on what installation options were chosen.

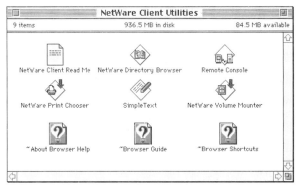

Figure 16-21: Several very useful utilities are installed with the NetWare Client.

The following items are installed into the NetWare Client Utilities folder as part of the Easy Install option:

- **NetWare Directory Browser**, for browsing NDS trees and their objects, such as volumes, printers, and users.

- **NetWare Print Chooser**, for selecting print queues and attaching to networked printers.

- **NetWare Volume Mounter**, for creating shortcuts to log in to IntranetWare and NetWare servers.

- **README** and **AppleGuide** files, to teach users how to utilize NetWare and the various client utilities.

In addition to these items, network administrators should probably also install the Remote Console program, a fully functional Mac OS implementation of the Rconsole program for DOS.

Users as well as systems administrators will find these utilities very useful, especially the NetWare Directory Browser, which is shown in Figure 16-22. From here, users will be able to get information about NDS objects and create shortcuts to them by dragging their icons to the desktop.

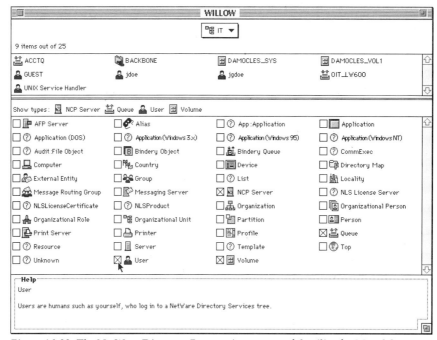

Figure 16-22: The NetWare Directory Browser is a very useful utility for Mac OS users as well as administrators.

The main difference bewteen the Mac OS client and the various Windows clients is the Mac OS client's comparatively easy installation and configuration. There's very little to change from the default installation, and the utilities that are installed make the Mac OS client a great addition to any NetWare or IntranetWare network.

Moving On

In the past two chapters, we have covered a wide variety of NetWare clients that will allow you to authenticate to the NetWare environment and use the resources on your network. This is obviously important because without your users and the client workstations, a central file server would be useless. Your network needs both components.

In the next chapter, we will discuss the file server in more detail. You already know enough about installing and configuring NetWare 4.11 to have a network up and running; however, an in-depth look at your file server and its management will provide you with some insight that will be helpful as you administer your company's IntranetWare environment.

17

NetWare 4.11 Server Architecture

So far in this section of the book, we have discussed the client software. You should have a thorough understanding of how to set up and configure the client. Of course, the client connects to a NetWare file server on the network to access the NDS database and NetWare file and print services. The server itself plays a critical role in the functionality of your network.

To make the performance of you network more efficient, it is important to understand how the server works. In the next chapter, we will discuss how you actually fine-tune the server to maximize its efficiency, but before we get to the actual tweaking, we need to take a look at the architecture of the NetWare 4.11 NOS to understand its components and how they interrelate.

In Chapter 1, we talked about the hardware components you should consider when you are selecting a server for your network. From a sheer hardware-performance standpoint, we provided you with some guidelines to pick the best server; however, that did not take into account how the software that is loaded on the machine will make use of the hardware. You could have the fastest hardware around but still have a slow server if the software does not make use of the hardware efficiently. Fortunately, NetWare 4.11 is an operating system that can be configured to run efficiently on your server to provide the best network performance possible.

In this chapter, we will talk about the main operating system files that load on the NetWare 4.11 server and what their functions are. These files lay the foundation for the rest of the network operating system and play a key role in the initial configuration of the server parameters. Once the files load, the NetWare 4.11 server is ready to go.

How the NetWare 4.11 server accesses its peripherals has an impact the performance of the server itself. NetWare is able to access components like the network card and the hard disk controller through modular pieces of software that are loaded individually. We will discuss how NetWare 4.11 loads this software, which is called NetWare Loadable Modules (NLMs). Specifically, we will address the NLMs that are responsible for providing the interface to the file system and the network. Without them, the server would be useless.

Another important component that affects the server performance is the memory. We learned that more memory in a server is better, but how the server uses that memory is also important. The memory management scheme used in NetWare 4.11 is different than the scheme used by all previous versions of NetWare. There is only one memory pool in NetWare 4.11 instead of the multiple memory pools in NetWare 3.x.

As we all know, the NetWare file system is organized in terms of volumes. There is always a SYS volume on every NetWare file server. Other volumes on the server are initially defined by you to help you organize the data in your file system. How NetWare stores files in the file system plays an important role in the performance of the file server. In this chapter, we will discuss both the volume structure and file system structure of the NetWare 4.11 server.

Finally, to communicate with other machines on the network, the NetWare 4.11 server by default uses the IPX/SPX protocol family, also known as the NetWare Core Protocol suite. We will cover the family of protocols and their functions in helping the server communicate with other NetWare servers and NetWare clients on the network.

The best place to start discussing the architecture of the NetWare 4.11 server is with the files that are required for the operating system. The operating system itself loads from a file called SERVER.EXE, which resides in the DOS partition. From this simple file, the powerful, complex NOS is started.

The Core Operating System Files & Their Roles

One of NetWare's biggest advantages over other network operating systems is its modularity. NetWare has several components that work together to perform the operating system's functions. The benefits of modularity are that third-party companies can develop additional functionality for NetWare and LAN administrators can use only the components they need, thus saving money and resources.

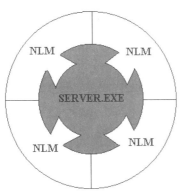

Figure 17-1: The modular architecture of NetWare 4.11.

The core of the NetWare operating system is the SERVER.EXE program. This portion of NetWare provides the foundation for the modular portions to "snap" into (Figure 17-1). The modules are called NetWare Loadable Modules (NLMs) and will be discussed in detail later in this chapter in the section "NLMs, Disk Drivers & Network Interfaces".

As we have mentioned previously (Chapter 1), NetWare 4.11 does not have its own bootstrap files. In order for the server to boot, it requires a small "kick" to get it going. It gets this kick from DOS. DOS must be booted first on the server; then SERVER.EXE can be launched from the DOS partition to load the NetWare OS.

When SERVER.EXE is executed, it takes over operating system functionality from DOS and loads any NLMs that it needs in order to function. At this point, DOS is no longer needed and can be removed from memory if desired. The memory that DOS was using will then be given to NetWare.

Tip

The NetWare 4.11 server can be automatically loaded as soon as you boot your server. Just add the line C:\NWSERVER\SERVER.EXE at the end of your AUTOEXEC.BAT file.

Just like most operating systems, NetWare has the ability to automatically load programs and drivers upon startup. NetWare accomplishes this with two files, the STARTUP.NCF and the AUTOEXEC.NCF. Both of these files are ASCII text files that contain NetWare commands, one per line, that are auto-matically executed by SERVER.EXE when it loads.

STARTUP.NCF

The first configuration file to load on the NetWare 4.11 server is the STARTUP.NCF file. It generally contains information concerning the NetWare disk drivers, memory management parameters, and filename space parameters.

The STARTUP.NCF file is located on the server's DOS partition in the C:\NWSERVER directory (or whatever directory the NetWare server files are stored in). The functions of this file are to set startup parameters for the server and to load disk driver NLMs so that NetWare can access disk subsystems.

Obviously, STARTUP.NCF has to exist in the DOS partition. Because NetWare 4.11 depends upon a disk driver to be loaded before it can access the NetWare file system, SERVER.EXE must load the disk driver from the DOS partition. It cannot load the disk driver from the NetWare file system to which it does not yet have access.

STARTUP.NCF is generally a small file. Here is an example of a typical STARTUP.NCF:

```
SET MINIMUM PACKET RECEIVE BUFFERS=200
SET RESERVED BUFFERS BELOW 16 MEG=200
LOAD CPQS710
LOAD CPQSDISK
```

Tip

*If necessary, the STARTUP.NCF can be prevented from automatically loading by starting SERVER.EXE with the -ns switch. At the DOS prompt, type **server -ns**.*

Two commands are commonly found in STARTUP.NCF files, SET and LOAD:

- **SET** Sets parameters that are used by the server as long as it is up.
- **LOAD** Loads NLMs (specifically disk drivers) into memory.

Once the STARTUP.NCF has finished executing its commands and mounting the SYS volume, it looks for a file on the SYS volume called AUTOEXEC.NCF and executes it. This file is located in the SYS:SYSTEM directory.

AUTOEXEC.NCF

The second file to load, AUTOEXEC.NCF, sets parameters and loads NLMs, which is similar to STARTUP.NCF's function. Typically the AUTOEXEC.NCF file configures things like the server's name, IPX numbers, and time zone. It also loads LAN drivers and other utility NLMs. The AUTOEXEC.NCF file executes after the STARTUP.NCF has run and the SYS volume has been mounted.

The following is an example AUTOEXEC.NCF:

```
FILE SERVER NAME FS_1
IPX INTERNAL NET 1AB23F222
SET BINDERY CONTEXT = O=USA

LOAD CPQNF3 SLOT=4 FRAME=ETHERNET_802.2
BIND IPX TO CPQNF3 NET=00000011

LOAD PSERVER USA_PS
LOAD MONITOR
```

Tip

If necessary, the AUTOEXEC.NCF can be prevented from automatically loading by starting SERVER.EXE with the na switch. At the DOS prompt, type **server -na**.

Since the AUTOEXEC.NCF file contains a long list of single commands that are normally executed from the server's console, we can add any of the many console commands that we would type in manually to this file. This automates the loading of NLMs and the configuration of the file server parameters (see Chapter 18). An explanation of some common commands used here can be found in Table 17-1.

Once the AUTOEXEC.NCF has finished executing, the server has finished loading. At this point you will be able to access the server with your client workstations. The server console prompt is displayed at the server console, indicating that the server is waiting for commands. This prompt (Figure 17-2) is shown as the server's name followed by a colon. Often referred to as the colon prompt, it is the interface to the NetWare server. If you need to issue server commands (like loading NLMs), it is done from the server console prompt.

Disk Drivers

The first type of NLM is the disk driver. The phrase "disk driver" is actually a misnomer. The disk driver NLM is not a driver for a disk drive but rather for the disk subsystem. Older disk driver NLMs (from NetWare 3.x days) have the extension DSK. NetWare 4.11 can use the older-style disk drivers, but it's optimized for components that conform to the NetWare Peripheral Architecture (NWPA).

NWPA drivers come in two parts. The first part, the Host Adapter Module (HAM), is the driver associated with host adapter (or disk controller). Once it is loaded, NetWare can route requests from the system to the specific disk device. The second part, Custom Device Module (CDM), is the driver associated with specific disk devices attached to the disk system. One CDM must be loaded for each disk device attached to the adapter.

Instead of loading one generic .DSK file for the whole disk subsystem, load a .HAM file for the adapter and one or more .CDM file(s) for the disk devices. If you have an SCSI adapter, an SCSI CD-ROM, and two SCSI hard disks, load one HAM for the adapter, a CDM for the CD-ROM, and two CDMs for the two hard disks.

Figure 17-3 shows the difference between the older and newer generations of physical device access. In the old NetWare 3.x environment, the device channel was specified by one driver. If this driver failed, the entire disk channel could not be accessed. In NetWare 4.11, the path to the data is defined by multiple drivers. If one device driver fails (a CDM), you can still access the other devices.

This modularity is beneficial to the developers of the physical devices and their drivers. Instead of having to make the new device compatible with an old driver, all they need to do is create a new CDM for the device. It will then just plug into the system.

Tip

Although NetWare includes support for IDE and other ISA-based disk technologies, it is not recommended that they be used. These technologies cannot handle multiple read/write requests simultaneously and thus have a detrimental impact on network performance.

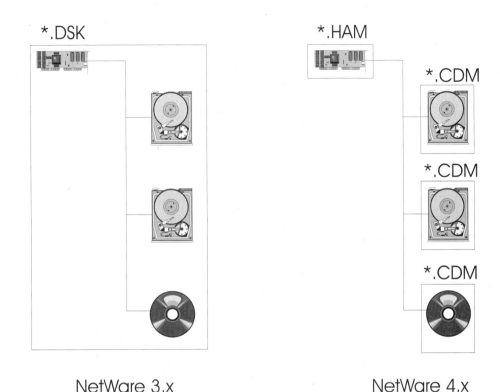

Figure 17-3: NetWare 4.11 uses a modular implementation to define the physical data channels.

When NetWare is installed, it automatically selects the appropriate disk driver NLM for your disk subsystem. If NetWare doesn't have the disk driver available for your server's hardware, or it can't detect the disk system, it will ask for the location of the proper disk driver NLM.

Once the disk driver has been loaded, the volumes can be mounted and file system access can be provided. By default, only DOS file system access is provided. This constrains users to use the DOS naming convention of up to eight letters followed by a period and a three-letter extension (commonly referred to as 8.3). For those file systems that need to use other filename conventions (like Macintosh, Windows 95, OS/2, UNIX, and so forth), you need to load another type of NLM, called a name space module.

Name Space Modules

Name space modules allow files from operating systems other than DOS to be stored in their native format on NetWare volumes. These NLMs typically have the NAM extension. The format for using them is slightly different than a regular NLM. First, the module must be loaded into memory using the standard LOAD command syntax. Then you use the ADD NAME SPACE command to add the name space module to a volume. The following series of commands will add the Macintosh name space to the SYS volume:

```
LOAD MAC.NAM
ADD NAME SPACE MAC TO SYS
```

After these commands have been issued, Macintosh computers will be able to save their files on the NetWare server. Other name space files include LONG.NAM for Windows 95, Windows NT, and OS/2 filename support, NFS.NAM for UNIX filename support, and FTAM.NAM for FTAM support. FTAM filename support must be purchased separately.

Tip

> *OS2.NAM was required for OS/2 name space in NetWare 4.1. In NetWare 4.11, support for OS/2 has been combined into LONG.NAM and OS2.NAM is no longer required.*

It should be noted that when name spaces are added to a volume, the number of directory entries supported by that volume is reduced by the number of name spaces loaded (by 1/2 for two name spaces, by 1/3 for three, and so on) because there has to be as many entries in the Directory Entry Table (DET) as there are name spaces. Also, adding each extra name space doubles the amount of memory required to mount that volume. Finally, once a name space is added, it cannot be removed without either deleting the volume and re-creating it (losing all data on the volume in the process) or by using VREPAIR.NLM. For more information on VREPAIR.NLM, refer to Chapter 18.

LAN Drivers

The next type of NLM is the LAN driver. The LAN driver is loaded to provide access to the network. It typically has the extension of LAN. Once loaded, the LAN driver provides a link between the network operating system and the network board. One LAN driver should be loaded for each network card installed in the file server. Each LAN driver can and must be loaded multiple times for multiple frame types running on the same network board. For example, if a server is running both ETHERNET_802.2 and ETHERNET_802.3 frame types on a single network card, the LAN driver will have to be loaded twice—once for each instance of the frame type as shown in the following example:

```
LOAD 3C59X SLOT=2 FRAME=ETHERNET_802.2 NAME=E822
LOAD 3C59X SLOT=2 FRAME=ETHERNET_802.3 NAME=E823
```

The first time the LAN driver is loaded, it will report its configuration as well as information like the driver name and frame type. Each subsequent time the driver is loaded, the server will respond, "The module has been used re-entrantly." This means the LAN driver has been reloaded successfully with another set of settings.

You'll notice from the preceding example that there is a *name* option at the end of the LOAD statement. This is to uniquely identify each instance of the LAN driver. If board instance names were not used, NetWare would have stopped and asked for the board instance to bind. This would be a bad thing if the AUTOEXEC.NCF were executing! You'll usually want your server to come up automatically (so you can reboot if from remote), which is why you should put these items in the AUTOEXEC.NCF in the first place.

Once a LAN driver is loaded, it does not mean the NetWare server can communicate with the rest of the network. A protocol needs to be logically attached, or *bound*, to an instance of the LAN driver. The most commonly bound protocol for NetWare servers is IPX, or Internetwork Packet Exchange. When binding IPX to an instance of a LAN driver, we need to specify an *IPX network number* so that all entities that are running IPX on the same network segment have a common address. The network address is an eight-digit hexa-decimal number. This parameter is set using the BIND command, as in the following example:

```
BIND IPX to E822 NET=A0000014
BIND IPX to E823 NET=A0000015
```

Once the protocol has been bound to the network board, the server will be able to communicate with the network. When NetWare 4.11 is installed, it automatically detects the appropriate LAN drivers and binds IPX. We will cover changing the LAN configuration in Chapter 18.

Once the disk drivers and the LAN drivers have been loaded on the server, it is ready to service user requests from the network. The remaining types of NLMs that can be loaded on the NetWare 4.11 server are generally enhance-ment or management NLMs, which are not required to provide basic services. We will cover these NLMs in the next section.

Management & Enhancement NLMs

We will discuss the management and enhancement NLMs together. Since the category is so broad, we couldn't possibly cover each NLM here, so we will discuss some general NLMs that are commonly loaded. For more information about Novell supplied NLMs, refer to the on-line documentation included with IntranetWare. Third party NLMs should come with instructions on how to use them.

Management and enhancement NLMs usually have the extension NLM and are loaded in the same manner as most NLMs. NLMs that fall under these two categories function as backup services, print services, management services (like SNMP, Managewise, and so forth), and server monitoring tools. Some commonly loaded NLMs are listed in Table 17-2. Use the LOAD command at the server console prompt (colon prompt) to load these NLMs into server memory.

NLM	NLM NAME	NLM Function
MONITOR.NLM	NetWare 4.11 Monitor Utility	Monitors NetWare functions and statistics. (See Chapter 18.)
INSTALL.NLM	NetWare 4.11 Installation Utility	Installs or reinstalls NetWare and its components. (See Chapter 18.)
SERVMAN.NLM	NetWare 4.11 Server Manager	Sets server parameters with a friendly interface (instead of using the SET command). (See Chapter 18.)
INETCFG.NLM	NetWare 4.11 Internetworking Configuration Utility	Used to dynamically configure LAN drivers, protocols, remote access, and bindings. (See Chapter 18.)
VREPAIR.NLM	NetWare 4.11 Volume Repair Utility	Used to repair corrupted volumes. Automatically run when a volume can't be mounted (this feature can be turned off, if needed). (See Chapter 18.)
PSERVER.NLM	NetWare 4.11 Print Server	Monitors print queues and shared printers. Sends print jobs from the queues to the printers. (See Chapter 7.)

Table 17-2: Commonly used NLMs and their functions.

Each time you load an NLM, it takes up a piece of server memory proportional to its size. An NLM that takes up approximately 500K of disk space will also require 500K of server memory for the duration it is loaded. As you can see, memory and NLMs are intertwined. In the next section, we will discuss NetWare 4.11 memory management.

Understanding NetWare 4.11 Memory Management

NetWare 4.11 has much better memory management and allocation than previous versions. Because of this, it is the most stable version of NetWare to date. If an NLM misbehaves and tries to take more memory than is allocated to it, NetWare management steps in. Rather than causing the server to abnormally end (ABEND) and crash, NetWare will just shut the offending process down, make a note in the ABEND.LOG file, and continue doing its job.

To discuss NetWare's memory management, we must discuss two concepts:

- Memory configuration
- Memory allocation

Memory Configuration

NetWare 4.11 keeps memory in one large memory pool rather than five pools as previous versions did. Memory is kept in this pool in 4K chunks known as *pages*. Pages are used for the main SERVER.EXE file when it is loaded into memory. They are also used for loading NLMs, caching files and directories, and caching packets from the network. The Directory Entry Table (DET) and File Allocation Table(s) (FAT) are also cached in memory pages. That's quite a bit of caching!

In NetWare 4.1, the memory structure differed from the memory structure in the old NetWare 3.x world. In NetWare 4.1, the memory was organized into memory rings. Ring 0 was reserved for operating system files, and Ring 3 could be used with DOMAIN.NLM to test NLMs. Due to the enhancements made to NetWare 4.11, the ring memory structure has been discarded. There are no memory rings—only one memory pool—in NetWare 4.11.

It is commonly said that when a workstation requests some information, 95 percent of the time it's already in server RAM. This is one of the features that makes NetWare the fastest NOS in networks today. It's also the reason to give NetWare as much RAM as possible.

There is actually a program that helps calculate the RAM requirements for a NetWare server. It is a freeware program, and you can get it from http:// www.connectotel.com/ctsoft.html. Table 17-3 offers a very general (as well as very generous) guideline for NetWare 4.11 server memory.

Component	Memory Required
Core OS	8MB
4GB disk (w/64K block size)	16MB
Support NLMs (CLIB, etc.)	4MB
Other NLMs	varies
PSERVER.NLM	4MB
Total (approx.)	32+MB

Table 17-3: Memory requirements for NetWare 4.11.

Again, we believe that the more server RAM, the better. If you are interested in specifically calculating the server RAM required for your setup, refer to Appendix A, "Calculate RAM Requirements" in the Installation manual. This manual can be found under the NetWare 4.11 Getting Started collection of your online documentation.

Memory Allocation

When an NLM loads, it is allocated memory from the pool of pages. An NLM performs best if its memory is in contiguous 4K blocks, so NetWare will try to allocate memory in one contiguous block. Memory is given to NLMs as 77 linked lists composed of the following memory blocks:

- 64 16-byte blocks for allocating memory space of up to 1K
- 12 25-byte blocks for allocating memory space of up to 4K
- 1 block for allocating memory spaces of 4K and larger.

Figure 17-4 shows the way memory is allocated for each NLM.

When an NLM is unloaded or has memory it doesn't need, it calls a memory API called FREE, which marks all or a portion of the NLM's memory as "not needed." When another NLM requests memory, the memory allocation routine scans each NLM's list for a chunk of memory equal to or greater than the size of the chunk requested. If it finds one, it just allocates that "not needed" memory to the NLM. If it can't find a "not needed" segment of the right size, it will get a new 4K block from the pool of pages.

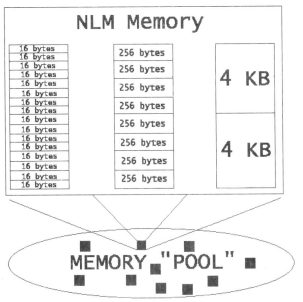

Figure 17-4: NLM memory allocation.

The problem is that this causes memory to be in noncontiguous blocks. After several NLM loads and unloads, the memory may become so fragmented that it may be impossible to assign enough contiguous memory blocks for another NLM to load even though there are plenty of blocks available. They may just be too far apart too allocate contiguously.

To solve this problem, NetWare has a routine called *garbage collection* that runs at either specified intervals or after certain conditions have been met. This routine examines all the free blocks on an NLM's lists, consolidates blocks on the smaller lists, and places them on the appropriate list for the new block's size. If the new block is larger than 4K, it is returned to the Cache Buffer pool.

With these features, NetWare's memory can operate very efficiently and have much fewer ABENDs or crashes. This is yet another case for upgrading from previous versions of NetWare to NetWare 4.11.

An In-Depth Look at the File System

NetWare has a very efficient file system. In previous versions, it was referred to as the directory tree. It is now referred to as the file system to prevent confusion with the NDS Directory. There is a definite hierarchy in the NetWare file system, as shown in Figure 17-5. A user's files are stored in the file system in directories, which are stored on volumes, which are made from partitions, which are part of physical disk drives.

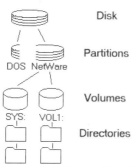

Figure 17-5: The NetWare file system hierarchy.

In this section, we will discuss the main components of the NetWare file system. Data on NetWare servers are logically stored in volumes. These volumes allow the network administrator to organize the data on the server. Once the volumes have been assigned, information about the files on the volume is stored in both the Directory Entry Table (DET) and File Allocation Table (FAT).

When a user requests information from the server, NetWare looks to the DET and FAT on the volume specified for the file. It retrieves the appropriate information about the physical location of the file on the volume and then accesses the file system to retrieve it. We will cover each one of these file system components—volumes, DET and FAT, and the file system itself—to provide a better understanding of the NetWare file system.

Understanding Volume Configuration

The lowest level of our hierarchy is the disk drive. NetWare is capable of using any type of disk drive but is optimized for use with SCSI-based hard drives (SCSI, SCSI-2, etc.). Before NetWare can be installed, at least one disk drive must be installed in the server. Redundant Array of Inexpensive Disks (RAID) systems may also be configured at this point to provide fault tolerance for your data.

The next level is the partition level. All NetWare servers have at least two partitions, one DOS partition and one NetWare partition. A server with this configuration would only have one volume. NetWare manages its own resources and only needs DOS to start up; therefore, the DOS partition is almost always the first partition. All subsequent partitions will be NetWare partitions. It is from these NetWare partitions that NetWare volumes are created.

NetWare volumes are the lowest unit of disk storage that users have access to. Volumes are created during system install time or afterward using INSTALL.NLM and can be named at your discretion. For more information concerning INSTALL.NLM, refer to Chapter 18.

Tip

The first volume is always *called SYS. It cannot be renamed or deleted (without destroying all of the information on it).*

There are several different ways of configuring volumes. The first is to create one volume per partition, illustrated in Figure 17-6. This has the advantage of being the best compromise between performance and redundancy.

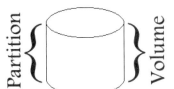

Figure 17-6: One volume per partition.

Another option is to have several volume segments stored on different partitions, making one big volume (Figure 17-7). This has the advantage of allowing volume sizes that are much larger than the largest physical disk size. However, since there are more partitions per disk, there is a higher probability that the volume will fail because if one partition fails, the entire volume fails.

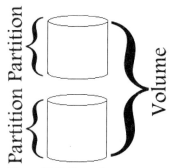

Figure 17-7: One volume over several partitions.

The last possibility for configuring volumes is to have more than one volume per partition. This has the advantage of maximizing the use of volume space while allowing for separation of volumes (Figure 17-8). This configuration is most commonly found if the server only has one disk drive and two volumes are needed to keep files off of the SYS volume.

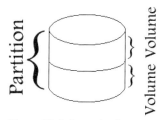

Figure 17-8: Several volumes on one partition.

There are a few limitations on the creation of volumes:

- A hard disk can contain up to 8 volume segments.
- Each volume can consist of up to 32 volume segments.
- Minimum size of the SYS volume is 2.5MB.
- There can be 16 million directory entries per volume.
- There can be up to 64 volumes per server.

At the time of this writing, these limitations affect only a few people. The largest commonly available hard disks currently hold around 9GB. That would give a "limitation" of 18432GB, or about 18 terabytes (9 GB X 32 segments and 64 volumes). Of course, people once thought that 20MB disks would have more than enough space.

Once they are created, volumes need to be *mounted* so that NetWare can access them. This is done using the MOUNT command at the server console prompt (colon prompt). The syntax is as follows:

```
MOUNT <volume name>
```

Once the command is issued, the server will tell you that it is "Mounting Volume *<volume name>*" and will tell you its status. NetWare and users can then access the files stored on that volume.

The final level of the filing system hierarchy comprises the files and directories themselves. (We covered the structure of file system in Chapter 6.) The way files and directories are accessed is rather efficient.

Directory Entry Table & File Allocation Table

There are two special files on each volume, the File Allocation Table (FAT) and the Directory Entry Table (DET). They can't be seen because they are stored at the partition level. These two files work together to provide access to the files stored on the hard disk. The FAT stores information on where the parts of a particular file are stored. The FAT is cached in RAM on the server, so the files on the volume can be accessed quickly and efficiently.

The Directory Entry Table is located on the volume and contains information about files, directories, or other items on the volume. The DET is contained within several directory blocks on a volume. A directory block is a 4K chunk of file system space. Each entry in the DET is 128 bytes long. So there can be up to 32 directory entries (4096 bytes/128 bytes per entry=32 entries) in each DET. When a directory is created, the server allocates a 4K block for that directory. All files stored within that directory have entries in the DET. The maximum number of directory entries per volume is 2,097,152.

When there gets to be more than 32 entries in the DET, another directory block is allocated to accommodate the new entries. The DET is particularly important in terms of the NetWare file system. It stores information like the directory's name and location, but it stores information about the file system trustee assignments for that directory as well. Without the DET, the file system security would be compromised.

In addition to the DET and FAT, which are stored in a special location on the physical disk drive, all other files in the file system are stored on the physical disk. The operating system is responsible for processing the user requests and fetching the files, which is transparent to the user. However, how the operating system stores the information on the hard drive and processes it is quite interesting.

Understanding the NetWare File System

The NetWare file system has several features in addition to its structure that make it very efficient for storing files—block suballocation, file compression, disk read ahead, and the elevator seek algorithm.

Block Suballocation

The first item of importance in the file system architecture is the block suballocation routine. When a volume is created, a block size is specified. The block size determines the smallest block of disk space allocated for each file stored. Common choices are 4K, 16K, 32K, 64K, and 128K. One problem with block sizes concerns smaller files. If a small file (like 1K) is saved, NetWare allocates a whole disk block for the file. If the block size was set to 32K, 31K of disk space would be wasted, as illustrated in Figure 17-9. The solution is to use block suballocation.

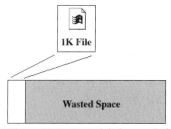

Figure 17-9: Wasted disk space before block suballocation.

When a file smaller than the disk block size needs to be stored, NetWare allocates a full disk block to the file. Whatever is left over is divided up into 512-byte suballocation blocks. Together, all the suballocated blocks make up the suballocation pool for the entire file system.

When a file larger than the block size is saved (for instance, a 33K file with a 32K block size), rather than allocate a full disk block, NetWare will grab suballocation blocks from the suballocation pool to allocate enough space for the file, as shown in Figure 17-10.

With block suballocation enabled, more efficient use of disk space for smaller files is attained. It can only be enabled or disabled at system install time. It is enabled by default. Unused blocks are recycled by the operating system and used for other files instead of wasting a portion of your file system.

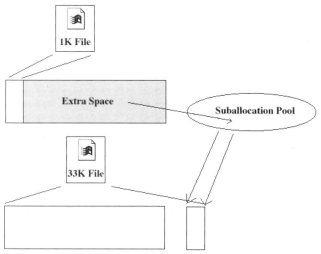

Figure 17-10: A dramatic amount of disk space is saved by using block suballocation.

File Compression

Another feature of NetWare 4.11 that makes file storage more efficient is file compression. With this feature enabled on a volume, it will commonly provide space gains of 60-70 percent.

When a file has not been accessed for a particular amount of time (typically a week), it is marked by the server as ready for compression. Then, during the time period set up for compression, all the files that have been marked are compressed. This does, however, have side effects of increased server processor utilization and extra load on the server.

Tip

There is a SET parameter on the server that controls when the server starts and stops compressing files. The parameters are:

```
SET DAILY COMPRESSION CHECK START HOUR=0
SET DAILY COMPRESSION CHECK STOP HOUR=6
```

The default times are shown (with 0 being midnight and 6 being 6:00 a.m.). This also happens to be the time many businesses do their backups. If backup and compression happen at the same time, it is possible that the server may lock up, the backup will take an extremely long time, or both. It is best to schedule both of these events so that they do not coincide.

To compress a file, the server reads and analyzes it. Once the file as been analyzed, a temporary file is built from the information in the original file. If any disk space can be saved by compressing the file, the server will continue. If not, the server deletes the temporary file and continues on to the next file. Once a compressed version of the file has been built, the compressed file and original file change places. When the compressed version has been determined to be error free, the original is deleted.

When accessed again, the files aren't decompressed immediately; that will put an undue load on the server. The operating system can leave the file compressed always, uncompress after the second access, or uncompress always. As the network administrator, you can set the parameters for file compression.

Disk Read Ahead

When it asks to retrieve a file, a workstation normally tells the server which file to get. The server checks to see if the file exists and if the user has the rights to get that file. If all requirements are met, the server retrieves the first part of the file and sends it to the workstation. The workstation receives it and asks for the second part. The server then goes and retrieves the second part and sends it to the workstation. This process continues until the workstation has the entire file.

NetWare improves on this process with a little bit of intelligence. If a workstation requests the first part of a file, there is a good chance that it's going to need the rest of it. So NetWare reads ahead and gets the rest of the file into memory. When the workstation asks for the second part of the file, rather than have to go to the disk to get it, NetWare gets it from RAM. Since RAM is faster than hard disks (nanoseconds compared to milliseconds), file reads are much more efficient.

Retrieving Files: The Elevator Seek Algorithm

The last feature of the NetWare file system is its ability to efficiently manage disk requests with the feature known as the *elevator seek algorithm*. Since NetWare caches everything, including disk reads and writes, it can put them in a logical order. It can then make retrieval more efficient. To understand how this works, let's take a look at how an elevator works.

Rather than service each request to go to a floor as it receives it, an elevator will stop at requested floors on the way up and on the way down. It can then move the passengers more quickly and efficiently. NetWare does the same with disk requests. Rather than read each file as it is requested, NetWare will reorder the disk requests with the elevator seek algorithm so that the read/write head is handling requests in order from sector to sector and from track to track; thus, head movement is not wasted.

Figure 7-11 shows an example of the elevator seek algorithm. Let's say the NetWare 4.11 server gets the request for resources in the following locations: 4, 27, 13, 1, 35, 22, and 6 in that order. Instead of going to each one individually and wasting precious seek time, it looks at the hard drive read head's initial position and orders the request for the most efficient file access. In our diagram, the read head is at position 20 going down. It will access the resources in the order 13, 6, 4, 1, 22, 27, 35. This eliminates unnecessary seek time and retrieves the data faster.

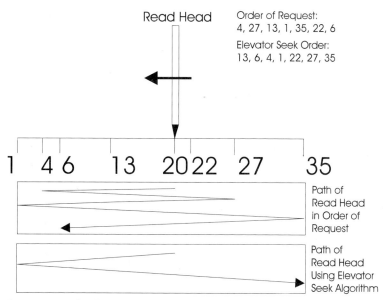

Figure 17-11: The elevator seek algorithm orders the requests for most efficient file access.

Combined with the lack of a heavy, graphical interface, these features make NetWare one of the most efficient file servers on the market today. It is common to have a NetWare file server servicing hundreds of users. It's a lean, mean, networking machine! But just as important as its ability to access data efficiently is the fact that the NetWare 4.11 server must be able to communicate that information to the client workstations. It is able to do so through the Novell NetWare Core Protocol (NCP) suite.

The NetWare Core Protocol Suite

When humans communicate, there is a need for everyone involved to understand a common set of rules. For example, if they choose to speak English, they all have to understand that short groupings called sentences must be used. Also, they have to understand that there needs to be at least one noun and one verb in every sentence. And they need to use a common set of words to make up those sentences. Anyone who does not follow the rules will not be able to communicate with the others.

The same idea applies to networks. All entities on the physical network that want to communicate will have to "speak" the same protocols. On a NetWare network, the server uses the following protocols to communicate:

- Internetwork Packet Exchange (IPX)
- Sequenced Packet Exchange (SPX)
- NetWare Core Protocol (NCP)
- Routing Information Protocol (RIP)
- Service Advertising Protocol (SAP)

Each one of these protocols provides a specific service on the network. For instance, IPX and SPX are used almost exclusively for NetWare file and print services. On the other hand, RIP and SAP are used to communicate important network information between the NetWare servers on your network. Each one provides a specific function, and together they can provide comprehensive networking services.

The IPX & SPX Protocols

Internetwork Packet Exchange (IPX) is the primary protocol that NetWare "speaks." It is based on Xerox's Internetwork Datagram Protocol (IDP) and corresponds to the Network layer of the Open Systems Interconnection (OSI) model. It is connectionless, meaning the protocol has no error, packet sequence, or flow control built in. This has the benefit of being a very efficient protocol but the disadvantage of reducing the reliability of the communication session.

To solve this problem, Sequenced Packet Exchange (SPX) was implemented as an extension of IPX. Based on Xerox's Sequenced Packet Protocol, SPX is connection oriented and uses connection identifiers (connection IDs) placed in the SPX header of an IPX datagram to establish a reliable end-to-end connection.

When network entities communicate via IPX, each entity needs to have its own address. These addresses are given in the format:

```
[SEGMENT IPX ADDRESS:LOCAL MAC ADDRESS]
```

The segment IPX address is an eight-digit hexadecimal number given to each network segment (a shared medium not crossing any bridges or routers). The local Media Access Control (MAC) address is the physical address given to a network card when it's manufactured. In addition to this address, each server has an internal IPX address, which is an eight-digit hexadecimal number that uniquely identifies each server.

Tip

Each internal IPX network number on the entire network must be unique. If there is a duplicate internal IPX network number, neither server can be seen by a workstation.

Connecting to the Internet seems to be the "in" thing to do to networks these days, so most programs and operating systems are being written to support TCP/IP, the primary protocol used on the Internet. NetWare 4.11 has native support for TCP/IP built in. Protocols like SNMP, FTP, HTTP, and TELNET are supported by NetWare 4.11. It is possible to communicate from client to server in a NetWare environment with TCP/IP, but not without an addition to the TCP/IP stack on both client and server. For more information on TCP/IP, refer to Chapters 15 and 18.

NetWare Core Protocol (NCP)

Communication with IPX between NetWare and its servers and workstations relies on a subset of IPX called the NetWare Core Protocol (NCP). All requests for services and resources from workstation to server use NCP calls.

If we compare NCP running over IPX to our U.S. mail system, we can see that NCP is like the letter and IPX is like the mail carrier. When we send mail, we put our message in an envelope and hand it off to the mail carrier. From there the mail carrier (eventually) hands off the mail to the recipient. The recipient opens the envelope and reads the message.

NCP works in a similar manner. A workstation makes a request for a file from a particular file server. An NCP request is handed to an IPX packet to deliver to the server. When the packet gets to the server, the server opens the IPX packet and reads the NCP request. It then responds by sending an NCP reply with the file attached.

We can change the mail system and still get the letter to its destination. We just use a mail carrier like UPS or Federal Express. We can also get our NCP requests to the NetWare server by encapsulating those requests in TCP/IP headers. By doing this, we can standardize on one protocol for both internal and Internet networks.

The software that allows us to encapsulate NCP requests in IP header is called NetWare/IP and is covered in Chapter 19. The benefits of using IP instead of NCP are tremendous because IP reduces the amount of traffic on your network and can increase its performance significantly.

The RIP & SAP Protocols

The Routing Information Protocol (RIP) is another subset of IPX that performs a special function. RIP is the protocol that discovers network addresses and the paths to them. To explain RIP, we'll extend the mail carrier analogy.

In smaller communities, rural mail addresses have a route number and a box number, such as RR2 Box 180a, which tells us very little about where someone actually lives. How does the mail carrier know how to deliver the mail? Hypothetically, there could be one person whose job is to go out and find the physical locations for all the rural addresses. He or she could also share this information with other communities in return for similar information from them.

RIP is similar in concept. Routers on the network (including NetWare servers) will send out RIP packets to discover nodes on its own network segments. Once a router compiles this information, it broadcasts it to other routers. RIP also receives these broadcasts and adds the other routers' information to its own. It will then rebroadcast the new information. Eventually, every router on the network knows about every other router and node. This is the way RIP and other *distance vector* protocols discover routing information.

The last part of the IPX/SPX protocol suite is the Service Advertising Protocol (SAP). SAP, as its name implies, advertises services on the network. Using SAP broadcasts, a server will send out periodic advertisements saying what services it is hosting. It will also poll other items that are SAPing and record what services they are hosting.

NetWare provides a feature that allows us to track RIP and SAP events so we can better understand the communication between NetWare 4.11 servers— the TRACK feature. To turn it on, type the following at the server console prompt (colon prompt):

```
TRACK ON
```

Once this command has been issued, you will see two screens like the ones in Figure 17-12 and 17-13.

```
OUT [00000778:00A02466C100]  5:53:13am    32E7C5B9  1/2
IN  [00000777:00A02466C100]  5:53:15am    Specific Route Request
OUT [00000778:00A02466C100]  5:53:15am    32E7C5B9  1/2
IN  [00000778:00A02466C100]  5:53:15am    Specific Route Request
OUT [00000778:00A02466C100]  5:53:15am    32E7C5B9  1/2
IN  [00000778:00A02466C100]  5:53:16am    Specific Route Request
OUT [00000777:00A02466C100]  5:53:16am    32E7C5B9  1/2
IN  [00000778:00A02466C100]  5:53:16am    Specific Route Request
OUT [00000778:00A02466C100]  5:53:16am    32E7C5B9  1/2
IN  [00000777:00A02466C100]  4:02:00pm    Specific Route Request
OUT [00000777:00A02466C100]  4:02:00pm    32E7C5B9  1/2
IN  [00000778:00A02466C100]  4:02:00pm    Specific Route Request
OUT [00000778:00A02466C100]  4:02:00pm    32E7C5B9  1/2
IN  [00000777:00A02466C100]  4:23:35pm    Specific Route Request
OUT [00000777:00A02466C100]  4:23:35pm    32E7C5B9  1/2
IN  [00000777:00A02466C100]  4:23:35pm    Specific Route Request
OUT [00000777:00A02466C100]  4:23:35pm    32E7C5B9  1/2
IN  [00000777:00A02466C100]  4:23:35pm    Specific Route Request
OUT [00000777:00A02466C100]  4:23:35pm    32E7C5B9  1/2
IN  [00000777:00A02466C100]  4:23:38pm    Specific Route Request
OUT [00000777:00A02466C100]  4:23:38pm    32E7C5B9  1/2
IN  [00000777:00A02466C100]  4:23:38pm    Specific Route Request
OUT [00000777:00A02466C100]  4:23:38pm    32E7C5B9  1/2
<Use ALT-ESC or CTRL-ESC to switch screens, or any other key to pause>
```

Figure 17-12: RIP TRACK screen.

In Figure 17-12, you'll see the TRACK screen, which displays RIP information. You'll notice that the majority (in fact all) of the items are *route requests*, which are requests from other routers on the network looking for new networks. The INs and OUTs on the left side are requests coming in or their responses going out, respectively. The next column (to the right) shows either the IPX network address of the initiating entity (for IN entries) or the IPX network address of the destination entity (for OUT entries).

The column to the right of the IPX addresses is the time the request was processed. And finally, the last column contains either the type of request (specific route request in this case) or the internal IPX number of the server responding and how many hops/ticks away from its destination the server is. A *hop* is a router and a *tick* is approximately 1/18th of a second. These values indicate if the server is local or across a WAN.

Figure 17-13 displays the information commonly found on the SAP TRACK screen. Just like with the RIP TRACK screen, the leftmost column indicates whether a request was IN to or OUT from the server. The next two columns show the source of the request or the destination of the response and the time of the request or response, respectively. The last column describes the request or response and what information it returned (if any). In this case, the request is for the name of the nearest server and for the server to send all of its information.

```
IN   [00000777:00A02466C100]   5:53:12am   Send All Server Info
OUT  [00000777:00A02466C100]   5:53:12am   DAVE_411        1
IN   [00000778:00A02466C100]   5:53:12am   Send All Server Info
OUT  [00000778:00A02466C100]   5:53:12am   DAVE_411        1
IN   [00000777:00A02466C100]   5:53:13am   Get Nearest Server
OUT  [00000777:00A02466C100]   5:53:13am   Give Nearest Server
  DAVE_411
IN   [00000777:00A02466C100]   5:53:13am   Get Nearest Server
OUT  [00000777:00A02466C100]   5:53:13am   Give Nearest Server
  DAVE_TREE_____ù ┌W┌K@@@@@DàPJ
IN   [00000778:00A02466C100]   5:53:14am   Get Nearest Server
OUT  [00000778:00A02466C100]   5:53:14am   Give Nearest Server
  DAVE_TREE_____ù ┌W┌K@@@@@DàPJ
IN   [00000777:00A02466C100]   5:53:15am   Send All Server Info
OUT  [00000777:00A02466C100]   5:53:15am   DAVE_TREE___    1
IN   [00000778:00A02466C100]   5:53:15am   Send All Server Info
OUT  [00000778:00A02466C100]   5:53:15am   DAVE_TREE___    1
IN   [00000777:00A02466C100]   5:53:16am   Get Nearest Server
OUT  [00000777:00A02466C100]   5:53:16am   Give Nearest Server
  DAVE_TREE_____ù ┌W┌K@@@@@DàPJ
IN   [00000777:00A02466C100]   4:23:35pm   Get Nearest Server
OUT  [00000777:00A02466C100]   4:23:35pm   Give Nearest Server
  DAVE_411
<Use ALT-ESC or CTRL-ESC to switch screens, or any other key to pause>
```

Figure 17-13: SAP TRACK screen.

Together, these protocols allow communication between workstations and servers and allow the mail, to use our analogy, in all of its forms to be delivered to the appropriate places.

Moving On

NetWare has several features that make it one of the most efficient network operating systems on the market today. The basic modular design of NetWare has remained unchanged over the past few years. But because of its efficiency, it will still be the design that other network operating systems are modeled after for years to come. A summary of the NetWare architecture is shown in Figure 17-14.

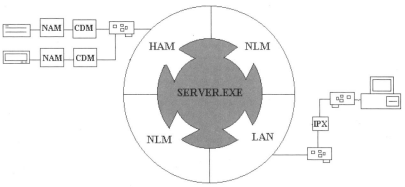

Figure 17-14: The NetWare architecture.

In the next chapter, we will take a step away from the architecture of the server and talk more about the management of the server. Once you understand the architecture and the function of the NetWare 4.11 operating system, you can appropriately "tweak" specific parameters to improve the performance of your server.

18

NetWare 4.11 Server Management

In the last chapter, you learned about the architecture of the NetWare 4.11 server. You know which files are required to start the server. You also know about the modularity of the NetWare 4.11 server. Programs called NetWare Loadable Modules (NLMs) are loaded on the server and build upon the core operating system to enhance the functionality of the server.

You know the basic functions NLMs provide; however, there is much more to managing the NetWare 4.11 server than just understanding the purpose of NLMs. The server is the main shared resource on your network. Assuming the network cabling itself is fine, the performance of the network is directly attributed to the server. If it is not performing up to an acceptable standard, then steps must be taken to see that it does.

Servers are just like children. They require constant attention and management. They also grow up and eventually move out (the latter applies more to children than to servers, but servers do grow). And yes, they do throw the occasional tantrum. This chapter deals with the parenting of our "children." We'll discuss the care and feeding of the server (adding options to the server) as well as the baby-sitting (performance monitoring) you perform as a network administrator.

In this chapter, we will cover the main utilities which are used to help you configure the NetWare 4.11 server. These utilities include INSTALL.NLM, SERVMAN.NLM, MONITOR.NLM, and INETCFG.NLM and are responsible for everything from installing and configuring IntranetWare components to configuring the network. As a network administrator, you will become intimate with these utilities.

Changing Installation Options & Editing System Files: INSTALL.NLM

A NetWare server is a dynamic entity just like the business it serves. From time to time, you need to add functionality to your servers to meet the growing demands of your business. NetWare has a common way of adding options to a server. That way is INSTALL.NLM.

The INSTALL.NLM is used during the installation of NetWare to guide the installer through the copying and initial setup of NetWare. It can also be used after the initial installation to perform other server functions. To load INSTALL.NLM, follow the same syntax as most other NLMs and type the following at the server console prompt:

```
LOAD INSTALL
```

Once loaded, INSTALL presents us with several options (see Figure 18-1). As with most NetWare NLMs, the gray bar at the bottom of the screen gives help as to what to do next. In this NLM utility, you navigate using the arrow keys and select using Enter or F10. F1 gives you some generic help information, and Alt+F10 will exit from anywhere in the menu system (although changes will not be saved).

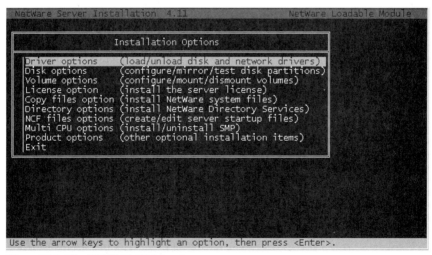

Figure 18-1: The INSTALL.NLM main menu.

As you can see, INSTALL.NLM gives you the ability to perform a wide variety of tasks. You can do everything from modify disk and LAN driver options to install new products. INSTALL.NLM will allow you to configure the following options:

- Driver Options
- Disk Options
- Volume Options
- License Option
- Copy Files Option
- Directory Options
- NCF Files Options
- Multi CPU Options
- Product Options

We will discuss these options one at a time to get you familiar with the INSTALL.NLM interface. As the network administrator, you will use the INSTALL.NLM utility frequently. Acquaint yourself with the available options.

Driver Options

By choosing Driver Options from the Installation Options menu of INSTALL.NLM, you have the ability to add additional drivers to NetWare (Figure 18-2). When you add new hardware, especially disks, you need to load a driver to access the new hardware. We discussed why you need to add drivers in Chapter 17. It is easiest to load them with INSTALL.NLM.

Figure 18-2: The INSTALL.NLM Driver Options screen.

NetWare has the ability to auto-detect both disk and LAN drivers. Select either Configure Disk and Storage Device Drivers or Configure Network Drivers, respectively. Once you select either option, a screen similar to Figure

18-3 will appear in which you can tell NetWare to either auto-detect a new driver or manually load or unload one. During that process, you can select the configuration settings for each respective driver.

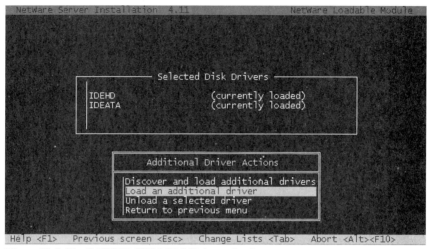

Figure 18-3: The INSTALL.NLM Disk Driver selection screen.

By having NetWare auto-detect the new driver, you take the difficulty out of determining exactly which driver is necessary for the piece of hardware you installed. NetWare 4.11 takes the guesswork out of the equation.

Disk Options

The next item in the Installation Options menu of INSTALL.NLM is the Disk Options selection. It brings up the screen in Figure 18-4, which you can use to make and delete disk partitions as well as to mirror disk partitions. When you mirror partitions, you increase the fault tolerance of the disk system. Whatever is saved to the volume(s) on the first partition is also saved to the second partition. If one partition fails, the other takes over automatically.

Figure 18-4: The INSTALL Disk Options screen.

When you select the first option, Modify Disk Partitions and Hot Fix, you will be asked for the device about which you want to view information. Select the appropriate device by highlighting it and pressing Enter. The partition information for the physical disk will be displayed as in Figure 18-5. You can make NetWare partitions out of free, unpartitioned disk space. If any disk space is available, highlight Create NetWare Disk Partition and select the free space by pressing Enter. NetWare will ask you how big to make the partition.

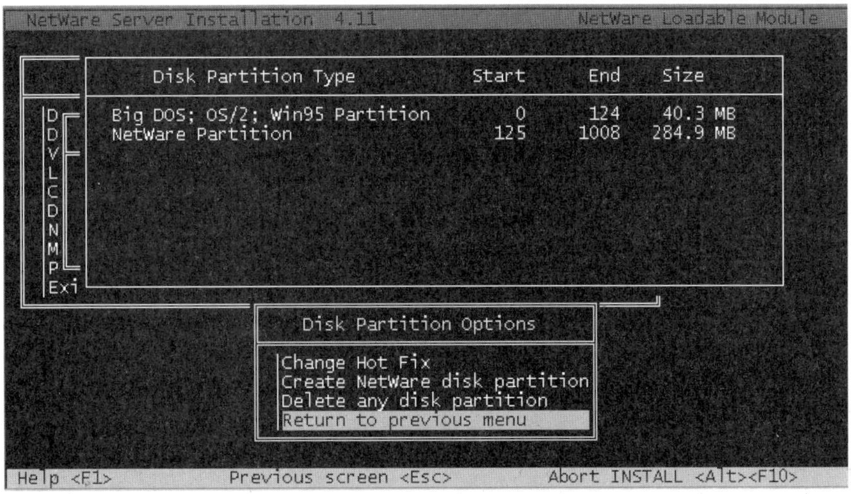

```
NetWare Server Installation  4.11                    NetWare Loadable Module

        Disk Partition Type          Start      End     Size

  D   Big DOS; OS/2; Win95 Partition      0      124    40.3 MB
  D   NetWare Partition                 125     1008   284.9 MB
  V
  L
  C
  D
  N
  M
  P
  Exi

                    Disk Partition Options

                Change Hot Fix
                Create NetWare disk partition
                Delete any disk partition
                Return to previous menu

 Help <F1>       Previous screen <Esc>       Abort INSTALL <Alt><F10>
```

Figure 18-5: Disk partition information.

Normally you would make it as big as the disk drive (minus any other partitions on the drive). NetWare will also ask how much of the partition to use as the Hot Fix area. Less than 1 percent of the available disk space is typically used for Hot Fix areas. You can use the arrow keys to move between the fields and the Enter key to accept the value. When you are finished specifying partition sizes, press either F10 or Escape to save the changes and continue.

Tip

Normally, the Hot Fix area is handled by NetWare, but some disk systems handle Hot Fix redirection at the hardware level. Hot Fix happens when NetWare writes a block of data to disk and reads it back to check its integrity. If the disk block is bad, NetWare marks it as such and saves the block of data to the Hot Fix area.

The next option on the Available Disk Options menu is Mirror/Unmirror Disk Partitions. It allows you to select a partition and then to select another partition to be mirrored to the first. Once the partitions are mirrored, any volumes created on the first partition will also be created on the second. Any data saved to any volume on the first partition will also be saved to the same volume on the second. The second partition is a mirror of the first.

You can also perform a surface test from the Available Disk Options menu (which is unnecessary with today's disk systems). The surface scan tests the physical media of the hard disk to see if there are any imperfections which exist on it. You can also scan for additional devices (which is mostly unnecessary—if NetWare can't see the drive, there's probably something else wrong). To return to the Installation Options menu, press Escape.

Volume Options

The next item on the Installation Options screen of INSTALL.NLM is Volume Options. With this option, you can create and mount NetWare volumes. When you select Volume Options and press Enter, the screen in Figure 18-6 will be displayed. All of the currently configured volumes will be shown.

If you need to create a volume on a new NetWare partition, press the Insert key. The Volume Segment List will be displayed showing all volume disk segments. Select the free space by pressing Enter to create the new volume. INSTALL.NLM will then ask if you want to make this segment a whole new volume or add this free space to an existing volume.

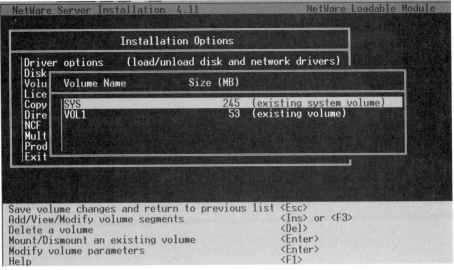

Figure 18-6: The Volume Options screen.

To make a new volume, select Make This Segment a New Volume. You will be prompted for the volume's name and how much of the free space you want to appropriate for the volume's use. Enter the value and press F10. You will be returned to the Volume Segment List screen where you can make additional volume assignments or delete existing volume assignments. To delete an existing volume, highlight the volume you want to delete and press the Delete key.

Tip

If you delete a volume, all the data on that volume is gone! *It can't be retrieved. Make sure this is what you want to do before committing to it.*

Once you have made or changed volume assignments, press Escape and select Yes from the menu that appears to save the changes. NetWare will ask you to log in so that it can make, delete, or change objects in NDS. When you log in to the NDS tree, the user account you use must have sufficient rights to make the modifications required. For example, if you have added a new volume, you will need to have the Create object right to the appropriate container to which you are adding the volume object.

Once NetWare has made the necessary changes, it will ask you if you want to mount the newly created volume. Select Mount Volumes if you want your users to be able to access that volume immediately. If you want to mount it manually, you can press Alt+Escape until you reach the server console prompt. To mount the volume manually, type **mount all** at the server console prompt. This will cause all NetWare volumes on that server to be mounted.

License Option

The next option on the INSTALL.NLM Installation Options menu is the License Option, which allows you to add or remove NetWare licenses from the server. Since NetWare uses additive licensing, also called stackable licensing, you can combine licenses to arrive at the total number of licensed connections required.

For example, if you need 35 user licenses, you would install a 10-user license and a 25-user license. The licenses must have different license numbers (located on the back of the license diskette) and must be specifically for NetWare 4.11. Combining licenses is more cost-effective because you will not need to purchase a 50-user license to accommodate a lesser number of connections. You can just buy the specific amount of licenses you need.

When the License Option is selected in the Installation Options menu, the screen shown in Figure 18-7 will appear. If you press Enter, INSTALL.NLM will look in the A:\ (floppy) drive of the server for the IntranetWare license disk. If one is found, INSTALL.NLM will add it to the server. You can also press F3 from the screen shown in Figure 18-7 to specify the location of the SERVER.MLS file. Type in the location and press Enter. You can delete the last installed license by pressing the F8 key.

Tip

You cannot selectively delete licenses. If you have 4 licenses installed in, for example, this order—5-user, 100-user, 50-user, 25-user—you cannot remove the 5-user license without first removing the 25-, 50-, and 100-user licenses in that order.

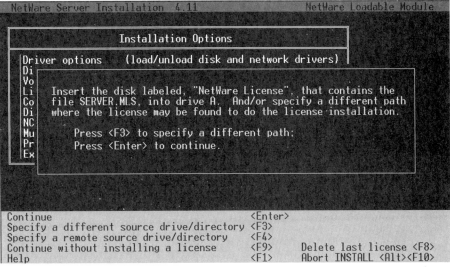

```
NetWare Server Installation 4.11                    NetWare Loadable Module

┌──────────────────────────────────────────────────────┐
│                Installation Options                    │
│ Driver options    (load/unload disk and network drivers) │
│ Di┌─────────────────────────────────────────────────────┐
│ Vo│                                                       │
│ Li│  Insert the disk labeled, "NetWare License", that contains the │
│ Co│  file SERVER.MLS, into drive A.  And/or specify a different path │
│ Di│  where the license may be found to do the license installation. │
│ NC│                                                       │
│ Mu│      Press <F3> to specify a different path;          │
│ Pr│      Press <Enter> to continue.                       │
│ Ex│                                                       │
   └─────────────────────────────────────────────────────┘



Continue                                  <Enter>
Specify a different source drive/directory <F3>
Specify a remote source drive/directory   <F4>
Continue without installing a license     <F9>    Delete last license <F8>
Help                                      <F1>    Abort INSTALL <Alt><F10>
```

Figure 18-7: The License Option screen.

IntranetWare licenses are sold in 5-, 10-, 25-, 50-, 100-, 250-, 500-, and 1,000-user packages. Your total number of user connections is the sum of these licenses. For instance, you could not have a 78-user license connection. You would have to buy a 50-user, 25-user, and 5-user license to allow the 78 users to connect to your network.

Copy Files Option

The Copy Files Option is really only used in two cases. It is used when the system is first installed to copy all of the operating system files to the SYS volume. If some of the files get corrupted, you can also use the Copy Files Option to restore them from the original installation CD.

To select this option, highlight it and press Enter. You will be presented with a screen that asks you for the location of the NetWare 4.11 installation CD. You can either accept the default location (the location from which the server was originally installed) by pressing Enter, or you can press F3 to specify a different path. Once the files have been located, INSTALL.NLM will start copying them to their appropriate location. As it copies the files, INSTALL.NLM will display a status bar indicating its progress. When it is finished, INSTALL.NLM will indicate whether or not the file copy was successful.

Tip

After the files have been copied, it is usually a good idea to down the server and restart it so that fresh copies of the NLMs will be loaded.

Directory Options

The next option in the Installation Options menu is Directory Options. This selection allows you to add, remove, and modify NDS on the NetWare 4.11 server. When Directory Options is selected, the screen in Figure 18-8 will be displayed. If NetWare 4.11 has already been installed, the first option in the Directory Services Options menu, Install Directory Services Onto This Server, won't do you any good. You need to use the second option, Remove Directory Services From This Server, before installing NDS again.

```
                 Directory Services Options
  Install Directory Services onto this server
  Remove Directory Services from this server
  Upgrade NetWare 3.x bindery information to the Directory
  Upgrade mounted volumes into the Directory
  Directory backup and restore options
  Return to the previous menu
```

Figure 18-8: The Directory Services Options screen.

Install Directory Services Onto This Server

If you have removed NDS from the server, select Install Directory Services Onto This Server to reinstall it. NetWare will walk you through the installation of Directory Services following the same procedure used when you installed the server for the first time. For more information on installing Directory Services, see Chapter 2.

Remove Directory Services From This Server

The next option, Remove Directory Services From This Server, is one that should be handled carefully. Remember that NDS is the backbone of your network. All of your users, servers, printers, and other network resources have an entry in the Directory. If there is only one server on the network, you will lose all of the information in the Directory when you remove NDS.

If you have multiple servers in an NDS tree, you can remove NDS without any major effect to the health of the tree; however, no one will be able to access any of the resources hosted by a server once NDS is removed from it.

To remove Directory Services, select that option from the Directory Services Options menu. Once selected, INSTALL.NLM will warn you not to remove NDS unless it is necessary to do so. To pass this screen, press Enter. INSTALL.NLM will confirm the request. To continue, highlight Yes and press Enter.

Tip

To make the removal of NDS easier, especially when trying to force it, type the following at the server console prompt:

```
LOAD INSTALL -DSREMOVE
```

This is not necessary every time, but it will make the removal easier on servers where mistakes in partitioning and replication have been made.

After selecting Yes, you have to log in to NDS so INSTALL.NLM can confirm that you have the authority to remove it. Log in as a user (or Admin) who has the Supervisor object right to [Root]. After you log in successfully, INSTALL asks you *again* if you want to remove NDS from the server. Continue with the removal by highlighting Yes and pressing Enter.

The next screen that appears warns you about the time server type. If this server is a Single Reference time server, the removal of NDS will corrupt the time synchronization environment. Reconfigure the time environment so that no servers are getting their time from this server. Once you are sure the time environment is set up properly to handle the removal of this server, press Enter to remove NDS.

Tip

Prior to the removal of NDS in a multiple server environment, you should remove all partition replica information. This will help you prevent NDS database corruption.

Upgrade NetWare 3.x Bindery Information to the Directory

The next option, Upgrade NetWare 3.x Bindery Information to the Directory, is used during the upgrade of a NetWare 3.x server. This option, when selected, will migrate the bindery information from a NetWare 3.x server and place it into the NDS database. Instead of having to input all of the data from the old server into NDS manually, you can use this option to have INSTALL.NLM do it for you automatically.

Upgrade Mounted Volumes Into the Directory

Another option in the Directory Services Options menu is the Upgrade Mounted Volumes Into the Directory option, which is mostly used during an upgrade from NetWare 3.x to NetWare 4.x. The bindery IDs of the volumes need to be changed to NDS IDs. This selection will allow you to do that. INSTALL.NLM will dismount the volumes, change the IDs, and upgrade the volume information into the Directory. This must be done before you can access the volume and its file system through NDS.

Directory Backup & Restore Options

The last option in the Directory Services Options menu gives you the option to save NDS information to diskette and retrieve it later in the event you need to replace the SYS volume on your server. What once required a tape backup or other archiving utility can now be accomplished through INSTALL.NLM. When you select this option, a new menu, DS Backup and Restore Options, will appear as in Figure 18-9.

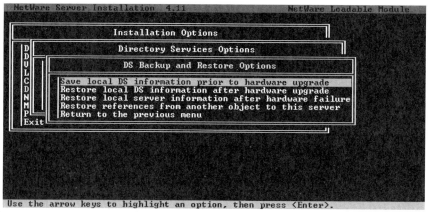

Figure 18-9: The DS Backup and Restore Options menu.

If you need to replace the physical disk that contains the SYS volume and you don't have backup software that can back up the NDS database, you can use the first option in the DS Backup and Restore Options menu to save the

NDS information to a disk. Once you select Save Local DS Information Prior to Hardware Upgrade, INSTALL.NLM will inform you that a temporary file containing your NDS information (BACKUP.NDS) will be placed in the SYS:SYSTEM directory. Once this occurs, NDS will be inaccessible. Press Enter to continue or Escape to cancel.

If you continue, INSTALL.NLM will ask you to log in to the NDS tree as Admin. After INSTALL.NLM has finished creating BACKUP.NDS, it will ask you where to place the copied file (the default is A:\). Press Enter to accept the default location or F3 to specify a different one. INSTALL.NLM will copy the BACKUP.NDS file to the desired location. At this point, the NDS is disabled on the server. You can now take the server down and replace the SYS volume.

Tip

Do not choose the Save Local DS Information Prior to Hardware Upgrade to perform a normal backup. NDS will be disabled on that server after the NDS database is archived to floppy disk.

After the SYS volume upgrade, reinstall NetWare and restore the file system. Then load INSTALL.NLM. Select Directory Options | Backup and Restore Options | Restore Local DS Information After Hardware Upgrade. This will copy NDS information from the BACKUP.NDS file you created and reinstall NDS exactly as it was before the hardware upgrade.

When the Restore Local DS Information After Hardware Upgrade option is chosen, INSTALL.NLM asks you where the BACKUP.NDS file is located. Once the location of BACKUP.NDS has been verified and accepted, INSTALL.NLM will copy the NDS information back to the SYS volume. Once the copy is complete, INSTALL.NLM will prompt you to log in as Admin. When you are authenticated, INSTALL.NLM will make the restoration permanent.

The next option in the DS Backup and Restore Options menu is similar to the previous option; however, you must have backed up NDS with an SMS-compliant backup program. After the server has been brought back up, you can restore NDS by retrieving the SERVDATA.NDS file from the SMS-compliant backup program to a directory on the file server. Select the Restore Local Server Information After Hardware Failure option to complete the restoration.

INSTALL.NLM will ask you for the location of either BACKUP.NDS or SERVDATA.NDS. Enter the location of either file and press Enter. INSTALL.NLM will copy the NDS information back to the server. To finalize the restoration, INSTALL.NLM will ask you to log in as Admin.

The last option under the DS Backup and Restore Options menu is Restore References From Another Object to This Server. When a server is removed from an NDS tree temporarily, INSTALL.NLM gives you the option to Assign References for This Server to Another Object. When you reinstall NDS, you can then use this option to assign those same references back to the server object.

When the Restore References From Another Object to This Server option is selected, INSTALL.NLM displays a warning screen. After this screen, log in as Admin. Once successfully authenticated, INSTALL.NLM will ask for the name of the placeholder object. Enter it as the typeful, distinguished name of the object and press Enter. INSTALL.NLM will restore the references to the server object.

NCF Files Options

The next option in the main menu of INSTALL.NLM is NCF Files Options. When this option is selected, the screen shown in Figure 18-10 appears showing the Available NCF Files Options menu, from which you can create and edit the AUTOEXEC.NCF and STARTUP.NCF files. You can also select the option to upgrade a NetWare v3.1x AUTOEXEC.NCF file.

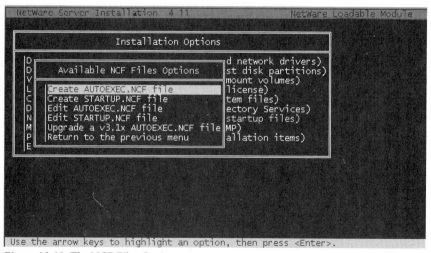

Figure 18-10: The NCF Files Options screen.

The first option in the Available NCF Files Options menu allows you to create an AUTOEXEC.NCF from the currently loaded configuration. By pressing Enter when this option is highlighted, you will create an AUTOEXEC.NCF file reflecting the current server configuration including server name, internal IPX number, currently loaded LAN drivers, and NDS configuration information. Once the AUTOEXEC.NCF file is created, INSTALL.NLM will present it and allow you to edit it. When you are finished reviewing it, press F10 to save it and continue.

You must reboot the server for the settings in the new AUTOEXEC.NCF file to take effect. The second option in the Available NCF Files Options menu, Create STARTUP.NCF File, works in the same manner, but it creates a new STARTUP.NCF file for the server instead of the AUTOEXEC.NCF file.

You most likely will not need to create these files since they are created for you during the installation of the operating system; however, you will need to modify them during the operation of your server. From the Available NCF Files Options menu, you can edit both AUTOEXEC.NCF and STARTUP.NCF. To do so, choose to edit the desired file by highlighting the appropriate option and pressing Enter. You will be taken to a text editing screen where the current file is displayed. Make the appropriate changes to the file and press F10 to save those changes.

The final selection in the Available NCF Files Options menu allows you to upgrade a v3.1x AUTOEXEC.NCF File. You can check the NetWare 3.1x AUTOEXEC.NCF for compatibility with NetWare 4.x. INSTALL.NLM will look for things like the 802.2 frame type (the default for NetWare 3.12 and above) and time and Directory information. INSTALL.NLM will also indicate if changes need to be made.

When the Upgrade v3.1x AUTOEXEC.NCF File option is selected, it displays an informational screen. Press Enter to continue. INSTALL.NLM will then read the 3.1x AUTOEXEC.NCF file and present any necessary changes. Inspect the changes, make modifications, and press F10 to continue.

NCF Files Options is particularly important because it allows you to manipulate NetWare 4.11's critical startup files. You will need to use this editing feature frequently to effectively manage your server.

Multi CPU Options

The Multi CPU options are only used on NetWare servers that have more than one CPU. In previous versions of NetWare, NetWare SMP (Symmetric Multi-Processing) was an extra-cost option with limited vendor support. In NetWare

4.11, SMP support is included with much better support from vendors such as Compaq, Corollary, Intel MPS, NetFRAME, and Tricord. Each company that creates support for NetWare SMP will write a Platform Support Module (PSM) that is compatible with NetWare.

When Multi CPU Options is selected, INSTALL.NLM presents the screen shown in Figure 18-11. If you choose Select a Platform Support Module, you will be given a list of PSMs. Once you select the appropriate PSM, INSTALL.NLM will modify the server's STARTUP.NCF with the commands to load NetWare SMP. You must reboot the server for the SMP feature to be loaded. Once the server has rebooted, you will need to use MONITOR.NLM to configure the SMP parameters for the server. For more information on MONITOR.NLM, refer to the section "Monitoring Server Performance & Statistics: MONITOR.NLM" later in this chapter.

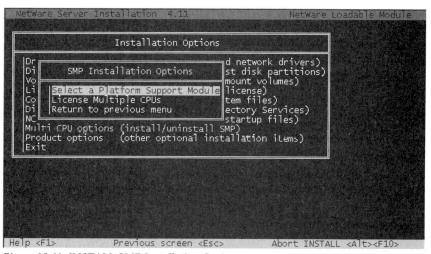

Figure 18-11: INSTALL SMP Installation Options.

The second option in the SMP Installation Options menu (Figure 18-11) is License Multiple CPUs. When there are more than four CPUs in your server, you need to add another SMP license. After you select this option, INSTALL.NLM will ask you for the location of the new license. See "License Option" earlier in this chapter for more information on installing additional licenses.

Product Options

The last option in the main menu of INSTALL.NLM is Product Options. This option allows you to install and configure additional enhancement products for NetWare. Since several hundred of these products exist, it would not be feasible to discuss each one. However, we will cover the generic procedures involved in adding a new product to a NetWare server using INSTALL.NLM.

Select Product Options by highlighting it and pressing Enter. The Other Installation Items/Products menu (Figure 18-12) will be displayed. From this screen you can see all the products for which NetWare has built-in installation options. However, you are not limited to only installing products that appear on the list.

To install an item that is listed, use the arrow keys to navigate through the list of products. Using the arrow keys does the same thing as selecting Choose an Item or Product Listed Above from the Other Installation Actions menu. Press Enter to select a product to install. From there, INSTALL.NLM will usually load another, separate installation NLM (normally PINSTALL.NLM) and continue the installation of the new product.

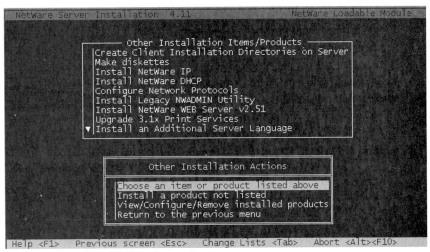

Figure 18-12: Other Installation Items/Products menu.

You can install products other than those listed by choosing Install a Product Not Listed from the Other Installation Actions menu. Select it by highlighting it and pressing Enter. INSTALL.NLM will prompt you for the location of the software you want to install. Once the location has been specified,

INSTALL.NLM will then start the installation by loading another NLM (usually the aforementioned PINSTALL.NLM). When complete, the installation program will return you to the Other Installation Actions screen.

Not only can you add products to the NetWare server, you can also view the products currently installed and remove them using the View/Configure/Remove Installed Products option. When this option is chosen, you are presented with a list of all products that were installed with INSTALL.NLM. If you select any of the products from this list, INSTALL.NLM will transfer control to the product's installation and configuration program. When finished, the product's configuration program will return you to INSTALL.NLM.

You can also remove an installed product by highlighting it and pressing the Delete key. INSTALL.NLM will remove the product from the server, but it will not unload it. You must reboot the server for the removal of the product to take effect.

The Product Options menu is important to understand because it plays a key role in installing the other products you might use with IntranetWare, including NetWare/IP and the Novell Web Server. If you do not see the product you want to install listed in the default list, follow the instructions included with the product to install it.

While INSTALL.NLM is a useful utility that you will use frequently, its main function is to install the operating system for the first time and configure some basic parameters. You also use it to install and remove enhancement products. However, it does not allow you to configure the parameters that will help you fine-tune the server. Server parameters that affect server performance are configured using a utility called SERVMAN.NLM. We will discuss this utility in the next section.

Optimizing Server Performance: SERVMAN.NLM

In previous versions of NetWare, it was necessary to change server parameters with the SET console command in order to tune server performance. With NetWare 4.x, Novell has included a special utility NLM called SERVMAN.NLM to assist in this function. SERVMAN allows you to change any SET parameter as well as view disk and LAN configuration settings. It has a graphical interface that allows you to browse all of the SET parameters easily so you do not have to remember them as you did with NetWare 3.x.

To load SERVMAN at the server, you need to issue the following command at the server console prompt (colon prompt):

```
LOAD SERVMAN
```

Once SERVMAN has been loaded, you will see the screen shown in Figure 18-13. From this screen you can view some general server information including server uptime, processor utilization, processor speed, number of server processes, number of loaded NLMs, number of mounted volumes, number of active queues, number of logged-in users, and number of loaded name spaces.

Besides viewing this general statistical information about your server, you can also set server parameters and view volume, storage, and LAN information from the Available Options menu. To select any of these options, use the arrow keys to highlight the desired choice and press Enter.

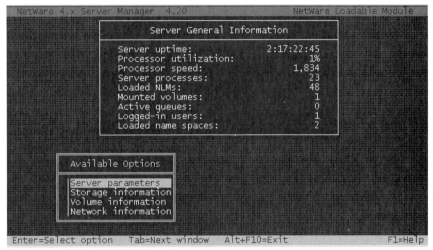

Figure 18-13: The SERVMAN main screen.

Setting Server Parameters

When Server Parameters is selected, a new menu, Select a Parameter Category, is displayed in which you are presented with several categories of parameters you can select to change (Figure 18-14). We will cover each of the following server parameters to describe the types of things you can configure on your server:

- Communications

- Directory Caching

- Directory Services

- Disk

- Error Handling
- File Caching
- File System
- Locks
- Memory
- Miscellaneous
- NCP
- Time
- Transaction Tracking

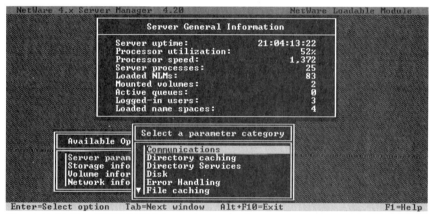

Figure 18-14: The SERVMAN Select a Parameter Category menu.

Communication

The first category of server parameters is Communications. This category contains parameters that deal with how the server communicates with the rest of the network. From the Select a Parameters Category menu, highlight Communications and press Enter. The screen in Figure 18-15 will be displayed.

You will want to modify the Communications parameters to improve the efficiency of the server's communication with the network. For example, the Minimum Packet Receive Buffers parameter controls the minimum resources allocated to store incoming network traffic. If you begin to get error messages from the server indicating that it is dropping packets, you will want to increase the value of the Minimum Packet Receive Buffers parameter.

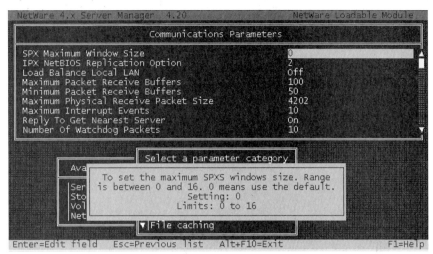

Figure 18-15: The SERVMAN Communications Parameters screen.

From the SERVMAN Communications Parameters screen, use the arrow keys to select a parameter. Press the Enter key to modify the parameter. Press the Enter key again to accept the modification. When you are finished editing parameters, press Escape until you see the screen shown in Figure 18-16. To make your changes permanent, you must update the server's startup files to reflect the changes. Select Update AUTOEXEC.NCF and STARTUP.NCF Now from the Update Options menu to cause your changes to take effect every time the server boots.

SERVMAN will update the appropriate file with a line to change the parameter and activate the change immediately, if possible. This same procedure works for any parameter and you can assume this is the case for the rest of this section.

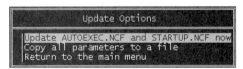

Figure 18-16: The SERVMAN Update Options menu.

You probably will not need to use every parameter in the Communications category. Table 18-1 lists the most common Communications parameters you might need to change on your server.

Parameter	Description
Minimum and Maximum Packet Receive Buffers	Sets how many packet receive buffers (a 4K page allocated for receiving information from the network card) are allocated at system startup time. This parameter is important because if the network traffic is busy and NetWare can't allocate enough packet receive buffers, server responses will be slow. Default for minimum is 50 and default for maximum is 100. It is recommended that these parameters be increased to at least 200 for minimum and 500 for maximum.
Maximum Physical Receive Packet Size	Sets the maximum packet size, in bytes, that the server will accept. If a packet is received that is larger than the value of this parameter, the server will reject it. Common values are 1514 for Ethernet, 4202 for Token Ring (both speeds—4 and 16 Mbps), 512 for ARCnet, and 4202 for ARCnet (turbo). The default is 4202 bytes to account for all network types. It can be set lower to decrease memory usage.
Reply to Get Nearest Server	Sends out a "get nearest server" packet when a workstation wants to attach to the network. Whichever server is fastest to respond with a kind of "here I am" packet is the one the workstation attaches to. Set Off if you don't want a workstation to attach to a particular server (for instance, it only has a 5-user license). The default is On.
Number of Watchdog Packets	Sets the number of times the server asks a suspect workstation if it's still attached to the network. A kind of "are you alive" packet. The default is 10.
Delay Before First Watchdog Packet	Sets how long the server waits between when the last packet is received from that workstation and when it sends the first watchdog packet. The default is 4 Min 56.6 Sec.

Table 18-1: Communications parameters.

Directory Caching

The next category of parameters in the Select a Parameter Category list is Directory Caching. This category contains parameters that control how the server handles the caching of directories. To modify these parameters, select Directory Caching by highlighting it and pressing Enter. The Directory Caching Parameters screen will be displayed.

Follow the same procedure you did for modifying the Communication parameters. You will want to modify the Directory Caching Parameters to adjust the amount of resources devoted to the update of the Directory Entry Table (DET). Remember that the DET is responsible for keeping track of file system information on your hard disk. When the file system is updated, the DET needs to be updated. Directory Caching Parameters control how many updates are written at a time and how frequently they are written.

The most common parameter you would want to modify is the Maximum Concurrent Directory Cache Writes. It sets the maximum number of directory cache buffers that can be written to disk simultaneously. The default value is 10.

Directory Services

One of the most discussed and most highly promoted features of NetWare 4.11 is NDS. The next category of parameters contains settings that affect the performance of NDS, including synchronization parameters and DSTRACE settings. For more information on DSTRACE, refer to Chapter 13.

To get to the directory services parameters, highlight Directory Services in the Select a Parameter Category menu and press Enter. The Directory Services Parameters box will be displayed. Table 18-2 summarizes the parameters that are commonly modified. For example, you would want to access the Directory Services Parameters screen to modify the bindery context to set up Bindery Services on the server.

Parameter	Description
NDS Trace to Screen	Activates the NDS tracing function that monitors and logs NDS events to the screen. The default is Off. Changing this setting to On will activate a screen labeled Directory Services that displays NDS events.
NDS Trace to File	Same as above, but will trace NDS events to a file, the name of which is specified in the next parameter. The default is Off.
NDS Trace Filename	Sets the location and name of the DSTRACE display file on the SYS: volume. The default is SYSTEM\DSTRACE.DBG.
NDS Inactivity Synchronization Interval	Sets the amount of time, in minutes, that is allowed to elapse with no NDS sync activity before a full sync is performed. Increasing this number will reduce network traffic but cause NDS information to become out of sync. Decreasing this value will have the opposite effect. The default is 30 min.
NDS Do Not Synchronize With	A stability factor for NDS. If a server with a new version of NDS tries to sync with a very old (one or more major revisions between versions) version, NDS could become corrupt. If set to Off, NDS can sync with any version. If set to On, variables must also specify which versions *not* to sync with. The default is On, with variable values (versions) of 290, 291, 296, 332, 463, and 477.
Bindery Context	Provides for backward compatibility with bindery-based clients and applications. Enter a typeful, distinguished name (no leading period) as a value here, although several simultaneous values are permitted. The default is the container in which the server was installed.

Table 18-2: NDS parameters.

Disk

The next category is a set of parameters that often causes problems for the inexperienced. Disk parameters affect low-level disk driver settings and can greatly enhance or detract from a server's performance. Before you modify these parameters, consider the impact of the changes you are about to make. The disk parameters you would most likely want to modify are listed in Table 18-3.

Parameter	Description
Enable Disk Read After Write Verify	Controls how data is verified after being written to disk. With this parameter enabled, NetWare will write a block of data to the disk and then read it back and compare the contents. If they are different, NetWare will know that the write was unsuccessful. Some disk controllers do this automatically and if NetWare has this enabled, it can detract from performance. The default is Off.
Mirrored Devices Are Out of Sync Message Frequency	Sets how often NetWare checks to see if devices are out of sync (like mirrored partitions). Values are in minutes. The default is 30 minutes. Increasing this value will decrease reliability but increase performance.
Ignore Disk Geometry	When set to On, the server will ignore the disk's geometry when creating a partition. Primarily applies to ISA-based disk system. The default is Off.

Table 18-3: Disk parameters.

Error Handling

One of the most important categories of parameters is the one that deals with how a server handles error messages. The Error Handling category does just that. When there was a problem with an NLM in previous versions of NetWare, the server might abnormally end (ABEND), taking down the whole server (and possibly the whole network). With NetWare 4.11, as mentioned earlier, the server will attempt to shut down the offending process and/or restart the server. If the workstations are using the VLM client or Client32 (one or the other is required for NDS network attachments anyway), the client will detect a problem with the network and try to reconnect in the background. Most times, the user won't even know a server ABEND has occurred.

There are two parameters within this category that affect this ABEND recovery feature; they are summarized in Table 18-4.

Parameter	Description
Auto Restart After ABEND	Controls whether or not the server restarts after an ABEND. When the parameter is set to 1, the server will wait for a specified period of time after an ABEND (see next parameter) and then restart the server. The default is 1.
Auto Restart After ABEND Delay Time	Sets how long, in minutes, after an ABEND the server waits before restarting. The default is 2.

Table 18-4: Error Handling parameters.

File System

Since file serving performance is of prime concern, there is a category of parameters that control file caching. As previously mentioned, a NetWare server caches just about everything, so if we can increase the performance of file caching, we will increase the performance of the file server. Table 18-5 lists the most commonly configured File Caching parameters. For more information on the File Caching parameters, refer to the Utilities Reference manual in the NetWare 4.11 Reference collection of the online documentation.

Parameter	Description
File Delete Wait Time	Sets how long the server waits between when a file is deleted and when it is purged from the system. The default is 5 Min 29.6 Sec. (Kind of a strange default, but this is nothing new.)
Fast Volume Mounts	When set to On, relaxes how many things NetWare checks when a volume is mounted. (When a volume mounts, NetWare checks to see if the volume is healthy.) The default is On.
Immediate Purge of Deleted Files	When set to On, NetWare will immediately purge any deleted files. The benefit is increased security (files are gone for good, especially sensitive ones). The downside is decreased performance and increased reliance on good backups. The default is Off.

Compression Daily Check Starting Hour	Sets the hour of the day (0-23) that the server checks for files to be compressed. If files that are ready to be compressed are found, the server will compress them. The default is 0 (midnight).
Compression Daily Check Stop Hour	Sets the hour of the day (0-23) that the server stops checking for and compressing files that are ready for compression. The default is 6 (6:00 A.M.).
Minimum Compression Percentage Gain	Sets the minimum amount of disk space that must be saved for a file to stay compressed. Values are given in %. The default is 20.
Enable File Compression	When set to Off, will prevent files from being compressed on all the volumes hosted by that server. The default is On.
Convert Compressed to Uncompressed Option	Controls how files are converted from compressed to uncompressed. If this parameter is set to 0, the file will always stay compressed. If it is set to 1, the first time the compressed file is accessed, it will stay compressed; the second time it will be uncompressed. If it is set to 2, the file will be decompressed the first time it is accessed after compressed. The default is 1.
Days Untouched Before Compression	Controls how long a file can remain "untouched," or unaccessed, before the file is marked as ready for compression. The default is 14.

Table 18-5: File System parameters.

Locks

When users access files on a NetWare server, the server has to keep track of those files so that two or more people can't change a file at the exact same time. This is accomplished through features called file locking and record locking. *File locking* prevents multiple users from accessing a file at the same time. *Record locking* works primarily with database files. It prevents users from accessing or changing an individual record in a database file at the same instant.

Table 18-6 shows the important File System parameters that you might want to set using SERVMAN.

Tip

If you run Windows 95, a DOS-based database such as Clipper or DBASE, and the Microsoft Client for NetWare networks, beware. The Microsoft Client overrides the record locking of NetWare. In order to solve this "feature," you have to install Novell's Client32 software and turn off the Opportunistic Record Locking setting.

Parameter	Description
Maximum Record Locks per Connection	Sets the maximum number of record locks per user logged in to that server. The default is 500.
Maximum File Locks per Connection	Sets the maximum number of files that can be open per connection. The default is 250.
Maximum Record Locks	Sets the maximum number of records that can be locked (total). The default is 20,000.
Maximum File Locks	Sets the maximum number of files that can be open on the server. The default is 10,000. This parameter can be monitored from the MONITOR main screen. See the information on MONITOR later in this chapter.

Table 18-6: Locks parameters.

Memory

The Memory category of parameters deals with the way NetWare manages its own memory. As mentioned in Chapter 17, NetWare uses its memory very efficiently, and there is a category of parameters to help control the server's memory management. Table 18-7 displays the most commonly modified memory parameters on a NetWare 4.11 server.

Parameter	Description
Garbage Collection Interval	Sets the number of minutes, maximum, that a server will wait before doing Garbage Collection (see Chapter 17). The default is 15.
Number of Frees for Garbage Collection	Sets the number of times the Free API is called, maximum, before the Garbage Collection routine is called. The default is 5,000. Lowering this number may be necessary if the server is low on memory.

Minimum Free Memory for Garbage Collection	Sets the minimum amount of memory, in bytes, that must be available before the Garbage Collection routine will run. The default is 8,000. It's generally not a good idea to change this parameter.
Auto Register Memory Above 16 Megabytes	Allows EISA servers to automatically add recognized memory above 16MB. The default is On.
Reserved Buffers Below 16MB	Sets the number of buffers to reserve for those device drivers that cannot access memory above 16MB (primarily ISA devices). The default is usually too small for ISA-bus machines.

Table 18-7: Memory parameters.

Miscellaneous

This category contains parameters that don't quite fit into any other parameter category—hence the name Miscellaneous. Most people will ignore these parameters, but there are a few that can affect server performance. They are summarized in Table 18-8.

Parameter	Description
Sound Bell for Alerts	Sets whether or not the server "beeps" when there's a problem. The default is On.
Minimum Service Processes	Controls the number of "wee beasties" that actually do work inside a server. The default is 10. When the server needs more, it can allocate them up to the maximum number allowed by the Maximum Service Processes parameter.
Maximum Service Processes	Sets the maximum number of processes that can be allocated by the server. If a server constantly reaches the maximum, this number should be set higher. The default is 50.
Automatically Repair Volumes	When set to On, automatically runs VREPAIR to repair a volume and then mount it (if the server detects a problem when mounting a volume). The default is On.
Enable SECURE.NCF	SECURE.NCF can be run manually from the command line. It is a server batch file that sets various Security parameters (see "Other Server Console Tools" later in this section). When Enable SECURE.NCF is set to On, the server will automatically execute it from the AUTOEXEC.NCF. The default is Off.
Allow Unencrypted Passwords	When set to On, allows workstations to send their passwords over the network in an unencrypted form. Macintoshes don't have any way of encrypting their passwords without adding additional software. This should be set to Off if higher security is desired. The default is Off.

Table 18-8: Miscellaneous parameters.

NCP

The next category deals with the parameters associated with the NCP portion of IPX/SPX on the server (see Chapter 17, "NetWare 4.11 Server Architecture"). Since NetWare uses NCP requests to do everything, these parameters have a lot to do with security. If someone on your network introduces packets with invalid NCP parameters, the server might execute them, crash, or both.

To help prevent this, you will want to modify the NCP server parameters. Table 18-9 summarizes the most important parameters you might need to modify.

Parameter	Description
Reject NCP Packets With Bad Components	When set to On, allows the server to reject all NCP packets that have bad components. Since these packets may take unnecessary processor time to try and process, set this parameter to On to prevent "NCP packet bombs." The default is Off.
Reject NCP Packets With Bad Lengths	Performs a function similar to the previous one. When set to ON, allows the server to reject packets that are too long or too short. The default is Off.

Table 18-9: NCP parameters.

Time

The Time category deals with parameters affecting the time synchronization environment. These parameters are covered thoroughly in Chapter 11. Refer to this chapter for more information on the time server parameters.

Transaction Tracking

The last category of parameters is Transaction Tracking. NetWare contains many fault-tolerant systems, and one of them is the Transaction Tracking System. When a workstation sends a file to be written to the server's disk, NetWare caches it. It then writes it to the disk. During the write process, the file is written to a temp file marked as "pending." Once the file is completely written and considered "good," it is marked as such and switches places with the older file (if one exists). Finally, the server deletes the old file.

If a server crashes during a file write, you have to restart the server. When the server comes back up, it mounts each volume, and TTS scans the volume for any incomplete transactions. If any are found, it "backs them out" to their last known state and makes an entry in the TTS$LOG.ERR file at the root of the SYS volume.

Table 18-10 lists some important parameters affecting the Transaction Tracking System. In the majority of cases, the default values are sufficient. Only change these parameters if you have a compelling reason to do so.

Parameter	Description
Auto TTS Backout Flag	When set to On, causes the server to automatically "back out" incomplete disk transactions to their last-known good point. The default is On.
TTS Abort Dump Flag	When set to ON, causes the server to log all incomplete transactions to the TTS$LOG.ERR file. The default is Off.
Maximum Transactions	Sets the maximum number of concurrent transactions that can happen on the server at any one time. The default is 10,000.

Table 18-10: Transaction Tracking parameters.

Although SERVMAN's primary function is to modify server parameters, you can also use it to view server statistic information. If you recall from Figure 18-13, there are other options available from the main menu of SERVMAN. In the next section, we will briefly discuss these options.

Retrieving Other File Server Information

From the Available Options menu of SERVMAN, you can also retrieve other statistical information concerning your server. The last three menu options are Storage Information, Volume Information, and Network Information. By highlighting one of these items and pressing Enter, you can retrieve important information about each one of these areas. Most of these statistics are covered in the section about the MONITOR.NLM. MONITOR.NLM allows you to view more server statistics that will give you a better picture of your server's overall performance.

Monitoring Server Performance & Statistics: MONITOR.NLM

Use the MONITOR.NLM on a NetWare server to find what is going on with the server. MONITOR is one of the most commonly loaded NLMs, probably because it's so important to keep track of the server's performance and status.

In order to get the MONITOR active, you need to load it into memory. Just as you do with other NLMs, use the load command at the server console prompt (colon prompt) to start MONITOR:

```
LOAD MONITOR.NLM
```

Once the MONITOR is loaded, you are presented with the screen in Figure 18-17. You can either shrink or expand the main window to view more options. If you wait long enough, the window will expand by itself, and if you press any key, the window will shrink to its former size. Pressing the Tab key will force the window to shrink and expand.

Tip

In most NetWare NLM screens, the key commands work the same: F1 for help, Enter to select, and so on. Whenever you see a pop up window that has a scroll bar and two arrows on the right, you can press the Tab key to enlarge the window.

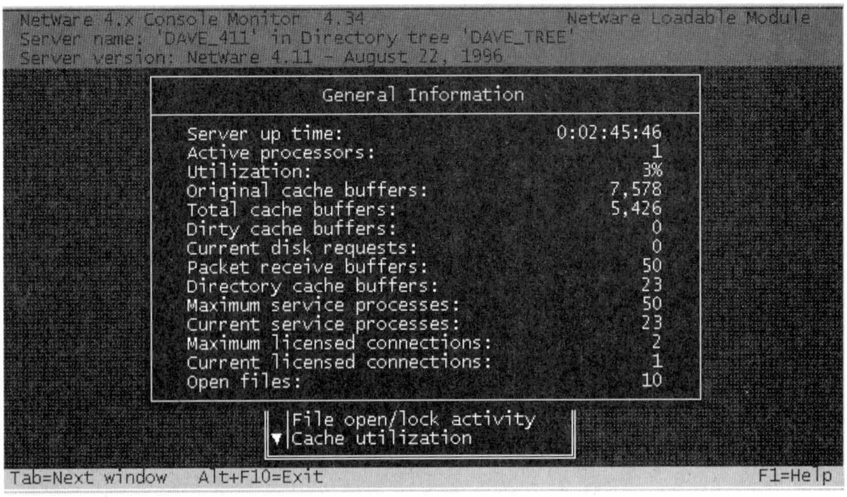

```
NetWare 4.x Console Monitor 4.34                    NetWare Loadable Module
Server name: 'DAVE_411' in Directory tree 'DAVE_TREE'
Server version: NetWare 4.11 - August 22, 1996
                     ┌─────────────── General Information ───────────────┐
                     │  Server up time:                    0:02:45:46  │
                     │  Active processors:                          1  │
                     │  Utilization:                               3%  │
                     │  Original cache buffers:                 7,578  │
                     │  Total cache buffers:                    5,426  │
                     │  Dirty cache buffers:                        0  │
                     │  Current disk requests:                      0  │
                     │  Packet receive buffers:                    50  │
                     │  Directory cache buffers:                   23  │
                     │  Maximum service processes:                 50  │
                     │  Current service processes:                 23  │
                     │  Maximum licensed connections:               2  │
                     │  Current licensed connections:               1  │
                     │  Open files:                                10  │
                     └───────────────────────────────────────────────────┘
                          ┌──│File open/lock activity
                          ▼ │Cache utilization
Tab=Next window    Alt+F10=Exit                                    F1=Help
```

Figure 18-17: The MONITOR.NLM main screen.

From the main screen shown in Figure 18-17, you can see and monitor several of the server's key statistics. Table 18-11 explains most of the statistics seen here.

Tip

One thing to note about MONITOR statistics is that each statistic can be "colored." For example, is a statistic that shows 10 errors serious? It depends on how long the server has been up. If it has been up for a minute, then yes, it is probably pretty serious; if it has been up for 100 days, it's probably not.

Statistic	Description
Server Up Time	The total time the server has been "up" in days, hours, minutes, and seconds.
Active Processors	The number of processors that are currently active. (Relates to NetWare SMP with more than one processor.)
Utilization	The average percentage of time that the processor is doing work. Most of the time, this statistic should be less than 50%. If it's consistently at 80%-100%, some work needs to be offloaded to another server or another processor. (This number will be very high during a backup or during file compression activity.)
Original Cache Buffers	The total number of cache buffers (4K pages) that were available when the server was brought up.
Total Cache Buffers	The total number of cache buffers that are currently available. (If this number is less than 50% of the original cache buffers, *run*, don't walk, to the computer store and buy more RAM! Your server is almost out of memory.)
Dirty Cache Buffers	The number of cache buffers that currently have data in them or have not been written to disk. If this number rises quickly and remains high, then there aren't enough service processes and more need to be allocated. (See "Optimizing Server Performance: SERVMAN.NLM" earlier in this chapter for information about setting maximum service processes.)

Statistic	Description
Current Disk Requests	The total number of requests that have not been serviced by the server. If this number rises quickly and stays high, then you either need to allocate more service processes or upgrade the disk subsystem hardware.
Packet Receive Buffers	The current number of packet receive buffers that the system uses. (See "Optimizing Server Performance: SERVMAN.NLM" earlier in this chapter for information about minimum and maximum packet receive buffers.)
Directory Cache Buffers	The number of cache buffers used for caching the DET.
Maximum Service Processes	The maximum number of service processes that the server can allocate.
Current Service Processes	The number of service processes that the server has currently allocated (if this statistic is the same as the maximum, you should increase the Maximum Service Processes value in SERVMAN).
Maximum Licensed Connections	The maximum number of users that can simultaneously be using the resources on this server (number of licenses).
Current Licensed Connections	The number of users currently attached to and using the resources of this server. If this number is the same as Maximum Licensed Connections, it's probably time to buy some more licensed connections.
Open Files	The total number of files that are currently open on the server.

Table 18-11: MONITOR main screen statistics.

If you leave the MONITOR screen up and don't touch the server's console for a few minutes, the built-in screen saver will come up (Figure 18-18). The screen saver also serves a useful purpose. The length of the snake gives an indication of processor utilization. The harder the processor is working, the longer the tail of the snake will be.

Figure 18-18: The server console screen saver.

From the MONITOR main screen, you are presented with a menu of available options. You can use the arrow keys to move up and down the list and the Enter key to select a category of statistics and information. From the Available Options menu, you can see statistics and information concerning the following categories:

- Connection Information
- Disk Information
- LAN/WAN Information
- System Module Information
- Lock File Server Console
- File Open/Lock Activity
- Cache Utilization
- Processor Utilization
- Resource Utilization
- Memory Utilization
- Scheduling Information
- Multiprocessor Information
- Server Parameters

Connection Information

The first category is Connection Information (Figure 18-19). The Connection Information screen shows who is connected to this server—both licensed and unlicensed connections. A *licensed* connection is an entity that is logged in to and using the resources of that server. The total number of licensed connections is dictated by the license that was installed at system install time (5-user, 25-user, and so on). The unlicensed connections are marked with a *.

```
       Active Connections
   1  *DAVE_411.corp.ema
   2  *DAVE_411.corp.ema
   3   NOT-LOGGED-IN
   4   DGROTH
```

Figure 18-19: The Connection Information screen.

Tip

The list of connected users can be sorted by either connection name or connection number by pressing F3 from the main screen.

If you want to get statistics about a particular connection, you can highlight the connection and press Enter. The statistics for each user are explained in more detail in Table 18-12.

Tip

If you need to disconnect anyone from the server (in case their machine locks up and you need to close their files safely), you can do so by highlighting the connection and pressing the Delete key.

Statistic	Description
Status	Whether the user is Normal, Authenticated, or Not-logged-in.
Network Address	The IPX Network number and address of the connected client.
Connection Time	How long the client has been connected in days, hours, and minutes.
Requests	The number of requests to the server this client has made.
Kilobytes Read	The number of kilobytes read by this client.
Kilobytes Written	The number of kilobytes written by this client.
Open Files	The files that this client currently has open. Select a file and press Enter to see its status (whether or not it's being held open). If the screen is blank, the file is not being locked by NetWare.

Table 18-12: Connection Information statistics.

Disk Information

If you highlight Disk Information and press Enter, you can get statistics about your disk subsystem (you can get some of the same information from INSTALL.NLM). You will see information about the model and type of disk installed as well as the configuration of the disk. Once you press Enter, you can choose from a list of the disk drives that can be accessed by the server. If you press Enter after selecting any of these entries, the Drive Status menu will appear where you can get specific statistics about that disk drive. The information includes the number of partitions on that drive, the size of the disk, the driver for that disk that is loaded on the server, whether or not the disk has partitions that are mirrored, and the volumes that are being hosted by that disk drive.

Tip

The Drive Status screen will also show the number of redirection/redirected blocks. If the number of redirected blocks gets close to the number of redirection blocks, it means that the disk is about to fail.

LAN/WAN Information

The next group of statistics that can be monitored are those dealing with the performance of network cards. If you press Enter on the LAN/WAN Information option, you will see a list of LAN drivers. For each LAN driver loaded, there will be an entry with its frame type and associated card settings (interrupt number, port number, or slot number). Select an instance of LAN driver to be presented with a screen like the one in Figure 18-20.

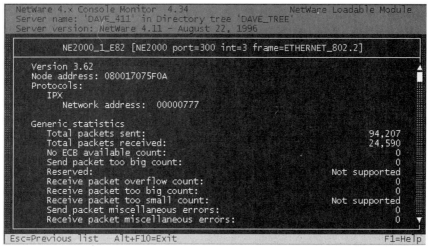

Figure 18-20: The MONITOR.NLM LAN driver statistics screen.

The MONITOR.NLM LAN driver statistics screen shows several LAN-related statistics. This screen can give you valuable information about the network and the performance of the server's network-related hardware. In addition, it shows the version of driver being used, the MAC address of the network card, and the protocols bound to that driver. Table 18-13 details some of the statistics found on this screen.

Statistic	Description
Total Packets Sent	The total number of packets sent through this network interface.
Total Packets Received	The total number of packets received by this network interface.
No Event Control Block (ECB) Available Count	The number of times a packet was received and rejected because there was no packet receive buffer available. If this number rises quickly, you need to increase either the number of minimum and maximum packet receive buffers or the number of service processes (so packet receive buffers are freed more quickly).
Send and Receive Packet Miscellaneous Errors	Increases in value when the network card reports an error that does not fall under any of these other categories. If this statistic increases over the course of a couple of minutes, there's a good chance that the card is "chattering" (sending more packets than are needed) and is faulty.
Receive Packet Too Big/ Too Small Count	The number of times a packet was received that was too big or too small. Most often this parameter increases steadily when the wrong packet size has been specified. If you specified 1514 bytes (Ethernet's packets) for a Token Ring card (4202 bytes), this statistic will increase quickly (you also won't be able to log in until you reset that parameter).
Send Abort From Excess Collisions	Applies to Ethernet networks. If the network has a lot of traffic, this number will increase over the course of a few days or weeks. It will also increase rapidly if the network card is "chattering."
Custom Statistics	This whole section includes statistics particular to the brand of LAN driver installed. To get the details of a particular driver's statistics, consult the manufacturer's documentation.

Table 18-13: MONITOR LAN driver statistics.

System Module Information

The next category of MONITOR statistics that is of interest is System Module Information. Select this entry and press Enter to be presented with a list of all the modules (NLMs) that are currently loaded in memory. Further, when you select a listed module and press Enter, MONITOR will show you the name of the NLM that is loaded, its size, its version, and what resource tags it is currently using. This information is useful if you need to find out if a version of an NLM needs to be updated.

Lock File Server Console

One of the most important aspects of security is server security. Without it, someone could come to the console and load an NLM that records transactions, or they could load a virus NLM. To prevent this, you can select the next entry, Lock File Server Console. Once selected, MONITOR will ask for a password. After a password is entered, it will ask for it to be reentered in order to confirm it. Once the password is reentered, the screen in Figure 18-21 will appear. Any time anyone tries to access the server console, either directly or through RCONSOLE, they will see this screen. They won't be able to change to any other screen without entering the correct password.

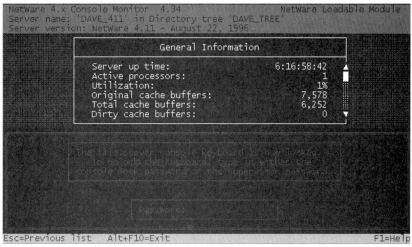

Figure 18-21: The Locked MONITOR screen.

File Open/Lock Activity

When corruption problems occur, one of the easiest ways to check if a file is in use is to use File Open/Lock Activity from the MONITOR screen. When selected, it will show you a list of all the volumes on that server. From there, you can navigate through the volumes, directories, and subdirectories to select the suspect file.

Once you have selected a file, you will see a screen like the one in Figure 18-22. This screen shows that the file EXAMPLE.DOC in the SYS:PUBLIC directory is being used by connection 4. The file is not locked, its use is not logged, it's been opened once for reading and once for writing, and only one connection is using it currently. Once you have found the connection number, you can go to the Connection Information screen and find out who has that file open. We can then either have the user log out or delete the connection.

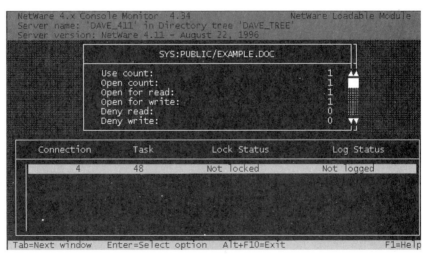

Figure 18-22: The File Open/Lock Activity screen.

Cache Utilization

The next four statistics—Cache Utilization, Processor Utilization, Resource Utilization, and Memory Utilization—indicate how well the server is using its resources. The first one, Cache Utilization, indicates how efficiently NetWare is using its memory. As you'll remember, NetWare caches almost everything.

When you select Cache Utilization, you are presented with the screen shown in Figure 18-23.

Cache hit means that the server has found the data it was looking for in RAM. The most important statistic here is Long Term Cache Hits. If this statistic falls below 90 percent, it is definitely time to add more RAM to a server. The LRU Sitting Time statistic shows how long, in days, hours, minutes, and seconds, the oldest block in the cache has been there. If this number is small, more RAM is probably needed.

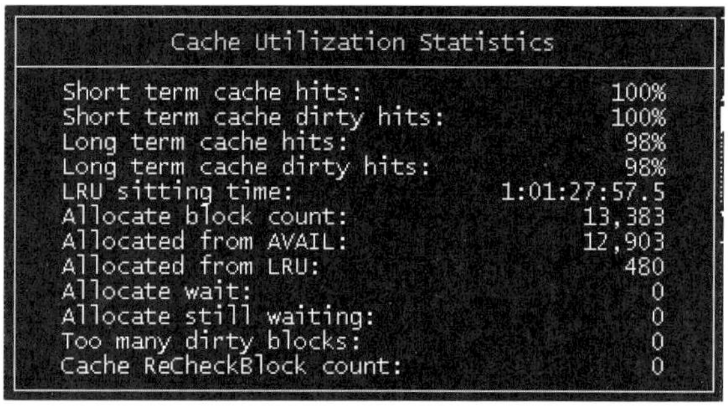

```
          Cache Utilization Statistics
   Short term cache hits:              100%
   Short term cache dirty hits:        100%
   Long term cache hits:                98%
   Long term cache dirty hits:          98%
   LRU sitting time:            1:01:27:57.5
   Allocate block count:              13,383
   Allocated from AVAIL:              12,903
   Allocated from LRU:                   480
   Allocate wait:                          0
   Allocate still waiting:                 0
   Too many dirty blocks:                  0
   Cache ReCheckBlock count:               0
```

Figure 18-23: The MONITOR Cache Utilization Statistics screen.

Processor Utilization

In addition to the utilization statistic on the main screen of MONITOR, there is a page that will give detailed processor utilization statistics on a per-module basis. If you select Processor Utilization, you will see a list of all the application programming interfaces (APIs) currently using processor time. If you select any of them and press Enter you can see the percentage of total processor time that particular API is using. There is one API called IDLE Loop that is always going to show a high percentage (usually greater than 70 percent) because most of the time, the processor in a NetWare server does nothing.

Tip

If you view processor utilization statistics, remember that the MONITOR also will take a certain percentage of processor time to perform this monitoring. The time is listed underneath the API's percentages as Histogram Overhead Time.

If you want to see the totals of several APIs, press F5 to select multiple APIs, or F3 to select all of them.

Resource Utilization

The next category of statistics lists the server's various resources and how it uses them. Figure 18-24 shows the Tracked Resources screen. You can get to this screen by selecting Resource Utilization from the main menu.

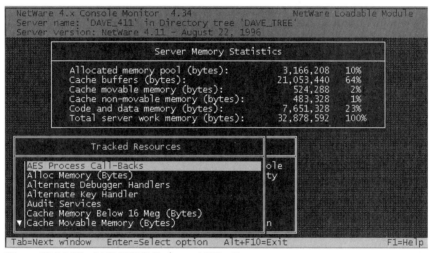

Figure 18-24: The MONITOR Resource Utilization screen.

One of the biggest resources you need to track is memory. The Resource Utilization screen will give you the best statistic used to track server health—the percentage of cache buffers; that is, the percentage of total memory that is used for caching information. For optimal performance, this number should be above 70 percent.

Tip

If the percentage of cache buffers ever falls below 30 percent of total memory, run, don't walk, to a computer store and buy more RAM.

If you select any of the resources listed in the Resource Utilization screen, you can see which services are using resources and how many resources are being used. This is useful if you suspect one NLM is misbehaving and taking more resources than it should.

Memory Utilization

The next category of MONITOR statistics will tell you exactly how much memory a particular NLM is using and how efficiently that NLM uses the memory that is given to it. When you select Memory Utilization, you will see the screen in Figure 18-25, which shows the total statistics for all modules. Selecting an individual module will show the statistics for that module. The statistics are explained in Table 18-14; both the summary screen and the statistics for each individual module display the same parameters.

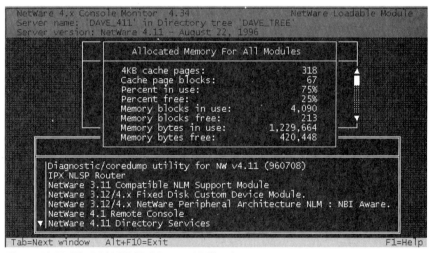

Figure 18-25: The MONITOR Memory Utilization screen.

These statistics need to be watched to see if the NLMs that are loaded are using all the memory that is given to them. If there are consistently high "in-use" statistics (>90%), then the NLMs are efficiently using their allocated memory. If not, you probably need to increase the Garbage Collection interval.

Statistic	Description
4K Cache Pages	The number of "pages" in the memory pool that has been allocated to a particular module.
Cache Page Blocks	The number of pages actually being used by the module.
Percent in Use	The percentage of the total memory given to an NLM that the NLM is actually using.
Percent Free	The percentage of the total memory given to an NLM that is not being used.
Memory Blocks in Use	The number of blocks of memory an NLM is currently using.
Memory Blocks Free	The number of blocks of memory that an NLM is not using.
Memory Bytes in Use	The exact number of bytes allocated to an NLM that it is currently using.
Memory Bytes Free	The total number of bytes allocated to an NLM that it is not currently using.

Table 18-14: MONITOR Memory Utilization statistics.

Scheduling Information

One area in MONITOR where you can actually change how the server performs is in the Scheduling Information option. When you select it, you will see a screen similar to the one in Figure 18-26. This screen shows all the major processes using processor time and how much time they are using. The name of the process being monitored is on the left-hand side. The next column shows the scheduling delay. If all numbers are 0, all processors handle all requests equally.

If, for example, you see that the IPXRTR Timer is using a large amount of processor time, you can increase the number next to it so that the processor handles the IPXRTR Timer's requests less often. If you set this number to 2, the processor handles its requests 1/2 as often, 3 will make the processor handle its requests 1/3 as often, and so on.

To schedule delay parameters, use the arrow keys to highlight the number next to the process and press the plus sign (+) key to increase the value and the minus sign (-) key to decrease the value. The default for all processes is 0. If you want these values to be permanent, load the SCHDELAY.NLM and use that to configure scheduling delay parameters.

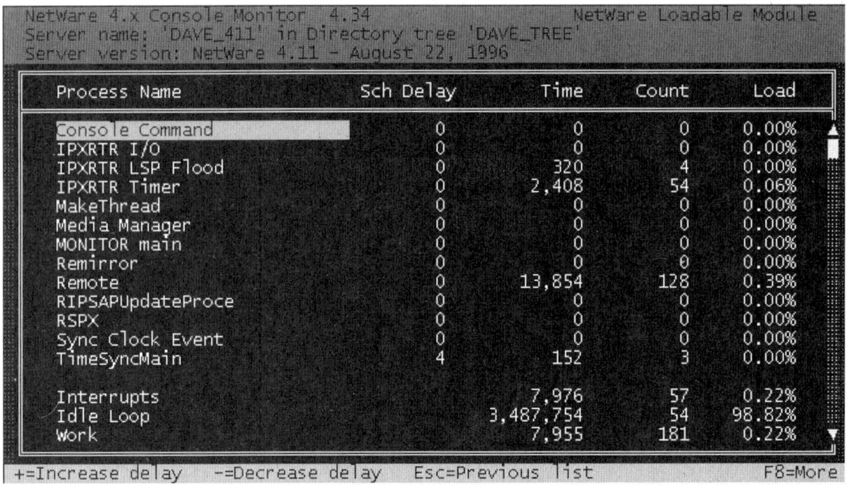

```
NetWare 4.x Console Monitor  4.34                NetWare Loadable Module
Server name: 'DAVE_411' in Directory tree 'DAVE_TREE'
Server version: NetWare 4.11 - August 22, 1996

 ┌─────────────────────────┬───────────┬──────────┬────────┬─────────┐
 │ Process Name            │ Sch Delay │     Time │  Count │   Load  │
 ├─────────────────────────┼───────────┼──────────┼────────┼─────────┤
 │ Console Command         │     0     │        0 │      0 │  0.00%  │
 │ IPXRTR I/O              │     0     │        0 │      0 │  0.00%  │
 │ IPXRTR LSP Flood        │     0     │      320 │      4 │  0.00%  │
 │ IPXRTR Timer            │     0     │    2,408 │     54 │  0.06%  │
 │ MakeThread              │     0     │        0 │      0 │  0.00%  │
 │ Media Manager           │     0     │        0 │      0 │  0.00%  │
 │ MONITOR main            │     0     │        0 │      0 │  0.00%  │
 │ Remirror                │     0     │        0 │      0 │  0.00%  │
 │ Remote                  │     0     │   13,854 │    128 │  0.39%  │
 │ RIPSAPUpdateProce       │     0     │        0 │      0 │  0.00%  │
 │ RSPX                    │     0     │        0 │      0 │  0.00%  │
 │ Sync Clock Event        │     0     │        0 │      0 │  0.00%  │
 │ TimeSyncMain            │     4     │      152 │      3 │  0.00%  │
 │                         │           │          │        │         │
 │ Interrupts              │           │    7,976 │     57 │  0.22%  │
 │ Idle Loop               │           │3,487,754 │     54 │ 98.82%  │
 │ Work                    │           │    7,955 │    181 │  0.22%  │
 └─────────────────────────┴───────────┴──────────┴────────┴─────────┘
 +=Increase delay   -=Decrease delay   Esc=Previous list           F8=More
```

Figure 18-26: The MONITOR Scheduling Information screen.

Multiprocessor Information

Until recently, most NetWare servers could not make use of multiprocessor machines without additional software. Even with recent versions (NetWare 4.1 in particular), Novell sold its support for multiprocessor machines as a separate product. With IntranetWare, Symmetric Multiprocessing (SMP) is built-in. You can use the Multiprocessor Information screen to view the various thread, lock, and processor options for SMP.

Server Parameters

The last option in the MONITOR.NLM is also one that allows you to change the way the server operates. When you select Server Parameters, you are presented with a screen identical to the one you are presented with when you select Server Parameters in SERVMAN. For more information on setting server parameters with SERVMAN, refer to "Optimizing Server Performance: SERVMAN.NLM" earlier in this chapter.

Of course, a server is useless if it is not connected to a network. During the installation of NetWare 4.11, INSTALL.NLM was able to detect the network card and bind the appropriate protocols to it; however, if you need to modify how your server actually communicates with the network, you will want to use the INETCFG.NLM to help you. This NLM (which did not exist in NetWare 3.x) provides a menu-based utility to help you configure how the server talks to the network.

Network Configuration: INETCFG.NLM

In previous versions of NetWare, the networking configuration was complex. It required the operator to load network LAN drivers and bind protocols to them in various configurations. NetWare 4 and above (including IntranetWare 4.11) includes an NLM utility known as INETCFG.NLM that allows you to dynamically configure several of the network-related parameters (when you change a parameter, you don't have to restart the server for the changes to take effect).

In order to get INETCFG loaded and running, start it in the same manner as other NLMs. Type the following command at the server console prompt (colon prompt):

```
LOAD INETCFG
```

The first time you load INETCFG, you will be presented with the screen shown in Figure 18-27 asking you if you want to transfer all the LAN configuration commands (and related commands) to INETCFG so that it can manage them. INETCFG will edit the AUTOEXEC.NCF file, comment out the lines that it can now manage, and add the INITSYS.NCF entry that initializes the INETCFG configuration you have set up. Most of the time, you will want to select Yes here. The only time you might want to select No is if you want to manually manage these commands (in that case, you can't use INETCFG for anything).

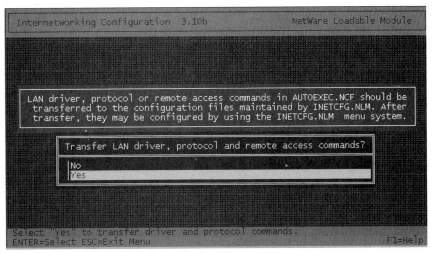

Figure 18-27: The INETCFG Command Transfer screen.

The INETCFG Configure Protocols screen lists some of the protocols available to NetWare. Next to each protocol, you will see its status, either unconfigured, enabled, or disabled. *Enabled* means that the protocol has been configured and can be bound to a LAN driver instance. *Disabled* means that you have configured the protocol as not being available for networking. *Unconfigured* means that protocol has not been configured for use yet. By default, IPX is enabled because it is the native protocol for NetWare.

If you select IPX and press Enter, you will see the screen in Figure 18-31. This screen gives you the option of configuring the way the server responds over IPX. The details of each command are given in Table 18-15. Although there are more commands than are listed, we will cover the most often used ones. For more information on INETCFG, refer to the Utilities Reference manual in the NetWare 4.11 Reference collection of the online documentation.

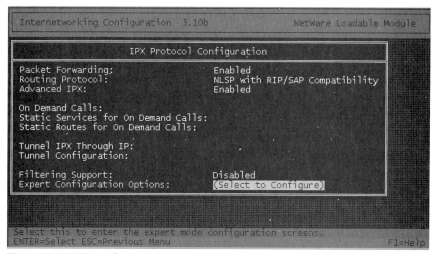

Figure 18-31: IPX configuration options.

The next protocol that INETCFG lets you configure is TCP/IP, which has gotten a lot of attention lately because of the Internet. NetWare has always been able to support TCP/IP services. In the past, it was available as a separate package, but now that support comes free with IntranetWare.

Option	Description
Packet Forwarding	If set to Enabled, allows the server to act as an IPX router (as long as there are two interfaces installed in this server). If disabled, causes the server to act as an end node. It is enabled by default.
Routing Protocol	Sets the routing protocol, either RIP/SAP only or NLSP with RIP/SAP capability.
Advanced IPX	If enabled, allows the server to use the advanced features of IPX, like NLSP. The default is Enabled.
Filtering Support	When enabled, allows filtering of IPX packets (you need to LOAD FILTCFG to configure these parameters). The default is Disabled.
Expert Configuration Options	Brings up the next group of parameters (Table 18-16).

Table 18-15: IPX Protocol Configuration options.

Option	Description
Get Nearest Server Requests	When set to Off, prevents this server from responding to workstation requests for the "nearest server." Can also set this feature with SERVMAN (see "Optimizing Server Performance: SERVMAN.NLM" earlier in this chapter). The default is Accept.
Override Nearest Server	Allows the server to return the name of another server instead of its own name. The default is Disabled. If enabled, it will also enable the next parameter, Server Name, where the name of a different server must be specified.
Advanced Packet Type 20 Flooding	When disabled, allows the server to replicate NetBIOS packets received on one interface to all interfaces. It may happen that the server will replicate the packet back to the workstation that originated it. By enabling this option, you prevent that. The default is Disabled.
Hop Count Limit	Sets the number of times a packet can cross a router before the packet "dies" and can't be routed any more. Also called the TTL (Time To Live). The default is 64.

Table 18-16: IPX Advanced Configuration options.

To configure TCP/IP, select the TCP/IP protocol from the Protocols menu. You will see the screen shown in Figure 18-32.

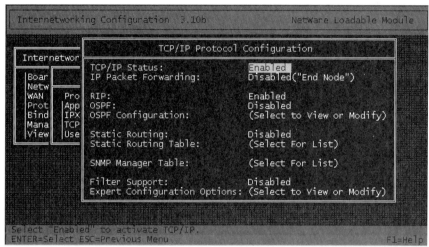

Figure 18-32: The TCP/IP Protocol Configuration screen.

A list of the configuration options and their explanations is given in Table 18-17. Again, we'll cover the most often used parameters. For more information on setting TCP/IP parameters, refer to INETCFG in the Utilities Reference manual in the NetWare 4.11 Reference collection of the online documentation.

Tip

Most often, even with dynamic route configurations, you must enter a "default route" into the static route configuration in order for TCP/IP to work properly. From the Static Route Configuration table, press Insert, and under the Route to Network or Host, press Enter and select Default Route. After that, enter the appropriate IP address for the gateway.

Since NetWare supports several operating systems natively, it couldn't leave out support for Macintosh networks. As a matter of fact, in some people's opinion, a NetWare server makes a better Mac file server than Apple's server does. So, NetWare supports AppleTalk protocol (running over LocalTalk, Ethernet, and Token Ring).

Option	Description
TCP/IP Status	Enables or disables the TCP/IP protocol on the server. The default is Disabled.
IP Packet Forwarding	As with IPX, when enabled, turns the server into an IP router. The default is Disabled, or End Node.
RIP	Enables or disables the RIP routing protocol. If the IP routers on your network only handle other routing protocols (NLSP), you can disable this. The default is Enabled.
OSPF	Enables or disables the OSPF routing protocol. The default is Disabled. OSPF is configured with the OSPF Configuration option.
Static Routing	Lets you configure routes to other networks or hosts. Set to Enabled if the IP routers on your network can't understand any of the dynamic routing protocols. The default is Disabled.
Static Routing Table	Presents a list of the configured routes. To add a new route, press the Insert key and enter the information for that route.
Filter Support	Enables or disables IP packet filtering on the server. If Filter Support is enabled, FILTCFG.NLM must be used to configure it. The default is Disabled.
Expert Configuration Options	Allows enabling and configuring BootP forwarding as well as EGP.

Table 18-17: TCP/IP Configuration options.

To configure it, select AppleTalk from the Protocol Configuration screen. You will be presented with a screen like the one in Figure 18-33. The options for configuring AppleTalk are listed in Table 18-18.

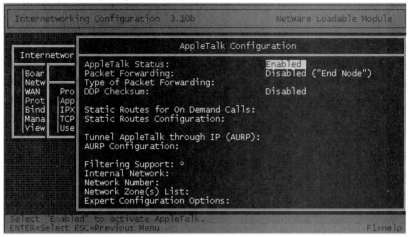

Figure 18-33: The AppleTalk Configuration screen.

Option	Description
AppleTalk Status	If enabled, allows the server to use AppleTalk. The default is Disabled.
Packet Forwarding	If enabled, turns the server into an AppleTalk router.
Filtering Support	If enabled, works similar to the filtering for IPX and TCP/IP. Allows certain AppleTalk packets to be filtered. Must use FILTCFG.NLM to configure the filtering options. The default is Disabled. This option is only available if Packet Forwarding (Router) has been enabled.
Tunnel AppleTalk Through IP (AURP)	Allows tunneling or encapsulating AppleTalk packets within IP packets. Must have TCP/IP configured to allow enabling of this option. The default is Disabled. This option is only available if Packet Forwarding (Router) has been enabled.
Internal Network	When enabled, allows the assigning of an AppleTalk network number to the internal network. The default is Disabled. This option is only available if Packet Forwarding (Router) has been enabled.
Network Number	Sets the actual network number assigned to the internal network. The default is blank. This option is only available if Internal Network has been enabled.
Network Zone(s) List	Shows a list of the zones in which this server will appear. If you press Enter with this item selected, you will be presented with a blank list. If you press Insert, you can enter the name of the zone in which that network should appear. This option is only available if Internal Network has been enabled.

Table 18-18: AppleTalk Configuration options.

You can, if necessary, configure other protocols using INETCFG. There is a User-Specified Protocol option for this purpose. If you select it, it will ask you the name of the protocol's NLM. It will then present a screen with the options for that particular protocol (see the software's documentation for the specifics of how to configure it).

Now that you have your protocols configured, you can press the Escape key (answering yes to "Save Changes?" when appropriate) and get back to the main menu. You must now select Bindings to bind, or logically attach, your protocol to the LAN driver(s) you have configured.

Bindings

When you select Bindings, you will see a screen like the one in Figure 18-34. This screen shows the current bindings (as you can see, only IPX is bound to any LAN drivers). If you select an instance and press Enter, you will be able to see the way that particular instance of LAN driver was bound (with all the options that were used).

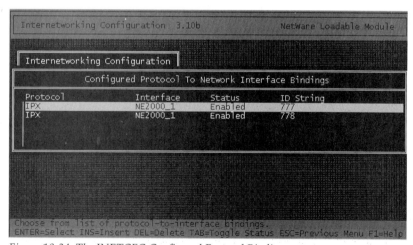

Figure 18-34: The INETCFG Configured Protocol Bindings screen.

If you want to make an additional binding, press Insert. INETCFG will ask you to pick from a list of the configured protocols. Once you select the protocol you want to bind, INETCFG will ask you to pick a LAN driver to bind the protocol to from a list of LAN drivers. After that, it will ask you the specific parameters of the bindings (network numbers, services, frame types, and so on). Table 18-19 shows IPX binding options; Table 18-20 shows TCP/IP binding options; and Table 18-21 shows AppleTalk binding options.

Option	Description
Network Interface	This field is automatically filled in and cannot be changed from this screen.
IPX Network Number	The logical IPX number given to the segment that the particular LAN driver is talking to. If there are no other servers on the network, any hexadecimal number can be entered here.
Frame Type	The network frame type assigned to this binding. See Chapter 17 for more information on frame types.
Expert Bind Options	When selected, presents a menu of advanced options. Do not modify these options unless you know exactly what you are doing. Some of these parameters can drastically change the performance of a NetWare server. See your NetWare documentation for details.

Table 18-19: IPX Binding options.

Option	Description
Network Interface	This field is automatically filled in and cannot be changed from this screen.
Local IP Address	The IP address you want to give to the network card to which you are binding. Make sure it is valid, especially if you are connected to the Internet.
Subnetwork Mask of Connected Network	Enter the subnetwork mask (subnet mask) of the network segment this network card is connected to. The format can be either FF.FF.FF.FF (hex) or 255.255.255.255 (decimal). If none is specified, the default (255.255.255.0) will be used.
RIP Bind Options	Options for binding RIP to the specified interface. If you are not using RIP, ignore this section. Contains items for the type of RIP (I or II), cost of interface (hops), and the manually configured neighbor list.
OSPF Bind Options	Options for binding OSPF to the specified interface. If you only use RIP, ignore this section. Contains items for the cost of the interface (hops), area IP address, and the manually configured neighbor list.
Expert Bind Options	When selected, presents a menu of advanced options. Do not modify these options unless you know exactly what you are doing. Some of these parameters can drastically change the performance of a NetWare server. See your NetWare documentation for details.

Table 18-20: TCP/IP Binding options.

Option	Description
Network Interface	This field is automatically filled in and cannot be changed from this screen.
Provide Applications Through This Interface	If set to Yes, an AppleTalk address will be assigned to this interface. If set to No, you must have had an internal network defined so that applications (such as AFP) can have an address on the server. The default is Yes.
Applications Zone Name	The zone name that this binding will provide services on. This option is only available when Extended Network is chosen as the type of binding.
Network Range and Zone Configuration	This option has two parameters: Learn From Network (Non-Seed) or Define Here (Seed). The first listens to the network and figures out what zone the server is in based on its own configuration and what the "seed" routers (those that have been manually configured with network range and zone information) say. The second option lets you specify the network range and zone that this interface is in, in effect, turning the NetWare server into a "seed" router. The default is Learn From Network (Non-Seed). This option is only available if AppleTalk was configured as a router in the Protocols section.
Network Range/Number	The network range assigned to this interface. If you have a nonextended network, enter a single number from 1-65,279. If you have an extended network, enter a range of numbers (i.e., 10-99), each number being from 1 to 65,279. This option is only available when Network Range and Zone configuration has been set to Define Here (Seed).
Zone(s) List	A list of the AppleTalk zone's that this server will appear in. If you need to select a zone, press Insert and define the zone(s) in which this server will appear. This option is only available when Network Range and Zone configuration has been set to Define Here (Seed).
Expert Bind Options	When selected, this option presents a menu of advanced options. Do not modify these options unless you know exactly what you are doing. Some of these parameters can drastically change the performance of a NetWare server. See your NetWare documentation for details.

Table 18-21: AppleTalk binding options.

You must know whether you have an extended or nonextended network to bind AppleTalk. When you select AppleTalk as the protocol to bind, a menu will appear asking if this is an extended or nonextended network. An extended

AppleTalk network is one that supports AppleTalk Phase 2 extensions such as AppleTalk zones and network ranges; nonextended networks don't. Also, the AppleTalk binding options will change if you have the server set up to route AppleTalk (it will add the option of configuring the routing and network number protocols).

When we're finished configuring the bindings and protocols, press Escape and answer Yes to the questions asking you to save the configurations.

Manage Configuration

From INETCFG, there are a few miscellaneous parameters you can configure. It is possible to configure them from the command line, but they are easier to configure with a menu-driven interface. Select Manage Configuration from the INETCFG main menu to see the screen shown in Figure 18-35.

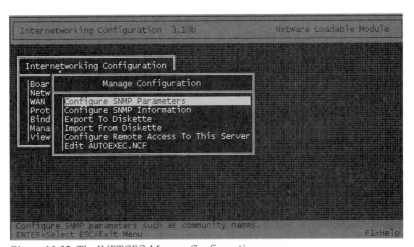

Figure 18-35: The INETCFG Manage Configuration screen.

From the INETCFG Manage Configuration screen, you can configure the parameters and information for Simple Network Management Protocol (SNMP), export the WAN call configuration to a disk, import the same configuration from a diskettonfigure remote access to the server's console, and edit the AUTOEXEC.NCF. Since most server's don't use WAN call configurations, we will omit the discussion of Export to Diskette and Import From

Diskette. The rest of the options are detailed in Table 18-22. For more information, refer to INETCFG in the Utilities Reference manual in the NetWare 4.11
Reference collection of the online documenation.

Option	Description
Configure SNMP Parameters	Allows you to set SNMP parameters such as which communities get monitored, which communities can be controlled, and which communities can be "trapped." Also allows you to specify additional miscellaneous parameters for SNMP.
Configure SNMP Information	Allows you to give detailed SNMP information about this server—the Node Name, the description of the hardware, the physical location, and the person to be contacted for information.
Configure Remote Access to This Server	Brings up the screen shown in Figure 18-36. See Table 18-23 for more information on the commands in this screen.
Edit AUTOEXEC.NCF	Presents the server's current AUTOEXEC.NCF. You can use this option like a text editor to make changes to the AUTOEXEC.NCF. F10 or Escape will save changes and continue.

Table 18-22: INETCFG Manage Configuration options.

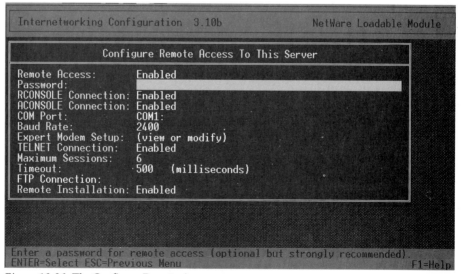

Figure 18-36: The Configure Remote Access screen.

Option	Description
Remote Access	When enabled, allows users to use RCONSOLE.EXE to access the server's console. The default is disabled.
Password	Enter a password to be used with RCONSOLE. The default is blank. Can only be accessed when Remote Access has been enabled.
RCONSOLE Connection	Allows RCONSOLE to function over SPX (network) connections. The default is Enabled. Can only be accessed when Remote Access has been enabled.
ACONSOLE Connection	Allows RCONSOLE to function over asynchronous (modem) connections. Once ACONSOLE Connection is enabled, you must fill out regarding the COM port, modem speed, and modem string information for the server's modem. The default is Disabled. Can only be accessed when Remote Access has been enabled.
TELNET Connection	Allows users to Telnet (using a VT100-compatible terminal) into a server and use the server console. TCP/IP must be configured first. If TELNET Connection is enabled, you must specify the maximum number of simultaneous connections and the timeout for each connection. The default is Disabled.
Remote Installation	When you install software on the server, normally the server asks for either a local drive letter (A: through C:) or a network path for the files it is installing. However, if this parameter is enabled, the server can copy files from a drive letter local to the machine running RCONSOLE.EXE. The default is Disabled.

Table 18-23: Remote Access options.

View Configuration

The last option in INETCFG is View Configuration, which lets you view all the console commands that are happening "behind the scenes." You can also view the commands by category, save the configuration summary to disk, and view the console command log. Table 18-24 details these options. You can only view these options from this menu; to edit them, you must go back into the appropriate menu in INETCFG.

Option	Description
All INETCFG Commands	View all the commands INETCFG uses to configure the server.
LAN Board Commands	View any commands that load LAN drivers and bind protocols.
WAN Board commands	View any WAN call commands (most servers don't have any).
Protocol Commands	View any commands used to load and configure protocols.
Protocol Bind Commands	View any commands used to bind protocols to a LAN driver (duplicates some of the information in LAN Board Commands).
Configuration Summary	Either view or save the configuration summary to a file.
Console Messages	View the console log. This option will show a history of all commands and messages that have been recently shown at the console screen (useful for troubleshooting).

Table 18-24: View Configuration options.

Once you have used INETCFG to configure your server, press Escape until INETCFG asks if you want to exit. At this point, you will be told that the changes are not made active immediately. You need to either "bounce" the server (issue the DOWN command and restart it) or type **reinitialize system**. INETCFG will make active any changes that have been made. If you decide to use the reinitialize system command, be careful as it may interrupt server network communications for an instant.

Tip

The reinitialize system command doesn't always work. Many times, you will be asked if you want to add a frame type for a previously loaded board. A way to prevent the server from asking you about bindings is to UNLOAD your LAN drivers that have changed and then issue the reinitialize system command. An even better way is to "bounce" the server. Basically, some changes don't respond well to the reinitialize system command.

Other Server Console Tools

There are a few commands besides LOAD that you can use at the server console to provide additional information and functionality to the server. Writing an NLM to perform some simple function might be a waste of time, money, and energy, so Novell decided to make these extra commands part of SERVER.EXE.

To find out a list of these extra commands, type **HELP** at the server's console. To get more information on any command, type **HELP** and then the command; HELP will give the syntax for using the command (but not always everything about the command). We will cover a few of these commands. For more information about a particular command, see the NetWare documentation.

ALIAS

The ALIAS command is a little-known console command that can be used as a security measure. ALIAS allows you to make shortcuts for longer commands. For example, you can ALIAS the letter D to DISPLAY SERVERS, like so:

```
ALIAS D DISPLAY SERVERS
```

To use the ALIAS command as a security feature, ALIAS a console command to a garbage string. If you do not want anyone LOADing NLMs on the server, you can ALIAS the LOAD command so that it sends a message to the administrator:

```
ALIAS LOAD SEND "Load attempt on Damocles server" to ADMIN
```

This will send the message "Load attempt on Damocles server" (without the quotes) to the user logged in as Admin. You can tell if someone is LOADing NLMs without your permission. You can change it back to the way it's supposed to work by doing the following:

```
ALIAS LOAD LOAD
```

You can ALIAS the LOAD command to perform other functions instead of loading NLMs. For instance, aliasing the LOAD command to ; (comment) would cause the LOAD command to do nothing when it was executed. Any console command can be ALIASed.

BROADCAST

Whenever you take the server down during the day, your users need to know. After all, they're *using* the server. You can send messages from the server to individual users using the SEND command. Or you can send a single message to everyone by using the BROADCAST command:
BROADCAST "server going down in 5 minutes"

Each workstation will receive the message, and they must either press Ctrl+Enter (for DOS users) or click OK (for most others—Windows 3.1, 95, NT, and Mac).

DISPLAY SERVERS

When you execute the DISPLAY SERVERS command, it will show a list of all of the services advertising on the network. There may be more than one listing for a single item because some network entities have support for more than one frame type or protocol. This command will also show a number after each service. The number is the number of router "hops" away the service is. If the number is 0, the service is located on that server (the one you typed DISPLAY SERVERS on).

DSTRACE

Since NDS is talked about so much but seen so little, it is often said that NDS "exists everywhere and nowhere" in that it is present in every activity, but its activity cannot be seen directly. There is a way to see the various activities of NetWare Directory Services. By typing SET DSTRACE=ON, you activate the screen shown in Figure 18-37. This screen, labeled Directory Services, shows the NDS synchronization that is happening in the background.

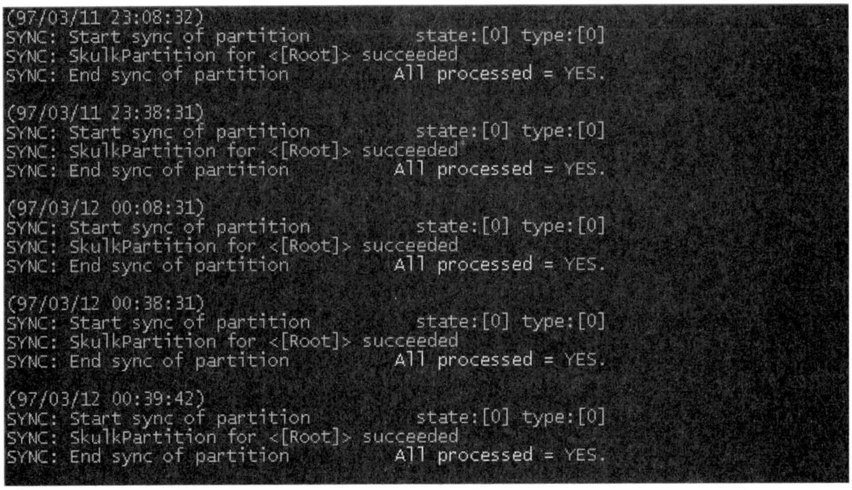

```
(97/03/11 23:08:32)
SYNC: Start sync of partition          state:[0] type:[0]
SYNC: SkulkPartition for <[Root]> succeeded
SYNC: End sync of partition            All processed = YES.

(97/03/11 23:38:31)
SYNC: Start sync of partition          state:[0] type:[0]
SYNC: SkulkPartition for <[Root]> succeeded
SYNC: End sync of partition            All processed = YES.

(97/03/12 00:08:31)
SYNC: Start sync of partition          state:[0] type:[0]
SYNC: SkulkPartition for <[Root]> succeeded
SYNC: End sync of partition            All processed = YES.

(97/03/12 00:38:31)
SYNC: Start sync of partition          state:[0] type:[0]
SYNC: SkulkPartition for <[Root]> succeeded
SYNC: End sync of partition            All processed = YES.

(97/03/12 00:39:42)
SYNC: Start sync of partition          state:[0] type:[0]
SYNC: SkulkPartition for <[Root]> succeeded
SYNC: End sync of partition            All processed = YES.
```

Figure 18-37: The DSTRACE screen.

If you SET DSTRACE=ALL, you can see *every* activity, from logins and logouts to the various cryptic things NetWare does to keep NDS functioning. The most important thing to look for on the DSTRACE screen is the green [YES] item. This means that an NDS action was successful. If you see a red [NO], you will also see a number that indicates an NDS error code (for example, -625, a common error). The error may or may not be a serious one. For more information on NDS error codes, refer to Appendix C.

Most of the time, the errors you see do not need to be acted upon (like the aforementioned -625 error; if left alone, this error will correct itself). A general rule of thumb is, if you see a red [NO] for a whole day, it may be time to take some action.

MEMORY

One thing that all servers can generally use more of is memory. Memory is used not only for loading SERVER.EXE and NLMs, but also for caching files and directories. There are a few console commands you can use to see how much memory your server has and to manipulate it. The MEMORY command will show you the total amount of memory (in kilobytes) that the server recognizes.

RCONSOLE

The RCONSOLE tool is actually used from a workstation to get access to a NetWare server's console. RCONSOLE.EXE is a DOS program that will allow you to use, either over a network or a modem connection, the server's console without actually being there. When you run RCONSOLE from the SYS:PUBLIC directory, you will see a screen like the one in Figure 18-38. From this screen, select either Asynchronous (Modem) Connection or SPX (LAN) Connection.

Tip

If you are using an Asynchronous connection, you won't have access to the server, so you will have to copy the following RCONSOLE files to your local hard drive: RCONSOLE.EXE, RCONSOLE.HEP, RCONSOLE.MSG, IBM_RUN.OVL, _RUN.OVL, IBM_AIO.OVL, _AIO.OVL, TEXTUTIL.HEP, TEXTUTIL.IDX, TEXTUTIL.MSG.

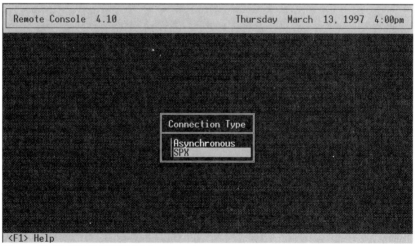

Figure 18-38: The RCONSOLE connection screen.

If you select SPX, you are presented with a list of NetWare servers that have the REMOTE.NLM and RSPX.NLM loaded. If you can't see a server on your network in this list, it is because that server does not have one of these two NLMs loaded. If you select a server and press Enter, RCONSOLE asks us for a password. This is the REMOTE console password configured in INETCFG (or the password entered when the REMOTE NLM was loaded).

Tip

> *In previous versions of NetWare, the password for the Supervisor or Admin users could be used if an administrator didn't know the remote console password. In NetWare 4.11, this is not the case. The only password that can be used is the password entered for the REMOTE.NLM*

Once the password has been entered and you press Enter, the server will beep and the workstation's screen and keyboard will function just as if you were at the server's console, with a few exceptions. Table 18-25 explains the keystrokes used to maneuver in RCONSOLE. Note: When a user RCONSOLEs in to the server, the server console displays a message, "RCONSOLE connection granted for . . ." with an IPX address of the workstation running RCONSOLE. When a connection is refused, the same message appears (except instead of "granted" you see "refused").

To do this . . .	Press . . .
Switch between the various server screens	Alt+F3 to cycle backward, Alt+F4 to cycle forward.
To show the RCONSOLE options menu	Alt+F1 and then select the option you wish to perform or press Escape to close the window.
To quit the RCONSOLE session to a server	Alt+F2 and then answer yes to "Quit Remote Console Session?" This will return you to the screen where you can pick a server to RCONSOLE to.
To show your workstation address	Alt+F5.

Table 18-25: RCONSOLE commands.

Once you finish your RCONSOLE session, you may press Escape or Alt+F10 to quit RCONSOLE.

Tip

> *If you run RCONSOLE under Windows 3.1, 95, or NT, RCONSOLE will complain that "MS Windows may cause RCONSOLE to behave erratically." Just press Enter to continue.*

REMOTE ENCRYPT

If you use remote access to a NetWare server, it is possible to see the remote console password in either INETCFG or the AUTOEXEC.NCF. There is a console command that will allow you to encrypt the console password and use a secured .NCF file to load RCONSOLE. The name of the command is REMOTE ENCRYPT. Once you execute it, it will ask for a password to encrypt (see Figure 18-39). Once the password is entered, it will generate an encrypted password and ask if you want to write that long number and the LOAD commands for it to the LDREMOTE.NCF. If you call LDREMOTE.NCF from AUTOEXEC.NCF or execute it manually, it will provide remote access, but the password that you encrypted will have to be entered (not the long string of letters, but the word or words used as the password).

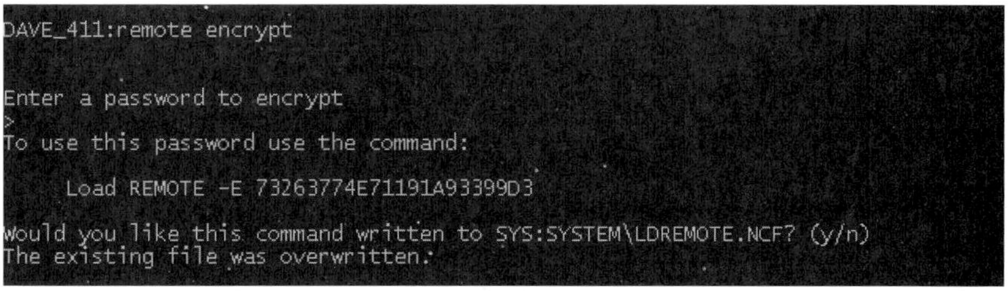

```
DAVE_411:remote encrypt

Enter a password to encrypt
>
To use this password use the command:

    Load REMOTE -E 73263774E71191A93399D3

Would you like this command written to SYS:SYSTEM\LDREMOTE.NCF? (y/n)
The existing file was overwritten.
```

Figure 18-39: The REMOTE ENCRYPT console command execution.

REMOVE DOS

If you ever run short of memory (less than 30 percent cache buffers available), there is a console command that allows you to remove DOS from memory and release the memory DOS used to NetWare's cache buffer pool. To do so, issue the REMOVE DOS command at the console. NetWare will respond by telling you, "DOS removed and its memory given to the disk cache." Once this has been done, there is no going back. When you type DOWN and then EXIT, the server normally brings you back to DOS. But, because REMOVE DOS was issued, the server can't do that, so it reboots.

Tip

Very often, you need to reboot a server remotely. You can accomplish this by making an .NCF file that has the following commands in this order: REMOVE DOS, DOWN, EXIT. After doing so, when you type REBOOT at the console, NetWare will automatically down the server and reboot it (assuming you have SERVER.EXE in the AUTOEXEC.BAT on the server).

SECURE CONSOLE

As previously mentioned, console security is one of the most important aspects of NetWare security. In addition to a command to lock the console, there is a console command you can issue to "tidy up" a few of the loose ends. The SECURE CONSOLE command, when executed, will take care of several issues that can threaten security. It will allow you to load modules from the search path only. It will also allow only the console operator to change the time and date. Finally, it will not let anyone into the internal "debug" program (where possible security holes exist) from the keyboard. However, the best way to secure the server console is to lock the server in a climate-controlled room (not a broom closet) to which only a few people have access.

Moving On

In this chapter, we covered the utilities you can use to manage a NetWare server. The nicest feature about all of these utilities is that they come with the server software; they don't have to be purchased separately. The server itself also has some options to configure but you don't have to change every option in the course of installing and configuring a NetWare server. The best guideline is to leave the default settings alone and change only the parameters that need to be changed. Generally speaking, if we didn't cover it in this chapter, it probably can be left at the default setting and your server will function properly with no problems.

19

NetWare/IP

U p to this point, we have been talking about the default configuration for NetWare 4.11 and NDS. We know that machines load a specific set of client software to talk to the network. They load the Internetwork Packet Exchange (IPX) protocol to communicate with the servers on the network.

While the IPX protocol is sufficient to handle basic services on your network, it does have some disadvantages as a communication protocol. It is a broadcast protocol. Every time a client requests data from a server, the IPX packet is broadcast to all corners of the network. It is not directed specifically to the server from which it is requesting services. When there are many servers and workstations on the same network segment, the performance of the network can be adversely affected by all of the traffic required to communicate.

This has serious repercussions in an enterprise network. Because of its unroutable, broadcast nature, IPX must be passed through all of the routers on your network. It cannot be filtered if you need to provide IPX-based services to every network segment. If your network spans WAN links, IPX must be broadcast across the WAN links to the IPX machines on the other side. This will seriously decrease the amount of available bandwidth for user transactions. Even requests for data between a client and server located on the same side of the WAN link will need to be broadcast across the WAN due to the nature of IPX.

Enter NetWare/IP. This package, which comes bundled with IntranetWare, will allow the clients on your network to request IPX-based services while using the TCP/IP protocol. This connection-based, routable protocol will help reduce the amount of base traffic on your network and isolate traffic to local sides of WAN links. There are many applications of NetWare/IP that will allow you to make your network more efficient.

In this chapter, we will cover the basics of NetWare/IP. We will show you the benefits of using it on your network and provide some sample network configurations that will highlight its many uses. We will also examine the basic services that are related to NetWare/IP, which you must understand before implementing it—Domain Name System (DNS), Domain SAP/RIP Service (DSS), and Dynamic Host Configuration Protocol (DHCP).

After discussing the theory behind NetWare/IP, we will dive into the installation and configuration of the NetWare/IP server. This server is the key to the implementation of NetWare/IP. Running on a NetWare 4.11 server, the NetWare/IP server will allow you to provide the normal IPX-based NetWare file and print services over the TCP/IP protocol.

Once the software has been installed and configured on the NetWare/IP server, the client workstations must be configured to use it. We will discuss the installation and configuration of the NetWare/IP software at the DOS/Windows and Windows 95 client workstations.

Before embarking upon the installation of NetWare/IP, you should have a thorough understanding of the TCP/IP protocol. We will give you a brief overview in this chapter; however, NetWare/IP is not for the faint at heart. Install and configure NetWare/IP on your network only if you need it. For more information on the TCP/IP protocol, refer to the NetWare 4.11 TCP/IP Reference manual in the NetWare 4.11 Communication collection of the on-line documentation. Enough said. Let's get on to the fundamentals of NetWare/IP.

NetWare/IP Basics

When NetWare was created, Novell based the communication between the client workstations and the servers upon a proprietary protocol called Internetwork Packet Exchange (IPX) and its partner protocol Sequential Packet Exchange (SPX). As later versions of NetWare were released, the IPX/SPX communications protocol was kept as the standard for communication on a Novell network. As NetWare applications were developed by third-party software designers, the applications were written to accommodate the IPX/SPX protocol in the Novell network environment.

At the same time that NetWare was growing and evolving, other types of networks were also proliferating. One of them is the Internet, which relies upon the Transmission Control Protocol/Internet Protocol (TCP/IP) for communication. TCP/IP is a connection-based protocol. When a machine is requesting services from another machine on a TCP/IP network, the requesting machine's information packets are directed to the machine providing services. Information is exchanged between only those two machines on the network. All of the other machines ignore TCP/IP packets that are not directly addressed to them.

Because TCP/IP is an address-specific protocol, it is also a routable protocol. Using a complex system of hardware and software, TCP/IP packets can be routed to their final destination. This leads to network segmentation and efficiency. TCP/IP network traffic is directed toward its target by the hardware on the network, unlike IPX/SPX packets, which are not routable due to the broadcast nature of the protocol.

The TCP/IP protocol has gained popularity in networks besides the Internet because of its efficient, routed nature. A lot of the hardware that is used to provide WAN connections for networks is only able to handle TCP/IP packets. If you have networks connected via WAN links that support only TCP/IP, then IPX/SPX-based NetWare services can only be used locally.

This is where NetWare/IP plays a key role in extending the services of your NetWare network. A NetWare/IP server can straddle both the IPX and TCP/IP worlds to provide a complete set of services to both types of clients. Because NetWare/IP is TCP/IP based, you must thoroughly understand the TCP/IP protocol and its related services. However, before we discuss those services, we will take a look at the reasons for using NetWare/IP on your network and the server and clients you will be using.

NetWare/IP

NetWare/IP version 2.2 is a product included in IntranetWare that allows you to provide NetWare services on TCP/IP-based networks. Instead of using the default IPX/SPX protocol to communicate between the clients and the servers, you can use the Internet-standard, more-efficient TCP/IP protocol. You might want to set up a NetWare/IP network for your company for the following reasons:

- Your company wants to standardize on a single protocol for the enterprise network. TCP/IP is an obvious choice because it is the protocol of the Internet. NetWare/IP will allow you to provide NetWare file and print services along with Internet services using only one protocol stack on the client workstation.

- Your WAN links do not support IPX/SPX-based protocols, and you want to extend the services of your NetWare network to all users in your company on both sides of the WAN link.

- You want to eliminate the Service Advertising Protocol (SAP)/Routing Information Protocol (RIP) broadcast traffic on your network because it is adversely affecting the performance of your network.

- You want to integrate separate IPX and TCP/IP networks so that users on either network can access NetWare resources.

When you use NetWare/IP, the protocol the machines use to communicate with one another is independent of the service. IPX applications will still work properly on a TCP/IP-based network with NetWare/IP because the communication is transparent to the applications running on the client workstation.

NetWare/IP can reduce the amount of workstation support required on your network because you can provide all of your NetWare services and Internet services using only one protocol stack. In addition, only one protocol will be active on your network, which makes it more efficient. Unfortunately, the price for this efficiency is the initial setup of NetWare/IP on your network. Each server and client must be configured to run NetWare/IP.

NetWare/IP Servers

On the server side, the NetWare/IP software must be loaded on a NetWare 4.x server. This enables the server to accept TCP/IP packets with requests for "normal" NetWare file and print services. It takes the packets from the client workstation, removes the TCP/IP wrapper, and processes the NetWare file and print service request like it normally would. When the information requested is ready to go out, it is placed inside a TCP/IP packet and sent back out to the client workstation that originally requested the information.

NetWare/IP Clients

At the client, NetWare/IP software must be loaded to enable the client to request traditional IPX/SPX services from the file server using TCP/IP. When information is to be sent to the network, the IPX header is encapsulated in the TCP/IP packet being sent. This provides backward compatibility, which is required for IPX-based applications to function using NetWare/IP.

Once loaded, the client will not be able to transmit any IPX packets. All IPX information will be encapsulated in the TCP/IP packets through NetWare/IP. By modifying the NET.CFG at the client workstation, you can configure the workstation to talk directly to the DSS server on the network so it can get the normal NetWare services it needs. We will discuss the modifications that need to be made to the client to enable NetWare/IP later in this chapter in the section "The NetWare/IP Client."

Besides setting up the client and server with the appropriate software, the other cost associated with setting up NetWare/IP is the service configuration that must be present before it can be run. As we have mentioned in Chapter 17, servers use protocols called SAP and RIP to communicate information about themselves to the rest of the network. Because you will no longer be broadcasting these packets to the network, you must provide an alternate means by which servers are able to track service type information on your network. Novell has done just that with a set of interdependent services included in NetWare/IP.

NetWare/IP-Related Services & Concepts

Before we can actually discuss the installation and configuration of NetWare/IP on your network's clients and servers, it is important that you understand the interdependent services provided with NetWare/IP. These services are responsible for taking the place of the RIP and SAP packets that are normally transmitted by NetWare servers to communicate information regarding servers' services and availability.

When RIP and SAP are employed on an IPX-based network, servers broadcast information about themselves to the rest of the network. In turn, these servers listen to the RIP and SAP packets from other servers and begin to store a table internally that is based upon the information received in the RIP and SAP packets. Servers are able to keep track of the names of the other servers on the network and the shortest distance across the network to each of the servers. Without these internal tables built upon the RIP and SAP traffic, servers would not be able to "see" the other servers on the network.

When you install and configure NetWare/IP, you are replacing the broadcast IPX protocol with the connection-oriented TCP/IP protocol. You are also replacing RIP and SAP as a means of communication between servers. In place of RIP and SAP, there are two services, called Domain Name System (DNS) and Domain SAP/RIP Service (DSS), that allow servers to be able to communicate with one another. These services must be in place before NetWare/IP can be run on your network.

But before we even get to those concepts, it is important to understand the communications protocol that will be employed when NetWare/IP is up and running. The first thing we need to understand is the TCP/IP protocol itself.

Transmission Control Protocol/Internet Protocol (TCP/IP)

TCP/IP is one of the oldest communication protocols in existence, and it is by far the most popular and widely used on today's networks. Most networking hardware available will support the TCP/IP protocol, and it is the "official" protocol of the Internet, although many other types of networks use TCP/IP as a primary method of communication.

TCP/IP was first proposed in the early 1970s as a communication protocol. It was the foundation for a network called Defense Advanced Research Projects Agency (called DARPAnet or ARPAnet). TCP/IP was designed with efficiency in mind from the start. Its first functions were to easily transfer files and e-mail from one place to another.

As ARPAnet grew, TCP/IP as a protocol suite grew with it. TCP/IP was developed in stages and refined over the period of a decade until it was finally standardized in 1982. To this day, it is still being revised and improved. In terms of the main network on which TCP/IP is used, ARPAnet has faded into history. It was one of the precursors to the Internet, which has since grown in leaps and bounds, beyond anyone's wildest imagination.

Those of you who are familiar with the Internet will know that every machine connected to the Internet has a unique *IP address*. This is the address by which the machine is known in the TCP/IP world. The IP address is a 32-bit number that is included in the header of every TCP/IP packet to properly route the information to the destination computer.

However, we do not normally refer to the IP address of our machine as 011010110101010000101010001010110. For convenience's sake, the 32-bit number is broken up into four 8-bit pieces referred to as *octets*. When these octets are converted from binary into decimal form, they must translate into a valid number from 0 to 255. This may begin to look familiar to you now.

The four octets of an IP address are strung together and separated by a period to achieve the *dotted quad* name format with which we are familiar. For instance, 172.54.91.5 is the dotted quad IP address of a TCP/IP-based machine. This is much easier to remember than the 32-bit string of zeros and ones.

The IP address can actually be broken up into two parts that logically describe the machine. It consists of a network number and a host number. Two machines with the same host number must have different network numbers. Likewise, two machines with the same network number must have different host numbers. Many times when you configure TCP/IP, you will need to specify a *subnet mask* for your network. Simply put, the subnet mask is the network number for your TCP/IP network. Common subnet masks would be, for example, 255.255.255.0 and 255.255.0.0. In the first case, the first three octets refer to the network number; in the second case, the first two octets refer to the network number.

Depending upon the size of your network, you will be assigned an IP address within a specific range, as we will discuss later in this section. There are three classes of IP addresses in use on the Internet today, and these three classes determine the network number and host number for your IP address:

- **Class A** IP addresses use the first 8 bits of the 32-bit IP address to determine the network number. The first bit is always 0. Thus, the first octet of a Class A IP address always has the value 0-127. The remaining 24 bits of the IP address are used for the host number. Because of this definition, there can only be 128 Class A TCP/IP networks, but there can be more than 16 million hosts.

- **Class B** IP addresses use the first 16 bits of the 32-bit IP address to determine the network number. The first bit is always 1, and the second bit is always 0. Thus, the first octet of a Class B IP address always has the value 128-191. The remaining 16 bits of the IP address are used for the host number. By definition, there can be over 16,000 Class B TCP/IP networks, which can accommodate over 65,000 hosts on each one.

- **Class C** IP addresses use the first 24 bits of the 32-bit IP address to determine the network number. The first bit is always 1, the second bit is always 1, and the third bit is always 0. Thus, the first octet (8 bits) of a Class C IP address will always be 110$xxxxx$ where each x can have the value of 1 or 0. Translated into decimal, this octet will always have the value 192-223. The remaining 8 bits of the IP address are used for the host number. By definition, there are over 2 million Class C TCP/IP networks, which can accommodate 254 hosts (0 and 255 are reserved host numbers) on each one.

The most common types of TCP/IP networks are Class B and Class C networks. Class C networks are generally used for small businesses and organizations that do not have a large number of hosts needing TCP/IP services. A lot of universities and larger corporations use Class B networks. Class A networks are reserved for very large networks.

If your network is connected to the Internet, then you must use a unique IP address. IP addresses are given out by the Internet Network Information Center (InterNIC) and must be registered. This prevents duplicate IP addresses from being issued. If you are not connected to the Internet, then you can choose any IP address you want; however, if you do connect your network to the Internet later, you will need to reconfigure all of your machines to their assigned IP addresses.

We have mentioned before that TCP/IP is a routable protocol, which is by nature directly related to the IP addressing scheme. Figure 19-1 shows a sample Class B network (152.7.0.0). The host machines have been logically grouped into subnets defined by the third octet of the IP address. All machines whose third octet is 10 are located on one network segment. All machines whose third octet is 20 are located on a different network segment. When the machine with the IP address 152.7.10.10 wants to communicate with the machine 152.7.20.16, the message can be sent from the 10 subnet directly to the 20 subnet because the routing hardware on the network understands the relationship between the IP addresses and the physical network.

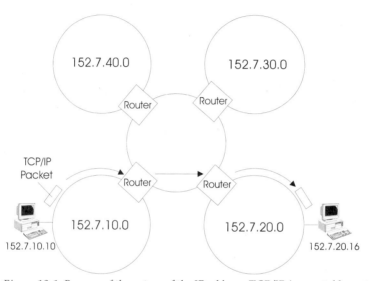

Figure 19-1: Because of the nature of the IP address, TCP/IP is a routable protocol.

You will notice something else looking at Figure 19-1. The network traffic generated by the machine 152.7.10.10 in its request to 152.7.20.16 only impacts the 10 and 20 subnets. Machines on the 30 and 40 subnets never see the packets generated in this transaction. This is unlike an IPX/SPX transmission where the packets would be transmitted to all four network segments.

Every machine that will be using your NetWare/IP network must have the TCP/IP protocol stack loaded on it. This means that each machine using the NetWare/IP network must also have a unique IP address. It does not matter whether the machine is a workstation or a client; the machines need to have an IP address to be able to talk to one another.

Unfortunately, the dotted quad addressing scheme does not lend itself easily to memorization. You might have one machine whose IP address is 156.29.46.31 and another whose IP address is 156.29.31.186. Will you be able to remember these off of the top of your head when asked? Probably not. Fortunately, there is a naming scheme that is used in conjunction with the dotted quad notation that does lend itself to memorization. It is called Domain Name System.

Domain Name System (DNS)

As we have said, the IP address can be broken up into network number and host number. Remembering these numbers can be very confusing; you'll need to make sure that you keep good records. Fortunately, there is another name by which your machines can be known. Each machine can have a hostname associated with it, which also uniquely identifies it.

As the IP address is composed of two pieces, so is the full TCP/IP name of a machine. The network number is given a specific domain name. This name is registered with InterNIC and uniquely identifies your company or organization on the Internet. The host number is given a specific hostname. This is the "pet name" for your machine. For example, Rambell, Inc., has been given Class C IP addresses starting with 204.32.75.0. That range of addresses has been registered with InterNIC as rambell.com. The TCP/IP protocol stack has been loaded on the file server Damocles, and it has been given the IP address 204.32.75.1. This machine can now be referred to in the TCP/IP world as either 204.32.75.1 or damocles.rambell.com. The second name is much easier to remember.

While it is easier for a human to remember the name damocles.rambell.com, it is not how the machines communicate with one another. When a machine communicates via TCP/IP, it must include the IP address of the machine it is communicating with—not its hostname. So if you sit at a machine and request TCP/IP services from damocles.rambell.com, the machine will not be able to contact Damocles unless there is an intermediate translation between the hostname and IP address. This is where the DNS server comes into play.

Every site that uses Domain Name System must have a DNS server. This server stores a database that provides the translation between the hostname and the IP address. When a hostname is issued in conjunction with a TCP/IP request, the machine first looks to the DNS server to resolve the hostname into an IP address. The DNS server takes the hostname, looks it up in its database of names and addresses, and returns the IP address associated with the hostname if it exists. Only then can the workstation contact the other machine for TCP/IP services.

The communication between the workstation, the DNS server, and the target machine is shown in Figure 19-2. The arrow labeled 1 is the first request the TCP/IP workstation must send out to the network. It is directed to the DNS server so the name damocles.rambell.com can be resolved. The arrow labeled 2 is the response from the DNS server. It has found damocles.rambell.com in its database of names and is returning the IP address of that machine. The arrow labeled 3 is the actual service request to the host.

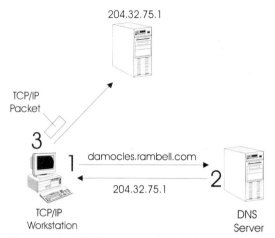

Figure 19-2: A DNS server resolves the hostname and returns the IP address for the requested TCP/IP resource.

When you have DNS services set up on your network, all of the TCP/IP machines must be configured to point to it for hostname resolution. If the host-name-to-IP-address translation does not occur, your users will not be able to communicate with other TCP/IP machines on your network unless they explicitly specify the IP address of the machines from which they are request-ing services.

NetWare/IP requires DNS services on your network to be able to function properly. Upon booting, the NetWare/IP server requests information from the DNS server on your network about the Domain SAP/RIP Service (DSS) servers. If this information is not returned, NetWare/IP will not load on your server.

There are two ways you can provide DNS services for NetWare/IP:

- **Install DNS services on a NetWare 4.11 server.** NetWare/IP comes with the software necessary for creating a DNS server, including installation and management utilities.

- **Tap into existing DNS services.** If there is already a DNS server running on your network, you can configure the NetWare/IP server to use it for hostname resolution. In this case, you will probably need help from the DNS administrator on your network.

NetWare/IP comes with the necessary software for installing and configur-ing a DNS server on your network. DNS is required for NetWare/IP because NetWare/IP servers request DSS information from the DNS server to commu-nicate information about NetWare services. NetWare/IP also requires a special NDS domain (called the *NetWare/IP domain*).

If you are implementing your own DNS services on your network, you may need more than one DNS server. This could be due to geographical constraints or fault tolerance. Two types of DNS servers are included with NetWare/IP to help you facilitate a more efficient NetWare/IP environment:

- **Master DNS name server.** This DNS server keeps the master database that lists the hostnames and IP addresses for all machines in your NetWare/IP domain. It also includes information concerning the DSS servers in your NetWare/IP domain.

- **Replica DNS name server.** This DNS server keeps a read-only copy of the Master DNS name server's DNS database. There can be multiple Replica DNS name servers on your network to provide fault tolerance or reduce network traffic across WAN links.

Besides DNS, there are other interdependent services that must be implemented to successfully create a NetWare/IP network. Just like the DNS servers keep a database of machines' hostnames and IP addresses, another type of server keeps a database of NetWare service-related information. This is the Domain SAP/RIP Service (DSS) server.

Domain SAP/RIP Service (DSS)

From our discussion of the TCP/IP protocol and DNS, it should be evident that the TCP/IP network environment does not easily support the broadcasting of information to all machines on the network. This presents a formidable obstacle for providing NetWare services over the TCP/IP protocol.

In the IPX/SPX NetWare environment, NetWare servers broadcast RIP and SAP information once a minute. This is how the servers communicate with one another and determine the layout of the network. Without this RIP and SAP information, NetWare servers are essentially blind to one another. Fortunately, Novell has come up with a solution to the absence of the RIP/SAP information in the TCP/IP environment.

When using NetWare/IP, you are required to have at least one DSS server on your network. All NetWare/IP servers are configured to point to this DSS server. On a periodic basis, all of the NetWare/IP servers send the DSS server their RIP and SAP information via TCP/IP. This way, all of the information concerning the NetWare services on the network is maintained by the DSS server(s). It is able to keep an accurate database concerning the NetWare server availability.

Besides sending RIP and SAP information to the DSS server, all NetWare/IP servers periodically download a copy of the database for themselves. This way, they are able to process requests concerning NetWare services without having to query the DSS server regularly. Thus, each NetWare server on the network has a copy of the RIP and SAP information, but the network is not flooded with the broadcasting of RIP and SAP packets. The information is provided through the DSS server(s) and is centrally maintained. Figure 19-3 shows how the DSS server assembles and disseminates the RIP and SAP information to the network.

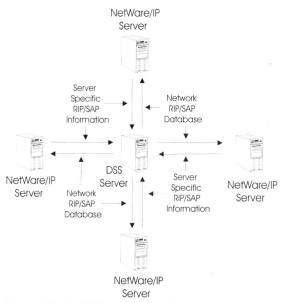

Figure 19-3: The DSS server centrally maintains the network RIP/SAP information and distributes it to the NetWare/IP servers.

There can be more than one DSS server on your network to handle the RIP and SAP information. There are two types of DSS servers provided with NetWare/IP:

- ■ **Primary DSS server.** The Primary DSS server maintains the master copy of the RIP and SAP information for your network. Also included in this database of network information is the NetWare/IP domain name, the NetWare/IP network number, and the UDP port information required by NetWare/IP. We will discuss these concepts later in this chapter when we discuss the installation and configuration of the NetWare/IP software.

- ■ **Secondary DSS server.** The Secondary DSS server provides support for the Primary DSS server. It keeps a read/write copy of the DSS database and shares the load of providing NetWare/IP information to the machines on the NetWare/IP network.

From our knowledge of NDS, we can see that the DSS database is a distributed database. As with all distributed databases, there are always questions of synchronization. The Primary and Secondary DSS servers synchronize their databases at a rate determined by the Primary DSS server. During this process, the Secondary DSS server uploads any changes to the Primary DSS server's DSS database that have occurred since the last synchronization. Then, the Secondary DSS server downloads the modifications to the DSS database from the Primary DSS server. The default interval for synchronization is five minutes.

Every NetWare/IP network must have at least one DSS server. It does not have to be functioning as a NetWare/IP server; however, the DSS server is necessary to provide the central point of data gathering for RIP and SAP information on the network. If you have only one DSS server, it is automatically the Primary DSS server. Other Secondary DSS servers that replicate the information contained in the Primary DSS server's database can be brought up. Secondary DSS servers should only be used on large networks or networks with WAN link considerations.

Tip

On networks with multiple DSS servers, there is only one Primary DSS server; the other DSS servers are Secondary DSS servers.

Dynamic Host Configuration Protocol (DHCP)

One of the frustrating aspects of implementing a TCP/IP network is the maintenance of the TCP/IP addresses. Every machine on your network has a unique address, which is configured manually. In addition, the subnet mask, gateway, and DNS information also need to be manually configured. It is a time-consuming process that requires great organization. You also need to keep track of which machine has which IP address in the event there is a problem on your network.

DHCP is a service that tries to resolve many of the frustrations involved in setting up a TCP/IP network. Through this protocol, a DHCP server can be set up to be responsible for disseminating IP addresses to machines on the network requesting them. When a client machine needs TCP/IP services, a request is sent by the client to the DHCP server. The DHCP server not only returns the IP address for the machine, it also returns information concerning the subnet mask, the relevant gateway, and the DNS information. It is a way to automatically configure the client workstations.

The beauty of DHCP is that the pool of IP addresses the server has available is predetermined by the network administrator. The network administrator defines a set of IP addresses in the DHCP server, and the server hands out the addresses as they are requested. The method of assignment varies from DHCP installation to DHCP installation. For more information on DHCP, refer to Chapter 12 in the NetWare/IP Administrator's Guide. This manual can be found in the NetWare 4.11 Communication collection located in the online documentation.

Figure 19-4 shows a sample network with a DHCP server and some client machines. When TCP/IP services are requested by the client workstations, a DHCP request is sent to the DHCP server, which responds with the appropriate TCP/IP information. In the sample in the figure, the DHCP server has a pool of five addresses to give out. When the IP address is returned to the requesting machine, all of the appropriate TCP/IP information is also returned.

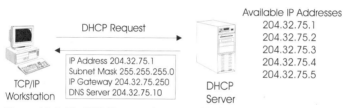

Figure 19-4: The DHCP server is responsible for dynamically allocating IP addresses to client machines requesting them.

Note that when DHCP services are provided on your network, it does not eliminate the need for a TCP/IP stack on each client workstation. This protocol stack is still required for the machine to communicate with other TCP/IP machines on the network. The only difference is that an initial request is sent to the DHCP server, which returns the TCP/IP configuration information required for the stack. After that point, the client workstation runs just like any other TCP/IP-based workstation.

NetWare/IP version 2.2 includes the software to turn your NetWare 4.11 server into a DHCP server. It can be installed using the INSTALL.NLM utility on the server. To install the software, perform the following steps:

1. At the server console prompt (colon prompt), type **load install** and press Enter. The Installation Options menu of INSTALL.NLM appears.

2. Select Product Options from the Installation Options menu by highlighting it and pressing Enter. The Other Installation Actions menu will appear.

3. Use the Up arrow key to reach the top menu on the screen, Other Installation Items/Products. Once the highlight bar is in this top menu, select Install NetWare DHCP by highlighting it and pressing Enter.

4. INSTALL.NLM will prompt you for the NetWare 4.11 Operating System CD (CD1 in the IntranetWare CD package). Once the DHCP server files have been copied from the CD, the Installation Options menu will appear.

5. Select Install Product from the Installation Options menu to install the DHCP server on your NetWare 4.11 server. A list of servers will appear once you press Enter. Select the server on which you want to install DHCP and press Enter.

6. After installation, down the server and restart it.

Once the server has been restarted, just type **load dhcpsrvr** at the server console prompt (colon prompt) to start DHCP services on your NetWare 4.11 server. For more information on configuring the DHCP server software on your IntranetWare server, refer to the NetWare/IP Administrator's Guide in the 4.11 Communication collection of the online documentation. DHCP can help you tremendously in the administration of your TCP/IP environment. It can also be run independently of NetWare/IP. You can provide the dynamic assignment of IP addresses to non-NetWare/IP networks using the DHCP server software.

It is important that you understand the NetWare/IP interdependent services and how they relate to one another before you attempt to set up a NetWare/IP network. DNS and DSS are absolutely necessary on your network for NetWare/IP to work properly. DHCP is an added product that comes with NetWare/IP that can help you in the administration of your TCP/IP network. But before we actually set up the NetWare/IP services, we will take a look at some common network models for NetWare/IP to help gain a better understanding for how you might implement it.

Sample NetWare/IP Network Configurations

Previously in this chapter, we discussed the reasons why you might want to implement NetWare/IP on your network. Whether you want to standardize on a single network protocol or extend NetWare services across a WAN, it is important for you to be familiar with some basic NetWare/IP network configurations. These configurations will help you plan what your network will look like after you decide that NetWare/IP is the way you want to go.

There are three basic models for implementing NetWare/IP on your network:

- Single protocol configuration
- Packet forwarding configuration
- WAN connector configuration

Each of the preceding configurations employs NetWare/IP servers in critical locations to facilitate efficient communication and distribution of NetWare services on your network.

Single Protocol Configuration

The single protocol configuration for NetWare/IP assumes you are going to replace the IPX protocol on your network with TCP/IP as a method for communication. All of the NetWare servers on your network must be NetWare/IP servers, and all of the clients on your workstation must be using the TCP/IP protocol stack in addition to the NetWare/IP client layer, which will encapsulate IPX headers in the TCP/IP packets.

Figure 19-5 shows a graphical representation of the single protocol configuration. Notice the benefit of using only TCP/IP on your network. Not only can the NetWare client workstations access the NetWare servers on the network, they can also access the Internet directly because they are using the TCP/IP protocol. The network administrator does not have to bother with the hassle of loading multiple protocol stacks at the client workstation or the server.

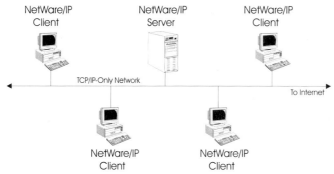

Figure 19-5: The single protocol configuration assumes TCP/IP will be the only allowed protocol on the network segment.

Tip

In a single protocol environment, IPX packets will not be transmitted on your network. For printing services, you must configure the NetWare-to-UNIX print environment to provide print services for your users over TCP/IP. See Chapter 7 for more information.

Packet Forwarding Configuration

In the packet forwarding configuration (also called the forwarding gateway configuration), the NetWare/IP server acts as a bridge between two different types of networks. In this model, the NetWare/IP server has two network cards in it. One of the cards is connected to a TCP/IP network, and the other card is connected to an IPX network. On the NetWare/IP server itself, the IPX protocol is bound only to the NIC connected to the IPX network. The TCP/IP protocol is bound only to the NIC connected to the TCP/IP network.

Figure 19-6 shows the packet forwarding configuration. Notice toward the bottom of the figure that there are NetWare 4.11 servers and clients using IPX and on the top of the figure there are NetWare/IP servers and clients using TCP/IP. Because one NetWare/IP server is connected to both the TCP/IP and IPX networks, the TCP/IP client workstations can access the NetWare resources on the IPX-based NetWare file servers and vice versa.

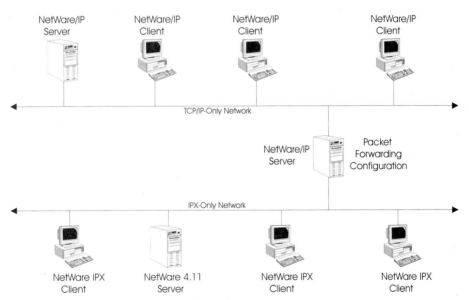

Figure 19-6: The packet-forwarding NetWare/IP server acts as a translator between the TCP/IP and IPX networks.

If an IPX-based client workstation needs to access the file system on a TCP/IP-based NetWare/IP server, the packet-forwarding NetWare/IP server will translate the IPX packet into a TCP/IP packet and forward it to the appropriate NetWare/IP server. When the information is returned through the gateway, the packet-forwarding NetWare/IP server will translate the TCP/IP packet into an IPX packet the client workstation can understand.

WAN Connector Configuration

The WAN connector configuration is really an extension of the packet forwarding configuration, but it is implemented in a special way. As we have already seen, WAN links on your network deserve special attention. They are generally expensive, and the bandwidth is precious. You want to minimize the amount of traffic that crosses WAN links, especially traffic that is administrative overhead.

In the WAN connector configuration, two NetWare/IP servers are set up, one at each end of the WAN link, and configured as packet-forwarding NetWare/IP servers. At each side of the WAN, the local network can use either IPX or TCP/IP as a method of communication; however, the NetWare/IP servers only put TCP/IP traffic across the WAN link. Figure 19-7 provides a graphic representation of the WAN connector configuration.

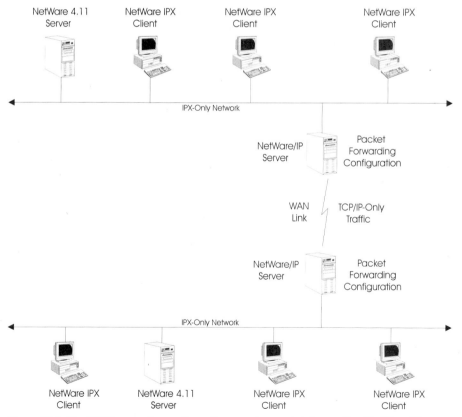

Figure 19-7: The WAN connector configuration uses two packet-forwarding NetWare/IP servers to control the traffic across the WAN link.

This configuration prevents RIP and SAP traffic from flooding the WAN link, which reserves the bandwidth of the WAN link for data traffic. This maximizes the overall performance of your network as well. RIP, SAP, and general IPX traffic are isolated to the local sides of the WAN.

There are many other configurations of NetWare/IP that can be employed on your network; however, these basic models will provide you with an understanding and plan for implementing NetWare/IP. Once you have decided upon a configuration for NetWare/IP on your network, you will need to install and configure the NetWare/IP software. We will cover the installation and configuration in the next section.

The NetWare/IP Server

Now that you have chosen to set up the NetWare/IP environment on your network, it is time to install and configure the software necessary to provide NetWare/IP services. The NetWare/IP software must be installed on a NetWare 4.x server, but once it is installed, the server will be able to provide the standard NetWare file and print services over TCP/IP instead of IPX.

Before you install and configure the software, it is a good idea to plan out your NetWare/IP environment. Previously, we have discussed the interdependent services that are required for NetWare/IP to work on your network. These services must be in place on your network before the NetWare/IP server can be brought up. If you do not have DNS and DSS servers in place, you must install and configure those environments first.

Also, all of your NetWare/IP, DNS, and DSS servers must have the TCP/IP protocol loaded and bound to the network board. Without this base method of communication, you will not be able to set up the NetWare/IP environment. Figure 19-8 shows a flowchart with the preliminary steps required for installing NetWare/IP successfully.

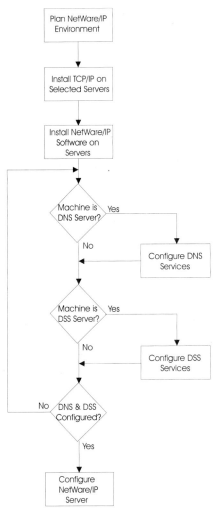

Figure 19-8: The interdependent services must be installed before bringing up the NetWare/IP servers.

After TCP/IP has been installed on the servers, you must set up the DNS environment. If there is an existing DNS environment on your network, you will be able to use it for NetWare/IP services. Otherwise, you must create and configure your own DNS servers. Plan the DNS environment for your network if you need to create it. Determine which server will be the Master DNS name server and, if you need them, which servers will be Replica DNS name servers.

Once the DNS servers have been planned, installed, and configured, you should apply the same process to the DSS environment for your network. If this is your first installation of NetWare/IP, you will need to create your own DSS environment. Determine which server on your network will be the Primary DSS server and which servers will be Secondary DSS servers. If you have WAN links, you will want to strategically place your DSS servers in locations where they can share the DSS workload and minimize the amount of traffic crossing the WAN.

To help you with this planning process, Novell has included some planning worksheets in Appendix A of the NetWare/IP Administrator's Guide. This manual can be found in the online documentation under the NetWare 4.11 Communication collection. Fill in the information on the worksheets concerning the DNS, DSS, and NetWare/IP environment. Have those worksheets available as you are installing NetWare/IP and the interdependent services. It will make the installation easier.

Only when the interdependent services have been configured can the NetWare/IP server be brought up. Through the rest of this section of the chapter, we will briefly discuss the installation and configuration of the interdependent services as well as the installation and configuration of the NetWare/IP server itself. But first we need to review the hardware and software required to implement your NetWare/IP environment.

System Requirements

Because the interdependent services are required to set up NetWare/IP, they are included in the system requirements. This means that you may need multiple servers to implement your NetWare/IP environment. The system requirements for the interdependent services are as follows:

- **DNS server.** There must be at least one DNS server on your network to provide NetWare/IP services. If you have an existing DNS environment, you can use it; otherwise, you will need a NetWare server on which DNS services will be configured.

- **DSS server.** A NetWare server is required for DSS services on your NetWare/IP network. This server must have at least 4MB of free disk space to accommodate the NetWare/IP software files. The DSS server also needs to have (n x 520) + 835,000 bytes of additional memory available, where n is the number of servers on the network.

The DSS server is one of the most critical pieces of the NetWare/IP environment. Its performance can adversely affect the performance of the entire network. If you have a large NetWare/IP network, consider making the server on which the DSS software is loaded a dedicated server for DSS services.

The NetWare/IP server itself has hardware requirements that must be met as well. The system requirements for the NetWare/IP server are as follows:

- The NetWare/IP server must have at least 4MB of free disk space available to store the NetWare/IP software.

- The NetWare/IP server must have (n x 380) + 258,000 bytes of additional memory available to provide NetWare/IP services, where n is the number of servers on the network.

For example, if you have 10 servers on your network, then each NetWare/IP server must have at least 261,800 bytes of memory available.

In terms of the actual number of physical servers that must be present on your network, you can configure one NetWare 4.11 server to be the Master DNS name server, the Primary DSS server, and the NetWare/IP server. Or you can split the load of these services across multiple machines. Loading too many services on a single server can adversely affect the performance of the machine.

Besides the hardware requirements, there are some other items you need to define before you actually install and configure NetWare/IP. You need to choose the name of the NetWare/IP domain as it will be known to all machines using NetWare/IP. For example, if your normal domain name were rambell.com, we would recommend that you name the NetWare/IP domain nwip.rambell.com.

You will also need a unique network number on which the NetWare/IP services will run. Choose an eight-character hexadecimal number (such as 62FA7BE1) to represent the NetWare/IP network. After the installation of the software, the NetWare/IP network will look like an IPX network even though it is running TCP/IP.

When you have chosen the servers that will provide the interdependent services and the servers that will be your NetWare/IP servers, make sure TCP/IP is loaded and bound to the network cards in those servers. In the next section, we will recap the installation and configuration of the TCP/IP protocol stack on the NetWare 4.11 server.

TCP/IP Installation

When you install NetWare 4.11, all of the files are in place to enable your server to communicate with the TCP/IP protocol. The only thing you have to do as the server administrator is configure it properly. To configure it, you must have some preliminary information for the server:

- IP address
- Subnet mask

If you are using static routing on your TCP/IP network, you will also need to get the IP address of the IP router on your subnet. This router's IP address will be placed in the server's static routing table. Simply put, it means that when the server addresses a packet that needs to leave the immediate subnet, it can send the packet to the IP router, which will forward it to another router so it can get to its final destination.

You can configure the TCP/IP protocol and bind it to the server's network board using the INETCFG.NLM utility. To start INETCFG, type the following command at the server console prompt (colon prompt):

```
LOAD INETCFG
```

The main menu of the INETCFG utility will appear. It is called Internetworking Configuration. From this menu, select Protocols by highlighting it and pressing Enter. The Protocol Configuration menu appears. Select TCP/IP from this menu by highlighting it and pressing Enter. The TCP/IP Protocol Configuration menu will appear (Figure 19-9). From this menu, you can configure the TCP/IP protocol as it pertains to your particular networking environment.

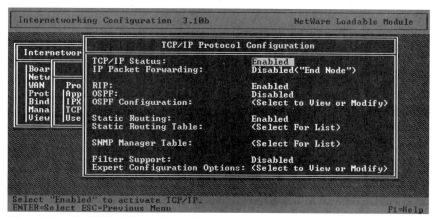

Figure 19-9: The TCP/IP Protocol Configuration menu allows you to customize your TCP/IP environment.

Make sure the TCP/IP Status parameter is set to Enabled. This will allow your server to generate TCP/IP packets. If you use static routing on your network, make sure the Static Routing parameter is set to Enabled as well. You will also need to configure the Static Routing Table to specify the next hop on your network.

Once you have configured the protocol, you need to bind it to the network board in the server. To do so, return to the Protocol Configuration menu by pressing Escape twice from the TCP/IP Protocol Configuration menu. To bind the protocol to the network board, perform the following steps:

1. Select Bindings from the Protocol Configuration menu by highlighting it and pressing Enter. The Configured Protocol to Network Interface Bindings menu will appear.

2. Press the Insert key to add a binding. The Select From the List of Configured Protocols menu appears. Choose TCP/IP by highlighting it and pressing Enter.

3. A new menu will appear with your network boards listed. Choose the appropriate network board by highlighting it and pressing Enter.

4. The Binding TCP/IP to a LAN Interface menu will appear (Figure 19-10). On this screen, specify the IP address and subnet mask for the protocol. When finished, press the Escape key.

5. You will be asked if you want to update the TCP/IP configuration. Select Yes. The new binding will appear in the bindings list.

6. Exit INETCFG by pressing escape twice from the bindings list and select Yes. At the server console prompt, type **reinitialize system**. This will restart your network interface configuration.

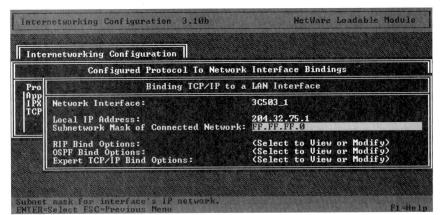

Figure 19-10: When binding TCP/IP to the network board, specify the IP address and subnet mask for the server.

For more information on the INETCFG utility and configuring the TCP/IP protocol on the NetWare 4.11 server, refer to Chapter 18. After TCP/IP has been installed and configured on the server, you can install the NetWare/IP software, configure the interdependent services, and bring up your NetWare/IP servers.

NetWare/IP Installation

The flowchart in Figure 19-8 indicates that the next step after installing and configuring TCP/IP is the installation of the NetWare/IP software. The NetWare/IP software that comes with IntranetWare also includes the interdependent services on which NetWare/IP is based. So before you can configure the interdependent services, you need to install the NetWare/IP software from the IntranetWare CDs.

After the software has been installed, then you can configure the interdependent services and start the NetWare/IP server. In this section, we will cover the installation of the NetWare/IP software, briefly describe the configuration of the interdependent services, and discuss the configuration of the NetWare/IP server itself. Buckle up; it's going to be a bumpy ride.

Tip

The NetWare/IP software installation program tries to configure the interdependent services and the NetWare/IP server. We recommend not *letting the installation program do this. Simply install the software, exit the installation program, and then configure all of the services.*

NetWare/IP Software Installation

The NetWare/IP software is included on the first IntranetWare CD labeled NetWare 4.11 Operating System. Make sure you have this CD available before attempting the installation of NetWare/IP. To install the NetWare/IP software, perform the following steps:

1. At the server console prompt (colon prompt), type **unistop** and press Enter. This executes an NCF file that stops all TCP/IP services that might interfere with the installation of the NetWare/IP software.

2. At the server console prompt, type **load install**. This will load INSTALL.NLM, which will help you install the NetWare/IP software.

3. From the main menu of INSTALL.NLM, Installation Options, select Product Options by highlighting it and pressing Enter. A new menu will appear called Other Installation Actions.

4. From the Other Installation Actions menu, select Choose an Item or Product Listed Above by highlighting it and pressing Enter. The Other Installation Items/Products menu will be highlighted.

5. Select Install NetWare IP by highlighting it and pressing Enter. You will be asked to insert the CD or specify the path from which NetWare/IP can be installed. Once the path has been specified, press Enter.

6. After the main file copies from the CD to the server, the installation program will notify you of a README.TXT file that may contain important information concerning NetWare/IP. Press Escape to continue and select whether or not you want to read this file.

7. The installation program will unpack the files that were copied from the CD and place them in the appropriate place on the server. Wait for the files to finish unpacking. If TCP/IP has not been configured by this point, you will be required to install and configure TCP/IP before the files will unpack. After installing and configuring TCP/IP, specify a hostname for the server.

8. Once the files have been unpacked, you will be notified that NetWare/IP 2.2 has been installed successfully, as shown in Figure 19-11. At this point, the installation program has opened myriad applications to help you install and configure the product. Press Escape to continue. You will be asked if you want to configure the NetWare/IP server. Select No and press Enter.

9. You will be warned that the NetWare/IP server has not been configured yet. Don't worry. We will get to that after ensuring the interdependent services have been set up properly. Press Escape; a new menu will appear asking you if you want to leave the NetWare/IP server configuration utility. Select Yes and press Enter.

10. You will be presented with the UNICON utility used to manage the NetWare/IP environment. We will use this utility a little later. Just press Escape to exit.

11. Press Escape again, and the installation will finish. The temporary files will be deleted, and you will be returned to the Other Installation Actions menu in INSTALL.NLM. Exit INSTALL.NLM.

12. We recommend you down your server and restart it after the NetWare/IP software has been installed.

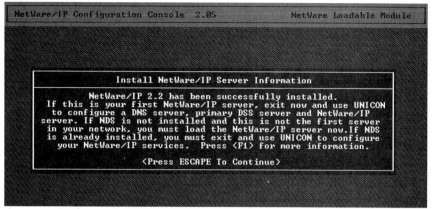

Figure 19-11: You will be notified after the NetWare/IP software has been successfully installed.

Once the software has been installed, you are ready to configure the inter-dependent services that are the foundation for NetWare/IP. The next step is to configure DNS services for your NetWare/IP network. This is done using the UNICON utility we saw briefly during the installation of the NetWare/IP software.

Starting DNS Services

The first step in setting up the NetWare/IP environment is the creation of DNS services on your network. If DNS services are already available on your network, you will need to integrate your NetWare/IP environment into the existing DNS system. Consult the NetWare/IP Administrator's Guide for more information. This manual can be found in the NetWare 4.11 Communication collection of the online documentation.

If you need to set up DNS services on a NetWare 4.11 server, you will need to do so using the UNICON utility on the server. At the server console prompt (colon prompt), type **load unicon** to start the UNICON utility. You will need to log in to the NDS tree as Admin to be able to manage the services through UNICON, as shown in Figure 19-12.

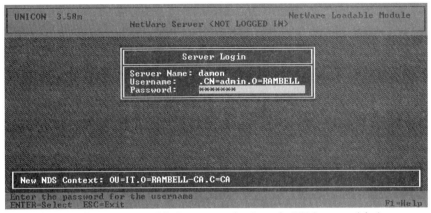

Figure 19-12: Before using UNICON, you must log in to the NDS tree as Admin.

After you successfully authenticate to the NDS tree through the UNICON utility, the main menu will appear. From this main menu you will be able to manage all of the server components of the NetWare/IP environment loaded on that specific server. If you need to create the NDS environment, perform the following steps:

1. From the main menu of the UNICON utility, select Manage Services by highlighting it and pressing Enter. The Manage Services screen will appear.

2. From the Manage Services screen, select DNS by highlighting it and pressing Enter. The DNS menu will appear (Figure 19-13).

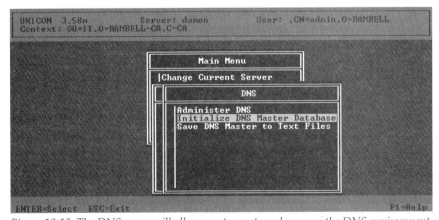

Figure 19-13: The DNS menu will allow you to create and manage the DNS environment.

3. From the DNS menu, select Initialize DNS Master Database. UNICON will initialize the DNS database and present you with the Select Name Servers menu. Specify your DNS domain. This domain is the network name for your TCP/IP environment; it is not the NetWare/IP domain name! Once the domain name has been specified, press Escape to continue.

4. You will be asked if you want to limit the DNS service to specific subnetworks. Select Yes or No depending upon your specific TCP/IP configuration. If you need help, press F1 for more details.

5. Once you have finished with the previous four steps, the Master DNS name server database will be created and started. Press Escape to continue when prompted.

At this point, the DNS service has been started on the NetWare server; however, you are still not finished configuring the DNS service for the NetWare/IP environment. You still must complete the following steps:

1. Specify the NetWare/IP domain name.

2. Create records in the database for the DSS servers that will exist on your network.

3. Add name server records for all of the TCP/IP hosts on your network. Once these records are entered into the DNS database, machines will be able to resolve hostnames into IP addresses to communicate on the network.

All of these things can be done using UNICON. From the DNS menu in Figure 19-13, select Administer DNS by highlighting it and pressing Enter. The DNS Server Administration menu will appear. From this screen you can manage the Master DNS name server database if you have loaded UNICON on the Master DNS name server by selecting Manage Master Database as shown in Figure 19-14.

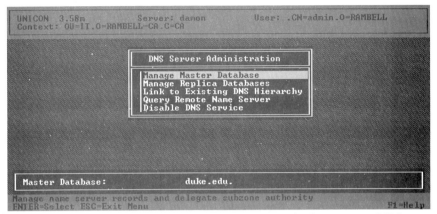

Figure 19-14: UNICON will allow you to manage the NDS databases on your NDS servers.

For more information on setting up the Master NDS database for your TCP/IP environment, refer to Chapter 7 of the NetWare/IP Administrator's Guide. This manual can be found in the online documentation in the NetWare 4.11 Communication collection.

Once you have configured the Master DNS name server, you can perform the same procedure on the Replica DNS name servers to deploy your DNS services. Again, refer to the NetWare/IP Administrator's Guide for setting up the Replica DNS name servers on your network.

After the DNS services have been set up on the DNS servers you have chosen, the next step is to enable DSS services on your network. DSS services rely upon an already existing DNS service; if DNS services do not exist on your network, you must create and configure them before proceeding to set up DSS services.

Implementing DSS Services

The second step in setting up NetWare/IP services on your network is the implementation of the DSS servers. As you will remember from our discussion, DSS is how servers are able to retrieve information about each other and about the network. It replaces the RIP and SAP broadcasts used on an IPX-based network. The first DSS server you set up should be the Primary DSS server for your NetWare/IP network.

To configure the DSS servers on your network, you must load UNICON at the server console of the DSS server. Type **load unicon** at the server console prompt (colon prompt) to start the UNICON utility. You will have to log in to the NDS tree as Admin to be able to configure the DSS server. To configure the DSS server, perform the following steps:

1. From the UNICON Main Menu, select Manage Services by highlighting it and pressing Enter. The Manage Services menu will appear.

2. Select NetWare/IP from the Manage Services menu by highlighting it and pressing Enter. The NetWare/IP Administration menu will appear.

3. From the NetWare/IP Administration menu, select Configure Primary DSS by highlighting it and pressing Enter. The Primary DSS Configuration menu will appear (Figure 19-15).

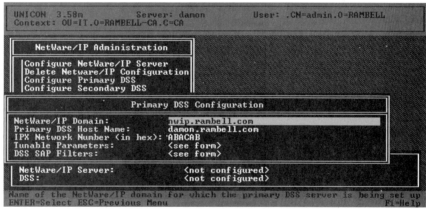

Figure 19-15: The Primary DSS Configuration screen will allow you to customize your Primary DSS server.

In the Primary DSS Configuration screen, you will be asked to input information concerning your NetWare/IP and TCP/IP environments. The three most important parameters on this screen are the NetWare/IP Domain, the Primary DSS Host Name, and the IPX Network Number, which will be used for NetWare/IP services. In Figure 19-15, the name of the NetWare/IP Domain is nwip.rambell.com, the Primary DSS Host Name is damon.rambell.com, and the IPX network number is ABACAB. Notice that the IPX network number does not need to be eight characters in length; eight characters is just the maximum limit.

Once you have specified the information for the DSS server, press Escape. You will be asked if you want to save the changes. Select Yes. You will be greeted with a DSS Configuration Reminder. Press Escape to continue. You will be returned to the NetWare/IP Administration menu. Notice at the bottom of the screen that the DSS is now reporting the status Configured as Primary.

Once the DSS server has been configured, it must be started. To start the DSS service on your NetWare 4.11 server, press Escape twice from the NetWare/IP Administration menu. This will return you to the UNICON main menu. Perform the following steps to implement the DSS server:

1. Select Start/Stop Services from the UNICON main menu by highlighting it and pressing Enter.

2. The Running Services menu will appear. Press the Insert key to add a new service to the list. The Available Services menu will appear.

3. Select Domain SAP/RIP Server from the Available Services menu by highlighting it and pressing Enter. After a brief pause, the Running Services menu will reappear with the Domain SAP/RIP server listed.

If you switch from the UNICON utility to the server console screen, you will see the results of your labor. The server console should display a message similar to the one in Figure 19-16 telling you that the DSS is ready to service your NetWare/IP domain.

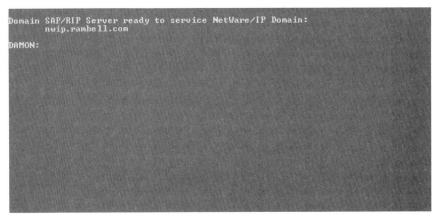

Figure 19-16: When the DSS server successfully starts, the server console displays a ready message.

You can follow a similar procedure for setting up the Secondary DSS servers on your network. For more information on setting up these backup DSS servers, consult the NetWare/IP Administrator's Guide in the online documentation.

Configuring the NetWare/IP Server

It was a long, circuitous route, but we've finally gotten here. Now that the interdependent services have been properly configured, we can actually configure and start the NetWare/IP server. We will access the configuration utility once again through UNICON. If UNICON was not loaded after the DSS server configuration, type **load unicon** at the server console prompt and log in to the NDS tree as Admin to manage the NetWare/IP server.

From the Main Menu of UNICON, select Manage Services by highlighting it and pressing Enter. Select NetWare/IP from the Manage Services menu by highlighting it and pressing Enter. The NetWare/IP Administration menu will appear. From this point, perform the following steps to configure the NetWare/IP server:

1. Select Configure NetWare/IP Server from the NetWare/IP Administration menu. The NetWare/IP Server Configuration menu will appear (Figure 19-17).

2. In the NetWare/IP Server Configuration menu, enter the name of the NetWare/IP Domain.

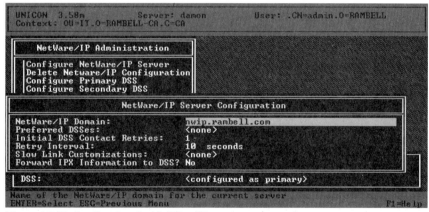

Figure 19-17: Configuring the NetWare/IP server.

In Figure 19-17, you can see that the name of the NetWare/IP domain has been entered. It is nwip.rambell.com. In this screen, you can also specify any preferred DSS servers you want the NetWare/IP server to contact. In addition, you can turn the NetWare/IP server into a Packet Forwarding server (Forwarding Gateway server) by setting the Forward IPX Information to DSS? parameter to Yes. After you are finished configuring the server, press Escape. You will be asked if you want to save the changes. Select Yes, and you will be returned to the NetWare/IP Administration screen.

Once the NetWare/IP server has been configured, it is time to start it. The NetWare/IP server is started in the same manner the DSS servers are started. From the main menu of UNICON, perform the following steps:

1. Select Start/Stop Services from the main menu of UNICON by highlighting it and pressing Enter. The Running Services menu will appear.

2. Press the Insert key. The Available Services menu will appear.

3. In the Available Services menu, select NetWare/IP Server from the list by highlighting it and pressing Enter. The NetWare/IP Server will now appear in the Running Services list.

You will need to confirm that the NetWare/IP server has started correctly. To do this, switch to the server console screen. If the NetWare/IP server has successfully started, you will see a message to that effect displayed on the screen, as shown in Figure 19-18. Otherwise, an error message will appear, which means you have to go back through the steps outlined in this chapter to make sure you have followed the correct procedure and filled in the appropriate information. Once the NetWare/IP server is "initialized and functional," you have successfully installed and configured your NetWare/IP environment. The only thing left to do is configure the NetWare/IP clients.

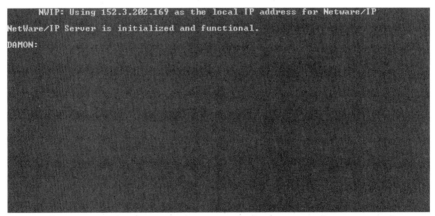

Figure 19-18: Confirm the NetWare/IP server has successfully started by looking for this message on the server console screen.

Setting up the initial NetWare/IP environment can be confusing; just refer to the flowchart shown in Figure 19-8. You must install the interdependent services and the NetWare/IP server in the following order due to how these services relate to one another:

1. DNS service

2. DSS service

3. NetWare/IP server

If you only need to set up NetWare/IP servers on your network, you are finished at this point; however, if you need to migrate your workstation clients from the IPX protocol to the TCP/IP protocol, then you must install the NetWare/IP client software at each workstation that will be using NetWare/IP services. You must have a NetWare/IP server up and running before you install the NetWare/IP client software. In the next section, we will discuss the installation and configuration of the client software that will allow you to access NetWare services over TCP/IP.

The NetWare/IP Client

If you want to provide NetWare services to your client workstations over TCP/IP, then a modification must be made to the client workstation to support the NetWare services. After NetWare/IP has been installed and configured on the server, the client workstation can be configured. Once it is configured, the client will use TCP/IP to communicate with the NetWare/IP server.

The user cannot tell the difference between an IPX workstation using NetWare services and a NetWare/IP workstation using TCP/IP for NetWare services. On the surface, there is no difference; however, on the network, the method of communication is completely different.

This section on the installation and configuration of the NetWare/IP workstation client assumes you have already installed TCP/IP on the client workstation. If you have not installed TCP/IP, then you must do so before trying to install and configure the NetWare/IP client. For more information on installing TCP/IP, refer to Chapters 15 and 16, which deal with the various IntranetWare workstation clients.

Once the NetWare/IP client software is installed on a machine, it will no longer be generating IPX packets and placing them on the network. The machine does need to know how to construct IPX packets because it must encapsulate the IPX header in the TCP/IP packet for NetWare/IP to work properly;

however, the packet placed on the network wire by the client workstation is definitely TCP/IP. Client workstations cannot concurrently run IPX and TCP/IP when the NetWare/IP client software is installed.

The NetWare/IP support at the client workstation is built into the Client32 NetWare shells that come bundled with IntranetWare. You can specify support for NetWare/IP when you install these clients on the workstation. Currently, Novell provides NetWare/IP client software for the following NetWare shells:

- NetWare Client32 for Windows NT (IntranetWare Client for Windows NT)

- NetWare Client32 for Windows 95

- NetWare Client32 for DOS/Windows

- NetWare DOS Requester Client (VLM 16-bit Client)

- NetWare Client for MacOS

In this section, we will cover the installation and configuration of the NetWare/IP client software for both Client32 for DOS/Windows and Client32 for Windows 95. They are the two most likely clients you will need to install on your network workstations. For more information regarding the configuration of the workstation client and NetWare/IP, refer to the online help for the workstation client or go to the Novell Web site (http://support.novell.com) and search Novell's knowledge base.

NetWare/IP Support in Client32 for DOS/Windows

As mentioned, the NetWare/IP client software is bundled with the Client32 for DOS/Windows NetWare shell included with IntranetWare. When this client is installed at the workstation, you just need to make sure you choose the appropriate options to install the NetWare/IP client software.

To install the NetWare/IP client software with the Client32 for DOS/Windows NetWare shell, perform the following steps:

1. Run INSTALL.EXE from the SYS:PUBLIC\CLIENT\DOSWIN32\IBM_6 directory of your NetWare 4.11 server. This assumes you have selected the option to install the client software installation files to your NetWare 4.11 server.

2. Press Enter to accept the license agreement. The main screen for the installation of Client32 for DOS/Windows appears. This screen is displayed in Figure 19-19.

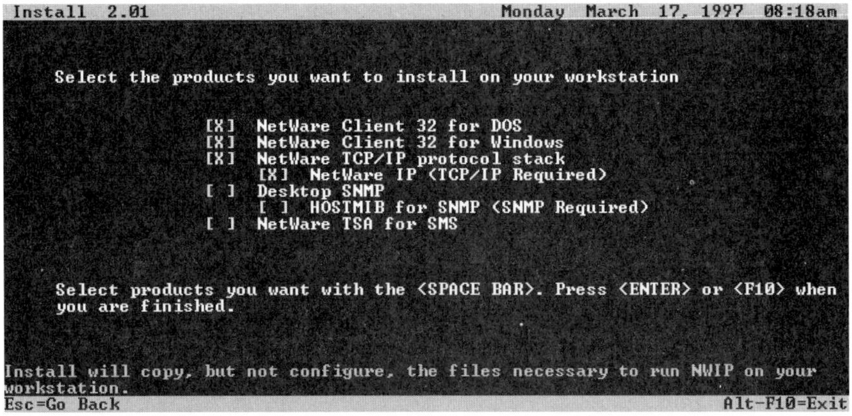

```
Install 2.01                              Monday  March  17, 1997  08:18am


   Select the products you want to install on your workstation

              [X]  NetWare Client 32 for DOS
              [X]  NetWare Client 32 for Windows
              [X]  NetWare TCP/IP protocol stack
                 [X]  NetWare IP (TCP/IP Required)
              [ ]  Desktop SNMP
                 [ ]  HOSTMIB for SNMP (SNMP Required)
              [ ]  NetWare TSA for SMS



   Select products you want with the <SPACE BAR>. Press <ENTER> or <F10> when
   you are finished.


Install will copy, but not configure, the files necessary to run NWIP on your
workstation.
Esc=Go Back                                                       Alt-F10=Exit
```

Figure 19-19: Make sure NetWare IP is marked during the installation of Client32 for DOS/Windows.

3. On this main screen, make sure there is an X in the box to the left of the NetWare IP selection. You must also install the TCP/IP protocol stack to get the NetWare/IP client software.

4. Press Enter or F10 to continue with the installation of Client32 for DOS/Windows. A new screen will appear.

5. Press F10 to accept the values on that screen. They do not pertain to the NetWare/IP client software. After you press F10, the Configure TCP/IP & NetWare/IP screen will appear.

6. Input the values for the IP address, router address, subnet mask, DNS domain name, DNS server address, and NetWare/IP domain name. Press F10 when you have finished modifying these parameters.

7. Select the LAN driver type and press Enter. You will then be provided with a summary of the installation configuration. Press F10 to continue with the installation. The Client32 for DOS/Windows software will be installed with NetWare/IP client support.

Once the configuration is complete, you should be able to reboot the workstation and connect to your NetWare/IP environment. As mentioned, the workstation now only speaks TCP/IP to the network. The only IPX communication generated by the workstation is the IPX header, which is encapsulated in the TCP/IP packet.

The difference between a workstation client with NetWare/IP support and one without it is minor; however, whether or not NetWare/IP is installed makes a world of difference in how the workstation communicates with the network. During the installation of Client32 for DOS/Windows with NetWare/IP support, a modification is made to the STARTNET.BAT and NET.CFG files located in the C:\NOVELL\CLIENT32 directory of the client workstation.

In the STARTNET.BAT file, an extra program called NWIP.NLM is loaded. This is the software responsible for providing the translation between IPX and TCP/IP. It must be loaded after the TCPIP.NLM program and before the IPX.NLM program. Figure 19-20 shows a sample STARTNET.BAT file from a client workstation with the NetWare/IP client software loaded.

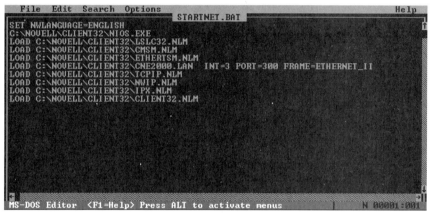

Figure 19-20: NWIP.NLM must load after TCPIP.NLM but before IPX.NLM in STARTNET.BAT.

When the client software is loading at the workstation, it looks to a configuration file called NET.CFG to get pertinent information about that workstation's setup. The installation program also makes a modification to the client's NET.CFG file when NetWare/IP client software support is installed. In the NET.CFG file, there is a new section titled NWIP that contains all of the NetWare/IP client software parameters. Figure 19-21 shows a sample NET.CFG file with the added NWIP section.

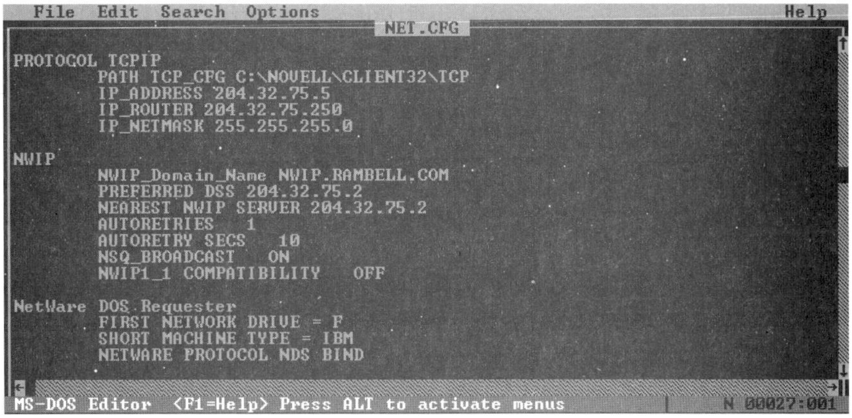

```
 File  Edit  Search  Options                              Help
                              NET.CFG
PROTOCOL TCPIP
        PATH TCP_CFG C:\NOVELL\CLIENT32\TCP
        IP_ADDRESS 204.32.75.5
        IP_ROUTER 204.32.75.250
        IP_NETMASK 255.255.255.0
NWIP
        NWIP_Domain_Name NWIP.RAMBELL.COM
        PREFERRED DSS 204.32.75.2
        NEAREST NWIP SERVER 204.32.75.2
        AUTORETRIES  1
        AUTORETRY SECS   10
        NSQ_BROADCAST   ON
        NWIP1_1 COMPATIBILITY   OFF

NetWare DOS Requester
        FIRST NETWORK DRIVE = F
        SHORT MACHINE TYPE = IBM
        NETWARE PROTOCOL NDS BIND

MS-DOS Editor  <F1=Help> Press ALT to activate menus      N 00027:001
```

Figure 19-21: NWIP is a new section in the NET.CFG file and defines the NetWare/IP client software configuration parameters.

This new section comes with several parameters you can use to reflect your particular NetWare/IP environment. Table 19-1 summarizes these new parameters that can be used in the NWIP section of the NET.CFG file.

Parameter	Values	Description
AUTORETRIES	0-10	Specifies the number of times a NetWare/IP client will attempt to contact a DSS server without receiving a response.
AUTORETRY SECS	5-60	Specifies the number of seconds between retries.
NEAREST NWIP SERVER	Valid IP addresses of NetWare/IP servers	Lists up to five NetWare/IP servers for the client workstation to contact.
NSQ BROADCAST	ON, OFF	Determines the nearest server.
NWIP DOMAIN NAME	Valid NetWare/IP domain name	Specifies the NetWare/IP domain name for your NetWare/IP environment.
NWIP 1_1 COMPATIBILITY	ON, OFF	Determines client's backward compatibility with NetWare/IP 1.1 and DSS servers.
PREFERRED DSS	Valid IP address of DSS servers	Lists up to five DSS servers the client considers "preferred."

Table 19-1: NetWare/IP parameters for the DOS/Windows Client32 NET.CFG file.

Once the NWIP section is configured, you will be able to access the NetWare services on the network with the NetWare/IP client just as you would with a traditional IPX-based client workstation. The only difference is that the machines are communicating via TCP/IP instead of IPX.

NetWare/IP Support in Client32 for Windows 95

Client32 for Windows 95 also comes with built-in NetWare/IP support; however, it is a little bit trickier to get the NetWare/IP client services configured after the installation program places the necessary files on the workstation's local hard disk. Just like you did for Client32 for DOS/Windows, you have to install the client, but you will have a few more steps to take after the installation is finished to completely configure the NetWare/IP client software.

To install the NetWare/IP client software with the Client32 for Windows 95 NetWare shell, perform the following steps:

1. Run SETUP.EXE from the SYS:PUBLIC\CLIENT\WIN95\IBM_ENU directory of your NetWare 4.11 server. This assumes you have selected the option to install the client software installation files to your NetWare 4.11 server.

2. The NetWare software license agreement will appear. Click on Yes to accept the agreement after you have read it. The main installation screen will appear.

3. Click on the Start button to install Client32 for Windows 95 on your machine. The installation program will install all of the appropriate files on your machine and configure the client for you.

4. When the client setup is finished, you will be presented with the final screen of the installation program. We recommend that you click on the Reboot button at this point to restart your machine with the new Client32 for Windows 95 NetWare shell.

Once the machine has rebooted, it is time to configure the NetWare/IP client software. This won't be as easy as the installation of the Client32 software, unfortunately. To configure the NetWare/IP client software, perform the following steps:

1. From the Windows 95 desktop, click on the Network Neighborhood icon once with the right mouse button and choose Properties from the menu that appears. This will bring up the Network Control Panel.

2. In the Network Control Panel, click on the Add button. A new dialog box will appear asking you which type of network component you want to add. Click on Protocol once with the left mouse button to highlight it. Then click on the Add button. The Select Network Protocol dialog box will appear.

3. In the Select Network Protocol dialog box, click on Novell in the Manufacturers box once with the left mouse button. The list of available Novell protocols appears in the Network Protocols box. Click on Novell NetWare/IP Protocol once with the left mouse button to highlight it, as in Figure 19-22. Click OK.

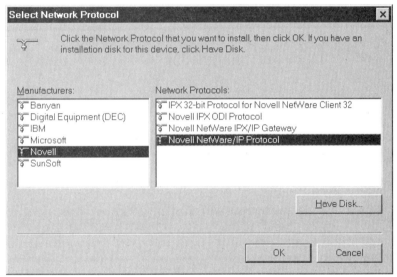

Figure 19-22: Select the Novell NetWare/IP Protocol from the list of available Novell protocols.

After clicking on the OK button, you will be returned to the main screen of the Network Control Panel. You will now see Novell NetWare/IP Protocol listed as a protocol. Although it is installed as a protocol, it is not yet configured. To configure it, click on it once with the left mouse button so it is highlighted, as in Figure 19-23. Then click on the Properties button.

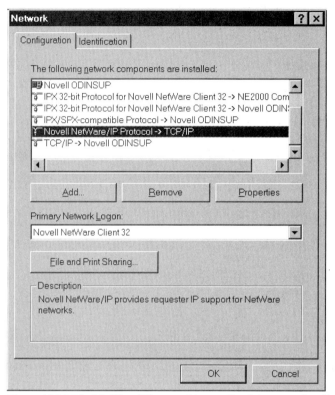

Figure 19-23: The NetWare/IP protocol is now listed; however, it still needs to be configured.

After you click on the Properties button, the Novell NetWare/IP Protocol Properties dialog box will appear (Figure 19-24). This is where the main configuration of the NetWare/IP client for Windows 95 takes place. Listed on the Parameters tab page are the general NetWare/IP parameters you can configure. These properties should look familiar because they are the same properties you could configure using the NET.CFG file for the DOS/Windows NetWare/IP client.

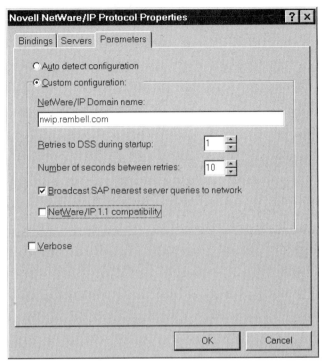

Figure 19-24: The Parameters tab lets you specify configuration information for the Windows 95 NetWare/IP client software.

The most important piece of information on this screen is the NetWare/IP domain name. You must specify the NetWare/IP domain name for the client to be able to locate your NetWare/IP environment. In Figure 19-24, you can see that the NetWare/IP domain name has been entered as nwip.rambell.com, as we have specified all along in this chapter.

The other important tab in the Novell NetWare/IP Protocol Properties dialog box is the Servers tab. To get to this page, click on the Servers tab once with the left mouse button. The Servers properties will appear (Figure 19-25). On this page, you can specify both the nearest NetWare/IP servers and the preferred Domain SAP/RIP servers. Each of these lists can accommodate up to five different servers. To add a server, just type the IP address in the appropriate text editing box and click on the Add button to the right. The specified address will be added to the list.

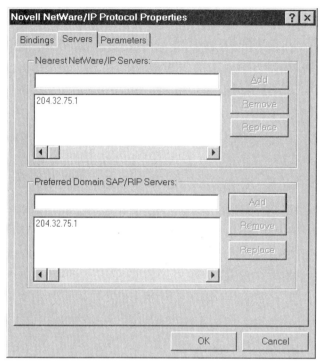

Figure 19-25: The Servers property tab lets you specify NetWare/IP servers and DSS servers on your network.

Once you are finished with the configuration of the NetWare/IP client software, click on the OK button at the bottom of the property page shown in Figure 19-25. You will be returned to the main screen of the Network Control Panel. Click on OK again. You will be asked to provide the diskette from which you installed Client32 for Windows 95. If you installed this across the network, specify the drive and path to the installation files (SYS:PUBLIC\ CLIENT\WIN95\IBM_ENU). Once the installation of the NetWare/IP client software is finished, restart your computer.

After you reboot, your machine will be using the NetWare/IP protocol to communicate with your NetWare/IP network. It will not be using the IPX protocol stack to get NetWare services. If you have problems connecting, review your NetWare/IP client software configuration for possible errors.

Moving On

Once you have configured your clients to use NetWare/IP, the NetWare/IP environment is complete. You have installed TCP/IP on the servers, set up the interdependent services, brought up the NetWare/IP servers, and installed and configured the NetWare/IP clients. Not too bad for a day's work!

Setting up NetWare/IP may be your first foray into physically accommodating a WAN environment on your network. There are many more ways to provide communications across WAN links using NetWare 4.11 servers. In the next chapter, we will talk about different methods of WAN connectivity and how you might apply them to the IntranetWare environment.

20

Wide Area Network (WAN) Connectivity

Even though you have your server up and running, additional functionality may be required to support your users' computer needs. For instance, your users may want to reach their branch offices, while the branch offices benefit from accessing the information stored on the server. In order to make this possible, you must create a wide area network (WAN). There are a number of different choices you can make to fulfill your users' needs. However, your choice is dependent upon the type of network connection available to the server. In this chapter, we will discuss the options that you have as well as what solutions Novell IntranetWare has to offer.

What Is a WAN?

A WAN is a set of computers and networked devices that are geographically separated but connected through a dedicated or switched connection. There are two ways to make a wide area connection: using a public network or using a private network built by your organization. A typical WAN is shown in Figure 20-1.

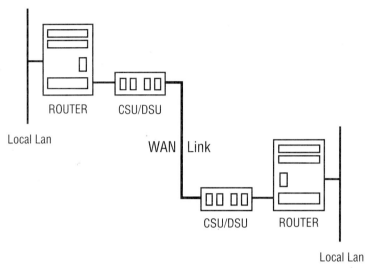

Figure 20-1: A typical wide area network.

In a typical WAN, a router sends local area network (LAN) traffic across the wide area connection to the remote destination. The router may be connected to an analog or digital line. For an analog line, the router uses a *modem* to attach to the wide area connection. Digital lines require the use of a *channel service unit/data service unit* (CSU/DSU). The type of equipment required to create a WAN depends on the *carrier service* used.

Connection Types

There are two types of connections that can be established for a WAN: dedicated and switched. A dedicated line is a permanent connection between two points. A switched line is a temporary connection among multiple points that lasts for the duration of the data transmission. Today, there are two types of switching services available: *circuit switching* and *packet switching*.

For a circuit switch, a dedicated channel is set up between two locations during the data transmission. Companies pay for a fixed amount of guaranteed bandwidth during the call. Because of the fixed amount of bandwidth, circuit-switching connections do not handle bursts of network traffic well. Another thing to note about circuit switching is that there is only one route available for the data. This means there is no redundant route for the data to take should the connection break, a limitation that led to the development of packet switching. Figure 20-2 shows an example of a circuit-switched network.

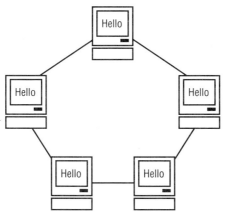

Figure 20-2: An example of a circuit-switching network.

Packet switching addresses the disadvantages of circuit switching by providing multiple routes for data to take and allowing for a variable amount of bandwidth. These two things allow packet switching to handle network traffic more efficiently. Picture an amorphous cloud when thinking of a packet-switching network, with multiple routes available to all the connected points, as shown in Figure 20-3.

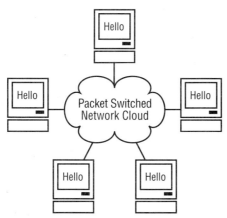

Figure 20-3: An example of a packet-switching network.

The type of switching service you will want will depend on two things:

- The type of network traffic you'll be generating
- Cost

If your data is delay sensitive, such as the data associated with video conferencing, then you will want to utilize a circuit-switching service. However, they tend to be more costly than packet switching because you pay for a guaranteed amount of bandwidth. Of course, if your data is not time sensitive or your traffic is more "bursty" in nature, then packet switching will be a better solution for you.

Where to Get a Connection

It is possible to get service from a multitude of places. An obvious place to start is your local exchange carrier (LEC), also known as a "regional Bell" operating company. Many exchange carriers have created public WANs that they then lease to companies. Of course, you share the network with other users, but this usually lowers the cost of the connection. In the past, LECs dealt only with connections in a company's service area; that is, local connections. However, due to deregulation in the telecommunications arena, LECs are now competing with interexchange carriers (IXC). An IXC, also known as a "long-haul carrier," is a company like AT&T that handles long distance communication. IXCs are now providing points of presence (POPs) to provide WAN services to companies and are directly competing with LECs for your business. Another option is a value added carrier (VAC) such as CompuServ or America Online. A VAC provides WAN services as a sideline to their core business. A value added carrier builds a private data network (PDN) for its own use and resells the excess bandwidth to other companies. The VAC handles all management and maintenance of the PDN and WAN services.

Carrier Services

Now that you know where to get the services needed to create your WAN, let's discuss the types of services available. Currently, you have a number of different options for developing your WAN. The types of services available today are:

- Switched analog lines
- Circuit-switching services

- Packet-switching services
- Cell-switched services
- Digital services

Switched analog lines, which include dial-up lines, use analog modems to connect to the remote site only when data needs to be transmitted. You can also have a dedicated line that is available at any time but still uses an analog modem to make and maintain the connection. This is a good solution when you have a minimal amount of data that needs to be transferred.

Circuit switching offers a faster solution through its switched 56 kilobits per second (kbps) service. Circuit switching is a digital service that uses a CSU/DSU instead of a modem to connect to the carrier. Integrated Services Digital Network, also known as ISDN, is a circuit-switching service, too. ISDN provides high-speed, digital circuit switching that can carry voice and data information. Currently, the basic ISDN line starts at 64 kbps, but it is possible to combine ISDN lines to establish faster connections.

Packet switching is a popular solution for public networks. Of the available packet-switching networks, *frame relay* is the most prevalent. Frame relay was initially developed as part of the ISDN standard. X.25 is another packet-switching service and is similar to frame relay. X.25 performs extensive error checking that ensures reliable delivery of packets, but the error checking increases the network bandwidth as well as slows down the connection.

One of the newer services beginning to be offered is cell-switched services. A cell-switched service uses a fixed size "cell" or packet rather than a variable size packet. Asynchronous Transfer Mode (ATM) is an example of a cell-switched service.

Digital services carry voice, video, and data. Digital lines are usually leased from the local exchange carrier and installed between two points to provide dedicated service. T1 and T3 lines are examples of digital services. A T1 line can handle 1.544 megabits per second (mbps) of data. In comparison, a T3 line can handle up to 45 mbps. This type of service is generally quite expensive.

Network Media Options for Connecting WANs

Now that you have an idea of the types of services available, it is time to introduce the services that IntranetWare supports. Many options exist for connecting your servers together to create your WAN. First you should decide on the type of connection that will be the most beneficial for your situation.

IntranetWare supports the following connection types: Asynchronous Transfer Mode (ATM), frame relay, ISDN, Point-to-Point Protocol (PPP), System Network Architecture (SNA) Links, and X.25.

Asynchronous Transfer Mode (ATM)

ATM is the newest media type gaining ground in today's network infrastructure. Because ATM networks handle voice and video as well as data communications, ATM can provide a single solution for all of a company's communication needs.

ATM contains many features that make it a desirable choice for creating WANs. The following is a list of ATM characteristics:

- **Controllable latency.** Due to the nature of ATM and its small cell size (53 bytes), the communications delay can be controlled.

- **Scalable for physical size, speed, and node count.** Because an ATM network can be any physical size, it tends to contain the features of a LAN and a WAN.

- **Bandwidth on demand.** Any bandwidth that the network may require can be acquired without having to reserve it in advance.

- **Virtual Circuit Multiplexing.** This allows multiple dialogs to occur over a single interface.

ATM networks use a high-speed cell-switching technology. A cell is composed of 53 bytes and is the standard form for ATM. Each cell has the necessary information for a switch to route the cell to its next switch; this process continues until the cell finally reaches its destination. When a cell arrives at a destination, the ATM adapter hardware creates a packet or byte stream. Any software that uses an ATM network is never aware of the ATM cells.

Although ATM is gaining popularity, it is not heavily used by many companies because the associated implementation costs are too high, although ATM hardware is readily available.

X.25

X.25, a packet-switching protocol, has been used since 1976 to provide remote terminal connections to mainframes. This protocol performs extensive error checking that ensures reliable delivery. Because of this error checking, X.25 is not recommended for most LAN-to-LAN traffic due to the time and bandwidth expended in checking every packet. A more popular alternative to the X.25 is frame relay.

Frame Relay

Frame relay initially started as a part of the Integrated Services Digital Network (ISDN) standard. The ISDN developers realized that the frame relay principles could be applied outside of ISDN. Therefore, frame relay was developed as an independent protocol.

Frame relay provides a high-speed, packet-switching service for devices that require high data transmittal within short periods of time. Routers are a perfect example of such a device. Frame relay connects two LANs over a public packet-switched network (a service that you may find from your local telephone company). The frame relay encapsulates the LAN packet (IPX, AppleTalk) in a frame relay frame (packet). The frame contains the packet's source and destination addresses. Using statistical multiplexing techniques, frame relay provides a way for multiple sources to use a single line to the frame relay network. This technique also provides the LAN with bandwidth on demand. Bandwidth on demand means that the network can get the bandwidth it needs without having to reserve it in advance. When the frame reaches its destination, the frame relay information is stripped off and the data is reassembled in its native packet format.

The difference between frame relay and X.25 lies in frame relay's lack of error checking. However, the advantage of frame relay is its more efficient use of bandwidth.

The Decision

Now that you have a better understanding of what types of services are available, you need to decide what services will best suit your situation. One thing to note is that your wide area connection is not the place to cut costs. Attempting to cut costs can lead to poor performance as well as data loss. Make sure that your wide area connection provides all of the necessary features; you can leave out the "extras" that can cause additional costs.

For the remainder of this chapter, we will be discussing the installation and configuration of Novell's MultiProtocol Router v3.1, IPX/IP Gateway, WAN Extensions, and NetWare Link Services Protocol, which come bundled with the IntranetWare package. These products work together to connect your LAN to a WAN.

MultiProtocol Router

IntranetWare provides a number of choices for connecting your server to other networks. In today's world, it is unusual to have a totally homogenous network containing only NetWare servers (although it would be nice!). Most companies have networks that run a multitude of different networking protocols. IntranetWare provides a way for your server to communicate and use these other protocols. IntranetWare offers the following options: a MultiProtocol Router (MPR), IPX/IP Gateway, and various WAN extensions. Using the tools provided by IntranetWare, you can expand your company's network reach.

What Is a Router?

A router is a device used to "route" network packets between networks. Routers read the network "address" information in a network packet and decide where to send the packet so that it reaches its final destination. You can think of a router as a post office. When a letter arrives at the post office, someone examines the address on the letter and determines where to send it next, as illustrated in Figure 20-4.

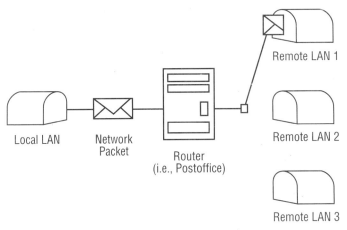

Figure 20-4: An example of a router.

Installing the MultiProtocol Router

Now you have your server up and running and are familiar with the ins and outs of IntranetWare and the INSTALL.NLM (if you need to review the operation of the INSTALL.NLM, please see Chapter 19). You are now ready to install the MultiProtocol Router (MPR) to accommodate your multiple protocol network.

Tip

> *Make sure you have your license diskette (which comes with the IntranetWare CD-ROMs when you purchase the package) or know where the license files are stored before you begin the installation. You will need the license information to complete the installation of the MPR.*

To begin the installation process, go to the system console and type **LOAD INSTALL**.

This will load the installation NLM. From the main menu, choose Product Options. This will take you to the Other Installation Actions menu shown in Figure 20-5.

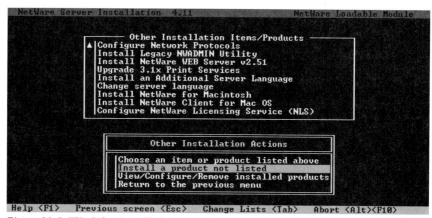

Figure 20-5: The Other Installation Actions screen.

The Other Installation Actions menu allows you to install and configure products that come with the IntranetWare package. It also allows you to install add-on products, such as the MultiProtocol Router. To install a product not listed in the available products list, choose the Install a Product Not Listed option from the menu.

You will be presented with a dialog box that asks for the product's location. If the product you are going to install is located on A:\, then all you need to do is press Enter. However, to install from the CD-ROM, you'll need to specify a different path. The CD for the MPR needs to be mounted at this point. If the CD is not currently mounted, do not worry. Press Ctrl+Esc, pick the system console from the system menu, and mount the CD from the console. Use Ctrl+Esc to return to the installation program. Press F3 and enter the path to the RINSTALL directory, which exists off the root of the CD-ROM. Press Enter to begin the installation. The installation program will begin by copying the files that it needs to the server. This takes a few minutes, so now is a good time to get a soda.

When the system finishes copying the files from the CD-ROM, you will be presented with the Installation Options menu for the MPR. There are three options available within this menu: Install Product, Display Log File, and Exit (see Figure 20-6). Choosing Exit will exit the installation program and delete the files copied from the previous operation. Choosing Display Log File will bring up a log file containing the installation status of any previously installed product. If you have not installed any other products, then an error message will inform you that it can not find the log file. Don't worry; this is normal. Use the arrow keys to select the Install Product option.

Figure 20-6: The Installation Options menu.

From the Install Product menu (Figure 20-7), you can pick the server(s) to which you want to install the software. The current server is listed within this menu. To install the software to multiple servers, press the Insert key and select the other servers from the list presented. If the server to which you want to install is not listed, make sure that it is running the latest version of RSPAWN.NLM. After choosing the server(s) to be installed with the MPR software, press Enter.

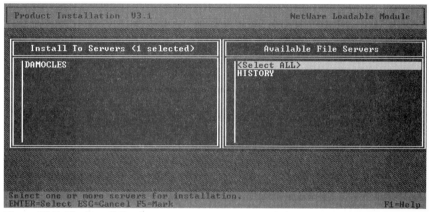

Figure 20-7: The Install Product menu.

Next you will see a dialog box that asks if you wish to use a set of previously created configuration files. This option allows you to copy the configuration of a previously configured MPR. If you select Yes, you will be prompted with the path to the configuration files. Since we are setting up a new MultiProtocol Router, choose No.

The next dialog box that is shown will ask you for the path to your license. You *must* have the license diskette or the path to the license files! If you do not, then you cannot continue the installation. Enter the path to the license file and press Enter.

After the license information is assimilated, the system will copy the files that are required for the installation. Afterward, a dialog box will inform you that the installation process was successful. At this point, you must down and restart the server for the changes to take effect. Press Enter and the system will tell you to take any disks out of the floppy drive. Press Enter again and you are back at the Install Product menu. From here, select Exit. This will remove any excess files and take you back to the Product Options menu. At this point, exit the INSTALL.NLM and down and reboot the server.

To recap this procedure, the following is a summarized list of steps required to install MPR on your server:

1. Load INSTALL.NLM on your NetWare 4.11 server.

2. Select Product Options from the main menu of INSTALL.NLM. The Other Installation Actions menu will appear.

3. Select Install a Product Not Listed from the Other Installation Actions menu.

4. Specify the location of the installation files for the MPR product.

5. Once the files have copied, select Install Product from the MPR Installation Options menu.

6. Select the server on which you will install MPR.

7. Choose whether or not you want to use existing MPR configuration information. If this is your first installation, select No.

8. Install the license from your license diskette. Once the license has been installed, MPR will delete all of the installation files that were initially copied to your server and exit the installation.

Once MPR has been successfully installed on the selected server(s), it is time to configure the product for your networking environment. We will discuss the configuration of the MultiProtocol Router in the next section.

Configuring the MPR

Configuring the MPR takes a little planning and patience. There are five utilities that help with the MPR configuration: Internetworking Configuration (INETCFG), Filter Configuration (FILTCFG), Static Routing Configuration (STATICON), Call Manager (CALLMGR), and Customer Premises Equipment Configuration (CPECFG). Also included are two new console commands: Initialize System and Reinitialize System. This will start and restart the router without you having to reboot the entire system.

Tip

When you install the MultiProtocol Router, IPX will be automatically configured.

Internetworking Configuration (INETCFG)

Most of your configuration needs will be covered by INETCFG. It allows you to configure the MultiProtocol Router for IPX, PPP, IP, AppleTalk, and the source route bridge. INETCFG allows you to:

- Select and configure a network board.
- Select and configure a network interface.
- Create a WAN call directory.
- Create a backup call association.
- Select and configure a network protocol.
- Bind a network protocol to an interface.
- Manage the configuration of the MPR.
- View the configuration of the MPR.
- Reinitialize the system.
- Switch to the fast setup method.

Figure 20-8 shows the INETCFG configuration menu. For more information on using the INETCFG utility, refer to Chapter 18.

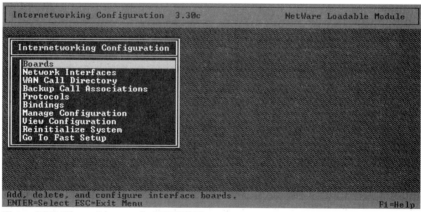

Figure 20-8: The main menu for INETCFG.

The INETCFG stores its configuration information in various configuration files (*.CFG) located in the SYS:\ETC directory. These files are used by INETCFG; do not change or delete them.

To start INETCFG, type **LOAD INETCFG** at the system console. When you start INETCFG, it checks the AUTOEXEC.NCF for commands that it can convert to INETCFG commands. Let INETCFG do this. Basically, it comments out all of your load and bind commands from your AUTOEXEC.NCF, and copies them into INITSYS.NCF. INETCFG will then be able to manage all your LAN and WAN interfaces. If you don't allow INETCFG to manage your LAN and WAN interfaces, it is possible that you will receive errors on the server due to multiple loading of a LAN/WAN driver.

INETCFG will also ask you if you wish to use the fast setup method. If you will be setting up a WAN connection, answer no. The fast setup feature provides a set of menus for configuring the MPR for simple router configurations. You can switch between the fast setup and the standard INETCFG menu.

Filter Configuration (FILTCFG)

FILTCFG is used to set up and configure filters (Figure 20-9). A filter will allow you to discriminatingly control which packets are sent and received by your router. How you configure a filter will depend on what you wish to accomplish. You can use filters to increase the security of your network by limiting what services are advertised. A filter can also be used to reduce the amount of bandwidth wasted by unnecessary or unwanted packets. For more information on using FILTCFG, refer to the MultiProtocol Router 3.1 collection found in the online documentation packaged with IntranetWare. This particular collection can be found on the third CD of the IntranetWare package, "Internet Access Server 4."

Tip

To configure a filter, filter support must be turned on within INETCFG. This is an option for each protocol supported by the MPR.

Figure 20-9: The Filter Configuration main menu.

Static Routing Configuration (STATICON)

STATICON is used to open connections to remote routers and configure static routes and services. STATICON performs the following tasks:

- Initiates configuration of static routing tables with a remote router.
- Configures local static services from gatekeepers.
- Configures local and remote static services and routes.
- Saves static routing tables.
- Restores static routing tables.

Use STATICON if you plan to use any uncommon services. STATICON will help you avoid creating routing loops. With STATICON, it is possible to manually add and remove routes and services that aren't listed in the routing table. You can also automatically configure static routes and services between a local router and a remote router. This configuration option will copy all missing routes from the local router to the remote router and from the remote router to the local router. Finally, STATICON allows you to configure local static services from a gatekeeper. A gatekeeper is a special file server located in an internetwork that is able to see all the public services from all of the connected sites. Using STATICON, you can obtain a list of advertised services and configure them to be advertised by your local router. Figure 20-10 shows the

STATICON menu. For more information on using STATICON, refer to the MultiProtocol Router 3.1 collection found in the online documentation packaged with IntranetWare. This particular collection can be found on the third CD of the IntranetWare package, "Internet Access Server 4."

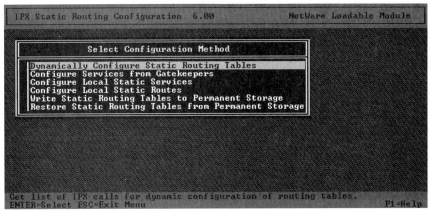

Figure 20-10: The STATICON menu.

Call Manager (CALLMGR)

CALLMGR initiates and terminates WAN connections. The CALLMGR provides a list of the current connections and each connection's status and network bindings. This utility can help you to debug problems with your WAN connection. Detailed error information for a call is available, but unfortunately, you must be in CALLMGR to see the error information because CALLMGR does not store error messages. Figure 20-11 shows the Call Manager menu.

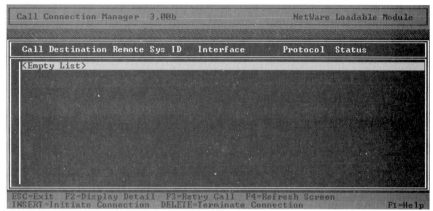

Figure 20-11: The Call Manager main screen.

Customer Premises Equipment Configuration (CPECFG)

Use CPECFG to configure and manage your communications equipment. This includes modems and CSU/DSUs. The CPECFG will allow you to connect to your equipment through an existing serial port on the server. The CPECFG main screen is shown in Figure 20-12.

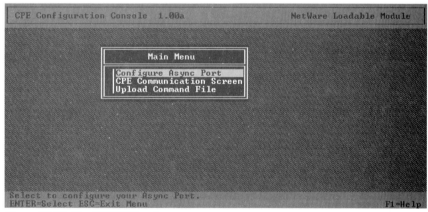

Figure 20-12: The CPECFG main screen.

A Simple Example Using IPRELAY

IntranetWare provides IPRELAY.LAN and IPTUNNEL with the MultiProtocol Router. IPRELAY acts as an IP tunnel driver for WAN connections. IPTUNNEL is a LAN driver that allows the router to see an IP internetwork as an IPX LAN that you can then tunnel IPX packets through. A tunnel driver works by encapsulating a packet of one type into the packet of a second type. The encapsulated packet is then transmitted over the medium that supports it. On the receiving end, the encapsulation is stripped off and the original packet is left intact.

For a more concrete example, let's say that we have an IPX packet. The IPX packet reaches a router that is running IPRELAY where it is encapsulated inside an IP packet. This new IP packet is then transmitted across the Internet where the receiving router strips off the IP encapsulation and broadcasts the original IPX packet over its local IPX network, shown in Figure 20-13.

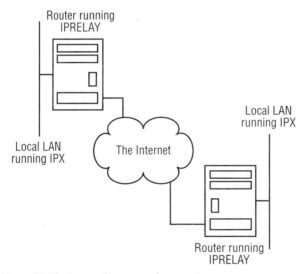

Figure 20-13: A tunneling example.

To provide an example of when you might want to use IPRELAY, let us assume you have decided on the type of WAN connection your company needs. You have also installed and configured NetWare/IP (see Chapter 19 for information on IP). Therefore, TCP/IP is enabled and bound to an interface. You know the IP address of the remote peer with whom you will be creating your IPRELAY. You are now ready to configure the MultiProtocol Router to support IPRELAY over your WAN connection.

At the server's console, type **LOAD INETCFG** to begin the configuration process. When the main menu appears, select the Protocols option.

From the Protocols option, choose IPX; the IPX protocol configuration screen will be displayed. Set the Tunnel IPX Through IP option to Enabled.

Select the Tunnel Configuration to configure the IP relay.

The relay needs to know where it should send its packets. Pick the Remote Peers option to add remote systems to your relay. Pressing Ins will allow you to enter the IP address for a remote peer. It is important to note that you can add more than one remote peer. Press Esc when you are done. This will return you to the Tunnel Configuration screen.

If your clients have trouble reaching a remote server, try increasing the Transport Time parameter. Valid values for this parameter are from 1 to 65535.

Tip

Do not change the UDP port number. This could cause the connection to the remote system to fail. Also, the UDP Checksum should not be changed from its default, Enabled. This default improves data reliability.

Press Esc to return to the Internetworking Configuration screen. When you press Esc, you will be prompted to select Yes to save your changes. Restart the router by selecting Reinitialize System from the main Internetworking Configuration menu. This will dynamically unload and reload the drivers without having to shut down the server.

NetWare IPX/IP Gateway for Internet Access

The IPX/IP Gateway provides a way for users to use Winsock-compliant services without having to install IP on their local workstations. Conceptually, this is similar to the way a proxy server works. A proxy server operates by receiving packets from a local workstation and redirecting the packets to their real destination. The remote server responds back to the proxy server, and the proxy server handles the redirection of the packets back to the original workstation. Proxy servers are sometimes used as a security measure because remote servers cannot communicate with anything on the other side of the proxy server.

Note that although the IPX/IP Gateway works like a proxy server, it is *not* a proxy server. It provides a way for IPX clients to access IP services such as the World Wide Web without requiring an IP stack on their computer. This eliminates the need for the systems administrator to configure IP on all workstations. IP will be set up once on the server to serve all the clients. The IPX/IP Gateway consists of two pieces: a server piece and a client piece.

The Server Piece

The server piece receives IPX packets from the LAN and redirects them over the IP interface to the remote destination. When the IPX/IP Gateway is configured, it extends the NDS schema by creating a new server object in the NDS tree. The new object's name consists of the name of the server and the ending -*GW*. For instance, if the name of the machine is *Betty*, then the gateway object would be *Betty-GW*. The gateway object can also be set up to restrict access to the IP link and to log who accesses what data across the link.

Configuring the IPX/IP Gateway

The IPX/IP software (including the IPX/IP Gateway client software) is installed along with the MultiProtocol Router software. To configure the gateway, you must have TCP/IP installed and bound to an interface on the server. The following steps describe the process of configuring the IPX/IP Gateway:

1. To start the configuration, you must enable the IPX/IP Gateway option through INETCFG. At the system console, type **LOAD INETCFG** and press Enter.

2. From the Internetworking Configuration menu, choose Protocols. This will open the Protocol Configuration menu. Choose TCP/IP to open the TCP/IP Configuration screen.

3. In the TCP/IP Configuration screen, pick IPX/IP Gateway Configuration. The Gateway Configuration screen will open; it contains two parts: Gateway Configuration and DNS Client Configuration, shown in Figure 20-14.

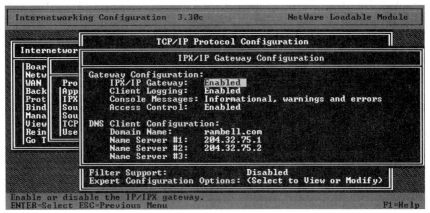

Figure 20-14: The IPX/IP Gateway Configuration screen.

4. In the Gateway Configuration portion, select the IPX/IP Gateway option and enable the gateway.

5. The Client Logging option is enabled by default. The logging option will record a client's access information. The log file identifies the client, the service used, and the amount of time taken for the service. The log file can be found in SYS: GW_AUDIT.LOG.

6. The Console Messages option controls the type of messages that are sent to the IPX/IP Gateway console and stored in the SYS: GW_INFO.LOG log file.

7. Enable the Access control option if you want to control access to the gateway on a per-user basis. It is disabled by default to allow all users access to the gateway. Configuration of user access is handled by the NetWare Administrator utility.

8. In the DNS Client Configuration portion, choose the Domain Name option, enter a valid domain name, and press Enter. The domain name can be provided by your Internet Service Provider or it can be a name that you have registered with InterNIC. For the Name Server# options, enter a valid IP address for a DNS server. You must enter at least one DNS server.

9. Press Esc to exit the IPX/IP Gateway Configuration screen. Press Esc again to exit the TCP/IP Configuration screen. At this point, you will be asked if you wish to update your TCP/IP configuration; select Yes.

To finish the configuration of the IPX/IP Gateway, the system needs to create a gateway server object within your NDS tree. You will be asked to log in as an administrator with rights to the Organizational context of your NDS tree. After you log in, the gateway server object will be created for you.

Tip

If this is the first IPX/IP Gateway that has been enabled, then you will need to log in as a user with the Supervisor object right to [ROOT]. This is because the gateway configuration extends the NDS schema for the user, group, organization, and organizational unit objects. This is only required for the first gateway.

If the configuration finishes correctly, a message will appear notifying the user that the name of the gateway server is the name of the file server with -GW appended to it. Should the configuration fail, the gateway will automatically be disabled. Check the username and password used to log in and reenable the gateway to try again.

Tip

Note that the gateway is automatically active for all interfaces.

To start the IPX/IP Gateway, it is now necessary to bring down and restart the server.

After the server has restarted, ensure that the HOSTS file located in SYS:ETC has an entry for the server by using EDIT.NLM to view the file. For instance, if the hostname is wakae and the IP address is 192.1.16.1, then there should be an entry in the HOSTS file that looks like:

```
192.1.16.1 wakae
```

If this entry exists, your gateway should be up and running. If it does not exist, you will need to add the server to the HOSTS file in the SYS:ETC directory of your server. You can edit this file using the EDIT.NLM utility. To edit the HOSTS file, type **load edit sys:etc\hosts** at the server console prompt (colon prompt).

The last thing you need to do to complete your IPX/IP Gateway configuration is use the NWADMIN utility. The gateway server object needs to be configured to read all of the access control information set up for the objects in the NDS tree. To accomplish this, you will need to grant specific objects in the NDS tree trustee assignments. For more information on NDS security and granting trustee assignments, refer to Chapter 9:

1. Make the [Public] object a trustee of the gateway object. Give the [Public] object the Browse object right. Also grant the [Public] object Read and Compare property rights (for all properties).

2. Make the [Public] object a trustee of the file server object that is running the IPX/IP Gateway. Grant the [Public] object the Browse object right. Also assign [Public] the Read and Compare property rights for the Network Address property only.

3. In order to make the gateway object a trustee in the [Root] object, grant the gateway object the Browse object right. Also, assign it the Read and Compare property rights (for all properties).

That is all there is to the server installation. To use the newly configured gateway object, you need to install the IPX/IP Gateway client software on each workstation that requires access to it. This will be covered in the next section.

The Client Piece

All that's left to do at this point is to configure the workstation clients to make use of the IPX/IP Gateway. The client software is included in the NetWare Client32 network client. For more information on installing Client32 on your workstations, refer to Chapters 15 and 16.

Essentially, the workstation needs to be configured to use the IPX/IP Gateway server for its IP services. Because the client workstation itself does not have an IP address, it "piggy-backs" off of the server for all of its IP interaction. When the client software is installed, it also installs a modified WINSOCK.DLL file, which is aware of this configuration and allows the IP applications to use the IPX/IP Gateway server as the required IP address.

Tip

The client software for the IPX/IP Gateway is not supported in DOS. You must be running Windows to use the IPX/IP Gateway.

If you have chosen to install support for IPX/IP Gateway on a Windows 3.x machine, two new icons will be created in the NetWare Tools program group. They are the IPX/IP Gateway: Switcher and IPX/IP Gateway: WinPing applications. They are shown in Figure 20-15.

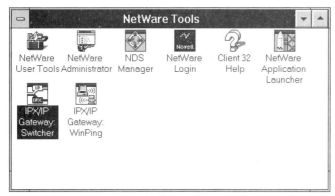

Figure 20-15: Two icons are added to NetWare Tools for IPX/IP Gateway client support.

To enable IPX/IP Gateway services at the workstation client, double-click on the IPX/IP Gateway: Switcher icon in the NetWare Tools program group. The Novell NetWare IPX/IP Gateway dialog box will appear (Figure 20-16). To enable the services, just click on the Enable IPX/IP Gateway radio button and specify the name of the preferred gateway server. Once you have entered this information, just click on the OK button.

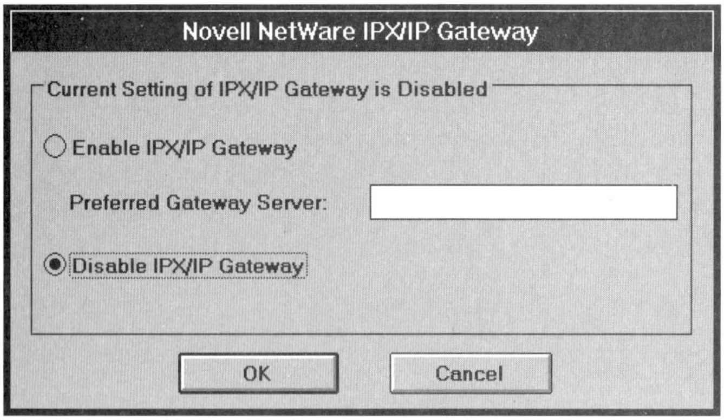

Figure 20-16: Enabling IPX/IP Gateway services at the Windows 3.x client.

Once you have enabled the services at the client, you can test them by double-clicking on the IPX/IP Gateway: WinPing icon in the NetWare Tools program group. This is your typical TCP/IP ping utility that allows you to see if any other TCP/IP-based machine is active on the network. Just type in the name of the host or provide the host's IP address in the Host box and click on the Ping button (Figure 20-17). You will know immediately if your client configured properly.

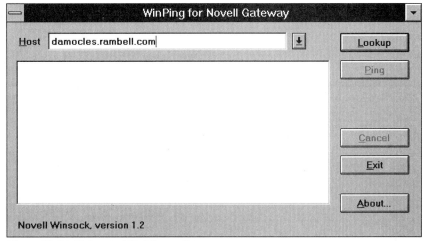

Figure 20-17: Using the WinPing utility.

To configure the client software for the IPX/IP Gateway on a Windows 95 machine, the process is a little more involved. You must install NetWare Client32 for Windows 95 initially. For more information on installing this client, refer to Chapter 16.

Once the client software is installed, perform the following steps:

1. On the Windows 95 desktop, click on the Network Neighborhood icon once with the right mouse button and choose Properties from the menu that appears. This will bring up the Network Control Panel.

2. In the Network Control Panel, click on the Add button. A new dialog box will appear asking you which type of network component you want to add. Click on Protocol once with the left mouse button to highlight it. Then click on the Add button. The Select Network Protocol dialog box will appear.

3. In the Select Network Protocol dialog box, click on Novell in the Manufacturers box once with the left mouse button. The list of available Novell protocols appears in the Network Protocols box. Click on Novell NetWare IPX/IP Gateway once with the left mouse button to highlight it, as shown in Figure 20-18. Click OK.

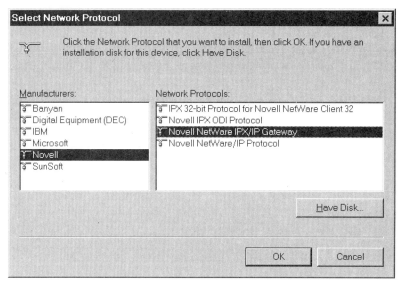

Figure 20-18: Select the Novell NetWare IPX/IP Gateway from the list of available Novell protocols.

4. After clicking on the OK button, you will be returned to the main screen of the Network Control Panel. You will now see Novell NetWare IPX/IP Gateway listed as a protocol. Although it is installed as a protocol, it is not yet configured. To configure it, click on it once with the left mouse button so it is highlighted, as shown in Figure 20-19. Then click on the Properties button.

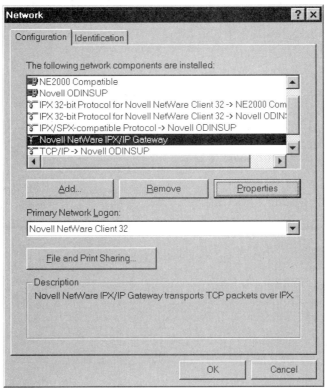

Figure 20-19: The NetWare IPX/IP Gateway is now listed; however, it still needs to be configured.

5. After clicking on the Properties button, the Novell NetWare IPX/IP Gateway Properties dialog box will appear (Figure 20-20). This is where the main configuration of the NetWare IPX/IP Gateway client for Windows 95 takes place. Listed on the IPX/IP Gateway tab is the important information required for the IPX/IP Gateway client software to work properly. Just enter the name of the preferred gateway server in the box and click on OK at the bottom of the screen. You will be returned to the Network Control Panel.

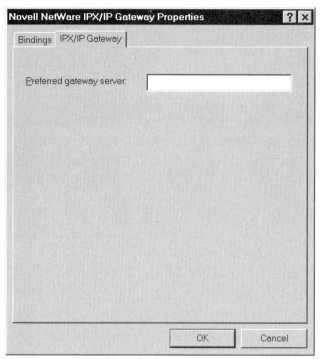

Figure 20-20: The IPX/IP Gateway Properties dialog box.

6. Click on the OK button again. Windows 95 will prompt you for the location of the NetWare Client32 for Windows 95 installation disks. Provide the location and let Windows 95 finish installing the client software for the IPX/IP Gateway. Windows 95 will ask you to reboot the machine for the changes to take effect.

Once you reboot the machine, the IPX/IP Gateway Switcher application will automatically launch when Windows 95 starts. Here is where you can enable or disable the IPX/IP Gateway client services, just like you could for the Windows 3.x client. This screen is shown in Figure 20-21.

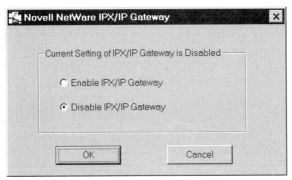

Figure 20-21: The IPX/IP Gateway Switcher for Windows 95.

Just as in Windows 3.x, there are two utilities that have been added to the client workstation. If you click on the Start button in Windows 95 and select Programs | Novell | IPXIP Gateway, you will see these applications. They are the Switcher and WinPing. They function exactly the same as the Windows 3.x clients do.

WAN Extensions

Along with the MultiProtocol Router and the IPX/IP Gateway, Novell also provides a set of WAN Extensions. The WAN Extensions contain the added connectivity needed to use an ATM, Frame Relay, or X.25 protocol to create a WAN. Before you configure a WAN Extension, make sure that you have planned out your network topology. Upon deciding on the kind of link needed, you must discover the limitations imposed by the service providers in your area. Taking the time to plan and coordinate with service providers will save time during the installation and configuration steps.

Configuring ATM, Frame Relay & X.25

Assuming that your service provider has provided you with a connection to their network and given you the information you need, you are now ready to configure the connection on your router. To configure the WAN Extensions, the MultiProtocol Router software should already be installed and configured.

To configure a Frame Relay or X.25 connection, first install any hardware that is needed to support the connection. Configure this hardware using INETCFG under the Boards option. This operation will be different depending on the type of hardware installed. After the hardware is installed, you will need to configure the network interface. This can be accomplished through the use of the INETCFG as well. Load INETCFG and select Network Interfaces from the Internetworking Configuration menu. From the available list of interfaces, select an unconfigured port on the WAN interface board. Select the type of media that you will be configuring. The upcoming screens depend on the type of media that you have selected here.

After the network interface is configured, you will need to configure a WAN call destination. Load INETCFG and select WAN Call Destination from the main menu. Press Ins to create a new WAN call destination. Enter a name for the WAN call destination when prompted and press Enter. A list of supported wide area media is presented; select the one that you wish to configure. You must configure a network interface before attempting to create a WAN call destination. Otherwise, the media type will not appear in the media list. After selecting a media type, you will be presented with configuration options that depend on the type of media you are configuring.

The same configuration procedure exists for ATM. The only difference is that ATM has its own logical interface for the ATM board. These logical boards will show up as ATMWAA1, ATMWAA2, and so on under the Network Interfaces option in INETCFG.

After the network interface and a call destination have been configured for a media, you can now use Bindings in INETCFG to bind a protocol to your new interface. This can be done by selecting an enabled protocol and then choosing an interface to bind to it. Restart the router and you are now ready to enjoy the growth of your network. For more information on configuring the MultiProtocol Router for these WAN protocols, refer to the NetWare MultiProtocol Router 3.1 Configuration manual in the MultiProtocol Router 3.1 collection of the online documentation. This collection can be found on the third CD-ROM of the IntranetWare package called "Internet Access Server 4."

NetWare Link Services Protocol (NLSP)

In this section, we will be discussing NetWare's Link Services Protocol (NLSP). NLSP is a link route protocol for IPX networks that exchanges information between routers and allows the routers to make decisions based on that information. Traditionally, NetWare servers have used the Routing Information

Protocol (RIP) to route IPX packets and the Service Advertising Protocol (SAP) to exchange service information between servers. NLSP provides the same functionality as RIP and SAP but does so in a more efficient manner.

So Why Should I Use NLSP?

NLSP provides a more efficient way to handle routing and service information. NLSP does this by building a logical map of the entire internetwork by exchanging information with its peers. NLSP transmits update packets only when there is a change or every two hours—whichever transpires first. This is unlike RIP and SAP, which periodically broadcast routing and service information whether it is needed or not. In large network topologies, this can lead to a significant amount of bandwidth being wasted on useless packets. This can be detrimental to the performance of WAN connections. NLSP provides a reliable delivery mechanism with decreased transmission rates to improve performance on WAN connections.

NLSP also provides faster network convergence than RIP. Convergence is the process that a routing protocol uses to discover the topology or a service change on a network and make that change known to all the other routers. A converged network is one in which all the routers have the same view of the network. This helps to discover problems more quickly than they can be discovered in a RIP environment and reduces the number of routing loops that would exist until the network converges.

Another feature of NLSP is its ability to load balance. It does this by spreading the network traffic across all available network interfaces given multiple equal-cost routes. The cost of a route is the number of hops that it has to make before it reaches its final destination. NLSP routers know the cost of every link, and they use this information to pick the most efficient route. If you use INETCFG, the cost of a particular link can even be changed so that NLSP will route packets differently.

Finally, NLSP is compatible with IPX RIP and SAP environments. NLSP will propagate routing and service information from RIP/SAP devices. This will allow you to migrate to NLSP without having to migrate your entire internetwork at the same time.

NLSP currently comes with all versions of NetWare 4.1 and above. It is also part of the MultiProtocol Router version 3.1 and above. An upgrade is available for NetWare 3.12 servers to allow them to run NLSP.

Moving On

In this chapter, we discussed topics concerning the creation and management of WAN connections. We also discovered that there are a number of decisions to make, such as the type of WAN connection to get and where to get it from. We looked at IntranetWare's MultiProtocol Router, IPX/IP Gateway, and WAN Extensions. Finally, we took a quick peek at NLSP, IntranetWare's replacement to RIP and SAP, which brings this section on LAN services to a close.

In the next section, we'll explore how to take advantage of IntranetWare's intranet services to configure and maintain Web and FTP services. We'll look at CGI scripts, how to publish secure documents, and how to provide anonymous FTP services.

Novell Intranet Services

Providing Web Services

Many companies initially provide Web services only as a means of advertising their products or services to the Internet community. In the early days of the Internet, especially on college campuses and in other academic-oriented organizations, Web services were used to provide simple, static information and documentation. In the early 1990s, however, the Web became a medium for more complex documentation, database interactivity, and online advertisements, as well as for interactive communication using a variety of multimedia resources. Now that we've covered all the basics of installing and configuring NetWare services, adding clients to the network, and building a secure NDS tree, it's time for the fun stuff: enabling your Novell Web Server.

Once installed and configured, your Novell Web Server (NWS) will be able to publish Web-based documents, images, sounds, movies, interactive forms, search engines, and databases, and provide access to just about any type of digital information imaginable. You will be able to provide these services to your internal LAN, your corporate intranet, or to the entire Internet. In fact, with version 3.0 of NWS, you will be able to host multiple "virtual" Web sites on a single IntranetWare server, each with its own domain name. This chapter will highlight the features of NWS 3.0 to show you how to install the various pieces of the server and how to manage the basic configuration options through the Web server's graphical interface management tool.

Features of Novell Web Server 3.0

Like the other component pieces of IntranetWare, Web services are provided through NetWare Loadable Modules (NLMs). The Novell Web Server is an NLM that was originally written to extend Web services to NetWare 4.x, and although it is included as part of IntranetWare, it is an optional service and does not have to be installed or enabled.

Features New to Version 3.0

NWS 3.0 provides all the features of a traditional Web server plus a few additional services that make NWS a unique Web server for use in an intranet environment. For those of you upgrading to version 3.0 of NWS here are the new features added from previous versions:

- Perl 5
- Secure Sockets Layer (SSL) 2 and 3
- Oracle database connectivity
- QuickFinder search engine
- Virtual directories
- Multihoming
- Twice the performance of NWS 2.5.1

You have the option to install and provide none, some, or all Web services and to manage these services you will use two types of tools:

- A graphical interface client for Windows 3.1, 95, or NT
- Any ASCII text editor

If you are installing NWS for the first time, you might be surprised at all the included features. For other Web server platforms, many of these services must be purchased separately and often don't integrate very well with your existing Web server. NWS 3.0 offers all the following features as part of the base installation package.

HyperText Markup Language Documents

NWS 3.0 is capable of serving any and all versions of HyperText Markup Language (HTML) documents. However, it is up to the individual Web browser, such as Netscape Navigator, to interpret these documents and display them properly to the person accessing them from your Web server. The first Web server was created in 1979 by Tim Berners-Lee and provided what came to be the basic set of Web services for the following 10 years—text and images that could be hyperlinked to other such documents anywhere on the Internet. HTML documents are simple ASCII text documents that contain document formatting instructions, the names and locations of other files that are to be imbedded within a document, as well as the names and locations of other documents and resources to which a user may be linked with the click of the mouse.

Image & Multimedia Files

Just about any type of image or multimedia file may be served by NWS 3.0, including Graphics Interchange Format (GIF) and Joint Photographic Experts Group (JPEG, or JPG) image files, Audio Interchange File Format (AIFF) and Waveform Audio Format (WAV) sound files, and QuickTime (QT or MOV) and Video for Windows (AVI) video files. Unlike HTML documents, most multimedia files are binary files and therefore considerably larger, taking up an average of 10MB of disk space for every 60 seconds of playing time.

GIFs are ideal for use as buttons and navigational aids because of their small file size. JPEG images, on the other hand, are capable of displaying millions of colors and are potentially much larger than GIFs. They are ideal for use on the Web to display photograph-quality images, but may place a higher load on your server. Images that are displayed within an HTML document are referred to as inline images, and most browsers are capable of viewing them individually as well.

Like image files, sound and movie files are considerably larger than HTML documents and may be found on most Web sites. Sound files may be recordings from compact discs; tape recordings; sampled from TV, cable TV, or VCR; or live recordings obtained using a computer or other digital device. Movie files are also quite popular on the Web today, and you may also serve them using your Novell Web Server. Where the different types of image and sound files number in the dozens, there are only a small handful of movie file types on the Web at this time. The most popular file formats include QuickTime,

AVI, and Motion Picture Experts Group (MPEG or MPG). All image, sound, and movie files served from your Web server are digital in format.

Clickable Image Maps

Clickable image maps are inline images divided into regions that are associated with other Web-based documents or services. Clickable image maps became very popular in the early 1990s, and since then a second, more efficient type of image map has become available. NWS is capable of serving images for use with both the old and the new types of image maps.

The first type of clickable image maps is referred to as a server-side image map, which means that the Web server is responsible for resolving which regions of the image map are associated to what document or resources. This can be a disadvantage to some Web servers because the server must burn CPU cycles to perform the calculations necessary to resolve image maps. To use server-side image maps on your Web server, you will have to place a map configuration file (which ends with the extension .MAP) for each image map in a special directory on your server. The HTML documents that use these image maps do not require special information or syntax in the body of the document.

The second type of clickable image map is called a client-side image map. As the name denotes, the browser is responsible for resolving image maps. This is a more efficient means of implementing clickable image maps because it is both faster from the user's perspective, and relieves the server of the burden of calculating which regions of an image map are linked to what document or resource. Not all Web browsers support client-side image maps, however, but the ones that do—Netscape Navigator and Microsoft's Internet Explorer—account for the vast majority of browsers in use today. Client-side image maps do not require configuration files to be placed in a special directory on your Web server, but each HTML document using a client-side image map will require special information and syntax in the body of the document.

Scripting Support

NWS 3.0 supports three different scripting languages to allow for the creation of dynamic Web server content: BASIC, NetBasic for Internet from the HiTecSoft Corporation, and Perl 5. The first two are based on the BASIC programming language and should be familiar to many NetWare administrators, engineers, and PC users. The last scripting language may be new to some, however. Perl is an industry-standard scripting language available for many platforms, most notably UNIX, Windows, and the Mac OS. Web server scripts are very useful in creating and manipulating text as well as querying databases. They are not as involved or complex as programming languages such as C++ or Java. However, because they are interpreted—not compiled—languages, they don't offer the performance of other solutions for providing interactivity with your Web server.

BASIC Scripts

BASIC scripts are not NLMs, but they do require the presence of an NLM to interpret the BASIC commands on behalf of the Web server. Moreover, not all the available BASIC commands are supported by the interpretive NLM, so you will find that you may not be able to accomplish everything you'd like using BASIC with the Novell Web Server.

NetBasic for Internet

NetBasic for Internet uses a version of the BASIC language customized for use with NetWare. You can use NetBasic for Internet to create scripts that interface with just about any aspect of the core NetWare NOS, including NDS management, creation of dynamic HTML documents, database lookup interfaces, and Simple Network Management Protocol (SNMP) routines. Several NLMs are required to implement NetBasic for Internet with your Web server, and the NetBasic for Internet installation comes with plenty of online documentation and examples to help get you started.

Perl 5 Scripts

Perl, an abbreviation for Practical Extraction and Report Language, is a scripting language that has wide support on a variety of platforms. Similar to the C programming language, Perl is capable of providing a variety of services, including the ability to serve as a gateway to TCP/IP–based resources such as online catalogs, phone book directories, Gopher servers, and search engines. The greatest advantage for writing scripts and CGIs in Perl is that it is a highly portable language and your work can easily be used on other platforms, such as UNIX. The reverse is true as well: there are thousands of Perl scripts that have been written for other platforms, and many of them could easily be modified to run on your Novell Web Server.

Common Gateway Interfaces

Web servers such as NWS 3.0 use Common Gateway Interfaces (CGIs) to connect Web browsers to resources, usually servers or applications, other than the Web server itself. These resources may reside on the same physical server as does the Web server or they may reside on a server elsewhere on your intranet or across the Internet. These resources can take the form of static data, dynamic databases, searchable indices, TCP/IP services, and just about anything else. CGIs are similar to scripts in that they are written to perform interactive functions on behalf of your Web server, but they differ in that they are compiled programs and run more efficiently than scripts, which are interpreted with each execution. NWS is a very powerful intranet solution because it provides several types of CGI interfaces.

Local Common Gateway Interface

The first type of CGI is called a Local Common Gateway Interface, or LCGI, and is unique to Novell NetWare and IntranetWare. LCGIs are NLMs written in one of two scripting languages and are capable of connecting to internal or external resources with great speed because they are more tightly integrated with the NetWare NOS than other types of CGIs. For example, because LCGIs are loaded as NLMs, they are not required to be launched or cloned like UNIX processes and stay in your server's memory awaiting the next request after processing each client's request. The disadvantage is that some NLMs require substantial server resources and cannot be efficiently run without additional memory and processing power. LCGIs run only under NetWare.

Remote Common Gateway Interface

Remote Common Gateway Interfaces (RCGIs) are unique to IntranetWare and perform tasks that are similar to the tasks LCGIs perform. Although they may be written to run on either NetWare servers or other servers (such as UNIX servers), they are designed to interface Novell Web Servers with remote services and resources. RCGIs are also written in the ANSI C programming language but are unlike LCGIs in that they are socketed and therefore slower and more resource hungry.

Secure Sockets Layer

NWS supports Secure Sockets Layer (SSL) levels 2 and 3, which are the industry standard for transacting business over the Internet. The SSL protocol allows your Web server to send and receive authenticated and encrypted data to and from Web browsers such as Netscape Navigator and Microsoft's Internet Explorer. Once a user has been authenticated and a trusted (secure) connection has been established, *keys* are exchanged and data flowing between your Web server and its clients is no longer in the form of clear ASCII text; rather, it is encrypted ASCII text. An additional level of security is provided by a Certificate Authority, a trusted third party who issues certificates of authenticity for secure Web servers. These certificates make it difficult, if not impossible, for other Web servers to masquerade as your secure server and intercept encrypted data. NWS includes the Key Manager program to assist you in managing keys and site certificates.

Oracle Database Connectivity

New to version 3.0 of NWS is an extended version of NetBasic that includes the ability to interface your Web server with Oracle 7 databases hosted on any platform. Oracle is an industry leader in database design and connectivity, and with NWS 3.0 you can design custom Web-based applications to query and update your Oracle databases from any computer on the Internet whose browser supports forms.

QuickFinder Search Engine

The Novell QuickFinder search engine adds the powerful ability to index the entire contents of your Web server and make the results available via the Web or to other applications by way of Perl, NetBasic, or LCGI scripts. Users looking for information on your Web server will be able to search using keywords (cat or dog), wildcards (ca? or do*), and Boolean operators (cat AND dog), as well as keywords in a particular order (dog AND cat) or proximity (cat in the same paragraph as dog).

Virtual Directories

NWS 3.0 enables access to directories located on other NetWare and IntranetWare servers. Virtual directories allow other departments in your company to publish on the Web without the overhead of maintaining their own Web servers. Virtual directories give users access to remote documents and resources outside of your Web server's document tree, saving storage space for your server's other tasks.

Multihoming

Multihoming enables a single IntranetWare server running Novell Web Server 3.0 to provide multiple Web sites, each with its own domain name. This feature has been most popular with professional Web site providers who have dozens of clients who have registered for unique domain names. For example, an NWS server accessible over the Web as http://www.rambell.com could also serve Web documents via http://www.yourcompany.com. For internal company use, you can enable multihoming for departments so they can each have their own Web site, such as http://accounting.rambell.com, http://engineering.rambell.com, or http://hr.rambell.com. Each Web site will have its own domain name, document tree, configuration set, and SSL.

Server-Side Includes

Server-side includes are commands that are embedded into HTML documents and executed by the server before the HTML documents are returned to a browser by the Web server. Before the advent of server-side includes, many of the actions now performed by server-side includes were performed by third-party scripts and CGIs. Among the more common actions now handled by server-side includes are page or "hit" counting, appending a document's modification date, and automatic indexing of a directory's contents. NWS 3.0 includes about a dozen server-side include commands that enable your documents to include information from other documents, modify date and other document information, and apply if-then conditional statements to documents.

Java Applets

NWS 3.0 is capable of serving Java applets, small binary applications written in Sun Microsystems's Java programming language. Java's chief advantage for use on the Web is that it is a flexible, hybrid, interpreted, compiled language that is platform independent. Few Web servers are capable of executing server-based Java applications at this time, so NWS, like most other Web servers, is only capable of serving Java applets to Java-enabled browsers such as Navigator that actually execute the applets. Java should not be confused with JavaScript, which is also used on the Web. Browsers such as Navigator and Internet Explorer are both JavaScript- and Java-enabled, and there are substantial differences between the two languages. JavaScript is an interpreted scripting language, it is only used on the Web, and it appears as ASCII text within an HTML document. Java applets are external, binary applications that are not embedded within an HTML document.

Long Filename Support

The Web got its start on the UNIX platform and was popularized by Macintosh computers, both of which support long filenames. Today, of course, long filenames are supported by all the major operating systems, including IntranetWare, which is capable of supporting filenames that exceed the 8.3 rule of popular DOS-based operating systems. While long filename support isn't required to provide basic Web services, it is required in order to provide Java support. Also, your intranet will probably include several computers whose operating systems utilize long filenames. Being able to develop content on your Web server using native-length filenames is a given factor these days.

Online Documentation

NWS 3.0 comes with a fair amount of online documentation and examples of clickable image maps, scripts, CGIs, server-side includes, and Java applets. When you install the Web server, a document called INDEX.HTM is placed in the root document directory and will be the default home page for your server until you change the default filename for your server, rename INDEX.HTM to another name, or delete INDEX.HTM from the DOC directory created by the Web server installation. Figure 21-1 shows the basic online documentation available on your server; you can access it by pointing a Web browser to the following address:

`http://www.`*`yourserver`*`.com`

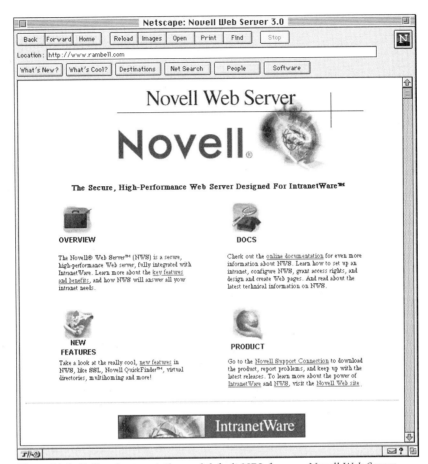

Figure 21-1: Online documentation and default URL for your Novell Web Server.

The basic online documentation will link you to many different examples, but one document in particular will be of great importance in creating CGI scripts and NLMs for your server. Figure 21-2 shows the main page of the Dynamic Web Page Programmer's Guide, available on your Web server at the following location:

```
http://your.server.name/online/wpguide/
```

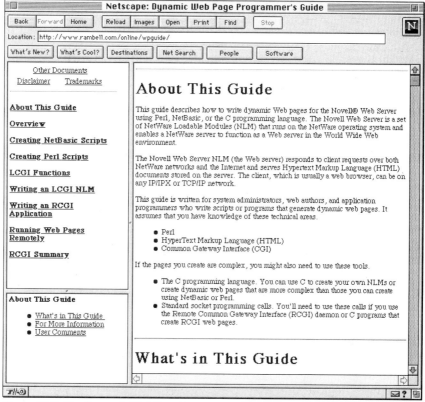

Figure 21-2: The Dynamic Web Page Programmer's Guide provides detailed documentation and examples for creating dynamic scripts, CGIs, and applications.

The Dynamic Web Page Programmer's Guide focuses on the intricacies involved in writing complex scripts, NLMs, and applications using the BASIC and ANSI C programming languages, and although programming novices will find it useful, it is really designed for advanced programmers. If you would like to access this documentation from CD-ROM instead of your Web server, you can use the following URL. However, you will not be able to run most of the demo scripts because they require the appropriate NLMs to be loaded and configured on an IntranetWare server:

```
file:///CD_DRIVE:/products/webserv/disk1/web/docs/online/wpguide/
```

Be sure to substitute your CD drive letter in place of CD_DRIVE in the above URL.

Installing the Server

The Novell Web Server is installed as an NLM during the IntranetWare installation process described in Chapter 2. However, like other optional NLMs, NWS must be loaded and activated from the server's console or remote console (Rconsole) before Web services are accessible over your intranet or the Internet. Providing Web services is a very easy process, and in this section we'll cover the requirements of NWS, which NLMs must be loaded, how to activate long filename support, a few DNS concerns, and the basic operation of the Web Manager program.

Tip

To access the NWS 3.0 Quick Start Card, see <VOL>:\WEB\DISK1\ INW_WEB\SHARED\DOCS\ONLINE\QSTART\QSTART.HTM.

Server Requirements

The Web server requirements are such that if your server is capable of running IntranetWare, then it will be adequate to provide Web services as well. However, before you add any additional service to your IntranetWare server, there are a few general considerations you should review:

- Increased load on the server.
- Additional server resources (RAM, disk storage).

With the activation of NWS, there are a few additional server resource concerns to consider:

- Requirements of secondary NLMs for long filename support and CGI scripting.
- Security of CGI execution.
- Overhead for multihoming.

Novell recommends that the following server hardware and software specifications be met prior to running NWS:

- 80486, Pentium, or Pentium Pro processor.
- 8MB of free disk space, not including user files.
- 24MB of total server RAM, minimum.
- 1.5MB additional RAM for minimal Web services.

■ IntranetWare.

■ Installation and configuration of the TCPIP NLM.

Additional RAM Requirements

In addition to the base 24MB of RAM required by IntranetWare, NWS 3.0 requires a base amount of RAM of 1.5MB plus additional RAM allocated for various performance issues and services. This amount of RAM should be installed above and beyond the 24MB recommended for IntranetWare. Figure 21-3 illustrates the various services and the RAM required.

```
                    1.5MB
            # of threads x 70KB
      # of virtual servers x 200 KB
  +     · # of virtual hosts x 20 KB
  _____

  additional RAM requirements
```

Figure 21-3: Additional memory requirements of NWS 3.0.

On the Rambell Web server, for example, we could have the standard number of threads (16), two virtual servers, and two virtual hosts, which would require a total of 3.06MB of RAM in addition to the 24MB required by IntranetWare. Figure 21-4 shows how this calculation adds up.

```
  1500      (1.5MB)
  1120      (16 x 70)
   400      (2 x 200)
    40      (2 x 20)
  _____
  3060      (total)
```

Figure 21-4: Additional memory requirement of NWS 3.0.

Long filename support places additional resource requirements on your IntranetWare server, so you'll need to do a quick calculation to determine if your server will be able to provide this type of support. Figure 21-5 illustrates the requirement in mathematical terms.

$$\frac{\text{volume-size} \times .032}{\text{block size}} = \begin{array}{c}\text{additional}\\\text{server memory}\end{array}$$

Figure 21-5: Additional memory requirement for adding long filename support.

Every volume for which long filename support is added needs additional memory. To figure out how much memory each volume needs:

1. Determine the block size in kilobytes.

2. Multiply the size of the volume in megabytes by .032.

3. Divide the result by the block size.

4. Round the result up to the closest megabyte.

5. Make sure the server has the memory available.

Adding long filename support to a volume 1GB in size, for example, would require that your server have an additional 8MB of RAM available, as illustrated in Figure 21-6.

$$\frac{1000 \times .032}{4} \; = \; 8MB$$

Figure 21-6: Additional memory requirement of adding long filename support to a 1GB volume.

Block Sizes

The size of your server's hard disk block allocation depends on the manufacturer of the hard disk and its interface. Moreover, operating systems use different methods of addressing blocks of data. For example, the Mac OS uses a variable block size, which depends on the overall size of the hard drive; the larger the hard drive, the larger the block size. Many UNIX systems use a technique called journaling. Block sizes of IntranetWare volumes can be obtained by loading the installation utility from the server console or via RCONSOLE and selecting Volume Options from the Installation Options menu. The block size will be shown for each volume along with the volume's name, status, and other information.

Installing the Software

Once you are sure your server hardware meets the minimal requirements, you are ready to install the Web server software. The core Web services are provided through several NLMs, which are loaded using the NetWare Server installation program from either the server console or using the RCONSOLE program.

Tip

You must install and configure TCP/IP prior to installing NWS 3.0, which will automatically update TCP/IP to the latest version.

To automatically install the NLMs and their associated files in their proper locations, run the installation utility as follows:

1. From the server console or by RCONSOLE, type **load install** to bring up the installation utility and the Installation Options menu.

2. Choose Product Options from the Installation Options menu.

3. If you purchased a version of IntranetWare that includes NWS 3.0, select the item or product you wish to install from the Other Installation Actions menu.

4. Highlight Install Novell Web Server from the Other Installation Items/ Products menu, as shown in Figure 21-7, and press Enter. If this option doesn't appear as a choice, skip "Upgrading the Software" later in the chapter.

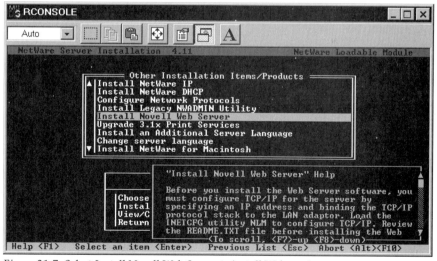

Figure 21-7: Select Install Novell Web Server to install Web services.

5. Select a product and server path by pressing the Enter key to accept the defaults paths. Select the default paths unless your needs require otherwise, in which case press the F3 key to choose alternative paths.

6. Choose an administrative password when prompted.

7. Finally, restart the system.

Once the system has been restarted, the Web server will be operational and several default configuration options will now be in effect. Therefore, it is important that you continue the installation process and pay close attention to the following sections.

Tip

The installation process automatically updates the AUTOEXEC.NCF file and requires that the server be restarted before Web services are provided.

Reconfiguring & Removing the Software

Once you have installed the Web server software, you may find it necessary to reinstall the software into another directory, onto another hard drive or volume, or to remove the product. To change the installation location of the server software, follow these steps:

1. From the server console or by RCONSOLE, type **load install** to bring up the installation utility and the Installation Options menu.

2. Choose Product Options.

3. Select View | Configure | Remove Installed Products from the Other Installation Actions menu.

4. Highlight Novell Web Server in the Currently Installed Products menu, as shown in Figure 21-8, and press Enter to view the available configuration options. If this option doesn't appear as a choice, go back to the previous section, "Installing the Software."

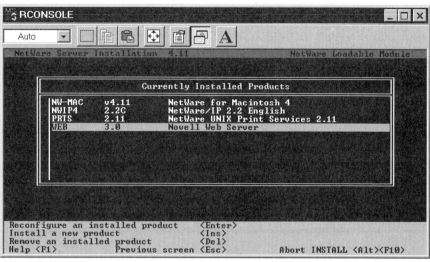

Figure 21-8: Selecting Novell Web Server for reconfiguration or deletion.

5. To delete the Web server software press the Del key, then follow the onscreen directions.

6. When you're done, restart the system if prompted.

Upgrading the Software

IntranetWare first shipped in October 1996 with version 2.5.1 of NetWare Web Server (also known as NWS). If you are upgrading to version 3.0, you must either download the product update from the Novell Web site (http:// www.novell.com/intranetware/webserver) or obtain the NWS installation CD-ROM disks from Novell. Once you have the installation software, follow these steps to upgrade your IntranetWare server:

1. From the server console or by RCONSOLE, type **load install** to bring up the installation utility and the Installation Options menu.

2. Choose Product Options from the Installation Options menu.

3. A list of currently installed products will appear in the upper window entitled Other Installation Items/Products. Select Install a Product Not Listed from the Other Installation Items/Products menu.

4. Press F3 (unless you are installing from the default path, the server's A:\ drive) and type in the path to the installation software, as in Figure 21-9.

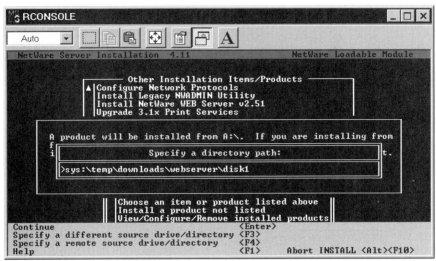

Figure 21-9: Upgrading to NWS 3.0.

5. You will need to answer several queries and provide a product and a server path. Select the default paths unless your needs require otherwise, in which case press the F3 key to choose alternative paths. Choosing SYS:WEB as the server root will install the new version in place of the older, but document, log, and configuration directories will not be replaced.

The recommended installation path of this version was SYS:WEB, and you may retain this path with version 3.0, although the default path for the new version uses a different root path. Actually, there are two root paths associated with NWS 3.0, a product root path and a server root path. The product root path specifies the location of the installation files and documentation, the default for which is SYS:INW_WEB. The server root path refers to the location of shared files and resources such as HTML documents, image map files, configuration files, scripting applications, as well as log files. You may accept the default root paths or you may specify alternatives by pressing F3 when prompted during the installation process.

6. Choose an administrative password when prompted.

7. Finally, restart the system.

Once the system has been restarted, the Web server will be operational and several default configuration options will now be in effect. Therefore, it is important that you continue the installation process and pay close attention to the following Web server configuration considerations.

Long Filenames

The first configuration consideration involves long filename support. As we've mention earlier in this chapter, most Web servers publish documents with filenames that excede the 8.3 rule. Long filename support is installed into the SYS:SYSTEM directory as part of IntranetWare, but like Web services, it is not automatically loaded. To activate long filename support, follow these steps:

1. From the server console or by RCONSOLE, type **load long.nam** and press Enter.

2. Type **add name space long to** *volume_name*, where volume_name is the name of the volume to which long filename support is to be added. This step must be repeated to add long filename support to any additional volumes.

3. To confirm that you have succeeded in adding long filename support to a volume, type **volumes** at the console or RCONSOLE prompt to list the currently mounted volumes and their options. Figure 21-10 shows the server console after long filename support has been added to two volumes on Rambell's IntranetWare server, Damocles.

Figure 21-10: Confirming long filename support on two volumes.

In addition to adding long filename support for IntranetWare users on the Windows 95, Windows NT, and OS/2 platforms, you'll need to add NetWare for Macintosh to provide an additional layer of long filename support, which will enable Mac OS and NFS users to store files on your IntranetWare server. Again, NetWare for Macintosh and NFS support are optional levels of support that come with IntranetWare but are not activated by default. To activate NetWare for Macintosh and NFS, follow the steps in the preceding section for adding long filename support, but in step 2, type **add name space mac** and **add name space nfs**. Each NLM-based service you add will be automatically loaded each time the server is restarted.

DNS Concerns

As we mentioned earlier in this chapter, TCP/IP must already be loaded and configured prior to bringing up the Web server, and installing NWS 3.0 will automatically update TCP/IP to the latest version. In addition to the concerns associated with TCP/IP configuration (IP name and number acquisition and registration, identifying the proper Domain Name System (DNS) server(s), routers, gateways, and subnet masks), there are a few additional things you should consider before loading the server.

First, the multihoming capabilities of NWS 3.0 can only be used in conjunction with properly registered domain names. If you aren't the primary contact for your organization's DNS administration, find out who is and present your intentions to him or her prior to enabling multihoming on your Web server. Second, if you'd like to register and add new domain names to your Web server, you will need to contact InterNIC, the organization charged with the administration of the Internet's domain names. InterNIC is a collaboration between the National Science Foundation, Network Solutions, Inc., and AT&T and provides several valuable services in addition to registering domain names, including public directory and database access services, Internet resource information, and Internet news and happenings.

InterNIC is responsible for administering only second-level domains. A top-level domain refers to one of seven root domains that identifies the type of organization (commercial, government, military, etc.) to which a host computer belongs. An example of a second-level domain under the top-level domain com would be yourcompany.com. Table 21-1 explains the types of top-level domains that are currently in use.

com	Commercial or business-oriented organizations
edu	Higher education institutions
gov	United States governmental organizations
mil	United States military organizations
net	Organizations involved with computer networking
org	Not-for-profit organizations
root	Reserved for a handful of special DNS servers called root DNS servers

Table 21-1: Top-level domains in use on the Internet.

InterNIC is responsible for coordinating all the second-level domains except those that fall under the root and mil domains (no way is Uncle Sam going to let anyone take on that responsibility!), as well as domains that fall under the United States (US) top-level domain. For information on obtaining a second-level US domain, see http://www.isi.edu/in-notes/usdnr/.

Tip

There is a move afoot to create new top-level domains to ease the crush on DNS systems struggling to keep up with the growing demand for domain names. See the Internet International ad hoc committee's home page at http://www.iahc.org/ for more information on the status of new top-level domains.

It is possible for you to query the InterNIC database to see if a domain name is in use. It is wise, of course, for you to check first before submitting a request for a domain name, which you may do by going to the InterNIC Whois database lookup page at http://rs.internic.net/cgi-bin/whois.

Tip

To see if a domain name is in use, open your browser to http://rs.internic.net/cgi-bin/whois and search the InterNIC domain registration database.

You may apply for a domain name for a fee of $100 (U.S.) and must renew it every year for a fee of $50 after the second year. Failure to renew your registration will result in a loss of all legal rights to the domain name, and InterNIC is known for invalidating domain names of delinquent accounts! Visit InterNIC's home page, shown in Figure 21-11, for details on how to register domain names.

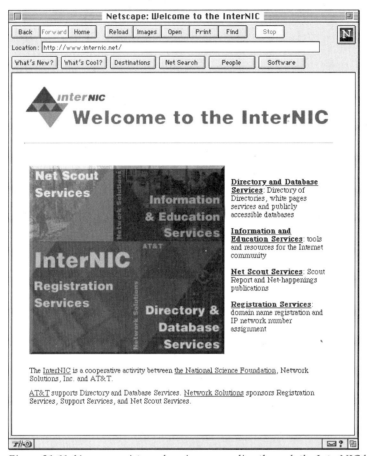

Figure 21-11: You can register a domain name online through the InterNIC home page.

Basic Server Configuration

Once restarted, your IntranetWare server will automatically be publishing on the World Wide Web using the Web server's default configuration. You will no doubt want to change several of the server's configuration options, and to do so you will need to access the Web Manager (WEBMGR.EXE) program located in the SYS:PUBLIC directory. Other configuration options are performed by manually editing several ASCII text files, and we'll cover these tasks in Chapter 22. It may be useful to create a folder in which you can create shortcuts to the essential programs you will use to manage the Web server. Figure 21-12 shows a collection of shortcuts to the server (Damocles), two volumes (SYS and VOL1), the Web server's root directory (WEB), a sample user's home directory (Jdoe), and two often-used programs (WEBMGR.EXE and RCONSOLE.EXE).

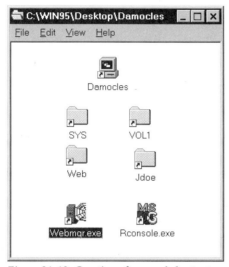

Figure 21-12: Creating often-used shortcuts can be a time saver.

The Web Manager program allows you to control dozens of configuration options through a typical Windows application interface, including the following tasks:

- Select a Web server to configure.
- Pause and/or restart a Web server.
- Enable or disable NDS browsing.
- Select the directories for a server's root, log files, and individual user files.
- View all the directories for the Web server, as well as enable automatic indexing and server-side includes.
- Configure user and system access.
- Create, modify, and delete virtual hosts.
- Enable and configure Secure Sockets Layers.

Client Requirements

The Web Manager program resides on your IntranetWare server in the SYS:PUBLIC directory, but it cannot be executed by all the clients that have access to the server. The following requirements must be met to run the Web Manager program:

- 386 or better processor
- 8MB system memory
- 1MB free disk space
- Windows 3.x or Windows 95
- NetWare client (VLM or Client 32) and TCP/IP stack

Prior to launching Web Manager, you must first log in to the NDS tree in which the Web server is located. If you don't, no virtual Web servers will be visible for you to select. To launch the Web Manager program under Windows 3.x, follow these steps:

1. Log in to the NDS tree.

2. Map an available drive letter to the SYS:PUBLIC directory, if you don't have one already mapped.

3. Create a Program Item called Web Manager that points to SYS:PUBLIC\WEBMGR.EXE.

4. Double-click the Web Manager icon.

5. Alternatively, choose File | Run and enter the path to WEBMGR.EXE every time you want to run the program.

If you're running Windows 95 on your client workstation, then follow these steps:

1. Log in to the NDS tree.

2. Open the SYS volume, then the Public directory, and double-click on the Webmgr.exe program.

3. To create a shortcut, instead of double-clicking on WEBMGR.EXE, single-click with the right mouse button and drag it to your Desktop. Release the mouse button and choose Create Shortcut when prompted.

Launching Web Manager

The Web Manager's main window is the starting point for all Web server configuration options. Here, you will have access to many configuration options for multiple Novell Web Servers through a standard Windows interface, shown in Figure 21-13.

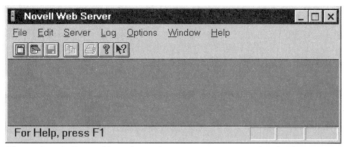

Figure 21-13: Launching the Web Manager program for the first time.

The main window allows you to perform several tasks. The menu items and their tasks include:

- **File Menu:** Choose a Web server to configure, print a log file, and exit the Web Manager application.
- **Edit Menu:** Copy text from a log file.
- **Server Menu:** Restart, or pause and then restart, a Web server.
- **Log Menu:** View, clear, and export access and error log files.
- **Options Menu:** Change the Web server's administrative password and contact e-mail address, view statistics, and specify the location of Web server databases.
- **Window Menu:** Change the way windows are viewed (Cascade, Tile, and Arrange Icons).
- **Help Menu:** Access the Web Manager's standard Windows-based online help.

Since the Web Manager program allows you to manage multiple Web servers, once the program is launched you will have to select a server to manage. To select a server:

1. Choose Select Server from the File menu (or Ctrl+O) and a dialog box will be presented asking you to locate a Web server.

2. Locate the ETC directory of the volume on which the Web server resides, usually the SYS volume.

3. The available Web servers will appear in the Select a Virtual Server to Configure window, shown in Figure 21-14. Select a server and choose the OK button.

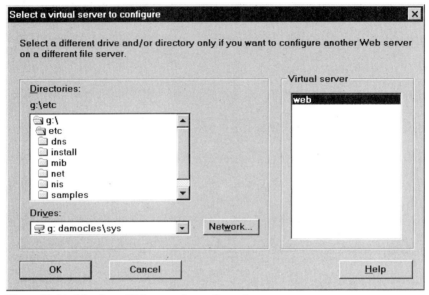

Figure 21-14: Selecting a Web server for configuration.

If the Network button in the Select a Virtual Server to Configure window (Figure 21-14) doesn't work, you may not have the proper version of COMMDLG.DLL located in your client's C:\WINDOWS or C:\WINDOWS\SYSTEM directory. You must delete the old version before installing the newer version; then restart the workstation and launch the Web Manager again.

You may also permanently map a drive letter for use with the Web Manager program by following these steps:

1. In the Select a Virtual Server to Configure window, shown in Figure 21-14, click the Network button.

2. Select a drive and path to the ETC directory of the SYS volume on which the Web server is installed.

3. Check the Reconnect at Logon check box and click OK, as shown in Figure 21-15.

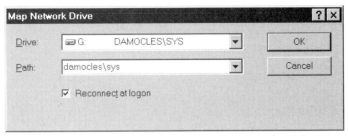

Figure 21-15: Mapping a network drive to reconnect to the Web Manager.

Once you have selected a Web server to configure, you'll use a familiar tabbed dialog box to make your configuration selections. The following sections briefly describe these tabs.

Server Tab

The Server tab, shown in Figure 21-16, provides information about the server and allows you to administer several of the server's basic configuration options.

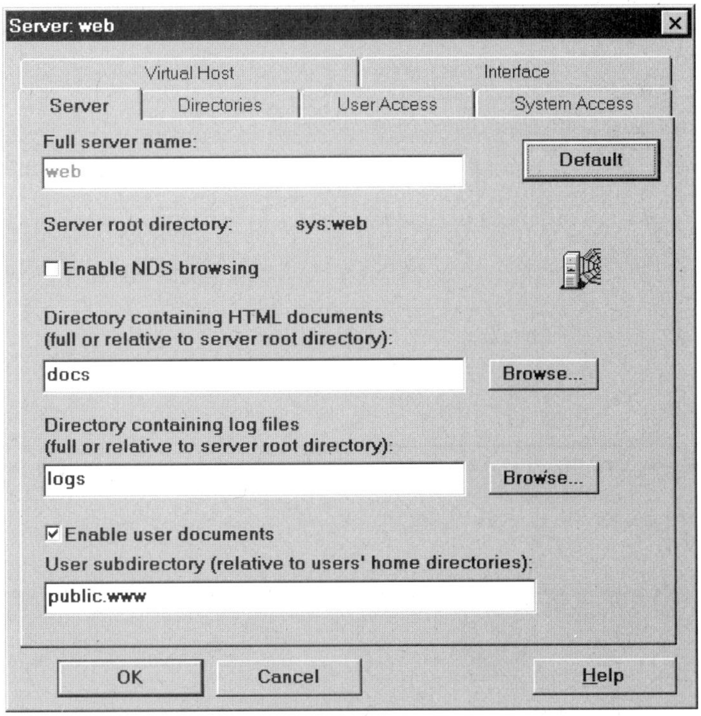

Figure 21-16: The Server configuration tab.

Full Server Name

The Full Server Name field is for a unique name assigned by the Web Manager program to a virtual Web server and may not be modified by the user. Since the Web Manager program allows anyone with the proper NDS privileges to configure other Novell Web Servers on your intranet, each will be identified using a different name. The default name for the first virtual Web server is "web."

Server Root Directory

The Server Root Directory line shows the location of the Web server root directory relative to your IntranetWare server, including the volume name and directory path. The default server root path is SYS:WEB.

Enable NDS Browsing

The Enable NDS Browsing check box allows you to either enable or disable the ability of users to browse your IntranetWare NDS tree. If enabled, users can view—but not edit—information about NDS objects such as users, groups, volumes, and printers, all through a Web browser.

Directory Containing HTML Documents

The Directory Containing HTML Documents field displays the name of the root directory used to serve HTML documents, referred to as the document root directory. The default directory is SYS:WEB\DOCS (for HTML documents) or SYS:INW_WEB\SHARED\DOCS (for online documentation). There is no need to change this field unless you want to change the default directory structure. For example, if you upgrade from an earlier version that doesn't use the same standard paths, you may want to change back to the original default directory root. Or you may want to change it because some of your CGI scripts have hard-coded path information that needs to be preserved. Use the Browse button to select a new directory.

Directory Containing Log Files

The Directory Containing Log Files field identifies the location where the server creates and updates Access.log and Error.log log files. Changing this field will cause the server to create new log files with the same names, but in the new location. Use the Browse button to select a new directory.

Enable User Documents

The Enable User Documents check box allows you to enable or disable the ability of individual users to publish HTML documents from within their home directories. This feature is useful to provide basic Web publishing capabilities to the authorized users of your IntranetWare server while ensuring user document security. An alternative—but less secure—method would be to create a single, shared directory under the HTML document root and assign all users the rights to create and modify documents in this directory. Checking the Enable User Documents check box ensures that a user's HTML documents cannot be modified or deleted by other users, an essential feature in today's Web publishing environments.

User Subdirectory

The User Subdirectory field allows you to identify the name of the subdirectory within a user's home directory in which the Web server will look for HTML documents, including a default HTML document (usually INDEX.HTM), images, and other multimedia files. The default directory name is PUBLIC.WWW, and to access the directory using a Web browser for a user whose username is jdoe, one would type in the server's base URL, a forward slash (/), a tilde (~), and the username; for example:

```
http://www.rambell.com/~jdoe
```

Directories Tab

The Directories tab helps you identify and manage the many directories used by the Web server. Shown in Figure 21-17, the Directories tab allows you to add, modify, and delete directories using the appropriate buttons at the bottom of the screen, as well as configure several features associated with a chosen directory.

Existing Directories

The Existing Directories list box contains the directories located on the Web server, including those under the document root and those that lay outside the document root, such as scripting directories. Select a directory to view, modify, or delete its attributes.

Directory Path

The Directory Path field displays a selected directory's path or the path to a newly created or proposed directory.

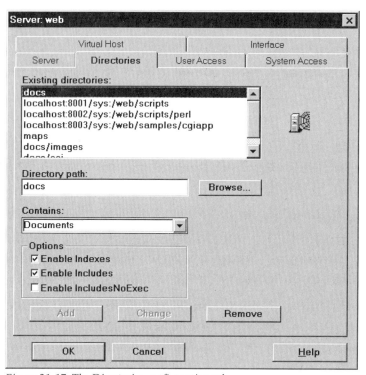

Figure 21-17: The Directories configuration tab.

Contains

The Contains field is a drop-down list that displays the commonly used purposes of directories on the Novell Web Server, including documents, scripts, image maps, and configuration files. You must select from this list when creating a new directory.

Options: Enable Indexes

When checked, the Enable Indexes option check box allows the Web server to automatically generate an index file for a directory that has no default HTML file, such as INDEX.HTM. In place of this file, the automatic indexing feature will scan the directory and create a simple HTML document that lists the directory's contents. The contents of the directory will be compared to a listing of the 20 or so most frequently accessed files, and a hyperlink and associated image will each be placed on a separate line for every item in the directory.

Option: Enable Includes

The Enable Includes option, when checked, will allow any server-side include commands contained in HTML documents residing in a directory to be executed. Older versions of NWS allowed you to select a single directory for documents containing server-side includes, but with the Enable Includes option, you can control them on a per-directory basis.

Option: Enable IncludesNoExec

The Enable IncludesNoExec option allows a new server-side include command called IncludesNoExec to be executed.

User Access Tab

The User Access tab allows you to manage which users may access your Web server. Many Web servers contain private information that must be shared only by authenticated users, and the User Access tab, shown in Figure 21-18, lets you control who has such access.

Figure 21-18: The User Access configuration tab.

Directory

The Directory field is a drop-down list that identifies all the directories that are currently available for user access control. Directories created using the Directories tab, described earlier, will automatically appear in this field when added.

Authentication Method

The Authentication Method field is a drop-down list that allows you to select what type of authentication method should be used in conjunction with a given directory. The default type of authentication, shown in Figure 21-18, is Directory Services, which allows you to use Novell's NDS to restrict access to a directory to individual users or groups.

Default NDS Context

The Default NDS Context field allows you to select the default context for authorized users so they don't have to enter the full context when they are accessing protected directories and are prompted for username and password information. You should set this field to match the context in which the majority of users reside.

Browse Network Users At

Entering a valid NDS context in the Browse Network Users At field will display a list of all valid NDS users and groups in the users list immediately below this field. In Figure 21-18, several groups are visible, and if you could scroll down, you would be able to see a list of individual users as well.

All Valid Users

The All Valid Users check box allows you to enable directory access to the entire list of available users and groups without having to select them individually. Checking this box will cause the list of available users to become inactive.

Authorized Users

The Authorized Users list box displays all users and groups that have been granted access to a directory. To add a user or group to this list, highlight the user or group name in the list immediately above and then click the Add to Authorized Users List button. To remove a user or group, click the Remove button after selecting the user or group from the Authorized User list box. By default, everyone is granted access to your Web server.

System Access Tab

The System Access tab, shown in Figure 21-29, allows you to globally restrict access to selected directories on your Web server based on the requesting Web client's full or partial IP number or domain or host name. The System Access tab is one of two ways you can control access to your server, the other being per-directory access control, described in Chapter 22.

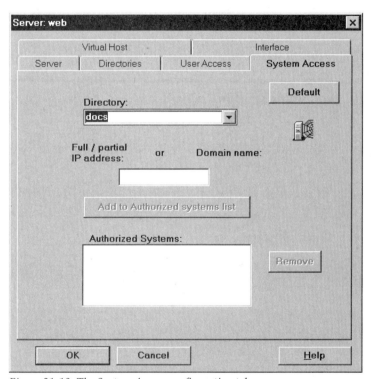

Figure 21-19: The System Access configuration tab.

Directory

The Directory drop-down list allows you to select the directory for which you may configure global access control. However, any directory selected here cannot utilize per-directory access control.

Full/Partial IP Address or Domain Name

The Full/Partial IP Address or Domain Name field is where you will enter either the full or partial IP number (or the system's domain or host name) of the system for which you wish to authorize access to a directory. For example, to restrict access to the DOCS directory to only those people in your company, you would enter your company's domain name, as in *yourcompany*.com. Likewise, you could enter IP number information here, which is a bit more tricky, to affect the same level of security. Typing 150.4 in this field would allow access for everyone whose IP number starts with 150.4, including 150.4.3.2 as well as 150.44.3.2 and 150.40.3.2. Restricting access by IP number and domain name is described in detail in Chapter 22.

Add to Authorized Systems List

The Add to Authorized Systems List button will add whatever IP name or number appears in the Full/Partial IP Address or Domain Name field to the list of systems that are authorized to access the selected directory.

Authorized Systems

The Authorized Systems display lists groups of users who have been granted access to selected directories based on their IP names and numbers. To remove a group from this list, highlight it and click the Remove button to the right of the list.

Virtual Host Tab

The Virtual Host tab allows you create, delete, modify, enable, and disable virtual hosts. A virtual host is used in conjunction with multihoming and allows a single virtual Web server to function as multiple Web servers. By default, when you install NWS 3.0, a single virtual Web server named web is created, and this virtual Web server may serve multiple virtual hosts, each with its own domain name. The number of virtual hosts you have is limited only by the amount of RAM available on your IntranetWare server. Figure 21-20 shows the Virtual Host configuration tab.

Create

To create a new virtual host, click the Create button to bring up the dialog box shown in Figure 21-21.

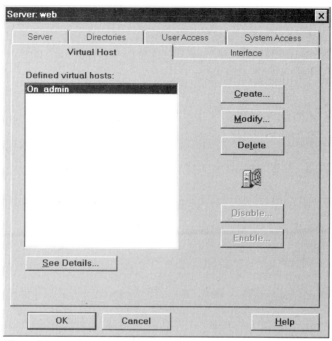

Figure 21-20: The Virtual Host configuration tab.

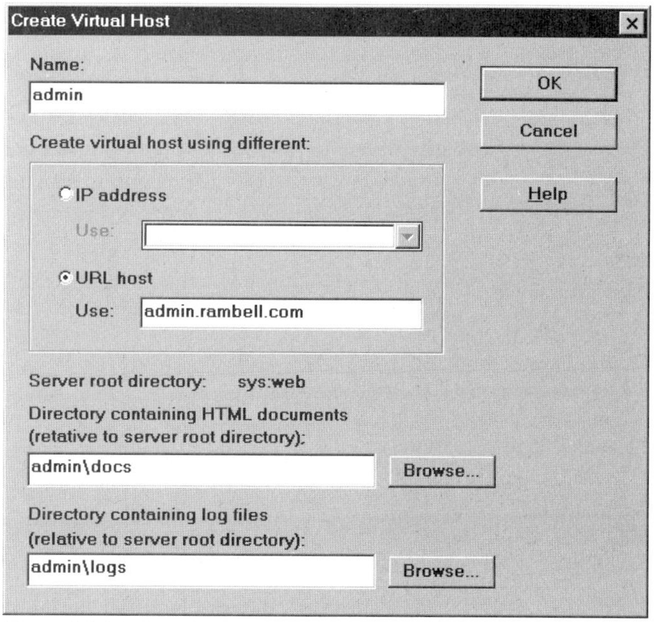

Figure 21-21: Creating a new virtual host.

Once the dialog box has opened, you will need to follow these steps to complete the creation of a virtual host:

1. Choose a name for the virtual host, such as admin.

2. Specify whether the virtual host is to be addressed by one or more IP addresses, or by a specific URL (i.e., a registered domain name). If the virtual host will be accessible using multiple IP addresses, enter the asterisk wildcard (*) in the IP Address field. If it will be accessible via a single uniform resource locator (URL), such as http://www.yourbusiness.com, then enter **www.*yourbusiness*.com** in the URL Host field.

3. Confirm the path to the document and log root directories, which will be automatically named \admin under the server root.

4. Click OK.

Interface Tab

Entries in the Interface tab allow you to control the network interface to a virtual server. Each virtual server must have a few unique settings to be properly identified by a URL, and the default Interface configuration options are shown in Figure 21-22.

Port

The TCP/IP protocol suite allows for multiple sessions of the same server application to run on the same server using different ports. The most popular server applications use well-defined, or standard, port numbers between 0 and 1000; the default port for Web servers is 80. If you change to a port other than port 80, you will need to advertise this port number in your server's URLs in order for the server to be accessed. For example, changing to port 8001 would require that your Web server's default URL be accessed as:

```
http://www.yourcompany.com:8001
```

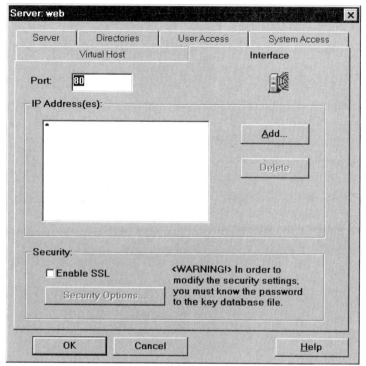

Figure 21-22: The Interface configuration tab.

IP Address(es)

Each virtual server can have one or more IP addresses assigned. However, the IP addresses must be registered with your IntranetWare server's DNS system or HOST file as well as be configured for use by the IntranetWare server itself through the TCPIP.NLM. By default, the asterisk (*) denotes that all IP addresses registered for use by your IntranetWare server are available for use by the Web server. Add and delete IP addresses using the Add and Delete buttons to the right of the IP Address(es) text box.

Security: Enable SSL

The Secure Sockets Layer (SSL) feature may be used with each virtual server, including the default "web" virtual server, and is enabled and disabled with the Enable SSL check box.

Moving On

The Novell Web Server is a powerful, and sometimes complex, means of providing Web publishing capabilities to your intranet users. NWS 3.0 has all the features of the most popular Web servers, as well as a few that are unique to the Novell NetWare environment. This chapter covered basic server features, how to install the server, and how to identify the basic configuration tasks. In the next chapter, "Advanced Web Server Configuration," we'll go into detail on such tasks as managing the most important configuration files on your Web server. We'll also cover various aspects of file management, as well as how to use your server's log files to ward off potential problems and diagnose errors reported by your users.

22

Advanced Web Server Configuration

Providing basic Web services on your IntranetWare server is as easy as installing the Web software. But your Web server is capable of doing so much more than serving HTML documents, and to prepare your server for the task, you'll need to pick up a few more advanced administrative skills. As far as Web servers go, the Novell Web Server is moderately complex in terms of features and ease of administration. It provides all the standard features of a modern Web server, plus several additional features that are unique to the Novell environment. Both of these feature levels require advanced knowledge to administer them properly and to protect the security of your Web server and its users.

Many basic elements of your Web server work together to comprise a complex whole, and while some of these elements are easily understood and administered, others may not be so quickly grasped and manipulated. In the previous chapter, we saw that many of the Web server's attributes are maintained through the Web Manager program, which uses a standard Windows-like program interface. This chapter will revisit many of the concepts introduced with the Web Manager program and show how they interact with more subtle configuration options that effect the manageability, configuration, and security of your intranet's Web server. Specifically, we'll look at the following issues:

- How to manage the several configuration files that control the Web server's behavior.
- How to manage the MIME types recognized by the Web server.

■ File and content management techniques.

■ Web server logging.

Managing Configuration Files

The Novell Web Server stores many configuration parameters and values in several configuration files that are located in the CONFIG directory under the server root, typically SYS:WEB\CONFIG. These configuration files are simple ASCII text files that are read when the server is loaded and are updated by the server and the Web Manager program when necessary. The information stored in these files ranges from the locations of certain files and directories to resource values that affect the performance of the Web server. You need to understand the purpose, structure, and use of each configuration file because you may have to edit them to achieve maximum performance and reliability.

You can edit the configuration files using text editors such as Notepad or the MS-DOS EDIT program as well as word processors such as Microsoft Word or WordPerfect. However, remember to save the files as ASCII text if you use a word processing program. When editing configuration files, keep these tips in mind:

■ Lines beginning with the pound sign (#) are treated as comments and are ignored by the Web server.

■ Blank lines (sometimes referred to as *white space* by programmers) and tabs are ignored by the Web server.

■ Paths in configuration files, unless otherwise noted, are relative to the server root, typically SYS:WEB.

The following sections detail the configuration files and the directives and values commonly used to control the behavior of the Web server, specifically the following files:

■ HTTPD.CFG, the master configuration file.

■ SRM.CFG, the server resource map file.

■ ACCESS.CFG, the server access control file.

■ SSL.CFG, the Secure Sockets Layer control file.

HTTPD.CFG

The HTTPD.CFG file is the master configuration file used by the Web server to control basic behavior and to locate other configuration files. The name comes from the UNIX world in which Web servers, which use HyperText Transfer Protocol (HTTP) to send and receive data over the Web, run as daemons (pronounced *dee-mons*) and are simply called httpd. The following are the important directives found in the HTTPD.CFG file and their default values. The order in which they appear is not important.

Port

```
Port 80
```

The Port directive instructs the Web server to listen for incoming HTTP connections on the selected port, the default being 80. If you change to a port other than 80, you will need to advertise this port number in your server's URLs in order for the server to be accessed. For example, changing to port 8001 would require that your Web server's default URL be accessed as:

```
http://www.yourcompany.com:8001
```

If you change to a nonstandard port, be sure there are no other TCP/IP services on your IntranetWare server communicating on the same port and that you select a number that is not considered to be a standard port number (the most popular server applications use well-defined, or standard, port numbers between 0 and 1000).

IPAddress

```
IPAddress *
```

The IPAddress directive tells the Web server to answer requests for the specified IP addresses. If your server is equipped with multiple Network Interface Cards (NICs) and multiple registered IP addresses, the NWS can serve Web documents using more than one IP address. The default is the wildcard asterisk (*), meaning that it will serve all the IP addresses registered for your Web server. If your server is using the multihoming and virtual host features, this directive may be edited through the Web Manager program to specify which specific IP addresses should be used by which virtual Web servers. For example, if your IntranetWare server is set up as several virtual servers, you can select which IP address(es) are to be used with which virtual Web servers.

SSL

```
SSL 0
```

The SSL directive uses a zero (0) or a one (1) to denote whether or not the Secure Sockets Layer feature is disabled (0) or enabled (1) at startup. By default, SSL is not enabled because there are many important configuration steps that must be completed prior to your Web server being able to serve secure documents using SSL. We'll talk more about the SSL feature later in this section when we discuss the role of the SSL.CFG file.

TransferLog

```
TransferLog logs/access.log
```

The TransferLog directive tells the server where to record information documenting what files were transferred by the Web server, the IP address of the requesting browser, what HTTP commands were issued, the result of the request, and the time and date of the transfer. See the "Logging" section later in this chapter for more information on log files.

ErrorLog

```
ErrorLog logs/error.log
```

The ErrorLog directive tells the server where to record information documenting what errors, if any, were encountered in the process of serving HTML documents. The time, date, specific error, and requesting browser are all recorded in this log file. See the "Logging" section later in this chapter for more information on log files.

SSLConfig

```
SSLConfig config/ssl.cfg
```

The SSLConfig directive determines where the Secure Sockets Layer configuration file is located. The Secure Sockets Layer configuration file, discussed in detail later in this section, stores configuration information for SSL, including certificate names, client authentication information, and SSL version support. It is typically located in the same directory as HTTPD.CFG.

ResourceConfig

```
ResourceConfig config/srm.cfg
```

The ResourceConfig directive determines where the server resource map file is located. The server resource map file, discussed in detail later in this section, tells the Web server where a variety of resources are located on your IntranetWare server and is typically located in the same directory as HTTPD.CFG.

AccessConfig

```
AccessConfig config/access.cfg
```

The AccessConfig directive determines where the access control file is located. The access control file, discussed in detail later in this section, controls multiple access policies for the Web server portion of your IntranetWare server and is typically located in the same directory as HTTPD.CFG.

TypesConfig

```
TypesConfig config/mime.typ
```

The TypesConfig directive determines where the MIME-type map file is located. This file, discussed in detail later in this chapter, tells the Web server how to serve various types of documents to Web browsers, such as text, binary, and multimedia files. This file is also typically located in the same directory as HTTPD.CFG.

SRM.CFG

The server resource map (SRM) file tells the Web server where a variety of resources are located on your IntranetWare server and is typically located in the same directory as HTTPD.CFG. However, you can change its location using the ResourceConfig directive in the HTTPD.CFG file. The following are the important directives found in the SRM.CFG file and their default values. The order in which they appear is not important.

DocumentRoot

```
DocumentRoot docs
```

The DocumentRoot directive identifies the root directory for HTML documents served by NWS. Documents in this directory, including your server's default home page, are accessed from your Web server using the URL http://www.yourserver.com.

DirectoryIndex

```
DirectoryIndex INDEX.HTM
```

The DirectoryIndex directive identifies the default HTML filename served when requesting URLs do not have a specific filename. Each directory under the document root may contain a different file with this same filename. On most UNIX and Mac Web servers, this value is index.html, but on most Novell- and Windows NT–based Web servers it is INDEX.HTM. This is a legacy of the 8.3 naming convention of MS-DOS, and as with DOS, filenames on the Novell Web Server are not case sensitive.

UserDir

```
UserDir public.www
```

The UserDir directive tells the Web server in which directory to search for individual user documents, if this feature has been enabled through the Web Manager program (discussed in the previous chapter in the section entitled "Basic Server Configuration"). In the "early" days, Web servers were usually dedicated servers that didn't have individual user accounts. However, because Novell servers are user-account oriented, it made sense to enable this type of feature. Documents placed in individual user directories are accessed using a Web server's base URL, a forward slash (/), a tilde (~), and the user's name; for example:

```
http://www.rambell.com/~jdoe
```

DefaultType

```
DefaultType text/plain
```

The DefaultType directive identifies the default Multipurpose Internet Mail Extensions (MIME) type for documents served by NWS. Every document is assigned a MIME type so it may be properly identified by a Web browser once it has been received from the server by the browser. The default MIME type is almost exclusively text/plain. See "MIME Management" later in the chapter for an in-depth review of managing MIME types.

FancyIndexing

```
FancyIndexing on
```

The FancyIndexing directive has two values, on and off, the default being off. In the previous chapter, we discussed the automatic indexing options that are controlled via the Web Manager program, and will go into more detail in Chapter 24.

MapAlias

```
MapAlias /maps/ maps
```

The MapAlias directive identifies the location of the directory containing the map files used in conjunction with clickable image maps. Map files contain the X- and Y-coordinates used in clickable image maps and the URLs that are returned to a Web browser after a user clicks on the image. These map files, discussed in Chapter 24, are also simple ASCII text files that are edited using any text editor.

RemoteScriptAlias

```
RemoteScriptAlias <local_dir> <remote_url>
```

The RemoteScriptAlias directive is used to locate CGI interpreters located on both the local Web server and remote Web servers. The values are <local_dir>, used to identify the local directory to which a URL has been requested, and <remote_url>, which identifies the name, port, and root directory of the machine on which the CGI resides. If the interpreter, such as BASIC or Perl, is running on the local machine, then substitute the machine name with the word **localhost**. For example, the following directive appears on a single line of the SRM.CFG file and points to the Perl interpreter located on the same computer as the Web server. Note that the nonstandard port (8002) is part of the remote_url variable:

```
RemoteScriptAlias /perl/ localhost:8002/sys:/web/scripts/perl
```

LoadableModule

```
LoadableModule <local_dir> <nlm_location>
```

The LoadableModule directive is used to locate NLMs used by the Web server to perform several functions. The <local_dir> variable indicates the local directory to which a URL has been requested, and <nlm_location> identifies the volume and root directory where the NLM resides. For example, the following directive tells the Web server where to look for the QuickFinder NLM:

```
LoadableModule /qfsearch/ SYS:\INW_WEB/shared/lcgi/qfsearch/qfsrch30.nlm
```

AccessFileName

```
AccessFileName access.www
```

The AccessFileName directive tells the Web server the name of the file used in per-directory access control. When the Web server retrieves a document from a directory, it first looks for this file and processes its security restriction information, and then it determines if the requesting browser has permission to receive the document in question. For more information on access control and security, see the next subsection discussing the ACCESS.CFG configuration file, and the section entitled "Restricting Access" in the next chapter.

ACCESS.CFG

The ACCESS.CFG file is the global access control file and is responsible for telling the Web server who may have access to what directories located under the server root. This file is maintained primarily through the Web Manager program discussed in the previous chapter, but there are several changes that are made manually. NWS allows you to restrict access either globally, using this file, or on a per-directory basis. You may restrict access to users based on authenticated user, group, or system. The following are the important directives found in the ACCESS.CFG file and their default values. Unlike previous configuration files, the order in which the directives appear is very important because of the way the Web server processes this data.

<Directory>...</Directory>

`<Directory directory_name>values </Directory>`

The <Directory>...</Directory> directive serves as a command set telling the Web server about the access controls for a specific directory. For example, <Directory docs>...</Directory> would control access to the docs directory. Directory name values in this directive are relative to the document root, usually SYS:WEB\DOCS. The following example entry illustrates the use of the following <Directory>...</Directory> values:

```
<Directory docs>
Options Indexes Includes
AllowOverride All
AuthGroupFile groups.www
AuthGroupMethod nds .web.admin.rambell
AuthName Web Users
AuthType Basic
AuthName Web Users
AuthUserFile users.www
AuthUserMethod nds .web.admin.rambell
<Limit GET>
order allow,deny
deny from all
</Limit>
</Directory>
```

Options

```
Options variables
```

The Options directive determines whether or not several special options, such as automatic directory indexing, are active or inactive for a specific directory whose access is controlled via ACCESS.CFG. Variables in this context include:

- Indexes (if exists, allows automatic directory indexing).
- Includes (if exists, allows server side includes).

AllowOverride

```
AllowOverride variables
```

The AllowOverride directive determines whether or not per-directory access control may override the global settings. The available variables are All and None.

AuthGroupFile

```
AuthGroupFile filename
```

The AuthGroupFile identifies a database file that contains information on groups and their members for file-based authentication.

AuthGroupMethod

```
AuthGroupMethod nds context
```

The AuthGroupMethod identifies the method used to authenticate a group; the only method supported at present is NDS. The variable used with this directive is the NDS context.

AuthName

```
AuthName string
```

The AuthName directive specifies a text string that appears in the request sent by the server to the user to provide the proper username and password for authentication. For example, using the string "Secret Web Administrators" would cause your Web browser to ask, "Enter username for Secret Web Administrators at web.admin.rambell."

AuthType

```
AuthType Basic
```

The AuthType directive identifies the type of user authentication. Currently, only basic is supported.

AuthUserFile

```
AuthUserFile filename
```

The AuthUserFile specifies the database file that contains the list of usernames and passwords for file-based authentication for a directory. It is used exactly like AuthGroupFile.

AuthUserMethod

```
AuthUserMethod nds context
```

The AuthUserMethod identifies the method used to authenticate a user; the only method supported at present is NDS. The variable used with this directive is the NDS context.

<Limit>...</Limit>

```
<Limit>values </Limit>
```

The <Limit>...</Limit> directive resides within <Directory>...</Directory> and lists the access control directives for the specified directory. For example:

```
<Directory web_admin>
Options Indexes Includes
AllowOverride All
AuthType Basic
AuthName Web Administrators
AuthUserMethod .web.admin.rambell
AuthGroupMethod .web.admin.rambell
<Limit GET>
order deny,allow
deny from all
allow from admin.rambell.com
require user president
require valid-user
require group webadmin
</Limit>
</Directory>
```

Like most of the other directives in ACCESS.CFG, the order of the directives and their variables is very important. The variables in this context include:

- **order** (allow,deny or deny,allow)
- **allow from** (all, full host name, domain name, partial IP address, or full IP address)
- **deny from** (all, full host name, domain name, partial IP address, or full IP address)
- **require** (user username, require valid-user, or require group groupname)

SSL.CFG

The SSL.CFG configuration file is used by the Secure Sockets Layer portion of the Web server and does not need to be manually edited. Information stored in this file includes the names of your site certificates, the level of SSL supported (2 or 3), and the number of clients that may be authenticated.

Familiarizing yourself with the preceding files is good practice for understanding the next section. The ability of your Web server to correctly identify and serve various file types depends upon the accuracy of your MIME.TYP configuration file, which has no graphical interface used for its maintenance. All the configuration tasks associated with this file must be made with a text editor.

MIME Management

The early days of the Web saw only a small number of file types being served to browsers, namely HTML documents, ASCII text files, and two types of image files, Graphics Interchange Format (GIF) files and Joint Photographic Experts Group (JPEG) files. Multimedia file formats such as QuickTime and Macromedia Director hadn't yet been invented, so there wasn't much need to worry about Web servers having to dish out multiple types of files.

Luckily for us, however, modern Web servers are programmed to use Multipurpose Internet Mail Extensions (MIME) as a means of delivering messages between Web servers and browsers. This allows information to flow freely between the two without users having to assist the browser when it receives a document, telling it what type of document it is, how many parts it comprises, and what helper application is required to view it if the browser itself isn't capable of reading it automatically.

Understanding MIME Types

In the early 1980s, there developed a need to extend the way e-mail servers and clients communicated with one another concerning the transmission of messages containing special characters. The 7-bit ASCII standard had become too limiting, and a new method of transmitting messages and attachments was needed. The MIME protocol was invented to overcome these limitations by creating a framework by which new types of e-mail message headers could be created. Header information is used by e-mail servers to communicate with one another. E-mail clients also use this information to receive messages and present them to the user in the correct manner. Early MIME specifications allowed for 8-bit characters and multipart messages to be delivered across the Internet.

Tip

See *http://www.oac.uci.edu/indiv/ehood/MIME/MIME.html* for more information on the history of MIME, as well as links to RFCs 1521 and 1522, which describe the technical specifications of MIME. If you have access to Usenet news, check out the comp.mail.mime newsgroup.

To effectively manage both your Web server and its contents, it is important that you understand the basics of MIME types and how they are used by the Novell Web Server, especially if you intend to use your Web server on an intranet. New document types are constantly springing up, and you won't be able to serve them if you don't know your MIME types.

There are seven different MIME types, and for every type there are multiple subtypes. The seven types describe the different forms a digital message may take, and the subtypes describe the dozens of examples these types represent. Table 22-1 illustrates the seven MIME types.

MIME Type	Description
Application	Describes a data format for an application, such as a word processor, usually in binary format.
Audio	Describes a data format for digital audio, such as AIFF.
Image	Describes a data format for a digital image, such as JPEG.
Message	Describes a data format for an encapsulated digital message, usually an e-mail message.
Multipart	Describes a format for two or more MIME types in the same message.
Text	Describes a data format for text, usually plain ASCII text.
Video	Describes a data format for digital video, such as MPEG.

Table 22-1: The seven MIME types.

Browser Configuration Issues

Not all MIME information is used by Web servers and browsers. Information that isn't used is simply ignored. The transaction between the two, as far as MIME information is concerned, goes like this:

1. A Web browser is configured to receive specific MIME information as part of a URL.

2. The browser requests a document from a Web server through a URL.

3. The Web server responds to the request and prefixes MIME information about the document prior to sending to the browser.

4. The browser receives the MIME information, processes it, and displays the document appropriately.

The HyperText Transfer Protocol borrows heavily from the protocols used by e-mail and Usenet news systems to transmit their data; the protocols are Simple Mail Transfer Protocol (SMTP) and Network News Transfer Protocol (NNTP), respectively. In all three of these protocols (HTTP, SMTP, and NNTP), the MIME-specific information is contained in a header message, which is seen by the end user. Information contained in the header includes the version of MIME being used (usually version 1.0), the MIME type and subtype of the document being transferred, the HTTP version used to make the transfer, and the character set and natural language of a text document (English, French, German, and so on).

Most Web browsers allow you to easily add, edit, and delete MIME types. Typically, they come preconfigured, but if you're a heavy user of the Web, you'll have to tinker with them at some point. To view MIME information in Navigator, for example, choose Options | General Preferences | Helpers and select an entry. Figure 22-1 shows the MIME configuration information used when receiving HTML documents. In this example, the default MIME type has been amended to allow documents ending in .ABS (an abbreviation for *abstract*) to be read by the browser as if they were HTML documents.

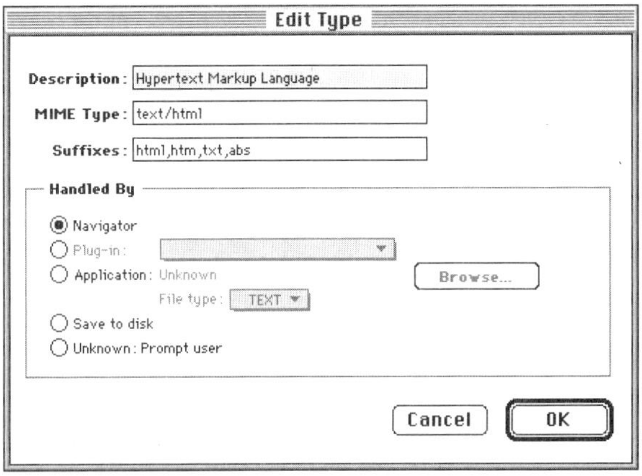

Figure 22-1: You may find it necessary to change a MIME type in your Web browser.

A common scenario on intranets is that multiple computer platforms must coexist peacefully—and gracefully, if possible—if they are to remain at all. Adding MIME information to browsers on your intranet must be completed before your Web server can serve new document types to your users. In Figure 22-2, for example, a Mac OS user needs to receive documents placed on the Rambell Web server by a UNIX programmer. To complicate matters, these files are in a compressed format. After deciding what helper application should be used to decompress the files, the systems administrator configures the Mac user's browser, in this case Microsoft's Internet Explorer, to use an application called StuffIt Expander to automatically decompress files downloaded from the Web server with the filename extension .Z.

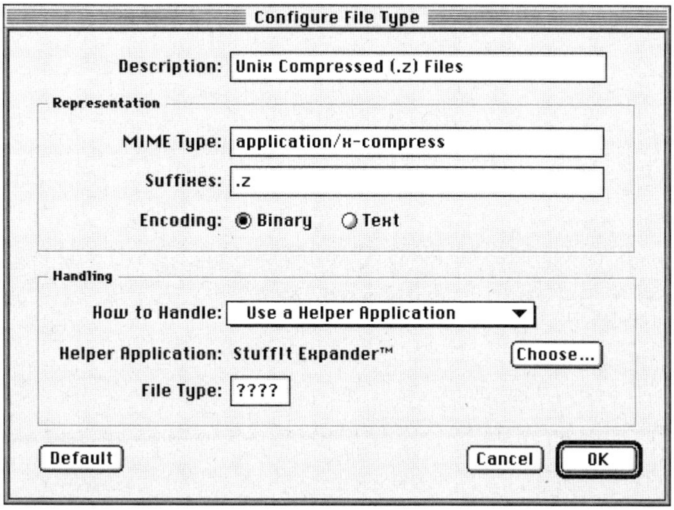

Figure 22-2: Adding a new MIME type to assist cross-platform communication.

The most important information you need to know about MIME and your Web server is contained in the MIME types configuration file.

MIME.TYP

The MIME types configuration file, MIME.TYP, is located in SYS:WEB\CONFIG by default. The location of this file is controlled by the TypesConfig directive in the HTTPD.CFG file, and the Web server must be able to find it upon startup. For every document type you wish to be able to serve, there must be an entry in the MIME type configuration file or the Web server will not function properly. The default MIME type is specified in the DefaultType directive of the server resource map file, SRM.CFG, and is usually text/plain or text/html. The directives in the MIME types configuration file are structured as follows, and the order in which the values appear is very important:

```
MIME type/MIME subtype    extensions
```

For example, the following directive allows you to serve QuickTime movies:

```
video/quicktime        qt mov
```

Tab spaces are allowed in this configuration file, and the possible filename extensions associated with an entry are separated by a single space. Table 22-2 lists the entries found in most MIME type configuration files.

MIME Type	Extension(s)
application/octet-stream	bin exe
application/oda	oda
application/pdf	pdf
application/postscript	ai eps ps
application/rtf	rtf
application/zip	zip
application/wordperfect	wp wpd
application/wordperfect6.0	wp5 w60
application/wordperfect6.1	w61
application/groupwise	vew
application/envoy	evy
audio/basic	au snd
audio/x-aiff	aif aiff aifc
audio/x-wav	wav
image/gif	gif
image/ief	ief
image/jpeg	jpeg jpg jpe
image/tiff	tiff tif
image/bmp	bmp
image/x-portable-bitmap	pbm
image/x-portable-graymap	pgm
image/x-portable-pixmap	ppm
image/x-rgb	rgb
text/html	html
text/html	htm
text/plain	txt
text/plain	bas
text/richtext	rtx
text/tab-separated-values	tsv
text/x-setext	etx
video/mpeg	mpeg mpg mpe
video/quicktime	qt mov
video/x-msvideo	avi
video/x-sgi-movie	movie
text/x-server-parsed-html	ssi

Table 22-2: The more common MIME types found in the MIME type configuration file.

Changing MIME Types

Your server's MIME type configuration file will need to be revised periodically to be able to serve new document types. To edit an existing entry or add a new one, follow these steps:

1. Locate the MIME type configuration file defined in the TypesConfig directive in the HTTPD.CFG configuration file, usually SYS:WEB\CONFIG.

2. Open the MIME.TYP file using a text editor.

3. Edit an entry by adding or changing the filename extensions, or add an entry on a new line.

4. Save the configuration file in the same location.

5. Restart the Web server.

For example, to add the ability to serve Macromedia Director movies from your Novell Web Server, you would add the following code to the MIME type configuration file:

```
application/x-director    dcr dir dxr
```

Of course, you will have to know the technical MIME type, subtype, and extension information for a type prior to editing the configuration file. There are two readily available sources to help you find information for this purpose, the hypertext version of RFC 1521 and 1522 located at http://www.oac.uci.edu/indiv/ehood/MIME/MIME.html, and your Web browser's helper application preferences.

File Management

File management is another common configuration task associated with managing a Web server in an intranet environment. Depending on the size of your intranet, the number of files on your Web server will range from a few hundred to tens of thousands. The default installation of NWS 3.0 places approximately 500 files on your server, and you are sure to add many more very quickly. It is very important that you keep track of these files as well as the files of those who use your server to publish on the Web both for personal reasons and in support of your company's mission. This section will offer you tips on reviewing files on your Web server and Webmaster etiquette to help you lay down ground rules for your users.

Reviewing Files

Periodically reviewing the files on your IntranetWare Web server is helpful to you, the Webmaster, users publishing on your Web server, and the Web server itself. Web servers require that documents be properly coded, located in specific locations, and appropriately named. HTML and HTTP are similar to other programming languages and TCP/IP protocols in that they require precision in syntax and configuration. Documents that are not properly coded, located, or named may suffer the following fates:

- Failure to be published by the Web server.
- Inability to be viewed by a Web browser.
- Increased security risk.
- Possible legal liability.

In addition to these concerns, what to do with all the old files on your Web server gives Webmasters something else to think about. Hard disk space is cheap these days, but not everyone can afford to keep unused files online.

Proper Coding

HTML documents are composed using a markup language rather than a true programming language. Markup languages consist of formatting instructions used by interpretive programs such as Web browsers to display information regarding formatted text, form entry fields, inline images, and other multimedia. Properly coded documents carry less risk of being improperly displayed, which decreases the effort you'll need to expend managing your Novell Web Server. Webmasters traditionally advertise their contact information, usually in the form of their e-mail address, as a means of inviting feedback from users to report broken links, bad images, and inaccessibility, not to mention poor taste in design. There are hundreds of Web sites that receive tens of thousands of "hits" per day, and Webmasters for these sites routinely receive dozens of messages per day from users reporting problems or soliciting assistance.

Webmasters should be aware of properly coded documents in at least three unique contexts to minimize unnecessary administrative work. First, the proper coding of an HTML document is important because it allows the document to be accurately displayed by visitors to your site. For example, Figure 22-3 shows an HTML document with multiple coding errors, each of which could generate problems for you. How many can you spot?

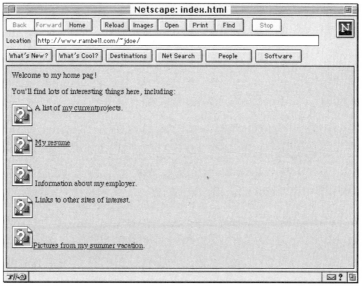

Figure 22-3: An improperly coded HTML document can have many consequences.

Hopefully, you spotted several coding errors. Did you notice all of these?

■ No information in the <TITLE></TITLE> tag.

■ A misspelled word.

■ Five broken images.

■ Inconsistent use of text alignment.

If you were to be able to review this document on the Web rather than in this printed version, you'd also find that the hyperlinks contain syntactical errors that prohibit them from properly linking to their intended destinations.

Next, improperly coded documents can divulge information you and your company would rather keep private. Sensitive documents and programs are frequently published unwittingly by Web content providers through hyperlinking mistakes and a lack of knowledge of HTML. When using SSL, for example, the only difference between a secure document and an insecure document can be the letter **s** in a hyperlink. In the three following lines of code, omitting the letter **s** could mean big trouble for someone in the Rambell organization:

```
<a href=shttp://www.rambell.com/payroll.html>
Payroll Database</a>

<a href=shttp://www.rambell.com/takeover.html>
Takeover Strategy</a>

<a href=shttp://www.rambell.com/bankruptcy.html>
Chapter 13 Records</a>
```

Because you are the Webmaster, these kinds of mistakes can have a negative impact on your career!

Finally, improperly coded documents can cause unnecessary security risks to the Web server itself. CGI scripts can perform a variety of tasks, including the wholesale erasure of files and directories. Today's Web servers include complex CGI scripts and applications that you can't possibly monitor at all times, so it is important that you thoroughly test these scripts as well as review the code used to create them. Programs that are written in languages such as BASIC and C are compiled into executable applications or NLMs, whereas CGI scripts are usually written in an interpreted language such as Perl. Scripts are easier to review for security concerns because you can easily read them. CGI applications, on the other hand, require that you see the source code. To ensure security for scripts you only need to open the code using a text editor. With applications, however, the safest route is to obtain the source code, review it, compile it yourself, and then thoroughly test it prior to allowing it to be used. You might also want to record the size and modification date of the application after it has been compiled and check periodically to ensure the same script is being used.

As the Webmaster, you are ultimately responsible for the documents served by your Web server. Take the necessary time and effort to ensure the accuracy of its content.

Proper Location

All the files on your Web server should be located in specific locations. Some Web servers are very uncaring about the location of documents, images, map files, configuration files, scripts, applications, and log files. In some cases, they may all be located in the same directory. Not so with the Novell Web Server. As you've seen in the Web Manager application and through discussion of configuration files, NWS is very sensitive about the locations of most files. The consequences of misplaced files include broken links, security risks, inoperable image maps, inaccurate MIME typing, and logging failures. The following list of directories will help you keep your documents in their proper locations.

SYS:ETC\

The SYS:\ETC\ directory contains a WEB.CFG file for each virtual Web server. The file is used to store the server's domain name, IP address, administrative password, number of threads used by the Web server, location of the product root, and name of the virtual Web server.

SYS:INW_WEB\

The SYS:INW_WEB\ directory is the default product root directory and contains the files and directories used when creating a new virtual server, including the default virtual server, *web*. This directory also contains a copy of the default HTML document for your Web server, INDEX.HTM, as well as a configuration file used by the SSL feature, SSLVER.CFG.

SYS:INW_WEB\SHARED\DOCS\

The SYS:INW_WEB\SHARED\DOCS\ directory contains the majority of documents—more than 300—that each virtual Web server comprises. Located in the DOCS directory are subdirectories for icons; a Java demo; LCGI files for the NDS browser, Net Basic, and the QuickFinder search engine; NetWare Web Server Performance Monitor files; and documents and images for the online publishing of administrative, QuickStart, and the Novell Web Server Dynamic Web Page Programmer guides.

SYS:INW_WEB\SHARED\LCGI\

The SYS:INW_WEB\SHARED\LCGI\ directory contains NLM and configuration files for the Web Server Monitor, NDS Browser, Net Basic, and QuickFinder search engines.

SYS:INW_WEB\SHARED\TEMPLATE\

The SYS:INW_WEB\SHARED\TEMPLATE\ directory contains copies of the main configuration files used by the virtual Web servers, including ACCESS.CFG, HTTPD.CFG, MIME.TYP, SRM.CFG, and SSL.CFG.

SYS:NETBASIC\NETBASIC\

The SYS:INW_WEB\SHARED\NETBASIC\ directory contains directories and files that support the Net Basic programming language.

SYS:PUBLIC\

The SYS:INW_WEB\SHARED\NETBASIC\ directory contains several dynamic link libraries (DLLs), help files, and Perl libraries.

SYS:\SYSTEM\

The SYS:SYSTEM\ directory contains more than a dozen NLMs that support many aspects of the Web server, including HTTP.NLM, KEYMGR.NLM, and TCPIP.NLM.

SYS:WEB\

The SYS:WEB\ directory contains about 100 files installed from the product root to create a virtual Web server. This directory serves as the server root directory for the default virtual server called *web*, including the following subdirectories:

- CONFIG\ (for the ACCESS.CFG, HTTPD.CFG, MIME.TYP, SRM.CFG, and SSL.CFG configuration files)
- DOCS\ (which serves as the document root for HTML documents and images, including Perl documents and SSL files)
- LOGS\ (for access and error log files)
- MAPS\ (for map files used to resolve URLs for clickable image maps)
- SCRIPTS\ (for CGI scripts, such as Perl scripts)

Misplaced documents, scripts, CGIs, and resources can cause your Web server to load improperly, to increase security risks, and more commonly, to return error messages such as the one shown in Figure 22-4. All of these situations will increase the amount of time you will spend administering your Web server.

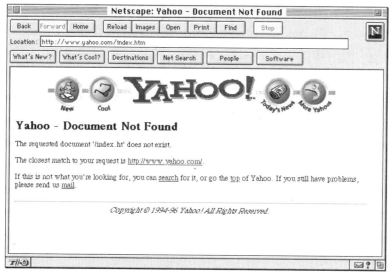

Figure 22-4: An improperly located document can cause you problems.

Proper Naming

Using proper document names is as equally important as their coding and location. Most of the files installed during the Web server installation process are automatically named and located in their proper locations. As users add content to your server, the likelihood that misnamed files will generate complaints will increase. Most filenaming mistakes are the result of using the wrong extension, which causes the server to be unable to deliver the document to a requesting browser. Table 22-3 lists the most common filename extensions and their associated file types.

Extension	File Type
AI, EPS, PS	PostScript
AIF, AIFF, AIFC	Audio-Audio Interchange File Format
AU, SND	Audio-basic
AVI	Movie-Video for Windows
BIN, EXE	Compressed file
BMP	Image: Windows Bitmap
GIF	Image: Graphics Interchange Format
HTM, HTML	HyperText Markup Language
JPEG, JPG, JPE	Image:Joint Photographic Experts Group
MPEG, MPG, MPE	Movie: Motion Picture Experts Group
PDF	Portable Document Format
QT, MOV	Movie: QuickTime
RTF	Rich Text Format
SSI	Secure Sockets Layer document
TIFF, TIF	Image: tiff
TXT	ASCII text
VEW	GroupWise
W61	WordPerfect6.1
WAV	Audio: Waveform Audio Format
WP, WPD	WordPerfect
WP5, W60	WordPerfect 5.0 or 6.0
ZIP	Compressed file

Table 22-3: Common file extensions and their associate file types.

Figure 22-5 shows another form of error message that visitors to your Web site may experience as a result of poorly named documents.

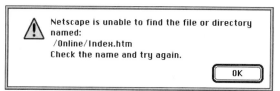

> ⚠ Netscape is unable to find the file or directory named:
> /Online/Index.htm
> Check the name and try again.
>
> [OK]

Figure 22-5: Improperly named documents will result in errors like this.

Old Files

Another aspect of file management to consider is what to do with all the files that are no longer relevant to the mission of your Web server. Web servers are designed to publish information, and the primary nature of information is its timeliness. Active Web sites generate hundreds or thousands of documents, and many of these documents will not have a very long shelf life. Periodically reviewing the content of your Web server for outdated documents will help make disk space available for other users and programs, as well as make the overall maintenance of your server an easier task. But what should you do with the old files? Your options are:

- Delete old files.
- Archive old files in case they are needed again.
- Create a placemarker for old files.

Do what is best for your organization when it comes to old or unused files, but it is a good idea to create a placemarker for pages that have either been removed or moved to another location. When someone looks for such a document, a placemarker will allow your visitors to receive a more informative error message than the standard "Error 404: File not found" message. How helpful is that? Figure 22-6 shows an example of a placemarker, which can be copied, moved, and renamed to take the place of documents that are no longer available on your Web server.

Figure 22-6: Creating a placemarker will help visitors to your site find the information they need.

File Management Etiquette

Managing the system files for a Web server is one task, but managing the files of your users is quite another story. A Webmaster is a type of systems administrator, and managing people is part of the job. In addition to checking up on the coding, location, and naming of files on your Web server, there are two other considerations to keep in mind when it comes to managing those who publish on your server.

Restricting Server Space

IntranetWare allows the systems administrator to restrict the amount of disk space for users. Since a user's personal directory is located in their home directory, it's easy to keep track of where their files are located, but the only effective way to track how much space they are using is through the Administrator utility. It is a good idea to restrict disk space because publishing on the Web is very storage-space intensive. Image and other multimedia files can be enormous, and one of the most insidious habits of Web publishers is to never throw away unwanted image files, such as buttons, backgrounds, and navigational icons. Make a disk space limit part of your standard operating procedure.

Acceptable Use Policy

Many large organizations have found it necessary to publish an acceptable use policy for their Web servers. The Web is a powerful medium for publishing, not to mention extremely accessible to the general public. The Web offers an easy means for just about anyone to present their thoughts, images, and dirty laundry to the world. Having an acceptable use policy is important because it places the expectation of responsible behavior on those who use your server, which will reduce the likelihood of an administrative showdown with your users. When creating an acceptable use policy, consider the following points:

- Whether or not users can publish materials not relating to the primary mission of the organization.

- The amount of traffic and disk space personal Web pages may utilize before server performance constraints become an issue.

- Whether or not users can promote goods or services for personal profit.

- The tone of personal Web pages, and whether or not they conflict with the corporate image.

Many users have come to expect limitations when publishing on corporate intranets, so to avoid confusion and make your administrative efforts run smoothly, post your company's acceptable use policy in an obvious place on your Web site. You'll save yourself a lot of trouble by investing in such as policy.

Logging

Your Web server records all the transactions that occur between the server and browsers requesting connections. You can use the log files generated by the server to monitor the following aspects of your server:

- The IP numbers or domain names of users accessing your server.

- The time and date of each transaction.

- The documents being requested.

- Whether or not a request was fulfilled.

- The size of the documents served.

You can gain valuable insight from the information contained in the log files, including:

- The most and least commonly requested files on your server.
- The frequency of requests, including peak access periods.
- Possible server or document access errors.
- Attempts to gain unauthorized access to your system.

The frequency with which you monitor your log files depends on whether you are monitoring the server's performance or troubleshooting a problem that may have been reported by a user. Analyzing your log files can give you vital information on your server's performance and assist you as you fine-tune your server by making configuration changes. Knowing access times and load data is crucial to configuring your server to perform at its best. You should also analyze your log files if users report problems relating to the failure of the server to deliver documents or process other requests. The status portion of each log entry will tell you if errors are present, and you'll have a good starting point to correct the problem.

Location & Settings

Two log files are generated by your Web server, ACCESS.LOG and ERROR.LOG. These files are generated for each virtual Web server and are located in the LOGS directory under the server root, the default being SYS:WEB\LOGS\. You may choose a different location for your log files by using the Web Manager program or by editing the HTTPD.CFG file located in SYS:\DOS\CONFIG\. To change the location of the log files using the Web Manager program, follow these steps:

1. Launch the Web Manager program as described in the previous chapter and select a virtual server.

2. Select the Server tab.

3. Edit the Directory Containing Log File field with the new location, using either the full path or a path relative to the virtual Web server's server root directory.

4. Restart the Web server.

Alternatively, you can manually edit the HTTPD.CFG file and change the following directives using a path relative to the server root directory:

```
TransferLog logs/access.log
ErrorLog logs/error.log
```

Several log configuration options are available that allow you to control the size of the log files and whether or not the files are archived or if they just roll over to the same filename. To edit the configuration options, follow these steps:

1. Open the Web Manager program as described in the previous chapter and select a virtual server.

2. Choose Log | Log File Handling from within the Web Manager program and the dialog box shown in Figure 22-7 will open.

3. In the Log File Handling section, select whether or not to roll log files.

4. If you opt to roll log files, in the Maximum Log Size field, choose the maximum size (in kilobytes) of a log file before it is either archived or rolled over.

5. In the Maximum Number of Old Logs field, select the maximum number of log files the server will store before deleting the oldest log files and creating new files.

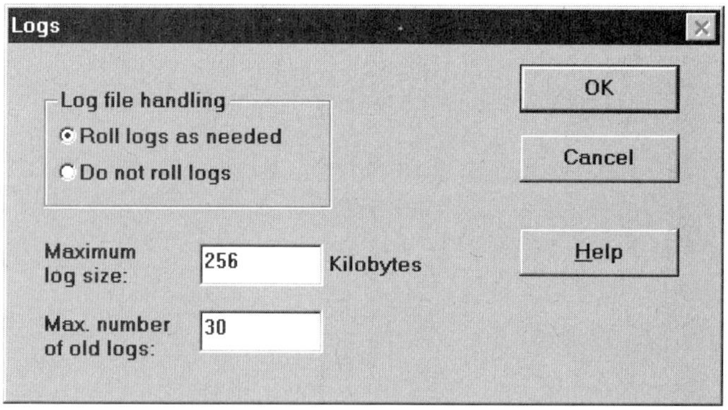

Figure 22-7: Configuring logging options for a virtual Web server.

By default, both the ACCESS.LOG and ERROR.LOG files record the requesting browser's IP address instead of domain name. You may change the Web server's configuration to use domain names instead by either DNS or the HOSTS file, whichever method is used by your server. To use DNS for name resolution, follow these steps:

1. Open the SYS:ETC\RESOLV.CFG file using a text editor.

2. Enter the following information:

   domain *domain_name*

   nameserver *IP_address*

3. Restart the Web server.

For example, on the Rambell server the RESOLV.CFG file would have the following information, where *domain_name* is the fully qualified domain name and *IP_address* is the IP number of the DNS server:

```
domain rambell.com
nameserver 123.4.5.67
```

To use the HOSTS file for name resolution instead of DNS, follow these steps:

1. Open the SYS:ETC\HOSTS file using a text editor.

2. Enter the following information:

   IP_address hostname alias

3. Restart the Web server.

For example, on the Rambell server the HOSTS file would have the following information, where *IP_address* is the IP number of the Web server, *hostname* is the domain name of the Web server, and *alias* is the short name (or alias) of the domain name:

```
123.4.5.60 www.rambell.com www
```

ACCESS.LOG

The ACCESS.LOG file logs transactional information for each access to your Web server. Figure 22-8 shows a section of the ACCESS.LOG file for the Rambell Web server.

Figure 22-8: A sample section of an ACCESS.LOG file.

Each log entry contains several pieces of information, with one entry for each transaction. The communication between a Web browser and Web server is said to be *stateless*, which means that the client and server only communicate when a request is sent by the client and the server replies. Other TCP/IP-based protocols use a *stateful* means of communication, where the client and server pass information back and forth on a more continuous basis. Because of this stateless relationship, the HTTP protocol must issue a separate request for each file or image. This means that a Web page containing four inline images will require a total of five requests to the Web server. Therefore, your ACCESS.LOG files will log every request for every HTML document and every image, which can cause the files to become quite large very quickly. The following is a description of each element of the first line of Figure 22-8:

- 152.3.202.140
  The requesting user's IP address.

- [04/Jan/1997:14:53:29-0500]
  The date and time of the request.

- "GET Online/oview/images/logo24.gif? HTTP/1.0"
  The HTTP method of request (usually GET, HEAD, or POST), the path to the requested document, and the HTTP version used by the requesting browser.

- 304
  The HTTP version 1.0 result code.

- 0
  The size of the file (in kilobytes) requested by the browser.

HTTP Version & Status Codes

All of the elements of a log entry should be easily understood, with the exception of the HTTP version information and HTTP status codes. The HTTP version is almost always version 1.0 or 1.1. There are a few UNIX-based Web servers out there that use version .9x, but since most Web servers in use today are running server software less than two to four years old, they use a more modern version.

The three-digit HTTP result code indicates whether or not the Web server was able to honor the browser's request. There are several categories of result codes, with the first digit indicating the category and the last two digits identifying the status. Table 22-4 explains the status codes used by NWS 3.0 and HTTP 1.0.

Result Code	Explanation
1xx	Not used at this time.
200	Success. The browser's request was fulfilled.
201	Created. The browser's request to create a new resource was accepted.
202	Accepted. The browser's request has been accepted.
204	No content. The browser's request has been fulfilled, but no new data was returned to the browser.
300	Redirection. The browser's request was received, but additional processing is required to complete the request.
301	Moved permanently. The document requested by the browser has been permanently moved and a new URL for the document has been returned to the browser for the user to act upon.
302	Moved temporarily. The document requested by the browser has been temporarily moved, but the browser should still use the current URL.
304	Not modified. The document has been requested using a modified GET command, which asks the server to return a file only if it has changed in size or modification date since the last request.
400	Illegal request. The browser's request is not valid.
401	Unauthorized request. The browser requesting the document has not yet been authorized to request the document.
403	Forbidden. The browser requesting the document will not be authorized to request the document.

Result Code	Explanation
404	Not found. The requested document cannot be found.
500	Server error. The browser's request cannot be honored because of an internal error.
501	Not implemented. The browser's request cannot be honored because the server cannot perform the required task.
502	Bad gateway. The browser's request cannot be completed because the Web server, acting as a gateway to an external service, is unable to connect to the external service hosting the requested document.
503	Service unavailable. The browser's request cannot be fulfilled because of a temporary server error.

Table 22-4: HTTP 1.0 status codes used by NWS 3.0.

ERROR.LOG

The ERROR.LOG log file logs the errors encountered by your Web server while it is responding to requests from Web browsers. Periodically reviewing this file can help you find various problems relating to the documents or services on the server before they become public knowledge. Figure 22-9 shows a section of the ERROR.LOG file for the Rambell Web server.

```
Error log for web                                                    _ □ X
[Sat Jan 11 23:37:58 1997] Access to sys:web/docs/docs.html failed for 152.3.202.140, reason: file does not exist
[Sat Jan 11 23:38:05 1997] Access to sys:web/docs/letters.html failed for 152.3.202.140, reason: file does not exist
[Sat Jan 11 23:38:14 1997] Access to sys:web/docs/brad.html failed for 152.3.202.140, reason: file does not exist
[Sat Jan 11 23:38:20 1997] Access to sys:web/docs/ellen.html failed for 152.3.202.140, reason: file does not exist
[Sat Jan 11 23:38:29 1997] Access to sys:web/docs/michael.html failed for 152.3.202.140, reason: file does not exist
[Sat Jan 11 23:39:47 1997] Access to sys:web/docs/dan.html failed for 152.3.202.140, reason: file does not exist
[Sat Jan 11 23:39:53 1997] Access to sys:web/docs/ben.html failed for 152.3.202.140, reason: file does not exist
[Sat Jan 11 23:39:59 1997] Access to sys:web/docs/ghosts.html failed for 152.3.202.140, reason: file does not exist
[Sat Jan 11 23:40:04 1997] Access to sys:web/docs/ctd.html failed for 152.3.202.140, reason: file does not exist
[Sat Jan 11 23:40:10 1997] Access to sys:web/docs/works.html failed for 152.3.202.140, reason: file does not exist
[Sat Jan 11 23:40:14 1997] Access to sys:web/docs/worms.html failed for 152.3.202.140, reason: file does not exist
[Sat Jan 11 23:40:25 1997] Access to sys:web/docs/shuffled.html failed for 152.3.202.140, reason: file does not exist
```

Figure 22-9: A sample section of an ERROR.LOG file.

Unlike the ACCESS.LOG file, ERROR.LOG file entries are made only if a browser's request cannot be fulfilled by the Web server. The following is a description of each element of the first line of Figure 22-9:

- [Sat Jan 11 23:37:58 1997]
  The date and time of the request (slightly different than in ACCESS.CFG).

- Access to sys:web/docs/docs.html failed for 152.3.202.140,
  The path to the requested document based on the server root of the virtual Web server and the IP address of the requesting browser.

- Reason: file does not exist.
  This explains why the error occurred. The reason for an error could be anything in the 4xx or 5xx result codes listed in Table 22-4, but the most common error is 404, file not found.

Saving, Clearing & Printing

Having an archived copy of your log files is a good idea, and the Web Manager program offers two options: save the log files to another filename or print a log file. It's probably best to save log files rather than print them because log files can become quite large, but you may need to use the print option for a selected log file. You may also clear a log file from the Web Manager program. To save, clear, or print a log file, follow these steps:

1. Start the Web Manager program as outlined in the previous chapter.

2. Select a virtual Web server.

3. Select a server or virtual host log from the Log menu.

4. To save the file to another filename, choose Log | Save Log As.

5. To clear the log file (erase the log, but not delete the file itself), choose Log | Clear Log.

6. To print the log file, choose File | Print.

Moving On

While the default Web server installation provides a basic level of configuration upon installation, you'll want to tweak your server's configuration to suit the needs of your intranet. The default configuration is easily modified via the Web Manager program, but a working knowledge of the server's configuration files, content, and logging options give you more opportunities to provide powerful Web services. Whereas the first generation of intranets offered only basic Web services, today's intranets must be capable of providing advanced security. In the next chapter, we'll show you how the Rambell Web server can be enhanced to provide secure HTML services using Secure Sockets Layer and basic password security.

23

SSL & Web Server Security

Providing secure documents from a Web server is an essential component of today's intranets. First-generation Web servers were not nearly as secure as today's servers, primarily because there wasn't a need for a secure environment. Their content was not about commercial enterprise; instead it was about sharing basic information, such as product descriptions, company profiles, personal home pages, and a whole lot of HTML documents not considered to be mission critical. However, as companies moved to the Web as a medium for conducting business, Web security has become *the* most important issue for Webmasters and intranet managers.

In two major ways, Novell Web Server 3.0 offers an extremely secure environment for conducting business transactions. First, it provides support for Secure Sockets Layer 3, the industry standard for providing a secure environment for Web browsers and Web servers to share information. Next, NWS 3.0 leverages the NetWare Directory Services built into the core network operating system to provide authentication and password protection to its files and directories. By creating usernames and passwords, you can extend the level of authentication NDS users get to other users as well.

In this chapter, we'll cover everything you'll need to know about the Secure Sockets Layer technology, how to restrict access to your server to protect its contents, and how to configure your users' browsers to provide the highest level of security possible.

Secure Sockets Layer

Secure Sockets Layer (SSL) is a security protocol developed by Netscape Communications Corporation to create a secure environment in which Web browsers and servers can communicate and share sensitive, or potentially sensitive, information. There is a need for this type of ability because the Web, and the Internet, are inherently unsecure environments. There have been several versions of SSL used on the Web, with each successive version offering increased levels of security and features. At the time of this writing, the current version of SSL is SSL 3, which is fully supported by Novell Web Server 3.0.

Tip

> *The Web, and the Internet, are inherently unsecure environments, and to provide a secure environment for your intranet, you should enable the Secure Sockets Layer ability of your Novell Web Server.*

Web Security Issues

To many IS managers and administrators, there may not be an apparent need for increased Web security because most Web servers are not "hacked," especially those that are not UNIX-based. Web servers that are UNIX-based are often the most vulnerable for attack because of their dependence on user and root accounts that are accessible over networks or the Internet and that allow command-line operation. An enterprising criminal can easily "sniff" packets that cross the network, wait for an unencrypted password to go by, and use this information to illegally log in and compromise the computer's integrity. Novell networks generally do not lend themselves to this type of situation because they do not use a command line interface or the Telnet access protocol, and are therefore often more secure than UNIX-based systems.

Why then, exactly, would you need to use SSL on your Web server? There are several reasons, including:

- ■ To prevent someone from masquerading as an authentic user of your Web site.

- ■ To prevent someone from modifying the data on your Web server.

- ■ To prevent unwanted users or computers from listening in on transactions between your users and Web servers.

Another good, but less tangible, reason to use SSL is to promote confidence in the use of your Web site. AT&T, for example, uses SSL to serve not only sensitive documents, but an entire Web site. Figure 23-1 shows the secure version of the AT&T home page.

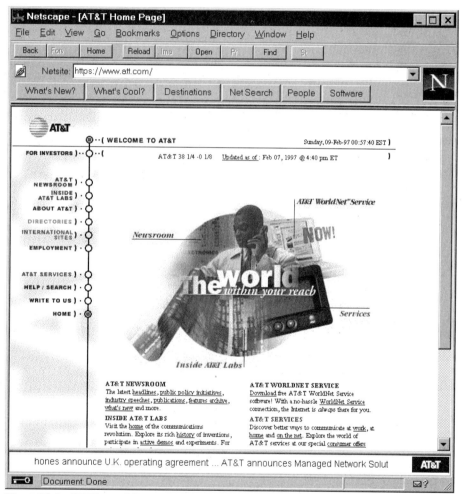

Figure 23-1: AT&T uses SSL to serve not just sensitive documents, but an entire Web site.

There are several ways you know you are visiting a site that has implemented SSL, and the actual number of hints depends on which Web browser you are using. Most full-featured browsers, such as Netscape Navigator, offer several visual clues in addition to warnings when you are about to enter or submit documents to a secure server. Figure 23-2 highlights the following three major visual signs indicating the use of SSL on the AT&T home page:

■ The use of HTTPS in the URL instead of HTTP.

■ The use of a blue bar across the top of the page.

■ An unbroken security key in the lower left-hand corner of the page.

Figure 23-2: Three visual indicators of SSL.

Tip

See Netscape's On Internet Security Web page at http://home.netscape.com/info/ security-doc.html for more information on security issues as they relate to the Internet and Netscape Navigator.

Depending on how Navigator's security preferences have been configured, a visitor may optionally have a warning dialog, shown in Figure 23-3, displayed every time he or she enters a Web site protected by SSL.

In addition to these hints and warnings, visitors to your secure Web site may also view information concerning a document's security by clicking on the security key. Figure 23-4 shows two possible responses by your Web server, unsecure and secure, superimposed over one another.

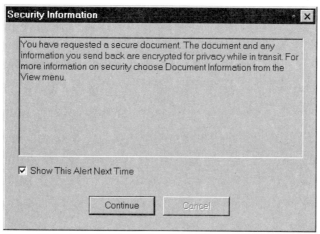

Figure 23-3: An optional warning dialog informs a visitor to your site that SSL has been enabled.

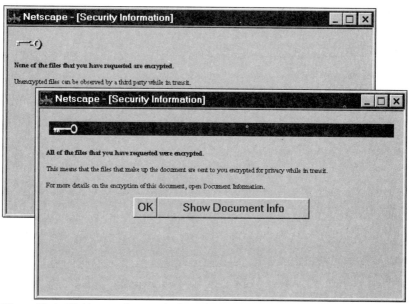

Figure 23-4: Clicking on the security key of any document view in Navigator reveals security information for that document.

Clicking on the Show Document Info button links the visitor's browser to the same information found in the View | Document Info menu option. Figure 23-5 shows the security information for the RSA Data Security home page.

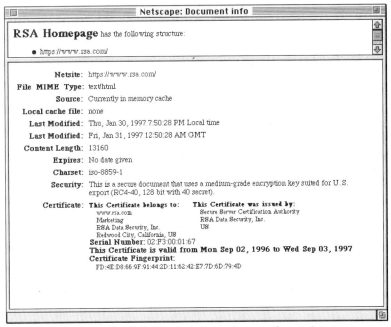

Figure 23-5: Viewing detailed information on a document's security status.

The Document Info dialog box contains the nitty-gritty details of a document's security status as well as a good amount of its general content. There are two parts to the Document Info dialog box in Figure 23-5; the security information is in the lower half. The fields in this section contain the following information:

- The document's URL.

- The MIME type used by the Web server to serve the document.

- The source of the document, either in memory or disk cache.

- The document's modification date and time.

- The size of the document in bytes.

- The expiration date as defined in an optional header tag.

- The character set used by the server to deliver the document.

- The level of security protecting the document, measured by the strength of the key used to encrypt the document. Domestic SSL servers are permitted by law to use 128-bit encryption, but export versions of SSL are only permitted to use 40-bit encryption. Figure 23-5 shows the use of a middle ground of encryption strength: 128-bit with only 40 bits used to secure the document, which is suitable for export outside the United States.

- Certificate information (described in detail in the next section).

Site Certificates & Keys

Site Certificates and keys are the most important concepts regarding the use of SSL on your intranet. Site Certificates are issued by trusted third parties for use with a specific Web server as a means of validating and uniquely identifying that Web server on the Internet. The exchange of keys between a Web server and a browser enable secure client-server transactions. The keys are used to encrypt and decrypt data transmitted between the server and browser, thereby protecting the data from misuse. The following sections outline the concepts of Site Certificates and keys as they relate to the Web and SSL.

Tip

For more information on the protocols used by Navigator to provide secure transactions, see Netscape's The SSL Protocol page at http://home.netscape.com/newsref/std/SSL.html.

Site Certificates

Site Certificates, electronic documents that are made available to visitors of your Web server, are issued by third-party organizations called Certificate Authorities (CAs). A CA investigates requests for Site Certificates to confirm that the requesting site is a legitimate entity, and if so, will issue a Site Certificate for a fee. The Site Certificate consists of your Web server's public key (discussed in the following section), information concerning your organization, an expiration date, and a digital signature belonging to the organization that has issued the Site Certificate.

In Figure 23-5, you can see the certificate-related information in the bottom third of the figure. The certificate provides information on:

- Ownership of the certificate itself, including the organization's name and address.
- The serial number of the certificate, which is used as part of the validation process.
- The period of time for which the certificate is valid.
- A certificate fingerprint, also used as part of the validation process.
- What CA issued the certificate.

While there are multiple CAs doing business on the Internet, the most popular company at this time is VeriSign, which is also the only company that has produced Site Certificates for use with Netscape products. To see which CAs are recognized by the Navigator Web browser, choose Options | Security Preferences | Site Certificates and select a certificate to view and edit. Figure 23-6 shows the information for RSA.

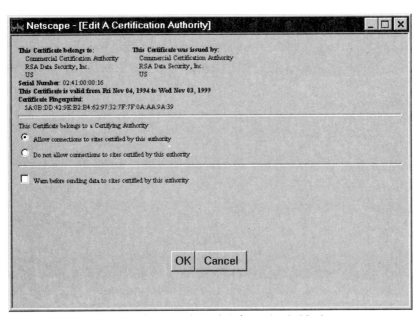

Figure 23-6: Viewing a Certificate Authority's information in Navigator.

The information contained in a CA's certificate is similar to the information viewed in Figure 23-5, but the Edit a Certification Authority dialog not only allows you to view this information, you can change several settings as well.

For each CA, you may choose to not make connections to Web sites certified by this CA, to allow a connection without a warning, or to be warned before making a connection to a Web site (and you can make these choices for each CA).

Public & Private Keys

The second important component to providing SSL on your intranet's Web server is the use of encryption keys, which allow the encryption and decryption of data once a server has been authenticated by a CA. SSL uses encryption keys much in the same way you use a key to unlock a door; only one key will unlock the door and permit entry. On the Web, data is encrypted to prevent someone who may have the ability to monitor or capture data from ever being able to read it.

Key encryption uses mathematical algorithms to scramble data, such as an HTML document, using two or more keys. Each key represents part of the formula required to decipher the scrambled message, and the strength of the encryption depends on the size of these keys measured in bits. The larger the number of bits used to create the encryption algorithm, the longer it will take a computer to crack the code and decipher the data.

SSL uses a two-key encryption scheme, with a public key and a private key. Data that is encrypted using one of these keys can only be deciphered with the other. Web servers using SSL retain the private key, information about which is never transmitted across a network, but freely give out the public key to any Web browser requesting an SSL connection. To increase the level of security, a new key, called a symmetric key, is created for each SSL connection based on the public and private keys. This makes it nearly impossible for someone monitoring a network to be able to decrypt any information because the encryption scheme is constantly being changed.

How SSL Works

SSL is probably the most complicated aspect of providing Web services for an intranet. Before enabling SSL on your Novell Web Server, let's go through the steps of a single SSL connection so you'll have a better idea of what is involved.

1. A Web browser requests a secure connection from a Web server using HTTPS instead of HTTP in the URL.

2. The Web server, which must be running SSL, checks the information sent by the browser to see if it includes information about CAs, and if it does, checks to see if any of the CAs, such as VeriSign, is recognized by the server.

3. The server sends its certificate to the browser, which either accepts or rejects the server's connection.

4. If the browser and server agree on a CA, the server's public key is sent to the browser.

5. The browser and server exchange information about encryption keys to negotiate the strongest level of encryption.

6. The server then delivers the requested URL.

Enabling SSL

Since enabling SSL is not a free option, you will need to decide whether or not you really need to provide SSL through your intranet's Web server prior to enabling and configuring SSL. Chances are, however, that you will need to provide SSL if your company's intranet will be used in any significant way. There are many steps involved in providing SSL, and you should plan to take several days to complete the process, which includes three main steps:

■ Requesting a Site Certificate

■ Installing a Site Certificate

■ Configuring SSL

Before you begin, however, there's just one more question you need to answer: How many Site Certificates will you need? Although you may have only one physical Web server, you may have multiple virtual servers, and although it is possible to use one Site Certificate for all these servers, you shouldn't do so. You will need a unique Site Certificate for:

■ Each virtual Web server

■ Each unique domain, if multihoming is used

■ Each company served by your server if you are hosting other's Web servers

Requesting a Site Certificate

The first major step toward providing SSL is requesting a Site Certificate from a Certifying Authority such as VeriSign, the cost for which at the time of this writing is under $300 (U.S.). However, you must first prepare a bit to be able to submit your request for a certificate. You'll need to create a new key database file and then create a signing request for the certificate.

Tip

See the Entrust home page at http://www.entrust.com for a free sample certificate for demonstration purposes.

Creating a Key Database File   Before you can submit your application for a Site Certificate, you must first use the Novell Web Server's Key Manager program (KEYMGR.NLM) to generate a file that contains important information about your public and private keys and their certificates. These are the keys that, when combined, allow data to be encrypted and properly decrypted. To generate this information, follow these steps:

1. From either the server console or Rconsole, execute the Key Manger program by executing the following command:

   load keymgr

2. In the spaces provided in the Key Manager program, type the path and filename of your key database file; then press the Enter or Return key twice to enter a password, as shown in Figure 23-7. Be sure to name your key file with no more than eight characters and without an extension; press the Esc key to exit and save your options.

Figure 23-7: Generating a key database file.

Keep the password in a secure location, as it will be required to modify the keys and certificates, and it will be used by the Web Manager program.

Creating a Certificate Signing Request   The next step in the process of requesting a Site Certificate is to create what is known as a Certificate Signing Request. This document contains information unique to your Web server, including your server's public and private keys. Your private key never leaves your server, but the public key is submitted as part of the Certificate Signing Request. To generate this information:

1. Load the Key Manager program as described in the previous section.

2. Enter the path, filename, and password for the key database file as described in the previous section. Press Esc and then choose Yes.

3. Select the KeyPair Generation/Certificate Request option and then press Enter.

4. Choose a Certificate Authority such as VeriSign and press the Enter key.

5. Type the letter **Y** in the field named New Certificate, press the Enter key, press Esc, and then select Yes.

6. Next, type in your server's common name, such as www.rambell.com, which is the same name used in a URL to access your Web server's default home page.

7. Enter all the information asked by Key Manager, including company name and contact information. When complete, press Esc and select Yes.

8. Review the information, make any necessary changes, press Y when asked if the information is correct, and then press Esc and Yes.

9. Document the location and filename of the certification request file along with the password for future reference.

After generating the Certificate Signing Request, you need to begin filling out the online form. Open your browser to https://digitalid.verisign.com/ss_intro.html and read the information. You will be asked the following questions or required to perform the following tasks:

1. Generate a Certificate Signing Request, outlined in the previous set of steps.

2. Copy and paste information from the file created by the Key Manager program into the online Web registration form. Find the file generated by the Key Manager and open it using your Web browser or text editor. It will look something like this:

```
Webmaster: webmaster@www.rambell.com
Phone : 919-123-4567
Server : www.rambell.com
```

```
Common-Name : www.rambell.com
Organization Unit : Rambell Incorporated
Organization : Information Technology
Locality : Durham
State : NC
Country : US

----BEGIN NEW CERTIFICATE REQUEST----
MIIBSzCB9gIBADCBkDELMAkGA1UEBhMCVVMxCzAJBgNVBAgTAk5DMQ8wDQYDVQQH
EwZEdXJoYW0xGDAWBgNVBAoTDOR1a2UgVW5pdmVyc210eTEpMCcGA1UECxMgT2Zm
aWN1IG9mIE1uZm9ybWF0aW9uIFR1Y2hub2xvZ3kxHjAcBgNVBAMTFWRhbW9jjbGVz
Lm9pdC5kdWt1LmVkdTBcMA0GCSqGSIb3DQEBAQUAA0sAMEgCQQC6RSFZXLh3Qkva

PyeVUDmOgtf8dsf+YuCVONfLWZqlFTQH7S2svtlCJDsxV1DkZn+xFm8SRfoxSG7Y
6CkAE1LZAgMBAAGgADANBgkqhkiG9w0BAQQFAANBAHz/ePrMW8hDiOhmVVnFMLgb
uu58uBO/ib9TYYtGJCNiFjNYI6Akc4tPrgKIgH3cbjGe185FVQhEOFp5hT4Pc4g=
----END NEW CERTIFICATE REQUEST----
```

3. Copy only the information between (and including) the BEGIN/END NEW CERTIFICATE lines, and paste it into the text area provided, as shown in Figure 23-8. Then click Continue.

4. Choose Novell Web Server from a drop-down list of Web servers that support SSL.

5. Provide a challenge phrase, in case you need to call VeriSign for help if you lose your keys or if you believe your certificate has been compromised. A challenge phrase can be any word or phrase (without punctuation) that is meaningful to you, but not easily guessed (such as your mother's maiden name or your father's birthplace).

6. Provide contact information for an authorized representative of your organization.

7. Provide information on how you will pay for the certificate.

8. Provide a Dun & Bradstreet (DUNS) business number. If you do not have a DUNS, you will be required to fax or mail additional information as proof of your company's existence. See the Web page for details.

Once you have gone online and submitted this information, the Site Certificate (also referred to as a Digital ID) will be e-mailed to you or the contact person named in the request.

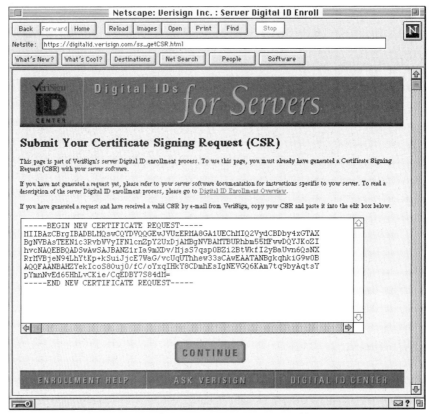

Figure 23-8: Submitting a Certificate Signing Request to VeriSign.

Installing Your Site Certificate

Once you have received your Site Certificate, you are ready to move on to the second step, installing it. Your certificate will probably arrive in the form of an e-mail message or may be retrieved from a secure Web site, and it will be saved in the form of a text file on your IntranetWare server. Follow these steps to install your Site Certificate:

1. Load the Key Manager program as described earlier, specifying a path and filename for your key database file.

2. Press the Esc key and select Yes, as directed by the onscreen instructions. The Key Manager program will search the key file for certificates and load the Key Database File Menu, as shown in Figure 23-9.

Figure 23-9: Using the Key Manager to install a Site Certificate.

3. Select Install Certificate from the menu and answer the following questions:

- **Certificate Chain.** Answer Yes if your certificate instructions indicate this particular certificate is part of a chain. The default is No.

- **Install Certificate.** Answer Yes.

- **Trusted Root.** A Trusted Root represents a Web server whose certificates are given an added level of trust by a browser. By default, only RSA's Low Assurance CA, RSA's Commercial CA, and RSA's Security Server CA are Trusted Roots, so unless you are instructed to do so, answer No to this question.

- **Location of Certificate to Install.** Type in the path and filename of the certificate to be installed, which should normally be found in the same directory as the key file database.

4. Press the Esc key and choose Yes to complete the installation process. You will be alerted when the installation has been completed.

Configuring SSL

The final step in being able to provide SSL with Novell Web Server is to configure SSL through the Web Manager program. Once you have requested and installed a Site Certificate, you must tell the Web server what port is used for SSL, what levels of SSL are to be supported, and several other pieces of information. The first step is to locate the key database file for a virtual Web server:

1. Launch the Web Manager program, as described in Chapter 21.

2. Choose Options | Set Key Database File and either enter the path to the file or select the Browse button to locate the file, as shown in Figure 23-10.

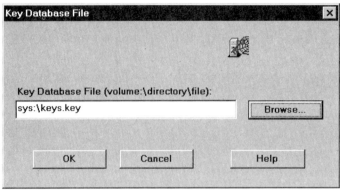

Figure 23-10: You must select a key database file prior to enabling SSL for a virtual Web server.

3. When prompted, enter the password for the key database file and choose Restart. You must also know the password to restart the Web server.

Tip

You must know the passwords for, and restart, both the key database file and the Web server before enabling SSL.

Once the key database file has been properly selected, you may proceed to enable SSL for a virtual Web server:

1. Choose a virtual Web server for which SSL is to be enabled. Remember, if you have only a single virtual Web server it will be called simply *web*. Refer to Chapter 21 for instructions on how to select a virtual Web server.

2. Choose the Interface tab and select the Enable SSL check box, as shown in Figure 23-11 below. If you have not yet completed the selection of the key database, you will be unable to proceed until doing so.

Figure 23-11: Enabling SSL for the default virtual Web server, web.

3. The default port for SSL is 443 instead of 80, which is used by HTTP. You may manually edit the Port field if needed.

4. Select the IP addresses that are to be used for this virtual Web server, if you have more than one IP address bound to your IntranetWare's network interface card. The default address of * will not need to be edited unless you have more than one IP address in use.

5. Click the Security Options button.

6. In the Security Options dialog, shown in Figure 23-12, select a Site Certificate to configure from the drop-down list. If you only have a single certificate installed, it will be called Default, as in Figure 23-12.

7. Select which levels of SSL you want to enable. The default is both SSL 2.0 and 3.0.

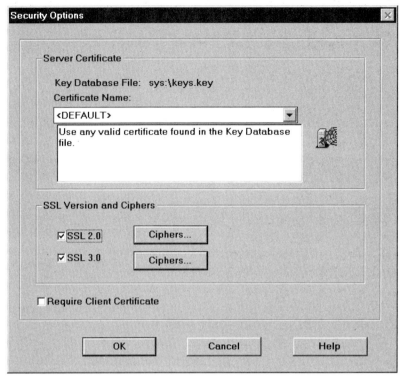

Figure 23-12: Configuring a Site Certificate's SSL for a virtual Web server.

Tip

Which levels of SSL should you enable? A good rule of thumb is to enable both SSL 2.0 and 3.0 to ensure older browsers that don't support SSL 3.0 can still take advantage of your secure Web server.

8. Click on the Ciphers buttons to review the levels of encryption a version of SSL supports. When a browser requests a secure connection, it sends a listing of the ciphers it is capable of supporting, and the Web server will choose the most secure form of encryption that can be mutually supported by both browser and server. Figure 23-13 shows the cipher information for SSL 3.0.

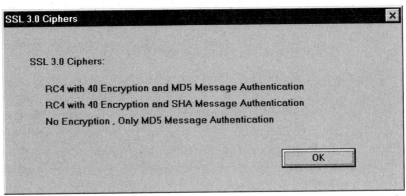

Figure 23-13: Review the levels of encryption a version of SSL supports for a virtual Web by clicking on the Ciphers button.

9. Finally, check the Require Client Certificate check box (see Figure 23-12) if you want the Web server to request client authentication before allowing a connection (described in detail in "Browser Configuration" later in this chapter).

Your NetWare Web Server is now ready to serve secure documents using the SSL protocol. Be sure to rest your Web server before making this service available to your users. You can test your server by opening a browser that uses SSL, such as Navigator 2.x or higher, and entering the URL for the server's default home page using HTTPS instead of HTTP.

Restricting Access

Many intranet environments require that portions of a Web server be restricted for departmental or special use. Next to using Secure Sockets Layer, the second best method of providing secure access to your Web server is through the use of your NetWare Web Server's built-in access controls. NetWare Web Server 3.0 provides two methods of access control:

■ Global access restrictions, based on entries in your Web server's global access control file, ACCESS.CFG. You'll use the Web Manager to configure most of these settings.

■ Directory access restrictions, which allow you to control access to specific directories with username and password requirements using individually created access control files, ACCESS.WWW. You'll use an ASCII text editor to configure these settings.

Both of these methods are designed to keep out unwanted users and offer a much different kind of security than SSL offers. By restricting access to your Web server, you can allow some users to have access to your server while keeping others out. SSL, on the other hand, uses encryption and client-server authentication to secure the integrity of data rather than authenticate a particular user (although this is possible, as we'll show you in the "Browser Configuration" section later in this chapter) or secure access to a particular directory. Between these two methods of restricting access, you may protect your Web server using the following three approaches:

- Restrict access by user, which allows only authorized users to access your Web server or certain areas in your server.

- Restrict access by group, which allows only authorized NDS-defined groups to access your Web server or certain areas in your server.

- Restrict access by system, which allows only authorized systems, defined by either domain name or IP address, to access your Web server or certain areas in your server.

Access restrictions are configured using a graphical interface, any ASCII text editor, and an executable program. The tools used to perform these tasks are:

- Web Manager, discussed in previous chapters, which is quick and easy to use and handles most of your access restriction configuration tasks.

- Individual access files, defined in the server resource map file (usually SYS:WEB\CONFIG\SRM.CFG). They are manually created using a text editor and saved in the directory for which the restrictions are intended.

- A name and password file.

- PWGEN.EXE, a DOS-based executable program that encrypts the name and password file for use by the Web server and access control files.

Tip

Directories that are not located under the Web server's document tree are not capable of being restricted by either the Web Manager program or individual access control files. All documents in these directories, such as individual users' directories, are therefore publicly available.

The following subsections describe how you can protect your intranet's Web server using these access restrictions and their associated tools.

Using Web Manager

As we've seen in Chapter 21 the basic tasks for configuring your Web server are accomplished through the Web Manager program and include basic security access restrictions, which are stored in your Web server's global access control file, usually SYS:WEB\CONFIG\ACCESS.CFG. To launch the Web Manager program, follow the steps that are appropriate for your operating system. Unfortunately, unless you are running a Windows emulation program such as SoftWindows, you cannot run Web Manager from a Macintosh computer.

For Windows 3.x users:

1. Log in to the NDS tree.

2. Map an available drive letter to the SYS:PUBLIC directory, if you don't have one already mapped.

3. Create a Program Item called Web Manager that points to SYS:PUBLIC\ WEBMGR.EXE.

4. Double-click the Web Manager icon.

5. Alternatively, choose File | Run and enter the path to WEBMGR.EXE every time you want to run the program.

If you're running Windows 95 or Windows NT on your client workstation, then follow these steps:

1. Log in to the NDS tree.

2. Open the SYS volume, then the Public directory, and double-click on the WEBMGR.EXE program.

To create a shortcut, instead of double-clicking on WEBMGR.EXE, single-click with the right mouse button and drag it to your Desktop. Release the mouse button and choose Create Shortcut when prompted.

When the Web Manager program is launched, choose the User Access tab and then the System Access tab and familiarize yourself with the available options. Refer to "Basic Server Configuration" in Chapter 21 for a brief explanation of each.

Creating Access Files & Using PWGEN.EXE

The second method to configure access restrictions involves the use of an ASCII text editor to create individual access control files for specific directories on your Web server. The access control files may use either of the following sources for information on what users and/or groups may have authorized access:

- A manually created list of users and groups and their passwords
- Existing NDS users and groups

For manually created lists, the usernames and passwords of users and groups are added to a separate file, and a DOS-based program called PWGEN.EXE is run to generate an encrypted version of the usernames and passwords for use by the Web server. NDS users and groups, which are managed through the NWADMIN program, are simply referenced in an access control file, and no name and password file management is necessary.

Tip

Unlike the ACCESS.CFG file, which stores information about all directories in a single file, the ACCESS.WWW files do not use the <DIRECTORY> tag since each directory can have its own access file.

The Access Control File

The filename used for each directory's access control file is always the same, although the contents of each file are directory specific. The server resource map configuration file (SRM.CFG), described in the previous chapter, contains a directive that identifies this filename to the Web server on startup. The default entry, which identifies ACCESS.WWW as the file containing directory-specific configuration information, is:

```
AccessFileName access.www
```

When the Web server retrieves a document from a directory, it first looks for this file, processes its security restriction information, and determines if the requesting browser has permission to receive the document in question. If it does, then the browser's request is honored. If it is not honored, a generic error message will be returned to the requesting browser. The directives and variables used in the access control file are described in the following sections.

AuthGroupFile

`AuthGroupFile` *filename*

The AuthGroupFile identifies a database file that contains information on groups and their members for file-based (not NDS) authentication.

AuthGroupMethod

`AuthGroupMethod nds` *context*

The AuthGroupMethod identifies the method used to authenticate a group, the only method supported at present being NDS. The variable used with this directive is the NDS context.

AuthName

`AuthName` *string*

The AuthName directive specifies a text string that appears in the request sent by the server to the user to provide the proper username and password for authentication. For example, using the string variable "Secret Web Administrators" would cause your Web browser to ask, "Enter username for Secret Web Administrators at web.admin.rambell."

AuthType

`AuthType Basic`

The AuthType directive identifies the type of user authentication. Currently, only basic is supported.

AuthUserFile

`AuthUserFile` *filename*

The AuthUserFile specifies the database file that contains the list of usernames and passwords for file-based authentication for a directory. It is used exactly like AuthGroupFile, and an explanation of how to create this file follows these descriptions of variables and directives.

AuthUserMethod

`AuthUserMethod nds` *context*

The AuthUserMethod identifies the method used to authenticate a user, the only method supported at present being NDS. The variable used with this directive is the NDS context.

\<Limit GET\>...\</Limit\>

`<Limit GET>values </Limit>`

Like most of the other directives in ACCESS.WWW, the order of the directives and their variables is very important. The variables in this context include:

- order (allow,deny or deny,allow)
- allow from (all, full host name, domain name, partial IP address, or full IP address)
- deny from (all, full host name, domain name, partial IP address, or full IP address)
- require (user *username*, require valid-user, or require group *groupname*)

Tip

Only the GET method is supported by directory access control files at this time.

Creating & Encrypting Password Files

The Web server knows what users to allow by looking for username entries in the ACCESS.WWW file and comparing them with the output of a password file created by the program that generates encrypted passwords (PWGEN.EXE), the location for which is also identified in ACCESS.WWW by the AuthUserFile directive. Directory restrictions made with the Web Manager program, on the other hand, use IntranetWare's NDS authentication to look up usernames and passwords. Follow these steps to create a list of usernames for use with directory access:

1. Using any ASCII text editor, create a file with entries that follow this scheme, where each entry is on a separate line:

   ```
   <username1>:<password1>
   <username2>:<password2>
   <username3>:<password3>
   ```

2. Save the file somewhere other than in the product root (i.e., not in SYS:WEB).

3. Map an available drive to SYS:PUBLIC on your IntranetWare server.

4. Open a DOS Prompt window and type the following command followed by Enter, where G represents the drive you've just mapped:

   ```
   G:PWGEN <SOURCEFILE> <TARGETFILE>
   ```

For example, Figure 23-14 shows PWGEN.EXE used to create a password file called PASSWD.BIN from an ASCII text file called PASSWD.TXT.

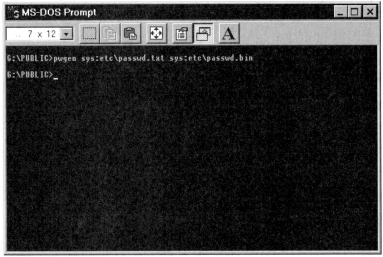

Figure 23-14: Generating an encrypted username and password file using PWGEN.EXE.

Creating a name and password file for groups is exactly the same except groups are identified instead of individual users:

1. Using any ASCII text editor, create a file with entries that follow this scheme, where each group entry is on a separate line:

```
<group1>:<user1> <user2> <user3>
<group2>:<user1> <user2> <user3>
<group3>:<user1> <user2> <user3>
```

2. Save the file somewhere other than in the product root (i.e., not in SYS:WEB).

3. Map an available drive to SYS:PUBLIC on your IntranetWare server.

4. Open a DOS Prompt window and type the following command followed by Enter, where G represents the drive you've just mapped:

```
G:PWGEN <SOURCEFILE> <TARGETFILE>
```

Once the file has been created, move it into a location that is specified in the ACCESS.WWW AuthUserFile directive, which was described earlier in the chapter.

Tip

Do not store the clear text versions of your username and password access control files in a Web server's product root. Since most Web servers allow the serving of text files, you risk the file being accidentally made available and therefore compromising your server's security.

Restricting Access by User

You may restrict access to your Web server based on individual users who can be authenticated via NDS or by a directory's access control file. On the Rambell Web server, for example, we can make the entire server, a single directory, or anywhere in between, accessible to a specific user based on his or her NDS entry. This is an easy and very secure method of controlling access to users known to your system. For documents whose access needs to be secured for users who are not part of your NDS tree, you can add them manually.

Tip

You may disable directory access restrictions for every directory under your Web server's document root except for the document root directory itself, usually SYS:WEB\DOCS.

Using Web Manager

The Web Manager utility is used to control access for users who are part of your NDS tree. For example, follow these steps to add the user JDOE to the list of users who are allowed to access documents in a directory called SECRETS on the root of the Rambell Web server.

1. Launch the Web Manager program and select a virtual Web server as described in the "Basic Server Configuration" section of Chapter 21.

2. Select the User Access tab, shown in Figure 23-15.

3. Choose the directory for which access is to be restricted, in this case SYS:WEB\DOCS\SECRETS.

4. Choose an authentication method, in this case Directory Services.

5. The Default NDS Context field will indicate the default context for the IntranetWare server on which the virtual Web server is running.

6. Choose an NDS context in which the user resides. In our example the user resides in the same context as does the Web server, but you can authenticate users on other NetWare servers that are members of your NDS tree.

7. Select a user to authenticate, such as JDOE.

8. Select the Add to Authorized Users List button to add this user, or check the All Valid Users box to add all the users in this NDS context.

9. Choose OK and enter the virtual Web server's password when prompted.

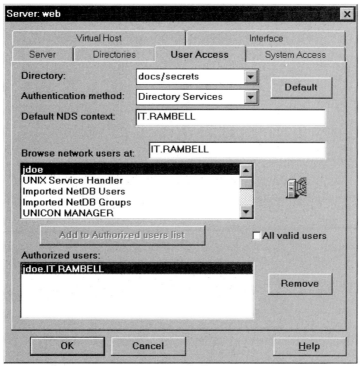

Figure 23-15: Authorizing user access for an NDS-authenticated user via the Web Manager.

Using ACCESS.WWW

Enabling access for a user who is not part of your NDS tree is a bit more tricky with NWS 3.0, but that will probably change in the future as Novell moves to incorporate more Web server configuration and management tasks through a graphical interface like the Web Manager. For now, follow these steps to enable a user to access a restricted directory.

1. Open a blank document using any ASCII text editor and type the following lines:

```
AuthType Basic
AuthName Secret Documents
AuthUserFile passwd.www
<LIMIT GET>
require user jdoe
</Limit>
```

Tip

To grant directory access to all valid users, type **require valid-user** *in place of* **require user jdoe** *in the above example.*

2. Save the file as ACCESS.WWW (identified in SRM.CFG) in the directory SYS:WEB\DOCS\SECRETS.

3. Add the username JDOE and a password to a text file such as SYS:ETC\PASSWD.TXT and run the PWGEN.EXE program described above in the section entitled "Creating & Encrypting (PWGEN.EXE)." Remember to output the password file as PASSWD.WWW and move to the directory SYS:WEB\DOCS\SECRETS. Figure 23-16 shows the end result of this example.

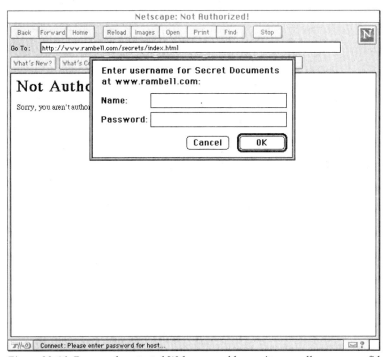

Figure 23-16: Password-protected Web pages add security as well as user confidence to your Web site.

You may also create an ACCESS.WWW file and specify that NDS authentication be used in place of the password file generated using PWGEN.EXE. To use NDS authentication, follow these steps:

1. Open a blank document using any ASCII text editor and type the following lines, where the default NDS context is it.rambell:

```
AuthType Basic
AuthName Secret Document
AuthUserMethod nds .IT.RAMBELL
<LIMIT GET>
require user jdoe
</Limit>
```

2. Save the file as ACCESS.WWW (identified in SRM.CFG) in the directory SYS:WEB\DOCS\SECRETS.

Access restrictions to this directory will go into effect immediately, and the Web server will not require restarting.

Restricting Access by Group

You may restrict access to your Web server based on groups of users created within an NDS context or by an access control file in the same way you would restrict access to individual users. On the Rambell Web server, for example, we can make the entire server, a single directory, or anywhere in between, accessible to a specific group (or groups) of users.

Using Web Manager

The Web Manager utility is used to control access to groups of users who are part of your NDS tree. For example, follow these steps to add the Rambell accounting department, whose members belong to the NDS group ACCT, to the list of users who are allowed to access documents in a directory called BUDGET on the root of the Rambell Web server.

1. Launch the Web Manager program and select a virtual Web server as described in the "Basic Server Configuration" section of Chapter 21.

2. Select the User Access tab.

3. Choose the directory for which access is to be restricted, in this case SYS:WEB\DOCS\BUDGET.

4. Choose an authentication method, in this case Directory Services.

5. The Default NDS Context field will indicate the default context for the IntranetWare server on which the virtual Web server is running.

6. Choose an NDS context in which the user resides. In our example the user resides in the same context as does the Web server, but you can authenticate groups of users on other NetWare servers that are members of your NDS tree.

7. Select a group to authenticate, such as ACCT.

8. Select the Add to Authorized Users List button to add this user, or check the All Valid Users box to add all the users in this NDS context.

9. Choose OK and enter the virtual Web server's password when prompted.

Using ACCESS.WWW

Enabling access for a groups of users who are not part of your NDS tree is exactly like enabling access to an individual user, except an additional entry is created to identify the group name:

1. Open a blank document using any ASCII text editor and type the following lines:

```
AuthType Basic
AuthName Secret Documents
AuthGroupFile group.www
<LIMIT GET>
require group acct
</Limit>
```

2. Save the file as ACCESS.WWW in the directory SYS:WEB\DOCS\ BUDGET.

3. Add the members of the group ACCT and their passwords to a text file such as SYS:ETC\GROUP.TXT and run the PWGEN.EXE program described earlier in this chapter. Remember to output the password file as GROUP.WWW and move to the directory SYS:WEB\DOCS\BUDGET.

You may also grant access to an existing NDS group specified in the ACCESS.WWW file and specify that NDS authentication be used in place of the password file generated using PWGEN.EXE. To use NDS authentication, follow these steps:

1. Open a blank document using any ASCII text editor and type the following lines, where the default NDS context is it.rambell:

```
AuthType Basic
AuthName Secret Document
AuthGroupMethod nds .it.rambell
<LIMIT GET>
require group acct
</Limit>
```

2. Save the file as ACCESS.WWW (identified in SRM.CFG) in the directory SYS:WEB\DOCS\SECRETS.

Access restrictions to this directory will go into effect immediately, and the Web server will not require restarting.

Restricting Access by System

Finally, you may restrict access to your Web server based on a requesting browser's full or partial IP address or domain name. This type of access control is especially helpful for managers of intranets whose users publish two main types of data on a Web server:

- Data for internal corporate use
- Data for public consumption

Examples of internal data may include budget information, training documentation, contact information, or employee schedules. Public data could include product information, corporate contact information, customer feedback forms, and ordering information. To better protect sensitive data, Novell Web Server allows you to control which systems have access to what types of data.

Identifying a full IP address or domain name for a specific host is easy enough. However, identifying a partial IP address can be a bit tricky because of they way IP addresses use four sets of from one to three characters to identify a specific address. Use the following examples as a guide to identifying IP addresses and domains for allowing access to directories on your Web server:

- **Full IP Address.** Identifies a specific computer, as in 123.4.5.6 or 123.456.789.100.

- **Partial IP Address.** Identifies computers on a specific subnet, as in 123.4 or 123.4.5.

- **Hostname.** Identifies a specific computer, as in www.good-company.com or mac32.employees.best-company.com.

- **Domain Name.** Identifies computers belonging to a specific domain, such as competition.com or smart.edu.

By default, all IP addresses and domain names are implicitly allowed access to all directories on your Novell Web Server. Granting access to one or more IP address or domain name for a particular directory will cause all others to therefore be explicitly denied access to this directory.

Using Web Manager

The Web Manager utility may be used to control access to all the directories on your Web server (located under the document root) based on a requesting browser's IP address or domain name. When a request is sent from a browser to the server, the HTTP header contains the requesting browser's IP address, which the Web server identifies and resolves using NDS. It then checks for access restrictions and either allows or denies the connection. Figure 23-17 shows what a denied connection from Novell Web Server looks like in Netscape Navigator.

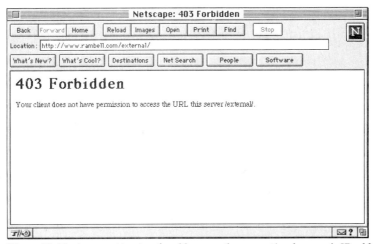

Figure 23-17: A connection is refused because the requesting browser's IP address is not allowed access to the directory named external.

Follow these steps to allow no one but those on the 123.4.5 subnet to have access to the URL http://www.rambell.com/internal.

1. Launch the Web Manager program and select a virtual Web server as described in the "Basic Server Configuration" section of Chapter 21.

2. Select the System Access tab.

3. Choose the directory for which access is to be restricted, in this case SYS:WEB\DOCS\INTERNAL.

4. Enter a full or partial IP address or a domain name, as shown in Figure 23-18.

5. Select the Add to Authorized Systems List button.

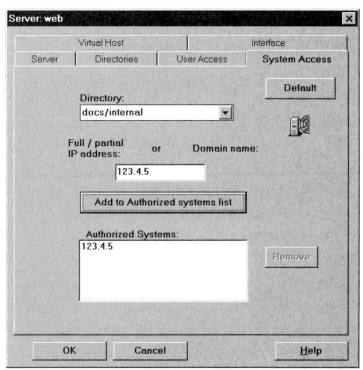

Figure 23-18: Adding a subnet to the list of systems authorized to access documents at http://www.rambell.com/internal.

6. Choose OK and enter the virtual Web server's password when prompted.

Using ACCESS.WWW

Authorizing access to systems using an access control file is very similar to other types of access control, but with a few exceptions. First, all of the directives and variables that precede the <LIMIT> section are omitted. Next, you will add several variables to the <LIMIT> section that are not needed in the previous sections. The following procedure performs the same access restrictions as does the previous example:

1. Open a blank document using any ASCII text editor and type the following lines:

```
<LIMIT GET>
order deny,allow
deny from all
allow from 123.4.5
</LIMIT>
```

2. Save the file as ACCESS.WWW in the directory SYS:WEB\DOCS\ INTERNAL.

If necessary, you may include multiple ALLOW statements following an explicit DENY ALL. For example, this is useful if departments on your intranet are spread across several cities and use different Internet Service Providers (ISPs). In such a case, your users will most likely have IP addresses on different networks and subnets. If they are all to have access to a secure directory, then you should obtain their IP addresses and create an access control file like this:

```
<LIMIT GET>
order deny,allow
deny from all
allow from 123.4.5
allow from 234.56.7
allow from 235.6.78
</LIMIT>
```

Of course, you may also reverse the order in which the Web server interprets the ALLOW and DENY statements, which makes it easier if you have a directory for which you want to allow access to all users except perhaps a particular user or domain. For example:

```
<LIMIT GET>
order allow,deny
allow from all
deny from 152.3.100.71
deny from vantg.com
deny from thor.com
</LIMIT>
```

Access restrictions to this directory will go into effect immediately, and the Web server will not require restarting.

Browser Configuration

Netscape Navigator 3, which is included with IntranetWare, is the industry leader when it comes to incorporating the latest security features. Your NetWare Web Server can take advantage of all the security features built into Navigator, including SSL, Site Certificates, and Personal Certificates as well as username and passwords. There are several security options that may be configured in Navigator, and knowing how to use them will help you better configure your NetWare Web Server to provide the best level of security for your intranet.

General Configuration Options

Users of Netscape Navigator on your intranet will benefit from a little tweaking of their browsers' general configuration options in terms of convenience and security. Most browsers, including Navigator, store recently accessed documents in memory cache (Windows only) and/or in disk cache (Mac and Windows) for faster loading when they are accessed again during the same session. Figure 23-19 shows the caching options that are available in both the Mac and Windows versions of Navigator 3 and their ability to cache documents retrieved through an SSL connection.

It is recommended that if your users are in a secure environment, they should cache documents retrieved through your SSL–enabled Web server to provide quicker access and fewer connections to your server. The only risk that you need to be aware of is that if a secured page is accessed and a user walks away from his or her desk without quitting Navigator, it is possible that someone else can easily view these documents because a new connection to your SSL server is not required. They might simply be able to click the Back and Forward buttons to view these pages, thereby circumventing the benefits of SSL's encryption. Figure 23-20 shows the two most common warning dialogs your users will see when entering and exiting Web sites that are SSL-secured.

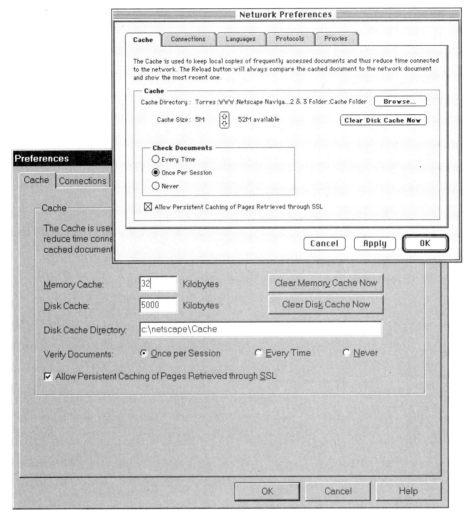

Figure 23-19: Configuring Navigator for the Mac OS and Windows 95 to cache documents retrieved via SSL connections.

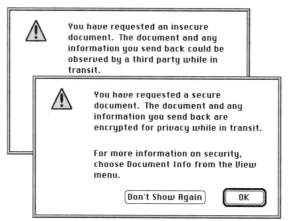

Figure 23-20: Two of the more common warnings Navigator uses involving SSL-protected Web sites.

You will find several additional client-side SSL configuration options under the Options I Security Preferences menu tab, which contains identical configuration options for both the Mac and Windows platforms of Navigator 3. The Mac version, shown in Figure 23-21, allows you to configure the following options:

- **Entering a Secure Document Space (Server).** Displays an alert when you request a document protected by SSL 2 or 3 linked from an insecure document.

- **Leaving a Secure Document Space (Server).** Displays an alert when you link to an insecure document from within a document protected by SSL 2 or 3.

- **Viewing a Document With a Secure/Insecure Mix.** Displays an alert when you request a document that is partially protected by SSL 2 or 3.

- **Submitting a Form Insecurely.** Displays an alert when you click the Submit button on any form, including search engines and many CGIs.

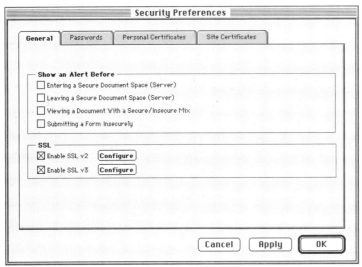

Figure 23-21: Configuring Navigator's general security preferences to effectively use your Web server's SSL features.

In addition to these configuration options, you may also enable or disable the browser's ability to communicate using either SSL 2 or 3. Also, as shown in Figure 23-22, you may enable or disable ciphers used to establish varying levels of encryption strength with an SSL server.

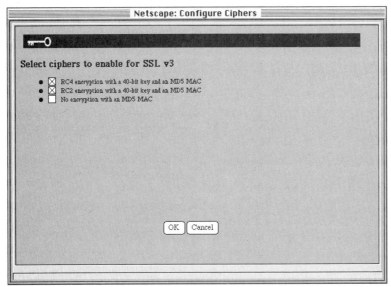

Figure 23-22: Configuring Navigator's SSL 3 features.

Passwords

Navigator can be configured to provide an extra level of security for your intranet users who do not have a secure work environment. The Passwords tab, shown below in Figure 23-23, allows users to enter a password that protects both Personal and Site Certificates, described in the following two sections. These certificates are worthy of protection, not only because of the risk to your Web server and browser, but also because users are charged a fee for many of these certificates and replacing them will cost even more money.

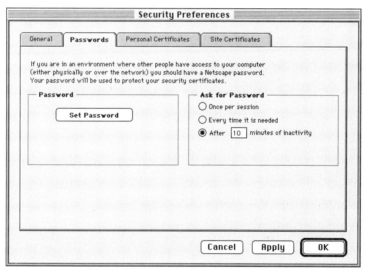

Figure 23-23: Setting a personal password is advisable for your users who are in an unsecure environment.

Personal Certificates

Personal Certificates function in a way that is similar to the way Site Certificates do when used in conjunction with SSL, which is described above. A *Personal Certificate* is an electronic ID card you either purchase or are given by a Certifying Authority (CA) such as VeriSign. Personal Certificates are used to *authenticate a user* to an SSL-enabled Web server that requests such authentication. Web sites that handle financial transactions or other sensitive information are more likely to use this feature as a means of adding another level of security to their Web server.

Novell Web Server 3.0 is capable of requesting that your users have, and submit, a Personal Certificate when connecting to your server via SSL. To enable this capability, follow these steps:

1. Launch the Web Manager program and select a virtual Web server as described in the "Basic Server Configuration" section of Chapter 21.

2. Select the Interface tab.

3. Select the Security Options button and check the Require Client Certificate check box, as shown in Figure 23-14. Click the Security Options tab.

4. Check the Require Client Certificate check box, as shown in Figure 23-24

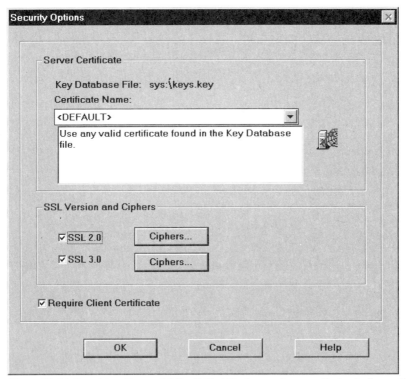

Figure 23-24: Requiring Personal (client) Certificates can increase the level of security of your Web server.

5. Choose OK to close the Security Preferences dialog window; then choose OK again to close the virtual Web server's configuration screen.

6. Save your changes and restart the Web server and SSL when prompted.

Tip

VeriSign is the only company at this time that issues Personal Certificates for use with Netscape browsers and servers.

To obtain or edit a Personal Certificate, open the Options I Security Preferences I Personal Certificates tab, shown in Figure 23-25. In this figure, there is one certificate installed named J. Doe's VeriSign, Inc. ID, whose properties can be viewed or deleted. To request a new Personal Certificate, click on the Obtain New Certificate button and follow the instructions on how one might be obtained.

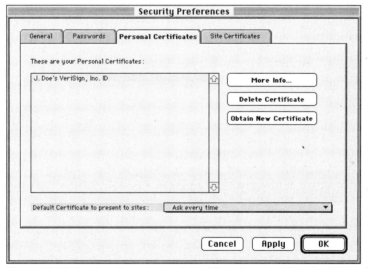

Figure 23-25: Configuring a Personal Certificate for use with a Novell Web Server.

Your users may eventually need several Personal Certificates, including future certificates that are customized to work in conjunction with only your Web server. In this example, the Rambell user named JDOE has configured Navigator to ask every time to choose which certificate to present to a Web server when one is requested. The options are:

- Ask Every Time
- Let Navigator Choose Automatically
- J. Doe's VeriSign, Inc. ID (because it is highlighted)

Tip

To pick up a Digital ID from VeriSign, open your browser to http://digitalid. verisign.com and choose Request a Digital ID.

Finally, to view the details of the Personal Certificate, including to whom it belongs and from whom it was issued, click on the More Info button in the Personal Certificates tab.

Site Certificates

The Site Certificates configuration tab allows your users to configure how Navigator is to respond to SSL-enabled Web sites and Certificate Authorities. Users may choose to view certificate information in three ways:

■ All Certificates

■ Site Certificates

■ Certificate Authorities

In Figure 23-26, for example, the user is viewing All Certificates, where the only Site Certificate (www.rambell.com) is displayed first.

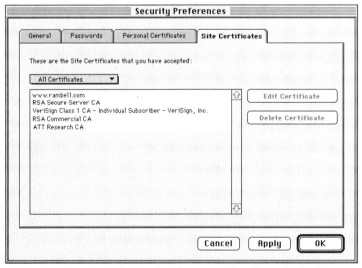

Figure 23-26: Configuring Site Certificates and Certificate Authorities.

Site Certificates are issued by SSL-enabled Web servers when a browser requests a connection. For example, when a browser first connected to the Rambell Web server, the certificate shown in Figure 23-27 was issued.

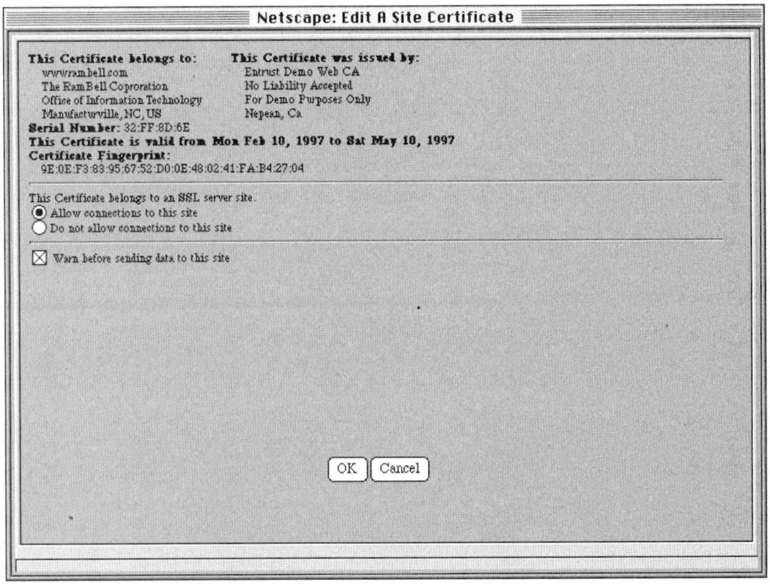

Figure 23-27: Editing a Site Certificate already accepted by a Web browser.

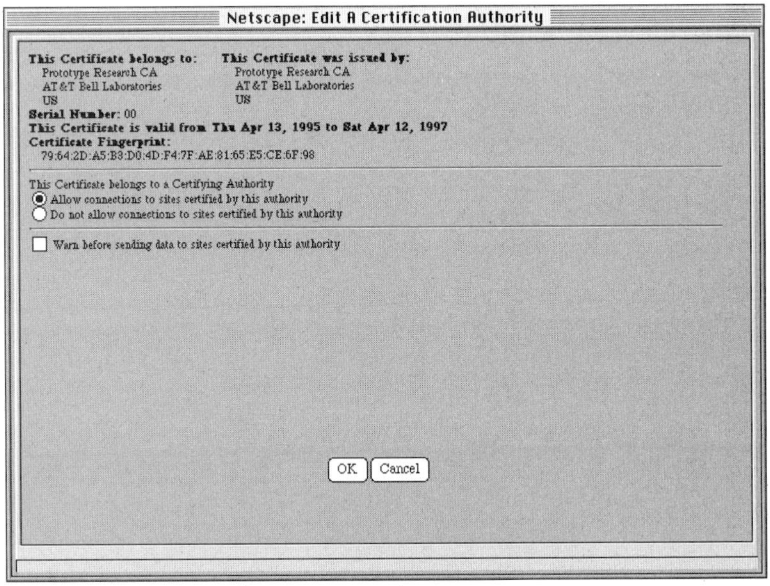

Figure 23-28: Editing a Certification Authority.

Note this certificate is a demo certificate and therefore the Warn Before Sending Data to This Site check box is selected. For even more security, users or network administrators may select the Do Not Allow Connections to This Site option. Similarly, users can configure Navigator to allow, disallow, or give a warning before SSL connections are made to Web sites whose Site Certificates are issued by a particular Certifying Authority, as illustrated in Figure 23-28.

Moving On

In this chapter we've discussed protecting your Novell Web Server and network from infiltration and attack by hackers. As Web browsers and servers become increasingly more sophisticated in their abilities to access and share information, the possible avenues for misdeeds and pilfering of sensitive information and resources grow as well. Your Novell Web Server provides you with several tools with which to defeat hackers and secure sensitive data and communications:

- Secure Sockets Layers 2 and 3
- Site Certificates
- Personal Certificates
- NDS-based access restrictions
- Directory-based access restrictions

Use these tools liberally as you continue to develop your Novell-based Web site. The chances are greater than not that somebody will attempt to hack into your system, so it really is common sense to secure important information on your Web server.

In the next chapter, "Providing Web Content," we'll explore a bit deeper the mechanics of how HTTP and HTML work, user documents and directories, clickable image maps, server-side includes, and how to browse your NDS tree through a Web browser.

24

Providing Web Content

Installing and configuring your Novell Web Server (NWS) is only half the battle. You or your company must also provide interesting and meaningful content on your Web server to make the time and energy spent installing and configuring the server worthwhile. Your NetWare Web Server is very unique among Web servers in that it is capable of serving many types of documents for which other Web servers require special CGI scripts. Most all Web servers are capable of cranking out HTML document and image files, but NWS is capable of serving much more.

Many large corporations might employ one or more full-time Web content developers to fill the Web server you will have spent so much time installing and configuring. Other companies, however, may not provide this level of staffing. Either way, this chapter is designed to help you, in the role of an intranet or Internet Webmaster, to understand not only the basics of serving HTML documents, but also how you can utilize the strengths of your Novell Web Server to provide more attractive Web content. Here's what we'll cover in this chapter:

- The basics of how HTTP and HTML work to provide easy access to documents and resources to anyone on the Web.

- How your Web server is organized to make providing content as easy a task as possible.

- How to provide server-side and client-side clickable image maps to make navigating your site more flexible.

- How to incorporate server-side includes (SSI) in the HTML documents published on your server.
- How to enable users to browse the NDS objects on your IntranetWare server.

Figure 24-1 shows you the default home page included with your Web server, and after reading this chapter, you'll have a much better idea of the capabilities of your server to publish on the Web.

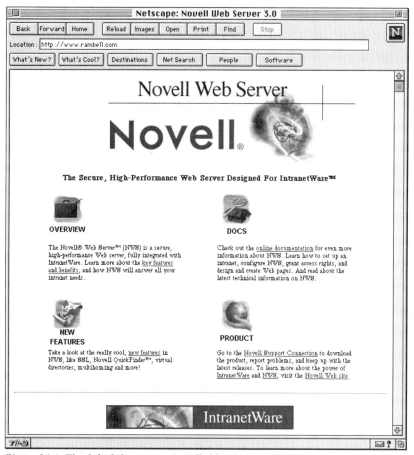

Figure 24-1: The default home page installed by the Novell Web Server.

Web Essentials

For the most part, Web clients and Web servers interact in a stateless client-server relationship, meaning a Web server doesn't serve anything that is not requested by a browser. There are emerging technologies that allow certain types of servers to deliver Web-like content on a prescheduled basis, such as *PointCast*; but your Novell Web Server only delivers content when it is requested. Users of your intranet can request documents from your Web server(s) in two ways:

- By using the HyperText Transfer Protocol (HTTP).

- By opening a file on the hard drive of your server or the local hard drive of the user's workstation.

We're obviously concerned with the files located on your server and accessing them via HTTP.

HTTP Interaction

The duties of listening, receiving, processing, and replying to HTTP requests are the same for an NWS as for any other Web server. The use of the TCP/IP-based client-server protocol is one of the greatest reasons for the presence of Web servers, as well as NetWare and IntranetWare, on so many platforms, and the description of HTTP 1.0 that follows is applicable to Web servers on all platforms that support it.

Listening

The Web server listens for a connection request continuously until it is instructed to stop listening, has reached the maximum number of connections it is permitted to allow, is unloaded from memory, or is otherwise disconnected from the network. So that it can allocate its memory resources accordingly, NWS is preconfigured to listen for a certain number of connections, called threads, rather than to listen for an unlimited number of connections. See Chapter 21 for the details on how much memory is required to run NWS 3.0 as well as how much memory is required for additional connections.

Tip

Your Web server's memory requirements must be properly calculated in order to provide effective and efficient access.

Receiving

When a Web server receives a request from Web browsers using the HTTP protocol, it allocates a thread (one of many concurrent processes) to the connection with the Web browser and reduces the number of threads available for new connections. To be able to be received by a Web server, a request must be made in the proper HTTP format and on the correct port, the default being port 80.

Tip

A port refers to a number that identifies a specific server process or application. There are more than 65,000 possible unique 16-bit numbers that can be used as port assignments. Ports 0-1024 are referred to as privileged ports and their assignment is controlled by the Internet Assigned Numbers Authority (IANA), a division of the University of Southern California's Information Sciences Institute.

HTTP uses two type of messages for each transaction between Web server and client: request (from the client to the server) and response (from the server to the client). Each message consists of three optional header fields (referred to as headers) plus an additional field. Headers include information on:

- The protocol (HTTP) version number.
- The date and time of the HTTP transaction.
- The MIME type supported.
- Whether the transaction is a request for the delivery of data or a request for the acceptance of data (see the next section, "Processing").

The Web server will return the appropriate error message and refuse the connection if it does not receive the correct header information.

Processing

After a connection has been received, the Web server processes the browser's requests. Processing a request can include the execution of one of several commands based on the first word that appears in the HTTP header, but not all commands are supported by all Web servers. HTTP requests supported by NWS consist mainly of three basic commands that are requested of the Web server by the browser: GET, HEAD, and POST (see Table 24-1).

Command	Description
GET	Requests a document from a server.
HEAD	Requests all but the body of a document from a server.
POST	Requests acceptance of data from the client by a server.

Table 24-1: HTTP commands.

Other commands could include PUT, to receive a file using the HTTP protocol instead of the File Transfer Protocol (FTP), or DELETE, to remove a file, for example. The GET command represents the vast majority of Web requests and is used whenever a browser requests a document specified in a URL. The HEAD command is used by programs that seek HTML document information without needing the contents of an HTML document's body. Some indexing programs use only the header information of an HTML document, although other indexing programs will request the entire document using the GET command so they can do a full-text search of it. Finally, the POST command is sent by a browser when it is requesting that the server accept input data from a browser for processing. Whenever you fill in a form using a browser, the POST command is issued and the values you entered are sent to the server.

Returning

After the Web server listens for, receives, and then processes a connection and request, it returns the information to the browser. At the HTTP level, a server response includes much of the same header information as is sent by the browser when it submits an HTTP request to the server, including date, time, MIME type, and HTTP version. In addition, the server response includes a three-digit status code, many of which you've probably encountered in your browsing experience. See Table 22-4 in Chapter 22 for a list of the various HTTP 1.0 status codes used by NWS 3.0. Figure 24-2 shows the results returned from a request sent by the Mosaic Web browser using the Header Mode feature.

Figure 24-2: Results of an HTTP request as seen in Mosaic.

If an HTTP request is successfully received by the server, the server returns a 2xx status code to the browser prior to sending the requested HTML file, script, image, or document. A browser doesn't display the "successful" 2xx status code to the user unless the requested HTML document is an empty file (literally, containing 0 bytes of data), in which case the 204 "the document is empty" status code is displayed by the browser. Otherwise, the proper document would be returned. Such a document could be an HTML document, a file, or perhaps the results of a CGI script. If, however, an HTTP request resulted in a 3xx or 5xx status code, the appropriate error message would then be returned to the browser and displayed to the user.

How It All Works

To review the process of Web client-server transactions, let's sample an HTTP transaction between a Web browser and your Novell Web Server. Because HTTP uses TCP/IP as the basis for its IP addressing and communications control, any of the following steps could be temporarily halted and restarted depending on the flow of traffic across the network and other factors such as data integrity and communication.

1. The server listens for a connection request.

2. A client sends a request to either GET, HEAD, or POST data.

3. The server receives the request, which it either accepts or rejects.

4. The server processes the request.

5. The server returns the results of the request.

6. The client receives, processes, and displays the results.

This series of transactions is repeated every time a user clicks a hyperlink in an HTML document or otherwise selects a linking command using the keyboard. In addition, every time an inline image is requested by an HTML document, the process is repeated. Have you ever noticed that when you request a document with numerous small images such as little colored round balls or icons, it can take a long time to load the entire document? That's because the browser must submit a new request to the server for every image and thereby start the transaction process.

The proposed successor to HTTP 1.x is called HTTP-NG, or Next Generation, and its proponents seek to correct the one-request/one-connection limitation. HTTP-NG proposes to allow for asynchronous transmission of HTTP requests for every connection, meaning that once a connection is established between a Web server and a client, multiple requests will be allowed before the connection is closed and the need for another is requested. This method of transmission will allow for less overhead for each request and a shorter startup time.

HTML

HTML is a markup language that defines the format in which Web documents are displayed and how other HTML documents and access protocols are linked. HTML uses English-like commands embedded within the text of a document that are interpreted by a browser for display and for action by helper applications. HTML can be both an exact programming language and a fairly forgiving markup language, depending on the browser used to view an HTML document. That is to say that one can be relatively slack when it comes to writing HTML documents and still create documents for the Web that appear properly formatted when viewed through certain Web browsers. Keep in mind that not all browsers are as forgiving as others, though. Some browsers will not properly display a document if it lacks even a single element of HTML, such as a closing quotation mark, for example, whereas another browser might display it properly.

Formatting Instructions

Web browsers receive and display HTML documents by discerning the difference between HTML formatting instructions and the content of a document. In the current versions of HTML and HTTP, this data is in the form of the 8-bit ISO8859-1 (Latin) character set or the 7-bit character set we know and love as ASCII text. To differentiate between formatting commands and document text, HTML reserves certain ASCII characters for use as interpretive symbols that direct browsers on how to identify formatting instructions. These special characters, called reserved characters, are few in number but enable HTML to specify a virtually unlimited number of formatting instructions.

The two most important HTML reserved characters are the mathematical symbols for less than (<) and greater than (>); the others are the double quote (") and the ampersand (&). The HTML formatting commands that are contained between these special characters are referred to as markup characters. All other data contained in an HTML document is considered to be text and is referred to as data characters. If an HTML document contains incorrectly placed reserved characters, your documents may be improperly interpreted and displayed by the browser.

Tip

See http://www.w3.org/pub/WWW/ for links to more information about Web standards and the ISO8859 character set.

If you want to use reserved characters as data characters in the body of your HTML documents, you're in luck. There are two methods for specifying the use of reserved characters, as well as foreign language, special, and 7-bit characters, within the body of an HTML document. Both methods instruct the browser to read special characters as data characters instead of markup characters. A special character can be identified as a character entity by using the ampersand (&) followed by either its associated keyword or ASCII code equivalent and a semicolon. Table 24-2 lists the four HTML reserved characters and two symbols often used in HTML with their keyword and ASCII code equivalents.

Character	Keyword	ASCII Code
<	<	<
>	>	>
"	"	"
&	&	&
©	©	¸
®	®	®

Table 24-2: Reserved characters used in HTML.

Basic HTML Tags

The current standardized version of HTML is 3.2, which consists of a surprisingly small number of formatting commands. All HTML documents, even the most simple, should contain certain basic tagging information, which usually appears in pairs that are often referred to as *tagged pairs*. HTML formatting commands are encased between the less-than (<) and greater-than (>) brackets and typically tell a browser where to start and stop a particular formatting attribute. Other tags, however, called *stand-alone tags*, are used one at a time and do not appear in pairs. Tags can also appear with attributes and arguments within the opening tag of a tagged pair. Here are the recommended HTML formatting tags that should be present in all HTML documents on your Web server:

```
<!DOCTYPE>
<HTML></HTML>
<HEAD></HEAD>
<TITLE></TITLE>
<BODY></BODY>
```

Tip

HTML formatting tags are not case sensitive, but paths and filenames in URLs are case sensitive.

Some tagged pairs need not appear together in the same section of the HTML document yet they are supposed to be nested, as in the <HTML></HTML> tag. So it's important to check your document for dangling tags. You'll be surprised by the number of errors out there where authors forget to close a tagged pair with a concluding tag! The following tags determine the basic structure of an HTML document.

<!DOCTYPE> The <!DOCTYPE> tag informs anyone who views the HTML source code what version of HTML the document has been created for. Not all Web servers and browsers use this information, however.

<HTML></HTML> The <HTML> tag denotes the beginning of an HTML document and the </HTML> tag concludes the document. Naturally, these tags do not appear together, and all other information in your HTML document will be nested between them.

<HEAD></HEAD>   Data within the <HEAD></HEAD> tags contains descriptive information about an HTML document—the title and comments the author may wish to insert concerning, for example, the content, location, and purpose of the document. These comments are not read by the browser but can be manually viewed by anyone who saves the document as a text file. Here is an example of a comment that has been broken into several short lines:

```
<HTML>
<HEAD>
<!--Created 1/1/97-->
<!--Last edited 2/15/97-->
<!--Author: webmaster@www.rambell.com-->
```

<TITLE></TITLE>   Nested within the <HTML> and <HEAD> tags is the <TITLE></TITLE> tagged pair. The title you give your document should be short and to the point for several reasons. First, many browsers, such as Netscape Navigator, use the information in the <TITLE></TITLE> to name the bookmark created for your document. Second, this information appears in the title bar of your browser. If you fail to give your document a title, its filename might appear in the title bar as well as in any bookmarks users create.

<BODY></BODY>   Everything not contained in the header belongs within the <BODY></BODY> section of your document. This includes all of its text, images, and hyperlinks. The closing </BODY> tag should always be the next to the last tag in your document.

In the following example of a properly coded HTML document, a blank line enables the user to easily distinguish between the header and body sections of the document. Comments have been inserted and the code is written in a hierarchically nested fashion to better illustrate how tags are nested:

```
<!DOCTYPE HTML PUBLIC "-//W3C//DTD HTML 3.2 Final//EN">
<HTML>
 <HEAD>
 <TITLE>Test HTML Document</TITLE>
 <!--Created 1/1/97-->
 <!--Last edited 2/15/97-->
 <!--Author: webmaster@www.rambell.com-->
 </HEAD>

 <BODY>
         <H1>This is a Level 1 heading.</H1>
         <H2>This is a Level 2 heading.</H2>
         <H3>This is a Level 3 heading.</H3>
```

```
                <H4>This is a Level 4 heading.</H4>
                <H5>This is a Level 5 heading.</H5>
                <H6>This is a Level 6 heading.</H6>
    </BODY>
</HTML>
```

Keep in mind that HTML ignores not only blanks lines but also all white space, so we could place a blank line between each line of text without changing the end result of our document as far as the browser is concerned. Likewise, our document could be one long run-on sentence, and again we would see the same result in the browser. It's our opinion that just as in a good essay, HTML documents should be as concise and to the point as possible without sacrificing grace and clarity. To this end, we suggest that you write your HTML documents with as little white space as possible; nesting your tags as in the preceding example is completely optional. Do what works for you, but be consistent.

The W3 Consortium

The W3 Consortium is an organization whose purpose is to promote and develop specifications and reference software for the Web and to ensure that the Web has every opportunity to fulfill its potential as a global networking resource. To this end, the W3C acts as a public repository for Web information, proposed standards, sample client and server software, and prototype and sample applications for use in Web development.

Numerous areas of interest exist within the W3C for users and developers to exchange ideas and concerns relating to the development of the Web, and visitors to the W3C home page are invited to contact W3C developers with their own concerns. As someone interested in creating Web resources, you should make time to explore the unique role of the W3C and the resources it has to offer. New and experienced users alike should regularly visit the W3C Web site at http://www.w3.org/ for the latest information about the Web and HTML standards.

Hyperlinks

Hyperlinks are to HTML and the Web as capital is to Wall Street—everything! Because of their ability to link one document or resource to another, hyperlinks are what make the Web useful. Without them, you would have just another word processing document. The mechanics of a hyperlink are very simple and there is very little variation in usage, so they are easily memorized. Table 24-3 illustrates the elements of a hyperlink.

Begin hyperlink	Target of hyperlink	Clickable text	End
<A HREF=	http://www.rambell.com>	click here	</a>

Table 24-3: Elements of a hyperlink.

Figure 24-3 illustrates each of the protocols in an HTML document entitled hyperlinks.html.

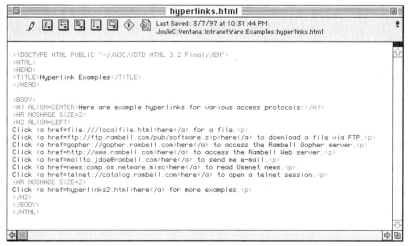

Figure 24-3: An HTML document illustrating the use of hyperlinks.

We're using an HTML editor in Figure 24-3 that color-codes the various elements of an HTML document; the hyperlinks are red and HTML text and clickable text are black. Figure 24-4 shows what this document looks like when viewed in Navigator, with the hyperlinks in a darker shade of gray than the body text. The figure above shows these colors as lighter and darker shades of gray.

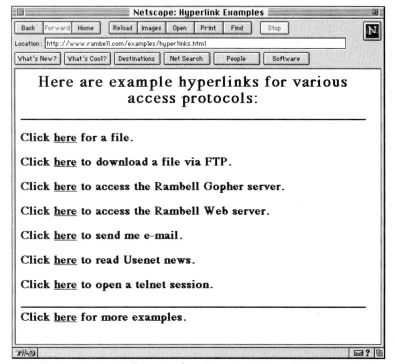

Figure 24-4: The HTML document from Figure 24-3 viewed in Navigator.

See Tables 24-6 and 24-7 later in this chapter for further explanations and examples of the various access protocols referenced in Figures 24-3 and 24-4.

Absolute vs. Relative Paths

Hyperlinks to other documents use either an absolute or a relative path to identify a document (file, image, CGI script) on either the same or a different Web server. A relative path, like those in our examples, excludes the access protocol, the separator, and a machine name (and/or path and document). Think of the term *absolute* as meaning that you must enter absolutely everything there is to know about a document's URL and the term *relative* as meaning that you have to know relatively little about the location of a document.

If you are linking to a series of documents located in the same directory on the Web server, then you should use a relative path. A path is considered to be relative when you don't need to enter the access protocol because the document being targeted is located on the same Web server as the currently opened document. In our example of an HTML document in Figures 24-3 and 24-4, we used a relative path in the last hyperlink to illustrate a relative link:

```
Click <a href=hyperlinks2.html>here</a> for more examples
```

Had hyperlinks2.html been located on another server (and hence a different file system), then we would have had to use an absolute path instead. Relative paths can point to any directory on the same file system as the Web server; you will need to use the forward slash to indicate the directory location in your HTML document. Here is the same line of HTML, but with the document located two directories deeper than in the previous line:

```
Click <a href=/test/HTML/examples/hyperlinks2.html>here</a> for more
examples
```

There is no need to use the absolute path in these examples because the document hyperlinks2.html is located on the same file system as the Web server. Had it been located on another server, the code might look like this:

```
Click <a href=http://www.yourserver.com/hyperlinks2.html>here</a> for more
examples
```

or this:

```
Click <a href=http://www.yourserver.com/test/examples/
hyperlinks2.html>here</a> for more examples
```

Linking documents together using text-based hyperlinks is the easiest way to create a functional HTML document, but why not add images and make them hyperlinks as well? After all, the Web was created with this in mind, and your Web server is capable of serving images and server-side clickable image maps as well as client-side clickable image maps.

URL Anatomy

A Uniform Resource Locator (URL) is used by the browser to locate an HTML document on your intranet's Web server, as well as a specific point within a particular HTML document. Like telephone numbers, URLs have to be entered precisely or you'll get what amounts to a wrong number (or at least the Web's version of the error message from the operator telling you that the number you just dialed doesn't exist). Where phone numbers consist of an area code, dialing prefix, and extension, a URL consists of:

- An access protocol
- A separator
- A machine name
- A path
- A document name

Not every URL contains all these elements, but they all must have the first three. Figure 24-5 illustrates these elements with a graphical representation.

http://www.rambell.com/book/lists.html

http:*//*www.rambell.com/book/lists.html

http://*www.rambell.com*/book/lists.html

http://www.rambell.com/*book*/lists.html

http://www.rambell.com/book/*lists.html*

Figure 24-5: The elements of a URL.

Directories & Documents

NWS 3.0 allows you to add as many documents in as many directories as your server has disk space to store. Users with accounts on your server may easily publish documents on the Web as well. This capability eliminates the need for multiple Web servers for your departments and users, freeing up valuable resources for your company.

Adding & Removing Directories

Each virtual Web server has its own directory tree in which documents are stored, and all documents located outside this tree are inaccessible to the Web server except for those stored in individual users' directories (which is described in more detail below). Figure 24-6 illustrates the default document tree for each virtual Web server.

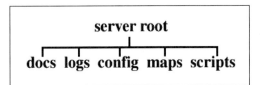

Figure 24-6: The default document tree for a virtual Web server.

The Web server looks for directories when loaded and expects to find certain types of document in them, as defined through the Web Manager program. Table 24-4 highlights the document types the Web server expects to find in a default server root configuration.

Directory	Contents
SERVER_ROOT\DOCS	Documents and images
SERVER_ROOT\LOGS	Server log files
SERVER_ROOT\CONFIG	Server configuration files
SERVER_ROOT\MAPS	Image map configuration files
SERVER_ROOT\SCRIPTS	CGI scripts

Table 24-4: Default directories in a server root and their contents.

In addition to the directories listed in Table 24-4, the subdirectories listed in Table 24-5 are usually located within the DOCS directory, where the majority of documents will probably be stored on your Web server.

Subdirectory	Contents
\DOCS\IMAGES	Image files
\DOCS\PERLDOCS	Documents that call Perl scripts
\DOCS\SSI	Server-side include documents

Table 24-5: Contents of subdirectories typically found in the DOCS directory.

Adding and deleting directories is an everyday occurrence on most active Web servers. To add directories to a virtual Web server, you must:

■ Create a new directory using a client such as Mac OS, Windows, or OS/2.

■ Add the directory using the Web Manager program, as described next. Figure 24-7 shows the Web Manager program assigning the proper document type for the newly added DOCS\INTERNAL directory.

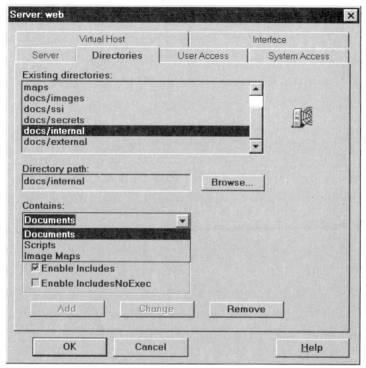

Figure 24-7: Making a directory available via the Web Manager program.

To make a newly added directory available to the virtual Web server's document tree, follow these steps:

1. Open the Web Manager program, as described in Chapter 21.

2. Select a virtual server, such as *web*.

3. Select the Directories tab.

4. Select a directory by either clicking on an existing directory or by clicking the Browse button and manually locating a directory.

5. Select an item from the Contains drop-down menu that best identifies the contents of the directory (usually Documents).

6. Click OK and restart the server when prompted.

To remove a directory, follow these steps up through step 4 and then click the Remove button.

User Directories

Users on your IntranetWare server may also publish Web documents through special directories in their home directories. In Chapter 21, we showed you how to enable this capability by checking the Enable User Documents check box through the Web Manager, as shown in Figure 24-8.

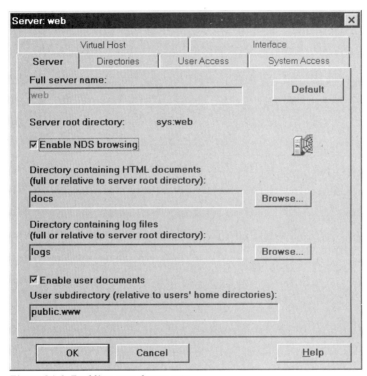

Figure 24-8: Enabling user documents.

To enable access to users' documents, follow these steps:

1. Open the Web Manager program, as described in Chapter 21.

2. Select a virtual server, such as *web*.

3. Select the Server tab.

4. Check the Enable User Documents check box.

5. Enter a directory name in the User Subdirectory field.

6. Click OK and restart the server.

Users and visitors may access these directories, as well as any subsequent subdirectories created under a user's public Web subdirectory, without any further interaction from you because they are located outside the server root and are therefore not manageable. The capability to provide user directories is either on or off; it is not configurable beyond the steps just outlined. Figure 24-9 shows the user jdoe's home page on the Rambell Web server, which is accessible via the following URL:

```
http://www.rambell.com/~jdoe
```

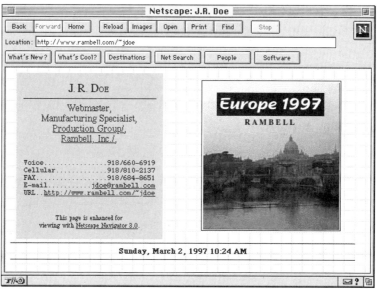

Figure 24-9: A user's home directory Web page.

Adding & Removing Documents

As the Webmaster, you control which users and groups have the ability to add and remove documents from your Web server. Using the NetWare Administrator, described in Chapters 3 and 4, you may grant access to selected directories for users and groups to add, modify, or delete documents as well as create subdirectories. Documents located in individual user directories, however, do not require further administration because a user automatically has full control of the contents of that directory.

Access Protocols

Documents located on your Web server can link to documents other than those on your server, however. There are many types of servers that can be accessed from a Web page by specifying the proper type of access protocol in the URL. Table 24-6 lists the access protocols that are currently used on the Web.

Access Protocol	Purpose
file	Links to a local or remote text file for viewing.
ftp	Links to a file on a remote FTP server for downloading.
gopher	Displays files on a remote Gopher server.
http	Links to local or remote HTML documents.
mailto	Sends Internet e-mail using SMTP.
news	Accesses Usenet newsgroup articles.
telnet	Connects to a Telnet service.

Table 24-6: Other access protocols in use on the Web today.

HTML specifies a standard syntax for evoking a hyperlink to another access protocol and/or document. The URL is the element of HTML that indicates the type and location of the document to be linked. Table 24-7 lists examples of each access protocol listed in Table 24-6.

Access Protocol	Example
file	file:///<local hard drive>filename.html
ftp	ftp://ftp.novell.com/
gopher	gopher://mtsu.edu
http	http://www.novell.com/
mailto	mailto:jdoe@rambell.com
news	news:comp.infosystems
telnet	telnet://ducatalog.lib.duke.edu

Table 24-7: Example URLs for access protocols currently used in HTML documents.

As with any other programming language, the syntax of a URL must be exact and contain only valid characters, or the hyperlink will not connect your users to the intended destination. Furthermore, most Web browsers are not capable of receiving all the types of data that the URL is capable of requesting.

A URL is capable of requesting the Telnet protocol, for example, but most Web browsers cannot display it. In this situation, a *helper application* is launched by the Web browser to handle the Telnet request on behalf of the browser. In the future, however, Web browsers may be able to handle all aspects of URL requests and will no longer require external TCP/IP-based helper applications to complete a URL request. The latest version of Netscape Navigator, for example, has completely integrated news and e-mail client capability built in to the browser.

Nonstandard Ports

As we mentioned in Chapters 21 and 22, most Web servers run on port 80, a port that is well known in the Internet community to be reserved for HTTP. If your server will be running on a nonstandard port, it is recommended that you assign a port numbered 8001 or higher. To specify a nonstandard port in a URL, insert a colon after the machine name and then enter the port number before any additional path information.

Since port 80 is the standard port for HTTP, both the Web browser and server will assume port 80 unless you specify a different port in the Web Manager and in a requesting URL. For example, the URL for the Novell home page, which uses the standard port of 80, is http://www.novell.com. Duke University's Online Phonebook Directory, on the other hand, uses a nonstandard port:

```
http://phonebk.duke.edu:8001
```

Other well-known ports used by TCP/IP-based server applications include Telnet (23), Simple Mail Transfer Protocol or SMTP (25), Gopher (70), FTP (20 for default data, 21 for control), and NNTP (119).

Local Files

One of the many access protocols mentioned previously is the file protocol. Users can use their Web browsers to open a file locally from their hard drives or from a network drive mapped to your IntranetWare server. The syntax is similar to both the absolute and relative URL examples, but with one exception: You must enter a third forward slash after file://. To open the file called test.html in jdoe's user directory, you might enter the following URL:

```
FILE:///DAMOCLES.VOL1/USERS/JDOE/PUBLIC.WWW/TEST.HTM
```

Images: Inline, Clickable & Maps

Adding images to your server's HTML documents is extremely easy, not to mention addictive. Images may be used simply as pictures, such as vacation photos, or they may be used as hyperlinks and navigational aids. You've no doubt seen and used them for all these purposes, so why not add a few to your Web site? When you installed the Web server, a directory was created for images and more than 30 images were placed in it. The path to this directory is as follows:

```
SERVER_ROOT/DOCS/IMAGES
```

Many Webmasters feel it's a good idea to keep all images in a single directory because it's easier to manage them. Image files probably take up the vast majority of disk space on most Web servers, especially files for consumer-oriented Web sites that sell products or services online. This is simply because image and multimedia files are what make most Web sites interesting to visitors.

Other Webmasters, however, don't want to give read/write access to a single directory to everyone with an account on the Web server for fear that one user might delete or edit the images of another. It's also much easier for HTML authors to be able to store their image files in the same directory as their documents and other resources. Not only is it easier to keep track of files this way, but authoring HTML documents is easier as well because relative paths with no changes in directory paths may be used in place of absolute or complex paths.

Inline Images

Inline images are not used as hyperlinks, but as static pictures. The basic HTML syntax to add an inline image is as follows:

```
<IMG SRC=IMAGE.TYP width=x height=y ALT="Alternative text goes here">
```

There are other HTML syntax considerations for adding inline images, but these are the attributes that are most often used. The syntax for inserting an image is much like the syntax for inserting a hyperlink. The following code inserts and centers an image of Lower Cathedral Rock in Yosemite National Park; the image measures 240 pixels wide by 320 pixels high:

```
<CENTER>
<IMG SRC=CathedralRock.JPG WIDTH=240 HEIGHT=320 ALT="Lower Cathedral Rock,
Yosemite Valley, Yosemite National Park">
</CENTER>
```

Figure 24-10 shows what this image looks like when placed in an HTML document.

Figure 24-10: An inline image centered in an HTML document.

The alternative text, mentioned in the syntax example for inline images, is important for visitors to your Web site who have not checked Navigator's Options | Auto Load Images configuration option. People who use dial-up instead of direct Internet connections often leave this option unchecked because the time spent downloading images may be too costly, and bypassing the images not only saves connection time, but it greatly improves the speed with which Web pages are downloaded and displayed in a browser. Figure 24-11 shows how the image in Figure 24-10 looks without having been automatically loaded.

Figure 24-11: Providing alternative text in the ALT field of an inline image is helpful in many ways.

There are many other considerations for using inline images in your HTML documents—too many to be covered here. For more information on creating HTML documents and using inline images, see the following titles from Ventana and Netscape Press:

■ *Looking Good Online*, by Steve Bain with Daniel Gray.

■ *The HTML Programmer's Reference*, by Robert Mullen.

■ *Official Multimedia Publishing for Netscape*, by Gary David Bouton.

Clickable Images

Images can be more than just something to look at; they can also be hyperlinks in the same way that text can be links to other Web pages or resources. You've probably see zillions of images used as navigational aids, including the images used in the default home page for your Novell Web Server (shown in Figure 24-1 at the beginning of this chapter). Any image that can be viewed in a Web browser may also be used as a clickable (or hyperlinked) image, but virtually all such images are either in the GIF or JPEG file formats.

A clickable image must have a target URL, just as text-based hyperlinks have. The format is as follows:

```
<A HREF=TARGET_URL><IMG SRC=IMAGE_FILE></A>
```

The construction of a clickable image is exactly the same as for a text-based hyperlink except that an image is inserted in place of the text. The following source code is used with the image at the bottom of the default home page shown in Figure 24-1. When clicked, it takes one to the IntranetWare home page on Novell's Web site:

```
<A HREF=http://www.novell.com/intranetware>
<IMG SRC=images/footer.gif WIDTH=284 HEIGHT=35 BORDER=0></A>
```

Figure 24-12 shows what this image looks like when placed in an HTML document all by itself, with the cursor poised to activate the hyperlink.

Figure 24-12: A clickable inline image linking to the IntranetWare home page.

You may also add a textual hyperlink as part of the clickable image, as in the following example code.

```
<A HREF=http://www.novell.com/intranetware>
<IMG SRC=images/footer.gif WIDTH=284 HEIGHT=35 BORDER=0><P>The IntranetWare
Home Page</A>
```

We've inserted a paragraph mark (<P>) between the image and the text so the hyperlinked text doesn't line up on the right side of the image. This way, as shown in Figure 24-13, both the hyperlinked image and the text are centered.

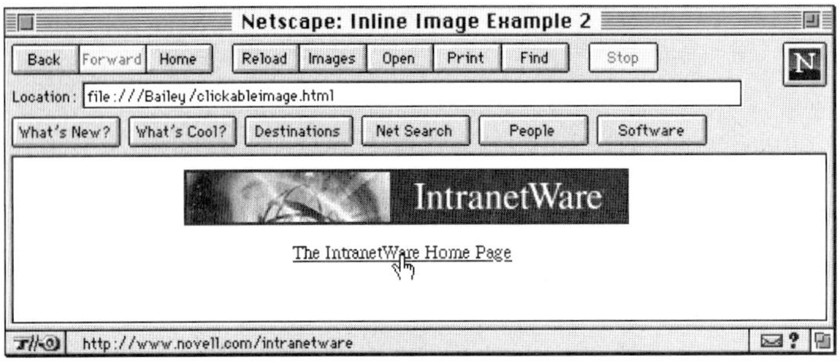

Figure 24-13: A clickable inline image and text.

A final variation on the inline image theme is for Web browsers that support JavaScript, including Navigator 2.x and 3.x. One of the many functions supported is the MOUSEOVER command, which allows you to replace the text displayed in Navigator's status line, usually the targeted URL of the hyperlink, with text you'd like visitors to your Web site to see. The MOUSEOVER command serves much the same purpose as the alternative text in the ALT field for browsers that are not automatically loading inline images; it provides additional information to visitors of your Web site before they load or link from an image. The MOUSEOVER command is inserted after the target URL but before the closing bracket (>) immediately preceding the image:

```
OnMouseover="window.status='Click here to visit the IntranetWare home
page...';return true"
```

The MOUSEOVER command is not case sensitive, so in the following example code we've changed the capitalization a bit to make it more readable. Also, the quote string between the opening and closing partial quotation marks may not contain certain characters reserved by JavaScript, such as an apostrophe:

```
<A HREF=http://www.novell.com/intranetware
OnMouseover="window.status='Click here to visit the IntranetWare home
page...';return true">
<IMG SRC=images/footer.gif WIDTH=284 HEIGHT=35 BORDER=0></A>
```

Figure 24-14 shows what the MOUSEOVER command looks like when placed in the example document.

Figure 24-14: A clickable inline image using a JavaScript command to display additional information on the destination of the hyperlink.

For more information on using JavaScript on your Web site, see the *Official Netscape JavaScript 1.2 Book, 2nd edition* by Peter Kent and John Kent (Netscape Press).

Clickable Image Maps

A more complex use for images is as clickable image maps. Instead of clicking anywhere on an image and being hyperlinked to a single location, a clickable image map allows you to divide an image into regions that each link to multiple locations when clicked, not just a single location. There are two kinds of image maps, and you may use them both on your Novell Web Server:

- Server-side image maps, which are hosted on your Web server and rely upon the server to process them.

- Client-side image maps, which are hosted on your server but rely on a Web browser such as Navigator to do the processing.

The advantage to using client-side image maps is that it relieves the Web server of having to process both the HTTP and the image map request. When a user clicks on a server-side image map, the server is responsible for processing the information that reconciles which region of the image, called a *hot spot*, has been clicked and to what location the user should be taken. It receives the location of the hyperlink that has been clicked based upon the X- and Y-coordinates of the mouse when it was clicked and then looks at a .MAP file associated with that image to decide where to redirect the Web browser.

Client-side image maps, unlike server-side image maps, contain all the information found in the .MAP file and instruct the Web browser to calculate where to take the user. No connection or processing requests are made to your Web server, which makes this form of clickable image map more desirable. However, what if you can't guarantee that all the visitors to your Web site are using client-side-enabled Web browsers? Simple: Write your HTML documents that utilize clickable image maps to do both. This way, when a document is requested by a browser that can process client-side image maps, it can be retrieved, and those browsers that can't can rely on your Novell Web Server to take care of the task.

There are three tasks associated with creating a clickable image map:

- Map the regions of an image that are to be hyperlinked.

- Create the necessary .MAP file for server-side image mapping.

- Add the information contained in the .MAP file to the HTML document utilizing client-side image mapping.

Each of these tasks is easy, but as with all HTML, one typographical error may cause it to not work properly. Also, you must first obtain a software program that maps the regions of an image and translates these regions into X- and Y-coordinates required by image maps. For a really good listing of commercial, shareware, and freeware image mapping utilities, including utilities that convert existing .MAP files into client-side image map data, see the following URL on the Yahoo Web site:

```
http://www.yahoo.com/Computers_and_Internet/Internet/World_Wide_Web/
Imagemaps/Software/
```

There are two main types of image .MAP files: CERN and NCSA. The NCSA file format, which we'll demonstrate for you shortly, is the most popular. Basically, the .MAP file contains information on three types of shapes:

- **Rectangles.** The coordinates of the upper left and lower right corners of a hot spot.

- **Circles.** The coordinates of the center and the radius of a hot spot.

- **Polygons.** The coordinates of up to 99 points of a multisided hot spot.

Most image maps use rectangular hot spots, which are also the easiest to learn how to create. For example, Figure 24-15 shows the hot spots of a clickable image map in the new home page of Rambell's faithful employee, J. Doe.

Figure 24-15: Mapping out the hot spots for a clickable image map.

J. Doe has run his image through a program that allows the user to resize or adjust the hot spots; it then exports the hot spot coordinates as a .MAP file for either the CERN or NCSA format, the latter of which is as follows:

```
#
# CREATED BY WEBMAP 1.0.1
# MONDAY, MAY 10, 1997 AT 4:05 PM
# FORMAT: NCSA
#

DEFAULT INDEX.HTML
RECT WORK.HTML 31,47 81,99
RECT BOOKS.HTML 86,48 137,100
RECT MANUALS.HTML 148,49 203,101
RECT EUROPE.HTML 61,100 111,150
RECT MACINTOSH.HTML 118,99 182,151
RECT CRASHTESTDUMMIES.HTML 54,152 173,201
```

In this example .MAP file, a default URL of INDEX.HTML is specified, so if a user clicks on an undefined region of the image map, he or she will be taken to the default URL instead of nowhere at all. Next, the hot spots (which are all rectangles), their associated URLs, and then finally their X- and Y-coordinates are declared. This file must be saved with the extension .MAP in the MAP directory on your Web server, usually located as follows:

```
SERVER_ROOT/MAPS
```

Once the .MAP file is placed in this directory, you'll need to inform your HTML document that the image is a clickable image map and tell it where to find the .MAP file. Hint: It is a good idea to name the image and its .MAP file with the same name (except for the extension) because they are easier to manage this way. Here is the code from J. Doe's home page that uses an image map, where the code relating to the image map is in boldface:

```
<!DOCTYPE HTML PUBLIC "-//W3C//DTD HTML 3.2 Final//EN">
<HTML>
<HEAD>
<TITLE>J. Doe's Home Page</TITLE>
</HEAD>

<BODY BGCOLOR=FFFFFF BACKGROUND=TILE.GIF>
<BR><BR>
<CENTER>

<A HREF=/MAP/JDOE.MAP>
<IMG SRC=JDOE.GIF WIDTH=254 HEIGHT=232 BORDER=0 ALT="Welcome to J. Doe's
home page. This image is a clickable image map and is about 50K in size"
ISMAP></A>

</CENTER>
</BODY>
</HTML>
```

Figure 24-16 shows the result of this code as viewed though Navigator. Note that using a server-side image map displays the X- and Y-coordinates of the mouse as it travels across the image and doesn't indicate whether or not you have located a hot spot.

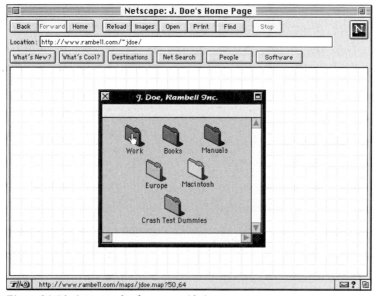

Figure 24-16: An example of a server-side image map.

In this example, instead of specifying a "normal" URL in the <A HREF> tag, the location of the .MAP file is used instead. The only other distinguishing feature of the code required to utilize a clickable image map is the presence of the ISMAP command in the <IMG SRC> tag, which indicates to the browser that the image that follows is more than just an inline image; it is a clickable image as well.

Finally, to use this image as a client-side image map you must incorporate the data in the .MAP file concerning the shapes, coordinates, and associated URLs into the HTML document, with a few formatting changes. Using a text editor, you can easily cut and paste the data to put it into the proper format. The only other change will be to include the USEMAP command in the <IMG SRC> tag identifying the map information that would otherwise reside on the Novell Web Server. These changes are shown in boldface in the following code:

```
<!DOCTYPE HTML PUBLIC "-//W3C//DTD HTML 3.2 Final//EN">
<HTML>
<HEAD>
<TITLE>J. Doe's Home Page</TITLE>
</HEAD>

<BODY BGCOLOR=FFFFFF BACKGROUND=TILE.GIF>
<BR><BR>
<CENTER>

<A HREF=/MAP/JDOE.MAP>
<IMG SRC=JDOE.GIF WIDTH=254 HEIGHTt=232 BORDER=0 ALT="Welcome to J. Doe's
home page. This image is a clickable image map and is about 50K in size"
USEMAP="#JDOE_MAP" ISMAP></A>

<MAP NAME=JDOE_MAP>
<AREA SHAPE=RECT COORDS="31,47 81,99"      HREF=WORK.HTML>
<AREA SHAPE=RECT COORDS="86,48 137,100"    HREF=BOOKS.HTML>
<AREA SHAPE=RECT COORDS="148,49 203,101"   HREF=MANUALS.HTML>
<AREA SHAPE=RECT COORDS="61,100 111,150"   HREF=EUROPE.HTML>
<AREA SHAPE=RECT COORDS="118,99 182,151"   HREF=MACINTOSH.HTML>
<AREA SHAPE=RECT COORDS="54,152 173,201"   HREF=CRASHTESTDUMMIES.HTML>
</MAP>

</CENTER>
</BODY>
</HTML>
```

Figure 24-17 shows the above HTML document after the addition of the client-side clickable image map information.

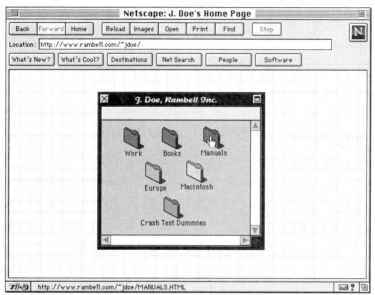

Figure 24-17: An example of a client-side image map.

Note the absence of X- and Y-coordinates of the mouse in the status line of Navigator's window; instead the target URL is shown as it travels across the image. When the mouse isn't located over a hot spot, the cursor will not change into the pointing finger that is used by Navigator and other Web browsers to indicate that a hyperlink has been located. You can also use the MOUSEOVER command described earlier to display alternative information about a hyperlinked hot spot on a clickable image map. For example, you would add the MOUSEOVER information to each hyperlink in the USEMAP section of the HTML document, as in the following code taken from the example of J. Doe's home page. This code links to the Manuals section:

```
<AREA SHAPE=RECT COORDS="148,49 203,101" HREF=MANUALS.HTML
OnMouseover="window.status= 'Click here to learn more about software manuals
available from Rambell...';return true">
```

Figure 24-18 illustrates how this would look when viewed through Navigator.

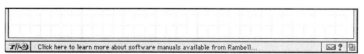

Figure 24-18: You can also use the MOUSEOVER option to display alternative information about a hot spot in a client-side image map.

Images can be put to very good use on your Web server to help it look more attractive, be more user-friendly, and enable additional navigational capabilities that would otherwise be unavailable to visitors to your site. Another way to provide alluring and useful content to your Web site is through the use of server-side includes, described and illustrated in the next section.

Server-Side Includes

Server-side include (SSI) documents are regular HTML documents that contain one or more special commands that enable users of your Web server to author more dynamic documents. These commands are easily included in a document and provide a great amount of flexibility and creativity without requiring advanced knowledge of programming languages. With SSI, HTML authors will be able to include in their documents such things as:

- The time and date a document was last updated.
- Selected text from an external document.
- The size of a document.
- A hit counter that displays the number of times a document has been retrieved.

The SSI commands used by NWS 3.0 include the standard SSI commands supported by most NCSA HTTP-compliant Web servers as well as many more commands that have been enabled for use with this particular Web server. For example, to display the size of a file called USERS.TXT within the body of the document itself, you would use the following command:

```
<!--#FSIZE file="USERS.TXT"-->
```

SSI commands are encapsulated within what is otherwise interpreted by Web browsers as the comment command (<!comments go here >). How does the Novell Web Server know to execute these commands if they are contained within a comment? There are two conditions that must be met before NWS can execute SSI commands:

- SSI documents must end with the .SSI extension.
- SSI documents must be located in the directory known to your Web server as the directory containing SSI documents, usually SERVER_ROOT\DOCS\SSI.

The following HTML document calls several of the NCSA HTTP-supported SSI commands, which are highlighted in boldface type:

```
<!DOCTYPE HTML PUBLIC "-//W3C//DTD HTML 3.2 Final//EN">
<HTML>
```

```
<HEAD>
<TITLE>SSI Examples</TITLE>
</HEAD>

<BODY>
<H3>NCSA HTTP-supported SSI Commands</H3>
<HR NOSHADE SIZE=2>

CONFIG:    Set to MM/DD/YY using the
                     <I>CONFIG TIMEFMT</I> option.
                     <!--#CONFIG TIMEFMT="%D %r %p"-->
<P>
INCLUDE:  <!--#INCLUDE file="USERS.TXT"-->
<p>
ECHO:       <!--#ECHO var="SERVER_SOFTWARE"-->
<P>
FLASTMOD: <!--#FLASTMOD file="USERS.TXT"-->
<P>
FSIZE:      <!--#FSIZE file="USERS.TXT"-->
<P>

</BODY>
</HTML>
```

Figure 24-19 shows how this document is served by Rambell's Novell Web Server.

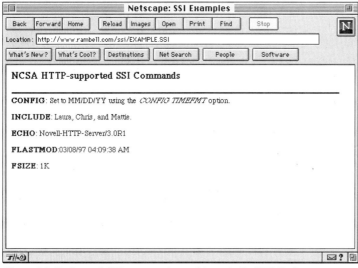

Figure 24-19: Several SSI commands used in a single HTML document.

Most of the SSI commands supported by NWS are very straightforward, but a few may be more familiar to those with just a hint of programming experience. Don't fear, however, because the online documentation that comes with the server explains them all in sufficient detail. The following list briefly explains the SSI commands supported at this time by NWS 3.0.

APPEND

```
<!--#APPEND FILE="filename" LINE="lines"-->
```

The APPEND command is used to take information from a Web page that uses forms to submit information to the Web server. It appends the information to an external file for future reference.

BREAK

```
<!--#BREAK-->
```

The BREAK command tells the Web server to stop sending the document when this command is encountered and to terminate the HTTP connection.

CALC

```
<!--#CALC VARNAME="operation"-->
```

The CALC command tells the Web server to perform the following mathematical calculations: addition, subtraction, multiplication, division.

CONFIG

```
<!--#CONFIG TIMEFMT="descriptors"-->
```

The CONFIG command allows you to change the way the date and time are displayed by the FLASTMOD and FSIZE commands when it is used prior to these commands in an SSI document.

COUNT

```
<!--#COUNT FILE="filename"-->
```

The COUNT command displays the number of "hits" a page has received.

ECHO

```
<!--#ECHO VAR="variable"-->
```

The ECHO command displays one of several environment variables that has been declared in the body of the same document, as in a form, or that it gets from a list of declared variables, such as the document's URL, the date and time, or the Web server version used to serve the document.

EXE CGI

```
<!--#EXE CGI="QFSearch?query"-->
```

The EXE CGI command interfaces with the Novell QuickFinder search engine, described in the next chapter, and allows you to display a list of documents that meet the search criteria without a user having to actually construct a search.

FLASTMOD

```
<!--#FLASTMOD FILE(VIRTUAL)="filename(path/filename)"-->
```

The FLASTMOD command displays the date on which either the current file or another file was last modified.

FSIZE

```
<!--#FSIZE FILE(VIRTUAL)="filename"-->
```

The FSIZE command displays the size of either the current file or another file.

GOTO

```
<!--#GOTO LABEL="labelname"-->
```

The GOTO command causes the Web server to stop sending data from a specific point in a Web page, jump to another location, and resume sending data from that point.

IF

```
<!--#IF "variable1" operator "variable2" operation-->
```

The IF command allows you to build Web pages that perform functions or return data after a simple if-then calculation has been processed, as in "If this page is requested between the hours of 8:00 A.M. and 5:00 P.M., then return the following special greeting at the top of the document."

INCLUDE

```
<!--#INCLUDE VIRTUAL="path/filename"-->
```

The INCLUDE command displays the contents of an external file within the body of the current SSI document.

LABEL

```
<!--#LABEL "label_name"-->
```

The LABEL command identifies a section within an SSI document that may be referenced by the GOTO command.

The SSI commands available to you are very easy to use, but there is much more information to learn about their use. See the online documentation that comes with NWS for this information as well as examples to help you get started.

NDS Browsing

The NDS Browser gives users the ability to view objects in your NDS tree using any Web browser, including Navigator. This is a helpful feature for large organizations who employ large numbers of employees and maintain numerous networked devices, such as NetWare and IntranetWare servers, printers and print queues, users, groups, volumes, and partitions. As the Webmaster, you can restrict what information users may see when browsing your NDS tree via the Web as well as decide what users and groups can have access to this information. This section will show you how to configure your Web server to enable NDS browsing, as well as how to browse NDS objects and what information users may find useful while browsing.

Configuring the Browser

Your Novell Web Server is able to perform NDS browsing with the help of an NLM called NDSOBJ.NLM, which is installed into the following directory as part of the Web server installation process:

```
SYS:INW_WEB/SHARED/LCGI/NDSOBJ
```

To enable NDS browsing, follow these steps:

1. Load the Web Manager program, as detailed in Chapter 21.

2. Select a virtual Web server for which NDS Browsing is to be enabled.

3. Choose the Server tab and confirm that the Enable NDS Browsing option is selected, as shown in Figure 24-20.

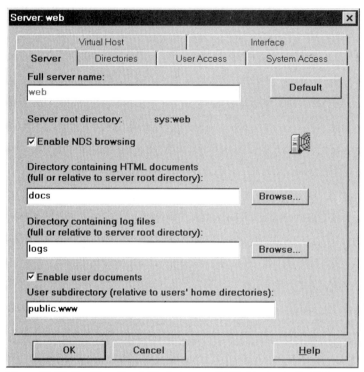

Figure 24-20: Enabling the ability to browse NDS objects via the Web.

4. Click OK and restart the server if prompted to do so.

Once NDS Browsing has been enabled, you may optionally configure the leaf objects in your NDS tree to have the following additional information available when viewed through a Web browser:

■ An associated home page (URL)

■ An associated image file

An associated home page or image file may be useful for large companies—the location of a printer could be represented using a diagram, a scanned photograph of an employee could be featured, or a clipping from your favorite Dilbert cartoon could be available for your users. These features are added to a user's leaf information using the NetWare Administrator utility. However, you must first install a snap-in to add these two fields to the NetWare Administrator by following the steps outlined next.

Windows 3.x Users

1. Open your \WINDOWS\NWADMIN.INI file using a text editor such as Notepad.

2. Add this line to the Snapin Objects DLLs WIN3X section:

    `WEBSNP3X.DLL=WEBSNP3X.DLL`

3. Save and close the file.

Windows 95 Users

1. Open the Registration Editor by executing C:\WINDOWS\REGEDIT.EXE.

2. From the Registry | Import Registry menu, choose SYS:PUBLIC\WIN95\ WEBREGED.REG.

3. Click OK and quit the Registration Editor.

   Once you have made the necessary changes, you may then add a URL for a leaf object's home page or an image file by using the NetWare Administrator.

Browsing the Tree

Browsing your organization's NDS tree using any Web browser is very easy. Unlike most other resources on your Web server, however, there isn't a collection of HTML documents that represent your tree's leaf objects. Instead, the NDS Browser creates HTML output on the fly in response to requests from Web browsers. Once the information has been sent to a browser, it is deleted from memory. Therefore, HTML files for these objects do not exist. To browse an NDS tree, enter the following URL, replacing www.*yourserver*.com with your Novell Web Server's address and the number 80 with your server's default port number:

`http://www.yourserver.com:80/nds`

   Figure 24-21 shows what the first level of an organization's NDS tree looks like when viewed via the Web.

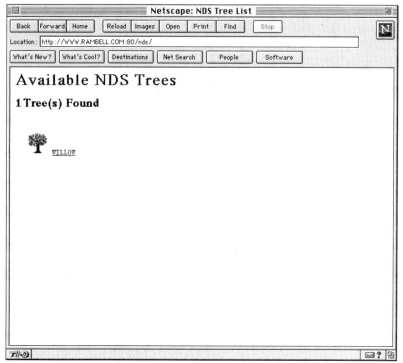

Figure 24-21: Browsing an NDS tree using Navigator.

You may proceed to navigate your NDS tree, its branches, and leaves by clicking on an object name. For example, the Rambell NDS tree begins with WILLOW, shown in Figure 24-22, whose organizational unit is divided among three countries: Bermuda, Canada, and the United States.

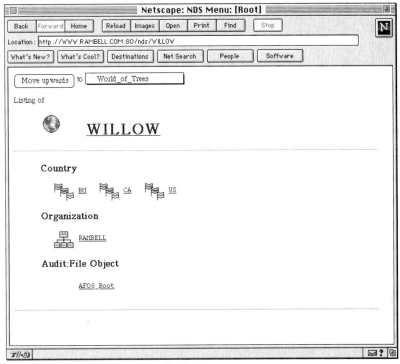

Figure 24-22: Exploring an organization's structure.

Selecting the RAMBELL leaf reveals a three-part organization, Accounting (ACCT), Information Technology (IT), and Manufacturing (MANUF), as well as a user named Administrator (ADMIN), shown in Figure 24-23.

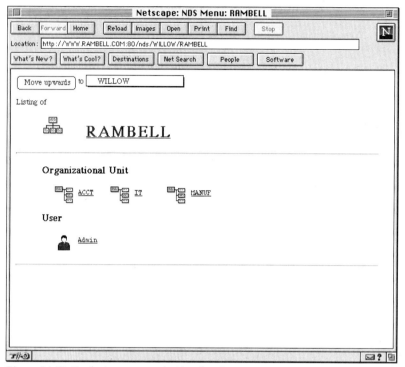

Figure 24-23: Exploring an organizational unit.

Finally, selecting the IT container reveals greater detail about its leaves, including its users, groups, organizational role, printing services, and volume information, shown in Figure 24-24.

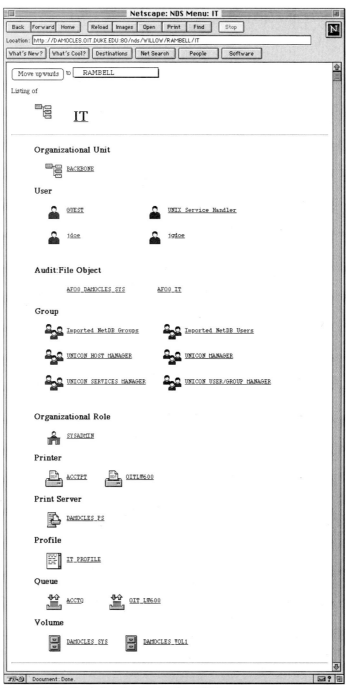

Figure 24-24: Browsing the details of an NDS tree.

Notice that using the NDS Browser reveals one of the important traits of a well-designed NDS tree: an NDS tree should have only a single object at the root, with more containers and leaves added as the tree grows. Enabling NDS Browsing helps network administrators, as well as users, understand the structural roles of the various departments in an organization and keep track of an organization's containers and objects.

Moving On

This chapter has covered a lot of ground in an attempt to help you provide better content in your Web server. We've covered all the basics of HTTP and HTML; the structure of server and user directories; how to use all the different types of URLs in hyperlinks; the use of images as pictures, hyperlinks, and image maps; and finally, how to enable users to browse your NDS tree using a Web browser. These are just the basics for providing Web content, so you should consider investing in a handful of more detailed reference materials that can help you create attractive, interesting, and useful content for your Web server. You need to look no further than the home page of the publisher of this book for this information:

```
http://www.vmedia.com
```

In the next chapter, we'll cover the basics of another hot topic for Webmasters, CGI scripting. The Novell Web Server comes with several very powerful solutions for CGI support, including several scripts that are ready for use and information on how to write your own.

25

CGI Scripting

In the past, corporate intranets have relied heavily upon the ability to publish static documentation on the Web, documentation such as product lists, contact information, and customer support resources. A corporate presence on today's Web, however, demands a more dynamic and interactive means of publishing on the Web. Novell Web Server can provide this type of interactivity with your users on a level that exceeds the capabilities of most of its competition. We've seen in the previous chapter that Server Side Includes (SSIs) can provide a limited dynamic element to your Web site by allowing HTML authors to include a dozen or so commands that insert data, the date, or time or hide data from users based on simple IF-THEN conditions.

With Common Gateway Interface (CGI) scripts and applications, however, you can provide a much higher level of interactivity to your Web site's visitors.

The first Web servers were designed to include CGI capabilities, but it hasn't been until fairly recently that programmers developed truly useful CGIs that take advantage of these capabilities to the benefit of corporations and corporate intranets. In fact, CGIs are now so plentiful that it often makes more business sense to purchase a prepackaged CGI instead of having a programmer develop one from scratch. There are also hundreds, if not thousands, of CGIs that are either freeware or in the public domain and that can accomplish a task that you might otherwise spend days or weeks developing.

This chapter will introduce you to the CGI capabilities of the Novell Web Server. We're presupposing that you have copious knowledge of NetWare, of course, but we're not making the same assumption about your knowledge of HTML, forms on the Web, and programming. Many, many books have been written on CGI programming, and it would be foolish for us to think that we can do justice to this topic in just one chapter. Instead, we'll introduce you to CGIs and the Novell Web Server as they relate to your intranet. Specifically, the goals for this chapter are as follows:

■ To introduce you to how CGIs and forms work and to the limits of their usefulness.

■ To provide a quick overview of the various types of CGIs you can use on your Novell Web Server and intranet.

■ To demonstrate a few of these CGIs, showing you in detail how they work.

■ To show you where to go for further assistance.

What Is a CGI?

Some of you may be wondering what exactly a CGI is, and that is a good question. Many people mistakenly believe a CGI is a type of program that interfaces a Web browser, such as Navigator, with a Web server such as Novell Web Server 3.0. In reality, the term Common Gateway Interface, or CGI, refers to a set of standards by which programmers may create applications that interface with Internet servers such as Web servers. There are very few applications that use the CGI standard to communicate with Internet servers other than Web servers at this time. However, there are a number of CGI-based applications that are designed to allow Web browsers and Internet servers to communicate with the assistance of Web servers. For simplicity's sake, we'll refer to these as CGI applications, or just CGIs.

The CGI standard defines three major areas to allow applications to communicate with Internet servers such as Web servers:

■ The method of encoding data sent from a Web browser to a CGI.

■ The information passed from a Web server to a CGI.

■ Tasks to be performed by a CGI.

CGIs are complex programs created by programmers, and describing how they work and why a Web site needs them can also be complex. However, we've come up with an alternative way of describing the concept of CGIs to those persons in your organization who are technologically challenged:

■ **Common.** CGIs use standard programming languages.

■ **Gateway.** CGIs have the ability to pass information between clients, servers, and applications.

■ **Interface.** CGIs rely on easy-to-use Web browsers to interface with complex Internet servers and applications.

As more companies rely on intranets and the Web as mission-critical components of their daily operations, more and more CGIs are developed to aid companies to accomplish their goals. The first CGIs were fairly simple programs, usually written in Perl, that served as gateways from Web browsers to other Internet services, such as Wide Area Information Service (WAIS) and Finger servers, and that made it possible to send e-mail and serve clickable image maps. Now many of the services that used to require CGIs have been integrated into Web browsers such as Navigator and Internet Explorer, so today's CGIs are designed to perform more complex tasks. Here is a list of services, past and present, that can be provided with CGIs:

- Text input forms
- Clickable image maps
- Searchable indices
- Discussion or "white" boards
- Database access
- Archie gateways
- WAIS gateways
- Usenet news gateways
- Dynamic documents
- Random image and hyperlink generators
- Hit counters
- Guestbooks
- Time and date stampers
- GIF animations
- Credit card verification
- Server-Side Includes
- Online order forms
- Shopping cart processors
- Chat room messaging
- Problem reports
- Product information requests
- On-the-fly HTML page creation
- Sending faxes
- Secure banking

Thousands of CGIs have been written over the past few years, some of which are still very useful, some of which are now obsolete, and still others that never saw the light of day. A great resource for information on CGIs is Matt's Script Archive, which can be found on the Web at the following URL:

```
http://www.worldwidemart.com/scripts/
```

There are plenty of useful CGIs to be found, but there are many more that have yet to be created. CGI development is probably the most important concern to Webmasters today because of the ever-increasing new uses for data. The trick, therefore, is to create CGIs to allow users access to this data over the Web. The first step is to create an HTML document that allows users to input data that will be sent to a CGI.

HTML Tags & Syntax for CGIs

HTML limits the ways in which data is sent to a CGI for processing as well as the ways in which CGIs can return data to a Web browser. All data passing between a browser and a CGI must pass through a Web server, which is capable of understanding only HTML-compliant data. Data created by a CGI must likewise go through a Web server on its way back to a browser. In the process of execution, a CGI may also pass data on to another application or service and not need to return any information to a Web browser other than a message like: "Your submission has been accepted. Thanks for visiting!" In the majority of cases, however, a CGI processes a request and returns a dynamically created HTML document (meaning it takes information you've entered or submitted, passes it through a CGI, and a new document is then created and sent back to your browser).

What this means for you, therefore, is that you must not only be proficient in HTML, but in the creation of *forms* as well. And only when you have mastered these skills can you write a CGI, which requires programming skills. However, since there are so many CGIs that are available for free or commercially, programming skills are not as necessary as they once were. The remainder of this section will focus on how to create HTML documents that invoke CGIs. Later on in this chapter, we'll cover the types of CGIs that are supported by the Novell Web Server and look at a few examples.

Searching With <ISINDEX> & GET

There are several methods available to submit data to a CGI over the Web. We'll only spend a few minutes on two of these methods, <ISINDEX> and GET, because they are very limited in capability and have been largely replaced by the POST method. Both <ISINDEX> and GET are still useful, however.

In Chapter 22, we mentioned the three basic commands sent by a browser to a Web server, GET, HEAD, and POST. The <ISINDEX> tag uses the GET method to send a simple search request from the Web browser to a CGI by appending the search terms onto the end of the CGI's URL. The benefit of using the <ISINDEX> method is that you don't need to create a form to prompt users to enter the data: the <ISINDEX> tag performs this function for you by automatically separating the search term(s) from the target CGI's URL with a question mark (?), and blank spaces between multiple search terms are replaced with the plus (+) sign.

The following HTML code is from a CGI used for Duke University's Departmental Directory and uses the <ISINDEX> method to pass small amounts of data to a CGI that searches a very large data file:

```
<HEAD>
<TITLE>Duke Departmental Directory Search</TITLE>
<ISINDEX>
</HEAD>

<BODY>
<H1>Search the Departmental Directory</H1>
Enter a search string in the search field. You will be informed if any
departmental listings in the Duke Departmental Directory have words that
match.
<P><HR><BR>
<A HREF="http://www.duke.edu/deptdir/">Return to Departmental Directory
</A><P>
Questions or problems with this service should be sent to
<A HREF="mailto:webmaster@www.duke.edu">
<ADDRESS>webmaster@www.duke.edu</ADDRESS></A>
</BODY>
</HTML>
```

Figure 25-1 shows the preceding HTML document when viewed in Navigator.

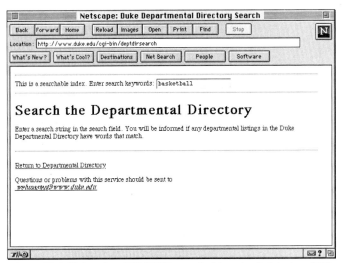

Figure 25-1: Using the <ISINDEX> method to submit data to a CGI.

The <ISINDEX> tag automatically inserts "This is a searchable index. Enter search keywords:" as well as a single-line text entry field. Also, you don't have to use a Submit button with the <ISINDEX> tag because pressing the Return key will activate the default action of submitting the search query to the CGI's URL (http://www.duke.edu/cgi-bin/deptdirsearch). Figure 25-2 shows the results of the user typing the word *basketball* into the preceding CGI.

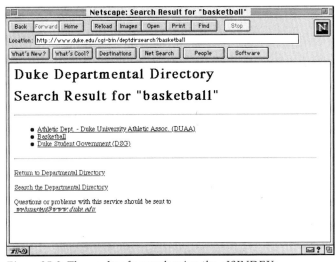

Figure 25-2: The results of a search using the <ISINDEX>.

Tip

When the <ISINDEX>/GET method is used, the entire URL (URL plus request) cannot exceed 1024 bytes of data, or 1K; it is therefore a very limited method to implement a complex form that sends a lot of text. CGI-based forms that use the POST method can exchange upwards of 30-60K of data per form.

The following HTML document uses the GET method to perform a simple search for the phrase "IntranetWare and Novell" on the Lycos search engine (http://www.lycos.com):

```
<!DOCTYPE HTML PUBLIC "-//W3C//DTD HTML 3.2 Final//EN">
<HTML>
<HEAD>
<TITLE>GET Sample Form</TITLE>
</HEAD>

<BODY BGCOLOR=#99FF99>
<CENTER>
<H2>Select the "Go Get It" button to begin a Lycos search using the GET form
submission method:</H2>
</CENTER>
<P>
<FORM ACTION="http://www.lycos.com/cgi-bin/pursuit" METHOD="get">
<P>
<input size="35" type="text" name="query" value="IntranetWare and Novell">
<input type="submit" value="Go Get It"> <p>
<input checked type=radio name=ab value=the_catalog> Lycos catalog <p>
<input type=radio name=ab value=a2z> A2Z directory <p>
<input type=radio name=ab value=point> Point reviews <p>
</FORM>
</BODY>
</HTML>
```

Figure 25-3 shows the get.html document as viewed in Netscape Navigator.

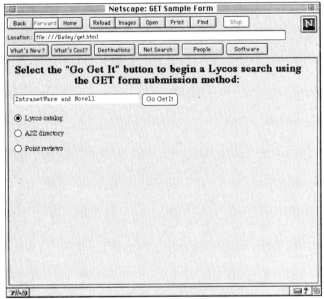

Figure 25-3: Using the GET method to submit data to a CGI.

Figure 25-4 shows the results of the search for "IntranetWare and Novell" using the GET method on the Lycos search engine.

These previous two HTML documents use the GET method and represent a very simple submission to a CGI on the Web. The document using the <ISINDEX> tags is the simplest of HTML forms, and the one using the GET method is also a simple example. Let's move on and explain how to create more complex HTML documents using the POST method and the many different types of input fields.

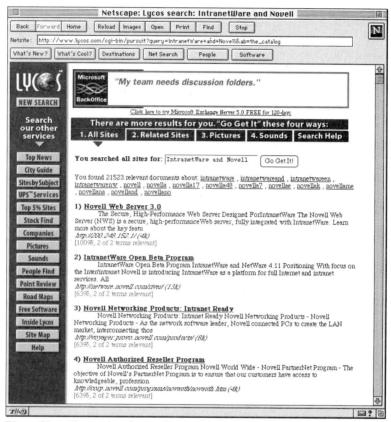

Figure 25-4: The results of a search using the GET method.

Using the POST Method

In HTML, the <FORM> tag is a tagged pair like most other tags, with the following usage:

```
<FORM ACTION=value METHOD=value>
input_fields
</FORM>
```

In the opening tag you must specify two things. First, the ACTION specifies the path (relative or absolute) and filename of the CGI to be executed by the form. Next, the <FORM> tag specifies, in the METHOD field, a method of transferring the form's data to the Web server. There are only two options for this field, GET and POST, and for almost all your needs, you must use the POST method. The following is an example of an opening <FORM> tag:

```
<FORM ACTION="/perldocs/cruncher.pl" METHOD="post">
```

All other elements of a form will be entered between the opening <FORM> tag and the closing </FORM> tag, including the HTML tags that define the number and types of text fields, buttons, and boxes. The last item in a form, however, will typically be the Submit and optional Reset buttons, although they do not actually need to appear on the form as the last items. Figure 25-5 illustrates the many types of input fields that may appear within the <FORM></FORM> tags.

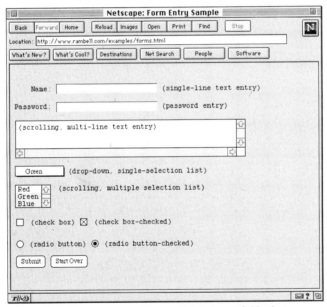

Figure 25-5: There are several types of data input fields that you may use in a form.

The NAME Element

All of the following elements that appear in a form must declare a NAME variable if they are to be able to pass data from the browser to the CGI. Each NAME element identifies a specific variable that has a corresponding element in the CGI for which the form is written. In the Lycos example earlier in this

chapter, there are four input fields, one for the text string and three that identify which database to search. The text field uses the name="query" variable
and the three radio buttons use the name="ab" variable.

The <INPUT> Tag

The <INPUT> tag is used to create entry fields and buttons; it is the tag used
most often in forms. The <INPUT> tag has several options, or types; the default is visible text and the other options are hidden text, password, check box,
radio button, submit button, and reset button. You do not need to define
TYPE=text as it is the default, but we suggest that you declare it anyway to
avoid confusion down the road.

Single-Line Text Fields

Several options are available when using the <INPUT> tag to create entry
fields for single-line text entries. The following HTML code and its output to
Netscape Navigator (Figure 25-6) show a sample HTML document that has
two types of single-line text entry fields—text and password:

```
<!DOCTYPE HTML PUBLIC "-//W3C//DTD HTML 3.2 Final//EN">
<HTML>
<HEAD>
<TITLE>One Line Entry Sample Form</TITLE>
</HEAD>

<BODY BGCOLOR=#99FF99>
<H1>Single-line Text Entry Form</H1>
<P>
This is a sample form that demonstrates several single-line text entry
fields.
</P>
<HR SIZE=3>
<PRE>
<FORM ACTION="/perldocs/submission.pl" METHOD="post">
Name: <INPUT TYPE="text" NAME="name" SIZE=40> <P>
Password: <INPUT TYPE="password" NAME="pwd" SIZE=8
                 MAXLENGTH=8> <P>
Street: <INPUT TYPE="text" NAME="str" SIZE=40> <P>
City: <INPUT TYPE="text" NAME="cty" SIZE=42> <P>
State: <INPUT TYPE="text" NAME="st" SIZE=2
                 MAXLENGTH=2>
```

```
Zip: <INPUT TYPE="text" NAME="zip" SIZE=10> <P>
E-mail: <INPUT TYPE="text" NAME="em" SIZE=20> <P>
 <INPUT TYPE="submit" VALUE="Submit"><INPUT TYPE="reset" VALUE="Start Over">
</PRE>
</FORM>

<HR SIZE=3>
</BODY>
</HTML>
```

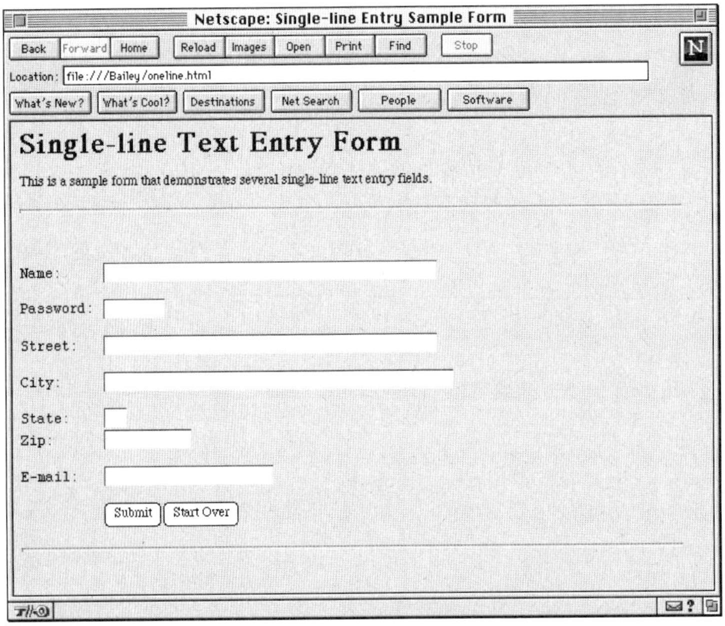

Figure 25-6: A sample form using several single-line text entry fields.

In the preceding example, we are using the POST method to send several lines of form data to a CGI named submission.pl in a folder called PERLDOCS on the same Web server as the CGI resides. It is possible to direct the form input data to another Web server, which could look like this:

```
<FORM ACTION="http://www.rival.com/bin/submission.pl" METHOD="post">
```

Using the SIZE value, you are able to control the length of the text fields, which can be a handy feature when you need to have more control over what your users are able to enter. For example, the State field of this example is limited to a two-character entry, and in the password field, which is encrypted, we are also capable of limiting the number of characters. Without the MAXLENGTH value, a line of text could stretch on far beyond the length of the visible text field, although in the case of the zip code field, you would only see 10 characters of such a long line of text.

Tip

The characters entered into the PASSWORD input type field are always encrypted.

Check Boxes & Radio Buttons

The <INPUT> field is also used to create check boxes and radio buttons, which use fewer options than the text fields use. The following HTML code, and Figure 25-7, shows a group of check boxes for dogs and a group of radio buttons for cats:

```
<!DOCTYPE HTML PUBLIC "-//W3C//DTD HTML 3.2 Final//EN">
<HTML>
<HEAD>
<TITLE>Check Boxes & Radio Buttons</TITLE>
</HEAD>

<BODY BGCOLOR=#99FF99>
<H1>Check Boxes & Radio Buttons</H1>
This is a sample form that demonstrates check boxes and radio buttons.
<HR SIZE=3>

<FORM ACTION="/cgi/test_script.acgi" METHOD="post">
<INPUT TYPE="checkbox" NAME="dogs" VALUE="american" CHECKED> American Cocker
Spaniel <P>
<INPUT TYPE="checkbox" NAME="dogs" VALUE="english"> English Cocker Spaniel
<P>
<INPUT TYPE="checkbox" NAME="dogs" VALUE="springer"> Springer Spaniel <P>
<INPUT TYPE="checkbox" NAME="dogs" VALUE="water"> Water Spaniel <P>

<CENTER>
```

```
<INPUT TYPE="radio" NAME="cats" VALUE="siam"> Siamese
<INPUT TYPE="radio" NAME="cats" VALUE="tab"> Tabby
<INPUT TYPE="radio" NAME="cats" VALUE="mainc" CHECKED> Main Coon
<INPUT TYPE="radio" NAME="cats" VALUE="Mnx"> Manx
</CENTER>
<P>
<INPUT TYPE="submit" VALUE="Submit">
<INPUT TYPE="reset" VALUE="Start Over">
</FORM>

<HR SIZE=3>
</BODY>
</HTML>
```

Tip

In the case of check boxes, you may have more than one box checked by default. With radio buttons, however, you may choose or default-check only one.

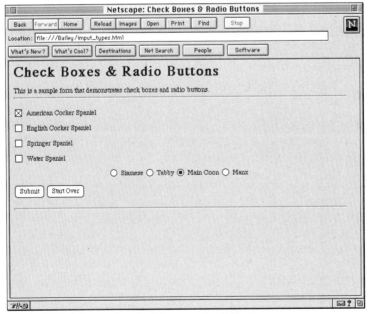

Figure 25-7: A form using check boxes and radio buttons.

Drop-Down, Scrolling & Multiple-Selection Lists

A drop-down list is created in a form using the <SELECT></SELECT> tagged pair option instead of the <INPUT> tag. A drop-down list is configurable to show one or more list choices; the default is one, as in the following code and Figure 25-8:

```
<!DOCTYPE HTML PUBLIC "-//W3C//DTD HTML 3.2 Final//EN">
<HTML>
<HEAD>
<TITLE>Drop-down Lists</TITLE>
</HEAD>

<BODY BGCOLOR=#99FF99>
<H1>Drop-down List Example</H1>
This is a sample form that demonstrates a drop-down list.
<HR SIZE=3>
<P><P>
<FORM ACTION="/PERLDOCS/LISTS.PL" METHOD="POST">
<SELECT NAME="email_software" VALUE="">
<OPTION> Emailer
<OPTION SELECTED> Bluto
<OPTION> Eudora
<OPTION> Pine
<OPTION> POPmail
</SELECT>
<INPUT TYPE="submit" VALUE="Submit">
<INPUT TYPE="reset" VALUE="Start Over">
</FORM>
<HR SIZE=3>
</BODY>
</HTML>
```

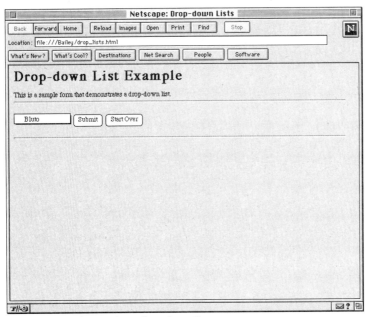

Figure 25-8: A form using a drop-down list.

In the preceding example, Bluto is the default choice, but only one option may be chosen using this type of input field. If we were to change the <SELECT> tag to include the following options, however, our drop-down list would become a scrolling, multiple-selection list, as seen in Figure 25-9:

```
<SELECT NAME="email_software" MULTIPLE SIZE=5 Value="">
<OPTION SELECTED> Emailer
<OPTION SELECTED> Bluto
<OPTION SELECTED> Eudora
```

The addition of the MULTIPLE and SIZE options creates a list that can have more than one item viewed and selected, as in the preceding example. Carlos Varela uses several of these options in his multisource phonebook directory at http://fiaker.ncsa.uiuc.edu:8080/cgi-bin/phfd, shown in Figure 25-10.

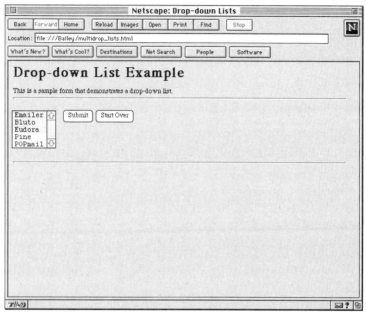

Figure 25-9: A scrolling, multiple-selection list.

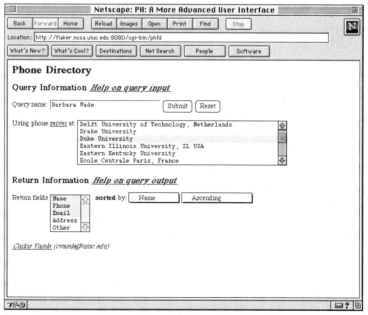

Figure 25-10: Several types of input fields working together.

The <TEXTAREA> Tag

The <TEXTAREA> tag allows you to add a large scratch space to a form, enabling your users to write a more lengthy message that just the single-line entry used with the <INPUT> tag. The <TEXTAREA> tag has two elements that control its size, ROWS and COLS, in addition to the mandatory NAME element. You cannot set a maximum number of rows and columns as in some of the other tags, however. If your users continue to type beyond the area that is provided, the text will scroll up. You may also enter default text into the window area, which your users may delete and write over, as in Figure 25-11. The following is an example of a document with a <TEXTAREA> tag:

```
<!DOCTYPE HTML PUBLIC "-//W3C//DTD HTML 3.2 Final//EN">
<HTML>
<HEAD>
<TITLE>Multiple Rows & Columns</TITLE>
</HEAD>

<BODY BGCOLOR=#99FF99>
<H1>Multiple Rows & Columns</H1>
This is a sample form that demonstrates multiple rows & columns.
<HR SIZE=3>
<P>
<FORM ACTION="/PERLDOCS/ROWS.PL" METHOD="POST">
<TEXTAREA NAME="comments" ROWS=6 COLS=60 WRAP>
Enter your comments here!
</TEXTAREA>
<P>
<INPUT TYPE="submit" VALUE="Submit">
<INPUT TYPE="reset" VALUE="Start Over">
</FORM>
<HR SIZE=3>
</BODY>
</HTML>
```

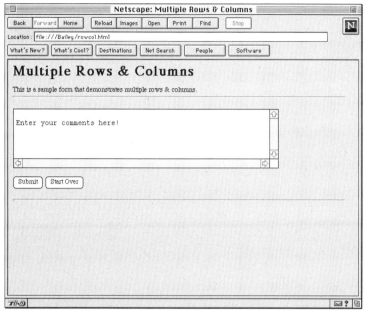

Figure 25-11: A form using a large text area with multiple columns and rows.

Submit & Reset

The last, but not least, important items included in the <FORM></FORM> tags are the Submit and Reset buttons, which are elements of the <INPUT> tag. They appear in all our previous examples except the <ISINDEX> example, where they are not required. Carlos Varela's phonebook form places these buttons near the top instead of at the bottom where they usually appear. You have the option of changing the text that appears on the face of these two buttons, and you may delete the VALUE statements altogether as well. If you do so, the buttons will default to being labeled Submit Query and Reset.

Supported CGIs

As we mentioned in Chapter 21, Novell Web Server 3.0 supports several different types of CGIs for the creation of dynamic Web server content. The CGI specification provides a set of standards by which programmers may create applications that interface with Internet servers, but it is up to the creators of each type of Web server to integrate these standards into a particular platform such as IntranetWare. Some of the methods used by NWS to integrate CGI support with IntranetWare may be more familiar to you than others. However, NWS offers so many different CGI integration methods that you or one of your company's programmers will most likely already be familiar with at least one of them:

- Remote Common Gateway Interface
- Local Common Gateway Interface
- Perl 5 scripts
- NetBasic scripts

In addition to these types of CGIs that some may be familiar with, a new CGI has been added to provide searching and indexing capabilities, called the QuickFinder Search Engine.

Local Common Gateway Interface

NWS uses two categories of CGIs, one that runs on the Web server itself and another that interfaces with a CGI located on another Web server. The first type, called a Local Common Gateway Interface (LCGI), is by far the most common. CGIs are typically written in one of several scripting languages that are interpreted by an NLM (NetWare Loadable Module) upon execution. Perl 5 and NetBasic for Internet from the HiTecSoft Corporation are two such languages. As we mentioned in Chapter 21, Perl is an industry-standard scripting language available for many platforms, most notably UNIX, Windows, and the Mac OS. Many Webmasters feel Perl is to CGI scripting as Gilligan is to Gilligan's Island—inseparable. NetBasic is based on the BASIC programming language and should be familiar to many NetWare administrators, engineers, and PC users. Web server scripts are very useful for creating and manipulating text as well as querying databases. Perl and NetBasic are not as involved or complex as programming languages such as C++ or Java. However, because they are interpreted—not compiled—languages, they don't offer the performance of other solutions for providing interactivity with your Web server.

Remote Common Gateway Interface

Remote Common Gateway Interface (RCGI) programs, the second type of CGI supported by NWS, are NLMs written in the ANSI C programming language. Unlike the NLMs used by Perl and NetBasic LCGIs, which are provided as part of the default Web server installation, RCGI NLMs are individually written to meet your needs and are provided as "canned" programs. RCGIs are unique to IntranetWare and perform tasks similar to those LCGIs perform, and although they may be written to run on either NetWare or other servers (such as UNIX servers), they are designed to interface Novell Web Servers with remote services and resources. Currently, RCGIs may be written for the following UNIX-based platforms:

- UnixWare 2 (Novell)
- Solaris 2.x (Sun Microsystems)
- SunOS 4.x (Sun Microsystems)

RCGIs are written in the ANSI C programming language and are unlike LCGIs in that they are socketed and therefore slower and more resource hungry.

Perl 5 Scripts

Perl, an abbreviation for Practical Extraction and Report Language, is a scripting language that has wide support on a variety of platforms. Similar to the C programming language, Perl is capable of providing a variety of services, including the ability to serve as a gateway to other TCP/IP-based resources such as online catalogs, phone book directories, Gopher servers, and search engines. The greatest advantage to writing scripts and CGIs in Perl is that it is a highly portable language and your work can easily be used on other platforms, such as UNIX, Windows, and the Mac OS. The reverse is true as well: there are thousands of Perl scripts that have been written for other platforms, and many of them could easily be modified to run on your Novell Web Server. See the link to Matt's Script Archive at http://www.worldwidemart.com/ scripts/ for several hundred examples.

NetBasic Scripts

NetBasic for Internet uses a Net2000-compliant version of the BASIC language customized for use with IntranetWare via an NLM. You can use NetBasic for Internet to create scripts that interface with just about any aspect of the core NetWare NOS, including NDS management, the creation of dynamic HTML documents, database lookup interfaces, and Simple Network Management Protocol (SNMP) routines. Several NLMs are required to implement NetBasic for Internet with your Web server, and the NetBasic for Internet installation comes with plenty of online documentation and examples to help get you started.

QuickFinder Search Engine

The Novell QuickFinder search engine is an NLM-based CGI that has the powerful ability to index the entire contents of your Web server and make the results available via the Web or to other applications by way of Perl, NetBasic, or other LCGI scripts.

QuickFinder is capable of indexing and allowing full-text searches of more than 20 file formats, including the following:

- Ami Pro
- ASCII
- HyperText Markup Language (HTML)
- Microsoft Excel
- Microsoft Word for Windows
- OLE Compound Document
- Presentations
- Quattro Pro
- Rich Text Format (RTF)
- Unicode
- WordPerfect

Loading the NLMs

The NLMs required to run all the preceding CGIs are included as part of the default Novell installation. However, you may find it necessary to change the ways in which the various NLMs are configured in order for them to work with your Web server's virtual Web servers. Each virtual Web server hosted on your IntranetWare server has its own directory structure that includes a set of configuration files, as discussed in Chapter 22. For security purposes, the directories containing the CGI scripts and applications are excluded from the document tree that contains HTML documents and images (the DOCS directory and its subdirectories).

The configuration file that defines the locations of your LCGIs and RCGIs is the Server Resource Map file, or SRM.CFG, which is itself located in SYS:WEB\CONFIG by default. Specifically, the directives inform a virtual Web server of the following:

- Whether it is an LCGI or an RCGI.
- The path to the local NLM or script.
- The URL used by a browser to invoke the CGI.

There are two directives used to configure CGIs, the LoadableModule directive, for LCGIs, and the RemoteScriptAlias directive, for use with RCGIs.

LCGIs & the LoadableModule Directive

The LoadableModule directive is for locating NLMs used by the Web server to perform LCGI functions. The directive is used as follows:

```
LoadableModule <local_dir> <nlm_location>
```

The *<local_dir>* variable indicates the local directory to which a URL has been requested, relative to the Web server's default URL. And *<nlm_location>* identifies the volume and root directory where the NLM resides. The default SRM.CFG entries are as follows:

QuickFinder
```
LoadableModule /qfsearch/ SYS:/INW_WEB/shared/lcgi/qfsearch/qfsrch30.nlm
```

NetBasic
```
LoadableModule /netbasic/ SYS:\INW_WEB/shared/lcgi/netbasic/cgi2nmx.nlm
```

Perl 5
```
LoadableModule /perl/ SYS:\INW_WEB/shared/lcgi/perl5/perl5.nlm
```

RCGIs & the RemoteScriptAlias

The RemoteScriptAlias directive is used to find CGI interpreters located on both the local Web server and the remote Web servers. The directive is used as follows:

```
RemoteScriptAlias <local_dir> <remote_url>
```

The values are *<local_dir>*, used to identify the local directory to which a URL has been requested, relative to the Web server's default URL, and *<remote_url>*, which identifies the name, port, and root directory of the machine on which the CGI resides. If the interpreter, such as BASIC or Perl, is running on the local machine, then substitute the machine name with the word *localhost*. For example, the following entry points to a sample RCGI located on the same computer as the Web server. Note that the nonstandard port (8003) is part of the *remote_url* variable:

```
RemoteScriptAlias /cgiproc/ localhost:8003/sys:/web/samples/cgiapp
```

A Few Examples

Writing your own CGI scripts and applications isn't for the faint of heart. The NWS installation places hundreds of pages of information documenting the various application programming interfaces (APIs) that you must master before writing a CGI. We'll conclude the chapter by pointing out the URLs for the APIs and other resources for more information on writing your own CGIs. The NWS installation also includes several telling examples of CGIs that are easy to understand and are very useful to help familiarize yourself with exactly how CGIs work under IntranetWare. Now we'll work through several examples of CGIs, including Perl, NetBasic, QuickFinder, and Java applet examples.

A Perl Example

One of the great strengths of Perl is how easy it is to manipulate text, which is why Perl has lent itself for use on the Web as the CGI scripting language of choice. A very basic example of this type of use can be seen in Figure 25-12, which shows a sample greeting card that comes as part of the Novell Web Server installation.

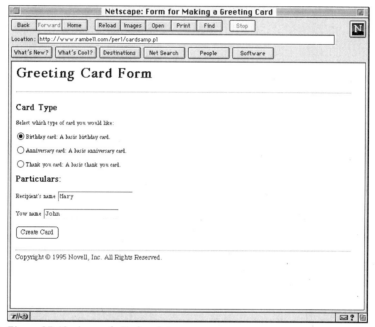

Figure 25-12: A sample Perl script.

This example takes data from two kinds of input fields, radio buttons and single-line text entry fields, and generates a dynamic HTML document by combining the input to create a greeting card of your choice. Figure 25-13 shows the output of the CGI script.

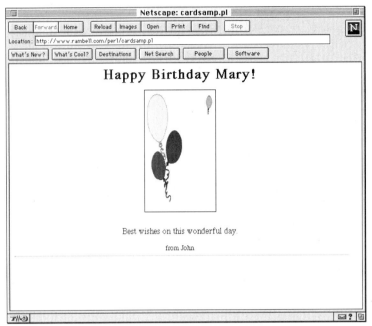

Figure 25-13: The output of the sample Perl script.

There are two ways you can invoke this particular script. First, you can call the script directly by using the following URL, shown here on the Rambell Web server:

```
http://www.rambell.com/perl/cardsamp.pl
```

The code used in this example Perl script includes both the HTML code used to create the form in Figure 25-12, as well as the code used by the Perl interpreter to create the greeting card in Figure 25-13. Here is the code:

```
require("cgi-lib.pl");
print &PrintHeader;
&ReadParse;

if ($ENV{"ARGC"} eq "0") {

print "<HTML><HEAD><TITLE>Form for Making a Greeting Card</TITLE></HEAD>\n";
print "<BODY>\n";
print "<H1>Greeting Card Form</H1>\n";
print "<HR>\n";
print "<FORM ACTION=\"/perl/cardsamp.pl\">\n";
print "<H3>Card Type</H3>\n";
```

```perl
print "<font size=-1>\n";
print "Select which type of card you would like:<P>\n";
print "<INPUT TYPE=\"radio\" NAME=\"type\" VALUE=\"1\" CHECKED>Birthday
card:\n";
print "A basic birthday card.<P>\n";
print "<INPUT TYPE=\"radio\" NAME=\"type\" VALUE=\"2\">Anniversary card:\n";
print "A basic anniversary card.<P>\n";
print "<INPUT TYPE=\"radio\" NAME=\"type\" VALUE=\"3\">Thank you card:\n";
print "A basic thank you card.<P>\n";

print "<H3>Particulars:</H3>\n";
print "Recipient's name <INPUT TYPE=\"text\" NAME=\"who\" MAXLENGTH=\"32\"
value=\"Mary\"><P>\n";
print "Your name <INPUT TYPE=\"text\" NAME=\"name\" MAXLENGTH=\"32\"
value=\"John\"><P>\n";

print "<INPUT type=\"submit\" VALUE=\"Create Card\">\n";
print "</font>\n";
print "</FORM>\n";
print "<hr>\n";
print "Copyright &#169; 1995 Novell, Inc. All Rights Reserved.\n";
print "</BODY></HTML>\n";


}
else {
        if ($in{"type"} == 1) {
            print "<CENTER><H1>";
            print "Happy Birthday ",$in{"who"},"!";
            print "</H1>";
            print "<IMG SRC=\"/images/art.gif\" width=120 height=200
border=1>";
            print "<font size=+1>";
            print "<P>Best wishes on this wonderful day.<BR>";
            print "</font>";
            print "<P>from " , $in{"name"},"<br>";
            print "</CENTER>";
            print "<hr>";
        }
        elsif ($in{"type"} == 2) {
            print "<IMG SRC=\"/images/vase.gif\" align=\"right\"
hspace=20>";
            print "<CENTER><H1>";
            print "Happy Anniversary ", $in{"who"}, "!";
            print "</H1>";
```

```
        print "<font size=+1>";
        print "<P>You mean so much to me.<BR>";
        print "</font>";
        print "<P>Love, ", $in{"name"}, "<br>";
        print "</CENTER>";
        print "<P><P><hr>";
    }
    else {
        print "<center>";
        print "<H1>Thank you ", $in{"who"}, "!";
        print "</H1>";
        print "<IMG SRC=\"/images/pen.gif\" width=200 height=200>";
        print "<P>your good friend, ", $in{"name"}, "<br>";
        print "</center>";
    }
}
```

Another way to use this example code, although the documentation that comes with the Perl interpreter doesn't tell you this, is to run the script using the URL to the Rambell Web server (which appears just before the preceding code) and then view the HTML source code after it has been loaded by your browser. In Navigator, choose View | Document Source, which will reveal the following HTML form document:

```
<HTML><HEAD><TITLE>Form for Making a Greeting Card</TITLE></HEAD>
<BODY>
<H1>Greeting Card Form</H1>
<HR>
<FORM ACTION="/perl/cardsamp.pl" METHOD="POST">
<H3>Card Type</H3>
<font size=-1>
Select which type of card you would like:<P>
<INPUT TYPE="radio" NAME="type" VALUE="1" CHECKED>Birthday card:
A basic birthday card.<P>
<INPUT TYPE="radio" NAME="type" VALUE="2">Anniversary card:
A basic anniversary card.<P>
<INPUT TYPE="radio" NAME="type" VALUE="3">Thank you card:
A basic thank you card.<P>
<H3>Particulars:</H3>
Recipient's name <INPUT TYPE="text" NAME="who" MAXLENGTH="32"
value="Mary"><P>
Your name <INPUT TYPE="text" NAME="name" MAXLENGTH="32" value="John"><P>
<INPUT type="submit" VALUE="Create Card">
</font>
</FORM>
```

```
<hr>
Copyright &#169; 1995 Novell, Inc. All Rights Reserved.
</BODY></HTML>
```

The result of the preceding code is the same document that you get when the Perl script is called directly. You may even save this document as you would any other HTML document and put it on your server. For example, we used the following URL:

```
http://www.rambell.com/perl/cardsamp.html
```

A NetBasic Example

The advantages of using NetBasic to write CGI scripts are that the BASIC programming language, on which NetBasic is based, is well known, and the Net2000 extensions that are included provide wide-ranging networking connectivity. Several example scripts come with the Web server. For a demo, open your Web browser to the following URL on your Web server, substituting the Rambell portion of the URL with your own:

```
http://www.rambell.com/lcgi/netbasic/docapi.htm
```

Figure 25-14 shows several areas of information regarding NetBasic that are provided with your Web server.

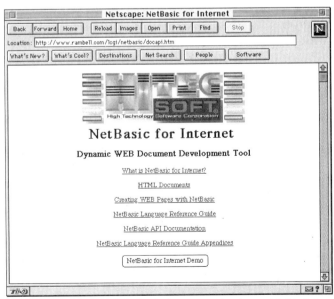

Figure 25-14: Plenty of NetBasic documentation is provided to help get you started.

Two example NetBasic scripts that are included illustrate these two strengths of NetBasic. Clicking on the NetBasic for Internet Demo button (Figure 25-14) takes you to a page on your Web server that demonstrates NetBasic's network interconnectivity and its usefulness as a processor of form-based CGI data. Figure 25-15 shows the page from which you may launch these two demos.

Figure 25-15: Two of the demos that are provided as part of the NetBasic installation.

Clicking on the View Server Version button invokes a script that queries your Web server for basic version information. The following code is all that's required for the script that generates the result shown in Figure 25-16:

```
#include "html.h"

Sub Main

 DOC:Heading("Server Information");
 DOC:Body(DOC_WHITE,DOC_BLACK,"",IMG("nbibg.gif"))

 STDHEADING()

 sinfo = NET:Server:Description
 DOC:Tag:Begin(DOC_TAG_PREFMT)
 DOC:Print(" Server: ", NET:Server:Name); NewLine
```

```
DOC:Print(" Company: ", sinfo.company) ; NewLine
DOC:Print(" Revision: ", sinfo.revision) ; NewLine
DOC:Print(" Date: ", sinfo.date) ; NewLine
DOC:Print("Copyright: ", sinfo.Copyright); NewLine
DOC:Tag:End(DOC_TAG_PREFMT)


End Sub
```

Figure 25-16: Only a small amount of NetBasic code is required for many scripts.

Like with Perl, the first line in this CGI calls a library required by the script to function as a Web-based CGI. In Perl, the first line reads like this:

```
require("cgi-lib.pl");
```

NetBasic performs a similar task when it calls a header file that is used with HTML documents:

```
#include "html.h"
```

Another NetBasic example provided with the installation of Novell Web Server 3.0 is similar to the Perl greeting card example. It provides several data input fields to construct a simple exchange of data from the user to an HTML document. Figure 25-17 illustrates this example.

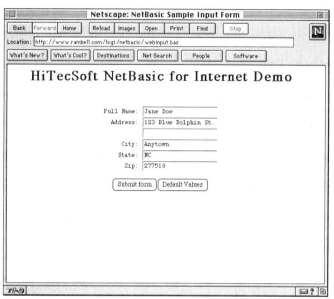

Figure 25-17: A second NetBasic script provided with the Web server performs a task similar to the Perl script greeting card example.

However, this example differs in that only one type of data input field is used and that it calls a second script to process the data once it has been submitted. The code for the example shown in Figure 25-17 is as follows:

```
#include "html.h"

Sub Main

DOC:Heading("NetBasic Sample Input Form");
DOC:Body(DOC_WHITE,DOC_BLACK,"",IMG("nbibg.gif"))

STDHEADING()
CENTERON()

DOC:Form:Begin( URL("webipost.bas") )
DOC:Tag:Begin(DOC_TAG_PREFMT)
DOC:Form:Input:Text("Name", "", " Full Name: ")
DOC:Form:Input:Text("Add1", "", " Address: ")
DOC:Form:Input:Text("Add2", "", "")
DOC:Form:Input:Text("City", "", " City: ")
DOC:Form:Input:Text("Stat", "AZ"," State: ")
DOC:Form:Input:Text("Zipc", "", " Zip: ")
```

```
DOC:Paragraph
DOC:Format(FALSE)
DOC:Form:Input:Submit("Submit form")
DOC:Form:Input:Reset("Default Values")
DOC:Tag:End(DOC_TAG_PREFMT)
DOC:Form:End


CENTEROFF()

End Sub
```

Unlike the Perl script, it must call a second script to perform a similar task, in this case " webipost.bas.

```
#include "html.h"

Sub Main

DOC:Heading("NetBasic Input Post");
DOC:Body(DOC_WHITE,DOC_BLACK,"",IMG("nbibg.gif"))

STDHEADING()

data = doc:var()
DOC:Print("You entered the following values:"); NewLine
DOC:Tag:Begin(DOC_TAG_PREFMT)
DOC:Print(" Name: ", data.name); NewLine
DOC:Print("Address1: ", data.add1); NewLine
DOC:Print("Address2: ", data.add2); NewLine
DOC:Print(" City: ", data.city); NewLine
DOC:Print(" State: ", data.stat); NewLine
DOC:Print(" Zip: ", data.zipc); NewLine
DOC:Tag:End(DOC_TAG_PREFMT)
DOC:Form:End

End Sub
```

Figure 25-18 shows the HTML output of this script.

Figure 25-18: The output of the second example NetBasic script.

A QuickFinder Example

Perhaps the CGI used most often on the Web today is the search engine. There are many different types of search engines available, and you've probably had firsthand experience with several of them. The search engine provided with your Novell Web Server is an excellent search engine, and, luckily for us, Novell made a CGI that provides access to it over the Web.

Many people don't even realize a search engine isn't part of the Web. There are a few combined search engine/Web servers, such as Maxum Development's Phantom (for Mac OS and Windows NT), but most search engines are applications that need the assistance of a CGI to allow users to submit queries and receive HTML documents in return. The Novell QuickFinder is actually a set of NLMs, some of which search and index the contents of the server, while another serves as a CGI (QFSRCH30.NLM, located in the SYS:WEB/INW_WEB/LCGI/QFSEARCH directory). Figure 25-19 shows the QuickFinder for the Rambell Web server.

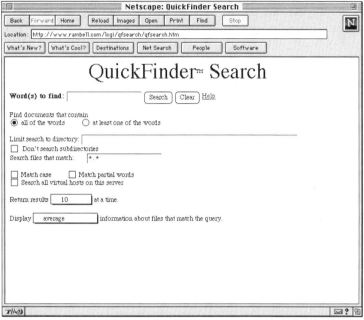

Figure 25-19: The QuickFinder CGI allows you to search over 20 different types of documents on your Web server.

Looking at the HTML source code, a portion of which is shown next, reveals the <FORM> action and method used to invoke the CGI. You can modify this document if you'd like to change the way the page looks, and you can insert the code between the <FORM></FORM> tags in other documents to create search links from these documents.

```
<HTML><TITLE>QuickFinder Search</TITLE>

<BODY>
<CENTER><FONT SIZE=8>QuickFinder<SUP><FONT SIZE=-2>TM</FONT></SUP> Search
</FONT></CENTER>

<FORM ACTION="/qfsearch" METHOD=GET>
<STRONG>Word(s) to find:</STRONG> <INPUT TYPE=TEXT NAME="Query">

<INPUT TYPE=SUBMIT VALUE="Search">
<INPUT TYPE="reset" VALUE="Clear">
<A HREF="qfhelp.htm">Help</A>
```

For example, users on your Web site could include this information on a Web page concerning manufacturing practices and fill in the form with the appropriate keywords so a user only needs to click the Search button to initiate a search on this topic. Figure 25-20 shows the results of a search on the phrase "novell and web."

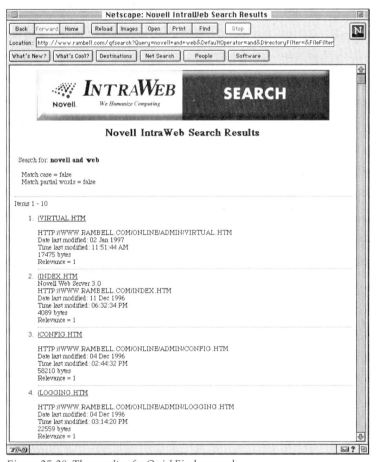

Figure 25-20: The results of a QuickFinder search.

A Java Applet Example

The hottest ticket on the Web today is Java, and for good reason: Java is a much more robust programming language than most scripting languages. All the major players in the software industry, including Netscape and Microsoft, are vigorously pursuing ways in which their products can support Java. The Novell Web Server comes with a Java demonstration applet, although it is not automatically installed with the Web server. Instead, it arrives as a compressed file that you must manually decompress. In addition, you must also install long filename support to accommodate the lengthy filenames used by many Java developers. They don't all use long filenames, but for the purpose of this demo, long filename support is required. Refer to Chapter 21 for details on setting up long filename support, which is the first step in preparing the Java demo.

The second step is to decompress the JAVADEMO.EXE file, as follows:

1. Map a network drive to the volume containing the Web server.

2. Locate the SYS:WEB\DOCS\JAVADEMO folder.

3. Double-click on the JAVADEMO.EXE file.

4. The files will be extracted in the proper order and in the correct location to begin the demo.

Once the file has been decompressed, open the following URL in Navigator, substituting your Web server's URL in place of the Rambell Web server:

```
http://www.rambell.com/javademo/javademo.htm
```

The Java demo is a plain-looking HTML document with an animated image in the upper left corner (Figure 25-21).

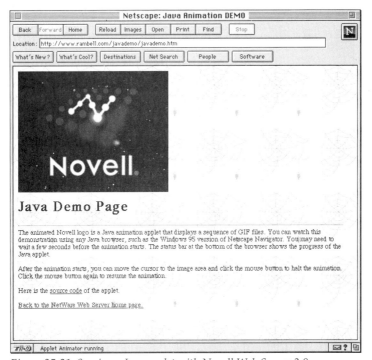

Figure 25-21: Serving a Java applet with Novell Web Server 3.0.

What is unique about the image in this HTML document is that once the Java applet has been loaded, the animation can be started and stopped at will by clicking the mouse anywhere on the image. What is not impressive, however, is the large number of files required to execute this script. No less than 15 files (HTML, images, and Java class libraries) is what it takes to make this interactive animation work (Figure 25-22). Also, what you can't see is the extremely large file entitled Animator.java, which is almost 1,000 lines in length.

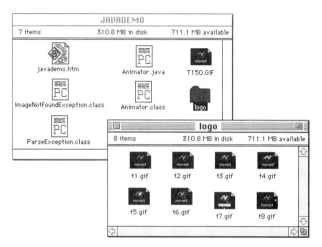

Figure 25-22: All but one of the 15 files required by the Java demo applet.

The syntax that invokes the applet is similar to the syntax in the JavaScript example in Chapter 24. The Java-specific information is contained between the <APPLET></APPLET> tags, which is in boldface in the following code. As with JavaScript, information in the <APPLET></APPLET> tags is ignored by Web browsers that do not understand Java:

```
<HTML><HEAD>
<TITLE>Java Animation DEMO</TITLE>
</HEAD><BODY>
<!body bgcolor="#C0C0C0">
<BODY BACKGROUND="images/image1.gif">
<PRE><P>

<APPLET CODE="Animator.class" WIDTH=258 HEIGHT=200>
<PARAM NAME="IMAGESOURCE" VALUE=logo>
<PARAM NAME="ENDIMAGE" VALUE=8>
<PARAM NAME="PAUSE" VALUE=100>
<PARAM NAME="REPEAT" VALUE=TRUE>
<PARAM NAME="STARTUP" VALUE=t1.gif>
<IMG SRC="T150.gif" ALIGN=LEFT ALT="Novell Logo">
</APPLET>

</P></PRE>
<H1>Java Demo Page</H1>
<HR>
```

```
The animated Novell logo is a Java animation applet that displays a sequence
of GIF files.
You can watch this demonstration using any Java browser, such as the Windows
95 version of
Netscape Navigator. You may need to wait a few seconds before the animation
starts.
The status bar at the bottom of the browser shows the progress of the Java
applet.
</P>
<P>
After the animation starts, you can move the cursor to the image area and
click the mouse
button to halt the animation. Click the mouse button again to resume the
animation.
<P>
Here is the <a href=Animator.java>source code</a> of the applet.
</P>
<P>
<A HREF = /novell.htm>Back to the NetWare Web Server home page.</A>
</P>
</BODY></HTML>
```

Moving On

CGI support is essential in the world of Web servers, and there is not a shortage of CGI support in Novell Web Server 3.0. You can not only provide CGIs based on Perl, the industry's most popular scripting language, but CGIs based on NetBasic and ANSI C as well. You also have the ability to serve Java applets and allow users to do ultrafast, full-text searches of more than 20 types of documents on your IntranetWare server.

The biggest drawback to providing CGI support, however, is the need for experienced programming skills. Not all Webmasters possess these kinds of skills, and those that do are often faced with the challenge of learning a new programming language such as Perl. For some, this is an easy task after struggling with C and C++, but it's not so easy for others. We've used several resources to do CGI work in our years on the Web, and what follows is a list of the "best-in-class" resources that you'll no doubt find very helpful.

- *CGI Programming on the World Wide Web*, by Shishir Gundavaram (O'Reilly & Associates, 1996).

- *Learning Perl*, by Randal L. Schwartz (O'Reilly & Associates, 1993).

- *Programming Perl,* by Larry Wall & Randal L. Schwartz (O'Reilly & Associates, 1991).

- comp.lang.perl.misc

- comp.infosystems.www.authoring.cgi

- comp.infosystems.www.authoring.html

- http://www.yahoo.com/Computers_and_Internet/Internet/ World_Wide_Web/CGI___Common_Gateway_Interface/

- http://www.w3.org/pub/WWW/

- http://hoohoo.ncsa.uiuc.edu/cgi/

These resources should get you started, but for information about your Novell Web Server's capabilities, refer to the Dynamic Web Page Programmer's Guide on your Web server at the following URL, where the URL for your Web server replaces the Rambell server URL:

```
http://www.rambell.com/Online/wpguide/index.htm
```

Many people who will be creating content for your server may not be located directly on your LAN, however, so in the next chapter, we'll discuss how to set up and maintain File Transfer Protocol (FTP) support on your IntranetWare server, which gives anyone on the Internet the ability to contribute to your Web server's content.

26

FTP Services

The final task in providing intranet services is to enable FTP services on your IntranetWare server. The File Transfer Protocol (FTP) is a valuable service because it enables a wide range of clients to access your server regardless of what operating system they are using. FTP clients and servers use the TCP/IP protocol to allow remote users to copy, add, delete, and rename files and directories (folders). Moreover, IntranetWare allows limited access to files and folders on other IntranetWare or NetWare servers even if they aren't running FTP services. Local users may not need FTP access, relying on NetWare's IPX/IP protocol to perform these tasks instead. FTP provides only a fraction of the functionality a locally connected user has, but there will be users who need FTP access, especially remote users who might otherwise not be able to connect to the server.

FTP services grew out of UUCP (UNIX-to-UNIX Copy Protocol) and are available for just about any operating system you can think of. Likewise, there are FTP clients for just about every platform, some of which use a graphical interface and others that use an old-style command-line interface. This chapter will show the nuts and bolts of how to:

- Install and configure FTP services.
- Manage the FTP server.
- Provide access to NDS-authenticated users.
- Provide anonymous FTP services.
- Link to other IntranetWare servers in your NDS tree.
- Serve different types of files.

Installing FTP Services

FTP services are provided as part of the UNIX Print Services, described in Chapter 7. Installing UNIX Print Services automatically installs FTP services with its default values. Once it is installed, you'll want to review the configuration and optimize it for use on your intranet. To load UNIX Print Services, or to determine if it is already loaded, follow these steps:

1. Type **LOAD INSTALL** from either the server console or an RCONSOLE session.

2. Select Product Options.

3. Select View | Configure | Remove Installed Products. The UNIX Print Services is called PRTS, and the current version is 2.11. If you see this in the Currently Installed Products window, skip on down to the section entitled Configuring FTP Services. Although the NetWare Server Installation program says you can configure an installed product, you cannot do so for UNIX printing or FTP services.

4. To install UNIX Print Services, go back to the Product Options window and select Install a Product Not Listed. Type the path to the UNIX Print Services software, called PINSTALL.NLM. For example, if you are installing from a CD (it should be CD #4 of the IntranetWare set of CDs) and the CD-ROM is mounted as the NWUXPS volume on the server, you would type the path **NWUXPS:\NWUXPS** after pressing F3 to provide NetWare with the location of the files. The installation program will find PINSTALL.NLM in this directory and proceed with the installation of the software.

5. The files will be copied into a temporary directory. You will be asked to provide the drive letter of the server's boot volume (usually C) and whether or not you want to install the online documentation.

6. The commands in the UNISTART.NCF file will be automatically executed. Once finished, UNICON.NLM (discussed in Chapter 19) is launched.

7. Provide the username and password for UNICON when prompted.

8. Next, you will be prompted to configure DNS services for your server. This must be done before FTP services can be initialized.

9. When prompted, press the Escape key to remove the temp files.

When the installation process has been completed, the server will be ready for access by registered users, but not anonymous users. You'll want to configure several aspects of FTP services and then reconfigure them only when needed. Managing FTP services, however, is an ongoing task that you'll need to perform on a very regular basis.

Configuring FTP Services

Configuring and managing FTP services is accomplished through the UNICON program and an ASCII text file, which may also be edited via UNICON. To begin configuring FTP services, follow these steps:

1. Type **LOAD UNICON** from either the server console or an RCONSOLE session.

2. Supply the necessary username and password information.

3. Select Manage Services.

4. Select FTP Server.

You'll be presented with the FTP Administration window, shown in Figure 26-1.

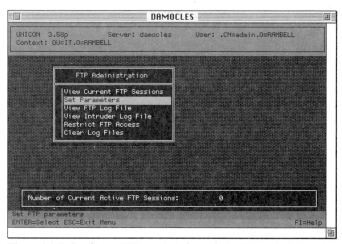

Figure 26-1: Configure FTP services through the FTP Administration window in the UNICON application.

The FTP Administration window allows you to configure as well as manage several aspects of FTP services. For the purpose of configuring FTP services, we'll look at these two menu options:

- Set Parameters
- Restrict FTP Access

Configuring FTP services is similar to configuring certain aspects of Web services. These two services are similar because you have a limited amount of server resources to share with both registered and anonymous users. You can't just sling the door wide open and invite everyone in for as long as they'd like to stay. You have to set some ground rules and limit the amount of time your guests may stay for the party.

Set Parameters

The Set Parameters menu option provides several important configuration options that directly affect the security and performance of your intranet and IntranetWare server. The options discussed in the following sections are applicable to version 2.11 of UNIX Print Services. To change any of these settings, just type in the new value in the appropriate field, and the changes will take place when you close the window. Figure 26-2 shows the options that may be configured, which are then described below.

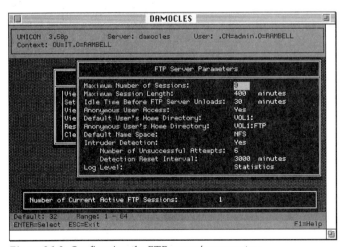

Figure 26-2: Configuring the FTP server's parameters.

Maximum Number of Sessions

The Maximum Number of Sessions setting determines how many concurrent users may access the FTP server at one time. Users attempting to connect after the limit has been reached will be refused. The default setting is 9, and the maximum number may equal up to the number of concurrent users for which your server is licensed. You may not need to enable a session for every user on your network; it's extremely unlikely that all 500 of your users will be using FTP at the same time, for example. You may want to limit the number of maximum sessions based on the amount of available resources.

Maximum Session Length

The Maximum Session Length setting determines how long a given FTP session may remain active before timing out and disconnecting the client. The default setting is 400 minutes.

Idle Time Before FTP Server Unloads

The Idle Time Before FTP Server Unloads setting measures how long the FTP server will remain on standby waiting for a connection before it unloads itself to conserve server resources. When unloaded, it will automatically reload itself when a connection is requested, which makes for a slower response time. The default setting is 30 minutes.

Anonymous User Access

The Anonymous User Access setting is a Yes/No option that determines whether or not anonymous FTP access is allowed. The default is No.

Default User's Home Directory

The Default User's Home Directory setting allows you to identify a home directory for users who do not have a home directory assigned. You may only have one such directory, and to configure this option, you will need to identify a volume and a directory. The default setting is the SYS volume; there is no default directory setting.

Anonymous User's Home Directory

The Anonymous User's Home Directory setting allows you to identify a home directory for anonymous users. When you install UNIX Print Services, an NDS object named anonymous is created for which you may edit properties. Editing this option only effects the directory to which the anonymous user has access via FTP. The default setting is the SYS volume; there is no default directory setting.

Default Name Space

The Default Name Space option allows you to select what type of name space is made available to FTP users. Both NFS (Network File System) and DOS are available to FTP; Mac Name Space (MAC.NAM) is not available even though it may be installed. The default option is DOS, but you should change this to NFS, which is a superset of DOS.

Intruder Detection

The Intruder Detection setting is a Yes/No option that determines whether or not the FTP server logs access attempts by intruders. Failed login attempts are recorded in the intruder log file, and a warning message is sent to the server console when an intruder has been detected. The default is Yes.

Number of Unsuccessful Attempts

The Number of Unsuccessful Attempts setting tells the Intruder Detection feature how many failed login attempts are allowed before an intrusion is logged. You shouldn't set this number too low because we all make mistakes when typing our usernames and passwords, but setting this option too high will give more latitude to hackers attempting to break into your system. The default setting is six unsuccessful attempts.

Detection Reset Interval

The Detection Reset Interval setting determines how long the Intruder Detection feature should keep track of a connection attempt from a specific computer based on that computer's IP address. This setting works in conjunction with the Number of Unsuccessful Attempts setting, and the default is 3000 minutes (a little over two days).

Log Level

The Log Level setting allows you to choose at what level of detail the FTP log is maintained. The options are:

- **None.** No information is logged.
- **Statistics.** Records login and file transfer information only.
- **Logins.** Records login information only.
- **File.** Records login, statistics, and file transfer information.

Restrict FTP Access

The second option that you may edit to configure FTP services is the Restrict FTP Access option. The Restrict FTP Access option edits an ASCII text file called RESTRICT.FTP located in SYS:ETC. This file functions like the configuration files for the Web server discussed in Chapter 22. Figure 26-3 shows this option as it is chosen in the FTP Administration window.

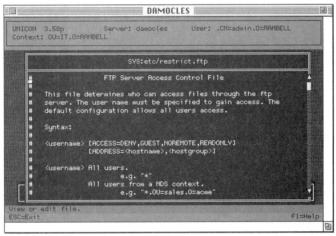

Figure 26-3: Restricting access to FTP services through the FTP Administration program.

Entries to this file allow you to control access to the FTP server in several ways; each entry has the following form and is on a single line:

`username access=variable address=hostname`

By default, access is permitted to all but anonymous users, and changes to this file override NDS attributes. The examples in Table 26-1 explain the options available for use in the username field.

Explanation	Example
All users	*
All users within an NDS context	*.OU=IT.O=RAMBELL
NDS username relative to the default context	JDOE
Typeful distinguished NDS name	.CN=JDOE.OU=IT.O=RAMBELL

Table 26-1: Usernames and their uses for restricting FTP access.

The variables that may be used with the ACCESS statement are described in Table 26-2. Multiple variables may be used in conjunction with a single entry, in which case they are separated by the pipe symbol (|).

ACCESS Variable	Explanation
DENY	Prevents users from accessing the FTP server even if the global variable * (all users) is used elsewhere in the RESTRICT.FTP file.
GUEST	Prevents a user from accessing any area of the FTP server other than the default user's home directory.
NOREMOTE	Prevents FTP access to other NetWare servers in the same NDS tree.
READONLY	Prevents users from uploading files to the FTP server.

Table 26-2: Explanation of ACCESS restrictions.

For example, the user JDEER will be denied access to the entire FTP server regardless of from which computer he or she is using with the following entry:

```
.JDEER.O=RAMBELL ACCESS=DENY
```

Finally, the ADDRESS command allows you to restrict the machine from which a user is allowed to connect. This is an optional setting; without it, the FTP server allows all computers to connect. You may want to set this option for critical usernames, such as Supervisor or others with unlimited access to your server. The ADDRESS variable can be either an IP number or name. For example, to restrict access to the FTP server for the organization unit called ACCT and require that they connect from a single computer, an entry would contain the following line:

```
*.OU=ACCT.O=RAMBELL ADDRESS=153.202.1
```

Client Access

There are two basic types of clients that may be used to access your IntranetWare server via FTP: command-line and graphical interface FTP clients. In the early days of FTP, the only clients that were available were command-line clients. These clients were very basic and required that users issue commands by typing them in a command line. For example, to view the contents of a directory on a remote FTP server, a user might type **ls** to *list* the contents, or **ls -a** to *list all* the contents, including hidden files. Figure 26-4 shows such a command-line interface connecting to the Rambell FTP server.

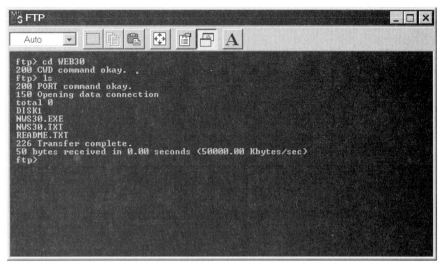

Figure 26-4: Using a command-line interface to connect to an FTP server.

Today, there are dozens of FTP clients, and most of them use a graphical interface to make uploading and downloading files to and from an FTP server much easier. Although these clients are easy to use, they are also complex in their capabilities to bookmark frequently used FTP servers, store user preferences, automatically decode and decompress files, and autodetect whether a file to be downloaded is ASCII or binary. Figure 26-5 shows the most popular FTP client for the Mac OS, called Fetch.

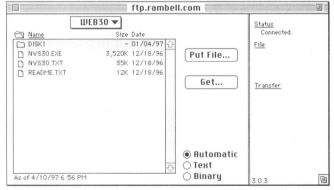

Figure 26-5: Using an FTP client with a graphical interface to connect to an FTP server.

Of course, you and your users should use an FTP client with which you feel most comfortable. The FTP server component of your IntranetWare server will accept connections from any FTP client, regardless of the platform on which it is used.

Managing FTP Services

In addition to the configuration tools, several management-oriented tools are available to help you keep tabs on your FTP users and their activities. You'll want to keep track of users to ensure they aren't trying to hack your system or gain access to restricted directories and files. From the FTP Administration window, you can perform the tasks discussed in the following sections.

View Current FTP Sessions

If you suspect a user who is currently logged in is abusing your FTP server, you can gain detailed information about the connection by choosing the View Current FTP Sessions menu item, which is shown in Figure 26-6.

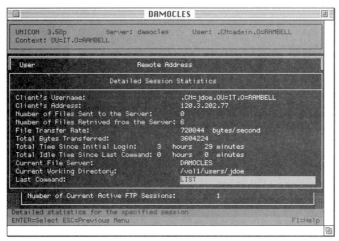

Figure 26-6: Monitoring a current FTP session.

If you determine that a person is abusing your FTP server, monitor their connections and review the FTP log file and Intruder log file to see if this user, or other users, have been in violation of your server in the past.

View FTP Log File

You can gain very important information about the use of your FTP server by viewing the FTP log file, located as follows:

`SYS:ETC/FTPSERV.LOG`

FTP log entries contain only the information you have chosen in the Log Level option in the FTP Server Parameters shown in Figure 26-2. Here's a sample log entry:

```
--------------------------------------------------------------------
Tue Mar 25 22:57:21 1997 FTP Session Starts from 155.77.202.77.
Tue Mar 25 23:07:35 1997 5 files copied from server.
22 files copied to server.
Tue Mar 25 23:07:35 1997 FTP Session Ends from 155.77.202.77.
--------------------------------------------------------------------
```

View Intruder Log File

The intruder log file maintains a history of failed FTP server access attempts, an example of which is shown below:

```
Intruder Alert. Host spooky.mulder.rambell.com at address 155.77.202.77 has
exceeded the limit
Time 3-26-97 6:47:29am User .CN=jdoe.OU=IT.O=RAMBELL used password vent .
Time 3-26-97 6:47:21am User .CN=jdoe.OU=IT.O=RAMBELL used password vent .
Time 3-26-97 6:47:15am User .CN=jdoe.OU=IT.O=RAMBELL used password vent .
Time 3-26-97 6:47:06am User .CN=jdoe.OU=IT.O=RAMBELL used password vent .
Time 3-26-97 6:47:00am User .CN=jdoe.OU=IT.O=RAMBELL used password vent .
Time 3-26-97 6:46:54am User .CN=jdoe.OU=IT.O=RAMBELL used password vent .
Time 3-26-97 6:46:48am User .CN=jdoe.OU=IT.O=RAMBELL used password vent .

8 unsuccessful logins from spooky.mulder.rambell.com at address
155.77.202.77
Time 3-26-97 6:47:37am User .CN=jdoe.OU=IT.O=RAMBELL used password vent .

9 unsuccessful logins from spooky.mulder.rambell.com at address
155.77.202.77
Time 3-26-97 6:47:45am User .CN=jdoe.OU=IT.O=RAMBELL used password vent .
```

The intruder log file is located as follows:

`SYS:SYSTEM/INTRUDER.FTP`

Refer to this file if you believe someone is trying to hack your system. Although you can view this file from the FTP Server Administrator utility, it's probably a better idea to open the log file using a text editor and use a Find All command to count the number of times a particular host or user has been denied access. Some hackers' attempts to gain access to a server will be in rapid succession, while others will wait several days or weeks to try again. In this case, you'll have to search the entire log file to know exactly how many times a particular host or user has attempted to connect, which you can't find out by viewing it through the View Intruder Log File menu option. When you detect such activities, follow your normal procedures to protect your server. Here are a few steps that you might take in such a situation:

- If the hacker is connecting from a specific domain, restrict access to your FTP server for this particular domain following the steps outlined above in the section entitled "Restrict FTP Access."

- Contact the system administrator(s) of the domain or organization from which the hacker is launching the attacks.

- Attempt to identify anyone in your organization that might have any information concerning the attacker or the object of the attack.

Clear Log Files

The Clear Log Files option allows you to delete either the FTP and the intruder log files (or both), which causes the FTP server to create a new file on the fly. To archive the files, you must first copy the files to a new location before deleting them. Log files can grow very large over time (we've see a log file that was over 180MB!) and can take up valuable disk space.

Linking to Other NetWare Servers

One of the unique features provided as part of the IntranetWare FTP services is the ability to link FTP users to other NetWare servers even if they aren't running an FTP server. The requirements for remote access are:

- Users must have an account on the remote server with the same password as on the IntranetWare server.

- The remote server must be located in the same NDS tree.

- Only DOS-style name spacing is supported.

- You must issue the following command at the server console of the IntranetWare server running FTP services:
  SET REPLY To GET NEAREST SERVER=ON

To access the remote server, open an FTP session to your IntranetWare server and issue the following change-directory command:
//REMOTE_SERVER_NAME /VOLUME/PATH

For example, to open a connection to the DOCS directory on the SYS volume of the server Thanatos, you would change directories as follows:
//THANATOS/SYS/DOCS

File Types & Compression Schemes

Once you have FTP services up and running, you'll probably get questions from your users about the different types of files that may upload and download from your FTP server. Your FTP server is capable of hosting any type of file that is also supported by the name spacing modules loaded on the server. For the purposes of FTP, there are only two types of files:

- ASCII text files

- Binary files

In addition to these types of files, your FTP server can host compressed files. Users often compress their files, using many different types of compression programs, to save space on the server and to minimize the upload and download times.

The main destination between ASCII and binary files for the purpose of FTP is that an ASCII file will look the same no matter what platform it is copied to and opened. An ASCII text file will look the same on a Windows machine, a Mac, or an SGI workstation. Binary files, on the other hand, are not so forgiving and are sometimes not transferable between platforms. Even if they do transfer, they are often platform-specific, where ASCII text files represent the lowest common denominator of files that may be transferred between platforms and successfully opened. However, you can easily use FTP to transfer most word processing documents between systems with no effect on your ability to open them successfully once transferred. Most modern FTP clients are capable of autodetecting if a file that has been selected for downloading or uploading is ASCII or binary; the FTP server will only transfer a binary file as a binary, and an ASCII text file as ASCII text (although the file would not be affected if it were transferred as binary at the request of the FTP client).

In addition to an understanding of file transfer types, knowledge of file compression is very important in the process of administering an FTP server. Compressed files are not only good for the user, because they cut down on transfer times, but also for the FTP server administrator, because they free up valuable server resources. The downside of file compression is that there is no single compression standard, and users will no doubt become confused over what program to use to compress and decompress file. It is the user's responsibility to decompress a file once it has been downloaded, but it is more or less your responsibility to help users properly compress the files before they are placed on your FTP server. A great source for more information on compression is Yahoo's compression page, which lists links to shareware and commercial software for all kinds of compression and decompression tasks:

```
http://www.yahoo.com/Computers_and_Internet/Software/System_Utilities/
Compression/
```

Many of the compression programs in use today are "smart" and are able to compress and decompress different types of files. Table 26-3 attempts to detangle the many types of file compression in use on the Internet based on platform.

Platform	Compression	Decompression	Extension(s)
Mac OS	DropStuff	StuffIt, StuffIt Expander, Compact Pro	SIT, SEA, HQX, CPT
Windows	PKZIP, WinZIP	PKUNZIP, WinZIP	ZIP, EXE
UNIX	gzip, tar	gunzip, untar	z, gz, tar.Z

Table 26-3: Compression and decompression programs by platform.

Providing FTP services is an essential element on today's intranets, so you should take the time to evaluate your need for FTP and install it if necessary. If you provide Web services and want to provide large text and binary files to your visitors, then enabling FTP makes good sense. You can easily configure and manage FTP services through the FTP Administration utility, as well as track usage and monitor potential problems.

Conclusion

Novell's IntranetWare is the most powerful network operating system available. But because it does so much, it can be hard to keep track of all of IntranetWare's intricacies as you try to use it to build and manage an intranet. We've tried to demystify the process of building a secure intranet that can scale from a small company to a large corporation. Along the way we've attempted to document and explain all of the IntranetWare features and idiosyncracies, a herculean task unto itself. Building an intranet that can easily grow with your organization is a huge commitment of time and resources. Hopefully, this book makes that job a lot easier.

SECTION V
Appendices

appendix A

Getting Help

IntranetWare is a very complex network operating system with a long history in the industry. There are millions of Novell networks around the world and countless individuals who interact with these networks on a daily basis. It stands to reason that there must have been an equally dizzying array of questions asked over the years, and in so many languages that a lot of time and effort have been spent answering them. Knowing where to get *your* questions answered, therefore, shouldn't be too difficult because with all that experience, surely your question has already been asked several dozen times. Knowing how, and where, to ask your questions is an important detail.

There are several ways to get help on installing, configuring, and maintaining your IntranetWare network. Some of these options are not without cost, however, and for the really, really, really tough questions, there may be no escaping the cost of a professional solution to your problem. But before you pay for help, give these avenues a chance:

- **Online documentation.** CD-ROM #2 of the IntranetWare installation, NetWare 4.11 Online Documentation, comes with hundreds of pages of detailed documentation and step-by-step procedures that can guide you through most issues. The Documentation Viewer program, shown in Figure A-1, has an intuitive interface and allows you to print the results of your sessions and queries.

- **Novell Support Connection Web site (ht.//support.novell.com/).** Search Novell's Knowledge Base for the latest information on a particular product, such as IntranetWare, or a specific subject, such as "web," shown in Figure A-2.

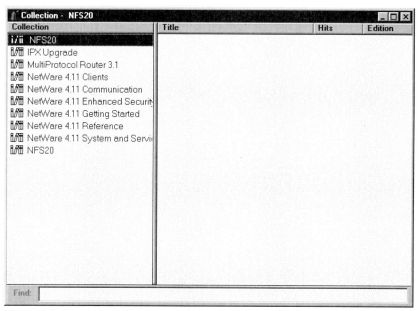

Figure A-1: Search the online documentation that comes with IntranetWare first.

- **Novell Support Connection CD-ROM.** The information on the Web site is on the CD-ROM for your own personal use. The CD-ROMs are updated monthly, but this one will cost you between $300 and $1100, depending on how many copies you purchase. See http://support.novell.com/c_option/connection_cd.htm for more information.

- **NetWire on CompuServe.** Again, the information on the Novell Support Connection Web site and CD-ROM is available here, but there is no charge for CompuServe customers. Type **GO NETWIRE** to access this option once you've logged in to CompuServe.

- **FaxBack.** This is a toll-free fax-back service that provides technical support as well as product information, developer notes, and educational information. Dial 800-209-3500 to access this service or ask for a catalog.

- **Premium Services.** Novell's three-tiered service plan option is designed to meet the needs of the smallest to the largest organizations. See http://support.novell.com/c_option/PremiumPackages.htm for more information.

- **Telephone Support.** Purchase technical support from Novell on a case-by-case basis for users in North America (800-858-4000), Europe (49-211-5632-743), Japan (81-3-5481-1050), and Asia-Pacific (61-2-9925-3194).

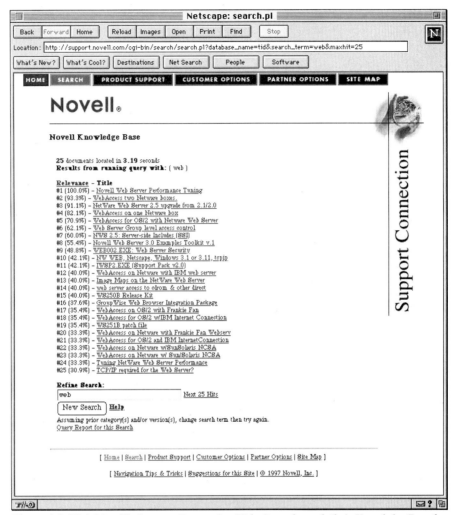

Figure A-2: Visit Novell's Support Connection Web site and search their Knowledge Base for more information on a product or topic.

appendix B

NetWare 4.11 New Features

If you are an experienced NetWare administrator, you probably don't need a lot of explanation about the nuts and bolts of NetWare. Sometimes, you are just looking for a quick-and-dirty explanation of the differences between the old versions and the new version of the NetWare operating system. We've been in that situation ourselves, so we've included this appendix to help you quickly identify the differences between NetWare 4.11 and previous versions of the NetWare operating system.

This appendix is essentially broken up into two parts. The first section is for the NetWare 3.x administrator who is considering upgrading his or her server to NetWare 4.11 by purchasing the IntranetWare package. It briefly describes the major differences between NetWare 3.x and NetWare 4.x. The differences represent a fundamental change in the way we think about networks.

The second section is for the NetWare 4.0x or NetWare 4.1 administrator who is considering purchasing IntranetWare. We briefly discuss the major differences between NetWare 4.1 and IntranetWare, including extra products bundled with IntranetWare and the differences between the NetWare 4.1 and NetWare 4.11 operating systems. So without further ado, let's get on with why you should upgrade to IntranetWare and NetWare 4.11.

From NetWare 3.x to NetWare 4.x

The differences between the NetWare 3.x and NetWare 4.x can effectively be summarized by the following categories:

- Operating system installation
- Operating system features
- Networking features
- File services
- Print services
- Security
- Backup services

Novell has made significant improvements in each one of these categories, making NetWare 4.x a more powerful and robust network operating system. The key to NetWare 4.x is the paradigmatic shift in the concept of a network. With NetWare 3.x, LANs were server centric. With NetWare 4.x, the network is viewed as one giant shared resource pool with a single point of access. All NetWare servers and services are integrated into one single environment that provides an efficient means of sharing data and printing resources. Beyond this new and innovative way of defining a network, Novell has also enhanced many other features of NetWare 4.x.

Operating System Installation

The installation of the NetWare 4.x operating system is more flexible and tends to be faster than the installation of NetWare 3.x. First, Novell has completely done away with the installation of NetWare from floppy disk. The installation of NetWare 4.x is accomplished through CD-ROM media, which makes for a much quicker and efficient installation of the operating system.

Second, NetWare 4.x comes with options that make the installation of the operating system customizable. There is a simple installation in which the installation program makes certain assumptions about your network for you. This is an excellent way of getting the server up and running quickly. Conversely, there is a custom installation that allows the advanced installer to customize the installation options to suit his or her network needs. This choice of installation was not included in NetWare 3.x.

Operating System Features

Because NetWare 4.x is a true enterprise network operating system, Novell planned on it being used internationally. Thus, NetWare 4.x comes with support for other languages in addition to English. You can install the server so that it displays all of its messages and utilities in a different language. NetWare 3.x came with support for the English language only.

With NetWare 3.x, you needed to have a DOS box, which would boot the DOS operating system before loading NetWare. This is also true with NetWare 4.x; however, NetWare 4.x also comes with support for OS/2. Through a product called NetWare Server for OS/2, you can install a NetWare server on an OS/2 box and have it run as a nondedicated server.

Memory management has also been improved since the days of NetWare 3.x. In NetWare 3.x, memory was divided into pools, and certain pools did not give back memory once they had appropriated it. This forced the network administrator to manually refresh the memory pools on a periodic basis by taking down the server and rebooting it. This is no longer the case with NetWare 4.x. The memory management involves only one pool of memory. When modules release memory, there is a garbage-collection process that frees all of the released memory, which makes that memory available to other modules that might need it.

Networking Features

Of course, the paradigmatic shift we already discussed is one of the most important changes that have occurred, but there have also been important changes in the networking features. With the advent of NDS—an object-oriented, distributed database—information about the resources on the network is stored in a central location where all users on the network have access to it. The network administrator restricts rights to users on a networkwide basis instead of having to manage multiple accounts on multiple servers to provide access to required resources.

In addition, NetWare 4.x provides more comprehensive support for the installation and configuration of multiple protocols and network boards in the server than NetWare 3.x did. Through additional utilities like INETCFG.NLM, you can configure and bind protocols easily and efficiently instead of having to manually load and bind protocols through server console commands like you do for NetWare 3.x.

NetWare 4.x also supports additional communication services like Large Internet Packets (LIP) and Packet Burst protocol to increase the performance of your network and help you maximize network bandwidth and throughput. These communication services are not featured in NetWare 3.x.

File Services

NetWare 4.x comes with some additional file system features that make it more attractive in terms of performance and efficiency. Such features as automatic file compression and block suballocation allow the server to maximize the usage of the physical capacity of your server hard drives. The file compression on NetWare 4.x servers can average a compression rate of over 60 percent. Suballocation also eliminates the waste of file blocks because unused portions of file blocks are recycled to store parts of other files that don't fall neatly into their assigned file blocks.

NetWare 4.x also comes with support for high capacity storage system (HCSS). This technology, when used with data migration, will allow you to migrate, on the fly, older data from your servers' hard drives to online HCSS devices. This way, data that is old and seldom used will be moved off of the server to make room for data that is used more frequently; however, it is still accessible on the HCSS if you need it.

Print Services

In addition to being more complex, the NetWare 4.x print environment is more robust and flexible than its NetWare 3.x counterpart. The printing environment is based upon the NDS tree, which means that the printing resources are also centralized instead of being server based. This allows any user in the NDS tree to print to any printer assuming he or she has the appropriate rights to use that printer.

Also, a single NetWare 4.x print server can accommodate 256 printers. The NetWare 3.x print server could only handle the concurrent connections of 16 printers. This increase in the number of available network printers can make a huge difference in your network printing environment.

Security

Although it is a fairly secure network operating system, NetWare 3.x pales in comparison to the security features of NetWare 4.x. NetWare 4.x includes both Rivest, Shamir, and Adleman (RSA) public/private key encryption services and a utility called AUDITCON, which allows an independent auditor to audit your network's security. These tools are invaluable in helping you secure your network environment.

Backup Services

Both NetWare 3.x and NetWare 4.x come with a packaged backup utility called SBACKUP; however, the SBACKUP for NetWare 4.x is more robust and efficient. It consistently provides faster backup speeds. SBACKUP also has an improved utility that will help you configure backup services for your networking environment.

Another drawback to SBACKUP in the NetWare 3.x environment is how the utility writes its data to the backup device. The data is written to the backup media in a proprietary format that can not be read by any other backup software. SBACKUP for NetWare 4.x is SMS compliant, and the data is written to the backup media in a system independent data format (SIDF)-compliant format. All other SIDF-compliant backup utilities will be able to read the files that SBACKUP writes.

As you can see, there are distinct benefits to upgrading from NetWare 3.x to NetWare 4.x. The only reason you might not want to perform this upgrade would be the cost. However, we recommend that you make the investment because the time and effort saved by upgrading to this new and improved network operating system will more than make up for the money you spend.

From NetWare 4.0x/4.1 to IntranetWare/NetWare 4.11

Of course, if you are going to upgrade to NetWare 4.11, it makes sense to upgrade to IntranetWare instead. IntranetWare costs as much as NetWare 4.11, but with IntranetWare you get NetWare 4.11 in addition to a wide variety of products that will allow you to turn your IPX-based network into a TCP/IP-based intranet. The additional products you get with the purchase of IntranetWare include:

- NetWare Directory Services (NDS)
- NetWare Print Services for UNIX
- FTP Services
- NetWare Web Server
- NetWare MultiProtocol Router
- IPX/IP Gateway
- WAN Extensions
- NetWare/IP

Even this is not a complete list of products you get with IntranetWare. If you are going to upgrade your NetWare 4.1 system, choose to upgrade to IntranetWare instead of just upgrading to NetWare 4.11. But why would you want to upgrade to IntranetWare/NetWare 4.11 anyway when your NetWare 4.1 server works just fine? There have been some enhancements made to the NetWare 4.11 environment that make upgrading your file server an attractive option. NetWare 4.11 provides better integration with other operating systems, including Windows 95, Windows NT, and Macintosh, and extra features to ease the administration of your network.

The differences between the NetWare 3.x and NetWare 4.x can effectively be summarized in the following categories:

- Operating system installation
- Operating system features
- Networking
- File services
- Print services
- Security
- Backup services
- Miscellaneous services

Again, Novell has made improvements in each one of these categories to help make NetWare 4.11 even more robust and efficient than its predecessor, NetWare 4.1. Also, Novell has taken steps to help NetWare be more compatible with other operating systems so it can integrate more seamlessly into a diverse network environment. With these enhancements, NetWare 4.11 is an attractive choice to deploy as the network operating system.

Operating System Installation

The installation of the NetWare 4.11 operating system is even more simple than the installation of NetWare 4.1. Both come with the simple and custom installation options; however, the NetWare 4.11 installation program has much better hardware-detection capabilities than the NetWare 4.1 installation program. We were pleasantly surprised when the NetWare 4.11 installation program completely detected our server hardware and configured itself without us having to press a key.

Also, NetWare 4.11 comes with some added support for migration from older NetWare environments to NetWare 4.11. Although NetWare 4.1 does have some limited support for migration and upgrade, it is not as good as the support included with NetWare 4.11.

Operating System Features

NetWare 4.11's most notable improvement in the operating system is the enhanced abnormal end (ABEND) recovery options. It used to be that when a NetWare server ABENDed, it had to be taken down and restarted by flipping off the power switch. That is no longer true with NetWare 4.11, which is able to identify offending processes and shut those processes down before they corrupt server memory. If the machine does happen to ABEND, it has an auto-restart feature through which it will reboot itself. These recovery options make NetWare 4.11 more robust.

With today's newer servers, it is not uncommon to have multiple CPUs in a machine. With older versions of NetWare, you had to rely on third-party vendors to provide support for Symmetric MultiProcessing (SMP). With NetWare 4.11, SMP support is included. You can now run a multiprocessor server and expect it to be supported by the operating system.

Once again, memory management has been improved with this release of NetWare. In NetWare 4.1, memory was conceptualized as rings, where all NLMs loaded in Ring 0 were operating system NLMs. Third-party NLMs could be tested in Ring 3 using DOMAIN.NLM. The separation of memory could be advantageous because you could isolate errant NLMs. However, with NetWare 4.11's improved ABEND recovery features, this memory management scheme is no longer needed. All NLMs share the same pool of memory, and the concept of memory rings has been discarded.

Networking

Of course, since NetWare is a network operating system, you would expect some enhancements concerning networking. You would expect correctly. Networking enhancements included with NetWare 4.11 include client and server connectivity services. First, NetWare/IP comes fully incorporated into NetWare 4.11. When you set up a NetWare/IP environment on your network, you create an environment in which NetWare services are provided using TCP/IP. You can completely eliminate the IPX protocol.

Second, NetWare 4.11 comes with client software for a wide array of clients, including DOS/Windows, Windows 95, Windows NT, OS/2, and Macintosh. In addition, the NetWare Client for Mac OS allows the Macintosh computer to communicate with the NetWare server over IPX or IP. AppleTalk is not re-quired for communication with the NetWare 4.11 server as it was with older versions of NetWare 4.x.

Management of the network environment also becomes easier. With NetWare 4.1, only DOS/Windows workstations could administer the network, using a utility called NetWare Administrator. With NetWare 4.11, Windows 95 and Windows NT machines can also perform administrative duties, using customized versions of NetWare Administrator tailored specifically for those operating systems.

A new version of NetWare Administrator for Windows 3.x is also included with NetWare 4.11. These three new versions of NetWare Administrator (Windows 95, Windows NT, and Windows 3.x) also support connections to multiple NDS trees. This is incredibly useful if you have an NDS environment where you need to access more than one NDS tree at a time. Also, these versions of NetWare Administrator are customizable, so you can adjust your view of the network and its resources to your taste.

File Services

NetWare 4.11 boasts increased volume capacities over previous versions of NetWare 4.x. The older versions had a limit of 2 million directory entries per volume. NetWare 4.11's limit is 16 million directory entries for each volume, which should accommodate most file system environments.

To increase efficiency, one of the name spaces for the file system has been discontinued. You no longer need to use OS2.NAM to provide long filename support to OS/2 client workstations. This support is now included in the LONG.NAM name space. LONG.NAM allows Windows 95, Windows NT, and OS/2 client workstations to take advantage of long filenames on the NetWare 4.11 server.

Print Services

With older versions of NetWare 4.x, NPRINTER.EXE was the only printing station software available to run a printer attached to a client workstation as a network printer. Printers attached to Windows 95 client workstations could not be used as network printers due to incompatibilities. With the client software included in NetWare 4.11, you can now use printers connected to Windows 95 workstations as network printers through a program called NPTWIN95.EXE. Again, this is another example of how NetWare 4.11 is better able to integrate different operating systems.

Also, setting up the NetWare printing environment in NDS can get complicated and confusing. To help network administrators set up and configure the printing environment, the new versions of NetWare Administrator packaged with the NetWare 4.11 client software have an option to perform a "quick setup" of print services.

Security

You can never have too much security in your networking environment. That is why Novell is constantly striving to create a more secure network operating system to keep your confidential data confidential. As we have mentioned, NetWare 4.x comes with built-in RSA public/private key encryption; however, NetWare 4.11 takes a step toward employing an even more secure network. NetWare 4.11 was designed to meet C2 network specifications.

NetWare 4.11 also comes with a file called SECURE.NCF that can be run to create an enhanced security server. This option is unavailable with older versions of NetWare 4.x. Also, the version of AUDITCON included with NetWare 4.11 expands the types of events on your network that can be audited. It provides a more comprehensive auditing environment to help you identify and eliminate security holes in your network.

Backup Services

The SMS-compliant backup utility, SBACKUP, has been enhanced to provide better backup services for NDS. You can protect your NDS database to give yourself a safety net in the event your NDS database becomes corrupt beyond repair. Just use your backed-up copy to restore the database to its original state.

As we have learned, SBACKUP can be used to back up client workstations running the appropriate Target Service Agent (TSA). In older versions of NetWare 4.x, the only TSAs available for client workstations were for DOS, Windows 3.x, and OS/2. NetWare 4.11 includes TSAs for Mac OS and Windows 95, allowing you to back up these types of client workstations as well.

Miscellaneous Services

NetWare 4.11 comes with some other added services that enhance the functionality of your networking environment. These services, which were not available in older versions of NetWare 4.x, include the following products:

- NetWare Application Manager (NAM) allows the network administrator to centrally manage network applications. Application objects are created in the NDS tree, and users are given access to them. Through an adjunct program called NetWare Application Launcher (NAL), users are able to access these network applications, and the network administrator can control which applications the user can access.

■ NetWare Licensing Services (NLS) allows the network administrator to implement license management services on the network. He or she can buy a specific number of licenses for an application and install NetWare Licensing Services to keep track of how many copies of that application are running on the network. It will not allow running copies of an application to exceed the total number of software licenses available.

■ Novell Workstation Manager helps integrate the NetWare 4.11 and Windows NT environments. You can create NT Configuration objects in your NDS tree, which controls user access to the Windows NT machines on your network at the same time it controls access to your NetWare environment.

As you can see, NetWare 4.11 provides a lot of improvements and enhancements over previous versions of NetWare 4.x. These features will allow you to provide a more efficient and robust network environment that integrates more completely with the diverse set of computers you are likely to have on your network.

appendix C

NDS Error Codes

In maintaining the health of your NDS tree, you are bound to encounter errors either through NDS Manager, DSTRACE, or DSREPAIR. These errors will be reported to you as a numeric value which you will need to reference in a manual for translation. Included in this appendix (Table C-1) are the NDS error codes and a brief description of their meaning.

This appendix is not meant to be an NDS troubleshooting reference, it is merely a quick index to NDS error codes. For more information on these errors and a description of the action(s) you should take when you encounter these errors, refer to the NDS Manager online help. You can also view these error codes in Appendix A, "Error Codes," of the System Messages manual. This manual can be found in the NetWare 4.11 Reference collection of the online documentation.

Error Code	Description
-601	Entry not found
-602	Value not found
-603	Attribute not found
-604	Class not found
-605	Partition not found
-606	Duplicate entry
-607	Noneffective class
-608	Attribute not allowed

Error Code	Description
-609	Mandatory attribute omitted
-610	Invalid NDS name
-611	Containment rule violation
-612	Multiple values not allowed
-613	Invalid property value syntax
-614	Value already exists
-615	Duplicate attribute
-616	NDS object limit reached—maximum of 16,777,220 objects are allowed in the NDS tree
-617	Invalid database format
-618	Database inconsistency found
-619	Illegal comparison
-620	Failed comparison
-621	TTS Disabled
-622	Transport not supported
-623	Bad name syntax
-624	Duplicate replica
-625	Communication failure
-626	Referral not found
-627	Cannot delete naming value
-628	Object class violation
-629	Deletion of nonleaf object attempted
-630	Other tree
-631	Required replica type not found
-632	Process failure
-633	Invalid object for partition root
-634	Referral not found
-635	Remote failure
-636	Server not reachable
-637	Move in progress
-638	Character not mapped
-639	Authentication not complete
-640	Certificate not valid
-641	Request not valid
-642	Iteration not valid
-643	Schema not removable
-644	Schema in use

-645	Duplicate class
-646	Naming attributes invalid
-647	Object not partition root
-648	Stack not sufficient
-649	Buffer not sufficient
-650	Containment rule vague
-651	Vague containment name
-652	Mandatory already exists
-653	Optional already exists
-654	Partition operation in progress
-655	Multiple replicas
-656	Illegal master replica operation
-657	Process failed due to synchronizing schema
-658	Process failed due to replica synchronization
-659	Network time not in sync
-660	Record not available, currently in use
-661	NDS volume not available/mounted
-662	I/O to DS volume failed
-663	NDS database locked
-664	Time stamp error—old partition
-665	Time stamp error—new partition
-666	NDS incompatibility
-667	Illegal partition root manipulation
-668	Illegal leaf object operation
-669	Authentication failure
-670	Context not found
-671	Parent not found
-672	Access denied
-673	Replica in intermediate state
-674	Name service not found
-675	Invalid NDS operation
-676	CONN handle invalid
-677	Object identity not found
-678	Already existing ACL
-679	Duplicate partition
-680	Reference not subordinate
-681	Attempt to create alias of alias

Error Code	Description
-682	Auditing process failure
-683	API invalid
-684	Packet signature security violation
-685	Replica move pending
-686	Attempt to move nonleaf partition
-687	Unable to abort
-688	Cache limit exceeded
-689	Subordinate count invalid
-690	RDN not valid
-691	Noncurrent MOD time
-692	Base class incorrect
-693	Reference missing
-694	Lost entry
-695	Duplicate agent registration
-696	Busy DS loader
-697	Unable to reload DS
-698	Synchronizing replica
-699	Unrecoverable (fatal) error

Table C-1: NDS error codes.

appendix D

X.500 Country Codes

When you use Country objects in your NDS tree for organization, it is a good idea to name those objects after the X.500 standard country naming convention. This will ensure the compatibility of your NDS tree with other networks using X.500-based directory services. Provided in Table D-1 are the two letter country codes as defined by the CCITT for the X.500 standard.

Country	Abbreviation	Country	Abbreviation
AFGHANISTAN	AF	AZERBAIJAN	AZ
ALBANIA	AL	BAHAMAS	BS
ALGERIA	DZ	BAHRAIN	BH
AMERICAN SAMOA	AS	BANGLADESH	BD
ANDORRA	AD	BARBADOS	BB
ANGOLA	AO	BELARUS	BY
ANGUILLA	AI	BELGIUM	BE
ANTARCTICA	AQ	BELIZE	BZ
ANTIGUA AND BARBUDA	AG	BENIN	BJ
ARGENTINA	AR	BERMUDA	BM
ARMENIA	AM	BHUTAN	BT
ARUBA	AW	BOLIVIA	BO
AUSTRALIA	AU	BOSNIA AND HERZEGOVINA	BA
AUSTRIA	AT	BOTSWANA	BW

Country	Abbreviation
BOUVET ISLAND	BV
BRAZIL	BR
BRITISH INDIAN OCEAN TERRITORY	IO
BRUNEI DARUSSALAM	BN
BULGARIA	BG
BURKINA FASO	BF
BURUNDI	BI
CAMBODIA	KH
CAMEROON	CM
CANADA	CA
CAPE VERDE	CV
CAYMAN ISLANDS	KY
CENTRAL AFRICAN REPUBLIC	CF
CHAD	TD
CHILE	CL
CHINA	CN
CHRISTMAS ISLAND	CX
COCOS (KEELING) ISLANDS	CC
COLOMBIA	CO
COMOROS	KM
CONGO	CG
COOK ISLANDS	CK
COSTA RICA	CR
COTE D'IVOIRE	CI
CROATIA	HR
CUBA	CU
CYPRUS	CY
CZECH REPUBLIC	CZ
DENMARK	DK
DJIBOUTI	DJ
DOMINICA	DM
DOMINICAN REPUBLIC	DO
EAST TIMOR	TP
ECUADOR	EC
EGYPT	EG
EL SALVADOR	SV
EQUATORIAL GUINEA	GQ

Country	Abbreviation
ERITREA	ER
ESTONIA	EE
ETHIOPIA	ET
FALKLAND ISLANDS (MALVINAS)	FK
FAROE ISLANDS	FO
FIJI	FJ
FINLAND	FI
FRANCE	FR
FRANCE, METROPOLITAN	FX
FRENCH GUIANA	GF
FRENCH POLYNESIA	PF
FRENCH SOUTHERN TERRITORIES	TF
GABON	GA
GAMBIA	GM
GEORGIA	GE
GERMANY	DE
GHANA	GH
GIBRALTAR	GI
GREECE	GR
GREENLAND	GL
GRENADA	GD
GUADELOUPE	GP
GUAM	GU
GUATEMALA	GT
GUINEA	GN
GUINEA-BISSAU	GW
GUYANA	GY
HAITI	HT
HEARD AND MCDONALD ISLANDS	HM
HONDURAS	HN
HONG KONG	HK
HUNGARY	HU
ICELAND	IS
INDIA	IN
INDONESIA	ID
IRAN (ISLAMIC REPUBLIC OF)	IR

Country	Abbreviation
IRAQ	IQ
IRELAND	IE
ISRAEL	IL
ITALY	IT
JAMAICA	JM
JAPAN	JP
JORDAN	JO
KAZAKHSTAN	KZ
KENYA	KE
KIRIBATI	KI
KOREA, DEMOCRATIC PEOPLE'S REPUBLIC OF	KP
KOREA, REPUBLIC OF	KR
KUWAIT	KW
KYRGYZSTAN	KG
LAO PEOPLE'S DEMOCRATIC REPUBLIC	LA
LATVIA	LV
LEBANON	LB
LESOTHO	LS
LIBERIA	LR
LIBYAN ARAB JAMAHIRIYA	LY
LIECHTENSTEIN	LI
LITHUANIA	LT
LUXEMBOURG	LU
MACAU	MO
MACEDONIA, THE FORMER YUGOSLAV REPUBLIC	MK
MADAGASCAR	MG
MALAWI	MW
MALAYSIA	MY
MALDIVES	MV
MALI	ML
MALTA	MT
MARSHALL ISLANDS	MH
MARTINIQUE	MQ
MAURITANIA	MR
MAURITIUS	MU

Country	Abbreviation
MAYOTTE	YT
MEXICO	MX
MICRONESIA (FEDERATED STATES OF)	FM
MOLDOVA, REPUBLIC OF	MD
MONACO	MC
MONGOLIA	MN
MONTSERRAT	MS
MOROCCO	MA
MOZAMBIQUE	MZ
MYANMAR	MM
NAMIBIA	NA
NAURU	NR
NEPAL	NP
NETHERLANDS	NL
NETHERLANDS ANTILLES	AN
NEW CALEDONIA	NC
NEW ZEALAND	NZ
NICARAGUA	NI
NIGER	NE
NIGERIA	NG
NIUE	NU
NORFOLK ISLAND	NF
NORTHERN MARIANA ISLANDS	MP
NORWAY	NO
OMAN	OM
PAKISTAN	PK
PALAU	PW
PANAMA	PA
PAPUA NEW GUINEA	PG
PARAGUAY	PY
PERU	PE
PHILIPPINES	PH
PITCAIRN	PN
POLAND	PL
PORTUGAL	PT
PUERTO RICO	PR
QATAR	QA

Country	Abbreviation
REUNION	RE
ROMANIA	RO
RUSSIAN FEDERATION	RU
RWANDA	RW
ST. HELENA	SH
SAINT KITTS AND NEVIS	KN
SAINT LUCIA	LC
ST. PIERRE AND MIQUELON	PM
SAINT VINCENT AND THE GRENADINES	VC
SAMOA	WS
SAN MARINO	SM
SAO TOME AND PRINCIPE	ST
SAUDI ARABIA	SA
SENEGAL	SN
SEYCHELLES	SC
SIERRA LEONE	SL
SINGAPORE	SG
SLOVAKIA	SK
SLOVENIA	SI
SOLOMON ISLANDS	SB
SOMALIA	SO
SOUTH AFRICA	ZA
SOUTH GEORGIA AND THE SOUTH SANDWICH ISLANDS	GS
SPAIN	ES
SRI LANKA	LK
SUDAN	SD
SURINAME	SR
SVALBARD AND JAN MAYEN ISLANDS	SJ
SWAZILAND	SZ
SWEDEN	SE
SWITZERLAND	CH
SYRIAN ARAB REPUBLIC	SY
TAIWAN, PROVINCE OF CHINA	TW
TAJIKISTAN	TJ

Country	Abbreviation
TANZANIA, UNITED REPUBLIC OF	TZ
THAILAND	TH
TOGO	TG
TOKELAU	TK
TONGA	TO
TRINIDAD AND TOBAGO	TT
TUNISIA	TN
TURKEY	TR
TURKMENISTAN	TM
TURKS AND CAICOS ISLANDS	TC
TUVALU	TV
UGANDA	UG
UKRAINE	UA
UNITED ARAB EMIRATES	AE
UNITED KINGDOM	GB
UNITED STATES	US
UNITED STATES MINOR OUTLYING ISLANDS	UM
URUGUAY	UY
UZBEKISTAN	UZ
VANUATU	VU
VATICAN CITY STATE (HOLY SEE)	VA
VENEZUELA	VE
VIETNAM	VN
VIRGIN ISLANDS (BRITISH)	VG
VIRGIN ISLANDS (U.S.)	VI
WALLIS AND FUTUNA ISLANDS	WF
WESTERN SAHARA	EH
YEMEN	YE
YUGOSLAVIA	YU
ZAIRE	ZR
ZAMBIA	ZM
ZIMBABWE	ZW

Table D-1: Country codes as defined by ISO 3166.

Glossary

ACCESS.CFG A file that controls who may have access to what directories under the Web server's root. Maintained by the Web Manager utility.

Access Control List (ACL) A property that controls the trustees and the rights of the trustees. The ACL exists in every object.

access time The amount of time required for data to be retrieved from a resource (i.e., a hard drive or RAM). Consists of the seek time and the read time.

aliased object An object to which an alias points. This object can be a user, container, or leaf object. An alias, in computer terms, refers to an object that has a name and references another object.

alias leaf object An object that points to another leaf object in the NDS tree and appears to be that object. Used to provide access to resources in other parts of the NDS tree.

Application leaf object An NDS object used with the NetWare Application Manager (NAM). Allows the network administrator to manage network-based software applications as NDS tree objects.

AppleTalk Filing Protocol (AFP) server object A leaf object in the NDS tree representing the location of a server that has AFP installed.

ASCII Acronym for American Standard Code for Information Interchange. ASCII is a coding method that assigns a numerical value to all alphanumeric characters.

asynchronous transfer mode (ATM) A cell-based switching technology designed to handle voice, video, and data communications. ATM can handle a large volume of data over a wide area network (WAN) link.

attribute   A characteristic of some data record. An attribute can refer to a field within a database record.

application programming interface (API)   A programming library that provides access to lower-level functions. Almost all programs are built on top of some type of API.

ARCnet   A local area network topology that combines star and bus topologies. ARCnet uses the token concept to operate. See also **Token Ring**.

auditing leaf object   An object that helps to provide auditing capabilities in NetWare 4.11. Contains the auditing file object (AFO).

AUTOEXEC.NCF   The second configuration file read by SERVER.EXE upon loading. It is a text file that contains configuration information like the server's name, IPX numbers, and time zone. It is also responsible for loading utility NLMs and LAN drivers. This file is read after STARTUP.NCF has been processed and the SYS volume is mounted.

base schema   The NDS schema that comes with NetWare 4.11. Includes all of the objects and their properties.

block suballocation   A 512-byte block used by NetWare to provide a way to handle data that is just a little too big or too small for the defined block size. Saves space from being wasted.

bindery   A database used by earlier versions of NetWare that provides information about users, groups, and other network devices. IntranetWare provides bindery emulation for backward compatibility.

bindery leaf object   Provides backward compatibility for older bindery-based utilities. Usually placed in the NDS tree by a migration or upgrade utility.

bindery leaf queue   Provides backward compatibility for older bindery-based print queues and users relying on bindery services to print. These leaf objects are placed in the NDS tree by migration or upgrade utilities.

bit   The smallest unit of information a computer can manipulate. Short for binary digit. A bit can have a value of 0 or 1.

byte   A unit of information containing 8 bits. Byte, short for binary term, is equal to a single character in computer processing and storage.

cache hit   A situation in which a server finds the requested data in RAM.

CAPTURE.EXE   A DOS utility used to send print jobs to the network printer.

CD-ROM   An abbreviation for compact disc read-only memory. A storage medium that can hold approximately 600MB of data. CD-ROMs use laser optics instead of magnets to read data.

cell   A network packet that is 53 bytes long used with asynchronous transfer mode protocol. A cell contains all the routing information necessary for it to be routed to its final destination.

central processing unit (CPU)   The brains of a computer. Handles computations and control of the computer. The Pentium Pro is an example of a CPU.

child object   An object that exists within another object.

circuit switching   A method of creating a dedicated, physical channel between two locations during data transmission. This link is maintained only as long as required. An example of circuit switching is a modem-type communication.

clickable image map   An inline image broken up into regions. Web-based documents or services are associated with each region. Selecting a region selects the associated service.

client   A machine on a local area network that uses the shared resource of another computer on the network.

clock speed   The oscillating rate at which the clock in a computer operates. This rate is usually measured in hertz (Hz), kilohertz (KHz), or megahertz (MHz). This speed is a factor of how fast a processor is able to operate.

command statement block   A list of command statements following an if-then statement. The last command must be followed by the END statement.

Common Gateway Interface (CGI)   Refers to a set of standards designed to allow programmers to create applications that can interface with a server. Currently, Web servers are the target of these applications.

common name   The name that identifies a leaf object within its context. All leaf objects have a common name.

concurrent routing   The ability to route more than one protocol at a time. Allows for multiple protocols to be used at the same time.

container   A container object holds leaf objects or other container objects. Containers exist to provide organization in the NDS tree.

container login script   The first login script to be executed for a user when he or she logs in. The location of the user in the NDS tree determines the script that is run. Organization and organizational units may hold container login scripts.

context   The exact position of an object within an NDS tree.

Country object   A type of container object that is designed to be used with large international companies. The Country object exists directly below [Root]. A Country object contains an organization container object or an alias leaf object.

current context   The up-to-date position of a client workstation within an NDS tree. This context will change depending on the exact position of the workstation at that specific point in time.

Custom Device Module (CDM)   Part of Novell's NetWare Peripheral Architecture (NWPA). This is the device driver that works with the specific disk devices attached to the disk subsystem. One CDM is required for each device.

CX utility   A DOS utility used to discover a user's current context in the NDS tree. With this utility, a user can change his or her context in the NDS tree.

data bus   A set of electrical lines that is used by the different components of a computer system to transfer data between one another. Access to the bus is supervised by the central processing unit.

database inconsistency   A situation where replicas contain different information and their differences cannot be resolved through synchronization.

data migration   A method provided by NetWare that allows least recently used files to be transferred to a high capacity storage subsystem. The files are still accessible, but access is extremely slow.

decrypt   The process of restoring encrypted data to a usable form. See also **encrypt**.

default login script   The last login script to run when a user logs in. It is compiled into LOGIN.EXE. The default login script does not run if a user has a user login script, but it will run if the user only has a profile login script and/or a container login script.

default partition   Created during installation and exists in every NDS tree. Also known as the [Root] partition.

Direct Memory Access (DMA)   Memory access that does not require the intervention of the CPU between a peripheral and memory.

directory   A logical grouping of related files within a file system.

Directory Entry Table (DET)   Located on a volume, the DET is a table that contains information about files and directories. Used to help retrieve a file from a volume.

Directory Map object   A leaf object in the NDS tree that points to a specific directory on any NetWare file server. A common use for Directory Maps is in login scripts.

disabled protocol   A protocol that has been configured but is not read for networking.

distinguished name   A combination of an object's common name and its context. Periods are used to separate objects in a distinguished name, and distinguished names always start with a leading period.

Domain Name System (DNS)   A system that resolves a domain name into an IP address. DNS uses a distributed database system with full-qualified domain names and addresses. DNS is the system used by the Internet for name/address resolution.

Domain SAP/RIP Service (DSS)   The DSS server acts as a central location for routing information for LANs running NetWare/IP. Servers running NetWare/IP send their RIP/SAP packets to the DSS server. The DSS server updates its database based on the newly acquired information. Periodically, the servers download a copy of the database to update themselves. A NetWare/IP network must have one DSS server.

DOS   Abbreviation for disk operating system.

dotted quad   The combination of four octets with periods in between them to form an IP address. See also **IP address, octet**.

drivers   A hardware device or software program that regulates another device. A device driver is a device-specific program that allows a computer to work with a particular device.

duplexing   A method used to provide data redundancy for hard disks. Data is stored on two hard disks. Each hard disk is attached to its own hard disk controller. See also **mirroring**.

Dynamic Host Control Protocol (DHCP)   A TCP/IP service that handles a pool of available IP addresses. The server dynamically assigns IP address as they are requested. IP addresses are returned to the pool when they are no longer in use.

EDIT.NLM   A NetWare Loadable Module (NLM) that can be used to edit the various text files used by NetWare.

effective rights   All of the security privileges granted for an object. These rights can be received from inheritance, from an association with another object, or by direct trustee assignments.

enabled protocol   A protocol that has been configured for use and is bound to a LAN driver instance. IPX is defaulted as an enabled protocol.

Ethernet   Developed in 1976 by Xerox, Ethernet is a local area network protocol. Ethernet cabling can connect stations approximately 300 meters apart. Information on an Ethernet network is contained in variable length frames containing control information plus 1500 bytes of data.

elevator seek algorithm   A routine used by NetWare to efficiently handle reads and writes to the server's disks.

encrypt   The process by which digital information is made unreadable/viewable to protect it from unauthorized use.

Enhanced Integrated Drive Electronics (EIDE)   A prevalent interface technology used to control hard disks and similar devices. EIDE can handle up to four devices and has a maximum device capacity of 2GB.

Enhanced Small Device Interface (ESDI)   An interface technology used to connect computers to hard drives and other peripherals.

Extended Industry Standard Architecture (EISA)   A bus system that uses a 32-bit data path and accepts Industry Standard Architecture (ISA) cards. EISA was designed by a consortium of nine companies in 1988 to compete with IBM's micro channel architecture. See also **Industry Standard Architecture (ISA)**.

extended memory (XMS)   On a machine using a processor above a 80286, extended memory is the memory above 1 megabyte. Memory managers handle access to this memory.

fault tolerance   The ability of a computer system to respond to a catastrophic error without data loss. Fault tolerance may be implemented in hardware or software.

FIFO   First in, first out. Refers to a queue processing method in which the first items added to the queue are the first items to be processed.

File Allocation Table (FAT)   A file located at the partition level that contains information about where a file is stored on the hard disk. This information is cached by the server to speed file access requests.

file locking   The process of preventing multiple users from using the same file. Usually, the first person who accesses the file will have the ability to make changes. Once the file is unlocked, other users may make changes to the file.

File Transfer Protocol (FTP)   An application, service, and protocol provided by TCP/IP that permits the copying of files between computers.

frame relay   A packet-switching service that is similar to X.25 but does not employ the extensive error checking that X.25 uses. Frame relay is employed as a WAN connection service. See also **X.25**.

frame type   Describes the structure used to create a physical packet. Frame types differ depending on the network architecture being used.

free space   A portion of the hard disk that contains no data or partition information. This area is available for use to create a new partition or volume.

Garbage Collection   A NetWare routine that defragments the free memory blocks on the server. Makes contiguous memory blocks available so that NLMs can be loaded.

Graphics Interchange Format (GIF)   Developed by CompuServe, GIF is a graphics file format.

Graphical User Interface (GUI)   An interface that interacts with the user. Uses pictorial representations and menus to allow interaction with the system.

group object   A user-related leaf object that allows an administrator to control many users under one object. Allows the administrator to grant/remove access rights once and have it affect many people.

hard disk   A storage device that consists of one or more inflexible platters that are coated with a magnetic material. The platters rotate at speeds starting at 3600 revolutions per minute; a read/write head is used to examine the data on the platter. A common size for a hard disk is 4 gigabytes.

hard disk controller   A computer subsystem that controls access to one or more disk drives. The controller manages physical and logical access to a drive.

hardware bottleneck   Created when the performance of a machine is degraded due to limitations of one component in the system. This can be severely detrimental to a server.

hexadecimal   A base-16 numbering system using the numerals 0 through 9 and the alpha characters A through F. Hexadecimal numbers are used in computers as a compact way to represent a binary number.

home directory   A directory on the file server that a user has complete access to. A user's home directory is not usually accessible to other users.

host machine   The main machine in a group of machines that is connected by a communication link. The host provides all the processing, while the connected machines provide an interface to the host machine.

Host Adapter Module (HAM)   Part of Novell's NetWare Peripheral Architecture (NWPA). A device driver that is used with a specific disk controller.

HTTPD.CFG   An ASCII text file that is the master configuration file for the Novell Web Server. This file is located in the SYS:WEB directory.

HyperText Markup Language (HTML)   A language used in the development of Web pages. The language allows for the embedding of text, images, fonts, and hypertext links. Hypertext links allow pages to be interconnected with one another.

HyperText Transfer Protocol (HTTP)   The protocol used by Web servers to communicate with Web browsers over the World Wide Web.

hyperlink   An HTML code that allows a document to reference or link another document or Web resource. An example would be: "<A HREF=http://www.rambell.com> Example hyperlink command </a>".

Integrated Drive Electronics (IDE)   An interface technology popular with PCs that is able to connect two devices to the computer. The controller electronics are located on the devices, removing the need for a separate adapter card.

Industry Standard Architecture (ISA)   A designation for the bus design of an IBM PC/XT. The design allows various adapters to be added to a computer system by plugging them into expansion slots.

informational leaf object   Contains the computer leaf object. Used to store information about specific workstations.

inheritance   An object-oriented term that refers to the method of passing properties between a parent object and a child object. The child object receives its properties from the parent object.

Integrated Service Digital Network   A digital communication network that is able to carry both voice and data.

interexchange carriers (IXC)   A company, such as AT&T, that provides long-distance telephone and telecommunication connections. IXCs are now able to compete against local exchange carriers (LECs) due to deregulation. See also **local exchange carrier**.

Internetwork Packet Exchange (IPX)   A core protocol used by NetWare to exchange information between machines. IPX is the default protocol installed when a new server or client is set up.

InterNIC   The organization in charge of administering the Internet's domain names. This is the organization that must be contacted to register a new domain name.

interrupt mode   Used to specify the exact interrupt where a device can be found. Specifying the wrong interrupt can cause system lockups. This option can be found on the communications screen for parallel printers.

IP address   A 32-bit number that is used by TCP/IP to route information to its final destination. Every machine on a TCP/IP network has its own unique IP address.

IPX network number   A hexadecimal number that identifies a piece of a network cable. This number is usually eight digits long.

Java   A programming language developed by Sun Microsystems that is platform independent. Java is used on the Web in the form of Java applets, which are small binary programs that are executed by a Web browser.

leaf   Any node in the hierarchy that is farthest away from the root node. In a tree structure, a leaf node has no descendants and is the last node on a branch in the tree.

leaf object   Part of the NDS tree that represents a logical or physical network resource. Users, printers, servers, print queues, and volume objects are all valid leaf objects. There are 23 different leaf objects that ship with NetWare 4.11.

licensed connection   An entity that is logged into and utilizes the server's resources.

Link Support Layer (LSL)   A component used to help implement the Open Datalink Interface (ODI) specification. Directs incoming network packets to their intended protocol stacks. Sits between the MLID driver and the protocol stack for the NetWare DOS Requester.

LOAD   A console command that is used to load NLMs into memory. The usual format is: LOAD <NLM NAME> <OPTIONS>.

local area network (LAN)   A set of devices located in the same geographical area that are able to communicate and exchange information through a communication link. The devices may consist of PCs, printers, and network devices such as routers.

Local Common Gateway Interface (LCGI)   A type of CGI program supported by Novell's Web server that runs on the local Web server. See also **Remote Common Gateway Interface** and **Common Gateway Interface**.

local exchange carrier (LEC)   A company that provides local telephone and telecommunication connections. Until recently, these companies were restricted by federal law from providing long-distance solutions. Due to deregulation, this is no longer true.

LOGIN.EXE   A DOS utility used to gain access to a NetWare server. When LOGIN.EXE is executed, it will prompt you for a username and password.

login script   A script used to map network resources at logon for a user. The same script may be used for multiple users, making it easy for users to gain access to network resources.

MAP utility   A utility used to map a workstation's drive letter to a volume on a file server. MAP can also be used to delete a drive mapping as well as manipulate search drive mappings.

mandatory property   A specific characteristic of an object that must have a value. An NDS object cannot be created or exist without mandatory properties.

megahertz (MHz)   One million cycles per second; a measure of frequency.

message-related leaf object   Leaf objects that are installed as a part of Novell's MHS messaging services. MHS messaging services are not included with IntranetWare and must be purchased with Novell's GroupWise.

Micro Channel Architecture (MCA)   A proprietary hardware bus designed by IBM in the late 1980s. Although MCA was an improvement over the ISA bus because it was faster and able to handle more data, MCA was not accepted by the computer industry.

Modified Frequency Modulation (MFM)   An interface technology for communicating with a hard disk. MFM was popular in the early 1980s.

Multipurpose Internet Mail Extensions (MIME)   An encoding scheme that embeds type codes into a document. The document is still ASCII text and therefore transferable over the Internet using Simple Mail Transfer Protocol (SMTP). There are seven MIME types: Application, Audio, Image, Message, Multipart, Text, and Video.

mirroring   A method used to provide redundant protection for hard disks. Mirroring works by creating an exact duplicate of a disk as it is being used. If the primary disk fails for some reason, the mirrored disk can be used until the primary disk is replaced. The hard disks are connected to a single disk controller.

Multiple Link Interface Driver (MLID)   A proprietary device driver developed for every network card. Responsible for interfacing directly with a network card. The lowest part of the NetWare DOS Requester client.

multihoming   The ability of a single Web server to serve multiple Web sites, each with its own domain name.

multivalued property   A specific attribute of an object that can have multiple values.

name space   A group of NLMs that provides file system compatibility with different operating systems such as OS/2, Macintosh, or a UNIX-based system.

nesting   The embedding of a construct inside of another construct.

NetBasic for Internet   Uses BASIC as the programming language for implementing CGI programs. An NLM is provided that acts as an interpreter for the basic programs.

NetWare Administrator utility   A GUI-based application that provides a centralized management solution for controlling file servers, users, groups, printers, and other network resources.

NETADMIN.EXE   A DOS utility that can be used to perform basic network administrative tasks.

NetWare Core Protocol (NCP)   A protocol used by NetWare to communicate information between clients and servers. Requests for services and resources use NCP. NCP information is encapsulated inside other protocols such as IP or IPX.

NetWare Directory Services (NDS)   A centralized database that is used to store information about a network. The NDS also handles users' security access to various network resources.

NetWare DOS Requester   Client software used by machines running DOS/Windows 3.x. It is NDS-aware and authenticates users to the NDS tree on a network. The DOS Requester is made up of four pieces: MLID driver, Link Support Layer, Protocol Stacks, and the VLM.EXE executable.

NetWare licensing services leaf object   Contains the LSP Server object that is created when the NetWare Licensing Services (NLS) NLM is loaded.

NetWare Link Services Protocol (NLSP)   A replacement for the RIP and SAP protocols. NLSP provides a more efficient way to handle routing and service information between routers. See also **Routing Information Protocol (RIP)** and **Service Advertising Protocol (SAP)**.

NetWare Loadable Module (NLM)   Used by NetWare to provide a modular plug-in style interface to the server software. To provide a service, you only need to load the correct NLM. Services not needed are not loaded and therefore memory is saved.

NetWare Server object   A leaf object that represents a file server in the NDS tree. This object is essential for accessing a file system on a server.

network   A logical grouping of machines connected by any communication medium. The communication link may be permanent or temporary.

network address   A 12-digit hexadecimal number that is used to identify the NIC address. See also **network interface card (NIC)**.

network drive mapping   Assigns a workstation's available drive letter to a volume on the server.

network interface card (NIC)   Provides the hardware interface to the local network. An NIC is required for a machine to communicate on a network. Also called a network adapter.

NPRINT.EXE   A Terminate and Stay Resident program that handles print jobs sent from the network printer server. NPRINT is loaded on workstations that are connected directly to a printer to allow them to act as printer stations. See also **Terminate and Stay Resident (TSR)**.

object A discrete NDS unit that contains information about a specific network resource. An object is the building block of the NDS tree.

object collision A situation where two NDS objects that have the same common names cannot be distinguished from one another when using Bindery Services.

object rights Composed of five attributes: Supervisor, Browse, Create, Delete, and Rename. Determines how a trustee can use an object.

octets Four sets of 8-bit numbers that comprise an IP address. An octet is converted from a binary form to a digital form and is a number from 0 to 255. See also **IP address**.

Open Datalink Interface (ODI) A standard developed by Apple and Novell in 1989 for network adapter specifications. Allows for the loading of multiple network adapters on one machine. Also responsible for allowing multiple protocols to run on one adapter.

organization object A type of container object that provides the tree with an identity. This is the first type of container object that may contain leaf objects. Cannot contain another Organization object and only exists below the [ROOT] object.

organizational role object A user-related leaf object that is used to create a specific position that exists in an organization. The user associated with this object inherits all the appropriate security rights for that position.

organizational unit object A container object that provides another level of organization for the NDS tree. Exists beneath an Organization object. Cannot exist immediately below the [ROOT] object. Able to contain other organizational units and all leaf objects.

packet switching A method of communication that sends smaller packets along the best route to their final destination. Multiple routes are available to ensure reliable delivery.

pages A 4KB chunk of memory from NetWare's memory pool.

parallel port A port on a computer that provides an input/output connection for a parallel interface. A parallel interface is able to send multiple data and control bits at the same time. A parallel port is extremely popular for connecting print devices.

parent object An object that contains other objects.

parity An error-checking procedure in which all the 1's in a given transmission must be equivalent. Parity is one of the parameters that must be decided on before a modem-to-modem communication can occur.

partition A logical division on a hard disk that acts like it is a physically separate device. When you create a volume with Novell, you are partitioning the hard disk.

partitioning The act of breaking up a database and spreading the pieces across multiple servers.

partition root The topmost container object in an NDS tree partition.

path Represents the directions necessary to navigate through a structured collection of data. The data may be a database, file system, or even a network.

PCONSOLE.EXE A DOS utility used to set up and configure printers and print queues. PCONSOLE can also be used to manage established printers and queues. PCONSOLE has been updated from NetWare 3.x to be NDS aware.

Peripheral Component Interface (PCI)   A local bus design created by Intel that provides a high-speed bus for peripherals.

peripheral device   A device that is connected to a computer and is controlled by its microprocessor. Peripheral devices include disk drives, printers, and modems.

Perl (Practical Extraction and Report Language)   A scripting language with large cross-platform support. Used extensively on the Internet to support CGI scripts for the Web. Supported by the IntranetWare Web server. See also **Common Gateway Interface (CGI)**.

port   A 16-bit number that identifies a specific server process. The numbers 0-1024 are privileged ports; the assignment of ports is handled by the Internet Assigned Numbers Authority (IANA).

Primary time server   A type of time provider that utilizes a democratic process for network time synchronization. The Primary time server asks for the network time from all other time providers in the NDS tree, and a vote is made to determine the correct network time. The Primary time servers change their times and provide the corrected time to all of the time consumers.

print driver   A software program designed to allow other programs to use a specific printer without having to know the printer's software and hardware specifics.

print data   Information that can be printed by a printer.

print server   A computer system dedicated to managing printers and the data sent to them. A Novell file server may also act as a print server.

print server object   A leaf object in the NDS tree that represents a print server.

print queue   Uses print image files to hold pending print jobs. Print jobs are processed as the printer becomes available.

print queue object   A leaf object in the NDS tree that represents a print queue.

printer object   A leaf object in the NDS tree that is associated with a physical network printer.

printer station   The workstation or machine that is directly connected to a printer and is on the network. Additional software allows the printer to act as a "network printer."

private key   See **public key**.

polled mode   Causes the software on the printing station to look for a connected printer by polling all interrupts. Slows down printing but keeps the system from possibly locking up due to interrupt conflicts. This option is found on the communications screen for parallel printers. See also **interrupt mode**.

power on self-test (POST)   A set of diagnostic routines stored in ROM that test various system components during power up. If a problem is found, the user is alerted by a message or an auditory alert.

profile object   A user-related leaf object. This NDS object acts as a way to execute a group login script. The profile object can be assigned trustee rights to the file system and other network resources. These assignments are then inherited by associated objects.

profile login script   Associated with the profile object, this is the second login script run by a user logging into the network. Profile login scripts are optional.

property   Describes a specific characteristic of an object. See also **object**.

property rights   Allows a trustee to use the data located in an NDS object. There are five property rights: Supervisor, Compare, Read, Write, and Add Self.

protocol   A set of rules designating how a group of computer systems may communicate with one another. IPX and TCP/IP are examples of a protocol.

protocol stack   The protocol stack exists above the Link Support Layer (LSL). Responsible for creating network packets on the way out of the machine and interpreting incoming network packets.

proxy server   A machine that shields the local LAN from the outside network by keeping the outside network from seeing anything other than the proxy server. The server handles all network traffic between the outside world and the local LAN by directing network packets to their appropriate destinations.

public key   Part of an encryption scheme based on two keys: a public key and a private key. Each key represents part of the answer for a mathematical formula that was used to scramble a message. Both keys are required to descramble a message.

QuickFinder   An NLM-based CGI search engine provided by Novell as part of IntranetWare. QuickFinder can index the entire contents of a Web server and publish that information to the Web.

random access memory (RAM)   A volatile storage space used by the central processing unit to execute programs. The storage locations in RAM may be read or written in any order.

read time   The amount of time required to read data from a hard disk after the data has been located on the physical medium.

record locking   The process that prevents multiple users from using the same database record. Similar to file locking. The first person to access the database record will have the ability to make changes.

Reference time server   A time provider that acts similarly to the Primary time server. However, the Reference time server will not make changes to its clock to reflect the voting outcome. The main responsibility of the Reference time server is to provide input to the voting process for the accuracy of the network time.

relative distinguished name   A name that is created by appending the current NDS context to another NDS context to create a distinguished name. Relative distinguished names are not written with a leading period and can have a trailing period. See also **distinguished name**.

Remote Common Gateway Interface (RCGI)   A type of CGI program supported by Novell Web Server (NWS). An RCGI is an NLM written in ANSI C and is unique to IntranetWare.

replica   A physical copy of a partition.

replica ring   A backup scheme that provides fault tolerance by ensuring that multiple copies of a partition exist on a network.

replica synchronization   A process in which replicas in a partition's replica ring exchange data. This ensures that all replicas within a replica ring contain any changes that are made.

replication   The process of copying parts of an NDS database to other IntranetWare servers to provide a redundant backup.

Routing Information Protocol (RIP)   A protocol used by servers to gather routing information about their network and to disseminate that information to other servers.

root   The highest level in a hierarchy of data. The root contains all subsets of the data in the hierarchy.

root directory   The highest level in a file system. The root directory represents the entry point into the file system. All other directories are located below the root directory. See also **root**.

router   A device that receives transmitted messages from a network and redirects those messages toward their destination, possibly on another network.

schema   Defines a view of a database. Also refers to the attributes contained within the database.

search drive mapping   A way to add a specified path to the local workstation's PATH environment variable. Search drives are only applicable on a DOS workstation.

search engine   A CGI program that can submit search requests and return any hits found on the local Web server. Search engines are used to locate information on a Web server. Novell provides a search engine with IntranetWare called QuickFinder.

Secondary time server   A type of time consumer whose sole responsibility is to reflect changes in the network time as dictated by the time providers.

Secure Sockets Layer (SSL)   A secure protocol used to transact business over the Internet. SSL enables your Web server to use encrypted data to interact with Web browsers. SSL was developed by Netscape Communications.

seek time   The amount of time required to move a hard disk's read/write head into a specified position.

Service Advertising Protocol (SAP)   A broadcast protocol that announces a server's services to the network.

server   A program that provides services to other computers. A server is another reference for the machine that provides services for other computers.

SERVER.EXE   NetWare's server executable program that is launched from the DOS partition. This executable represents the base of NetWare's modular network operating system.

server console prompt   A prompt received after the server has processed AUTOEXEC.NCF. At this point, the server is ready to accept commands. The prompt is the server's name followed by a colon.

server-side includes   Commands in an HTML document that are executed by the server before the document is served to a Web browser.

Sequenced Packet Exchange (SPX)   To provide a reliable connection, SPX was implemented to support connection-oriented communication and connection IDs. This information is encapsulated inside an IPX packet.

Single Reference time server   A type of time provider that is the only source of network time. Since this type of timer server controls the network time, all other servers are time consumers.

Site Certificates   A document made available to visitors of your Web site that confirms a server's identity. This certificate is issued by a third-party organization called a Certifying Authority (CA). Site Certificates are used with SSL transactions.

Small Computer System Interface (SCSI)   A popular interface technology used to connect hard drives and other devices to a computer. SCSI controllers can handle up to seven devices and support transfer rates up to 40 MB/sec. SCSI can also handle multiple read/write requests simultaneously.

source tree   An NDS tree that is merged with another NDS tree to create a target tree.

SRM.CFG   The server resource map file. An ASCII text file used by the Novell Web Server to locate various resources on your IntranetWare server. Usually located in the SYS:WEB directory.

SSL.CFG   A file that is used by the Secure Sockets Layer. It should not need to be manually edited. Information stored in this file includes your Site Certificate names, the level of SSL supported, and the number of clients supported for authorization.

STARTUP.NCF   The first configuration file read by SERVER.EXE upon startup. It is a text file that contains information about disk drivers, memory management, and name space parameters.

stateless   Communication on the Web is said to be stateless. Web servers respond to requests from Web browsers but don't keep track of what was served and to whom it was served.

subdirectory   A directory within another directory. In a hierarchical file system, a subdirectory has one parent directory that may have multiple subdirectories. See also **directory**.

subnet mask   Used to separate the host and network pieces of an IP address. A 32-bit number that can be used to subdivide an IP network into smaller pieces.

synchronization radius   The acceptable margin of error that a server's time can have with respect to the network's time.

SYSCON.EXE   A DOS-based utility used to manipulate bindery properties. This utility must be used to manipulate bindery properties; the NetWare Administrator utility cannot make any changes.

tagged pairs   HTML commands encased in less-than and greater-than symbols that tell a browser where a particular command begins and ends.

target   Refers to an objective of a computer command. A target can be a directory, file, or device.

target tree   An NDS tree comprising merging source trees. The target tree will have the objects from the source trees.

TCP/IP   An acronym for Transmission Control Protocol/Internet Protocol. Developed by the U.S. Department of Defense (DoD) as a software protocol to be used on DoD computers for communication. TCP/IP is a routable protocol and is used extensively on the Internet.

Terminate and Stay Resident (TSR)   A program that loads into conventional memory and then exits. A TSR will remain in memory until used or unloaded from memory.

time consumers   Time servers that set their clocks to the Universal Time Coordinated (UTC) time dictated by the time providers.

time provider group   A group of time servers in the NDS tree that collectively calculates a network's time for the NDS tree.

time providers   Time servers that dictate the correct Universal Time Coordinated (UTC) time to other servers.

Token Ring   A ring topology local area network that uses token passing to regulate network traffic. A Token Ring network is governed by a token that determines when a station can transmit data.

topology   The configuration created by connecting devices together on a LAN. The three common types of topologies are star, ring, and bus.

Topology Specific Module (TSM)   Part of the Client32 software; TSM provides specific network topology information to the client. There are different TSMs for different network topologies.

transaction   A discrete activity in a computer system. A transaction may be updating a customer order or creating a new entry in a database.

Transaction Tracking System (TTS)   A system that allows the server to log all events as they occur; it can then re-create them if the server crashes. Using TTS can increase NetWare's reliability.

tree walking   The process by which the NDS tree looks for information or a resource in the NDS tree. The NDS tree will query itself as to the location of the resource and continue up the tree until the resource is located.

trustee assignment   A user object that is granted a security assignment to the file system. An example would be a user's home directory.

typeful name   A name that includes the object attribute type abbreviations in the name of the NDS object. Useful when specifying a context.

typeless name   A concise way to specify context in an NDS tree that doesn't include the object attribute type abbreviations. See also **typeful name**.

Uniform Resource Locator (URL)   The address of a Web document. Every document on the Web has its own URL. All URLs contain the following elements: an access protocol, a separator, and a machine name. The URL is a part of HTML that describes the type and location of a document.

Uninterrupted Power Supply (UPS)   A device between a computer and a power source that ensures that the computer does not lose power in the event of a power loss. A UPS also provides protection against power surges and brownouts from the power source.

Universal Time Coordinated (UTC)   A standard time for the NDS network. Calculated to adjust for time zones in which the servers are located.

UNIX   Developed at Bell Laboratories in 1969, UNIX is a multitasking, multiuser operating system. A version of UNIX is available for almost all PCs today.

unknown leaf object   An object that appears in the NDS tree when an NDS object cannot be identified as any other type of leaf object. This is usually an indication that something is wrong with the NDS tree.

user login script   Associated with the user object, this is the third script to run when a user logs in. User login scripts can be maintained by the user. This script is optional.

user object   A leaf object in the NDS tree that represents an actual user on the network. There are 55 properties associated with this NDS object.

value   Information that describes a property within an object. See also **object** and **property**.

virtual directories   A feature that allows directories from other NetWare servers to be published by a Novell Web Server.

volume   Another name for a disk partition. Novell uses named volumes to represent disk partitions. In a Novell file system, a volume may span multiple disks.

volume object   A leaf object that represents a volume on a NetWare file server. A volume object is automatically installed for all volumes created during the NetWare 4.11 installation.

volume block   A value that represents the minimum amount of data that NetWare will read/write from a volume.

volume segment   Space on a storage device that has been appropriated for a volume's use. Multiple volume segments can be defined for a NetWare partition.

Web Manager utility   A GUI-based utility used to configure the Novell Web Server. You must have TCP/IP on your client workstation to run the Web Manager utility.

Web server   Part of IntranetWare, the Web server provides the ability to publish HTML documents, images, sounds, movies, and other digital information to the Internet or an internal LAN.

wide area network (WAN)   A communication network that connects local area networks that are geographically separated.

World Wide Web   A service provided on the Internet that uses hypermedia information. Also known as "the Web." Access to the World Wide Web is provided by a Web browser.

X.25   An old packet-switching technology originally used to connect terminals to mainframes over WAN links. X.25 provides extensive error checking to ensure the reliable delivery of network packets.

index

A

A (ARCHIVE) file attribute   226
Access control file
   directives   905–906
   location   853
Access Control Lists (ACLs)
   and property rights   337
Access files, creating   904–907
Access protocols   946–947
Access restrictions
   FTP (File Transfer Protocol)   1019–1020
   Web
      access files, creating   904–907
      by group   911–913
      overview   901–903
      PWGEN.EXE file   904
      by system   913–916
      by user   908–911
      Web Manager   903, 908–909, 911–912, 914–915
      WEBMGR.EXE   903
   Web server   841–844
Access time   12–13
ACCESS.CFG file   856–858
AccessConfig directive   853
AccessFileName directive   855
ACCESS.LOG file   877–878
ACCESS_SERVER identifier variable   182
ACCESS.WWW program
   access restrictions
      by group   911–912
      by system   915–916
      by user   909–911
ACLs (Access Control Lists)
   and property rights   337
Add Self rights   336–337
AFP (AppleTalk Filing Protocol)   81
AFP server object   81
ALIAS command   724
Alias object   83

Aliases
   ALIAS command   724
   Alias object   83
   for commands   724
   for directories   82
   Directory Map object   82
   for image maps   854
   for leaf objects   83
   overview   139–140
AllowOverride directive   857
AM_PM identifier variable   179
Anonymous FTP, enabling   1017
Anonymous User Access, FTP parameter   1017
Anonymous User's Home Directory, FTP parameter   1017
APPEND, SSI command   961
AppleTalk   293–298
AppleTalk Filing Protocol (AFP)   81
AppleTalk Print Services (ATPS)   294
Application leaf objects   80
Applications
   associating objects with users   512–513
   creating application objects   509–512
   granting rights to users   514
   launching   514–517
   managing   80
ARCHIVE (A) file attribute   226
Assignments tab
   Print Queue Properties dialog box   254
   Print Server Properties dialog box   264–265
   Printer Properties dialog box   258–259
Asynchronous Transfer Mode (ATM)   782
ATM (Asynchronous Transfer Mode)   782
   WAN extensions   805–806
ATPS (AppleTalk Print Services)   294
ATPSCON.NLM program   294
ATPS.NLM program   294–298
ATTACH login script command   158
Attributes
   See directory attributes
   See file attributes

Attributes tab   196–197
ATXRP.NLM   296–298
Audible alerts   691
Auditing   80
Auditing leaf objects   80
Auditing Log tab   266–267
AuthGroupFile directive   905
AuthGroupMethod directive   857, 905
AuthName directive   857, 905
AuthType directive   858, 905
AuthUserFile directive   858, 905
AuthUserMethod directive   858, 905
AUTOEXEC.BAT, editing during installation   22–23
AUTOEXEC.NCF file
    common commands   638
    defined   637
    editing   638–639
    editing during installation   37, 66
    example   637
    time synchronization   430
    time synchronization parameters   430, 434–435

B

Backing up NDS databases   500–506
Banner option   289
Banner Type tab   262
Banners, specifying   262, 289
Base schema   314–315
BASIC scripts   815
Battery power   16
Beeps   691
Bindery
    backward compatibility   315–316
    container limitations   318
    NDS tree as   316–317
    NetWare 3.x architecture   309–311
    object collision   318
    object limitations   318
    SERVMAN.NLM utility   319–320
    setting up   319–320
    SYSCON.EXE *vs.* NetWare Administrator   318
    See also NDS (NetWare Directory Services)
Bindery object   83
Bindery queue object   83
Bindery services
    connecting to   158
    and replicas   406–407
Bindings, configuring   717–720
Block sizes, NWS (Novell Web Server)   824
Block suballocation   652–653

BLOCK.NDS file   313
<BODY> </BODY>, HTML tags   936–937
Booting from a floppy diskette   20
Bootstrap files   30
Bottlenecks   12–13
BREAK, SSI command   961
BROADCAST command   725
Browse rights   334
Bus mastering   10
Buttons, in CGI scripts   981

C

CA (Certificate Authorities)   889
Cache hit   704
Cache utilization   703–704
CALC, SSI command   961
CALLMGR utility   792–793
CAN'T COMPRESS (Cc) file attribute   226
CAPTURE.EXE utility
    Banner option   289
    Default Queue option   286
    End Capture option   289
    Form Feed option   289
    Keep option   289
    Notify option   290
    options, reference summary   286–288
    printing station software   292
    redirecting print data   239, 285–286
    Show option   290–291
Case sensitivity
    HTML tags   935
    URLs (Uniform Resource Locators)   935
Cc (CAN'T COMPRESS) file attribute   226
CDM (Custom Device Module)   640
CD-ROM
    incompatibility with IntranetWare   24
    installing IntranetWare from   23–24
    requirements for IntranetWare   15
Cell-switched services   781
Central processing unit (CPU)
    See CPU (central processing unit)
Certificate Authorities (CA)   889
CGI (Common Gateway Interface)
    buttons   981
    check boxes   983–984
    drop-down lists   985–987
    entry fields   981
    GET command   975–979
    getting data to   975–979

HTML tags and
    \<INPUT> 981
    \<ISINDEX> 975–979
    \<TEXTAREA> tag 988–989
Java Applet example 1007–1010
LCGI (Local Common Gateway Interface)
    defined 990
    and LoadableModule directive 993
multiple-selection lists 985–987
NAME element 980–981
NetBasic scripts
    defined 992
    example 999–1004
NLMs, loading 993
NWS (Novell Web Server) 816
overview 971–974
Perl 5 scripts
    defined 991
    example 995–999
POST method 979–980
QuickFinder search engine
    defined 992
    example 1004–1006
radio buttons 983–984
RCGI (Remote Common Gateway Interface)
    defined 991
    and RemoteScriptAlias directive 994
Reset button 989
scratch-pad space 988–989
scrolling lists 985–987
sending data from 979–980
single-line text fields 981–983
Submit button 989
URL length restriction 977
variable names 980–981
CGI interpreters, locating 855
Check boxes, in CGI scripts 983–984
Child objects 80
Child partitions 377–378
Ci (COPY INHIBIT) file attribute 227
Circuit switching 778, 781
Clickable image maps
    NWS (Novell Web Server) 814
    overview 953–959
Clickable images 950–953
Client workstations
    storing information about 80
Client workstations, DOS/Windows
    installation, preparing for 556–559
    NetWare Client32
        architecture 569–579

configuration file 575–579
    customizing 588–593
    file relationships 574–575
    hardware requirements 579–580
    installing 580–586
    NET.CFG file 575–579
    NetWare Login 587–588
    NetWare User Tools 586–587
    overview 568–569
    software requirements 579–580
    STARTNET.BAT file 570–574
    startup file 570–574
    TCP/IP 593–594
    utilities 586–593
    NetWare DOS Requestor
        connecting to NetWare 4.11 server 566–568
        hardware requirements 563–564
        installation 564–566
        LSL (Link Support Layer) 562
        MLID (Multiple Link Interface Driver) 562
        ODI (Open Datalink Interface) 560–561
        overview 559–560, 563
        protocol stacks 562–563
        software requirements 563–564
        VLM workstation client architecture
            560–561
    VLM client 555
Client workstations, Mac OS
    configuring 626–627
    hardware requirements 625–626
    installing 626–627
    logging in 627–629
    NetWare Directory Browser 631–632
    NetWare Print Chooser 631–632
    NetWare Volume Mounter 631–632
    overview 624–625
    servers, installing and configuring 629–630
    software requirements 625–626
    utilities 631–632
Client workstations, Windows 95
    See NetWare Client32, Windows 95
Client workstations, Windows NT
    See IntranetWare Client, Windows NT
CLIENT32.NLM module 600
Clock speed 6–7
CMSM.NLM module 599
CN identifier variable 179
CNE2000.LAN module 600
Co (COMPRESSION) file attribute 226
Code page 37
Command shortcuts 724
Commenting script code 174–175

Common Gateway Interface (CGI)
    See CGI (Common Gateway Interface)
Common names   88
Communications equipment, configuring   793
Compare rights   336
COMPRESSION (Co) file attribute   226
Conditional processing   161–165
CONFIG, SSI command   961
CONFIG.SYS, editing during installation   22–23
Configuration tab   259–260
Console commands, viewing   722–723
Container limitations   318
Container login script   145–146
Container objects
    as file system trustees   211–212
    overview   76–78, 320–325
Container operations with NDS Manager   371
Containers, default rights   347
Context
    current context   85
    defined   84
Copy files options   671–672
COPY INHIBIT (Ci) file attribute   227
COUNT, SSI command   961
Country codes   37, 1049–1052
Country objects   77, 321–322
CPECFG utility   793
CPU (central processing unit)
    clock speed   6–7
    data bus   6–7
    processor evolution   6
    processor types   6–7
    and server performance   5–8
Create Alias dialog box   139–140
Create Group dialog box   134–136
Create rights   334
Custom Device Module (CDM)   640
CX command   85–87

D

Data bus   6–7
Data redundancy   50–53
Database files, viewing   313
Databases
    backing up   500–506
    inconsistencies   473–474
    local, repairing   485
    loosely consistent   473
    network addresses, repairing   484–485
    partition continuity   479–482

remote server IDs, verifying   483–484
repairing   495–499
replica synchronization   475–479
    monitoring   489–495
replicas
    assigning new Master   485–486
    repairing   484
    servers, removing   487–488
    volume objects, repairing   486–487
Date identifier variable   178
DAY identifier variable   178
Daylight Saving Time Offset parameter   442
DAY_OF_WEEK identifier variable   178
Dc (DON'T COMPRESS) directory attribute   230
Dc (DON'T COMPRESS) file attribute   227
Dedicated lines   778
Default login script   150–152
Default Name Space, FTP parameter   1018
Default partitions   376
Default Queue option   286
Default Time Server Type parameter   441
Default User's Home Directory, FTP parameter   1017
DefaultType directive   854
DEL option   170
DELETE INHIBIT (Di)
    directory attribute   230
    file attribute   227
Delete rights   334
Desktops, standardizing   507
DET (Directory Entry Table)   651
Detection Reset Interval, FTP parameter   1018
DHCP (Dynamic Host Control Protocol)   743–745
Di (DELETE INHIBIT)
    directory attribute   230
    file attribute   227
Directories
    copying   223
    creating   223
    deleting   223
        inhibiting   230
    displaying information about   224–225
    hiding   230
    managing with Web Manager   839–841
    marking as operating system   230
    moving   223
    renaming   223
        inhibiting   230
    Web servers, adding/deleting   941–943
Directories tab   839–841
Directory access controls   856–857

Directory access rights
   See rights, directory access
Directory attributes   230
Directory caching, effects on server
   performance   685
Directory entry allocations, displaying
   number of   192
Directory Entry Table (DET)   651
Directory Map object   81
Directory options   672–676
Directory services
   backup & restore options   674–676
   effects on server performance   685–686
   expanding networks   328
   installing   672
   removing   672–673
   upgrading bindery information   673–674
   upgrading volumes   674
Directory structure, Web server   869–870
Directory tree
   See file system
<Directory>...</Directory> directive   856
DirectoryIndex directive   853
Disk drivers
   NLMs (NetWare Loadable Modules)   640–641
   selecting   39–40
   setting parameters for   41–42
Disk options   666–668
Disk read ahead   654
Disk space, displaying   191
Disk statistics   699
Disks, effects on server performance   686–687
DISPLAY login script command   159
DISPLAY SERVERS command   725
Displaying text to screen   159, 175–177
Distinguished naming   89
Dm (DON'T MIGRATE)
   directory attribute   230
   file attribute   227
DNS (Domain Name System)
   NWS (Novell Web Server)   830–832
   overview   739–741
   starting   757–760
<!DOCTYPE>, HTML tag   935
Document security status, displaying   888–889
DocumentRoot directive   853
Domain Name System (DNS)
   See DNS (Domain Name System)
Domain SAP/RIP Service (DSS)   741–743, 760–762
DON'T COMPRESS (Dc)
   directory attribute   230

file attribute   227
DON'T MIGRATE (Dm)
   directory attribute   230
   file attribute   227
DON'T SUBALLOCATE (Ds) file attribute   227
DOS environment
   NetWare/IP clients   766–770
   print service configuration   277–280
   printer station software   277–280
   printing   277–280
   releasing memory   729–730
DOS environment identifier variable   181
DOS partitions, creating   20–22
DOS startup files, editing   22–23
Dotted quad names   736
Drive not ready error   24
Driver options   665–666
Drop-down lists, in CGI scripts   985–987
Ds (DON'T SUBALLOCATE) file attribute   227
DSREPAIR utility
   Advanced Options menu   498–499
   DSREPAIR.LOG file, viewing   498
   overview   494–495
   replicas, synchronization status   497
   time synchronization   496–497
   unattended full repair   495
DSREPAIR.LOG file, viewing   455, 498
DSS (Domain SAP/RIP Service)   741–743, 760–762
DSS servers   742–743
DSTRACE command   725–726
DSTRACE utility
   messages   491–493
   NDS error codes   493
   options   490
   overview   491
   replica state codes   492
Duplexing   50–53
Dynamic Host Control Protocol (DHCP)   743–745

E

ECHO, SSI command   962
Effective rights
   calculating   354–355
   excessive   357–360
   overview   217–221, 352–353
   troubleshooting   357–360
   viewing   356–357
EIDE (Enhanced Integrated Drive Electronics)
   11–12
8086 processor   6

8088 processor 6
80386 processor 6
80486 processor 6
EISA (Extended Industry Standard
    Architecture) 10
Elevator seek algorithm 654–655
ELSE option login script command 163–164
E-mail services 81, 330
Encryption keys 891
End Capture option 289
End of Daylight Saving Time parameter 442
Enhanced Integrated Drive Electronics (EIDE)
    11–12
Enhanced Small Drive Interface (ESDI) 11
Enhancement NLMs 645
Entry fields, in CGI scripts 981
ENTRY.NDS file 313
Error handling, effects on server performance
    687–688
ERROR_LEVEL identifier variable 182
ErrorLog directive 852
ERROR.LOG file 880–881
ESDI (Enhanced Small Drive Interface) 11
ETHERTSM.NLM module 599
Everyone group
    See public trustee
EXE CGI, SSI command 962
Execute external (#) command 158
EXECUTE ONLY (X) file attribute 227
EXIT login script command 159–160
Explorer (Windows 95), replacing 515
Extended Industry Standard Architecture
    (EISA) 10
External programs, executing from scripts 158
External time sources 432

F

Failed login attempts, limiting 1018
FancyIndexing directive 854
FAT (File Allocation Table) 651
FDISPLAY login script command 159
File access rights
    See rights, file access
File Allocation Table (FAT) 651
File attributes
    ARCHIVE (A) 226
    CAN'T COMPRESS (Cc) 226
    COMPRESSION (Co) 226
    COPY INHIBIT (Ci) 227
    DELETE INHIBIT (Di) 227

DON'T COMPRESS (Dc) 227
DON'T MIGRATE (Dm) 227
DON'T SUBALLOCATE (Ds) 227
EXECUTE ONLY (X) 227
execute-only status 227
file compression
    immediate 227
    inhibiting 226–227
    marking completion 226
file copying, inhibiting (Macintosh) 227
file deletion
    inhibiting 227
    without recovery 228
file migration
    inhibiting 227
    marking as migrated 228
file renaming, inhibiting 228
HIDDEN (H) 227
hiding files 227
IMMEDIATE COMPRESS (Ic) 227
marking files as operating system 228
marking files for backup 226
MIGRATED (M) 228
NORMAL (N) 228
preventing partial updates 228
PURGE (P) 228
READ ONLY (Ro) 228
READ WRITE (Rw) 228
read-only status 228
read-write status 228
RENAME INHIBIT (Ri) 228
SHAREABLE (S) 228
sharing files on a network 228
suballocation, inhibiting 227
SYSTEM (Sy) 228
TRANSACTIONAL (T) 228
File compression
    FTP 1025–1026
    immediate 227, 230
    inhibiting 226–227, 230
    marking completion 226, 230
    overview 653–654
File extensions, list of 871
File locking 689
File management
    acceptable use policy 874
    file extensions 871
    naming conventions 871–872
    old or unused files 872–873
    organizing by directory 868–870
    restricting server space 872–873

reviewing HTML coding 866–868
File retrieval 654–655
File server console, locking 702
File services 327
File system
    block suballocation 652–653
    child directory, defined 198
    default directories 199–201
    DET (Directory Entry Table) 651
    disk read ahead 654
    effects on server performance 688–689
    elevator seek algorithm 654–655
    FAT (File Allocation Table) 651
    file compression 653–654
    file retrieval 654–655
    naming conventions 198
    parent directory, defined 198
    paths, defined 198–199
    root directory, defined 198
    subdirectories, defined 198
    SYS:DELETED.SAV directory 200
    SYS:DOC directory 200
    SYS:ETC directory 200
    SYS:LOGIN directory 200
    SYS:MAIL directory 200
    SYS:_NETWARE directory 201
    SYS:PUBLIC directory 200
    SYS:SYSTEM directory 200
    volume configuration 648–651
File system rights
    See rights, file system
File system security 111–112
File Transfer Protocol (FTP)
    See FTP (File Transfer Protocol)
File types, FTP 1025–1026
File-based authentication 857
Files
    attributes 225–229
    checking if in use 703
    compressed, displaying number of 192
    copying 223
    copying, inhibiting (Macintosh) 227
    creating 223
    date/time stamps 411
    deleted
        displaying number of 191
        storage directory 200
    deleting 223
        without recovery 228
    deletion, inhibiting 227
    displaying information about 224–225

execute-only status 227
hiding 227
marking as operating system 228
marking for backup 226
migrated, displaying number of 193
migration
    inhibiting 227
    marking as migrated 228
moving 223
preventing partial updates 228
purging 231–232
read-only status 228
read-write status 228
recovering deleted 231–232
renaming 223
    inhibiting 228
salvaging 231–232
sharing on a network 228
FILE_SERVER identifier variable 180
FILTCFG utility 790–791
Filters, configuring 790–791
FIRE PHASERS login script command 160
FLASTMOD, SSI command 962
Form feed at job end 289
Form Feed option 289
486DX-4/100 processor 7
Frame relay
    carrier service 781
    example 794–795
    overview 783
    WAN extensions 805–806
Frame types
    default 45
    and protocols 44–45
FSIZE, SSI command 962
FTAM file support
    See name space modules
FTAM.NAM file 642
FTP (File Transfer Protocol)
    access restriction 1019–1020
    anonymous access, enabling 1017
    client access 1020–1022
    configuring 1015–1016
    failed login attempts, setting 1018
    file compression 1025–1026
    file types 1025–1026
    home directories 1017
    idle time, setting 1017
    installing 1014–1015
    intruder detection, enabling 1018
    intruder detection interval 1018

intruder log, viewing   1023–1024
linking to other NetWare servers   1024–1025
logs
   clearing   1024
   detail level   1018
   viewing   1023
name space, selecting   1018
parameters   1017–1018
sessions
   length, setting   1017
   number of, setting   1017
   viewing   1022
FULL_NAME identifier variable   179

G

Garbage collection   647
GET command   975–979
GOTO, SSI command   962
GOTO login script command   160–161
Graphics formats, NWS (Novell Web Server)
   813–814
GREETING_TIME identifier variable   179
Group information   857
Group objects
   adding members   135
   creating   133–134
   detailing   134
   overview   82
   trustee assignments   136
   viewing members   134
Groups
   overview   82
   vs. organizational roles   138

H

H (HIDDEN)
   directory attribute   230
   file attribute   227
HAM (Host Adapter Module)   640
Hard disk controllers
   EIDE (Enhanced Integrated Drive
      Electronics)   11–12
   ESDI (Enhanced Small Drive Interface)   11
   IDE (Integrated Drive Electronics)   11
   MFM (Modified Frequency Modulation)   11
   SCSI (Small Computer System Interface)   11–12
   and server performance   11–12
Hard disks
   access time   12–13

configuring   47–53
data redundancy   50–53
duplexing   50–53
Hot Fix area   50
IntranetWare requirements   14–15
mirroring   50–53
read time   12–13
seek time   12–13
and server performance   12–13
Hardware bottlenecks   12–13
Hardware buses
   bus mastering   10
   EISA (Extended Industry Standard
      Architecture)   10
   ISA (Industry Standard Architecture)   9–10
   local bus technology   10–11
   MCA (Micro Channel Architecture)   10
   PCI (Peripheral Component Interface)   11
   and server performance   9–11
   VESA (Video Electronics Standards
      Association)   11
Hardware compatibility   19
<HEAD> </HEAD>, HTML tags   936
Help   1031–1033
HIDDEN (H)
   directory attribute   230
   file attribute   227
Host Adapter Module (HAM)   640
Host machine, defined   502
Hot Fix area   50, 668
HOUR identifier variable   179
HOUR24 identifier variable   179
HTML documents
   NWS (Novell Web Server)   813
   root directory for   853
   user directory for   854
HTML filenames, default   853
<HTML> </HTML>, HTML tags   935
HTML (Hyper Text Markup Language)
   blank lines, ignoring   937
   character entities   934
   defined   933
   reserved characters   934
   special characters   934
HTML tags
   <BODY> </BODY>   936–937
   case sensitivity   935
   and CGI scripts   975–979, 981, 988–989
   <!DOCTYPE>   935
   <HEAD> </HEAD>   936
   <HTML> </HTML>   935

<INPUT> 981
<ISINDEX> 975–979
stand-alone tags 935
tagged pairs 935
<TEXTAREA> tag 988–989
<TITLE> </TITLE> 936
HTTP status codes 879–880
HTTP versions 879–880
HTTPD.CFG file 851–853
HTTPS, in URLs 886
Hyper Text Markup Language (HTML)
  See HTML (Hyper Text Markup Language)
Hyperlinks
  absolute *vs.* relative paths 939–940
  image maps 953–959
  images 950–953
  text 937–939

I

Ic (IMMEDIATE COMPRESS)
  directory attribute 230
  file attribute 227
IDE (Integrated Drive Electronics) 11, 640
Identification tab
  Print Queue Properties dialog box 254
  Print Server Properties dialog box 263–264
  Printer Properties dialog box 257
  volume object property dialog box 190
Identifier variables
  ACCESS_SERVER 182
  AM_PM 179
  CN 179
  date 178
  DAY 178
  DAY_OF_WEEK 178
  DOS environment 181
  ERROR_LEVEL 182
  FILE_SERVER 180
  FULL_NAME 179
  GREETING_TIME 179
  HOUR 179
  HOUR24 179
  LAST_NAME 179
  LOGIN_ALIAS_CONTEXT 179
  LOGIN_CONTEXT 180
  LOGIN_NAME 180
  MACHINE 181
  MEMBER OF 180
  MINUTE 179
  MONTH 178
  MONTH_NAME 178
  NDAY_OF_WEEK 178
  NETWARE_REQUESTOR 181
  network 180
  NETWORK_ADDRESS 180
  NOT MEMBER OF 180
  object properties 182
  OS 181
  OS_VERSION 181
  overview 177–178
  PASSWORD_EXPIRES 180
  PLATFORM 181
  P_STATION 181
  REQUESTOR_CONTEXT 180
  SECOND 179
  SHELL_TYPE 181
  SHORT_YEAR 178
  SMACHINE 181
  STATION 181
  time 179
  user 179–180
  USER_ID 180
  workstation 181
  YEAR 178
Idle Time Before FTP Server Unloads, FTP
  parameter 1017
IF, SSI command 962
IF-THEN login script command 161–165
Image files, NWS (Novell Web Server) 813–814
Image maps
  aliases 854
  clickable
    NWS (Novell Web Server) 814
    overview 953–959
  hyperlinks 953–959
IMMEDIATE COMPRESS (Ic)
  directory attribute 230
  file attribute 227
INCLUDE, SSI command 963
Indexing, automatic 854
Industry Standard Architecture (ISA) 9–10
INETCFG.NLM utility
  bindings 717–720
  defined 644
  internetworking configuration 789–790
  network boards 710–711
  overview 709–710
  protocols, binding
    AppleTalk 719
    IPX 718
    TCP/IP 718

protocols, setting
    AppleTalk   716–717
    IPX   712–713
    TCP/IP   714–715
  remote access   721–722
  SNMP (Simple Network Management
    Protocol)   720–721
  viewing console commands   722–723
Informational leaf objects   80
Inherited Rights Filter (IRF)
  See IRF (Inherited Rights Filter)
Inline images   948–950
INS option   169–170
INSTALL.BAT file   30–38
Installing client workstations, Mac OS   626–627
Installing FTP   1014–1015
Installing IntranetWare
  from another server   24–26
  AUTOEXEC.BAT, editing   22–23
  battery power   16
  booting from a floppy diskette   20
  from a CD-ROM   23–24
  CD-ROM incompatibility   24
  CD-ROM requirements   15
  CONFIG.SYS file, editing   22–23
  DOS partitions, creating   20–22
  Drive not ready error   24
  editing DOS startup files   22–23
  gathering server information   17–19
  hard disk requirements   14–15
  hardware compatibility   19
  MLID (Multiple Link Interface Driver)   25
  NIC (network interface card)   17
  RAM requirements   14–15
  setting up the server   17
  software requirements   19–20
  STARTNET.BAT file   25
  surge protection   16
  technical manuals   19–20
  UPS (uninterrupted power source)   16
  from a Windows 95 partition   20
Installing IntranetWare Client, Windows NT
  611–614
Installing NDS (NetWare Directory Services)   62–65
Installing NetWare 4.11
  AUTOEXEC.NCF file   37, 66
  bootstrap files   30
  code page   37
  country code   37
  custom installation   34–35
  data redundancy   50–53

disk drivers
  selecting   39–40
  setting parameters for   41–42
duplexing   50–53
experienced user's guide   66–68
fault tolerance   50
frame types   44–45
hard disks
  configuring   47–53
  Hot Fix area   50
Hot Fix   50
installation file destination   36
INSTALL.BAT file   30–38
internal IPX numbers   34–35
IPX network number   45–47
IPX network numbers   35
keyboard mapping   37
LAN drivers
  re-entrant loading   45
  selecting   40–41
  setting parameters for   42–43
language, choosing   30
license   65
license agreement   31–32
locale information   36–37
mirroring   50–53
NDS (NetWare Directory Services)   62–65
NETWARE.NLM file   644
network drivers
  re-entrant loading   45
  selecting   40–41
  setting parameters for   42–43
partitions (NetWare), creating   47–50
product selection   32–33
readme files, displaying   33
serial number   65
server drivers
  activating   43–47
  loading   38–39
servers
  increasing capacity of   58–59
  naming conventions   34–35
  starting at DOS startup   38
  time   63–65
simple installation   34–35
startup files   66
STARTUP.NCF file   37, 66
time servers   63–65
time zones, configuring for   63–65
upgrades   34–35
users, setting number of   65

volumes
    block size   56–57
    block suballocation   58
    creating assignments   61–62
    data migration   58–59
    deleting assignments   61
    file compression   57
    maximum capacity   53
    names   56
    segment size   59–60
    spanning hard disks   54
    status   57
    SYS   54
    viewing parameters of   54–55
    See also INSTALL.NLM utility
Installing NetWare Client32, DOS/Windows   580–586
Installing NetWare Client32, Windows 95   602–603
Installing NetWare DOS Requestor   564–566
Installing NetWare/IP   755–757
Installing NWS (Novell Web Server)   822–826
Installing TCP/IP   753–755
INSTALL.NLM utility
    copy files options   671–672
    defined   644
    directory options   672–676
    directory services
        backup & restore options   674–676
        installing   672
        removing   672–673
        upgrading bindery information   673–674
        upgrading volumes   674
    disk options   666–668
    driver options   665–666
    Hot Fix area   668
    license options   670–671
    Multi CPU options   677–678
    NCF files options   676–677
    product options   679–680
    volume options   668–670
Integrated Drive Electronics (IDE)   11, 640
Intel processors   6
Interface tab   846–847
Internal IPX numbers   34–35
Internet Packet Exchange (IPX) protocol
    See IPX (Internet Packet Exchange) protocol
Internet time sources   432
IntranetWare Client, Windows NT
    configuring   614–616
    hardware requirements   610–611
    installing   611–614

IntranetWare Login   617
IntranetWare Send Message   617–619
NetWare Administrator for Windows NT   621
NetWare Application Launcher   621
Novell Workstation Manager   621–624
overview   609–610
software requirements   610–611
utilities   616–619
IntranetWare Client for Windows NT utility   616–619
IntranetWare Login utility   617
IntranetWare Send Message utility   617–619
Intruder detection, FTP   1018, 1023–1024
Intruder Detection, FTP parameter   1018
Intruder lockout   125–127
IP addresses
    defined   736
    Web server   851
IPAddress directive   851
IPX (Internet Packet Exchange) protocol
    overview   656–657
    using with TCP/IP
        See NetWare/IP
IPX network numbers   35, 45–47
IPX/IP Gateway
    client piece   799–805
    configuring   796–799
    defined   795–796
    server piece   796
    Windows 95 environment   801–805
IPX.NLM module   600
IRF (Inherited Rights Filter)
    modifying   350–351
    overview   349–350
    and Supervisor rights   351–352
ISA (Industry Standard Architecture)   9–10

J

Java applets
    example   1007–1010
    NWS (Novell Web Server)   819
Job List tab   255–257

K

Keep option   289
Key database file, creating   893
Key icon on Web pages   886
Keyboard mapping   37
KEYMGR.NLM program   893

L

LABEL, SSI command   963
LAN drivers
   NLMs (NetWare Loadable Modules)   642–643
   re-entrant loading   45
   selecting   40–41
   setting parameters for   42–43
LAN statistics   700–701
Language, choosing   30
LAST_NAME identifier variable   179
LCGI (Local Common Gateway Interface)
   defined   990
   and LoadableModule directive   993
Leaf objects   78–83, 326
License Service Provider (LSP) object   81
Licenses
   agreement   31–32
   deleting   670
   installing   65, 670–671
   License Product object   325
   managing   81
   options   670–671
   required for MPR installation   787
<Limit GET>...<Limit> directive   906
<Limit>...</Limit> directive   858
Link Support Layer (LSL)   562
LoadableModule directive   855
   and LCGI (Local Common Gateway
      Interface)   993
Local bus technology   10–11
Local Common Gateway Interface (LCGI)
   See LCGI (Local Common Gateway Interface)
Locale information   36–37
Locality object   325
Locks, effects on server performance   689–690
Log files
   clearing   881
   location   875–877
   printing   881
   saving   881
   settings   875–877
Log level, FTP parameter   1018
Logging
   errors   852
   transferred files   852
   Web server
      ACCESS.LOG file   877–878
      ERROR.LOG file   880–881
      HTTP status codes   879–880
      HTTP versions   879–880

log files, clearing   881
log files, location   875–877
log files, printing   881
log files, saving   881
log files, settings   875–877
overview   874–875
Login files, directory for   200
Login restrictions   120–121
Login script commands
   # (execute external)   158
   associating user objects with login scripts   174
   ATTACH   158
   bindery services, connecting to   158
   comments   174–175
   conditional processing   161–165
   DISPLAY   159
   displaying text to screen   159, 175–177
   ELSE option   163–164
   executing external programs   158
   executing multiple scripts   165–166
   EXIT   159–160
   FDISPLAY   159
   FIRE PHASERS   160
   GOTO   160–161
   IF-THEN   161–165
   looping   160–161
   MAP
      DEL option   170
      display options   167
      drive mappings   167–169
      error options   167
      INS option   169–170
      overview   166–167
      ROOT option   170–171
   mapping drives
      deleting a mapping   170
      displaying error messages   167
      displaying maps   167
      explicit assignments, disadvantages of   171
      hiding upper tree levels   170–171
      local device conflicts   172
      mapping workstations to volumes   168
      modifying the search path   168–170
      to NDS Directory Map objects   172–173
      network drive mapping   168
      search drive mapping   168
      substitute for the [Root] object   170–171
   NO_DEFAULT   174
   overview   152–155
   phaser sound effect   160
   prevent script execution   174

PROFILE   174
quick reference table   155–158
REMARK   174–175
terminating a login script   159–160
WRITE   175–177
Login scripts
container type   145–146
creating   124–125
default type   150–152
generalizing
   See identifier variables
location of   83
for multiple users   173
order of execution   144, 151
overview   144–145
profile type   146–149
user type   149–150
Login security   108–109
Login time restrictions   122–123
LOGIN_ALIAS_CONTEXT identifier variable   179
LOGIN_CONTEXT identifier variable   180
LOGIN_NAME identifier variable   180
Logs, FTP
clearing   1024
detail level   1018
viewing   1023
Long filenames, NWS (Novell Web Server)   819,
829–830
LONG.NAM file   642
Looping in scripts   160–161
Loosely consistent database   473
LSL (Link Support Layer)   562
LSLC32.NLM module   599
LSP (License Service Provider) object   81

M

M (MIGRATED) file attribute   228
Mac OS
file support
   See name space modules
printing
   AppleTalk   293–298
   ATPS (AppleTalk Print Services)   294
   ATPSCON.NLM program   294
   ATPS.NLM program   294–298
   ATXRP.NLM   296–298
   PSERVER.NLM program   294–298
utility   631–632
MACHINE identifier variable   181
Mail files, directory for   200

Management NLMs   644
MAP command   201–203
MAP login script command
DEL option   170
display options   167
drive mappings   167–169
error options   167
INS option   169–170
overview   166–167
ROOT option   170–171
MapAlias directive   854
Mapping drives
deleting a mapping   170
displaying error messages   167
displaying maps   167
explicit assignments, disadvantages of   171
hiding upper tree levels   170–171
local device conflicts   172
mapping workstations to volumes   168
modifying the search path   168–170
to NDS Directory Map objects   172–173
network drive mapping   168
overview   201–203
search drive mapping   168
substitute for the [Root] object   170–171
Master replicas   390
Maximum Number of Sessions, FTP
parameter   1017
Maximum Session Length, FTP parameter   1017
MCA (Micro Channel Architecture)   10
Media types
ATM (Asynchronous Transfer Mode)   782
frame relay   783
frame relay, example   794–795
X.25 protocol   782
MEMBER OF identifier variable   180
Memory
   See RAM (random access memory)
MEMORY command   726
Memory utilization   706–707
Merging partitions   383–384
Message-Related leaf objects   81
Messages, broadcasting   725
Messaging services   330
MFM (Modified Frequency Modulation)   11
Micro Channel Architecture (MCA)   10
MIGRATED (M) file attribute   228
MIME (Multipurpose Internet Mail Enhancement)
browser configuration   861–863
configuration file   863–864

MIME types
   changing   865
   default   854
   list of   864
   overview   860–861
MIME.TYP file   863–864
MIME type, default   854
MIME types
   changing   865
   default   854
   list of   864
   overview   860–861
MIME-type file map location   853
MINUTE identifier variable   179
Mirroring   50–53
MLID (Multiple Link Interface Driver)   25, 562
Modified Frequency Modulation (MFM)   11
Monitoring the network, NLMs for   644
MONITOR.NLM utility
   cache utilization   703–704
   checking if a file is in use   703
   defined   644
   disk statistics   699
   displaying server connections   698–699
   LAN statistics   700–701
   locking the file server console   702
   memory utilization   706–707
   multiprocessor information   708
   overview   694–697
   processor utilization   704–705
   resource utilization   705–706
   scheduling information   707–708
   server parameters   708
   system module statistics   702
   WAN statistics   700–701
MONTH identifier variable   178
MONTH_NAME identifier variable   178
MPR (MultiProtocol Router)
   CALLMGR utility   792–793
   configuring   788–794
   CPECFG utility   793
   FILTCFG utility   790–791
   INETCFG utility   789–790
   installing   785–788
   license requirements   787
   STATICON utility   791–792
Multi CPU options   677–678
Multihoming   818
Multimedia files, NWS (Novell Web Server)
   813–814
Multiple Link Interface Driver (MLID)   25, 562

Multiple-selection lists   985–987
Multiprocessor information   708
MultiProtocol Router (MPR)
   See MPR (MultiProtocol Router)
Multipurpose Internet Mail Enhancement (MIME)
   See MIME (Multipurpose Internet Mail
      Enhancement)

N

N (NORMAL) file attribute   228
NAL (NetWare Application Launcher)
   launching applications   514–517
   standardizing desktops   507
   as Windows shell   515
NAM (NetWare Application Manager)
   defining network applications
      associating objects with users   512–513
      creating application objects   509–512
      granting rights to users   514
      overview   507–508
NAME element   980–981
Name space modules   642
Name spaces
   displaying   192
   selecting in FTP   1018
Naming conventions, files   871–872
Navigating the NDS tree
   NDS (NetWare Directory Services)   85–87
   NetWare Administrator   95–97
NCF files options   676–677
NCP (NetWare Core Protocol)
   effects on server performance   692
   overview   657–658
NDAY_OF_WEEK identifier variable   178
NDS database transactions   412–413
NDS error codes   493, 1045–1048
NDS level security
   effects on file system security   188
   overview   109–110
NDS Manager
   container operations   371
   navigating   366–370
   NDS tree, viewing   366–368
   with NetWare Administrator   365
   overview   364–365
   partitioning operations   374
   Partitions & Servers view   368–370
   partitions, viewing   368–370
   replication operations   374
   server operations   371–374

servers, viewing   368–370
Tree view   366–368
NDS (NetWare Directory Services)
AFP (AppleTalk Filing Protocol)   81
aliases   82
applications, managing   80
auditing   80
context   84–85
current context   85
CX command   85–87
e-mail services   81
groups   82
installing   62–65
international divisions
See country objects
licenses, managing   81
login scripts   83
navigating the NDS tree   85–87
object classes
AFP server object   81
Alias object   83
Application leaf objects   80
Auditing leaf objects   80
bindery object   83
bindery queue object   83
child objects   80
container objects   76–78
country objects   77
Directory Map object   81
group object   82
Informational leaf objects   80
leaf objects   78–83
LSP (License Service Provider) object   81
Message-Related leaf objects   81
NCP (NetWare Core Protocol)   82
NetWare Licensing Services leaf objects   81
NetWare Server object   82
organization objects   77
organization unit objects   78
organizational role object   82
parent objects   80
Printer-Related leaf objects   81
profile object   83
[Root] object   76
Server-Related leaf objects   81–82
unknown object   83
user object   83
User-Related leaf objects   82–83
volume objects   82
object naming conventions
common names   88
distinguished naming   89

examples   90
relative distinguished naming   89
typeful naming   90
typeless naming   90
uniqueness   88
organizational rules   82
overview   72–74
paths
See context
printing environment   81
replica synchronization
overview   399–401
partition continuity   404–405
performance   401–403
viewing information about   403–404
replicas
adding to servers   393–394
and Bindery Services   406–407
changing types   396
Master   390
overview   387–389
Read-Only   391
Read/Write   390
removing from servers   395
replica rings   392–393
Subordinate Reference   391–392
updating   397–399
viewing information about   406
servers, storing information about   81–82
structure   74–75
tracing   725–726
user profiles   83
volumes, pointers to   82
workstations, storing information about   80
See also bindery
NDS partitions
See partitions, NDS
NDS replicas
See replicas, NDS
NDS security   109–110
NDS special trustees
See special trustees
NDS trees
administration models
centralized administration   524
distributed administration   524–525
exclusive distributed administration   525–527
as bindery   316–317
browsing from the Web   963–970
default rights   346

finding resources in 378–379
hiding the upper levels 171
merging
  checking server status 457–458
  checking time synchronization 459–461
  container placement 467
  disabling logins during 453
  DSMERGE.NLM utility 456–457
  DSREPAIR.LOG file, viewing 455
  local source trees 451
  local trees 451
  merging two trees 461–463
  modification log 455
  multiple Admin accounts from 468
  NDS version compatibility 454
  overview 450–452
  partitioning 464–467
  prerequisites 452–456
  replica status 454
  replication 464–467
  [Root] subordinates 453
  schema compatibility 454–455
  security 466, 468
  source trees 451
  target trees 451
  tree name, default 466
  tree name, renaming 463–464
  unique object identification 453
  user connections 453
  workstation connectivity 468–469
navigating
  with NDS (NetWare Directory Services)
    85–87
  with NetWare Administrator 95–97
planning structure of 518–520
structure of
  Bindery Services 527–528
  combinational structure 523
  example 545–546
  geographic structure 522
  naming conventions 528–529
  network topology 527
  organizational chart structure 520–521
  planning 518–520, 543–544
  workflow structure 521–522
tree walking 378–379
viewing with NDS manager 366–368
NDS utilities
  See utilities
NDSMGR16.EXE program 364
NDSMGR32.EXE program 364

NDSMGRNT.EXE program 364
NDSOBJ.NLM file 963
NETADMIN utility 113
NetBasic for Internet scripts 815
NetBasic scripts
  defined 992
  example 999–1004
NET.CFG file 575–579
Netscape Navigator
  configuration options 917–920
  passwords 921
  personal certificates 921–924
  site certificates 924–926
NetWare 3.x
  bindery architecture 309–311
  limitations of 311
  scalability 311
  security 311
NetWare 4.11 servers
  See servers, NetWare 4.11
NetWare 4.x architecture 313–314
NetWare Administrator
  creating an icon for 92
  file system management 222–232
  navigating the NDS tree 95–97
  NWADMN3X.EXE vs. NWADMIN.EXE 93
  objects
    creating 98–99
    deleting 102–103
    detailing 100–102
    filtering display of 103–105
    moving 99
    renaming 99
    searching for 105–106
  starting 94
  view filtering 103–105
  vs. SYSCON.EXE 318
  for Windows 95 608–609
  for Windows NT 621
NetWare Application Launcher (NAL)
  See NAL (NetWare Application Launcher)
NetWare Application Manager (NAM)
  See NAM (NetWare Application Manager)
NetWare Client32, DOS/Windows
  architecture 569–579
  configuration file 575–579
  customizing 588–593
  file relationships 574–575
  hardware requirements 579–580
  installing 580–586
  NET.CFG file 575–579

NetWare Login   587–588
NetWare User Tools   586–587
overview   568–569
software requirements   579–580
STARTNET.BAT file   570–574
startup file   570–574
TCP/IP   593–594
utilities   586–593
NetWare Client32, Windows 95
architecture   599–600
CLIENT32.NLM module   600
CMSM.NLM module   599
CNE2000.LAN module   600
configuring   603–604
ETHERTSM.NLM module   599
hardware requirements   601
installing   602–603
IPX.NLM module   600
LSLC32.NLM module   599
NetWare Administrator for Windows 95
   608–609
NetWare Application Launcher   609
NetWare Login   606–608
NIOS.VXD module   599
overview   598–599
software requirements   601
utilities   605–609
NetWare Core Protocol (NCP)
   See NCP (NetWare Core Protocol)
NetWare Directory Browser   631–632
NetWare Directory Services (NDS)
   See NDS (NetWare Directory Services)
NetWare DOS Requestor
connecting to NetWare 4.11 server   566–568
hardware requirements   563–564
installation   564–566
LSL (Link Support Layer)   562
MLID (Multiple Link Interface Driver)   562
ODI (Open Datalink Interface)   560–561
overview   559–560, 563
protocol stacks   562–563
software requirements   563–564
VLM workstation client architecture   560–561
NetWare Licensing Services leaf objects   81
NetWare Link Services Protocol (NLSP)   806–807
NetWare Loadable Modules (NLMs)
   See NLMs (NetWare Loadable Modules)
NetWare Login   587–588, 606–608
NetWare Peripheral Architecture (NWPA)   640
NetWare Print Chooser   631–632

NetWare Server object
defined   82
file system security   187–188
NetWare User Tools   586–587
NetWare Volume Mounter   631–632
NetWare/IP
clients
   DOS   766–770
   overview   734–735
   Windows 3.x   766–770
   Windows 95   770–774
DHCP (Dynamic Host Control Protocol)
   743–745
DNS (Domain Name System)   739–741
dotted quad names   736
DSS (Domain SAP/RIP Service)   741–743
IP addresses   736
octets   736
overview   731–734
packet forwarding configuration   747
servers
   configuring   763–765
   DNS (Domain Name System), starting
      757–760
   DSS (Domain SAP/RIP Service)   760–762
   NetWare/IP installation   755–757
   overview   734, 749–751
   system requirements   751–752
   TCP/IP installation   753–755
single protocol configuration   746
subnet masks   736
TCP/IP (Transmission Control Protocol/Internet
   Protocol)   736–738
WAN connector configuration   748–749
NETWARE_REQUESTOR identifier variable   181
Network Address Restriction tab   262
Network address restrictions   123–124
Network addresses, repairing   484–485
Network boards, configuring   710–711
Network configuration
   See INETCFG.NLM utility
Network drivers
re-entrant loading   45
selecting   40–41
setting parameters for   42–43
Network identifier variable   180
Network interface card (NIC)
installing   17
and server performance   12–13
NETWORK_ADDRESS identifier variable   180
New feature summary

1086 Novell IntranetWare: The Comprehensive Guide

IntranetWare
  backup services 1043
  file services 1042
  NAM (NetWare Application Manager) 1043
  networking 1041–1042
  NLS (NetWare Licensing Services) 1044
  Novel Workstation Manager 1044
  operating system features 1040
  operating system installation 1040
  print services 1042
  security 1043
NetWare 4.11
  backup services 1039
  file services 1038
  networking features 1037
  operating system features 1036–1037
  operating system installation 1036
  print services 1038
  security 1038
New Time With Daylight Saving Time Status
  parameter 442
NFS.NAM file 642
NIC (network interface card)
  installing 17
  and server performance 12–13
NIOS.VXD module 599
NLMs (NetWare Loadable Modules)
  CDM (Custom Device Module) 640
  defined 639
  disk drivers 640–641
  enhancement 645
  GUI parameter interface 644
  HAM (Host Adapter Module) 640
  IDE (Integrated Drive Electronics) 640
  INETCFG.NLM 644
  installing NetWare 4.11 644
  INSTALL.NLM 644
  LAN drivers 642–643
  loading 993
  locating 855
  management 644
  monitoring the network 644
  MONITOR.NLM 644
  name space modules 642
  non-DOS file support 642
  NWPA (NetWare Peripheral Architecture) 640
  print services 644
  PSERVER.NLM 644
  repairing corrupted volumes 644
  SERVMAN.NLM 644
  VREPAIR.NLM 644

NLSP (NetWare Link Services Protocol) 806–807
NO_DEFAULT login script command 174
Non-DOS file support 642
Non-parity RAM 8–9
NORMAL (N) file attribute 228
NOT MEMBER OF identifier variable 180
Notification tab 262
Notify option 290
Novell Web Server (installing NWS) 822–826
Novell Web Server (NWS)
  See NWS (Novell Web Server)
Novell Workstation Manager 621–624
NPRINTER.EXE program 246
NPRINTER.NLM 244
NPRINT.EXE utility 239
NTPWIN95.EXE program 281–284
Number of Unsuccessful Attempts, FTP
  parameter 1018
NWADMN3X.EXE vs. NWADMIN.EXE 93
NWPA (NetWare Peripheral Architecture) 640
NWS (Novell Web Server)
  BASIC scripts 815
  block sizes 824
  CGI (Common Gateway Interface) 816
  clickable image maps 814
  DNS (domain name service) 830–832
  graphics formats 813–814
  HTML documents 813
  image files 813–814
  installing 822–826
  Java applets 819
  long filenames 819, 829–830
  multihoming 818
  multimedia files 813–814
  NetBasic for Internet scripts 815
  online document 819–821
  Oracle database connectivity 817
  Perl 5 scripts 815
  QuickFinder search engine 817
  RAM requirements 823–824
  reconfiguring 826–827
  removing 826–827
  scripting languages 814–815
  server configuration
    See Web Manager
  server requirements 822–823
  server-side includes 818
  SSL (Secure Sockets Layer) 817
  upgrading 827–829
  virtual directories 818

O

Object classes
   AFP server object   81
   Alias object   83
   Application leaf objects   80
   Auditing leaf objects   80
   bindery object   83
   bindery queue object   83
   child objects   80
   container objects   76–78
   country objects   77
   Directory Map object   81
   group object   82
   Informational leaf objects   80
   leaf objects   78–83
   LSP (License Service Provider) object   81
   Message-Related leaf objects   81
   NCP (NetWare Core Protocol)   82
   NetWare Licensing Services leaf objects   81
   NetWare Server object   82
   organization objects   77
   organization unit objects   78
   organizational role object   82
   parent objects   80
   Printer-Related leaf objects   81
   profile object   83
   [Root] object   76
   Server-Related leaf objects   81–82
   unknown object   83
   user object   83
   User-Related leaf objects   82–83
   volume objects   82
Object collision   318
Object limitations   318
Object naming conventions
   common names   88
   distinguished naming   89
   examples   90
   relative distinguished naming   89
   typeful naming   90
   typeless naming   90
   uniqueness   88
Object properties identifier variable   182
Object rights
   Browse   334
   Create   334
   defined   109–110
   Delete   334
   Rename   335
   Supervisor   334

Objects
   aliases   139–140
   creating   98–99
   defined   74
   deleting   102–103
   detailing   100–102
   filtering display of   103–105
   moving   99
   renaming   99
   searching for   105–106
   See also user objects
Octets   736
ODI (Open Datalink Interface)   560–561
Online documentation
   directory for   200
   NWS (Novell Web Server)   819–821
Open Datalink Interface (ODI)   560–561
Operating system files, directory for   200
Operator tab
   Print Queue Properties dialog box   254
   Print Server Properties dialog box   266
Options directive   857
Oracle database connectivity   817
Organization objects   77, 322–324
Organization unit objects   78
Organizational role object   82
Organizational roles
   creating   137–138
   security   137
   vs. groups   138
Organizational rules   82
Organizational units   324–325
OS identifier variable   181
OS/2 environment
   directory for login files   200
   file support
      See name space modules
   print service configuration   277–280
   printer station software   277–280
   printing   277–280
OS_VERSION identifier variable   181
Overview   971–974

P

P (PURGE) file attribute   228
Packet forwarding configuration   747
Packet switching   778–779, 781
Pages   645
Parallel port status, displaying   290–291
Parent objects   80

Parent partitions 377–378
Parity RAM 8–9
Partition continuity 404–405, 479–482
Partition root 376
PARTITIO.NDS file 313
Partitions
    DOS 20–22
    NDS
        child 377–378
        creating 381–383
        default 376
        example 547–548
        merging 383–384
        moving 385–386
        network topology 530–531
        number of 532–533
        overview 374–376
        parent 377–378
        partition root 376
        and physical network layout 381
        placing boundaries 530
        [Root] 376
        rules for 379–380
        size 381, 531–532
        viewing 368–370
        viewing information about 386–387
    NetWare 47–50
Partitions & Servers view, NDS Manager 368–370
Password restrictions 121–122
PASSWORD_EXPIRES identifier variable 180
Passwords
    allowing unencrypted 691
    encrypting 729, 904, 906–907
    list of 858
    login 109
    in login scripts 158
    Netscape Navigator 921
PCI (Peripheral Component Interface) 11
PCONSOLE.EXE utility 271–272
Pentium processors 6
Peripheral Component Interface (PCI) 11
Perl 5 scripts
    defined 991
    example 995–999
    NWS (Novell Web Server) 815
Personal certificates 921–924
Phaser sound effect 160
PLATFORM identifier variable 181
Port assignment 851
Port directive 851
POST method 979–980

Preconditions have been met message 382
Primary time server 417
Print queue object
    creating 251–253
    current jobs, displaying 255–257
    detailing 253–257
    general information, displaying 254
    print servers, displaying 254
    printers, displaying 254
    queue operators, displaying 254
    queue users, displaying 254–255
Print Queue Properties dialog box
    Assignments tab 254
    Identification tab 254
    Job List tab 255–257
    Operator tab 254
    Users tab 254–255
Print queues
    adding to printer objects 258–259
    current jobs, displaying 255–257
    defined 239
    listing 276
    operators, displaying 254
    print servers, displaying 254
    printers, displaying 254
    queue operators, displaying 254
    service interval, setting 262
    users, displaying 254–255
Print request handling
    CAPTURE.EXE utility 239
    flow diagram 237
    issuing the request 238
    NPRINT.EXE utility 239
    print server services the queue 240
    print station prints the job 240–241
    redirecting requests to print queue 238–240
Print server
    displaying information about 273–274
    loading 273–274
    print jobs, aborting 275
    printer status, displaying 274–275
    printers, pausing 275
    printers, starting/stopping 275
    queues, listing 276
    unloading 274
Print server object
    creating 263
    detailing 263–269
    general information 263–264
    logging audit information 266–267
    operators, listing 266

print layout 268–269
printers, assigning 264–265
users, listing 265
Print Server Properties dialog box
    Assignments tab 264–265
    Auditing Log tab 266–267
    Identification tab 263–264
    Operator tab 266
    Users tab 264–265
Print service configuration
    network-ready printers
        external print server mode 248–249
        remote printer mode 249–250
    NPRINTER.EXE program 246
    NPRINTER.NLM 244
    printers connected to NetWare 4.11 servers
        243–245
    printers connected to workstations 245–247
    PSERVER.NLM program 244
Print service configuration, back end
    DOS environment 277–280
    NTPWIN95.EXE program 281–284
    OS/2 environment 277–280
    print server
        displaying information about 273–274
        loading 273–274
        print jobs, aborting 275
        printer status, displaying 274–275
        printers, pausing 275
        printers, starting/stopping 275
        queues, listing 276
        unloading 274
    printing station software
        NPRINTER.EXE program 277–280
        NPRINTER.NLM program 276–277
    Windows 95 environment 281–284
Print service configuration, client workstations
    banner, specifying 289
    CAPTURE.EXE program 285–286
        Banner option 289
        Default Queue option 286
        End Capture option 289
        Form Feed option 289
        Keep option 289
        Notify option 290
        options, reference summary 286–288
        printing station software 292
        Show option 290–291
    ending data capture 289
    form feed at job end 289
    keeping data until job end 289

notify on job completion 290
parallel port status, displaying 290–291
printing station software 292
printing to multiple network printers 291–292
redirecting data to parallel ports 285–291
Print service configuration, front end
    PCONSOLE.EXE utility 271–272
    physical location independence 269
    print queue object
        creating 251–253
        current jobs, displaying 255–257
        detailing 253–257
        general information, displaying 254
        print servers, displaying 254
        printers, displaying 254
        queue operators, displaying 254
        queue users, displaying 254–255
    Print Queue Properties dialog box
        Assignments tab 254
        Identification tab 254
        Job List tab 255–257
        Operator tab 254
        Users tab 254–255
    print server object
        creating 263
        detailing 263–269
        general information 263–264
        logging audit information 266–267
        operators, listing 266
        print layout 268–269
        printers, assigning 264–265
        users, listing 265
    Print Server Properties dialog box
        Assignments tab 264–265
        Auditing Log tab 266–267
        Identification tab 263–264
        Operator tab 266
        Users tab 264–265
    printer object
        banner type, specifying 262
        creating 257
        detailing 257–262
        general information 257
        network address restrictions 262
        notice of job completion 262
        print queues, adding 258–259
        printer type, specifying 260–261
        printers, associating with 258
        printers, configuring 259–260
        priority, setting 259
        queue service interval, setting 262

Printer Properties dialog box
    Assignments tab   258–259
    Banner Type tab   262
    Configuration tab   259–260
    Identification tab   257
    Network Address Restriction tab   262
    Notification tab   262
    Printer Type tab   260–261
    Priority tab   259
    Service Interval tab   262
Print services
    LANs (local area networks)   327
    NLMs (NetWare Loadable Modules)   644
Printer object
    banner type, specifying   262
    creating   257
    detailing   257–262
    general information   257
    network address restrictions   262
    notice of job completion   262
    print queues, adding   258–259
    printer type, specifying   260–261
    printers, associating with   258
    printers, configuring   259–260
    priority, setting   259
    queue service interval, setting   262
Printer Properties dialog box
    Assignments tab   258–259
    Banner Type tab   262
    Configuration tab   259–260
    Identification tab   257
    Network Address Restriction tab   262
    Notification tab   262
    Printer Type tab   260–261
    Priority tab   259
    Service Interval tab   262
Printer Type tab   260–261
Printer-Related leaf objects   81
Printers
    adding print queues   258–259
    assigning to print server objects   264–265
    associating with printer objects   258
    configuring   259–260
    connected to NetWare 4.11 servers   243–245
    connected to workstations   245–247
    displaying   254
    network address restrictions   262
    network-ready
        external print server mode   248–249
        remote printer mode   249–250
    notice of job completion   262

    parallel, polled mode *vs.* interrupt mode   261
    pausing   275
    printer type, specifying   260–261
    setting priorities   259
    starting/stopping   275
    status, displaying   274–275
Printing
    DOS environment   277–280
    Macintosh environment
        AppleTalk   293–298
        ATPS (AppleTalk Print Services)   294
        ATPSCON.NLM program   294
        ATPS.NLM program   294–298
        ATXRP.NLM   296–298
        PSERVER.NLM program   294–298
    to multiple network printers   291–292
    notice of job completion   262
    OS/2 environment   277–280
    UNIX environment   298–299
        printing NetWare to UNIX   299–300
        printing UNIX to NetWare   300–301
Printing environment
    hardware requirements   242
    printer-related leaf objects   81
    quick setup option   270–271
Printing station software
    CAPTURE.EXE program   292
    NPRINTER.EXE program   277–280
    NPRINTER.NLM program   276–277
Priority tab   259
Private keys   891
Processor evolution   6
Processor types   6–7
Processor utilization   704–705
Product options, INSTALL.NLM utility   679–680
Product selection   32–33
Profile login script   146–149
PROFILE login script command   174
Profile object   83
Program Manager (Windows), replacing   515
Properties
    defined   74
    mandatory   75
    multivalued   75
Property rights
    and ACLs (Access Control Lists)   337
    Add Self   336–337
    Compare   336
    defined   110
    overview   335
    Read   336

Supervisor   336
Write   336–337
Protocol stacks   562–563
Protocols
    binding
        AppleTalk   719
        IPX   718
        TCP/IP   718
    defined   44
    and frame types   44–45
    IPX (Internet Packet Exchange)   656–657
    NCP (NetWare Core Protocol)   657–658
    RIP (Routing Information Protocol)   658–660
    SAP (Service Advertising Protocol)   658–660
    setting
        AppleTalk   716–717
        IPX   712–713
        TCP/IP   714–715
    SPX (Sequenced Packet Exchange)   656–657
PSERVER.NLM program   244, 294–298, 644
P_STATION identifier variable   181
[Public] as a file system trustee   212
Public keys   891
[Public] rights   345
Public trustee   212
PURGE (P) file attribute   228
PWGEN.EXE file   904

Q

QuickFinder search engine
    defined   992
    example   1004–1006
    NWS (Novell Web Server)   817

R

Radio buttons   983–984
RAM (random access memory)
    allocation   646–647
    configuration   645–646
    defragmenting   647
    displaying   726
    DOS, releasing   729–730
    effects on server performance   691
    garbage collection   647
    IntranetWare requirements   14–15
    non-parity   8–9
    parity   8–9
    requirements for NetWare 4.11   646
    and server performance   8–9

Random access memory (RAM)
    See RAM (random access memory)
RCGI (Remote Common Gateway Interface)
    defined   991
    and RemoteScriptAlias directive   994
RCONSOLE command   727
RCONSOLE.EXE utility   313
READ ONLY (Ro) file attribute   228
Read rights   336
Read time   12–13
READ WRITE (Rw) file attribute   228
Readme files, displaying   33
Read-Only replicas   391
Read/Write replicas   390
Record locking   689
Reference time server   417
Relative distinguished naming   89
REMARK login script command   174–175
Remote access, configuring   721–722
Remote Common Gateway Interface (RCGI)
    defined   991
    and RemoteScriptAlias directive   994
REMOTE ENCRYPT command   729
Remote server IDs, verifying   483–484
RemoteScriptAlias directive
    overview   855
    and RCGI (Remote Common Gateway
        Interface)   994
REMOVE DOS command   729–730
RENAME INHIBIT (Ri)
    directory attribute   230
    file attribute   228
Rename rights   335
Replica rings
    administering   537
    number of replicas in   535–536
    number of replicas on a single server   536
    overview   392–393
    types of replicas in   536
Replica synchronization
    monitoring   489–495
    overview   399–401, 475–479
    partition continuity   404–405
    performance   401–403
    viewing information about   403–404
Replicas, NDS
    adding to servers   393–394
    assigning new Master   485–486
    and Bindery Services   406–407
    changing types   396
    defined   313

example 547–548
managing 374
Master 390
and merging NDS trees 464–467
network topology 534–535
overview 387–389
Read-Only 391
Read/Write 390
removing from servers 395
repairing 484
replica rings
administering 537
number of replicas in 535–536
number of replicas on a single server 536
overview 392–393
types of replicas in 536
state codes 492
Subordinate Reference 391–392
synchronization status 497
updating 397–399
viewing information about 406
REQUESTOR_CONTEXT identifier variable 180
Reset button, in CGI scripts 989
Resource utilization 705–706
ResourceConfig directive 852
Restoring NDS databases 505–506
Ri (RENAME INHIBIT)
directory attribute 230
file attribute 228
Rights
default for
containers 347
new NDS trees 346
servers 346
user objects 346–347
determining for an object 217–221
directory access
creating new directories 205
deleting directories 205
renaming directories 205
supervisor rights 206–208
effective
calculating 219–221, 354–355
excessive 357–360
overview 217–219, 352–353
troubleshooting 357–360
viewing 356–357
file access
applied to individual files 207
creating new files 205
deleting files 205

displaying file names 205–206
granting access rights 206
reading file contents 204
renaming files 205
supervisor rights 206–208
writing to existing files 204
file system
Access Control 206
Create 205
Erase 205
File Scan 205–206
Modify 205
Read 204
Supervisor 206–208
Write 204
granting equivalent 353
object
Browse 334
Create 334
defined 109–110
Delete 334
Rename 335
Supervisor 334
overview 332–333
property
and ACLs (Access Control Lists) 337
Add Self 336–337
Compare 336
defined 110
overview 335
Read 336
Supervisor 336
Write 336–337
[Public] 345
security equivalence 353
See also trustee assignments
Rights inheritance
blocking 214–216, 349–352
defined 213–214
IRF (Inherited Rights Filter)
defined 214–215
modifying 215–216, 350–351
overview 349–350
and Supervisor rights 216–217, 351–352
overview 347–349
RIP (Routing Information Protocol) protocol
658–660
Ro (READ ONLY) file attribute 228
Root directory, displaying attributes of 196–197
[Root] object
defined 76, 320

substituting lower level for   170–171
ROOT option   170–171
[Root] partitions   376
Routers, defined   784
Routing Information Protocol (RIP) protocol
    658–660
Rw (READ WRITE) file attribute   228

S

S (SHAREABLE) file attribute   228
Salvaging deleted files   231–232
SAP (Service Advertising Protocol)
    defined   541–542
    overview   658–660
    time server communication   422
    turning on and off   439
SBACKUP.NLM program
    defined   502
    loading   504–505
Scalability   311, 313, 327–329
Scheduling information   707–708
Schema   314–315
Schema extensions   315
Scripting languages, NWS (Novell Web
    Server)   814–815
Scrolling lists, in CGI scripts   985–987
SCSI (Small Computer System Interface)   11–12
SECOND identifier variable   179
Secondary time server   418, 428
SECURE CONSOLE command   730
Secure Sockets Layer (SSL)
    See SSL (Secure Sockets Layer)
Security
    ALIAS command   724
    command shortcuts   724
    file-system level   111–112
    intruder lockout   125–127
    locking the file server console   702
    login level   108–109
    login restrictions   120–121
    login time restrictions   122–123
    NDS level   109–110
    and NDS tree structure   328
    NetWare 3.x   311
    network address restrictions   123–124
    object rights   109–110
    organizational roles   137
    password restrictions   121–122
    passwords   109
    passwords in login scripts   158

property rights   110
    restrictions   855
    security equivalences   129–130
    server naming conventions   34–35
    trustee assignments   109–110
        assigning rights to   132–133
        creating   130–132
        finding   131–132
        viewing rights   132–133
    trustee properties   130–131
    See also rights
    See also SSL (Secure Sockets Layer)
    See also trustee assignments
Security equivalence   129–130, 353
Seek time   12–13
Select Object dialog box   96
Sequenced Packet Exchange (SPX) protocol
    656–657
Serial number   65
Server drivers
    activating   43–47
    loading   38–39
Server operations, NDS Manager   371–374
Server parameters   708
Server requirements, NWS (Novell Web
    Server)   822–823
Server resource map location   852
Server tab   837–839
Server time parameters, defined   434–435
SERVER.EXE program   635
Server-Related leaf objects   81–82
Servers, DSS   742–743
Servers, NetWare 4.11
    booting from a floppy diskette   20
    consoles
        locking   730
        remote   727–728
    default rights   346
    displaying connections   698–699
    displaying information about   187–188
    displaying list of   725
    finding volume for   253
    gathering installation information   17–19
    increasing capacity of   58–59
    loading at startup   635
    naming conventions   34–35
    performance
        clock speed   7
        CPU (central processing unit)   5–8
        data bus   7
        hard disk   12–13

hard disk controller 11–12
hardware bottlenecks 13–14
hardware bus 9–11
NIC (network interface card) 13–14
processor speed 7
RAM (random access memory) 8–9
See also MONITOR.NLM utility
See also SERVMAN.NLM utility
removing 487–488
sample configuration files 200
setting up 17
starting at DOS startup 38
storing information about 81–82
time 63–65
Servers, NetWare/IP
configuring 763–765
DNS (Domain Name System), starting 757–760
DSS (Domain SAP/RIP Service) 760–762
NetWare/IP installation 755–757
overview 734, 749–751
system requirements 751–752
TCP/IP installation 753–755
Servers, viewing with NDS Manager 368–370
Servers, Web
virtual servers
enabling SSL 847
IP addresses 847
ports 846
Server-side includes, NWS (Novell Web
Server) 818
Server-side includes (SSI) 959–963
Server-to-server installation 24–26
Service Advertising Protocol (SAP)
See SAP (Service Advertising Protocol)
Service Interval tab 262
Service processes, effects on server
performance 691
SERVMAN.NLM utility
defined 644
setting server parameters
allowing unencrypted passwords 691
audible alerts 691
beeps 691
communications 682–684
directory caching 685
directory services 685–686
disk 686–687
error handling 687–688
file system 688–689
locks 689–690
maximum service processes 691

memory 691
minimum service processes 691
NCP 692
repairing corrupted volumes 691
time 692
transaction tracking 692–693
setting up bindery services 319–320
time synchronization parameters, viewing 435
Sessions, FTP
length, setting 1017
number of, setting 1017
viewing 1022
SHAREABLE (S) file attribute 228
SHELL_TYPE identifier variable 181
SHORT_YEAR identifier variable 178
Show option 290–291
Simple Network Management Protocol
(SNMP) 720–721
Single protocol configuration 746
Single reference time servers 416
Single SSL connection 891–892
Site certificates
cost 892
defined 889–891
installing 896–897
Netscape Navigator 924–926
requesting 892
signing requests, creating 893–896
SMACHINE identifier variable 181
Small Computer System Interface (SCSI) 11–12
SMS Technology
backing up 505
device drivers, loading 503–504
host machine, defined 502
restoring 505–506
SBACKUP.NLM program
defined 502
loading 504–505
target, defined 502
TSA (Target Service Agent)
defined 501–502
loading on target 503
SNMP (Simple Network Management
Protocol) 720–721
Special trustees 344–345
SPX (Sequenced Packet Exchange) protocol
656–657
SRM.CFG file 853–855
SSI commands 961–963
SSI (server-side includes) 959–963
SSL directive 852

SSL (Secure Sockets Layer)
  blue bar on Web page 886
  CA (Certificate Authorities) 889
  configuration file 859
  configuration file location 852
  configuring 897–901
  document security status, displaying 888–889
  enabling/disabling 852
  encryption keys 891
  HTTPS, in URLs 886
  key database file, creating 893
  key icon 886
  KEYMGR.NLM program 893
  NWS (Novell Web Server) 817
  private keys 891
  public keys 891
  purpose of 884–885
  single SSL connection 891–892
  site certificates
    cost 892
    defined 889–891
    installing 896–897
    requesting 892
    signing requests, creating 893–896
  visual cues to 885–886
  warning dialogs 886–887
SSL.CFG file 859
SSLConfig directive 852
Start of Daylight Saving Time parameter 441–442
STARTNET.BAT file 25, 570–574
Startup files 66
STARTUP.NCF file
  defined 636
  editing
    after installation 638–639
    during installation 37, 66
  example 636
  location 636
  preventing automatic loading 636
Static routers, configuring 791–792
STATICON utility 791–792
STATION identifier variable 181
Statistics tab 190–193
Storing information about 80
Suballocation, inhibiting 227
Submit button, in CGI scripts 989
Subnet masks 736
Subordinate Reference replicas 391–392
Supervisor rights
  and IRF (Inherited Rights Filters) 216–217
  objects 334

  properties 336
Surge protection 16
Switched analog lines 781
Switched lines 778
SX *vs.* DX processors 6
Sy (SYSTEM)
  directory attribute 230
  file attribute 228
Synchronization radius 418–420
SYSCON.EXE *vs.* NetWare Administrator 318
SYS:ETC\ directory 869
SYS:INW_WEB\ directory 869
SYS:INW_WEB\SHARED\DOCS\ directory 869
SYS:INW_WEB\SHARED\LCGI\ directory 869
SYS:INW_WEB\SHARED\TEMPLATE\ directory 869
SYS:NETBASIC\NETBASIC\ directory 869
SYS:PUBLIC\ directory 869
SYS:\SYSTEM\ directory 870
System Access tab 843–844
System module statistics 702
SYSTEM (Sy)
  directory attribute 230
  file attribute 228
SYS:WEB\ directory 870

T

T (TRANSACTIONAL) file attribute 228
Target, defined 502
Target Service Agent (TSA)
  defined 501–502
  loading on target 503
TCP/IP (Transmission Control Protocol/Internet
  Protocol)
  in NetWare Client32 593–594
  NetWare/IP 736–738
Text, displaying to screen 159
Time, setting 692
Time consumers
  correcting time 429
  defined 416
Time correction
  custom method 428–429
  default method 422–423
Time identifier variable 179
Time provider group 423–425
Time providers
  correcting time 428–429
  defined 416
Time servers
  adding 437, 440

communicating with external 438
communication 422, 426–428
communication strategies 541–542
communication with
    custom method 426–428
    default method 422
default type, setting 441
defined 415–416
external time sources 432
Internet time sources 432
network topology considerations 540
overview 63–65
primary time server 417
reference time server 417
removing 439
secondary time server 418, 428
setting time 432–433
single reference 416
time consumers
    correcting time 429
    defined 416
time correction
    custom method 428–429
    default method 422–423
time providers
    correcting time 428–429
    defined 416
    determining number of 539
time zone location, specifying 441
type, specifying 440
viewing time 433
Time synchronization
AUTOEXEC.NCF file
    overview 430
    time synchronization parameters 434–435
custom method
    guidelines 426
    time provider group 423–425
    time server communication 426–428
    time server time correction 428–429
    TIMESYNC.CFG file 426–428
default configuration 410
default method
    defined 420–421
    disadvantages 421–422
    SAP (Service Advertising Protocol) 422
    time server communication 422
    time server time correction 422–423
example 549–551
file date/time stamps 411

margin of error
    See synchronization radius
NDS database transactions 412–413
repairing 496–497
server time parameters, defined 434–435
SERVMAN.NLM file 435
synchronization radius 418–420
time parameters, configuring 429–431
TIMESYNC.CFG file 430
TIMESYNC.NLM file 429–430
transactional databases 410
transactions 410
UTC (Universal Time Coordinated) 412–414
See also time synchronization parameters
Time synchronization parameters
changing network time 440
configuring 429–431
daylight saving time 441–442
Daylight Saving Time Offset 442
Default Time Server Type 441
End of Daylight Saving Time 442
ignoring SAP packets 438
New Time With Daylight Saving Time
    Status 442
polling 438
quick reference summary 436–437
rebooting after changes 439
resetting default configuration 439
SAP (Service Advertising Protocol) 439
saving synchronizations 443
Start of Daylight Saving Time 441–442
synchronization radius, setting 439
synchronizing the hardware clock 438
Time Zone 441
Time zone location, specifying 441
Time Zone parameter 441
Time zones, configuring for 63–65
TIMESYNC ADD parameter 437
TIMESYNC ADD 437
TIMESYNC Configuration File 437
TIMESYNC Configured Sources 438
TIMESYNC Directory Tree Mode 438
TIMESYNC Hardware Clock 438
TIMESYNC Polling Count 438
TIMESYNC Polling Interval 438
TIMESYNC REMOVE Time Source 439
TIMESYNC RESET 439
TIMESYNC Restart Flag 439, 443
TIMESYNC Service Advertising 439
TIMESYNC Synchronization Radius 439
TIMESYNC Time Adjustment 440

TIMESYNC Time Source   440
TIMESYNC Type   440
TIMESYNC Write Parameters   440, 443
TIMESYNC Write Value   440
TIMESYNC.CFG file
    rebooting after changes   439
    resetting default configuration   439
    saving changes to   440, 444–446
    specifying location of   437
    viewing   435
    See also time synchronization
TIMESYNC Configuration File parameter   437
TIMESYNC Configured Sources parameter   438
TIMESYNC Directory Tree Mode parameter   438
TIMESYNC Hardware Clock parameter   438
TIMESYNC Polling Count parameter   438
TIMESYNC Polling Interval parameter   438
TIMESYNC REMOVE Time Source parameter   439
TIMESYNC RESET parameter   439
TIMESYNC Restart Flag parameter   439, 443
TIMESYNC Service Advertising parameter   439
TIMESYNC Synchronization Radius
    parameter   439
TIMESYNC Time Adjustment parameter   440
TIMESYNC Time Source parameter   440
TIMESYNC Type parameter   440
TIMESYNC Write Parameters parameter   440, 443
TIMESYNC Write Value parameter   440
TIMESYNC.CFG file
    overview   430
    time server communication   426–428
TIMESYNC.NLM file   429–430
<TITLE> </TITLE>, HTML tags   936
Transaction tracking, effects on server
    performance   692–693
Transactional databases   410
TRANSACTIONAL (T) file attribute   228
Transactions   410
TransferLog directive   852
Transmission Control Protocol/Internet Protocol
    (TCP/IP)
    See TCP/IP (Transmission Control Protocol/
    Internet Protocol)
Tree view, NDS Manager   366–368
Tree walking   378–379
Trustee assignments
    assigning rights to   132–133
    container objects as file system trustees   211–212
    creating   130–132, 195
    defined   109–110, 209
    deleting   196

finding   131–132
granting   209–211
    from the target   342–344
    from the trustee   339–342
overview   338
[Public] as a file system trustee   212
public trustee   212
viewing rights   132–133
See also rights
Trustee properties   130–131
Trustees, adding self to a property   337
Trustees of the Root Directory tab   194–196
TSA (Target Service Agent)
    defined   501–502
    loading on target   503
Typeful naming   90
Typeless naming   90
TypesConfig directive   853

U

Uniform Resource Locators (URLs)
    See URLs (Uniform Resource Locators)
Uninterrupted power source (UPS)   16
Universal Time Coordinated (UTC)   412–414
UNIX environment
    file support
        See name space modules
    printing   298–299
        NetWare to UNIX   299–300
        UNIX to NetWare   300–301
Unknown object   83
UPS (uninterrupted power source)   16
URLs (Uniform Resource Locators)
    case sensitivity   935
    examples   946
    length restriction with CGI scripts   977
    syntax   940–941
User Access tab   841–842
User authentication   858
User dialog box
    Environment tab   119
    Group Membership tab   128–129
    Identification tab   119
    Intruder Detection tab   125–126
    Intruder Lockout tab   126–127
    Login Restrictions tab   120–121
    Login Script tab   124–125
    Login Time Restrictions tab   122–123
    Network Address Restrictions tab   123–124
    Password Restrictions tab   121–122

Postal Address tab   119
Rights to Files and Directories tab   131–133
Security Equal To tab   129–130
User identifier variable   179–180
User interface
    See NDS (NetWare Directory Services)
    See NETADMIN utility
    See NetWare Administrator
User login script   149–150
User objects
    associating with login scripts   174
    creating
        home directory   117–118
        login name   114–115
        templates for   115–117
        user's last name   115
    default rights   346–347
    defined   83
    detailing
        group membership   128–129
        intruder lockout   125–127
        login restrictions   120–121
        login scripts   124–125
        login time restrictions   122–123
        network address restrictions   123–124
        overview   118–119
        password restrictions   121–122
        security equivalences   129–130
        trustee assignments, assigning rights to
            132–133
        trustee assignments, creating   130–132
        trustee assignments, finding   131–132
        trustee assignments, viewing rights   132–133
        trustee properties   130–131
User profiles   83
User space limits, displaying   193–194
User Space Limits tab   193–194
UserDir directive   854
USER_ID identifier variable   180
User-Related leaf objects   82–83
Users, setting number of   65
Users tab
    Print Queue Properties dialog box   254–255
    Print Server Properties dialog box   264–265
UTC (Universal Time Coordinated)   412–414
Utilities
    bindery services, NetWare 4.x   319–320
    CALLMGR   792–793
    CAPTURE.EXE
        Banner option   289
        Default Queue option   286

End Capture option   289
Form Feed option   289
Keep option   289
Notify option   290
options, reference summary   286–288
printing station software   292
redirecting printer data   239, 285–286
Show option   290–291
copy files options   671–672
CPECFG   793
directory for   200
directory options   672–676
directory services
    backup & restore options   674–676
    installing   672
    removing   672–673
    upgrading bindery information   673–674
    upgrading volumes   674
DSMERGE.NLM   456–457
DSREPAIR
    Advanced Options menu   498–499
    DSREPAIR.LOG file, viewing   498
    overview   494–495
    replicas, synchronization status   497
    time synchronization   496–497
    unattended full repair   495
DSTRACE
    messages   491–493
    NDS error codes   493
    options   490
    overview   491
    replica state codes   492
FILTCFG   790–791
INETCFG.NLM
    bindings   717–720
    MPR (MultiProtocol Router)   789–790
    network boards   710–711
    overview   709–710
    protocols, binding   718–719
    protocols, setting   713–717
    remote access   721–722
    SNMP (Simple Network Management
        Protocol)   720–721
    viewing console commands   722–723
INSTALL.NLM
    copy files options   671–672
    defined   644
    directory options   672–676
    disk options   666–668
    driver options   665–666
    Hot Fix area   668

license options   670–671
Multi CPU options   677–678
NCF files options   676–677
product options   679–680
volume options   668–670
IntranetWare Client for Windows NT   616–619
IntranetWare Login   617
IntranetWare Send Message   617–619
Mac OS   631–632
MONITOR.NLM
   cache utilization   703–704
   checking if a file is in use   703
   disk statistics   699
   displaying server connections   698–699
   LAN statistics   700–701
   locking the file server console   702
   memory utilization   706–707
   multiprocessor information   708
   overview   694–697
   processor utilization   704–705
   resource utilization   705–706
   scheduling information   707–708
   server parameters   708
   system module statistics   702
   WAN statistics   700–701
MPR (MultiProtocol Router)   789–793
NDS trees, merging   456–457
NETADMIN   113
NetWare Administrator for Windows 95
   608–609
NetWare Administrator for Windows NT   621
NetWare Application Launcher   609, 621
NetWare Client32, Windows 95   605–609
NetWare Client32, Windows NT   616–619
NetWare Directory Browser   631–632
NetWare Login   606–608
NetWare Print Chooser   631–632
NetWare Volume Mounter   631–632
network configuration
   See INETCFG.NLM
Novell Workstation Manager   621–624
NPRINT.EXE   239
PCONSOLE.EXE   271–272
print request handling
   CAPTURE.EXE   239
   NPRINT.EXE   239
print service configuration, front end
   PCONSOLE.EXE   271–272
product options
   INSTALL.NLM   679–680
protocols, binding

AppleTalk   719
IPX   718
TCP/IP   718
protocols, setting
   AppleTalk   716–717
   IPX   712–713
   TCP/IP   714–715
RCONSOLE.EXE   313
remote consoles   313
SERVMAN.NLM   319–320, 682–693
setting server parameters
   allowing unencrypted passwords   691
   audible alerts   691
   beeps   691
   communications   682–684
   directory caching   685
   directory services   685–686
   disk   686–687
   error handling   687–688
   file system   688–689
   locks   689–690
   maximum service processes   691
   memory   691
   minimum service processes   691
   NCP   692
   repairing corrupted volumes   691
   time   692
   transaction tracking   692–693
STATICON   791–792
user interface
   See NETADMIN
volume options   668–670
WAN (wide area networks)   789–793

V

VALUE.NDS file   313
Values, defined   74
VESA (Video Electronics Standards Association)   11
Video Electronics Standards Association (VESA)   11
Virtual directories, NWS (Novell Web Server)   818
Virtual Host tab   844–846
Virtual hosts, Web Manager   844–846
VLM client   555
VLM workstation client architecture   560–561
Volatile memory
   See RAM (random access memory)
Volume blocks   56–57
Volume object property dialog box
   Attributes tab   196–197
   Identification tab   190

Statistics tab   190–193
Trustees of the Root Directory tab   194–196
User Space Limits tab   193–194
Volume objects
   attributes for root directory   196–197
   compressed file count   192
   creating   189
   defined   82
   deleted file count   191
   directory entries allocated   192
   disk space   191
   file system security   188–190
   installed features   192
   migrated file count   193
   name spaces   192
   and physical volume names   190
   repairing   486–487
   trustee assignments
      creating   195
      deleting   196
   user space limits   193–194
   viewing properties of
      physical volume association   190
      statistics   191
Volume options, INSTALL.NLM utility   668–670
Volumes
   block size   56–57
   block suballocation   58
   configuration   648–651
   creating assignments   61–62
   data migration   58–59
   deleting assignments   61
   file compression   57
   maximum capacity   53
   names   56
   pointers to   82
   repairing corrupted   644, 691
   segment size   59–60
   spanning hard disks   54
   status   57
   SYS   54
   viewing parameters of   54–55
VREPAIR.NLM   644

W

W3 Consortium   937
WAN connector configuration   748–749
WAN extensions
   ATM (Asynchronous Transfer Mode)   805–806
   frame relay   805–806

X.25   805–806
WAN statistics   700–701
WAN (wide area networks)
   communications equipment, configuring   793
   connection types
      cell-switched services   781
      circuit switching   778, 781
      dedicated lines   778
      frame relay   781
      packet switching   778–779, 781
      sources for   780–781
      switched analog lines   781
      switched lines   778
   connectivity   328
   defined   777–778
   filters, configuring   790–791
   Internet access
      See IPX/IP Gateway
   IPX/IP Gateway
      client piece   799–805
      configuring   796–799
      defined   795–796
      server piece   796
      Windows 95 environment   801–805
   media types
      ATM (Asynchronous Transfer Mode)   782
      frame relay   783
      frame relay, example   794–795
      X.25 protocol   782
   MPR (MultiProtocol Router)
      CALLMGR utility   792–793
      configuring   788–794
      CPECFG utility   793
      FILTCFG utility   790–791
      INETCFG utility   789–790
      installing   785–788
      license requirements   787
      STATICON utility   791–792
   NLSP (NetWare Link Services Protocol)
      806–807
   routers, defined   784
   static routers, configuring   791–792
   video support   782
   voice support   782
   WAN connections, starting/stopping   792–793
Web browsers
   browsing NDS trees   963–970
   configuring   963–965
   See also Netscape Navigator
Web Manager
   access restrictions

by group 911–912
by system 843–844, 914–915
by user 841–842, 908–909
client requirements 834
Directories tab 839–841
directory management 839–841
Interface tab 846–847
launching 835–837
overview 832–833
Server tab 837–839
System Access tab 843–844
User Access tab 841–842
Virtual Host tab 844–846
virtual hosts 844–846
virtual servers
enabling SSL 847
IP addresses 847
ports 846
Web pages
blue bar on 886
clickable image maps 953–959
clickable images 950–953
hyperlinks
absolute *vs.* relative paths 939–940
image maps 953–959
images 950–953
text 937–939
inline images 948–950
Web security
See SSL (Secure Sockets Layer)
Web server configuration files
ACCESS.CFG 856–858
blank lines 850
comments 850
editing 850
HTTPD.CFG 851–853
paths 850
SRM.CFG 853–855
SSL.CFG 859
Web servers
access control file directives 905–906
access protocols 946–947
access restrictions
access files, creating 904–907
by group 911–913
overview 901–903
PWGEN.EXE file 904
by system 913–916
by user 908–911
Web Manager 908–909, 911–912, 914–915
with Web Manager 903

WEBMGR.EXE 903
ACCESS.WWW program
access restrictions by group 911–912
access restrictions by system 915–916
access restrictions by user 909–911
directories, adding/deleting 941–943
local files 947
nonstandard ports 947
passwords, encrypting 904, 906–907
Web Manager
access restrictions by group 911–912
access restrictions by system 914–915
access restrictions by user 908–909
Web servers, configuring
access control file location 853
aliases for image maps 854
automatic indexing 854
CGI interpreters, locating 855
directory access controls 856
overriding 857
directory structure
SYS:ETC\ 869
SYS:INW_WEB\ 869
SYS:INW_WEB\SHARED\DOCS\ 869
SYS:INW_WEB\SHARED\LCGI\ 869
SYS:INW_WEB\SHARED\TEMPLATE\ 869
SYS:NETBASIC\NETBASIC\ 869
SYS:PUBLIC\ 869
SYS:\SYSTEM\ 870
SYS:WEB\ 870
file management
acceptable use policy 874
file extensions 871
naming conventions 871–872
old or unused files 872–873
organizing by directory 868–870
restricting server space 872–873
reviewing HTML coding 866–868
file-based authentication 857
group information 857
HTML documents, root directory for 853
HTML documents, user directory for 854
HTML filenames, default 853
IP addresses 851
logging
ACCESS.LOG file 877–878
ERROR.LOG file 880–881
HTTP status codes 879–880
HTTP versions 879–880
log files, clearing 881
log files, location 875–877

log files, printing 881
log files, saving 881
log files, settings 875–877
overview 874–875
logging errors 852
logging transferred files 852
MIME (Multipurpose Internet Mail
  Enhancement)
  browser configuration 861–863
  configuration file 863–864
  MIME types 860–861
  MIME types, changing 865
  MIME types, list of 864
  MIME types, overview 860–861
  MIME.TYP file 863–864
MIME type, default 854
MIME-type file map location 853
NLMs, locating 855
passwords, list of 858
port assignment 851
security restrictions 855
  See also SSL (Secure Sockets Layer)
server resource map location 852
SSL (Secure Sockets Layer)
  configuration file 859
  configuration file location 852
  enabling/disabling 852
text for login prompt 857
user authentication 858
Web services
  See NWS (Novell Web Server)
WEBMGR.EXE program
  See Web Manager
Wide area networks (WAN)
  See WAN (wide area networks)
Windows 3.x environment
  clients
    See NetWare Client32, DOS/Windows
  NetWare/IP clients 766–770
  Program Manager, replacing 515

Windows 95 environment
  clients
    See NetWare Client32, Windows 95
  Explorer, replacing 515
  file support
    See name space modules
  installing IntranetWare from 20
  IPX/IP Gateway 801–805
  NetWare/IP clients 770–774
  print service configuration 281–284
Windows NT environment
  clients
    See IntranetWare Client, Windows NT
  file support
    See name space modules
Workstation identifier variable 181
Workstations
  See client workstations
World Wide Web (WWW) services 329
WRITE login script command 175–177
Write rights 336–337
WWW (World Wide Web) services 329

X

X (EXECUTE ONLY) file attribute 227
X.25 protocol
  overview 782
  WAN extensions 805–806
X.500 compliance 325
X.500 country codes 1049–1052

Y

YEAR identifier variable 178

VENTANA

Java Programming for the Internet

$49.95, 816 pages, illustrated, part #: 1-56604-355-7

Master the programming language of choice for
Internet applications. Expand the scope of your
online development with this comprehensive, step-
by-step guide to creating Java applets. The CD-ROM
features Java Developers Kit, source code for all the
applets, samples and programs from the book, and
much more.

The Visual Basic Programmer's Guide to Java

$39.99, 450 pages, part #: 1-56604-527-4

At last—a Java book that speaks your language!
Use your understanding of Visual Basic as a
foundation for learning Java and object-oriented
programming. This unique guide not only relates
Java features to what you already know—it also
highlights the areas in which Java excels over
Visual Basic, to build an understanding of its
appropriate use. The CD-ROM features compara-
tive examples written in Java & Visual Basic, code
for projects created in the book and more

VENTANA

Principles of Object-Oriented Programming in Java

$39.99, 400 pages, illustrated, part #: 1-56604-530-4

Move from writing programs to designing solutions—with dramatic results! Take a step beyond syntax to discover the true art of software design, with Java as your paintbrush and objects on your palette. This in-depth discussion of how, when and why to use objects enables you to create programs—using Java or any other object-oriented language that not only work smoothly, but are easy to maintain and upgrade. The CD-ROM features the Java SDK, code samples and more.

The Comprehensive Guide to Visual J++

$49.99, 792 pages, illustrated, part #: 1-56604-533-9

Learn to integrate the Java language and ActiveX in one development solution! Master the Visual J++ environment using real-world coding techniques and project examples. Includes executable J++ sample projects plus undocumented tips and tricks. The CD-ROM features all code examples, sample ActiveX COM objects, Java documentation and an ActiveX component library.

VENTANA

The Comprehensive Guide to Visual Basic 5

$49.99, 600 pages, illustrated, part #: 1-56604-484-7

From the author of Ventana's bestselling *Visual Guide to Visual Basic for Windows*! Command and syntax descriptions feature real-world examples. Thoroughly covers new features, uses, backward compatibility and much more. The CD-ROM features a complete, searchable text version of the book including all code.

Visual C++ X Power Toolkit, Second Edition

$49.99, 800 pages, part #: 1-56604-528-2

Completely updated to cover all new features in the latest version of Visual C++ — including graphics, animation, sound, connectivity and more. Class libraries, tutorials and techniques offer programmers a professional edge. The CD-ROM features fully compiled class libraries, demo programs and complete standards files for all major picture formats.

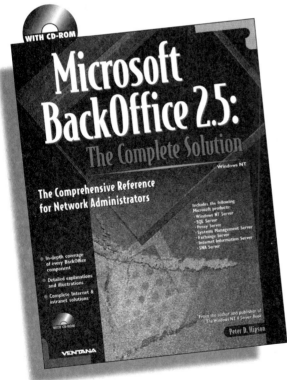

HTML Publishing on the Internet, Second Edition

$39.99, 700 pages, illustrated, part #: 1-56604-625-4

Take advantage of critical updates and technologies that have emerged since this book's bestselling predecessor was published. Learn to create a home page and hyperlinks, and to build graphics, video and sound into documents. Highlighted throughout with examples and templates, and tips on layout and nonlinear organization. Plus, save time and money by downloading components of the new technologies from the Web or from the companion CD-ROM. The CD-ROM also features HTML authoring tools, graphics and multimedia utilities, textures, templates and demos.

The HTML Programmer's Reference

$39.99, 376 pages, illustrated, part #: 1-56604-597-5

The ultimate professional companion! All HTML categories, tags and attributes are listed in one easy-reference sourcebook, complete with code examples. Saves time and money testing—all examples comply with the top browsers! Provides real-world JavaScript and HTML examples. The CD-ROM features a complete hyperlinked HTML version of the book, viewable with most popular browsers.

TO ORDER ANY VENTANA TITLE, COMPLETE THIS ORDER FORM AND MAIL OR FAX IT TO US, WITH PAYMENT, FOR QUICK SHIPMENT.

TITLE	PART #	QTY	PRICE	TOTAL

SHIPPING

For orders shipping within the United States, please add $4.95 for the first book, $1.50 for each additional book.
For "two-day air," add $7.95 for the first book, $3.00 for each additional book.
Email: vorders@kdc.com for exact shipping charges.
Note: Please include your local sales tax.

SUBTOTAL = $ _____

SHIPPING = $ _____

TAX = $ _____

TOTAL = $ _____

Mail to: International Thomson Publishing • 7625 Empire Drive • Florence, KY 41042
☎ US orders 800/332-7450 • fax 606/283-0718
☎ International orders 606/282-5786 • Canadian orders 800/268-2222

Name _____

E-mail _____ Daytime phone _____

Company _____

Address (No PO Box) _____

City_____ State_____ Zip_____

Payment enclosed ___VISA ___MC ___ Acc't # _____ Exp. date_____

Signature _____ Exact name on card _____

Check your local bookstore or software retailer for these and other bestselling titles, or call toll free:

800/332-7450

8:00 am - 6:00 pm EST